# Miller & Levine Biology

# Study Workbook A

PEARSON

Boston, Massachusetts Chandler, Arizona Glenview, Illinois Upper Saddle River, New Jersey

**Photo Credits:** p 1 ©istockphoto.com/Linda Fleurin; p 13 ©Comstock/Jupiter Images; p 27 ©Flip Nicklin/Minden Pictures; p 29 ©istockphoto.com/John Woodworth; p 45 © Jeff Rotman/www.jeffrotman.com; p 65 ©George McCarthy/Nature Picture Library; p 79 ©Eric Wanders/ Foto Natura/Minden Pictures; p 95 ©SIME s.a.s / eStock Photo; p 97 ©istockphoto.com/Andrey Prokhorov; p 113 © simple stock shots/Age Fotostock; p 127 Watering can (earthenware), English School, (16th century) / © Museum of London, UK, / The Bridgeman Art Library International; p 141 ©Flip Nicklin/Minden Pictures; p 157 © Joe McDonald /CORBIS; p 159 ©istockphoto.com/Andrey Prokhorov; p 177 blickwinkel/Alamy; p 191 t. ©Pearson Education, Photo by Heather Wright; b. ©aliciahh/istockphoto.com; p 211 EYE OF SCIENCE / SPL/Photo Researchers, Inc.; p 225 BL: ©arlindo71/istockphoto.com, BM: Kenneth Eward/BioGrafx/Photo Researchers, Inc., BR: PR NEWSWIRE, TL: Biophoto Associates / Photo Researchers, Inc.; p 227 © Dr. Stanley Flegler / Visuals Unlimited; p 245 ©David Parker / Photo Researchers, Inc.; p 247 ©istockphoto.com/Lorraine Benjamin; p 265 ©Chris Johns/National Geographic Image Collection; p 283 ©Pearson Education. Photo by Heather Wright; p 297 © Mark Hamblin/age footstock; p 311 © Marvin Dembinsky Photo Associates / Alamy; p 313 ©istockphoto.com/Joe Biafore; p 323 © Peter Cade/Getty Images; p 339 © Nigel Cattlin / Visuals Unlimited; p 355 © Vienna Report Agency/Sygma/Corbis; p 375 © Ted Mead/PhotoLibrary; p 391 ©Martin Perez/istockphoto.com; p 393 ©istockphoto.com/alle12; p 405 ©Kelly McGann Hebert; p 419 © O. LOUIS MAZZATENTA /National Geographic Society; p 435 ©Anastasiya Maksymenko/istockphoto.com; p 451 © 2002 Masa Ushioda/Image Quest 3-D; p 463 ©Ariadne Van Zandbergen/africanpictures.net; p 465 ©istockphoto.com/Svetlana Prikhodko; p 481 © Walter Smith/Workbook Stock/Jupiter Images; p 497 © Private Collection/Bridgeman Art Library; p 511 © The Schlesinger Library/Radcliffe; p 527 ©Libby Chapman/istockphoto.com; p 543 ©Nicholas Monu/istockphoto.com; p 559 © Christopher Wheeler



ISBN-13: 978-0-13-368718-7

ISBN-10: 0-13-368718-X

1 2 3 4 5 6 7 8 9 10 12 11 10 09 08

# Contents

# How to Use Study Workbook A

Did you know that learning to study more effectively can make a real difference in your performance at school? Students who master study skills are more confident and have more fun learning. *Study Workbook A* for *Miller & Levine Biology* is designed to help you acquire skills that will allow you to study biology more effectively. Your active participation in class and use of this workbook can go a long way toward helping you achieve success in biology.

This study workbook can be used to

- preview a chapter
- learn key vocabulary terms
- master difficult concepts
- review for chapter and unit tests
- practice 21st Century Skills

Here are some suggestions for how to use this workbook to help you study more effectively.

### Start with the Big Idea

Each chapter in your workbook begins with the Big Idea and Essential Question from your textbook. Use the guiding questions provided in the graphic organizer to help you develop an answer to the Essential Question. Fill in the first column of the graphic organizer before you begin. Then as you finish each lesson, come back and fill in the second column.

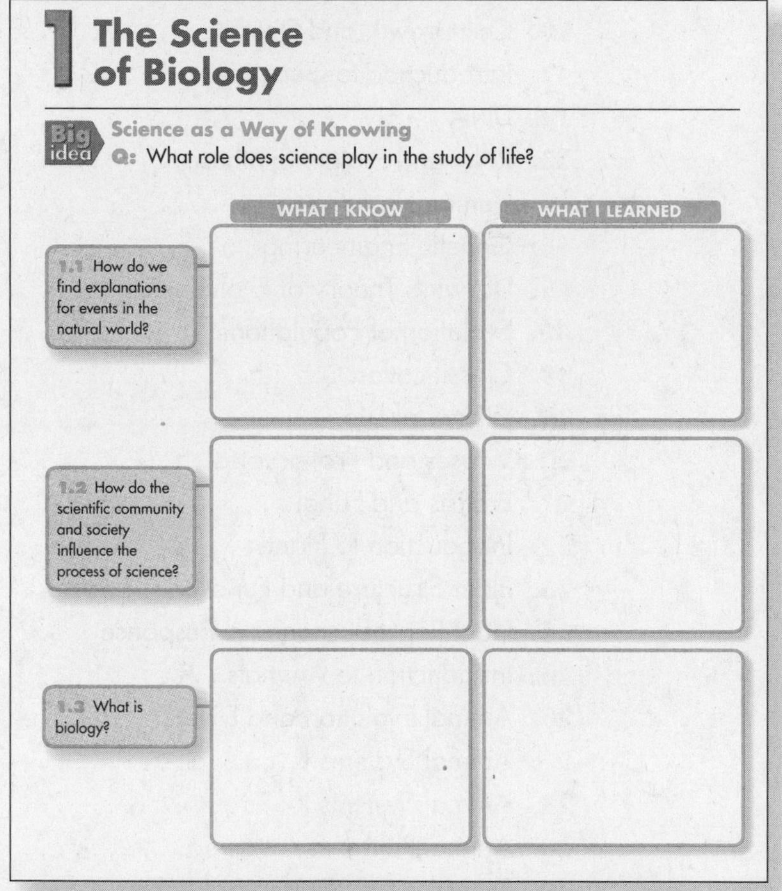

1 The Science of Biology
Big idea
Science as a Way of Knowing
Q: What role does science play in the study of life?
WHAT I KNOW
WHAT I LEARNED
1.1 How do we find explanations for events in the natural world?
1.2 How do the scientific community and society influence the process of science?
1.3 What is biology?

## Preview Each Lesson

Each lesson opens with a list of Lesson Objectives that state the goals of the lesson. Use the Lesson Summary that follows to preview the lesson, then read the corresponding lesson in your textbook. You can also use this page for a quick review before a test or quiz.

### 3.4 Cycles of Matter

**Lesson Objectives**

- Describe how matter cycles among the living and nonliving parts of an ecosystem.
- Describe how water cycles through the biosphere.
- Explain why nutrients are important in living systems.
- Describe how the availability of nutrients affects the productivity of ecosystems.

**Lesson Summary**

**Recycling in the Biosphere** Matter, unlike energy, is recycled within and between ecosystems. Elements pass from one organism to another and from one part of the biosphere to another through **biogeochemical cycles**, which are closed loops powered by the flow of energy.

**The Water Cycle** Water moves between the ocean, the atmosphere, and land.

- Evaporation is the process in which water changes from a liquid to a gas.
- Transpiration is the process in which water evaporates from the leaves of plants.

**Nutrient Cycles** The chemical substances that an organism needs to survive are called **nutrients**. Like water, nutrients pass through organisms and the environment.

- **Carbon Cycle:** Carbon is a key ingredient of all organic compounds. Processes involved in the carbon cycle include photosynthesis and human activities such as burning.
- **Nitrogen Cycle:** Nitrogen is needed by all organisms to build proteins. Processes involved in the nitrogen cycle include nitrogen fixation and denitrification.
  - In **nitrogen fixation**, certain bacteria convert nitrogen gas into ammonia.
  - In **denitrification**, other soil bacteria convert nitrogen compounds called nitrates back into nitrogen gas.
- **Phosphorus Cycle:** Phosphorus is needed for molecules such as DNA and RNA. Most of the phosphorus in the biosphere is stored in rocks and ocean sediments. Stored phosphorus is gradually released into water and soil, where it is used by organisms.

## Work Through the Lesson

Following the lesson summary, you will find different workbook activities designed to help you understand and remember what you read in your textbook. Completing these worksheets will help you master the key concepts and vocabulary of each lesson. The questions are written in a variety of formats.

### Summary of Mendel's Principles

*For Questions 16–20, complete each statement by writing the correct word or words.*

16. The units that determine the inheritance of biological characteristics are ______________.
17. A form of a gene is a(n) ______________.
18. If two or more forms of a gene exist, some may be dominant and others may be ______________.
19. The offspring of most sexually reproducing organisms have two copies of each gene. One came from each ______________.
20. Alleles from different genes usually ______________ independently from each other when gametes form.

*For Questions 21–25, match the term with its description.*

| | | |
|---|---|---|
| ______ | **21.** Determine traits | **A.** parents |
| ______ | **22.** Can be two of these in one gene | **B.** alleles |
| ______ | **23.** Allele that is expressed | **C.** dominant |
| ______ | **24.** Where genes come from | **D.** segregate |
| ______ | **25.** What genes do during gamete formation | **E.** genes |

### An Overview of Photosynthesis

*For Questions 11–13, write the letter of the correct answer on the line at the left.*

______ **11.** What are the reactants of the photosynthesis reaction?

**A.** chlorophyll and light **C.** carbohydrates and oxygen
**B.** carbon dioxide and water **D.** high-energy electrons and air

______ **12.** What are the products of the light-dependent reactions?

**A.** chloroplasts and light **C.** oxygen and ATP
**B.** proteins and lipids **D.** water and sugars

______ **13.** Where do the light-independent reactions occur?

**A.** stroma **C.** chlorophyll
**B.** thylakoids **D.** mitochondria

## Organize Your Thoughts

In addition to different types of questions, you will also find graphic organizers to help you pull together your thoughts.

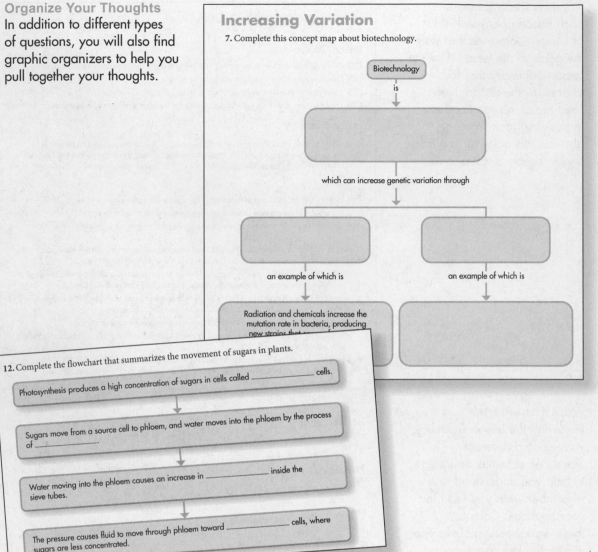

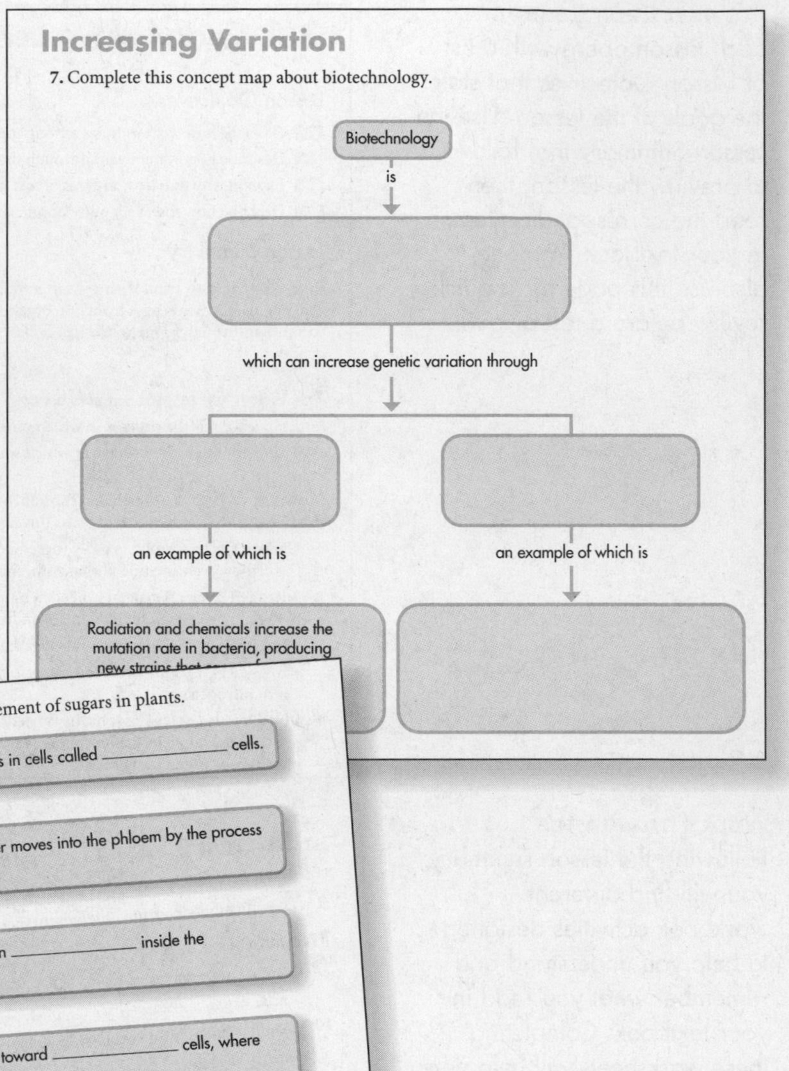


12. Complete the flowchart that summarizes the movement of sugars in plants.

Photosynthesis produces a high concentration of sugars in cells called ____________ cells.

Sugars move from a source cell to phloem, and water moves into the phloem by the process of ____________.

Water moving into the phloem causes an increase in ____________ inside the sieve tubes.

The pressure causes fluid to move through phloem toward ____________ cells, where sugars are less concentrated.

## Think Visually

You will also work with a variety of visuals that reinforce the concepts of the lesson.

5. VISUAL ANALOGY In the visual analogy of the growing town, what does the library represent? Identify two characteristics that make it a good choice for this analogy.

____________________

____________________

____________________

____________________

17. THINK VISUALLY The four circles below represent the nucleus of a cell going through mitosis. Draw four chromosomes as they go through each phase. Label each phase and describe what is happening to the DNA.

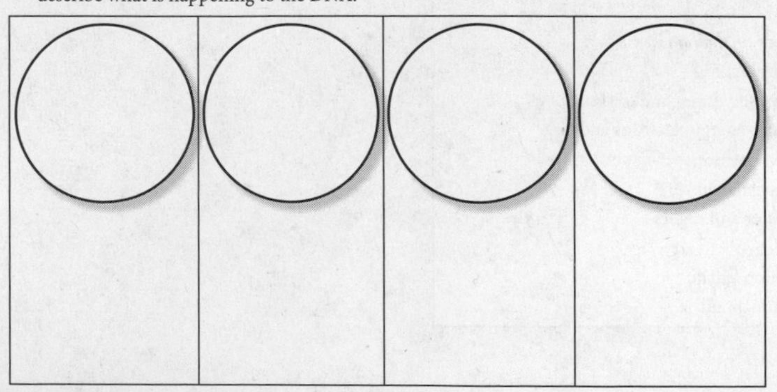

**Put It Together** Each lesson ends with a question that brings you back to the Big Idea and gives you an opportunity to apply what you've learned.

**Apply the Big idea**

39. Some housecats have orange fur with darker orange stripes. The traits of these *tabby* cats are usually seen in male cats. *Tortoiseshell* cats have patches of many different colors. "Torties," as they are called, are almost always female. What does this tell you about the way cellular information about color and sex are passed on in cats?

______________________________________________

______________________________________________

______________________________________________

______________________________________________

**Apply the Big idea**

8. The left side of the heart is larger and more muscular than the right side. Also, artery walls are thicker than those of veins. Explain how those differences in structure are important to function.

______________________________________________

______________________________________________

______________________________________________

______________________________________________

**Review the Vocabulary** Following the lessons, you will be able to review the vocabulary from the chapter.

## Chapter Vocabulary Review

**Crossword Puzzle** *Complete the puzzle by entering the term that matches each numbered description.*

**Across**

1. a specific characteristic
4. physical traits
6. the separation of alleles during formation of sex cells
9. containing two identical alleles for a trait
11. the likelihood of an event occurring
12. scientific study of heredity
13. the union of male and female sex cells

**Down**

2. one form of a gene
3. the offspring of a cross between parents with different, true-breeding traits
4. word that describes a trait controlled by two or more genes
5. containing two different alleles for a trait
7. genetic makeup
8. a phenotype in which both alleles are expressed
10. reproductive cell, egg or sperm

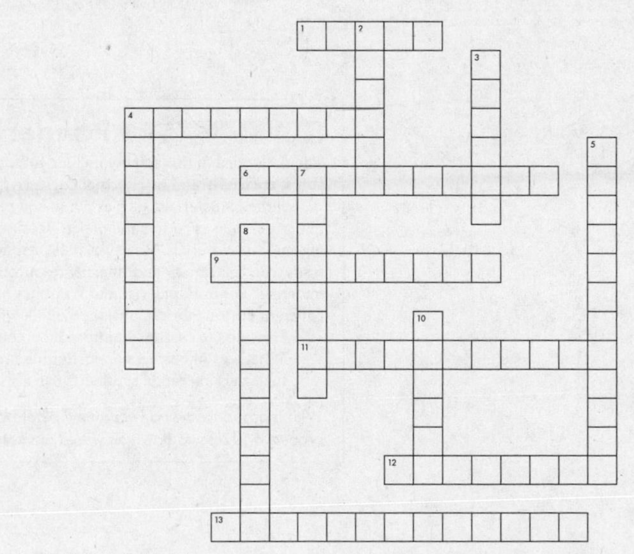

**Broaden Your Perspective**

The Chapter Mystery in your textbook introduces you to a real-world application of biology. At the end of the chapter in your workbook, you are given an opportunity to consider the mystery from another perspective. See where the mystery leads while practicing 21st Century skills, such as putting together a presentation, preparing a business plan, and even writing a resume!

CHAPTER **MYSTERY**

**STONE AGE STORYTELLERS**

In the Chapter Mystery, you learned about Iceman, who died 5300 years ago. His body is the oldest naturally preserved mummy ever recovered. Many plant materials were preserved along with Iceman. It's very unusual for plant materials to survive that long.

21st Century Learning

## Iceman of the Future?

The environmental conditions where Iceman died were unique. The glacial ice he was found in helped to preserve him and many of his belongings for thousands of years before hikers discovered him in 1991. Consider what might happen to a climber today who died on a mountaintop and whose body became trapped in ice. The article below is a fictional broadcast account of the discovery of Iceman II in the year 3008.

**Afternoon Mindcast, January 8, 3008—**Hikers on Pike's Glacier literally stumbled upon a major anthropological discovery this morning. When Klendon Deel, 85, tripped over something in the trail, his hiking companion and mother, Mender Yayv Akong, 122, helped him up and then looked for the partially hidden obstacle. It turned out to be an ancient electronic device called a "Hype-Odd," which was used for listening to music aurally. But the most amazing part of the discovery was the skeletal hand still clutching the device.

Akong and Deel beamed the authorities, and within an hour scientists had uncovered the remains of an adult male human. Preliminary tests indicate the man died in February or March of 2016. At that time the glacier did not cover the mountain, which is in an area that was then called "Colorado."

Scientists say that unfortunately most of the man's soft tissue disintegrated through the 100-Year Heat Wave of the 22nd century, the Crustal Shocks of the 24th century, and the Kelvin Ice Age of the 29th century. But according to spokesbeing Nkavrjdn*w, the skeleton, nails, hair, and many of the belongings were all remarkably well preserved. "The lead scientist studying the find is particularly fascinated with the objects remaining in the man's pack," Nkavrjdn*w says. "For example, she thinks she has found what is left of an ancient apple. While the actual fruit is gone, a stem and a pile of seeds remained in the pack."

In addition, a clear bottle was found in the pack. Scientists are planning on doing tests to try to determine what the bottle contained. The only marking they could find on the bottle was a small triangular shape composed of three arrows. Scientists are unsure what this mysterious symbol meant.

## 21st Century Skills Pondering Plant Products

The skills used in this activity include **information and media literacy, communication skills, creativity and intellectual curiosity,** and **social responsibility.**

Synthetic materials, such as nylon and plastic, tend to be more durable than plant-based materials, such as cotton and paper. Because of this, many modern products are made out of synthetic materials. However, most synthetic materials are made from nonrenewable resources. Use library and Internet resources to compare plant-based materials to synthetic materials. For example, visit the Web sites of companies that manufacture plastic, nylon, paper, or cotton fabric. Consider the following questions:

- How do the costs of plant products compare with those of synthetic products?
- What sort of business opportunities are there in manufacturing products out of plant materials instead of synthetic materials?

*With a group, come up with a new plant-based product. Identify potential customers for the product and discuss how you would market the product to them.*

Name ______________________ Class ______ Date ______

# 1 The Science of Biology

## Science as a Way of Knowing

**Q:** What role does science play in the study of life?

| | WHAT I KNOW | WHAT I LEARNED |
| --- | --- | --- |
| **1.1** How do we find explanations for events in the natural world? | | |
| **1.2** How do the scientific community and society influence the process of science? | | |
| **1.3** What is biology? | | |

# 1.1 What Is Science?

## Lesson Objectives

- State the goals of science.
- Describe the steps used in scientific methodology.

## Lesson Summary

**What Science Is and Is Not** **Science** is an organized way of gathering and analyzing evidence about the natural world. The goals of science are to provide natural explanations for events in the natural world and to use those explanations to make useful predictions. Science is different from other human works in the following ways:

- Science deals only with the natural world.
- Scientists collect and organize information about the natural world in an orderly way.
- Scientists propose explanations that are based on evidence, not belief.
- They test those explanations with more evidence.

**Scientific Methodology: The Heart of Science** Methodology for scientific investigation involves:

- Making an **observation**. Observation involves the act of noticing and describing events or processes in a careful, orderly way. Scientists use their observations to make inferences. An **inference** is a logical interpretation based on what scientists already know.
- Suggesting hypotheses. A **hypothesis** is a scientific explanation for a set of observations that can be tested in ways that support or reject it.
- Testing the hypothesis. Testing a hypothesis often involves designing an experiment. Whenever possible, a hypothesis should be tested by a **controlled experiment**—an experiment in which only one variable (the **independent variable**, or manipulated variable) is changed. The variable that can change in response to the independent variable is called the **dependent variable**, or responding variable. The **control group** is exposed to the same conditions as the experimental group except for one independent variable.
- Collecting, recording, and analyzing **data**, or information gathered during the experiment.
- Drawing conclusions based on data.

## What Science Is and Is Not

**1.** What is science?

_______________________________________________

_______________________________________________

**2.** What are the goals of science?

_______________________________________________

_______________________________________________

_______________________________________________

 

# Scientific Methodology: The Heart of Science

*Questions 3–10 refer to spontaneous generation, the idea that life can arise from nonliving matter. Spontaneous generation was accepted by many in the scientific community up until the mid-nineteenth century. A series of simple experiments tested the validity of this idea.*

**3.** Evidence used to support spontaneous generation was the observation that foods over time become covered in maggots or fungal and bacterial growth. The inference behind spontaneous generation is that there is no "parent" organism. Write this inference as a hypothesis using an if–then sentence that suggests a way of testing it.

______________________________________________________________________

______________________________________________________________________

**4.** In 1668, Francesco Redi proposed a different hypothesis to explain the specific example of maggots that appear on spoiled food. He had observed that maggots appear on meat a few days after flies have been seen on the food. He inferred that the flies had left behind eggs too small to see. Redi's experiment is shown below. What conclusion can you draw from Redi's experiment?

______________________________________________________________________

______________________________________________________________________

**5.** In the late 1700s, Lazzaro Spallanzani designed a different experiment to show that life did not arise spontaneously from food. He inferred that some foods spoil because of growing populations of microorganisms. Fill in the information requested below.

Independent variable:

______________________________________

Dependent variable:

______________________________________

Controlled variables (identify three):

______________________________________

______________________________________

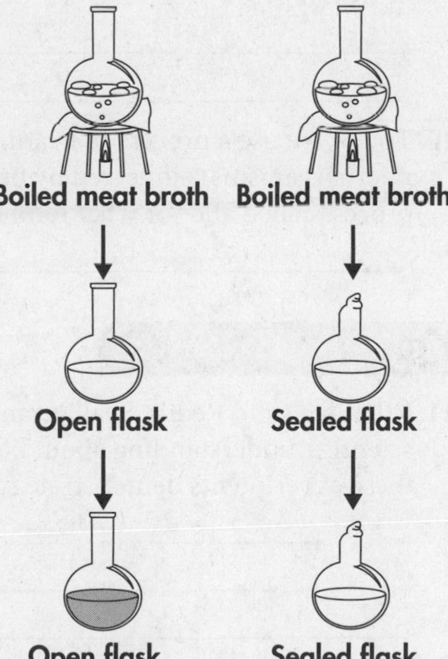

6. THINK VISUALLY Critics of Spallanzani said that he showed only that organisms cannot live without air. In 1859 Louis Pasteur designed an experiment to address that criticism, an experiment that reproduced Spallanzani's results.

*Draw in the third and final steps in the experiment. Use an arrow to show the path of travel of the microorganisms. Shade the broth in the flask(s) in which microorganisms grew.*

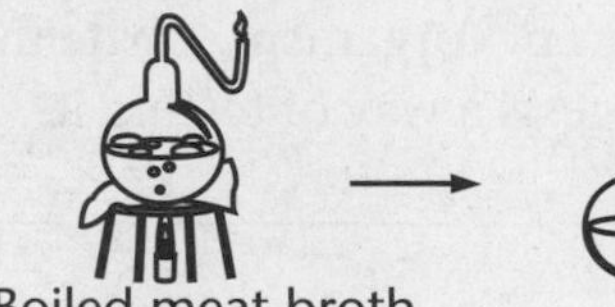


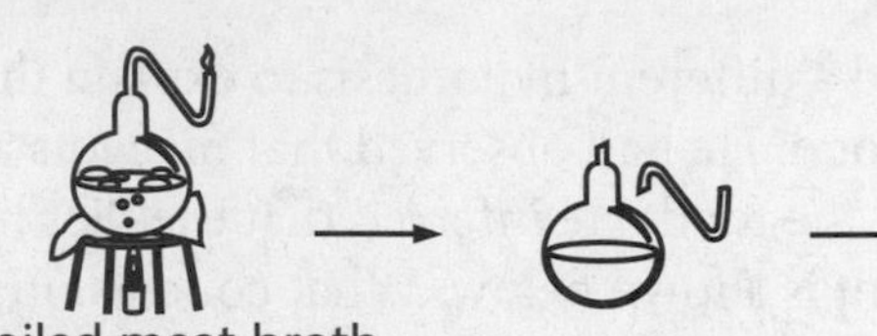


7. How did Pasteur solve Spallanzani's problem of limiting exposure to air?

8. What purpose did boiling the meat broth serve in both the Spallanzani and Pasteur experiments?

9. How do the Redi, Spallanzani, and Pasteur experiments disprove the hypothesis you wrote in Question 3?

10. Today, we use a process of heating liquids to prevent spoiling by bacteria and other microorganisms, pioneered by one of the three scientists mentioned above. What is that process called and for what food is it used?

## Apply the Big idea

11. What facts did Redi's, Spallanzani's, and Pasteur's experiments establish? What broader scientific understanding about life did the experiments explore? How does the example of these experiments demonstrate science as a way of knowing?

# 1.2 Science in Context

## Lesson Objectives

- Explain how scientific attitudes generate new ideas.
- Describe the importance of peer review.
- Explain what a scientific theory is.
- Explain the relationship between science and society.

## Lesson Summary

**Exploration and Discovery: Where Ideas Come From** Scientific methodology is closely linked to exploration and discovery. Good scientists share scientific attitudes, or habits of mind, that lead them to exploration and discovery. New ideas are generated by curiosity, skepticism, open-mindedness, and creativity.

- Ideas for exploration can arise from practical problems.
- Discoveries in one field of science can lead to new technologies; the new technologies give rise to new questions for exploration.

**Communicating Results: Reviewing and Sharing Ideas** Communication and sharing of ideas are vital to modern science. Scientists share their findings with the scientific community by publishing articles that undergo peer review. In peer review, scientific papers are reviewed by anonymous, independent experts. Publishing peer-reviewed articles in scientific journals allows scientists to

- share ideas.
- test and evaluate each other's work.

Once research has been published, it enters the dynamic marketplace of scientific ideas. New ideas fit into scientific understanding by leading to new hypotheses that must be independently confirmed by controlled experiments.

**Scientific Theories** In science, the word **theory** applies to a well-tested explanation that unifies a broad range of observations and hypotheses and that enables scientists to make accurate predictions about new situations.

- No theory is considered absolute truth.
- Science is always changing; as new evidence is uncovered, a theory may be reviewed or replaced by a more useful explanation.

**Science and Society** Using science involves understanding its context in society and its limitations. Understanding science

- helps people make decisions that also involve cultural customs, values, and ethical standards.
- can help people predict the consequences of their actions and plan the future.

Scientists strive to be objective, but when science is applied in society, it can be affected by **bias**, a point of view that is personal rather than scientific.

 

# Exploration and Discovery: Where Ideas Come From

**1.** Describe how new ideas are generated.

______________________________

**2.** How are science and technology related?

______________________________

______________________________

**3.** It took hundreds of years of discussion and the experiments of Louis Pasteur in the nineteenth century for the larger scientific community to accept that spontaneous generation of life was not a valid scientific concept. Referring to the diagram, describe how modern methods of communication have changed the scientific process.

______________________________

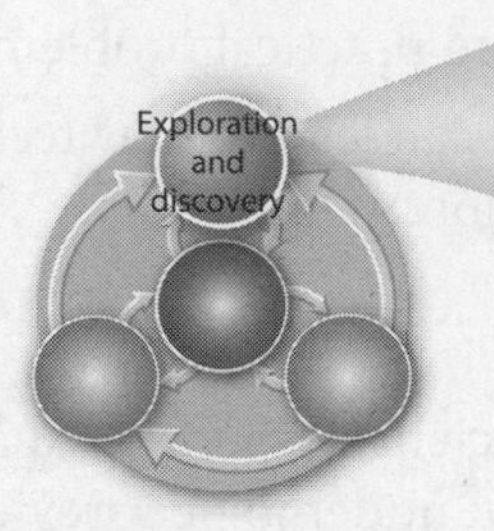


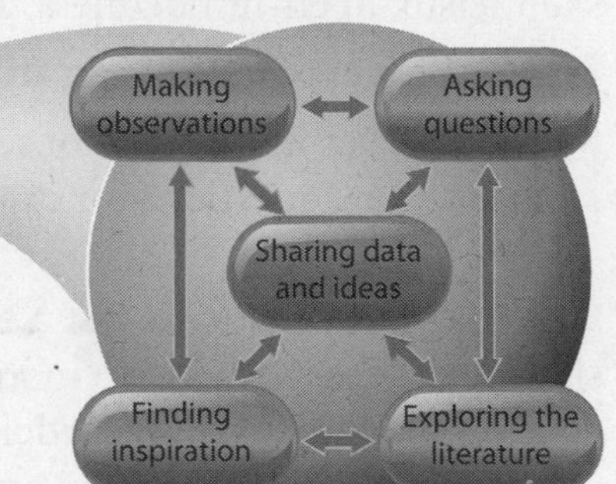


Adapted from *Understanding Science*, UC Berkeley, Museum of Paleontology

# Communicating Results: Reviewing and Sharing Ideas

**4.** **THINK VISUALLY** Use lesson concepts to complete the diagram to show the outcome of communication among scientists. Why are "New Ideas" placed at the center of the diagram?

______________________________

______________________________

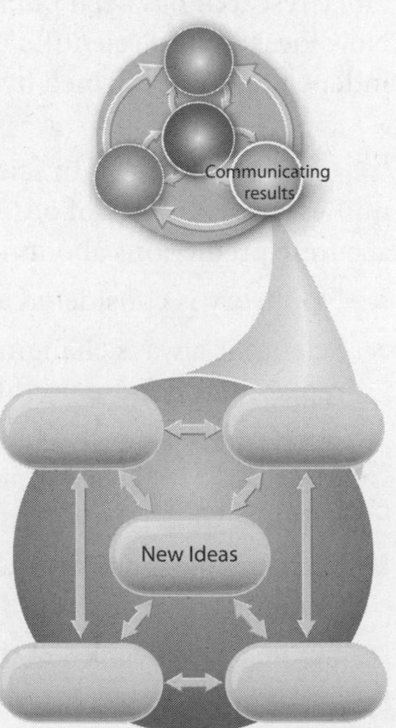


Adapted from *Understanding Science*, UC Berkeley, Museum of Paleontology

**5.** Of the four types of communication you added, identify the one that is critical to ensuring communication among the scientific community.

______________________________

## Scientific Theories

**6.** A typical dictionary will have different definitions for the word *theory*. It will include a definition that describes how scientists use the term, but it will also define *theory* as speculation, or an assumption, or a belief. Are these common definitions of *theory* synonyms (words similar in meaning) or antonyms (words opposite in meaning) to the definition of a scientific theory? Explain your thinking.

______________________________________________

______________________________________________

______________________________________________

______________________________________________

*For Questions 7–11, identify whether each statement is a hypothesis or a theory. For a hypothesis, write an "H" on the line. For a theory, write a "T."*

______ **7.** The rate that grass grows is related to the amount of light it receives.

______ **8.** All life is related and descended from a common ancestor.

______ **9.** The universe began about 15 billion years ago.

______ **10.** New tennis balls bounce higher than old tennis balls.

______ **11.** Caffeine raises blood pressure.

## Science and Society

**12.** How can bias affect the application of science in society? What role does a good understanding of science play in this phenomenon?

______________________________________________

______________________________________________

______________________________________________

______________________________________________

### Apply the Big idea

**13.** What is it about science, as a way of knowing, that makes it self-correcting?

______________________________________________

______________________________________________

______________________________________________

______________________________________________

# 1.3 Studying Life

## Lesson Objectives

- List the characteristics of living things.
- Identify the central themes of biology.
- Explain how life can be studied at different levels.
- Discuss the importance of a universal system of measurement.

## Lesson Summary

**Characteristics of Living Things** **Biology** is the study of life. Living things share these characteristics: They are made of cells and have a universal genetic code; they obtain and use materials and energy to grow and develop; they reproduce; they respond to signals in their environment (**stimuli**) and maintain a stable internal environment; they change over time.

**Big Ideas in Biology** The study of biology revolves around several interlocking big ideas:

- **Cellular basis of life.** Living things are made of cells.
- **Information and heredity.** Living things are based on a universal genetic code written in a molecule called **DNA**.
- **Matter and energy.** Life requires matter that provides raw material, nutrients, and energy. The combination of chemical reactions through which an organism builds up or breaks down materials is called **metabolism**.
- **Growth, development, and reproduction.** All living things reproduce. In **sexual reproduction**, cells from two parents unite to form the first cell of a new organism. In **asexual reproduction**, a single organism produces offspring identical to itself. Organisms grow and develop as they mature.
- **Homeostasis**. Living things maintain a relatively stable internal environment.
- **Evolution.** Taken as a group, living things evolve, linked to a common origin.
- **Structure and function.** Each major group of organisms has evolved structures that make particular functions possible.
- **Unity and diversity of life.** All living things are fundamentally similar at the molecular level.
- **Interdependence in nature.** All forms of life on Earth are connected into a **biosphere**—a living planet.
- **Science as a way of knowing.** Science is not a list of facts but "a way of knowing."

**Fields of Biology** Biology includes many overlapping fields that use different tools to study life. These include biotechnology, global ecology, and molecular biology.

**Performing Biological Investigations** Most scientists use the metric system as a way to share quantitative data. They are trained in safe laboratory procedures. To remain safe when you are doing investigations, the most important rule is to follow your teacher's instructions.

# Characteristics of Living Things

**1.** Complete the graphic organizer to show the characteristics living things share.

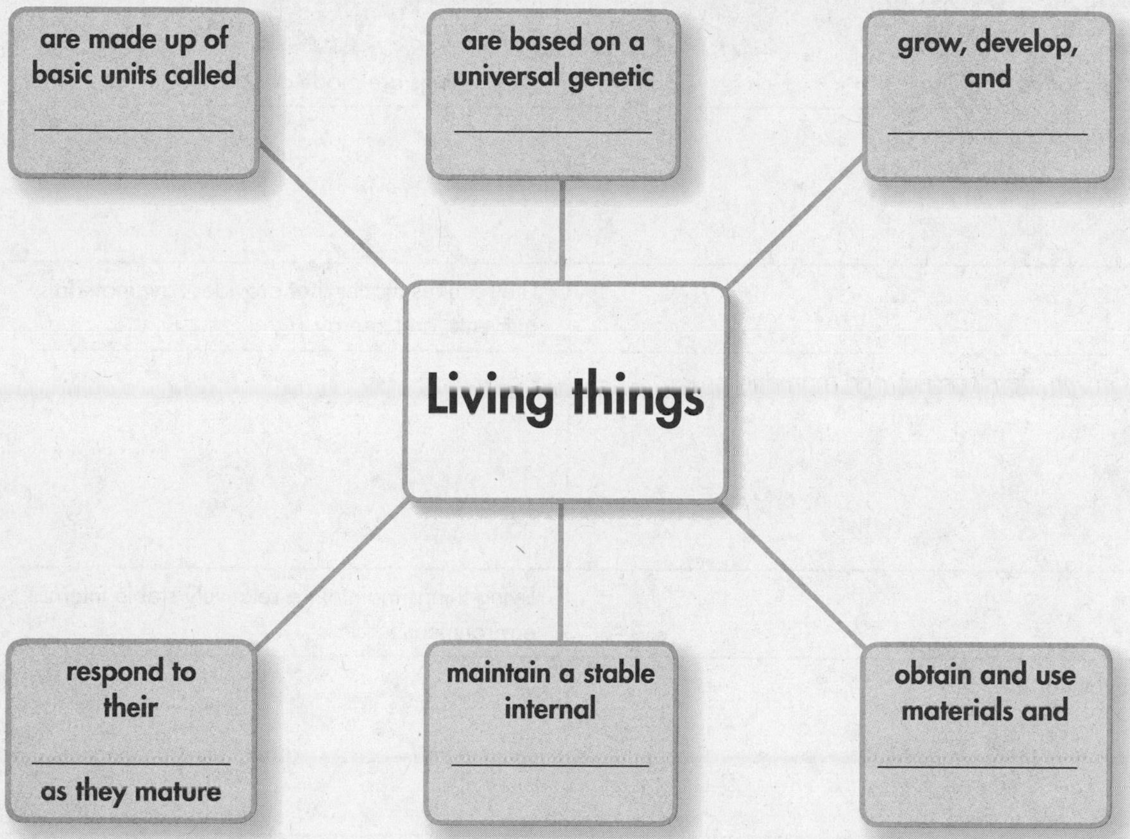


**2.** The genetic molecule common to all living things is ______.

**3.** The internal process of ______ enables living things to survive changing conditions.

**4.** Living things are capable of responding to different types of ______.

**5.** Living things have a long history of ______ change.

**6.** The continuation of life depends on both ______ and ______.

**7.** The combination of chemical reactions that make up an organism's ______ help to organize raw materials into living matter.

## Big Ideas in Biology

**8.** Complete the table of Big Ideas in Biology. The first row is filled in for you.

| Big Idea | Description |
|---|---|
| Cellular basis of life | Living things are made of cells. |
| Information and heredity | |
| | Life requires matter that provides raw materials, nutrients, and energy. |
| Growth, development, and reproduction | |
| | Living things maintain a relatively stable internal environment. |
| Evolution | |
| | Each major group of organisms has evolved structures that make particular functions possible. |
| | All living things are fundamentally similar at the molecular level. |
| | All forms of life on Earth are connected into a biosphere—a living planet. |
| Science as a way of knowing | |

**9.** Pick two of the big ideas from the chart and describe how the ideas interlock.

______________________________________________

______________________________________________

______________________________________________

______________________________________________

______________________________________________

 

## Fields of Biology

**10.** Biology is made up of many overlapping fields, each of which uses different tools to gather information about living things. Fill out the table below with information about two fields of biology—one that appeals to you, and one that does not. Include a description of each field and the tools scientists in the field use, as well as your impressions of each.

| Field of Biology | Description of Field | Why It Does or Does Not Appeal to Me |
|---|---|---|
| | | |
| | | |

## Performing Biological Investigations

**11.** Describe the system of measurement most scientists use when collecting data and doing experiments.

______________________________________________

______________________________________________

**12.** Why do scientists need a common system of measurement?

______________________________________________

______________________________________________

______________________________________________

**13.** What is the most important safety rule for you to follow in the laboratory?

______________________________________________

______________________________________________

### Apply the Big idea

**14.** Your teacher is doing a long-term experiment by having you and your classmates grow plants at home. You are testing the hypothesis that plant growth is affected by the amount of water a plant receives. All the data will be compiled in three weeks. Why isn't it a good idea to use the 8-ounce measuring cup from your kitchen or the 12-inch ruler you have on your desk?

______________________________________________

______________________________________________

______________________________________________

______________________________________________

# Chapter Vocabulary Review

*For Questions 1–8, complete each statement by writing the correct word.*

**1.** The act of noticing and describing events or processes in a careful, orderly way is called ____________.

**2.** The information gathered during an experiment is called ____________.

**3.** A(n) ____________ is a logical interpretation based on what scientists already know.

**4.** A(n) ____________ is a scientific explanation for a set of observations that can be tested in ways that support or reject it.

**5.** A(n) ____________ is a well-tested explanation that unifies a broad range of observations and hypotheses.

**6.** In ____________ reproduction, the new organism has a single parent.

**7.** A(n) ____________ is a signal to which an organism responds.

**8.** ____________ is an organized way of gathering and analyzing evidence about the natural world.

*For Questions 9–17, write the letter of the definition that best matches each term on the line provided.*

**Term**

_____ **9.** biology

_____ **10.** bias

_____ **11.** homeostasis

_____ **12.** metabolism

_____ **13.** DNA

_____ **14.** control group

_____ **15.** independent variable

_____ **16.** dependent variable

_____ **17.** biosphere

**Definition**

**A.** in an experiment, the group exposed to the same conditions as the experimental group except for one independent variable

**B.** the study of life

**C.** living things maintaining a relatively stable internal environment

**D.** a molecule containing the universal genetic code

**E.** a point of view that is personal rather than scientific

**F.** a living planet

**G.** the combination of chemical reactions through which an organism builds up or breaks down materials

**H.** in an experiment, the variable that is manipulated

**I.** in an experiment, the responding variable

 

Name ______ Class ____ Date ______

HEIGHT BY PRESCRIPTION

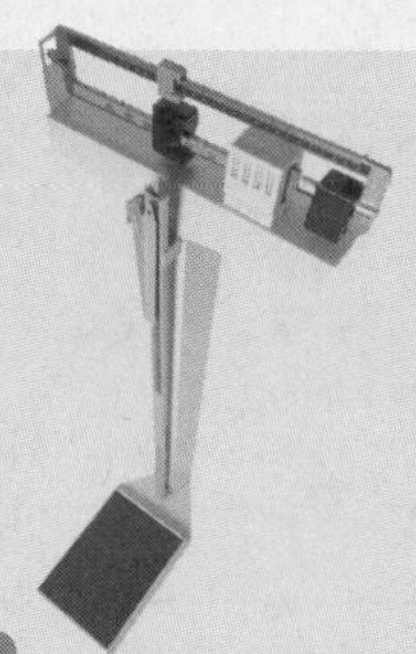

In the Chapter Mystery, you read about parents who had their healthy son injected with HGH hormones in the hope the treatment would increase his height. You also read that there is no evidence that treatment will make a child grow taller.

21st Century Learning

## Should Pharmaceuticals Be Advertised on Television?

Today, medical consumers often make the final decision about their or their child's treatment. It was not always like that. Not that long ago, patients were far more accepting of treatments prescribed by their doctor. They listened to the doctor's advice and did not demand a particular treatment. Why have the roles of doctor and patient changed today? One reason has to do with pharmaceutical advertising on television and in magazines. Drug ads are aimed at consumers, not doctors. Is it a good idea to advertise prescription drugs on television? Two viewpoints are presented below.

### Want some fries with that?

By: The Opinionator

I was watching TV last night, and I counted 14 ads for drugs. That's right, 14! I think things have gotten a bit out of hand. I mean, I'm all in favor of informed consumers, but I think this goes far beyond that.

I did some research this morning. Turns out that of all the people who go to their doctor and say, "Please write me a prescription for Drug X," 80% of them get it! Apparently, the doctor is just following the patients' orders.

Here's the thing. All drugs, all medicines, can be dangerous under certain circumstances. Doctors know if a patient should be taking a particular drug or not, and how much the patient should take. Doctors, not patients, should be making the decisions about medical treatments and what drug a patient should take.

### Responses to "Want some fries with that?"

**Posted at 9:17 by Dragonfly**

Believe it or not, this humble blogger still reads newspapers. I read an OpEd piece in the paper this morning that was all about how dangerous TV ads for drugs are. Here's a link to it. I couldn't find one point in the OpEd that I agreed with. What's wrong with letting people know what's out there? Nothing. Doctors are still the gatekeepers. They still have to write the prescription. If a drug is dangerous for people who have kidney problems, and you have kidney problems, your doctor won't write the prescription. But you probably wouldn't ask for it because you heard that little voice at the end of the ad say, "Do not take Drug X if you have kidney problems." Doctors can't possibly keep up with all the medical journals and stuff they get. TV advertising lets doctors know about new medications, too. So when it comes to drug ads, I say bring 'em on.

*Continued on next page* ▶

## 21st Century Themes Science and Civic Literacy

*Answer the following questions.*

**1.** What is the main point made by the first blogger?

______________________________________________

______________________________________________

**2.** How does the second blogger address the first blogger's point of view?

______________________________________________

______________________________________________

**3.** What argument does second blogger use to support his or her viewpoint?

______________________________________________

**4.** Which blogger do you agree with? Give reasons for your answer.

______________________________________________

______________________________________________

______________________________________________

______________________________________________

**5.** More than 200 medical school teachers, as well as 39 medical and senior citizens' groups, have supported an end to all medical advertising aimed at consumers. They want to ban these ads on television, on the radio, in newspapers and magazines, and online. Does this change the opinion you expressed in the previous answer? Why or why not?

______________________________________________

______________________________________________

______________________________________________

______________________________________________

## 21st Century Skills Evaluating Sources of Information

The skills used in this activity include **social responsibility, critical thinking and systems thinking, information and media literacy,** and **communication skills.**

Use Internet resources to find additional arguments in favor of and against advertising pharmaceuticals to consumers. "DTCA" (which stands for "direct to consumer advertising") might be a helpful keyword to use in your search. Make two lists, one containing arguments that support DTCA for drugs and one containing reasons for opposing drug DTCA. Then, for each source, evaluate the accuracy of the Web site and the usefulness of the information. HINT: Sites with URLs that end in ".gov" or ".edu" are usually fairly reliable. Sites put up by organizations or individuals who have a financial interest in the issue may be biased.

 

# 2 The Chemistry of Life

**Big idea** **Matter and Energy**

**Q:** What are the basic chemical principles that affect living things?

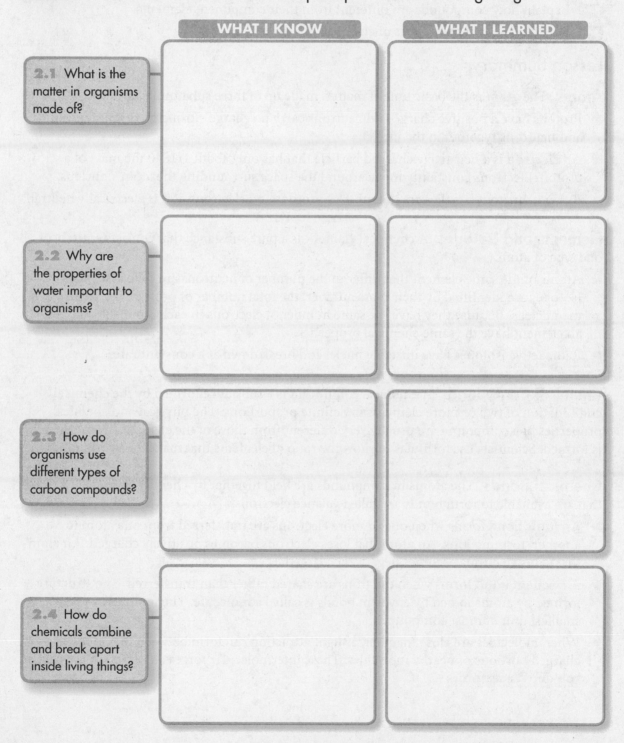

| | WHAT I KNOW | WHAT I LEARNED |
|---|---|---|
| **2.1** What is the matter in organisms made of? | | |
| **2.2** Why are the properties of water important to organisms? | | |
| **2.3** How do organisms use different types of carbon compounds? | | |
| **2.4** How do chemicals combine and break apart inside living things? | | |

# 2.1 The Nature of Matter

## Lesson Objectives

- Identify the three subatomic particles found in atoms.
- Explain how all of the isotopes of an element are similar and how they are different.
- Explain how compounds are different from their component elements.
- Describe the two main types of chemical bonds.

## Lesson Summary

**Atoms** The **atom** is the basic unit of matter, made up of three subatomic particles.

- Protons have a positive charge and neutrons carry no charge. Strong forces bind protons and neutrons together in the **nucleus**.
- An **electron** is a negatively charged particle that has only about 1/1840 the mass of a proton. Electrons constantly move around the space surrounding the atom's nucleus.
- Because an atom has the same number of protons and electrons, if it is electrically neutral.

**Elements and Isotopes** A chemical **element** is a pure substance that consists entirely of one type of atom.

- Atoms of the same element that differ in the number of neutrons are called **isotopes**. Isotopes are identified by their mass number, the total number of protons and neutrons in the nucleus. Because they have the same number of electrons in each atom, all isotopes of an element have the same chemical properties.
- Radioactive isotopes have unstable nuclei and break down at a constant rate.

**Chemical Compounds** A chemical **compound** is a substance formed by the chemical combination of two or more elements in definite proportions. The physical and chemical properties of a compound are usually very different from those of the elements from which it is formed. Scientists use formulas to show the ratio of elements that make up a compound.

**Chemical Bonds** The atoms in compounds are held together by chemical bonds. Electrons that are available to form bonds are called valence electrons.

- An **ionic bond** forms when one or more electrons are transferred from one atom to another, forming **ions**. An atom that loses electrons becomes positively charged. An atom that gains electrons becomes negatively charged.
- A **covalent bond** forms when electrons are shared rather than transferred. The structure formed by atoms joined by covalent bonds is called a **molecule**. The molecule is the smallest unit of most compounds.
- When molecules are close together, a slight attraction can form between the oppositely charged portions of nearby molecules. These intermolecular forces of attraction are called **van der Waals forces**.

 

Name ______________________ Class ______ Date ______

# Atoms

**1.** THINK VISUALLY The diagram shows a model of a carbon atom, with an atomic number of 6. Complete the diagram by drawing in the rest of the atomic particles, including their charges. Label all particles and the nucleus.

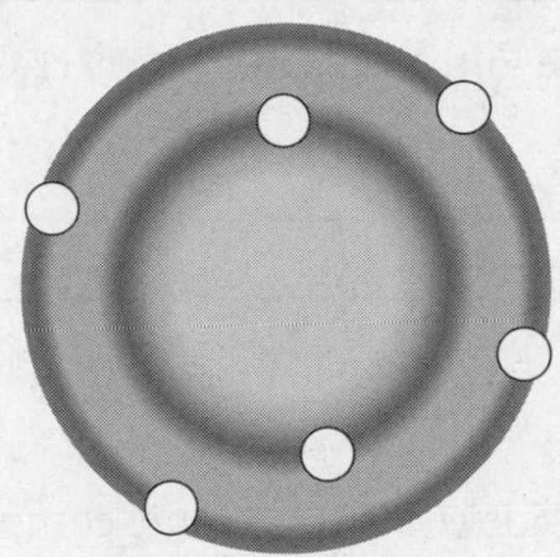

# Elements and Isotopes

**2.** THINK VISUALLY The diagrams show models of carbon isotopes. Complete the diagrams by drawing in the rest of the atomic particles, including their charges.

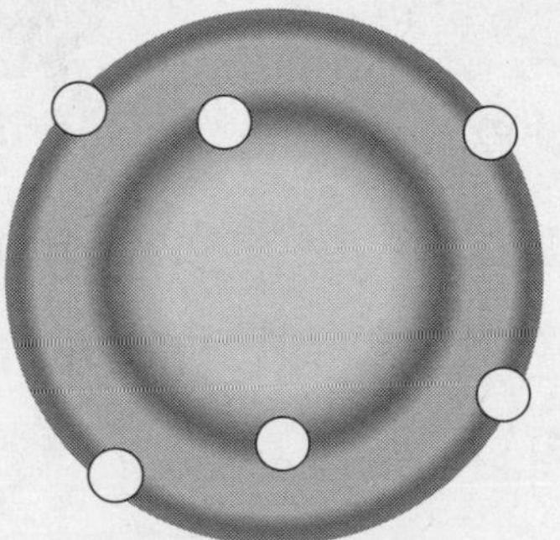

**Nonradioactive carbon-13**

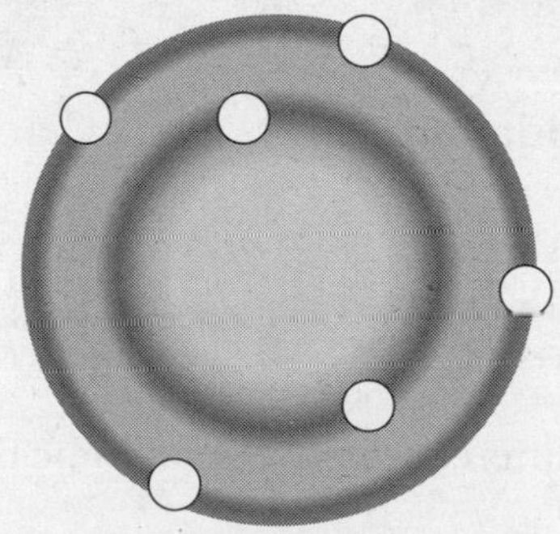

**Radioactive carbon-14**

*Use your completed diagrams to answer Questions 3–4.*

**3.** Identify two differences between carbon-12 and carbon-14.

______________________________________________

______________________________________________

**4.** Identify two ways in which carbon-12, carbon-13, and carbon-14 are alike.

______________________________________________

______________________________________________

*For Questions 5–7, complete each statement by writing the correct word or words.*

**5.** A chemical element is a pure substance that consists entirely of one type of ______________.

**6.** Atoms of the same element that differ in the number of neutrons they contain are called ______________.

**7.** An atom is made up of protons, neutrons, and ______________.

Name ______________________ Class _____ Date _________

## Chemical Compounds

**8.** What is a chemical compound?

______________________________________________

______________________________________________

**9.** What do the formulas for table salt, NaCl, and water, $H_2O$, indicate about these compounds?

______________________________________________

______________________________________________

## Chemical Bonds

**10.** Sea salt contains calcium chloride ($CaCl_2$), an ionic compound similar to table salt. One atom of calcium (atomic number 20) bonds to two atoms of chlorine (atomic number 17). Fill in the number of protons and electrons in each ion.

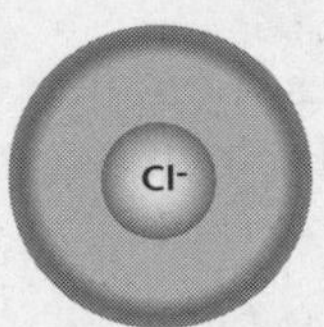


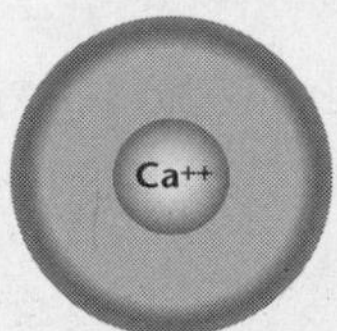


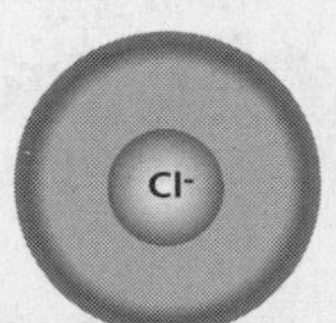


| **Chloride ion** | **Calcium ion** | **Chloride ion** |
|---|---|---|
| Protons _____ | Protons _____ | Protons _____ |
| Electrons _____ | Electrons _____ | Electrons _____ |

**11.** What is the difference between an ionic bond and a covalent bond?

______________________________________________

______________________________________________

**Apply the Big idea**

**12.** How are chemical bonds important in metabolism?

______________________________________________

______________________________________________

______________________________________________

 

# 2.2 Properties of Water

## Lesson Objectives

- Discuss the unique properties of water.
- Differentiate between solutions and suspensions.
- Explain what acidic solutions and basic solutions are.

## Lesson Summary

**The Water Molecule** Water molecules ($H_2O$) are polar because of an uneven distribution of electrons, creating a slight negative (–) charge in the oxygen atom and a slight positive (+) charge in each hydrogen atom. The attraction between a hydrogen atom of one water molecule and the oxygen atom of another water molecule is called a **hydrogen bond**.

- **Cohesion** is an attraction between molecules of the same substance. It causes water molecules to be drawn together, producing surface tension.
- **Adhesion** is an attraction between molecules of different substances. It causes capillary action, an effect that causes water to rise in a narrow tube against the force of gravity.

**Solutions and Suspensions** A **mixture** is a material composed of two or more elements or compounds that are physically mixed together but not chemically combined. A **solution** is a mixture in which all the components are evenly spread out: the substance dissolved is the **solute**; the substance that causes the dissolving is the **solvent**. Mixtures of water and undissolved materials are **suspensions**.

**Acids, Bases, and pH** A water molecule ($H_2O$) can split apart to form a hydrogen ion ($H^+$) and a hydroxide ion ($OH^-$).

- The **pH scale** measures the concentration of hydrogen ions in a solution. The scale ranges from 0 to 14. Pure water has a pH of 7.
- An **acid** is any compound that forms $H^+$ ions in solution. Acidic solutions have pH values below 7. A **base** is a compound that forms $OH^-$ ions in solution. Basic, or alkaline, solutions have pH values above 7.
- **Buffers** are weak acids or bases that can react with strong acids or bases to prevent sudden changes in pH.

## The Water Molecule

*For Questions 1–4, write True or False on the line provided.*

______ **1.** Water is a polar molecule.

______ **2.** Hydrogen bonds are an example of adhesion.

______ **3.** Covalent bonds give water a low heat capacity.

______ **4.** A hydrogen bond is stronger than a covalent bond.

Name ______________________ Class ______ Date ______

## Solutions and Suspensions

**5.** Complete the table.

| Substance | Definition | Example(s) |
|---|---|---|
| | Physical combination of two or more substances | Cinnamon sugar |
| Solute | | Salt in saltwater |
| | | |
| | Mixture of water and nondissolved substance | Blood |
| Solution | | |

## Acids, Bases, and pH

**6.** What makes pure water neutral?

______________________

______________________

**7.** What does the pH scale measure?

______________________

**8.** On the pH scale, indicate which direction is increasingly acidic and which is increasingly basic.

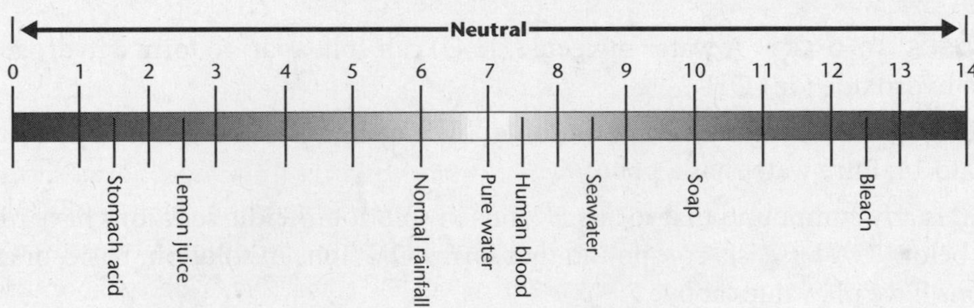


**9.** Identify two solutions that have more $H^+$ ions than $OH^-$ ions.

______________________

**10.** Identify two solutions that have more $OH^-$ ions than $H^+$ ions.

______________________

**11.** How would you buffer a solution that has a pH of 12?

______________________

**Apply the Big idea**

**12.** Why are buffers important to living things?

______________________

______________________

# 2.3 Carbon Compounds

## Lesson Objectives

- Describe the unique qualities of carbon.
- Describe the structures and functions of each of the four groups of macromolecules.

## Lesson Summary

**The Chemistry of Carbon** Organic chemistry is the study of compounds with bonds between carbon atoms. Carbon atoms have four valence electrons, allowing them to form strong covalent bonds with many other elements, including hydrogen, oxygen, phosphorus, sulfur, and nitrogen. Living organisms are made up of molecules made of carbon and these other elements.

- One carbon atom can bond to another to form chains and rings.
- Carbon can form millions of different large and complex structures.

**Macromolecules** Many of the carbon molecules in living things are so large they are called macromolecules. Macromolecules form by polymerization, in which smaller units called **monomers** join together to form **polymers**. Biochemists sort the macromolecules in living things into groups based on their chemical composition.

- **Carbohydrates** (starches and sugars) are composed of carbon, hydrogen, and oxygen. Carbohydrates are the main energy source for living things. Plants and some animals also use carbohydrates for structural purposes. Molecules with one sugar monomer are **monosaccharides**. A disaccharide is made of two monosaccharides.
- **Lipids** (fats, oils, and waxes) are made mostly of carbon and hydrogen atoms. Lipids can be used to store energy and form parts of biological membranes and waterproof coverings. Steroids manufactured by the body are lipids as well.
- **Nucleic acids** contain hydrogen, oxygen, nitrogen, carbon, and phosphorus. They are polymers of **nucleotides**. A nucleotide has three parts: a 5-carbon sugar, a phosphate ($-PO_4$) group, and a nitrogenous base. Nucleic acids store and transmit hereditary (genetic) information. There are two kinds of nucleic acids: DNA (deoxyribonucleic acid) and RNA (ribonucleic acid).
- **Proteins** are made up of nitrogen, carbon, hydrogen, and oxygen. Proteins are polymers of **amino acids**. An amino acid molecule has an amino group ($-NH_2$) on one end and a carboxyl group ($-COOH$) on the other end. Proteins control the rate of reactions, regulate cell processes, form cellular structures, carry substances into or out of cells, and help fight disease.
  - More than 20 different amino acids are found in nature. Any amino acid can bond with any other.
  - Covalent bonds called peptide bonds link amino acids together to form a polypeptide.
  - Amino acids are assembled into polypeptide chains according to instructions coded in DNA.

Name ______________________ Class ______ Date ______

## The Chemistry of Carbon

**1.** How many valence electrons does each carbon atom have?

_______________________________________________

**2.** What gives carbon the ability to form chains that are almost unlimited in length?

_______________________________________________

## Macromolecules

*For Questions 3–5, complete each statement by writing the correct word or words.*

**3.** Many of the molecules in living cells are so large they are called ____________.

**4.** ____________ is the process that forms large organic molecules.

**5.** When two or more ____________ join together, a polymer forms.

**6.** Create a table in which you compare the components and functions of the following macromolecules: carbohydrates, lipids, nucleic acids, and proteins.

**Apply the Big idea**

**7.** How did organic compounds get their name? How is the word related to its meaning?

_______________________________________________

_______________________________________________

_______________________________________________

Name ______________________ Class ______ Date ______

# 2.4 Chemical Reactions and Enzymes

## Lesson Objectives

- Explain how chemical reactions affect chemical bonds.
- Describe how energy changes affect how easily a chemical reaction will occur.
- Explain why enzymes are important to living things.

## Lesson Summary

**Chemical Reactions** Everything that happens in an organism is based on chemical reactions. A **chemical reaction** is a process that changes one set of chemicals into another set of chemicals.

- The elements or compounds that enter into the reaction are the **reactants**.
- The elements or compounds produced by the reaction are the **products**.
- Chemical reactions involve changes in the chemical bonds that join atoms in compounds.

**Energy in Reactions** Some chemical reactions release energy; others absorb energy.

- Chemical reactions that release energy often occur on their own.
- Chemical reactions that absorb energy require a source of energy. The energy needed to get a reaction started is called the **activation energy**.

**Enzymes** An **enzyme** is a protein that acts as biological catalyst. A **catalyst** is a substance that speeds up the rate of a chemical reaction. Catalysts work by lowering a reaction's activation energy.

- In an enzyme-catalyzed reaction, the reactants are known as **substrates**. Substrates bind to a part of an enzyme called the active site and remain bound to the enzyme until the reaction is complete, when the products are released.
- Temperature, pH, and regulatory molecules can affect the activity of enzymes.

# Chemical Reactions

**1.** What is a chemical reaction?

_______________________________________________

**2.** Complete the table about chemicals in a chemical reaction.

| Chemicals in a Chemical Reaction | |
|---|---|
| **Chemicals** | **Definition** |
| Reactants | |
| Products | |

Name ______ Class ______ Date ______

## Energy in Reactions

3. THINK VISUALLY The graphs below show the amount of energy present during two chemical reactions. One of the reactions is an energy-absorbing reaction, the other is an energy-releasing reaction. Label the type of reaction for each, label the energy level for the reactants and products, then draw an arrow on each to show the energy of activation.

Energy →
Course of Reaction →

Energy →
Course of Reaction →

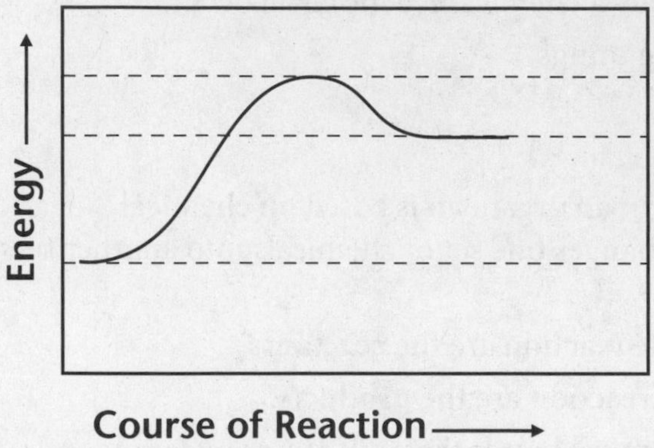

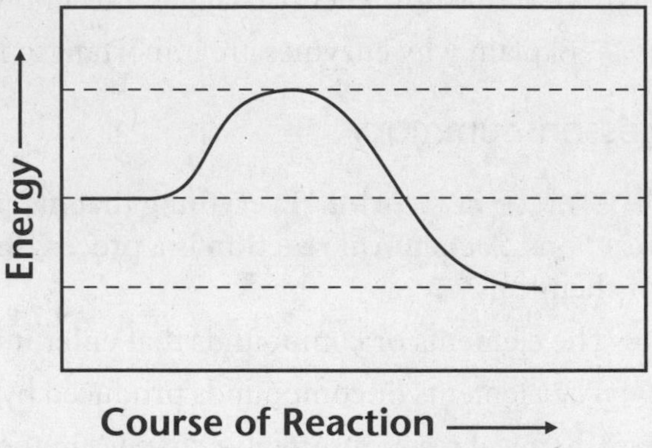

Type of reaction: ______ Type of reaction: ______

4. What is released or absorbed whenever chemical bonds form or are broken?

______

5. What is the energy of activation?

______

6. Of the two reactions shown, which one is more likely to start spontaneously and why?

______

______

## Enzymes

7. How does the addition of a catalyst affect the energy of activation of a chemical reaction?

______

______

8. What type of catalysts affect biochemical reactions?

______

9. What makes proteins the ideal types of compounds to act as enzymes?

______

______

______

*Use the diagram to answer Questions 10–11.*

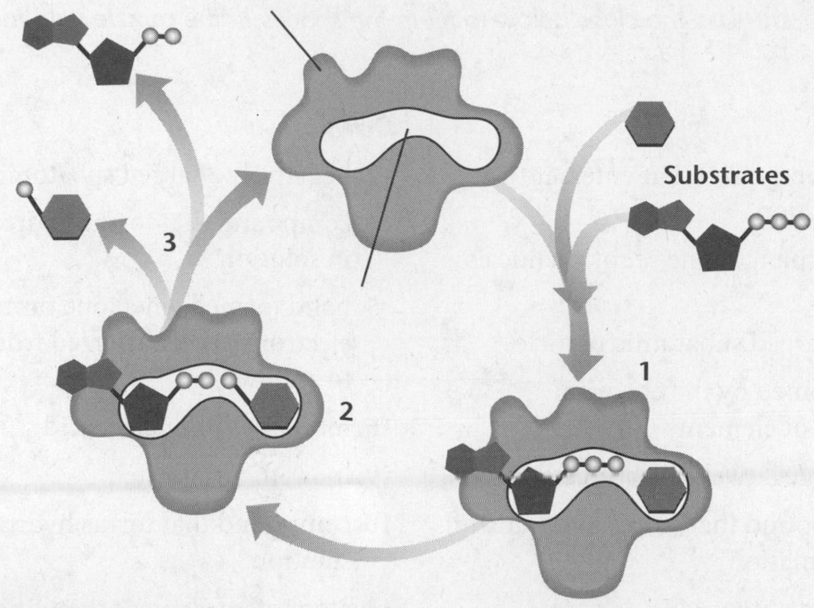


10. **THINK VISUALLY** Label the enzyme, the active site, and the products in the diagram.

11. Write what is happening at each numbered part of the diagram.

(1) ____________________

(2) ____________________

(3) ____________________

*For Questions 12–13, refer to the Visual Analogy comparing the action of enzymes to a lock and key.*

12. **VISUAL ANALOGY** How is a substrate and its enzyme like a lock and its key?

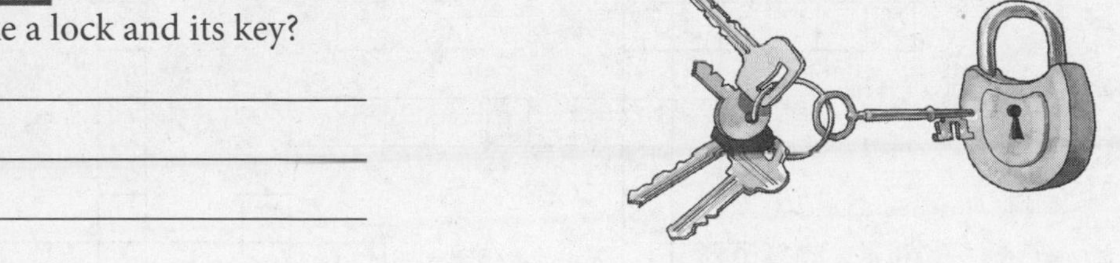

____________________

____________________

____________________

____________________

13. What is being unlocked in this analogy?

____________________

## Apply the Big idea

14. In terms of an organism and how it interacts with its environment, what is the benefit of having controls on the chemical reactions that take place in its body?

____________________

____________________

____________________

 

# Chapter Vocabulary Review

**Crossword Puzzle** *Use the clues below to fill in the spaces in the puzzle with the correct words.*

### Across

**1.** element or compound that enters into a chemical reaction

**4.** process that changes one set of chemicals into another

**7.** positively charged subatomic particle

**8.** substance formed by the chemical combination of elements

**11.** positively or negatively charged atom

**12.** carbon compound that stores and transmits genetic information

**14.** the center of an atom

**16.** bond formed when electrons are shared between atoms

**17.** macromolecule formed when monomers join together

### Down

**2.** negatively charged subatomic particle

**3.** compound that forms hydroxide ions in solution

**5.** bond formed when one or more electrons are transferred from one atom to another

**6.** monomer of nucleic acid

**9.** monomer of protein

**10.** compound that forms hydrogen ions in solution

**13.** atom of an element that differs in the number of neutrons compared with other atoms of the same element

**15.** basic unit of matter

CHAPTER MYSTERY

THE GHOSTLY FISH

In the Chapter Mystery, you learned about a fish whose body produces an "antifreeze" protein. Several other species of fish, as well as species of insects and plants, produce similar proteins. The proteins' structure and chemical makeup are different, but all function as an effective "antifreeze."

21st Century Learning

## Marketing a Natural "Antifreeze"

A protein able to prevent organic matter from freezing could have enormous commercial value. As with other inventions and innovations, a company that develops such a protein—or devises a unique method for producing such a protein—should have the right to patent it. A patent is a government order that grants an inventor exclusive rights to the use of the invention. In other words, a patent prevents anyone other than the inventor from profiting from the invention. A patent application may be hundreds of pages long. That's why every application must start with a brief description of the invention. This brief description is called an abstract. An abstract that might be written for a patent application for an antifreeze production process is shown below.

### Abstract

**Description of Invention:** A method for producing a protein that lowers the freezing temperature of water. Such proteins are not unusual in nature. Called "antifreeze proteins" (AFPs) or "Ice Structuring Proteins" (ISPs), they are produced in certain species of fish, plants, and insects. One AFP, produced in nature by fish but commercially by genetically modified yeast, is already being used in frozen products such as ice cream and sherbet.

The method described herein produces a type of insect-derived AFP. Fish-derived AFPs can reduce the freezing point of water by as much as 1.5° Celsius. This insect-derived AFP reduces the freezing point of water to –10° C. The process uses genetically modified algae to produce a threonine- and cysteine-rich 9 kDa protein that is produced naturally by the spruce budworm (*Choristoneura fumiferana*).

Continued on next page ▶

 

## 21st Century Themes Science and Economic Literacy

**1.** What is the inventor trying to patent?

**2.** What commercial application does AFP already have? How is this AFP produced commercially?

**3.** Why do you think the patent applicant wants to use insect-derived AFP rather than fish-derived AFP?

**4.** Why would this process need algae?

**5.** Why did the patent applicant research the spruce budworm?

## 21st Century Skills AFP Ad Campaign

The skills used in this activity include **information and media literacy, critical thinking and systems thinking,** and **creativity and intellectual curiosity.**

Work with a partner to use Internet or library resources to research the effects of extreme cold on the human body. Think about how these reactions would change if the body contained the AFP described in the patent application. What safety concerns would have to be addressed if a person had to ingest an AFP? What are the commercial applications for an AFP treatment that is safe for humans to ingest? Who would want to use it? Choose one type or group of potential users.

*Create an ad campaign aimed specifically at that group of people and designed to convince them to get the AFP treatment.*

 

Name ______________________ Class ______ Date ______

# 3 The Biosphere

## Matter of Energy, Interdependence in Nature

**Q:** How do living and nonliving parts of the Earth interact and affect the survival of organisms?

| | WHAT I KNOW | WHAT I LEARNED |
| --- | --- | --- |
| **3.1** How do we study life? | | |
| **3.2** How do different organisms get the energy they need to survive? | | |
| **3.3** How does energy move through an ecosystem? | | |
| **3.4** Why is the cycling of matter important to life on Earth? | | |

 

# 3.1 What Is Ecology?

## Lesson Objectives

- Describe the study of ecology.
- Explain how biotic and abiotic factors influence an ecosystem.
- Describe the methods used to study ecology.

## Lesson Summary

**Studying Our Living Planet** **Ecology** is the scientific study of interactions among organisms and between organisms and their environment.

- Earth's organisms live in the **biosphere**. The biosphere consists of the parts of the planet in which all life exists.
- Ecologists may study different levels of ecological organization:
  - Individual organism
  - An assemblage of individuals that belong to the same species and live in the same area is called a **population**.
  - An assemblage of different populations that live together in an area is referred to as a **community**.
  - An **ecosystem** includes all the organisms that live in a particular place, together with their physical environment.
  - A group of ecosystems that have similar climates and organisms is called a **biome**.

**Biotic and Abiotic Factors** Ecosystems include biotic and abiotic factors.

- A **biotic factor** is any living part of an environment.
- An **abiotic factor** is any nonliving part of an environment.

**Ecological Methods** Ecologists use three basic methods of research: observation, experimentation, and modeling:

- Observation often leads to questions and hypotheses.
- Experiments can be used to test hypotheses.
- Modeling helps ecologists understand complex processes.

## Studying Our Living Planet

**1.** What is ecology?

______________________________________________

______________________________________________

______________________________________________

**2.** What does the biosphere contain?

______________________________________________

______________________________________________

**3.** How are human economics and ecology linked?

_______________________________________________

_______________________________________________

_______________________________________________

_______________________________________________

*Use the diagram to answer Questions 4–5.*

**4.** Label each level of organization on the diagram.

**5.** Explain the relationship between ecosystems and biomes.

_______________________________________________

_______________________________________________

_______________________________________________

 

Name ______________________________ Class ______ Date ________

## Biotic and Abiotic Factors

**6.** Use the terms in the box to fill in the Venn diagram. List parts of the environment that consist of biotic factors, abiotic factors, and some components that are a mixture of both.

| | | |
|---|---|---|
| **air** | **heat** | **precipitation** |
| **animals** | **mushrooms** | **soil** |
| **bacteria** | **plants** | **sunlight** |

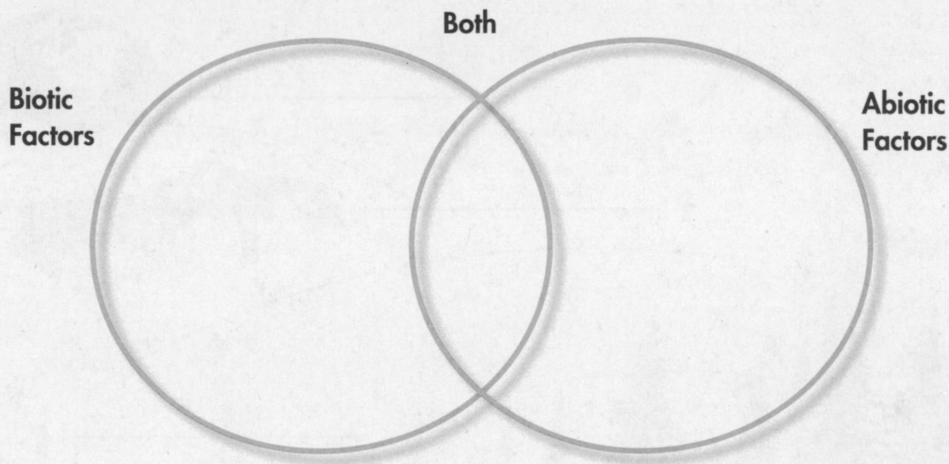


## Ecological Methods

**7.** Why might an ecologist set up an artificial environment in a laboratory?

______________________________________________________________

______________________________________________________________

**8.** Why are many ecological phenomena difficult to study?

______________________________________________________________

______________________________________________________________

**9.** Why do ecologists make models?

______________________________________________________________

______________________________________________________________

### Apply the Big idea

**10.** What makes a planet living? Explain your answer by comparing Earth with Mars.

______________________________________________________________

______________________________________________________________

______________________________________________________________

______________________________________________________________

______________________________________________________________

# 3.2 Energy, Producers, and Consumers

## Lesson Objectives

- Define primary producers.
- Describe how consumers obtain energy and nutrients.

## Lesson Summary

**Primary Producers** Sunlight is the main energy source for life on Earth. Organisms that can capture energy from sunlight or chemicals and use that energy to produce food are called **autotrophs**, or **primary producers**.

- The process in which autotrophs capture light energy and use it to convert carbon dioxide and water into oxygen and sugars is called **photosynthesis**.
- The process in which autotrophs use chemical energy to produce carbohydrates is called **chemosynthesis**.

**Consumers** Organisms that rely on other organisms for their energy and food are called **heterotrophs**. Heterotrophs are also referred to as consumers. There are many different types of heterotrophs:

- **Herbivores**, such as cows, obtain energy by eating only plants.
- **Carnivores**, such as snakes, eat only animals.
- **Omnivores**, such as humans, eat both plants and animals.
- **Detritivores**, such as earthworms, feed on dead matter.
- **Decomposers**, such as fungi, break down organic matter.
- **Scavengers**, such as vultures, consume the carcasses of other animals.

# Primary Producers

1. What do autotrophs do during photosynthesis?

_______________________________________________

_______________________________________________

2. Can some organisms survive without energy from the sun? Explain your answer.

_______________________________________________

_______________________________________________

_______________________________________________

_______________________________________________

3. Can organisms create their own energy? Explain your answer. ______________

_______________________________________________

_______________________________________________

_______________________________________________

## Consumers

**4.** Complete the table about types of heterotrophs.

| Types of Heterotrophs | | |
|---|---|---|
| **Type** | **Definition** | **Examples** |
| Herbivore | | cows, rabbits |
| | Heterotroph that eats animals | |
| Omnivore | | humans, bears, pigs |
| Detritivore | | |
| Decomposer | | |
| | Heterotroph that consumes the carcasses of dead animals but does not typically kill them itself | |

**5.** What is a consumer?

______

**6.** How would you categorize a consumer that usually catches and eats prey, but also eats dead animal carcasses? ______

Apply the Big idea

**7.** What role do producers play in establishing Earth as a living planet? ______

______

______

______

______

______

______

# 3.3 Energy Flow in Ecosystems

## Lesson Objectives

Trace the flow of energy through living systems.

Identify the three types of ecological pyramids.

## Lesson Summary

**Food Chains and Food Webs** Energy flows through an ecosystem in one direction from primary producers to various consumers.

- A **food chain** is a series of steps in which organisms transfer energy by eating and being eaten. Producers, such as floating algae called **phytoplankton**, are at the base of every food chain.
- A **food web** is a network of all the food chains in an ecosystem. Food webs are very complex. Small disturbances to one population can affect all populations in a food web. Changes in populations of **zooplankton**, small marine animals that feed on algae, can affect all of the animals in the marine food web.

**Trophic Levels and Ecological Pyramids** Each step in a food chain or food web is called a **trophic level**. Producers make up the first trophic level. Consumers make up higher trophic levels. Each consumer depends on the trophic level below it for energy.

An **ecological pyramid** is a diagram that shows the relative amounts of energy or matter contained within each trophic level in a food chain or food web. Types of ecological pyramids are pyramids of energy, pyramids of biomass, and pyramids of numbers:

- Pyramids of energy show relative amounts of energy available at different trophic levels.
- Pyramids of **biomass** show the total amount of living tissue at each trophic level.
- A pyramid of numbers shows the relative numbers of organisms at different trophic levels.

# Food Chains and Food Webs

**1.** Complete the table about feeding relationships.

| Feeding Relationships | |
|---|---|
| **Relationship** | **Description** |
| Food Chain | |
| Food Web | |

 

*Use the food chain to answer Questions 2–4.*

**2.** Draw arrows between the organisms to show how energy moves through this food chain. Write *producer, herbivore,* or *carnivore* under each organism.

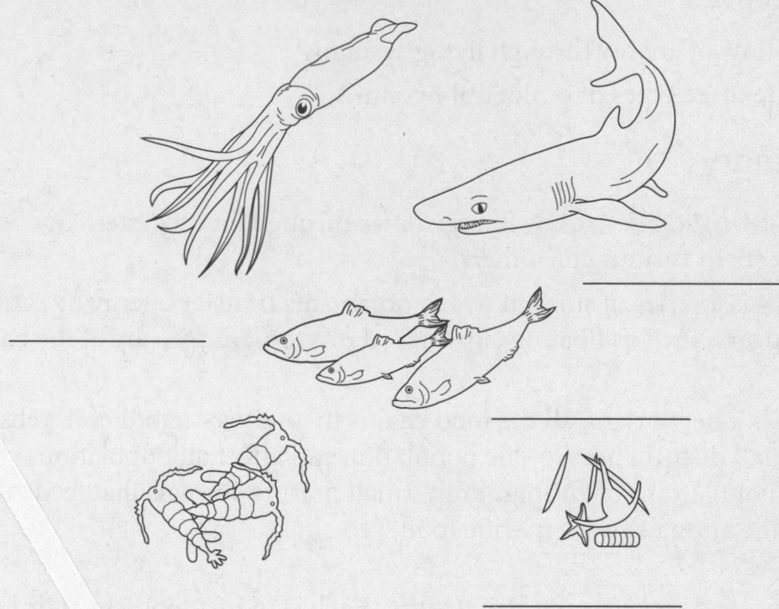

**3.** Explain how energy flows through this food chain. ______________________

**4.** What would happen to this food chain if a disturbance caused a serious decline in the shark population? ______________________

**5.** VISUAL ANALOGY What role does energy play in the diagram, and how is it represented? ______________________

Name ______________________ Class ______ Date ______

# Trophic Levels and Ecological Pyramids

*Write True or False on the line provided.*

______ **6.** Primary consumers always make up the first trophic level in a food web.

______ **7.** Ecological pyramids show the relative amount of energy or matter contained within each trophic level in a given food web.

______ **8.** On average, about 50 percent of the energy available within one trophic level is transferred to the next trophic level.

______ **9.** The more levels that exist between a producer and a given consumer, the larger the percentage of the original energy from producers is available to that consumer.

*Use the diagram to answer Questions 10–17.*

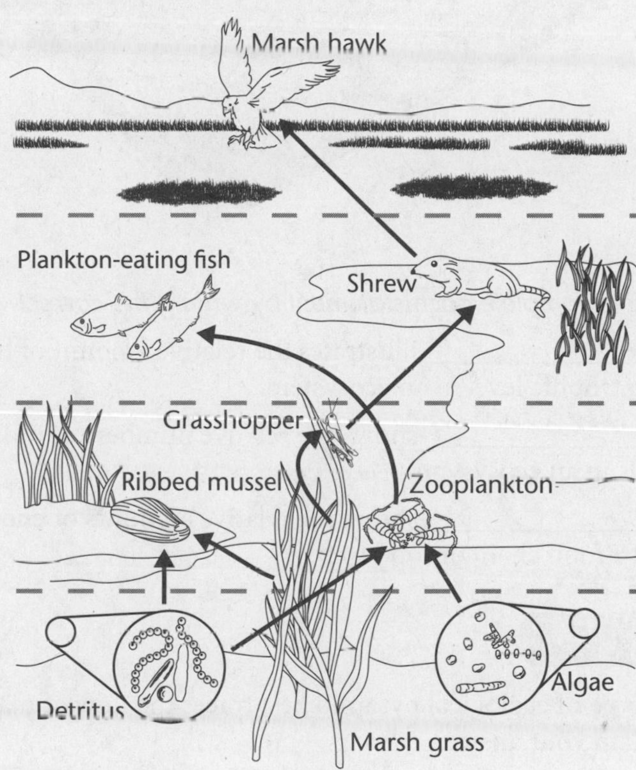


*Match the organism with its trophic level. A trophic level may be used more than once.*

**Organism**

______ **10.** algae

______ **11.** grasshopper

______ **12.** marsh grass

______ **13.** marsh hawk

______ **14.** plankton-eating fish

______ **15.** ribbed mussel

______ **16.** shrew

______ **17.** zooplankton

**Trophic Level**

**A.** primary producer

**B.** first-level consumer

**C.** second-level consumer

**D.** third-level consumer

 

**18.** Complete the energy pyramid by writing the source of the energy for the food web a[nd] how much energy is available to first-, second-, and third-level consumers.

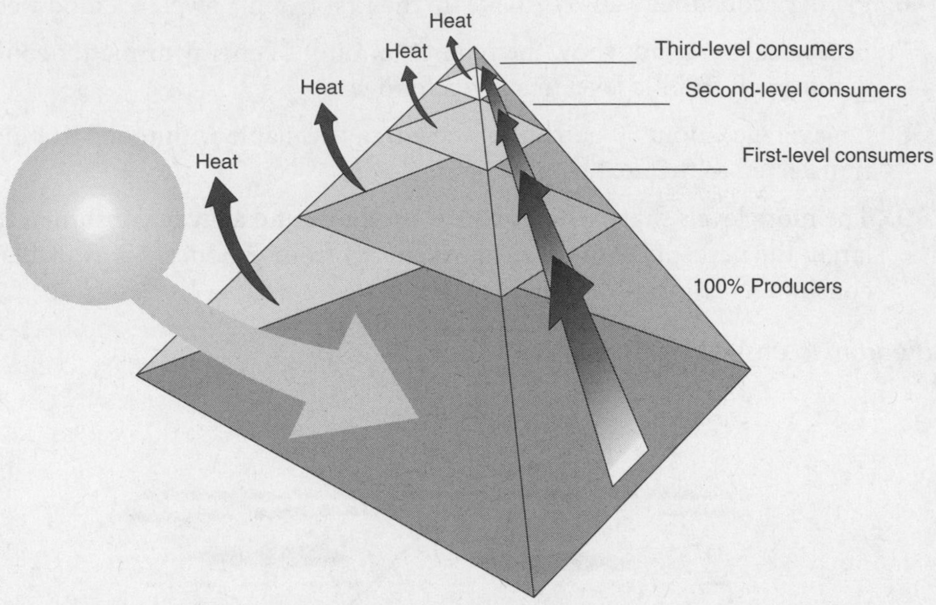


*For Questions 19–21, complete each statement by writing the correct word or words.*

**19.** A pyramid of ________________ illustrates the relative amount of living organic matter available at each trophic level in an ecosystem.

**20.** A pyramid of ________________ shows the relative numbers of individual organisms at the trophic levels in an ecosystem.

**21.** A pyramid of ________________ shows the relative amounts of energy available at the trophic levels of a food chain or food web.

## Apply the Big idea

**22.** Identify which type of ecological pyramid best traces the flow of matter through an ecosystem. Explain your answer.

______________________________________________________________________

______________________________________________________________________

______________________________________________________________________

______________________________________________________________________

______________________________________________________________________

______________________________________________________________________

Name ______________________________ Class _____ Date _________

# 3.4 Cycles [illegible] Matter

## Lesson Objectives

- Describe how matt[illegible] cycles among the living and nonliving parts of an ecosystem.
- Describe how wat[illegible] cycles through the biosphere.
- Explain why nutri[illegible]s are important in living systems.
- Describe how the [illegible]ailability of nutrients affects the productivity of ecosystems.

## Lesson Summary

**Recycling in the B[illegible]phere** Matter, unlike energy, is recycled within and between ecosystems. Elemen[illegible] pass from one organism to another and from one part of the biosphere to another through [illegible] **geochemical cycles**, which are closed loops powered by the flow of energy.

**The Water C[illegible]** Water moves between the ocean, the atmosphere, and land.

- Evapor[illegible] the process in which water changes from a liquid to a gas.
- T[illegible] is the process in which water evaporates from the leaves of plants.

**[illegible] Cycles** The chemical substances that an organism needs to survive are called **nutrients**. Like water, nutrients pass through organisms and the environment.

- **Carbon Cycle:** Carbon is a key ingredient of all organic compounds. Processes involved in the carbon cycle include photosynthesis and human activities such as burning.
- **Nitrogen Cycle:** Nitrogen is needed by all organisms to build proteins. Processes involved in the nitrogen cycle include nitrogen fixation and denitrification.
  - In **nitrogen fixation**, certain bacteria convert nitrogen gas into ammonia.
  - In **denitrification**, other soil bacteria convert nitrogen compounds called nitrates back into nitrogen gas.
- **Phosphorus Cycle:** Phosphorus is needed for molecules such as DNA and RNA. Most of the phosphorus in the biosphere is stored in rocks and ocean sediments. Stored phosphorus is gradually released into water and soil, where it is used by organisms.

**Nutrient Limitation** A nutrient that, in short supply, can limit the productivity of an ecosystem is called a **limiting nutrient**.

## Recycling in the Biosphere

*For Questions 1–3, write True if the statement is true. If the statement is false, change the underlined word or words to make the statement true.*

_______________ **1.** The four elements that make up over 95 percent of the body in most organisms are oxygen, <u>sulfur</u>, nitrogen, and hydrogen.

_______________ **2.** Matter moves through an ecosystem in <u>cycles</u>.

_______________ **3.** Chemical and physical processes include the formation of clouds and precipitation, <u>"burning" food</u>, and the flow of running water.

Name ______________________ Class ______ Date ________

4. **VISUAL ANALOGY** The illustration draws an analogy between the way energy drives matter to cycle in an ecosystem and the way water causes a waterwheel to turn. Give an example of another analogy that could be used to show the relationship between energy and the cycles of matter.

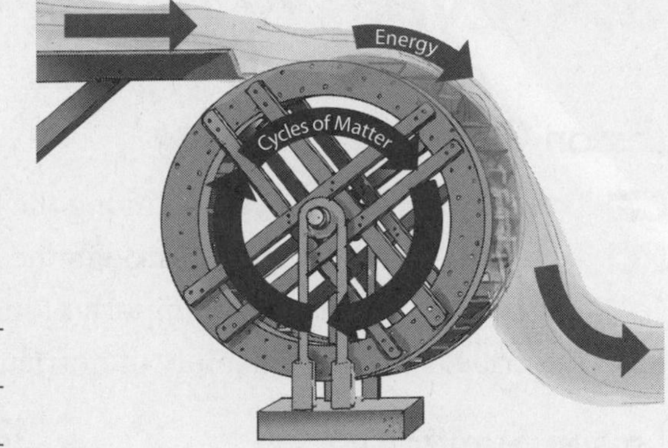


______________________________________________

______________________________________________

______________________________________________

5. Explain why Earth is considered a closed system.

______________________________________________

______________________________________________

6. How might building a new highway affect the cycles of matter?

______________________________________________

______________________________________________

______________________________________________

______________________________________________

## The Water Cycle

7. What role do plants play in the water cycle?

______________________________________________

______________________________________________

______________________________________________

8. **THINK VISUALLY** Draw a diagram explaining the water cycle. Label the processes involved as biological or physical/chemical.

 

# Nutrient Cycles

**9.** Complete the chart about the carbon cycle.

| Processes That Cause Carbon to Move into the Atmosphere | | Processes That Cause Carbon to Move out of the Atmosphere | |
|---|---|---|---|
| **Process** | **Description** | **Process** | **Description** |
| Respiration | | Photosynthesis | |
| | the release of $CO_2$ and other gases into the atmosphere through vents in Earth's crust | | |

*For Questions 10–12, write the letter of the correct answer on the line at the left.*

______ **10.** The carbon in coal, oil, and natural gas came from

**A.** the combustion of fossil fuels.

**B.** the remains of dead organisms.

**C.** carbon-fixing bacteria in swamp soil.

**D.** carbon dioxide dissolved in ocean water.

______ **11.** How does most of the carbon in an organism's body return to the environment after the organism dies?

**A.** Decomposers break the body down into simpler compounds.

**B.** Heat from the sun causes the carbon in the body to evaporate.

**C.** Geological processes cause the body to turn into a fossil fuel.

**D.** Rainwater dissolves the carbon in the body and carries it to the ocean.

______ **12.** Human processes mainly contribute to the

**A.** release of carbon dioxide into the atmosphere.

**B.** decrease of the total amount of carbon found on Earth.

**C.** depletion of carbon dioxide reserves in the atmosphere.

**D.** increase in the amount of carbon contained in rock materials.

 

Name ______________________ Class ______ Date ________

*Write True if the statement is true. If the statement is false, change the underlined word or words to make the statement true.*

______________ **13.** Nitrogen, in the form of ammonia, <u>nitrate</u>, and nitrite, is found in the soil.

______________ **14.** Nitrogen fixation is the process in which certain bacteria convert nitrogen gas into <u>nitrates</u>.

______________ **15.** <u>Denitrification</u> is the process by which some soil bacteria convert nitrates into nitrogen gas.

______________ **16.** All organisms require nitrogen to make amino acids, which in turn are used to build <u>carbohydrates</u>.

______________ **17.** Phosphate is released as <u>rocks and sediments</u> wear down.

______________ **18.** Plants absorb phosphate from the <u>soil</u> or from water.

______________ **19.** <u>Phosphorus</u> is the most abundant gas in the atmosphere.

______________ **20.** <u>Organic phosphate</u> is taken up by producers during photosynthesis and released by cellular respiration.

______________ **21.** <u>Phosphorus</u> forms part of the important life-sustaining molecules such as DNA and RNA.

______________ **22.** Plants absorb phosphorus from <u>the atmosphere</u> or water.

**23.** List and describe the biological steps in the nitrogen cycle.

______________________________________________

______________________________________________

______________________________________________

______________________________________________

______________________________________________

______________________________________________

**24.** What is atmospheric nitrogen fixation, and how does it affect organisms?

______________________________________________

______________________________________________

______________________________________________

**25.** How do humans add nitrogen to the biosphere?

______________________________________________

______________________________________________

**26.** Which parts of the phosphorus cycle are geological processes?

______________________________________________

______________________________________________

______________________________________________

 

# Nutrient Limitation

*Use the diagram of the interlocking nutrients to answer Question 27.*

**27.** VISUAL ANALOGY The visual analogy compares interlocking gears to the major nutrients—potassium, phosphorus, and nitrogen. What other "gears" would be affected if these gears stopped working together?

Micronutrients
Potassium
Phosphorus
Nitrogen

**28.** If a nutrient were in short supply in an ecosystem, how might it affect an organism?

**29.** When is a substance a limiting nutrient?

## Apply the Big idea

**30.** Compare and contrast the flow of energy through an environment with the flow of matter through that same environment.

# Chapter Vocabulary Review

*Match the term with its definition.*

| Term | Definition |
|---|---|
| _____ **1.** nutrient | **A.** all the organisms in one area and their physical environment |
| _____ **2.** chemosynthesis | **B.** a process in which producers use chemical energy to make carbohydrates |
| _____ **3.** consumer | **C.** an organism that feeds on other organisms |
| _____ **4.** ecosystem | **D.** a chemical substance that an organism needs to survive |
| _____ **5.** photosynthesis | **E.** an organism that uses chemical or light energy to produce its own food supply |
| _____ **6.** ecology | **F.** the study of the biosphere |
| _____ **7.** primary producer | **G.** the portion of Earth and its atmosphere that contains organisms |
| _____ **8.** biosphere | **H.** a process in which producers use light energy to make carbohydrates |

*For Questions 9–12, complete the analogies.*

**9.** omnivore : human :: carnivore : ______________

**10.** detritivore : earthworm :: herbivore : ______________

**11.** autotroph : heterotroph :: phytoplankton : ______________

**12.** biotic factor : elephant :: abiotic factor : ______________

**13.** What is the difference between a food chain and a food web?

______________________________________________________________

______________________________________________________________

______________________________________________________________

*Complete each statement by writing the correct word or words.*

**14.** There are several hundred squirrels living in an oak forest. The squirrels make up a(n) ______________.

**15.** Fungi and some kinds of bacteria are ______________ that obtain nutrients by chemically breaking down organic matter.

**16.** Ecologists measure ______________ in grams of organic matter per unit area.

**17.** In a process known as ______________, some types of soil bacteria obtain energy by converting nitrates into nitrogen gas.

 

Name ______________________________ Class ______ Date ________

CHAPTER
MYSTERY
CHANGES IN THE BAY
21st Century Learning


Rhode Island's Narragansett Bay is not the only ecosystem that suffers from changes in abiotic factors such as temperature. This is happening within many biomes and ecosystems around the world.

## Rising Temperatures in a Lake

The northwest coniferous forest is a small biome along the coast of the northwestern United States. It experiences seasonal variations in temperature and precipitation. Close to Seattle, Washington, is Lake Washington, which is a freshwater ecosystem in peril from decades of sewage dumping and rising water temperatures. The following is a brief summary of an environmental report on Lake Washington.

**ENVIRONMENTAL REPORT:** Lake Washington Sta

**PREPARED BY:** Environmental Sub-Com

**SUMMARY:** While it has been m years since sewage has been dumped into Lake W ton, problems still exist in this freshwater ecosystem. Th e's overall temperature has increased by 0.5°C in the past 4( ears. Its upper layer, which is 9 meters deep, has experience temperature increase of 1.25°C. These rising temperatures e negatively affecting the ecosystem's food chain. Zooplankt numbers are declining. These microscopic organisms eat a e, which are at the base of the food chain. Zooplankton also prey for salmon. Higher temperatures are generating re frequent algal blooms, which are starting to create eutrophic nditions in the lake. Eutrophication is a condition in which a dy of water is very high in nutrients, but low in oxygen. Salmc populations are also declining due to these conditions. Spri turnover in the lake, a process by which warmer surface wa sinks and mixes with deep, cold water, is occurring a month later than in the past. The result is that some fish that prefer colder water are migrating into deeper waters, where they encounter more predatory species than they would in shallow water. Studies indicate that global warming is the major contributor to the rising temperatures.

Continued on next page ▶

 

## 21st Century Themes Science and Global Awareness, Science and Civic Literacy

1. What abiotic factor is changing the ecosystem of Lake Washington, and how has this factor changed over time?

______

______

2. Explain how this change has affected the mixing of warm and cold water in the lake. How does this in turn affect fish?

______

______

______

3. This report suggests that global warming is a primary contributor to the increased temperature in the lake. What does this suggest about other lake ecosystems in the northwest coniferous forest?

______

______

______

4. Briefly describe a food chain in Lake Washington.

______

______

5. If the zooplankton population is decreasing in Lake Washington, what do you think is happening to the salmon population? Explain your answer.

______

## 21st Century Skills Lake Presentation

The skills used in this activity include **critical thinking and systems thinking; problem identification, formulation, and solution; communication; information literacy;** and **leadership and responsibility.**

Working with a small group, research information about Lake Washington's past issues with sewage disposal and current trends in increasing water temperature. Or, conduct research about a body of water in your community or state. You may find it helpful to start your research at the Web sites of federal and state environmental agencies. Visiting your local public library and inquiring at government offices can offer valuable information, too. Find evidence about the relationship between global warming and these rising temperatures. Prepare a presentation describing the information that you find. In your presentation, provide at least one example and show the effects of changing conditions on this ecosystem. Present your findings to the class in an oral report, using figures, tables, and illustrations.

Name ______________________ Class ______ Date ______

# 4 Ecosystems and Communities

**Big idea** **Interdependence in Nature**

**Q:** How do abiotic and biotic factors shape ecosystems?

| | WHAT I KNOW | WHAT I LEARNED |
|---|---|---|
| **4.1** What factors affect global climate? | | |
| **4.2** How do organisms interact with one another? | | |
| **4.3** How do ecosystems change over time? | | |
| **4.4** What are the characteristics of the major biomes? | | |
| **4.5** What are the characteristics of aquatic ecosystems? | | |

 

Name ______________________ Class ______ Date ______

# 4.1 Climate

## Lesson Objectives

- Differentiate between weather and climate.
- Identify the factors that influence climate.

## Lesson Summary

**Weather and Climate** **Weather** is the condition of Earth's atmosphere at a particular time and place. Climate is the average condition of temperature and precipitation in a region over long periods.

- Climate can vary over short distances.
- These variations produce **microclimates**.

**Factors That Affect Climate** Climate is affected by solar energy trapped in the biosphere, by latitude, and by the transport of heat by winds and ocean currents.

- Temperature on Earth stays within a range suitable for life due to the greenhouse effect. The **greenhouse effect** is the trapping of heat by gases in the atmosphere.
- Earth's curvature causes different latitudes to receive less or more intense solar energy. The unequal distribution of the sun's heat on Earth's surface results in three main climate zones: polar, temperate, and tropical.
- Unequal heating of Earth's surface also causes winds and ocean currents. Winds and currents move heat and moisture through the biosphere.

## Weather and Climate

**1.** How is weather different from climate?

______________________________________________

______________________________________________

______________________________________________

______________________________________________

______________________________________________

**2.** What causes microclimates to form?

______________________________________________

______________________________________________

______________________________________________

**3.** In the Northern Hemisphere, why are the south-facing sides of buildings often warmer and drier than the north-facing sides?

______________________________________________

______________________________________________

 

Name ______________________ Class ______ Date ________

# Factors That Affect Climate

**VISUAL ANALOGY** *For Questions 4–5, refer to the Visual Analogy comparing the Earth's atmosphere to a greenhouse.*

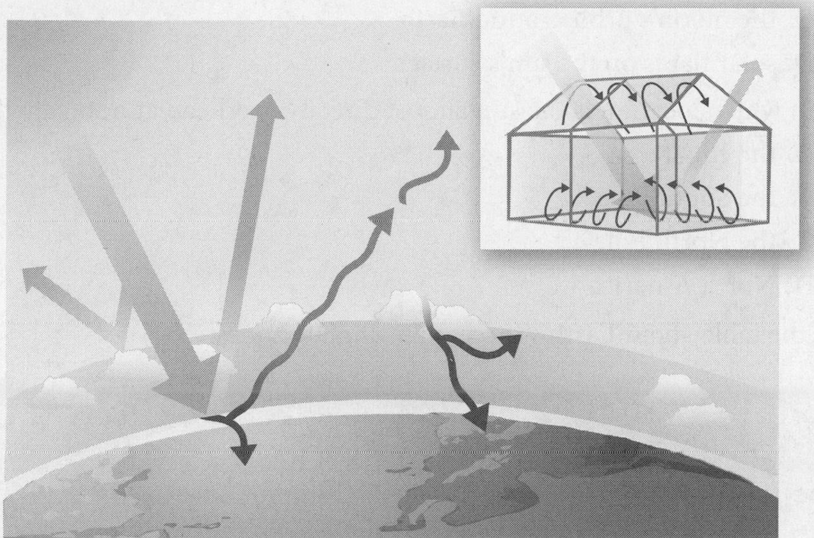

**4.** What is the source of radiation for both the Earth's atmosphere and the greenhouse?

______________________________________________

**5.** What happens to sunlight that hits Earth's surface?

______________________________________________

______________________________________________

______________________________________________

______________________________________________

______________________________________________

*For Questions 6–9, write the letter of the correct answer on the line at the left.*

_____ **6.** What effect do carbon dioxide and methane have on Earth's temperature?

- **A.** They trap heat in the atmosphere.
- **B.** They release heat from the atmosphere.
- **C.** They block heat from entering the ocean.
- **D.** They block heat from reaching Earth's surface.

_____ **7.** How would the temperature on Earth change without the greenhouse effect?

- **A.** The temperature at the equator would be warmer.
- **B.** The temperature would stay the same.
- **C.** It would be 30°C warmer.
- **D.** It would be 30°C cooler.

 

______ **8.** What causes solar radiation to strike different parts of Earth's surface at an angle that varies throughout the year?

**A.** Earth's tilted axis

**B.** Earth's erratic orbit

**C.** the moon's orbit around Earth

**D.** solar flares on the sun's surface

______ **9.** In which location is the sun almost directly overhead at noon all year?

**A.** the equator

**B.** the South Pole

**C.** the North Pole

**D.** North America

**10.** Complete the table about Earth's three main climate zones.

| Main Climate Zones | | |
|---|---|---|
| **Climate Zone** | **Location** | **Climate Characteristics** |
| | Areas around North and South poles | |
| | Between the polar zones and the tropics | |
| | Near the equator | |

*For Questions 11–14, write True if the statement is true. If the statement is false, change the underlined word or words to make the statement true.*

______ **11.** Patterns of heating and cooling result in <u>ocean currents</u>.

______ **12.** Warm air is <u>less</u> dense than cool air.

______ **13.** Surface water moved by <u>winds</u> results in ocean currents.

______ **14.** Deep ocean currents are caused by the sinking of <u>warm</u> water near the poles.

## Apply the Big idea

**15.** Describe how a change in the temperature of an ocean current might affect the climate of a nearby coastal area.

Name ______________________ Class ______ Date ______

# 4.2 Niches and Community Interactions

## Lesson Objectives

- Define niche.
- Describe the role competition plays in shaping communities.
- Describe the role predation and herbivory play in shaping communities.
- Identify the three types of symbiotic relationships in nature.

## Lesson Summary

**The Niche** Every species has its own **tolerance**, or a range of conditions under which it can grow and reproduce. A species' tolerance determines its **habitat**, the place where it lives.

- A **niche** consists of all the physical and biological conditions in which a species lives and the way the species obtains what it needs to survive and reproduce.
- An organism's niche must contain all of the resources an organism needs to survive. A **resource** is any necessity of life, such as water, nutrients, light, food, or space.

**Competition** Competition occurs when organisms try to use the same limited resources.

- Direct competition between species often results in one species dying out. This is the basis of the **competitive exclusion principle**. This principle states that no two species can occupy exactly the same niche in exactly the same habitat at the same time.
- Competition helps to determine the number and type of species in a community.

**Predation, Herbivory, and Keystone Species** Predator-prey and herbivore-plant interactions help shape communities.

- **Predation** occurs when one organism (the predator) captures and eats another (the prey).
- **Herbivory** is an interaction that occurs when an animal (the herbivore) feeds on producers (such as plants).
- Sometimes changes in the population of a single species, often called a **keystone species**, can cause dramatic changes in the structure of a community.

**Symbioses** **Symbiosis** occurs when two species live closely together in one of three ways: mutualism, commensalism, or parasitism.

- In **mutualism**, both species benefit from the relationship.
- In **parasitism**, one species benefits by living in or on the other and the other is harmed.
- In **commensalism**, one species benefits and the other is neither helped nor harmed.

# The Niche

**1.** What is a niche?

______________________________________________

______________________________________________

2. Give an example of resources a squirrel might need.

_______________________________________________

_______________________________________________

3. Three different warbler species live in the same tree. One species feeds at the top of the tree, the second species feeds in the middle part of the tree, and the third species feeds at the bottom of the tree. Do all three species occupy the same niche? Explain.

_______________________________________________

_______________________________________________

_______________________________________________

## Competition

*For Questions 4–8, write True if the statement is true. If the statement is false, change the underlined word or words to make the statement true.*

__________ 4. Competition occurs when organisms attempt to use the same resources.

__________ 5. Competition between members of the same species is known as interspecific competition.

__________ 6. The competitive exclusion principle states that no two organisms can occupy exactly the same niche in exactly the same habitat at exactly the same time.

__________ 7. If two species of bacteria are grown in the same culture, one species will always outcompete the other.

__________ 8. Members of the same species tend to divide resources instead of competing over them.

## Predation, Herbivory, and Keystone Species

*Write the letter of the correct answer on the line at the left.*

______ 9. A lion eating a zebra is an example of

**A.** herbivory.
**B.** habitat destruction.
**C.** predation.
**D.** a keystone species.

______ 10. A cow eating grass is an example of

**A.** herbivory.
**B.** predation.
**C.** habitat destruction.
**D.** a keystone species.

______ 11. A keystone species is one that

**A.** eats a mixture of plants and animals.
**B.** is introduced into a community after a major disturbance.
**C.** causes the amount of diversity in a community to decrease.
**D.** helps to stabilize the populations of other species in the community.

 

# Symbioses

**12.** Complete the table about main classes of symbiotic relationships.

| Main Classes of Symbiotic Relationships | |
|---|---|
| **Class** | **Description of Relationships** |
| Mutualism | |
| Commensalism | |
| Parasitism | |

*Match the example with the type of relationship. A relationship type may be used more than once.*

**Example**

______ **13.** a tick living on the body of a deer

______ **14.** a bee eating a flower's nectar and picking up the flower's pollen

______ **15.** a barnacle living on a whale's skin

______ **16.** a tapeworm living in a person's intestines

______ **17.** an aphid providing food to an ant in exchange for protection

**Type of Relationship**

**A.** mutualism

**B.** commensalism

**C.** parasitism

## Apply the Big idea

**19.** How do keystone species illustrate the interdependence of organisms living in a community? Give an example.

 

Name ______________________ Class ______ Date ______

# 4.3 Succession

## Lesson Objectives

- Describe how ecosystems recover from a disturbance.
- Compare succession after a natural disturbance with succession after a human-caused disturbance.

## Lesson Summary

**Primary and Secondary Succession** The series of predictable changes that occurs in a community over time is called **ecological succession**. Over the course of succession, the number of different species usually increases.

- **Primary succession** begins in areas with no remnants of an older community. It occurs on bare rock surfaces where no soil exists. The first species to live in an area of primary succession are called **pioneer species**.
- **Secondary succession** occurs when a disturbance changes a community without completely destroying it.

**Climax Communities** A climax community is a mature, relatively stable ecosystem.

- Secondary succession in healthy ecosystems following natural disturbances often reproduces the original climax community.
- Ecosystems may or may not recover from extensive human-caused disturbances.

# Primary and Secondary Succession

**1.** What is ecological succession?

______________________________________

______________________________________

**2.** What is primary succession?

______________________________________

______________________________________

**3.** When a disturbance changes a community without removing the soil, what type of succession follows?

______________________________________

**4.** Describe the process of succession in an ecosystem.

______________________________________

______________________________________

**5.** Why does secondary succession typically proceed faster than primary succession?

______________________________________

______________________________________

Name ______________________ Class _____ Date _____

# 4.4 Biomes

## Lesson Objectives

- Describe and compare the characteristics of the major land biomes.
- Identify the areas that are not classified into a major biome.

## Lesson Summary

**The Major Biomes** A biome is a group of terrestrial regional climate communities that covers a large area and is characterized by soil type, climate, and plant and animal life.

- In tropical rain forests, the tops of tall trees form a covering called the **canopy**. Shorter trees and vines form another layer called the **understory**. It is hot and wet all year.
- Tropical dry forests are found in areas with alternating wet and dry seasons. The trees in these forests may be **deciduous**, meaning they shed their leaves during a particular season.
- In a tropical grassland, grassy areas are spotted with isolated trees.
- Deserts have less than 25 centimeters of precipitation annually.
- Temperate grasslands have warm summers, cold winters, and deep soil.
- Temperate woodlands and shrublands are large areas of grasses and wildflowers such as poppies interspersed with trees or shrubs.
- Temperate forests are made up of deciduous and evergreen coniferous trees. **Coniferous** trees produce seed-bearing cones and most have waxy needles. Temperate forests have soils rich in **humus**, which forms from decaying leaves and makes soil fertile.
- Northwestern coniferous forests have mild temperatures with cool, dry summers and abundant precipitation in fall, winter, and spring.
- Boreal forests, or **taiga**, are dense forests of coniferous evergreens.
- Tundra is characterized by **permafrost**, a layer of permanently frozen subsoil.

**Other Land Areas** Some areas, such as mountains and polar ice caps, do not fall neatly into the major biomes.

# The Major Biomes

*For Questions 1–4, complete each statement by writing the correct word or words.*

1. The side of a mountain range that faces the wind often receives more ______________ than the downwind side of the same range.
2. A(n) ______________ is a group of terrestrial communities that covers a large area and is characterized by certain soil and ______________ conditions and particular types of plants and animals.
3. Organisms within each biome can be characterized by ______________ that enable them to live and reproduce successfully in the environment.
4. In a tropical rain forest, the layer formed by the leafy tops of tall trees is called the ______________ and the layer of shorter trees and vines is called the ______________.

Name ______________________________ Class ______ Date __________

5. **THINK VISUALLY** In the box below, draw and label a diagram showing how a coastal mountain range can affect a region's climate.

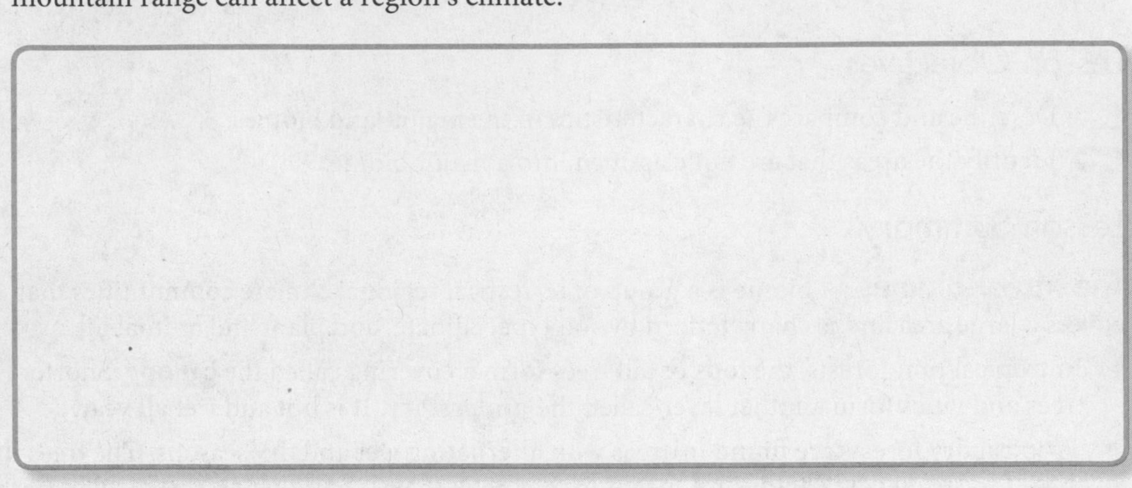

*Use the graph to answer Questions 6–9.*

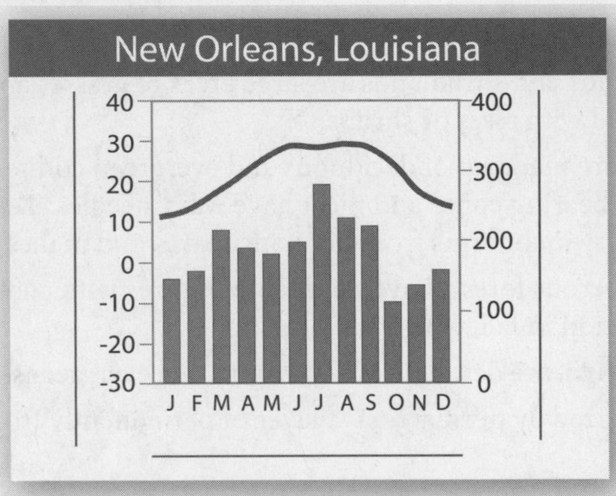


6. Complete the climate diagram by adding labels to the bottom and both sides of the graph to show what the variables are.

7. Describe what a climate diagram summarizes.

_______________________________________________

_______________________________________________

8. Explain what the line plot on a climate diagram shows.

_______________________________________________

_______________________________________________

9. Explain what the vertical bars on a climate diagram show.

_______________________________________________

_______________________________________________

## Population Growth

*For Questions 6–10, write True if the statement is true. If the statement is false, change the underlined word or words to make the statement true.*

______ **6.** If the death rate is <u>less</u> than the birthrate, the population is likely to shrink.

______ **7.** <u>Immigration</u> increases population size.

______ **8.** Young animals may <u>immigrate</u> from the place where they were born to establish new territories.

______ **9.** A high birthrate and immigration <u>decrease</u> population size.

______ **10.** Populations grow if <u>more</u> individuals are born than die in a period of time.

**11.** **THINK VISUALLY** The dots in the box represent individuals in a population with a random pattern of distribution. Use arrows and dots to show what will happen to this population if emigration is greater than immigration. (Assume birthrate and death rate are equal.) On the lines below, explain your drawing.

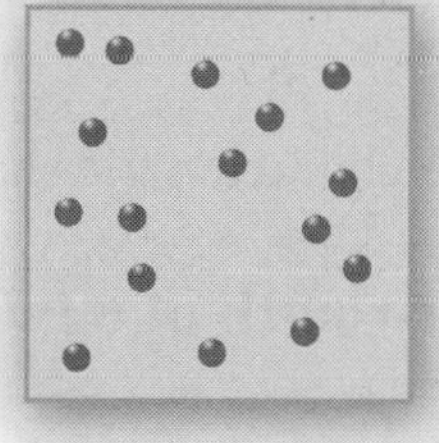

______________________________________________

______________________________________________

______________________________________________

## Exponential Growth

**12.** Describe the conditions in which exponential growth occurs.

______________________________________________

______________________________________________

**13.** Can exponential growth occur in a population of organisms that take a long time to reproduce? Why or why not?

______________________________________________

______________________________________________

 

**14.** Complete the graph by drawing the characteristic shape of exponential population growth.

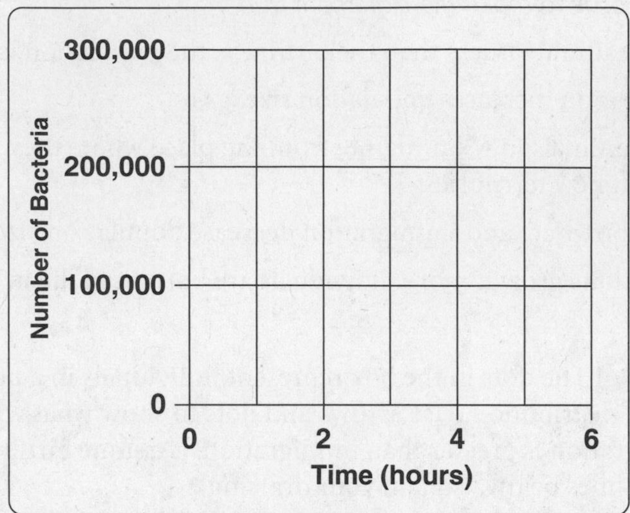


**15.** What letter is used to refer to the characteristic shape of an exponential growth curve?

______________________________________________

## Logistic Growth

**16.** Complete the graph by drawing the characteristic shape of logistic population growth.

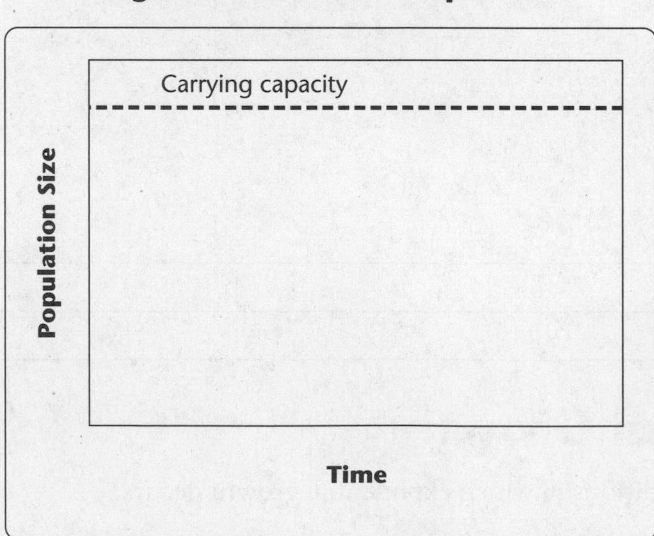


**17.** What letter is used to refer to the characteristic shape of the logistic growth curve?

______________________________________________

 

**18.** When real-world populations of plants and animals are analyzed, why do they most often have the logistic growth curve?

______________________

______________________

______________________

**19.** What does the term carrying capacity refer to?

______________________

______________________

**20.** Complete the table to name and explain three phases of logistic growth. Use the terms *growth rate, population size,* and *carrying capacity* in your explanations.

| Phases of Logistic Growth | | |
|---|---|---|
| **Phase** | **Phase name** | **Explanation** |
| 1 | | |
| 2 | | |
| 3 | | |

## Apply the Big idea

**21.** What is an example of a limiting factor that humans use to control the carrying capacity of an environment for a particular type of organism? Explain your answer.

______________________

______________________

______________________

______________________

______________________

 

Name ______________________ Class _____ Date _________

# 5.2 Limits to Growth

## Lesson Objectives

Identify factors that determine carrying capacity.

Identify the limiting factors that depend on population density.

Identify the limiting factors that do not depend on population density.

## Lesson Summary

**Limiting Factors** A **limiting factor** is a factor that controls the growth of a population.

- Some factors depend on the density of the population. Others do not.
- Acting separately or together, limiting factors determine an environment's carrying capacity.
- Limiting factors produce the pressures of natural selection.

**Density-Dependent Limiting Factors**

- **Density-dependent limiting factors** operate strongly when the number of individuals per unit area reaches a certain point.
- Examples include:
  - competition
  - predation and herbivory
  - parasitism and disease
  - stress from overcrowding

**Density-Independent Limiting Factors** Some limiting factors do not necessarily depend on population size.

- **Density-independent limiting factors** depend on population density, or the number of organisms per unit area.
- Examples include severe weather, natural disasters, and human activities.
- Some of these factors may have more severe effects when population density is high.

# Limiting Factors

*For Questions 1–6, write True if the statement is true. If the statement is false, change the underlined word to make the statement true.*

_______ **1.** Limiting factors determine the <u>immigration</u> capacity of a population.

_______ **2.** A limiting factor controls the growth of a <u>population</u>.

_______ **3.** Limiting factors operate when growth is <u>exponential</u>.

_______ **4.** Populations grow too large in the <u>absence</u> of limiting factors.

_______ **5.** <u>Competition</u> is an example of a limiting factor.

_______ **6.** Population <u>size</u> can be limited by factors such as predation.

 

Name ______________________ Class ______ Date ______

# Density-Dependent Limiting Factors

**7.** What is a density-dependent limiting factor?

______________________________________________

**8.** When do density-dependent factors operate most strongly?

______________________________________________

**9.** What are four density-dependent limiting factors?

______________________________________________

______________________________________________

*Use the graph to answer Questions 10–13.*

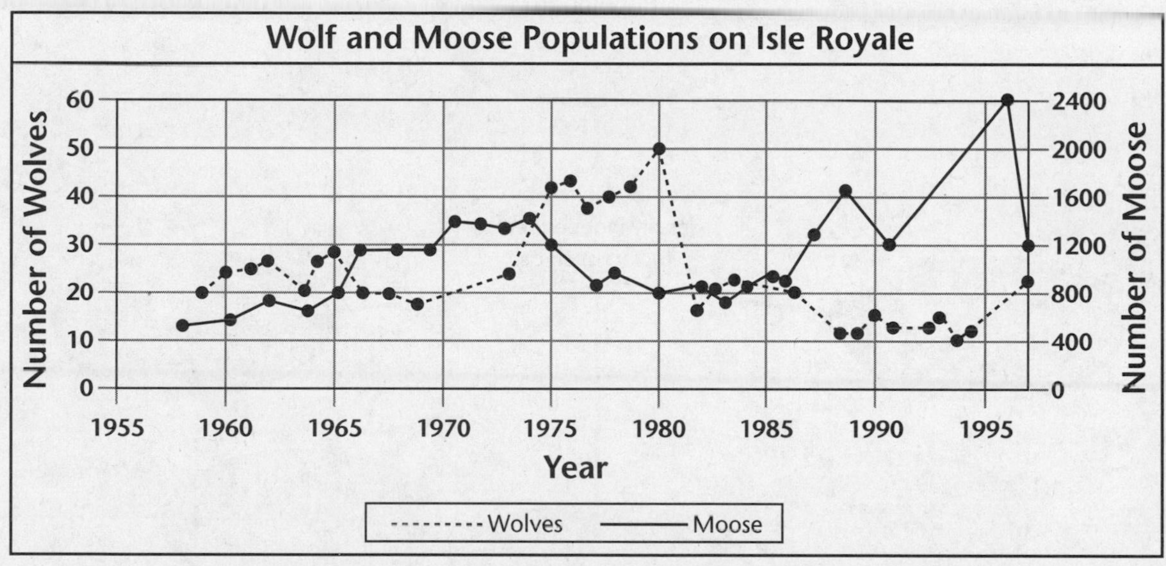


**10.** What happened to the number of wolves on Isle Royale between 1975 and 1985?

______________________________________________

**11.** What happened to the moose population when the number of wolves was low?

______________________________________________

**12.** What is the relationship between the moose and the wolves on Isle Royale?

______________________________________________

**13.** Is the number of moose on the island a density-dependent or density-independent limiting factor for the wolf? Explain your answer.

______________________________________________

______________________________________________

______________________________________________

# Density-Independent Limiting Factors

**14.** What term describes a limiting factor that affects all populations in similar ways, regardless of population size?

______________________________________________

**15.** What is the usual response in the population size of many species to a density-independent limiting factor?

______________________________________________

**16.** Complete the graphic organizer with examples of density-independent limiting factors.

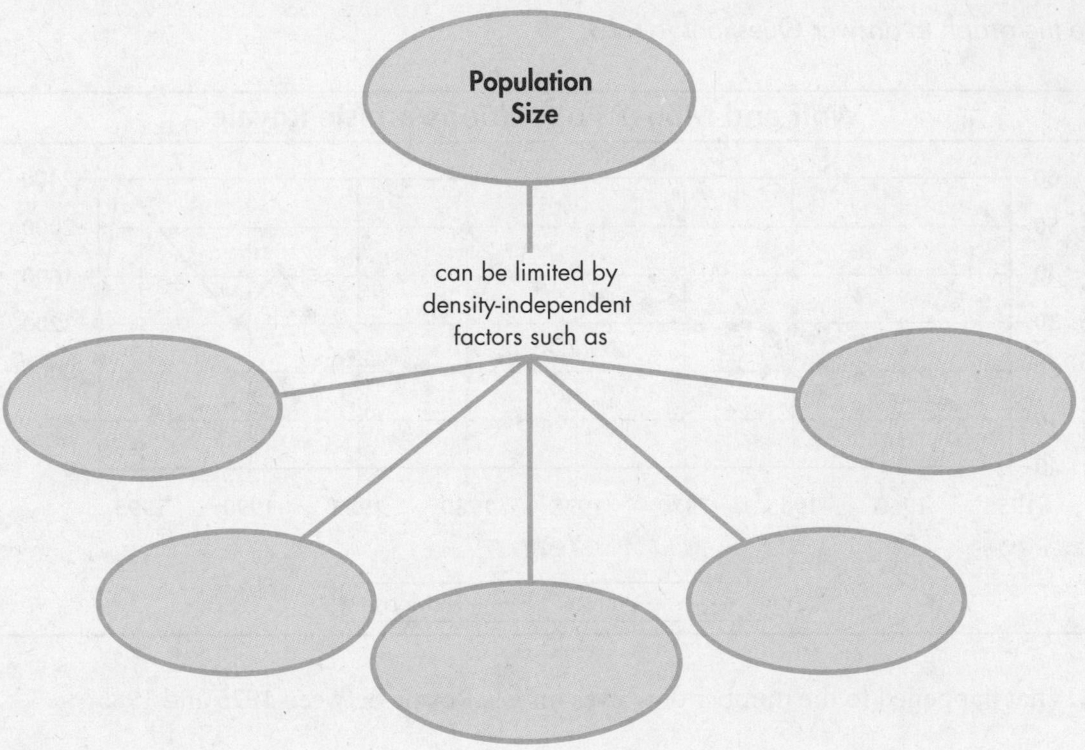


## Apply the Big idea

**17.** A population continues at a stable size for many years. Suddenly, in a single season, the population size drops by half. Is the cause more likely to be density-dependent, density-independent, or both? Explain your answer.

______________________________________________

______________________________________________

______________________________________________

______________________________________________

______________________________________________

 

Name ______________________ Class ______ Date ________

# 5.3 Human Population Growth

## Lesson Objectives

Discuss the trend of human population growth.

Explain why population growth rates differ in countries throughout the world.

## Lesson Summary

**Historical Overview** The size of the human population has increased over time.

- For most of human existence, limiting factors such as the scarcity of food kept death rates high.
- As civilization advanced, agriculture, industry, improved nutrition, sanitation, and medicine reduced death rates. Birthrates stayed high in most places. This led to exponential growth.
- Today, the human population continues to grow exponentially, although the doubling time has slowed.

**Patterns of Human Population Growth** **Demography** is the scientific study of human populations. Demographers try to predict how human populations will change over time.

- Over the past century, population growth in developed countries slowed. As death rates dropped, birthrates dropped also. Demographers call this shift the **demographic transition**. Most people live in countries that have not undergone the demographic transition.
- An age-structure graph shows how many people of each gender are in each age group in a population. Demographers use such graphs to predict how a population will change. More people of reproductive age usually means faster growth.
- Many factors, including disease, will affect human population growth in the twenty-first century. Current data suggest the human population will grow more slowly over the next 50 years than it did for the last 50 years.

# Historical Overview

*For Questions 1–5, write True if the statement is true. If the statement is false, change the underlined word or words to make the statement true.*

______________ **1.** Over the last 1000 years, the size of the human population has decreased.

______________ **2.** Since the 1800s, human population growth has been logistic.

______________ **3.** The human population has increased because birthrates have dropped.

______________ **4.** The combination of low death rates and high birthrates led to exponential growth.

______________ **5.** Charles Darwin suggested that human populations are regulated by war, famine, and disease.

**6.** Complete the table below to explain how each factor affected the size and growth rate of the human population over the last 10,000 years.

| Factors That Affected Human Population Growth | |
|---|---|
| **Cause** | **Effect** |
| Agriculture | |
| Improved health care and medicine | |
| Improved sanitation | |
| Bubonic plague | |
| Industrial Revolution | |

# Patterns of Human Population Growth

**7.** THINK VISUALLY Complete the diagram below by adding the information for stages II and III of the demographic transition. Draw bars to represent the birthrate and the death rate and describe the stages on the lines provided. Stage I is done for you.

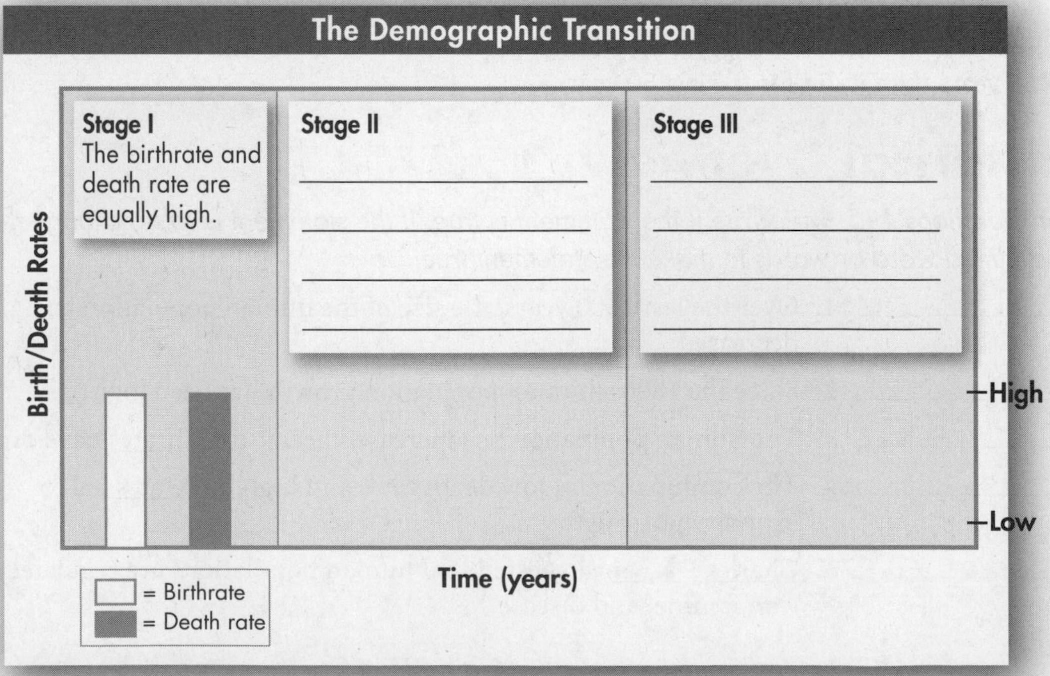


 

*Use these age structure diagrams to answer Questions 8–11.*

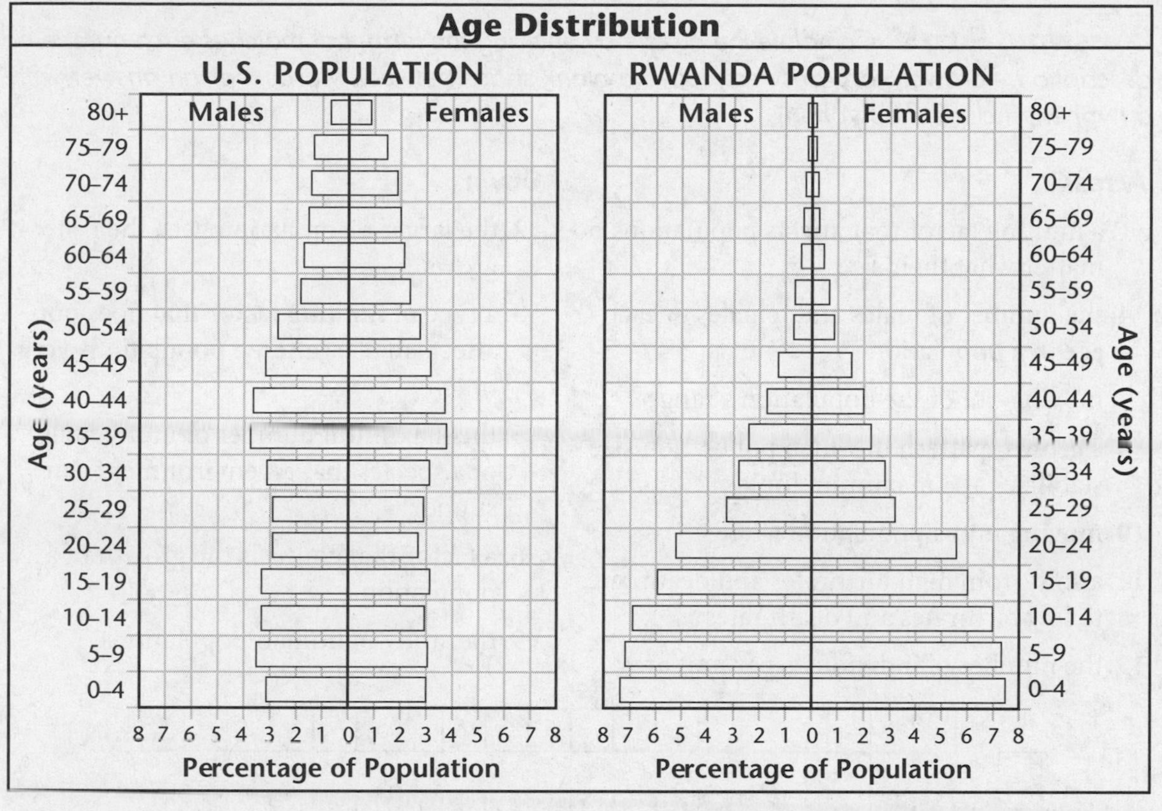


**8.** Which country has gone through the demographic transition? How do you know?

______________________________________________

______________________________________________

**9.** Which country do you predict will experience a slow and steady growth rate in the near future? Why? ______________________________________________

______________________________________________

**10.** Which country is most likely to grow exponentially in the near future? Why?

______________________________________________

**11.** Suggest three factors that might slow population growth in Rwanda.

______________________________________________

______________________________________________

## Apply the Big idea

**12.** Explain why human population size is likely to increase in the twenty-first century, but not as rapidly as it did in the twentieth century.

______________________________________________

______________________________________________

______________________________________________

Name ______________________ Class ______ Date ________

# Chapter Vocabulary Review

**Crossword Puzzle** *Complete the puzzle by entering the term that matches each numbered description. For two-word answers, leave a blank space between words. For an answer with a hyphen, include the hyphen.*

**Across**

**1.** a limiting factor that affects populations no matter what their size

**4.** the number of males and females of each age in a population

**7.** moving out of the population's range

**8.** a growth pattern in which population size stabilizes at a maximum limit

**10.** moving into a population's range

**11.** a shift from high birthrates and death rates to low birthrates and death rates

**12.** the number of individuals per unit area

**Down**

**2.** the larger a population gets, the faster it grows

**3.** a type of limiting factor that does not affect small, scattered populations very much

**5.** the maximum number of individuals of a species that an environment can support

**6.** a factor that controls the growth of a population

**9.** the study of human populations

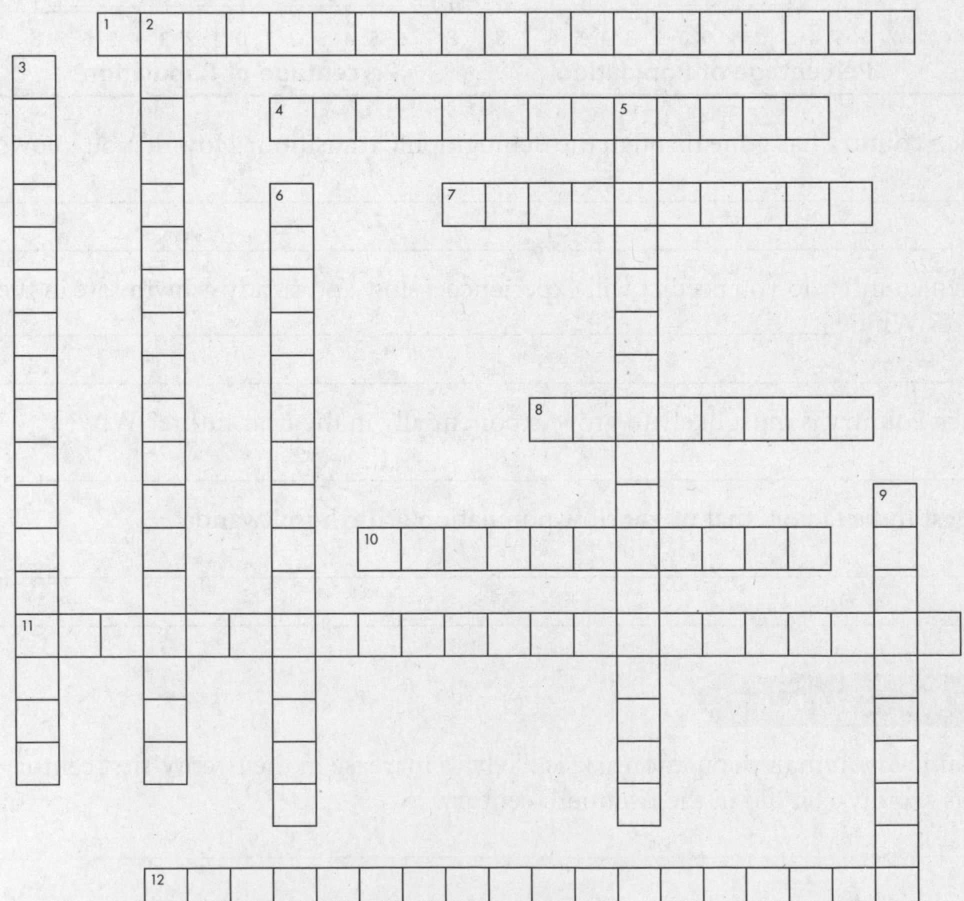

Name ______________________ Class ______ Date ______

In the Chapter Mystery, you learned about the effects of the deliberate release of the European rabbit by an Australian farmer. With few predators and plentiful food, the rabbit population exploded. Animal populations rise and fall even in the healthiest ecosystems.

21st Century Learning

## Deer, Deer, Everywhere

White-tailed deer were hunted almost to extinction a little over 100 years ago. Today, many regions of the United States are home to large populations of this species. This increase is the result of the disappearance of predators, the use of conservation practices, and the deer's ability to thrive in a variety of habitats.

Like all species, white-tailed deer have characteristics that set them apart from other species. Field guides describe the characteristics of organisms, enabling people to identify them. The following is a description that might appear in a field guide.

### White-tailed deer, *Odocoileus virginianus*

**SIZE:** Size can vary. Weight varies from 50–300 lbs.

**IDENTIFICATION:** Color changes with the seasons. The upper body is reddish or yellowish in warmer months and gray in the winter. The underside and inside of the legs are white. The tail is long and bushy. It is brown with white along the edges of the tail. Male white-tail deer grow antlers, which are shed after the mating season.

**HABITAT:** Habitat will vary. It includes woodland areas, farmland, gardens, and pastures.

**FOOD:** Grasses, shrubs, tree leaves and buds, and other plants provide food.

**PREDATORS:** Primary predators are wolves and mountain lions, but the populations of these species have been eradicated in many areas of the United States.

**BREEDING:** Offspring are born in litters of 1 to 3 in the early spring. Fawns have white spots and are active within a few days of birth. Where resources are plentiful, populations may double every few years.

**RANGE:** Most of North America

*Continued on next page* ▶

## 21st Century Themes Science and Health Literacy

*Answer the following questions.*

**1.** Based on the field guide excerpt, what animals prey on deer?

______________________________________________

______________________________________________

______________________________________________

**2.** How might the habitat conditions in which deer thrive play a role in increasing their numbers?

______________________________________________

______________________________________________

**3.** How many offspring do white-tailed deer have each year? How might these numbers influence their population?

______________________________________________

______________________________________________

______________________________________________

**4.** What do you think might happen if expanding human development led to a serious decrease in the amount of food available to white-tailed deer?

______________________________________________

______________________________________________

______________________________________________

______________________________________________

## Controlling Deer Populations 21st Century Learning

The skills used in this activity include **information and media literacy; critical thinking and systems thinking; problem identification, formulation, and solution;** and **self-direction.**

Work in a group to determine why white-tailed deer populations are increasing and to find out about the different techniques to manage these populations. Consult state and government Web sites, science articles, and newspaper articles. Present your findings in a report that describes the advantages and disadvantages of different methods of control. You might also want to present opposing viewpoints on the approach. Use maps, charts, and diagrams in your presentation.

 

Name ______________________ Class ______ Date ______

# 6 Humans in the Biosphere

**Big idea** **Interdependence in Nature**

**Q:** How have human activities shaped local and global ecology?

| | WHAT I KNOW | WHAT I LEARNED |
|---|---|---|
| **6.1** How does human activity affect the environment? | | |
| **6.2** How can we use our natural resources wisely? | | |
| **6.3** Why is it important to protect and conserve biodiversity? | | |
| **6.4** How can we change our behaviors to help protect our planet? | | |

# 6.1 A Changing Landscape

## Lesson Objectives

Describe human activities that can affect the biosphere.

Describe the relationship between resource use and sustainable development.

## Lesson Summary

**The Effect of Human Activity** Humans and other organisms change the environment when they obtain food, eliminate wastes, and prepare places to live.

- Because Earth is like an island, life is limited to the resources that are here.
- Humans affect regional and global environments through three major activities:
  - agriculture, particularly **monoculture**, which is the cultivation of a single crop
  - development of cities and suburbs, including conversion of farmland and destruction of habitats for other organisms
  - industrial growth, which consumes energy and emits pollutants

**Sustainable Development** In economic terms, ecosystems are providers of goods and services (natural resources).

- Healthy ecosystems produce or replace **renewable resources**.
- Humans must be careful about the use of **nonrenewable resources**, such as fossil fuels, which cannot be replaced.
- **Sustainable development** provides for human needs while preserving the ecosystems that provide renewable resources.

## The Effect of Human Activity

**1.** What three human activities have transformed the biosphere?

______________________________________________

**2.** What is monoculture?

______________________________________________

______________________________________________

**3.** List three resources used in agriculture.

______________________________________________

**4.** How does urban and suburban development affect the environment and habitats?

______________________________________________

______________________________________________

**5.** What source provides most of the energy for industrial production?

______________________________________________

**6.** Complete the table to show some consequences of human activities on global ecology.

| Consequences of Some Human Activities | | |
|---|---|---|
| **Activity** | **Positive Consequences** | **Negative Consequences** |
| Agriculture | | |
| Development | | |
| Industrial Growth | | |

## Sustainable Development

**7.** Complete the Venn diagram to compare renewable and nonrenewable resources.

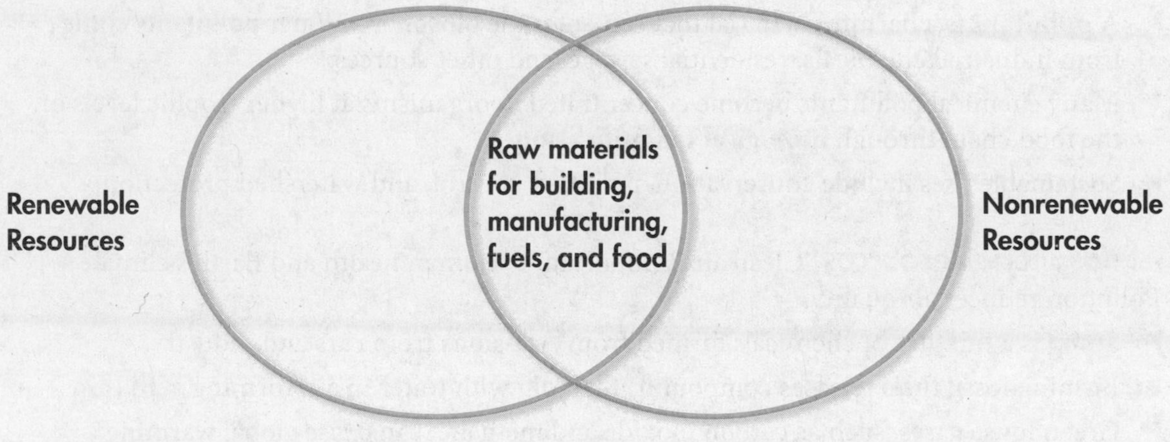


**8.** How can development be sustainable?

______________________________________________

______________________________________________

**Apply the Big idea**

**9.** The human population (currently around 7 billion) may reach 9 billion by 2100. Most of those people will live in cities. Predict the impact of city growth on natural ecosystems and farmland. What will happen if sustainable development is not achieved?

______________________________________________

______________________________________________

______________________________________________

 

Name ____________________ Class _____ Date _________

# 6.2 Using Resources Wisely

## Lesson Objectives

- Describe how human activities affect soil and land.
- Describe how human activities affect water resources.
- Describe how human activities affect air resources.

## Lesson Summary

**Soil Resources** Soil is a renewable resource, but it must be managed properly.

- **Soil erosion** is the wearing away of surface soil by water and wind.
- In dry climates, farming and overgrazing change farmland into deserts, a process called **desertification**.
- **Deforestation** is loss of forests. Because healthy forests hold soil in place, deforestation increases erosion.
- Sustainable uses include leaving stems and roots of previous crops in place, crop rotation, contour plowing, terracing, selectively harvesting mature trees, and tree farms.

**Freshwater Resources** The amount of fresh water is limited, and some sources cannot be replaced.

- A **pollutant** is a harmful material that can enter the biosphere. Water pollutants come from industrial chemicals, residential sewage, and other sources.
- Many chemical pollutants become concentrated in organisms at higher trophic levels of the food chain through **biological magnification**.
- Sustainable uses include conservation, pollution control, and watershed protection.

**Atmospheric Resources** Clean air is important to human health and Earth's climate. Pollution reduces air quality.

- **Smog** is a mixture of chemicals formed from emissions from cars and industry.
- Burning fossil fuels releases compounds that join with water in air, forming **acid rain**.
- Greenhouse gases, such as carbon dioxide and methane, can cause global warming.
- Particulates are microscopic particles that cause health problems.
- One way of sustaining air quality is controlling automobile emissions.

## Soil Resources

**1.** What is topsoil?

_______________________________________________

**2.** How does topsoil form?

_______________________________________________

_______________________________________________

3. What is soil erosion?

______________________________________________

4. How does plowing land increase the rate of soil erosion?

______________________________________________

5. What happens to farmland during desertification?

______________________________________________

______________________________________________

6. Are mature forests a renewable resource? Why or why not?

______________________________________________

7. What happens to soil when rain forest is cut down?

______________________________________________

8. Complete the graphic organizer to give examples of sustainable uses of soil.

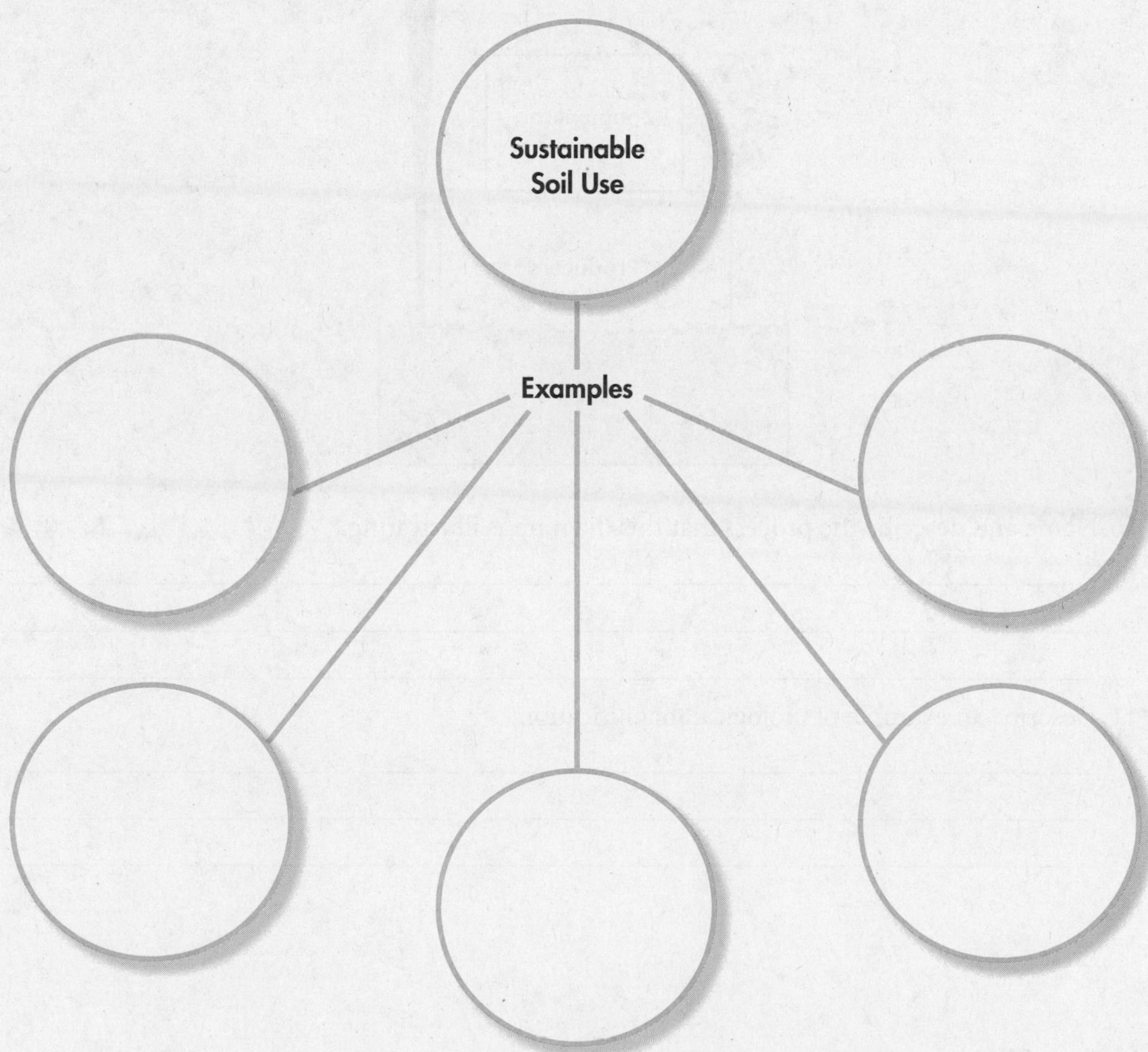


 

# Freshwater Resources

*Use this diagram to answer Questions 9–11.*

**9.** THINK VISUALLY The diagram shows the typical impact of a chemical pollutant in an aquatic ecosystem.

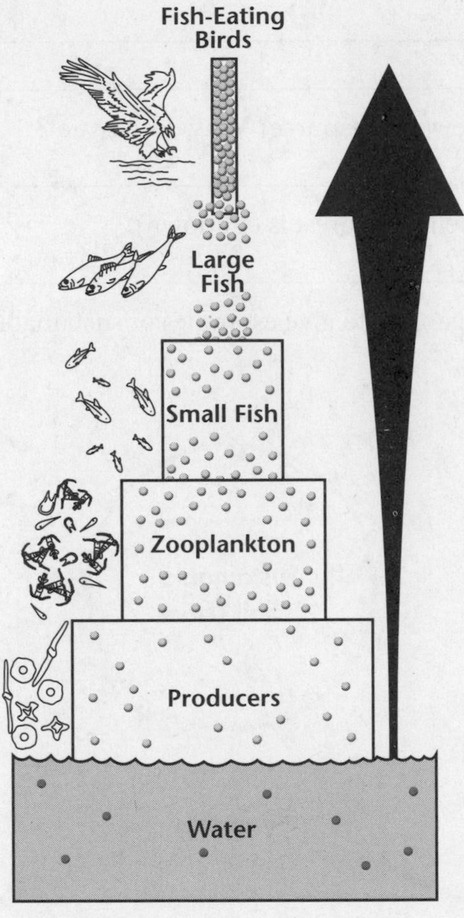


**10.** Name and describe the process that this diagram is illustrating.

______________________________________________

______________________________________________

______________________________________________

**11.** Describe an example of biological magnification.

______________________________________________

______________________________________________

______________________________________________

**12.** What is a "dead zone," and what is its cause?

______________________________________________

______________________________________________

______________________________________________

**13.** Why is watershed management important to maintaining good water quality in a large river or lake?

______________________________________________

______________________________________________

______________________________________________

## Atmospheric Resources

*For Questions 14–17, write the letter of the correct answer on the line at the left.*

______ **14.** Which is the name for the mixture of chemicals that forms as a gray-brown haze in the atmosphere?

**A.** dust
**B.** smog
**C.** ozone
**D.** radiation

______ **15.** Which component of acid rain kills plants and harms soil?

**A.** carbon dioxide and water
**B.** CFCs and fossil fuels
**C.** nitric and sulfuric acids
**D.** ozone and particulates

______ **16.** Which is the name for the bits of ash and dust put into the air by certain kinds of diesel engines?

**A.** particulates
**B.** precipitation
**C.** ozone layer
**D.** greenhouse gases

______ **17.** Which is a pollutant of soil and water that is now dropping steadily due to laws that affected the automobile industry?

**A.** carbon
**B.** lead
**C.** nitrogen
**D.** ozone

## Apply the Big idea

**18.** The citizens of Ecotown want to protect the quality of their soil, fresh water, and air. Suggest a plan for Ecotown that includes steps for achieving sustainable use of each of those three categories of resources.

______________________________________________

______________________________________________

______________________________________________

______________________________________________

Name ______________________ Class ______ Date ______

# 6.3 Biodiversity

## Lesson Objectives

- Define biodiversity and explain its value.
- Identify current threats to biodiversity.
- Describe how biodiversity can be preserved.

## Lesson Summary

**The Value of Biodiversity** The sum of all the genetic diversity among all the organisms in the biosphere is called **biodiversity**. There are three general types of biodiversity:

- **Ecosystem diversity** is the variety of habitats, communities, and ecological processes in the biosphere.
- **Species diversity** is the number of different species in an area or in the biosphere.
- **Genetic diversity** is the total of all genetic information carried in living things.

Biodiversity benefits humans through its contributions to medicine and agriculture and through the provision of ecological goods and services.

**Threats to Biodiversity** Human activities threaten biodiversity.

- Development splits ecosystems into pieces, resulting in **habitat fragmentation**. The smaller the pieces of a habitat, the less likely that species in the habitat can survive.
- Other threats to biodiversity include hunting, introduced species, pollution, and climate change.

**Conserving Biodiversity** Conservation efforts are focused on three things:

- Protecting single species is the focus of groups such as the Association of Zoos and Aquariums (AZA), which oversees species survival plans (SSPs).
- Protecting habitats and ecosystems is the main thrust of global efforts. Biologists are particularly concerned about **ecological hot spots**, which are places where significant numbers of habitats and species are in immediate danger of extinction.
- Considering local interests is part of developing plans to replace harmful activities with ones that conserve environments and biodiversity.

# The Value of Biodiversity

**1.** What is biodiversity?

______________________________________________

**2.** Why is biodiversity one of Earth's greatest natural resources?

______________________________________________

______________________________________________

______________________________________________

Name ______________________ Class ______ Date ______

**3.** Complete the table to define the types of biodiversity.

| Diversity in the Biosphere | |
|---|---|
| **Type of Diversity** | **Definition** |
| Ecosystem diversity | |
| Species diversity | |
| Genetic diversity | |

## Threats to Biodiversity

*For Questions 4–8, write True if the statement is true. If the statement is false, change the underlined word or words to make the statement true.*

______ **4.** The current rate of species loss is <u>10</u> times the typical rate of extinction.

______ **5.** The smaller a habitat "island," the <u>larger</u> the number of species that can live there.

______ **6.** Habitat fragmentation <u>increases</u> the impact of hunting on endangered species.

______ **7.** <u>Endangered</u> species can become invasive and threaten biodiversity.

______ **8.** The increased concentration of carbon dioxide in air is making oceans <u>more acidic</u> and putting stress on coral reefs.

**9.** What are five ways that human activity reduces biodiversity?

______________________

______________________

______________________

**10.** Identify three reasons why endangered species are hunted.

______________________

______________________

**11.** How can introduced species lead to economic losses?

**12.** How does climate change threaten biodiversity?

## Conserving Biodiversity

**13.** What is the main purpose of biodiversity conservation today?

**14.** Why have ecologists identified ecological hot spots?

**15.** What are some of the challenges that conservationists face?

**16.** What are some strategies that encourage conservation? Provide an example of one of these strategies.

### Apply the Big idea

**17.** Why is preserving entire ecosystems a better idea than protecting single species from extinction?

 

Name ______________________ Class _____ Date ________

# 6.4 Meeting Ecological Challenges

## Lesson Objectives

- Explain the concept of ecological footprint.
- Identify the role of ecology in a sustainable future.

## Lesson Summary

**Ecological Footprints** The **ecological footprint** of an individual or a population is the amount of land and water needed to provide resources, absorb wastes, and render the wastes harmless.

**Ecology in Action** Three case studies illustrate the three steps of ecology in action: (1) recognize a change in the environment, (2) determine the cause of that change, and (3) change behavior to have a positive impact.

▶ **Case Study 1: Atmospheric Ozone** This gas blocks ultraviolet (UV) radiation.

- Ozone gas blocks ultraviolet (UV) rediation.
- The ozone layer is an area of relatively high concentration of ozone in the atmosphere, between 20 and 50 kilometers above Earth's surface. In the 1970s, a hole in the layer was observed.
- Regulations reduced CFC use, and the hole may be slowly disappearing.

▶ **Case Study 2: North Atlantic Fisheries**

- Commercial fish catches have declined in recent years.
- The cause is overfishing.
- Regulations closed some fishing grounds to allow fish stocks to replenish. In the mean time, **aquaculture**, or fish farming, also can provide food for people.

▶ **Case Study 3: Climate Change**

- **Global warming**, the rise in the biosphere's average temperature, and climate change, a shift in Earth's overall weather patterns, has occurred.
- Physical evidence includes rising sea levels due to melting ice. Biological evidence includes temperature-related behavior changes in organisms.
- Using less fossil fuel will reduce greenhouse gases in the atmosphere.

# Ecological Footprints

*For Questions 1–2, refer to the Visual Analogy that shows examples of factors that contribute to a population's ecological footprint.*

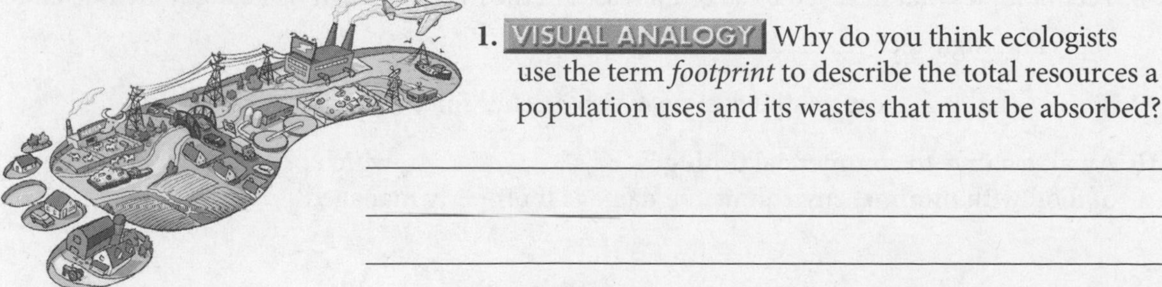

1. **VISUAL ANALOGY** Why do you think ecologists use the term *footprint* to describe the total resources a population uses and its wastes that must be absorbed?

______________________________

______________________________

______________________________

2. Explain this statement: The average American has an ecological footprint more than four times larger than the global average.

______________________________________________

______________________________________________

## Ecology in Action

3. List three factors that will affect the future of the biosphere.

______________________________________________

______________________________________________

4. Complete the table to summarize how the basic principles of ecology can lead to positive impacts on the environment.

**Examples of Ecology in Action**

| Environmental Change | Cause | Behavior Change Needed |
|---|---|---|
| Hole in the ozone layer | | |
| Declining numbers of fish in the oceans | | |
| Global warming and climate change | | |

## Case Study 1: Atmospheric Ozone

*For Questions 5–7, complete each statement by writing the correct word or words.*

5. The ozone layer is a high concentration of ozone at about ______________ above Earth's surface.

6. The ozone layer is important to humans because it protects against exposure to ______________ from the sun.

7. UV radiation causes ______________, damages eyes, and reduces resistance to disease.

## Case Study 2: North Atlantic Fisheries

*For Questions 8–10, complete each statement by writing the correct word or words.*

8. Technologies that have led to large increases in the mass of ocean fish caught include large boats and high-tech ______________ equipment.

9. ______________ caused the decline in fish catches since 1997.

10. An alternative to commercial fishing is ______________, which produces large amounts of food with minimal environmental damage if properly managed.

# Case Study 3: Climate Change

*Use the graph to answer Questions 11–12.*

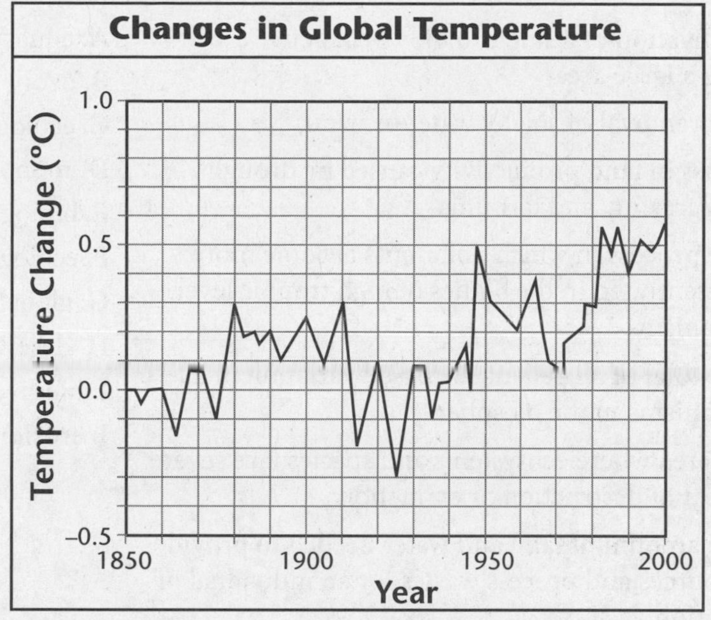


**11.** How does the change in global temperature between 1850 and 2000 compare with the change that occurred between 1850 and 1880?

______________________________________________

______________________________________________

______________________________________________

**12.** List three factors that may have contributed to the trend shown in the graph.

______________________________________________

______________________________________________

**13.** Suggest three possible effects of global warming on the future of the biosphere.

______________________________________________

______________________________________________

## Apply the Big idea

**14.** Explain why populations with the largest ecological footprints change the biosphere the most.

______________________________________________

______________________________________________

______________________________________________

______________________________________________

Name ______________________ Class _____ Date _______

# Chapter Vocabulary Review

*For Questions 1–10, match the term with its definition.*

| Definition | Term |
|---|---|
| _____ **1.** Cultivation of a single, highly productive crop over a large area | **A.** aquaculture |
| _____ **2.** The removal of soil by water or wind | **B.** ozone layer |
| _____ **3.** A loss in land productivity caused by drought, overgrazing, and farming | **C.** ecological footprint |
| _____ **4.** The process in which pollutants become more concentrated in the bodies of high trophic level organisms | **D.** monoculture |
| _____ **5.** The total of all genetically based variation in all organisms in the biosphere | **E.** biological magnification |
| _____ **6.** An area where ecosystems and species face severe threat of destruction or extinction | **F.** ecological hot spot |
| _____ **7.** The amount of land and water needed to provide resources and process wastes for an individual or a nation | **G.** global warming |
| _____ **8.** A part of the atmosphere that blocks UV rays of the sun from reaching Earth's surface | **H.** desertification |
| _____ **9.** The farming of fish and other aquatic organisms for food | **I.** biodiversity |
| _____ **10.** A rise in Earth's average temperature | **J.** erosion |

*For Questions 11–17, complete each statement by writing in the correct word or words.*

**11.** A resource that can be produced or replaced by a healthy ecosystem is a(n) ______________ resource.

**12.** Fossil fuels are examples of ______________ resources.

**13.** ______________ can lead to severe soil erosion, especially on mountainsides.

**14.** Any harmful material that enters the biosphere is a(n) ______________.

**15.** The mixture of chemicals that forms a gray-brown haze in the air of cities is ______________.

**16.** The variety of habitats, communities, and ecological processes in the biosphere is ______________.

**17.** The number of different species in an area is ______________.

 

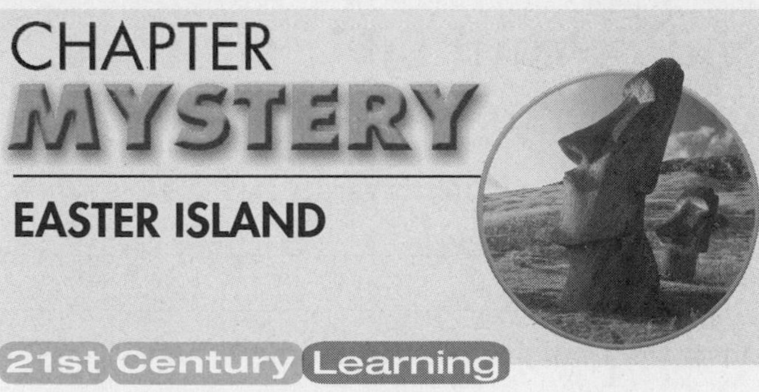


The lessons of Easter Island can serve as a guide to help the citizens of the world live as stewards of their environment. Even after the disaster that occurred on Easter Island, people and cultures around the world often continued to devastate their environment, though not always so drastically.

## Creating a Butterfly Haven

Today, some people actively work to improve their environment to help wildlife. For example, butterflies and their larvae depend on vegetation for survival. When this vegetation is destroyed to develop suburban areas, butterflies are threatened. Some citizens have designed and planted gardens to attract butterflies and aid in their survival. Below is a brief guide that explains the steps necessary for creating a successful butterfly garden.

### Getting Started on Your Own Community Butterfly Garden

**STEP 1:** Research the butterfly species that live in your area.

**STEP 2:** Based on your results from Step 1, research what plants these butterflies and their larvae are attracted to and use for survival. Plant species should vary and choices should be based on color, nectar, and bloom time. Remember that adult butterflies and their larvae may have different plant preferences.

**STEP 3:** Determine what other attractants would be appropriate for local butterflies.

**STEP 4:** Choose an ideal location based on your research.

**STEP 5:** Map out your location with a blueprint. This blueprint should include placement of vegetation and other landscaping projects.

**STEP 6:** Now build your garden! Plant vegetation for butterflies based on your blueprint.

Continued on next page ▶

 

Name ______________________ Class _____ Date _______

## 21st Century Themes Science and Civic Literacy, Science and Economic Literacy

**1.** What variables should one study when developing a butterfly garden?

______________________________________________

______________________________________________

**2.** Why do you think butterfly species may vary from one place to another?

______________________________________________

______________________________________________

**3.** After choosing vegetation for a butterfly garden, are there other considerations that should be addressed regarding plant or shrub survival? What are they?

______________________________________________

______________________________________________

**4.** Are there any steps that should be added to the list above?

______________________________________________

______________________________________________

**5.** What might happen if you don't choose the location of the butterfly garden carefully?

______________________________________________

______________________________________________

## 21st Century Skills Collaborate on a Garden

The skills used in this activity include **communication skills; critical thinking and systems thinking; problem identification, formulation, and solution; interpersonal and collaborative skills; and accountability** and **adaptability.**

Work as a class to follow the steps above to design, implement, and build a community butterfly garden. Plan your work by assigning specific tasks to individual students or small groups. Start by researching other communities that have successfully accomplished this. Sources of information may include local garden clubs, Audubon societies, and conservation organizations. Make sure you seek permission from your school principal or local government officials. After completing the steps above, compile a list of materials you will need and determine the quantity of these materials you will need for the garden. Then comparison shop for the best prices. Based on your results, develop a budget. Think about how you can raise money to fund the garden. Present your findings to your school board as a proposal. Once the proposal is accepted, begin fundraising and building your garden.

Name ____________________ Class ______ Date ________

# 7 Cell Structure and Function

**Big idea** **Cellular Basis of Life, Homeostasis**

**Q:** How are cell structures adapted to their functions?

| | WHAT I KNOW | WHAT I LEARNED |
|---|---|---|
| **7.1** Why is it important to study cells? | | |
| **7.2** How do cell structures enable a cell to carry out basic life processes? | | |
| **7.3** How does a cell transport materials across the cell membrane? | | |
| **7.4** How does a cell maintain homeostasis both within itself and as part of a multicellular organism? | | |

Name ______________________ Class _____ Date _______

# 7.1 Life Is Cellular

## Lesson Objectives

- State the cell theory.
- Describe how the different types of microscopes work.
- Distinguish between prokaryotes and eukaryotes.

## Lesson Summary

**The Discovery of the Cell** The invention of the microscope in the 1600s enabled researchers to see cells for the first time.

- Robert Hooke named the empty chambers he observed in cork "cells."
- Anton van Leeuwenhoek was the first to observe living microorganisms.
- **Cells** are the basic units of life.
- Discoveries by German scientists Schleiden, Schwann, and Virchow led to the development of the **cell theory**, which states:
  - All living things are made of cells.
  - Cells are the basic units of structure and function in living things.
  - New cells are produced from existing cells.

**Exploring the Cell** Scientists use light microscopes and electron microscopes to explore the structure of cells.

- Compound light microscopes have lenses that focus light. They magnify objects by up to 1000 times. Chemical stains and fluorescent dyes make cell structures easier to see.
- Electron microscopes use beams of electrons focused by magnetic fields. They offer much higher resolution than light microscopes. There are two main types of electron microscopes—transmission and scanning. Scientists use computers to add color to electron micrographs, which are photos of objects seen through a microscope.

**Prokaryotes and Eukaryotes** Cells come in an amazing variety of shapes and sizes, but all cells contain DNA. Also, all cells are surrounded by a thin flexible barrier called a **cell membrane**. There are two basic categories of cells based on whether they contain a nucleus. The **nucleus** (plural: nuclei) is a large membrane-enclosed structure that contains DNA.

- **Eukaryotes** are cells that enclose their DNA in nuclei.
- **Prokaryotes** are cells that do not enclose their DNA in nuclei.

# The Discovery of the Cell

*For Questions 1–6, complete each statement by writing the correct word or words.*

1. The invention of the ______________ made the discovery of cells possible.
2. Robert Hooke used the name ______________ to refer to the tiny empty chambers he saw when he observed magnified cork.

Name ______________________ Class ______ Date ______

3. German botanist Matthias Schleiden concluded that ______________ are made of cells.

4. German biologist Theodor Schwann concluded that ______________ are made of cells.

5. Rudolph Virchow concluded that new cells are produced from ______________.

6. The ______________ combines the conclusions made by Schleiden, Schwann, and Virchow.

## Exploring the Cell

*For Questions 7–9, write True if the statement is true. If the statement is false, change the underlined word or words to make the statement true.*

__________ **7.** The size of the image formed by a light microscope is <u>unlimited</u> because light that passes through matter is diffracted.

__________ **8.** Fluorescent dyes help scientists see the movement of <u>compounds and structures</u> in living cells.

__________ **9.** <u>Transmission</u> electron microscopes form a 3-D image of the surface of a specimen.

**10.** **THINK VISUALLY** In the second row of the table, draw diagrams to show how a sample of three yeast cells would look in the types of micrographs indicated in the top row of the table. Then, in the third row, describe how each image would be formed.

**A Comparison of Detail in Basic Types of Micrographs**

| **Light Micrograph** (LM 500×) | **Transmission Electron Micrograph** (TEM 4375×) | **Scanning Electron Micrograph** (SEM 3750×) |
| --- | --- | --- |
| | | |
| A light microscope image is formed by ______________ ______________ ______________. | A transmission electron microscope image is formed by ______________ ______________ ______________. | A scanning electron microscope image is formed by a ______________ ______________ ______________. |

Name ______________________ Class ______ Date ______

11. To study cells with a light microscope, different types of stains are usually available. Why is it generally more useful to stain eukaryotic cells than prokaryotic cells?

## Prokaryotes and Eukaryotes

12. Complete the table about the two categories of cells.

**Two Categories of Cells**

| Category | Definition | Size range | Examples |
|---|---|---|---|
| Prokaryotic cells | | | |
| Eukaryotic cells | | | |

13. Which category of cells—prokaryotic or eukaryotic—is your body composed of?

### Apply the Big idea

14. Recall that in science, a theory is a well-tested explanation that unifies a broad range of observations and hypotheses and enables scientists to make accurate predictions about new situations. How does the cell theory demonstrate this definition of theory?

Name ______________________ Class ______ Date ________

# 7.2 Cell Structure

## Lesson Objectives

- Describe the structure and function of the cell nucleus.
- Describe the role of vacuoles, lysosomes, and the cytoskeleton.
- Identify the role of ribosomes, endoplasmic reticulum, and Golgi apparatus in making proteins.
- Describe the function of the chloroplasts and mitochondria in the cell.
- Describe the function of the cell membrane.

## Lesson Summary

**Cell Organization** Eukaryotic cells contain a nucleus and many specialized structures.

- **Cytoplasm** is the fluid portion of a cell.
- **Organelles** are structures that have specialized functions in eukaryotic cells.
- The nucleus contains DNA and controls the activity of a cell.

**Organelles That Store, Clean Up, and Support** These structures include:

- **vacuoles:** membrane-enclosed saclike structures that store water, salts, and organic molecules
- **lysosomes:** small organelles filled with enzymes that break down large molecules and organelles that are no longer useful
- the **cytoskeleton:** a network of protein filaments; it helps the cell maintain its shape and is involved in movement
- **centrioles:** organelles made from tubulins; they help organize cell division in animal cells

**Organelles That Build Proteins** Three kinds of organelles work with the nucleus to make and distribute proteins:

- **ribosomes:** small particles of RNA and protein found throughout the cytoplasm in all cells; they produce proteins by following coded instructions from DNA
- the **endoplasmic reticulum (ER):** an internal membrane system where lipid components of the cell membrane are assembled, along with proteins and other materials
- the **Golgi apparatus:** an organelle that appears as a stack of flattened membranes; it modifies, sorts, and packages proteins and other materials from the ER for storage in the cell or release outside the cell

**Organelles That Capture and Release Energy** Two types of organelles act as power plants of the cells. Both types are surrounded by two membranes.

- **Chloroplasts** capture the energy from sunlight and convert it into food that contains chemical energy in a process called photosynthesis. Cells of plants and some other organisms contain chloroplasts, which contain chlorophyll.
- **Mitochondria** are found in nearly all eukaryotic cells; they convert the chemical energy stored in food to a usable form.

Name ______________________ Class ______ Date ________

**Cellular Boundaries** All cells are surrounded by a cell membrane. Many cells also have a cell wall. Both cell membranes and cell walls separate cells from the environment and provide support.

- **Cell walls** support, shape, and protect the cell. Most prokaryotes and many eukaryotes have them. Animals do not have cell walls. Cell walls lie outside the cell membrane. Most cell walls allow materials to pass through them.
- A cell membrane consists of a **lipid bilayer**, a strong but flexible barrier between the cell and its surroundings. The cell membrane regulates what enters and leaves the cell and also protects and supports the cell. Most biological membranes are **selectively permeable**, allowing some substances, but not others, to pass across them.

## Cell Organization

**1.** Describe the relationship between the cytoplasm and the nucleus of a cell.

______________________________

______________________________

______________________________

**2.** What does the term *organelle* mean literally?

______________________________

*For Questions 3–5, refer to the Visual Analogy comparing the cell with a factory.*

**3.** VISUAL ANALOGY In the visual analogy of a cell as a factory, what two functions of the nucleus are represented? How are these functions illustrated?

______________________________

______________________________

______________________________

______________________________

______________________________

______________________________

______________________________

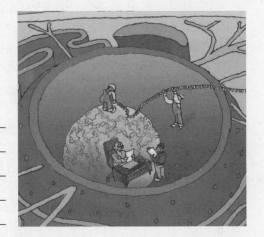

**4.** Which feature of the nucleus is *not* clearly shown by the visual analogy?

______________________________

**5.** What is another possible analogy that could be compared with the structure and function of a cell? ______________________________

______________________________

______________________________

Name ______________________ Class ______ Date ______

# Organelles That Store, Clean Up, and Support

**6.** What are vacuoles?

______________________

______________________

**7.** What are the two roles of the central vacuole in plant cells?

______________________

**8.** How are contractile vacuoles different from other types of vacuoles?

______________________

______________________

**9.** In the diagrams of the animal cell and the plant cell, label the structures indicated by the lines.

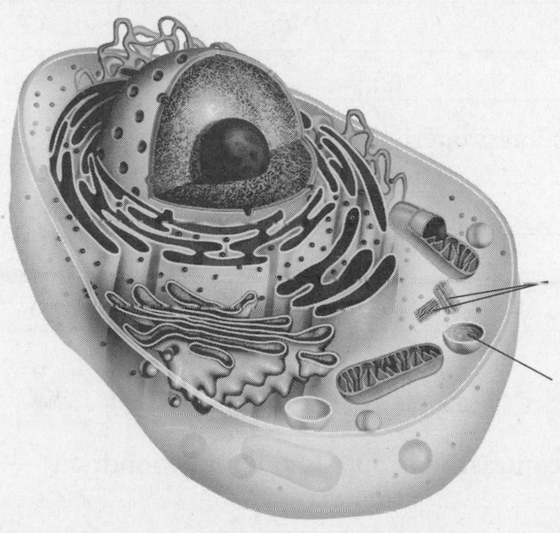

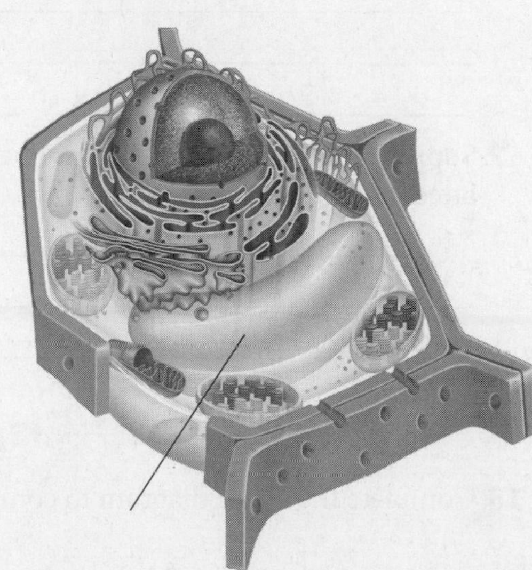

**10.** What is the role of lysosomes in the cell? Why is this a vital role?

______________________

______________________

______________________

**11.** Which structures of the cytoskeleton are found in animal cells but not in plant cells?

______________________

**12.** What other structures of the cytoskeleton would show the same pattern of microtubules as a flagellum?

______________________

 

Name ________________ Class ______ Date ________

## Organelles That Build Proteins

**13.** What are ribosomes? What do they do?

______________________________

______________________________

______________________________

**14.** In which organelle are the lipid components of the cell membrane assembled?

______________________________

**15.** What is the difference between rough ER and smooth ER?

______________________________

______________________________

**16.** Using the cell as a factory analogy, describe the role of the Golgi apparatus in cells.

______________________________

______________________________

______________________________

**17.** Suppose a cell's Golgi apparatus does not function properly. How might this problem affect other cells?

______________________________

______________________________

______________________________

## Organelles That Capture and Release Energy

**18.** Complete the Venn diagram to compare and contrast chloroplasts and mitochondria.

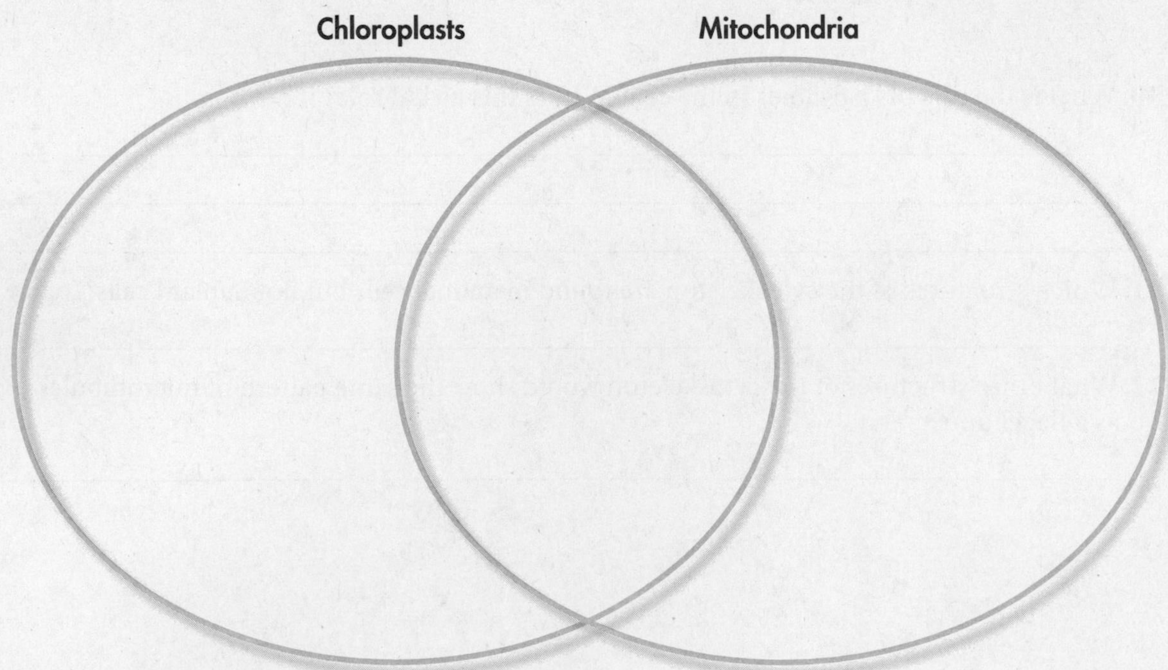

Name ______________________ Class ______ Date ______

*For Questions 19–22, write True if the statement is true. If the statement is false, change the underlined word or words to make the statement true.*

________ **19.** Chloroplasts are never found in animal cells.

________ **20.** Unlike chloroplasts, mitochondria are surrounded by a double membrane.

________ **21.** Nearly all of the mitochondria in your cells were inherited from your mother.

________ **22.** Both chloroplasts and mitochondria lack genetic information in the form of DNA.

## Cellular Boundaries

*For Questions 23–25, complete each statement by writing the correct word or words.*

**23.** Most cell ____________ are porous to water and other materials but strong enough to support and protect cells.

**24.** Nearly all of the plant tissue called ____________ is made up of cell walls.

**25.** Besides supporting and protecting a cell, the cell membrane ____________ what enters and leaves the cell.

**26.** Complete the diagram of a section of a cell membrane. Then, on the line below the diagram, write the name of the model that describes the cell membrane's structure.

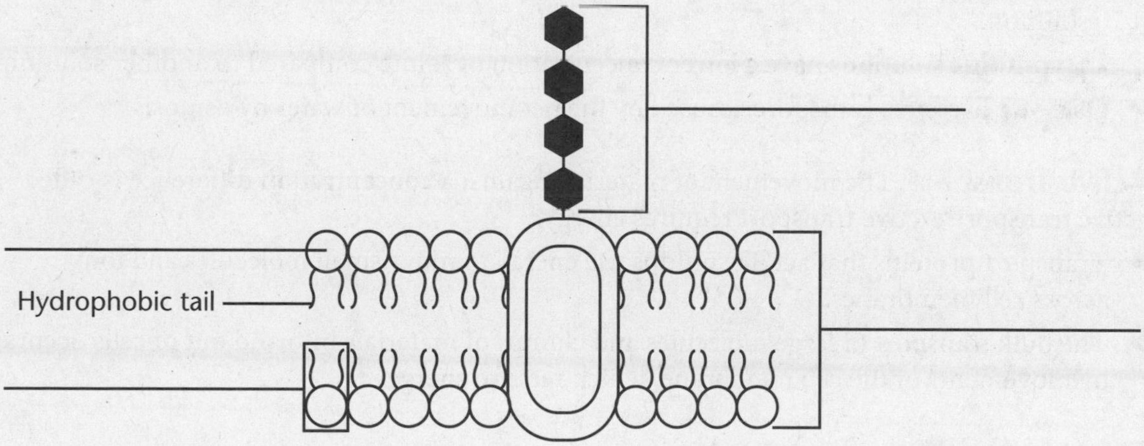

Hydrophobic tail

______________________

### Apply the Big idea

**27.** What is the function of vesicles in the synthesis of proteins and the release of those proteins outside the cell?

______________________________________________

______________________________________________

______________________________________________

______________________________________________

Name ____________________ Class ______ Date ________

# 7.3 Cell Transport

## Lesson Objectives

- Describe passive transport.
- Describe active transport.

## Lesson Summary

**Passive Transport** The movement of materials across the cell membrane without using cellular energy is called passive transport.

- **Diffusion** is the process by which particles move from an area of high concentration to an area of lower concentration.
- **Facilitated diffusion** is the process by which molecules that cannot directly diffuse across the membrane pass through special protein channels.
- **Osmosis** is the facilitated diffusion of water through a selectively permeable membrane.
  - **Aquaporins** are water channel proteins that allow water to pass through cell membranes.
  - Two adjacent solutions are **isotonic** if they have the same concentrations of solute.
  - **Hypertonic** solutions have a higher concentration of solute compared to another solution.
  - **Hypotonic** solutions have a lower concentration of solute compared to another solution.
- **Osmotic pressure** is the force caused by the net movement of water by osmosis.

**Active Transport** The movement of materials against a concentration difference is called active transport. Active transport requires energy.

- Transport proteins that act like pumps use energy to move small molecules and ions across cell membranes.
- The bulk transport of large molecules and clumps of materials into and out of cells occurs by movements of the cell membrane, which require energy.

# Passive Transport

*For Questions 1–4, write the letter of the correct answer on the line at the left.*

______ **1.** Which of the following must be true for diffusion to occur?

**A.** Molecules or particles must have different sizes.

**B.** Special protein channels must always be available.

**C.** There must be areas of different concentrations.

**D.** Energy must be available.

 

______ **2.** Which term refers to the condition that exists when *no* net change in concentration results from diffusion?

**A.** concentration  **C.** osmosis
**B.** equilibrium  **D.** randomness

______ **3.** Air has a higher concentration of oxygen molecules than does the cytoplasm of your lung cells. Where in your lungs will there be a net increase of oxygen?

**A.** in the air breathed in  **C.** outside of the lung cells
**B.** in the air breathed out  **D.** inside of the lung cells

______ **4.** Which of the following statements tells how facilitated diffusion differs from simple diffusion?

**A.** Particles move through cell membranes without the use of energy by cells.
**B.** Particles tend to move from high concentration to lower concentration
**C.** Particles move within channel proteins that pass through cell membranes.
**D.** Particles tend to move more slowly than they would be expected to move.

*For Questions 5–7, match the situation with the result. Write the letter of the correct answer on the line at the left.*

| **Situation** | **Result** |
|---|---|
| ______ **5.** Cells are in an isotonic solution. | **A.** The cells lose water. |
| ______ **6.** Cells are in a hypertonic solution. | **B.** The cells gain water. |
| ______ **7.** Cells are in a hypotonic solution. | **C.** The cells stay the same. |

**8.** THINK VISUALLY In the table below, draw how each type of cell will look after being placed in a hypertonic solution.

**Appearance of Cells in a Hypertonic Solution**

| Animal Cells | Plant Cells |
|---|---|
| | |

## Active Transport

**9.** What is the function of active transport in moving small molecules and ions across cell membranes? Give an example.

**10.** How does ATP enable transport proteins to move ions across a cell membrane?

**11.** What are the proteins used in active transport called? ______________

**12.** Complete the table to summarize the types of bulk transport.

| Types of Bulk Transport | |
|---|---|
| **Type** | **Description** |
| Endocytosis | |
| Phagocytosis | |
| Exocytosis | |

### Apply the Big idea

**13.** Most sports drinks are isotonic in relation to human body fluids. Explain why athletes should drink solutions that are isotonic to body fluids when they exercise rather than ones that are hypotonic to body fluids (contain a greater proportion of water in comparison to the fluids in and around human body cells).

 

Name ________________________________ Class ______ Date ________

# 7.4 Homeostasis and Cells

## Lesson Objectives

- Explain how unicellular organisms maintain homeostasis.
- Explain how multicellular organisms maintain homeostasis.

## Lesson Summary

**The Cell as an Organism** Sometimes a single cell is an organism. Single-celled organisms must be able to carry out all the functions necessary for life.

- Unicellular organisms maintain **homeostasis**, relatively constant internal conditions, by growing, responding to the environment, transforming energy, and reproducing.
- Unicellular organisms include both prokaryotes and eukaryotes.
- Unicellular organisms play many important roles in their environments.

**Multicellular Life** Cells of multicellular organisms are interdependent and specialized.

- The cells of multicellular organisms become specialized for particular tasks and communicate with one another to maintain homeostasis.
- Specialized cells in multicellular organisms are organized into groups.
  - A **tissue** is a group of similar cells that performs a particular function.
  - An **organ** is a group of tissues working together to perform an essential task.
  - An **organ system** is a group of organs that work together to perform a specific function.
- The cells of multicellular organisms communicate with one another by means of chemical signals that are passed from one cell to another.
  - Certain cells form connections, or cellular junctions, to neighboring cells. Some of these junctions hold cells together firmly.
  - Other cells allow small molecules carrying chemical signals to pass directly from one cell to the next.
  - To respond to a chemical signal, a cell must have a **receptor** to which the signaling molecule can bind.

## The Cell as an Organism

*For Questions 1–5, complete each statement by writing the correct word or words.*

**1.** The term ______________ refers to the relatively constant internal physical and chemical state of a living cell.

**2.** Unicellular prokaryotes, called ______________, are adapted to living in a remarkable number of different places.

**3.** Some unicellular eukaryotes, called ______________, contain chloroplasts.

**4.** Yeasts are unicellular ______________, which are eukaryotes.

**5.** Other unicellular eukaryotes include ______________ and algae.

 

Name ______________________ Class ______ Date ______

6. How do single-celled organisms maintain homeostasis?

______________________________________________

______________________________________________

7. Why is maintaining homeostasis particularly important to single-celled organisms?

______________________________________________

______________________________________________

______________________________________________

## Multicellular Life

8. How are the cells of a multicellular organism like a baseball team?

______________________________________________

______________________________________________

______________________________________________

______________________________________________

______________________________________________

9. How does a multicellular organism maintain homeostasis?

______________________________________________

______________________________________________

______________________________________________

______________________________________________

______________________________________________

10. Complete the table by describing the functions of the specialized cells.

**Examples of Specialized Cells**

| Type of Cell | Name of Specialized Cell Part | Function of Specialized Cell Part |
|---|---|---|
| cells that line the upper air passages in humans | cilia | |
| pine pollen grains | wings | |

Name ______________________ Class ______ Date ________

11. The Venn diagram below consists of four concentric circles. Complete the diagram to show the relationships among four levels of organization of life. Use the terms *cells, organ, organ system,* and *tissue.*

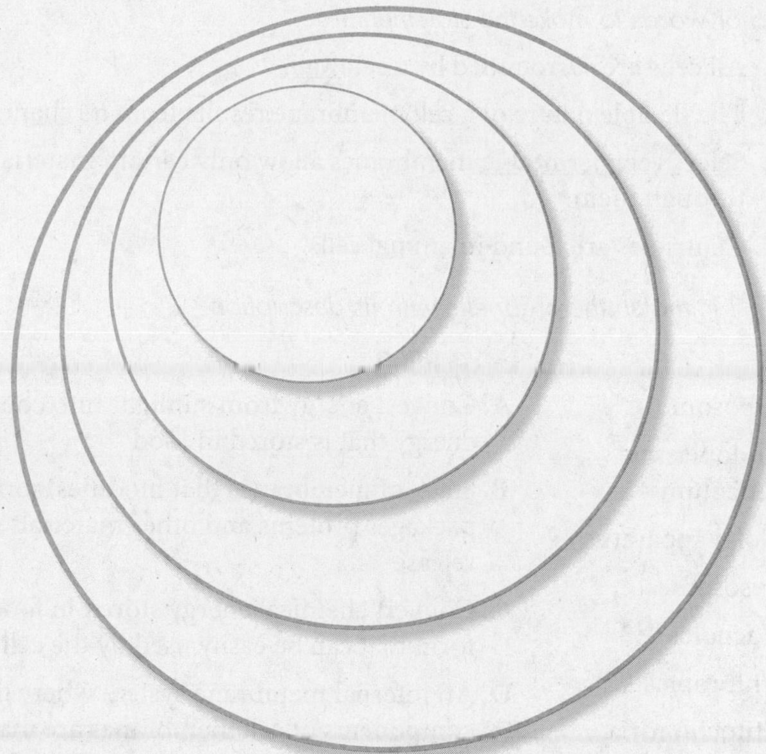

12. Starting with the outermost circle of the diagram, explain how each level is related to the next level within each circle.

_______________________________________________

_______________________________________________

_______________________________________________

13. What is the name of the areas that hold adjacent cells together and enable them to communicate?

_______________________________________________

## Apply the Big idea

14. On the Venn diagram above, where would you add a circle that represents the organism level of life? Where would you add a circle that represents another organ of the same organ system?

_______________________________________________

_______________________________________________

_______________________________________________

_______________________________________________

_______________________________________________

# Chapter Vocabulary Review

*For Questions 1–4, write True if the statement is true. If the statement is false, change the underlined word or words to make the statement true.*

________ **1.** All cells are surrounded by a cell <u>wall</u>.

________ **2.** The flexible nature of a cell membrane results from its <u>channel proteins</u>.

________ **3.** <u>Selectively permeable</u> membranes allow only certain materials to pass through them.

________ **4.** Centrioles are found in <u>animal</u> cells.

*For Questions 5–11, match the organelle with its description.*

| Organelle | Description |
|---|---|
| ____ **5.** Ribosomes | **A.** Convert energy from sunlight into chemical energy that is stored in food |
| ____ **6.** Endoplasmic reticulum | **B.** Stack of membranes that modifies, sorts, and packages proteins and other materials for storage or release |
| ____ **7.** Golgi apparatus | **C.** Convert chemical energy stored in food into a form that can be easily used by the cell |
| ____ **8.** Lysosomes | **D.** An internal membrane system where lipid components of cell membranes are made |
| ____ **9.** Vacuoles | **E.** Saclike structures that store materials |
| ____ **10.** Chloroplasts | **F.** Small particles of RNA and protein on which proteins are assembled using instructions from DNA |
| ____ **11.** Mitochondria | **G.** Filled with enzymes used to break down carbohydrates into smaller molecules |

*For Questions 12–15, complete each statement by writing the correct word or words.*

**12.** Osmosis occurs through water channel proteins called ________.

**13.** The force created by the net movement of water through a cell membrane is called ________ pressure.

**14.** Red blood cells are able to maintain homeostasis because they are bathed in blood, which is ________ to the fluid in the cells themselves.

**15.** To respond to a chemical signal, a cell must have a ________ to which the signaling molecule can bind.

 

Name ______________________ Class ______ Date ________

# CHAPTER MYSTERY

## DEATH BY ... WATER?

In the Chapter Mystery, you learned how the body's salt balance can be disrupted during periods of exertion, in this case a marathon. Running a marathon can disrupt other aspects of the body's homeostasis.

21st Century Learning

# Preparing for, Completing, and Recovering From a Race

Marathon running poses some challenges to cellular homeostasis. Dehydration can occur due to sweating. Exercising muscles demand more oxygen and produce excess heat. But if participants take precautions, marathon running is generally a safe activity. The plan below explains some of the things that runners should do.

**Six Weeks Before the Race**
Do not try any new training techniques. Limit your strength training to exercises with minimal external resistance (that means no weights).

**Three Weeks Before the Race**
Reduce the length of long training runs by 25%.

**Two Weeks Before the Race**
Reduce the length of long training runs by another 25%.

**The Week Before the Race**
Stop all long training runs—just do light ones. Stop strength training. Do not try any unfamiliar foods, and that means ordinary meals as well as training foods. If you plan to use any new electrolyte drinks, nutrition bars, gel supplements, etc. during the race, start consuming them now. Get extra sleep every night.

**The Day Before the Race**
Stay off your feet. Take it easy. Eat lots of complex carbohydrates. Do not eat much fiber. Drink a lot of water. Do not drink any caffeine. Do not eat anything late at night.

**The Day of the Race**
Get up early. Eat a light breakfast. Drink a large glass of water two hours before the race. Do not drink again until after the race starts.

**During the Race**
Start slowly—you can pick up speed later in the race. Drink at every water station. Drink electrolyte drinks as well as water.

**Within Two Hours of the End of the Race**
Drink water or electrolyte drinks. Walk for 60 of the 120 minutes (not necessarily all at once, though). Eat something with carbohydrates and a little protein. Do not eat anything high in fat or sugar.

**After That**
Put ice on any sore muscles. Get lots of sleep. Do not run for the next week. Do not do any strength training for two weeks.

Continued on next page ▶

## 21st Century Themes Science and Health Literacy

1. When should a runner stop doing long training runs?

2. What should an athlete do after a marathon?

3. What should a runner do six weeks before a race? Why do you think that is advisable?

4. Should a runner eat nothing, a light, meal, or a heavy meal before the race? Why do you think this advice is given?

5. What advice does the article give about eating the week before the race? Why might that advice be appropriate?

## 21st Century Skills Race for a Cause

The skills used in this activity include **problem identification, formulation, and solution; interpersonal and collaborative skills; accountability and adaptability;** and **social responsibility.**

Use library and Internet resources to research different ideas about what an athlete should do the week prior to a race, the day of the race, and the day after. Combine the tips you find with the ones presented here, and then write them up in the form of a calendar or schedule for prospective athletes.

Working with a group, choose a charity or non-profit organization in your community. Plan, organize, and stage a race to benefit that organization.

Have a sports physician and a gym teacher review your training calendar. Make any changes they suggest, and then mail a copy to each entrant.

Things you will need to do include determining the length of the race, planning the course, getting permits for the race, and finding sponsors. You will need to publicize the event twice—first to attract entrants, and later to attract spectators.

*You will also need to check that entrants do not have any physical conditions that rule out their participation.*

 

Name ______________________ Class ______ Date ________

# Photosynthesis

## Cellular Basis of Life

**Q:** How do plants and other organisms capture energy from the sun?

| | WHAT I KNOW | WHAT I LEARNED |
|---|---|---|
| **8.1** How do organisms store energy? | | |
| **8.2** What cellular structures and molecules are involved in photosynthesis? | | |
| **8.3** How do photosynthetic organisms convert the sun's energy into chemical energy? | | |

Name ______________________ Class _____ Date _________

# 8.1 Energy and Life

## Lesson Objectives

Describe the role of ATP in cellular activities.

Explain where plants get the energy they need to produce food.

## Lesson Summary

**Chemical Energy and ATP** Energy is the ability to do work. Organisms need energy to stay alive.

- **Adenosine triphosphate (ATP)** is a chemical compound cells use to store and release energy.
  - An ATP molecule consists of adenine, the sugar ribose, and three phosphate groups.
  - Cells store energy by adding a phosphate group to adenosine diphosphate (ADP) molecules.
  - Cells release energy from ATP molecules by subtracting a phosphate group.
- Energy provided by ATP is used in active transport, to contract muscles, to make proteins, and in many other ways.
- Cells contain only a small amount of ATP at any one time. They regenerate it from ADP as they need it, using energy stored in food.

**Heterotrophs and Autotrophs** The energy to make ATP from ADP comes from food. Organisms get food in one of two ways.

- **Heterotrophs** get food by consuming (eating) other organisms.
- **Autotrophs** use the energy in sunlight to make their own food.
- **Photosynthesis** is the process that uses light energy to produce food molecules.

# Chemical Energy and ATP

*For Questions 1–6, complete each statement by writing the correct word or words.*

1. ______________________ is the ability to do work.

2. The main chemical compound cells use for energy is ______________________ (ATP).

3. ______________________ is a 5-carbon sugar molecule that is part of an ATP molecule.

4. The ______________________ of ATP are the key to its ability to store and supply energy.

5. ATP releases energy when it ______________________ bonds between its phosphate groups.

6. Most cells only store enough ATP for ______________________ of activity.

7. **THINK VISUALLY** Label each part of the diagram of an ATP molecule below.

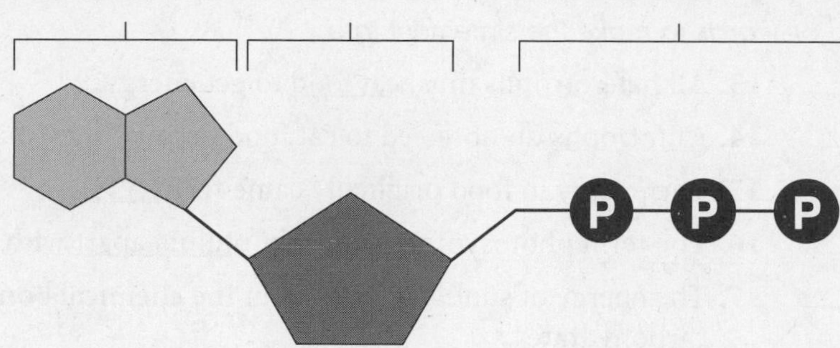


*For Questions 8–10, refer to the Visual Analogy comparing ATP to a charged battery.*

8. **VISUAL ANALOGY** In the visual analogy, what chemical is represented by the low battery?

_______________________________________________

_______________________________________________

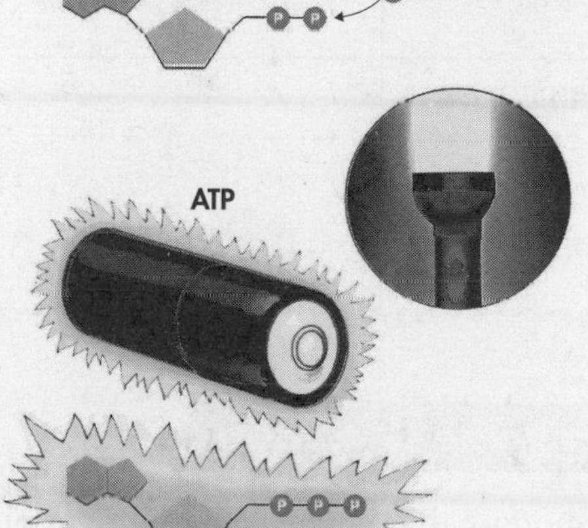


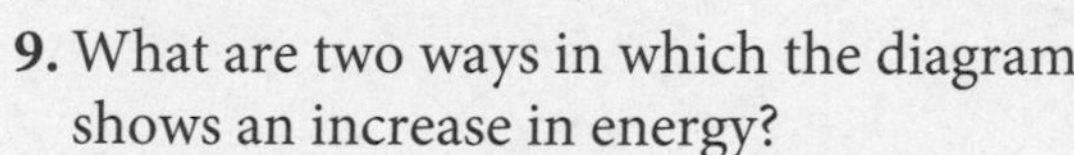

9. What are two ways in which the diagram shows an increase in energy?

_______________________________________________

_______________________________________________

10. Describe the concepts shown in the diagram.

_______________________________________________

_______________________________________________

_______________________________________________

_______________________________________________

_______________________________________________

_______________________________________________

_______________________________________________

11. What are two ways in which cells use the energy temporarily stored in ATP?

_______________________________________________

_______________________________________________

12. Energy is needed to add a third phosphate group to ADP to make ATP. What is a cell's source of this energy?

_______________________________________________

_______________________________________________

 

Name ________________________ Class ______ Date ________

## Heterotrophs and Autotrophs

*For Questions 13–17, write True if the statement is true. If the statement is false, change the underlined word or words to make the statement true.*

________ **13.** All heterotrophs must eat food to get energy.

________ **14.** Autotrophs do not need to eat food because they make food.

________ **15.** The energy in food originally came from ATP.

________ **16.** The term photosynthesis means "pulling apart with light" in Greek.

________ **17.** The energy of sunlight is stored in the chemical bonds of carbohydrates.

**18.** Complete the table comparing two types of organisms.

| Autotrophs and Heterotrophs | | |
|---|---|---|
| **Type** | **Description** | **Examples** |
| Autotrophs | | |
| Heterotrophs | | |

### Apply the Big idea

**19.** Suppose that you ate a hamburger on a wheat roll with lettuce, tomatoes, and onions for lunch. As you ate, you took in food molecules from plants and animals. Explain why all the energy in the food molecules of this hamburger could be traced back to the sun.

 

# 8.2 Photosynthesis: An Overview

## Lesson Objectives

- Explain the role of light and pigments in photosynthesis.
- Explain the role of electron carrier molecules in photosynthesis.
- State the overall equation for photosynthesis.

## Lesson Summary

**Chlorophyll and Chloroplasts** In eukaryotes, photosynthesis occurs in organelles called chloroplasts. Chloroplasts house light-absorbing chemicals.

- Light is a form of energy. Sunlight is a mixture of all the different colors of visible light.
- Light-absorbing molecules called **pigments** capture the sun's energy.
- **Chlorophyll** is the principal pigment in photosynthetic organisms. Chlorophyll absorbs blue-violet and red light but reflects green light.
- Chloroplasts have a complex internal structure that includes:
  - **thylakoids:** saclike photosynthetic membranes that contain chlorophyll and other pigments and are arranged in stacks called grana.
  - **stroma:** the fluid portion outside of the thylakoids.

**High-Energy Electrons** The energy in light raises some of the electrons in chlorophyll to higher energy levels. These high-energy electrons are used in photosynthesis.

- Electron carriers are used to transport the electrons from chlorophyll to other molecules during photosynthesis.
- **$NADP^+$** is a compound that can accept and hold 2 high-energy electrons and 1 hydrogen ion. This process converts $NADP^+$ into NADPH.

**An Overview of Photosynthesis** Usually summarized by a simple chemical reaction, photosynthesis is a complex process that involves two interdependent sets of reactions.

- The **light-dependent reactions** require light, light-absorbing pigments, and water to form NADPH, ATP, and oxygen.
- The **light-independent reactions** do not use light energy. They use carbon dioxide from the atmosphere, NADPH, and ATP to make energy-rich carbon compounds.

## Chlorophyll and Chloroplasts

*For Questions 1–6, complete each statement by writing the correct word or words.*

1. The ______________ of light determines its color.
2. Chemicals that absorb light are called ______________.
3. Chlorophyll makes plants look green because it ______________ green light.
4. Chloroplasts contain an abundance of saclike photosynthetic membranes called

______________.

**5.** The ______________ is the fluid portion of the chloroplast located outside the thylakoids.

**6.** The visible light absorbed by chlorophyll ______________ the energy level of the chlorophyll's electrons.

**7.** THINK VISUALLY Label the internal parts of the chloroplast below.

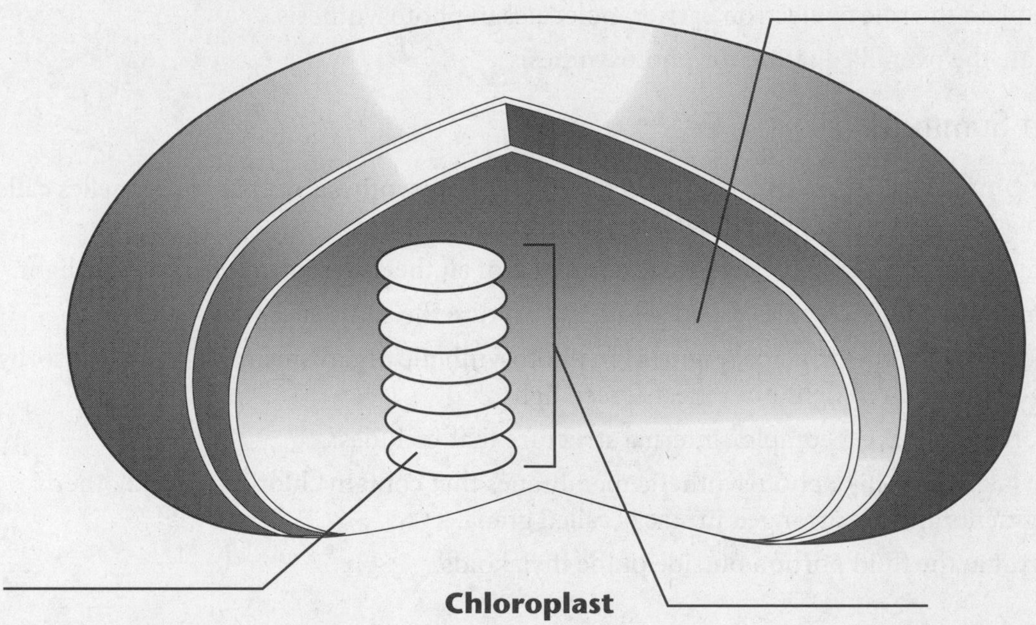

**Chloroplast**

## High-Energy Electrons

*For Questions 8–9, refer to the Visual Analogy comparing electron carriers to oven mitts.*

**8.** VISUAL ANALOGY In the visual analogy of carrying electrons, what represents the high-energy electrons?

______________________________

______________________________

______________________________

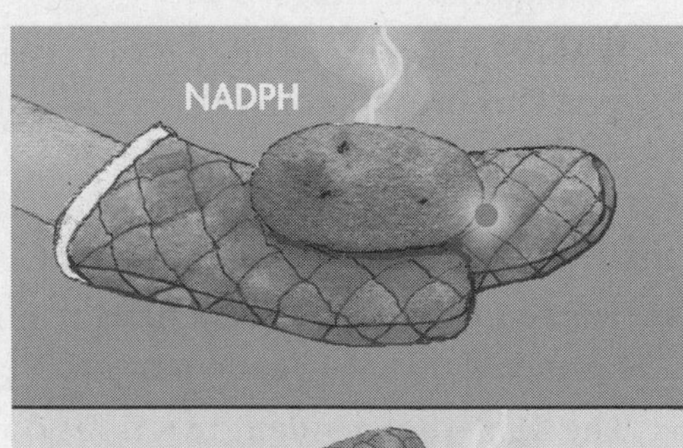

**9.** Write another analogy that describes the process of electron carriers.

______________________________

______________________________

______________________________

______________________________

______________________________

______________________________

**10.** Where do the high-energy electrons carried by NADPH come from?

______________________________

______________________________

# An Overview of Photosynthesis

*For Questions 11–13, write the letter of the correct answer on the line at the left.*

_____ **11.** What are the reactants of the photosynthesis reaction?

**A.** chlorophyll and light
**B.** carbon dioxide and water
**C.** carbohydrates and oxygen
**D.** high-energy electrons and air

_____ **12.** What are the products of the light-dependent reactions?

**A.** chloroplasts and light
**B.** proteins and lipids
**C.** oxygen and ATP
**D.** water and sugars

_____ **13.** Where do the light-independent reactions occur?

**A.** stroma
**B.** thylakoids
**C.** chlorophyll
**D.** mitochondria

**14.** Complete the illustration by writing the reactants and products of the light-dependent and light-independent reactions. Also, fill in the energy source that excites the electrons.

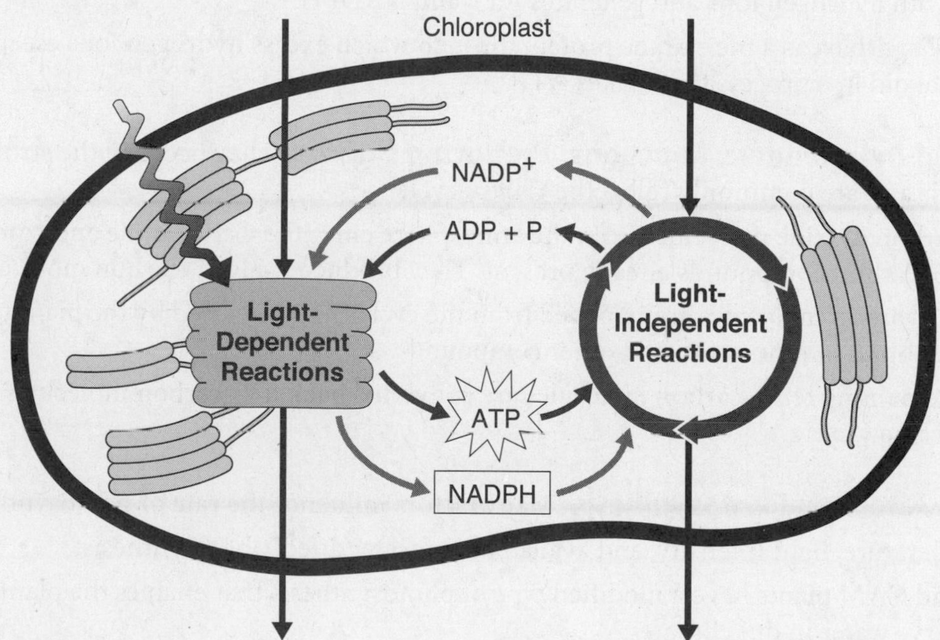


## Apply the Big idea

**15.** Solar power uses cells or panels to absorb the sun's energy. That energy is then used to create electricity. How does this compare to the light dependent reactions of photosynthesis?

______________________________________________

______________________________________________

______________________________________________

______________________________________________

______________________________________________

 

Name ______________________ Class ______ Date ________

# 8.3 The Process of Photosynthesis

## Lesson Objectives

- Describe what happens during the light-dependent reactions.
- Describe what happens during the light-independent reactions.
- Identify factors that affect the rate at which photosynthesis occurs.

## Lesson Summary

### The Light-Dependent Reactions: Generating ATP and NADPH

Photosynthesis begins with these reactions, which occur in thylakoid membranes.

- **Photosystems** are clusters of proteins and chlorophyll in thylakoid membranes.
- High-energy electrons form when pigments in photosystem II absorb light. The electrons pass through **electron transport chains**, a series of electron carrier proteins.
  - The movement of electrons through an electron transport chain causes a thylakoid to fill up with hydrogen ions and generates ATP and NADPH.
  - **ATP synthase** is a membrane protein through which excess hydrogen ions escape a thylakoid in a process that makes ATP.

**The Light-Independent Reactions: Producing Sugars** They occur in the stroma of thylakoids and are commonly called the **Calvin cycle**.

- Six carbon dioxide molecules from the atmosphere enter the Calvin cycle and combine with 5-carbon compounds already present. They produce twelve 3-carbon molecules.
- Two 3-carbon molecules are removed from the cycle. They are used by the plant to build sugars, lipids, amino acids, and other compounds.
- The remaining ten 3-carbon molecules are converted back to 5-carbon molecules and begin a new cycle.

**Factors Affecting Photosynthesis** Many factors influence the rate of photosynthesis.

- Temperature, light intensity, and availability of water affect photosynthesis.
- C4 and CAM plants have a modified type of photosynthesis that enables the plants to conserve water in dry climates.

## The Light-Dependent Reactions: Generating ATP and NADPH

*For Questions 1–5, write True if the statement is true. If the statement is false, change the underlined word or words to make the statement true.*

______________ 1. Photosystems are clusters of chlorophyll and <u>proteins</u>.

______________ 2. The light-dependent reactions begin when <u>photosystem I</u> absorbs light.

______________ 3. Electrons from <u>water</u> molecules replace the ones lost by photosystem II.

______________ 4. <u>ATP</u> is the product of photosystem I.

______________ 5. ATP and NADPH are two types of <u>protein</u> carriers.

Name ______________________ Class ______ Date ________

6. How does ATP synthase produce ATP? ______________________

______________________

______________________

7. When sunlight excites electrons in chlorophyll, how do the electrons change?

______________________

______________________

8. Where do the light-dependent reactions take place? ______________________

______________________

9. Complete the table by summarizing what happens in each phase of the light-dependent reactions of photosynthesis.

| Light-Dependent Reactions | Summary |
|---|---|
| Photosystem II | |
| Electron Transport Chain | |
| Photosystem I | |
| Hydrogen Ion Movement and ATP Formation | |

 

# The Light-Independent Reactions: Producing Sugars

**10.** What does the Calvin cycle use to produce high-energy sugars?

______________________________________________

______________________________________________

**11.** Why are the reactions of the Calvin cycle called light-independent reactions?

______________________________________________

______________________________________________

**12.** What makes the Calvin cycle a cycle?

______________________________________________

______________________________________________

**13.** Complete the diagram of the Calvin cycle by filling in the missing labels.

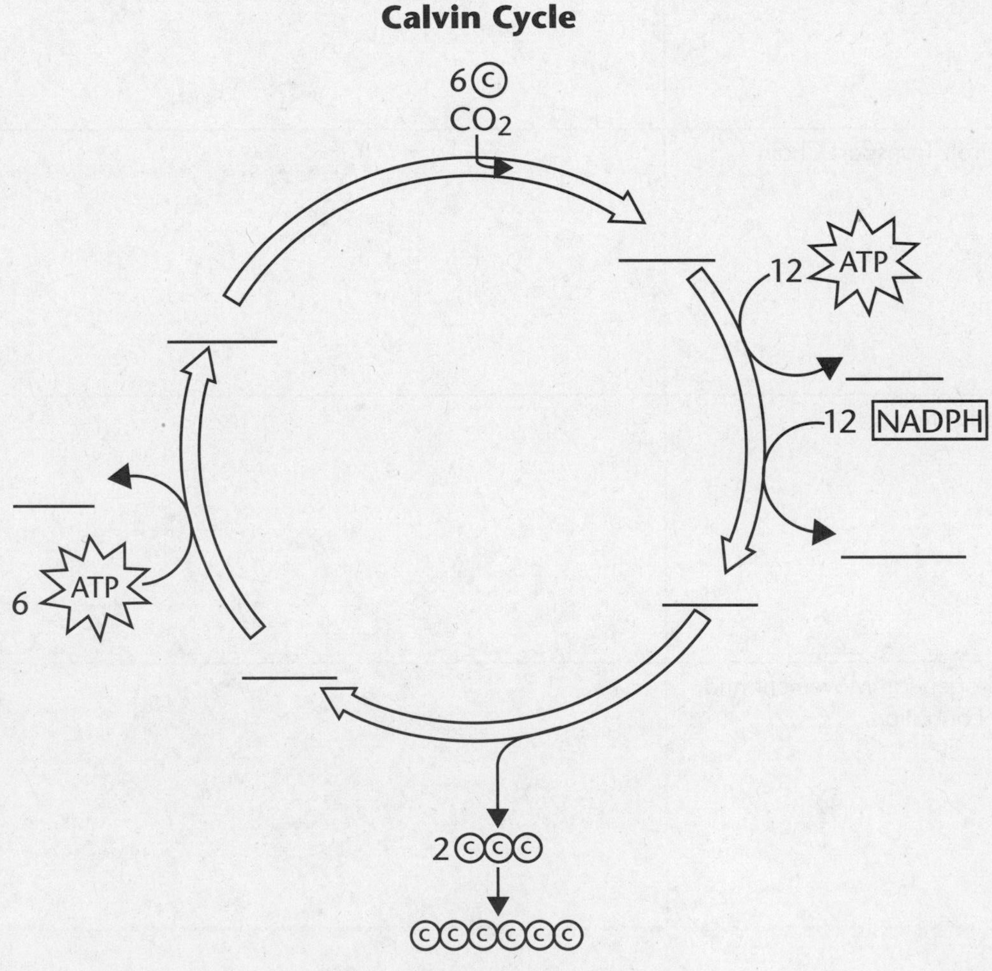

Name ______________________ Class ______ Date ______

# Factors Affecting Photosynthesis

**14.** What are three factors that affect the rate at which photosynthesis occurs?

______________________

______________________

______________________

**15.** Would a plant placed in an atmosphere of pure oxygen be able to conduct photosynthesis? Explain your answer.

______________________

______________________

______________________

**16.** Complete the table about variations of photosynthesis.

| Type | Description | Examples |
|---|---|---|
| | Occurs in plants that have a specialized chemical pathway that allows them to capture even very low levels of carbon dioxide and pass it to the Calvin cycle. | |
| | | pineapple trees, many desert cacti, and "ice plants" |

## Apply the Big idea

**17.** Photosynthesis plays an important role in supplying energy to living things. Considering what the products of photosynthesis are, what is another way in which photosynthesis is vital to life?

______________________

______________________

______________________

______________________

______________________

______________________

______________________

Name ____________________ Class ______ Date ________

# Chapter Vocabulary Review

**Crossword Puzzle** *Complete the puzzle by entering the term that matches the description.*

**Across**

**4.** energy carrier cells use to transport high-energy electrons

**6.** cluster of pigments and proteins that absorbs light

**7.** a saclike photosynthetic membrane found in chloroplasts

**8.** energy carrier made as a result of photosystem II

**9.** process of using the sun's energy to make food

**10.** man who worked out the light-independent reactions

**Down**

**1.** liquid part of the inside of a chloroplast

**2.** chemical that absorbs light for photosynthesis

**3.** light-absorbing chemical

**5.** organism that makes its own food

*For Questions 11–16, complete each statement by writing the correct word or words.*

**11.** The light-____________ reactions occur in thylakoid membranes.

**12.** Carbon dioxide is used to make sugars in the light-____________ reactions.

**13.** The light-independent reactions are also called the ____________.

**14.** ____________ spins to provide the energy for adding a phosphate group to ADP.

**15.** Electron ____________ move high-energy electrons between photosystems.

**16.** An animal that obtains food by eating other organisms is called a(n) ____________.

Name ______________________ Class ______ Date ________

In the Chapter Mystery, you read about a five-year-long experiment that Jan van Helmont performed in the middle of the seventeenth century. That experiment is a milestone in the history of science and is taught in high schools and colleges around the world.

# Explore and Teach van Helmont's Experiment

But, van Helmont's experiment, as famous as it is, led him to the wrong conclusion. In the end, he did not know where the tree's mass came from. He guessed that it came from the water he'd added. It turns out he was wrong.

The problem was the way van Helmont set up his experiment. He set up his experiment to prove that the tree's extra mass came from the soil, and he did not consider other possible explanations of where the extra mass might come from. Therefore, the experiment, as carried out, could not prove where the tree's extra mass came from. In the 1600s, science and the scientific method were in their infancy. Now we know that an experiment should take all the variables into account and consider every possible outcome. An experiment should be done to find out what happens, or at least to find out if something happens, not to "prove" that the scientist's preconceived notion is correct.

Consider how you could modify van Helmont's procedures if you were to carry out the experiment today. Start with van Helmont's original hypothesis: A tree's mass comes from absorbing matter from the soil. What variable(s) would you need to control in this experiment?

_______________________________________________

_______________________________________________

What procedure would you follow in your experiment?

_______________________________________________

_______________________________________________

_______________________________________________

_______________________________________________

_______________________________________________

_______________________________________________

_______________________________________________

What materials and tools would you need for your experiment?

_______________________________________________

_______________________________________________

Continued on next page ▶

 

## 21st Century Themes Science Literacy

1. How does your experimental procedure make sure that nothing comes into contact with the tree without your being aware of it?

2. How would you account for the mass of the water that comes into contact with the tree during the five-year experiment?

3. How would you account for the mass of the air that comes into contact with the tree over the five years?

4. How would you account for the gases that would be released by the tree over the five years?

5. Are there any variables you would not be able to account for? If so, what are they?

## 21st Century Skills Communicating Results

The skills used in this activity include **communication skills; critical thinking and systems thinking; problem identification, formulation, and solution;** and **creativity** and **intellectual curiosity.**

How might you change your experiment to improve it? List any alterations you would make to ensure your results would be more valid. Then prepare a lesson plan that you could use to teach another student about van Helmont's experiment. The lesson plan should include an outline of what you would say, as well as any diagrams or pictures you would show to the student.

*Ask your teacher to arrange for a time when you can meet with a middle-school student and teach him or her the lesson.*

 

Name ____________________ Class ______ Date ________

# Cellular Respiration and Fermentation

**Big idea** **Cellular Basis of Life**

**Q:** How do organisms obtain energy?

| | WHAT I KNOW | WHAT I LEARNED |
|---|---|---|
| **9.1** Why do most organisms undergo the process of cellular respiration? | | |
| **9.2** How do cells release energy from food in the presence of oxygen? | | |
| **9.3** How do cells release energy from food without oxygen? | | |

 

# 9.1 Cellular Respiration: An Overview

## Lesson Objectives

- Explain where organisms get the energy they need for life processes.
- Define cellular respiration.
- Compare photosynthesis and cellular respiration.

## Lesson Summary

**Chemical Energy and Food** Chemical energy is stored in food molecules.

- Energy is released when chemical bonds in food molecules are broken.
- Energy is measured in a unit called a **calorie**, the amount of energy needed to raise the temperature of 1 gram of water 1 degree Celsius.
- Fats store more energy per gram than do carbohydrates and proteins.

**Overview of Cellular Respiration** **Cellular respiration** is the process that releases energy from food in the presence of oxygen.

- Cellular respiration captures the energy from food in three main stages:
  - glycolysis
  - the Krebs cycle
  - the electron transport chain
- Glycolysis does not require oxygen. The Krebs cycle and electron transport chain both require oxygen.
  - **Aerobic** pathways are processes that require oxygen.
  - **Anaerobic** pathways are processes that occur without oxygen.

**Comparing Photosynthesis and Cellular Respiration** The energy in photosynthesis and cellular respiration flows in opposite directions. Their equations are the reverse of each other.

- Photosynthesis removes carbon dioxide from the atmosphere, and cellular respiration puts it back.
- Photosynthesis releases oxygen into the atmosphere, and cellular respiration uses oxygen to release energy from food.

## Chemical Energy and Food

*For Questions 1–4, complete each statement by writing the correct word or words.*

**1.** A calorie is a unit of ______________.

**2.** The Calorie used on food labels is equal to ______________ calories.

**3.** A Calorie is also referred to as a ______________.

**4.** Cells use the energy stored in chemical bonds of foods to produce compounds that directly power the cell's activities, such as ______________.

Name ______________________ Class _____ Date _______

# Overview of Cellular Respiration

*For Questions 5–10, complete each statement by writing the correct word or words.*

**5.** The equation that summarizes cellular respiration, using chemical formulas, is ______________________.

**6.** If cellular respiration took place in just one step, most of the __________ would be lost in the form of light and __________.

**7.** Cellular respiration begins with a pathway called __________, which takes place in the __________ of the cell.

**8.** At the end of glycolysis, about __________ percent of the chemical energy is locked in the bonds of the __________ molecule.

**9.** Cellular respiration continues in the __________ of the cell with the __________ and electron transport chain.

**10.** The pathways of cellular respiration that require oxygen are said to be __________. Pathways that do not require oxygen are said to be __________.

**11.** **THINK VISUALLY** Complete the illustration by adding labels for the three main stages of cellular respiration.

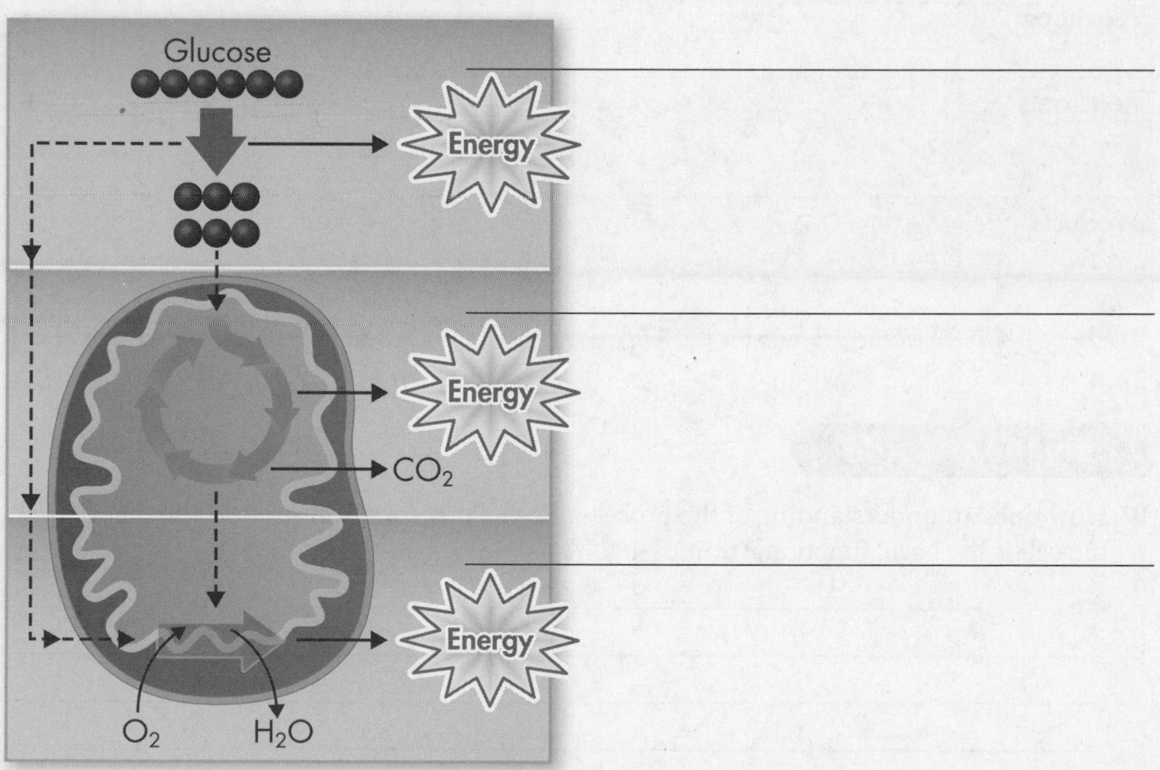

Name ______________________________ Class ______ Date ________

# Comparing Photosynthesis and Cellular Respiration

*For Questions 12–15, write True if the statement is true. If the statement is false, change the underlined word or words to make the statement true.*

______________ **12.** The energy flow in photosynthesis and cellular respiration occurs in the <u>same</u> direction.

______________ **13.** Photosynthesis <u>deposits</u> energy in Earth's "savings account" for living organisms.

______________ **14.** Cellular respiration removes <u>carbon dioxide</u> from the air.

______________ **15.** <u>Photosynthesis</u> takes place in nearly all life.

**16.** Complete the table comparing photosynthesis and cellular respiration.

**A Comparison of Photosynthesis and Cellular Respiration**

| Aspect | Photosynthesis | Cellular Respiration |
|---|---|---|
| Function | energy capture | |
| Location of reactions | chloroplasts | |
| Reactants | | |
| Products | | |

## Apply the Big idea

**17.** How does an understanding of the process of cellular respiration support the theory that the cell is the basic functional unit of life?

________________________________________________________________

________________________________________________________________

________________________________________________________________

________________________________________________________________

________________________________________________________________

________________________________________________________________

Name ______________________ Class ______ Date ________

# 9.2 The Process of Cellular Respiration

## Lesson Objectives

- Describe what happens during glycolysis.
- Describe what happens during the Krebs cycle.
- Explain how high-energy electrons are used by the electron transport chain.
- Identify how much ATP cellular respiration generates.

## Lesson Summary

**Glycolysis** The word **glycolysis** literally means "sugar-breaking." The end result is 2 molecules of a 3-carbon molecule called pyruvic acid.

- 2 ATP molecules are used at the start of glycolysis to get the process started.
- High-energy electrons are passed to the electron carrier **$NAD^+$**, forming two molecules of NADH.
- 4 ATP are synthesized during glycolysis for a net gain of 2 ATP.

**The Krebs Cycle** The second stage of cellular respiration is the **Krebs cycle**, which operates only when oxygen is available. The Krebs cycle is a series of energy-extracting reactions.

- Pyruvic acid produced by glycolysis enters mitochondria. In the innermost compartment of a mitochondrion, or the **matrix**, pyruvic acid molecules are broken down into carbon dioxide and acetyl-CoA molecules.
- Acetyl-CoA combines with a 4-carbon compound, producing a 6-carbon molecule—citric acid. Energy released by the breaking and rearranging of carbon bonds is captured in ATP, NADH, and $FADH_2$.
- The Krebs cycle produces four types of products:
  - high-energy electron carriers (NADH and $FADH_2$)
  - carbon dioxide
  - 2 ATP molecules (per glucose molecule)
  - the 4-carbon molecule needed to start the cycle again

**Electron Transport and ATP Synthesis** The electron transport chain uses the high-energy electrons from glycolysis and the Krebs cycle to convert ADP into ATP.

- The electron carriers produced during glycolysis and the Krebs cycle bring high-energy electrons to the electron transport chain. Oxygen is the final electron acceptor.
- The passing of electrons through the electron transport chain causes $H^+$ ions to build up in the intermembrane space, making it positively charged relative to the matrix.
- The charge difference across the membrane forces $H^+$ ions through channels in enzymes known as ATP synthases. As the ATP synthases spin, a phosphate group is added to ADP, generating ATP.

**The Totals** Together, glycolysis, the Krebs cycle, and the electron transport chain generate about 36 molecules of ATP per molecule of glucose.

 

# Glycolysis

1. **THINK VISUALLY** Complete the diagram by writing on the lines provided the names and numbers of molecules used and produced during glycolysis.

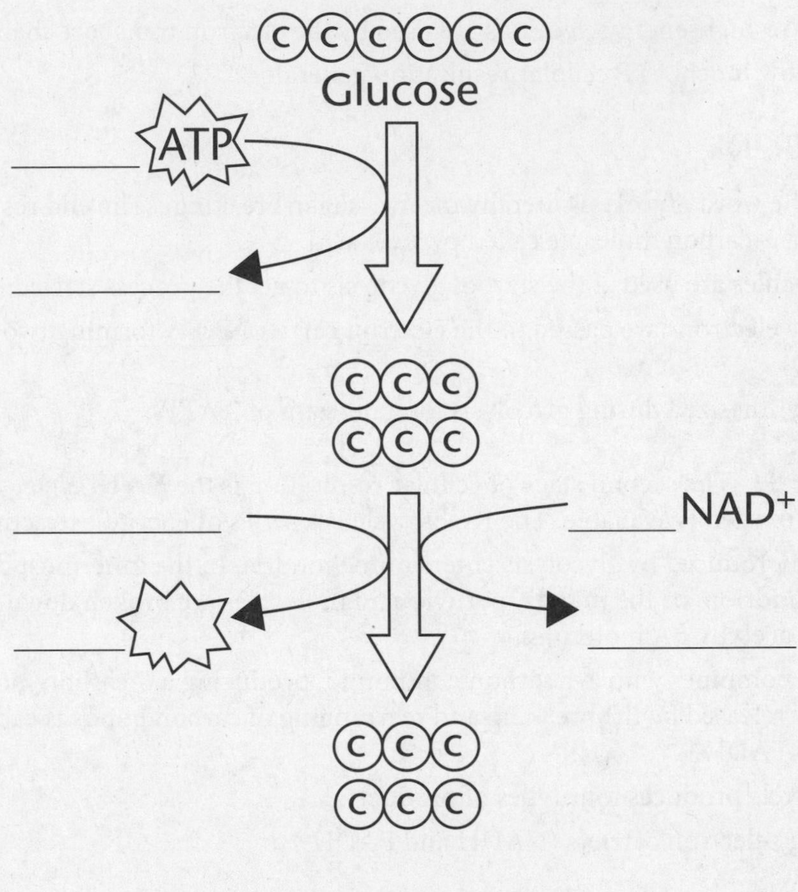


2. Why is it an investment for the cell to use two ATP at the beginning of glycolysis?

3. What are two advantages of glycolysis?

Name ______________________________ Class ______ Date ________

## The Krebs Cycle

*For Questions 4–7, write True if the statement is true. If the statement is false, change the underlined word or words to make the statement true.*

______________ **4.** The pyruvic acid produced in glycolysis enters the <u>chloroplasts</u> if oxygen is present in a cell.

______________ **5.** In the matrix, pyruvic acid is converted to <u>lactic</u> acid before the Krebs cycle begins.

______________ **6.** The compound that joins with a 4-carbon molecule in the Krebs cycle is called <u>acetyl-CoA</u>.

______________ **7.** <u>Carbon dioxide</u> is the only product of the Krebs cycle that is not re-used or used in other stages of cellular respiration.

**8.** Complete the flowchart to show which of the Krebs cycle's many products go on to the third stage of cellular respiration.

## Electron Transport and ATP Synthesis

*For Questions 9–14, complete each statement by writing the correct word or words.*

**9.** In eukaryotes, the electron transport chain is composed of a series of electron carriers located in the ______________ of the mitochondrion.

**10.** In prokaryotes, the electron transport chain is in the ______________.

**11.** ______________ serves as the final electron acceptor of the electron transport chain.

**12.** ______________ and ______________ pass high-energy electrons to the electron transport chain.

**13.** The transfer of high-energy electrons down the electron transport chain causes ______________ to be transported across the mitochondrial membrane.

**14.** ATP synthases produce the force needed to add one ______________ to each ADP molecule by spinning when hydrogen ions flow through them.

Name ______________________ Class ______ Date ________

## The Totals

**15.** How many ATP molecules per glucose molecule does a cell gain from each of the three stages of cellular respiration?

**16.** Besides glucose, what other kinds of molecules can be used to produce ATP in cellular respiration?

**17.** Why is cellular respiration considered an efficient process?

### Apply the Big idea

**18.** Where does the heat that warms your body come from? Explain your answer.

 

Name ______________________ Class ______ Date ________

# 9.3 Fermentation

## Lesson Objectives

Explain how organisms get energy in the absence of oxygen.

Identify the pathways the body uses to release energy during exercise.

## Lesson Summary

**Fermentation** **Fermentation** releases energy from food molecules by producing ATP without oxygen. Cells convert NADH to the electron carrier $NAD^+$. This allows glycolysis to produce a steady stream of ATP. There are two forms of fermentation. Both start with the reactants pyruvic acid and NADH.

- alcoholic fermentation produces ethyl alcohol and carbon dioxide
  - occurs in yeast and a few other microorganisms
  - produces alcoholic beverages and causes bread dough to rise
- lactic acid fermentation produces lactic acid
  - occurs in most organisms, including humans
  - used to produce beverages such as buttermilk and foods such as cheese, yogurt, and pickles

**Energy and Exercise** The body uses different pathways to release energy.

- For short, quick bursts of energy, the body uses ATP already in muscles as well as ATP made by lactic acid fermentation.
- For exercise longer than about 90 seconds, cellular respiration is the only way to continue generating a supply of ATP.

## Fermentation

*For Questions 1–6, write True if the statement is true. If the statement is false, change the underlined word or words to make the statement true.*

______ 1. Glycolysis provides the pyruvic acid molecules used in fermentation.

______ 2. Fermentation allows glycolysis to continue by providing the NADPH needed to accept high-energy electrons.

______ 3. Fermentation is an aerobic process.

______ 4. Fermentation occurs in the mitochondria of cells.

______ 5. Alcoholic fermentation gives off carbon dioxide and is used in making bread.

______ 6. Most organisms perform fermentation using a chemical reaction that converts pyruvic acid to lactic acid.

 

**7.** Compare and contrast fermentation and cellular respiration by completing the compare/contrast table. Write your answers in the empty table cells.

| Aspect | Fermentation | Cellular Respiration |
|---|---|---|
| Function | | |
| Reactants | | |
| Products | | |

**8.** Compare and contrast alcoholic fermentation and lactic acid fermentation by completing the compare/contrast table. Write your answers in the empty table cells.

| Type of Fermentation | Summary Equation | Use in Industry |
|---|---|---|
| Alcoholic | | |
| Lactic acid | | |

**9.** What causes humans to become lactic acid fermenters?

______

______

______

 

Name ______________________ Class ______ Date ______

## Energy and Exercise

**10.** What are three main sources of ATP available for human muscle cells?

**11.** During a race, how do your muscle cells produce ATP after the store of ATP in muscles is used?

**12.** Why does a sprinter have an oxygen debt to repay after the race is over?

**13.** A runner needs more energy for a longer race. How does the body generate the necessary ATP?

**14.** Why are aerobic forms of exercise so beneficial for weight control?

### Apply the Big idea

**15.** Compare and contrast the role of fermentation and cellular respiration in the actual production of ATP. In your response, consider which process produces ATP and which process contributes to its production.

Name ______________________ Class ______ Date ______

# Chapter Vocabulary Review

*For Questions 1–7, match the term with its definition.*

| Term | Definition |
|---|---|
| ______ **1.** anaerobic | **A.** Innermost compartment of a mitochondrion |
| ______ **2.** glycolysis | **B.** Process that forms either lactic acid or ethyl alcohol when no oxygen is present |
| ______ **3.** Krebs cycle | **C.** Stage of cellular respiration that starts with pyruvic acid and produces carbon dioxide |
| ______ **4.** calorie | **D.** Process in which glucose is broken down into two molecules of pyruvic acid |
| ______ **5.** matrix | **E.** "In air" |
| ______ **6.** aerobic | **F.** "Without air" |
| ______ **7.** fermentation | **G.** Amount of energy needed to raise the temperature of 1 gram of water 1°C |

*For Questions 8–10, write the letter of the correct answer on the line at the left.*

______ **8.** Which is the process that releases energy by breaking down food molecules in the presence of oxygen?

**A.** cellular respiration
**B.** electron transport
**C.** glycolysis
**D.** photosynthesis

______ **9.** Which is the electron carrier that accepts electrons during glycolysis?

**A.** ADP
**B.** ATP
**C.** $NAD^+$
**D.** $NADP^+$

______ **10.** When comparing cellular respiration and photosynthesis, these two processes are best described as

**A.** energy-releasing processes.
**B.** energy-storing processes.
**C.** opposite processes.
**D.** similar processes.

**11.** Complete the illustration by adding the words "aerobic" or "anaerobic" on the lines provided.

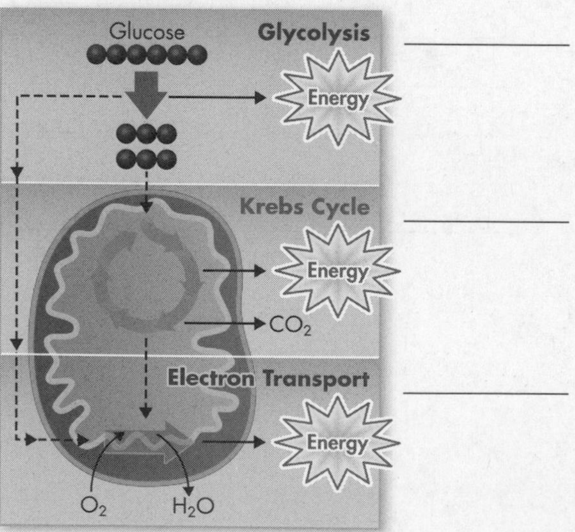

Name ______________________ Class _____ Date ________

CHAPTER
MYSTERY

DIVING WITHOUT A BREATH

In the Chapter Mystery, you read about the traits that allow a whale to stay underwater for 45 minutes. The human body doesn't have any of those traits, so while swimming, we must stay near the surface where we have access to oxygen.

21st Century Learning

# Does Carbon Sink?

You have learned about the ways in which photosynthesis and cellular respiration are different. To put it simply, during respiration, animals and plants take in oxygen and release carbon dioxide and water; during photosynthesis, plants take in carbon dioxide and release oxygen.

As you may already know, many human-made machines burn fossil fuels, such as coal and oil that release large quantities of carbon dioxide into the air. People began building carbon-emitting machines in the mid-1700s when the Industrial Revolution began. More and more of them, including factories and cars, have been built ever since. As a result, much more carbon dioxide is being released into Earth's atmosphere than in the past. Carbon dioxide absorbs and retains heat near Earth's surface, and the additional carbon dioxide in the atmosphere contributes to global warming.

Scientists and governments around the world are trying to find ways to reduce and eventually reverse global warming. This article presents one possible method for reducing carbon dioxide emissions to the atmosphere.

## We'll Try Everything—Including Making New Carbon Sinks

These days everyone is talking about reducing carbon dioxide emissions. Reducing carbon emissions is important. But we also could use a reliable way to dispose of the $CO_2$ we create. Nature does it every day, through carbon reservoirs, also known as carbon sinks. The word *sink* has many definitions, including "something that stores or disposes of something else."

In fact, Earth has two major types of carbon sinks: oceans and trees. The world's oceans absorb and store $CO_2$ from the air. All the world's plants take in carbon dioxide and release the oxygen we breathe. The catch is, these natural carbon sinks may not last. Studies indicate that oceans are reaching the limit of the carbon dioxide they can hold. And trees? Well, you've probably heard how quickly we're cutting down rain forests.

Perhaps people can make new carbon sinks. We've been pumping oil and natural gas out of the ground for more than 150 years. What if we could pump $CO_2$ back into the ground to take their place? We have the technology to convert old oil and gas wells into carbon dioxide storage units that can hold the $CO_2$ we pump into them. It would be expensive to retrofit existing power plants, or to build pipelines to carry the gas away. But if we can find underground storage areas near fossil-fuel burning power plants, then transport would not be an issue. Also, building new carbon-disposal plants near power plants would be a relatively inexpensive way to store carbon emissions near their source.

Continued on next page ▶

 

## 21st Century Themes Science and Global Awareness

**1.** What are two main natural carbon sinks?

**2.** What type of carbon sink does the author propose people use?

**3.** Most power plants are not located near sites where fossil fuels are mined. How do you think this would affect the practicality of this proposal?

**4.** According to the article, costs can be kept down if new plants are built "in the right places." What are the right places?

**5.** Do you think what the author proposes is a good long-term solution? Why or why not?

## 21st Century Skills Planning a Carbon Sink

The skills used in this activity include **communication skills, creativity and intellectual curiosity, interpersonal and collaborative skills, accountability and adaptability,** and **social responsibility.**

What types of carbon sinks or carbon dioxide storage can be used to dispose of $CO_2$ in your community? Find out who in your local government is in charge of the trees on city property. Interview that person to identify places where trees could be planted. Can all new trees be planted in one place or must they be scattered around town? Get an estimate for the number of trees that might be planted on all sites in your community. Try to obtain as many trees as you can, either by asking local nurseries to donate them or by holding fundraisers to get the money to buy them. Then assemble a group of volunteers to spend "Carbon Sink Day" planting the trees. Make sure you get the necessary permits and oversight from your community government before you start planting. You might also have to prepare a plan for taking care of the small trees as they grow.

Name ______________________ Class _____ Date _________

# 10 Cell Growth and Division

**Big idea** **Growth, Development, and Reproduction**

**Q:** How does a cell produce a new cell?

| | WHAT I KNOW | WHAT I LEARNED |
|---|---|---|
| **10.1** Why do cells divide? | | |
| **10.2** How do cells divide? | | |
| **10.3** How does a cell control the process of cell division? | | |
| **10.4** How does a single, undifferentiated cell lead to a complex multicellular organism? | | |

# 10.1 Cell Growth, Division, and Reproduction

## Lesson Objectives

- Explain the problems that growth causes for cells.
- Compare asexual and sexual reproduction.

## Lesson Summary

**Limits to Cell Size** There are two main reasons why cells divide:

- Information "overload": The larger a cell gets, the more demands it places on its DNA. Eventually, the cell's DNA cannot meet the cell's needs.
- Exchange of materials: Cells take in nutrients and eliminate wastes through the cell membrane.
  - The larger a cell's volume, the more materials it needs to function and the more waste it creates.
  - A cell's volume increases at a faster rate than its surface area. As a cell grows, its surface-area-to-volume ratio becomes too small.
  - The larger a cell gets, the harder it is for enough materials to move across its cell membrane.
- **Cell division** solves the information overload and materials exchange problems.

**Cell Division and Reproduction** Cell division is part of both types of reproduction:

- **Asexual reproduction**:
  - produces genetically identical organisms.
  - occurs in many single-celled organisms and in some multicellular organisms.
  - allows rapid reproduction of organisms in favorable environments.
- **Sexual Reproduction**:
  - produces organisms with genetic information from both parents.
  - occurs in most animals and plants and in many single-celled organisms.
  - increases genetic diversity, which aids species survival in changing environments.

## Limits to Cell Size

*For Questions 1–4, write True if the statement is true. If the statement is false, change the underlined word or words to make the statement true.*

__________ **1.** As a cell's size increases, its amount of DNA <u>also increases</u>.

__________ **2.** The amount of activity in a cell is related to its <u>volume</u>.

__________ **3.** The smaller the cell, the <u>smaller</u> its ratio of surface area to volume.

__________ **4.** The <u>information crisis</u> in a cell is solved by the replication of the DNA before cell division.

Name ______________________ Class ______ Date ________

5. VISUAL ANALOGY In the visual analogy of the growing town, what does the library represent? Identify two characteristics that make it a good choice for this analogy.

______________________________

______________________________

______________________________

______________________________

# Cell Division and Reproduction

*For Questions 6–8, complete each statement by writing the correct word or words.*

6. ______________ is the formation of new individuals.

7. For single-celled organisms, cell division is a form of ______________ reproduction.

8. Most multicellular organisms reproduce by ______________ reproduction.

9. Use the table to compare and contrast asexual and sexual reproduction.

| Asexual and Sexual Reproduction | |
|---|---|
| **Similarities** | **Differences** |
| | |

## Apply the Big idea

10. Vascular tissue helps plants transport water against the force of gravity. Because of this, plants that lack vascular tissue do not grow very tall. How is this situation similar to the information you have learned in this lesson? Explain.

______________________________

______________________________

______________________________

______________________________

______________________________

 

Name ______________________ Class ______ Date ________

# 10.2 The Process of Cell Division

## Lesson Objectives

- Describe the role of chromosomes in cell division.
- Name the main events of the cell cycle.
- Describe what happens during the four phases of mitosis.
- Describe the process of cytokinesis.

## Lesson Summary

**Chromosomes** Packages of DNA called **chromosomes** hold a cell's genetic information.

- Prokaryotic chromosomes consist of a single, circular strand of DNA.
- Eukaryotic chromosomes are highly organized structures.
  - The DNA winds around histone proteins, forming **chromatin**.
  - Chromosomes make the precise separation of DNA possible during cell division.

**The Cell Cycle** The **cell cycle** is the series of events in the growth and division of a cell.

- In the prokaryotic cell cycle, the cell grows, duplicates its DNA, and divides by pinching in the cell membrane.
- The eukaryotic cell cycle has four stages (the first three of which are referred to as **interphase**):
  - In the $G_1$ phase, the cell grows.
  - In the S phase, the cell replicates its DNA.
  - In the $G_2$ phase, the cell produces organelles and materials for division.
  - In the M phase, the cell divides in two stages—**mitosis**, the division of the nucleus, and **cytokinesis**, the division of the cytoplasm.

**Mitosis** The division of the nucleus, mitosis, occurs in four stages:

- **Prophase**: a cell's genetic material condenses, a spindle starts to form, and the nuclear envelope breaks down.
- **Metaphase**: the duplicated chromosomes line up and spindle fibers connect to the **centromeres**.
- **Anaphase**: sister **chromatids** separate and move toward the **centrioles**.
- **Telophase**: the chromosomes begin to unwind and a nuclear envelope reforms.

**Cytokinesis** Division of the cytoplasm differs in plant cells and animal cells.

- In animal cells, the cell membrane draws in and pinches off.
- In plant cells, a cell plate forms, followed by a new cell membrane, and finally a new cell wall forms.

 

Name ______________________ Class ______ Date ________

# Chromosomes

*For Questions 1–5, complete each statement by writing the correct word or words.*

**1.** Cells carry genetic information in packages of DNA called ____________.

**2.** Most ____________ have only one circular strand of DNA.

**3.** In eukaryotic cells, the genetic structure consists of DNA and a tightly wound protein, which together form a substance called ____________.

**4.** The beadlike structures formed by DNA wrapped around ____________ molecules are called nucleosomes.

**5.** ____________ make possible the precise separation of DNA during cell division.

# The Cell Cycle

**6.** What is the name of the type of cell division that occurs in the prokaryotic cell cycle?

______________________________________________

**7.** What happens during interphase?

______________________________________________

______________________________________________

**8.** Complete the cell cycle diagram by writing the correct name of a phase on each line.

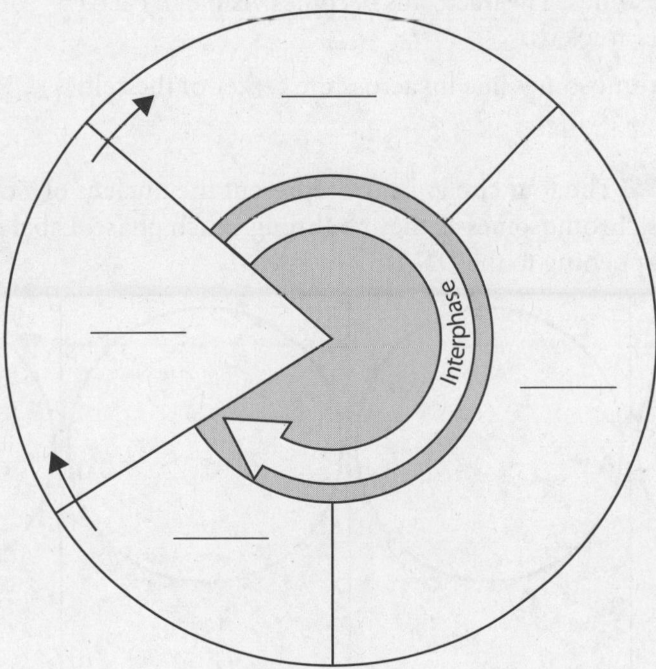


**9.** In eukaryotic cells, what happens in the $G_1$ phase that differs from the $G_2$ phase?

______________________________________________

**10.** In eukaryotic cells, what are the two main stages of cell division?

______________________________________________

# Mitosis

**11.** During prophase, when cell chromosomes become visible, what are the duplicated strands of DNA called? What is the name for the area in which these duplicated strands are joined?

______________________________________________

______________________________________________

**12.** What structures are spindle fibers attached to that help pull the paired chromosomes apart?

______________________________________________

______________________________________________

*For Questions 13–16, match the description of the event with the phase of mitosis in which it occurs. Each phase may be used more than once.*

| Event | | Phase of Mitosis |
|---|---|---|
| _____ | **13.** The chromosomes separate and begin to move to opposite sides of the cell. | **A.** Telophase |
| _____ | **14.** The chromosomes become visible. The centrioles take up positions on opposite sides of the nucleus. | **B.** Prophase |
| _____ | **15.** A nuclear envelope re-forms around each cluster of chromosomes. The nucleolus becomes visible in each daughter nucleus. | **C.** Metaphase |
| _____ | **16.** The chromosomes line up across the center of the cell. | **D.** Anaphase |

**17.** **THINK VISUALLY** The four circles below represent the nucleus of a cell going through mitosis. Draw four chromosomes as they go through each phase. Label each phase and describe what is happening to the DNA.

# Cytokinesis

**18.** What is cytokinesis?

---

---

---

**19.** Use the Venn diagram to compare and contrast cytokinesis in animal cells with cytokinesis in plant cells.

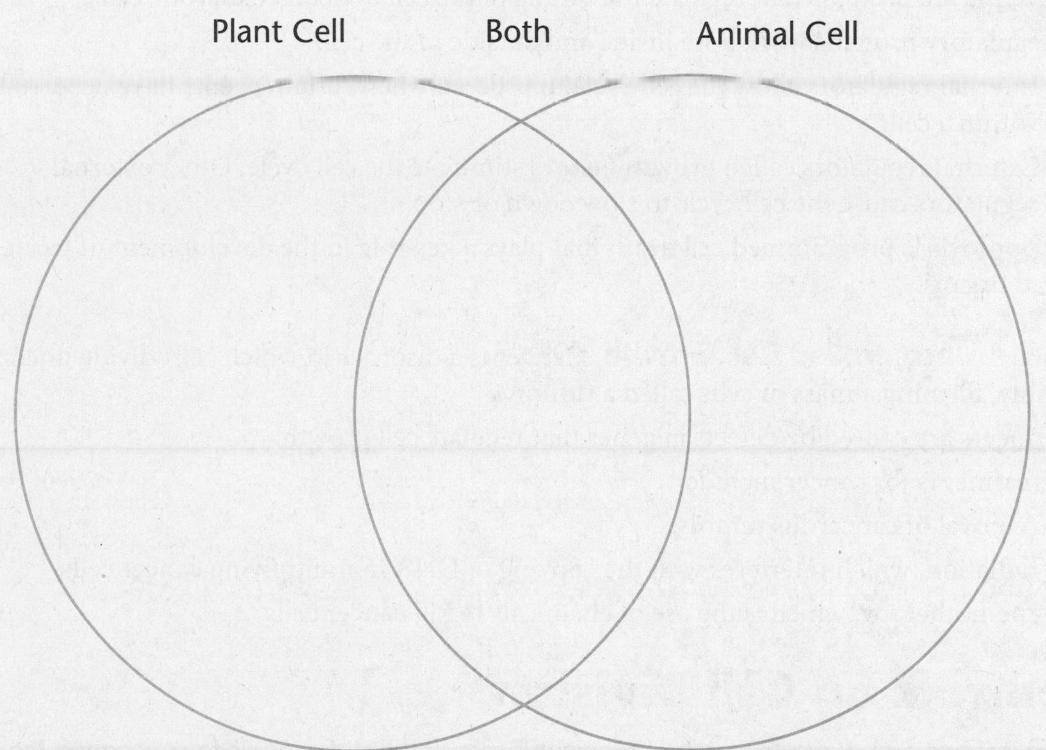


## Apply the Big idea

**20.** During certain stages of their life cycle, some cells repeatedly undergo mitosis but do not undergo cytokinesis. What would you expect to see if you looked at such cells, or a tissue made up of such cells, under a microscope? Explain your answer.

---

---

---

---

Name ______________________ Class ______ Date ________

# 10.3 Regulating the Cell Cycle

## Lesson Objectives

Describe how the cell cycle is regulated.

Explain how cancer cells are different from other cells.

## Lesson Summary

**Controls on Cell Division** Dozens of proteins regulate the cell cycle.

- **Cyclins** are proteins that regulate the timing of the cell cycle in eukaryotic cells.
- Regulatory proteins work both inside and outside of the cell.
  - Internal regulators allow the cell cycle to proceed when certain events have occurred within a cell.
  - External regulators called **growth factors** stimulate the cell cycle. Other external regulators cause the cell cycle to slow down or stop.
- **Apoptosis** is programmed cell death that plays a key role in the development of tissues and organs.

**Cancer: Uncontrolled Cell Growth** **Cancer** is a disorder in which cells divide uncontrollably, forming a mass of cells called a **tumor**.

- Cancers are caused by defects in genes that regulate cell growth.
- Treatments for cancer include:
  - removal of cancerous tumors.
  - radiation, which interferes with the copying of DNA in multiplying cancer cells.
  - chemotherapy, which is the use of chemicals to kill cancer cells.

# Controls on Cell Division

*For Questions 1–6, write True if the statement is true. If the statement is false, change the underlined word or words to make the statement true.*

______ **1.** Cells tend to <u>continue</u> dividing when they come into contact with other cells.

______ **2.** Cell division <u>speeds up</u> when the healing process nears completion.

______ **3.** Proteins called <u>growth factors</u> regulate the timing of the cell cycle in eukaryotic cells.

______ **4.** If chromosomes have not attached to spindle fibers during metaphase, an <u>internal</u> regulatory protein will prevent the cell from entering anaphase.

______ **5.** Growth factors are external regulatory proteins that <u>slow down</u> the cell cycle.

______ **6.** Once apoptosis is triggered, a cell proceeds to <u>self-destruct</u>.

 

Name ______________________________ Class ______ Date ________

7. Complete the cause-and-effect chart by giving an example of an effect caused by each type of regulatory protein.

| Factors Affecting the Cell Cycle | |
|---|---|
| **Cause** | **Effect** |
| Cyclins | |
| Internal regulatory proteins | |
| External regulatory proteins | |

## Cancer: Uncontrolled Cell Growth

8. What is cancer?

______________________________________________

______________________________________________

9. What are the two basic types of tumors? Explain how they are different.

______________________________________________

______________________________________________

______________________________________________

______________________________________________

______________________________________________

10. Why can cancer be life threatening?

______________________________________________

______________________________________________

______________________________________________

______________________________________________

 

**11.** What is the cause of cancer?

______

**12.** How do radiation and chemotherapy affect cancer cells?

______

______

**13.** Fill out the flowchart by completing each statement with the correct word or words.

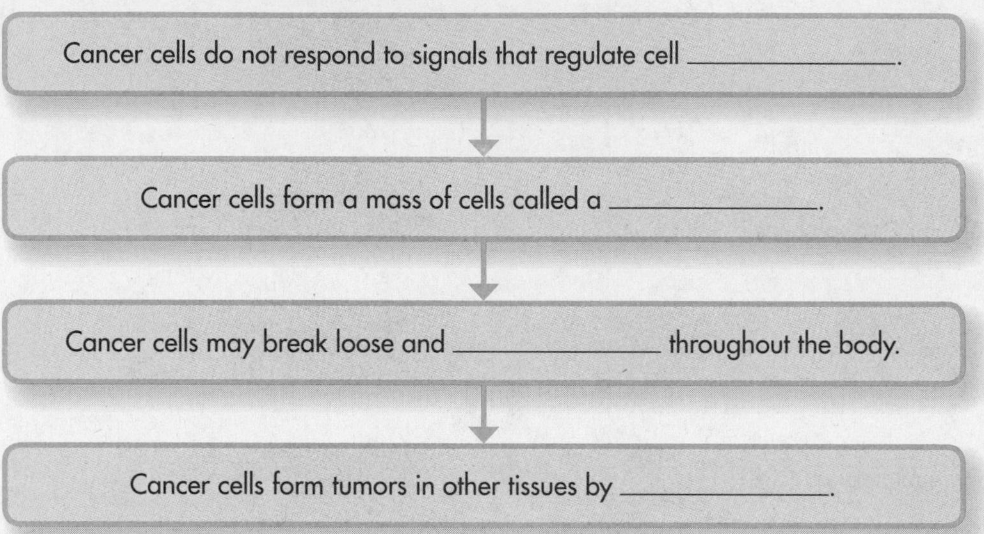

Cancer cells do not respond to signals that regulate cell ______.
Cancer cells form a mass of cells called a ______.
Cancer cells may break loose and ______ throughout the body.
Cancer cells form tumors in other tissues by ______.


## Apply the Big idea

**14.** Hair grows from hair follicles, pockets of continually dividing cells in the outer layer of the skin. New cells are added to the base of a hair shaft, inside each follicle. Use what you have learned in this lesson to explain why cancer patients often lose their hair when receiving chemotherapy and grow more hair after chemotherapy stops.

______

______

______

______

______

______

 

Name ______________________ Class ______ Date ________

# 10.4 Cell Differentiation

## Lesson Objectives

- Describe the process of differentiation.
- Define stem cells and explain their importance.
- Identify the possible benefits and issues relating to stem cell research.

## Lesson Summary

**From One Cell to Many** Multicellular organisms produced via sexual reproduction begin life as a single cell.

- Early cell divisions lead to the formation of an **embryo**.
- Then, individual cells become specialized in both form and function through the process of **differentiation**.
- Once cells of a certain type, such as nerve cells or muscle cells, have formed, the cells cannot develop into a different type of cell.

**Stem Cells and Development** During an organism's development, some cells differentiate to become a wide variety of body cells.

- A fertilized egg and the first few cells in an embryo are able to form any kind of cell and tissue. Such a cell is termed **totipotent**.
- A **blastocyst** is an embryonic stage that consists of a hollow ball of cells. These cells are able to become any type of body cell. Such cells are termed **pluripotent**.
- Unspecialized cells that can develop into differentiated cells are called **stem cells**. Stem cells are found in embryos and in adults.
  - Embryonic stem cells are the pluripotent cells of an early embryo.
  - Adult stem cells are **multipotent**, which means they can produce many, but not all, types of differentiated cells.

**Frontiers in Stem Cell Research** Scientists want to learn about the signals that tell a cell to become either specialized or multipotent.

- Potential benefits of stem cell research include the repair or replacement of damaged cells and tissues.
- Research with human stem cells is controversial because it involves ethical issues of life and death.

## From One Cell to Many

*For Questions 1–4, complete each statement by writing the correct word or words.*

**1.** Humans, pets, and petunias all pass through an early stage of development called a(n) ______________.

**2.** Cells become ______________ through the process of differentiation.

 

Name ______________________ Class ______ Date ______

3. Scientists have mapped the outcome of every ______________ that leads to differentiation in the development of the microscopic worm *C. elegans*.

4. Most cells in the adult body are no longer capable of ______________.

## Stem Cells and Development

*For Questions 5–7, write the letter of the correct answer on the line at the left.*

______ **5.** Which is an example of a totipotent cell?

**A.** blastocyst
**B.** bone cell
**C.** fertilized egg
**D.** lymphocyte

______ **6.** Cells that are pluripotent are unable to develop into the tissue that

**A.** forms the skin.
**B.** lines the digestive tract.
**C.** produces blood cells.
**D.** surrounds an embryo.

______ **7.** Adult stem cells are best described as

**A.** multipotent.
**B.** pluripotent.
**C.** totipotent.
**D.** unable to differentiate.

8. Complete the concept map by identifying some of the types of cells that embryonic stem cells give rise to. Then explain how stem cells are like the stem of a plant.

______________________________________________

______________________________________________

______________________________________________

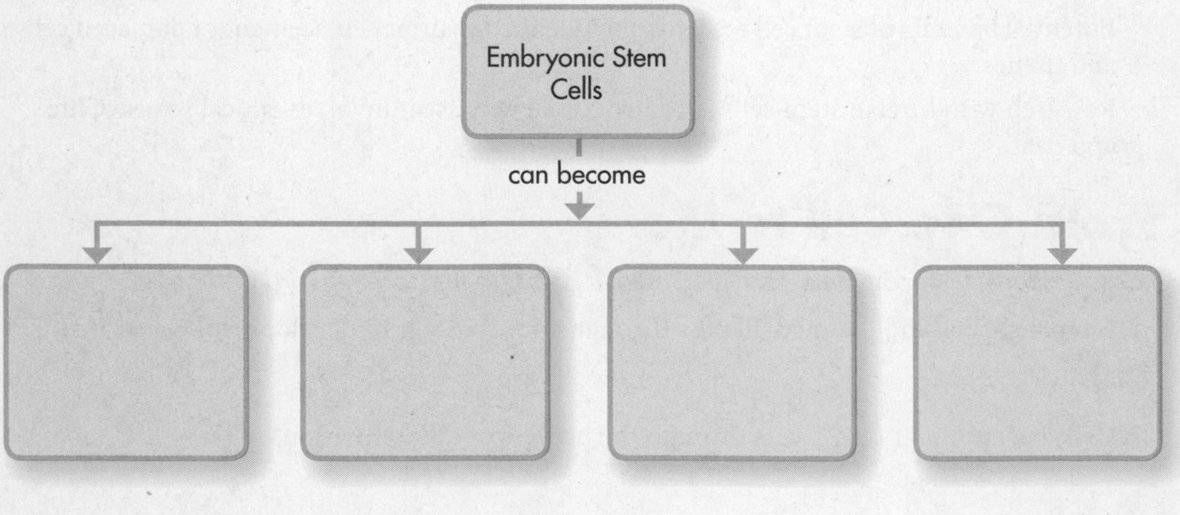

Embryonic Stem Cells

can become

[ ] [ ] [ ] [ ]

Name ______________________ Class _____ Date _______

# Frontiers in Stem Cell Research

*For Questions 9–11, write the letter of the correct answer on the line at the left.*

_____ **9.** Which is not a new, potential benefit of stem cell research?

**A.** growing new skin cells to repair a cut

**B.** replacing heart cells damaged by heart attacks

**C.** repairing breaks between nerve cells in spinal injuries

**D.** preventing suffering and death caused by cellular damage

_____ **10.** What is the main reason that embryonic stem cell research is considered ethically controversial?

**A.** Embryos contain totipotent cells.

**B.** Embryos are the result of sexual reproduction.

**C.** Embryos from many different organisms must be used.

**D.** Embryos are destroyed in the process.

_____ **11.** What is one new technology that could make stem cell research less controversial?

**A.** implanting skin cells instead of stem cells in damaged tissue

**B.** developing the ability to switch on the genes that make an adult cell pluripotent

**C.** replacing stem cells with cancer cells

**D.** using the Internet to get more people to accept stem cell research

## Apply the Big idea

**12.** Many plants such as orchids are grown by a technique called tissue culture. Small pieces of plant tissue from a leaf, stem, or root of a mature plant are placed in a medium that contains the proper nutrients. The cells first form a mass of undifferentiated cells, from which tiny roots, stems, and leaves eventually grow. How do the plant cells placed in a medium for tissue culture change in terms of their degree of specialization? What types of animal cells are most similar to the undifferentiated plant cells in a tissue culture? Explain your answer.

________________________________________

________________________________________

________________________________________

________________________________________

________________________________________

________________________________________

________________________________________

________________________________________

Name ______________________ Class ______ Date ________

# Chapter Vocabulary Review

**1.** Describe how the following terms are related to one another.

asexual reproduction, sexual reproduction: ______________________

chromosome, centrioles: ______________________

centromere, chromatid: ______________________

binary fission, mitosis: ______________________

*For Questions 2–9, match the event with the phase of the cell cycle in which it takes place. A phase may be used more than once.*

**Event**

_____ **2.** A nuclear envelope forms around chromosomes.

_____ **3.** The cell grows and replicates DNA.

_____ **4.** A spindle forms.

_____ **5.** Chromosomes line up across the center of the cell.

_____ **6.** The genetic material condenses and chromosomes become visible.

_____ **7.** Chromosomes move to opposite sides of the cell.

_____ **8.** The cytoplasm divides.

_____ **9.** Sister chromatids separate.

**Phase of the Cell Cycle**

**A.** anaphase

**B.** cytokinesis

**C.** interphase

**D.** metaphase

**E.** prophase

**F.** telophase

*For Questions 10–13, complete each statement by writing the correct word or words.*

**10.** ____________ and growth factors are examples of regulatory proteins that control the cell cycle.

**11.** ____________ is the controlled series of steps that lead to cell death.

**12.** The first few cells that form a(n) ____________ are said to be ____________ because they can become any type of cell.

**13.** The hollow ball of cells that forms in early embryonic development is called the ____________.

Name ______________________ Class ______ Date ______

# CHAPTER MYSTERY

## PET SHOP ACCIDENT

In the Chapter Mystery, you learned that stem cells make it possible for salamanders to regrow limbs. Developments in stem cell research tend to produce excitement in the media, particularly when the research might lead to a remedy for human health problems.

21st Century Learning

## Stem Cells in the Media

When you read an article about stem cells, as with any scientific topic, you need to consider the source and whether the reporter is giving an accurate account of the facts. You should also try to determine whether the article shows bias. Bias is a preference for a particular point of view, and it may involve distorting facts or slanting information so that it seems to support the preferred point of view.

*Read the following two articles. Determine to what degree each article uses facts to back up its conclusions. Also look for evidence of bias or distorted facts.*

### World News Daily

**Stem Cells Improve Memory in Brain-Damaged Mice**

From the Science Desk—A research team at Watson University today announced that stem cells can improve the memory of mice with brain injuries. The researchers were interested in how an injection of stem cells might affect mice that had injuries in the area of the brain involved in memory.

Working with 100 mice, the scientists injected 50 of the mice with stem cells known to give rise to mouse nerve cells. The other 50 mice did not receive any treatment. After three months, the scientists tested the memory of both groups of mice by seeing whether they recognized objects. The group that did not receive the stem cells remembered the objects about 40 percent of the time. In contrast, the group that received the stem cells remembered the objects about 70 percent of the time.

The scientists hope that their research will one day lead to a treatment for human diseases and conditions, such as Alzheimer's disease, in which people suffer significant memory loss. "We are very excited by our results," said Diane Brandon, the leader of the research team. "But we are not ready to try this treatment with humans."

LOOKING AHEAD
A Weekly Guide for People in the Know


**Alzheimer's Disease—Is a CURE for Memory Loss Just Around the Corner?**

Don't look now, but those mice that you hate to see scurry across the kitchen floor might just provide a cure for the thousands of people afflicted with Alzheimer's Disease. Scientists at Watson University are reporting that stem cells injected into brain-damaged mice can cure memory loss. The researchers suspected that the stem cells would give rise to new mouse nerve cells. Indeed, the mice that received the stem cells were found to have greatly improved memories. "We are very excited by our results," said Diane Brandon, the leader of the research team. The scientists are confident that, since stem cells can treat memory loss in mice, stem cells can also be used to cure Alzheimer's disease in humans.

Continued on next page ▶

 

## 21st Century Themes Science and Health Literacy

**1.** Which article provides the reader with the most facts that describe the procedure of the research team and the result of the experiment? Give examples.

**2.** Carefully look at the words that each article uses to describe the results of the research. According to the first article, how did the injected stem cells affect memory loss in mice?

According to the second article, how did the injected stem cells affect memory loss in mice?

**3.** Compare the titles of both articles. Which of the two titles more accurately describes the results of the research? Explain your answer.

**4.** Both articles use quotations from one of the scientists. Compare the use of quotations in the two articles. Which of the two articles omits something important that the scientist said? How does this omission affect the reader's impression of the implication of this research for humans?

**5.** Which of the two articles do you trust more? Which would attract more attention? Explain your answers.

## 21st Century Skills Comparing Articles

The skills used in this activity include **information and media literacy** and **critical thinking and systems thinking.**

Use Internet or library resources to find two articles that evaluate the treatments for a specific type of cancer, such as leukemia or prostate cancer. Compare the articles by answering the following questions: How easy is the article to understand? Are opinions supported by facts? Is there evidence of bias? Does the article omit important information? On the basis of your analysis, write an essay comparing the effectiveness of the two articles.

 

Name ____________________ Class ______ Date ______

# 11 Introduction to Genetics

**Big idea** Information and Heredity

**Q:** How does cellular information pass from one generation to another?

| | WHAT I KNOW | WHAT I LEARNED |
|---|---|---|
| **11.1** How does an organism pass its characteristics on to its offspring? | | |
| **11.2** How can you predict the outcome of a genetic cross? | | |
| **11.3** How can interactions between alleles, genes, and the environment affect an organism's traits? | | |
| **11.4** How does a cell divide to create cells with exactly half of the original cell's genetic information? | | |

 

# 11.1 The Work of Gregor Mendel

## Lesson Objectives

Describe Mendel's studies and conclusions about inheritance.

Describe what happens during segregation.

## Lesson Summary

**The Experiments of Gregor Mendel** The delivery of characteristics from parents to offspring is heredity. The scientific study of heredity is **genetics**. Gregor Mendel founded modern genetics with his experiments on a convenient model system, pea plants:

- **Fertilization** is the process in which reproductive cells (egg from the female and sperm from the male) join to produce a new cell.
- A **trait** is a specific characteristic, such as (in peas) seed color or plant height.
- Mendel prevented self-pollination in the peas. He controlled fertilization so he could study how traits passed from one generation to the next.
- He created **hybrids**, which are crosses between true-breeding parents (the P generation) with different traits.
  - These hybrids were the $F_1$ (first filial) generation.
  - They each showed the characteristic of only one parent.
- Mendel found that traits are controlled by factors that pass from parent to offspring. Those factors are **genes**. The different forms of a gene are **alleles**.
- Mendel's **principle of dominance** states that some alleles are dominant and others are recessive. The recessive allele is exhibited only when the dominant allele is not present.

**Segregation** Mendel allowed members of the $F_1$ generation to self-pollinate. The trait controlled by the recessive allele appeared in the next generation ($F_2$) in about one-fourth of the offspring—even when it did not appear in the $F_1$ generation.

- Separation of alleles is **segregation**.
- When **gametes** (sex cells) form, alleles segregate so that each gamete carries only one allele for each gene.
- The $F_2$ generation gets a new combination of alleles: one from each parent.

# The Experiments of Gregor Mendel

*Match the term with its definition.*

| | Term | Definition |
|---|---|---|
| ______ | **1.** genes | **A.** Specific characteristics that vary among individuals |
| ______ | **2.** hybrids | **B.** The offspring of true-breeding parents with different traits |
| ______ | **3.** traits | **C.** Factors that determine traits |
| ______ | **4.** alleles | **D.** Sex cells, egg or sperm |
| ______ | **5.** gametes | **E.** The different forms of a gene |

Name ______________________ Class ______ Date ________

6. Why are peas a good model system for studying heredity?

_______________________________________________

_______________________________________________

7. How did Mendel cross-pollinate flowers?

_______________________________________________

_______________________________________________

8. What is the difference between a gene and an allele?

_______________________________________________

_______________________________________________

9. State the principle of dominance.

_______________________________________________

_______________________________________________

*The table shows some crosses between true-breeding parents that carry pairs of dominant alleles (such as SS) or pairs of recessive alleles (such as ss). Complete the table to show the combination of alleles in the offspring. Then use it to answer Questions 10–11.*

| **Dominant and Recessive Forms of Pea Plant Traits** | | | | |
|---|---|---|---|---|
| **Trait** | **Parent Plants (P Generation)** | | | **Offspring ($F_1$ Generation)** |
| Seed Color | Yellow *YY* | X | Green *yy* | Yellow *Yy* |
| Seed Coat Color | White *gg* | X | Gray *GG* | Gray ______ |
| Pod Shape | Constricted *ss* | X | Smooth *SS* | Smooth ______ |
| Pod Color | Green *CC* | X | Yellow *cc* | Green ______ |

10. What is the dominant shape of a pea pod? How do you know?

_______________________________________________

_______________________________________________

11. What symbol represents the recessive allele for pod color?

_______________________________________________

Name ______________________ Class ______ Date ______

## Segregation

**12.** What is segregation? What is the result of segregation?

_______________________________________________

_______________________________________________

**13.** THINK VISUALLY The capital letter *G* represents the allele in peas that causes the dominant trait, gray seed coat. The lower-case letter *g* represents the recessive allele that causes the recessive trait, white seed coat.

*In the circles, show the alleles in the gametes of the parent generation. Show how the alleles recombine in the $F_1$ plants.*

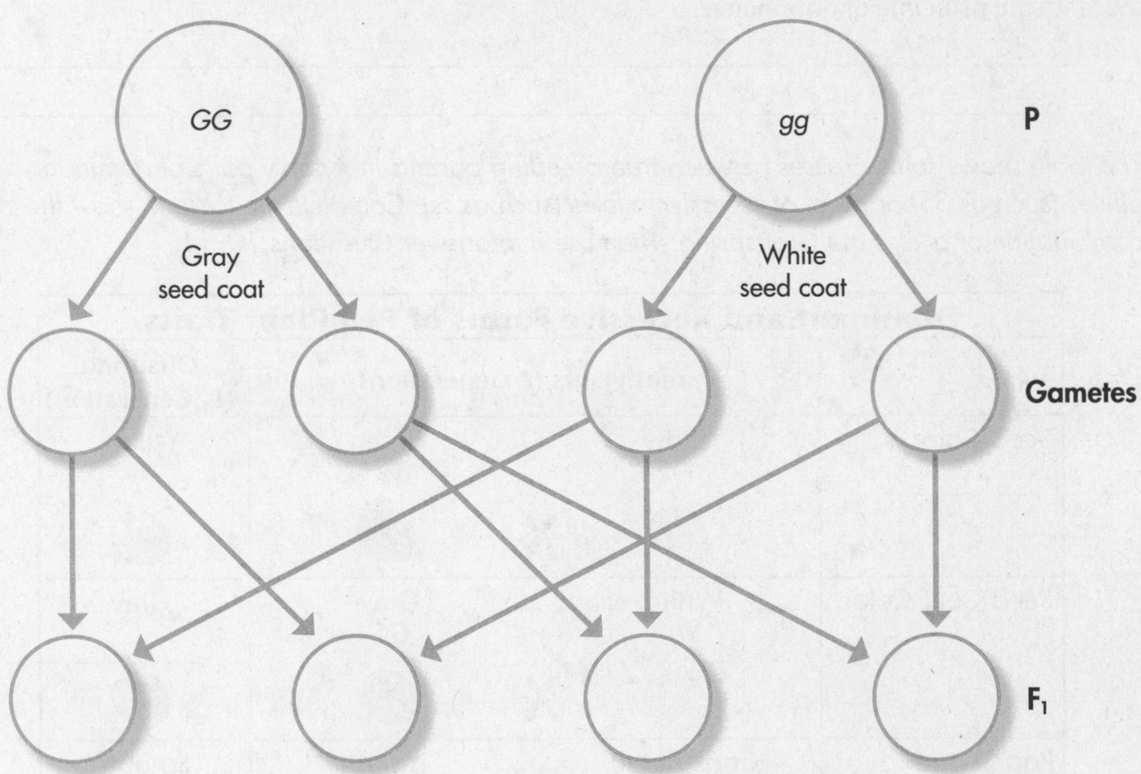


### Apply the Big idea

**14.** A black cat and a white cat have four black kittens in the $F_1$ generation. In the $F_2$ generation, there are three black kittens and one white kitten. Explain how the $F_2$ generation proves that genetic information passes unchanged from one generation to the next, even when a specific trait is not exhibited.

_______________________________________________

_______________________________________________

_______________________________________________

Name ______ Class ______ Date ______

# 11.2 Applying Mendel's Principles

## Lesson Objectives

- Explain how geneticists use the principles of probability to make Punnett squares.
- Explain the principle of independent assortment.
- Explain how Mendel's principles apply to all organisms.

## Lesson Summary

**Probability and Punnett Squares** **Probability** is the likelihood that a particular event will occur. Probability predicts the recombination of alleles:

- Of an allele pair, the probability of each allele in a gamete is ½, or 50 percent.
- When $F_1$ hybrid individuals are crossed, the probability of
  - two recessive alleles is ¼.
  - two dominant alleles is ¼.
  - one dominant allele and one recessive allele is ½ (¼ + ¼).
- Organisms that have two identical alleles for a gene are **homozygous** for that trait. If they have different alleles for the same gene, they are **heterozygous** for that trait.
- Physical traits are an organism's **phenotype**. Its **genotype** is its genetic makeup.
- A **Punnett square** is a mathematical tool that helps predict combinations in genetic crosses.

**Independent Assortment** The principle of **independent assortment** states that genes for different traits segregate independently during the formation of gametes. In two-factor crosses, the phenotypes of the $F_2$ offspring occur in a 9:3:3:1 ratio: 9 with with both traits dominant, 3 with the first trait dominant and the second trait recessive, 3 with the first trait recessive and the second trait dominant, and 1 with both traits recessive.

### A Summary of Mendel's Principles

- Genes are passed on from parents and determine traits.
- Where two or more alleles for a gene exist, some may be dominant and others recessive.
- In sexually reproducing organisms, offspring receive a copy of each gene from each parent. The alleles segregate when forming gametes.
- Alleles for different genes usually segregate independently.

## Probability and Punnett Squares

**1.** What is probability? ______________________________

______________________________

**2.** In a parent pea plant with the allele pair *Gg*, what is the probability that one gamete will contain the *G* allele? ______________________________

______________________________

**3.** Complete the graphic organizer to define the characteristics of homozygous and heterozygous genotypes and phenotypes.

| | **Homozygous** | **Heterozygous** |
|---|---|---|
| **Genotype** | | |
| **Phenotype** | | |

**4.** The dominant allele for smooth pod shape in peas is *S*. The recessive allele for constricted pod shape is *s*. In the Punnett square, show the result of crossing two heterozygous parents (*Ss*). Write the genotype and the phenotype of each type of offspring in the space provided.

| | **S** | **s** |
|---|---|---|
| **S** | Genotype: ________<br>Phenotype: ________ | Genotype: ________<br>Phenotype: ________ |
| **s** | Genotype: ________<br>Phenotype: ________ | Genotype: ________<br>Phenotype: ________ |

*For Questions 5–9, refer to the Punnett square above.*

**5.** What is the probability of a heterozygous offspring? Explain your answer.

______________________________________________

______________________________________________

**6.** What is the probability of a homozygous offspring? Explain.

______________________________________________

**7.** What is the probability of a homozygous recessive offspring?

______________________________________________

**8.** What is the probability of a smooth phenotype?

______________________________________________

**9.** What is the probability of a homozygous recessive individual (*ss*) producing a gamete with a dominant allele (*S*)? Explain.

______________________________________________

______________________________________________

 

## Independent Assortment

**10.** State the principle of independent assortment below.

______________________________________________

**11.** Using the principle of independent assortment, complete the Punnett square to show the results of an $F_1$ cross between two individuals heterozygous for both pod color ($C$ = green and $c$ = yellow) and pod shape ($S$ = smooth and $s$ + constricted). The gametes and some of the genotypes of the $F_2$ offspring are given.

| | **CS** | **cS** | **Cs** | **cs** |
|---|---|---|---|---|
| **CS** | CCSS | | | |
| **cS** | | | | ccSs |
| **Cs** | | | CCss | |
| **cs** | | ccSs | | |

*For Questions 12–15, refer to the Punnett square above.*

**12.** Which genotype belongs to an offspring that is homozygous recessive for both traits? What is the probability of that genotype?

______________________________________________

**13.** What is the phenotype of an individual heterozygous for both traits?

______________________________________________

**14.** What is the probability of an $F_2$ offspring having the green pod color and smooth pod shape? Explain. (Note: Remember that more than one genotype can produce this phenotype.)

______________________________________________

______________________________________________

**15.** The Punnett square predicts a 9:3:3:1 ratio for phenotypes. Explain what that ratio means.

______________________________________________

______________________________________________

______________________________________________

______________________________________________

______________________________________________

______________________________________________

 

## Summary of Mendel's Principles

*For Questions 16–20, complete each statement by writing the correct word or words.*

**16.** The units that determine the inheritance of biological characteristics are ____________.

**17.** A form of a gene is a(n) ____________.

**18.** If two or more forms of a gene exist, some may be dominant and others may be ____________.

**19.** The offspring of most sexually reproducing organisms have two copies of each gene. One came from each ____________.

**20.** Alleles from different genes usually ____________ independently from each other when gametes form.

*For Questions 21–25, match the term with its description.*

_____ **21.** Determine traits

_____ **22.** Can be two of these in one gene

_____ **23.** Allele that is expressed

_____ **24.** Where genes come from

_____ **25.** What genes do during gamete formation

**A.** parents

**B.** alleles

**C.** dominant

**D.** segregate

**E.** genes

**26.** Explain the importance of Thomas Hunt Morgan's experiments with fruit flies. Why was his work an important addition to Mendel's research?

___________________________________________

___________________________________________

### Apply the Big idea

**27.** Four sisters begin attending your school. One has brown hair and brown eyes. Another has brown hair and blue eyes. The third also has blue eyes, but blond hair. The fourth has blond hair, too, but she has brown eyes. Explain how the principle of independent segregation accounts for these sisters having four different phenotypes for two traits.

___________________________________________

___________________________________________

___________________________________________

___________________________________________

Name ______________________ Class ______ Date ______

# 11.3 Other Patterns of Inheritance

## Lesson Objectives

- Describe the other patterns of inheritance.
- Explain the relationship between genes and the environment.

## Lesson Summary

**Beyond Dominant and Recessive Alleles** Some alleles are neither dominant nor recessive:

- In cases of **incomplete dominance**, neither allele is completely dominant over the other. The phenotype is a blend of the two homozygous phenotypes.
- In cases of **codominance**, both alleles in the heterozygous genotype are expressed in the phenotype.
- Genes with **multiple alleles** have more than two forms of the same gene. There may be more than one dominant form and several different phenotypes.
- **Polygenic traits** are controlled by the interaction of two or more genes and exhibit a wide range of phenotypes.

**Genes and the Environment** The phenotype of an organism results only partly from its genotype. Environmental conditions can affect how genes are expressed.

## Beyond Dominant and Recessive Alleles

**1.** Complete the graphic organizer to summarize exceptions to Mendel's principles.

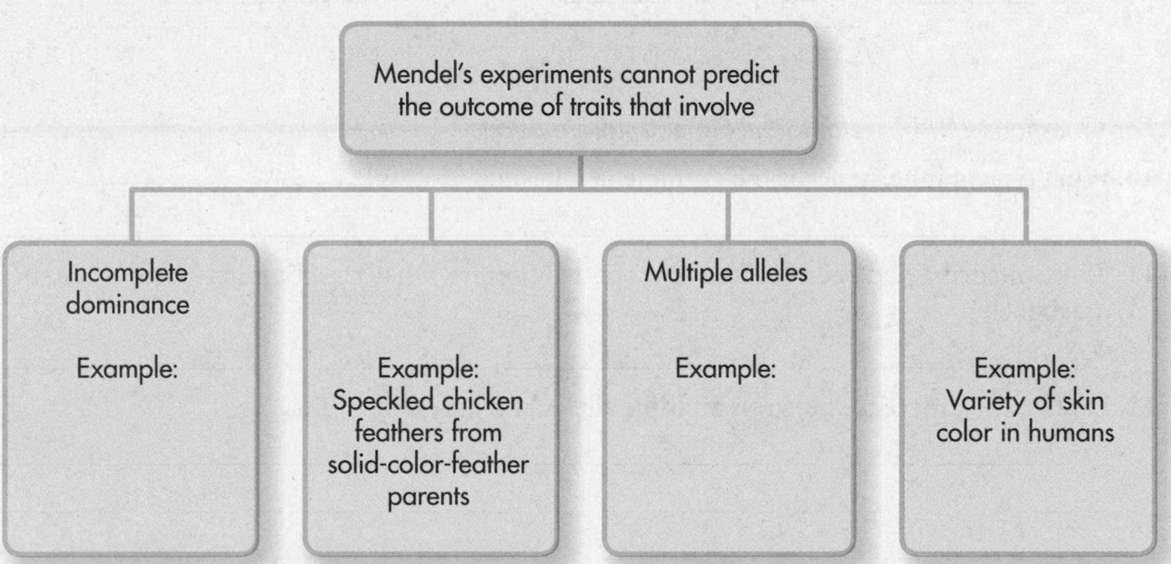

*For Questions 2–8, write True if the statement is true. If the statement is false, change the underlined word to make the statement true.*

______ **2.** When offspring show a blend of the parents' traits, <u>one</u> allele is dominant over the other.

______ **3.** In <u>complete</u> dominance, the heterozygous phenotype lies somewhere between the two homozygous phenotypes.

______ **4.** A heterozygous individual that exhibits the traits of both parents is an example of <u>codominance</u>.

______ **5.** Many genes exist in several forms and are said to have <u>codominant</u> alleles.

______ **6.** While multiple alleles may exist in a population, an individual usually carries only two alleles for each <u>gene</u>.

______ **7.** Traits produced by two or more genes are <u>codominant</u>.

______ **8.** Polygenic traits often show a wide range of <u>phenotypes</u>.

**9.** A plant breeder produced a purple flower by crossing a red parent with a blue parent. Use *RR* as the genotype for the red parent and *BB* for the blue parent. Complete the Punnett square to show the resulting genotypes and phenotypes of the offspring.

| | **Gamete allele:** ______ | **Gamete allele:** ______ |
|---|---|---|
| **Gamete allele:** ______ | Genotype: ______<br>Phenotype: ______ | Genotype: ______<br>Phenotype: ______ |
| **Gamete allele:** ______ | Genotype: ______<br>Phenotype: ______ | Genotype: ______<br>Phenotype: ______ |

*For Questions 10–11, refer to the Punnett square above.*

**10.** What type of inheritance is the example in Question 9?

______

**11.** If the offspring had been red and blue spotted flowers, what kind of inheritance would be most likely?

______

**12.** Explain the difference between multiple alleles and polygenic traits.

______

______

______

 

Name ____________________ Class ______ Date ________

# Genes and the Environment

*For Questions 13–16, complete each statement by writing in the correct word or words.*

**13.** An organism's ______________ results from its genotype and its environment.

**14.** Some ______________ produce variable traits depending on environmental conditions.

**15.** Western white butterflies vary in their wing color because their ______________ varies depending on when they hatch.

**16.** ______________ is an environmental variable that affects wing color in western white butterflies.

*For each of the following examples, write G if the trait is determined by genotype, and E if it is determined by environment.*

**17.** ______________ Turtles whose eggs hatch at higher temperatures tend to be female.

**18.** ______________ A blue-eyed girl is born to two blue-eyed parents.

**19.** ______________ Bees in a colony are assigned different jobs. As they develop, workers begin to look dramatically different.

**20.** ______________ A pair of twins is separated at birth. They grow up in different countries and speak different languages.

**21.** ______________ A litter of puppies is born. They are all gray except one, which is brown.

**22.** ______________ Tall pea plant seeds are planted in different locations around a yard. They produce plants of different heights.

**23.** ______________ A kitten is born with six toes.

**24.** ______________ A rabbit is born weak with hunger.

## Apply the Big idea

**25.** A dog gave birth to four puppies. The father has brown eyes, and the mother has green eyes. Two puppies have brown eyes. One has green eyes. One puppy has blue eyes. What does this tell you about how the cellular information for eye color is passed on? Explain.

______________________________________________________________

______________________________________________________________

______________________________________________________________

______________________________________________________________

______________________________________________________________

# 11.4 Meiosis

## Lesson Objectives

- Contrast the number of chromosomes in body cells and in gametes.
- Summarize the events of meiosis.
- Contrast meiosis and mitosis.
- Describe how alleles from different genes can be inherited together.

## Lesson Summary

**Chromosome Number** **Homologous** chromosomes are pairs of chromosomes that correspond in body cells. One chromosome from each pair comes from each parent.

- A cell that contains both sets of homologous chromosomes has a **diploid** number of chromosomes (meaning "two sets").
- **Haploid** cells contain only one set of chromosomes. Gametes are haploid.

**Phases of Meiosis** **Meiosis** is the process that separates homologous pairs of chromosomes in a diploid cell, forming a haploid gamete. The phases are as follows:

- Meiosis I, which is preceded by a replication of chromosomes. Its stages are
  - Prophase I: Each replicated chromosome pairs with its corresponding homologous chromosome forming a **tetrad**. During tetrad formation, alleles can be exchanged between chromatids, a process called **crossing-over**.
  - Metaphase I: Paired homologous chromosomes line up across the center of the cell.
  - Anaphase I: Spindle fibers pull each homologous pair toward opposite ends of the cell.
  - Telophase I: A nuclear membrane forms around each cluster of chromosomes. Cytokinesis then occurs, resulting in two new cells. The resulting daughter cells contain chromosome sets that are different from each other and the parent cell.
- Meiosis II: Chromosomes do not replicate.
  - Prophase II: Chromosomes, each consisting of two chromatids, become visible.
  - Metaphase II, Anaphase II, Telophase II, and Cytokinesis: These phases are similar to meiosis I. Four haploid cells form. They are the gametes. During fertilization, two gametes unite forming a **zygote**.

### Comparing Meiosis and Mitosis

- Mitosis is one cell division that results in two genetically identical diploid cells.
- Meiosis is two cell divisions that result in four genetically different haploid cells.

### Gene Linkage and Gene Maps

- Alleles tend to be inherited together if they are located on the same chromosome.
- Chromosomes, not genes, segregate independently.
- The farther apart genes are on a chromosome, the more likely is cross over.
- Information on linkage and the frequency of crossing-over lets geneticists construct maps of the locations of genes on chromosomes.

 

Name ______________________ Class ______ Date ______

## Chromosome Number

*For Questions 1–8, write True if the statement is true. If the statement is false, change the underlined word to make the statement true.*

______ **1.** The offspring of two parents obtains a single copy of every <u>gene</u> from each parent.

______ **2.** A <u>gamete</u> must contain one complete set of genes.

______ **3.** Genes are located at specific positions on <u>spindles</u>.

______ **4.** A pair of corresponding chromosomes is <u>homozygous</u>.

______ **5.** One member of each homologous chromosome pair comes from each <u>gene</u>.

______ **6.** A cell that contains both sets of homologous chromosomes is <u>haploid</u>.

______ **7.** The gametes of sexually reproducing organisms are <u>haploid</u>.

______ **8.** If an organism's haploid number is 6, its diploid number is <u>3</u>.

## Phases of Meiosis

*On the lines provided, identify the stage of meiosis I or meiosis II in which the event described occurs.*

______ **9.** Each replicated chromosome pairs with its corresponding homologous chromosome.

______ **10.** Crossing-over occurs between tetrads.

______ **11.** Paired homologous chromosomes line up across the center of the cell.

______ **12.** Spindle fibers pull each homologous chromosome pair toward an opposite end of the cell.

______ **13.** A nuclear membrane forms around each cluster of chromosomes and cytokinesis follows, forming two new cells.

______ **14.** Chromosomes consist of two chromatids, but they do not pair to form tetrads.

______ **15.** A nuclear membrane forms around each cluster of chromosomes and cytokinesis follows, forming four new cells.

 

**16.** THINK VISUALLY Draw two homologous pairs of chromosomes (in different colors if you have them) in these diagrams to illustrate what happens during these three phases of meiosis.

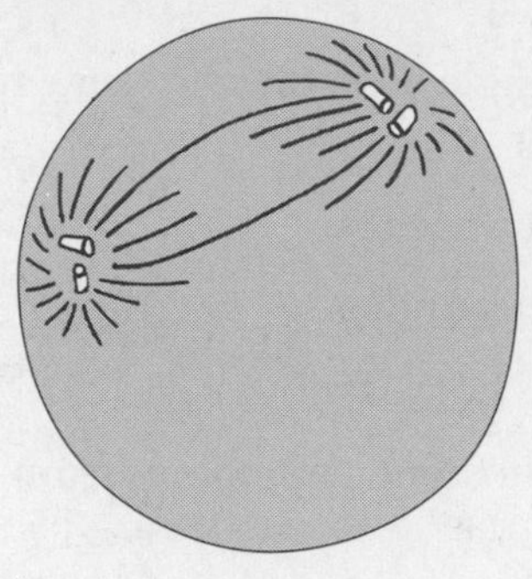

Prophase I

Metaphase I

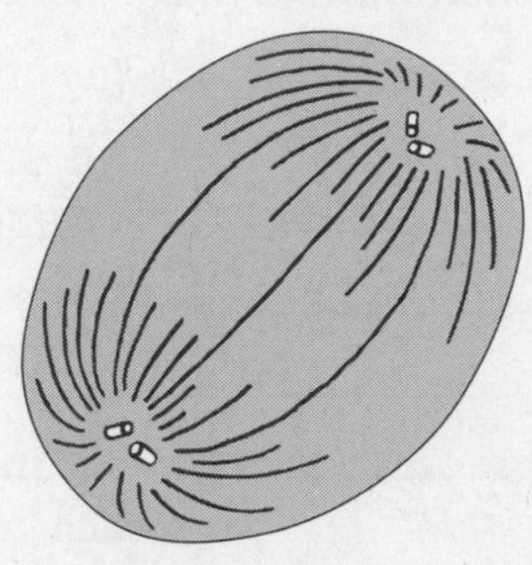

Anaphase II

**17.** Identify which phase of meiosis is shown in the diagrams below.

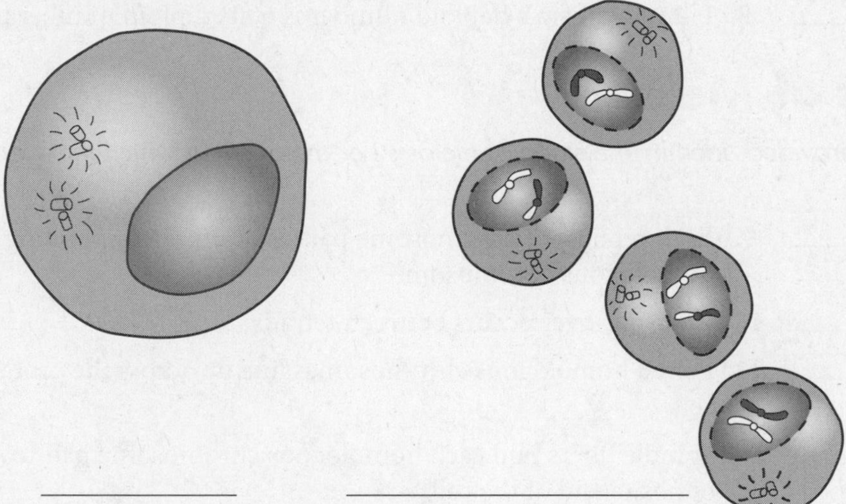

_______________ _______________

*Use this diagram to answer Questions 18–20.*

**18.** What does the diagram show?

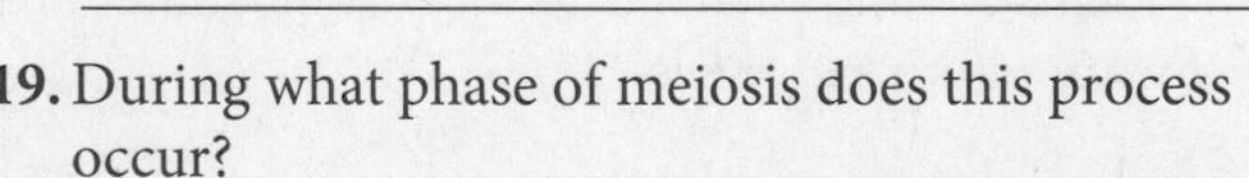

___________________________________________

___________________________________________

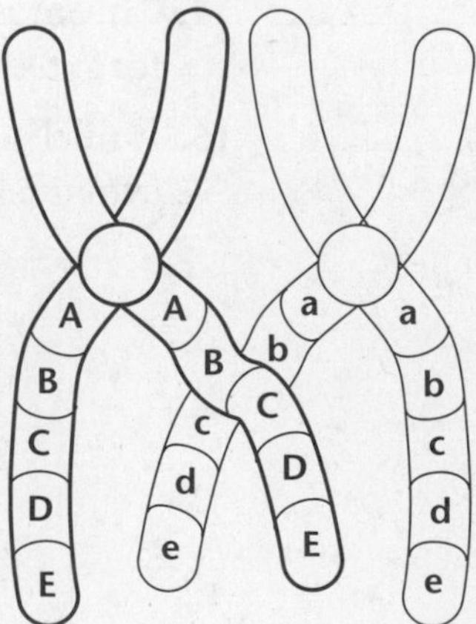


**19.** During what phase of meiosis does this process occur?

___________________________________________

___________________________________________

**20.** What is the result of this process?

___________________________________________

___________________________________________

# Comparing Meiosis and Mitosis

**21.** Complete the table to compare meiosis and mitosis.

| | Mitosis | Meiosis |
|---|---|---|
| Form of reproduction | | |
| Number of daughter cells | | |
| Change in chromosome number | | |
| Number of cell divisions | | |
| Difference in alleles between parent cell and daughter cells | | |

*For Questions 22–27, complete each statement by writing the correct word or words.*

**22.** A diploid cell that enters mitosis with 16 chromosomes will divide to produce ____________ daughter cells. Each of these daughter cells will have ____________ chromosomes.

**23.** If the diploid number of chromosomes for an organism is 16, each daughter cell after mitosis will contain ____________ chromosomes.

**24.** A diploid cell that enters meiosis with 16 chromosomes will pass through ____________ cell divisions, producing ____________ daughter cells, each with ____________ chromosomes.

**25.** Gametes have a ____________ number of chromosomes.

**26.** If an organism's haploid number is 5, its diploid number is ____________.

**27.** While a haploid number of chromosomes may be even or odd, a diploid number is always ____________.

 

# Gene Linkage and Gene Maps

**28.** What did Thomas Hunt Morgan discover that seemed to violate Mendel's principles?

______________________

______________________

**29.** How did Morgan explain his finding?

______________________

______________________

**30.** How did Alfred Sturtevant use gene linkage to create gene maps?

______________________

______________________

*Use this diagram to answer Questions 31–34.*

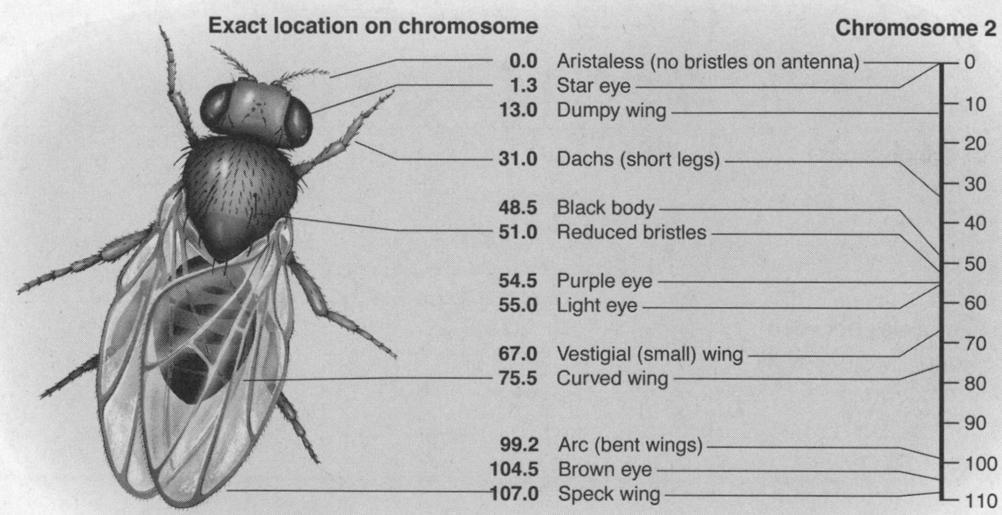


**31.** What does the diagram show?

______________________

**32.** How was the information in this diagram gathered?

______________________

**33.** Which pairs of characteristics are more likely to cross over: curved wing and dumpy wing; or curved wing and vestigial (small) wing? Why?

______________________

______________________

**34.** Which pair of genes shown is least likely to cross over? How do you know?

______________________

______________________

*Use this diagram to answer Questions 35–38.*

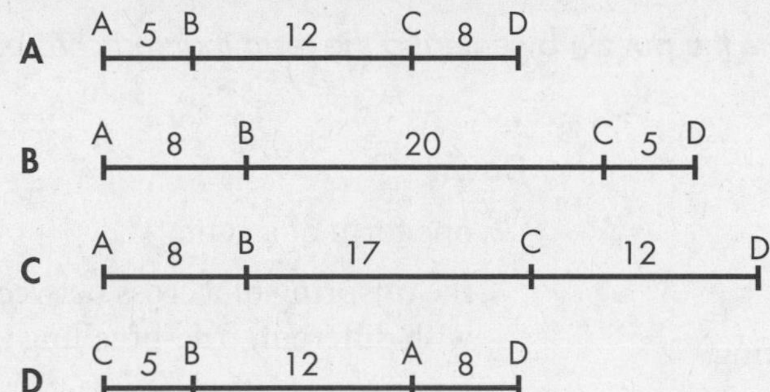


**35.** In which gene map is the probability of crossing-over between A and D greatest?

______________

**36.** In which gene map is the probability of crossing-over between A and D the least?

______________

**37.** In which map are genes C and D most closely linked? ______________

**38.** In map D, which genes are least likely to cross over? ______________

## Apply the Big idea

**39.** Some housecats have orange fur with darker orange stripes. The traits of these *tabby* cats are usually seen in male cats. *Tortoiseshell* cats have patches of many different colors. "Torties," as they are called, are almost always female. What does this tell you about the way cellular information about color and sex are passed on in cats?

______________________________________________

______________________________________________

______________________________________________

______________________________________________

 

# Chapter Vocabulary Review

**Crossword Puzzle** *Complete the puzzle by entering the term that matches each numbered description.*

**Across**

1. a specific characteristic
4. physical traits
6. the separation of alleles during formation of sex cells
9. containing two identical alleles for a trait
11. the likelihood of an event occurring
12. scientific study of heredity
13. the union of male and female sex cells

**Down**

2. one form of a gene
3. the offspring of a cross between parents with different, true-breeding traits
4. word that describes a trait controlled by two or more genes
5. containing two different alleles for a trait
7. genetic makeup
8. a phenotype in which both alleles are expressed
10. reproductive cell, egg or sperm

# CHAPTER MYSTERY

## GREEN PARAKEETS

In the Chapter Mystery, you read about a brood of parakeets that gave the owners results they didn't expect. Do you think Gregor Mendel ever got results he didn't expect?

21st Century Learning

## Can Results Be Too Good?

As odd as it sounds, if you perform a lot of experiments, you should expect to get results you don't expect. Random chance will cause some of the experiments to have different outcomes from the rest of the experiments. Scientists have a mathematical formula to express an experiment's deviation, or how much the actual results varied from the expected results. If an experiment has a deviation of 0, that means the results were exactly as was expected. If it has a deviation of 2 or –2, that means the results were quite different from what was expected. A negative deviation indicates that the actual observations were smaller than average. A positive deviation indicates that the actual observations were larger than average.

The table below was created for the number and type of experiments Mendel performed. Each number in the second column represents the number of experiments we would expect Mendel to have had with the deviation in the first column. For example, we would expect Mendel to have had 13 experiments in which the deviation was between 0 and 0.5, and two experiments with deviations between –2.0 and –2.5. Each number in the third column represents the actual number of experiments with the deviation in the first column. For example, Mendel recorded 16 experiments in which the deviation was between 0 and 0.5.

**An Analysis of Mendel's Data**

| Deviation | Expected Number of Experiments with This Deviation | Actual Number of Experiments with This Deviation |
|---|---|---|
| –2 to –2.5 | 2 | 0 |
| –1.5 to –2 | 3 | 0 |
| –1 to –1.5 | 6 | 4 |
| –0.5 to –1 | 10 | 12 |
| –0 to –0.5 | 13 | 14 |
| 0 to 0.5 | 13 | 16 |
| 0.5 to 1 | 10 | 20 |
| 1 to 1.5 | 6 | 2 |
| 1.5 to 2 | 3 | 1 |
| 2 to 2.5 | 2 | 0 |

Continued on next page ▶

Name ______________________ Class ______ Date ________

## 21st Century Themes Science Literacy

1. How many experiments with deviations between 1.5 and 2.0 would you expect Mendel to have had? How many did he have? ______________________

2. Look at the deviations between –1.0 and 1.0. Did Mendel have more or fewer experiments with deviations in this range than expected? ______________________

3. Look at the deviations beyond –1.0 and 1.0. Did Mendel have more or fewer experiments with deviations in this range than expected? ______________________

4. Do you think scientists ever throw out results that were quite different from expected? Why might a scientist be tempted to do this? ______________________

5. Mendel worked with an assistant, a gardener, and two other monks, all of whom helped count and record the results, and none of whom were scientists. These nonscientists spent years counting tens of thousands of peas. It wouldn't take them long to figure out what the usual results were. How might one or more of Mendel's helpers have caused the low number of high-deviation results?

6. Do you think that what you described in your answer to Question 4 is excusable? Is what you described in Question 5 excusable? Why or why not? ______________________

7. Would your answer to Question 6 be changed if you were considering a case in which a scientist altered data collected while testing a new medicine? Explain your answer.

## 21st Century Skills A Gardening Play

The skills used in this activity include **creativity and intellectual curiosity, self-direction,** and **accountability and adaptability.**

You described what one or more of Mendel's helpers might have done to skew the results of the experiments and how you felt about those actions. Now it's time to get creative. Write a one-act play about Mendel's gardener and what he may or may not have done. The gardener may be the main character, or one or more main characters may affect what the gardener does. The play may be a comedy, a drama, or a tragedy.

*When the play is finished, assign each of the roles to one of your classmates and have a play reading, either in class or after school.*

Name ______________________________ Class _____ Date ________

# 12 DNA

**Information and Heredity, Cellular Basis of Life**

**Q:** What is the structure of DNA, and how does it function in genetic inheritance?

| | WHAT I KNOW | WHAT I LEARNED |
|---|---|---|
| **12.1** How did scientists determine that DNA is responsible for storing, copying, and transmitting genetic information? | | |
| **12.2** How was the basic structure of DNA discovered? | | |
| **12.3** How do cells copy their DNA? | | |

 

# 12.1 Identifying the Substance of Genes

## Lesson Objectives

- Summarize the process of bacterial transformation.
- Describe the role of bacteriophages in identifying genetic material.
- Identify the role of DNA in heredity.

## Lesson Summary

**Bacterial Transformation** In 1928, Frederick Griffith found that some chemical factor from heat-killed bacteria of one strain could change the inherited characteristics of another strain.

- He called the process **transformation** because one type of bacteria (a harmless form) had been changed permanently into another (a disease-carrying form).
- Because the ability to cause disease was inherited by the offspring of the transformed bacteria, he concluded that the transforming factor had to be a gene.

In 1944, Oswald Avery tested the transforming ability of many substances. Only DNA caused transformation. By observing bacterial transformation, Avery and other scientists discovered that the nucleic acid DNA stores and transmits genetic information from one generation of bacteria to the next.

**Bacterial Viruses** A **bacteriophage** is a kind of virus that infects bacteria. When a bacteriophage enters a bacterium, it attaches to the surface of the bacterial cell and injects its genetic material into it.

- In 1952, Alfred Hershey and Martha Chase used radioactive tracers to label proteins and DNA in bacteriophages.
- Only the DNA from the bacteriophage showed up in the infected bacterial cell.
- Hershey and Chase concluded that the genetic material of the bacteriophage was DNA.
- Their work confirmed Avery's results, convincing many scientists that DNA was the genetic material found in genes—not just in viruses and bacteria, but in all living cells.

**The Role of DNA** The DNA that makes up genes must be capable of storing, copying, and transmitting the genetic information in a cell.

## Bacterial Transformation

1. What happened when Griffith injected mice with the pneumonia-causing strain of bacteria that had been heat-killed?

______________________________________________

2. What happened when Griffith injected mice with a mixture of heat-killed, pneumonia-causing bacteria and live bacteria of the harmless type?

______________________________________________

 

3. What was the purpose of Oswald Avery's experiments?

______________________________________________________________

______________________________________________________________

4. What experiments did Avery do?

______________________________________________________________

______________________________________________________________

______________________________________________________________

5. What did Avery conclude?

______________________________________________________________

## Bacterial Viruses

6. Fill in the blanks to summarize the experiments of Hershey and Chase. (Note: The circles represent radioactive labels.)

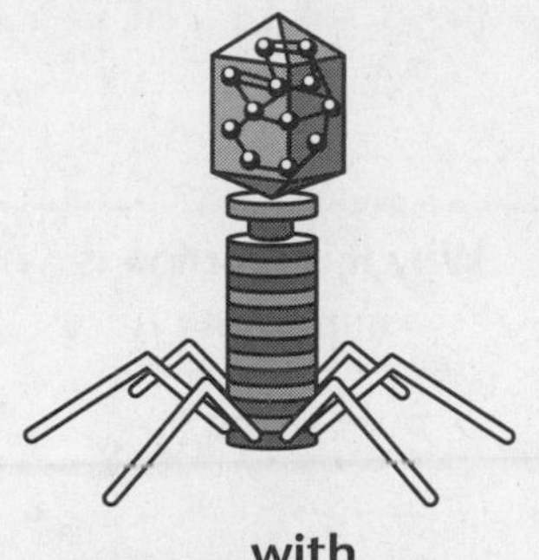

________ with radioactive label

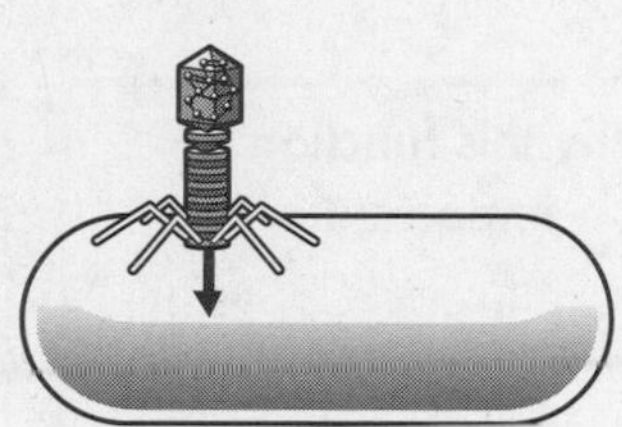

______________________

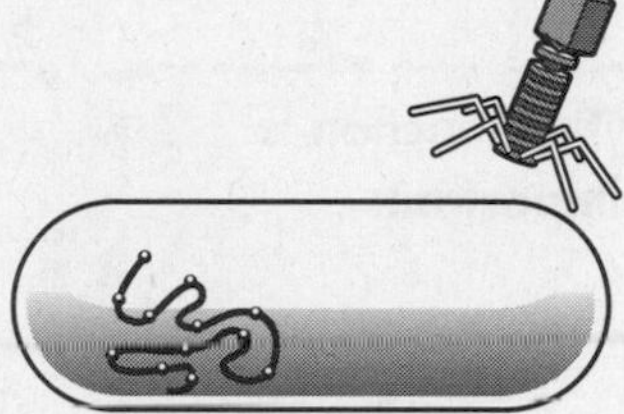

______________________

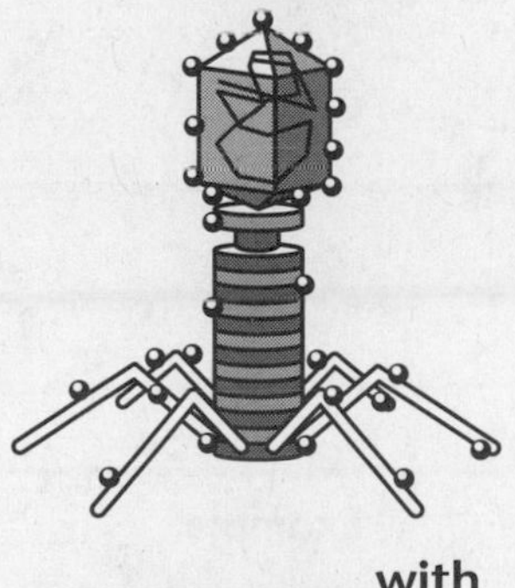

____________ with radioactive label

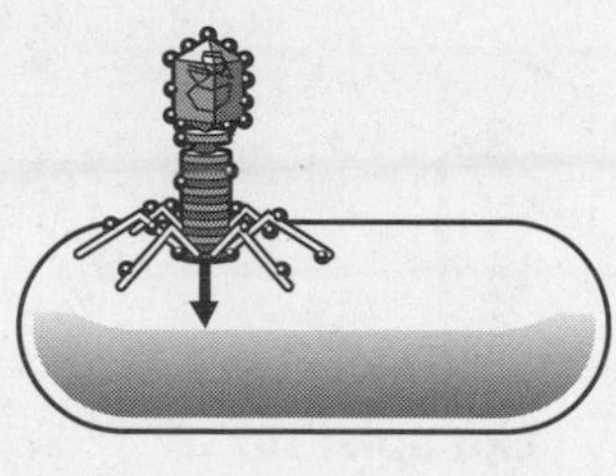

______________________

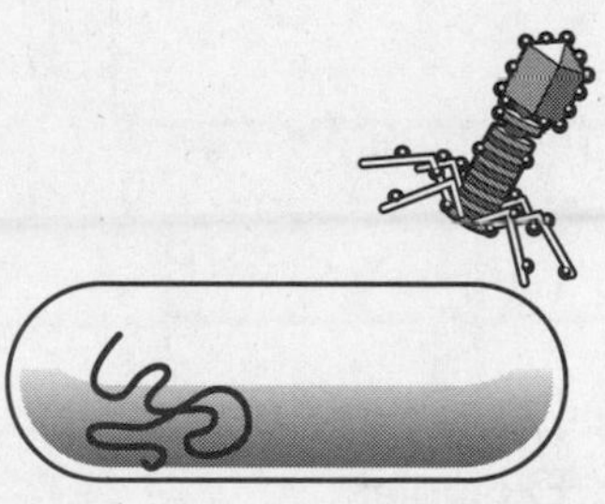

______________________

7. What did Hershey and Chase conclude? Why?

______________________________________________________________

______________________________________________________________

8. How did Hershey and Chase confirm Avery's results?

______________________________________________________________

______________________________________________________________

______________________________________________________________

 

Name ______________________ Class ______ Date ________

# The Role of DNA

**9.** Complete this graphic organizer to summarize the assumptions that guided research on DNA in the middle of the twentieth century. Use an oak tree to give an example of each function.

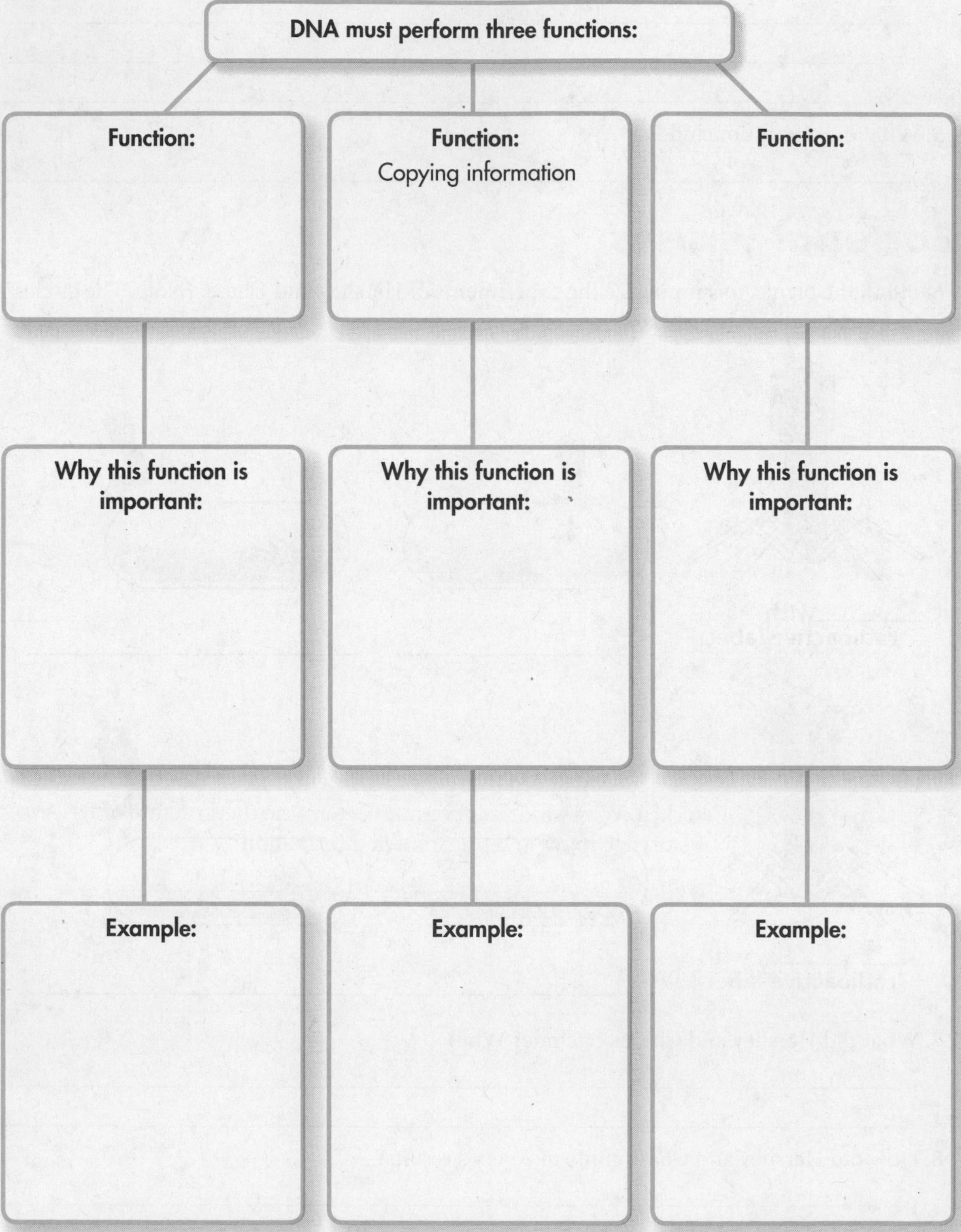


 

Name ______________________ Class ______ Date ________

VISUAL ANALOGY

**10.** DNA is like a book titled *How to Be a Cell.* Explain why that title is appropriate for each of DNA's three functions.



**a.** ______________________

______________________

______________________

______________________

**b.** ______________________

______________________

______________________

______________________

**c.** ______________________

______________________

______________________

______________________

______________________

______________________

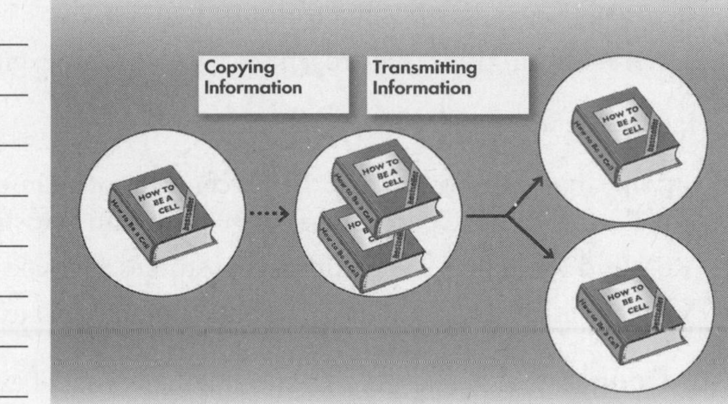

## Apply the Big idea

**11.** By 1952, many scientists were convinced that genes are made of DNA, but they did not yet know how DNA worked. Why was it important to determine the structure of DNA to understand how DNA stored, copied, and transmitted information?

______________________

______________________

______________________

**12.** Why was the fact of transformation so important to the study of DNA's role? What did transformation demonstrate?

______________________

______________________

______________________

 

Name ______________________ Class _____ Date _______

# 12.2 The Structure of DNA

## Lesson Objectives

- Identify the chemical components of DNA.
- Discuss the experiments leading to the identification of DNA as the molecule that carries the genetic code.
- Describe the steps leading to the development of the double-helix model of DNA.

## Lesson Summary

**The Components of DNA** DNA is a nucleic acid made up of nucleotides joined into long strands or chains by covalent bonds. Nucleotides may be joined in any order.

- A DNA nucleotide is a unit made of a nitrogenous base, a 5-carbon sugar called deoxyribose, and a phosphate group.
- DNA has four kinds of nitrogenous bases: adenine, guanine, cytosine, and thymine.

**Solving the Structure of DNA**

- Erwin Chargaff showed that the percentages of adenine and thymine are almost always equal in DNA. The percentages of guanine and cytosine are also almost equal.
- Rosalind Franklin's X-ray diffraction studies revealed the double-helix structure of DNA.
- James Watson and Francis Crick built a model that explained the structure of DNA.

**The Double-Helix Model** The double-helix model explains Chargaff's rule of base pairing and how the two strands of DNA are held together. The model showed the following:

- The two strands in the double helix run in opposite directions, with the nitrogenous bases in the center.
- Each strand carries a sequence of nucleotides, arranged almost like the letters in a fourletter alphabet for recording genetic information.
- Hydrogen bonds hold the strands together. The bonds are easily broken allowing DNA strands to separate.
- Hydrogen bonds form only between certain base pairs–adenine with thymine, and cytosine with guanine. This is called **base pairing**.

## The Components of DNA

*For Questions 1–5, complete each statement by writing in the correct word or words.*

1. The building blocks of DNA are ______________.
2. Nucleotides in DNA are made of three basic components: a sugar called ______________, a ______________, and a nitrogenous ______________.
3. DNA contains four kinds of nitrogenous bases: ______________, ______________, ______________, and ______________.
4. In DNA, ______________ can be joined in any order.
5. The nucleotides in DNA are joined by ______________ bonds.

 

# Solving the Structure of DNA

**6.** Complete the table to describe each scientist's contribution to solving the structure of DNA.

| Scientist | Contribution |
|---|---|
| Erwin Chargaff | |
| Rosalind Franklin | |
| James Watson and Francis Crick | |

**7.** Complete the table by estimating the percentages of each based on Chargaff's rules.

| DNA sample | Percent of adenine | Percent of thymine | Percent of guanine | Percent of cytosine |
|---|---|---|---|---|
| 1 | 31.5 | | | |
| 2 | | 30 | 20 | |
| 3 | | | | 17 |

# The Double-Helix Model

*For Questions 8–13, on the lines provided, label the parts of the DNA molecule that correspond to the numbers in the diagram.*

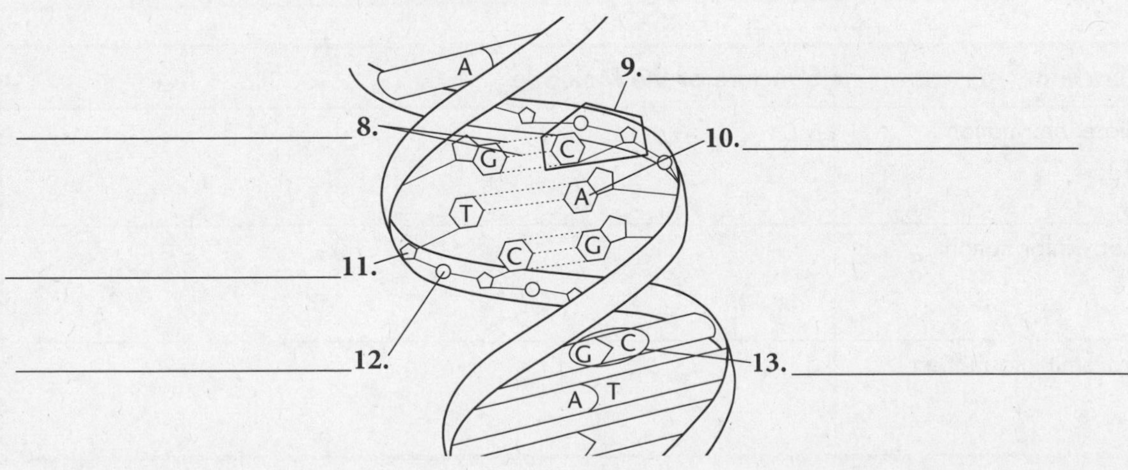


 

Name ______________________ Class ______ Date ______

14. THINK VISUALLY The drawing below shows half of a DNA molecule. Fill in the appropriate letters for the other half. Explain why you drew your sketch the way you did.

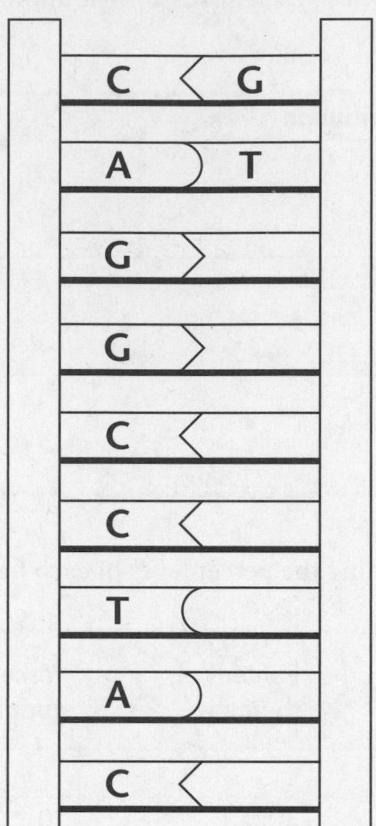


**Key**
A = Adenine
C = Cytosine
G = Guanine
T = Thymine

______________________________________________________________________

______________________________________________________________________

## Apply the Big idea

15. Complete this table to show how the structure of the DNA molecule allows it to perform each essential function.

| Function | Structure of the Molecule |
|---|---|
| Store information | |
| Copy information | |
| Transmit information | |

 

Name ______________________ Class ______ Date ______

# 12.3 DNA Replication

## Lesson Objectives

Summarize the events of DNA replication.

Compare DNA replication in prokaryotes with that of eukaryotes.

## Lesson Summary

**Copying the Code** Each strand of the double helix has all the information needed to reconstruct the other half by the mechanism of base pairing. Because each strand can be used to make the other strand, the strands are said to be complementary. DNA copies itself through the process of **replication**:

- The two strands of the double helix unzip, forming replication forks.
- New bases are added, following the rules of base pairing (A with T and G with C).
- Each new DNA molecule has one original strand and one new strand.
- **DNA polymerase** is an enzyme that joins individual nucleotides to produce a new strand of DNA.
- During replication, DNA may be lost from the tips of chromosomes, which are called **telomeres**.

**Replication in Living Cells** The cells of most prokaryotes have a single, circular DNA molecule in the cytoplasm. Eukaryotic cells have much more DNA. Nearly all of it is contained in chromosomes, which are in the nucleus.

- Replication in most prokaryotic cells starts from a single point and proceeds in two directions until the entire chromosome is copied.
- In eukaryotic cells, replication may begin at dozens or even hundreds of places on the DNA molecule, proceeding in both directions until each chromosome is completely copied.

# Copying the Code

**1.** Why are the strands of a DNA molecule said to be complementary?

______________________________________________

**2.** What is the first step in eukaryotic DNA replication?

______________________________________________

______________________________________________

**3.** If the base sequence on a separated DNA strand is CGTAGG, what will the base sequence on its complementary strand be?

______________________________________________

**4.** What enzyme joins individual nucleotides to produce the new strand of DNA?

______________________________________________

 

5. What enzyme makes it less likely that DNA will be lost from telomeres during replication?

______

6. How does this enzyme work?

______

______

7. What is a replication fork?

______

______

______

8. Does DNA replication take place in the same direction along both strands of the DNA molecule that is being replicated? Explain your answer. (Hint: Look at the illustration of DNA replication in your textbook.)

______

______

9. **THINK VISUALLY** Make a sketch of the double helix of DNA. Show how it unzips for replication and how complementary strands are built. Label the nitrogenous bases, replication fork, DNA polymerase, the original strand, and the new strand.

 

## Replication in Living Cells

**10.** Complete the table to compare and contrast DNA replication in prokaryotes and eukaryotes.

| | Prokaryotes | Eukaryotes |
|---|---|---|
| Location of DNA | | |
| Amount of DNA | | |
| Starting Point(s) for Replication | | |

**11.** Is DNA replication always a foolproof process? Explain your answer.

______________________________________________

______________________________________________

______________________________________________

### Apply the Big idea

**12.** Why is the pairing of bases during replication essential for the transmission of inherited traits from parent to offspring?

______________________________________________

______________________________________________

______________________________________________

______________________________________________

# Chapter Vocabulary Review

*For Questions 1–6, match the term with its definition.*

**Definition**

_____ **1.** In DNA, the fit between thymine and adenine and the fit between cytosine and guanine.

_____ **2.** An enzyme that joins individual nucleotides to produce a new strand of DNA

_____ **3.** The process that can change a harmless bacterial strain into a disease-causing strain

_____ **4.** The tip of a chromosome

_____ **5.** The process that copies a DNA molecule

_____ **6.** A kind of virus that infects bacteria

**Term**

**A.** transformation

**B.** bacteriophage

**C.** base pairing

**D.** replication

**E.** DNA polymerase

**F.** telomere

*For Questions 7–15, complete each statement by writing in the correct word or words.*

**7.** Each time a chromosome is replicated, some DNA may be lost from the tip of the chromosome, or ______________.

**8.** Griffith's experiments showed that some chemical compound in cells must be responsible for bacterial ______________.

**9.** Hershey and Chase studied a ______________ that was composed of a DNA core and a protein coat.

**10.** The center of the DNA strand exhibits ______________.

**11.** The enzyme that "proofreads" each new DNA strand so that each molecule is a near-perfect copy of the original is ______________.

**12.** In eukaryotic cells, ______________ can begin at dozens or even hundreds of places on the DNA molecule.

**13.** The double-helix model explains Chargaff's rule of ______________.

**14.** The DNA molecule separates into two strands during ______________.

**15.** The principal enzyme involved in DNA replication is ______________.

 

Name ______ Class ______ Date ______

# CHAPTER MYSTERY

## UV LIGHT

In the Chapter Mystery, you were introduced to the complex process by which radiation from the sun causes skin cancer. And there's even more to learn about the links between sun exposure and skin cancer. But you don't need to be a molecular geneticist to understand how to prevent skin cancer.

21st Century Learning

## The Sun and Your Skin

Even people who don't understand how radiation from the sun causes skin cancer know they should protect themselves. Even so, only 40 percent of Americans consistently use sunscreen when they're in the sun. And 20 percent of American adults actually sunbathe—that is, they deliberately expose their skin to solar radiation. This poster presents information everyone should know.

**What is ultraviolet radiation?**

- Ultraviolet (UV) rays are an invisible form of radiation.
  - They make up a part of sunlight.
- There are three types of UV rays.
  - ultraviolet A (UVA), ultraviolet B (UVB), and ultraviolet C (UVC)

**What are the results of exposure to ultraviolet radiation?**

- various types of skin cancer
- various eye conditions, including cataracts
- premature aging
- dry, sagging, and wrinkled skin
- yellowing of the skin

**How does UV radiation cause skin cancer?**

- Phase 1
  - UV radiation interferes with the mechanism by which cells repair damage.
  - These abnormal cells are more vulnerable to injury.
- Phase 2
  - Normal cells that are overexposed to UV radiation die.
  - Abnormal cells that are overexposed to UV radiation do not die.
  - Genetic damage accumulates.

**How can you protect yourself from UV radiation?**

- Seek shade, especially from 10:00 A.M. to 4:00 P.M. when UV rays are strongest.
- Cover exposed skin with clothing.
- Wear a hat with a wide brim that shades your face, head, ears, and neck.
- Wear sunglasses.
  - Wraparounds are best.
  - They should block as close to 100 percent of both UVA and UVB rays as possible.
- Use sunscreen.
  - Use one with a sun protective factor (SPF) of 15 or higher.
  - Use one that blocks both UVA and UVB radiation.
  - Reapply it every two hours, as well as right after you swim or sweat.

**These sunscreen ingredients block UVA radiation.**

- benzophenone
- oxybenzone
- sulisobenzone
- titanium dioxide
- zinc oxide
- butyl methoxydibenzoylmethane, also called avobenzone, also called Parsol 1789

**These sunscreen ingredients block UVB radiation.**

- Cinnamates, including octyl methoxycinnamate and cinoxate
- Salicylates, including homomenthyl salicylate, octyl salicylate, and triethanolamine salicylate
- Octocrylene
- Ensulizole, or PBSA

**Some risk factors make you more likely to contract skin cancer.**

- lighter natural skin, eye, or hair color
- family or personal history of skin cancer
- exposure to the sun
- history of sunburns early in life
- skin that burns, freckles, or reddens easily
- certain types of moles
- a large number of moles

**Skin cancer is an undeclared epidemic.**

- It's the most common of all the types of cancer.
- It's roughly as common as all other cancers combined.
- This year a million Americans will develop skin cancer.

**It's time to explode some myths.**

- UV radiation causes damage whether you get it from the sun or from a tanning bed.
- Damage done now will not become evident for many years.
- More frequent sun exposure at an early age results in a higher risk of skin damage; 80 percent of a person's lifetime sun exposure is acquired before age 18.
- There is no such thing as a healthy tan.

Continued on next page ▶

 

## 21st Century Themes Science and Health Literacy

**1.** How many types of ultraviolet radiation are there? What are they?

**2.** One form of ultraviolet radiation is absorbed by the ozone in the atmosphere and never reaches Earth's surface. Which one do you think that is? Why?

**3.** When is the sun's UV radiation strongest?

**4.** Your friend says she's going sunbathing. She says, "I've been in the sun all summer. I've tanned, but I haven't burned. My skin is still soft and it isn't dry at all. I have nothing to worry about." Is she right or wrong? Why?

**5.** Do you think that skin cancer can be inherited? Why or why not?

## 21st Century Skills Warning Signs of Skin Cancer

The skills used in this activity include **creativity and intellectual curiosity, information and media literacy,** and **social responsibility**.

The poster on the previous page was intended to educate people about how UV radiation in sunlight damages skin cells and show them how they can avoid exposure to UV. For some people, though, these warnings come too late. Use Internet and library resources to research the warning signs of skin cancer and what a person who detects one or more of these warning signs should do.

*Compile this information into a booklet that could be distributed in doctors' offices and drugstores.*

 

Name ______________________ Class ______ Date ______

# 13 RNA and Protein Synthesis

**Big idea** **Information and Heredity**

**Q:** How does information flow from the cell nucleus to direct the synthesis of proteins in the cytoplasm?

| | WHAT I KNOW | WHAT I LEARNED |
|---|---|---|
| **13.1** What is RNA? | | |
| **13.2** How do cells make proteins? | | |
| **13.3** What happens when a cell's DNA changes? | | |
| **13.4** How do cells regulate gene expression? | | |

# 13.1 RNA

## Lesson Objectives

Contrast RNA and DNA.

Explain the process of transcription.

## Lesson Summary

**The Role of RNA** **RNA** (ribonucleic acid) is a nucleic acid like DNA. It consists of a long chain of nucleotides. The RNA base sequence directs the production of proteins. Ultimately, cell proteins result in phenotypic traits. The main differences between RNA and DNA are:

- The sugar in RNA is ribose instead of deoxyribose.
- RNA is generally single-stranded and not double-stranded like DNA.
- RNA contains uracil in place of thymine.

RNA can be thought of as a disposable copy of a segment of DNA. Most RNA molecules are involved in protein synthesis. The three main types of RNA are:

- **Messenger RNA** (mRNA) carries copies of instructions for polypeptide synthesis from the nucleus to ribosomes in the cytoplasm.
- **Ribosomal RNA** (rRNA) forms an important part of both subunits of the ribosomes, the cell structures where proteins are assembled.
- **Transfer RNA** (tRNA) carries amino acids to the ribosome and matches them to the coded mRNA message.

**RNA Synthesis** Most of the work of making RNA takes place during transcription. In **transcription**, segments of DNA serve as templates to produce complementary RNA molecules. In prokaryotes, RNA synthesis and protein synthesis takes place in the cytoplasm. In eukaryotes, RNA is produced in the cell's nucleus and then moves to the cytoplasm to play a role in the production of protein. The following focuses on transcription in eukaryotic cells.

- The enzyme **RNA polymerase** binds to DNA during transcription and separates the DNA strands. It then uses one strand of DNA as a template from which to assemble nucleotides into a complementary strand of RNA.
- RNA polymerase binds only to **promoters**, regions of DNA that have specific base sequences. Promoters are signals to the DNA molecule that show RNA polymerase exactly where to begin making RNA. Similar signals cause transcription to stop when a new RNA molecule is completed.
- RNA may be "edited" before it is used. Portions that are cut out and discarded are called **introns**. The remaining pieces, known as **exons**, are then spliced back together to form the final mRNA.

Name ______________________ Class ______ Date ________

# The Role of RNA

**1.** Complete the table to contrast the structures of DNA and RNA.

| | Sugar | Number of Strands | Bases |
|---|---|---|---|
| DNA | | | |
| RNA | | | |

**2.** On the lines provided, identify each kind of RNA.

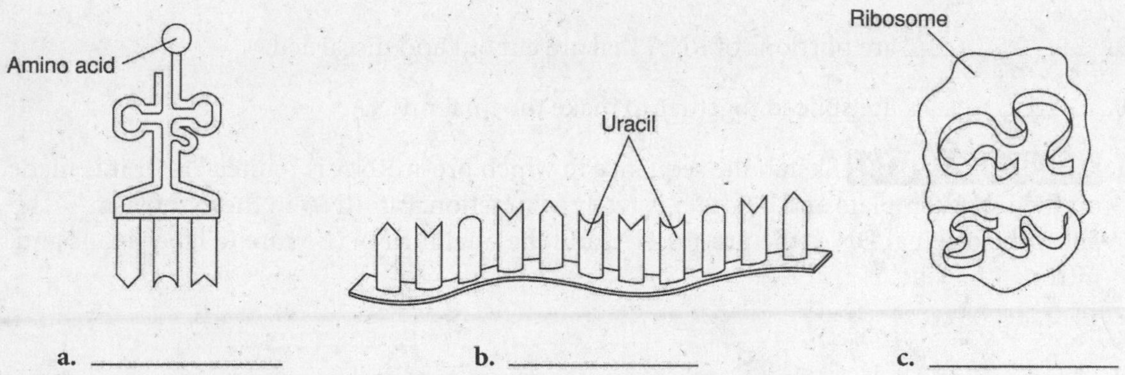


**a.** __________ **b.** __________ **c.** __________

**3.** **VISUAL ANALOGY** The master plan of a building shows how to build and place important parts of the building, such as walls, pipes, and electrical outlets. On the building site, workers use copies of the master plan called blueprints to show them what to do. The master plan is kept in the office. Explain how mRNA works like a blueprint in constructing proteins.

______________________________________________

______________________________________________

______________________________________________

## RNA Synthesis

*For Questions 4–10, complete each statement by writing the correct word or words.*

4. The process of using DNA to produce complementary RNA molecules is called ____________.

5. The sequence of ____________ in mRNA complements the sequence in the DNA template.

6. In eukaryotes, RNA is formed in the ____________ and then travels to the ____________.

7. The enzyme ____________ binds to DNA during transcription.

8. RNA polymerase binds to regions of DNA called ____________, which are "start" signals for transcription.

9. ____________ are portions of RNA that are cut out and discarded.

10. ____________ are spliced together to make the final mRNA.

11. **THINK VISUALLY** Sketch the sequence in which pre-mRNA is "edited" after it is made on the DNA template and before it is ready to function as mRNA in the cytoplasm. Show the original DNA, the pre-mRNA, and the final mRNA. Be sure to label exons and introns.

### Apply the Big idea

12. Use the analogy of the master plan and blueprints used by builders to identify what represents messenger RNA, where the "ribosome" is, and who performs the same kind of job as transfer RNA.

*Explain your reasoning.*

 

# 13.2 Ribosomes and Protein Synthesis

## Lesson Objectives

- Identify the genetic code and explain how it is read.
- Summarize the process of translation.
- Describe the "central dogma" of molecular biology.

## Lesson Summary

**The Genetic Code** A specific sequence of bases in DNA carries the directions for forming a **polypeptide**, a chain of amino acids. The types and order of amino acids in a polypeptide determine the properties of the protein. The sequence of bases in mRNA is the **genetic code**. The four bases, A, C, G, and U, act as "letters."

- The code is read three "letters" at a time, so that each "word" is three bases long and corresponds to a single amino acid. Each three-letter "word" in mRNA is known as a **codon**.
- Some codons serve as "start" and "stop" signals for protein synthesis.

**Translation** Ribosomes use the sequence of codons in mRNA to assemble amino acids into polypeptide chains. The process of decoding of an mRNA message into a protein is **translation**.

- Messenger RNA is transcribed in the nucleus and then enters the cytoplasm.
- On the ribosome, translation begins at the start codon. Each codon attracts an **anticodon**, the complementary sequence of bases on tRNA.
- Each tRNA carries one kind of amino acid. The match between the codon and anticodon ensures that the correct amino acid is added to the growing chain.
- The amino acids bond together, each in turn. The ribosome moves along the mRNA, exposing codons that attract still more tRNAs with their attached amino acids.
- The process concludes when a "stop code" is reached. The newly formed polypeptide and the mRNA molecule are released from the ribosome.

**The Molecular Basis of Heredity** Molecular biology seeks to explain living organisms by studying them at the molecular level, using molecules like DNA and RNA.

- The central dogma of molecular biology is that information is transferred from DNA to RNA to protein.
- **Gene expression** is the way in which DNA, RNA, and proteins are involved in putting genetic information into action in living cells.
- The genetic code is generally the same in all organisms.

 

Name _______________ Class _______ Date _______

# The Genetic Code

*Use the diagram to answer Questions 1–7.*

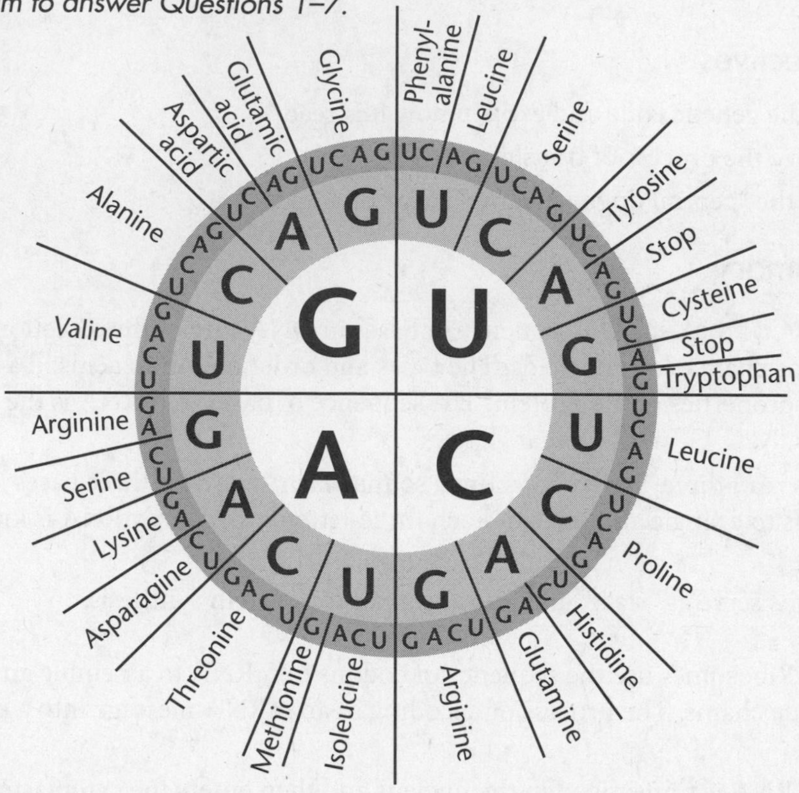


**1.** What are the words along the outside of the circle?

_______________________________________________

**2.** What can you find by reading this diagram from the inside out?

_______________________________________________

**3.** For which amino acid is AAA a codon?

_______________________________________________

**4.** What is the codon for tryptophan?

_______________________________________________

**5.** For which amino acid is GGA a codon?

_______________________________________________

**6.** What is a codon for alanine?

_______________________________________________

**7.** What are three other codons for alanine?

_______________________________________________

# Translation

*Use the diagram to answer Questions 8–10.*

**8.** What is the anticodon for leucine? ______

**9.** What is the codon for leucine? ______

**10.** List the amino acids in the order they would appear in the polypeptide coded for by this mRNA.

______________________________________

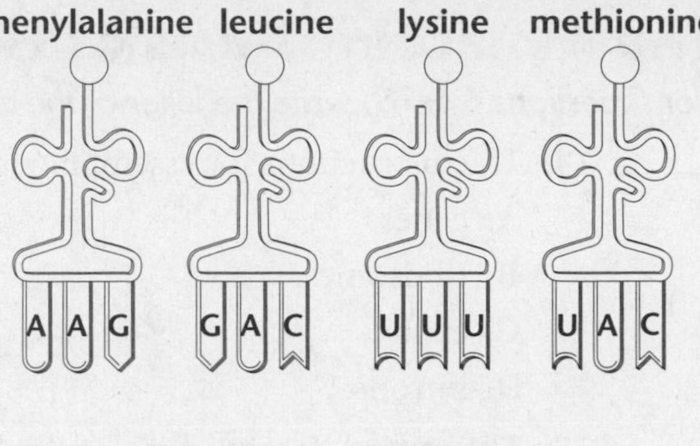

**11.** What is the difference between transcription and translation?

______________________________________

______________________________________

______________________________________

**12.** Complete the table to describe the steps in protein synthesis.

| Step | Description |
|---|---|
| Beginning of translation | |
| Assembly of polypeptide | |
| Completing the polypeptide | |

**13.** Describe the role of rRNA during translation.

______________________________________

______________________________________

______________________________________

 

## The Molecular Basis of Heredity

*For Questions 14–18, write the letter of the correct answer on the line at the left.*

______ **14.** The instructions for assembling proteins are contained in the
**A.** genes.
**B.** ribosomes.
**C.** exons.
**D.** introns.

______ **15.** The central dogma of molecular biology is that information is transferred from
**A.** RNA to protein to DNA.
**B.** DNA to protein to RNA.
**C.** protein to DNA to RNA.
**D.** DNA to RNA to protein.

______ **16.** An exception to the central dogma is
**A.** the infection of a virus by a bacteriophage.
**B.** the ability of some viruses to transfer information from RNA to DNA.
**C.** the expression of different genes during different stages of development.
**D.** the translation of the codon into the anticodon of tRNA.

______ **17.** The way in which DNA, RNA, and proteins are all involved in putting genetic information into action in living cells is called
**A.** translation.
**B.** transcription.
**C.** gene expression.
**D.** viral transfer.

______ **18.** All organisms are mostly the same in
**A.** the proteins they make on their ribosomes.
**B.** how their proteins catalyze chemical reactions.
**C.** the size of their genes.
**D.** the molecular biology of their genes.

### Apply the Big idea

**19.** Whether the organism is a pea plant or a human being, the information in the DNA of the cell's nucleus directs synthesis of proteins in the cytoplasm. Why, then, are pea plants and human beings so different?

______

______

______

______

 

# 13.3 Mutations

## Lesson Objectives

Define mutations and describe the different types of mutations.

Describe the effects mutations can have on genes.

## Lesson Summary

**Types of Mutations** **Mutations** are heritable changes in genetic information. There are two categories of mutations: gene mutations and chromosomal mutations.

- Gene mutations produce changes in a single gene. **Point mutations** involve only one or a few nucleotides. Substitutions, insertions, and deletions are all types of point mutations
  - In a substitution, one base is changed to a different base, which may affect only a single amino acid and have no effect at all.
  - In insertions and deletions, one base is inserted or removed from the DNA sequence. Insertions and deletions are called **frameshift mutations** because they shift the "reading frame" of the genetic message. Frameshift mutations can change every amino acid that follows the point of mutation and can have dramatic effects on the organism.
- Chromosomal mutations produce changes in the number or structure of chromosomes. They include deletions, duplications, inversions, and translocations.
  - Deletion involves the loss of all or part of a chromosome.
  - Duplication produces an extra copy of all or part of a chromosome.
  - Inversion reverses the direction of parts of a chromosome.
  - Translocation occurs when part of one chromosome breaks off and attaches to another.

**Effects of Mutations** Genetic material can be altered by natural events or by artificial means. Errors can be made during replication. Environmental conditions may increase the rate of mutation. **Mutagens** are chemical or physical agents in the environment that cause mutations.

The effects of mutations on genes vary widely:

- Some mutations have little or no effect.
- Some mutations produce beneficial variations. One example is **polyploidy** in plants, in which an organism has extra sets of chromosomes. Polyploid plants are often larger and stronger than diploid plants. Mutations can also produce proteins with new or altered functions that can be useful to organisms in different or changing environments.
- Some mutations negatively disrupt gene function or dramatically change protein structure. Genetic disorders such as sickle cell disease can result.

 

# Types of Mutations

*For Questions 1–8, match the term with its definition.*

**Definition**

_____ **1.** The change of one base to another in a DNA sequence

_____ **2.** A change in one or a few nucleotides that occur at a single point in the DNA sequence

_____ **3.** Part of one chromosome breaks off and attaches to another

_____ **4.** A heritable change in genetic information

_____ **5.** A mutation that produces an extra copy of all or part of a chromosome

_____ **6.** A chromosomal mutation that reverses the direction of parts of a chromosome

_____ **7.** A kind of mutation that can change every amino acid that follows the point of mutation

_____ **8.** The addition of a base to the DNA sequence

**Term**

**A.** mutation
**B.** substitution
**C.** point mutation
**D.** frameshift mutation
**E.** insertion
**F.** translocation
**G.** inversion
**H.** duplication

**9.** Complete the table to describe the processes and outcomes of the different types of gene (point) mutations.

| Type | Description | Outcome |
|---|---|---|
| Substitution | | |
| Insertion | | |
| Deletion | | |

**10.** Deletion can happen as a gene mutation or as a chromosomal mutation. What is the difference?

_______________________________________________

_______________________________________________

_______________________________________________

# Effects of Mutations

*For Questions 10–17, write the letter of the correct answer on the line at the left.*

______ **10.** The cellular machinery that replicates DNA inserts an incorrect base

**A.** most of the time.

**B.** about half the time.

**C.** roughly once in every million bases.

**D.** roughly once in every 10 million bases.

______ **11.** Small changes in genes

**A.** disappear quickly.

**B.** gradually accumulate over time.

**C.** prevent the next generation from developing

**D.** do not affect future generations.

______ **12.** A possible mutagen is

**A.** an anticodon.

**B.** translocation.

**C.** hemoglobin.

**D.** ultraviolet light.

______ **13.** What happens when cells cannot repair the damage caused by a mutagen?

**A.** The DNA base sequence changes permanently.

**B.** The DNA base sequence is not affected.

**C.** The organism is not affected.

**D.** The organism is affected temporarily.

______ **14.** Which of the following most accurately summarizes the effects of mutations on living things?

**A.** Most mutations are harmful, but some have little effect.

**B.** Many mutations have little or no effect, but some can be harmful or beneficial.

**C.** Most mutations are beneficial and a few are harmful.

**D.** About half of mutations are beneficial and half are harmful.

______ **15.** Mutations are important to the evolution of a species because they

**A.** happen over the long period of time that evolution requires.

**B.** cut out and replace damaged or useless genes.

**C.** are a source of genetic variability.

**D.** accelerate the transcription rate of DNA.

______ **16.** Cancer is the product of a mutation that

**A.** causes the uncontrolled growth of cells.

**B.** changes the structure of hemoglobin in the blood.

**C.** brings about stunted growth and severe pain.

**D.** causes a translocation in a pair of chromosomes.

 

_____ **17.** Polyploidy is the condition in which

**A.** a piece of a chromosome breaks off and reattaches to another chromosome.

**B.** an organism has an extra set of chromosomes.

**C.** a mutagen speeds the mutation rate.

**D.** an insect develops a resistance to a pesticide.

**18.** In the space below, draw an example of a normal blood cell and an example of a sickle cell.

## Apply the Big idea

**19.** A gene that codes for one of the polypeptide chains of the blood protein hemoglobin lies on chromosome 11 in humans. A substitution mutation in that gene causes the amino acid valine to be incorporated into hemoglobin in a place where glutamic acid would normally lie. The result is sickle cell disease. Explain how a change in a single base in DNA can bring about such a serious disorder.

# 13.4 Gene Regulation and Expression

## Lesson Objectives

- Describe gene regulation in prokaryotes.
- Explain how most eukaryotic genes are regulated.
- Relate gene regulation to development in multicellular organisms.

## Lesson Summary

**Prokaryotic Gene Regulation** Prokaryotes do not need to transcribe all of their genes at the same time. They can conserve energy and resources by regulating their activities, producing only those genes necessary for the cell to function. In prokaryotes, DNA binding proteins regulate genes by controlling transcription. An **operon** is a group of genes that are regulated together. An example is the *lac* operon in the bacterium *E. coli*:

- This group of three genes must be turned on together before the bacterium can use lactose as food.
- When lactose is not present, the DNA-binding protein called *lac* repressor binds to a region called the **operator**, which switches the *lac* operon off.
- When lactose binds to the repressor, it causes the repressor to fall off the operator, turning the operon on.

**Eukaryotic Gene Regulation** Transcription factors are DNA-binding proteins. They control the expression of genes in eukaryotes by binding DNA sequences in the regulatory regions. Gene promoters have multiple binding sites for transcription factors, each of which can influence transcription.

- Complex gene regulation in eukaryotes makes cell specialization possible.
- The process by which microRNA (miRNA) molecules stop mRNA molecules from passing on their protein-making instructions is **RNA interference (RNAi)**.
- RNAi technology holds the promise of allowing scientists to turn off the expression of genes from viruses and cancer cells, and it may provide new ways to treat and perhaps even cure diseases.

**Genetic Control of Development** Regulating gene expression is especially important in shaping the way a multicellular organism develops. Gene regulation helps cells undergo **differentiation**, becoming specialized in structure and function. Master control genes are like switches that trigger particular patterns of development and differentiation in cells and tissues.

- **Homeotic genes** are master control genes that regulate organs that develop in specific parts of the body.
- **Homeobox genes** share a similar 130-base DNA sequence called homeobox. They code for transcription factors that activate other genes that are important in cell development and differentiation in certain regions of the body.
- **Hox genes** are a group of homeobox genes that tell the cells of the body how to differentiate as the body grows.

Environmental factors can also affect gene expression.

 

# Prokaryotic Gene Regulation

**1.** How do prokaryotes conserve energy?

**2.** How do DNA-binding proteins in prokaryotes regulate genes?

**3.** What is an operon?

**4.** What is in the *lac* operon in *E. coli*?

**5.** What is the function of the genes in the *lac* operon of *E. coli*?

**6.** What turns the *lac* operon off?

**7.** How does a repressor protein turn off the *lac* operon?

**8.** How does lactose turn on the *lac* operon?

**9.** Complete the table to describe the role of each regulatory region or molecule in the operation of the *lac* operon.

| Regulatory Region or Molecule | What It Does |
|---|---|
| Repressor protein | |
| Operator | |
| RNA polymerase | |
| Lactose | |

Name ______________________ Class ______ Date ________

# Eukaryotic Gene Regulation

**10.** In what two ways is gene regulation in eukaryotes different from gene regulation in prokaryotes?

a. ______________________________

b. ______________________________

**11.** What is a TATA box? What does a TATA box do?

**12.** What are transcription factors and what do they do?

**13.** Explain how gene regulation makes cell specialization possible.

**14.** What is microRNA and how is it related to mRNA?

**15.** Explain how the process of RNA interference works.

 

# Genetic Control of Development

*For Questions 16–23, write the letter of the correct answer on the line at the left.*

______ **16.** As an embryo develops, different sets of genes are regulated by
- **A.** mRNA and *lac* repressors.
- **B.** operons and operators.
- **C.** transcription factors and repressors.
- **D.** promoters and operators.

______ **17.** The process through which cells become specialized in structure and function is
- **A.** transcription.
- **B.** gene expression.
- **C.** differentiation.
- **D.** RNA interference.

______ **18.** Homeotic genes are
- **A.** regulator genes that bind to operons in prokaryotes.
- **B.** master control genes that regulate organs that develop in specific parts of the body.
- **C.** parts of the silencing complex that regulates gene action through RNA interference.
- **D.** base sequences complementary to sequences in microRNA.

______ **19.** What role do homeobox genes play in cell differentiation?
- **A.** They code for transcription factors that activate other genes important in cell development and differentiation.
- **B.** They block certain gene expression.
- **C.** They cut double-stranded loops into microRNA.
- **D.** They attach to a cluster of proteins to form a silencing complex, which binds to and destroys certain RNA.

______ **20.** In flies, the group of homeobox genes that determines the identities of each segment of a fly's body is the group known as
- **A.** silencing complexes.
- **B.** promoters.
- **C.** operators.
- **D.** Hox genes.

______ **21.** Clusters of Hox genes are found in
- **A.** flies only.
- **B.** flies and frogs only.
- **C.** plants only.
- **D.** nearly all animals.

______ **22.** The "switches" that trigger particular patterns of development and differentiation in cells and tissues are
- **A.** mRNA molecules.
- **B.** master control genes.
- **C.** silencing complexes.
- **D.** Dicer enzymes.

______ **23.** Metamorphosis is
- **A.** a series of transformations from one life stage to another.
- **B.** the master switch that triggers development and differentiation.
- **C.** the product of interactions among homeotic genes.
- **D.** the process by which genetic information is passed from one generation to the next.

24. Environmental factors can influence gene expression. Fill in the table below to show how organisms respond to conditions in their environment.

| | Environmental Factor Influencing Gene Expression | How the Organism Responds |
|---|---|---|
| ***E. coli*** **with limited food supply** | nutrient availability | |
| **A tadpole in a drying pond** | | |

## Apply the Big idea

25. Many research studies have shown that different species may possess some of the exact same genes but show vastly different traits. How can that happen?

_______________________________________________

_______________________________________________

_______________________________________________

_______________________________________________

_______________________________________________

# Chapter Vocabulary Review

*For Questions 1–7, write True if the statement is true. If the statement is false, change the underlined word or words to make the statement true.*

______ **1.** <u>DNA</u> contains the sugar ribose.

______ **2.** <u>Messenger RNA</u> carries copies of the instructions for making proteins from DNA to other parts of the cell.

______ **3.** <u>RNA polymerase</u> transfers amino acids to ribosomes.

______ **4.** The process of <u>transcription</u> produces a complementary strand of RNA on a DNA template.

______ **5.** The enzyme that assembles a complementary strand of RNA on a DNA template is <u>RNA polymerase</u>.

______ **6.** The region of DNA where the production of an RNA strand begins is called the <u>intron</u>.

______ **7.** <u>Exons</u> are spliced together in forming messenger RNA.

*For Questions 8–16, match the term with its definition.*

**Definition**

______ **8.** The sequence of bases that serves as the "language" of life

______ **9.** A sequence of three bases on a tRNA molecule that is complementary to a sequence of bases on an mRNA molecule

______ **10.** How genetic information is put into action in a living cell

______ **11.** Having extra sets of chromosomes

______ **12.** The decoding of an mRNA message into a protein

______ **13.** A heritable change in genetic information

______ **14.** A chain of amino acids

______ **15.** The three consecutive bases that specify a single amino acid to be added to the polypeptide chain

______ **16.** A chemical or physical agent that causes a change in a gene

**Term**

**A.** polypeptide
**B.** genetic code
**C.** codon
**D.** translation
**E.** anticodon
**F.** gene expression
**G.** mutation
**H.** mutagen
**I.** polyploidy

*For Questions 17–19, complete each statement by writing the correct word or words.*

**17.** A group of genes that are regulated together is called a(n) ______________.

**18.** A region of DNA where a repressor can bind is a(n) ______________.

**19.** Master control genes, called ______________ genes, regulate organs that develop in specific parts of the body.

 

Name ______________________ Class ______ Date ______

In the Chapter Mystery, you learned about a fly that was genetically manipulated to grow eyes in different places on its body. Scientists continue to develop techniques to modify a variety of other animals. But should they?

21st Century Learning

# Should Genetic Experiments Be Performed on Animals?

Some people think that the type of research that produced the mouse-eyed fly is perfectly acceptable. Others think that it's a terrible thing to do even to a fly. In the biological sciences, animal testing has always been controversial, and it probably always will be.

## Perspectives on Animal Genetic Experiments

Animal rights groups have come a long way in recent years. More people are responding to the issues brought up by animal rights groups. For example, animal testing of cosmetics has been banned in a number of countries, and in the United States many companies have voluntarily stopped testing on animals. So what's the next frontier for animal rights activists? According to Edward Avellone of Animal Rights Now!, it's genetic experimentation. "What purpose is there in creating a mouse with six legs or a sheep with one eye in the middle of its forehead?" asks Avellone. "Scientists are just playing around with a new technology. They're creating horribly deformed animals for no real reason."

Some people disagree with this point of view. Says Ann Wilber of Scientists for the Ethical Treatment of Animals, "We're responsible professionals, not monsters." Wilber explains that the one-eyed sheep was the unintended result of an attempt to understand how the eye developed and how it works. "We've also developed a sheep whose milk contains a protein that might cure emphysema. There are reasons for what we do."

But to Avellone, the point is not simply the motivation behind the experimentation. It's also the process of the experiment. "Only 10 percent of the animals they breed have the gene they want to study. The remaining 90 percent [of the animals] are simply killed." Wilber admits that this situation is "sad, but true." Still, she says, "We're working every day to improve our techniques and therefore our success rate." Even if the success rate never tops 10 percent, she asks, "Isn't that a small price to pay for a cure for cancer, or multiple sclerosis, or Parkinson's disease?"

Continued on next page ▶

 

## 21st Century Themes Science and Civic Literacy

**1.** Edward Avellone makes several arguments against animal testing in genetics experiments. Why does he think the *process* of animal genetic experimentation is flawed?

**2.** Avellone argues that genetic experiments are unnecessary. What claim does he make about scientists' motivations for doing such experiments?

**3.** What is Ann Wilber's main argument in favor of genetic testing on animals?

**4.** Which of her arguments could be summed up as, "It's a necessary evil"?

**5.** Do you agree with Avellone, with Wilber, or with neither of them? Why?

## 21st Century Skills Evaluating an Issue

The skills used in this activity include **creativity and intellectual curiosity, communication skills, interpersonal and collaborative skills, information and media literacy,** and **social responsibility.**

The issue of experimenting on animals, especially genetic experimentation, is complex; you can't construct an informed opinion after reading just one article. Working with a group, use library and Internet resources to collect opinions on both sides of the issue. Work through the material thoroughly and then make up your mind about how you feel about the issue.

*If everyone in the group agrees, create a multimedia presentation for your class in which you present your point of view. If the members of your group disagree, stage a debate in front of the class, with the same number of students arguing each side of the issue.*

 

# 14 Human Heredity

**Big idea** **Information and Heredity**

**Q:** How can we use genetics to study human inheritance?

| | WHAT I KNOW | WHAT I LEARNED |
|---|---|---|
| **14.1** How does studying the human genome help us to draw conclusions about the inheritance of traits? | | |
| **14.2** What causes some human genetic disorders? | | |
| **14.3** How do we study the human genome and what have we learned so far? | | |

# 14.1 Human Chromosomes

## Lesson Objectives

- Identify the types of human chromosomes in a karotype.
- Describe the patterns of the inheritance of human traits.
- Explain how pedigrees are used to study human traits.

## Lesson Summary

**Karyotypes** A **genome** is the full set of all the genetic information that an organism carries in its DNA. Chromosomes are bundles of DNA and protein found in the nucleus of a eukaryotic cell. A **karyotype** is a picture that shows the complete diploid set of human chromosomes, grouped in pairs and arranged in order of decreasing size. A typical human diploid cell contains 46 chromosomes, or 23 pairs:

- Two of the 46 are the **sex chromosomes** that determine an individual's sex: XX = female and XY = male. The X chromosome carries nearly 10 times the number of genes as the Y chromosome.
- The other 44 are **autosomes**, or autosomal chromosomes.

**Transmission of Human Traits** Human genes follow the same Mendelian patterns of inheritance as the genes of other organisms:

- Many human traits follow a pattern of simple dominance.
- The alleles for many human genes display codominant inheritance.
- Many human genes, including the genes for blood group, have multiple alleles.
- A gene located on a sex chromosome is a **sex-linked gene**. The genes on sex chromosomes show a sex-linked pattern of inheritance, since females have two copies of many genes (located on X chromosomes) while males have just one.
- In females, most of the genes in one of the X chromosomes are inactivated in each cell.

**Human Pedigrees** A chart used to analyze the pattern of inheritance that shows the relationships in a family is a **pedigree**. Pedigrees can be used to determine the nature of genes and alleles associated with inherited human traits.

## Karyotypes

1. THINK VISUALLY Make a sketch of a human karyotype. Number the chromosome pairs. Label autosomes and sex chromosomes.

 

*For Questions 2–8, write the letter of the correct answer on the line at the left.*

______ **2.** The complete set of genetic information an organism carries in its DNA is its

**A.** karyotype.

**B.** genome.

**C.** chromosomes.

**D.** autosomes.

______ **3.** From what is a karyotype made?

**A.** A photograph of cells in mitosis

**B.** A series of X-ray diffraction images

**C.** A preparation of gametes on a microscope slide

**D.** A Punnett square

______ **4.** How many chromosomes are in a normal human karyotype?

**A.** 23

**B.** 46

**C.** 44

**D.** 2 (either XX or XY)

______ **5.** Which of the following genetic abbreviations denotes a male human?

**A.** 23, XX

**B.** 23, XY

**C.** 46, XX

**D.** 46, XY

______ **6.** Why is the ratio of male to female births roughly 50:50?

**A.** All egg cells carry an X chromosome.

**B.** Half of all egg cells carry a Y chromosome.

**C.** All sperm cells carry an X chromosome.

**D.** Half of all sperm cells carry a Y chromosome.

______ **7.** How are the X and Y chromosomes different?

**A.** Only one is an autosome.

**B.** The X is smaller than the Y.

**C.** The Y carries fewer genes than the X.

**D.** Only females have a Y.

______ **8.** All human cells carry

**A.** at least one X chromosome.

**B.** at least one Y chromosome.

**C.** a pair of X chromosomes.

**D.** one X and one Y chromosome.

 

# Transmission of Human Traits

**9.** Complete the graphic organizer to list, describe, and give examples of three types of inheritance patterns in humans:

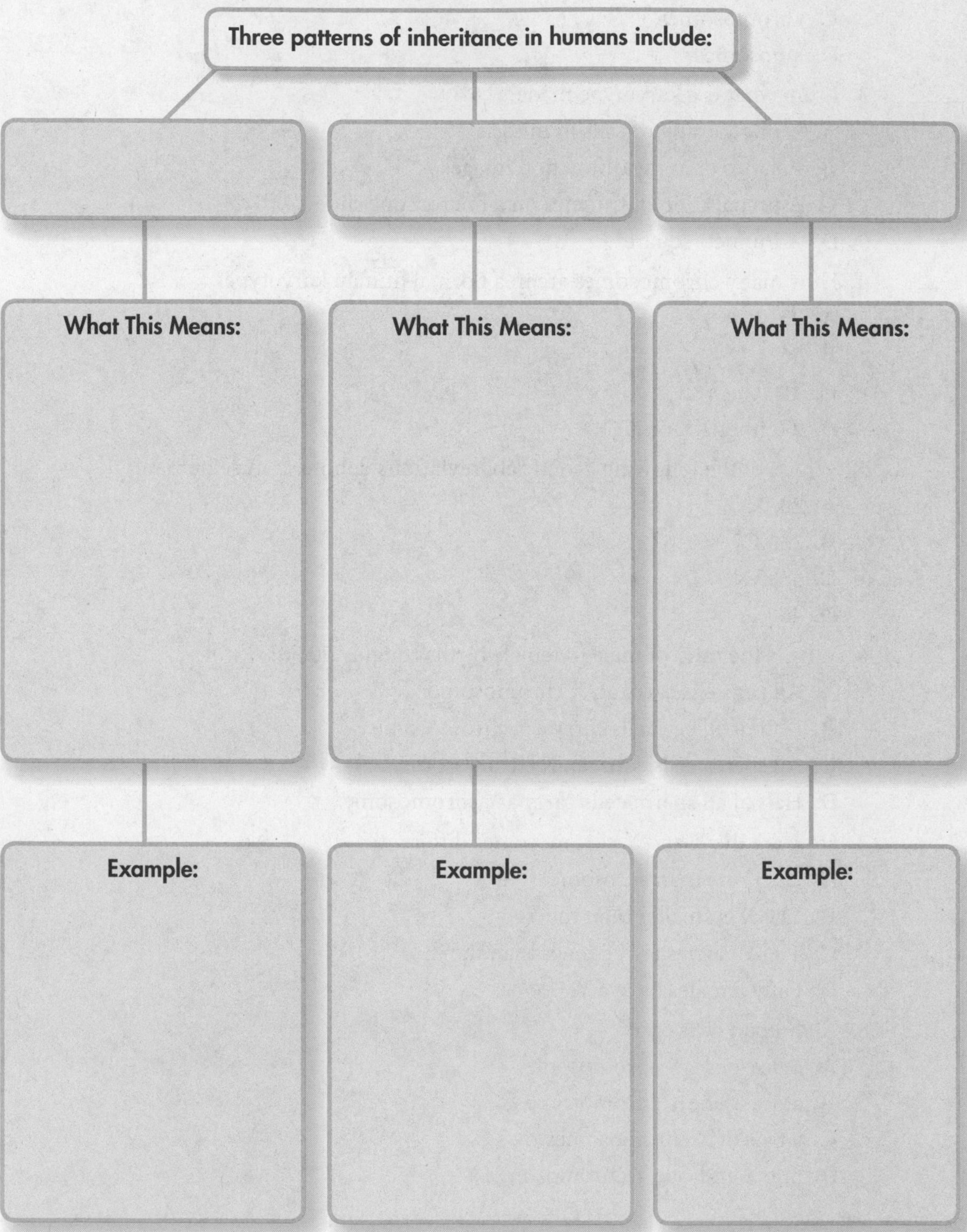

**10.** Colorblindness is a sex-linked trait. Let *C* represent an allele for normal color vision. Let *c* represent an allele for colorblindness. The genotype for a male with normal color vision is $X^CY$. The genotype for a female heterozygous for normal color vision is $X^CX^c$.

Complete the Punnett square to show the genotypes and phenotypes of their possible offspring.

| | **Male Gamete:** | **Male Gamete:** |
|---|---|---|
| Female Gamete: | Genotype:<br>Phenotype: | Genotype:<br>Phenotype: |
| Female Gamete: | Genotype:<br>Phenotype: | Genotype:<br>Phenotype: |

**11.** Use your Punnett square to explain why a female with one *c* allele has normal color vision but a male with one *c* allele is colorblind.

______________________________________________

______________________________________________

**12.** How does the cell "adjust" to the extra X chromosome in female cells?

______________________________________________

______________________________________________

**13.** What is a Barr body?

______________________________________________

______________________________________________

**14.** Why don't males have Barr bodies?

______________________________________________

______________________________________________

**15.** Is a cat with three colors of spots more likely to be male or female?

______________________________________________

______________________________________________

______________________________________________

 

# Human Pedigrees

*For Questions 16–21, match the labels to the parts of the pedigree chart shown below. Some of the labels may be used more than once.*

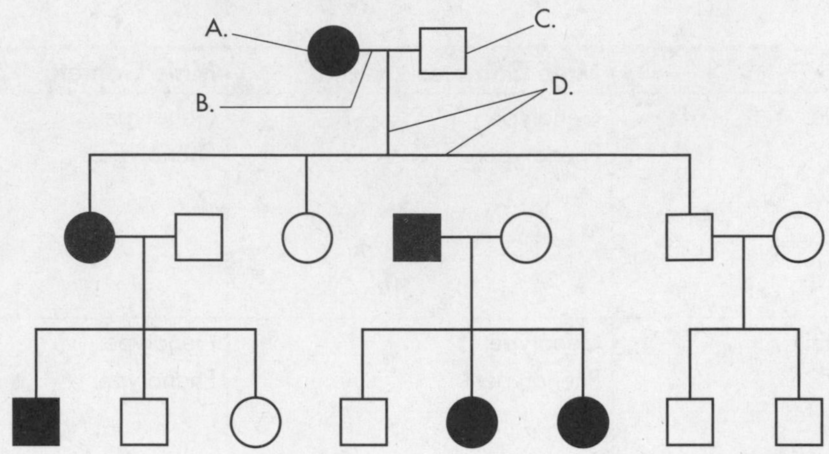


______ **16.** A person who expresses the trait

______ **17.** A male

______ **18.** A person who does not express the trait

______ **19.** A marriage

______ **20.** A female

______ **21.** A connection between parents and offspring

## Apply the Big idea

**22.** Dimples in the cheeks are inherited as a dominant trait on an autosome. Using the proper form and symbols, draw a pedigree chart, beginning with a heterozygous, dimpled father (*Dd*), and a nondimpled mother (*dd*). Show four children of the expected types: boys, girls, dimples, and no dimples. Label your pedigree with phenotypes and genotypes.

 

# 14.2 Human Genetic Disorders

## Lesson Objectives

- Explain how small changes in DNA cause genetic disorders.
- Summarize the problems caused by nondisjunction.

## Lesson Summary

**From Molecule to Phenotype** There is a molecular reason for genetic disorders. A change in DNA can alter an amino acid sequence, which can change a protein and therefore, the phenotype. Some common inherited disorders result from a change in DNA. They include:

- sickle cell disease, in which a defective polypeptide makes hemoglobin in the blood less soluble;
- cystic fibrosis, in which a deletion of three bases in a gene causes cell membranes to lose their ability to transport chloride ions;
- Huntington's disease, in which a single codon for a certain amino acid repeats more than 40 times, causing mental deterioration and uncontrolled movements.

Some alleles that cause disease in the homozygote can provide an advantage in the heterozygote. The geographic associations between sickle cell disease and malaria and between cystic fibrosis and typhoid demonstrate how the heterozygous state reduces the risk of infection.

**Chromosomal Disorders** Sometimes, during meiosis, homologous chromosomes fail to separate. This **nondisjunction** (not coming apart) can create a gamete with an abnormal number of chromosomes, leading to offspring with missing or extra chromosomes. Examples include:

- Down syndrome, most often a result of three copies of chromosome 21;
- Turner's syndrome, a female with a single X chromosome;
- Klinefelter's syndrome, a male with an extra X chromosome.

## From Molecule to Phenotype

**1.** The boxes below each show a step to explain how genetic disorders have a molecular basis. Number them so that the steps are in the correct order.

| A change in phenotype results. ______ | A gene's DNA sequence changes. ______ | The amino acid sequence that alters a protein changes. ______ |
|---|---|---|

 

*For Questions 2–7, write the letter of the correct answer on the line at the left.*

_____ **2.** How many human genetic disorders are known?

**A.** three
**B.** about 20
**C.** about 100
**D.** thousands

_____ **3.** The inherited disease in which hemoglobin molecules clump into long fibers, changing the shape of blood cells is

**A.** cystic fibrosis.
**B.** sickle cell disease.
**C.** Huntington's disease.
**D.** Klinefelter's syndrome.

_____ **4.** What happens to the CFTR gene in individuals who have cystic fibrosis?

**A.** The entire gene is deleted.
**B.** The entire gene is duplicated.
**C.** Three bases are deleted, causing one amino acid to be missing.
**D.** Three bases are duplicated, causing one amino acid show up about 40 times.

_____ **5.** Why are individuals who are heterozygous for the cystic fibrosis allele unaffected by the disease?

**A.** They have an extra copy of the allele on their X chromosome.
**B.** Cystic fibrosis only occurs in males, so females are unaffected.
**C.** They make enough of a particular protein to allow their cells to work properly.
**D.** Their cells can transport chloride ions through diffusion channels.

_____ **6.** How might the allele that causes a disease stay in the population if it is fatal to those who have the disease?

**A.** It is present only in heterozygotes.
**B.** It makes the heterozygote resistant to a fatal disease.
**C.** It disappears but is continuously replaced by mutations.
**D.** It occurs only in certain geographic areas.

_____ **7.** What advantage do individuals with one sickle cell allele have?

**A.** a stronger resistance to malaria
**B.** immunity to typhoid fever
**C.** more rigid red blood cells
**D.** no advantage

# Chromosomal Disorders

**8.** Complete this graphic organizer to explain the process and outcomes of nondisjunction.

| Definition: | Sketch of Process: |
|---|---|
| NONDISJUNCTION | |
| Example of Outcome (in genotype): | Example of Outcome (in phenotype): |

**9.** What is trisomy?

______

______

**10.** What happens when a male has XXY sex chromosomes?

______

______

## Apply the Big idea

**11.** Most of the genetic disorders you have learned about are the result of a change in DNA sequence, as with cystic fibrosis, or the presence of an extra chromosome, as with Down syndrome. The exception is Turner's syndrome. Women with Turner's syndrome have only 45 chromosomes. They are missing an X chromosome. This disorder is the *only* case in which a person can survive with one less chromosome. What does this tell you about how genetic information is inherited in humans?

______

______

______

 

# 14.3 Studying the Human Genome

## Lesson Objectives

- Summarize the methods of DNA analysis.
- State the goals of the Human Genome Project and explain what we have learned so far.

## Lesson Summary

**Manipulating DNA** Since the 1970s, techniques have been developed that allow scientists to cut, separate, and replicate DNA base-by-base. Using these tools, scientists can read the base sequences in DNA from any cell.

- **Restriction enzymes** cut DNA into smaller pieces, called restriction fragments, which are several hundred bases in length. Each restriction enzyme cuts DNA at a different sequence of bases.
- **Gel electrophoresis** separates different-sized DNA fragments by placing them at one end of a porous gel, then applying an electrical voltage. The electrical charge moves the DNA.
- Using dye-labeled nucleotides, scientists can stop replication at any point along a single DNA strand. The fragments can then be separated by size using gel electrophoresis and "read," base-by-base.

**The Human Genome Project** was a 13-year international effort to sequence all 3 billion base pairs in human DNA and identify all human genes. The project was completed in 2003.

- The researchers identified markers in widely separated strands of DNA.
- They used "shotgun sequencing," which uses a computer to match DNA base sequences.
- To identify genes, they found promoters, exons, and other sites on the DNA molecule.
- To locate and identify as many haplotypes (collections of linked single-base differences) in the human population as possible, the International HapMap Project began in 2002.
- The Human Genome Project identified genes associated with many diseases and disorders. From the project came the new science of **bioinformatics**, the creation and use of databases and other computing tools to manage data. Bioinformatics launched **genomics**, the study of whole genomes.
- The human genome project pinpointed genes and associated particular sequences in those genes with numerous diseases and disorders. It also found that the DNA of all humans matches base-for-base at most sites, but can vary at 3 million sites.
- The 1000 Genomes Project, launched in 2008, will catalogue the variation among 1000 people.

# Manipulating DNA

*For Questions 1–4, write True if the statement is true. If the statement is false, change the underlined word to make the statement true.*

_________ **1.** Bacteria produce restriction enzymes that cut the <u>DNA</u> molecule into smaller pieces.

_________ **2.** Restriction fragments are always cut at a particular sequence of <u>proteins</u>.

_________ **3.** The technique that separates differently sized DNA fragments is <u>gel electrophoresis</u>.

_________ **4.** The enzyme that copies DNA is DNA <u>restrictase</u>.

**5.** Complete the graphic organizer to summarize the steps used to determine the sequences of bases in DNA.

| Purpose | Tool or Technique Used | Outcome |
|---|---|---|
| Cutting DNA | | |
| Separating DNA | | |
| Reading DNA | | |

*For Questions 6–10, complete each statement by writing in the correct word or words.*

**6.** By using tools that cut, separate, and then replicate DNA, scientists can now read the _______________ sequence in DNA from any cell.

**7.** Restriction enzymes cut pieces of DNA sometimes called restriction _______________.

**8.** Each restriction enzyme cuts DNA at a different sequence of _______________.

**9.** The smaller the DNA, the _______________ and farther it moves during gel electrophoresis.

**10.** After chemically dyed bases have been incorporated into a DNA strand, the order of colored _______________ on the gel reveals the exact sequence of bases in DNA.

 

# The Human Genome Project

*For Questions 11–16, write the letter of the correct answer on the line at the left.*

_____ **11.** What technology made the Human Genome Project possible?

**A.** DNA sequencing
**B.** RNA replication
**C.** protein synthesis
**D.** enzyme activation

_____ **12.** What were the "markers" that the researchers of the Human Genome Project used?

**A.** restriction enzymes
**B.** gel electrophoresis
**C.** base sequences
**D.** restriction fragments

_____ **13.** What does "shotgun sequencing" do?

**A.** separate fragments using gel electrophoresis
**B.** find overlapping areas of DNA fragments
**C.** cut DNA into millions of "puzzle pieces"
**D.** bind colored dyes to base sequences

_____ **14.** What are SNPs?

**A.** points where a restriction enzyme cuts a DNA molecule
**B.** missing sequence of base pairs in a restriction fragment
**C.** proteins formed by a mutated gene
**D.** differences in a base between two individuals

_____ **15.** Bioinformatics would not have been possible without

**A.** microscopes.
**B.** genes.
**C.** computers.
**D.** genomics.

_____ **16.** In humans, single-base differences

**A.** occur at about 3 million sites.
**B.** occur rarely in the sex chromosomes.
**C.** seldom occur in normal DNA.
**D.** cannot be identified from DNA analysis.

**17.** What were the goals of the Human Genome Project?

________________________________________

________________________________________

________________________________________

________________________________________

 

**18.** THINK VISUALLY The field of bioinformatics combines both life sciences and modern technology. Fill in the Venn diagram to show how.

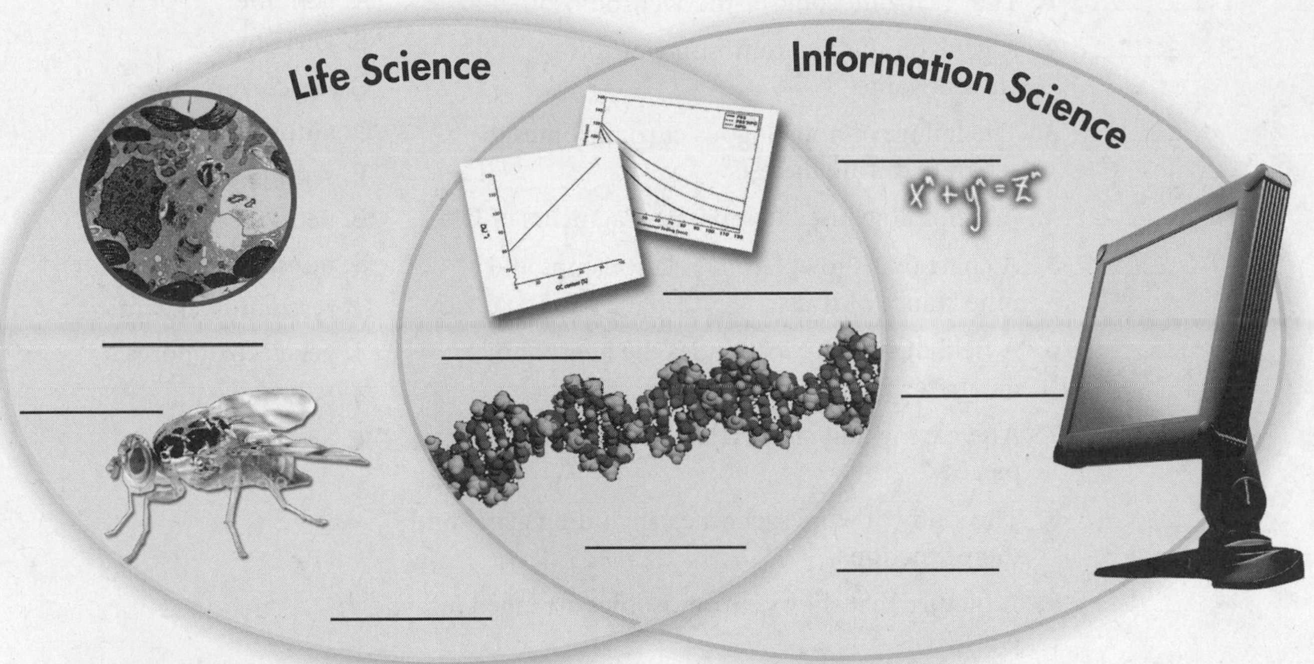


## Apply the Big idea

**19.** The Icelandic people have always placed high importance on knowing about their ancestors. In fact, 80% of all the Icelandic people who have ever lived can be added to a family tree. Medical records are just as detailed. The population is quite isolated, so the gene pool is considered to be homogeneous. Why would these conditions make the genome of the Icelandic population ideal for studying rare inherited disorders associated with gene sequencing errors?

_______________________________________________

_______________________________________________

_______________________________________________

_______________________________________________

_______________________________________________

Name ____________ Class ______ Date ______

# Chapter Vocabulary Review

*For Questions 1–11, match the term with its definition.*

**Definition**

_____ 1. The X chromosome or the Y chromosome

_____ 2. A gene on the X chromosome or the Y chromosome

_____ 3. The failure of homologous chromosomes to separate during meiosis

_____ 4. A technology used to separate fragments of DNA

_____ 5. A chart that shows family relationships and inheritance of traits

_____ 6. A field of study that includes the operation of databases

_____ 7. An enzyme that cuts a DNA molecule into small pieces

_____ 8. The study of whole genomes, including genes and their functions

_____ 9. A picture that shows chromosomes arranged in pairs

_____ 10. Any chromosome that is not a sex chromosome

_____ 11. The full set of genetic information in an organism's DNA

**Term**

A. genome
B. karyotype
C. sex chromosome
D. autosome
E. sex-linked gene
F. pedigree
G. nondisjunction
H. restriction enzyme
I. gel electrophoresis
J. bioinformatics
K. genomics

*For Questions 12–19, complete each statement by writing in the correct word or words.*

12. A circle represents a female in a(n) ____________.

13. The protein that cuts DNA into pieces is a restriction ____________.

14. An inherited disorder that appears more often in males than females is probably caused by a ____________.

15. The 23 pairs of human chromosomes are arranged from largest to smallest in a ____________.

16. Humans have 22 pairs of ____________.

17. The cause of Down syndrome is ____________ during meiosis.

18. Humans have 3 billion base pairs in their ____________.

19. The new field of ____________ resulted from the Human Genome Project.

 

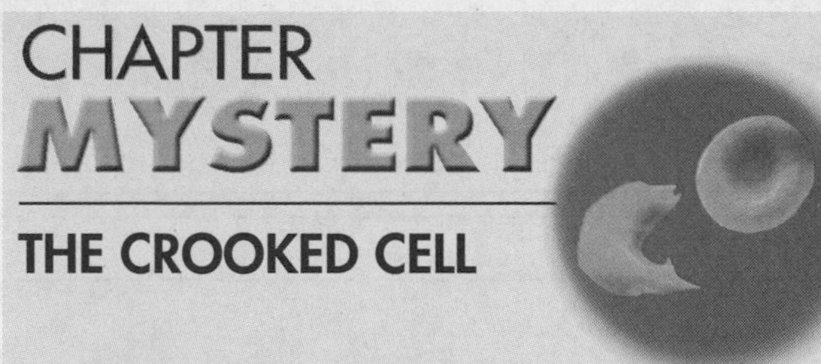


In the Chapter Mystery, you learned how genetic testing can help identify risk for an inheritable disease, such as sickle-cell anemia. Geneticists have made great strides in recent years to develop many more DNA-based genetic tests.

21st Century Learning

# Genetic Testing: A Personal Choice

Today, more than 1000 genetic tests are available to determine whether patients carry genes associated with diseases from breast cancer to the degenerative neurological disorder known as Huntington's disease. But the genetic tests pose a difficult dilemma for many people at risk for genetic disease.

The choice is especially difficult for those conditions, such as Huntington's disease, for which there are no treatments or cures. Recent polls have found that a significant majority of people say they would want to undergo genetic testing for a treatable disease. But respondents remain almost evenly split on whether they would undertake testing for an untreatable condition. Many people are concerned that testing positive for an untreatable genetic disease could lead to employment discrimination, denial of medical insurance, or other types of discrimination. The National Institutes of Health has issued the following information to help people make their decisions.

## How Do I Decide Whether to Be Tested?

People have many different reasons for being tested or not being tested. For many, it is important to know whether a disease can be prevented if a gene alteration causing a disease is found. For example, those who have inherited forms of breast or colon cancer have options such as screening or early treatment. Pharmacogenetic testing can find the best medicine or dose of a medicine for a certain person. (Pharmacogenetic testing involves the analysis of a person's genetic makeup in order to prescribe the most effective medications for that person.)

But in some cases, there is no treatment or cure available. There are no preventive steps or cures for Huntington's disease, for example. Some people simply do not want to know that they will develop a serious illness for which there is no treatment or cure. Others, however, feel that knowing the test results might help them make decisions such as career choices, family planning, or insurance coverage.

To help make such decisions, people can seek advice from a genetic counselor. Genetic counselors help individuals and families think about the scientific, emotional, and ethical factors that affect their decision whether or not to test. But the difficult decision is still up to the individual or family.

Continued on next page ▶

 

## 21st Century Themes Science and Health Literacy

**1.** What is a genetic test?

**2.** How many genetic tests are currently available?

**3.** According to the National Institutes of Health, why would someone want to undergo a genetic test?

**4.** What major factor, according to polls, affects the way people feel about a particular genetic test?

**5.** Do you think anti-discrimination laws should be put in place to protect people who test positive for an untreatable condition like Huntington's disease? Why or why not?

## 21st Century Skills An Individual's Case

The skills used in this activity include **information and media literacy; communication skills;** and **problem identification, formulation, and solution.**

Use Internet or library resources to research the case of neuropsychologist Nancy Wexler. Twenty years ago, Wexler identified the gene that causes Huntington's disease. She was spurred on in her research because Huntington's disease runs in her family. Wexler spent much of her career working to develop a genetic test for Huntington's disease. But when the test finally became available, she decided that she would rather not know whether she carried the gene because no treatment exists for the disease.

*Organize into groups to present your findings in a panel discussion about genetic testing.*

Here are some questions you might consider:

- What are the arguments that someone should consider about the decision to undergo genetic testing?
- Should a genetic test even be offered for an untreatable condition like Huntington's? If so, why?

 

Name ______________________ Class ______ Date ______

# 15 Genetic Engineering

**Big idea** **Science as a Way of Knowing**

**Q:** How and why do scientists manipulate DNA in living cells?

| | WHAT I KNOW | WHAT I LEARNED |
|---|---|---|
| **15.1** How do humans take advantage of naturally occurring variation among organisms? | | |
| **15.2** How do scientists study and work with specific genes? | | |
| **15.3** How do humans use genetic engineering? | | |
| **15.4** What are some of the ethical issues raised by genetic engineering? | | |

 

Name ______________________ Class ______ Date ________

# 15.1 Selective Breeding

## Lesson Objectives

Explain the purpose of selective breeding.

Explain how people increase genetic variation.

## Lesson Summary

**Selective Breeding** Through **selective breeding**, humans choose organisms with wanted characteristics to produce the next generation.

- This takes advantage of natural variation among organisms and passes wanted traits to offspring.
- The numerous breeds of dogs and varieties of crop plants and domestic animals are examples of selective breeding.

**Hybridization** crosses dissimilar individuals to bring together the best of both parents in the offspring. **Inbreeding** is the continued breeding of individuals with selected characteristics. It ensures that wanted traits are preserved, but can also result in defects being passed on.

**Increasing Variation** Mutations are the source of biological diversity. Breeders introduce mutations into populations to increase genetic variation. **Biotechnology** is the application of a technological process, invention, or method to living organisms. Selective breeding is one example of biotechnology.

- Radiation and chemicals can increase the mutation rate. Diverse bacterial strains have been bred from mutated lines.
- Drugs can prevent the separation of chromosomes during mitosis, leading to polyploidy in plants. Such plants may be larger or stronger than their diploid relatives.

# Selective Breeding

*For Questions 1–5, write True if the statement is true. If the statement is false, change the underlined word or words to make the statement true.*

______________ **1.** <u>Selective breeding</u> works because of the natural genetic variation in a population.

______________ **2.** Hybridization crosses <u>similar</u> individuals to bring together the best of both.

______________ **3.** The individuals produced by crossing dissimilar parents are <u>purebreeds</u>.

______________ **4.** The continued crossing of individuals with similar characteristics is <u>hybridization</u>.

______________ **5.** Inbreeding <u>increases</u> the risk of genetic defects.

6. Complete the table describing the types of selective breeding.

| Selective Breeding | | |
|---|---|---|
| **Type** | **Description** | **Examples** |
| | Crossing dissimilar individuals to bring together the best of both organisms | |
| | The continued breeding of individuals with similar characteristics | |

## Increasing Variation

7. Complete this concept map about biotechnology.

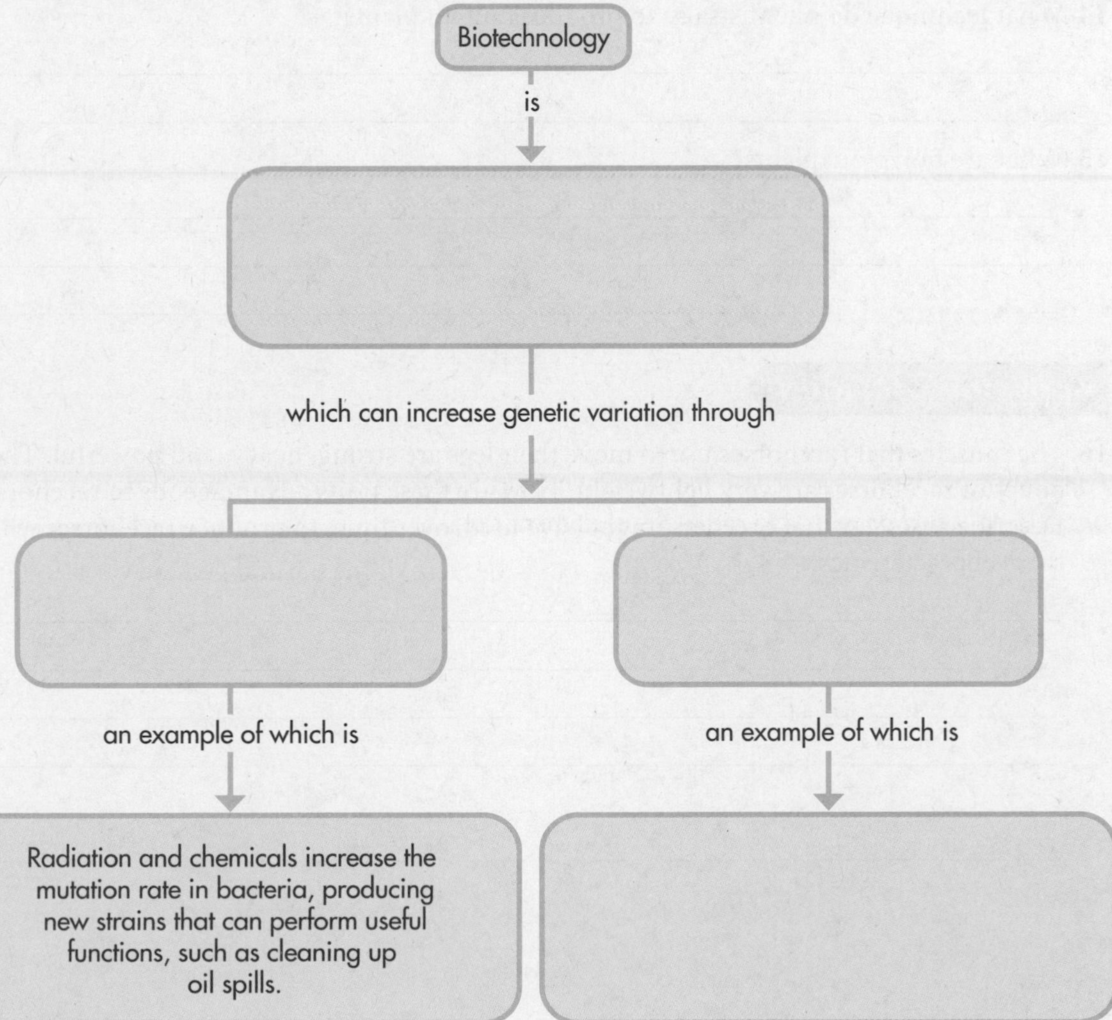

*For Questions 8–11, match the example with the probable method used to introduce the mutation. Each answer can be used more than once.*

______ **8.** Bacteria that clean up radioactive substances

______ **9.** Larger, stronger banana trees

______ **10.** Bacteria that clean up metal pollution

______ **11.** Watermelons that grow faster and larger

**A.** radiation or chemicals

**B.** polyploidy

**12.** Is it easy for breeders to produce mutants with desirable mutations? Explain.

**13.** Why are radiation and chemicals useful techniques for producing mutant bacteria?

**14.** What technique do scientists use to produce mutant plants?

**15.** What are polyploid plants?

## Apply the Big idea

**16.** The muscles that racehorses use to move their legs are strong, heavy, and powerful. The bones of racehorses are very lightweight. How are these traits advantageous in racehorses? Describe a process that breeders might have used, over time, to produce racehorses with these characteristics.

 

Name ______________________ Class ______ Date ________

# 15.2 Recombinant DNA

## Lesson Objectives

- Explain how scientists manipulate DNA.
- Describe the importance of recombinant DNA.
- Define transgenic and describe the usefulness of some transgenic organisms to humans.

## Lesson Summary

**Copying DNA** Genetic engineers can transfer a gene from one organism to another to achieve a goal, but first, individual genes must be identified and separated from DNA. The original method (used by Douglas Prasher) involved several steps:

- Determine the amino acid sequence in a protein.
- Predict the mRNA code for that sequence.
- Use a complementary base sequence to attract the predicted mRNA.
- Find the DNA fragment that binds to the mRNA.

Once scientists find a gene, they can use a technique called the **polymerase chain reaction** to make many copies.

- Heat separates the DNA into two strands.
- As the DNA cools, primers are added to opposite ends of the strands.
- DNA polymerase adds nucleotides between the primers, producing two complementary strands. The process can be repeated as many times as needed.

**Changing DNA** **Recombinant DNA** molecules contain DNA from two different sources. Recombinant-DNA technology can change the genetic composition of living organisms.

- **Plasmids** are circular DNA molecules found in bacteria and yeasts; they are widely used by scientists studying recombinant DNA, because DNA joined to a plasmid can be replicated.
- A **genetic marker** is a gene that is used to differentiate a cell that carries a recombinant plasmid from those that do not.

**Transgenic Organisms** **Transgenic** organisms contain genes from other species. They result from the insertion of recombinant DNA into the genome of the host organism. A **clone** is a member of a population of genetically identical cells.

# Copying DNA

*For Questions 1–5, complete each statement by writing in the correct word or words.*

1. Genetic engineers can transfer ______________ from one organism to another.
2. As a first step toward finding a gene, Douglas Prasher studied the ______________ sequence of part of a protein.
3. Prasher next found the ______________ base sequence that coded for the protein.

Name ______________________ Class ______ Date ________

4. Using the technique of ________________, Prasher matched the mRNA to a DNA fragment that contained the gene for GFP.

5. Southern blot analysis uses ________________ probes to bind to fragments with complementary base sequences.

6. **THINK VISUALLY** Make a sketch to show the steps in the polymerase chain reaction (PCR) method of copying genes. Label each part of your sketch.

## Changing DNA

*For Questions 7–10, write the letter of the correct answer on the line at the left.*

______ 7. Why is DNA ligase so important in recombinant DNA technology?

A. It causes DNA to make multiple copies of itself.

B. It joins two DNA fragments together.

C. It shapes bacterial DNA into a circular plasmid.

D. It cuts DNA into restriction fragments.

______ 8. A recombinant plasmid can be used to

A. prevent nondisjunction at meiosis.

B. double the number of chromosomes in a plant cell.

C. cut DNA into restriction fragments.

D. transform a bacterium.

 

______ **9.** What do genetic engineers use to create the "sticky ends" needed to splice two fragments of DNA together?

**A.** an amino acid sequence

**B.** DNA ligase

**C.** restriction enzymes

**D.** mRNA

______ **10.** Why must a genetically engineered plasmid contain a genetic marker?

**A.** to prevent the construction of an artificial chromosome

**B.** to separate cells that contain recombinant DNA from those that do not

**C.** to produce multiple copies of the recombined plasmid after heat treatment

**D.** to break apart the circular plasmid and introduce another DNA fragment

**11.** Give a reason why a plasmid is useful for DNA transfer.

______

______

______

______

## Transgenic Organisms

**12.** Complete the flowchart about how a transgenic plant is produced, using *Agrobacterium* as an example.

*Agrobacterium* can cause tumors in plants. The part of the DNA that causes tumors is deactivated and replaced with ______ DNA.

↓

The ______ bacteria are placed in a dish with plant cells. The bacteria infect the plant cells.

↓

Inside a plant cell, *Agrobacterium* inserts part of its DNA into the host cell ______.

↓

A ______ is generated from the transformed cell.

**13.** What is a transgenic organism?

______________________________________________

______________________________________________

**14.** What can happen when DNA is injected into the nucleus of an animal's egg cell?

______________________________________________

______________________________________________

**15.** How is a DNA molecule constructed so that it will eliminate a particular gene?

______________________________________________

______________________________________________

______________________________________________

**16.** What is a clone?

______________________________________________

______________________________________________

**17.** What kinds of mammals have been cloned in recent years?

______________________________________________

______________________________________________

*For Questions 18–22, write True if the statement is true. If the statement is false, change the underlined word to make the statement true.*

______________ **18.** An organism that contains one or more genes from another species is <u>inbred</u>.

______________ **19.** Transgenic organisms can be made by inserting recombinant DNA into the <u>genome</u> of the host organism.

______________ **20.** Examining the properties of a transgenic organism allows scientists to discover the function of the transferred <u>chromosome</u>.

______________ **21.** Plant cells will sometimes take up DNA on their own if their <u>cell walls</u> are absent.

______________ **22.** Carefully designed DNA molecules can achieve gene <u>replacement</u>.

*On the lines below, write* T *next to an example of a transgenic organism, and* C *next to an example of a clone.*

______________ **23.** A goat that produces spider's silk in its milk

______________ **24.** A plant that is grown from a cell into which *Agrobacterium* has incorporated recombinant DNA

______________ **25.** A lamb that is born with the same DNA as a donor cell

______________ **26.** A colony of bacteria that grows from one bacterium

______________ **27.** A bacterium that can produce human insulin

 

Name ______________________________ Class ______ Date ________

28. **THINK VISUALLY** Complete the sentences in the diagram below to show the steps in cloning a sheep.

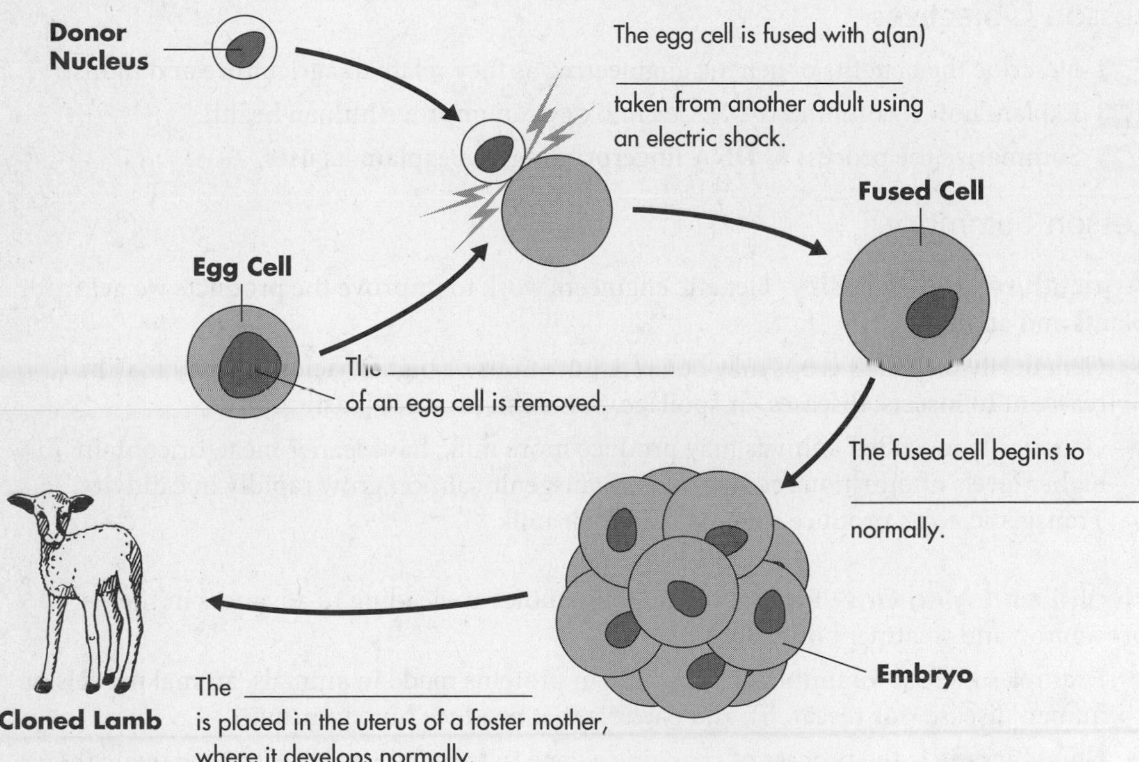

Donor Nucleus
The egg cell is fused with a(an) ________ taken from another adult using an electric shock.
Fused Cell
Egg Cell
The ________ of an egg cell is removed.
The fused cell begins to ________ normally.
Embryo
Cloned Lamb
The ________ is placed in the uterus of a foster mother, where it develops normally.

## Apply the Big idea

29. The most successful heart transplants occur when proteins in the donor heart closely match those of the recipient's original heart. If the proteins don't match, the recipient's immune system may reject the transplanted organ. Scientists would like to develop a strain of transgenic pigs that could provide donor hearts for humans. How might such an animal be developed? How might cloning help provide hearts for human recipients?

_______________________________________________

_______________________________________________

_______________________________________________

_______________________________________________

_______________________________________________

_______________________________________________

_______________________________________________

_______________________________________________

 

Name ______________________ Class ______ Date ______

# 15.3 Applications of Genetic Engineering

## Lesson Objectives

- Describe the benefits of genetic engineering as they relate to agriculture and industry.
- Explain how recombinant DNA technology can improve human health.
- Summarize the process of DNA fingerprinting and explain its uses.

## Lesson Summary

**Agriculture and Industry** Genetic engineers work to improve the products we get from plants and animals.

- Genetically modified crops may be more nutritious or higher yielding. They may be resistant to insects, diseases, or spoilage. Some can produce plastics.
- Genetically modified animals may produce more milk, have leaner meat, or contain higher levels of nutritious compounds. Transgenic salmon grow rapidly in captivity. Transgenic goats produce spider silk in their milk.

**Health and Medicine** Recombinant DNA studies are leading to advances in the prevention and treatment of disease.

- Examples include vitamin-rich rice, human proteins made in animals, animal models of human disease (for research), and bacteria that produce human insulin.
- **Gene therapy** is the process of changing a gene to treat a disorder. However, gene therapy is still an experimental and high-risk technique.
- Genetic testing can identify hundreds of inherited disorders.

Not all genes are active in every cell. **DNA microarray** technology lets scientists study thousands of genes at once to determine their activity level.

**Personal Identification** **DNA fingerprinting** analyzes sections of DNA that may have little or no function but that vary from one individual to another.

- DNA fingerprinting is used in **forensics**—the scientific study of crime-scene evidence—to identify criminals. It is also used to identify the biological father when paternity is in question.
- Common ancestry can sometimes be determined using mitochondrial DNA (mtDNA) and Y-chromosome analysis.

## Agriculture and Industry

**1.** Give two examples of how genetically modified organisms lead to more environmentally friendly agricultural practices.

a. ______________________________

b. ______________________________

**2.** Name two other benefits that may be gained from genetically engineering food crops.

a. ______________________

b. ______________________

**3.** Give two examples of how DNA modification has increased the importance of transgenic animals to our food supply.

a. ______________________

b. ______________________

## Health and Medicine

*For Questions 4–6, write True if the statement is true. If the statement is false, change the underlined word or words to make the statement true.*

__________ **4.** Human growth hormone is now widely available because it is mass produced by recombinant <u>viruses</u>.

__________ **5.** In <u>DNA fingerprinting</u>, an absent or faulty gene is replaced by a normal, working gene.

__________ **6.** Prospective parents can find out if they carry the alleles for a genetic disease through genetic <u>testing</u>.

**7.** Complete the flowchart to show the steps required to analyze gene activity using a microarray.

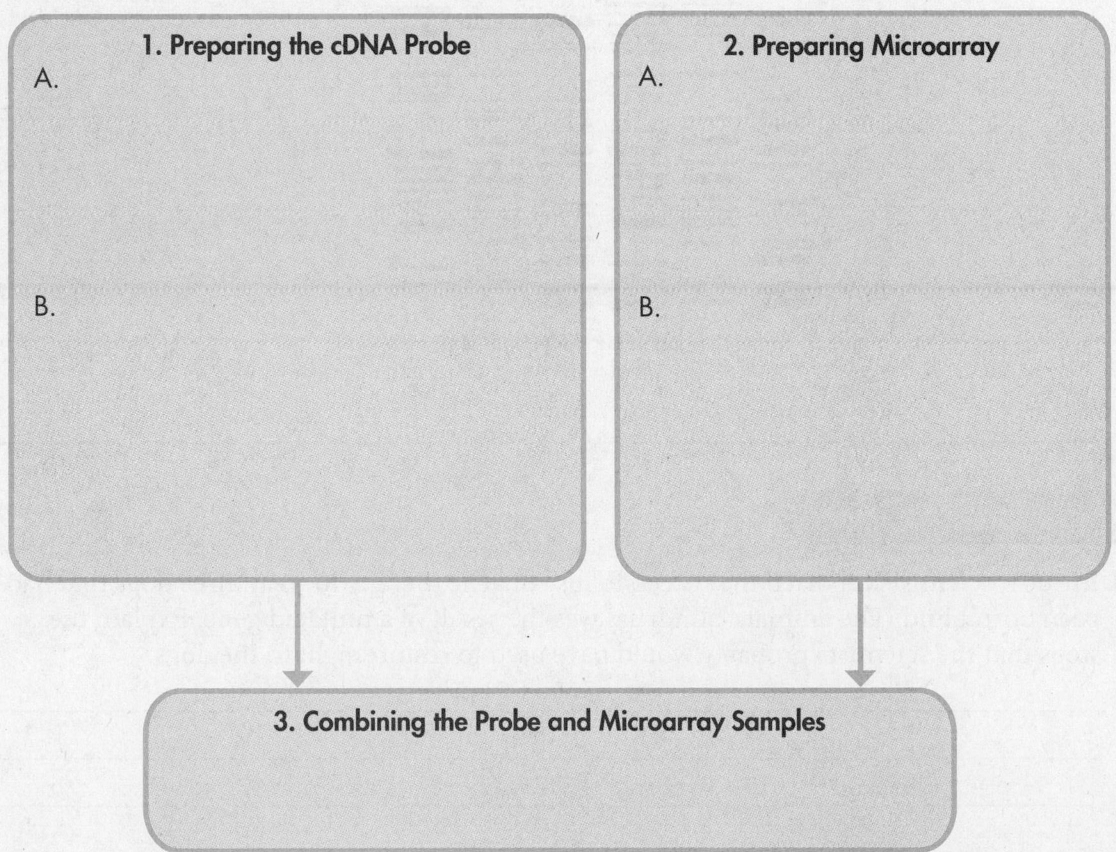

# Personal Identification

**8.** Complete the flowchart about how DNA fingerprints are made.

Restriction ______________ are used to cut the DNA into fragments containing genes and repeats.

↓

The restriction fragments are separated according to size using gel ______________.

↓

The DNA fragments containing repeats are then labeled using radioactive ______________. This labeling produces a series of bands—the DNA fingerprint.

**9.** Study the DNA fingerprint below. Which two samples may be from a set of identical twins? How do you know?

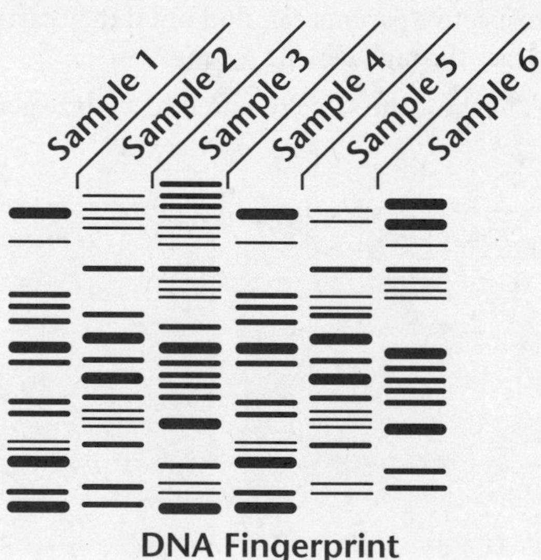


DNA Fingerprint

______________________________________________________________________

## Apply the Big idea

**10.** In 2001, scientists reported the successful use of gene therapy to treat three dogs that had been born blind. The animals' blindness was the result of a mutated gene. Explain the steps that the scientists probably would have used to restore sight to the dogs.

______________________________________________________________________

______________________________________________________________________

______________________________________________________________________

 

Name ______________________ Class ______ Date ______

# 15.4 Ethics and Impacts of Biotechnology

## Lesson Objectives

- Describe some of the issues that relate to biotechnology.
- Identify some of the pros and cons of genetically modified food.
- Describe some of the ethical issues relating to biotechnology.

## Lesson Summary

**Profits and Privacy** Most of the research in genetic engineering is done by private companies.

- They patent their findings and inventions to protect their investment and make a profit.
- The patents block other scientists from pursuing certain lines of research.
- In 2007, the Genetic Information Nondiscrimination Act was signed into law in the United States. It prohibits discrimination based on genetic information.

**Safety of Transgenics** There is controversy about the safety of GM foods.

- Proponents of genetically modified foods argue that GM crops are better, safer, and higher yielding than conventional crops. GM crops require less land and energy to grow, and insecticides need not be applied to insect-resistant strains. Careful studies have provided no support for concerns about the safety of GM crops.
- Opponents argue that the safety of GM crops has been neither adequately tested for long-term use, nor regulated. Patents on GM seeds may force small farmers out of business. The resistance of GM plants to insects may harm beneficial insect species. Resistance to herbicides may result in the overuse of toxic chemicals.
- Some states have introduced legislation to require that GM foods be labeled.

**Ethics of the New Biology** Few argue that gene therapy for curing disease is ethically wrong, but many ask the question of how far genetic modification should go.

- Is it right to try to engineer children to have certain characteristics?
- Should human cloning be allowed?

# Profits and Privacy

1. Should you be able to keep your genetic information confidential? State two answers: one giving a reason for a "yes" answer, and the other giving a reason for a "no" answer.

Yes ______________________________________________

______________________________________________

______________________________________________

No ______________________________________________

______________________________________________

______________________________________________

**2.** Explain what the Genetics Information Nondiscrimination Act is, and give an example of how it might protect people.

______________________________________________

______________________________________________

______________________________________________

## Safety of Transgenics

**3.** Complete the table to summarize the pros and cons of genetically modified foods. List at least four items in each column.

| Pros | Cons |
|---|---|
| | |

*For Questions 4–8, write True if the statement is true. If the statement is false, change the underlined word or words to make the statement true.*

______ **4.** Most GM plants are grown in the <u>United States</u>.

______ **5.** Growing GM crops requires <u>more</u> energy resources than growing traditional crops.

______ **6.** With all the questions raised about GM agriculture, the wider use of biotechnology <u>has been</u> blocked.

______ **7.** Federal laws in the U. S. <u>require</u> that GM foods be labeled as such.

______ **8.** GM foods are <u>required</u> to undergo safety testing before they enter the U. S. market.

 

**9.** Some proponents of GM agriculture argue that GM crops are safer than others. Explain what they mean.

**10.** Some critics of GM agriculture fear that GM plants' resistance to herbicides could result in the overuse of toxic chemicals. Explain why this may happen.

## Ethics of the New Biology

**11.** It is easy to move genes from one species to another. Is it right to do this? Explain your position.

### Apply the Big idea

**12.** Recent developments have resulted in the ability to clone cats. Many people argue that cloning offers pet owners comfort in a time of need. Others argue that there are many homeless pets at shelters in need of homes, and that adopting one of these animals is a better solution for owners who have lost a pet. Do you think that the cloning of pets is acceptable? Explain why or why not.

 

# Chapter Vocabulary Review

*For Questions 1–8, complete each statement by writing in the correct word or words.*

1. ______________ consists of allowing only those organisms with particular characteristics to produce the next generation.
2. In the process called ______________, dissimilar organisms are crossed in order to obtain bigger or stronger offspring.
3. When organisms that are genetically similar are crossed over and over to produce the next generation, the process is called ______________.
4. ______________ is the application of a technological process, invention, or method to living organisms.
5. The technology that makes copies of DNA is called ______________.
6. The DNA that results from the transfer of DNA from one organism into another is ______________.
7. The small, circular DNA molecule in a bacterial cell is a(n) ______________.
8. A gene that allows scientists to distinguish a cell that carries recombinant DNA from one that does not is a(n) ______________.

*For Questions 9–15, match the term with its definition.*

| Definition | Term |
|---|---|
| _____ **9.** One of a population of genetically identical cells produced from a single cell | **A.** transgenic |
| _____ **10.** A technique that allows the identification of individuals using differences in their DNA | **B.** clone |
| _____ **11.** A technique that allows scientists to study thousands of genes at once | **C.** gene therapy |
| _____ **12.** Containing genes from another species | **D.** DNA microarray |
| _____ **13.** Treating a disease by changing a gene | **E.** DNA fingerprinting |
| _____ **14.** The scientific study of evidence from a crime scene | **F.** forensics |
| _____ **15.** A gene that scientists use to find transformed bacteria | **G.** genetic marker |

*Write the letter of the correct answer on the line at the left.*

_____ **16.** Hybridization and inbreeding are both types of

**A.** gene therapy. **C.** transgenics.
**B.** forensics. **D.** selective breeding.

_____ **17.** Because of their replication process, plasmids are excellent carriers of

**A.** genetic markers. **C.** clones.
**B.** recombinant DNA. **D.** transgenics.

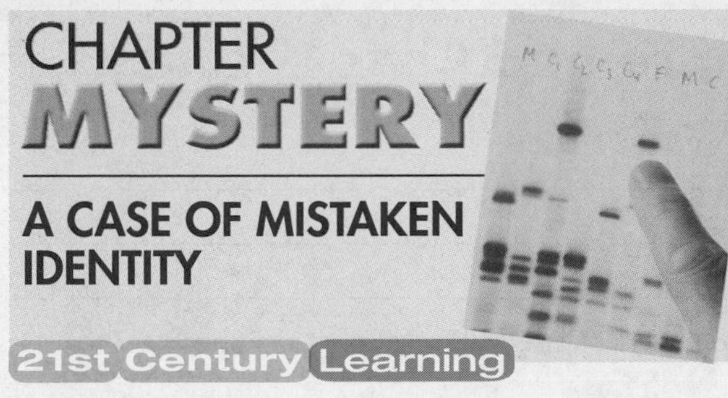


In the Chapter Mystery, as in tens of thousands of real-life cases, police used DNA fingerprinting to avoid arresting the wrong suspect. However, DNA fingerprinting is a very new technology.

21st Century Learning

# DNA Forensics: The Innocence Project

Many people in prison today were convicted of a crime before DNA fingerprinting was widely available. Should DNA forensic evidence be used to reopen such cases? At least one national legal group believes prisoners should have access to DNA testing. The Innocence Project has led the effort in the United States to use DNA forensic evidence to exonerate (or free from blame) and release wrongly convicted prisoners. They also work to improve evidence preservation techniques, to investigate possible wrongful executions based on DNA evidence, and to re-open cases based on today's more sensitive and modern methods of testing DNA evidence.

The group still faces obstacles in its battle to gain acceptance for its methods. For instance, the laws in six states still will not allow newly discovered DNA evidence to be introduced after a trial. But the power of this technology has already worked in many states. In some cases where doubts about a conviction remain, or where prisoners have steadfastly maintained that they have been wrongly convicted, scientists and lawyers from the Innocence Project have worked together to subject the cases' physical evidence to DNA forensic analysis. In more than 200 cases so far the DNA analysis has proved that innocent people have been mistakenly convicted and forced to spend many years in jail.

Learn more about the DNA exonerations by reading the fact sheet below, adapted from information provided by the Innocence Project.

## THE INNOCENCE PROJECT:

**Facts on Post-Conviction DNA Exonerations as of 2008**

- Number of post-conviction DNA exonerations in the United States: 223
- The year the first DNA exoneration took place: 1989
- Number of states in which exonerations have been won: 32
- Number of exonorees who served time on death row before being freed: 17
- Average length of time served by exonerees: 12 years
- Total number of years served by exonerees: approximately 2754
- The average age of exonerees at the time of their wrongful convictions: 26
- Cases in which the true suspects and/or perpetrators have been identified: 88

Continued on next page ▶

 

## 21st Century Themes Science and Civic Literacy

**1.** What is the mission of the Innocence Project?

______

______

______

**2.** By 2008, how many times had DNA evidence been used successfully to exonerate prisoners in the United States? ______

**3.** In what portion of the cases of people exonerated by the Innocence Project have the true suspects and/or perpetrators been identified? ______

**4.** Considering the Innocence Project's statistics, do you think prisoners jailed before DNA testing was widely available should be given access to the technology? Why or why not?

______

______

______

______

**5.** Do you think DNA evidence could be used to unintentionally convict an innocent person of a crime? Explain your answer.

______

______

______

______

## 21st Century Skills Letter to a Lawmaker

The skills used in this activity include **problem identification, formulation, and solution; critical thinking and systems thinking;** and **information and media literacy.**

Search newspapers' Web sites to read about cases in which the Innocence Project or DNA evidence has helped exonerate people. Then, find out about your own state's position on prisoner access to DNA testing by contacting your state legislature or doing research online. Use the information you find to take the part of a citizen activist.

If your state allows access, then find out about a case in your state in which DNA testing was used after a conviction. Write a letter to a newspaper expressing your opinion on the outcome of the case. If the case is pending, you can discuss in your letter what you think should happen.

If your state does not allow post-conviction access, express your opinion in a letter to a state lawmaker. Explain how DNA fingerprinting works and what position you think the lawmaker should take regarding legislation allowing prisoners access to DNA testing.

 

Name ______________________ Class ______ Date ______

# 16 Darwin's Theory of Evolution

**Big idea** **Evolution**

**Q:** What is natural selection?

| | WHAT I KNOW | WHAT I LEARNED |
|---|---|---|
| **16.1** What patterns of biodiversity did Darwin observe aboard the *Beagle*? | | |
| **16.2** How did other scientists' work help Darwin develop his theory of natural selection? | | |
| **16.3** What is Darwin's theory of evolution by natural selection? | | |
| **16.4** What are the main lines of scientific evidence that support Darwin's theory of evolution by natural selection? | | |

 

Name ______________________ Class ______ Date __________

# 16.1 Darwin's Voyage of Discovery

## Lesson Objectives

State Charles Darwin's contribution to science.

Describe the three patterns of biodiversity noted by Darwin.

## Lesson Summary

**Darwin's Epic Journey** Darwin developed a scientific theory to explain how **evolution**, or change over time, occurs in living things. Darwin's theory explains how modern organisms have evolved over long periods of time through descent from common ancestors.

**Observations Aboard the *Beagle*** During his five-year trip on the *Beagle*, Darwin made many observations and collected a great deal of evidence.

- He noticed that many different, yet ecologically similar, animal and plant species occupied different, yet ecologically similar, habitats around the globe.
- On the Galápagos Islands, Darwin noticed that the traits of many organisms—such as the shell shapes of tortoises—varied from island to island. He noticed that different, yet related, animal and plant species occupied different habitats within a local area.
- Darwin collected **fossils**, the preserved remains of ancient organisms. He noticed that some fossils of extinct species resembled living species.

Darwin's findings led him to think that species are not fixed and that they could change by some natural process.

## Darwin's Epic Journey

1. THINK VISUALLY On the map below, (1) find and label the Galápagos Islands (2) circle the names of three large land masses Darwin did not visit on his voyage.

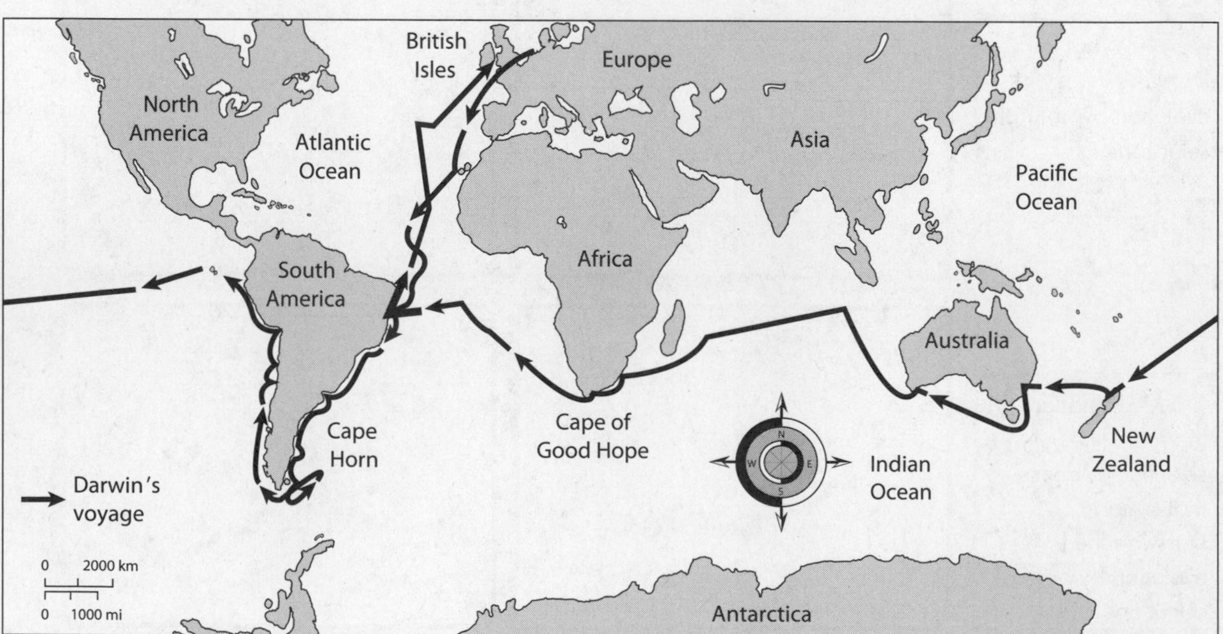

*For Questions 2–4, complete each statement by writing the correct word or words. Refer to the map on the previous page as needed.*

**2.** Darwin spent most of his time exploring the continent of ______________; he did not visit ______________, ______________, or ______________.

**3.** During Darwin's time, geologists were suggesting that Earth was ______________ ______________.

**4.** Darwin's work offers insight into the living world by showing organisms are constantly ______________.

## Observations Aboard the *Beagle*

*Use the drawings of the tortoises to answer Questions 5 and 6.*

**Isabela Island tortoise**

**Hood Island tortoise**

**5.** What important information about the Galápagos Islands tortoises did Darwin learn?

______________________________________________

______________________________________________

**6.** Given its body structure, which tortoise above would require a habitat where food is easy to reach?

______________________________________________

______________________________________________

*Use the map on the previous page to answer Questions 7 and 8.*

**7.** On the map, place the labels Rheas, Emus, and Ostriches on the continents where they are found. Why were the similarities among rheas, ostriches, and emus surprising to Darwin?

______________________________________________

______________________________________________

**8.** Why might Darwin come to think that the finches of the Galápagos Islands might be related to the finches of South America, despite how different the birds were in appearance?

______________________________________________

______________________________________________

**9.** Darwin observed that the birds he would eventually discover were finches had differently shaped beaks. What might this suggest about the eating habits of the birds? Explain.

______________________________________________

______________________________________________

 

**10.** What did the similarities between fossil animals and modern animals, like the glyptodont and armadillo, suggest to Darwin?

______________________________________________

______________________________________________

**11.** Complete the graphic organizer by listing three ways that species vary. For each pattern of biodiversity, list an example that Darwin observed.

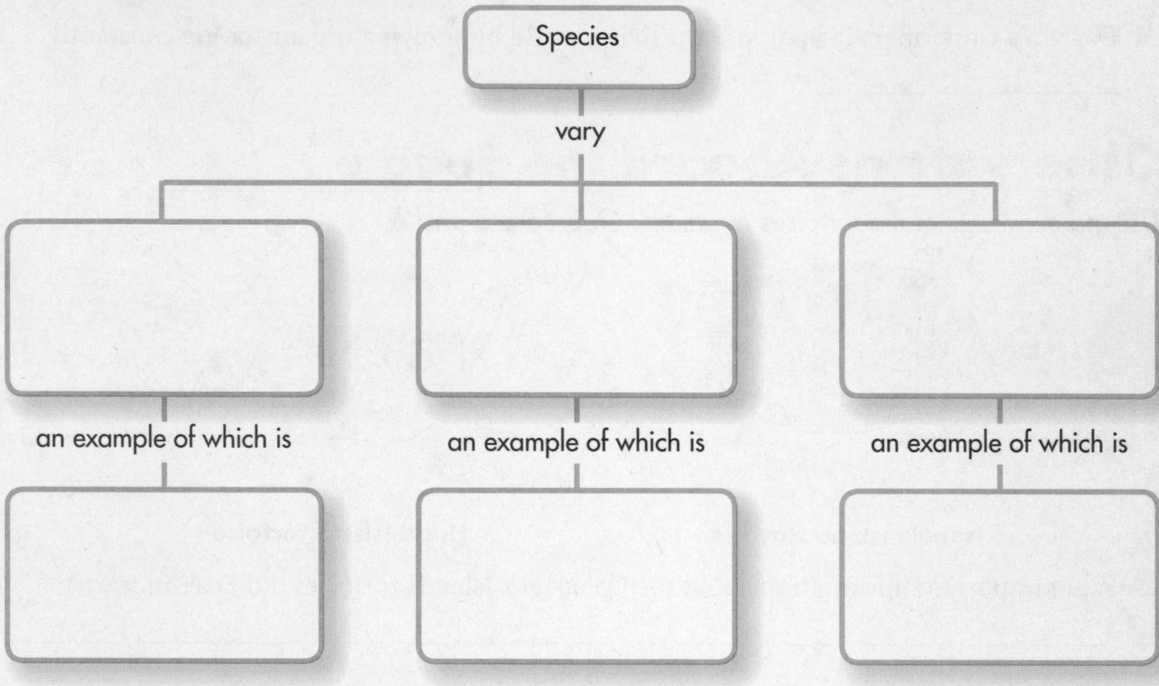


## Apply the Big idea

**12.** When Darwin returned to England, he learned that the small brown birds he observed on the Galápagos Islands were all finches. They resembled South American finches. What hypothesis does this observation support?

______________________________________________

______________________________________________

______________________________________________

______________________________________________

 

# 16.2 Ideas That Shaped Darwin's Thinking

## Lesson Objectives

- Identify the conclusions drawn by Hutton and Lyell about Earth's history.
- Describe Lamarck's hypothesis of evolution.
- Describe Malthus's view of population growth.
- Explain the role of inherited variation in artificial selection.

## Lesson Summary

**An Ancient, Changing Earth** In Darwin's day, most Europeans believed that Earth and all its life forms were only a few thousand years old and had not changed very much in that time. Several scientists who lived around the same time as Darwin began to challenge these ideas. These scientists had an important influence on the development of Darwin's theory of evolution.

- Geologists James Hutton and Charles Lyell argued that Earth is many millions of years old.
- They also argued that the processes changing Earth today, like volcanism and erosion, are the same ones that changed Earth in the past.

Knowing that Earth could change over time helped Darwin realize that species might change as well. Knowing that Earth was very old convinced Darwin that there had been enough time for life to evolve.

**Lamarck's Evolutionary Hypothesis** Jean-Baptiste Lamarck was one of the first scientists to propose hypotheses about how evolution occurred.

- To explain evolution, Lamarck hypothesized that all organisms have an inborn drive to become more complex and perfect. According to Lamarck, an organism could gain or lose traits during its lifetime by using or not using certain organs.
- Lamarck also hypothesized that acquired characteristics could be passed on to an organism's offspring leading to evolution of the species.

Scientists now know that most of Lamarck's ideas about evolution are incorrect. However, he correctly suggested that life is not fixed and was the first to offer a natural and scientific explanation for evolution. Further, he recognized that an organism's traits are linked to its environment.

**Population Growth** Thomas Malthus thought that if the human population continued to grow unchecked, it would run out of living space and food. Darwin realized that this was true of all organisms, not just humans.

**Artificial Selection** Plant and animal breeders in Darwin's time used a process now known as artificial selection to improve their crops and livestock. In **artificial selection**, nature provides the variations, and humans select those they find desirable. Darwin experimented with artificial selection. The results from his experiments indicated natural variation was very important because it provided the raw material for evolution.

Name ______________________ Class ______ Date ________

## An Ancient, Changing Earth

**1.** In what two ways did an understanding of geology influence Darwin?

______________________________________________

______________________________________________

______________________________________________

*For Questions 2–5, write True if the statement is true. If the statement is false, change the underlined word or words to make the statement true.*

________ **2.** Hutton realized that Earth was much younger than previously believed.

________ **3.** Lyell thought most geological processes operated extremely quickly.

________ **4.** The processes that changed Earth in the past are different from the processes that operate in the present.

________ **5.** Lyell's work explained how large geological features could be built up or torn down over long periods of time.

## Lamarck's Evolutionary Hypotheses

**6.** How did Lamarck propose that species change over time?

______________________________________________

______________________________________________

______________________________________________

______________________________________________

*Use the diagram to answer Questions 7–8.*

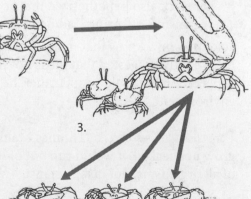

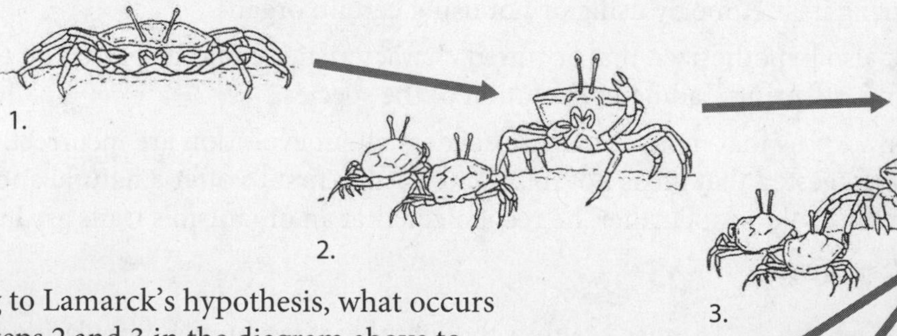


**7.** According to Lamarck's hypothesis, what occurs between steps 2 and 3 in the diagram above to make the crab's claw grow larger?

______________________________________________

______________________________________________

______________________________________________

**8.** Which step in the diagram above shows the inheritance of acquired traits as proposed by Lamarck?

______________________________________________

**9.** How did Lamarck pave the way for the work of later biologists?

______________________________________________

______________________________________________

______________________________________________

**10.** Which of Lamarck's ideas turned out to be true? Which turned out to be false?

______________________________________________

______________________________________________

______________________________________________

______________________________________________

**11.** How would Lamarck have explained the length of a giraffe's neck?

______________________________________________

______________________________________________

______________________________________________

______________________________________________

______________________________________________

## Population Growth

*For Questions 12–14, write the letter of the correct answer on the line at the left.*

_____ **12.** Which observation caused Thomas Malthus to form his theory about population growth?

**A.** Human birth rate was higher than the death rate.

**B.** War caused the death of thousands of people.

**C.** Famines were common in England in the 1800s.

**D.** The offspring of most species survived into adulthood.

_____ **13.** Which of the following is an idea attributed to Malthus?

**A.** As a population decreases in size, warfare and famine become more common.

**B.** As a population increases in size, the percentage of offspring that survive also increases.

**C.** If the human population grew unchecked, its rate of evolution would increase geometrically.

**D.** If the human population grew unchecked, there wouldn't be enough living space and food for everyone.

_____ **14.** Malthus's ideas led Darwin to conclude that

**A.** Earth is much older than previously thought.

**B.** the size of the human population can grow indefinitely.

**C.** many more organisms are born than will survive and reproduce.

**D.** organisms are able to evolve through a process known as artificial selection.

Name ______________________ Class ______ Date ________

## Artificial Selection

**15.** How do humans affect artificial selection? What role does nature play?

______________________________

______________________________

______________________________

**16.** What is another name for artificial selection?

______________________________

**17.** Describe how you could use artificial selection to breed pigeons with large beaks.

______________________________

______________________________

______________________________

**Apply the Big idea**

**18.** Complete the table about scientists who contributed to the development of the theory of evolution.

| Scientists Who Contributed to Darwin's Theory of Evolution | |
|---|---|
| **Scientist** | **Contribution to Darwin's Theory** |
| James Hutton | |
| Charles Lyell | |
| Jean-Baptiste Lamarck | |
| Thomas Malthus | |

 

Name ______________________ Class _______ Date _______

# 16.3 Darwin Presents His Case

## Lesson Objectives

- Describe the conditions under which natural selection occurs.
- Explain the principle of common descent.

## Lesson Summary

**Evolution by Natural Selection** Darwin published *On the Origin of Species* in 1859. In the book, Darwin describes and provides evidence for his explanation of how evolution occurs. He called this process **natural selection** because of its similarities to artificial selection. Darwin's theory of evolution by natural selection can be summed up as follows:

- More offspring are produced than can survive to reproduce. There is competition for limited resources, or a struggle for existence.
- Individuals exhibit variation in their traits and some of these differences can be passed on to their offspring.
- Inherited traits that increase an organism's ability to survive and reproduce are called **adaptations**.
- Differences among adaptations affect an individual's **fitness**—the ability to survive and reproduce in a specific environment.
- Only the fittest organisms live to reproduce and pass on their adaptive traits to offspring. This is known as the survival of the fittest.

From generation to generation, populations continue to evolve as they become better adapted, or as their environment changes.

**Common Descent** Darwin argued that all species are descended, with modification, from common ancestors. Through descent with modification, all organisms—living and extinct—are linked on a single tree of life.

## Evolution by Natural Selection

**1.** What does the phrase *struggle for existence* mean?

_______________________________________________

_______________________________________________

**2.** Why is camouflage considered an adaptation?

_______________________________________________

_______________________________________________

**3.** How does an animal's level of fitness relate to its chances of survival and reproduction?

_______________________________________________

_______________________________________________

*For Questions 4–6, write True if the statement is true. If the statement is false, change the underlined word or words to make the statement true.*

______________ **4.** Natural selection acts on <u>acquired</u> traits.

______________ **5.** Any inherited characteristic that increases an organism's chance of survival is considered <u>an adaptation</u>.

______________ **6.** <u>Natural selection</u> is the ability of an individual to survive and reproduce in its specific environment.

**7.** Below is a partially completed flowchart that models how natural selection drives evolution. The missing steps are listed below, out of order, and lettered A–D. Write the letter of the missing step in a blank box in the flowchart.

**A.** Adaptations are passed on to the next generation.

**B.** The accumulation of adaptations may lead to the evolution of a new species.

**C.** These offspring have few or no offspring of their own.

**D.** Some offspring inherit traits that increase fitness (adaptations).

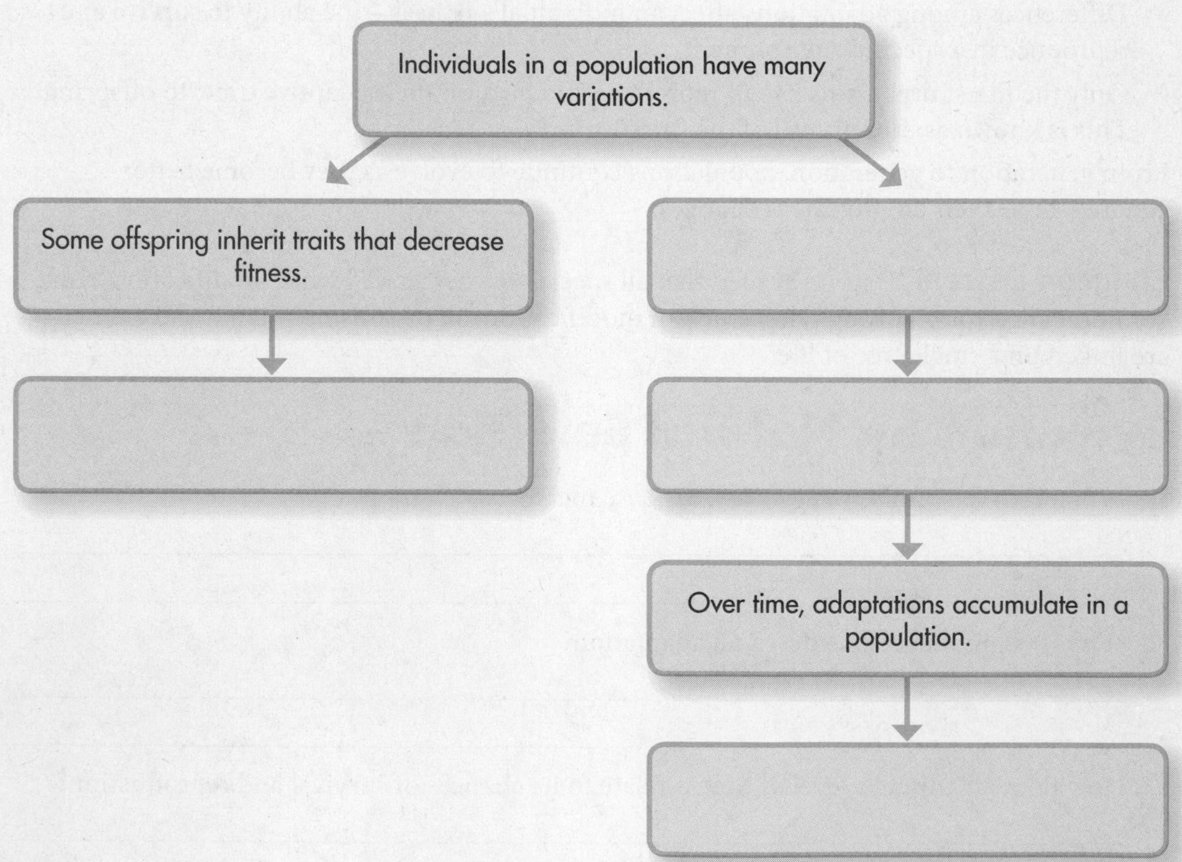

Name ______________________ Class ______ Date ______

## Common Descent

*For Questions 8–13, complete each statement by writing the correct word or words.*

**8.** Natural selection depends on the ability of organisms to ______________, which means to leave descendants.

**9.** Every organism alive today ______________ from ancestors who survived and reproduced.

**10.** Over many generations, adaptation could cause successful species to ______________ into new species.

**11.** Common descent suggests that all species, living and extinct, are ______________.

**12.** The principle that living species descend, with changes, from other species over time is referred to as ______________________________.

**13.** The ______________ provides physical evidence of descent with modification over long periods of time.

### Apply the Big idea

**14.** In the three boxes on the left, draw an example of natural selection that might occur in a population of frogs. Then, on the lines at right, describe each stage.

| Stage | Drawing | Description |
|---|---|---|
| The Struggle for Existence | | |
| Variation and Adaption/ Survival of the Fittest | | |
| Natural Selection | | |

# 16.4 Evidence of Evolution

## Lesson Objectives

- Explain how geologic distribution of species relates to their evolutionary history.
- Explain how fossils and the fossil record document the descent of modern species from ancient ancestors.
- Describe what homologous structures and embryology suggest about the process of evolutionary change.
- Explain how molecular evidence can be used to trace the process of evolution.
- Explain the results of the Grants' investigation of adaptation in Galápagos finches.

## Lesson Summary

**Biogeography** **Biogeography** is the study of where organisms live now and where they and their ancestors lived in the past. Two biogeographical patterns are significant to Darwin's theory:

- The first is a pattern in which closely related species differentiate in slightly different climates. The Galápagos tortoises and finches follow this pattern.
- The second is a pattern in which very distantly related species develop similarities in similar environments. The rheas, ostriches, and emus fall into this pattern.

### The Age of Earth and Fossils

- Radioactive dating techniques have confirmed that Earth is ancient—approximately 4.5 billion years old.
- Recent fossil finds document intermediate stages in the evolution of many groups including whales, birds, and mammals.

### Comparing Anatomy and Embryology

- **Homologous structures** are shared by related species and have been inherited from a common ancestor. Similarities and differences among homologous structures help determine how recently two groups shared a common ancestor.
  - Body parts that share a common function, but neither structure nor common ancestry, are called **analogous structures**. Analogous structures do not provide any evidence for evolutionary descent.
  - Homologous structures that are greatly reduced in size or have little to no function are called **vestigial structures**.
  - Many homologous structures develop in the same order and in similar patterns during the embryonic, or pre-birth, stages of related groups. These similarities provide further evidence that the animals share common ancestors.

**Genetics and Molecular Biology** At the molecular level, the universal genetic code and homologous molecules such as genes and proteins provide evidence of common descent.

**Testing Natural Selection** Scientists have designed experiments to test natural selection. Observations of Galápagos finches confirm that competition and environmental change drive natural selection.

## Biogeography

*For Questions 1–3, complete each statement by writing the correct word or words.*

1. Biogeographers study where organisms live now and where they and their ______________ lived in the past.

2. When individuals from a mainland bird population immigrate to various islands, natural selection may result in ______________, but different, island species.

3. Distantly related organisms may be similar if they live in ______________.

4. What explains the distribution of finch species on the Galápagos Islands?

______________________________________________

______________________________________________

5. What explains the existence of similar but unrelated species?

______________________________________________

______________________________________________

## The Age of Earth and Fossils

6. **THINK VISUALLY** The illustrations below show organisms whose fossils make up part of the fossil record. The organisms are in order from oldest to most recent. In the boxes, draw an animal that might have been an intermediate form between the shown organisms.

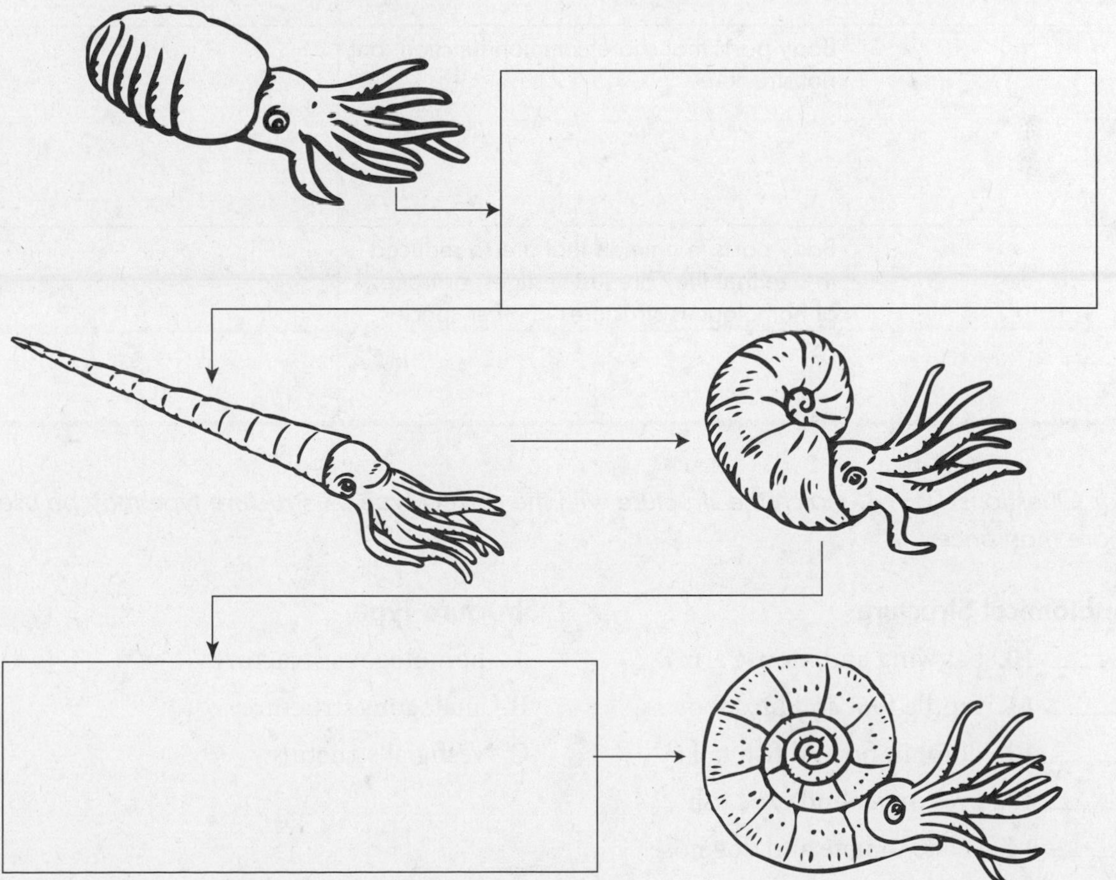

 

*Use the illustrations of the marine organisms on the previous page to answer Questions 7–8.*

**7.** Describe a situation in which organism 3 might have had an advantage over organism 2?

______________________________________________

______________________________________________

______________________________________________

**8.** How might these fossils provide evidence for evolution?

______________________________________________

______________________________________________

______________________________________________

## Comparing Anatomy and Embryology

**9.** Complete the table about types of anatomical structures.

| Types of Anatomical Structures | | |
|---|---|---|
| **Structure Type** | **Description** | **Example** |
| | Structures that are shared by related species and that have been inherited from a common ancestor | |
| | Body parts that share common function, but not structure | |
| | Body parts in animals that are so reduced in size that they are just vestiges, or traces, of homologous structures in other species | |

*For Questions 10–14, match the structure with the correct type. A structure type may be used more than once.*

**Anatomical Structure**

_____ **10.** bat wing and mouse arm

_____ **11.** reptile foot and bird foot

_____ **12.** dolphin fin and fish tail

_____ **13.** eyes on a blind cave fish

_____ **14.** snake tongue and dog nose

**Structure Type**

**A.** homologous structure

**B.** analogous structure

**C.** vestigial structure

 

*Use the illustrated homologous structures to answer Questions 15–17.*

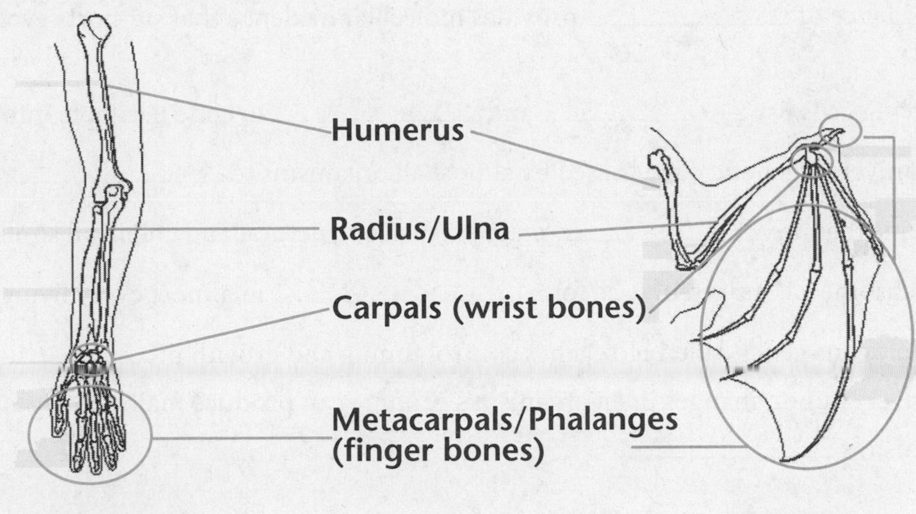


**15.** How are the forelimbs similar?

______________________________________________

______________________________________________

**16.** How are the forelimbs different?

______________________________________________

______________________________________________

______________________________________________

**17.** How are homologous structures such as forelimbs evidence for common descent?

______________________________________________

______________________________________________

______________________________________________

**18.** How does the pattern of embryological development provide further evidence that organisms have descended from a common ancestor?

______________________________________________

______________________________________________

______________________________________________

 

## Genetics and Molecular Biology

*For Questions 19–25, complete each statement by writing the correct word or words.*

**19.** The science of ______________ provides molecular evidence that supports evolutionary theory.

**20.** All living cells use ______________ and ______________ to code heritable information.

**21.** The universal genetic code is used by almost all organisms to ______________________.

**22.** Proteins that are ______________ share extensive structural and chemical similarities.

**23.** Cytochrome c is a protein used for ______________ in almost every living cell.

**24.** Homologous genes called Hox genes control timing and growth in ______________.

**25.** Relatively minor changes in an organism's genome can produce major changes in an organism's ______________.

## Testing Natural Selection

*Write the letter of the correct answer on the line at the left.*

_____ **26.** Which of the following hypotheses did the Grants test?

**A.** Differences in beak size and shape produce differences in fitness.

**B.** For beak size and shape to evolve, the birds must leave the islands.

**C.** For beak size and shape to evolve, the climate must change radically.

**D.** Differences in beak size and shape are not determined by genetic mutations.

_____ **27.** The data that the Grants collected proved that there is

**A.** no link between the environment and the shape of finch feet.

**B.** no link between the environment and the shape of finch beaks.

**C.** great variation of heritable traits among Galápagos finches.

**D.** very little variation of heritable traits among Galápagos finches.

_____ **28.** The Grants conducted their experiment to test which of the following processes?

**A.** Natural selection

**B.** Genetic mutation

**C.** Artificial selection

**D.** Sexual reproduction

 

**29.** VISUAL ANALOGY The art shows how finch beaks are similar to certain kinds of hand tools. Suppose a finch fed on insects that burrowed into small holes on tree trunks. What type of tool do you think this finch's beak would resemble? Explain your answer.

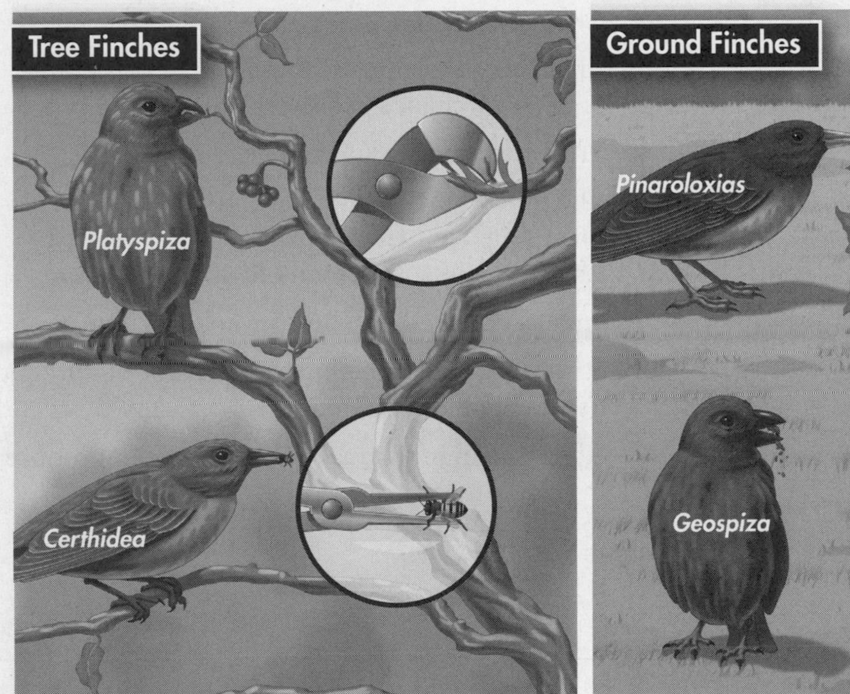


_______________________________________________

_______________________________________________

_______________________________________________

## Apply the Big idea

**30.** Complete the concept map.

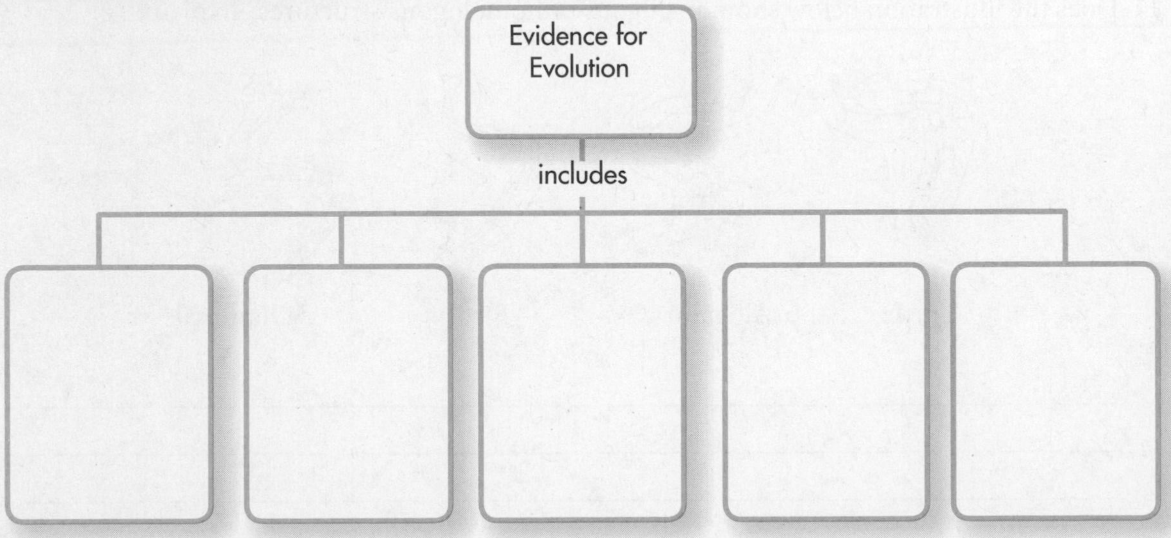

# Chapter Vocabulary Review

*Match the term with its definition.*

| Term | Definition |
|---|---|
| ______ 1. evolution | A. Change over time |
| ______ 2. fossil | B. Inherited characteristic that increases an organism's chance of survival |
| ______ 3. fitness | C. Preserved remains of an ancient organism |
| ______ 4. adaptation | D. The process by which organisms with variations most suited to their environment survive and leave more offspring than others |
| ______ 5. natural selection | E. Small structures with little or no function |
| ______ 6. homologous structures | F. Structures that develop from the same embryonic tissues but have different mature forms |
| ______ 7. vestigial structures | G. Ability of an individual to survive and reproduce in a specific environment |

*For Questions 8–10, write a definition for the vocabulary term.*

8. biogeography

______________________________________________

______________________________________________

9. artificial selection

______________________________________________

______________________________________________

10. analogous structures

______________________________________________

______________________________________________

11. Does the illustration below show analogous or homologous structures? Explain.

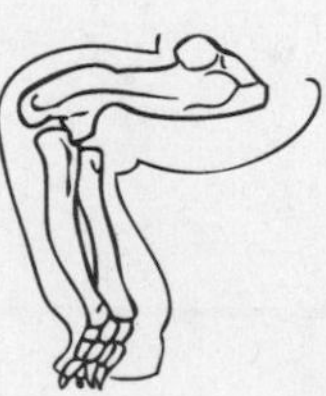

Turtle

Alligator

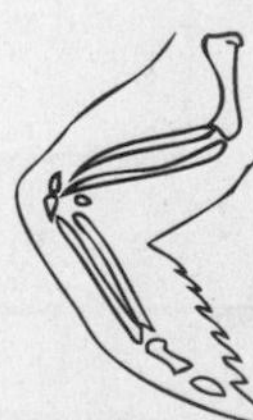

Bird

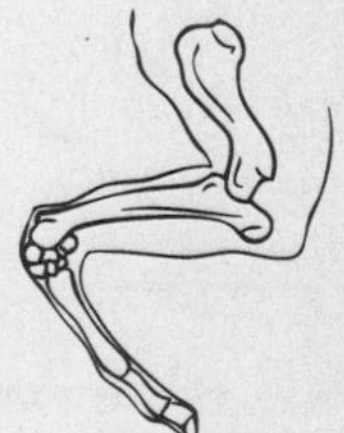

Mammals

______________________________________________

______________________________________________

______________________________________________

______________________________________________

 

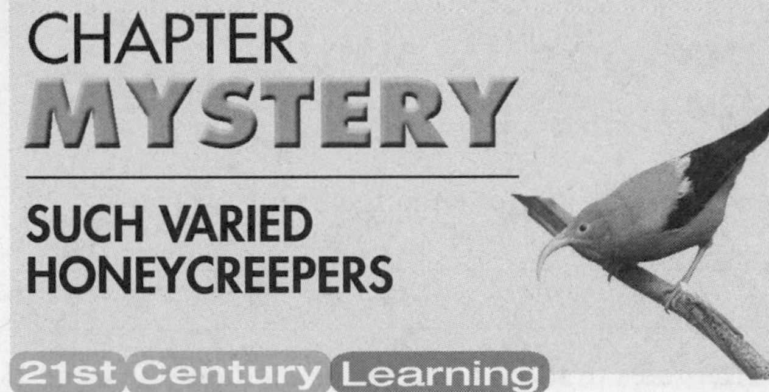


"The Chapter Mystery explained how the 'i'iwi and other Hawaiian honeycreeper species evolved adaptations suited to their specific habitats. What happens when species face a loss of their habitats due to urbanization or environmental degradation?

21st Century Learning

# Habitat Loss and Endangered Species

Scientists report that in the United States, habitat loss is the most widespread cause of species endangerment, affecting approximately 85 percent of imperiled species according to a recent estimate. Designed to combat the problem, the U.S. Endangered Species Act of 1973 is a federal law that protects threatened and endangered species. When a species is listed as endangered, the government enforces more stringent protections on the species' remaining habitats, especially when those habitats are on federal lands. In addition, the Act allows the government to purchase land containing important habitats and forbids the capture, killing, or sale of an endangered species. In addition, people who violate the Act can be prosecuted.

Unfortunately, threats to many species continue. Experts believe that fewer than half the species native to the United States—especially insect, plant, and fungi species—have yet been discovered and catalogued. Therefore, it is impossible to know whether these species are endangered. Another problem, other scientists emphasize, is that the regulations protecting endangered species are not effective enough and are based on an underestimation of the problem. One recent expert analysis suggests that, even within the pool of known species, the number now threatened with extinction may actually be as much as ten times greater than the number currently protected under the U.S. Endangered Species Act.

The table below, adapted from data compiled by the nonprofit scientific group NatureServe, assesses the current situation for vertebrate species in the United States.

**Vertebrate Species Data in the U.S.**

| Group: Imperiled U.S. Vertebrates | Total Number of Known Species | Number of Species Imperiled or Extinct/ Possibly Extinct | Percentage of Species Imperiled or Extinct/ Possibly Extinct |
|---|---|---|---|
| Mammals | 421 | 29 | 7 |
| Birds | 783 | 75 | 10 |
| Reptiles | 295 | 28 | 9 |
| Amphibians | 258 | 66 | 26 |
| Freshwater Fishes | 798 | 179 | 22 |
| Vertebrate Totals | 2555 | 377 | 15 |

Continued on next page ▶

 

Name ______________________ Class ______ Date ________

## 21st Century Themes Science and Global Awareness

**1.** What is believed to be the most widespread cause of species endangerment?

______________________________________________

______________________________________________

**2.** According to the table, which group of vertebrates in the United States includes the largest number of imperiled or extinct species?

______________________________________________

______________________________________________

**3.** According to the table, which group of vertebrates appears to be most endangered overall? How can you tell? Why do you think this group is most imperiled?

______________________________________________

______________________________________________

______________________________________________

______________________________________________

**4.** What is the U.S. Endangered Species Act?

______________________________________________

______________________________________________

______________________________________________

**5.** Some experts think that a significant number of species native to the United States have yet to be discovered. Some experts think that the U.S. Endangered Species Act underestimates the number of endangered species. How does the first problem lead to the second?

______________________________________________

______________________________________________

______________________________________________

## 21st Century Skills Species Presentation

The skills used in this activity include **information and media literacy; critical thinking and systems thinking;** and **problem identification, formulation, and solution.**

Visit the Web site of the U.S. Fish and Wildlife Service to learn more about the agency's efforts to protect endangered species in the United States. Choose one endangered species and investigate the threats it faces. Present the information to the class, including whether you believe the species deserves protection under the Act and, if so, why.

*Your presentation can be in the form of a video about the species or an illustrated guide.*

Name ______________________ Class ______ Date ______

# 17 Evolution of Populations

**Big idea** **Evolution**

**Q:** How can populations evolve to form new species?

| | WHAT I KNOW | WHAT I LEARNED |
|---|---|---|
| **17.1** How do genes make evolution possible? | | |
| **17.2** How do genes make evolution possible? | | |
| **17.3** How do new species form? | | |
| **17.4** What can genes tell us about an organism's evolutionary history? | | |

 

# 17.1 Genes and Variation

## Lesson Objectives

Define evolution in genetic terms.

Identify the main sources of genetic variation in a population.

State what determines the number of phenotypes for a trait.

## Lesson Summary

**Genetics Joins Evolutionary Theory** Darwin's original ideas can now be understood in genetic terms.

- Researchers discovered that traits are controlled by genes and that many genes have at least two forms, or alleles. The combination of different alleles is an individual's genotype. Natural selection acts on phenotype, not genotype.
- Genetic variation and evolution are studied in populations. Members of a population share a common group of genes, called a **gene pool**.
- **Allele frequency** is the number of times an allele occurs in a gene pool compared with the number of times other alleles for the same gene occur. In genetic terms, evolution is any change in the allele frequency in a population.

**Sources of Genetic Variation** The three main sources of genetic variation are mutations, genetic recombination during sexual reproduction, and lateral gene transfer.

- A mutation is any change in a sequence of DNA.
- Most heritable differences are due to genetic recombination during sexual reproduction. This occurs during meiosis when each chromosome in a pair moves independently. Genetic recombination also occurs during crossing-over in meiosis.
- Lateral gene transfer is the passing of genes from one organism to another organism that is not its offspring.

**Single-Gene and Polygenic Traits** The number of different phenotypes for a given trait depends on how many genes control the trait.

- A **single-gene trait** is controlled by one gene. An example in snails is the presence or absence of dark bands on their shells.
- A **polygenic trait** is controlled by two or more genes, and each gene often has two or more alleles. An example of a human polygenic trait is height.

## Genetics Joins Evolutionary Theory

*For Questions 1–4, complete each statement by writing the correct word or words.*

**1.** Natural selection works on an organism's ______________ rather than its ______________.

**2.** A(n) ______________ consists of all the genes, including the alleles for each gene, that are present in a population.

 

Name ______________________________ Class ______ Date ______

3. A gene pool typically contains different __________ for each heritable trait.

4. The number of times that an allele occurs in a gene pool compared with the number of times other alleles for the same gene occur is called the __________ of the population.

*Use the circle graph of a sample mouse population to answer Questions 5–8.*

5. **THINK VISUALLY** In the diagram below, use circles to represent the alleles within each segment of the population. Draw the *B* alleles as solid circles and the *b* alleles as outline circles. The total number of individuals in this population is __________; the total number of alleles is __________.

**Sample Population**

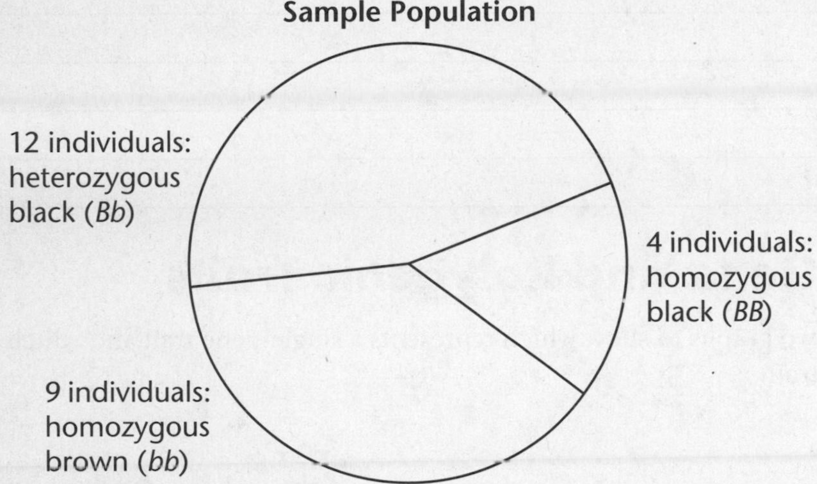


6. How many alleles for black fur are in the sample population and what percentage of allele frequency does that represent?

______________________________

7. How many alleles for brown fur are in the sample population and what percentage of allele frequency does that represent?

______________________________

8. Describe how a geneticist might be able to tell that this population is evolving.

______________________________

9. Can you determine whether an allele is dominant or recessive on the basis of the ratio of phenotypes in the population? Explain your answer.

______________________________

______________________________

______________________________

## Sources of Genetic Variation

10. What are mutations? When do they affect evolution?

______________________________

______________________________

______________________________

**11.** How does sexual reproduction affect a population's genetic variation?

______________________________________________

______________________________________________

______________________________________________

**12.** Identify two ways in which genes can be recombined during meiosis.

______________________________________________

______________________________________________

**13.** What is lateral gene transfer? How does it affect variation?

______________________________________________

______________________________________________

______________________________________________

______________________________________________

______________________________________________

## Single Gene and Polygenic Traits

**14.** Label the two graphs to show which represents a single-gene trait and which represents a polygenic trait.

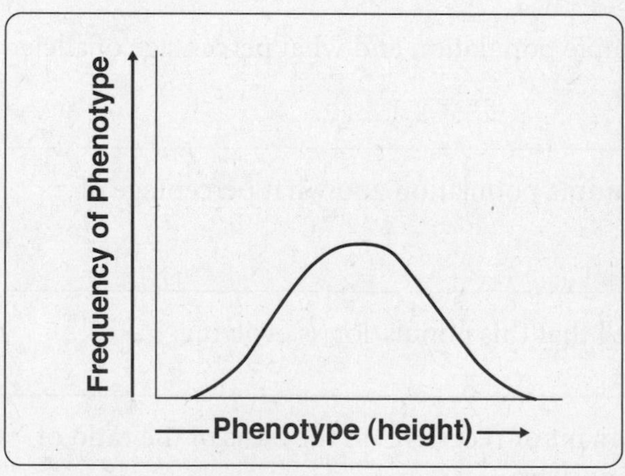


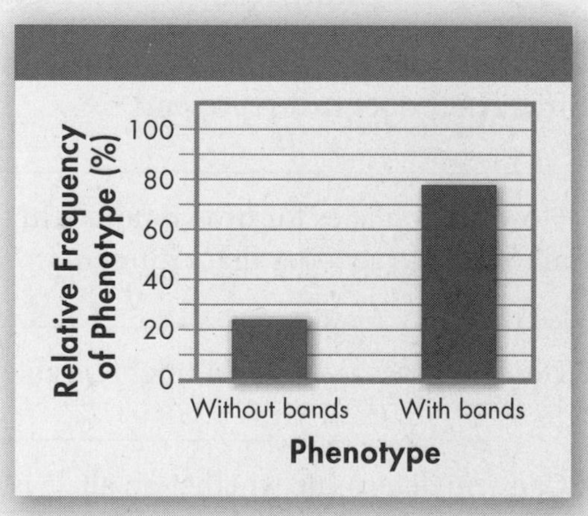


____________________ ____________________

*For Questions 15–19, write True if the statement is true. If the statement is false, change the underlined word or words to make the statement true.*

__________ **15.** The number of <u>phenotypes</u> produced for a given trait depends on how many genes control the trait.

__________ **16.** Height in humans is an example of a <u>single-gene</u> trait.

 

Name ______________________ Class ______ Date ______

______ **17.** Each gene of a polygenic trait often has two or more phenotypes.

______ **18.** A single polygenic trait often has many possible genotypes.

______ **19.** A symmetrical bell-shaped graph is typical of polygenic traits.

**20.** Use the Venn diagram to compare and contrast single-gene traits and polygenic traits.

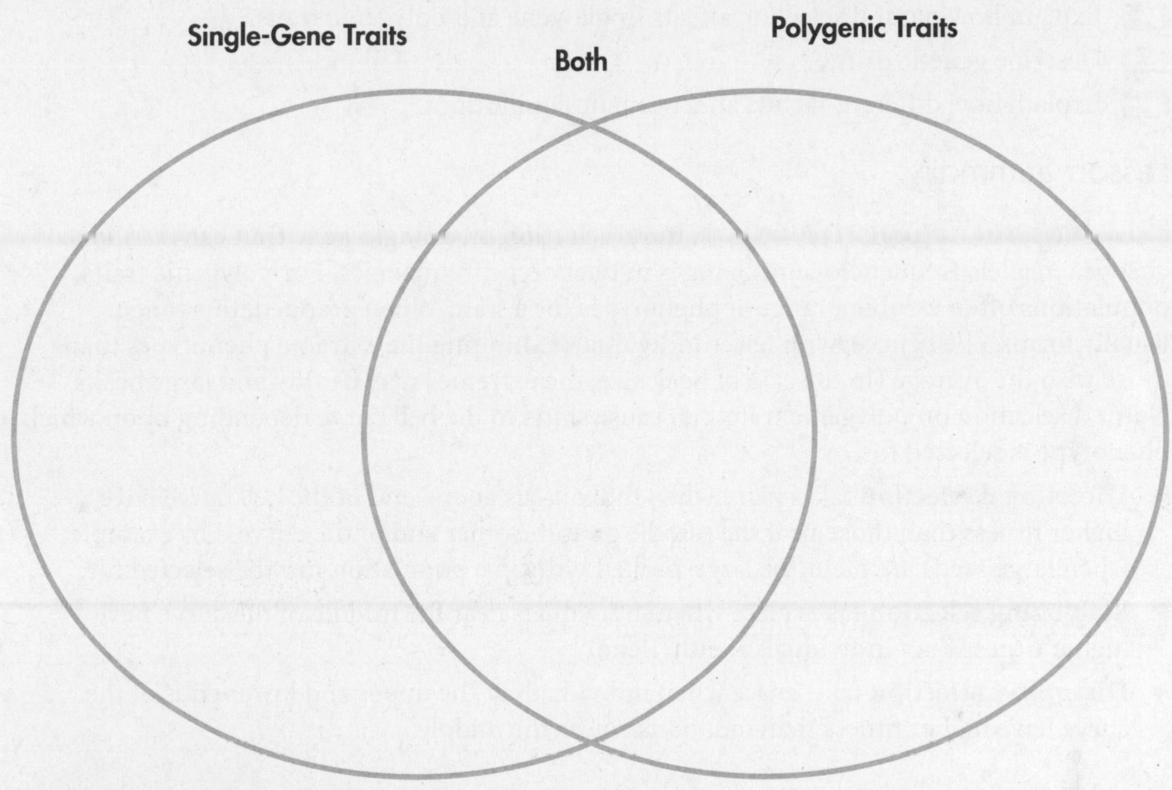


**Apply the Big idea**

**21.** Why is genetic variation important to the process of evolution?

______________________________________________

______________________________________________

______________________________________________

______________________________________________

______________________________________________

______________________________________________

 

# 17.2 Evolution as Genetic Change in Populations

## Lesson Objectives

- Explain how natural selection affects single-gene and polygenic traits.
- Describe genetic drift.
- Explain how different factors affect genetic equilibrium.

## Lesson Summary

**How Natural Selection Works** Natural selection on a single-gene trait can lead to changes in allele frequencies and changes in phenotype frequencies. For polygenic traits, populations often exhibit a range of phenotypes for a trait. When graphed, this range usually forms a bell curve, with fewer individuals exhibiting the extreme phenotypes than those with the average (in the case of beak size, the extremes may be tiny and large beaks). Natural selection on polygenic traits can cause shifts to the bell curve depending upon which phenotype is selected for.

- **Directional selection** takes place when individuals at one end of the bell curve have higher fitness than those near the middle or at the other end of the curve. For example, when large seeds are plentiful, large-beaked birds in a population may be selected for.
- **Stabilizing selection** takes place when individuals near the middle of the curve have higher fitness than individuals at either end.
- **Disruptive selection** takes place when individuals at the upper and lower ends of the curve have higher fitness than individuals near the middle.

**Genetic Drift** In small populations, alleles can become more or less common simply by chance. This kind of change in allele frequency is called **genetic drift**.

- The **bottleneck effect** is a change in allele frequency following a dramatic reduction in the size of a population.
- The **founder effect** is a change in allele frequency that may occur when a few individuals from a population migrate to and colonize a new habitat.

**Evolution Versus Genetic Equilibrium** If allele frequencies in a population do not change, the population is in **genetic equilibrium**. Evolution is not taking place.

- The **Hardy-Weinberg Principle** states that allele frequencies in a population should remain constant unless one or more factors cause those frequencies to change. These factors include: non-random mating, small population size, immigration or emigration, mutations, and natural selection.
- Populations are rarely in genetic equilibrium. Most of the time, evolution is occurring. For example, many species exhibit non-random mating patterns. **Sexual selection**, or the process in which an individual chooses its mate based on heritable traits (such as size or strength), is a common practice for many organisms.

 

# How Natural Selection Works

**1.** If a trait made an organism less likely to survive and reproduce, what would happen to the allele for that trait? ______________________

**2.** If a trait had no effect on an organism's fitness, what would likely happen to the allele for that trait? ______________________

*Use the table showing the evolution of a population of mice to answer Questions 3–5.*

| Initial Population | Generation 10 | Generation 20 | Generation 30 |
|---|---|---|---|
| 90% | 80% | 70% | 40% |
| 10% | 20% | 30% | 60% |

**3.** Is the trait for fur color a single-gene trait or a polygenic trait? Explain your answer.

______________________

**4.** Describe how the relative frequency of fur color alleles is changing in this population and propose one explanation for this change.

______________________

**5.** Suppose a mutation causes a white fur phenotype to emerge in the population. What might happen to the mouse population after 40 generations?

______________________

 

Name ______________________ Class ______ Date ________

6. What effect does stabilizing selection have on variation in a population?

_______________________________________________

_______________________________________________

*For Questions 7–9, match the type of selection with the correct situation.*

| Type of Selection | Situation |
|---|---|
| ______ 7. Directional | A. Individuals at the upper and lower ends of the curve have higher fitness than individuals near the middle. |
| ______ 8. Stabilizing | B. Individuals at one end of the curve have higher fitness than individuals in the middle or at the other end. |
| ______ 9. Disruptive | C. Individuals near the center of the curve have higher fitness than individuals at either end. |

10. **THINK VISUALLY** Draw the missing line in the graph on the right to show how disruptive selection affects beak size.

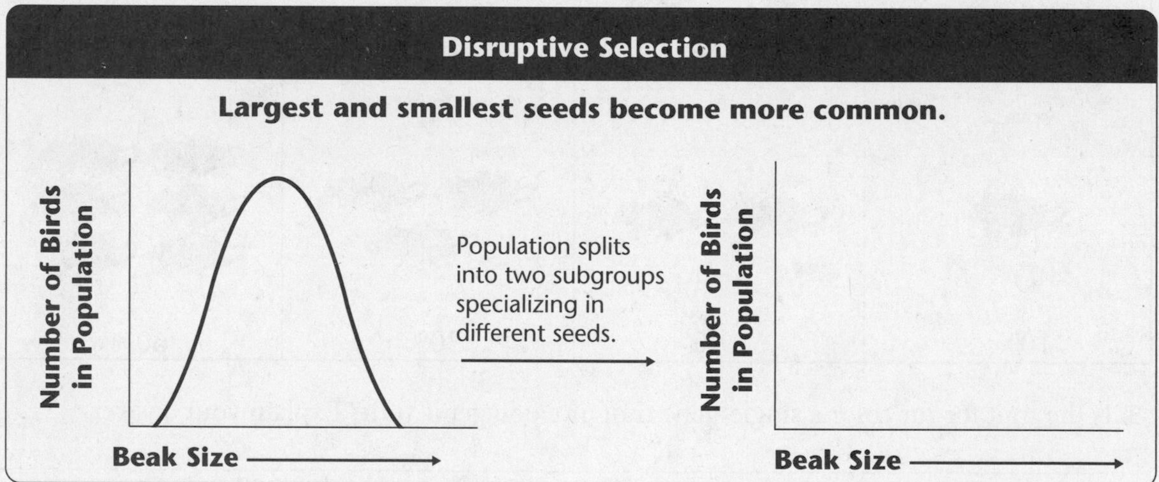


## Genetic Drift

*For Questions 11–13, complete each statement by writing the correct word or words.*

11. In small populations, random changes in ______________ is called genetic drift.

12. A situation in which allele frequencies change as a result of the migration of a small subgroup of a population is known as the ______________________.

13. The ______________________ is a change in allele frequency following a dramatic reduction in the size of a population.

 

**14.** Complete the concept map.

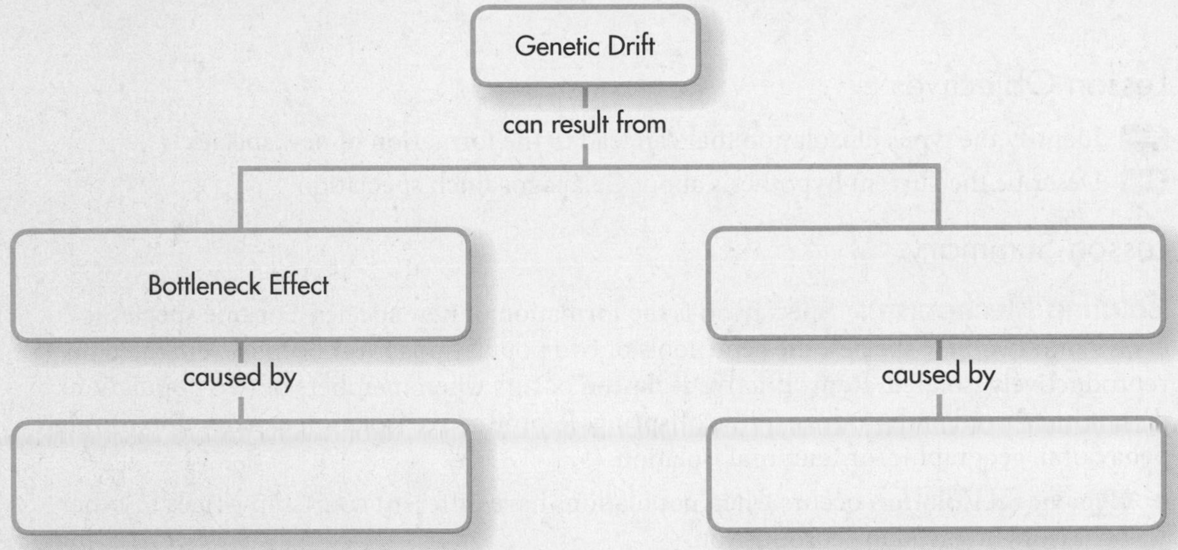


## Evolution Versus Genetic Equilibrium

**15.** What does the Hardy-Weinberg principle state? ______________________

**16.** What is genetic equilibrium? ______________________

**17.** List the five conditions that can disturb genetic equilibrium and cause evolution to occur.

______________________

**18.** Explain how sexual selection results in non-random mating.

______________________

### Apply the Big idea

**19.** Suppose a population of insects live in a sandy habitat. Some of the insects have tan bodies and some have green bodies. Over time, the habitat changes to a grass-filled meadow. Use the ideas of natural selection to explain how and why the insect population might change.

______________________

Name ________________________ Class ______ Date ________

# 17.3 The Process of Speciation

## Lesson Objectives

- Identify the types of isolation that can lead to the formation of new species.
- Describe the current hypothesis about Galápagos finch speciation.

## Lesson Summary

**Isolating Mechanisms** **Speciation** is the formation of new species. For one species to evolve into two new species, the gene pools of two populations must become separated, or reproductively isolated. **Reproductive isolation** occurs when members of two populations do not interbreed and produce fertile offspring. Reproductive isolation can develop through behavioral, geographic, or temporal isolation.

- **Behavioral isolation** occurs when populations have different courtship rituals or other behaviors involved in reproduction.
- **Geographic isolation** occurs when populations are separated by geographic barriers, such as mountains or rivers.
- **Temporal isolation** occurs when populations reproduce at different times.

**Speciation in Darwin's Finches** Peter and Rosemary Grant's work supports the hypothesis that speciation in the Galápagos finches was, and still continues to be, a result of the founder effect and natural selection.

- Speciation in Galápagos finches may have occurred in a sequence of events that involved the founding of a new population, geographic isolation, changes in the gene pool, behavioral isolation, and ecological competition.
- For example, a few finches may have flown from mainland South America to one of the islands. There, they survived and reproduced. Some birds may have crossed to a second island, and the two populations became geographically isolated. Seed sizes on the second island could have favored birds with larger beaks, so the population on the second island evolved into a population with larger beaks. Eventually, these large-beaked birds became reproductively isolated and evolved into a new species.

## Isolating Mechanisms

**1.** What is speciation?

________________________________________

**2.** What does it mean for two species to be reproductively isolated from each other?

________________________________________

________________________________________

**3.** What must happen in order for a new species to evolve?

________________________________________

________________________________________

4. List three ways that reproductive isolation occurs.

_______________________________________________

_______________________________________________

5. When does behavioral isolation occur?

_______________________________________________

_______________________________________________

_______________________________________________

6. When does geographic isolation occur?

_______________________________________________

_______________________________________________

_______________________________________________

7. What is an example of temporal isolation?

_______________________________________________

_______________________________________________

_______________________________________________

8. Suppose a seamount forms from an underwater volcano. Birds on the mainland colonize the island. How might this lead to speciation?

_______________________________________________

_______________________________________________

_______________________________________________

_______________________________________________

_______________________________________________

_______________________________________________

## Speciation in Darwin's Finches

*For Questions 9–13, complete each statement by writing the correct word or words.*

9. Peter and Rosemary Grant spent years on the Galápagos Islands studying changes in ______________ populations.

10. Many finch characteristics appear in bell-shaped distributions typical of ______________ traits.

11. The ancestors of the Galápagos Island finches originally came from the continent of ______________________.

12. The populations of finches on separate islands are ______________________ isolated from one another by large stretches of open water.

13. Big-beaked finches that prefer to mate with other big-beaked finches are ______________ isolated from small-beaked finches living on the same island.

 

**14.** Write a paragraph that summarizes how speciation likely occurred in the Galápagos finches. Use the following terms in your response: *geographic isolation, gene pools, behavioral isolation,* and *competition.*

## Apply the Big idea

**15.** Explain why reproductive isolation must occur for separate populations of the same species to evolve into different species.

Name ______________________________ Class ______ Date ________

# 17.4 Molecular Evolution

## Lesson Objectives

- Explain how molecular clocks are used.
- Explain how new genes evolve.
- Describe how Hox genes may be involved in evolutionary change.

## Lesson Summary

**Timing Lineage Splits: Molecular Clocks** A **molecular clock** uses mutation rates in DNA to estimate the length of time that two species have been evolving independently.

- Molecular clock models assume that neutral mutations, which do not affect phenotype, accumulate in the DNA of different species at about the same rate.
- Two species evolving independently from each other will accumulate different neutral mutations through time. The more differences between the DNA, the more time has passed since the two species shared an ancestor.

**Gene Duplication** New genes evolve through the duplication, and then modification, of existing genes.

- Organisms may carry multiple copies of the same gene. The extra copies of a gene may undergo mutations.
- The mutated gene may have a new function that is different from the original gene. In this way, new genes evolve.
- Multiple copies of a duplicated gene can turn into a gene family.

**Developmental Genes and Body Plans** Researchers study the relationship between evolution and embryological development.

- Some genes, called Hox genes, control the forms of animals' bodies.
- Small changes in Hox genes during embryological development can produce major changes in adult organisms.
- Some scientists think that changes in Hox genes may contribute to major evolutionary changes.

## Timing Lineage Splits: Molecular Clocks

**1.** What is a molecular clock?

______________________________________________________________

______________________________________________________________

**2.** Why are only neutral mutations useful for molecular clocks?

______________________________________________________________

______________________________________________________________

**3.** Why are there many molecular clocks in a genome instead of just one?

______________________________________________

______________________________________________

*Use the diagram of an ancestral species to answer Questions 4–5. Each picture in the diagram represents a gene. Each shaded portion of a gene represents a mutation.*

**4.** Which species is most closely related to Species B? Explain your answer.

______________________________________________

______________________________________________

______________________________________________

______________________________________________

______________________________________________

______________________________________________

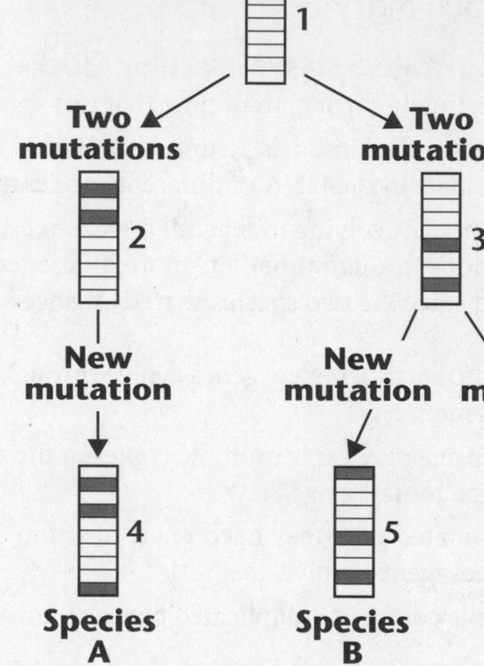


**5.** How can you tell that Species C is probably not a descendant of the organism with Gene 2?

______________________________________________

______________________________________________

______________________________________________

______________________________________________

______________________________________________

______________________________________________

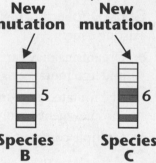

## Gene Duplication

*For Questions 6–7, write the letter of the correct answer on the line at the left.*

_____ **6.** Multiple copies of a duplicated gene can turn into a group of related genes called

- **A.** globins.
- **B.** duplicates.
- **C.** a Hox gene.
- **D.** a gene family.

_____ **7.** A chromosome may get several copies of the same gene during the process of

- **A.** crossing-over.
- **B.** gene mutation.
- **C.** gene expression.
- **D.** artificial selection.

**8.** Complete the flowchart to show how a new gene can evolve from a duplicated gene.

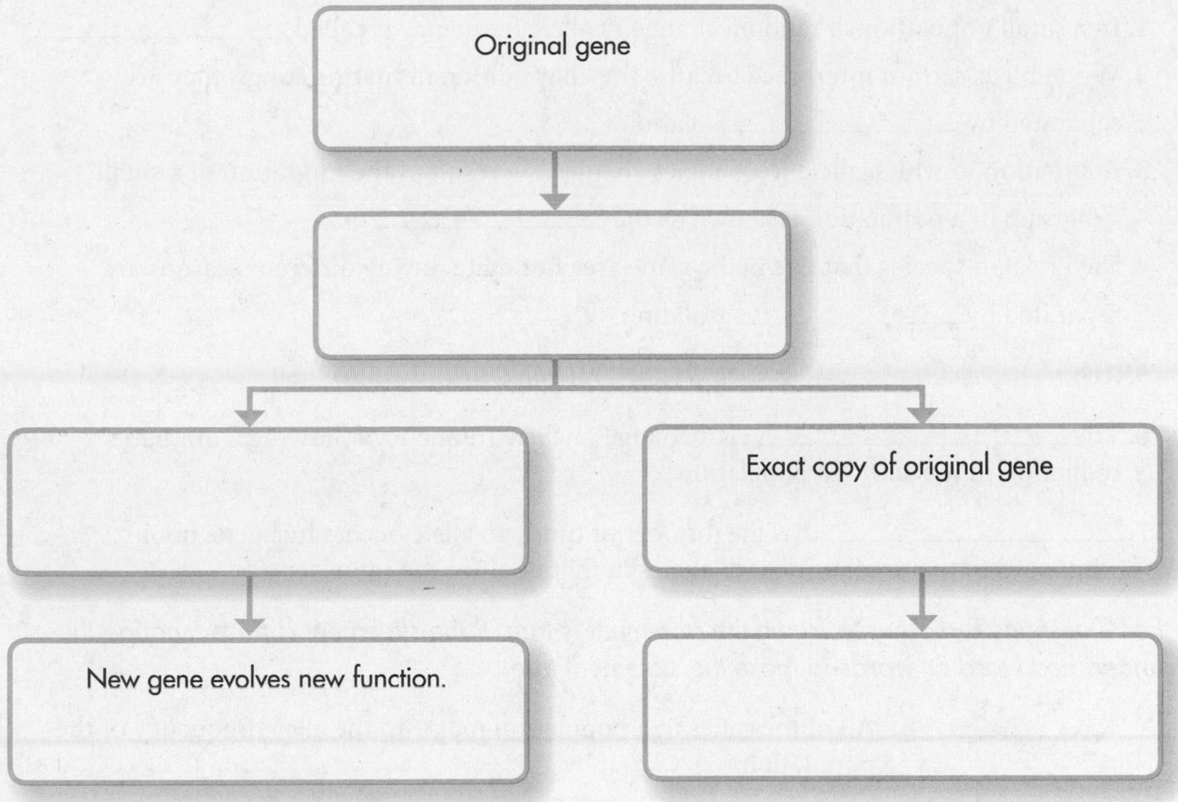


## Developmental Genes and Body Plans

**9.** What genetic factors might be responsible for a change in an organism's body plan?

______________________________________________

______________________________________________

______________________________________________

Apply the **Big** idea

**10.** How can Hox genes help reveal how evolution occurred?

______________________________________________

______________________________________________

______________________________________________

______________________________________________

______________________________________________

______________________________________________

Name ______________________ Class ______ Date ________

# Chapter Vocabulary Review

*For Questions 1–8, complete each statement by writing the correct word or words.*

1. In a small population, a random change in allele frequency is called ______________.
2. When birds cannot interbreed because they have different mating songs, they are separated by ______________ isolation.
3. A situation in which allele frequencies change as a result of the migration of a small subgroup of a population is known as the ______________.
4. Two related species that live in the same area but mate during different seasons are separated by ______________ isolation.
5. A(n) ______________ is a trait controlled by only one gene.
6. The ______________ is a change in allele frequency following a dramatic reduction in the size of a population.
7. ______________ is the number of times an allele occurs in a gene pool, compared to the total number of alleles in that pool for the same gene.

*For Questions 8–16, write True if the statement is true. If the statement is false, change the underlined word or words to make the statement true.*

______________ **8.** All of the genes in a population make up the <u>allele frequency</u> of the population.

______________ **9.** Traits controlled by two or more genes are <u>polygenic traits</u>.

______________ **10.** <u>Reproductive isolation</u> occurs when members of two populations do not interbreed and produce fertile offspring.

______________ **11.** The separation of two populations by barriers such as rivers or mountains results in <u>temporal</u> isolation.

______________ **12.** The <u>Hardy-Weinberg</u> principle states that allele frequencies in a population should remain constant unless one or more factors cause those frequencies to change.

______________ **13.** <u>Genetic drift</u> is the formation of new species.

______________ **14.** <u>The founder effect</u> occurs when the allele frequencies in a population remain constant.

______________ **15.** For polygenic traits, when individuals near the center of the bell curve have higher fitness than individuals at either end, <u>disruptive</u> selection takes place.

______________ **16.** When researchers use a <u>molecular clock</u>, they compare stretches of DNA to mark the passage of evolutionary time.

 

# CHAPTER MYSTERY

## EPIDEMIC

The Chapter Mystery focused on the emergence of the deadly strain of influenza that led to the cataclysmic flu epidemic of 1918. Today, teams of scientists, doctors, and other health specialists are working hard to prevent contagious diseases from spreading out of control.

21st Century Learning

# Preventing the Next Epidemic

The Global Outbreak Alert and Response Network, called "GOARN," is a vital and little-known group that serves as an international early warning system to prevent and contain disease outbreaks. It is based at the World Health Organization headquarters in Geneva, Switzerland. The World Health Organization is part of the United Nations system.

Read the following case study to learn more about GOARN's work fighting a disease outbreak known as SARS.

## How GOARN Helped Prevent a SARS Epidemic

In late 2002, an outbreak of an unusual and deadly type of pneumonia occurred in southern China. After additional cases appeared early in 2003 in Vietnam and Hong Kong, doctors named the mysterious ailment "severe acute respiratory syndrome," or SARS. It appeared to be spreading fast and no drug seemed effective against it. SARS killed many of the people it infected. Within months, cases of SARS had begun to occur in more than a dozen countries around the world.

From the start, the Global Outbreak Alert and Response Network (GOARN) quickly swung into action. GOARN staff mobilized partners in many countries to support scores of professionals in the field working to fight SARS. They lent support for tracking the disease and controlling its spread. While GOARN staff worked to coordinate quarantine efforts and take blood samples from infected patients, they also mobilized scientists in GOARN's network of laboratories. These laboratories, located in nine different countries, studied the blood samples to try to identify the underlying cause for SARS.

GOARN set up a secure Web site so that its worldwide network of researchers could keep in contact as they worked around the clock. The communications system was so well designed that scientists could display patient samples and electron microscope images in real time to colleagues continents away. Details of each lab's analysis and testing of samples were immediately posted online so researchers elsewhere could instantly act upon relevant information. Scientists at all these laboratories participated in daily teleconferences to discuss progress and obstacles. With the extraordinary global collaboration, scientists in GOARN's global network were able to identify the previously unknown mutant virus responsible for SARS *in less than two weeks.*

GOARN's network of scientists succeeded in identifying the culprit and containing the spread of SARS in record time. But researchers say that a virulent strain of flu could spread even faster than SARS. So, night and day, the GOARN staff remains on alert, carefully monitoring outbreaks of disease wherever they occur around the world.

Continued on next page ▶

 

Name ______________________ Class ______ Date ________

## 21st Century Themes Science and Global Awareness

**1.** What steps did GOARN take to fight SARS in the field?

______________________________________________

______________________________________________

______________________________________________

**2.** What steps did GOARN take to identify the underlying cause of SARS?

______________________________________________

______________________________________________

______________________________________________

**3.** Was the worldwide collaboration between the laboratories successful in identifying the virus responsible for SARS? If so, what were the key factors that led to its success?

______________________________________________

______________________________________________

______________________________________________

**4.** How do you think GOARN could improve their response time to an emerging disease?

______________________________________________

______________________________________________

______________________________________________

**5.** Today, emerging viruses can spread faster than ever before. What factors do you think contribute to this fast pace of transmission?

______________________________________________

______________________________________________

______________________________________________

______________________________________________

## 21st Century Skills Media Review

The skills used in this activity include **information and media literacy, critical thinking and systems thinking,** and **self-direction.**

A number of books and movies are based on the potential for, or the occurrence of, a disease outbreak. Two examples are Richard Preston's 1995 nonfiction thriller *The Hot Zone: A Terrifying True Story* and the 1995 Hollywood feature film "Outbreak." At the library or other local resource, find a book or a movie that dramatizes the threat of a disease epidemic. Also, find out more about how GOARN helps to fight epidemics. You may want to start by visiting the World Health Organization's Web site.

*After getting permission from your teacher, write a review discussing the work and how its treatment of the subject compares with what you have learned about GOARN's real-life monitoring and prevention activities.*

# 18 Classification

**Big idea** **Unity and Diversity of Life**

**Q:** What is the goal of biologists who classify living things?

| | WHAT I KNOW | WHAT I LEARNED |
|---|---|---|
| **18.1** Why do scientists classify organisms? | | |
| **18.2** How do evolutionary relationships affect the way scientists classify organisms? | | |
| **18.3** What are the major groups within which all organisms are currently classified? | | |

# 18.1 Finding Order in Diversity

## Lesson Objectives

- Describe the goals of binomial nomenclature and systematics.
- Identify the taxa in the classification system devised by Linnaeus.

## Lesson Summary

**Assigning Scientific Names** To study Earth's great diversity of organisms, biologists must give each organism a name. Biologists also must organize living things into groups in a logical way. Therefore, biologists need a classification system. The science of naming and grouping organisms is called **systematics**.

In the 1730s, Carolus Linnaeus developed a naming system, called **binomial nomenclature**. In binomial nomenclature, each species is assigned a two-part scientific name:

- The first part of the name refers to the **genus**, or a group of similar species.
- The second part of the name is unique to each species.

**Linnaean Classification System** Linnaeus's system of classification has seven different levels. From smallest to largest, the levels are species, genus, family, order, class, phylum, and kingdom. Each of the ranking levels is called a **taxon**.

- Just as a genus is a group of similar species, a **family** is a group of similar genera.
- An **order** is a group of similar families.
- A **class** is a group of similar orders.
- A **phylum** is a group of similar classes.
- A **kingdom** is a group of similar phyla.

# Assigning Scientific Names

**1.** Complete the graphic organizer.

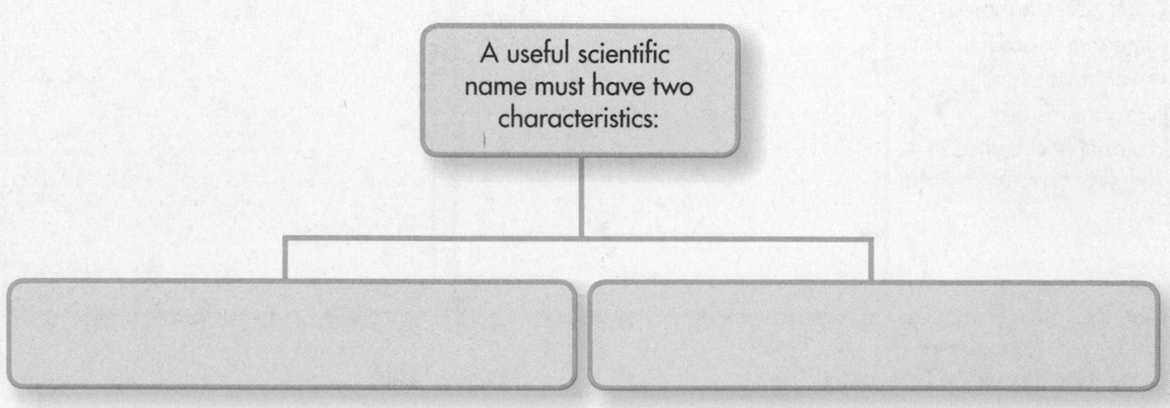

*For Questions 2–3, write the letter of the correct answer on the line at the left.*

______ **2.** What is the science of naming and grouping organisms called?

- **A.** genetics
- **B.** speciation
- **C.** systematics
- **D.** linnaeanology

______ **3.** Modern systematists try to group organisms based on

- **A.** size.
- **B.** evolutionary relationships.
- **C.** ecological niche.
- **D.** physical appearance.

**4.** Why is it confusing to refer to organisms by common names?

______________________________

______________________________

______________________________

**5.** What is binomial nomenclature?

______________________________

______________________________

**6.** What genus does the grizzly bear, *Ursus arctos*, belong to?

______________________________

**7.** What is the correct way to write scientific names in the binomial nomenclature system?

______________________________

______________________________

## Linnaean Classification System

*For Questions 8–10, complete each statement by writing the correct word or words.*

**8.** The goal of systematics is to organize living things into groups, called ______________, that have biological meaning.

**9.** The largest taxonomic category in the Linnaean system of classification is the ______________, while the smallest is the ______________.

**10.** Similar classes are grouped into a(n) ______________, and similar orders are grouped into a(n) ______________.

 

Name ______________________ Class ______ Date ______

11. **THINK VISUALLY** Fill in the name of each missing taxonomic category in the chart below.

**KINGDOM**
**Animalia**

______

**Chordata**

______

**Mammalia**

______

**Carnivora**

______

**Ursidae**

______

***Ursus***

**SPECIES**
***Ursus arctos***

## Apply the Big idea

12. How does Linnaeus's system of classification help establish the unity of life?

______________________________________________

______________________________________________

______________________________________________

______________________________________________

______________________________________________

______________________________________________

______________________________________________

# 18.2 Modern Evolutionary Classification

## Lesson Objectives

- Explain the difference between evolutionary classification and Linnaean classification.
- Describe how to make and interpret a cladogram.
- Explain the use of DNA sequences in classification.

## Lesson Summary

**Evolutionary Classification** The study of evolutionary relationships among organisms is called **phylogeny**. Classification based on evolutionary relationships is called phylogenetic systematics, or evolutionary classification.

- Evolutionary classification places organisms into higher taxa whose members are more closely related to one another than they are to members of any other group. The larger the taxon, the further back in time all of its members shared a common ancestor.
- In this system, organisms are placed into groups called clades. A **clade** is a group of species that includes a single common ancestor and all descendants of that ancestor. A clade must be a monophyletic group. A **monophyletic group** must include all species that are descended from a common ancestor, and cannot include any species that are not descended from that common ancestor.

**Cladograms** A **cladogram** is a diagram that shows how species and higher taxa are related to each other. A cladogram shows how evolutionary lines, or lineages, branched off from common ancestors.

- In a cladogram, the place where the ancestral lineage splits is called a fork, or a node. Nodes represent the point where new lineages last shared a common ancestor.
- The bottom of the diagram, or the root, represents the ancestor shared by all of the organisms on the cladogram.
- Cladistic analysis relies on specific shared traits, or characters. A **derived character** is a trait that arose in the most recent common ancestor of a particular lineage and was passed to all of its descendants.

**DNA in Classification** All organisms have DNA. Because DNA is so similar across all forms of life, this molecule can be compared in different species. In general, the more derived genetic characters two species share, the more recently the species shared a common ancestor and the more closely related they are.

# Evolutionary Classification

1. How did Darwin's theory of evolution change the way biologists thought about classification categories?

_______________________________________________

_______________________________________________

2. Describe the goal of phylogenetic systematics (evolutionary classification).

______________________________________________

______________________________________________

3. Which group of organisms would have the most recent common ancestor: the members of a clade corresponding to a genus or the members of a clade corresponding to an order? Explain your answer.

______________________________________________

______________________________________________

______________________________________________

______________________________________________

4. Use the Venn diagram to compare and contrast the definitions of the Linnaean class Reptilia and the clade Reptilia.

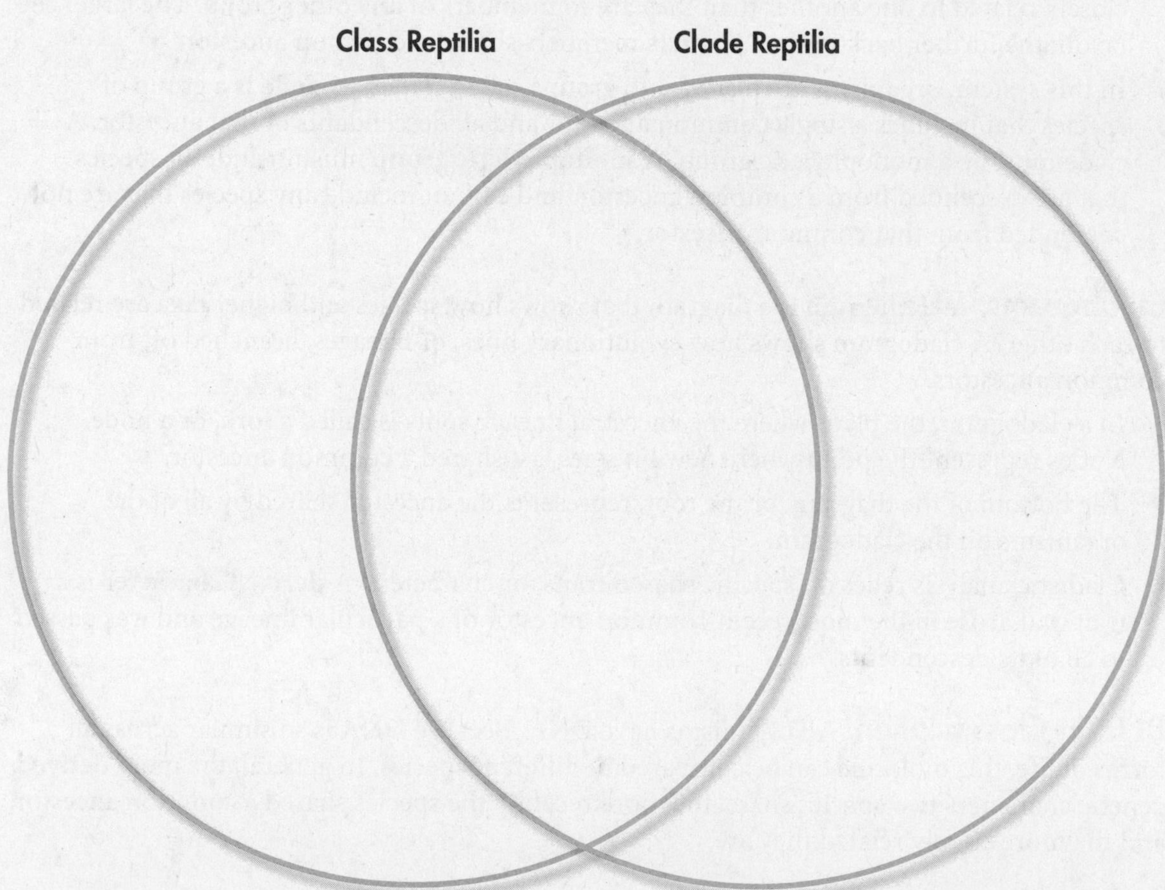


*For Questions 5–7, complete each statement by writing the correct word or words.*

5. All species descended from a(n) ________________ are part of a monophyletic group.

6. ________________ is the study of how living and extinct organisms are related to one another.

7. A clade includes a common ancestor and all its descendants, living or ________________.

 

# Cladograms

*For Questions 8–10, complete each statement by writing the correct word or words.*

**8.** A diagram that shows the evolutionary relationships among a group of organisms is called a(n) ______________.

**9.** The place where the ancestral lineage splits on a cladogram is called a fork, or a(n) ______________.

**10.** Characteristics shared by members of a clade and only by members of that clade are called ______________.

**11.** THINK VISUALLY Examine the cladogram below:

- Shade in the two organisms that belong to a clade that does not include the third organism. Cross hatch the organism that does not belong to the clade.
- Circle the point on the cladogram that shows the most recent common ancestor of the crab and the barnacle.
- Mark an X on the point on the cladogram that shows the most recent common ancestor of mollusks and crustaceans.
- Underline the characteristic that all three organisms have in common.

# DNA in Classification

**12.** Why can genes be considered derived characters?

_______________________________________________

_______________________________________________

_______________________________________________

*Use the figure below to answer Questions 13–15.*

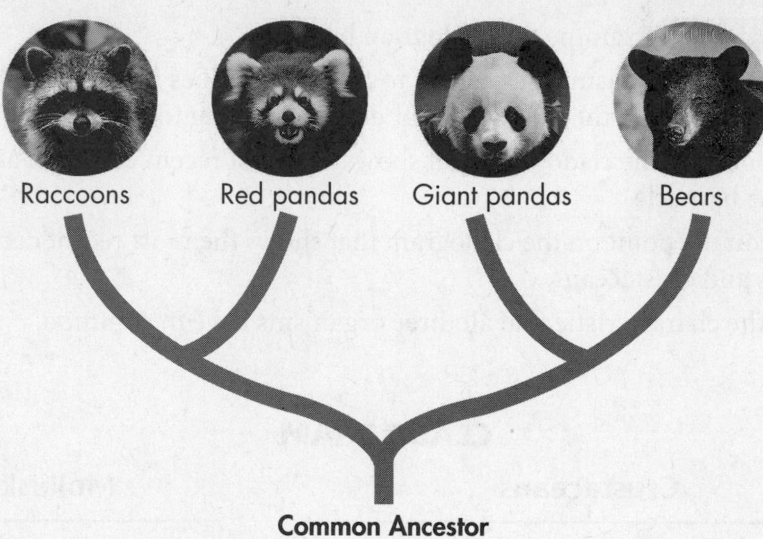


**13.** According to the figure, which species is most closely related to red pandas?

_______________________________________________

**14.** Although giant pandas and raccoons share some distinct anatomical similarities, they are in different clades. What type of evidence do you think was used to construct this diagram?

_______________________________________________

**15.** Biologists had previously classified giant pandas together with raccoons and red pandas. What did DNA analysis reveal about giant pandas and bears?

_______________________________________________

_______________________________________________

## Apply the Big idea

**16.** Both humans and yeasts have a gene that codes for a myosin protein. What does this indicate about their ancestry?

_______________________________________________

_______________________________________________

_______________________________________________

# 18.3 Building the Tree of Life

## Lesson Objectives

- Name the six kingdoms of life as they are currently identified.
- Explain what the tree of life represents.

## Lesson Summary

**Changing Ideas About Kingdoms** As biologists learned more about the natural world, they realized that Linnaeus's two kingdoms, Animalia and Plantae, did not represent all life.

- Researchers found that microorganisms were very different from plants and animals. They were placed in their own kingdom, called Protista.
- Then, yeast, molds, and mushrooms were separated from plants and placed in their own kingdom, called Fungi.
- Because bacteria lack nuclei, mitochondria, and chloroplasts, they were separated from Protista and placed in another new kingdom, called Monera.
- In the 1990s, kingdom Monera was divided into two kingdoms: Eubacteria and Archaebacteria. The six-kingdom system of classification includes the kingdoms Eubacteria, Archaebacteria, Protista, Fungi, Plantae, and Animalia.
- Genetic analysis revealed that two prokaryotic groups are even more different from each other, and from Eukaryotes, than previously thought. This discovery lead to the creation of a new taxon, called the domain. The **domain** is a larger, more inclusive category than a kingdom. The three domain system consists of: Bacteria, Archaea, and Eukarya.
- Domain Bacteria corresponds to the kingdom Eubacteria. Domain Archaea corresponds to the kingdom Archaebacteria. Domain Eukarya corresponds tokingdoms Fungi, Plantae, Animalia, and "Protista."
- Quotations are used for the old kingdom Protista to signify that it is not a valid clade.

**The Tree of All Life** The tree of life shows current hypotheses regarding evolutionary relationships among taxa within the three domains of life.

- The domain **Bacteria** includes unicellular organisms without a nucleus. They have cell walls containing a substance called peptidoglycan.
- The domain **Archaea** also includes unicellular organisms without a nucleus. These organisms have cell walls that do not contain peptidoglycan.
- The domain **Eukarya** includes the four remaining kingdoms: "Protista," Fungi, Plantae, and Animalia. All members of the domain Eukarya have cells with a nucleus.
  - Most members of the kingdom "Protista," are unicellular organisms. Some Protista are photosynthetic; others are heterotrophs.
  - Most members of the kingdom Fungi are multicellular, and all members of this kingdom are heterotrophs with cell walls containing chitin.
  - All members of the kingdom Plantae are multicellular and photosynthetic. Most plants cannot move about, and their cells have cell walls.
  - All members of the kingdom Animalia are multicellular heterotrophs. Most animals can move about, and their cells lack cell walls.

Name ______________________ Class ______ Date ______

# Changing Ideas About Kingdoms

**1.** What fundamental traits did Linnaeus use to separate plants from animals?

**2.** What types of organisms were first placed in the kingdom Protista?

**3.** What types of organisms were placed into the kingdom Fungi?

**4.** Why did scientists place bacteria in their own kingdom, the Monera?

**5.** What two kingdoms was kingdom Monera separated into?

**6.** Complete the concept map.

The Six-Kingdom System

includes

Animalia

**7.** What is a domain?

**8.** What did genomic analysis reveal about the two prokaryotic groups?

Name ______________________ Class ______ Date ______

# The Tree of All Life

**9.** Complete the chart below.

| Classification of Living Things | | |
|---|---|---|
| **Domain** | **Kingdom** | **Examples** |
| | Eubacteria | *Salmonella typhimurium* |
| Archaea | | *Sulfolobus archaea* |
| | "Protista" | |
| | | mushrooms, yeasts |
| | Plantae | |
| | | Sponges, worms, insects, fishes, mammals |

*Match the kingdom with the description that applies to members of that kingdom.*

**Kingdom**

_____ **10.** "Protista"

_____ **11.** Fungi

_____ **12.** Plantac

_____ **13.** Animalia

**Description**

**A.** They feed on dead or decaying organic matter.

**B.** They have no cell walls and they move about.

**C.** They are a "catchall" group of eukaryotes.

**D.** They include mosses and ferns.

## Apply the Big idea

**14.** What characteristics led camels to be classified in the same domain, kingdom, phylum, and class as dogs?

_______________________________________________

_______________________________________________

_______________________________________________

_______________________________________________

_______________________________________________

_______________________________________________

 

# Chapter Vocabulary Review

*Match the term with its definition.*

| Term | Definition |
|---|---|
| ______ **1.** phylogeny | **A.** The domain containing all organisms that have a nucleus |
| ______ **2.** Bacteria | **B.** The domain containing organisms that are prokaryotic and unicellular |
| ______ **3.** order | **C.** A group of classes |
| ______ **4.** phylum | **D.** A group of orders |
| ______ **5.** clade | **E.** A group of families |
| ______ **6.** class | **F.** A group of species that includes a single common ancestor and all descendents of that ancestor |
| ______ **7.** Eukarya | **G.** A larger, more inclusive category than a kingdom |
| ______ **8.** domain | **H.** The study of how living and extinct organisms are related to one another |

*For Questions 9–18, complete each statement by writing the correct word or words.*

**9.** Members of the domain ________________ live in some of the most extreme environments on Earth.

**10.** A(n) ________________ is a trait that arose in the most recent common ancestor of a particular lineage, and was passed along to its descendants.

**11.** Multicellular organisms that move about are placed in the ________________ Animalia.

**12.** Under Linnaeus' classification system, similar genera were placed into a larger category called a(n) ________________.

**13.** Families, Orders, Classes, and Phyla are all ________________.

**14.** The science of naming and grouping organisms is called ________________.

**15.** A(n) ________________ shows relative degrees of relatedness among lineages.

**16.** The name *Ursus arctos* is an example of the two-part scientific name given in the ________________________ system.

**17.** A(n) ________________ is a group of similar species.

**18.** A clade is made up of a(n) ________________.

# CHAPTER MYSTERY

## GRIN AND BEAR IT

As you learned from solving the mystery, the question of what defines a species is sometimes hard to answer. The distinction is not just important to scientists. It can also have legal ramifications.

21st Century Learning

## Legal Protection for a Threatened Species

WASHINGTON, D.C.—On May 14, 2008, the Secretary of the Interior Dirk Kempthorne announced that he would accept the recommendation of U.S. Fish and Wildlife Service to list the polar bear as a threatened species under the Endangered Species Act (ESA). Section 3 of the 1973 Endangered Species Act defines an endangered species as any species "which is in danger of extinction throughout all or a significant portion of its range." The opening paragraph of the rule is shown below.

> **AGENCY:** Fish and Wildlife Service, Interior
>
> **ACTION:** Final rule
>
> **SUMMARY:** We, the U.S. Fish and Wildlife Service (Service), determine threatened status for the polar bear *(Ursus maritimus)* under the Endangered Species Act of 1973, as amended (Act) (16 U.S.C. 1531 et seq.). Polar bears evolved to utilize the Arctic sea ice niche and are distributed throughout most ice-covered seas of the Northern Hemisphere.
>
> We find, based upon the best available scientific and commercial information, that polar bear habitat—principally sea ice—is declining throughout the species' range, that this decline is expected to continue for the foreseeable future, and that this loss threatens the species throughout all of its range. Therefore, we find that the polar bear is likely to become an endangered species within the foreseeable future throughout all of its range.

Continued on next page ▶

 

Name ______________________ Class ______ Date ________

## 21st Century Themes Science and Civic Literacy

**1.** Who wrote the document and who ruled on its findings?

**2.** How does the U.S. Government define an endangered species?

**3.** In making its ruling, the U.S. Government considered not only scientific information but also commercial information. What do you think this means?

**4.** What is the reason for listing the polar as a threatened species?

**5.** The Government lists the polar bear as a threatened species, not an endangered one. What is the threat facing a species that is listed as threatened?

## 21st Century Skills Update: Status of Polar Bears

The skills used in this activity include **information and media literacy, communication skills,** and **critical thinking and systems thinking.**

Working with a small group, report back to the class on what has happened to the status of the polar bear since the U.S. Government made its initial ruling in May 2008. Find out if the status of the polar bear has changed and comment on whether the Government was right to make the ruling when it did.

*Present your findings to the class using a digital slide show.*

 

Name ______________________ Class ______ Date ______

# 19 History of Life

**Big idea** **Evolution**

**Q:** How do fossils help biologists understand the history of life on Earth?

| | WHAT I KNOW | WHAT I LEARNED |
|---|---|---|
| **19.1** How do scientists use fossils to study Earth's history? | | |
| **19.2** What are some patterns in which evolution has occurred? | | |
| **19.3** What happened during Earth's early history? | | |

 

Name _______________ Class _____ Date _______

# 19.1 The Fossil Record

## Lesson Objectives

- Explain what information fossils can reveal about ancient life.
- Differentiate between relative dating and radiometric dating.
- Identify the divisions of the geologic time scale.
- Describe how environmental processes and living things have shaped life on Earth.

## Lesson Summary

**Fossils and Ancient Life** Fossils are preserved remains or traces of ancient life.

- Fossils are the most important source of information about extinct species. An **extinct** species is one that has died out.
- Most fossils are preserved in sedimentary rock. Sediments build up over time, and bury the remains and traces of dead organisms.
- Scientists who study fossils are called **paleontologists**.

**Dating Earth's History** Relative dating and radiometric dating are used to determine the age of fossils.

- **Relative dating** establishes the relative age of fossils. Fossils from deeper rock layers are assumed to be older than fossils from rock layers closer to the surface. **Index fossils** represent species that lived for a short period of time but over a wide geographic range. Index fossils can help determine the relative ages of rock layers and their fossils.
- **Radiometric dating** determines a fossil's approximate age in years by finding the proportion of radioactive to nonreactive isotopes in a sample. Radioactive isotopes in fossils and rock layers decay, or break down, at a steady rate, called a half-life. A **half-life** is the length of time needed for half of the radioactive atoms in a sample to decay. A fossil's age is calculated from the half-life and the amount of remaining radioactive atoms the fossil contains.

**Geologic Time Scale** The **geologic time scale** is a time line of Earth's history based on relative and absolute dating.

- The scale begins with the Precambrian.
- Geologic time is divided into four eons: the Hadean, Archean, Proterozoic, and Phanerozoic. The Phanerozoic eon is divided into three **eras**: the Paleozoic, Mesozoic, and Cenozoic.
- Each era is further divided into smaller lengths of time, called **periods**.

**Life on a Changing Planet** Climactic, geological, astronomical, and biological processes have affected the history of life on Earth.

- Earth's climate has changed often in the course of its history. Small temperature shifts can bring about heat waves and ice ages which have great effects on living things. **Plate tectonics** is a theory that Earth's outermost layer is divided into plates that move. The movement, called continental drift, has transformed life on Earth through the formation of mountain ranges, supercontinents, and other geologic features.
- The impact of objects from space has affected the global climate.

 

Name ______________________ Class ______ Date ________

# Fossils and Ancient Life

*For Questions 1–3, complete each statement by writing the correct word or words.*

**1.** Species that died out are said to be ______________.

**2.** Most fossils are found in layers of ______________ rock.

**3.** Scientists who study fossils are called ______________.

**4.** What is the fossil record?

______________________________________________

______________________________________________

**5.** What information does the fossil record provide?

______________________________________________

______________________________________________

______________________________________________

**6.** Fill in the flowchart to explain how fossils are formed.

| |
|---|
| |
| |
| The preserved fossil remains may later be discovered and studied. |

# Dating Earth's History

**7.** What is an index fossil? What do index fossils reveal about other material found with them?

______________________________________________

______________________________________________

______________________________________________

______________________________________________

**8.** Fossil A is found in a layer of rock above a layer containing Fossil B. Which fossil is probably older? Explain your answer. ______________________________

______________________________________________

**9.** List the two techniques paleontologists use to determine the age of fossils.

______________________________________________

 

**10.** What is a half-life? ____________________

____________________

**11.** How do scientists calculate the age of a sample using radiometric dating?

____________________

____________________

*For Questions 12–13, write the letter of the correct answer on the line at the left.*

_____ **12.** A species that is easily recognizable, existed for a relatively short period of time, and covered a wide geographic area may be used as a(n)

**A.** index fossil.
**B.** fossil record.
**C.** microfossil.
**D.** macrofossil.

_____ **13.** The same index fossil is found in rock layers A and B that are separated by several miles. What can you infer about the relationship between the rock layers?

**A.** Layer A is older than B.
**B.** The sediments in layer B were deposited before those in layer A.
**C.** Layers A and B are probably about the same age.
**D.** Layer B probably contains more radioactive isotopes than layer A.

## Geologic Time Scale

**14.** Fill in the missing eras and periods in the geologic time scale below.

| Time (millions of years ago) | Period | Era |
|---|---|---|
| 1.8–present | Quaternary | |
| 23–1.8 | | |
| 65.5–23 | Paleogene | |
| 146–65.5 | | |
| 200–146 | Jurassic | |
| 251–200 | | |
| 299–251 | Permian | Paleozoic |
| 359–299 | | |
| 416–359 | Devonian | |
| 444–416 | | |
| 488–444 | Ordovician | |
| 542–488 | | |
| 4600–542 | Precambrian Time | |

 

*For Questions 15–16, refer to the Visual Analogy of life as a clock.*

______ **15.** **VISUAL ANALOGY**
Which of the following appeared on Earth most recently?

**A.** chordates
**B.** tetrapods
**C.** dinosaurs
**D.** single-celled algae

______ **16.** Dinosaurs appeared before

**A.** mammals.
**B.** photosynthesis.
**C.** chordates.
**D.** land plants.

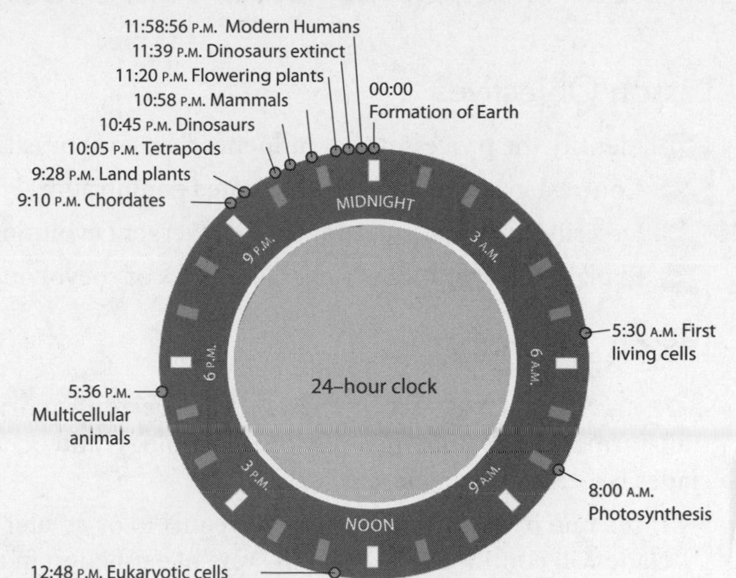


# Processes Affecting Life's History

**17.** How might an asteroid impact change Earth's climate?

______________________________________________________________

______________________________________________________________

______________________________________________________________

______________________________________________________________

**18.** Explain the theory of plate tectonics and tell how it has affected the distribution of fossils and organisms.

______________________________________________________________

______________________________________________________________

______________________________________________________________

______________________________________________________________

## Apply the Big idea

**19.** What are some aspects of a species' evolution that can't be studied using fossil evidence? Why don't fossils provide information about these characteristics?

______________________________________________________________

______________________________________________________________

______________________________________________________________

______________________________________________________________

______________________________________________________________

______________________________________________________________

 

Name ______________________ Class ______ Date ________

# 19.2 Patterns and Processes of Evolution

## Lesson Objectives

- Identify the processes that influenced survival or extinction of a species or clade.
- Contrast gradualism and punctuated equilibrium.
- Describe adaptive radiation and convergent evolution.
- Explain the evolutionary characteristics of coevolving organisms.

## Lesson Summary

**Speciation and Extinction** **Macroevolutionary patterns** are grand transformations in anatomy, phylogeny, ecology, and behavior that usually take place in clades larger than a single species.

- If the rate of speciation in a clade is equal to or greater than the rate of extinction, the clade will continue to exist. If the rate of extinction in a clade is greater than the rate of speciation, the entire clade will eventually become extinct.
- **Background extinction** is extinction caused by the slow process of natural selection. **Mass extinctions** affect huge numbers of species over a relatively short time.

**Rate of Evolution** Evidence shows that evolution has occurred at different rates for different organisms at different times.

- The idea that evolution occurs slowly and gradually is called **gradualism**.
- In **punctuated equilibrium**, long periods of little or no change are interrupted by short periods of rapid change.

**Adaptive Radiation and Convergent Evolution** **Adaptive radiation** is the process in which a single species evolves into diverse species that live in different ways. **Convergent evolution** is the process in which unrelated species come to look alike because they have evolved similar adaptations in response to similar environments.

**Coevolution** **Coevolution** is the process by which two species evolve in response to changes in each other over time. For example, plants evolved poisons that protected them from insects. In response, insects evolved ways of protecting themselves from the poisons.

# Speciation and Extinction

*For Questions 1–4, write True if the statement is true. If the statement is false, change the underlined word or words to make the statement true.*

______ **1.** Large-scale evolutionary changes that usually take place over long periods of time are referred to as <u>speciation</u>.

______ **2.** Many species disappear rapidly during a <u>background extinction</u>.

______ **3.** The <u>rate of speciation</u> in a clade must be equal to or greater than the rate of extinction in order for a clade to survive.

______ **4.** Immediately after a mass extinction, <u>biodiversity</u> is dramatically reduced.

**5.** What are possible causes of mass extinction?

______________________

______________________

**6.** What effects have mass extinctions had on the history of life?

______________________

______________________

## Rate of Evolution

**7.** Horseshoe crabs have changed little in structure from the time they first showed up in the fossil record. Which pattern of evolution do horseshoe crabs likely follow—gradualism or punctuated equilibirum? Explain your answer.

______________________

______________________

______________________

______________________

**8.** Why does rapid evolution occur more often in small populations?

______________________

______________________

**9.** Use the Venn diagram below to compare punctuated equilibrium with gradualism.

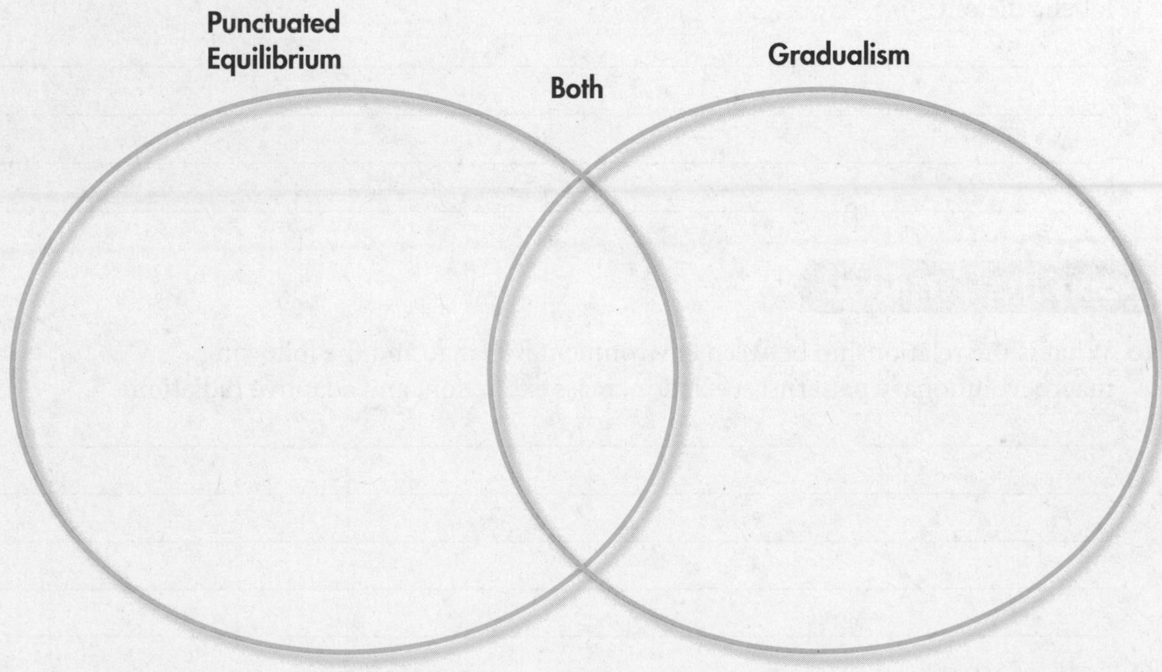

## Adaptive Radiation and Convergent Evolution

*Write the letter of the correct answer on the line at the left.*

______ **10.** The process in which a single species or a small group of species evolves into diverse forms that live in different ways is called

**A.** coevolution.
**B.** macroevolution.
**C.** adaptive radiation.
**D.** convergent evolution.

______ **11.** The process by which unrelated organisms come to resemble one another is

**A.** coevolution.
**B.** macroevolution.
**C.** adaptive radiation.
**D.** convergent evolution.

______ **12.** What contributed to the adaptive radiation of mammals?

**A.** the evolution of plants
**B.** the extinction of most dinosaurs
**C.** the decrease in ocean depth
**D.** continental drift

______ **13.** Which of the following is an example of convergent evolution?

**A.** bird's wing and fish's fin
**B.** human's arm and bird's wing
**C.** shark's fin and dolphin's limb
**D.** human's leg and dolphin's limb

## Coevolution

**14.** What is coevolution? ______________________________

______________________________

**15.** 'I'iwi birds have long, curved beaks that enable them to get nectar from tubular lobelia flowers. Explain how these two species might have coevolved. What might happen if the lobelia die out?

______________________________

______________________________

______________________________

______________________________

### Apply the Big idea

**16.** What is the relationship between environmental change and the following macroevolutionary patterns: speciation, mass extinction, and adaptive radiation?

______________________________

______________________________

______________________________

______________________________

______________________________

______________________________

______________________________

______________________________

 

Name ______________________ Class ______ Date ________

# 19.3 Earth's Early History

## Lesson Objectives

- Identify some of the hypotheses about early Earth and the origin of life.
- Explain the endosymbiotic theory.
- Explain the significance of sexual reproduction in evolution.

## Lesson Summary

**The Mysteries of Life's Origins** Earth's early atmosphere contained toxic gases. The atmosphere also contained little or no oxygen.

- In the 1950s, Stanley Miller and Harold Urey set out to determine if organic molecules could assemble under eartly Earth conditions. They filled a container with water and gases that they thought represented the composition of Earth's early atmosphere. They passed electric sparks through the mixture to simulate lightning. Soon, organic compounds formed. The experiment showed that molecules needed for life could have arisen from simpler compounds.
- Under some conditions, large organic molecules form tiny bubbles called proteinoid microspheres. Structures similar to proteinoid microspheres might have become the first living cells. RNA and DNA also could have evolved from simple organic molecules.
- The first known life forms evolved about 3.5 billion years ago. They were single celled and looked like modern bacteria. Eventually, photosynthetic bacteria became common. During photosynthesis, the bacteria produced oxygen. The oxygen accumulated in the atmosphere. The rise of oxygen drove some life forms to extinction. At the same time, other life forms evolved that depended on oxygen.

**Origin of Eukaryotic Cells** The first eukaryotes, or organisms with nuclei, evolved from prokaryotes that began to develop internal cell membranes. One explanation for how eukaryotes evolved is the **endosymbiotic theory**. This theory proposes that smaller prokaryotes began living inside larger cells and evolved a symbiotic relationship with the larger cells.

**Sexual Reproduction and Multicellularity** Sexual reproduction evolved after eukaryotic cells. Sexual reproduction increased genetic variation, so evolution could occur more quickly. Several hundred million years after sexual reproduction evolved, multicellular life evolved.

## The Mysteries of Life's Origins

**1.** What are protenoid microspheres?

______________________________________________

______________________________________________

**2.** Why do scientists think that RNA may have evolved before DNA?

______________________________________________

______________________________________________

*Use the diagram of the Miller-Urey experiment to answer Questions 3–5.*

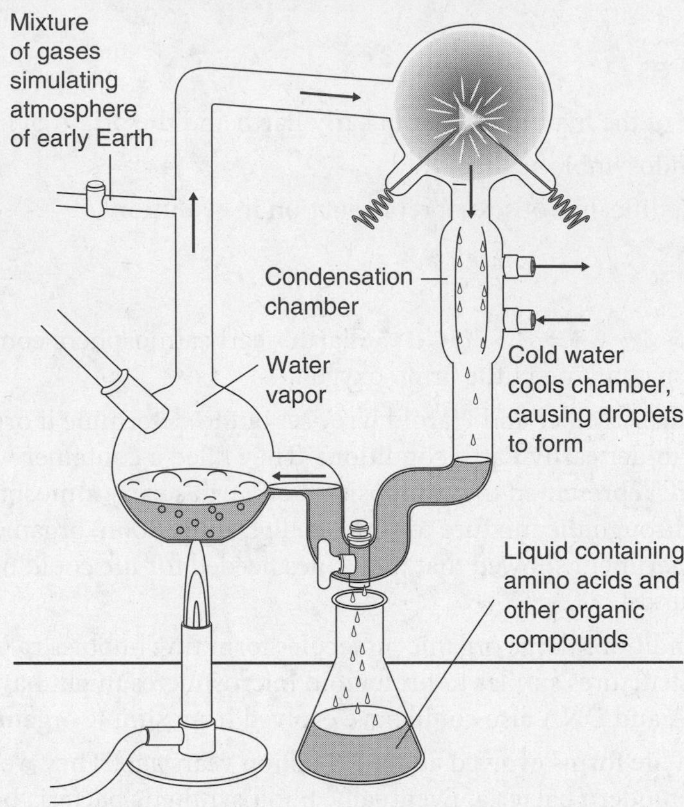


3. **THINK VISUALLY** Label the diagram to show which part of Miller and Urey's apparatus simulated lightning storms on early Earth.

4. What was the purpose of Miller and Urey's experiment? ______________________

5. Explain the results of the Miller-Urey experiment. What did these findings suggest?

______________________

## Origin of Eukaryotic Cells

6. Explain the endosymbiotic theory. ______________________

7. **THINK VISUALLY** Draw the step in the endosymbiotic theory that shows the origin of chloroplasts. Label the structures in your drawing.

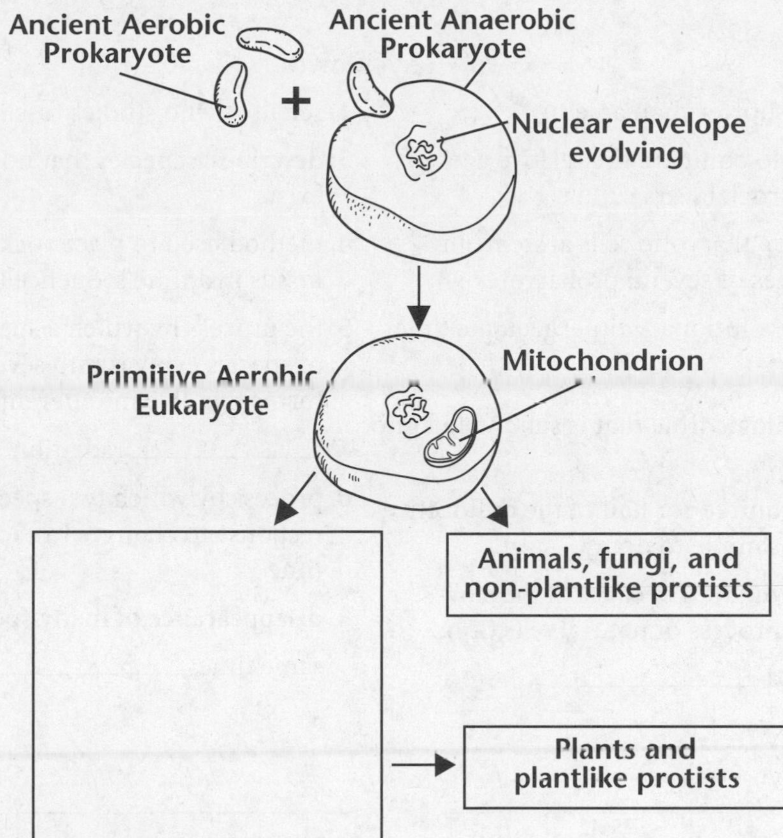


## Sexual Reproduction and Multicellularity

8. How did sexual reproduction speed up the evolutionary process?

9. What is the most likely cause of the great amount of diversity currently seen in multicellular life forms?

## Apply the Big idea

10. Once DNA evolved, what could have caused it to become the primary means of transmitting genetic information instead of RNA?

 

# Chapter Vocabulary Review

***Crossword Puzzle*** *Complete the puzzle by entering the term that matches the description.*

**Across**

1. time span shorter than an era
2. fossil used to compare the relative ages of fossils and rock layers
7. theory that eukaryotic cells arose from communities of several prokaryotes
9. measures evolutionary time: geologic time ____________
10. span of geologic time that is subdivided into periods
11. the time required for half of the radioactive atoms in a sample to decay
12. a species dying out because of the slow but steady process of natural selection: background ____________

**Down**

1. scientist who studies fossils
3. describes a species that no longer exists
4. method used to place rock layers and their fossils in a time sequence (2 words)
5. the process by which a species or group of species evolves into several different forms that live in different ways: ____________ radiation
6. process by which two species evolve in response to changes in each other over time
8. disappearance of many species at the same time: ____________ extinction

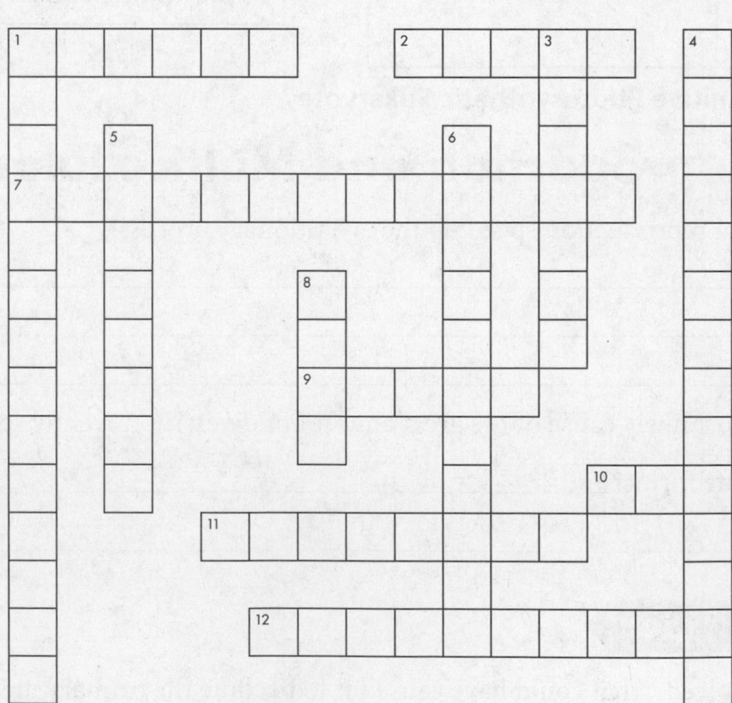

Name ______ Class ______ Date ______

# CHAPTER MYSTERY

## MURDER IN THE PERMIAN

21st Century Learning

Geologists are still working on solving the 250-million-year-old Permian murder mystery. To accomplish this, they piece together clues from the past that are preserved in rocks.

## The Story Is in the Rocks

In the Chapter Mystery, geologists and other scientists examine rocks to help them uncover the story behind a catastrophic destruction of species and ecosystems. Rocks are extremely useful in revealing what happened on Earth long ago.

The type of rock in a rock layer indicates how the rock formed. Rocks are made up of minerals. The minerals in rocks tell a story. For example, igneous rocks with small mineral crystals are formed during a volcanic eruption because the lava cooled too quickly for large crystals to form. In contrast, igneous rock with large crystals formed underground. Some types of mineral crystals can only form in open spaces, such as a cave, while other crystals can only be deposited in an aquatic environment.

When looking for clues about the past, geologists also look at the shape and size of a rock layer. An unconformity, or a disturbed sequence of rock layers, gives information about events that happened after a rock layer formed. For example, an earthquake can cause a rock layer to snap in two. And slanted rock layers may indicate that uplift occurred in the area.

Most of what we know about Earth's ancient past comes from Earth's rocks. Thus, as the interpretive sign below from Yellowstone National Park shows, discussions of Earth's history are typically based on geological information.

**From Yellowstone National Park**

### BURIED ALIVE

Excelsior Geyser's rugged crater was created by rare massive geyser eruptions. Surprisingly, it also preserves a record of early life.

For thousands of years, microbes have grown in the runoff channels extending from nearby Grand Prismatic Spring. These vast communities were buried alive as the flowing hot water deposited a crust of silica minerals. The resulting deposit, called sinter, preserves the shape of the microbial mat it entombed. As new mats grew, more layers developed. Today's formation is the result of this interplay between its living and nonliving components.

Yellowstone's hydrothermal features provide a glimpse into the distant past, when intense volcanism was widespread on the young Earth. The life forms found here help scientists understand the types of life that likely arose and diversified billions of years ago on our planet.

Continued on next page ▶

 

## 21st Century Themes Science Literacy

**1.** What is an unconformity?

______________________________

______________________________

______________________________

**2.** Using the information on the sign, infer how the crusts of silica minerals at Excelsior Geyser formed.

______________________________

______________________________

______________________________

______________________________

**3.** Why do the rocks around Excelsior Geyser give scientists information about the history of life on Earth?

______________________________

______________________________

______________________________

**4.** Suppose a massive volcanic eruption occurred millions of years ago near Excelsior Geyser. What sort of evidence of this eruption would you expect to find?

______________________________

______________________________

**5.** After studying these signs, what else would you have liked to learn about Excelsior Geyser and Grand Prismatic Springs?

______________________________

______________________________

______________________________

## 21st Century Skills Geology of Your Region

The skills used in this activity include **information and media literacy, communication skills, critical thinking and systems thinking, creativity and intellectual curiosity, interpersonal and collaborative skills,** and **accountability and adaptability.**

Working in small groups, research the geological history of your town or region. Choose one geological site that particularly interests you and research it. Your research should include geological information found in the library, on the Internet, and from other sources. List the geological conditions at the site and note any interesting or unique features it has and how they formed.

*Design a sign that would educate visitors to the site about its geology. Include text, photographs, and a map on your sign.*

 

Name ______________________ Class ______ Date ______

# 20 Viruses and Prokaryotes

**Big idea** Cellular Basis of Life

**Q:** Are all microbes that make us sick made of living cells?

| | WHAT I KNOW | WHAT I LEARNED |
|---|---|---|
| **20.1** What is a virus? | | |
| **20.2** What are prokaryotes and why are they important? | | |
| **20.3** How can we prevent bacterial and viral diseases from spreading? | | |

# 20.1 Viruses

## Lesson Objectives

Explain how viruses reproduce.

Explain how viruses cause infection.

## Lesson Summary

**The Discovery of Viruses** In 1935, the American biochemist Wendell Stanley isolated a virus for the first time.

- A **virus** is a particle made of nucleic acid, protein, and, in some cases, lipids.
- A typical virus is composed of a core of DNA or RNA surrounded by a protein coat called a **capsid**.
- Viruses that infect bacteria are called **bacteriophages**. They enter living cells and, once inside, use the machinery of the infected cell to produce more viruses.

**Viral Infections** Viruses have two methods of infection once inside a host cell.

- In a **lytic infection**, a virus enters a cell, makes copies of itself, and causes the cell to burst, releasing new virus particles that can attack other cells. In the case of bacteriophage *T4*, viral DNA directs the synthesis of new viruses using materials in the cell.
- In a **lysogenic infection**, a virus integrates part of its DNA called a **prophage** into the DNA of the host cell. The viral genetic information replicates along with the host cell's DNA. Eventually, the prophage will remove itself from the host cell DNA and make new virus particles.

In a **retrovirus**, the genetic information is copied backward—from RNA to DNA instead of from DNA to RNA. The virus that causes the disease AIDS is a retrovirus.
Viruses must infect a living cell in order to reproduce. Although viruses are parasites, they are not made of cells and are not considered living things.

## The Discovery of Viruses

**1.** What is a bacteriophage?

______________________________

**2.** What are viruses?

______________________________

______________________________

**3.** What is a capsid?

______________________________

**4.** How does a typical virus get inside a cell?

______________________________

**5.** What occurs when viruses get inside cells?

______________________________

 

# Viral Infections

**6.** **VISUAL ANALOGY** In the visual analogy, why is the outlaw locking up the sheriff, instead of the other way around?

______________________________

______________________________

______________________________

______________________________

**7.** **THINK VISUALLY** The diagram below shows the lytic cycle of a viral infection. Label the bacterial DNA, host bacterium, viral DNA, and virus. Then, circle the step that shows lysis of the host cell.

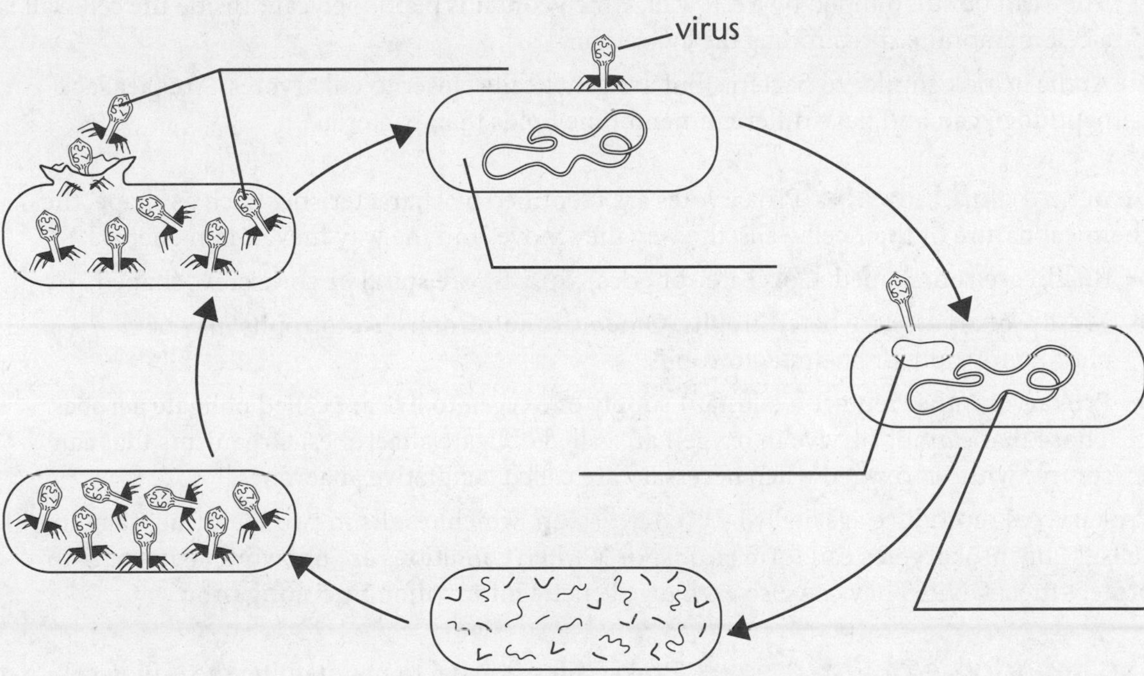


**8.** In a lysogenic infection, how can one virus infect many cells?

______________________________

______________________________

**9.** How is the common cold like the HIV virus?

______________________________

## Apply the Big idea

**10.** What would happen to a virus that never came in contact with a living cell? Explain your answer.

______________________________

______________________________

 

Name ______________________________ Class ______ Date ________

# 20.2 Prokaryotes

## Lesson Objectives

- Explain how the two groups of prokaryotes differ.
- Describe how prokaryotes vary in structure and function.
- Explain the role of bacteria in the living world.

## Lesson Summary

**Classifying Prokaryotes** The smallest and most common microorganisms are **prokaryotes**, which are unicellular organisms that lack a nucleus. Prokaryotes are classified either in domain Bacteria or domain Archaea.

- They can be surrounded by a cell wall, which contains peptidoglycan. Inside the cell wall is a cell membrane surrounding the cytoplasm.
- Archaea look similar to bacteria, but are genetically closer to eukaryotes. Archaea lack peptidoglycan and have different membrane lipids than bacteria.

**Structure and Function** Prokaryotes are identified by characteristics such as shape, the chemical nature of their cell walls, the way they move, and the way they obtain energy.

- **Bacilli** are rod-shaped. **Cocci** are spherical. **Spirilla** are spiral or corkscrew-shaped.
- Most prokaryotes are heterotrophs. Others are autotrophs. Autotrophs may be photoautotroph, or chemoautotrophs.
- Prokaryotes that require a constant supply of oxygen to live are called obligate aerobes. Those that cannot survive in oxygen are called obligate anaerobes. Organisms that can survive without oxygen when necessary are called facultative anaerobes.

Prokaryotes reproduce asexually by **binary fission**, which results in two identical "daughter" cells. Many prokaryotes can form **endospores** when conditions are unfavorable in order to protect their DNA. They can also exchange genetic information by **conjugation**.

**The Importance of Prokaryotes** Prokaryotes are vital to maintaining the ecological balance of the living world.

- Some are decomposers that break down dead matter.
- Others are producers that carry out photosynthesis.
- Some soil bacteria convert natural nitrogen gas into a form plants can use through a process called nitrogen fixation.
- Humans use bacteria in industry, food production, and other ways.

## Classifying Prokaryotes

*For Questions 1–5, complete each statement by writing the correct word or words.*

1. Unicellular organisms that lack a nucleus are called ________________.
2. The two different domains of prokaryotes are ________________ and ________________.
3. A cell wall made of ________________ protects some bacteria from damage.

Name ______________________ Class ______ Date ______

4. Archaea are more closely related to ______________ than ______________.

5. Some bacteria have a second ______________ outside the cell wall.

6. **THINK VISUALLY** Use the box to draw and label a diagram of a typical bacterium.

## Structure and Function

*Write the letter of the correct answer on the line at the left.*

_____ **7.** What are rod-shaped bacteria called?
**A.** cocci
**B.** bacilli
**C.** spirilla
**D.** endospores

_____ **8.** What are spherical bacteria called?
**A.** cocci
**B.** bacilli
**C.** spirilla
**D.** endospores

_____ **9.** Whiplike structures on a bacterium that produce movement are called
**A.** pilli.
**B.** capsids.
**C.** flagella.
**D.** endospores.

**10.** Complete the table about the different ways prokaryotes obtain energy.

| Energy Capture by Prokaryotes | |
|---|---|
| **Group** | **Description** |
| | Organism that carries out photosynthesis in a manner similar to that of plants |
| Chemoautotroph | |
| | Organism that takes in organic molecules and then breaks them down |
| Photoheterotroph | |

 

**11.** What occurs in the process of binary fission?

**12.** What occurs during conjugation?

## The Importance of Prokaryotes

**13.** How do decomposers help the ecosystem recycle nutrients when a tree dies?

**14.** What would happen to plants and animals if decomposers did not recycle nutrients?

**15.** Why do all organisms need nitrogen?

**16.** Why is the process of nitrogen fixation important?

**17.** What kind of relationship do many plants have with nitrogen-fixing bacteria?

**18.** Describe three different ways that humans use bacteria.

### Apply the Big idea

**19.** Suppose you were studying an infectious unicellular organism with a cell wall under a microscope. How could you confirm that the organism was a prokaryote? How could scientists determine whether it should be classified in domain Bacteria or domain Archaea?

 

Name ______________________ Class ______ Date ______

# 20.3 Diseases Caused by Bacteria and Viruses

## Lesson Objectives

- Explain how bacteria cause disease.
- Explain how viruses cause disease.
- Define emerging disease and explain why emerging diseases are a threat to human health.

## Lesson Summary

**Bacterial Diseases** Microorganisms that cause diseases are known as **pathogens**. Bacterial pathogens can produce many diseases that affect humans and other animals. They do so in one of two general ways:

- They destroy living cells and tissues directly or by causing an immune response that destroys tissue.
- They damage the cells and tissues of the infected organism directly by breaking down the cells for food.
- They release toxins (poisons) that travel throughout the body, interfering with the normal activity of the host.

Many bacterial pathogens can be controlled by washing, using disinfectants, preparing and storing food safely, or sterilizing exposed items. Bacterial diseases can be prevented and treated through the following methods:

- A **vaccine** is a preparation of weakened or killed pathogens or inactivated toxins. A vaccine can prompt the body to produce immunity to the disease. Immunity is the body's natural way of killing pathogens.
- When a bacterial infection does occur, **antibiotics** can be used to fight the disease. Antibiotics are compounds that block the growth and reproduction of bacteria.

**Viral Diseases** Viruses produce disease by directly destroying living cells or by affecting cellular processes in ways that disrupt homeostasis. In many viral infections, viruses attack and destroy certain body cells, causing the symptoms of the disease. Viral diseases in humans include the common cold, influenza, AIDS, chicken pox, and measles. Viruses produce other serious diseases in other animals and in plants. Protection against viruses, either by hygiene or vaccination, is the best way to avoid viral illness. A handful of antiviral drugs have been developed that help reduce the symptoms of specific viruses.

**Emerging Diseases** An unknown disease that appears in a population for the first time or a well-known disease that suddenly becomes harder to control is called an **emerging disease**. The increase of worldwide travel and food shipments is one reason new diseases are spreading. Another is virus and bacteria evolution. Scientists are struggling to keep up with changes. They recently discovered **prions**, which are disease-causing forms of proteins. Prions cause disease in animals, including humans.

Name ______________________ Class ______ Date ______

# Bacterial Diseases

*For Questions 1–5, complete each statement by writing the correct word or words.*

1. One way bacteria can cause disease is by breaking down and damaging ____________ of the infected organism.
2. Bacteria can also cause disease by releasing ____________ that harm the body.
3. A(n) ____________ is a disease-causing agent.
4. One way to control bacterial growth is by subjecting the bacteria to high temperatures during a process known as ____________ .
5. A(n) ____________ is a preparation of weakened or killed pathogens or inactivated toxins that can prompt the body to produce immunity to a disease.
6. What organs do the bacteria that cause tuberculosis typically damage?

______________________________________________

7. What are antibiotics?

______________________________________________

8. How are the causes of tuberculosis and diphtheria similar? How are they different?

______________________________________________

______________________________________________

9. Describe the similarities and differences of antibiotics and disinfectants.

______________________________________________

______________________________________________

10. Why should meat be cooked until it is well-done?

______________________________________________

______________________________________________

*Match the bacterial control method with an example of the method.*

| Bacterial Control Method | Example |
|---|---|
| ______ **11.** physical removal | **A.** Putting milk in a refrigerator |
| ______ **12.** disinfectant | **B.** Using bleach to clean a countertop |
| ______ **13.** safe food storage | **C.** Using boiling water to clean dishes |
| ______ **14.** safe food processing | **D.** Washing hands |
| ______ **15.** sterilization by heat | **E.** Boiling soup |

Name ______________________ Class ______ Date ______

## Viral Diseases

**16.** What are some human diseases caused by viruses?

______________________________________________

**17.** How do antiviral medications work? Why don't they also kill host cells?

______________________________________________

*Write the letter of the correct answer on the line at the left.*

_____ **18.** A person has a low helper-T cell count. What viral disease does he or she most likely have?

**A.** HPV
**B.** AIDS
**C.** hepatitis B
**D.** chicken pox

_____ **19.** A person has blister-like lesions on the skin. What viral disease does he or she most likely have?

**A.** HPV
**B.** AIDS
**C.** hepatitis B
**D.** chicken pox

## Emerging Diseases

*For Questions 20–24, write True if the statement is true. If the statement is false, change the underlined word or words to make the statement true.*

__________ **20.** Pathogens are able to <u>evolve</u> over time.

__________ **21.** A(n) <u>noninfectious</u> disease is an unknown disease that appears in a population for the first time.

__________ **22.** The widespread use of <u>vaccines</u> has led to the emergence of resistant strains of bacteria.

__________ **23.** Slight genetic changes would be needed for the bird flu virus to become infectious to <u>humans</u>.

__________ **24.** Scrapie is most likely caused by pathogens known as <u>viroids</u>.

### Apply the Big idea

**25.** RNA viruses have shown an ability to evade antiviral drugs. How do you suppose this is possible, when viruses are not alive? How may the reproductive methods of viruses help the process?

______________________________________________

______________________________________________

______________________________________________

______________________________________________

______________________________________________

Name ______________________ Class ______ Date ______

# Chapter Vocabulary Review

**1.** The picture shows three different bacteria shapes. Label each shape.

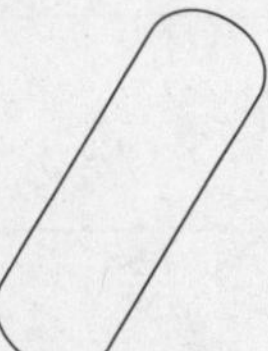

________________ ________________ ________________

*Match the term with its definition.*

| Term | Definition |
|---|---|
| _____ **2.** lysogenic infection | **A.** Compound that can block the growth and reproduction of bacteria |
| _____ **3.** prion | **B.** Misfolded protein that causes disease in animals |
| _____ **4.** bacteriophage | **C.** Bacteriophage DNA that is embedded in the host's DNA |
| _____ **5.** antibiotic | **D.** Protective structure formed by a prokaryote when growth conditions are unfavorable |
| _____ **6.** virus | **E.** A particle made of nucleic acid, protein, and in some cases, lipids that can replicate only by infecting living cells |
| _____ **7.** prokaryote | **F.** Process in which viral DNA becomes part of a host cell's DNA |
| _____ **8.** prophage | **G.** Disease-causing microorganism |
| _____ **9.** pathogen | **H.** Preparation of weakened or killed pathogens or inactivated toxins used to produce immunity |
| _____ **10.** lytic infection | **I.** Process in which a host cell bursts after being invaded by a virus |
| _____ **11.** endospore | **J.** Organism consisting of one cell that lacks a nucleus |
| _____ **12.** binary fission | **K.** Virus that infects bacteria |
| _____ **13.** vaccine | **L.** Process in which a bacterium replicates its DNA and divides in half |

*Complete each statement by writing the correct word or words.*

**14.** A protein coat surrounding a virus is a(n) ______________ .

**15.** Viruses that have RNA as their genetic material are called ______________ .

**16.** Some bacteria exchange genetic material through the process of ______________ .

**17.** SARS, MRSA, Ebola, and bird flu are all examples of ______________ .

 

Name ______ Class ______ Date ______

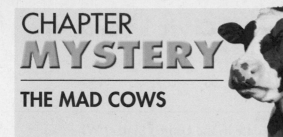

CHAPTER MYSTERY

THE MAD COWS

The Chapter Mystery investigated the 1986 outbreak of "mad cow" disease (also known as bovine spongiform encephalopathy, or BSE) in the United Kingdom. Subsequent outbreaks occurred around the world, and controversy about how to deal with the disease continues today.

21st Century Learning

## Assuring the Safety of the Beef Supply

The Kansas-based beef producer Creekstone Farms Premium Beef, Inc. filed a lawsuit against the United States Department of Agriculture (USDA) over BSE testing. Creekstone Farms claims that its export sales plummeted after a cow infected with BSE was found in the United States in 2003. To combat its losses, Creekstone sought to conduct its own BSE testing on every cow it slaughtered to assure consumers, and especially foreign buyers, of the beef's safety. Creekstone argued that this would be an improvement over the USDA's testing procedures because the USDA only tests approximately 1 percent of all U.S. beef.

However, the USDA argues that the regulation of U.S. beef falls solely under its jurisdiction and that it cannot allow a private company to conduct its own testing because the agency cannot oversee the testing to insure its reliability. Furthermore, a beef producer would have a conflict of interest in reporting accurate results of any BSE tests it conducts.

As it currently stands, the appeals court sided with the USDA, preventing Creekstone from conducting its own BSE tests on its meat. Read the document below, which is adapted and excerpted from the appeals court verdict:

### United States Court of Appeals

No. 07-5173
Creekstone Farms Premium Beef, L.L.C.
v.
Department of Agriculture

Bovine Spongiform Encephalopathy, or BSE, was first diagnosed in the United Kingdom in 1986. Since then, more than 189,000 confirmed cases of BSE in cattle worldwide have been reported. While almost all of the cases (95 percent) have occurred in the United Kingdom, BSE has been found in cattle raised in at least 25 other countries as well. Despite prevention efforts by the U.S. government, three BSE-infected cows have been found in the United States. The first was reported in December 2003 in Washington State. Two more BSE-infected cattle were found—one in Texas in June 2005 and one in Alabama in March 2006.

Following the discovery of the first BSE-infected cow in Washington State, several major beef importing countries, including Japan, South Korea and Mexico, (at the time, three of the four largest importers), banned the importation of U.S. beef. Creekstone claims to have suffered $200,000 per day in lost revenue as a result of the diminished export market.

To allay the concerns of consumers and importers, in 2004 Creekstone made a "business decision" to perform a rapid BSE test on each cow it slaughtered. Creekstone sought to purchase rapid BSE test kits from Bio-Rad Laboratories, Inc. Bio-Rad informed Creekstone, however, that it could not sell Creekstone the kits without USDA authorization. On February 19, 2004, Creekstone requested USDA permission to purchase the test kits. USDA denied Creekstone's requests. Creekstone challenged the USDA's action in court.

Continued on next page ▶

 

## 21st Century Themes Science and Civic Literacy; Science and Health Literacy

**1.** Where and when was BSE first diagnosed?

______________________________

**2.** How many BSE-infected cows have been found to date in the United States? When and where did the incidents occur?

______________________________

______________________________

______________________________

**3.** Which countries stopped importing beef from the United States after the first U.S. incident of a BSE-infected cow in December, 2003?

______________________________

______________________________

**4.** How much does Creekstone contend it lost in revenue each day from the drop in exports?

______________________________

**5.** Infer what the key arguments on each side of the case are. Why does Creekstone think it should be able to conduct its own additional BSE testing? Why does the USDA oppose the idea?

______________________________

______________________________

______________________________

______________________________

## BSE Testing Debate

**21st Century Skills** The skills used in this activity include **information and media literacy; communication skills; critical thinking and systems thinking; problem identification, formulation, and solution; and creativity and intellectual curiosity.**

Search the Internet to find the actual U.S. appeals court verdict in the Creekstone case. The verdict is filled with legal terminology, but it also offers a wealth of information about the case. Skim the main decision by Judge Karen Henderson, the concurring opinion by Judge Rogers, and the dissenting opinion by Chief Judge Sentelle. Then look for news articles about the case. The legal details might seem complicated, but the underlying issues in the case are clear. Both sides make strong arguments: Creekstone wants more testing to assure its customers; USDA feels that the safety of the beef supply must be regulated by a government agency because companies should not be trusted to regulate their own products. What do you think? Identify some of the different aspects of the problem raised in this case.

*Divide into working groups to debate the issue in class.*

 

Name ______________________ Class _____ Date _______

# 21 Protists and Fungi

**Interdependence in Nature**

**Q:** How do protists and fungi affect the homeostasis of other organisms and ecosystems?

| | WHAT I KNOW | WHAT I LEARNED |
|---|---|---|
| **21.1** Why are "protists" difficult to classify? | | |
| **21.2** How do protists move and reproduce? | | |
| **21.3** What roles do protists play in the environment? | | |
| **21.4** What are fungi, and what roles do they play in the environment? | | |

Name ______________________ Class ______ Date ______

# 21.1 Protist Classification—The Saga Continues

## Lesson Objectives

Explain what a "protist" is.

Describe how protists are related to other eukaryotes.

## Lesson Summary

**The First Eukaryotes** Protists are eukaryotes that are not members of the plant, animal, or fungi kingdoms. The first eukaryotes were protists.

- Most protists are unicellular.
- Protists are a very diverse group of species.
- Many species of protists are more closely related to plants, fungi, or animals than they are to other protists. Because of this, some scientists think the members of the kingdom Protista should be reclassified.

**Protists—Ancestors and Descendants** All eukaryotes are descended from early protists, but modern protists are very different from their ancestors. Like other eukaryotes, they have been evolving over the last 2.5 billion years.

## The First Eukaryotes

**1.** What is a protist?

______________________________________________

______________________________________________

**2.** Why are brown algae considered protists even though they are multicellular?

______________________________________________

______________________________________________

**3.** Why do scientists no longer use the categories of animal-like, plantlike, and funguslike protists to classify protists?

______________________________________________

*For Questions 4–7, complete each statement by writing the correct word or words.*

**4.** Most single-celled eukaryotes are currently classified as ______________.

**5.** Genetic analyses of protists indicate that they belong in six different ______________.

**6.** Protists were the first ______________.

**7.** Unlike most protists, which are unicellular, kelp has ______________ tissues.

 

Name ______________________ Class ______ Date ______

*For Questions 8–11, use the diagram and legend below.*

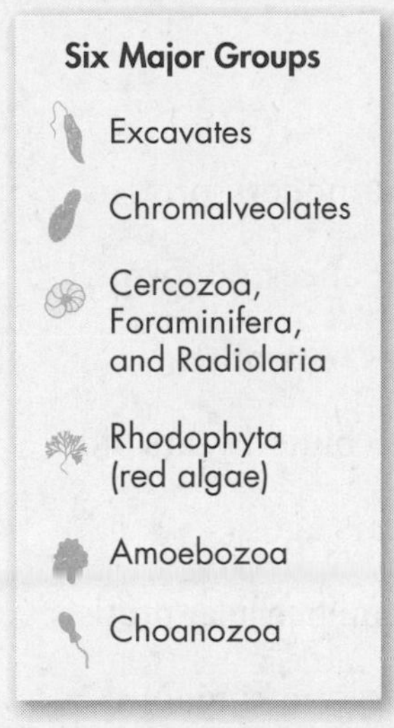

Six Major Groups
Excavates
Chromalveolates
Cercozoa, Foraminifera, and Radiolaria
Rhodophyta (red algae)
Amoebozoa
Choanozoa


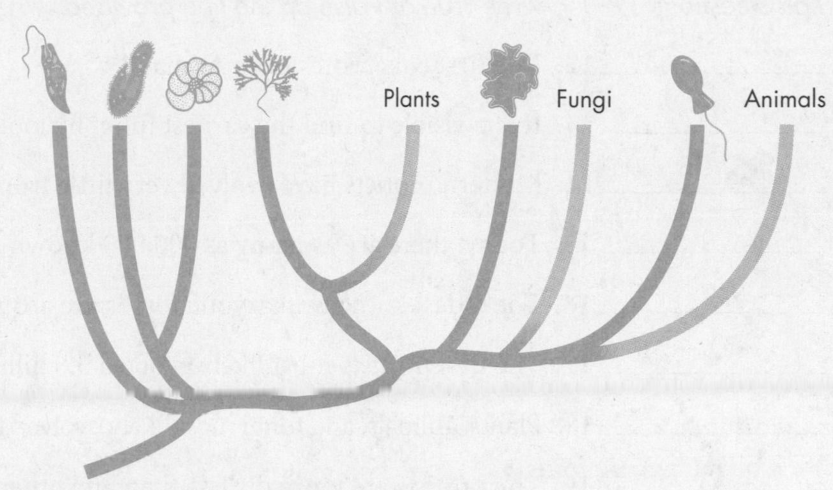


______ **8.** Plants are most closely related to which of the following groups?

**A.** Amoebozoa
**B.** Cercozoa
**C.** Rhodophyta
**D.** Choanozoa

______ **9.** Brown algae is a member of the clade Chromalveolates. Which of the following is its closest relative?

**A.** slime mold, an Amoebozoan
**B.** red algae, a Rhodophytan
**C.** *Giardia*, an Excavate
**D.** *Globigerina*, a Foraminiferan

______ **10.** Which clade is most primitive?

**A.** Excavates
**B.** Choanozoa
**C.** Cercozoa
**D.** Chromalveolates

______ **11.** Which statement is true?

**A.** Plants, fungi, and animals all emerged from a common protist ancestor.
**B.** Only fungi and animals emerged from a common protist ancestor.
**C.** Only animals and plants emerged from a common protist ancestor.
**D.** Plants, fungi, and animals all emerged from different protist ancestors.

 

# Protists—Ancestors and Descendants

*For Questions 12–19, write True or False on the line provided.*

_______________ **12.** The first eukaryotes were Archaea.

_______________ **13.** It is possible to find the earliest fungi by looking at modern protists.

_______________ **14.** Modern protists have evolved very little from their ancestral forms.

_______________ **15.** Today, there are as many as 300,000 known species of protists.

_______________ **16.** The oldest known eukaryotic fossils are around 1.5 billion years old.

_______________ **17.** The first protists most likely evolved 3.6 billion years ago.

_______________ **18.** Plants, animals, and fungi most likely evolved from multicellular protists.

_______________ **19.** The protists are more diverse than any other eukaryotic kingdom.

**20.** Complete the concept map below.

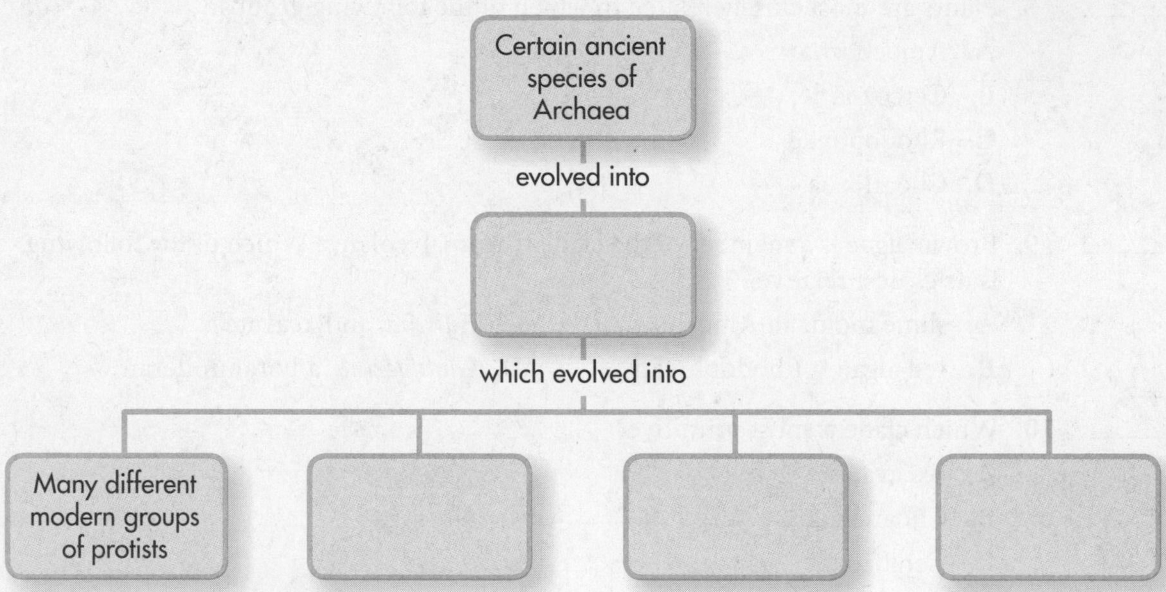


## Apply the Big idea

**21.** *Euglena* are photosynthetic protists that live in fresh water. How would their photosynthetic properties help stabilize a pond ecosystem? Suppose they and all the other photosynthetic organisms disappeared from the pond. How might their disappearance affect other organisms that lived in the pond?

_______________________________________________

_______________________________________________

_______________________________________________

_______________________________________________

_______________________________________________

 

Name ______________________ Class ______ Date ________

# 21.2 Protist Structure and Function

## Lesson Objectives

Describe the various methods of protist locomotion.

Describe how protists reproduce.

## Lesson Summary

**How Protists Move** Protists move in a wide variety of ways.

- Some protists move by extending temporary projections of cytoplasm known as **pseudopods**. These protists, such as amoebas, also use pseudopods for getting prey.
- Some protists swim using **cilia**, numerous short hairlike projections. Others swim using **flagella**, which are similar to cilia, but are longer and fewer in number.
- Some protists do not move on their own. They depend on wind, water, or another organism to move them. They reproduce by means of **spores**.

**Protist Reproduction** Protists reproduce in a wide variety of ways.

- Some protists reproduce asexually by mitosis.
- Some protists can undergo **conjugation**—a sexual process in which two organisms exchange genetic material. Conjugation helps produce genetic diversity.
- The life cycles of many protists include switching between a diploid and a haploid generation, a cycle called **alternation of generations**.
- Some protist species reproduce asexually by producing spores in a structure called a **sporangium**.

## How Protists Move

**1.** What are pseudopods? How do protists use them? ______________________

______________________________________________

**2.** How do amoebas capture and ingest food? ______________________

______________________________________________

**3.** What are cilia? How are they used by protists? ______________________

______________________________________________

**4.** THINK VISUALLY In the three boxes below, draw pictures of three organisms—one with a pseudopod, one with a flagellum, and one with cilia.

| **Pseudopod** | **Flagellum** | **Cilia** |
|---|---|---|

Name ______________________ Class ______ Date ______

5. **VISUAL ANALOGY** The visual analogy compares structures used by cells for movement to boat oars. Explain why a series of oars is compared to cilia, and why only one oar is used to represent flagella.

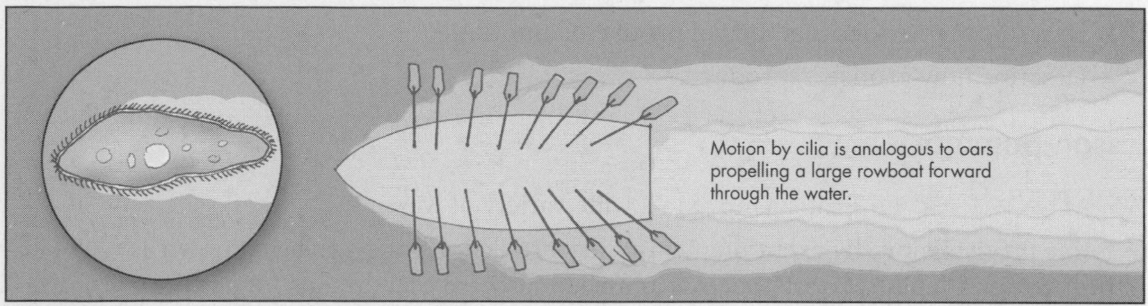

Motion by cilia is analogous to oars propelling a large rowboat forward through the water.


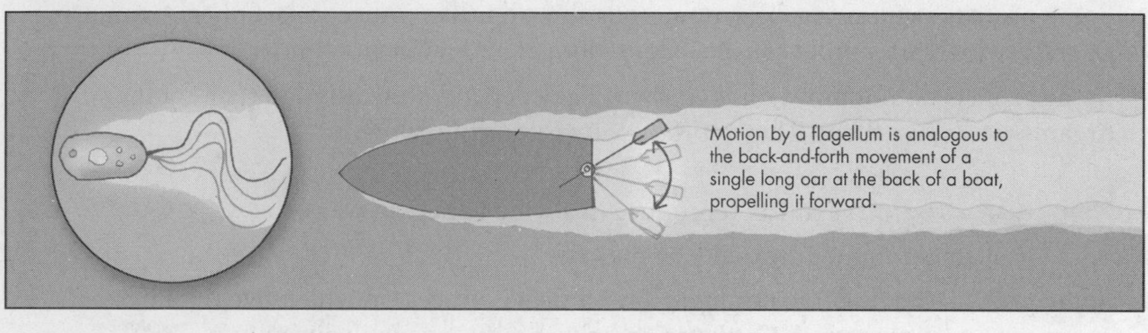

Motion by a flagellum is analogous to the back-and-forth movement of a single long oar at the back of a boat, propelling it forward.


______________________________________________

______________________________________________

______________________________________________

# Protist Reproduction

6. How do amoebas reproduce?

______________________________________________

7. What is conjugation?

______________________________________________

______________________________________________

8. Within a large population, how does conjugation benefit protists?

______________________________________________

______________________________________________

9. What occurs in the process known as alternation of generations?

______________________________________________

______________________________________________

______________________________________________

 

Name ______________________ Class ______ Date ______

10. Complete the flowchart to show the process of conjugation between two paramecia.

Conjugation begins when two paramecia attach to each other.

↓

______________________________

↓

In each cell, three of the micronuclei disintegrate.

↓

______________________________

↓

The two cells exchange one haploid micronucleus from each pair.

↓

In each cell, the micronuclei fuse to form a single diploid micronucleus, and the macronuclei disintegrate.

↓

______________________________

## Apply the Big idea

11. *Plasmodium* is the protist that causes malaria in humans. It is carried by mosquitoes, which transmit the parasite when they bite humans. In the human body, Plasmodia cause red blood cells to break and release spores in the evening. The spores can then travel through the bloodstream. How would this mechanism help spread the parasite throughout an ecosystem? What methods might help prevent its spread?

______________________________

______________________________

______________________________

______________________________

______________________________

______________________________

______________________________

 

Name ______________________ Class ______ Date ________

# 21.3 The Ecology of Protists

## Lesson Objectives

- Describe the ecological significance of photosynthetic protists.
- Describe how heterotrophic protists obtain food.
- Identify the symbiotic relationships that involve protists.

## Lesson Summary

**Autotrophic Protists** Protists that perform photosynthesis are autotrophic. The position of photosynthetic protists at the base of the food chain makes much of the diversity of aquatic life possible.

- They feed fish and whales, support coral reefs, and provide shelter to marine life.
- In areas where sewage is dumped, protists help recycle the waste. However, when the amount of waste is excessive, algae grow into enormous masses called **algal blooms**.

**Heterotrophic Protists** Some heterotrophic protists engulf and digest their food, while others live by absorbing molecules from the environment.

- Amoebas capture and digest their food, surrounding a cell or particle and then taking it inside themselves to form a food vacuole. A **food vacuole** is a small cavity in the cytoplasm that temporarily stores food.
- *Paramecia* and other ciliates use their cilia to sweep food particles into the **gullet**, an indentation in one side of the organism.
- Slime molds and water molds are important recyclers of organic material. At one stage of their life cycle, some slime molds fuse to form large cells with many nuclei. These structures are known as **plasmodia**. Sporangia develop from a plasmodium.

**Symbiotic Protists—Mutualists and Parasites** Some protists have symbiotic relationships with other organisms. *Trichonympha* has a mutualistic relationship with termites. It lives within their digestive system and helps them digest wood. Other protists are parasitic and cause disease. The protist *Trypanosoma* causes African sleeping sickness. The protist *Plasmodium* causes malaria.

# Autotrophic Protists

**1.** How do autotrophic protists make the diversity of aquatic life possible?

______________________________________________

**2.** What are phytoplankton?

______________________________________________

______________________________________________

**3.** How do protists help maintain homeostasis in coral reef ecosystems?

______________________________________________

______________________________________________

______________________________________________

Name ______________________ Class ______ Date ______

4. How can algal blooms be harmful?

______________________

______________________

______________________

## Heterotrophic Protists

5. What is the function of a food vacuole?

______________________

6. Label the illustration of a paramecium.

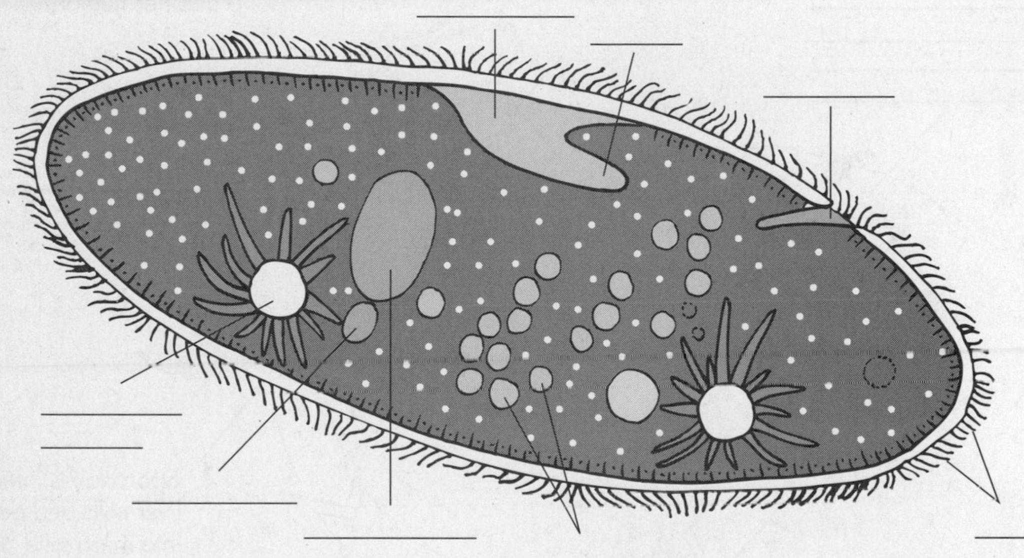

7. What are slime molds?

______________________

8. By what process are haploid spores made by a water mold? Where does the process occur?

______________________

9. What structure does a plasmodium eventually develop into and what is the function of that structure?

______________________

*For Questions 10–13, write True if the statement is true. If the statement is false, change the underlined word or words to make the statement true.*

______________ 10. In amoebas, indigestible materials remain inside <u>contractile</u> vacuoles.

______________ 11. A gullet is a structure used by a paramecium for <u>reproduction</u>.

______________ 12. In a slime mold's life cycle, germinating spores release <u>amoeba-like</u> cells.

______________ 13. <u>Water molds</u> grow on dead or decaying plants and animals.

Name ______ Class ______ Date ______

# Symbiotic Protists—Mutualists and Parasites

**14.** How does the protist *Trichonympha* make it possible for termites to eat wood?

______

______

______

______

**15.** What causes malaria? ______

**16.** Complete the flowchart showing the cycle of malarial infection.

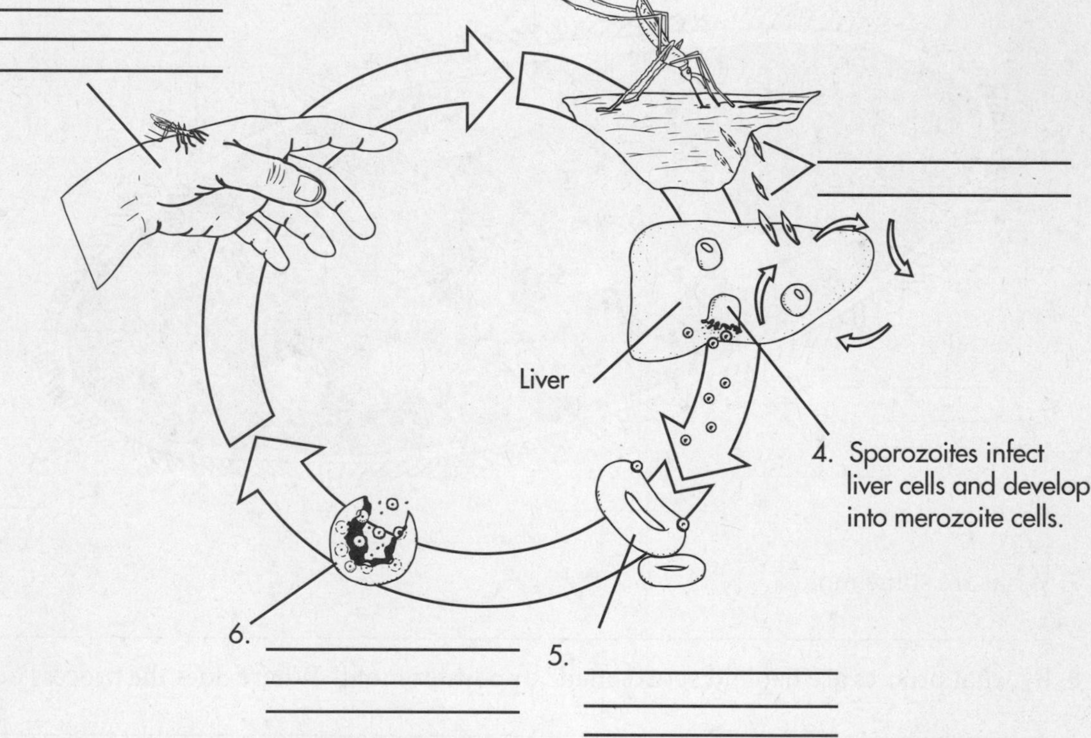

1.
2. Sexual phase of *Plasmodium* life cycle occurs in mosquito.
3. Mosquito bites another human.
Liver
4. Sporozoites infect liver cells and develop into merozoite cells.
5.
6.

## Apply the Big idea

**17.** Slime molds are heterotrophic protists that thrive on decaying matter. How would they help maintain homeostasis within their ecosystems? How do they benefit an ecosystem? Why is their role so important?

______

______

______

______

 

Name ____________________ Class ______ Date ________

# 21.4 Fungi

## Lesson Objectives

- Identify the defining characteristics of fungi.
- Describe how fungi affect homeostasis.

## Lesson Summary

**What Are Fungi?** Fungi are eukaryotic heterotrophs that have cell walls. The cell walls of fungi contain **chitin**, a complex carbohydrate.

- Most fungi are composed of thin filaments called **hyphae**. The **fruiting body** of a fungus—such as the above-ground part of a mushroom—is a reproductive structure that you can see. It grows from many hyphae tangled underground in a thick mass called a **mycelium**.
- Most fungi reproduce both asexually and sexually. Asexual reproduction can occur when cells or hyphae break off and begin to grow on their own. Some fungi also reproduce asexually by means of spores.
- Most fungi can also reproduce sexually. Spores are produced in structures called sporangia. Many fungi have minus (-) and plus (+) types that can reproduce sexually by fusing their nuclei when they meet.

**The Ecology of Fungi** Fungi do not ingest their food as animals do. Instead, fungi digest food outside their bodies and then absorb it. Many fungi feed by absorbing nutrients from decaying matter. Some fungi are parasites.

- Fungi help maintain equilibrium in nearly every ecosystem by recycling nutrients by breaking down the bodies and wastes of other organisms.
- Parasitic fungi cause serious plant and animal diseases. Fungal diseases in humans include athlete's foot, thrush, and yeast infections of the female reproductive tract.
- Some fungi form mutualistic relationships in which both partners benefit.
- **Lichens** are symbiotic associations between a fungus and a photosynthetic organism. The photosynthetic organism provides a source of energy. The fungus provides water and minerals.
- Mutualistic associations of plant roots and fungi are called **mycorrhizae**. The plant's roots are woven into a partnership with the web of fungal hyphae.

# What Are Fungi?

**1.** Why do scientists think that fungi are more closely related to animals than to plants?

______________________________________________________________

**2.** Describe two types of hyphae.

______________________________________________________________

______________________________________________________________

**3.** Label the parts of the fungus.

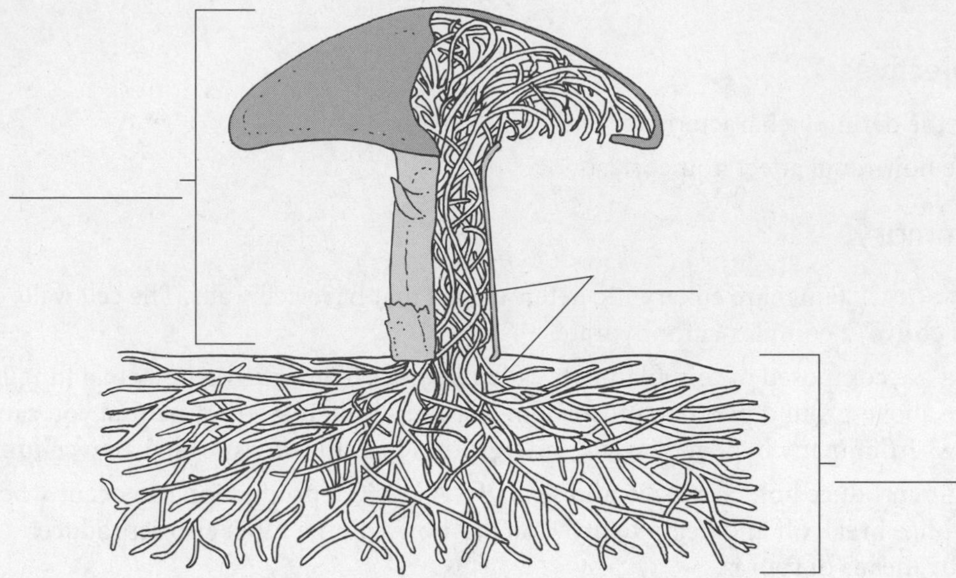

**4.** What is the function of a fruiting body?

______________________________________________

**5.** What is a fairy ring, and why does it form?

______________________________________________

______________________________________________

______________________________________________

______________________________________________

**6.** The diagram below shows the life cycle of *Rhizopus stolonifer* fungi. Shade the arrows that show sexual reproduction. Cross-hatch the arrows that show asexual reproduction.

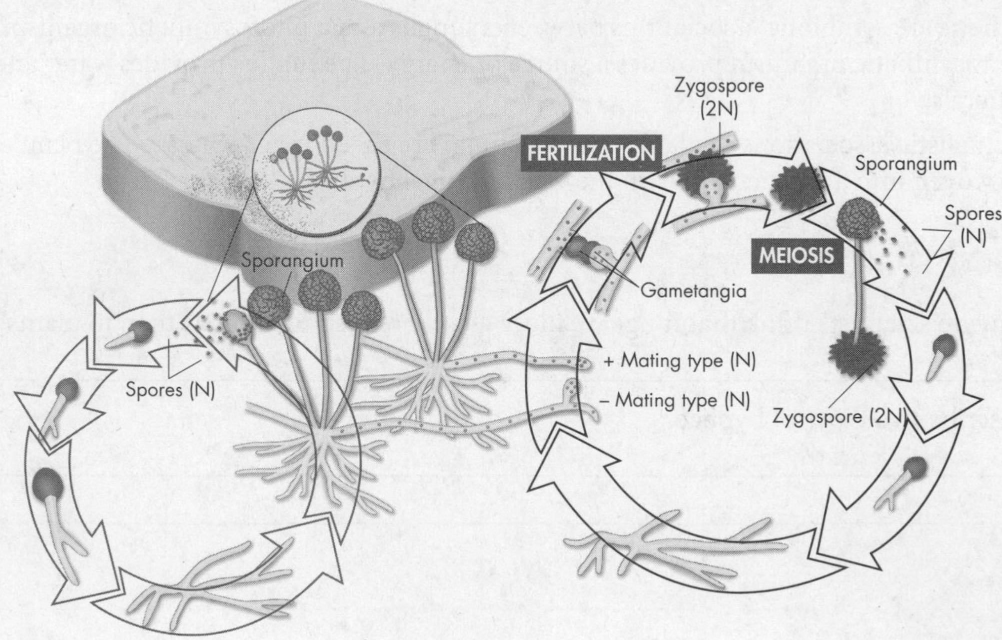

# The Ecology of Fungi

**7.** How do fungi break down leaves, fruit, and other organic material into simple molecules?

______________________________________________

______________________________________________

**8.** How can fungi disrupt the homeostasis of plants?

______________________________________________

**9.** Lichens and mycorrhizae are both examples of what kind of symbiotic relationship?

______________________________________________

**10.** How do plants benefit from mycorrhizae? How do fungi benefit?

______________________________________________

______________________________________________

______________________________________________

**11.** **THINK VISUALLY** In the diagram of a lichen, label the alga and the fungus. Then, on the lines below, describe what benefits the fungus and alga each derive from their association in the lichen.

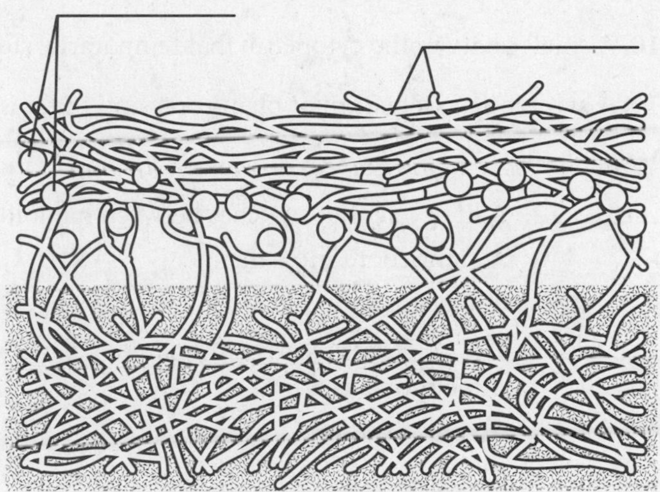

______________________________________________

______________________________________________

## Apply the Big idea

**12.** A fungus-killing chemical soaks into the ground and is absorbed through the roots of a plant with a fungal disease. How might this help infected plants regain homeostasis? How might it damage the homeostasis of other plants in the area?

______________________________________________

______________________________________________

______________________________________________

 

Name ______________________________ Class ______ Date ________

# Chapter Vocabulary Review

*Match the term with its definition.*

| Term | Definition |
|---|---|
| ______ **1.** mycelium | **A.** Complex carbohydrate that makes up the cell walls of fungi |
| ______ **2.** lichen | **B.** An example of a symbiotic association |
| ______ **3.** sporangium | **C.** A structure that contains spores |
| ______ **4.** chitin | **D.** Mass of tangled fungus hyphae |
| ______ **5.** algal bloom | **E.** A rapid growth in algae in a body of water with a great deal of sewage |
| ______ **6.** flagella | **F.** Structures that protists use for motion |

*Complete each statement by writing the correct word or words.*

**7.** Multicellular fungi are composed of thin filaments called ________________.

**8.** A(n) ________________ is a fungal reproductive structure growing from the mycelium.

**9.** Ciliates sweep food particles into their cell into a ________________.

**10.** A small cavity in the cytoplasm that temporarily stores food is a food ________________.

**11.** A symbiotic association of plant roots and fungi is called a(n) ________________.

*Write the letter of the correct answer on the line at the left.*

______ **12.** A life cycle that switches between haploid and diploid stages is called

**A.** amoeboid movement. **C.** meiotic binary fission.
**B.** conjugation. **D.** alternation of generations.

______ **13.** The single structure with many nuclei that is formed by a mass of amoeba-like slime molds is a(n)

**A.** plasmodium. **C.** pseudopod.
**B.** cilium. **D.** sporangium.

______ **14.** Amoebas move and feed by using their

**A.** pseudopods. **C.** cilia.
**B.** gullets. **D.** flagella.

______ **15.** Some ciliates exchange genetic material through a process called

**A.** amoeboid movement. **C.** fruiting bodies.
**B.** conjugation. **D.** alternation of generations.

______ **16.** A reproductive cell made by some protists is called a

**A.** spore. **C.** sporangium.
**B.** cilium. **D.** hypha.

______ **17.** A paramecium moves by using hairlike projections called

**A.** gullets. **C.** cilia.
**B.** contractile vacuoles. **D.** pseudopods.

 

Name ______________________ Class ______ Date ________

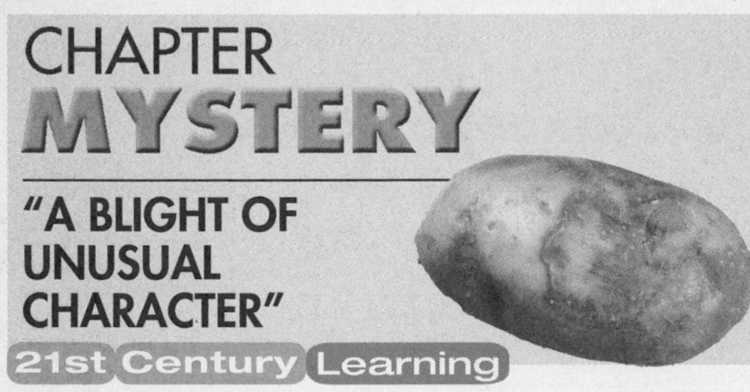

CHAPTER
MYSTERY
"A BLIGHT OF
UNUSUAL
CHARACTER"
21st Century Learning


In the Chapter Mystery you investigated the water mold *Phytophthora* that led to the Irish potato famine in the 1840s. In recent years, experts have warned that the modern-day banana crop might soon face a similar threat.

# A Threat to the World's Banana Crop

Juan Fernando Aguilar is a leading banana breeder at the Honduran Foundation for Agricultural Investigation (FHIA). He believes that the worldwide banana trade is currently highly vulnerable to a blight known as Fusarium wilt, or Panama disease, which is caused by the *Fusarium* fungus. As Aguilar explains, the modern-day banana, a variety known as the Cavendish, is highly susceptible to the disease, which has already destroyed plantations in Southeast Asia and now threatens crops elsewhere.

Read the fact sheet below, compiled from information from banana growers like Aguilar, to learn more about bananas and the threat they face from Fusarium wilt.

## Facts About the Banana Trade and the Threat Posed by Fusarium Wilt

- The Cavendish banana, nutritious and convenient, is a monoculture. Almost all commercial banana farming relies on the Cavendish.
- As many as 100 billion Cavendish bananas are consumed worldwide each year.
- The global trade in Cavendish bananas is a \$4-billion-per-year business.
- Americans eat more bananas than any other kind of fresh fruit. Average consumption in the U.S. equals 26.2 pounds of bananas per year.
- Fusarium wilt, once called Panama Disease, is caused by *Fusarium* fungi that invade young roots of the banana plant and cause its leaves to wilt and die.
- Some varieties of the fungus have proven resistant to existing fungicides and continue to thrive in surrounding soil, preventing the success of future plantings.
- Fusarium wilt wiped out the Gros Michel banana, which once was the most widely consumed banana. The Gros Michel became extinct by 1960.
- The Cavendish banana does not appear to be safe from the latest strain of Fusarium wilt which first appeared in 1992 and has spread throughout Southeast Asia. It has not reached the Western Hemisphere yet, but experts predict it will.
- Scientists have found no cure for Fusarium wilt.
- Fusarium wilt is so virulent that a single clump of dirt carried on a tire or shoe can spark an outbreak.

Continued on next page ▶

 

## 21st Century Themes Science and Global Awareness, Science and Economic Literacy

**1.** How big is the global trade in bananas? What figures illustrate the popularity of bananas and their commercial importance?

______

______

______

**2.** What characteristic of the current banana crop makes it particularly vulnerable to a blight?

______

______

______

______

**3.** What is Fusarium wilt? What causes it and how does it affect the banana crop?

______

______

______

**4.** What characteristics of the current strain of Fusarium wilt make banana growers particularly worried?

______

______

______

**5.** Based on the facts presented, how vulnerable do you think the world's banana crop is to a widespread blight? Why or why not?

______

______

______

## 21st Century Skills Investigate Fusarium Wilt

The skills used in this activity include **problem identification, formulation, and solution; information and media literacy;** and **communication skills**.

Use library and Internet resources to conduct further research about this topic. Try to find out more about the science of Fusarium wilt and expert assessment of the threat posed to the world's banana crops. How does the current situation compare to the Irish potato famine in the 1840s? Based on your research, write a newspaper article on the threat posed to the world trade in bananas and suggest what you think banana growers ought to do about it.

 

Name ______________________ Class _____ Date _______

# 22 Introduction to Plants

**Big idea** Unity and Diversity of Life

**Q:** What are the five main groups of plants, and how have four of these groups adapted to life on land?

| | WHAT I KNOW | WHAT I LEARNED |
|---|---|---|
| **22.1** What are the characteristics of plants? | | |
| **22.2** What are the characteristics of seedless plants? | | |
| **22.3** What are the characteristics of seed plants? | | |
| **22.4** What are the characteristics of flowering plants? | | |

Name ______________________ Class _____ Date ________

# 22.1 What Is a Plant?

## Lesson Objectives

- Describe what plants need to survive.
- Describe how the first plants evolved.
- Explain the process of alternation of generations.

## Lesson Summary

### Characteristics of Plants

- Plants are eukaryotes that have cell walls containing cellulose. Mostly autotrophs, plants use chlorophyll *a* and *b* to carry out photosynthesis.
- Without moving about, plants get what they need from the environment.
  - Sunlight: gathered by leaves arranged in ways that maximize absorption
  - Gas exchange: brings in oxygen and carbon dioxide and releases excess oxygen
  - Water: absorbed mostly from the soil and transported internally
  - Minerals: absorbed along with water from the soil

**The History and Evolution of Plants** Ancestors of today's land plants were water-dwellers similar to today's green algae. Over time, the demands of life on land favored the evolution of plants more resistant to the drying rays of the sun, more capable of conserving water, and more capable of reproducing without water.

- The first land plants were dependent on water and lacked leaves and roots.
- Five major groups of plants are classified based on four important features:
  - embryo formation
  - specialized water-conducting tissues
  - seeds
  - flowers

**The Plant Life Cycle** The life cycle of land plants has two alternating phases, a diploid (2N) phase and a haploid (N) phase. This shift between haploid and diploid is known as the **alternation of generations**.

- **Sporophyte**: the multicellular diploid phase, a spore-producing plant
- **Gametophyte**: the multicellular haploid phase, a gamete-producing plant

## Characteristics of Plants

*For Questions 1–8, write True if the statement is true. If the statement is false, change the underlined word or words to make the statement true.*

_______________ **1.** Both grasses and <u>mosses</u> are examples of plants.

_______________ **2.** Green algae are now considered to be <u>protists</u>.

_______________ **3.** <u>Most</u> plants are either parasites or saprobes.

_______________ **4.** In plants, chlorophyll *a* and *b* are located in <u>chloroplasts</u>.

______________ 5. Besides oxygen, plants need water and carbon dioxide for photosynthesis.

______________ 6. Plants require oxygen for cellular respiration.

______________ 7. Land plants evolved with structures that promote water loss.

______________ 8. Plants usually take in water and minerals through their leaves.

## The History and Evolution of Plants

*For Questions 9–12, complete each statement by writing the correct word or words.*

9. The ancestors of land plants lived in ______________.

10. The oldest fossils of land plants are roughly ______________ years old.

11. The greatest challenge faced by early land plants was obtaining ______________.

12. Early land plants obtained enough water because they grew close to the ground in ______________ places.

13. Describe why biologists now classify green algae as plants.

______________________________________________________________________

______________________________________________________________________

______________________________________________________________________

14. Describe three characteristics of plants that helped them meet the demands of life on land.

______________________________________________________________________

______________________________________________________________________

15. Identify the important features that separate the five major groups of plants by writing each correct answer on the corresponding line provided.

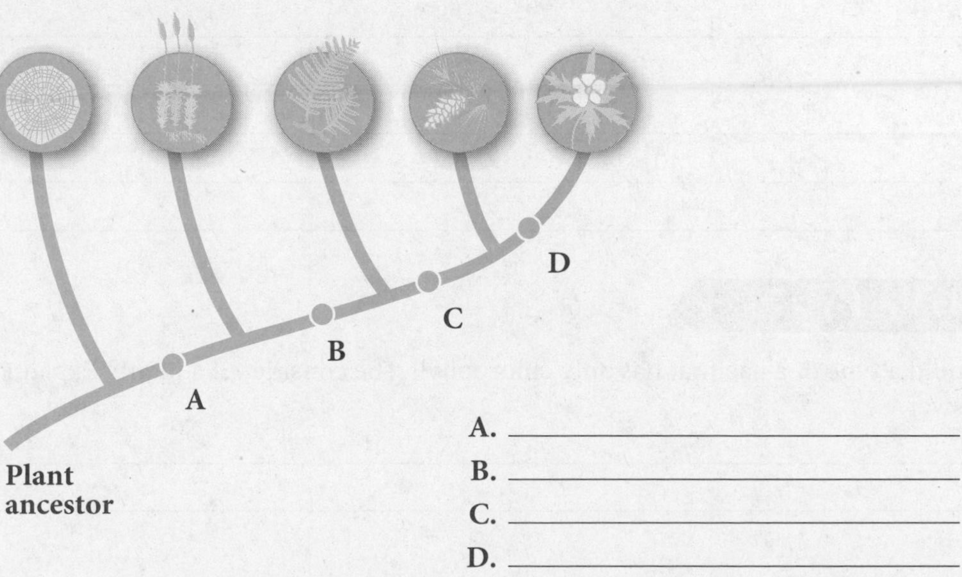


A. ______________________________

B. ______________________________

C. ______________________________

D. ______________________________

 

# The Plant Life Cycle

**16.** What is the shift between haploid and diploid phases in the sexual life cycle of a plant called?

______________________________

**17.** Complete the diagram below by writing the name of each phase in a plant's life cycle. Also indicate whether the phase is haploid (N) or diploid (2N).

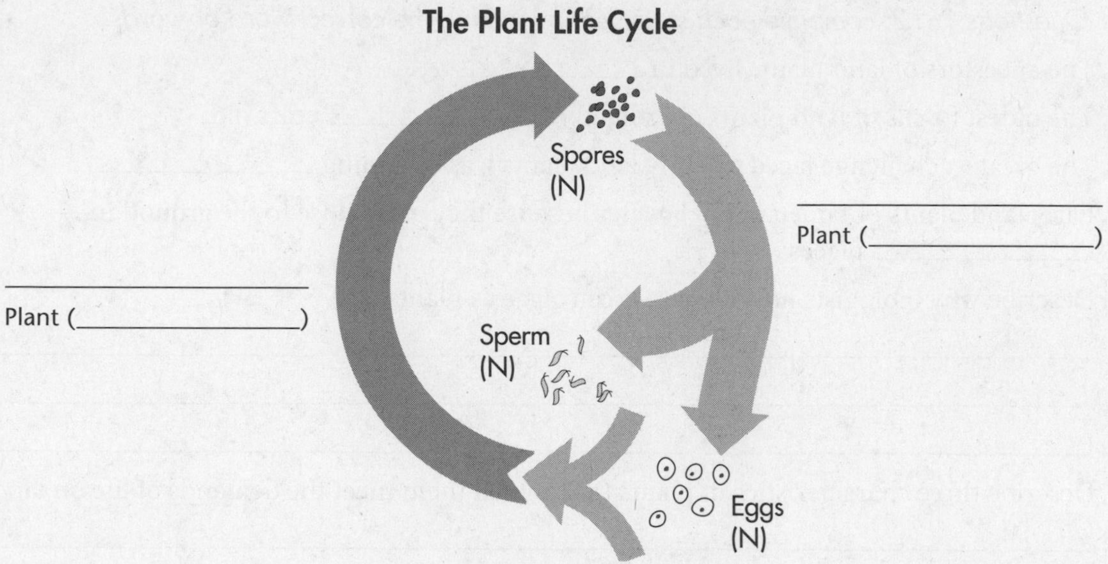


**18.** What evolutionary trend is observable in the relative sizes of the stages in the life cycles of plants, starting with green algae and ending with seed plants?

______________________________

______________________________

______________________________

______________________________

______________________________

______________________________

## Apply the Big idea

**19.** Would a type of algae that has only chlorophyll *a* be considered a plant? Explain your answer.

______________________________

______________________________

Name ____________________ Class ______ Date ________

# 22.2 Seedless Plants

## Lesson Objectives

- Identify the characteristics of green algae.
- Describe the adaptations of bryophytes.
- Explain the importance of vascular tissue.

## Lesson Summary

**Green Algae** Green algae are mostly aquatic. They are found in fresh and salt water, and in some moist areas on land.

- Most do not contain the specialized tissues found in other plants.
- Some may not alternate between haploid and diploid stages with every generation.
- Green algae form colonies providing a hint about how multicellular plants evolved. Although most cells in a *Volvox* colony are identical, a few are specialized for reproduction.

**Mosses and Other Bryophytes** The **bryophytes** have specialized reproductive organs.

- Bryophytes are small because they lack **vascular tissue**, which is specialized for conducting water.
- Bryophytes display alternation of generations:
  - Gametophytes produce eggs in **archegonia** and sperm in **antheridia**. Sperm and egg cells fuse to produce a diploid zygote.
  - The zygote is the beginning of the sporophyte stage. The sporophyte grows out of the gametophyte and develops a long stalk and a spore-producing capsule called a **sporangium**. Here, haploid spores are produced by meiosis. When the capsule opens, the haploid spores are scattered to start the cycle again.

**Vascular Plants** These plants are also known as **tracheophytes**.

- Vascular plants have vascular tissues that make it possible to move fluids through their bodies against the force of gravity.
  - **Tracheids** are hollow tubelike water-conducting cells with thick cell walls strengthened by lignin. Tracheids are found in **xylem**, a tissue that carries water upward from the roots to every part of a plant.
  - **Phloem** is a vascular tissue that carries nutrients and carbohydrates produced by photosynthesis.
- In a fern life cycle, spores grow into haploid gametophytes that produce eggs in archegonia and sperm in antheridia. The diploid zygote develops into a sporophyte. Haploid spores will develop on the undersides of a fern's fronds, actually the diploid sporophyte stage of the life cycle, and the cycle continues.

Name ______________________ Class ______ Date ______

# Green Algae

*For Questions 1–7, complete each statement by writing the correct word or words.*

1. *Alga* is the Latin word for ______________.
2. Large mats of green algae lived during the ______________ Period, more than 550 million years ago.
3. Green algae are mostly aquatic, but some live in ______________ areas on land.
4. ______________ is an example of a single-celled green alga.
5. The ______________ of a green alga are able to survive freezing or drying conditions.
6. ______________ is a colonial green alga shaped like a filament.
7. *Volvox* is a colonial green alga that shows some cell ______________.

# Mosses and Other Bryophytes

*For Questions 8–14, write True if the statement is true. If the statement is false, change the underlined word or words to make the statement true.*

______________ 8. Mosses and their relatives belong to a group called <u>sporophytes</u>.

______________ 9. The moss life cycle is highly dependent on <u>fertile soil</u>.

______________ 10. Bryophytes stay small because they lack true <u>vascular tissue</u>.

______________ 11. The <u>gametophyte</u> is the dominant stage of bryophytes.

______________ 12. Bryophytes must live in places where there is standing water for at least part of the year because, for fertilization to occur, <u>eggs</u> must swim.

______________ 13. The egg producing organs of bryophytes are called <u>antheridia</u>.

______________ 14. When a moss spore germinates, it grows into a <u>sporangium</u>.

15. **THINK VISUALLY** Label the gametophyte and sporophyte in the illustration of a moss plant below.

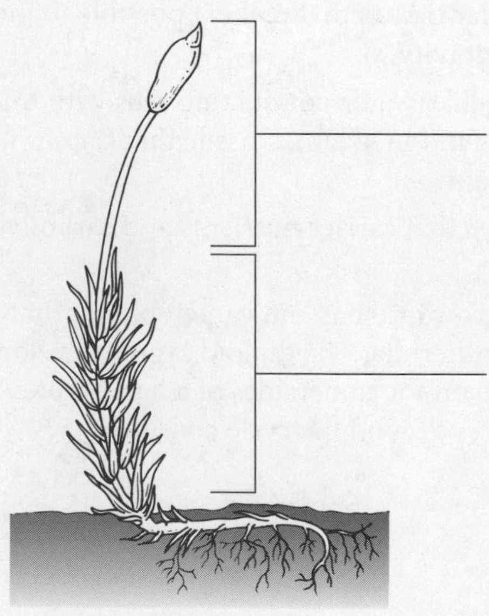

 

Name ______________________ Class ______ Date ______

# Vascular Plants

**16.** What is vascular tissue?

______________________________________________

______________________________________________

**17.** Complete the compare and contrast table for the two main types of vascular tissue.

| Xylem and Phloem | |
|---|---|
| **Similarities** | **Differences** |
| | |

**18.** What is the dominant stage in the life cycle of ferns?

______________________________________________

**19.** THINK VISUALLY Label the parts of a fern in the illustrations below. Then label each drawing as either the sporophyte or the gametophyte.

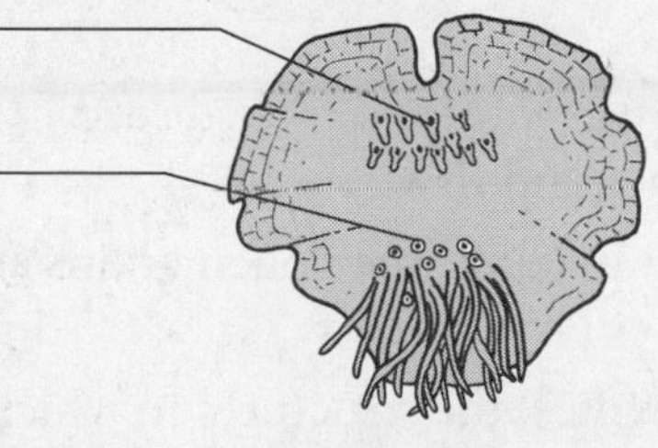

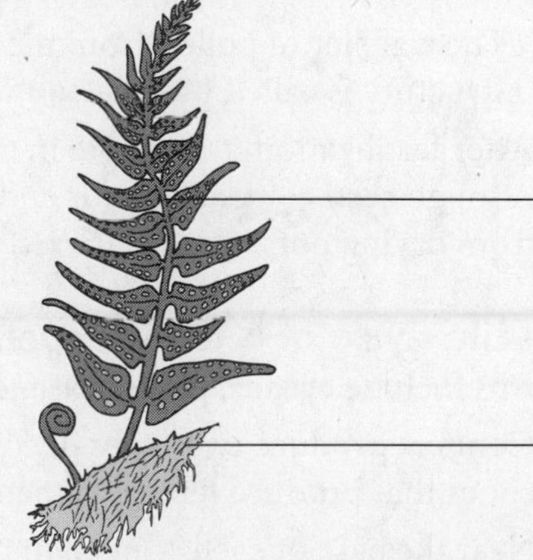

Apply the **Big** idea

**20.** Which type of plant reproductive cell—spore or gamete—is better adapted for dispersing, or spreading, bryophytes and ferns to other places? Justify your answer.

______________________________________________

______________________________________________

______________________________________________

# 22.3 Seed Plants

## Lesson Objectives

Describe the reproductive adaptations of seed plants.

Identify the reproductive structures of gymnosperms.

## Lesson Summary

**The Importance of Seeds** A **seed** is a plant embryo and a food supply, encased in a protective covering. The embryo is an early stage of the sporophyte.

- Ancestors of seed plants evolved with many adaptations that allow seed plants to reproduce without open water. These include a reproductive process that takes place in cones or flowers, the transfer of sperm by pollination, and the protection of embryos in seeds. These adaptations enabled plants to survive on dry land.
- The gametophytes of seed plants grow and mature within the sporophyte.
  - The **gymnosperms** are seed plants that bear their seeds directly on the scales of cones.
  - The **angiosperms** are seed plants that bear their seeds in flowers inside a layer of tissue that protects the seed.
- In seed plants, the entire male gametophyte is contained in a tiny structure called a **pollen grain**.
  - The sperm are produced inside pollen grains and do not have to swim.
  - Pollen grains are carried to female reproductive structures by wind or animals.
  - The transfer of pollen from the male reproductive structure to the female reproductive structure is called **pollination**.
- After fertilization, the zygote in the seed grows into a tiny plant—the sporophyte embryo. A tough **seed coat** surrounds and protects the embryo and keeps the contents of the seed from drying out.

**The Life Cycle of a Gymnosperm** The word *gymnosperm* means "naked seed." Gymnosperms include cycads, ginkgoes, and conifers such as pines and firs.

- Conifers produce two types of cones: pollen cones that produce the pollen grains and seed cones that produce female gametophytes.
- Near the base of each scale of the seed cones are two **ovules**, the structures in which the female gametophytes develop.
- Wind carries pollen from pollen cones to new female cones.
- In gymnosperms, the direct transfer of pollen to the female cone allows fertilization to take place without the need for open water.
- If a pollen grain lands near an ovule, the grain begins to grow a structure called a **pollen tube**, which allows the pollen to travel without water and which contains two haploid sperm nuclei.
- Once the pollen tube reaches the female gametophyte, one sperm nucleus disintegrates, and the other fertilizes the egg contained within the gametophyte.
- Fertilization produces a zygote, which grows into an embryo. The embryo is then encased in a seed and is ready to be dispersed.

## The Importance of Seeds

*For Questions 1–4, complete each statement by writing the correct word or words.*

**1.** Acorns, pine nuts, and beans are examples of ______________.

**2.** The living plant within a seed represents the early developmental stage of the ______________ phase of the plant life cycle.

**3.** In seed formation, fertilization does not require ______________.

**4.** The gametophytes usually develop in reproductive structures known as ______________ or ______________.

**5.** Complete the Venn diagram by correctly placing terms in the diagram. Use the terms that follow: cones, fertilization, flowers, pollen grains, pollination, seeds, and seed coats.

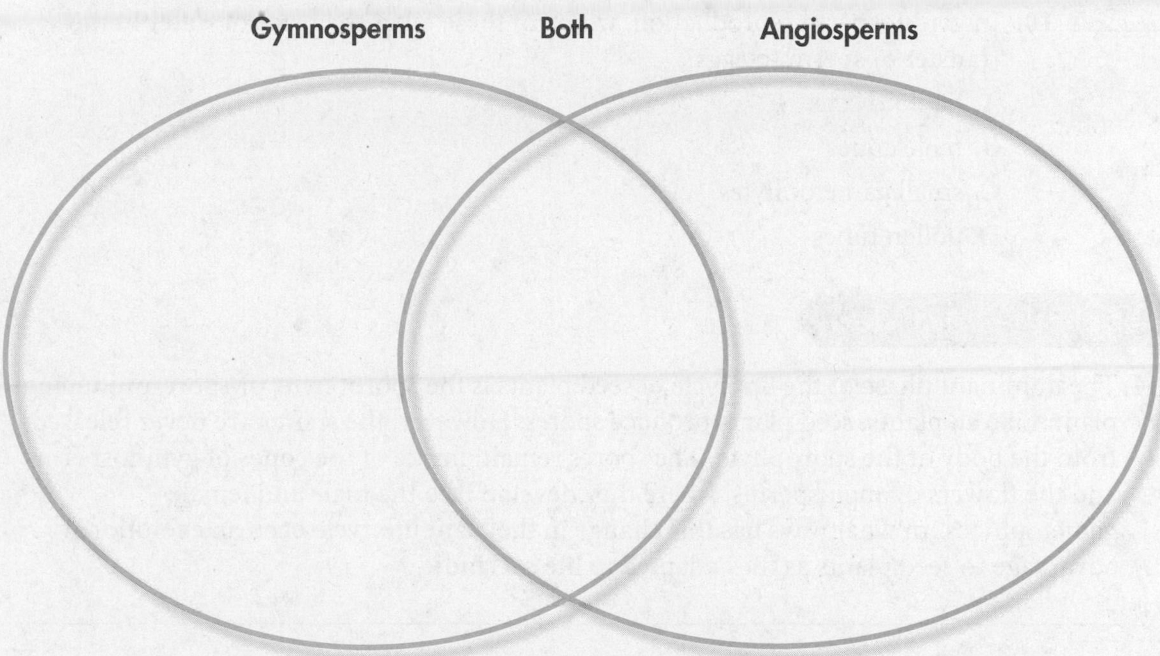


## The Life Cycle of a Gymnosperm

*For Questions 6–10, write the letter of the correct answer on the line at the left.*

______ **6.** In which part of a pine tree are pollen grains produced?

**A.** pollen cones
**B.** male flowers
**C.** seed cones
**D.** female flowers

______ **7.** Which is one entire male gametophyte of a gymnosperm?

**A.** a diploid cell
**B.** a haploid nucleus
**C.** a pollen cone
**D.** a pollen grain

 

______ **8.** The structures of gymnosperms in which the female gametophytes develop are called

**A.** needles.

**B.** ovules.

**C.** pollen grains.

**D.** pollen tubes.

______ **9.** How much time does the conifer life cycle typically take to complete?

**A.** 2 days

**B.** 2 months

**C.** 2 years

**D.** 2 centuries

______ **10.** In gymnosperm reproduction, which of these takes the place of water in the transfer of sperm to eggs?

**A.** haploid cells

**B.** male cones

**C.** small gametophytes

**D.** pollen tubes

## Apply the Big idea

**11.** The dominant phase of the life cycle of seed plants is the sporophyte, or spore-producing plant. Like all plants, seed plants produce spores. However, the spores are never released from the body of the sporophyte. The spores remain inside of the cones of gymnosperms and the flowers of angiosperms, where they develop into the male and female gametophytes. In what ways has this change in the plant life cycle been an evolutionary advantage to seed plants as they adapted to life on land?

 

Name ______________________ Class ______ Date ______

# 22.4 Flowering Plants

## Lesson Objectives

Identify the reproductive structures of angiosperms.

Identify some of the ways angiosperms can be categorized.

## Lesson Summary

**Flowers and Fruits** Angiosperms reproduce sexually by means of flowers.

- Flowers contain **ovaries**, which surround and protect the seeds. *Angiosperm* means "enclosed seed."
- Flowers are an evolutionary advantage because they attract animals that carry pollen with them as they leave flowers.
- After fertilization, ovaries within flowers develop into fruits that surround, protect, and help disperse the seeds.
- A **fruit** is a structure containing one or more matured ovaries.
- For many years, angiosperms were classified according to the number of seed leaves, or **cotyledons**.
  - **Monocots** have one seed leaf.
  - **Dicots** have two seed leaves.
  - Scientific classification now places the monocots into a single group and dicots in a variety of categories. Recent discoveries are used to place angiosperms in clades. Five of these clades are *Amborella*, water lilies, magnoliids, monocots, and eudicots.

**Angiosperm Diversity** Scientific classification reflects evolutionary relationships. Farmers, gardeners, and other people who work with plants group angiosperms according to the number of their seed leaves, the strength and composition of their stems, and the number of growing seasons they live.

- Monocots and dicots, grouped according to the number of cotyledons they produce, differ in several other characteristics, including:
  - the distribution of vascular tissue in stems, roots, and leaves
  - the number of petals per flower
- Plants are also grouped by the characteristics of their stems.
  - **Woody plants** have stems that are made primarily of cells with thick cell walls that support the plant body.
  - **Herbaceous plants** have smooth and nonwoody stems.
- Plants are grouped according to life span as annuals, biennials, or perennials. Annuals live one year; biennials live two years; and perennials can live for several years.

## Flowers and Fruits

*For Questions 1–4, complete each statement by writing the correct word or words.*

1. ______________ are seed plants that produce flowers and fruits.

 

Name ______________________________ Class ______ Date ________

2. Flowering plants first appeared during the ______________ Period.

3. The seeds of flowering plants are encased in ______________.

4. The success of angiosperms on land is attributed to their flowers, which attract animal ______________, and to their fruits, which disperse ______________.

*For Questions 5–6, write the letter of the correct answer on the line at the left.*

_____ 5. Which plant's discovery caused botanists to rearrange the classification of plants?

A. *Amborella*

B. *Archaefructus*

C. *Cooksonia*

D. *Magnolia*

_____ 6. Which major group of angiosperms is by far the largest?

A. *Amborella*

B. Eudicots

C. Magnoliids

D. Monocots

## Angiosperm Diversity

7. Complete the table about groups of angiosperms.

| Groups of Angiosperms Based on Seed Structure | | | |
|---|---|---|---|
| **Group** | **Number of Seed Leaves** | **Other Characteristics** | **Examples** |
| Monocots | | | |
| Dicots | | | |

 

Name ______________________ Class ______ Date ______

*For Questions 8–11, match each example with the type of plant it is. Each type may be used more than once.*

| Example | | Type of Plant |
|---|---|---|
| ______ | **8.** Rose shrubs | **A.** Herbaceous |
| ______ | **9.** Oaks | **B.** Woody |
| ______ | **10.** Sunflowers | |
| ______ | **11.** Dandelions | |
| ______ | **12.** Grape vines | |
| ______ | **13.** Petunias | |

**14.** Complete the table about plant life spans.

**Plant Types Based on Life Spans**

| Category | Definition | Examples |
|---|---|---|
| Annuals | | |
| Biennials | | |
| Perennials | | |

## Apply the Big idea

**15.** Could the terms *woody* and *herbaceous* be used to describe other types of plants besides angiosperms? Justify your answer.

______________________________________________

______________________________________________

______________________________________________

______________________________________________

# Chapter Vocabulary Review

**Crossword Puzzle** *Complete the puzzle by entering the term that matches the description.*

**Across**

5. a moss or its relative
8. plant with two seed leaves in seeds
9. sugar-conducting vascular tissue
10. structure in which a female gametophyte develops
11. sperm-producing organ of seedless plants
12. plant with vascular tissues
13. spore-producing structure of seedless plants

**Down**

1. egg-producing organ of seedless plants
2. spore-producing stage of plant life cycles
3. water-conducting vascular tissue
4. embryo plant, food supply, and protective covering
6. gamete-producing stage of the plant life cycle
7. the transfer of pollen
10. egg-containing structure of flowering plants

Name ______________________ Class ______ Date ________

CHAPTER
# MYSTERY

## STONE AGE STORYTELLERS

In the Chapter Mystery, you learned about Iceman, who died 5300 years ago. His body is the oldest naturally preserved mummy ever recovered. Many plant materials were preserved along with Iceman. It's very unusual for plant materials to survive that long.

21st Century Learning

## Iceman of the Future?

The environmental conditions where Iceman died were unique. The glacial ice he was found in helped to preserve him and many of his belongings for thousands of years before hikers discovered him in 1991. Consider what might happen to a climber today who died on a mountaintop and whose body became trapped in ice. The article below is a fictional broadcast account of the discovery of Iceman II in the year 3008.

**Afternoon Mindcast, January 8, 3008**—Hikers on Pike's Glacier literally stumbled upon a major anthropological discovery this morning. When Klendon Deel, 85, tripped over something in the trail, his hiking companion and mother, Mender Yayv Akong, 122, helped him up and then looked for the partially hidden obstacle. It turned out to be an ancient electronic device called a "Hype-Odd," which was used for listening to music aurally. But the most amazing part of the discovery was the skeletal hand still clutching the device.

Akong and Deel beamed the authorities, and within an hour scientists had uncovered the remains of an adult male human. Preliminary tests indicate the man died in February or March of 2016. At that time the glacier did not cover the mountain, which is in an area that was then called "Colorado."

Scientists say that unfortunately most of the man's soft tissue disintegrated through the 100-Year Heat Wave of the 22nd century, the Crustal Shocks of the 24th century, and the Kelvin Ice Age of the 29th century. But according to spokesbeing Nkavrjdn*w, the skeleton, nails, hair, and many of the belongings were all remarkably well preserved. "The lead scientist studying the find is particularly fascinated with the objects remaining in the man's pack," Nkavrjdn*w says. "For example, she thinks she has found what is left of an ancient apple. While the actual fruit is gone, a stem and a pile of seeds remained in the pack."

In addition, a clear bottle was found in the pack. Scientists are planning on doing tests to try to determine what the bottle contained. The only marking they could find on the bottle was a small triangular shape composed of three arrows. Scientists are unsure what this mysterious symbol meant.

Continued on next page ▶

 

Name ______________________ Class ______ Date ______

## 21st Century Themes Science and Global Awareness

**1.** Consider the items you take with you when hiking. Suppose Iceman II had these items. Which of these items do you think would survive?

______________________

______________________

**2.** Which of the items that Iceman II possibly took with him on his hike do you think would *not* survive? Explain your answer.

______________________

______________________

______________________

______________________

**3.** Describe what future scientists might be able to learn about the 21st century by studying Iceman II's belongings. What type of evidence would be difficult for them to interpret?

______________________

______________________

______________________

______________________

______________________

## 21st Century Skills Pondering Plant Products

The skills used in this activity include **information and media literacy, communication skills, creativity and intellectual curiosity,** and **social responsibility.**

Synthetic materials, such as nylon and plastic, tend to be more durable than plant-based materials, such as cotton and paper. Because of this, many modern products are made out of synthetic materials. However, most synthetic materials are made from nonrenewable resources. Use library and Internet resources to compare plant-based materials to synthetic materials. For example, visit the Web sites of companies that manufacture plastic, nylon, paper, or cotton fabric. Consider the following questions:

- How do the costs of plant products compare with those of synthetic products?
- What sort of business opportunities are there in manufacturing products out of plant materials instead of synthetic materials?

*With a group, come up with a new plant-based product. Identify potential customers for the product and discuss how you would market the product to them.*

 

Name ______________________ Class ______ Date ________

# 23 Plant Structure and Function

**Big idea** **Structure and Function**

**Q:** How are cells, tissues, and organs organized into systems that carry out the basic functions of a seed plant?

| | WHAT I KNOW | WHAT I LEARNED |
|---|---|---|
| **23.1** How are plant tissues organized? | | |
| **23.2** How do the structure and function of roots help a plant carry out life processes? | | |
| **23.3** How do the structure and function of stems help a plant carry out life processes? | | |
| **23.4** How do the structure and function of leaves help a plant carry out life processes? | | |
| **23.5** How do plants move materials through their bodies? | | |

 

# 23.1 Specialized Tissues in Plants

## Lesson Objectives

- Identify the principal organs of seed plants.
- Explain the primary functions of the main tissue systems of seed plants.
- Contrast meristems with other plant tissues.

## Lesson Summary

**Seed Plant Structure** All seed plants have three principal organs:

- Roots anchor plants in the ground and absorb water and dissolved nutrients.
- Stems provide a support system for the plant body, a transport system that carries nutrients, and a defensive system that protects the plant.
- Leaves conduct photosynthesis and exchange gases with the air.

**Plant Tissue Systems** Plants have three main tissue systems:

- Dermal tissue is the protective outer covering of a plant. In young plants it consists of a single layer of cells called the **epidermis**. A waxy cuticle often covers epidermis and protects against water loss. In older plants, dermal tissue may be many cell layers deep and may be covered with bark.
- Vascular tissue supports the plant body and transports water and nutrients throughout the plant. The two kinds are xylem, a water-conducting tissue, and phloem, a tissue that carries dissolved nutrients.
  - Xylem contains cells called tracheids, which have cell walls with **lignin**, a complex molecule that resists water and gives wood much of its strength. Angiosperms have a second form of xylem tissue called **vessel elements**, which are arranged end to end on top of one another.
  - Phloem contains **sieve tube elements**, which are arranged end to end. **Companion cells** support the phloem cells and aid in the movement of substances in and out of the phloem.
- Ground tissue produces and stores sugars, and helps support the plant.
  - **Parenchyma** cells have a thin cell wall and a large central vacuole.
  - **Collenchyma** cells have strong, flexible cell walls that help support plant organs.
  - **Sclerenchyma** cells have extremely thick, rigid cell walls that make ground tissue tough and strong.

**Plant Growth and Meristems** **Meristems** are regions of unspecialized cells in which mitosis produces new cells that are ready for differentiation.

- **Apical meristems** are found in the tips of stems and roots.
- Floral meristems produce the tissues of flowers.

Name ______________________________ Class ______ Date ________

# Seed Plant Structure

**1.** List the three principal organs of seed plants, and state the function of each one.

______________________________________________________________________

______________________________________________________________________

______________________________________________________________________

**2.** What adaptation helps leaves conserve water?

______________________________________________________________________

# Plant Tissue Systems

*For Questions 3–6, complete each statement by writing the correct word or words.*

**3.** The three main tissue systems of plants are ____________ tissue, ____________ tissue, and ____________ tissue.

**4.** The cuticle protects against ____________ loss.

**5.** Some epidermal cells have tiny projections known as ____________, which may give a leaf a fuzzy appearance.

**6.** Dermal tissue in roots contains ____________ cells that help absorb water.

*For Questions 7–11, match the vascular-tissue elements with their descriptions.*

| Vascular-Tissue Elements | Description |
|---|---|
| _____ **7.** Tracheids | **A.** The main phloem cells |
| _____ **8.** Lignin | **B.** Long, narrow xylem cells with openings in their cell walls |
| _____ **9.** Vessel elements | **C.** Cells that support the phloem cells and aid in the movement of substances |
| _____ **10.** Sieve tube elements | **D.** Xylem cells arranged end to end on top of one another |
| _____ **11.** Companion cells | **E.** The substance in the cell walls of dead tracheids that makes wood tough |

**12.** How can water move from one tracheid into a neighboring cell?

______________________________________________________________________

______________________________________________________________________

______________________________________________________________________

**13.** How can materials move from one sieve tube element into the next?

______________________________________________________________________

______________________________________________________________________

______________________________________________________________________

Name ______________________ Class ______ Date ______

**14.** Complete the table that compares ground-tissue cells.

| Ground-Tissue Cells | | |
|---|---|---|
| **Type of Cell** | **Structure** | **Function** |
| | | Photosynthesis in leaves |
| | Cells with strong, flexible cell walls | |
| | Cells with extremely thick, rigid cell walls | |

## Plant Growth and Meristems

*For Questions 15–19, write True if the statement is true. If the statement is false, change the underlined word or words to make the statement true.*

__________ **15.** Meristems are regions of the plant that produce new cells by mitosis.

__________ **16.** Apical meristems are found in the growing tip of a root or stem.

__________ **17.** The specialized cells that result from cell division in meristems have thin cell walls.

__________ **18.** Newly produced plant cells undergo fertilization as they mature into different cell types.

__________ **19.** An apical meristem changes into a floral meristem when its pattern of gene expression changes.

### Apply the Big idea

**20.** Plants are the source of many useful fibers, such as cotton and linen. Fibers are long, thin structures that have strength and flexibility. Which plant tissue system produces fibers such as cotton and linen? Justify your answer.

______________________________________________

______________________________________________

______________________________________________

______________________________________________

______________________________________________

______________________________________________

 

# 23.2 Roots

## Lesson Objectives

- Describe the main tissues in a mature root.
- Describe the different functions of roots.

## Lesson Summary

**Root Structure and Growth** The root is the first part of a plant to emerge from a seed.

- Plants have two main types of root systems:
  - Taproot systems are found mainly in dicots and consist of a large primary root that has many smaller branches.
  - Fibrous root systems are found mainly in monocots and consist of many equally sized branch roots. They help prevent topsoil from being washed away.
- Roots contain cells from the three tissue systems. A mature root has an outside layer, called the epidermis, and also contains vascular tissue and a large area of ground tissue. The root system is important to water and mineral transport.
  - The root's epidermis performs the dual functions of protection and absorption. Its surface is covered with thin cellular projections called **root hairs**, which produce a large surface area that allows water and minerals to enter.
  - Ground tissue called **cortex** stores products of photosynthesis, such as starch. Water and minerals move through the cortex. A layer called the **endodermis** encloses the vascular cylinder.
  - The xylem and phloem together make up a region called the **vascular cylinder** at the center of the root.
  - Apical meristems produce new cells near the root tip, which is covered by a tough **root cap** that protects the root tip as it grows into the soil.

**Root Functions** Roots support a plant, anchor it in the ground, store food, and absorb water and dissolved nutrients from the soil.

- Roots take in many essential inorganic nutrients, such as nitrogen and potassium.
- Active transport brings the mineral ions of dissolved nutrients from the soil into the plant.
- Cells of the root epidermis create conditions under which osmosis causes water to "follow" ions and flow into the root.
- The waterproof **Casparian strip** enables the endodermis to filter and control the water and nutrients that enter the vascular cylinder, as well as ensuring that nutrients do not leak out.
- Root pressure, produced within the vascular cylinder by active transport, forces water through the vascular cylinder and into the xylem.

Name ______________________ Class ______ Date ________

# Root Structure and Growth

**1.** Complete the table that compares the types of root systems.

| Types of Root Systems | | | |
|---|---|---|---|
| **Type of Root** | **Description** | **Mainly in Dicots or Monocots?** | **Examples** |
| | Long and thick primary roots that grow deep into the soil | | |
| | Equally sized branch roots that grow separately from the base of the stem | | |

*For Questions 2–6, complete each statement by writing the correct word or words.*

**2.** A mature root has a large area of ____________ tissue between its dermal and vascular tissues.

**3.** A root's surface area for absorption of water is increased by ____________.

**4.** One function of the ____________ is the storage of starch.

**5.** The ____________ cylinder, made up of xylem and phloem, is found at the center of a root.

**6.** A root's apical meristem can be found just behind the ____________.

**7.** THINK VISUALLY Complete the illustration of a cross section of a root by adding labels for the parts indicated.

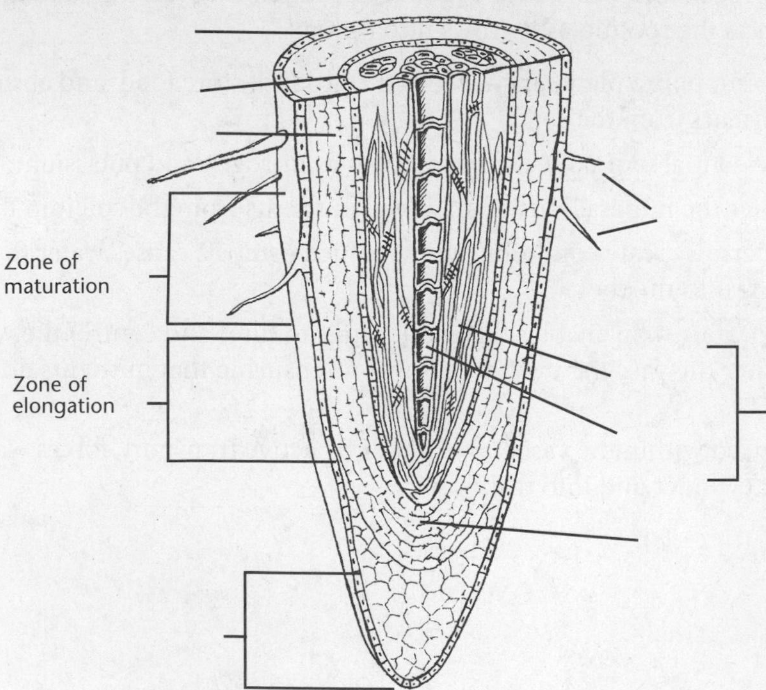

## Root Functions

**8.** Name at least two functions, besides uptake of water and nutrients, of a plant's roots.

______

**9.** What is the role of active transport in the uptake of water by plant roots?

______

**10.** Where in roots are active transport proteins located?

______

**11.** What happens to water and dissolved minerals after they move across the epidermis of a root?

______

**12.** Why is there a one-way passage of materials into the vascular cylinder in plant roots?

______

**13.** How do water and nutrients cross the endodermis that surrounds the vascular cylinder?

______

**14.** What is root pressure?

______

### Apply the Big idea

**15.** People often give potted houseplants more fertilizer than they need. As a result, the plants begin to wilt and eventually die instead of getting larger and healthier. What could be the reason for this result?

______

 

# 23.3 Stems

## Lesson Objectives

- Describe the main functions of stems.
- Contrast the processes of primary growth and secondary growth in stems.

## Lesson Summary

**Stem Structure and Function** Aboveground stems have three main functions:

- Stems produce leaves, branches, and flowers.
- Stems hold leaves up to the sun.
  - Growing stems contain distinct **nodes**, where leaves are attached.
  - **Buds** contain apical meristems that can produce new stems and leaves.
- Stems transport substances throughout the plant.
  - Vascular tissues are arranged in clusters of xylem and phloem called **vascular bundles**. In monocots, vascular bundles are scattered throughout the stem; in dicots they are arranged a cylinder, or ring.
  - In a young dicot, the parenchyma cells inside the ring of vascular tissue are known as **pith**.

**Growth of Stems** One type of growth adds length to a plant's stems and roots. The other adds width, or thickens stems and roots.

- **Primary growth** of stems is the result of elongation of cells produced in the apical meristem. It takes place in all seed plants.
- **Secondary growth** is an increase in the thickness of stems and roots that is common among dicots and gymnosperms but rare in monocots. In conifers and dicots, secondary growth takes place in meristems called the vascular cambium and cork cambium.
  - The **vascular cambium** produces vascular tissues and increases the thickness of stems over time.
  - The **cork cambium** produces the outer covering of stems.
  - "Wood" is actually layers of secondary xylem produced by the vascular cambium. **Heartwood**, near the center of the stem, contains old xylem that no longer conducts liquids. **Sapwood** surrounds heartwood and is active in fluid transport.
  - In most of the temperate zone, tree growth is seasonal. Tree rings can be used to estimate a tree's age and provide information about past climate and weather conditions. In a mature stem, all of the tissues found outside the vascular cambium make up the **bark**.

Name ______________________ Class ______ Date ______

# Stem Structure and Function

1. What are the three main functions of stems?

2. What is an example of a stem that conducts photosynthesis and stores water?

3. What is a node?

4. What kind of plant tissue does a bud contain?

5. What does a vascular bundle contain?

6. Complete the cross-section diagrams by writing labels for the structures indicated.

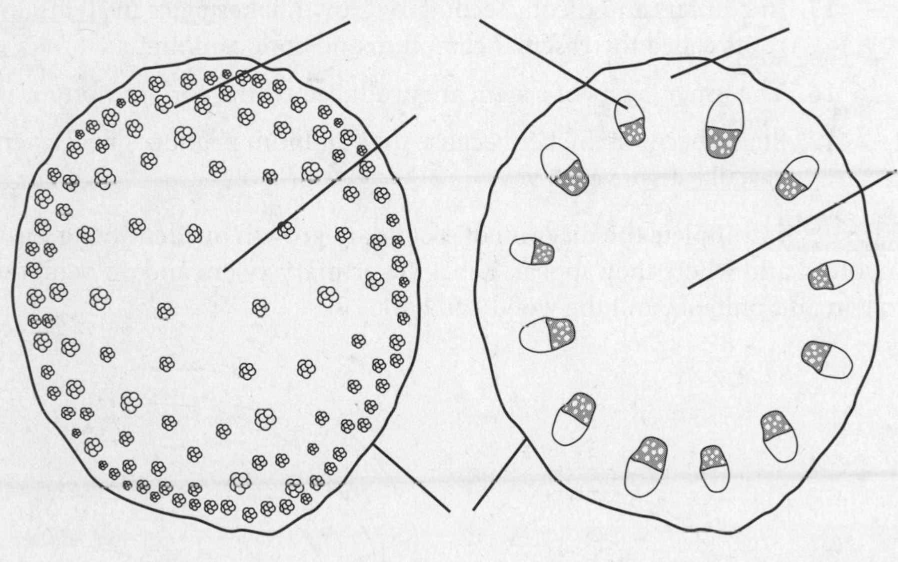

7. Complete the compare and contrast chart.

| Structure of Monocot Stems and Dicot Stems | |
|---|---|
| **Similarities** | **Differences** |
| | |

 

Name ______________________ Class ______ Date ______

# Growth of Stems

*For Questions 8–17, write True if the statement is true. If the statement is false, change the underlined word or words to make the statement true.*

__________ **8.** Plants grow in a way that is the same as the way animals grow.

__________ **9.** The number of legs an animal will have is predetermined, but the number of branches a plant will have is not predetermined.

__________ **10.** Primary growth of stems is the result of elongation of cells produced in the ground tissue.

__________ **11.** The increasing thickness of stems and roots in dicots and gymnosperms is called new growth.

__________ **12.** Secondary growth is common in monocots.

__________ **13.** Dicots can grow to great heights because the increase in width supports the weight.

__________ **14.** Vascular cambium forms between the xylem and phloem of the vascular bundles.

__________ **15.** In conifers and dicots, secondary growth takes place in stems and roots called the vascular cambium and cork cambium.

__________ **16.** The inner layers of a stem are produced by the cork cambium.

__________ **17.** Stems become thicker because the cambium produces new layers of vascular tissue each year.

**18.** THINK VISUALLY Complete the diagram of secondary growth by identifying the structures involved and where they appear. Label the primary xylem and phloem, the secondary xylem and phloem, and the wood and bark.

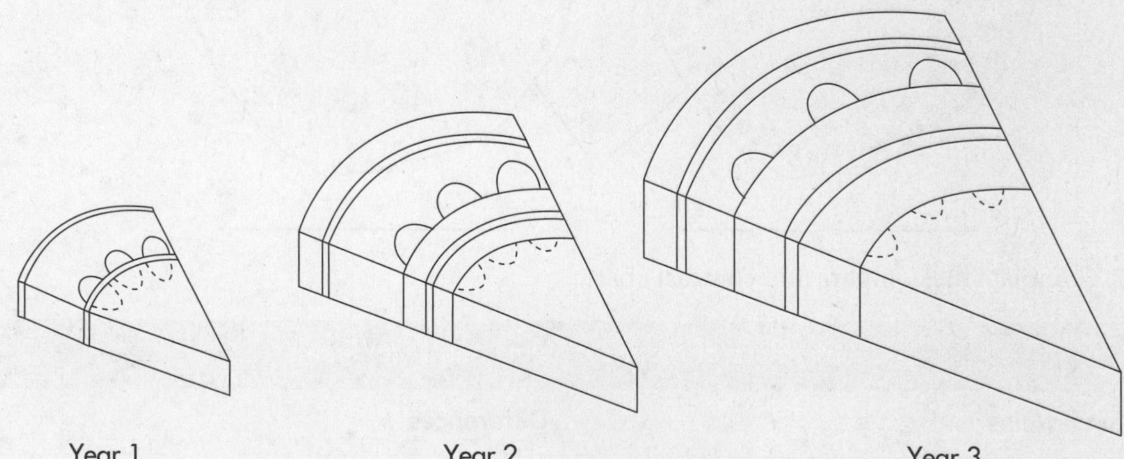

Name ______________________ Class ______ Date ______

*For Questions 19–23, complete each statement by writing the correct word or words.*

**19.** Most of what we call "wood" is made up of layers of ______________ xylem.

**20.** The dark wood that no longer conducts water is called ______________.

**21.** The wood that is active in fluid transport is called ______________.

**22.** The lighter wood in tree rings contains ______________ cells with thin cell walls compared with the cells in darker wood.

**23.** Alternating layers of light wood and dark wood are used to estimate a tree's ______________.

**24.** **THINK VISUALLY** Complete the illustration showing the formation of wood and bark. Use the following terms: wood, bark, cork, cork cambium, vascular cambium, phloem, heartwood, and sapwood.

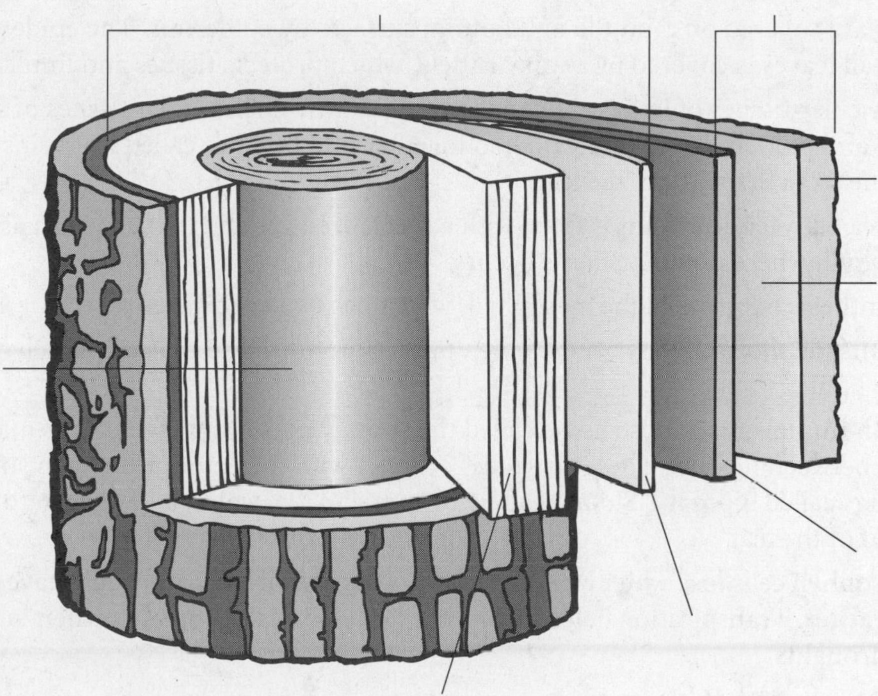

## Apply the Big idea

**25.** "Girdling" is a term that refers to removing the bark of a tree in a complete ring around the trunk or a branch. Predict the effect that girdling will have on a tree. Explain.

______________________________________________

______________________________________________

______________________________________________

______________________________________________

______________________________________________

 

# 23.4 Leaves

## Lesson Objectives

- Describe how the structure of a leaf enables it to carry out photosynthesis.
- Explain how gas exchange in leaves relates to homeostasis.

## Lesson Summary

**Leaf Structure and Function** The structure of a leaf is optimized to absorb light and carry out photosynthesis.

- Most leaves have a thin, flattened part called a **blade**, which is attached to the stem by a thin stalk called a **petiole**. Leaves are made up of the three tissue systems.
  - Leaves are covered on their top and bottom surfaces by epidermis. The epidermis of nearly all leaves is covered by a waxy cuticle, which protects tissues and limits water loss.
  - The vascular tissues of leaves are connected directly to the vascular tissues of stems. Xylem and phloem tissues are gathered together into bundles called leaf veins that run from the stem throughout the leaf.
  - The area between leaf veins is filled with a specialized ground tissue known as **mesophyll**, where photosynthesis occurs.
- Photosynthesis happens in the mesophyll, which has two specialized layers:
  - The **palisade mesophyll** is beneath the upper epidermis. The cells are closely packed and absorb light.
  - Beneath this layer is a loose tissue called the **spongy mesophyll**, which has many air spaces between its cells. These air spaces connect with the exterior through small openings called **stomata**. Stomata allow carbon dioxide, water, and oxygen to diffuse in and out of the leaf.
- The mesophyll cells lose water by evaporation. This loss of water through leaves is called **transpiration**. Transpiration helps to cool the leaves, but also threatens their survival during droughts.

**Gas Exchange and Homeostasis** A plant's control of gas exchange is one of the most important elements of homeostasis.

- Plant leaves allow gas exchange between air spaces in the spongy mesophyll and the exterior by opening their stomata.
- Plants maintain homeostasis by keeping their stomata open just enough to allow photosynthesis to take place but not so much that they lose an excessive amount of water.
- **Guard cells** are highly specialized cells that surround the stomata and control their opening and closing depending on environmental conditions.
- Wilting results from the loss of water and pressure in a plant's cells. The loss of pressure causes a plant's cell walls to bend inward. When a plant wilts, its stomata close so the plant can conserve water.

Name ______________________ Class ______ Date ________

# Leaf Structure and Function

*For Questions 1–4, complete each statement by writing the correct word or words.*

1. The structure of a leaf is optimized for the purposes of absorbing ____________ and carrying out ____________.
2. The ____________ of nearly all leaves is covered by a waxy ____________.
3. The vascular tissues of leaves are connected directly to the vascular tissues of ____________.
4. The area between leaf veins is filled with a specialized ground tissue known as ____________.

*For Questions 5–10, match the description with the leaf structure.*

| Description | Structure |
|---|---|
| ____ **5.** A layer of mesophyll cells that absorb light that enters the leaf | **A.** leaf vein |
| ____ **6.** Small openings in the epidermis | **B.** blade |
| ____ **7.** The thin, flattened part of a leaf | **C.** petiole |
| ____ **8.** A bundle of xylem and phloem tissues in a leaf | **D.** stomata |
| ____ **9.** A stalk that attaches a leaf to a stem | **E.** spongy mesophyll |
| ____ **10.** A loose tissue with many air spaces between its cells | **F.** palisade mesophyll |

# Gas Exchange and Homeostasis

11. Why can't stomata be kept open all the time?

______________________________________________

______________________________________________

12. Complete the flowchart that summarizes how guard cells help maintain homeostasis.

Guard cells are forced into a curved shape when water pressure ____________.

↓

The thick inner walls of the guard cells pull away from one another, opening the ____________. Water is lost by transpiration.

↓

Guard cells straighten out when water pressure ____________.

↓

The inner walls of the guard cells pull together, closing the ____________.

Name ____________________ Class ______ Date ________

*For Questions 13–17, write the letter of the correct answer on the line at the left.*

_____ **13.** Which is likely to happen to a plant if it starts losing more water than it can take in?

**A.** It will reproduce.
**B.** It will flower.
**C.** It will grow.
**D.** It will wilt.

_____ **14.** Which is a plant that has narrow leaves with a waxy epidermis?

**A.** cactus
**B.** spruce
**C.** rock plant
**D.** rose bush

_____ **15.** A pitcher plant's leaves are adapted for

**A.** conducting photosynthesis.
**B.** limiting transpiration.
**C.** catching and digesting insects.
**D.** pollination and fertilization.

_____ **16.** A rock plant adapts to hot, dry conditions by having very few

**A.** thorns.
**B.** leaves.
**C.** stomata.
**D.** nutrients.

_____ **17.** A cactus's thorns are actually its

**A.** leaves.
**B.** stems.
**C.** roots.
**D.** bark.

## Apply the Big idea

**18.** The inside of the glass or plastic walls of a greenhouse full of plants is very wet on cool days. Where does this water come from?

______________________________________________

______________________________________________

______________________________________________

Name ______________________ Class ______ Date ______

# 23.5 Transport in Plants

## Lesson Objectives

- Explain the process of water movement in a plant.
- Describe how the products of photosynthesis are transported throughout a plant.

## Lesson Summary

**Water Transport** The pressure created by water entering the tissues of a root push water upward in a plant stem, but this pressure is not enough. Other forces are much more important.

- The major force is provided by the evaporation of water from leaves during transpiration. Its pull extends into vascular tissue so that water is pulled up through xylem.
- Both the force of attraction between water molecules, cohesion, and the attraction of water molecules to other substances, **adhesion**, help with water transport. The effects of cohesion and adhesion of water molecules are seen in **capillary action**, which is the tendency of water to rise in a thin tube. Capillary action is important because xylem tissue is composed of tracheids and vessel elements that form hollow, connected tubes.

**Nutrient Transport** The leading explanation of phloem transport is known as the **pressure-flow hypothesis**.

- Active transport moves sugars into the sieve tube from surrounding tissues.
- Water then follows by osmosis, creating pressure in the tube at the source of the sugars.
- If another region of the plant needs sugars, they are actively pumped out of the tube and into the surrounding tissues. Pressure differences move the sugars to tissues where they are needed.
- Changes in nutrient concentration drive the movement of fluid through phloem tissue in directions that meet the nutritional needs of the plant.

# Water Transport

*For Questions 1–2, refer to the Visual Analogy of clowns being pulled up a ladder compared to water being pulled up a tree.*

**1.** VISUAL ANALOGY In the visual analogy of the climbing circus clowns, what makes it possible for the falling clowns to pull others up the ladder?

______________________________________

______________________________________

______________________________________

______________________________________

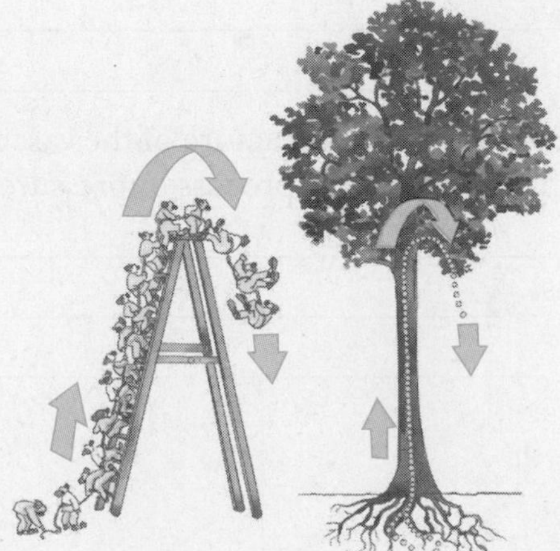

**2.** How are water molecules similar to the clowns?

______________________________________________

______________________________________________

______________________________________________

**3.** Complete the table about the types of attraction between molecules.

| Attraction Between Molecules | |
|---|---|
| **Type of Attraction** | **Definition** |
| Cohesion | |
| Adhesion | |

*For Questions 4–8, complete each statement by writing the correct word or words.*

**4.** Water cohesion is especially strong because water molecules tend to form ____________ bonds with each other.

**5.** The tendency of water to rise in a thin tube is called ____________.

**6.** The height to which water can rise in a tube is determined by its ____________.

**7.** ____________ in xylem form many hollow, connected tubes through which water moves.

**8.** The pull of transpiration extends from the leaves to the ____________ of a plant.

## Nutrient Transport

**9.** According to the pressure-flow hypothesis, why must sieve-tube elements in phloem be living cells?

______________________________________________

______________________________________________

______________________________________________

**10.** Where sugar concentration is high, what is the source of water taken in by phloem?

______________________________________________

______________________________________________

**11.** How does the structure of the vascular bundles in stems and roots and of the veins in leaves make the process of pressure-flow possible?

______________________________________________

______________________________________________

______________________________________________

 

12. Complete the flowchart that summarizes the movement of sugars in plants.

Photosynthesis produces a high concentration of sugars in cells called ______________ cells.

↓

Sugars move from a source cell to phloem, and water moves into the phloem by the process of ______________.

↓

Water moving into the phloem causes an increase in ______________ inside the sieve tubes.

↓

The pressure causes fluid to move through phloem toward ______________ cells, where sugars are less concentrated.

13. What is one importance of the cell walls of xylem to the capillary action that occurs during transpiration?

______________________________________________________________

______________________________________________________________

14. According to the pressure-flow hypothesis, what process prompts rapid spring growth in a plant?

______________________________________________________________

______________________________________________________________

## Apply the Big idea

15. Leaves range in size from very large to very tiny. In what type of environment would you expect to find the most plants with very large leaves? Very small leaves? Explain.

______________________________________________________________

______________________________________________________________

______________________________________________________________

______________________________________________________________

______________________________________________________________

 

Name ______ Class ______ Date ______

# Chapter Vocabulary Review

*For Questions 1–2, refer to the diagram.*

**1.** What are the names of the two parts of a leaf indicated in the diagram?

**A.** ______

**B.** ______

**2.** What process do the structures control?

______

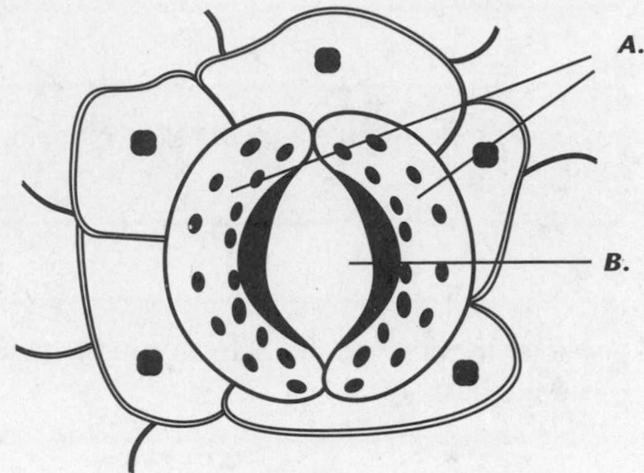


*For Questions 3–9, match the description with the tissue or cell type.*

| Description | | Tissue and Cell Types |
|---|---|---|
| ______ | **3.** Ground tissue specialized for photosynthesis | **A.** sclerenchyma |
| ______ | **4.** Layer of ground tissue that encloses the vascular cylinder | **B.** collenchyma |
| ______ | **5.** Thick-walled cells in ground tissue | **C.** parenchyma |
| ______ | **6.** Dermal tissue in leaves and young plants | **D.** mesophyll |
| ______ | **7.** Region of actively dividing unspecialized cells | **E.** meristem |
| ______ | **8.** Very thick-walled cells that make ground tissue such as seed coats tough and strong | **F.** epidermis |
| ______ | **9.** Thin-walled cells in ground tissue | **G.** endodermis |

*For Questions 10–16, complete each statement by writing the correct word or words.*

**10.** Most leaves have a flattened part called a ______, which is attached at a ______ on the stem by a ______.

**11.** The root ______ increase a root's surface area for absorption, while the root ______ protects the growing tip of the root.

**12.** The cells of the ______ mesophyll are tightly packed, but many air spaces separate the cells of the ______ mesophyll.

**13.** The meristem between xylem and phloem cells is called ______ and forms wood by ______.

**14.** In a mature stem, the tissues outside the vascular cambium make up the ______; the tissues include phloem, cork, and the ______.

**15.** Water is drawn to the material in cell walls by the process called ______.

**16.** Monocot stems have scattered ______ while dicots form a ringlike pattern around the ______.

 

CHAPTER
# MYSTERY
## THE HOLLOW TREE

In the Chapter Mystery, you learned about a tree that begins growing in the branches of other trees. Its roots get nutrients from materials that collect in the folds in the host tree's bark.

21st Century Learning

## Scale Drawings

Engineers often look to nature for inspiration. Early designers of airplane wings examined birds. Modern camera lens engineers are using the human eye for inspiration. Similarly, an engineer interested in extracting water or oil from the ground might look to a plant's roots for ideas. The engineer might start by making a model of a root.

Often, the first step in building a model is making a scale drawing of the object. A scale drawing is a drawing that is the same shape but not the same size as the actual object. Maps and blueprints are examples of scale drawings.

Scale drawings are often used to show objects that are too large or too small to be shown in detail in their actual sizes. For example, the root used for the blueprint below is actually 1/1,000 the size of the drawing. This makes the scale of the drawing 1 cm = 0.001 cm.

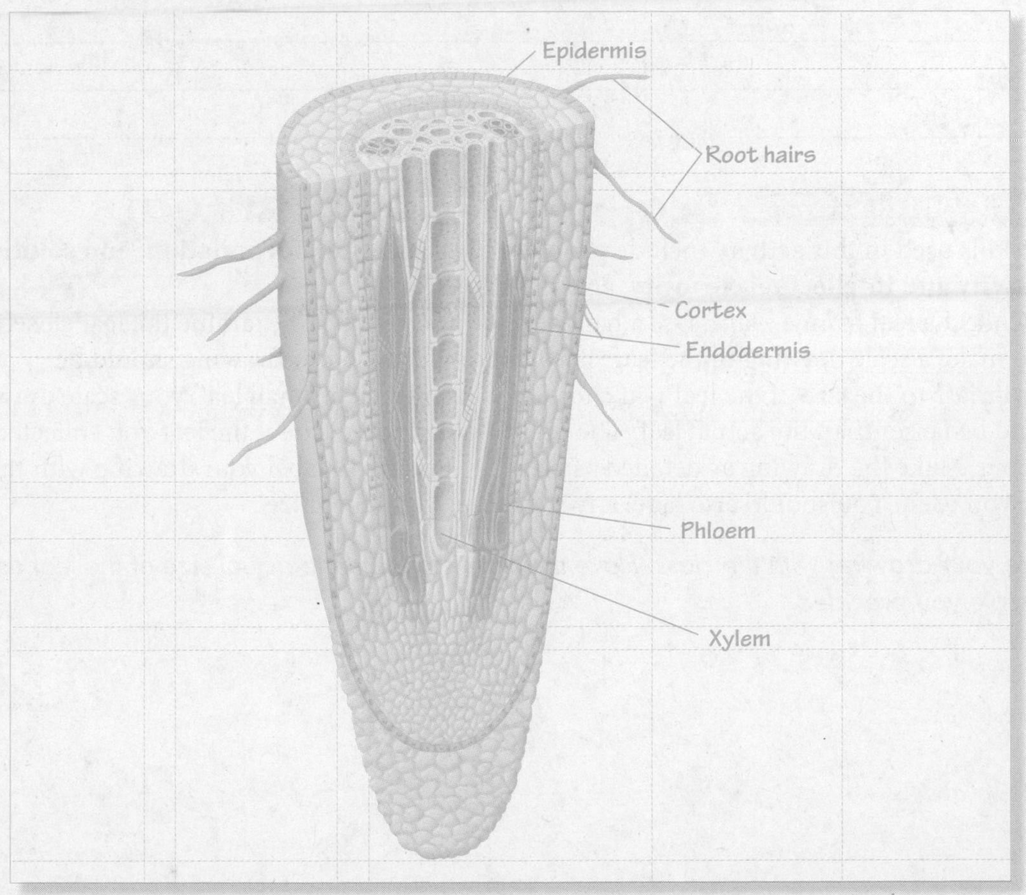


Continued on next page ▶

Name ______________________ Class ______ Date __________

## 21st Century Themes Science Literacy

1. Considering the scale of the root blueprint, approximately how long would the root hairs on the actual root be?

_______________________________________________

2. If you were building a working model of a root, what properties would you want the root hairs to have?

_______________________________________________

_______________________________________________

3. Suppose the root blueprint is reduced to half its current size. What would the scale then be?

_______________________________________________

4. The root used to draw the blueprint is very small, thus the drawing is bigger than the actual object. Give an example of a plant part that you would most likely need to draw on a smaller scale if you were making a blueprint of that part.

_______________________________________________

5. Suppose you were going to use the root blueprint to build a model. Give some examples of materials you might use when making your model. Explain your answer.

_______________________________________________

_______________________________________________

_______________________________________________

_______________________________________________

_______________________________________________

## 21st Century Skills Scale Drawing of a Leaf

The skills used in this activity include **problem identification, formulation, and solution**; **creativity and intellectual curiosity**; and **self-direction.**

Collect a leaf from a plant. Use a hand lens or microscope to examine the leaf closely. Then make a scale drawing of the leaf. The scale you use in your drawing should be appropriate to the size of the leaf you chose. If you collected a small leaf, your scale drawing should be larger than the actual leaf. The opposite should be true if the leaf you collected is very big. Make the drawing as detailed as possible. Be sure to label your drawing with the scale you used. You should also label any structures you recognize.

*Share your drawing with the class. Have the class calculate the actual size of the leaf using the scale you provided.*

Name ______________________ Class ______ Date ______

# 24 Plant Reproduction and Response

**Big idea** **Growth, Development, and Reproduction**

**Q:** How do changes in the environment affect the reproduction, development, and growth of plants?

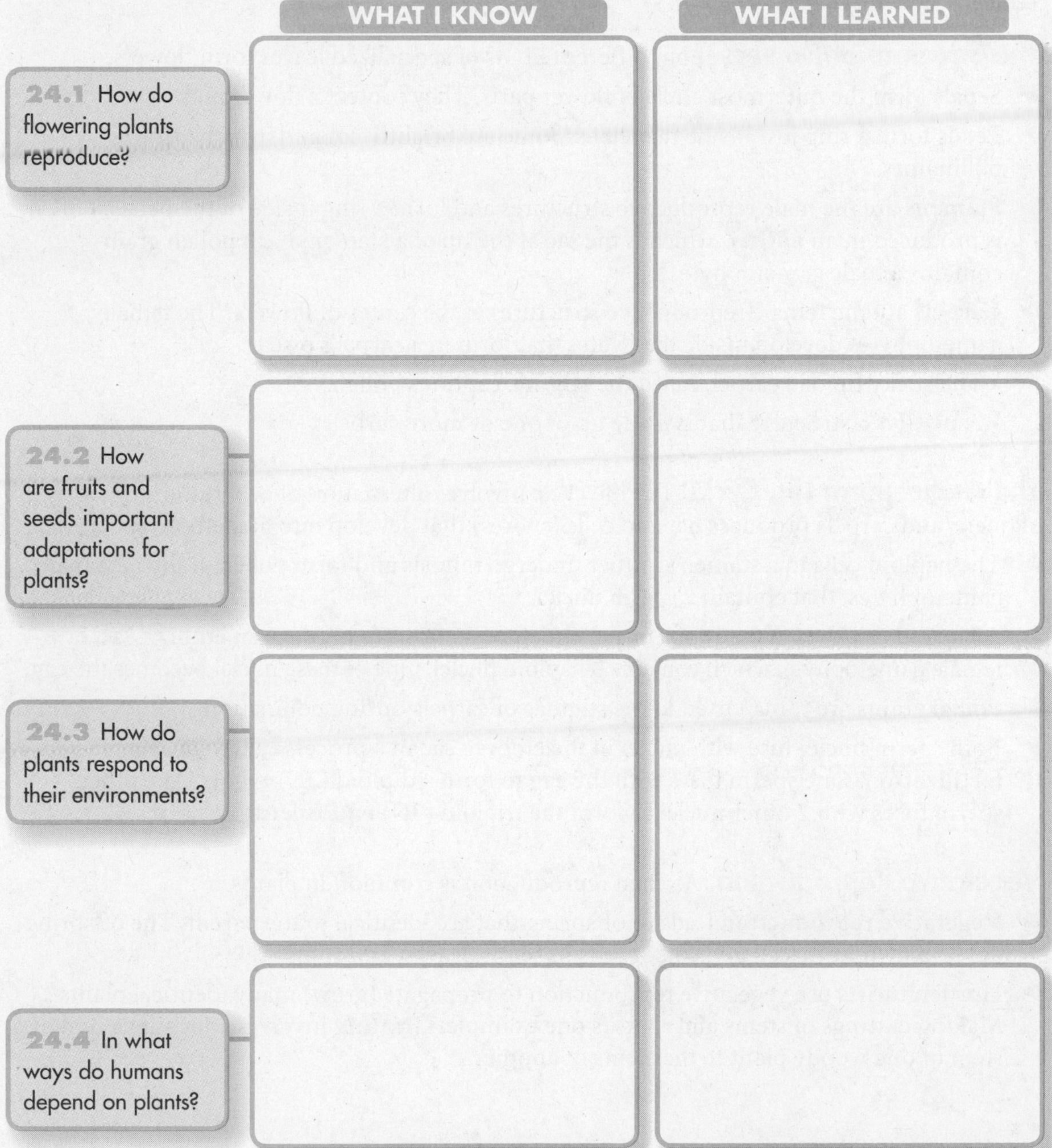

| | WHAT I KNOW | WHAT I LEARNED |
|---|---|---|
| **24.1** How do flowering plants reproduce? | | |
| **24.2** How are fruits and seeds important adaptations for plants? | | |
| **24.3** How do plants respond to their environments? | | |
| **24.4** In what ways do humans depend on plants? | | |

 

Name ______________________ Class ______ Date ______

# 24.1 Reproduction in Flowering Plants

## Lesson Objectives

- Identify the functions of various structures of a flower.
- Explain how fertilization differs between angiosperms and other plants.
- Describe vegetative reproduction.

## Lesson Summary

### The Structure of Flowers
Four different kinds of specialized leaves form flowers.

- Sepals form the outermost circle of flower parts. They protect a flower bud.
- Petals form a ring just inside the sepals. Some are brightly colored, which attracts pollinators.
- **Stamens** are the male reproductive structures and form a ring inside of the petals. Pollen is produced in an **anther**, which is the sac at the tip of a stamen. Each pollen grain contains a male gametophyte.
- **Carpels** are the female reproductive structures at the center of flowers. The female gametophytes develop inside the ovules that form in a carpel's ovary.
  - The sticky tip of a carpel, called the **stigma**, captures pollen.
  - A **pistil** is a structure that is made up of one or more carpels.

### The Angiosperm Life Cycle
The life cycle involves alternation of generations. Meiosis in stamens and carpels produces haploid cells (spores) that develop into gametophytes.

- The haploid cells in a stamen's anther undergo mitosis and form pollen grains, the male gametophytes, that contain 2 sperm nuclei.
- A haploid cell in each ovule of a carpel undergoes mitosis to produce an **embryo sac**, or female gametophyte, which contains 8 haploid nuclei. One of these nuclei becomes the egg.
- Pollen grains are transported to the stigmas of carpels during pollination.
- Both sperm nuclei fuse with nuclei in the embryo sac in a process called **double fertilization**. One sperm fuses with the egg to form a diploid (2N) zygote. The other sperm fuses with 2 other nuclei to form the triploid (3N) **endosperm**.

### Vegetative Reproduction
Asexual reproduction is common in plants.

- **Vegetative reproduction** leads to offspring that are identical to the parent. The offspring develop by mitotic cell division of cells in stems, leaves, and roots.
- Horticulturists use vegetative reproduction to propagate (grow) many identical plants. Making cuttings of stems and roots is one example. **Grafting** involves attaching a bud or a stem of one woody plant to the stems of another.

# The Structure of Flowers

*For Questions 1–10, match the floral part with its description.*

| Floral Part | Description |
|---|---|
| ______ **1.** anthers | **A.** Stalk with a stigma at the top |
| ______ **2.** carpels | **B.** Structures that produce male gametophytes |
| ______ **3.** filament | **C.** Structure that contains one or more ovules |
| ______ **4.** ovary | **D.** Outermost circle of green floral parts |
| ______ **5.** petals | **E.** Long, thin structure that supports an anther |
| ______ **6.** pollen | **F.** Floral parts that produce female gametophytes |
| ______ **7.** sepals | **G.** Yellowish dust that contains male gametophytes |
| ______ **8.** stamen | **H.** Male structure with an anther and a filament |
| ______ **9.** stigma | **I.** Brightly colored parts just inside the sepals |
| ______ **10.** style | **J.** Sticky, top portion of style |

**11.** Complete the illustration by labeling the parts of the flower indicated.

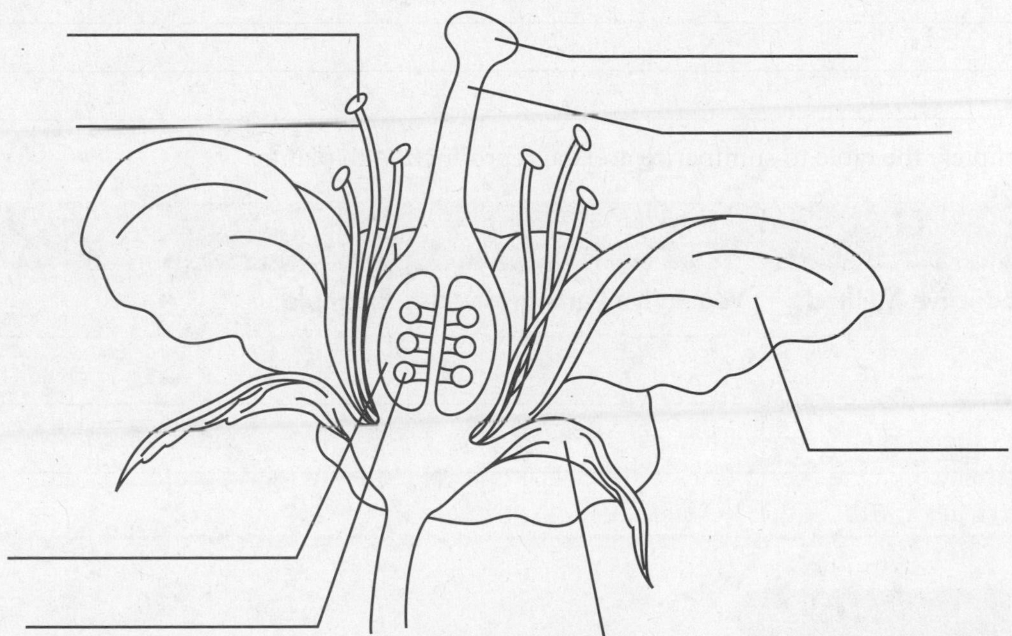

# The Angiosperm Life Cycle

*For Questions 12–15, complete each statement by writing the correct word or words.*

**12.** The body of an adult plant with flowers is the ______________ generation of the plant's life cycle.

**13.** The gametophytes of angiosperms have cells with nuclei that have the ______________ number of chromosomes.

 

14. A male ______________ of an angiosperm is a pollen grain.

15. A(n) ______________ contains a female gametophyte of an angiosperm.

*For Questions 16–20, write True if the statement is true. If the statement is false, change the underlined word or words to make the statement true.*

______________ **16.** In pollination, pollen grains are transferred to the <u>ovary</u> of a flower.

______________ **17.** A pollen tube delivers <u>one</u> sperm to an ovule.

______________ **18.** The fertilized egg in an ovule becomes the <u>zygote</u> of a new sporophyte.

______________ **19.** Triploid tissue, called <u>endosperm</u>, forms in double fertilization.

______________ **20.** A fertilized <u>embryo sac</u> then develops into a seed.

## Vegetative Reproduction

21. What is vegetative reproduction in plants?

______________________________________________

______________________________________________

22. Give an advantage and a disadvantage of vegetative reproduction to plants.

______________________________________________

______________________________________________

______________________________________________

23. Complete the table to summarize asexual reproduction in plants.

| Vegetative Reproduction in Plants | | |
|---|---|---|
| **Reproductive Method** | **Vegetative Parts Involved** | **Example** |
| Stolons | | |
| Tubers | | |
| Grafts | | |

### Apply the Big idea

24. How might a long period of rainy weather affect reproduction in wind-pollinated plants?

______________________________________________

______________________________________________

______________________________________________

______________________________________________

______________________________________________

 

Name ______________________ Class ______ Date ______

# 24.2 Fruits and Seeds

## Lesson Objectives

- Describe the development of seeds and fruits.
- Explain how seeds are dispersed.
- List the factors that influence the dormancy and germination of seeds.

## Lesson Summary

**Seed and Fruit Development** Seeds develop in the fruit of angiosperms.

- A seed protects and provides nourishment for a plant embryo.
- An ovary matures into a fruit as an embryo develops within each of its seeds. Some fruits are fleshy, and others are dry. Many foods are fruits.

**Seed Dispersal** Fruits are adaptations for seed dispersal that have been favored by natural selection.

- Animals disperse seeds for many plants that make edible fruits or fruits that cling to animal bodies.
- Wind and water disperse seeds for plants that make fruits with adaptations for gliding on the wind or floating on water.

**Seed Dormancy and Germination** Some seeds sprout right away, and others lie dormant for a period of time.

- In a period of **dormancy**, the embryo of a seed is alive but not growing.
- **Germination** is the resumption of growth by the embryo. Seeds absorb water before germinating. The water causes tissues in a seed to swell, causing the seed coat to crack. The embryonic root emerges first.
- Monocots and dicots have different patterns of germination.
- Dormancy helps the embryos in seeds survive until the environment is favorable for plant growth.

# Seed and Fruit Development

*For Questions 1–6, complete each statement by writing the correct word or words.*

**1.** The function of a seed is to nourish and ______________ a plant embryo.

**2.** After fertilization, ______________ flow into the flower to support the growing embryo.

**3.** A fruit is a matured ______________ of a flower.

**4.** Fruits are adaptations for ______________ seeds.

**5.** Peas, corn, green beans, tomatoes, and rice are all examples of the ______________ of angiosperms.

**6.** In a peanut, the ______________ is the fruit and the nut is the ______________.

Name ______________________ Class ______ Date ______

## Seed Dispersal

*For Questions 7–11, write the letter of the correct answer on the line at the left.*

______ **7.** Which tissue formed in plant reproduction nourishes the embryo?

**A.** nectar **C.** ovary wall

**B.** endosperm **D.** seed coat

______ **8.** In evolutionary terms, seed dispersal is important because it

**A.** allows plants to produce more offspring.

**B.** keeps the number of plants in an area high.

**C.** helps plants form new communities.

**D.** reduces competition with parent plants.

______ **9.** Seeds encased in fleshy, nutritious fruits are usually dispersed by

**A.** animals. **C.** water.

**B.** gravity. **D.** wind.

______ **10.** Which fruit would be adapted for dispersal by water?

**A.** a dry fruit with feathery branches

**B.** a greenish fruit with a sticky surface

**C.** a large, lightweight fruit with a thick, waxy covering

**D.** a small, round fruit with a sweet, jellylike covering

______ **11.** Which is an adaptation of a fruit for dispersal by wind?

**A.** a tough, hard seed coat

**B.** a ring of fleshy projections

**C.** a pair of papery wings

**D.** a hollow, air-filled center

## Seed Dormancy and Germination

**12.** Complete the flowchart to summarize the process of seed germination.

*For Questions 13–20, write True if the statement is true. If the statement is false, change the underlined word or words to make the statement true.*

______________ **13.** In most <u>monocots</u>, the cotyledon remains underground.

______________ **14.** In monocots, a <u>cotyledon</u> protects the young shoot as it emerges.

______________ **15.** The <u>hook</u> of the new shoot of a germinating dicot protects the new leaves from injury by the soil.

Name ______________________________ Class ______ Date ________

______ 16. The <u>primary</u> root is the first root of a new plant.

______ 17. Dormancy enables seeds to <u>live</u> under ideal growing conditions.

______ 18. The seeds of most plants in temperate regions germinate in the <u>fall</u>.

______ 19. For many seeds, a <u>long period of cold</u> is required before dormancy can end.

______ 20. The cones of some pine trees must be exposed to <u>light</u> in order to release their seeds.

21. **THINK VISUALLY** Complete the illustration comparing seed germination in corn (monocot) and a bean (dicot). Under each drawing, identify the kind of plant that is shown, and make a sketch of the missing stage for each in the appropriate circle.

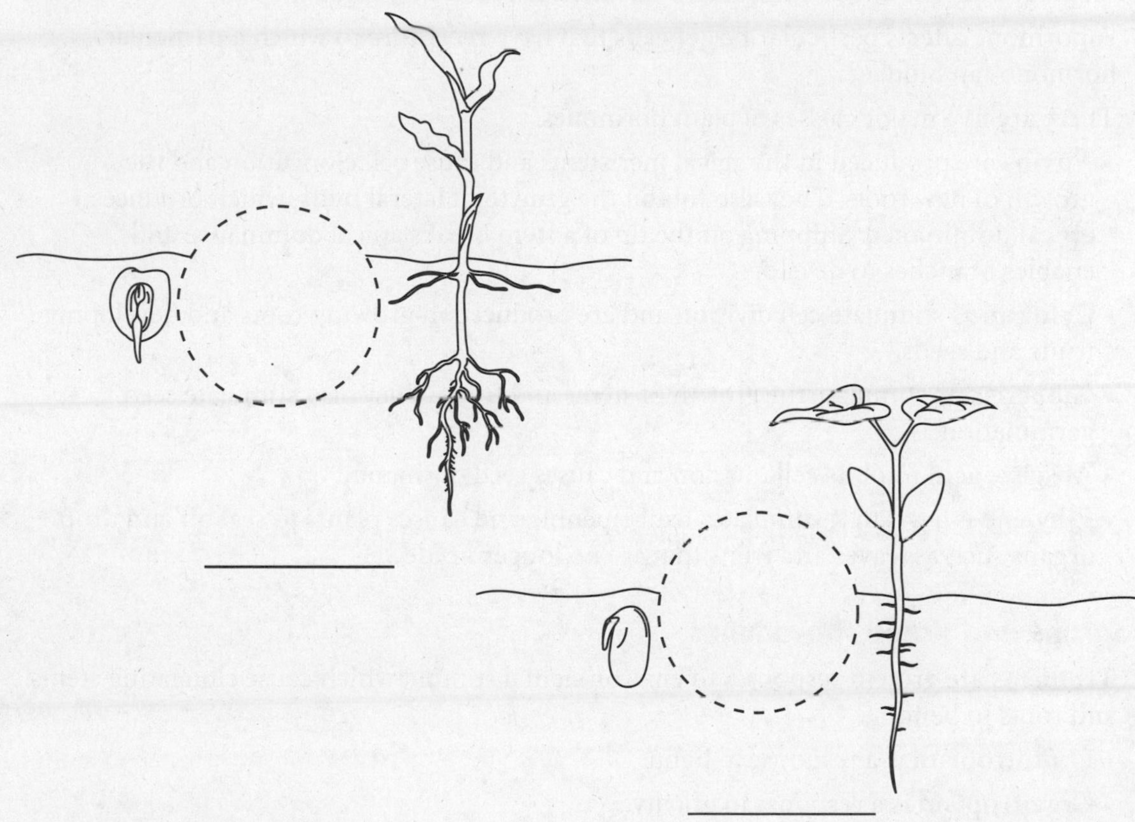

## Apply the Big idea

22. Lupines are flowering plants that make seeds with a thick, hard seed coat. Seeds collected from wild lupines are difficult to grow. What could be the cause of this difficulty? How might a hard seed coat be an adaptation that helps lupines survive?

______________________________________________

______________________________________________

______________________________________________

______________________________________________

______________________________________________

 

Name ______________________ Class ______ Date ________

# 24.3 Plant Hormones

## Lesson Objectives

- Describe the effects of hormones on plant growth and development.
- Identify three tropisms exhibited in plants.
- Describe how plants respond to seasonal change.

## Lesson Summary

**Hormones** Living organisms produce chemical signals that affect the growth, activity, and development of cells and tissues. Such a chemical is called a **hormone**.

- A hormone affects particular **target cells** that have **receptors** to which a particular hormone can bind.
- There are five major classes of plant hormones.
  - **Auxins** are produced in the apical meristems and cause cell elongation and the growth of new roots. They also inhibit the growth of lateral buds, which produces **apical dominance**. Snipping off the tip of a stem breaks apical dominance and enables branches to develop.
  - **Cytokinins** stimulate cell division and are produced in growing roots and developing fruits and seeds.
  - **Gibberellins** stimulate the growth of stems and fruits. They also stimulate seed germination.
  - **Abscisic acid** inhibits cell division and causes seed dormancy.
  - **Ethylene** is a gas that stimulates fruit ripening and causes plants to seal off and drop organs such as leaves and fruits that are no longer needed.

### Tropisms and Rapid Movements

- **Tropisms** are growth responses to environmental stimuli, which cause elongating stems and roots to bend.
  - **Phototropism** is a response to light.
  - **Gravitropism** is a response to gravity.
  - **Thigmotropism** is a response to touch.
- Rapid movements such as the closing of leaves when touched are caused by changes in cell walls and in osmotic pressure in certain cells.

**Response to Seasons** Plants have regular cycles in their patterns of growth, development, and flowering that are tied to seasonal changes. One environmental stimulus that changes with the seasons is the **photoperiod**, the relative length of the light and dark periods in a day. A plant pigment called phytochrome causes a plant's response to the photoperiod.

- The timing of flowering is one plant response to the photoperiod.
- Preparations for winter dormancy, which include leaf loss and the formation of scales around terminal buds, are also responses to the photoperiod.

 

Name ______________________ Class _____ Date _______

# Hormones

1. What is a hormone?

_______________________________________________

_______________________________________________

2. What are the functions of hormones in plants?

_______________________________________________

_______________________________________________

3. What is a target cell?

_______________________________________________

4. Briefly describe the experiments that Charles and Francis Darwin performed on grass seedlings.

_______________________________________________

_______________________________________________

_______________________________________________

_______________________________________________

*For Questions 5–19, match the action with the plant hormone that produces it. Hormones may be used more than once.*

| Action | Plant Hormone |
|---|---|
| _____ **5.** May oppose the effects of auxins | **A.** abscisic acid |
| _____ **6.** Promotes cell elongation | **B.** auxin |
| _____ **7.** Causes petals and leaves to drop | **C.** cytokinins |
| _____ **8.** Promotes seed germination | **D.** ethylene |
| _____ **9.** Promotes seed dormancy | **E.** gibberellin |
| _____ **10.** Stimulates cell division | |
| _____ **11.** Causes the enlargement of fruits | |
| _____ **12.** Causes apical dominance | |
| _____ **13.** Stimulates fruit ripening | |
| _____ **14.** Forms in growing roots | |
| _____ **15.** Forms in aging leaves and flowers | |
| _____ **16.** Opposes the effects of abscisic acid | |
| _____ **17.** Stimulates dramatic stem growth | |
| _____ **18.** Stimulates new root growth | |
| _____ **19.** Inhibits cell division | |

 

Name ______________________ Class ______ Date ______

# Tropisms and Rapid Movements

**20.** What is a tropism?

______________________

______________________

**21.** What causes the bending of stems and roots in tropisms? Give an example.

______________________

______________________

______________________

______________________

**22.** Complete the table about plant tropisms.

| Plant Tropisms | | |
|---|---|---|
| **Tropism** | **Definition** | **Example** |
| Gravitropism | | |
| Phototropism | | |
| | The response of a plant to touch | |

**23.** How are the speed and causes of rapid movements of plants different from the speed and causes of tropisms?

______________________

______________________

______________________

______________________

**24.** List two examples of rapid movements that occur in plants.

______________________

______________________

## Response to Seasons

*For Questions 25–28, complete each statement by writing the correct word or words.*

**25.** Plants that flower when nights are longer than days are called ______________ plants.

**26.** Irises that flower in summer when nights are short are called ______________ plants.

**27.** The relative lengths of the light and dark times in a day are a stimulus called the ______________.

**28.** The chemical that causes the seasonal responses of plants is a type of light-sensitive chemical called a(n) ______________.

**29.** Complete the concept map that summarizes the role of phytochrome in plants.

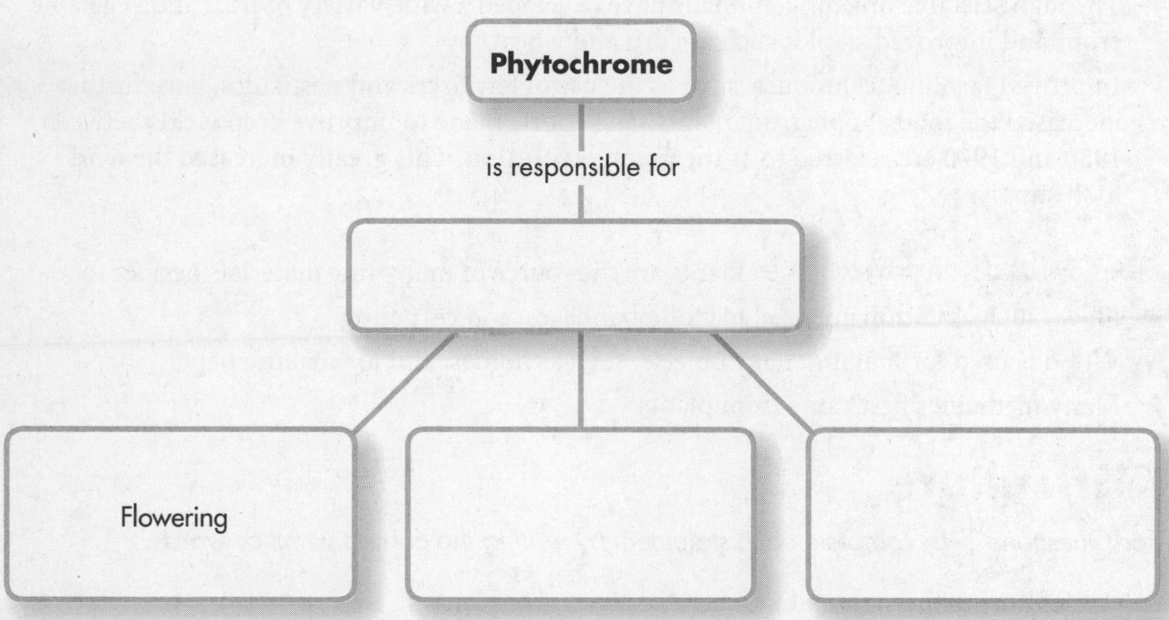


### Apply the Big idea

**30.** You have been asked to suggest a flowering plant that would bloom and beautify a lighted parking lot. The parking lot is only dark between midnight and sunrise. What information should you research about the plants you consider? Explain your answer.

_______________________________________________

_______________________________________________

_______________________________________________

_______________________________________________

_______________________________________________

 

Name ______________________ Class ______ Date ________

# 24.4 Plants and Humans

## Lesson Objectives

Identify the major food-supply crops for humans.

Describe how humans benefit from plants.

## Lesson Summary

**Agriculture** The systematic cultivation of useful plants is called agriculture.

- The beginning of human civilization is linked to the development of agriculture. Worldwide, a few crop plants such as rice, wheat, soybeans, and corn provide the bulk of the food supply for humans and livestock.
- Through selective breeding, humans have developed a wide variety of fruit and vegetable crops and improved staples such as corn and wheat.
- Improved farming techniques, such as the use of fertilizers and pesticides, have further increased the food supply from plants. The efforts made to improve crop yields between 1950 and 1970 are referred to as the **green revolution**. This greatly increased the world's food supply.

**Fiber, Wood, and Medicine** Plants are the source of many raw materials besides food.

- Fibers such as cotton are used in cloth, bandages, and carpeting.
- Wood is used for making many objects, such as homes, and for making paper.
- Many medicines first came from plants.

## Agriculture

*For Questions 1–8, complete each statement by writing the correct word or words.*

**1.** Agriculture is the systematic ______________ of plants.

**2.** The foundation on which human society is built is modern ______________.

**3.** Evidence suggests that agriculture developed between ______________ and ______________ years ago.

**4.** Nearly all agricultural plants belong to the group of plants called ______________.

**5.** The ______________ produced by crop plants such as wheat, rice, and corn are the source of most of the food humans eat.

**6.** Humans changed wild food plants into productive crops through the practice of ______________.

**7.** Cabbage, broccoli, and Brussels sprouts were all developed from the wild ______________ plant.

**8.** The green revolution greatly increased ______________.

Name ______________________ Class ______ Date ______

**9.** Complete the concept map.

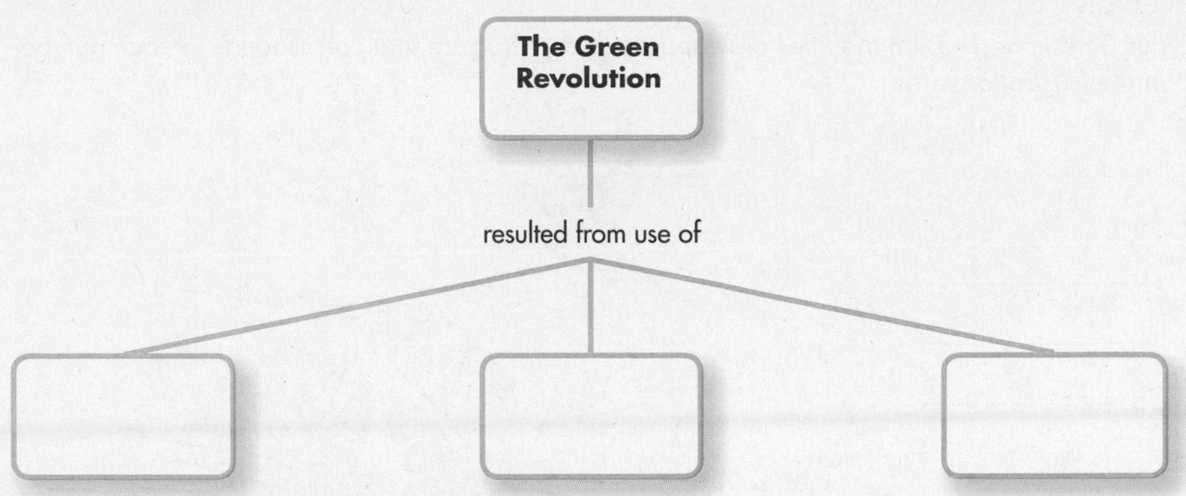


## Fiber, Wood, and Medicine

*For Questions 10–13, write the letter of the correct answer on the line at the left.*

______ **10.** Which is an example of a plant that is a source of food?

**A.** *Aloe vera* **C.** maize

**B.** cotton **D.** Sitka spruce

______ **11.** Cotton fibers are outgrowths of the

**A.** seed coat epidermis. **C.** vascular cambium.

**B.** ripened ovary wall. **D.** vascular bundles.

______ **12.** The wood used to make chairs and musical instruments is made up of which plant tissue?

**A.** the cortex **C.** the mesophyll

**B.** the cambium **D.** the xylem

______ **13.** Which plant contains chemicals that can help burns and other wounds?

**A.** *Aloe vera* **C.** maize

**B.** cotton **D.** Sitka spruce

## Apply the Big idea

**14.** What effect is global climate change likely to have on agriculture?

______________________________________________

______________________________________________

______________________________________________

______________________________________________

 

Name ______________________________ Class ______ Date __________

# Chapter Vocabulary Review

*For Questions 1–3, on the lines provided, label the structure that corresponds to each number in the illustration.*

1. ______________
2. ______________
3. ______________

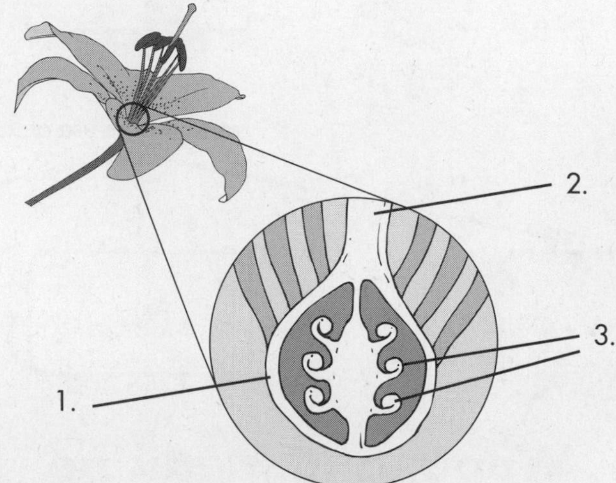


*For Questions 4–15, complete each statement by writing the correct word or words.*

**4.** The female structure of a flower that can be made up of a single carpel or two or more fused carpels is called a ______________.

**5.** A plant hormone that causes stem and fruit growth as well as seed ______________ is called ______________.

**6.** A ______________ cell has ______________ for a particular hormone.

**7.** The female gametophyte of an angiosperm is a small structure called the ______________.

**8.** The food storage tissue that results from double ______________ in angiosperms is called ______________.

**9.** Seed ______________ is a period during which a plant embryo stops growing.

**10.** ______________ is the method of propagating many identical woody plants using the buds of a desirable plant.

**11.** The ripening of fruits is one effect of the plant hormone called ______________.

**12.** Identical offspring produced by a single parent plant result from ______________ reproduction.

**13.** ______________ dominance is a major effect of the plant hormone ______________.

**14.** Pollination occurs when pollen grains land on the ______________ of a flower.

**15.** The ______________ of flowers are the tiny sacs that produce the male gametophytes of angiosperms.

 

# CHAPTER MYSTERY

## THE GREEN LEMONS

In the Chapter Mystery, you learned how one factor could disrupt a plant's ripening schedule. Many factors affect a plant's growth and reproduction, as well as its taste and nutrition. Today's consumers are becoming increasingly conscious of the factors that affect the food they eat.

21st Century Learning

## Organic Food Farming and Labeling

Organic farming is a type of agricultural production system that uses natural methods, such as compost instead of synthetic fertilizers, biological pest control instead of synthetic pesticides, and crop rotation instead of plant growth regulators. Organic farmers are not allowed to use certain products that conventional farmers use. All organic food products must be certified by independent state or private agencies accredited by the U.S. Department of Agriculture.

Many consumers think that organic food tastes better and is more nutritious and healthful. Therefore, they are willing to pay more for food labeled organic. Scientists, however, have not proven that organic food is more nutritious.

### Rules for Labeling Food as Organic

1. Animals producing meat, poultry, eggs, and dairy products must not be given antibiotics or growth hormones. They also cannot be fed animal byproducts, such as feathers and ground-up chicken parts.
2. Cows on organic farms must graze on grass that has not been treated with pesticides.
3. Vegetables must be grown without using conventional pesticides.
4. The use of conventional pesticides, petroleum-based fertilizers, bioengineering, and ionizing radiation is prohibited from all organic food production.

Before any food receives an organic label, a government-approved certifier must inspect the farm where the food is produced as well as the companies that process and transport the food.

## 21st Century Themes Science and Global Awareness

1. Why are organic food products considered more "natural" than conventional food products?

______________________________________________

______________________________________________

2. Why are many consumers willing to pay more for food items labeled "organic"?

______________________________________________

Continued on next page ▶

 

**3.** Why do you think the U.S. Department of Agriculture deems it important to regulate which foods get the "organic" label?

**4.** The first rule states that animals producing organic foods cannot be fed animal byproducts. Why do you think this rule is included? Give an example to support your reasoning.

**5.** Why is important to inspect companies transporting the food as well as those producing the food?

## 21st Century Skills History of Organic Food

The skills used in this activity include **information and media literacy, communication skills, critical thinking and systems thinking, creativity and intellectual curiosity,** and **interpersonal and collaborative skills.**

Work in a small group to find out about the history of organic food. Decide on a graphic to present to the class. For example, your group may want to make a graph to show how the amount of organic food produced in the U.S. has changed over the past few decades. Or, your group might choose to make a poster or a timeline that shows the evolution of what food is considered "organic." Then, present your graphic to the class.

Name ______________________ Class ______ Date ______

# 25 Introduction to Animals

**Big idea** **Unity and Diversity of Life**

**Q:** What characteristics and traits define animals?

| | WHAT I KNOW | WHAT I LEARNED |
|---|---|---|
| **25.1** What is an animal? | | |
| **25.2** How have different animal body plans evolved? | | |

# 25.1 What Is an Animal?

## Lesson Objectives

- List the characteristics that all animals share.
- Differentiate between invertebrates and chordates.
- List and discuss the essential functions that animals perform in order to survive.

## Lesson Summary

**Characteristics of Animals** All animals are multicellular, heterotrophic, and eukaryotic. Their cells lack cell walls.

**Types of Animals** Animals are often classified into two broad categories: invertebrates and chordates.

- **Invertebrates** do not have a backbone, or vertebral column.
  - More than 95 percent of all animal species are invertebrates.
  - Invertebrates are classified in at least 33 phyla, the largest taxonomic groups of animals. Examples of invertebrates are sea stars, jellyfishes, and insects.
- **Chordates** exhibit four characteristics during some stage of development: a dorsal, hollow nerve cord; a notochord; a tail that extends beyond the anus; and pharyngeal pouches.
  - A **notochord** is a supporting rod that runs through the body just below the nerve cord.
  - **Pharyngeal pouches** are paired structures in the throat region.
  - Most chordates develop a backbone, or vertebral column. They are **vertebrates**.

**What Animals Do to Survive** Animals must maintain homeostasis in order to survive. One important way to maintain homeostasis is **feedback inhibition**, also called negative feedback, in which the product or result of a process limits the process itself. In order to maintain homeostasis, animals must

- gather and respond to information;
- obtain and distribute oxygen and nutrients;
- collect and eliminate carbon dioxide and other wastes.

They also reproduce.

## Characteristics of Animals

**1.** Complete the graphic organizer to summarize the characteristics of animals.

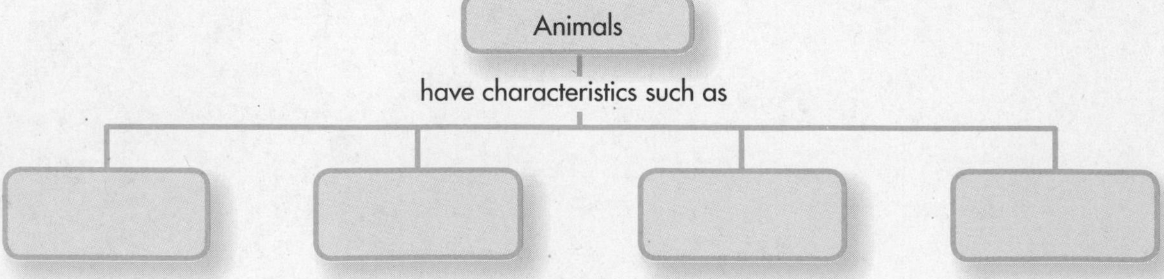

# Types of Animals

**2.** Are invertebrates rare? Explain your answer.

______________________________________________

______________________________________________

**3.** What is an invertebrate?

______________________________________________

______________________________________________

**4.** Why do invertebrates not form a clade?

______________________________________________

______________________________________________

**5.** What are some examples of invertebrates?

______________________________________________

**6.** Look at the diagram of a chordate. Write the name of the labeled structure on the lines below.

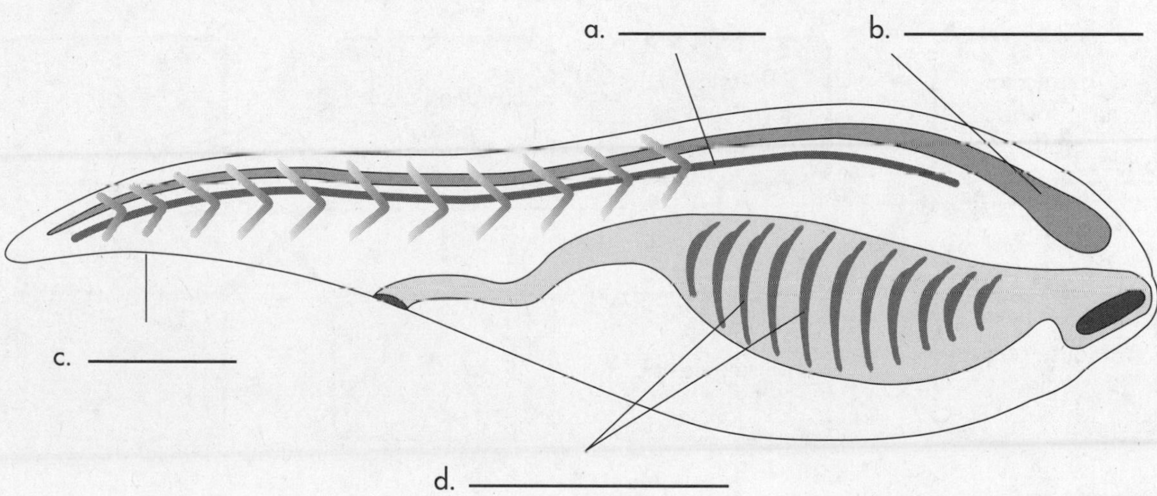


**7.** Are all chordates vertebrates? Explain your answer.

______________________________________________

______________________________________________

**8.** What groups of animals are vertebrates?

______________________________________________

______________________________________________

**9.** Both snakes and earthworms have long, streamlined body shapes, but snakes are vertebrates and earthworms are not. Why are they classified differently despite their similarity in appearance?

______________________________________________

______________________________________________

______________________________________________

 

## What Animals Do to Survive

**10.** Complete the graphic organizer to define three ways that animals maintain homeostasis.

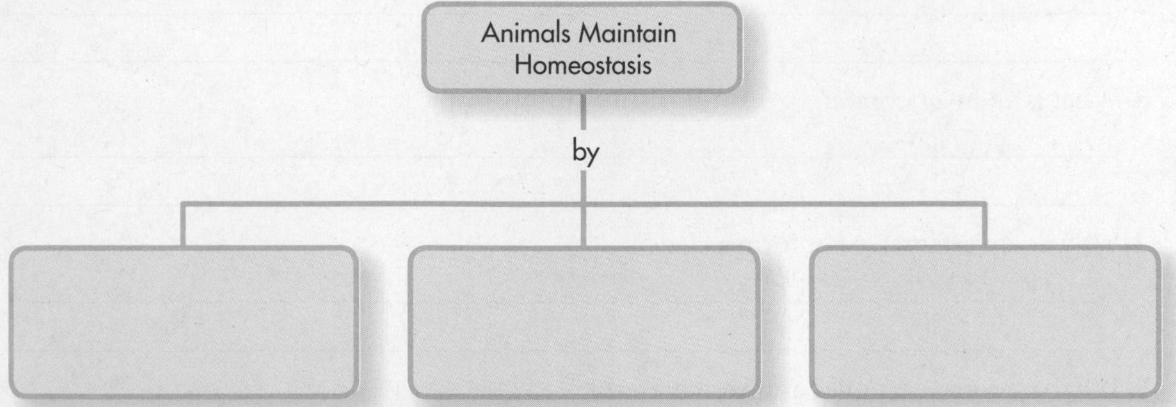


**11.** The diagram on the left below shows the feedback inhibition that maintains temperature in a house. Complete the blank boxes in the diagram on the right below to show how body temperature is maintained in a human being.

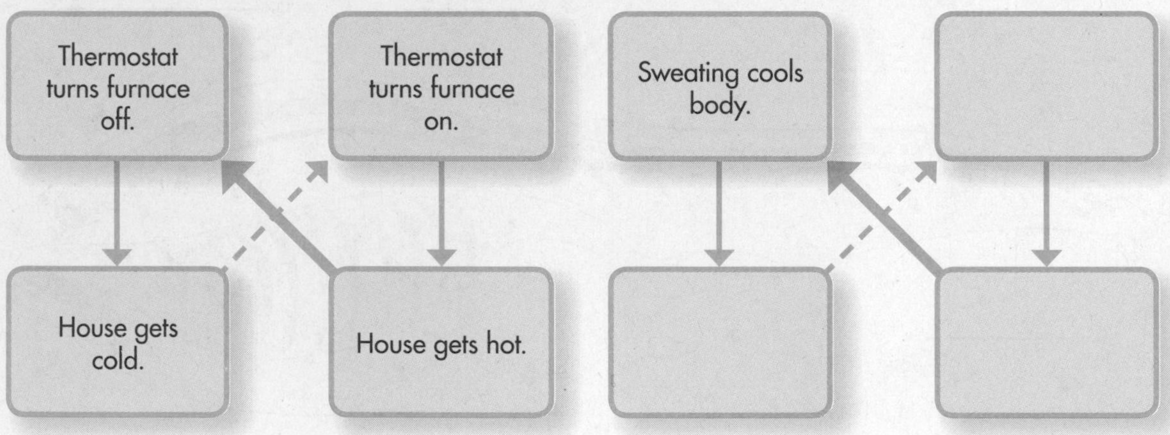


**12.** Describe generally how an animal's nervous and musculoskeletal systems work together to allow it to escape a predator.

______________________________________________

______________________________________________

______________________________________________

______________________________________________

**13.** In complex animals, what system collects metabolic wastes and delivers them to the respiratory and excretory systems?

______________________________________________

**14.** In complex animals, which three body systems work together to obtain and distribute oxygen and nutrients?

______________________________________________

 

Name ______________________ Class _____ Date _________

*For Questions 15–24, write the letter of the correct answer on the line at the left.*

_____ **15.** What system gathers information through receptors for sound, light, chemicals, and other stimuli?

**A.** respiratory
**B.** circulatory
**C.** musculoskeletal
**D.** nervous

_____ **16.** Most chordates have a large number of nerve cells concentrated into a

**A.** backbone.
**B.** notochord.
**C.** brain.
**D.** pharyngeal pouch.

_____ **17.** How does muscle tissue generate force?

**A.** It stretches.
**B.** It shortens.
**C.** It inflates.
**D.** It dilates.

_____ **18.** How do the skeletons of insects and vertebrates differ?

**A.** Insects have fluid skeletons. Vertebrates have external skeletons.
**B.** Insects have external skeletons. Vertebrates have internal skeletons.
**C.** Insects have internal skeletons. Vertebrates have external skeletons.
**D.** Insects have external skeletons. Vertebrates have fluid skeletons.

_____ **19.** What process allows some aquatic animals to "breathe" through their skin?

**A.** diffusion
**B.** digestion
**C.** excretion
**D.** circulation

_____ **20.** Which structure performs a function most similar to that of gills?

**A.** heart
**B.** intestine
**C.** blood vessel
**D.** lung

_____ **21.** Which of these functions requires the coordinated actions of the digestive, circulatory, and excretory systems?

**A.** gathering $O_2$ and distributing it to body systems
**B.** collecting and eliminating $CO_2$ from tissues
**C.** acquiring nutrients and distributing them to body systems
**D.** collecting and eliminating metabolic wastes

 

______ **22.** How do the respiratory system and excretory system differ in the wastes they eliminate?

**A.** The respiratory system eliminates carbon dioxide. The excretory system eliminates ammonia.

**B.** The respiratory system eliminates wastes that contain nitrogen. The excretory system eliminates carbon-based wastes.

**C.** The respiratory system eliminates oxygen and nitrogen. The excretory system eliminates ammonia.

**D.** The respiratory system eliminates ammonia. The excretory system eliminates carbon dioxide.

______ **23.** Which activity is required for survival of the species but not survival of the organism?

**A.** digestion

**B.** excretion

**C.** reproduction

**D.** circulation

______ **24.** What is an advantage of asexual reproduction?

**A.** It increases genetic diversity in a population.

**B.** It produces large numbers of offspring rapidly.

**C.** It increases a species' ability to evolve.

**D.** It produces offspring that are genetically different from the parents.

## Apply the Big idea

**25.** In what ways do invertebrates differ from vertebrates? Identify at least three groups of invertebrates.

______________________________________________

______________________________________________

______________________________________________

______________________________________________

**26.** Suppose you were studying the cell walls of a multicellular organism under a microscope. Were you studying an animal? Explain your answer.

______________________________________________

______________________________________________

 

# 25.2 Animal Body Plans and Evolution

## Lesson Objectives

- Discuss some trends in animal evolution.
- Explain the differences among the animal phyla.

## Lesson Summary

**Features of Body Plans** Each animal phylum has a unique organization of body structures called its "body plan." The features of a body plan include

- levels of organization: cells, tissues, organs, organ systems
- body symmetry:
  - **radial symmetry:** body parts extend from a central point
  - **bilateral symmetry:** left and right sides are mirror images, with front and back ends
- differentiation of germ layers:
  - **endoderm**, the innermost layer
  - **mesoderm**, the middle layer
  - **ectoderm**, the outermost layer
- formation of a cavity, or fluid-filled space between the digestive tract and the body wall:
  - a true **coelom** (found in most complex animal phyla) develops in the mesoderm and is lined with tissue derived from the mesoderm
  - a **pseudocoelom** is only partially lined with mesoderm
  - Some invertebrates lack a body cavity and some have only a primitive, jellylike layer between the ectoderm and endoderm.
- patterns of embryological development
  - Sexually reproducing animals begin life as a **zygote**, or fertilized egg.
  - The zygote develops into a hollow ball of cells, the **blastula**.
  - The blastula folds in on itself and creates a tube that becomes the digestive tract; the tube has a single opening, the blastopore:
    - In **protostomes** (most invertebrates), the blastopore becomes the mouth.
    - In **deuterostomes** (chordates and echinoderms), the blastopore becomes the anus.
- segmentation: repeated parts, such as the segments of worms
- **cephalization**: the concentration of sense organs and nerves near the anterior (head) end
- limb formation: external appendages such as legs, flippers, and wings

**The Cladogram of Animals** The features of body plans provide the evidence needed to build a cladogram, or phylogenetic tree, of all animals. Animal phyla are usually defined by their adult body plans and patterns of embryological development.

- The characteristics of animals vary within each phylum.
- Each phylum may be thought of as an "evolutionary experiment." Phyla with successful body plans have survived.

Name ______________________ Class ______ Date ________

# Features of Body Plans

**1.** Complete the table of main ideas and details about animal body plans. Use the boxes to list and summarize the features of animal body plans.

| Features of Body Plans | |
|---|---|
| **Main Idea: Feature of Body Plan** | **Details: Important structures or patterns of development** |
| Levels of organization | |
| | None, radial, or bilateral |
| Germ layers | |
| Body cavity | |
| Patterns of embryological development | |
| | Repeated parts, such as the segments of worms |
| Cephalization | |
| Limb formation | |

**2.** **THINK VISUALLY** Sketch two common objects that show the difference between radial symmetry and bilateral symmetry. Label your sketches and explain them.

 

3. THINK VISUALLY Label each of these organisms with the kind of symmetry it exhibits.

______________________ ______________________

______________________ ______________________

4. THINK VISUALLY Draw three sketches that show the difference between acoelomate, pseudocoelomate, and coelomate animals. Label ectoderm, mesoderm, and endoderm in your sketches.

 

5. Label the diagram showing the difference between deuterostomes and protostomes. Label the following structures: blastula, blastopore, ectoderm, endoderm, mesoderm, mouth, protostome.

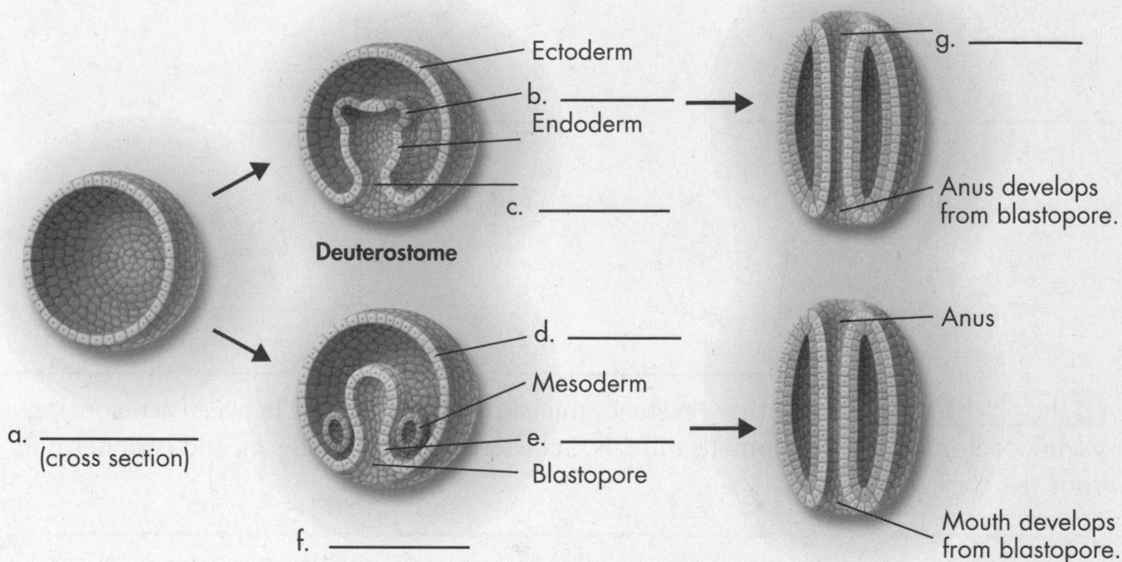


*For Questions 6–14, complete each statement by writing the correct word or words.*

6. Deuterostomes that show radial symmetry in their adult form are called ______________.

7. ______________ are bilaterally symmetrical animals with three germ layers and no coelom.

8. ______________ are protostomes with a true coelom and cephalization without segmentation.

9. Members of the ______________ phylum have no body symmetry.

10. Animals in the ______________ phylum have specialized cells and tissues, but no organs.

11. Both ______________ and ______________ are segmented protostomes with bilateral symmetry.

12. In addition to echinoderms, ______________ are also deuterostomes.

13. An important way in which the body plan of mollusks differs from that of arthropods is that mollusks lack ______________.

14. Only members of the ______________ phylum have a pseudocoelom.

 

# The Cladogram of Animals

*Use the cladogram to answer Questions 15–17.*

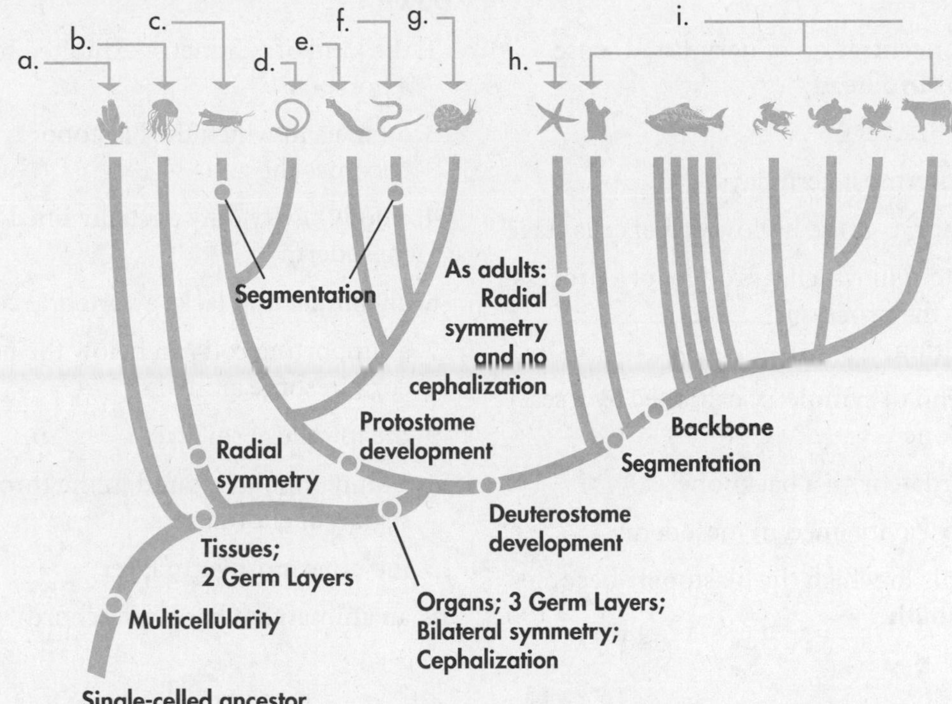


**15.** On the lines provided, label the names of the animal phyla that correspond to the letters in the diagram.

| | | |
|---|---|---|
| **a.** ______ | **d.** ______ | **g.** ______ |
| **b.** ______ | **e.** ______ | **h.** ______ |
| **c.** ______ | **f.** ______ | **i.** ______ |

**16.** What characteristics define the branch of the cladogram that leads to the mollusks?

______

______

**17.** Is a chordate a "better" animal than a sponge? Explain your answer.

______

______

## Apply the Big idea

**18.** Cows, hawks, and whales are all vertebrates. However, their forelimbs are noticeably different. Explain how "evolutionary experiments" that yield variations on a body plan have produced such diversity among vertebrates. Use forelimb structures as an example.

______

______

______

______

# Chapter Vocabulary Review

**Across**

2. the concentration of nerves and sense organs in a head
5. a fertilized egg
8. the outermost germ layer
10. an embryo at the hollow ball of cells stage
12. A system in which a product of a process limits the process is ____________ inhibition.
15. the kind of symmetry exhibited by a sea anemone
16. a chordate with a backbone
17. a body cavity lined in mesoderm
18. animals in which the blastopore becomes the mouth

**Down**

1. the kind of symmetry exhibited by a horse
3. animals in which the blastopore becomes the anus
4. a body cavity only partially lined with mesoderm
6. an animal that lacks a vertebral column
7. a supporting rod just below the nerve cord in some animals
9. the middle germ layer
11. a kind of pouch found in the throat region of chordates
13. the innermost germ layer
14. an animal that has a notochord

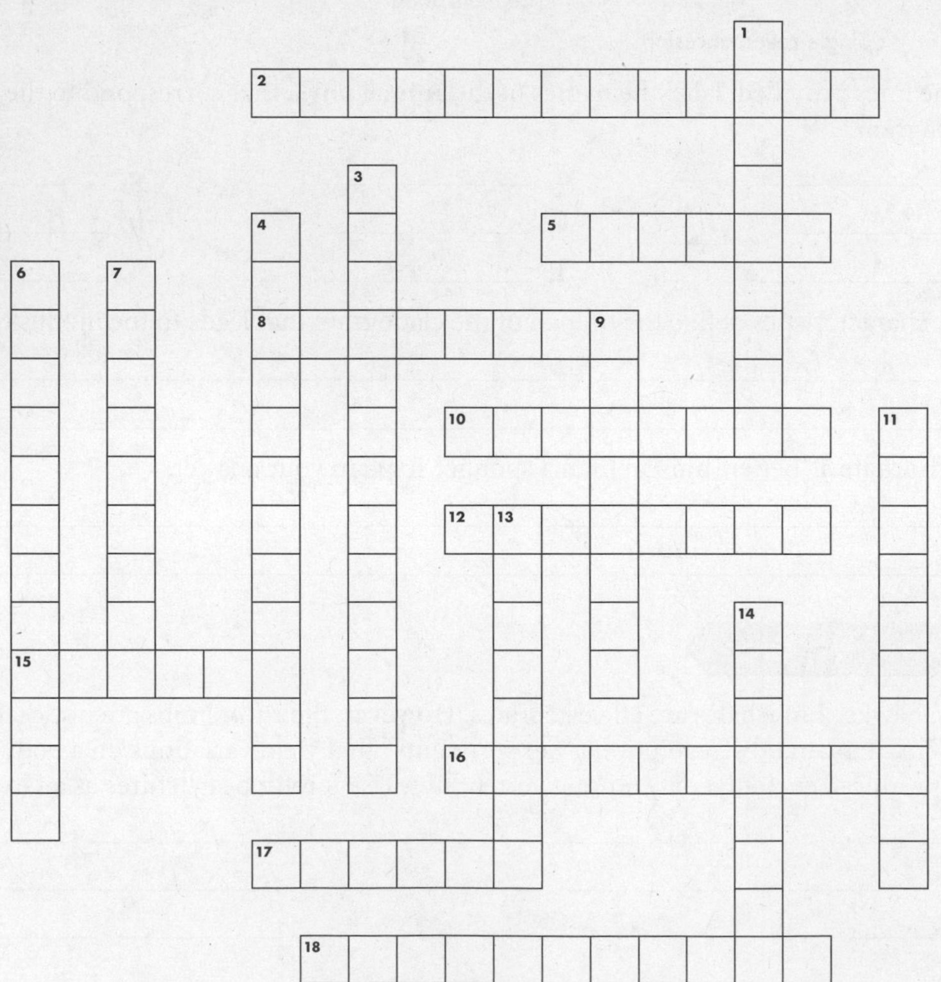

 

Name ______________________ Class _____ Date _______

CHAPTER
**MYSTERY**

**SLIME DAY AT THE BEACH**

The scientists who helped identify the salp in the Chapter Mystery probably studied animal biology or marine biology in college. The knowledge they acquired at school and their work experience helped them solve the mystery of the slime.

21st Century Learning

## Working with Animals

Some people who are interested in animals and love to be around them own pets or volunteer at local animal shelters. Other people, however, want to devote their careers to caring for or studying animals.

People who want to work with animals must decide what level of education and training they are willing to pursue to achieve their goal. Some jobs that involve caring for and understanding animals require extensive education or intensive training, such as that of the scientists in the Chapter Mystery. Other careers that involve working with animals require less experience and education. For example, animal control officers might be required to have a two-year degree, rather than a four-year degree or a graduate degree. Below is an example of a job description for an animal control officer.

### County Animal Control Officer Job Opening

**JOB DESCRIPTION**
Candidates will respond to different assignments while upholding the best animal control services in the county. Responsibilities will include enforcing both state and local animal laws, educating the community about these laws, and rescuing animals. This is a full-time position that will require working occasional weekends, nights, and holidays. Candidates will also be on-call at times. Continuing education provided on the job.

**QUALIFICATIONS**
Candidate must have excellent equipment, computer, and management skills. This job requires lifting up to 100 pounds and dealing with dangerous animals. Applicant must have a valid driver's license. Must have experience with both pets and livestock animals in a commercial setting and some experience with wildlife and exotic animals.

**EDUCATION**
Associate's Degree in Applied Science, Animal Health Technology, or similar field is preferred, with at least two years of work experience in animal control.

**STATUS**
Full time

**SALARY**
Depends on qualifications and experience

*Continued on next page* ▶

## 21st Century Themes Science and Economic Literacy

1. What work experience should a candidate for this job opening have?

2. What might be a commercial setting in which a candidate worked with animals?

3. Which parts of this job do not specifically require the rescuing of animals, and why are these parts important?

4. This ad states that an Associate's Degree is preferred. What do you think might be an alternative to this degree?

5. What danger might an animal control officer face when rescuing an animal?

## 21st Century Skills Investigate a Career

The skills used in this activity include **information and media literacy, critical thinking and systems thinking, creative and intellectual curiosity,** and **self-direction.**

Work with a group to investigate how a person would become an animal control officer. Then create a chronological plan to become an animal control officer. Do an online search to identify community colleges, state colleges, and private institutions that offer courses and degrees that satisfy the job description on the previous page. (Alternatively, you could call local animal shelters to discuss the educational programs completed by its staff members.) In your group's plan, identify the courses a person would need to complete the program. Include any high school experiences, internships, and summer jobs that would be helpful to secure a job after college graduation. Your group should also create a budget that includes tuition, room and board, application fees, meal plans, textbooks, and other supplies. Submit your group's plan and budget to your teacher.

 

Name ______________________ Class ______ Date ______

# 26 Animal Evolution and Diversity

**Evolution**

**Q:** How have animals descended from earlier forms through the process of evolution?

| | WHAT I KNOW | WHAT I LEARNED |
|---|---|---|
| **26.1** How did invertebrates evolve? | | |
| **26.2** How did chordates evolve? | | |
| **26.3** How did primates evolve? | | |

 

# 26.1 Invertebrate Evolution and Diversity

## Lesson Objectives

- Explain what fossil evidence indicates about the timing of the evolution of the first animals.
- Interpret the cladogram of invertebrates.

## Lesson Summary

**Origins of the Invertebrates** It is not known when the first multicellular animals evolved from single-celled eukaryotes.

- Animals probably evolved from ancestors they shared with choanoflagellates. Fossil evidence indicates that animals began evolving long before the Cambrian Explosion, which occurred between 530 and 515 million years ago.
- Fossils from the Ediacara Hills of Australia date from roughly 565 to 544 million years ago. Their body plans are different from those of anything alive today. Some seem to be related to invertebrates such as jellyfishes and worms.
- Cambrian fossils (dating back about 542 million years ago) show how animals evolved complex body plans over a span of 10–15 million years. Many had body symmetry, a front and back end, specialized cells, and **appendages**, structures such as legs or antennae protruding from the body. Some had hard body parts that became fossilized.
- By the end of the Cambrian, the basic body plans of the modern phyla were established.
- Today, invertebrates are the most abundant animals on Earth.

**Cladogram of Invertebrates** The cladogram of invertebrates presents current hypotheses about evolutionary relationships among major groups of modern invertebrates.

- The major invertebrate phyla are the sponges, cnidarians, arthropods, nematodes (roundworms), flatworms, annelids, mollusks, and echinoderms.
  - Sponges have pores in their bodies.
  - Cnidarians are radially symmetrical animals with stinging tentacles.
  - Arthropods have segmented bodies, a hard external skeleton, jointed appendages, and cephalization.
  - Nematodes, or roundworms, are nonsegmented worms with pseudocoeloms. Their digestive tracts have two openings.
  - Platyhelminthes, or flatworms, are the simplest animals to have three germ layers, bilateral symmetry, and cephalization.
  - Annelids are worms with segmented bodies and a true coelom.
- **Larvae** are the immature stages of development in some animals, such as mollusks. Many mollusks have a free-swimming larval stage called a **trochophore**. The trochophore is also characteristic of many annelids, indicating that annelids and mollusks are closely related.
  - Mollusks are soft-bodied animals that usually have a shell. They also have a true coelom and complex organ systems.
  - Echinoderms have spiny skin and exhibit radial symmetry.

 

Name ______________________ Class ______ Date ______

# Origins of the Invertebrates

**1.** How much time passed between the appearance of the first prokaryotic cells and the emergence of multicellular organisms?

______________________________________________

**2.** What are choanoflagellates? What is their significance in animal evolution?

______________________________________________

______________________________________________

**3.** How old is our oldest evidence of multicellular life?

______________________________________________

*For Questions 4–9, write the letter of the correct answer on the line at the left.*

______ **4.** The first animals were tiny and soft-bodied, so

**A.** no fossilized bodies exist.

**B.** few fossilized bodies exist.

**C.** fossilized bodies are plentiful.

**D.** the only fossils that exist are "trace fossils."

______ **5.** Fossil evidence indicates that the first animals began evolving

**A.** during the Cambrian Period.

**B.** before the Cambrian Explosion.

**C.** after the Cambrian Explosion.

**D.** after the Cambrian Period.

______ **6.** Why are the fossils of the Ediacara Hills of Australia important?

**A.** Their body plans are different from those of anything alive today.

**B.** Some had cells, tissues, and specialized organs.

**C.** Some were differentiated into a front and back end.

**D.** Some were autotrophic.

______ **7.** Over a period of 10–15 million years in the Cambrian Period, animals evolved

**A.** into eukaryotic, photosynthetic forms.

**B.** the ability to survive on the bottom of shallow seas.

**C.** complex body plans, including cells, tissues, and organs.

**D.** into modern, vertebrate forms.

______ **8.** Structures such as legs or antennae that protrude from the body are

**A.** trace fossils.

**B.** appendages.

**C.** shells, skeletons, and other hard body parts.

**D.** evidence of an extinct phylum.

______ **9.** Which animals are the most abundant on Earth?

**A.** arthropods

**B.** mollusks

**C.** sponges

**D.** invertebrates

 

# Cladogram of Invertebrates

**10.** Write "yes" or "no" to indicate how certain features distinguish each phylum of multicellular invertebrates. The first row is completed as an example.

| | Tissues | Radial | Bilateral symmetry | Protostome development | Deuterostome development |
|---|---|---|---|---|---|
| Sponges | no | no | no | no | no |
| Cnidarians | | | | | |
| Arthropods | | | | | |
| Nematodes (Roundworms) | | | | | |
| Flatworms | | | | | |
| Annelids | | | | | |
| Mollusks | | | | | |
| Echinoderms | | | | | |

## Apply the Big idea

**11.** Describe three evolutionary trends you see in invertebrates.

______________________________________________

______________________________________________

______________________________________________

______________________________________________

______________________________________________

 

Name ______________________ Class ______ Date ______

# 26.2 Chordate Evolution and Diversity

Describe the most ancient chordates.

Interpret the cladogram of chordates.

## Lesson Summary

**Origins of the Chordates** Embryological studies suggest that the most ancient chordates were related to the ancestors of echinoderms.

- Fossils of the earliest chordates (Cambrian Period) show muscles arranged in a series, traces of fins, sets of feathery gills, a head with paired sense organs, and a skull and skeletal structures likely made of **cartilage**, a strong connective tissue that is softer and more flexible than bone. Cartilage supports all or part of a vertebrate's body.
- Modern chordates are very diverse, consisting of six groups: the nonvertebrate chordates and the five groups of vertebrates—fishes, amphibians, reptiles, birds, and mammals.

**Cladogram of Chordates** The cladogram of chordates presents current hypotheses about relationships among chordate groups. Major groups are:

- Nonvertebrate chordates: The tunicates and the lancelets lack backbones.
- Jawless fishes: Lampreys and hagfishes lack vertebrae and have notochords as adults.
- Sharks and their relatives: They have jaws and skeletons made of cartilage.
- Bony fishes: These animals have skeletons made of true bone. Most modern bony fishes are ray-finned fishes. One group of ancient lobe-finned fishes evolved into the ancestors of **tetrapods,** which are four-limbed vertebrates.
- Amphibians: Amphibians live in water as larvae but on land as adults. They breathe with lungs as adults, but most require water for reproduction.
- Reptiles: Reptiles have dry, scaly skin, well-developed lungs, strong limbs, and shelled eggs that do not develop in water.
- Birds: Birds can regulate their internal body temperature. They have an outer covering of feathers, strong yet lightweight bones, two legs covered with scales that are used for walking or perching, and front limbs modified into wings.
- Dinosaurs and birds are now considered to be in one clade, which is part of the larger reptiles clade. Modern birds are, therefore, reptiles. The traditional class Reptilia, which is not a clade, includes living reptiles and dinosaurs but not birds.
- Mammals: Mammals produce milk from mammary glands, have hair, breathe air, have four-chambered hearts, and regulate their internal body temperature.

## Origins of the Chordates

*For Questions 1–8, write True if the statement is true. If the statement is false, change the underlined word to make the statement true.*

______________ **1.** Embryological evidence suggests that the most ancient chordates were related to the ancestors of <u>echinoderms</u>.

______________ **2.** *Pikaia* was an early <u>vertebrate</u> fossil.

______ **3.** The earliest known <u>chordate</u> fossil was *Myllokunmingia,* which had muscles arranged in a series, traces of fins, sets of feathery gills, a head with paired sense organs, and a skull and skeletal structures.

______ **4.** The earliest vertebrate fossils had skeletons made of <u>bone</u>.

______ **5.** Cartilage is a strong <u>connective</u> tissue that is more flexible than bone.

______ **6.** Most modern chordates are <u>vertebrates</u>.

______ **7.** Modern chordates include <u>five</u> groups of vertebrates.

______ **8.** The most numerous group of vertebrates today is the <u>mammals</u>.

## Cladogram of Chordates

**9.** Write "yes" or "no" to indicate how certain features distinguish each subphylum of chordates. The first row is completed as an example.

| | Vertebrae | Jaws and Paired Appendages | True Bone | Lungs | Four Limbs | Amniotic Egg | Endothermy |
|---|---|---|---|---|---|---|---|
| Nonvertebrate chordates | no | no | no | no | no | no | no |
| Jawless fishes | | | | | | | |
| Sharks and their relatives | | | | | | | |
| Bony fishes | | | | | | | |
| Amphibians | | | | | | | |
| Reptiles | | | | | | | |
| Birds | | | | | | | |
| Mammals | | | | | | | |

**10.** Sharks and their relatives are the first group of animals with jaws. Why are jaws a significant evolutionary development?

______________________________________________

______________________________________________

**11.** What three adaptations were needed for chordates to move from living in water to living on land?

______________________________________________

______________________________________________

 

**12.** One group of feathered dinosaurs led to modern birds. What advantage might feathers have given these dinosaurs?

______________________________________________________________

**13.** How do mammals differ from all other chordates on the cladogram?

______________________________________________________________

**14.** Which chordate groups can regulate their body temperatures?

______________________________________________________________

**15.** THINK VISUALLY Much evidence supports the hypothesis that modern birds share a common ancestor with dinosaurs. Make a sketch to show the probable evolutionary relationships among modern birds, modern reptiles, and extinct dinosaurs. Circle the clades shown in your diagram.

## Apply the Big idea

**16.** The order in which the major groups of chordates evolved makes sense. For example, a bony skeleton had to evolve before a vertebral column. A vertebral column had to develop before four limbs. Fish had to evolve before birds. Explain why certain traits had to evolve before the traits now seen in birds.

______________________________________________________________

______________________________________________________________

______________________________________________________________

______________________________________________________________

______________________________________________________________

______________________________________________________________

______________________________________________________________

 

Name ______________________________ Class ______ Date ______

# 26.3 Primate Evolution

- Identify the characteristics that all primates share.
- Describe the major evolutionary groups of primates.
- Describe the adaptations that enabled later hominine species to walk upright.
- Describe the current scientific thinking about the genus *Homo*.

## Lesson Summary

**What Is a Primate?** In general, a primate is a mammal that has relatively long fingers and toes with nails instead of claws, arms that can rotate around shoulder joints, a strong clavicle, and a well-developed cerebrum.

- Many primates have eyes that face forward, giving them **binocular vision**, which is the ability to combine visual images from both eyes to provide three-dimensional views.
- The well-developed cerebrum enables complex behaviors.

**Evolution of Primates** Humans and other primates evolved from a common ancestor that lived more than 65 million years ago. Early in their history, primates split into two groups:

- Primates in one group look very little like typical monkeys. This group contains the lemurs and lorises.
- Primates in the other group include tarsiers and **anthropoids**, or humanlike primates. Monkeys, great apes, and humans are anthropoids. Anthropoids split into two groups about 45 million years ago.
  - The New World monkeys have **prehensile tails**, which can coil tightly around a branch to serve as a "fifth hand."
  - Old World monkeys do not have prehensile tails. Great apes, also called **hominoids**, include gibbons, orangutans, gorillas, chimpanzees, and humans.

**Hominine Evolution** The hominoids in the lineage that led to humans are called **hominines**. The skull, neck, spinal column, hip bones, and leg bones of early hominine species changed shape in ways that enabled later species to walk upright.

- The evolution of **bipedal**, or two-footed, locomotion freed both hands to use tools.
- The hominine hand evolved an **opposable thumb** that could touch the tips of the fingers, enabling the grasping of objects and the use of tools.
- Hominines also evolved much larger brains.
- The oldest hominine fossil may be *Sahelanthropus*, roughly seven million years old.
- Fossils of one early group of hominines, *Australopithecus*, showed they were bipedal apes that probably spent some time in trees.
- *Paranthropus* probably had a diet like that of modern gorillas. This species lived two to three million years ago.

**The Road to Modern Humans** Many species of the genus *Homo* existed before *Homo sapiens* appeared. At least three other *Homo* species existed at the same time as early humans.

- *Homo neanderthalensis* survived in Europe until 28,000–24,000 years ago. *H. sapiens* coexisted with the Neanderthals for several thousand years.

 

Name ______________________ Class ______ Date ______

# What Is a Primate?

*For Questions 1–4, complete each statement by writing the correct word or words.*

**1.** Primates have ______________ on their fingers and toes.

**2.** Primates are good climbers because they have a strong shoulder joint attached to a strong ______________.

**3.** The ability to combine vision from both eyes is ______________ vision.

**4.** The "thinking" part of the brain is the ______________.

# Evolution of Primates

*For Questions 5–11, write the letter of the correct answer on the line at the left.*

_____ **5.** How long ago did the common ancestor of all primates live?

**A.** 65 million years ago | **C.** 45 million years ago
**B.** 56 million years ago | **D.** 28,000 years ago

_____ **6.** Which of these is NOT an anthropoid?

**A.** gibbon | **C.** human
**B.** orangutan | **D.** tarsier

_____ **7.** What factor contributed to the split of two groups of anthropoids about 45 million years ago?

**A.** One group developed a prehensile tail.
**B.** The continents where they lived moved apart.
**C.** They diverged from the lemurs and tarsiers.
**D.** The climate changed from warmer to colder.

_____ **8.** Which characteristic distinguishes the New World monkeys from the Old World monkeys?

**A.** prehensile tail | **C.** binocular vision
**B.** opposable thumb | **D.** mammary glands

_____ **9.** Which of these is a hominoid?

**A.** loris | **C.** tarsier
**B.** lemur | **D.** gibbon

_____ **10.** Which primate is the closest relative of humans?

**A.** gorilla | **C.** orangutan
**B.** gibbon | **D.** chimpanzee

_____ **11.** How did scientists confirm which primate was the closest primate relative to humans?

**A.** by comparing the skeletons
**B.** by studying behavior
**C.** by using DNA analyses
**D.** by using geographic analyses

 

Name ________________________ Class ______ Date ______

# Hominine Evolution

**12.** Complete the Venn diagram to compare human and gorilla skeletons.

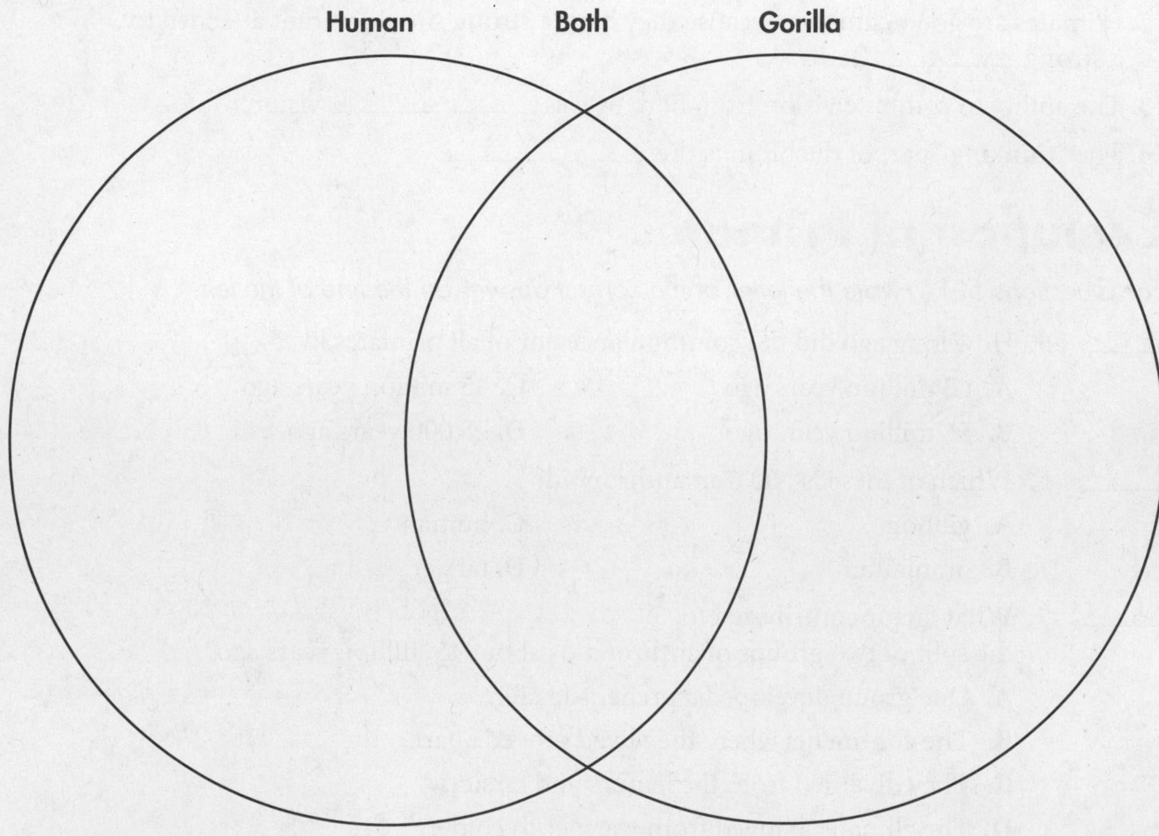


**13.** What do Lucy and the Dikika Baby have in common? Which one is more complete?

______________________________________________

______________________________________________

**14.** Why did scientists conclude that *Paranthropus* probably ate a diet that included coarse and fibrous plant foods?

______________________________________________

**15.** Why do we now think about human evolution as a shrub with multiple trunks rather than a family tree?

______________________________________________

______________________________________________

# The Road to Modern Humans

*For Questions 16–21, write True if the statement is true. If the statement is false, change the underlined word to make the statement true.*

_______ **16.** One species of our genus, *Homo*, existed before our species, *Homo sapiens*.

_______ **17.** The earliest fossils that can definitely be assigned to the genus *Homo* are from the species *H. ergaster*.

_______ **18.** Researchers agree that the genus *Homo* originated in Asia and migrated to other parts of the world.

_______ **19.** One way to discover the migration patterns of human ancestors is to compare the mitochondrial DNA of living humans.

_______ **20.** Early *Homo sapiens* lived at the same time as another, closely related species, *Homo neanderthalensis*.

_______ **21.** The only surviving species of the once large and diverse hominine clade is *Homo erectus*.

## Apply the Big idea

**22.** What evidence do scientists use to classify extinct species of the genus *Homo?* How do scientists differentiate extinct species of *Homo* from each other and from the modern species?

 

Name ______________________ Class ______ Date ______

# Chapter Vocabulary Review

For Questions 1–8, match the term with its definition.

| Definition | Term |
|---|---|
| _____ **1.** The ability to combine visual images from both eyes | **A.** appendage |
| _____ **2.** Any four-limbed vertebrate | **B.** larva |
| _____ **3.** Another name for the great apes | **C.** trochophore |
| _____ **4.** A structure such as an arm, a leg, or an antenna protruding from the body | **D.** cartilage |
| _____ **5.** The group of humanlike primates that includes monkeys and great apes | **E.** tetrapod |
| _____ **6.** An immature stage of life in some animals; many mollusks have one called a trochophore. | **F.** binocular vision |
| _____ **7.** Connective tissue that is more flexible than bone | **G.** anthropoids |
| _____ **8.** The free-swimming larval stage of some mollusks | **H.** hominoids |

*For Questions 9–12, complete each statement by writing the correct word or words.*

**9.** The appendage that can serve as a "fifth hand" in some primates is the ______________.

**10.** A hominoid in the lineage that led to humans is a(n) ______________.

**11.** The evolution of ______________, or two-footed, locomotion freed the hands for tool use.

**12.** The line that led to humans evolved a(n) ________________ that can touch the tips of the fingers.

**13.** What groups have a trochophore?

______________________________________________

**14.** What does the fact that these groups have a trochophore indicate about the relationships between them?

______________________________________________

**15.** What advantage does a primate with an opposable thumb have over a primate without an opposable thumb?

______________________________________________

**16.** What advantage does a primate with binocular vision have over a primate without binocular vision?

______________________________________________

______________________________________________

______________________________________________

______________________________________________

 

CHAPTER
# MYSTERY
## FOSSIL QUEST

Josh and Pedro, whom you read about in the Chapter Mystery, have a strong interest in fossils. It can be difficult, however, to pursue this interest if the local area is not rich in fossils.

21st Century Learning

## Fossil Education for the Nonscientist

Josh, who is interested in fossils that are over 600 million years old, learned that it was impossible for him to find these fossils nearby. In fact, he would have to travel to China or Australia to find such fossils. Alternatively, Josh could learn about ancient fossils by reading articles published in scientific journals. If he does, he will discover that many of the articles are technical and difficult to understand. But another pathway to such information exists: national park staff members and other science educators help convey complex scientific information to the public with their interpretive activities. They use presentations, workshops, pamphlets, and other materials to educate people about fossils. Below is an example of a pamphlet describing the Grampians mountain range in western Victoria, Australia.

### The Grampians Range, Western Victoria

**INTRODUCTION**

The Grampians Range was not always the incredible mountain range it is today. Over 400 million years ago, this area was actually a relatively flat coastline. To the east of this coastline was a deep ocean, and to the west was a mountain range that has now been eroded away. How did a flat coastline area become a mountain range hundreds of kilometers away from the sea? This pamphlet discusses the sedimentation, the pressure, and the forces that made the Grampians Range.

**SEDIMENTATION**

Over millions of years, rivers from the mountains and inlets along the shore deposited layers of gravel, sand, and mud. They deposited thousands of meters of material. Each layer of sediment tells a story about the past. Some layers contain fossils, including small plants, vertical worm holes, pieces of primitive jawless fish, brachiopods, and what scientists believe may be algal mats. Petrified ripples and mud cracks indicate the locations of ancient beaches, rivers, and other bodies of water that deposited sediments. These features and other geological evidence help explain the sedimentation story.

**PRESSURE AND PLATES**

As the layers of sediment accumulated or built up, the pressure and temperature increased, squeezing the water out and turning the sand to stone. Continental drift kept the Earth's tectonic plates moving. Tectonic forces buckled, folded, and uplifted the sediments, creating the Grampians Range, as well as other mountain ranges on Earth.

Continued on next page ▶

 

Name ______ Class ______ Date ______

## 21st Century Themes Science and Global Awareness

**1.** What evidence indicates that some of the land making up the Grampians Range was once under water?

______

______

**2.** What was the topography (surface characteristics) of the land in this region at that time?

______

______

**3.** What types of informational material do you think would help explain the geology of the Grampians Range other than what is described in the text?

______

______

**4.** Consider the evidence presented in the pamphlet to explain the formation of the Grampians. What type of similar evidence could you collect to study the geological history of landforms in your area?

______

______

______

______

**5.** Suppose you found a fossilized algal mat in a desert. What could you infer about the probably nature of the ancient environment of this area?

______

______

## 21st Century Skills Fossils Pamphlet

The skills used in this activity include **information and media literacy, communication skills, critical thinking and systems thinking, creativity and intellectual curiosity,** and **self-direction**.

Research the geology and fossils in your state or region online or by going to a visitor center of nearby state or national park. Museum Web sites are a good place to start, as is the National Park Service Web site. If possible, ask your teacher to arrange a field trip to help you with research. Based on your research, put together a pamphlet describing the fossils in your area. While designing and writing your pamphlet, remember that your audience includes people who may not know much about fossils and geology.

*The pamphlet should fold into three parts and include maps, figures, diagrams, and photographs that are appropriately labeled.*

 

Name ______ Class ______ Date ______

# 27 Animal Systems I

## Structure and Function

**Q:** How do the structures of animals allow them to obtain essential materials and eliminate wastes?

| | WHAT I KNOW | WHAT I LEARNED |
|---|---|---|
| **27.1** How do different animals obtain and digest food? | | |
| **27.2** How do animals in different environments breathe? | | |
| **27.3** How have animals evolved complex, efficient ways to move materials through their bodies? | | |
| **27.4** How do animals in different environments excrete metabolic wastes? | | |

 

Name ______________________ Class ______ Date ______

# 27.1 Feeding and Digestion

## Lesson Objectives

- Describe the different ways animals get food.
- Explain how digestion occurs in different animals.
- Describe how mouthparts are adapted for an animal's diet.

## Lesson Summary

**Obtaining Food** Animals obtain food in different ways.

- Most filter feeders catch algae and small animals by using modified gills or other structures as nets that filter food items out of water.
- Detritivores feed on detritus, or decaying bits of plant and animal material. Detritivores often obtain extra nutrients from the bacteria, algae, and other microorganisms that grow on and around the detritus.
- Carnivores eat other animals.
- Herbivores eat plants or parts of plants in terrestrial and aquatic habitats.
- Many animals rely upon symbiosis for their nutritional needs. Parasites live within or on a host organism, where they feed on tissues or on blood and other body fluids. In mutualistic relationships, both participants benefit.

**Processing Food** Some invertebrates break down food primarily by intracellular digestion, but many animals use extracellular digestion to break down food.

- In **intracellular digestion**, food is digested inside specialized cells that pass nutrients to other cells by diffusion.
- In **extracellular digestion**, food is broken down outside cells in a digestive system and then absorbed.
  - Some invertebrates, such as cnidarians, have a **gastrovascular cavity** with a single opening through which they both ingest food and expel wastes.
  - Many invertebrates and all vertebrates, such as birds, digest food in a tube called a **digestive tract**, which has two openings: a mouth and an anus. Food travels in one direction through the digestive tract.

**Specializations for Different Diets** The mouthparts and digestive systems of animals have evolved many adaptations to the physical and chemical characteristics of different foods.

- Carnivores typically have sharp mouthparts or other structures that can capture food, hold it, and "slice and dice" it into small pieces.
- Herbivores typically have mouthparts adapted to rasping or grinding.
- Some animals have specialized digestive organs that help them break down certain foods. For example, cattle have a pouchlike extension of their stomach called a **rumen**, in which symbiotic bacteria digest cellulose.

Name ____________________ Class ______ Date ______

# Obtaining Food

**1.** Complete the table about types of feeders.

| Types of Feeders | |
|---|---|
| **Type of Feeder** | **Description** |
| Filter feeder | |
| | feeds on decaying bits of plant and animal material |
| Carnivore | |
| | eats plants or parts of plants |
| Parasitic symbionts | |
| Mutualistic symbionts | |

**2.** Explain the difference between a parasite and a host.

______________________________________________

______________________________________________

**3.** Give an example of a mutualistic relationship involving a nutritional symbiont.

______________________________________________

______________________________________________

______________________________________________

# Processing Food

**4.** How is the digestion of food different in simple animals compared with more complex animals?

______________________________________________

______________________________________________

______________________________________________

______________________________________________

**5.** How is a one-way digestive track like a "disassembly line"?

______________________________________________

______________________________________________

**6.** Label the digestive structures of this cnidarian.

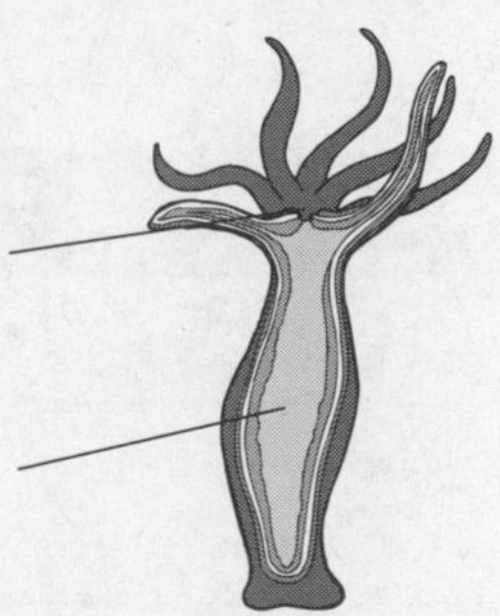

## Specializations for Different Diets

**7.** VISUAL ANALOGY

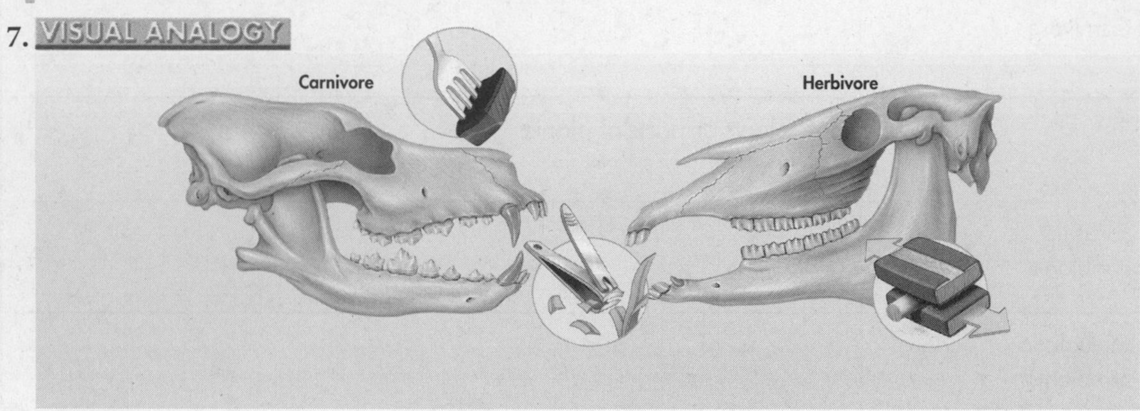


The visual analogy compares different types of teeth with common tools. Complete the table about the different kinds of teeth found in mammals and the tools they are like.

| Teeth Adaptations in Mammals | | |
|---|---|---|
| **Type of Teeth** | **Description** | **Tool Analogy** |
| Canines | | |
| | chisel-like teeth used for cutting, gnawing, and grooming | |
| Molars | | |

**Apply the Big idea**

**8.** Explain whether organisms with a gastrovascular cavity or organisms with a digestive tract obtain and process nutrients more efficiently.

 

# 27.2 Respiration

## Lesson Objectives

- Describe the characteristics of respiratory structures that all animals share.
- Explain how aquatic animals breathe.
- Identify the respiratory structures that enable land animals to breathe.

## Lesson Summary

**Gas Exchange** Animals have evolved respiratory structures that promote the movement of oxygen and carbon dioxide in the required directions by passive diffusion.

- Gases diffuse most efficiently across a thin, moist membrane.
- Respiratory structures maintain a difference in concentrations of oxygen and carbon dioxide on either side of the respiratory membrane, promoting diffusion.

**Respiratory Surfaces of Aquatic Animals** Many aquatic invertebrates and most aquatic chordates, other than reptiles and mammals, exchange gases through gills.

- **Gills** are feathery structures that expose a large surface area of thin, selectively permeable membrane to water.
- Aquatic reptiles and aquatic mammals, such as whales, breathe with **lungs**, organs that exchange oxygen and carbon dioxide, and must hold their breath underwater.

**Respiratory Surfaces of Terrestrial Animals** Terrestrial animals must keep their respiratory membranes moist in dry environments.

- Respiratory structures in terrestrial invertebrates include skin, mantle cavities, book lungs, and tracheal tubes.
- All terrestrial vertebrates breathe with lungs.
  - In mammalian lungs, **alveoli** provide a large surface for gas exchange.
  - In birds, a unique system of tubes and air sacs enables one-way airflow.

## Gas Exchange

*For Questions 1–5, write True if the statement is true. If the statement is false, change the underlined word or words to make the statement true.*

__________ **1.** In respiratory systems, gas exchange occurs through <u>active</u> diffusion.

__________ **2.** Substances diffuse from an area of <u>higher concentration</u> to an area of lower concentration.

__________ **3.** Gases diffuse most efficiently across thin, <u>dry</u> surfaces.

__________ **4.** Respiratory structures have a <u>selectively permeable</u> membrane.

__________ **5.** Respiratory structures maintain a difference in the relative concentrations of oxygen and <u>nitrogen</u> on either side of the membrane.

Name ______________________ Class ______ Date ______

**6.** Respiratory organs have large surface areas. How is this an advantage to an animal?

______________________________________________

______________________________________________

**7.** Respiratory surfaces are moist. How does this enable respiration to take place?

______________________________________________

## Respiratory Surfaces of Aquatic Animals

**8.** Complete the flowchart that describes the path of water as it moves through fish.

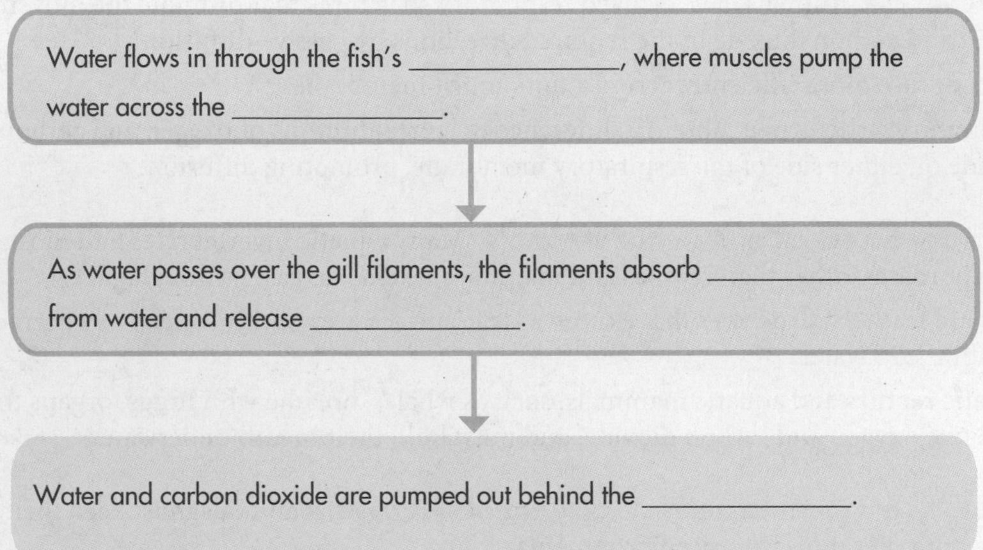
Water flows in through the fish's ______________, where muscles pump the water across the ______________.
As water passes over the gill filaments, the filaments absorb ______________ from water and release ______________.
Water and carbon dioxide are pumped out behind the ______________.

## Respiratory Surfaces of Terrestrial Animals

**9.** THINK VISUALLY Label the book lung, spiracles, and tracheal tubes in the organisms below. Write a description of these structures on the lines below the organisms.

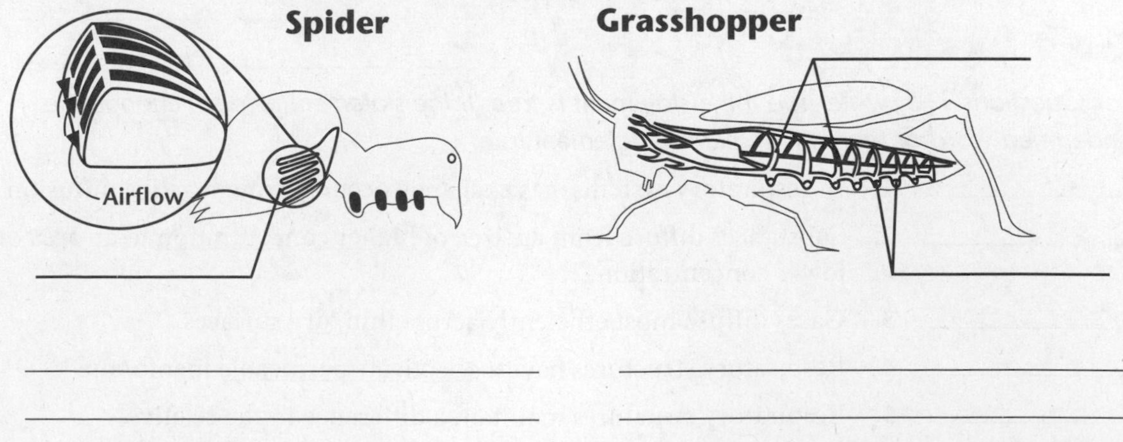
Spider
Grasshopper
Airflow

______________________ ______________________

______________________ ______________________

______________________ ______________________

 

10. THINK VISUALLY Label the nostrils, mouth, and throat; trachea; and lungs of the animals below.

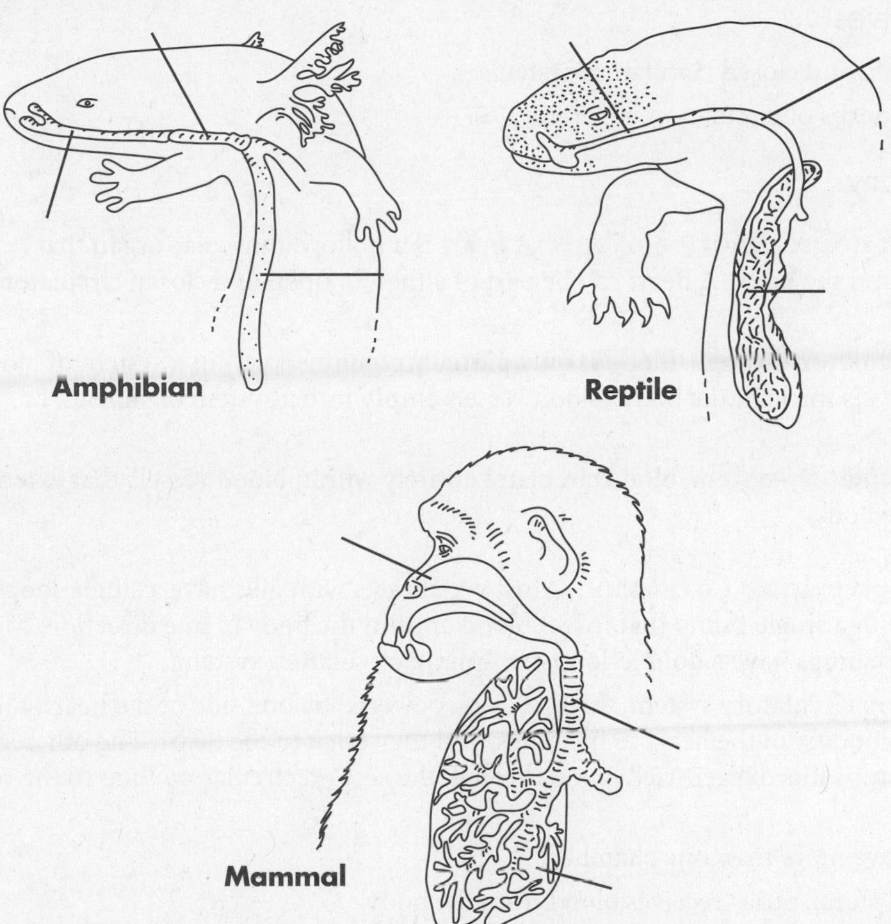


11. Describe the basic process of breathing among land vertebrates.

_______________________________________________

_______________________________________________

_______________________________________________

12. Why are the lungs of birds more efficient than those of most other animals?

_______________________________________________

_______________________________________________

## Apply the Big idea

13. Compare the structure and function of fish gills with the structure and function of bird lungs.

_______________________________________________

_______________________________________________

_______________________________________________

_______________________________________________

 

# 27.3 Circulation

## Lesson Objectives

- Compare open and closed circulatory systems.
- Compare patterns of circulation in vertebrates.

## Lesson Summary

**Open and Closed Circulatory Systems** A **heart** is a hollow, muscular organ that pumps blood around the body. A heart can be part of either an open or a closed circulatory system.

- In an **open circulatory system**, blood is only partially contained within a system of blood vessels as it travels through the body. Blood vessels empty into a system of sinuses, or cavities.
- In a **closed circulatory system**, blood circulates entirely within blood vessels that extend throughout the body.

**Single- and Double-Loop Circulation** Most vertebrates with gills have a single-loop circulatory system with a single pump that forces blood around the body in one direction. Most vertebrates that use lungs have a double-loop, two-pump circulatory system.

- In a double-loop circulatory system, the first loop, powered by one side of the heart, forces oxygen-poor blood from the heart to the lungs, and then back to the heart. The other side of the heart pumps this oxygen-rich blood through the second circulatory loop to the rest of the body.
- Some hearts have more than one chamber.
  - The **atrium** (plural: atria) receives blood from the body.
  - A **ventricle** pumps blood out of the heart to the rest of the body.
- Amphibian hearts usually have three chambers: two atria and one ventricle.
  - The left atrium receives oxygen-rich blood from the lungs.
  - The right atrium receives oxygen-poor blood from the body.
  - Both atria empty into the ventricle. Some mixing of oxygen-rich and oxygen-poor blood occurs in the ventricle.
- Most reptilian hearts have three chambers. However, most reptiles have a partial partition in the ventricle, so there is little mixing of oxygen-rich and oxygen-poor blood in the ventricle.
- Modern mammals have four-chambered hearts that are actually two separate pumps working next to one another.

 

Name ________________ Class ______ Date ______

# Open and Closed Circulatory Systems

**1.** Use the Venn diagram to compare and contrast open and closed circulatory systems.

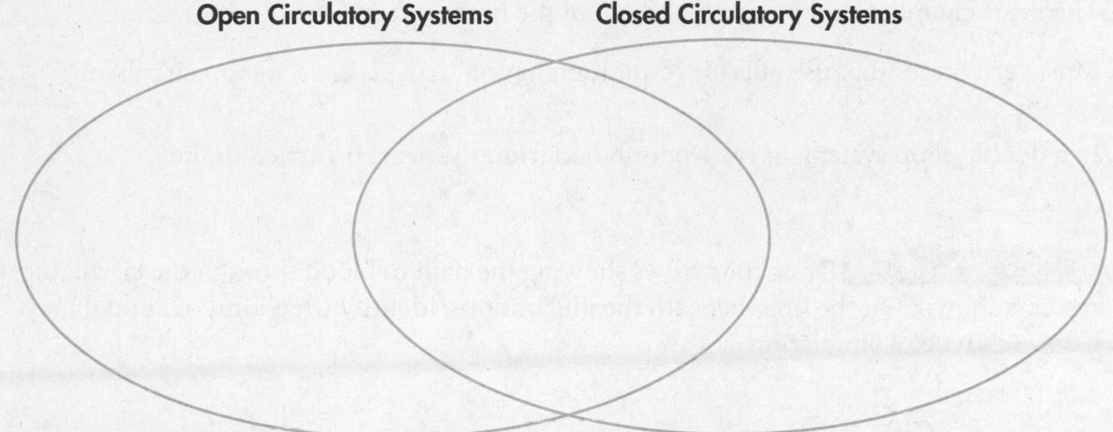


**2.** THINK VISUALLY Label the structures shown on each organism. Then write on the line below the organism whether the organism has an open or a closed circulatory system.

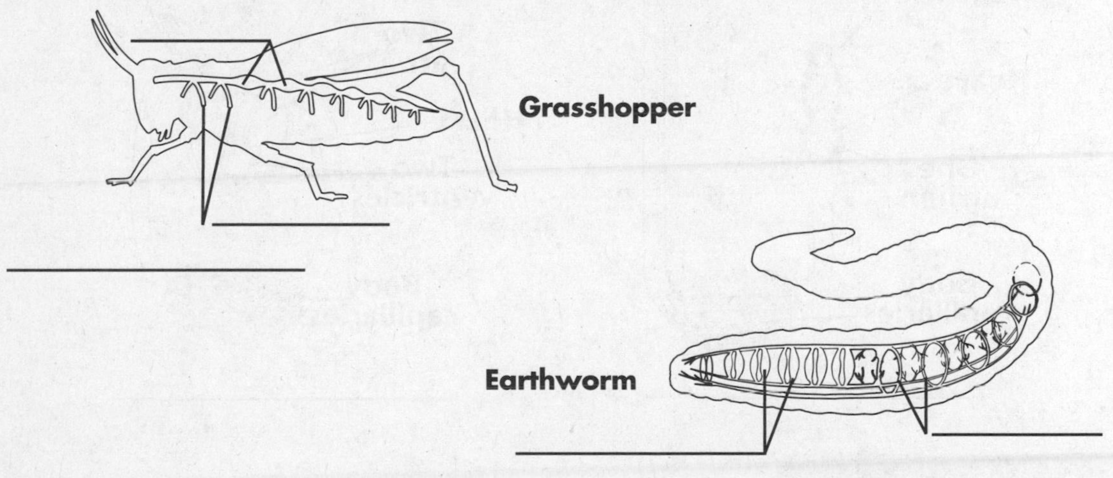


# Single- and Double-Loop Circulation

**3.** Identify where the blood is carried in each loop of a double-loop circulatory system.

______________________________________________

______________________________________________

**4.** Why is a four-chambered heart sometimes described as a double pump?

______________________________________________

______________________________________________

**5.** What is the difference between a reptilian heart and an amphibian heart?

______________________________________________

______________________________________________

 

*For Questions 6–9, complete each statement by writing the correct word or words.*

**6.** In most vertebrates with gills, the heart consists of ____________ chambers.

**7.** The heart chamber that pumps blood out of the heart is called the ____________.

**8.** Most vertebrates that use gills for respiration have a ____________ loop circulatory system.

**9.** In a double-loop system, oxygen-poor blood from the heart is carried to the ____________.

**10.** THINK VISUALLY Draw the arrows showing the path of blood through the circulatory systems shown. On the lines beneath the illustrations, identify what kind of animal may have each type of circulation.

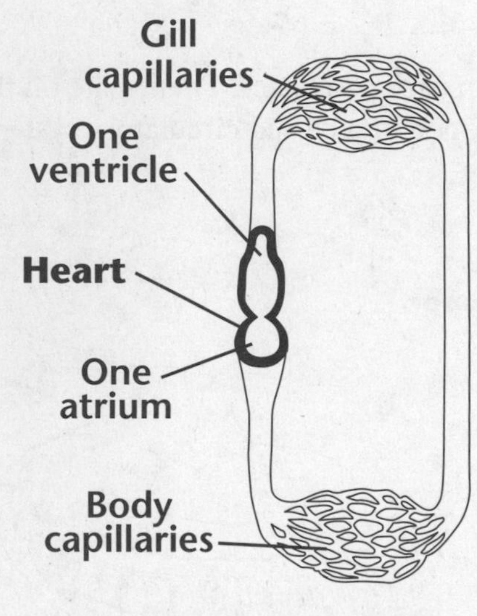


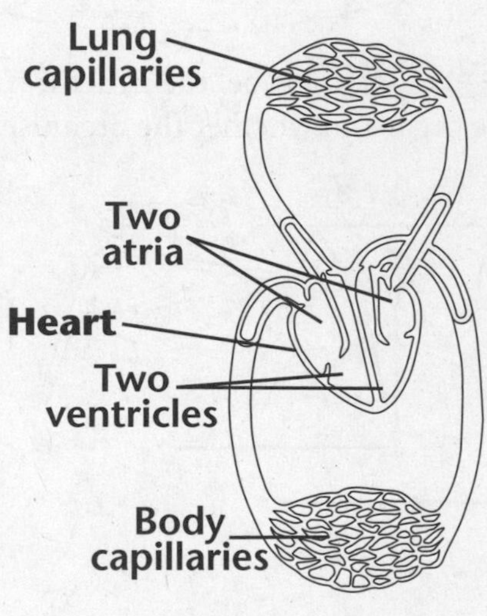


____________________ ____________________

## Apply the Big idea

**11.** On the basis of what you have learned about circulatory systems, infer how many chambers a bird's heart has. Explain your answer.

______________________________________________________________

______________________________________________________________

______________________________________________________________

______________________________________________________________

______________________________________________________________

______________________________________________________________

Name ________________ Class ______ Date ________

# 27.4 Excretion

## Lesson Objectives

- Describe the methods animals use to manage nitrogenous wastes.
- Explain how aquatic animals eliminate wastes.
- Explain how land animals eliminate wastes.

## Lesson Summary

**The Ammonia Problem** Ammonia is a waste product that can kill most cells, even in moderate amounts.

- Animals either eliminate ammonia from the body quickly or convert it into other nitrogenous compounds that are less toxic.
- The elimination of metabolic wastes, such as ammonia, is called **excretion**.
- Many animals use **kidneys** to separate wastes and excess water from blood.

**Excretion in Aquatic Animals** In general, aquatic animals can allow ammonia to diffuse out of their bodies into surrounding water, which dilutes the ammonia and carries it away.

- Many freshwater invertebrates lose ammonia to their environment by simple diffusion across their skin. Many freshwater fishes and amphibians eliminate ammonia by diffusion across the same gill membranes they use for respiration. Freshwater fishes also actively pump salt inward across their gills.
- Marine invertebrates and vertebrates typically release ammonia by diffusion across their body surfaces or gill membranes. These animals also actively excrete salt across their gills.

**Excretion in Terrestrial Animals** In dry environments, land animals can lose large amounts of water from respiratory membranes that must be kept moist. In addition, they must eliminate nitrogenous wastes in ways that require disposing of water.

- Some terrestrial invertebrates produce urine in **nephridia**, which are tubelike excretory structures that filter body fluid. Urine leaves the body through excretory pores.
- Other terrestrial invertebrates, such as insects and arachnids, convert ammonia into uric acid. Nitrogenous wastes, such as uric acid, are absorbed from body fluids by structures called **Malpighian tubules**, which concentrate the wastes and add them to digestive wastes traveling through the gut.
- Mammals and land amphibians convert ammonia into urea, which is excreted in urine. In most reptiles and birds, ammonia is converted into uric acid.

## The Ammonia Problem

**1.** Why does ammonia build up in organisms? ______________________________

______________________________________________

**2.** Why is ammonia a problem in the body of an animal?

______________________________________________

 

3. Complete the concept map.

**Ways to Store Nitrogenous Waste**

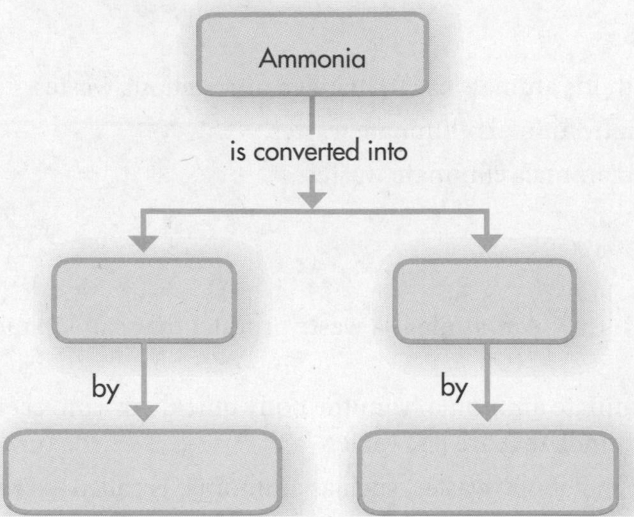


## Excretion in Aquatic Animals

4. How do many freshwater invertebrates rid their bodies of ammonia?

_______________________________________________

5. Describe how flatworms maintain water balance.

_______________________________________________

_______________________________________________

6. Why do freshwater fishes typically have very dilute urine and marine fishes have very concentrated urine?

_______________________________________________

_______________________________________________

_______________________________________________

_______________________________________________

_______________________________________________

*For Questions 7–8, write the letter of the correct answer on the line at the left.*

______ 7. Marine organisms tend to lose water to their surroundings because

A. their bodies are less salty than the water they live in.

B. their bodies are more salty than the water they live in.

C. their cells actively pump water across their membranes.

D. their cells actively pump ammonia across their membranes.

______ 8. Which of the following structures helps remove excess water from an organism's body?

A. a gill

B. a ventricle

C. a flame cell

D. an operculum

 

# Excretion in Terrestrial Animals

9. THINK VISUALLY Label the excretory organs on the organisms shown. Then, describe the function of the labeled organs on the lines below.

______________________________________________

______________________________________________

______________________________________________

______________________________________________

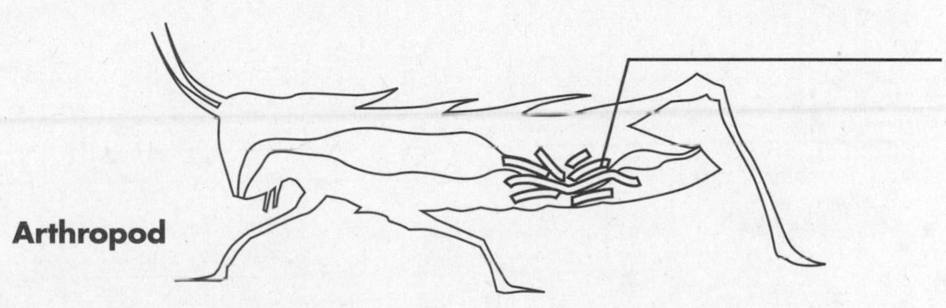


______________________________________________

______________________________________________

*For Questions 10–12, complete each statement by writing the correct word or words.*

10. In terrestrial vertebrates, excretion is carried out mostly by the __________.

11. In mammals, urea is excreted from the body in a liquid known as __________.

12. Most vertebrate kidneys cannot excrete concentrated __________.

## Apply the Big idea

13. How does the structure of a gill make it an ideal excretory organ?

______________________________________________

______________________________________________

______________________________________________

______________________________________________

 

# Chapter Vocabulary Review

*Match the image with the best term.*

| Image | | Term |
|---|---|---|
| ______ 1. | 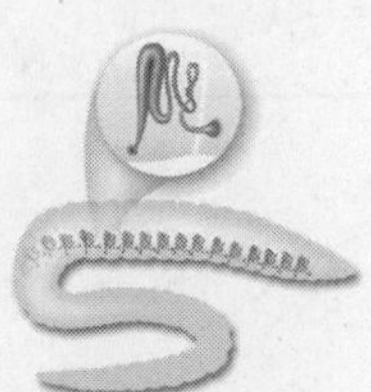 | **A.** lung |
| ______ 2. | 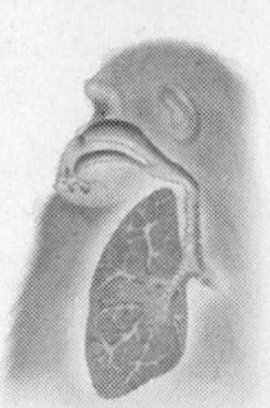 | **B.** gill |
| ______ 3. |  | **C.** closed circulatory system |
| ______ 4. | 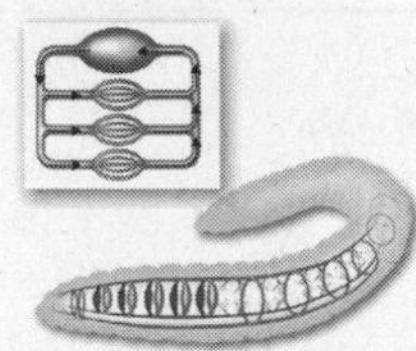 | **D.** open circulatory system |
| ______ 5. | 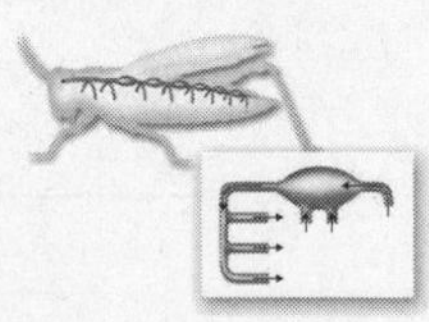 | **E.** nephridium |

*For Questions 6–13, write True if the statement is true. If the statement is false, change the underlined word or words to make the statement true.*

______________ **6.** <u>Intracellular</u> digestion is the process in which food is broken down outside cells and then absorbed.

______________ **7.** <u>Kidneys</u> concentrate the wastes and add them to digestive wastes traveling through the gut.

______________ **8.** Many invertebrates and all vertebrates digest food in a <u>gastrovascular cavity</u>, which has two openings.

______________ **9.** <u>Excretion</u> is the elimination of metabolic wastes from the body.

______________ **10.** A pouchlike extension of a stomach in which symbiotic bacteria digest cellulose is called a <u>rumen</u>.

______________ **11.** <u>Atria</u> pump blood out of the heart.

______________ **12.** Circulatory systems contain a pumplike organ called a <u>heart</u>.

______________ **13.** <u>Alveoli</u> in lungs provide an enormous surface area for gas exchange.

 

Name ______________________ Class ______ Date __________

CHAPTER
MYSTERY
(NEAR) DEATH BY SALT WATER
21st Century Learning


Drinking clean water is a vital part of maintaining your health. The Chapter Mystery showed that drinking the wrong water can have negative health effects.

## Why Clean Water?

Clear water may look clean, but it could possibly contain dissolved contaminants. Contaminants include pesticides or other agricultural chemicals, industrial chemicals, disease-causing microorganisms, and high concentrations of minerals. Contaminants often have no taste and can be toxic to humans. You could develop serious health problems by drinking contaminated water. Therefore, it is important to be aware of drinking water regulations and treatment methods. Below are some facts about drinking water.

### Important Facts about Clean Drinking Water

1. The Safe Drinking Water Act regulates the supply of public drinking water, or tap water. The regulations protect rivers, reservoirs, springs, and other sources so that the public water supply remains safe. The regulations also set guidelines for testing and treating the public water supply and detail which chemicals and the amount of each chemical that can be present in the supply.
2. The Federal Food, Drug, and Cosmetic Act and individual state laws regulate bottled water. All bottled water must be sampled and analyzed before it is considered safe for drinking.
3. Tap water is treated with filters and/or disinfecting agents such as chlorine. When water flows through filters, many contaminants are removed. Disinfectants such as chlorine help kill bacteria and fungi in water.
4. Bottled water is sealed in sanitary or sterilized plastic bottles according to both federal and state standards. Chemicals and sweeteners cannot be added to bottled water.
5. Bottled water sources include municipal supplies, springs, and wells. Springs and wells are considered natural sources. About 75% of bottled water comes from these natural sources.
6. The FDA has defined different kinds of bottled water. Definitions are based on the source of the water and on the chemicals in the water at its source. FDA classifications include artesian well water, mineral water, spring water, and well water.
7. Before water is bottled, it can be treated using distillation, reverse osmosis, filtration, and ozonation. Not all bottled water is treated this way. If a manufacturer treats water using these methods, the manufacturer can sell and label the water as purified.

Continued on next page ▶

## 21st Century Themes Science and Economic Literacy

**1.** What federal laws regulate public drinking water and bottled water, and how are these laws similar?

______________________________

______________________________

______________________________

**2.** How is tap water treated to prevent consumers from getting sick?

______________________________

______________________________

**3.** What do you think most public water is used for?

______________________________

______________________________

**4.** Suppose a city's tap water became temporarily unsafe. What would be the likely consequences?

______________________________

______________________________

**5.** If you wanted to start a bottled water company, what would be the first thing you would do?

______________________________

______________________________

______________________________

## 21st Century Learning Bottled Water Business Plan

The skills used in this activity include **information and media literacy; communication skills; critical thinking and systems thinking; problem identification, formulation, and solution; interpersonal and collaborative skills; accountability and adaptability;** and **social responsibility.**

Working in small groups, create a business plan to sell bottled water. Research and enhance the facts given on the previous page about bottled drinking water. Start by visiting the FDA's Web site to learn more about how the FDA regulates bottled water. Create a name for your company and assign roles to each team member. Your business plan should include the following: a summary description of the business, product description, an analysis of the bottled water market, strategy and implementation of the business plan, management team, and a financial or budgetary plan.

*Present your business plan to your class.*

 

Name ______ Class ______ Date ______

# 28 Animal Systems II

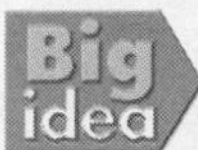

## Structure and Function

**Q:** How do the body systems of animals allow them to collect information about their environments and respond appropriately?

| | WHAT I KNOW | WHAT I LEARNED |
|---|---|---|
| **28.1** How do animals sense and respond to the environment? | | |
| **28.2** How are different animals adapted to move through their environments? | | |
| **28.3** What are the different strategies animals have evolved to help them produce offspring? | | |
| **28.4** How do animals maintain homeostasis? | | |

# 28.1 Response

## Lesson Objectives

- Describe how animals respond to stimuli.
- Summarize the trends in the evolution of nervous systems in animals.
- Describe some of the different sensory systems in animals.

## Lesson Summary

**How Animals Respond** Information in the environment that causes an organism to react is called a **stimulus**. A specific reaction to a stimulus is called a **response**. The nervous systems of animals help animals respond to stimuli. Nervous systems are composed of specialized nerve cells, or **neurons**.

- Neurons that respond to stimuli are **sensory neurons**.
- Neurons that typically pass information to still other neurons are called **interneurons**.
- **Motor neurons** carry "directions" from interneurons to muscles.

**Trends in Nervous System Evolution** Animal nervous systems exhibit different degrees of cephalization and specialization.

- Cnidarians, such as jellyfishes, have simple nervous systems called nerve nets.
- Other invertebrates have a number of interneurons that are grouped together into small structures called **ganglia**.
- Bilaterally symmetric animals often exhibit cephalization, the concentration of sensory neurons and interneurons in a "head."
- In some species, cerebral ganglia are further organized into a structure called a brain. Vertebrate brains include the following structures:
  - The **cerebrum** is the "thinking" region of the brain.
  - The **cerebellum** coordinates movement and controls balance.
  - The medulla oblongata controls the functioning of many internal organs.

**Sensory Systems** Sensory systems range from individual sensory neurons to sense organs that contain both sensory neurons and other cells that help gather information.

- Many invertebrates have sense organs that detect light, sound, vibrations, movement, body orientation, and chemicals in air or water.
- Most vertebrates have highly evolved sense organs. Many vertebrates have very sensitive organs of taste, smell, and hearing.

## How Animals Respond

**1.** What is a response?

______________________________________________

**2.** What body systems interact to produce a behavior in response to a stimulus?

______________________________________________

*Write the letter of the correct answer on the line at the left.*

_____ **3.** Which of the following is the best example of a stimulus?

**A.** sneezing | **C.** swallowing food
**B.** a bell ringing | **D.** holding your breath

_____ **4.** Which of the following is the best example of a response?

**A.** hunger pains | **C.** a breeze blowing
**B.** a hot sidewalk | **D.** answering a phone

**5.** Complete the table about types of neurons.

**Types of Neurons**

| Type of Neuron | Description |
|---|---|
| | neurons that pass information from one neuron to another |
| Sensory neurons | |
| Motor neurons | |

# Trends in Nervous System Evolution

**6.** THINK VISUALLY Label the nervous system structures in the following invertebrates. Circle the organism that does NOT show cephalization.

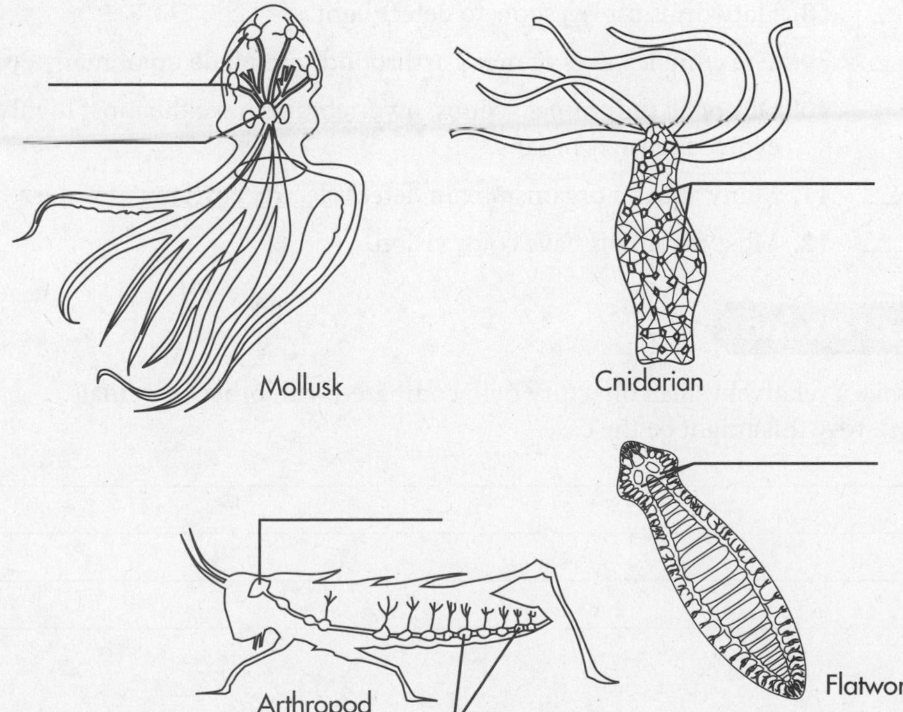

Name ______________________ Class ______ Date ______

7. **THINK VISUALLY** Use the terms in the box below to label the diagrams of the reptile, bird, and mammal brains. Then, circle the brain with the most complex cerebrum.

| Cerebellum | Cerebrum | Medulla oblongata | Olfactory bulb | Optic lobe |
|---|---|---|---|---|

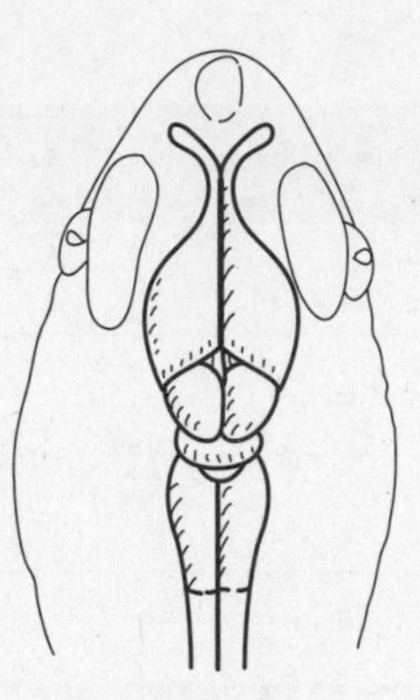

Reptile

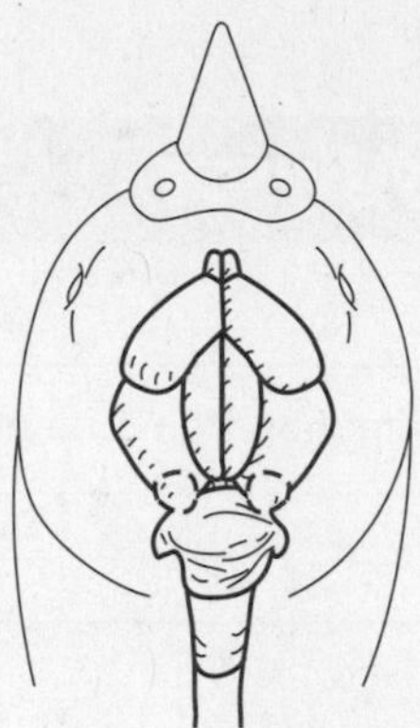

Bird

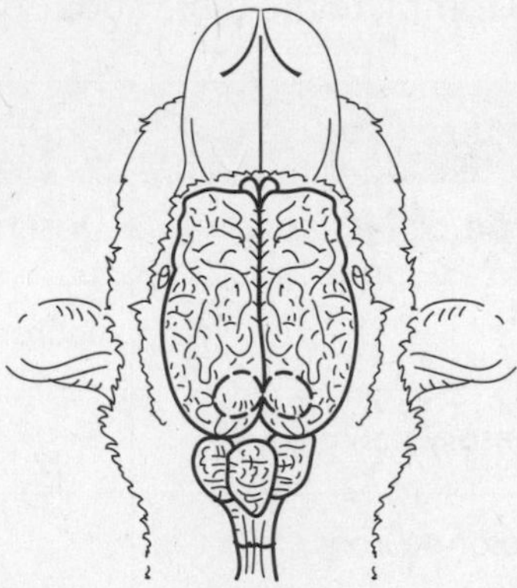

Mammal

## Sensory Systems

*For Questions 8–12, write True if the statement is true. If the statement is false, change the underlined word or words to make the statement true.*

______ **8.** Flatworms use <u>eyespots</u> to detect light.

______ **9.** The complex eyes of many arthropods are made up of many <u>eyespots</u>.

______ **10.** Out of all the animal groups, <u>invertebrates</u> have the most highly evolved sensory organs.

______ **11.** Many aquatic organisms can detect <u>electric currents</u> in water.

______ **12.** Most mammals have <u>color</u> vision.

### Apply the Big idea

**13.** Humans have a relatively small olfactory bulb compared with other mammals. Hypothesize why this might be the case.

______________________________

______________________________

______________________________

______________________________

Name ______________________ Class ______ Date ______

# 28.2 Movement and Support

## Lesson Objectives

- Describe the three types of skeletons in animals.
- Explain how muscles produce movement in animals.

## Lesson Summary

**Types of Skeletons** There are three main types of animal skeletons:

- Some invertebrates, such as cnidarians and annelids, have hydrostatic skeletons. A **hydrostatic skeleton** consists of fluids held in a gastrovascular cavity that can alter the animal's body shape drastically by working with contractile cells in its body wall.
- An **exoskeleton**, or external skeleton, of an arthropod is a hard body covering made of a protein called chitin. Most mollusks have exoskeletons, or shells, made of calcium carbonate. To increase in size, arthropods break out of their exoskeleton and grow a new one in a process called **molting**.
- An **endoskeleton** is a structural support system within the body. Vertebrates have an endoskeleton made of cartilage or a combination of cartilage and bone.
- Arthropods and vertebrates can bend because many parts of their skeletons are connected by **joints**. In vertebrates, bones are connected at joints by strong connective tissues called **ligaments**.

**Muscles and Movement** Muscles are attached to and pull on different parts of an organism's skeleton. This causes movement.

- Muscles are attached to bones around the joints by tough connective tissue called **tendons**.
- The shapes and relative positions of bones and muscles, and the shapes of joints, are linked very closely to the functions they perform.
- Muscles often work in opposing groups. Flexors bend a joint. Extensors straighten a joint.

## Types of Skeletons

**1.** What are the three main kinds of skeletal systems?

______________________________________________

______________________________________________

**2.** What does a cnidarian's hydrostatic skeleton consist of?

______________________________________________

______________________________________________

**3.** What is chitin?

______________________________________________

______________________________________________

**4.** Which invertebrates have endoskeletons?

______________________________________________

Name ______________________ Class ______ Date ________

*Match the organism with its skeleton. A skeleton type may be used more than once.*

**Organism**

_____ **5.** cow

_____ **6.** grasshopper

_____ **7.** jellyfish

_____ **8.** hawk

_____ **9.** sea star

_____ **10.** crab

_____ **11.** earthworm

_____ **12.** ant

_____ **13.** dog

**Skeleton Type**

**A.** hydrostatic skeleton

**B.** exoskeleton

**C.** endoskeleton

*For Questions 14–16, write the letter of the correct answer on the line at the left.*

_____ **14.** What is the process by which an arthropod breaks out of an exoskeleton it has outgrown?

**A.** molting
**B.** excreting
**C.** shedding
**D.** metamorphosing

_____ **15.** The pieces of an exoskeleton move against each other along

**A.** chitin.
**B.** joints.
**C.** tendons.
**D.** cavities.

_____ **16.** What type of structure connects one bone to another in a vertebrate skeleton?

**A.** a muscle
**B.** a tendon
**C.** a ligament
**D.** a tube foot

## Muscles and Movement

**17.** Explain how arthropods move.

______________________________

______________________________

______________________________

**18.** What are tendons?

______________________________

______________________________

**19.** What muscle pairs with the hamstring to move your leg?

______________________________

20. Complete the Venn diagram comparing arthropod movement with vertebrate movement.

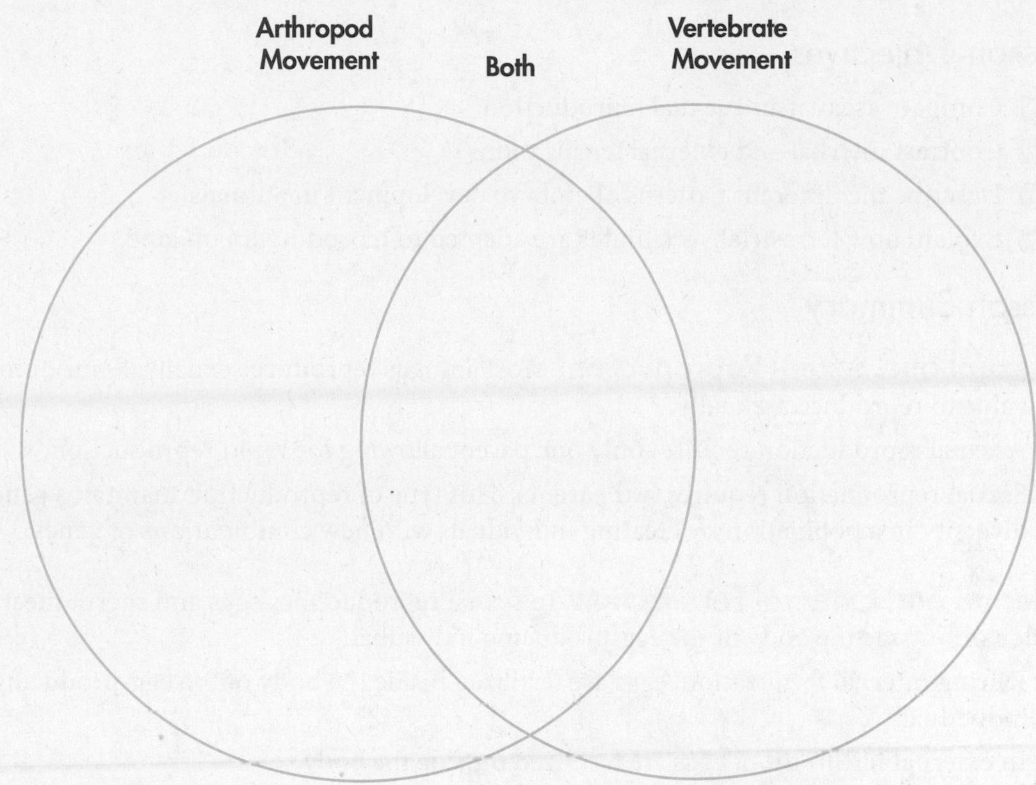


*For Questions 21–27, complete each statement by writing the correct word or words.*

21. Specialized tissues that produce physical force by contracting, or getting shorter, when they are stimulated are called ______________.

22. When they are not being stimulated, muscles ______________.

23. In many animals, muscles work in ______________ on opposites sides of a joint.

24. Muscles are attached to bones around the joints by tough connective tissue called ______________.

25. When muscles contract, tendons pull on ______________.

26. Arthropod muscles are attached to the inside of the ______________.

27. Paleontologists can reconstruct how an extinct mammal moved by looking at the shape of its ______________.

## Apply the Big idea

28. Hypothesize how a bird's skeleton might be different from reptile and mammal skeletons in order to help the bird fly.

______________________________________________

______________________________________________

______________________________________________

 

# 28.3 Reproduction

## Lesson Objectives

- Compare asexual and sexual reproduction.
- Contrast internal and external fertilization.
- Describe the different patterns of embryo development in animals.
- Explain how terrestrial vertebrates are adapted to reproduction on land.

## Lesson Summary

**Asexual and Sexual Reproduction** Most animals reproduce sexually. Some animals are also able to reproduce asexually.

- Asexual reproduction requires only one parent allowing for rapid reproduction.
- Sexual reproduction requires two parents. This type of reproduction maintains genetic diversity in a population by creating individuals with new combinations of genes.

**Internal and External Fertilization** In sexual reproduction, eggs and sperm meet either inside or outside the body of the egg-producing individual.

- During internal fertilization, eggs are fertilized inside the body of the egg-producing individual.
- In external fertilization, eggs are fertilized outside the body.

**Development and Growth** Embryos develop either inside or outside the body of a parent in various ways.

- **Oviparous** species are those in which embryos develop in eggs outside the parents' bodies.
- In **ovoviviparous** species, embryos develop within the mother's body, but they depend entirely on the yolk sac of their eggs.
- **Viviparous** species' embryos obtain nutrients from the mother's body. Some mammals nourish their embryos by means of a **placenta**—a specialized organ that enables exchange of respiratory gases, nutrients, and wastes between the mother and her developing young.
- As invertebrates, nonvertebrate chordates, fishes, and amphibians develop, they undergo **metamorphosis**, resulting in changes to their shape and form.
- Some insects undergo gradual or incomplete metamorphosis. Immature forms, or **nymphs**, resemble adults, but they lack functional sexual organs and some adult structures.
- Other insects undergo complete metamorphosis. Larvae change into a **pupa**, the stage in which an insect larva develops into an adult.

**Reproductive Diversity in Chordates** Chordates had to adapt to reproduction on land. Most chordates need a wet or moist environment for their eggs.

- The eggs of most aquatic organisms must develop in water. Reptiles, birds, and a few mammals have evolved **amniotic eggs** in which an embryo can develop outside its mother's body, and out of water, without drying out.
- Mammals have various reproductive adaptations. But all mammalian young are nourished by milk produced by the mother's **mammary glands**.

# Asexual and Sexual Reproduction

**1.** What does asexual reproduction allow animals to do?

______

**2.** What is an advantage of sexual reproduction?

______

**3.** THINK VISUALLY Shade the arrows showing haploid stage of the life cycle. Draw small dots in the arrows showing diploid stages.

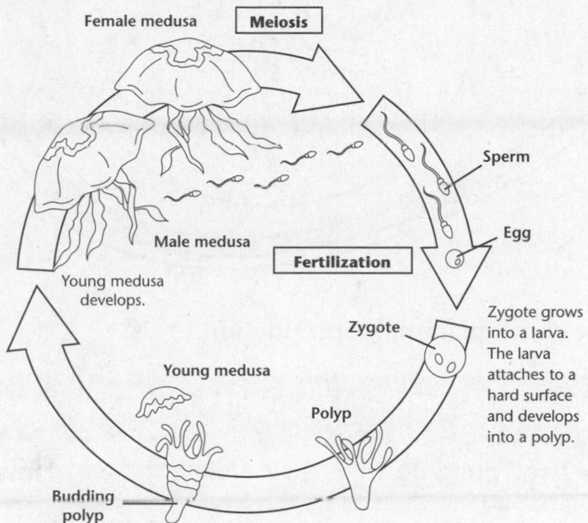


# Internal and External Fertilization

**4.** What is the difference between external and internal fertilization?

______

______

______

# Development and Growth

*Write the letter of the correct answer on the line at the left.*

______ **5.** In which mode of reproduction do the embryos develop inside the mother's body using the egg yolk for nourishment?

**A.** oviparous　　**C.** viviparous
**B.** ovoviviparous　　**D.** herbivorous

______ **6.** Organisms that develop placentas are

**A.** oviparous.　　**C.** viviparous.
**B.** ovoviviparous.　　**D.** herbivorous.

**7.** Explain the difference between complete and incomplete metamorphosis.

______

______

______

# Reproductive Diversity in Chordates

**8.** THINK VISUALLY

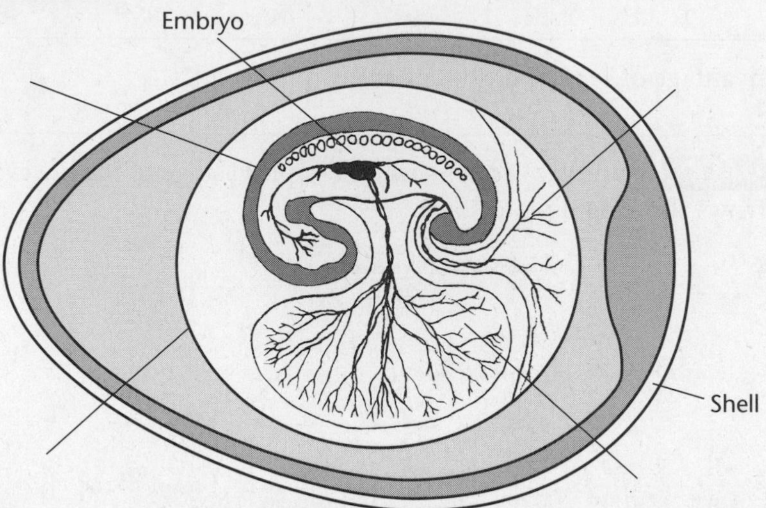


**9.** Complete the table about mammal reproduction.

| Types of Mammalian Reproduction and Development | | |
|---|---|---|
| **Group** | **How Are Young Born?** | **How Are Young Fed?** |
| | Young hatch from soft-shelled eggs laid outside the mother's body. | |
| Marsupials | | Young drink from a nipple inside the mother's pouch. |
| Placental mammals | | Young are generally nursed by the mother. |

## Apply the Big idea

**10.** How might the shape of an amniotic egg complement its function?

______________________________________________

______________________________________________

______________________________________________

______________________________________________

# 28.4 Homeostasis

## Lesson Objectives

- Explain how homeostasis is maintained in animals.
- Describe the importance of body temperature control in animals.

## Lesson Summary

**Interrelationship of Body Systems** Homeostasis is the maintenance of a relatively stable internal environment. All body systems work together to maintain homeostasis. Fighting disease-causing agents is a large part of maintaining homeostasis. Most animals have an immune system that attacks pathogens.

- Vertebrates and many invertebrates regulate many body processes using a system of chemical controls.
- **Endocrine glands**, which produce and release hormones, regulate body activities by releasing hormones into the blood.

**Body Temperature Control** Control of body temperature is important for maintaining homeostasis, particularly in areas where temperature varies widely with time of day and with season.

- An **ectotherm** is an animal whose regulation of body temperature depends mostly on its relationship to sources of heat outside its body. Most reptiles, invertebrates, fishes, and amphibians are ectothermic.
- An **endotherm** is an animal whose body temperature is regulated, at least in part, using heat generated by its body. Birds and mammals are endothermic.

## Interrelationship of Body Systems

**1.** Complete the graphic organizer about body systems working together.

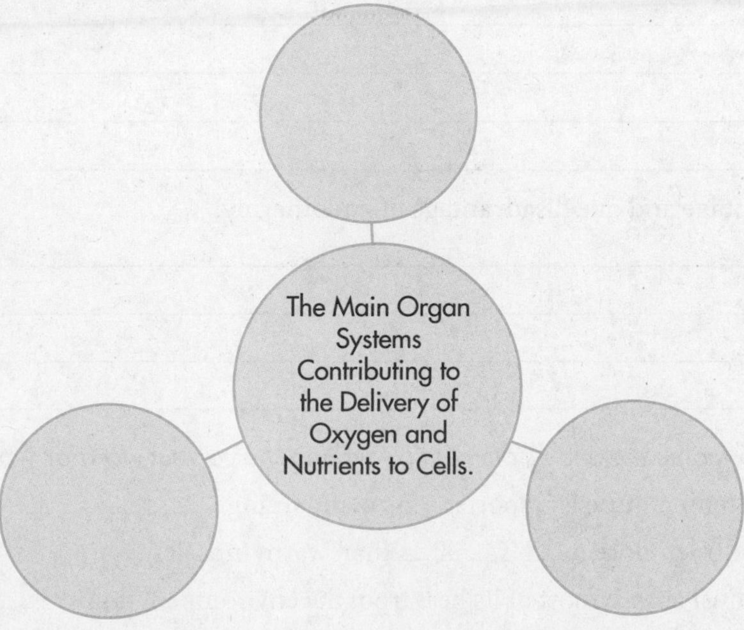

2. What is homeostasis?

3. Name the body system that helps protect mammals from disease and describe how it accomplishes this task.

4. What are endocrine glands?

## Body Temperature Control

5. List three features that animals need in order to control their body temperature.

6. How do ectotherms control their body temperature?

7. Explain how the human body cools itself.

8. Name one advantage and one disadvantage of endothermy.

*For Questions 9–15, complete each statement by writing the correct word or words.*

9. Control of body temperature is important for maintaining ____________.

10. Cold muscles contract more ____________ than warm muscles.

11. An animal that must absorb most of its heat from the environment is a(n) ____________.

 

Name ______________________ Class ______ Date ________

12. An animal that uses heat generated by its own body to maintain its body temperature is a(n) ____________.

13. Endotherms have a higher ____________ rate than ectotherms.

14. Endothermy evolved ____________ ectothermy.

15. Mammals use ____________ and ____________ as insulation in order to stay warm.

*Match each organism with the method of controlling body heat. Methods may be used more than once.*

| **Organism** | **Body Heating Method** |
|---|---|
| _____ 16. mammals | A. Ectothermy |
| _____ 17. fish | B. Endothermy |
| _____ 18. amphibian | |
| _____ 19. invertebrate | |
| _____ 20. birds | |
| _____ 21. reptiles | |

*For Questions 22–25, write True if the statement is true. If the statement is false, change the underlined word or words to make the statement true.*

__________ 22. The first land vertebrates were <u>ectotherms</u>.

__________ 23. Some scientists hypothesize that some <u>dinosaurs</u> were endotherms.

__________ 24. Current evidence suggests that endothermy evolved at least <u>four times</u>.

__________ 25. Most animals living in polar regions are <u>ectotherms</u>.

## Apply the Big idea

26. Explain how an organism's circulatory, digestive, or excretory system helps the organism maintain homeostasis.

Name ______________________ Class ______ Date ______

# Chapter Vocabulary Review

**1.** In the box below, draw a picture of the arrangement of a joint, including at least one ligament and at least one tendon. Label your picture.

*For Questions 2–7, complete each statement by writing the correct word or words.*

**2.** A single, specific reaction to a stimulus is a(n) ______________.

**3.** A structure called a(n) ______________ forms when an embryo's tissues join with the tissues from the mother's body.

**4.** One of the most important adaptations to life on land is the ______________, which protects the growing embryo and keeps it from drying out.

**5.** In ______________ animals, the eggs develop inside the mother's body, and the embryo uses the yolk for nourishment.

**6.** A(n) ______________ is a tough external covering of the body.

**7.** A(n) ______________ is an internal skeleton.

*For Questions 8–11, write True if the statement is true. If the statement is false, change the underlined word or words to make the statement true.*

______________ **8.** A <u>stimulus</u> is any kind of signal that carries information and can be detected.

______________ **9.** In <u>oviparous</u> animals, the embryos develop inside the mother's body and obtain their nourishment from their mother, not the egg.

______________ **10.** In complete metamorphosis, the stage in which an insect changes from larva to adult is called a(n) <u>nymph</u>.

______________ **11.** A group of nerve cells that control the nervous system in many invertebrates is called a(n) <u>ganglion</u>.

*Write the letter of the correct answer on the line at the left.*

______ **12.** Mammals are characterized by hair and

**A.** lungs.
**B.** prehensile tails.
**C.** mammary glands.
**D.** four-chambered hearts.

______ **13.** Animals that can generate their own body heat are known as

**A.** ectotherms.
**B.** endotherms.
**C.** chordates.
**D.** invertebrates.

 

Name ______________________ Class ______ Date ________

CHAPTER
# MYSTERY

## SHE'S JUST LIKE HER MOTHER

After the incredible birth of the bonnethead shark at the Doorly Zoo, the zoo's public relations department was probably working overtime. The birth of this shark provided a perfect opportunity to promote the zoo.

21st Century Learning

## Promoting Zoo Births

Zoos work responsibly to foster the reproduction of animals. The birth of a zoo animal is something to be celebrated and promoted, especially when it involves an endangered or threatened animal. Zoo births are helpful to zoos in many ways. For example, they can bring in additional visitors and encourage donations to the zoo.

A zoo's public relations department can find many ways to promote the birth of an animal. They may create and issue press releases, posters, pamphlets, commercials, and billboards. Their efforts may lead local television and radio stations to cover the animal birth in news reports. The following is an example of what a transcript of a live report by a local television station might have been like after a Sumatran tiger gave birth to triplets at the San Francisco Zoo.

### Live at 5 - San Francisco News
### REPORTING LIVE FROM THE SAN FRANCISCO ZOO

March 14, 2008 - I'm reporting live from the San Francisco Zoo. Zookeepers were in for a couple of surprises today at the San Francisco Zoo. The zoo has been buzzing with excitement and activity since their 230-pound Sumatran tiger, Leanne, gave birth to one cub on March 6. But just this week, the zoo revealed that Leanne actually had triplets! The zoo's chief veterinarian did not suspect that there was more than one cub until 6 days ago. How could this be? Well, Leanne had decided to take a tiger-size lick of the camera that was monitoring her, fogging up part of the lens. The birthing box was not completely visible, either. It was not until the thirsty new mom left the box to get a drink that the zookeeper noticed the two other cubs. Zookeepers do not want to disturb the mother and her young yet. Leanne is doing a great job of taking care of her babies—even protecting them from the camera lens. Sumatran tigers are an endangered species, with only about 600 remaining in the wild. Zoo officials hope that these web-footed cubs will soon be swimming just as fast as other Sumatran tigers.

Continued on next page ▶

 

Name ______________________ Class ______ Date ________

## 21st Century Themes Science and Global Awareness

1. What is the tone of this television report, and how is it intended to make you feel?

2. Suppose you were giving this report. What information would you add to the report? Explain your answer.

3. What do you think is the purpose of this television report?

4. What are some words and phrases in the broadcast that appeal to listeners' emotions and make them want to visit the zoo?

5. What are two facts you learned about Sumatran tigers from this report?

## 21st Century Skills Promote Zoo News

The skills used in this activity include **information and media literacy, creativity and intellectual curiosity.**

Find out about the latest news at a zoo close to your town or in your area by calling the zoo and asking to speak with its public relations department, visiting the zoo, or looking at the zoo's Web site. Choose an event, such as the recent birth or acquisition of an animal, that you can promote to encourage more people to visit the zoo. After researching the event, create a poster to promote it. Your poster should include persuasive text, photographs or illustrations, contact information, and how to visit the zoo.

*Display copies of your poster around your school. You may also want to contact the zoo and encourage them to use your poster.*

 

Name ______________________ Class ______ Date ______

# 29 Animal Behavior

**Big idea** **Evolution**

**Q:** How do animals interact with one another and their environments?

| | WHAT I KNOW | WHAT I LEARNED |
| --- | --- | --- |
| **29.1** What are the elements of animal behavior? | | |
| **29.2** How do the environment and other organisms affect an animal's behavior? | | |

 

Name ______________________ Class ______ Date ______

# 29.1 Elements of Behavior

## Lesson Objectives

- Identify the significance of behavior in the evolution of a species.
- Explain what an innate behavior is.
- Describe the major types of learning.
- Explain what types of behaviors are usually considered complex.

## Lesson Summary

**Behavior and Evolution** **Behavior** is the way an organism reacts to stimuli in its environment.

- Behaviors essential to survival and reproduction include finding and catching food, selecting a habitat, avoiding predators, and finding a mate.
- Some behaviors are influenced by genes and can be inherited.
- Certain behaviors evolve under the influence of natural selection:
  - If a behavior increases an individual's fitness and is influenced by genes, it tends to spread through a population.
  - Over many generations, adaptive behaviors can prove important in the survival of populations and species.

**Innate Behavior** An **innate behavior**, also called an instinct, is fully functional the first time it is performed, although the animal has no previous experience with the stimulus. All innate behaviors depend on patterns of nervous system activity that develop through complex interactions between genes and the environment.

**Learned Behavior** Acquiring changes in behavior during one's lifetime is called **learning**. There are four types:

- **Habituation** is the process by which an animal decreases or stops its response to a repetitive stimulus that neither rewards nor harms the animal.
- In **classical conditioning**, a certain stimulus comes to produce a particular response, usually through an association with a positive or negative experience.
- **Operant conditioning** (a form of trial-and-error learning) is the use of a reward or punishment to teach an animal to behave in a certain way through repeated practice.
- **Insight learning** occurs when an animal applies to a new situation something that it learned previously in another context.

**Complex Behaviors** Many complex behaviors combine innate behavior with learning. Imprinting is a complex behavior. **Imprinting** is the process by which some animals, such as birds, recognize and follow the first moving object they see during a critical period in their early lives.

 

# Behavior and Evolution

*For Questions 1–5, write True if the statement is true. If the statement is false, change the underlined word or words to make the statement true.*

__________ **1.** An adaptation is the way an animal responds to a stimulus in its environment.

__________ **2.** An animal's nervous system makes behaviors possible.

__________ **3.** Certain behaviors are influenced by genes and can therefore be inherited.

__________ **4.** If a behavior decreases fitness, it may spread in a population.

__________ **5.** Adaptive behaviors can play a role in the survival of a species.

**6.** How are behaviors affected by natural selection?

# Innate Behavior

**7.** Does learning play a role in innate behavior? Explain your answer.

**8.** Give three examples of innate behaviors.

# Learned Behavior

**9.** What is learning? Why is it important for survival?

 

Name ______________________ Class ______ Date ______

**10.** Complete the graphic organizer to summarize the four types of learning.

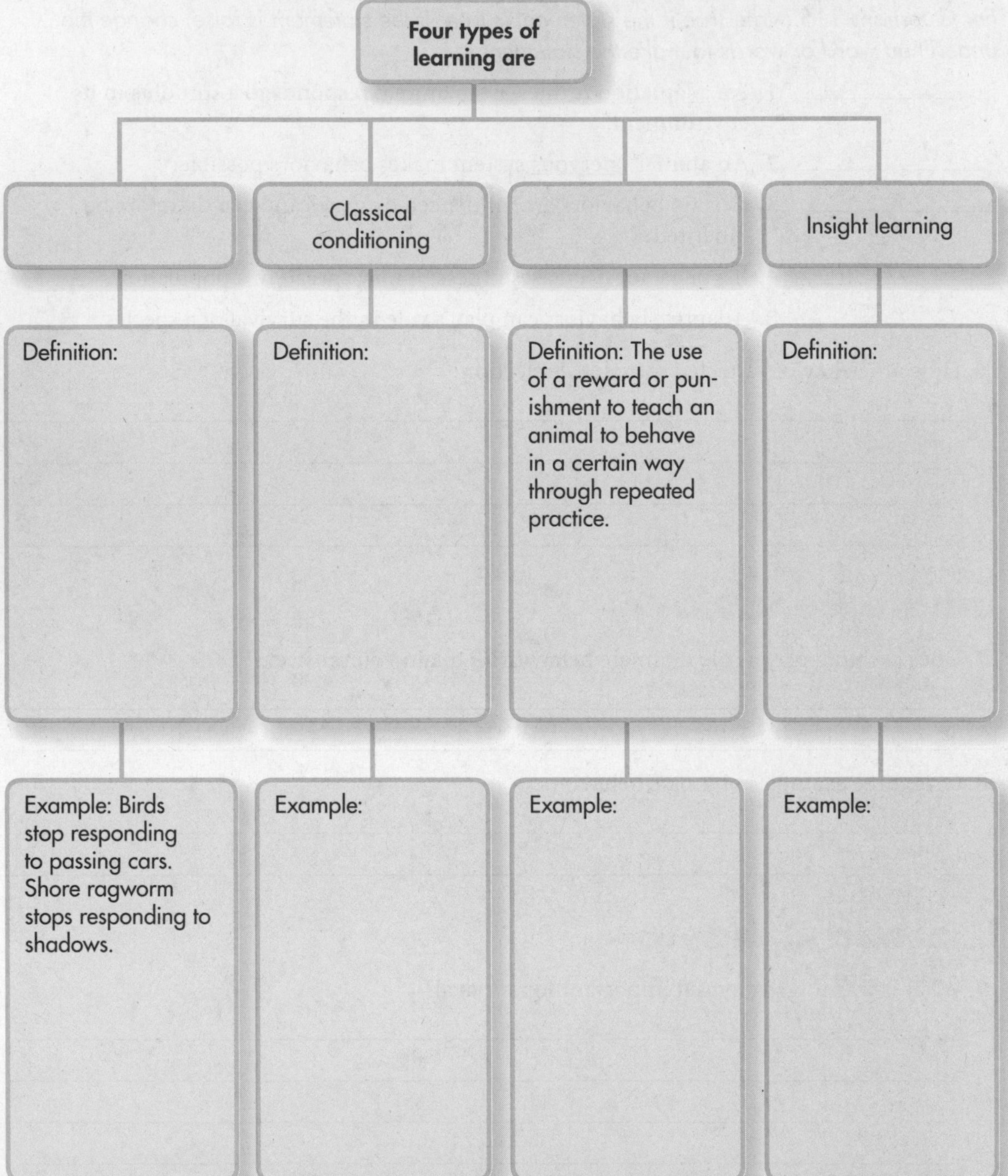
Four types of learning are
Classical conditioning
Insight learning
Definition:
Definition:
Definition: The use of a reward or punishment to teach an animal to behave in a certain way through repeated practice.
Definition:
Example: Birds stop responding to passing cars. Shore ragworm stops responding to shadows.
Example:
Example:
Example:

**11.** In Pavlov's experiment, a dog produced salivation in reaction to a bell associated with food. Which type of learning does this describe? Explain your answer.

______________________________________________

______________________________________________

______________________________________________

______________________________________________

 

Name ______________________ Class ______ Date ________

12. What is a "Skinner box"? Explain how it is used in learning.

______________________________________________

______________________________________________

______________________________________________

______________________________________________

______________________________________________

______________________________________________

## Complex Behavior

*For Questions 13–17, write the letter of the correct answer on the line at the left.*

_____ **13.** Birds that are born recognizing the songs of their own species are exhibiting

**A.** innate behavior. **C.** operant conditioning.

**B.** habituation. **D.** insight learning.

_____ **14.** Young birds following their mother is an example of

**A.** imprinting. **C.** operant conditioning.

**B.** classical conditioning. **D.** habituation.

_____ **15.** What do newly hatched salmon imprint on?

**A.** Sounds of the stream where they hatched

**B.** Sights of the stream where they hatched

**C.** Odors of the stream where they hatched

**D.** Feel of the stream where they hatched

_____ **16.** Imprinting is considered a complex behavior because

**A.** it is adaptive.

**B.** it is instinctual.

**C.** it combines classical conditional and instinct.

**D.** it combines innate behavior with learning.

_____ **17.** Once imprinting has occurred, the behavior becomes

**A.** complex. **B.** fixed. **C.** conditioned. **D.** innate.

## Apply the Big idea

18. Lloyd has two goldfish in a bowl he keeps on his desk. Every morning when he arrives at work, he turns on his office lights. The instant the lights come on, the fish rise to the surface of the water and move their mouths. Lloyd always feeds them before he begins work. What kind of behavior are the fish exhibiting before Lloyd drops food into the water? How is this type of behavior adaptive? Explain.

______________________________________________

______________________________________________

______________________________________________

______________________________________________

 

# 29.2 Animals in Their Environments

## Lesson Objectives

- Explain how environmental changes affect animal behavior.
- Explain how social behaviors increase the evolutionary fitness of a species.
- Summarize the ways that animals communicate.

## Lesson Summary

**Behavioral Cycles** Many animals demonstrate daily or seasonal cycles in their behavior.

- **Circadian rhythms** are behavioral cycles that occur daily.
- **Migration** is the seasonal movement from one environment to another. For example, many birds find food and nesting sites in the north in summer, but they fly south to warmer climates for the winter.

**Social Behavior** Interactions among animals of the same species are social behavior. There are several types:

- Animals (usually the males) perform **courtship** behaviors to attract a mate. An elaborate series of courtship behaviors is a courtship ritual.
- Many animals occupy a specific area, or **territory**, that they defend against competitors. Animals may use threatening behaviors, or **aggression**, to defend their territories. Animals also may use aggression when they compete for resources.
- Some animals form a **society**, or a group that interacts closely and often cooperatively. The theory that helping a relative survive increases the chance of transmitting one's own genes is **kin selection**.
- The most complex animal societies are those formed by social insects such as ants, bees, and wasps. All animals in the society cooperate closely to perform complex tasks, such as nest construction.

**Communication** The passing of information from one individual to another is **communication**.

- Animals use a variety of signals for communication, including visual, chemical, and sound.
- **Language** is a system of communication that combines sounds, symbols, and gestures according to rules about sequence and meaning.

# Behavioral Cycles

*For Questions 1–6, complete each statement by writing the correct word or words.*

1. Many animals respond to periodic changes with ______________ or ______________ cycles of behavior.
2. Behavioral cycles that occur daily are called ______________.
3. Seasonal dormancy in mammals is called ______________.
4. The seasonal movement from one environment to another is ______________.

5. Migration allows animals to take advantage of favorable ______________ conditions.

6. During northern winters, many birds live in tropical environments where ______________ is plentiful.

7. **THINK VISUALLY** Draw a diagram that shows the migration pattern of green sea turtles. Label your diagram. Then, on the lines below, describe the migration pattern followed by these animals.

______________________________________________

______________________________________________

______________________________________________

## Social Behavior

8. Complete the table of main ideas and details about the social behavior of animals. Explain and give an example of each type of social behavior.

**Social Behaviors of Animals**

| Type of Social Behavior | Definition | Example |
|---|---|---|
| | | |
| | | |
| | | |

**9.** What are rituals? How do rituals help a species' survival?

______________________________________________

______________________________________________

______________________________________________

______________________________________________

______________________________________________

**10.** Suppose you find a stray cat. As you approach, the cat begins to hiss, arch its back, and flatten its ears. Which type of behavior is this cat exhibiting? How would this behavior help this cat survive?

______________________________________________

______________________________________________

______________________________________________

______________________________________________

**11.** Coyotes are predators. Prairie dogs are prey. Prairie dogs live in large colonies. When a coyote nears, one prairie dog may spot the predator and make a high-pitched sound that alerts other members of the colony. In the process of making the sound, the alarm-calling prairie dog draws the coyote's attention, so that animal faces the greatest risk of predation. How does the theory of kin selection explain this behavior?

______________________________________________

______________________________________________

______________________________________________

______________________________________________

______________________________________________

## Communication

*For Questions 12–20, complete each statement by writing the correct word or words.*

**12.** ______________ is the passing of information from one individual to another.

**13.** Communication is important to ______________ behavior, which involves more than one individual.

**14.** The kinds of signals that animal species send and receive depend on the stimuli they can detect with their ______________.

**15.** Visual signals may be used by animals that can detect color, shape, or ______________.

**16.** Some animals may change ______________ to signal readiness to mate.

**17.** The use of chemical signals requires a well-developed sense of ______________.

**18.** A chemical messenger that affects the behavior or another individual of the same species is a(n) ______________.

**19.** Some animals send and receive sound signals that they do not hear but they can ______________.

 

**20.** Rules of sequence and meaning are required for the form of communication called ______________.

**21.** Complete the concept map to show the kinds of signals animals can use to communicate.

Apply the Big idea

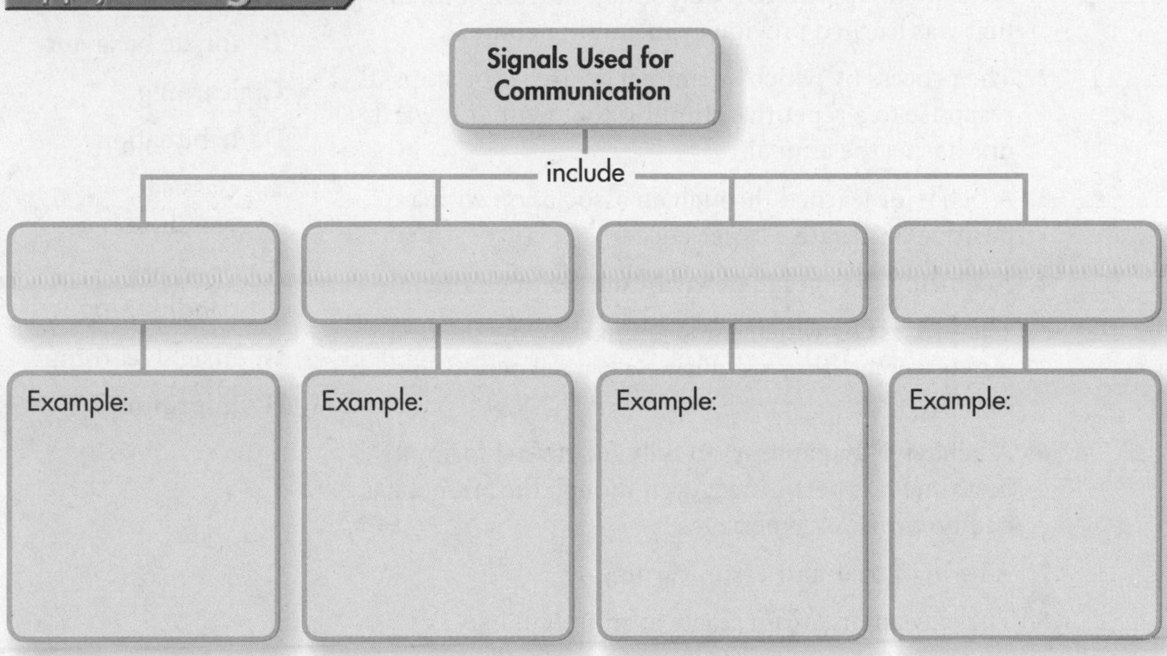


**22.** Explain how social behaviors can increase evolutionary fitness.

_______________________________________________

_______________________________________________

_______________________________________________

_______________________________________________

_______________________________________________

# Chapter Vocabulary Review

*For Questions 1–8, match the term with its definition.*

**Definition**

______ **1.** A behavior applied to a new situation from something that was learned previously in another context

______ **2.** The process by which an animal decreases or stops its response to a repetitive stimulus that neither rewards nor harms the animal

______ **3.** A behavior learned through an association with a positive or negative experience

______ **4.** Acquiring changes in behavior during one's lifetime

______ **5.** The process by which some animals follow the first moving object they see during a critical period in their early lives

______ **6.** A behavior that appears in fully functional form the first time it is performed, even though the animal has had no previous experience

______ **7.** A form of trial-and-error learning

______ **8.** The way an organism reacts to stimuli in its environment

**Term**

**A.** behavior
**B.** innate behavior
**C.** learning
**D.** habituation
**E.** classical conditioning
**F.** operant conditioning
**G.** insight learning
**H.** imprinting

*For Questions 9–13, complete each statement by writing the correct word or words.*

**9.** The behavior used to attract a mate is called ______________.

**10.** The area that animals occupy and defend against competitors is their ______________.

**11.** Any threatening behavior is a form of ______________.

**12.** A ______________ is the term for a group of animals of the same species that interact.

**13.** Helping a relative survive may be explained by the theory of ______________.

*Write the letter of the correct answer on the line at the left.*

______ **14.** What are behavioral cycles that occur daily?

**A.** circadian rhythms
**B.** courtship
**C.** migration
**D.** learned behaviors

______ **15.** Each year, green sea turtles travel back and forth between their feeding and nesting grounds. This is an example of

**A.** kin selection.
**B.** circadian rhythms.
**C.** hibernation.
**D.** migration.

______ **16.** The system that combines sounds, symbols, and gestures to communicate meaning is

**A.** society.
**B.** kin selection.
**C.** language.
**D.** territory.

 

Name ______________________ Class _____ Date _________

CHAPTER
MYSTERY

ELEPHANT CALLER ID

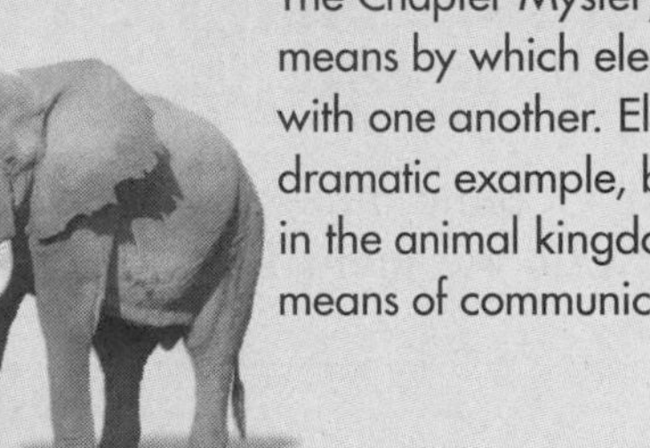

The Chapter Mystery revealed the subtle means by which elephants communicate with one another. Elephants offer a dramatic example, but they are not alone in the animal kingdom in their sophisticated means of communication.

21st Century Learning

# The Impact of Ocean Noise on Marine Mammals

Marine mammals and fish have sensitive hearing. They use sound for most of the important aspects of their survival, including reproduction, feeding, navigation, and the avoidance of predators.

For some time, ocean noise has been increasing because of huge ocean tankers, offshore oil drilling, naval sonar, and other human activity. Many marine biologists have worried about the impact of this noise on marine species. In 2004, the National Oceanic and Atmospheric Administration (NOAA) in the United States held the first international symposium to draw together experts from government, academia, and the commercial shipping industry to address this issue.

Read the symposium's summary report below to learn more about the effect of noise on marine mammals.

## Shipping Noise and Marine Mammals

2004 International Symposium
Sponsored by the U.S. National Oceanic and Atmospheric Administration
18-19 May 2004, Arlington, Virginia, USA

There is currently considerable interest in whether human-generated sound produced in the marine environment impacts animals and, if so, how. It is clear from scientific investigations of many marine mammals that the production and reception of certain sounds are critical to their survival and well being. It is also evident that ocean noise has the potential to interfere with these marine mammals' normal functioning.

The symposium found evidence that noise levels in the ocean have risen dramatically over the past several decades. Researchers reported, for instance, that the worldwide fleet of commercial shipping vessels, such as tankers and container ships, has more than doubled over the past several decades. In one study, scientists continuously sampled ocean noise in a single location off southern California and determined that noise levels have increased at a rate of approximately 3 decibels per decade over the past thirty years.

Although ocean noise is getting louder, it remains largely unclear exactly what kind of disruption and threat the noise pollution may cause to populations of marine mammals. Marine biologists have studied the hearing capabilities of at least 22 of the approximately 125 species of living marine mammals, although usually in very small sample sizes. Most of these studies have determined that these marine species can be very sensitive to sound. In addition, noise can induce physical trauma to non-auditory structures. In fish, noise can increase egg mortality.

One scientist argued that the most important effect of vessel noise on marine animals is that it masked sounds that were biologically significant. Nonetheless, the evidence remains sparse and limited. While participants at the symposium raised a number of issues about the possible effects of noise on marine life, they agreed that more research is badly needed to better understand the effects of ocean noise on marine mammals.

Continued on next page ▶

 

Name ______________________ Class ______ Date ______

## 21st Century Themes Science and Global Awareness

**1.** Why did the National Oceanic and Atmospheric Administration hold the meeting discussed above, and who was invited?

______________________

______________________

______________________

______________________

**2.** What evidence do scientists have that ocean noise is increasing?

______________________

______________________

______________________

______________________

**3.** What role does sound play in the survival of marine mammals?

______________________

______________________

**4.** What may be the most important effect of shipping-vessel noise on marine animals?

______________________

______________________

**5.** What has limited scientists' ability to learn more about the effect of noise on marine mammals?

______________________

______________________

______________________

## 21st Century Skills Listing Research Priorities

The skills used in this activity include **problem identification, formulation, and solution; creativity and intellectual curiosity;** and **self-direction.**

NOAA officials seek to spur new research on the impacts of noise on marine mammals. What research do you think is needed? Find the final report of the symposium on the Internet. It suggests many ideas for future research. Which ideas do you think should have the highest priority? Using the online symposium report, make a list of the top three ideas for possible research projects that you think could best help scientists learn more about this subject. Justify your choices in writing. Then work with three other students to arrive at one list of three priorities and present your list to the class.

 

Name ______________________ Class ______ Date ______

# 30 Digestive and Excretory Systems

**Big idea** **Homeostasis**

**Q:** How are the materials that go into your body and the materials that come from your body related to homeostasis?

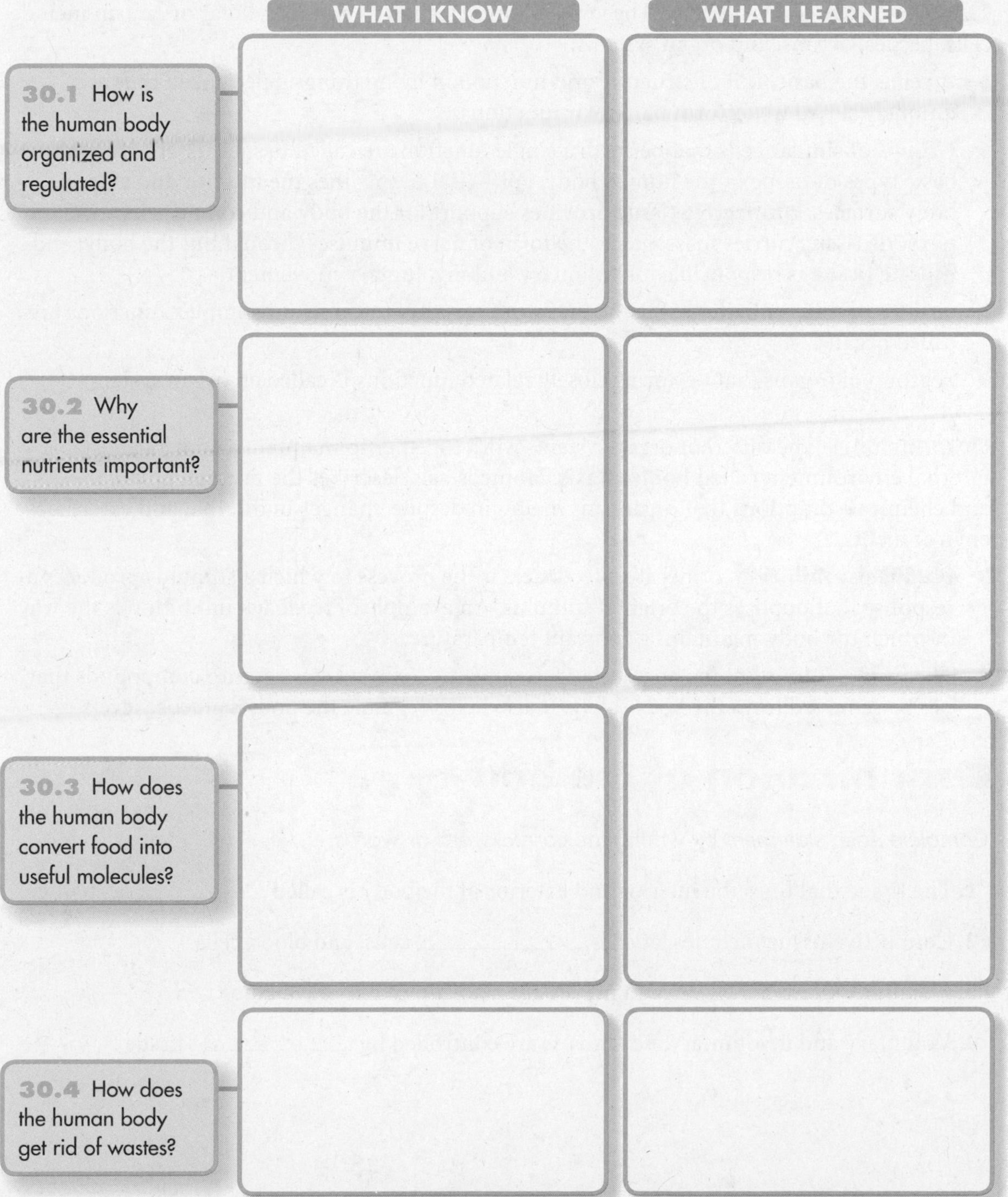

WHAT I KNOW
WHAT I LEARNED
30.1 How is the human body organized and regulated?
30.2 Why are the essential nutrients important?
30.3 How does the human body convert food into useful molecules?
30.4 How does the human body get rid of wastes?

# 30.1 Organization of the Human Body

## Lesson Objectives

- Describe how the human body is organized.
- Explain homeostasis.

## Lesson Summary

**Organization of the Body** The levels of organization in a multicellular organism include cells, tissues, organs, and organ systems.

- A cell is the basic unit of structure and function in living things. Specialized cells are uniquely suited to perform particular functions.
- Groups of similar cells that perform a single function are called tissues. There are four basic types of tissue in the human body: **epithelial tissue** lines the interior and exterior body surfaces; **connective tissue** provides support for the body and connects its parts; **nervous tissue** carries messages in the form of nerve impulses throughout the body; and **muscle tissue** is responsible for voluntary and involuntary movement.
- Groups of different kinds of tissue that work together to carry out complex functions are called organs.
- A group of organs that performs closely related functions is called an organ system.

**Homeostasis** The different organ systems work together to maintain a controlled, stable internal environment called **homeostasis**. Homeostasis describes the internal physical and chemical conditions that organisms maintain despite changes in internal and external environments.

- **Feedback inhibition**, or negative feedback, is the process in which a stimulus produces a response that opposes the original stimulus. An example of feedback inhibition is the way in which the body maintains a constant temperature.
- The liver is important for homeostasis. It converts toxic substances into compounds that can be removed from the body safely. It also helps regulate the body's glucose levels.

## Organization of the Body

*Complete each statement by writing the correct word or words.*

**1.** The tissue that lines the interior and exterior of the body is called ______________ tissue.

**2.** Connective tissue includes fat cells, ______________ cells, and blood cells.

**3.** The brain, ______________, and nerves are made up of nervous tissue.

**4.** Voluntary and involuntary movements are controlled by ______________ tissue.

 

**5.** Complete the table about the organization of the human body.

| Organization of the Human Body | | |
|---|---|---|
| **Level of Organization** | **Description** | **Example** |
| | Basic unit of structure and function in living things | |
| Tissue | | |
| | Group of different types of tissue that function together | |
| | | Nervous system |

*For Questions 6–16, match the function(s) with the organ system.*

**Function**

_____ **6.** Eliminates waste products from the body

_____ **7.** Produces gametes

_____ **8.** Breaks down food

_____ **9.** Protects the body from disease

_____ **10.** Recognizes and coordinates the body's response to changes

_____ **11.** Transports oxygen to cells

_____ **12.** Produces voluntary movement

_____ **13.** Guards against ultraviolet light

_____ **14.** Brings in oxygen for cellular respiration

_____ **15.** Protects internal organs

_____ **16.** Controls growth and metabolism

**Organ System**

**A.** nervous system

**B.** integumentary system

**C.** immune/lymphatic systems

**D.** muscular system

**E.** circulatory system

**F.** skeletal system

**G.** respiratory system

**H.** digestive system

**I.** excretory system

**J.** endocrine system

**K.** reproductive system

 

Name ______________________ Class ______ Date ______

## Homeostasis

**17.** All of the organ systems in the human body work together to maintain homeostasis. What is homeostasis?

______________________________________________

______________________________________________

**18.** What is a feedback inhibition? Give an example of how it is used in the human body.

______________________________________________

______________________________________________

**19.** Why is the liver important for homeostasis?

______________________________________________

______________________________________________

______________________________________________

**20.** THINK VISUALLY Fill in the missing labels in the diagram to show how a thermostat uses feedback inhibition to maintain a stable temperature in a house.

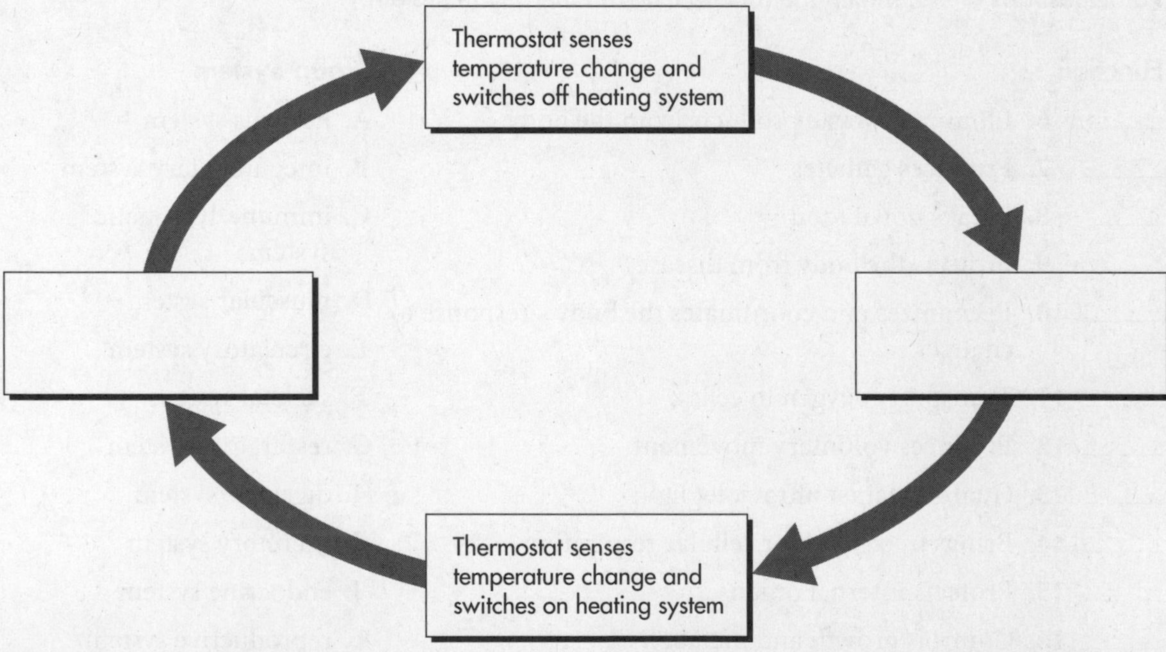


### Apply the Big idea

**21.** Which organ systems work together to maintain body temperature?

______________________________________________

______________________________________________

# 30.2 Food and Nutrition

## Lesson Objectives

- Explain how food provides energy.
- Identify the essential nutrients your body needs and tell how each is important to the body.
- Explain how to plan a balanced diet.

## Lesson Summary

**Food and Energy** Molecules in food contain chemical energy that cells use to produce ATP. Food also supplies raw materials cells need to build and repair tissues.

- The energy in food is measured in dietary Calories. One **Calorie** is equal to 1000 calories. A calorie is the amount of heat needed to raise the temperature of 1 gram of water by 1 degree Celsius.
- A healthy diet provides the body with raw materials to build and repair body tissues and make enzymes, lipids, and DNA.

**Nutrients** Nutrients are substances in food that supply the body with energy and raw materials needed for growth, repair, and maintenance. The nutrients that the body needs are water, carbohydrates, fats, proteins, vitamins, and minerals.

- Many of the body's processes take place in water. Water makes up a large part of blood and other body fluids.
- Simple and complex **carbohydrates** are the body's main source of energy. Complex carbohydrates, such as starches, must be broken down into simple sugars to be used for energy.
- **Fats** are formed from fatty acids and glycerol. Fats help the body absorb fat-soluble vitamins and are a part of cell membranes, nerve cells, and certain hormones.
- **Proteins** supply raw materials for growth and repair of structures such as skin and muscle. Many enzymes and hormones are proteins.
- **Vitamins** are organic molecules that the body needs in very small amounts. They are needed to help the body perform chemical reactions.
- **Minerals** are inorganic nutrients the body needs in small amounts. Examples of minerals include calcium and iron.

**Nutrition and a Balanced Diet** The science of nutrition is the study of food and its effects on the body. A balanced diet provides nutrients in adequate amounts and enough energy for a person to maintain a healthful weight.

- Food labels provide general information about nutrition as well as specific information about a food.
- Exercising about 30 minutes a day, eating a balanced diet, and controlling fat intake can help maintain a healthful weight.

 

Name ______________________________ Class ______ Date ______

## Food and Energy

*Write True if the statement is true. If the statement is false, change the underlined word or words to make the statement true.*

______ **1.** A calorie is the amount of heat needed to <u>lower</u> the temperature of 1 gram of water by 1 degree Celsius.

______ **2.** One dietary Calorie is equal to <u>2000</u> calories.

______ **3.** The energy stored in food molecules is used to produce <u>ATP</u>.

______ **4.** The body needs raw materials from food to build body tissues and make enzymes, lipids and <u>DNA</u>.

## Nutrients

*For Questions 5–16, match each description with the nutrient. Each nutrient may be used more than once.*

**Description**

______ **5.** Provide the body with building materials for growth and repair

______ **6.** Needed to build cell membranes, produce certain hormones, and store energy

______ **7.** Major source of food energy

______ **8.** Makes up the bulk of most body fluids

______ **9.** Inorganic nutrients

______ **10.** Organic molecules used by the body to help regulate body processes

______ **11.** May be saturated or unsaturated

______ **12.** Required to produce the compound that makes up bones and teeth

______ **13.** May be fat-soluble or water-soluble

______ **14.** Polymers of amino acids

______ **15.** May be monosaccharides, disaccharides, or polysaccharides

______ **16.** The most important nutrient

**Nutrient**

**A.** water
**B.** carbohydrates
**C.** fats
**D.** proteins
**E.** vitamins
**F.** minerals

**17.** What are three ways the body loses water?

______________________________________________

______________________________________________

 

# Nutrition and a Balanced Diet

**18.** What is the science of nutrition?

_______________________________________________

_______________________________________________

*Complete each statement by writing the correct word or words.*

**19.** A gram of fat has more Calories than a gram of carbohydrate because carbon atoms in fat have more carbon to ______________ bonds than the carbon atoms in carbohydrates.

**20.** Nutrient needs are affected by age, ______________, and lifestyle.

**21.** When a person stops growing or becomes less active, energy needs ______________.

**22.** Percent Daily Values found on food labels are based on a ______________ diet.

**23.** Eating a balanced diet and exercising ______________ a day can help maintain a healthful weight.

**24.** Physical activity can ______________ the heart, bones, and muscles.

**25.** Diets that are high in ______________ and trans fat increase a person's risk of developing heart disease and Type II diabetes.

## Apply the Big idea

**26.** How can poor food choices negatively affect a person's health?

_______________________________________________

_______________________________________________

_______________________________________________

_______________________________________________

_______________________________________________

_______________________________________________

 

# 30.3 The Digestive System

## Lesson Objectives

- Describe the organs of the digestive system and explain their functions.
- Explain what happens during digestion.
- Describe how nutrients are absorbed into the bloodstream and wastes are eliminated from the body.

## Lesson Summary

**Functions of the Digestive System** The digestive system converts food into small molecules that can be used by body cells. Food is processed by the digestive system in four phases: ingestion, digestion, absorption, and elimination.

- Ingestion is the process of putting food into your mouth.
- **Mechanical digestion** is the physical breakdown of large pieces of food into smaller pieces. During **chemical digestion**, enzymes break down food into molecules the body can use.
- Food molecules are absorbed into the circulatory system by cells in the small intestine.
- Materials the body cannot digest travel through the large intestine and are eliminated as feces.

**The Process of Digestion** During digestion, food travels through the mouth, esophagus, stomach, and small intestine.

- Mechanical digestion begins as teeth tear and grind food. Saliva contains **amylase**, an enzyme that breaks down starches into sugars. This begins the process of chemical digestion. Once food is chewed, it is pushed into the pharynx.
- The tube leading from the pharynx to the stomach is called the **esophagus**. Contractions of smooth muscles, called **peristalsis**, move food through the esophagus to the **stomach**, a large muscular sac that continues digestion.
  - Glands in the stomach lining release hydrochloric acid and the enzyme **pepsin**, which breaks proteins into smaller polypeptide fragments.
  - Contractions of stomach muscles churn the stomach contents, which forms **chyme**, a mixture with an oatmeal-like consistency.
- As chyme moves out of the stomach, it enters the duodenum, the uppermost portion of the **small intestine**. Here, digestive fluids from the pancreas, liver, and lining of the duodenum are added to the chyme.

**Absorption and Elimination** Most nutrients from food are absorbed by the small intestine. The large intestine absorbs water and prepares waste for elimination from the body.

- The small intestine has fingerlike projections (**villi**) that are covered with microvilli, which absorb nutrients. Most nutrients are absorbed into the blood, but fats are absorbed into the lymph.
- When chyme leaves the small intestine, it enters the **large intestine**, or colon. The large intestine absorbs water and some vitamins that are produced by bacteria in the large intestine. The remaining waste material leaves the body through the anus.

 

# Functions of the Digestive System

**1.** What is the function of the organs of the digestive system?

______________________________________________

______________________________________________

**2.** What are the four phases of digestion?

______________________________________________

**3.** What is mechanical digestion?

______________________________________________

______________________________________________

**4.** How do absorbed food molecules travel to the rest of the body?

______________________________________________

______________________________________________

# The Process of Digestion

*Write the letter of the correct answer on the line at the left.*

______ **5.** Where does chemical digestion begin?

**A.** the stomach  **C.** the mouth

**B.** the small intestine  **D.** the esophagus

______ **6.** Saliva eases the passage of food through the digestive system and contains

**A.** amylase.  **C.** sodium bicarbonate.

**B.** pepsin.  **D.** bile.

______ **7.** Which is the correct order of passage of food through the digestive system?

**A.** mouth, stomach, esophagus, large intestine, small intestine

**B.** mouth, stomach, esophagus, small intestine, large intestine

**C.** mouth, esophagus, stomach, small intestine, large intestine

**D.** mouth, esophagus, stomach, large intestine, small intestine

______ **8.** Which of the following is not a role of the pancreas?

**A.** produces sodium bicarbonate

**B.** produces bile

**C.** produces hormones that regulate blood sugar

**D.** produces enzymes that break down carbohydrates, proteins, lipids, and nucleic acids

Name ______________________ Class ______ Date ________

9. Complete the table about the effects of digestive enzymes.

| Active Site | Enzyme | Effect on Food |
|---|---|---|
| | | Breaks down starches into disaccharides |
| | Pepsin | |
| Small intestine (released from pancreas) | | Continues the breakdown of starch |
| | Trypsin | |
| | | Breaks down fat |
| Small intestine | Maltase, sucrase, lactase | |
| | | Breaks down dipeptides into amino acids |

10. **THINK VISUALLY** Draw and label the digestive system. Include the salivary glands, mouth, epiglottis, esophagus, stomach, liver, gallbladder, small intestine, and large intestine.

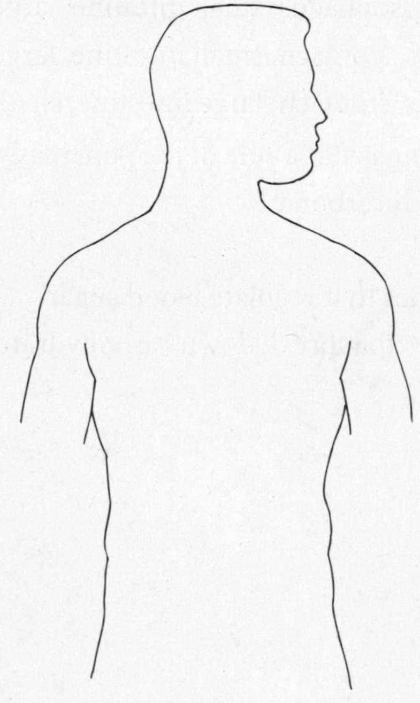

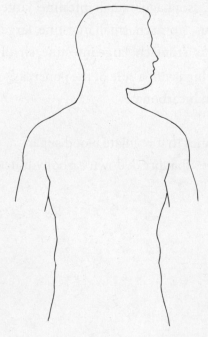

Name ______________________ Class ______ Date ______

# Absorption and Elimination

*For Questions 11–16, complete each statement by writing the correct word or words.*

**11.** The folded surface and fingerlike projections of the ______________ provide a large surface area for absorption of nutrient molecules.

**12.** The fingerlike projections are called ______________.

**13.** Capillaries in the villi absorb the products of ______________ and ______________ digestion.

**14.** Fats and fatty acids are absorbed by ______________.

**15.** In some animals, the ______________ processes cellulose, but not in humans.

**16.** Once chyme leaves the small intestine, it enters the large intestine, or ______________.

**17.** The small intestine is longer than the large intestine. How did the large intestine get its name?

______________________________________________

______________________________________________

**18.** What is the primary function of the large intestine?

______________________________________________

______________________________________________

**19.** What happens to waste materials when they leave the colon?

______________________________________________

______________________________________________

## Apply the Big idea

**20.** What role does the large intestine play in maintaining homeostasis?

______________________________________________

______________________________________________

______________________________________________

______________________________________________

 

# 30.4 The Excretory System

## Lesson Objectives

- Describe the structures of the excretory system and explain their functions.
- Explain how the kidneys clean the blood.
- Describe how the kidneys maintain homeostasis.

## Lesson Summary

**Structures of the Excretory System** Cells produce wastes such as salts, carbon dioxide, and ammonia. For homeostasis to be maintained, these wastes need to be removed from the body. **Excretion** is the process by which metabolic wastes are eliminated from the body.

- The skin excretes excess water, salts, and a small amount of urea in sweat.
- The lungs excrete carbon dioxide and water vapor.
- The liver converts potentially dangerous nitrogen wastes to urea.
- The kidneys are the major organs of excretion. They remove excess water, urea, and metabolic wastes from the blood. **Ureters** carry urine from the kidneys to the **urinary bladder**, where it is stored until it leaves the body through the **urethra**.

**Excretion and the Kidneys** The kidneys remove excess water, minerals, and other waste products from the blood. The cleansed blood returns to circulation. Each kidney has nearly a million processing units called **nephrons**. Filtration and reabsorption occur in the nephrons.

- **Filtration** is the passage of a fluid or gas through a filter to remove wastes. The filtration of blood in the nephron takes place in the **glomerulus**, a small, dense network of capillaries. Each glomerulus is encased by a cuplike structure called **Bowman's capsule**. Pressure in the capillaries forces fluids and wastes from the blood into Bowman's capsule. This fluid is called filtrate.
- Most of the material that enters Bowman's capsule is returned to circulation. The process by which water and dissolved substances are taken back into the blood is called **reabsorption**.
- A section of the nephron tubule, called the **loop of Henle**, conserves water and minimizes the volume of filtrate. The fluid that remains in the tubule is called urine.

**The Kidneys and Homeostasis** The kidneys remove wastes, maintain blood pH, and regulate the water content of the blood.

- The activity of the kidneys is controlled in part by the composition of blood. For example, if blood glucose levels rise well above normal, the kidneys excrete glucose into the urine.
- Disruption of kidney function can lead to health issues such as kidney stones and serious health issues such as kidney damage, and kidney failure.
  - Kidney stones occur when minerals or uric acid salts crystallize and obstruct a ureter.
  - Kidney damage is often caused by high blood pressure or diabetes.
  - When a patient's kidneys can no longer maintain homeostasis, the patient is said to be in kidney failure.

Name ______________________ Class ______ Date ________

# Structures of the Excretory System

**1.** Why does the body need an excretory system?

______________________________________________

______________________________________________

______________________________________________

**2.** What is excretion?

______________________________________________

______________________________________________

**3.** What waste compounds are produced by every cell in the body?

______________________________________________

**4.** What organs are included in the excretory system?

______________________________________________

______________________________________________

**5.** Complete the table about the excretory system.

**Organs of the Excretory System**

| Organ | Function |
|---|---|
| Skin | |
| Lungs | |
| | Converts dangerous nitrogen wastes into urea |
| Kidneys | |
| | Transport urine from kidneys to the bladder |
| | Stores urine |
| Urethra | |

Name ______________________ Class ______ Date ________

# Excretion and the Kidneys

**6.** Complete the concept map.

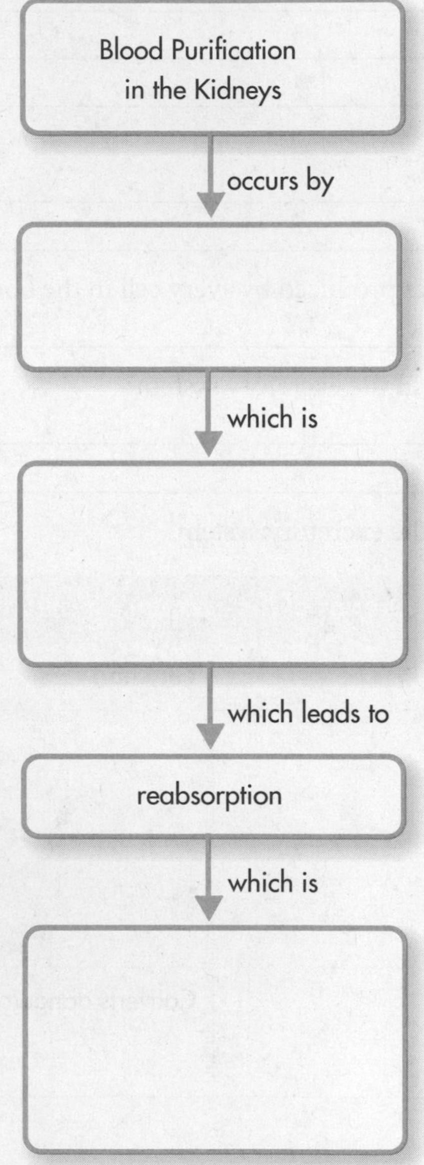


*For Questions 7–10, write True if the statement is true. If the statement is false, change the underlined word or words to make the statement true.*

_____________ **7.** Each kidney has nearly a million individual processing units called <u>capillaries</u>.

_____________ **8.** The material that is filtered from the blood contains water, urea, <u>glucose</u>, salts, amino acids, and some vitamins.

_____________ **9.** A number of materials, including salts, are removed from the filtrate by <u>osmosis</u> and reabsorbed by the capillaries.

_____________ **10.** The <u>glomerulus</u> is responsible for conserving water and minimizing the volume of the filtrate.

11. **THINK VISUALLY** Label the diagram of a nephron.

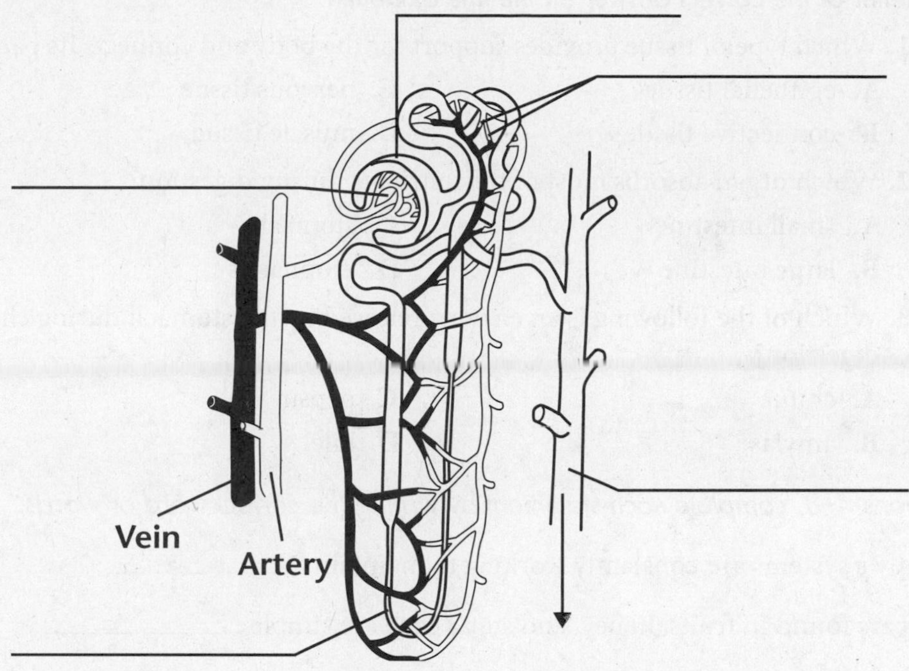


# The Kidneys and Homeostasis

12. Describe three ways that the kidneys help maintain homeostasis.

13. Explain how the kidneys regulate the levels of salt in the blood.

14. How does dialysis work?

## Apply the Big idea

15. Urine testing is a common way that doctors can monitor a patient's health. Suppose a urine test reveals that there are proteins in the patient's urine. What might be wrong with this patient? What part of the excretory system might not be functioning properly?

 

Name ____________________ Class ______ Date ______

# Chapter Vocabulary Review

*Write the letter of the correct answer on the line at the left.*

_____ **1.** Which type of tissue provides support for the body and connects its parts?

**A.** epithelial tissue
**B.** connective tissue
**C.** nervous tissue
**D.** muscle tissue

_____ **2.** Which organ absorbs most of the nutrients during digestion?

**A.** small intestine
**B.** large intestine
**C.** stomach
**D.** esophagus

_____ **3.** Which of the following is an enzyme released by the stomach during chemical digestion?

**A.** chime
**B.** amylase
**C.** pepsin
**D.** bile

*For Questions 4–8, complete each statement by writing the correct word or words.*

**4.** The body's systems are constantly working to maintain ____________.

**5.** The sugars found in fruits, honey, and sugar cane are simple ____________.

**6.** The ____________ is a long tube that connects the mouth and the stomach.

**7.** The ______________ absorbs water from undigested material that will be eliminated.

**8.** The process by which metabolic wastes are eliminated is called ______________.

*For Questions 9–18, match the term with its definition.*

| Terms | Definitions |
|---|---|
| _____ **9.** Calorie | **A.** Inorganic molecule needed by the body in small quantities |
| _____ **10.** proteins | **B.** Functional unit of the kidney |
| _____ **11.** vitamins | **C.** Mixture of stomach fluids and partially digested food |
| _____ **12.** amylase | **D.** Section of a nephron that conserves water and minimizes urine volume |
| _____ **13.** mineral | **E.** Enzyme that breaks down carbohydrates |
| _____ **14.** peristalsis | **F.** Organic molecules that regulate body processes |
| _____ **15.** chyme | **G.** Unit equal to 1000 calories of heat or 1 kilocalorie |
| _____ **16.** nephron | **H.** Smooth muscle contractions that squeeze food through the esophagus into the stomach |
| _____ **17.** Bowman's capsule | **I.** Cup-shaped structure that surrounds a glomerulus |
| _____ **18.** loop of Henle | **J.** Nutrients that provide the body with the building materials it needs for growth and repair |

Name ______ Class ____ Date ______

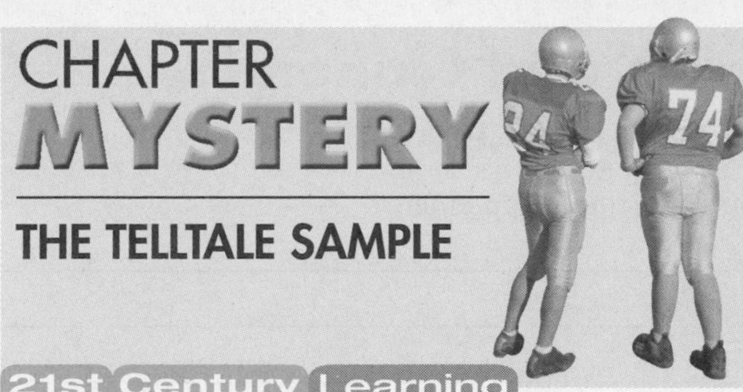


In the Chapter Mystery, you learned how evidence of illegal drug use can be found by testing a person's urine. In this activity, you'll learn about other substances that athletes should possibly be tested for.

# Dietary Supplements

Some athletic organizations test competing athletes for illegal drug use. Dietary supplements, on the other hand, are not tested for by most athletic organizations, because they are legal. But since many supplements claim to improve health or boost physical performance, should they be included in athletes' drug tests as well? Are dietary supplements even safe or effective? The following Web page presents one view on supplements.

SportsMedForum > Home > Fitness > Dietary Supplements

## Dietary Supplements: Helpful or Hazardous?

Do you agree with the following two statements about the safety and effectiveness of dietary supplements?

*"If it weren't safe, they wouldn't be allowed to sell it."*
*"They can't claim it in their ad if it's not true."*

The fact is, both statements are false an awful lot of the time. Neither statement is true, for instance, when you see an ad for a dietary supplement claiming that it will help you lose weight, build muscles, or be happier. Why?

Here's the thing. Before a drug—defined as any substances intended for use in the diagnosis, cure, mitigation, treatment, or prevention of disease—can be sold in this country, the manufacturer has to prove to the Food and Drug Administration that the drug is safe and effective. If it doesn't, the FDA won't approve the drug. But dietary supplements are not drugs, and so the rules are different.

Manufacturers are not allowed to sell dietary supplements—defined as substances that are added to a person's diet, but don't have proven disease-treating effects—that are unsafe and/or ineffective. However, the manufacturers don't have to prove to anyone that their product actually is safe and effective. The FDA can only ban a product if it performs its own tests to prove that the product is dangerous or fraudulent. Needless to say, the FDA can't afford to test all of the roughly 29,000 supplements on the market. This means unsafe and ineffective supplements may slip by.

The FDA does have rules about what a manufacturer can claim, but these rules are very easy to get around. For example, product labels are not allowed to include any "false or misleading claims." But is anybody going to test the claims to see if they are false or misleading? No. Manufacturers can't claim that a supplement will "treat, mitigate, or cure a disease," a label reserved for drugs. So they can't say a product will treat high blood pressure but to get around it, they can say it will "promote blood-vessel health." They can't say a supplement will treat depression, but they can say it will "promote a feeling of well-being."

And then there's the phrase I hate the most—"all natural." In how many ads does someone say, "It's all natural, so you know it's safe"? Oh yeah? Poison ivy is "natural," but I wouldn't eat it. Foxglove is "natural," but if you eat it, be prepared for nausea, diarrhea, vomiting, irregular heartbeat, convulsions, and maybe death. Monkshood is "natural," but you can die if you handle it, never mind ingest it.

As always, friends, don't believe everything you read. Even here.

Murray Gelb, D. Jur,. is a practicing attorney.

This column is for entertainment only. Nothing in it should be construed as legal advice.

Continued on next page ▶

Name ______________________________ Class ______ Date __________

## 21st Century Themes Science and Economic Literacy, Science and Health Literacy

**1.** What is the difference between a drug and a dietary supplement?

_______________________________________________

_______________________________________________

_______________________________________________

**2.** What are two FDA rules about labeling on packages of dietary supplements?

_______________________________________________

_______________________________________________

**3.** An ad for a dietary supplement says a product builds muscle mass and improves athletic performance. Why should you approach such claims with skepticism? Explain your answer.

_______________________________________________

_______________________________________________

**4.** A dietary supplement's label has the phrase "all natural." Can you assume that the product is safe? Explain your answer.

_______________________________________________

_______________________________________________

_______________________________________________

**5.** If a product label says it will "treat and prevent heartburn and acid indigestion," what does that tell you about the product?

_______________________________________________

_______________________________________________

## 21st Century Skills Race for a Cause

The skills used in this activity include **information and media literacy, communication skills, creativity and intellectual curiosity**, and **social responsibility.**

Go to a local mall, pharmacy, or health food store and look for products taken to improve one's health or well-being that are not FDA-approved. Read the labels. Look at any advertising you see nearby—signs, brochures, pamphlets, and so on. Look at the wording that is used, and how things are phrased.

*Write a short essay about these products, giving your opinion on what the products most likely can and cannot do.*

 

Name ______________________ Class ______ Date ______

# 31 The Nervous System

**Big idea** **Structure and Function**

**Q:** How does the structure of the nervous system allow it to control functions in every part of the body?

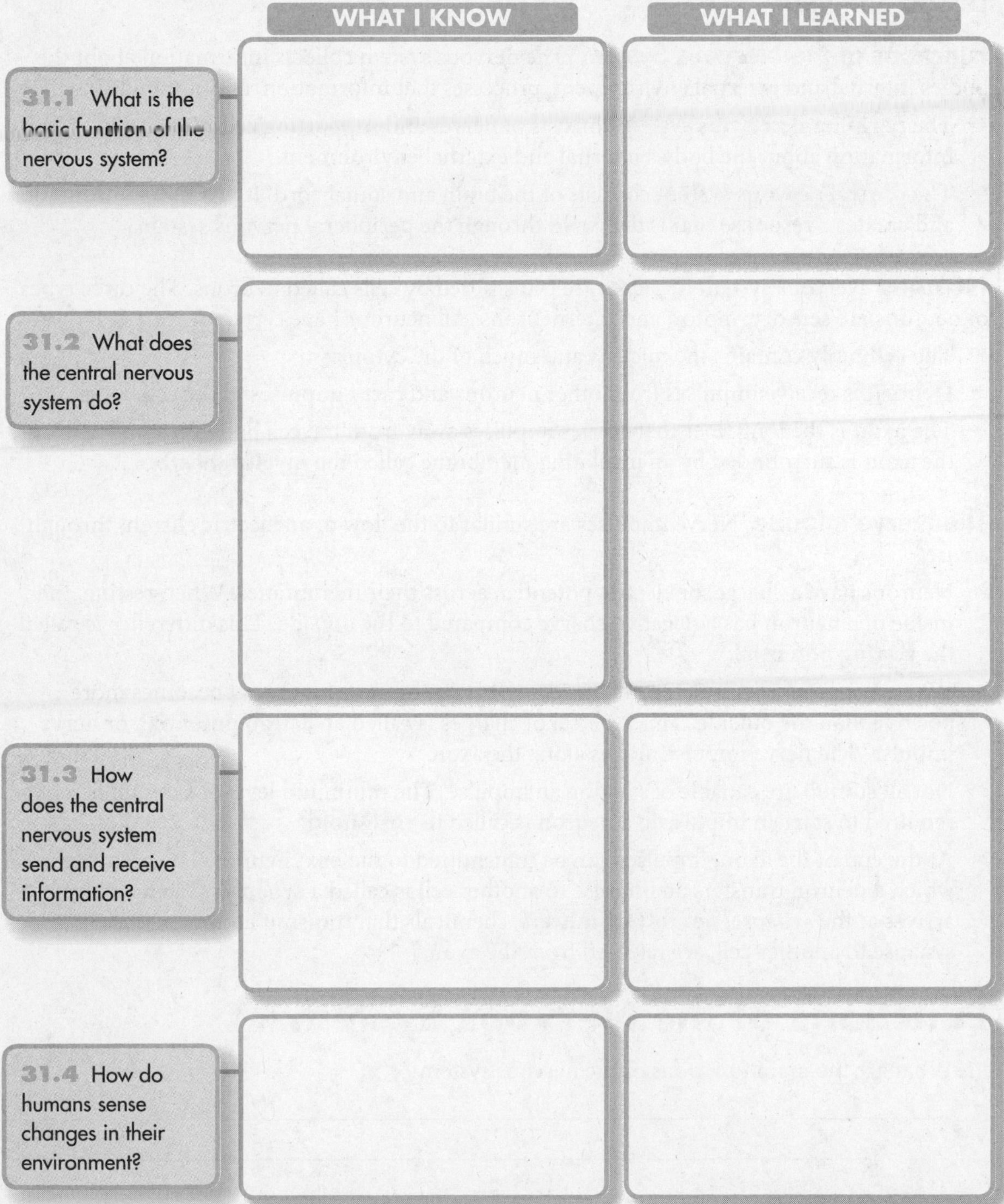

| | WHAT I KNOW | WHAT I LEARNED |
|---|---|---|
| **31.1** What is the basic function of the nervous system? | | |
| **31.2** What does the central nervous system do? | | |
| **31.3** How does the central nervous system send and receive information? | | |
| **31.4** How do humans sense changes in their environment? | | |

Name ______________________ Class _____ Date _________

# 31.1 The Neuron

## Lesson Objectives

- Identify the functions of the nervous system.
- Describe the function of neurons.
- Describe how a nerve impulse is transmitted.

## Lesson Summary

**Functions of the Nervous System** The nervous system collects information about the body's internal and external environment, processes that information, and responds to it.

- The **peripheral nervous system** consists of nerves and supporting cells. It collects information about the body's internal and external environment.
- The **central nervous system** consists of the brain and spinal cord. It processes information and creates a response that is delivered through the peripheral nervous system.

**Neurons** Nervous system impulses are transmitted by cells called neurons. The three types of neurons are sensory, motor, and interneurons. All neurons have certain features:

- The **cell body** contains the nucleus and much of the cytoplasm.
- **Dendrites** receive impulses from other neurons and carry impulses to the cell body.
- The **axon** is the long fiber that carries impulses away from the cell body. In some neurons, the axon is surrounded by an insulating membrane called the **myelin sheath**.

**The Nerve Impulse** Nerve impulses are similar to the flow of an electric current through a wire.

- Neurons have a charge, or electric potential, across their membranes. When resting, the inside of a neuron has a negative charge compared to the outside. This difference is called the **resting potential**.
- When a neuron is stimulated, the inside of its membrane temporarily becomes more positive than the outside. This reversal of charges is called an **action potential**, or nerve impulse. The nerve impulse moves along the axon.
- Not all stimuli are capable of starting an impulse. The minimum level of a stimulus that is required to start an impulse in a neuron is called its **threshold**.
- At the end of the axon, impulses can be transmitted to the next neuron. The point at which a neuron transfers an impulse to another cell is called a **synapse**. When an impulse arrives at the synapse, **neurotransmitters**, chemicals that transmit an impulse across a synapse to another cell, are released from the axon.

# Functions of the Nervous System

**1.** What are the main functions of the nervous system?

______________________________________________

______________________________________________

Name ______________________ Class ______ Date ________

2. Name the two parts of the nervous system and explain what each part does.

______________________________________________

______________________________________________

______________________________________________

______________________________________________

______________________________________________

## Neurons

3. **THINK VISUALLY** Draw and label a diagram of a neuron. Be sure to include the following features in your drawing: axon, axon terminals, cell body, dendrites, myelin sheath, nodes, and nucleus.

*For Questions 4–8, complete each statement by writing the correct word or words.*

4. Neurons that carry impulses from the eyes to the spinal cord and brain are called ________________.

5. Motor neurons carry impulses from the brain and spinal cord to ________________ and ________________.

6. The neuron's cell body has short, branched extensions called ________________ which receive impulses from other neurons.

7. In most animals, ________________ and ________________ of different neurons are clustered in bundles called nerves.

8. The insulating membrane that surrounds a single axon in some neurons is called the ________________.

Name ______________________ Class ______ Date ______

## The Nerve Impulse

**9.** Describe the role of sodium ions in propagating a nerve impulse.

*For Questions 10–11, use the Visual Analogy comparing falling dominoes to a moving impulse.*

**10.** **VISUAL ANALOGY** Dominoes require a push to begin falling. What "push" starts a nerve impulse?

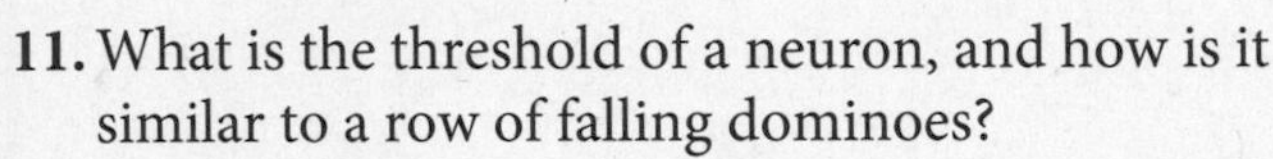

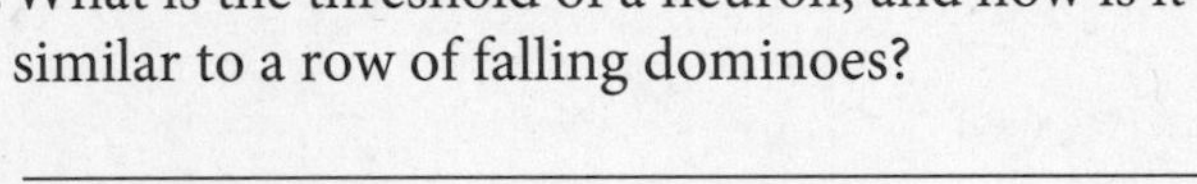

**11.** What is the threshold of a neuron, and how is it similar to a row of falling dominoes?

Action Potential

**12.** What are neurotransmitters, and how do they function?

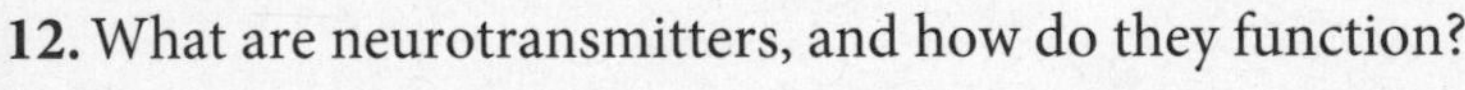

**Apply the Big idea**

**13.** How is the structure of a neuron suited to its function?

 

Name ________________________ Class _____ Date _________

# 31.2 The Central Nervous System

## Lesson Objectives

- Discuss the functions of the brain and spinal cord.
- Describe the effects of drugs on the brain.

## Lesson Summary

**The Brain and Spinal Cord** The central nervous system consists of the brain and spinal cord. Some kinds of information, including some reflexes, are processed directly in the spinal cord. A **reflex** is a quick, automatic response to a stimulus.

- The largest region of the human brain is the **cerebrum**, which controls learning, judgment, and voluntary actions of muscles.
  - The cerebrum is divided into right and left hemispheres. Each deals primarily with the opposite side of the body.
  - The outer layer of the cerebrum is the **cerebral cortex**. It processes information from the sense organs and controls body movements.
- The limbic system controls functions such as emotion, behavior, and memory.
- The **thalamus** receives messages from sensory receptors throughout the body and sends the information to the proper region of the cerebrum for processing.
- The **hypothalamus** controls the recognition and analysis of hunger, thirst, fatigue, anger, and body temperature. It helps coordinate the nervous and endocrine systems.
- The **cerebellum** is the second largest region of the brain. It receives information about muscle and joint position and coordinates the actions of these muscles.
- The **brain stem** connects the brain and spinal cord. It regulates the flow of information between the brain and the rest of the body.

**Addiction and the Brain** Almost all addictive substances affect brain synapses.

- Many drugs cause an increase in the release of the neurotransmitter **dopamine**. The brain reacts to high dopamine levels by reducing the number of receptors.
- With fewer dopamine receptors available, larger amounts of drugs are required to produce a high. This can result in an addiction.

# The Brain and Spinal Cord

*Write the letter of the correct answer on the line at the left.*

_____ **1.** What is the main link between the brain and the rest of the body?

**A.** cerebrum **B.** spinal cord **C.** cerebellum **D.** brain stem

_____ **2.** Which of the following is the best example of a reflex?

**A.** jumping up and down
**B.** running in a race
**C.** slowly putting your foot into cool water
**D.** pulling your hand away from a hot pot

_____ 3. Which part of the brain controls blood pressure, heart rate, breathing, and swallowing?

A. brain stem

B. limbic system

C. cerebral cortex

D. thalamus

_____ 4. Which of the following is a function of the frontal lobe?

A. making judgments

B. hearing and smelling

C. reading and speech

D. vision

_____ 5. Which part of the brain is the site of intelligence, learning, and judgment?

A. brain stem

B. cerebellum

C. cerebrum

D. limbic system

*For Questions 6–10, match the part of the brain with its function.*

| Part of Brain | Function |
|---|---|
| _____ 6. cerebrum | A. Coordinates and balances the actions of the muscles |
| _____ 7. cerebellum | B. Regulates the flow of information between the brain and the rest of the body |
| _____ 8. brain stem | C. Controls voluntary activities of the body |
| _____ 9. thalamus | D. Controls hunger, thirst, fatigue, anger, and body temperature |
| _____ 10. hypothalamus | E. Receives and relays messages from the sense organs |

11. What connects the two hemispheres of the brain?

_______________

12. Identify the four lobes of the brain and their functions.

_______________

_______________

_______________

13. What is the cerebral cortex and what is its function?

_______________

_______________

_______________

_______________

Name ______________________ Class ______ Date ______

# Addiction and the Brain

**14.** What parts of the brain are changed by drug use?

______________________

**15.** What is dopamine?

______________________

______________________

______________________

**16.** How do drugs cause addiction?

______________________

______________________

______________________

______________________

**17.** Complete the table.

| Effects of Drugs on the Body | |
|---|---|
| **Drug** | **Effects on the Body** |
| | Releases a flood of dopamine, produces an instant high |
| | Keeps dopamine in the synaptic region longer, intensifying pleasure and suppressing pain |
| Heroin | |
| Nicotine and alcohol | |

## Apply the Big idea

**18.** What might be the effects on someone who seriously injured his or her cerebellum? Explain your answer.

______________________

______________________

______________________

______________________

______________________

# 31.3 The Peripheral Nervous System

## Lesson Objectives

Describe the functions of the sensory division of the peripheral nervous system.

Describe the functions of the motor division of the peripheral nervous system.

## Lesson Summary

**The Sensory Division** The peripheral nervous system consists of all the nerves and associated cells that are not part of the brain or spinal cord. It is made up of the sensory division and the motor division.

- The sensory division transmits impulses from sense organs to the central nervous system.
- Sensory receptors are cells that transmit information about changes in the internal and external environment. Chemoreceptors respond to chemicals. Photoreceptors respond to light. Mechanoreceptors respond to touch, pressure, vibrations, and stretch. Thermoreceptors respond to temperature change. Pain receptors respond to tissue injury.

**The Motor Division** The motor division, which is divided into the somatic and autonomic nervous systems, transmits impulses from the central nervous system to muscles and glands.

- The **somatic nervous system** regulates processes under voluntary control.
- Actions of the somatic nervous system called reflexes occur automatically. The impulses controlling these actions travel on a pathway called a **reflex arc**. An impulse travels through a sensory neuron, to the spinal cord, and then back through a motor neuron.
- The **autonomic nervous system** regulates activities that are involuntary. It consists of two parts, the sympathetic nervous system and the parasympathetic nervous system.
  - In general, the sympathetic nervous system prepares the body for intense activity. It prepares the body to "fight or flee" in response to stress.
  - The parasympathetic nervous system causes the "rest and digest" response.

# The Sensory Division

**1.** Which nerves go through openings in the skull and stimulate the head and neck?

______

**2.** What are ganglia?

______

**3.** What is the function of the sensory division of the peripheral nervous system?

______

**4.** What are sensory receptors?

______

______

*Match the sensory receptor with the stimuli to which it responds.*

| **Sensory Receptor** | **Stimuli** |
|---|---|
| ______ **5.** chemoreceptor | **A.** light |
| ______ **6.** mechanoreceptor | **B.** touch and pressure |
| ______ **7.** pain receptor | **C.** temperature changes |
| ______ **8.** photoreceptor | **D.** tissue injury |
| ______ **9.** thermoreceptor | **E.** chemicals |

## The Motor Division

*For Questions 10–12, write True or False on the line provided.*

__________ **10.** The motor division of the peripheral nervous system transmits impulses directly from the sensory receptors to muscles or glands.

__________ **11.** The somatic nervous system regulates body activities that are under conscious control.

__________ **12.** Brain impulses are carried to motor neurons and then to muscles.

**13.** Complete a flowchart showing the reflex arc that occurs when you step on a sharp object.

Sensory receptors react to a stimulus and send an impulse to sensory neurons.

↓

↓

↓

↓

**14.** Complete the concept map.

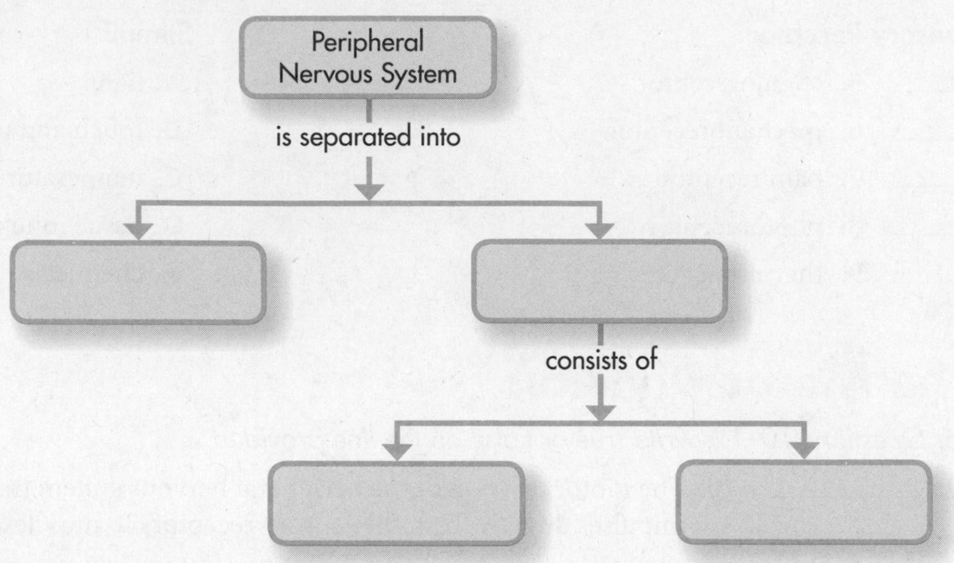


**15.** What is the function of the autonomic nervous system?

_______________________________________________

**16.** How might the autonomic nervous system prepare your body during rigorous exercise?

_______________________________________________

_______________________________________________

**17.** What is the function of the parasympathetic nervous system?

_______________________________________________

_______________________________________________

**18.** What situation might trigger a response from the sympathetic nervous system? Explain.

_______________________________________________

_______________________________________________

## Apply the Big idea

**19.** Suppose someone was playing baseball and trying to catch a pop fly ball. Explain how the different parts of the nervous system would respond in this situation.

_______________________________________________

_______________________________________________

_______________________________________________

_______________________________________________

_______________________________________________

_______________________________________________

_______________________________________________

 

# 31.4 The Senses

## Lesson Objectives

- Discuss the sense of touch and identify the various types of sensory receptors in the skin.
- Explain the relationship between smell and taste.
- Identify the parts of the ears that make hearing and balance possible.
- Describe the major parts of the eye and explain how the eye enables us to see.

## Lesson Summary

**Touch and Related Senses** Different sensory receptors in the body respond to touch, temperature, and pain.

- Skin contains at least seven types of sensory receptors that respond to touch.
- Thermoreceptors respond to heat and cold. They are found in the skin and hypothalamus.
- Pain receptors are found throughout the body. They respond to physical injuries.

**Smell and Taste** Sensations of smell and taste are the result of impulses sent to the brain by chemoreceptors. Sense organs that detect taste are called **taste buds**. Sensory cells in taste buds respond to salty, bitter, sweet, sour, and savory foods.

**Hearing and Balance** Mechanoreceptors found in parts of the ear transmit impulses to the brain. The brain translates the impulses into sound and information about balance.

- Vibrations cause pressure waves in the fluid-filled **cochlea** of the inner ear. Tiny hair cells in the cochlea are pushed back and forth by the pressure waves. The hair cells send nerve impulses to the brain, which interprets them as sound.
- The ears also help maintain balance. The **semicircular canals** and two fluid-filled sacs behind them monitor the position of the body in relation to gravity.

**Vision** Vision occurs when photoreceptors in the eyes transmit impulses to the brain, which translates these impulses into images.

- The **cornea** is a tough, transparent layer of cells. The cornea helps focus the light, which passes through a chamber filled with fluid called aqueous humor.
- The **iris** is the colored portion of the eye. In the middle of the iris is a small opening called the **pupil**, through which light enters the eye.
- The **lens** is located behind the iris. The shape of the lens is changed by tiny muscles to adjust the eye's focus.
- The lens focuses light on the **retina**, the inner layer of the eye. Photoreceptors in the retina convert light energy into nerve impulses that are carried to the brain via the optic nerve. There are two kinds of photoreceptors:
  - **Rods** are very sensitive to light but do not distinguish colors.
  - **Cones** are less sensitive to light, but do distinguish colors.

 

Name ______________________ Class ______ Date ______

## Touch and Related Senses

*Write True or False on the line provided.*

______ 1. Unlike other senses, the sense of touch is not found in one particular place.

______ 2. The greatest density of touch receptors is found on the arms and legs.

______ 3. Touch is detected by mechanoreceptors.

______ 4. Thermoreceptors which respond to heat and cold are found in the thalamus region of the brain.

______ 5. The brain has pain receptors that respond to chemicals released during infection.

## Smell and Taste

*Complete each statement by writing the correct word or words.*

6. Chemical-sensing cells known as ______ in the nose and mouth are responsible for the senses of ______ and ______.

7. The sense organs that detect taste are the ______.

8. Taste buds respond to ______, bitter, sweet, and ______ foods.

9. The ______ receptors are stimulated by MSG, meat, and cheese.

10. People with head colds may have difficulty tasting foods. Explain why this happens.

______

______

______

______

## Hearing and Balance

11. Name the two sensory functions of the human ear.

______

12. What is sound? ______

13. After you spin around and around, you usually become dizzy. What part of the ear is involved in this sensation? Explain.

______

______

______

______

______

 

Name ______________________ Class ______ Date ______

**14.** Complete the flowchart showing how we process sound.

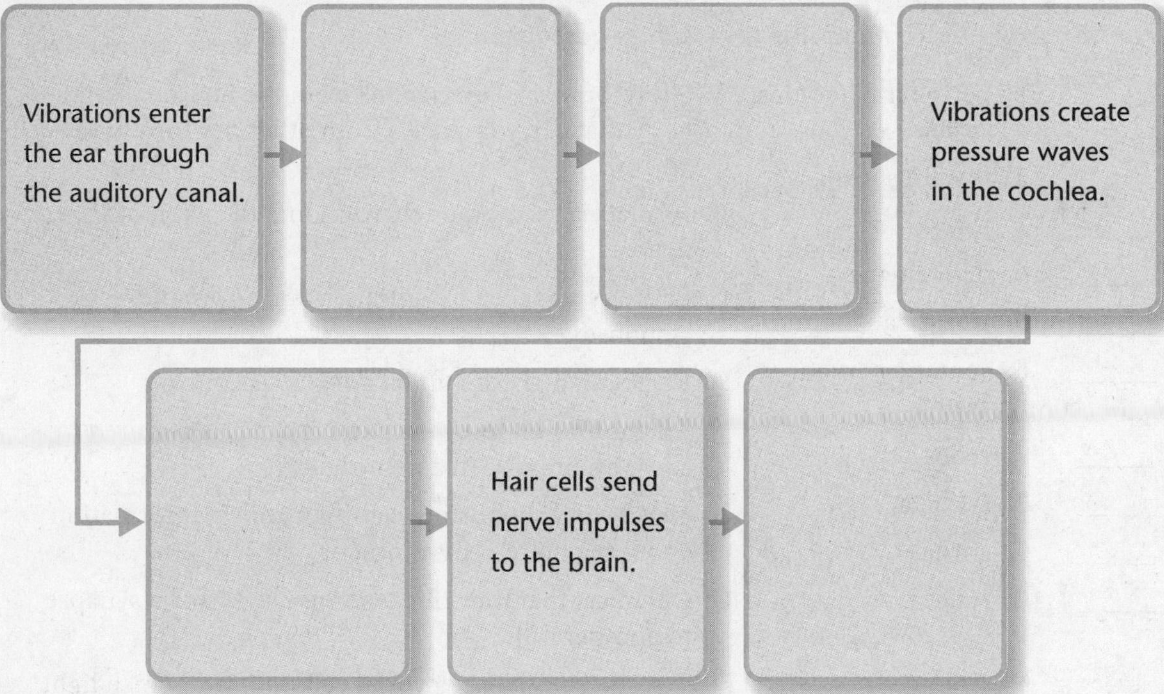
Vibrations enter the ear through the auditory canal.
Vibrations create pressure waves in the cochlea.
Hair cells send nerve impulses to the brain.

## Vision

**15.** Label the diagram of the eye.

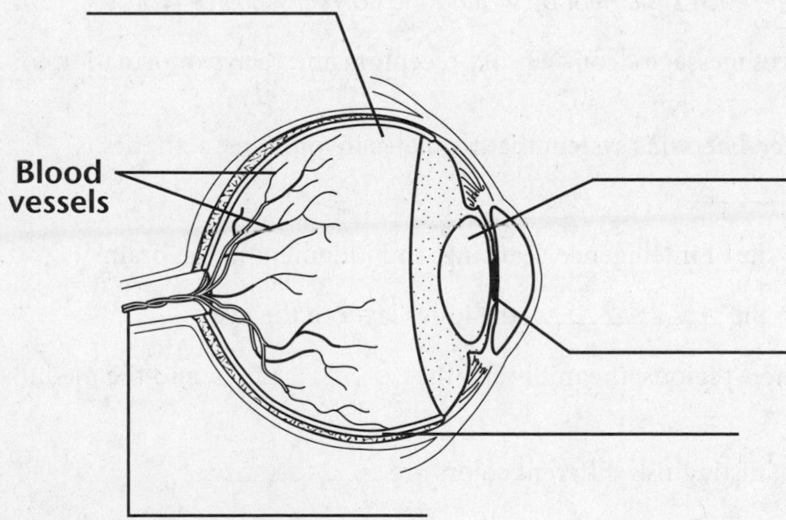
Blood vessels

**Apply the Big idea**

**16.** How does the shape and structure of the lens relate to its function in the eye?

_______________________________________________

_______________________________________________

_______________________________________________

 

Name ______ Class ______ Date ______

# Chapter Vocabulary Review

*For Questions 1–10, match the term with its description.*

| |  | |  |
|---|---|---|---|
| ____ | 1. peripheral nervous system | A. | Short, branched extensions from the neuron's cell body that carry impulses from other neurons to the cell body |
| ____ | 2. myelin sheath | B. | Insulating membrane surrounding the axon of a neuron |
| ____ | 3. threshold | C. | Pathway travelled by impulses during a rapid response |
| ____ | 4. dendrites | D. | Regulates activities under conscious control |
| ____ | 5. neurotransmitter | E. | The minimum level of a stimulus that is required to cause an impulse in a neuron |
| ____ | 6. somatic nervous system | F. | Nerves and supporting cells that collect information about the body's environment |
| ____ | 7. reflex arc | G. | Chemical that transmits an impulse across a synapse to another cell |
| ____ | 8. cochlea | H. | Tough, transparent layer of cells through which light enters the eye |
| ____ | 9. cornea | I. | Fluid-filled inner ear structure lined with hair cells |
| ____ | 10. reflex | J. | Quick, automatic response to a stimulus |

*For Questions 11–20, complete each statement by writing the correct word or words.*

**11.** The ______ receives messages from sensory receptors and relays information to the cerebrum.

**12.** The division of the peripheral nervous system that regulates involuntary activities is the ______.

**13.** The ______ is the site of intelligence, learning, and judgment in the brain.

**14.** The lens focuses light onto the ______, the inner layer of the eye.

**15.** The ______ has three regions, the midbrain, the ______, and the medulla oblongata.

**16.** Photoreceptors that do not distinguish different colors are ______.

**17.** The brain and the spinal cord make up the ______.

**18.** The ______ is made up of densely packed nerve cell bodies called gray matter.

**19.** Most addictive substances act on synapses that use ______ as a neurotransmitter.

**20.** A nerve impulse, or ______, begins when a neuron is stimulated by another neuron or the environment.

 

Name ______________________ Class _____ Date _________

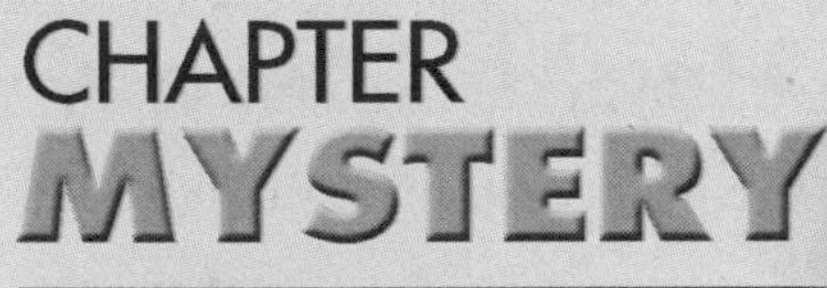

## POISONING ON THE HIGH SEAS

The Chapter Mystery focused on the likelihood that eating the Silverstripe blaasop may have poisoned the men on Captain James Cook's ship the HMS *Resolution* in 1774. Bacteria that live in the fish produce the poison tetrodotoxin.

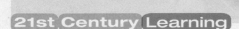

# Poison Safety at Home

The effects of tetrodotoxin are deadly and dramatic. Thankfully, tetrodotoxin poisoning is rare. Many other poisons however, while perhaps not as deadly, surround us each day. In fact, in the United States, roughly one million possible poisonings are reported each year for children under the age of six. Approximately 90 percent of poisonings occur in the home.

Small children may eat pills such as analgesics, or pain relievers, in doses that can be toxic to them. Other poisonings can occur when people accidentally ingest household cleaners, cosmetic or personal care products, pesticides, or prescription drugs.

The table below is adapted from the 2006 Annual Report of the American Association of Poison Control Centers. It shows the number of cases handled by poison control centers in the United States that year by poison category:

**Poisons Most Frequently Involved in Human Exposures**

| Substance | Number of cases/yr | % |
|---|---|---|
| Analgesics | 284,906 | 11.9 |
| Cosmetics/personal care products | 214,780 | 8.9 |
| Cleaning substances (household) | 214,091 | 8.9 |
| Sedatives/hypnotics/antipsychotics | 141,150 | 5.9 |
| Foreign bodies/toys/miscellaneous | 120,752 | 5.0 |
| Cold and cough preparations | 114,559 | 4.8 |
| Topical preparations | 108,308 | 4.5 |
| Pesticides | 96,811 | 4.0 |
| Antidepressants | 95,327 | 4.0 |
| Chemicals | 47,557 | 2.0 |

Continued on next page ▶

## 21st Century Themes Science and Health Literacy

1. How many possible poisonings are reported each year in the United States for children under the age of six?

2. Where do most poisonings tend to occur?

3. According to the table, what percent of poisoning cases in the United States involve household cleaning substances?

4. According to the table, what portion of all poisoning cases involve all the categories of drugs—analgesics, sedatives, cold medicines, and antidepressants? How many of these cases are reported each year?

5. Were you surprised to learn about the most common poisonings in the United States? Which category surprised you the most? Why?

## 21st Century Skills Letter to the FDA

The skills used in this activity include **problem identification, formulation, and solution; creativity and intellectual curiosity; information and media literacy;** and **social responsibility.**

Sometimes substances believed to be safe raise concerns about toxic effects. This happened recently with the chemical bisphenol-A (BPA). BPA was suspected of being hazardous to humans as early as the 1930s. But, until recently, it was widely used as a component in polycarbonate plastic water bottles and baby bottles. In 2008, concerns about the use of BPA in consumer products grabbed headlines when several governments issued reports questioning its safety, and some retailers voluntarily pulled products made with it off their shelves. The chemical is still widely used in the lining of cans and many other products. Scientists remain divided about the health risks posed by BPA. The Canadian government has moved to restrict it, but the U.S. Food and Drug Administration (FDA) has not. Using the Internet, find at least two news articles about the controversy over the potentially toxic effects of BPA. Weigh the evidence for yourself. Then write a letter to the FDA recommending what you think the FDA should do about BPA. Include your reasoning.

 

Name ______________________ Class ______ Date ________

# 32 Skeletal, Muscular, and Integumentary Systems

**Big idea** **Structure and Function**

**Q:** What systems form the structure of the human body?

| | WHAT I KNOW | WHAT I LEARNED |
|---|---|---|
| **32.1** How does the structure of the skeletal system allow it to function properly? | | |
| **32.2** How do muscles help you move? | | |
| **32.3** Why is the integumentary system a necessary organ system? | | |

 

Name ______________________ Class ______ Date ________

# 32.1 The Skeletal System

## Lesson Objectives

- List the structures and functions of the skeletal system.
- Describe the structure of a typical bone.
- List the different kinds of joints and describe the range of motion of each.

## Lesson Summary

**The Skeleton** The human skeleton, like that of other vertebrates, is an endoskeleton.

- The adult human skeleton consists of 206 bones. Some bones are considered part of the axial skeleton and others of the appendicular skeleton.
  - The skull, vertebral column, and rib cage form the **axial skeleton**, which supports the central axis of the body.
  - The bones of the arms, legs, shoulders, and hips make up the **appendicular skeleton**.
- The skeleton supports the body, protects internal organs, produces movement by acting as levers, stores minerals, and produces blood cells.

**Bones** A solid network of living cells and protein fibers surrounded by calcium salts forms the bones of the human body.

- Bones have a complex structure. A layer of tough connective tissue called the periosteum covers a bone. Bones are made up of two types of bone tissue.
  - Compact bone is a dense outer layer that is arranged around **Haversian canals**—channels through which blood vessels and nerves run.
  - Spongy bone is a less dense layer found at the ends of long bones and in the center of flat bones, which adds strength without adding excess mass.
  - Soft tissue called **bone marrow** fills cavities in some bones. Yellow marrow stores fat. Red marrow contains stem cells, which make most types of blood cells.
- In infants, the skeleton is almost all **cartilage**, which is a dense tissue built around protein fibers. Bone replaces cartilage by a process called **ossification**, during which cells called **osteoblasts** secrete minerals. Osteoblasts mature into cells called **osteocytes**, which maintain the minerals in bone and strengthen the bone.
- Mature bone contains some osteoblasts, which build new bone, and cells called **osteoclasts**, which break down bone minerals. These cells enable the repair of broken or damaged bones and keep bone from becoming brittle and weak.

**Joints** Bones meet at **joints**, which contain connective tissues that hold the ends together. Joints permit bones to move without damaging each other.

- Joints are classified into three types:
  - Immovable, or fixed, joints allow no movement. These joints are found between bones in the skull.
  - Slightly movable joints, such as those found between vertebrae, permit some movement.
  - Freely movable joints, such as those found in the elbows and knees, permit movement in two or more directions.

- Cartilage covers the ends of the bones in a joint. **Ligaments**, tough strips of connective tissue, hold bones together. Synovial fluid reduces friction between moving bones. Bursae are sacs of synovial fluid that also act as shock absorbers.
- Joint injuries include ligament damage, inflammation, or loss of cartilage. Bursitis is inflammation of the bursae. Osteoarthritis is a painful stiffening of joints caused by the breakdown of cartilage.

## The Skeleton

**1.** Complete the concept map that summarizes the parts of the human skeleton.

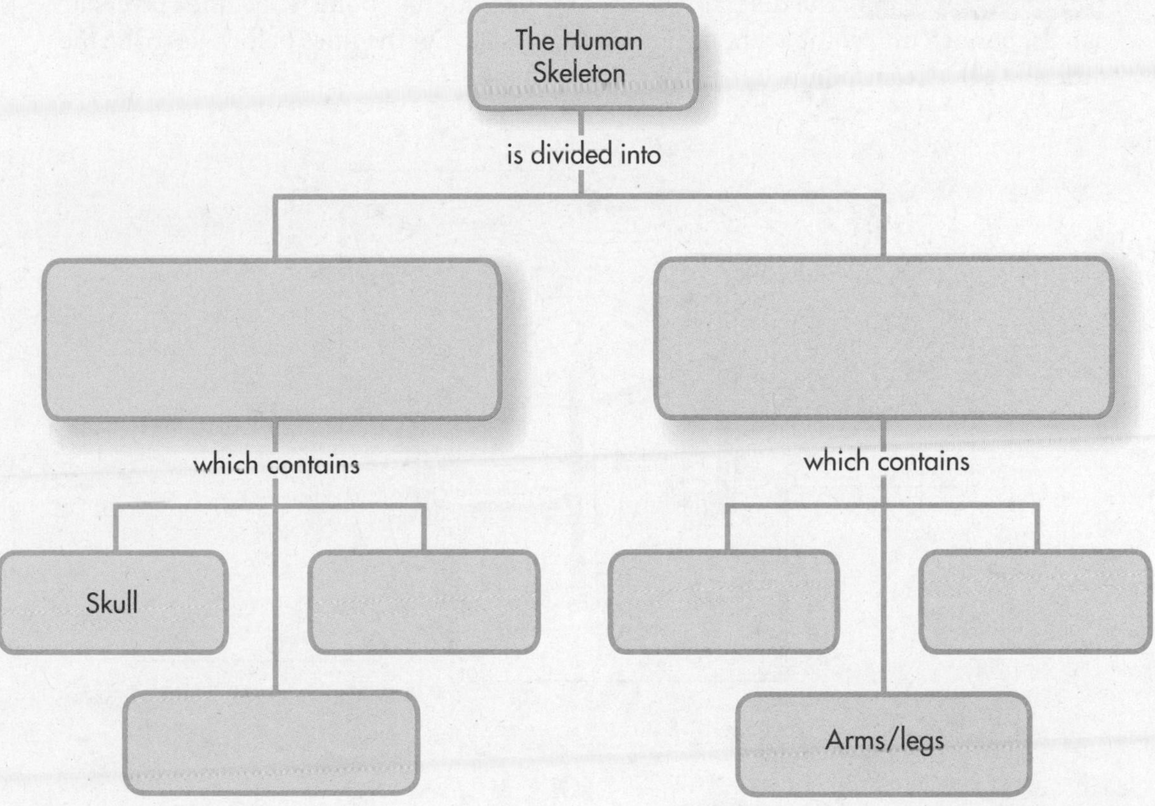


*For Questions 2–3, refer to the Visual Analogy comparing the skeleton to the wooden frame of a house.*

**2.** VISUAL ANALOGY What would happen to a house if its upright beams were not strong and sturdy? Compare that to what would happen in the human body if upright bones were not strong and sturdy.

______

______

______

______

______

**3.** Suggest another possible analogy for the structure and function of the skeleton.

______

**4.** List five functions of the skeletal system.

______

______

______

## Bones

**5.** THINK VISUALLY The diagram shows a cross-section of bone. Label the Haversian canals, periosteum, compact bone, and spongy bone. On the lines below, describe the difference between spongy bone and compact bone.

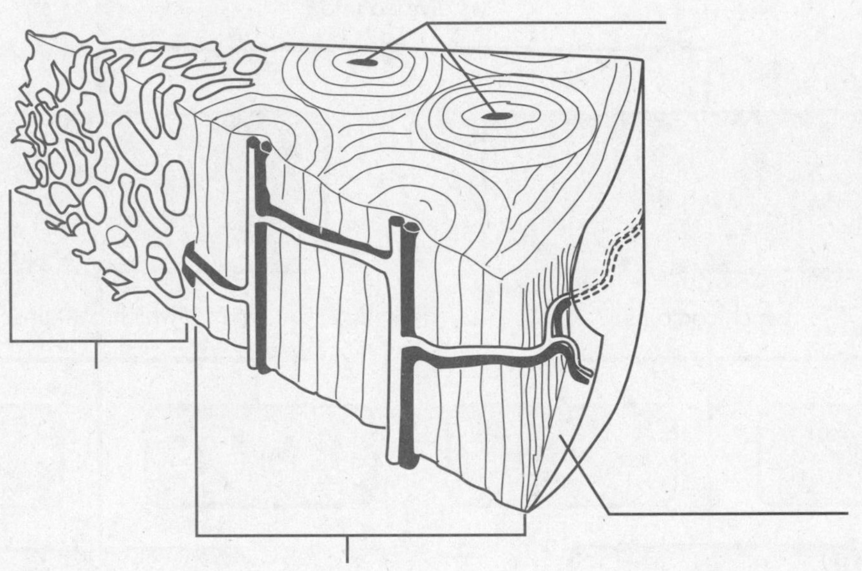

______

______

______

______

*For Questions 6–12, complete each statement by writing the correct word or words.*

**6.** A tough layer of connective tissue called the ______ surrounds a bone.

**7.** Nerves and blood vessels run through the ______ in bones.

**8.** Bone ______ is soft tissue in bone cavities that ______ (yellow) or produces blood cells (red).

**9.** Bone with a latticework structure is called ______ bone.

 

Name ____________________ Class ______ Date ______

10. During the process of ______________, cartilage is replaced by bone.

11. Cells that secrete mineral deposits that form bone are called ______________.

12. A disorder called ______________ results when ______________ break down bone minerals more quickly than they can be deposited.

## Joints

13. What is a joint?

______________________________________________

______________________________________________

14. List the three classifications of joints, based on their type of movement.

______________________________________________

______________________________________________

*For Questions 15–19, match each joint with the category of joints that it represents.*

| Joint | Category |
|---|---|
| ______ **15.** Ankle | **A.** Ball-and-socket joint |
| ______ **16.** Between two vertebrae | **B.** Hinge joint |
| ______ **17.** Shoulder | **C.** Immovable joint |
| ______ **18.** Elbow | **D.** Pivot joint |
| ______ **19.** Between skull bones | **E.** Slightly movable joint |

*For Questions 20–22, write True or False on the line provided.*

______________ **20.** Ligaments protect the ends of bones as they move against each other at joints.

______________ **21.** Synovial fluid prevents the ends of bones from slipping past each other at joints.

______________ **22.** Osteoarthritis is joint pain and stiffness caused by loss of cartilage.

### Apply the Big idea

23. Plumbers use the word *joint* to refer to the place where two pipes are joined together. How are the structure and function of pipe joints similar to and different from the skeletal system's joints?

______________________________________________

______________________________________________

______________________________________________

______________________________________________

Name ______________________ Class ______ Date ______

# 32.2 The Muscular System

## Lesson Objectives

- Describe the structure and function of each of the three types of muscle tissue.
- Describe the mechanism of muscle contraction.
- Describe the interaction of muscles, bones, and tendons to produce movement.

## Lesson Summary

**Muscle Tissue** About one third of the mass of the body is muscle. There are three different types of muscle tissue.

- Skeletal muscle, which has alternating light and dark bands called striations, makes up muscles that are usually attached to bones. Movements of most skeletal, or striated, muscle are consciously controlled by the central nervous system. The cells in skeletal muscle are often called **muscle fibers**.
- Smooth muscle, which lacks striations and is made up of spindle-shaped cells, lines the walls of hollow structures such as the stomach and blood vessels. Movements of smooth muscle are usually involuntary.
- Cardiac muscle, which is also striated but has smaller cells than skeletal muscle, is found only in the heart. The control of cardiac muscle is involuntary.

**Muscle Contraction** Skeletal muscles produce movements by contracting from end to end. The contractions result from the interaction of two kinds of muscle protein filaments—actin and myosin.

- Skeletal muscle fibers are tightly packed with **myofibrils**, which are bundles of protein filaments. Thick filaments of the protein **myosin** and thin filaments of the protein **actin** are arranged in an overlapping pattern, which creates the striations of skeletal muscle. Actin filaments are bound together in areas called Z lines. Two Z lines and the filaments between them make up a unit called a **sarcomere**.
- During a muscle contraction, myosin filaments (powered by ATP) form connections called cross-bridges with actin filaments. The cross-bridges change shape and pull the actin filaments toward the center of the sarcomere. This action decreases the distance between Z lines, and the sarcomere shortens.
- Motor neurons control muscle fiber contractions. A motor neuron meets a muscle fiber at a synapse called a **neuromuscular junction**. The neurotransmitter **acetylcholine** carries nerve impulses across the synapse to the muscle cell.

**Muscles and Movement** Muscles produce force by contracting in only one direction.

- Strips of connective tissue called **tendons** attach skeletal muscles to bones, which act like levers. Controlled movements are possible because muscles work in opposing pairs.
- Red muscles, or slow-twitch muscles, contain many mitochondria and can work for long periods of time. White muscles, or fast-twitch muscles, contain fewer mitochondria, but can generate more force than slow-twitch. They are used for quick bursts of strength or speed.
- Regular exercise helps maintain muscle strength and flexibility, which makes muscle injuries less likely to occur.

Name ____________________ Class ______ Date ______

# Muscle Tissue

*For Questions 1–6, write True if the statement is true. If the statement is false, change the underlined word or words to make the statement true.*

______ **1.** Large skeletal muscles have long, slender cells with multiple <u>nuclei</u>.

______ **2.** The light and dark bands in skeletal muscles are called <u>Z lines</u>.

______ **3.** The cells of smooth muscle are shaped like <u>boxes</u>.

______ **4.** Smooth-muscle tissue lines the <u>inside</u> of the blood vessels and the digestive tract.

______ **5.** Cardiac muscle is under <u>voluntary</u> control.

______ **6.** The cells in cardiac muscle are connected to each other by <u>gap</u> junctions that allow electrical impulses to pass from cell to cell.

**7.** Complete the table that compares and contrasts the three types of muscle tissue.

**Types of Muscle Tissue**

| Type of Muscle | Striated/Not Striated | Type of Control |
|---|---|---|
| | Striated | |
| | | Involuntary |
| Cardiac | | |

# Muscle Contraction

*For Questions 8–13, complete each statement by writing the correct word or words.*

**8.** Muscle fibers are filled with ______________, which are bundles of tightly packed protein filaments.

**9.** The thick protein filaments in muscle fibers are called ______________, and the thin protein filaments are called ______________.

**10.** The thick filaments in muscle fibers form ______________, which cause the filaments to slide past each other.

**11.** The energy used in muscle contraction is supplied by ______________.

**12.** Impulses passed from motor neurons release ______________ ions within the muscle fibers.

**13.** The difference between a strong muscle contraction and a weak muscle contraction is the ______________ muscle fibers that contract.

# Muscles and Movement

**14.** THINK VISUALLY Complete the illustration showing how the muscles of the upper arm produce movements of the forearm by adding labels for the structures indicated. Then, on the lines below the illustration, explain how the muscles cause the elbow to bend and straighten.

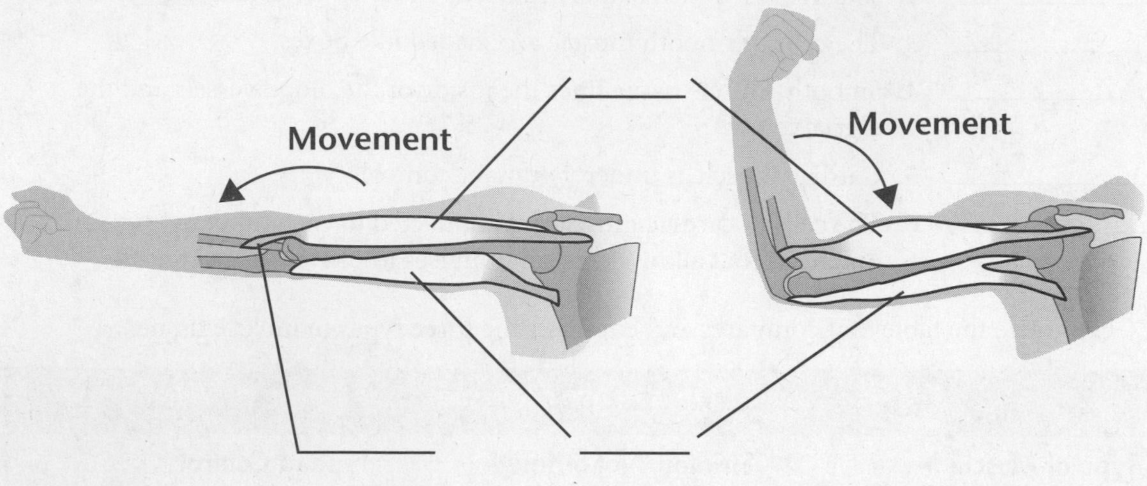


_______________________________________________

_______________________________________________

*For Questions 15–19, complete each statement by writing the correct word or words.*

**15.** While producing movements, muscles supply the force, bones act as ______________, and a joint acts as a(n) ______________.

**16.** Skeletal muscles work in ______________ pairs.

**17.** Red muscle fibers contain ______________, which stores oxygen.

**18.** White muscle is also called ______________ muscle.

**19.** Many mitochondria are found in the cells of ______________ muscle, which uses oxygen for aerobic respiration.

## Apply the Big idea

**20.** When viewed under a microscope, a sample of tissue reveals striations and long, thin fibers that contain many nuclei and mitochondria. What type of tissue is most likely being viewed? Explain your answer.

_______________________________________________

_______________________________________________

_______________________________________________

_______________________________________________

Name ______________________ Class ______ Date ______

# 32.3 Skin—The Integumentary System

## Lesson Objectives

- State the functions of the integumentary system.
- Identify the structures of the integumentary system.
- Describe some of the problems that affect the skin.

## Lesson Summary

**Integumentary System Functions** The skin, hair, and nails make up the integumentary system, which functions to protect internal organs, regulate body temperature, excrete wastes, gather information about the environment, and produce vitamin D.

**Integumentary System Structures** The system consists of skin and its related structures—hair, nails, and several types of glands. Skin consists of two main layers.

- The outer layer of the skin is the **epidermis**, which has an upper layer of dead cells and an inner layer of rapidly dividing living cells. Living epidermal cells make **keratin**, the tough fibrous protein that fills dead skin cells. The epidermis also contains cells called **melanocytes**, which make melanin. **Melanin** is the brown pigment that gives skin its color and protects the skin from ultraviolet radiation.
- The **dermis** is the thick inner layer of skin that contains structures that interact with other body systems to maintain homeostasis by regulating body temperature. **Sebaceous glands** in the dermis secrete sebum, an oily acidic substance that keeps the epidermis flexible and waterproof and kills bacteria.
- Hairs are large columns of cells that have filled with keratin and died. They are produced in **hair follicles**, pockets in the epidermis that extend into the dermis.
- Nails grow from rapidly dividing cells at the tips of fingers and toes. The cells fill with keratin and produce the tough, platelike nails.

**Skin Problems** Many external and internal factors affect the health of the skin.

- Acne is a condition that develops when sebum and dead skin cells plug hair follicles.
- Hives are red welts that result from allergies to food or medicines.
- Skin cancer, the abnormal growth of skin cells, results from excessive exposure to ultraviolet radiation in sunlight and in the lights of tanning beds.

# Integumentary System Functions

*For Questions 1–5, write True or False on the line provided.*

______ 1. Protection from pathogens, water loss, and ultraviolet radiation are functions of the dermis.

______ 2. The skin releases excess heat but holds in some body heat.

______ 3. Sweat contains salts and urea excreted by the skin.

______ 4. The skin has sensory receptors for both pressure and pain.

______ 5. The skin needs sunlight to produce vitamin B.

 

# Integumentary System Structures

6. **THINK VISUALLY** Label the structures of the skin.

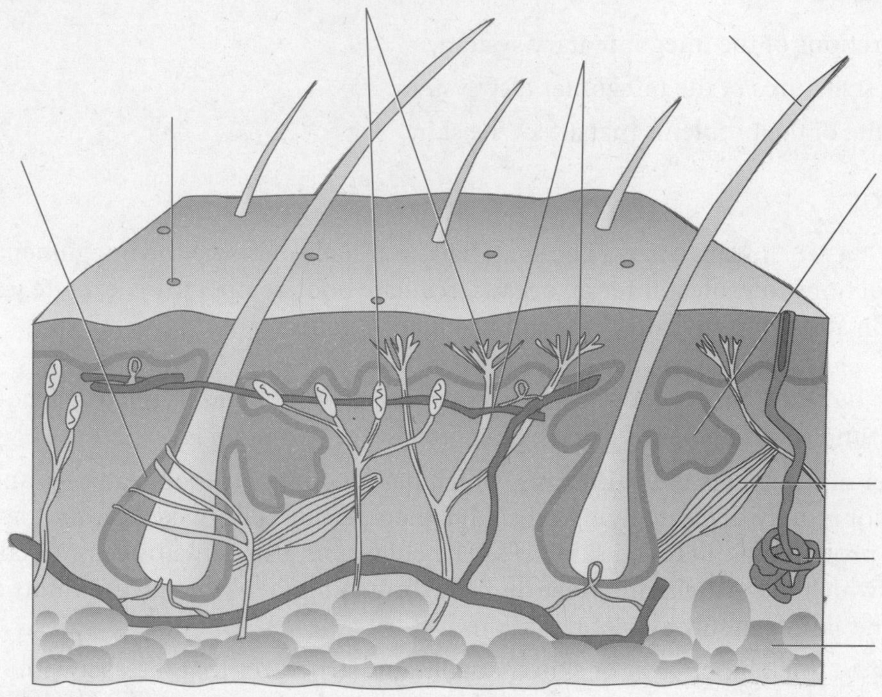

*For Questions 7–14, complete each statement by writing the correct word or words.*

7. The outer layer of the skin is called the ______________.
8. The inner layer of the epidermis includes ______________ cells that divide rapidly, producing new skin cells that push old ones to the surface.
9. Epidermal cells, called ______________, produce the brown pigment ______________.
10. The brown pigment in skin protects it by absorbing ______________.
11. The lower layer of skin that contains many specialized structures is the ______________.
12. Structures that help maintain homeostasis by excreting salts and urea from the skin are called ______________.
13. The ______________ produce a fluid that kills bacteria.
14. Both hair and ______________ contain ______________, the same tough, fibrous protein made by skin cells.
15. How does the dermis help regulate body temperature?

______________________________________________________________

______________________________________________________________

______________________________________________________________

16. How does sweat help keep you cool?

______________________________________________________________

 

**17.** What is the function of sebum?

**18.** How does the hair in the nose and ears and around the eyes help protect the body?

**19.** What causes hair to grow?

**20.** What is a nail root?

## Skin Problems

**21.** Complete the table that summarizes types of skin problems and their causes.

| Types of Skin Problems | | |
|---|---|---|
| **Skin Problem** | **Description** | **Cause** |
| | Bumps that become red, may contain pus, and may leave scars | |
| Hives | | |
| Skin cancer | | |

### Apply the Big idea

**22.** Why is a third-degree burn, which damages both the epidermis and the dermis of the skin, a very serious injury?

 

# Chapter Vocabulary Review

**1.** The diagram below shows muscle filaments in a relaxed muscle. Label the myosin, actin, and sarcomere. Then on the lines below, describe how the position of the actin filaments changes during muscle contraction.

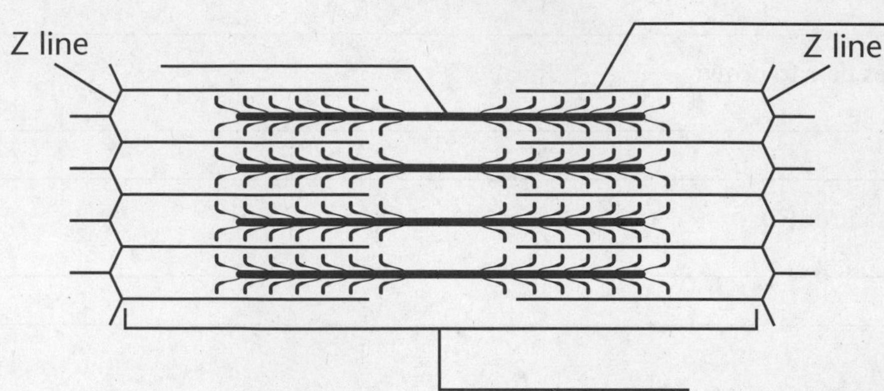


_______________________________________________

_______________________________________________

*For Questions 2–9, match the cell or tissue named with its description.*

| Cell/Tissue | Description |
|---|---|
| ______ **2.** Dermis | **A.** Attaches two bones at a joint |
| ______ **3.** Epidermis | **B.** Attaches muscles to bones |
| ______ **4.** Ligament | **C.** Bone cell that breaks down minerals in bone |
| ______ **5.** Melanocyte | **D.** Inner layer of the skin |
| ______ **6.** Osteoblast | **E.** Mature bone cell that maintains bone |
| ______ **7.** Osteoclast | **F.** Outer layer of the skin |
| ______ **8.** Osteocyte | **G.** Skin cell that produces a brown pigment |
| ______ **9.** Tendon | **H.** Bone cell that builds bone |

*For Questions 10–15, complete each statement by writing the correct word or words.*

**10.** A(n) ______________ is a section of a myofibril that includes two Z lines and the filaments between them.

**11.** A substance that waterproofs the skin and kills bacteria on it is produced by the ______________.

**12.** A(n) ______________ is a bundle of actin and ______________ filaments.

**13.** Hair and nails are both made of the protein ______________.

**14.** The neurotransmitter ______________ is released at neuromuscular junctions of motor neurons and muscle fibers.

**15.** Nerves and blood vessels in compact bone run through structures called ______________.

 

Name ______ Class ____ Date ______

CHAPTER
MYSTERY
THE DEMISE OF A DISEASE
21st Century Learning


In the Chapter Mystery, you unraveled the link between vitamin D and the scourge of rickets that afflicted many malnourished children in northern climates early in the twentieth century. Though this disease has been largely eradicated in this country, many millions of children worldwide still suffer from vitamin and mineral deficiencies.

## Fighting Malnutrition Around the World

The problem of child malnutrition is so pressing and dire that many governmental and nonprofit organizations have pledged to combat it. One such effort is by the nonprofit Bill and Melinda Gates Foundation. The Foundation has announced that it would award $25 million in grants to support "biofortification." This approach involves breeding crops that provide higher levels of micronutrients such as iron, zinc, and vitamin A.

Read the facts below, from a United Nations report, to learn more about the scope of the problem that spurred the Gates Foundation to action:

### Report on Childhood Vitamin and Mineral Deficiencies

### A Global Problem

- **Iron deficiency**, the most prevalent form of malnutrition worldwide, affects *billions* of people. Iron carries oxygen in the blood, so symptoms of a deficiency include tiredness and pallor. Lack of iron in large segments of the population severely damages a country's productivity. Iron deficiency also impedes cognitive development. In developing countries, it affects over half of children aged 6–24 months, a time when the brain is developing rapidly.
- **Vitamin A deficiency** affects 127 million preschool children and six million pregnant women in developing countries. It is also a leading cause of blindness in children in developing countries. Vitamin A deficiency weakens the immune system, increasing vulnerability to disease and risk of dying from diarrhea, measles, and malaria.
- **Iodine deficiency** affects 780 million people worldwide. The clearest symptom is a swelling of the thyroid gland called a goiter. But the most serious impact is on the brain, which cannot develop properly without iodine. According to UN research, each year 20 million children are born impaired because their mothers did not consume enough iodine. The most severe deficiencies result in mental retardation and physical stunting.
- **Zinc deficiency** contributes to growth failure and weakened immunity in young children. It is linked to a higher risk of diarrhea and pneumonia, resulting in nearly 800,000 deaths per year worldwide.

Continued on next page ▶

## 21st Century Themes Science and Global Awareness, Science and Health Literacy

1. What are some of the vitamin and mineral deficiencies other than vitamin D that affect children and adults around the world today?

2. What percentage of children aged six months to two years old are estimated to suffer from a deficiency in iron?

3. How many preschool children are thought to suffer from a vitamin A deficiency, and what are the health effects associated with it?

4. What is "biofortification" and how can it help combat vitamin and mineral deficiencies?

5. Do you agree that the problem of vitamin and mineral deficiencies among the world's children needs urgent attention? Explain.

6. Do you think that a focus on biofortification can help? Why or why not?

## 21st Century Skills Memo to the Gates Foundation

The skills used in this activity include **critical thinking and systems thinking; problem identification, formulation, and solution; creativity and intellectual curiosity; information and media literacy;** and **social responsibility.**

On the Internet, visit Web sites that map problems of hunger and malnutrition around the world. You might try the Web site of the World Food Program of the United Nations. Based on your research, draft a brief letter to the Gates Foundation. State where you think the need is greatest and outline the steps you think the foundation should consider taking to combat vitamin and mineral deficiencies.

 

Name ______________________ Class ______ Date ________

# 33 Circulatory and Respiratory Systems

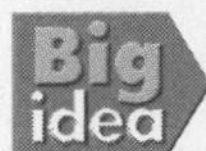

**Big idea** **Structure and Function**

**Q:** How do the structures of the circulatory and respiratory systems allow for their close functional relationship?

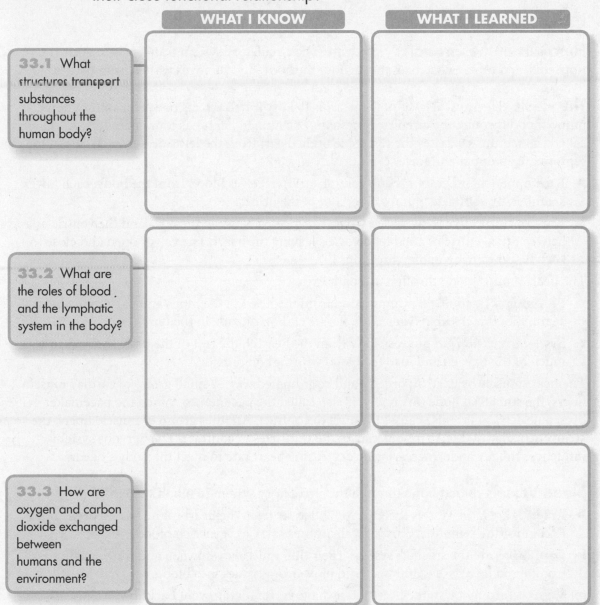

| | WHAT I KNOW | WHAT I LEARNED |
|---|---|---|
| **33.1** What structures transport substances throughout the human body? | | |
| **33.2** What are the roles of blood and the lymphatic system in the body? | | |
| **33.3** How are oxygen and carbon dioxide exchanged between humans and the environment? | | |

Name ______________________ Class ______ Date ______

# 33.1 The Circulatory System

## Lesson Objectives

- Identify the functions of the human circulatory system.
- Describe the structure of the heart and explain how it pumps blood through the body.
- Name three types of blood vessels in the circulatory system.

## Lesson Summary

**Functions of the Circulatory System** The circulatory system transports oxygen, nutrients, and other substances throughout the body, and removes wastes from tissues.

**The Heart** The muscle layer of the heart is the **myocardium**. Its powerful contractions pump blood through the circulatory system. The human heart has four chambers. A wall called the septum separates the right side of the heart from the left side. On each side of the septum are an upper and lower chamber.

- Each upper chamber, or **atrium** (plural: atria), receives blood from the body; each lower chamber, or **ventricle**, pumps blood out of the heart.
- Flaps of connective tissue called **valves** are located between the atria and the ventricles and between the ventricles and blood vessels leaving the heart. The valves open and close to keep blood moving in one direction.

The heart pumps blood through two pathways:

- **Pulmonary circulation** pumps blood from the heart to the lungs and back to the heart again. Blood picks up oxygen and releases carbon dioxide in the lungs.
- **Systemic circulation** pumps blood from the heart to the rest of the body. Cells absorb much of the oxygen and load the blood with carbon dioxide.

The heart muscle beats in an orderly and coordinated way. A small group of cardiac muscle fibers, the sinoatrial node (SA node), is also called the **pacemaker**. When the pacemaker fires, an electrical impulse causes the atria to contract. Another group of muscle fibers, the atrioventricular node (AV node), causes the ventricles to contract. The nervous system influences the SA node, increasing or decreasing heart rate to meet the body's needs.

**Blood Vessels** Blood flows through the circulatory system in blood vessels:

- **Arteries** are large vessels that carry blood away from the heart to the tissues of the body. Except for the pulmonary arteries, all arteries carry oxygen-rich blood.
- **Capillaries** are the smallest vessels. Their thin walls allow oxygen and nutrients to pass from blood into tissues and wastes to move from tissues into blood.
- **Veins** return blood to the heart. Many have valves that prevent backflow.

The contractions of the heart produce a wave of fluid pressure in the arteries, known as blood pressure. Without that pressure, blood would stop flowing through the body. The body regulates blood pressure through actions of the brain and the kidneys.

 

# Functions of the Circulatory System

**1.** Why do animals with millions of cells "need" a circulatory system while animals with few cells can do without one?

**2.** VISUAL ANALOGY Marie lives in a large city. She is disabled and cannot leave her home. Everything she needs must be delivered to her, and all her garbage must be hauled away. Compare how the streets and highways of the city supply Marie's needs with how the circulatory system supplies the needs of individual cells of the human body.

# The Heart

**3.** Complete the table.

| Circulation Pathway | Side of Heart Pumping | Destination After Leaving Heart | Blood Change |
|---|---|---|---|
| Pulmonary | | | |
| Systemic | | | |

 

Name ______________________________ Class ______ Date __________

4. Label the diagram at the points indicated to show the structures of the human circulatory system. Add arrows to show the direction of blood flow.

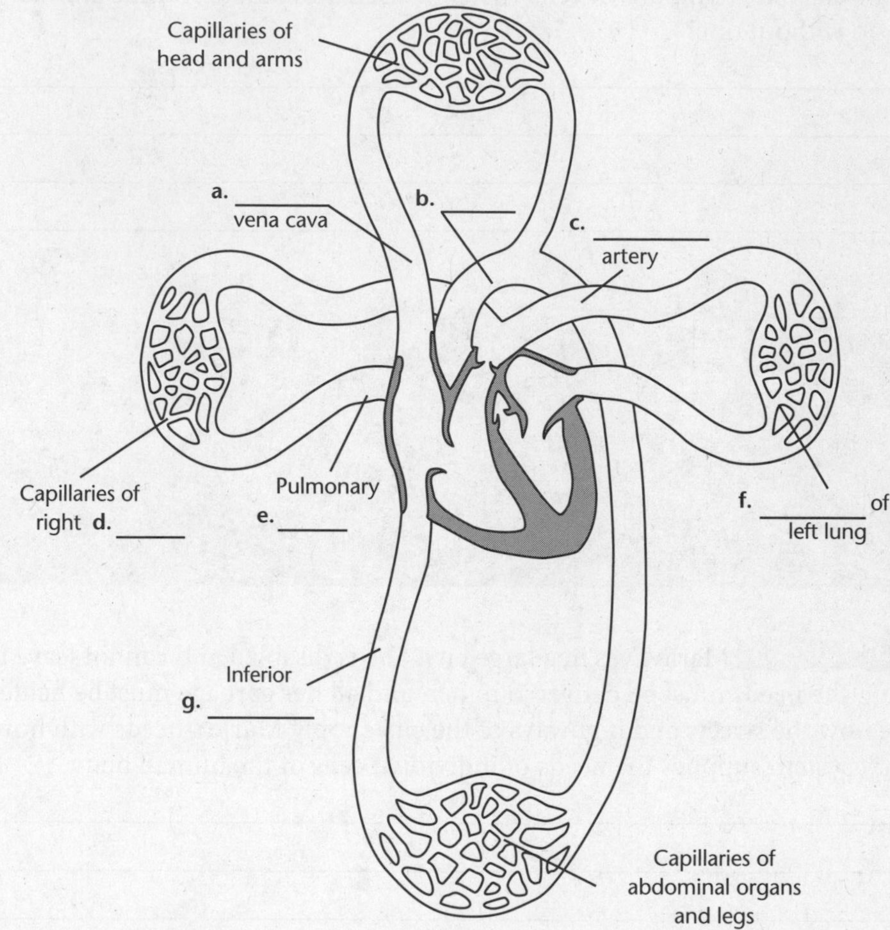


5. Complete the flowchart to show the actions that keep the heart beating in an orderly way.

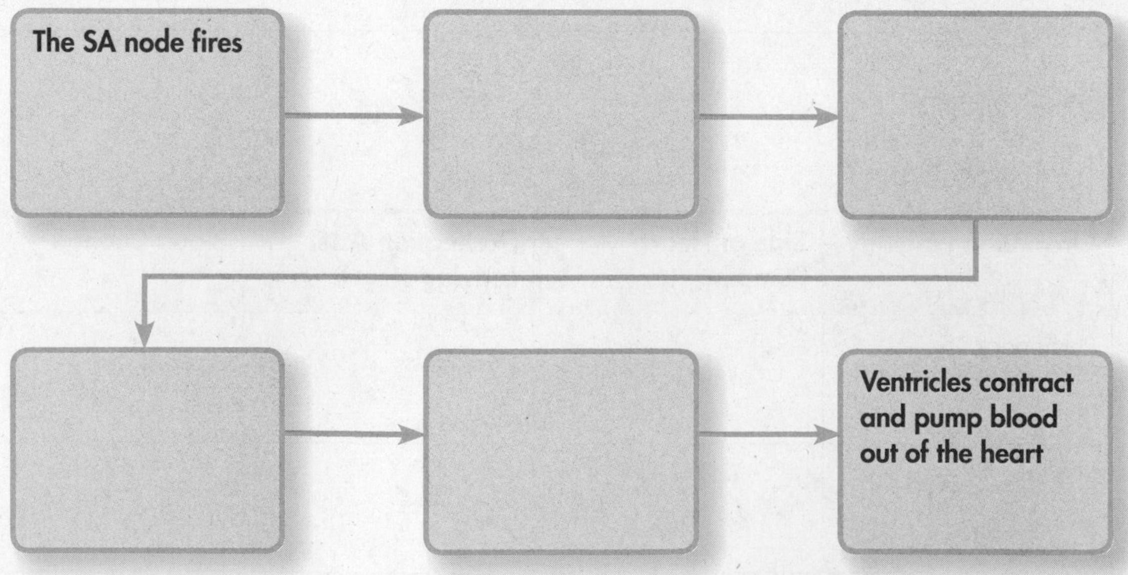

# Blood Vessels

**6.** As blood flows through the body, it passes through three types of blood vessels. Complete the table by naming each type and describing its structure and function.

| Blood vessels | Structure | Function |
|---|---|---|
| | | |
| | | |
| | | |

**7.** Complete the feedback diagram to show how the nervous system regulates blood pressure.

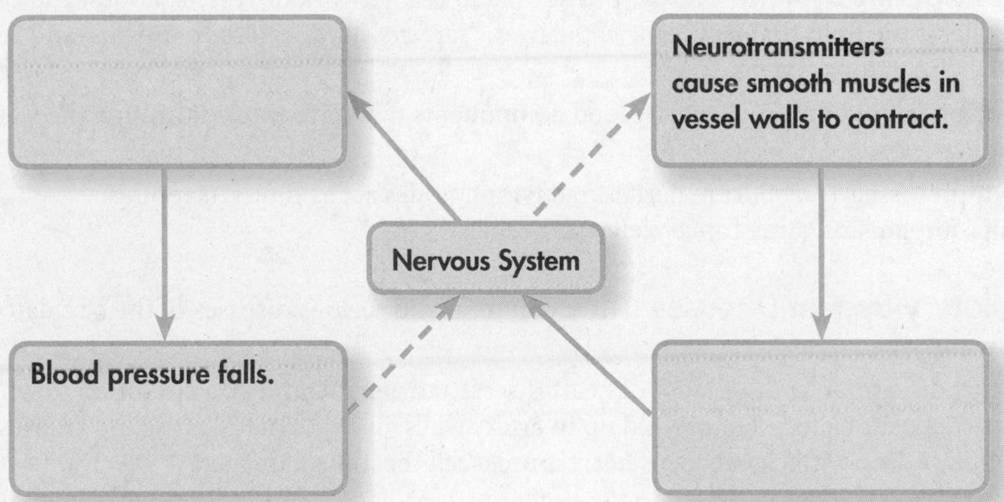
Neurotransmitters cause smooth muscles in vessel walls to contract.
Nervous System
Blood pressure falls.

## Apply the Big idea

**8.** The left side of the heart is larger and more muscular than the right side. Also, artery walls are thicker than those of veins. Explain how those differences in structure are important to function.

______

______

______

______

 

# 33.2 Blood and the Lymphatic System

- Explain the functions of blood plasma, red blood cells, white blood cells, and platelets.
- Describe the role of the lymphatic system.
- List three common circulatory diseases.
- Describe the connection between cholesterol and circulatory disease.

## Lesson Summary

**Blood** Blood has four main components:

- **Plasma** is a straw-colored fluid. It is about 90 percent water and 10 percent dissolved gases, salts, nutrients, enzymes, hormones, waste products, plasma proteins, cholesterol, and other important compounds. Parts of plasma help control body temperature, transport substances, and fight infection. Plasma proteins are involved in blood clotting.
- **Red blood cells** transport oxygen. Blood gets its red color from the iron in **hemoglobin**, a protein that binds oxygen in the lungs and releases it in the capillaries.
- **White blood cells** guard against infection, fight parasites, and attack bacteria.
- **Platelets** are cell fragments involved in blood clotting.

**The Lymphatic System** The lymphatic system is a network of vessels, nodes, and organs that collects the fluid that leaves the capillaries, "screens" it for microorganisms, and returns it to the circulatory system.

- **Lymph** is fluid that consists of blood components that have moved through the walls of capillaries.
- Lymph vessels transport materials and lymph nodes act as filters, trapping microorganisms, stray cancer cells, and debris.

**Circulatory System Diseases** Three common and serious diseases of the circulatory system are:

- Heart disease: A leading cause of heart disease is **atherosclerosis**, a condition in which fatty deposits called plaque build up in artery walls and eventually cause the arteries to stiffen. A heart attack occurs as heart muscle cells become damaged.
- Stroke: A clot that blocks a blood vessel in the brain may cause a stroke, which is the sudden death of brain cells when their blood supply is interrupted. A stroke can also occur if a weak vessel breaks and causes bleeding in the brain.
- High blood pressure, or hypertension, is usually defined as blood pressure higher than 140/90. Uncontrolled high blood pressure can damage the heart and blood vessels. It can also lead to heart attack, stroke, and kidney damage.

**Understanding Circulatory Disease** Cholesterol is a lipid that is part of animal cell membranes. It is transported in the blood primarily by two types of lipoproteins: low-density lipoprotein (LDL) and high-density lipoprotein (HDL). The liver manufactures cholesterol, but it also comes from animal product foods. High cholesterol levels, along with other risk factors, lead to atherosclerosis and higher risk of heart attack.

 

Name ______________________ Class ______ Date ______

# Blood

*For Questions 1–5, write True if the statement is true. If the statement is false, change the underlined word or words to make the statement true.*

______ **1.** Blood helps regulate body temperature and fight infections.

______ **2.** The human body contains 8–10 liters of blood.

______ **3.** Plasma is about 50 percent water.

______ **4.** Albumin, globulins, and fibrinogen are nucleic acids in blood.

______ **5.** Fibrinogen is necessary for blood clotting.

**6.** Complete the table to describe the characteristics and functions of blood.

| Component | Characteristics | Function |
|---|---|---|
| Plasma | | |
| Red blood cells | | |
| White blood cells | | |
| Platelets | | |

 

Name ______________________ Class _____ Date _________

# The Lymphatic System

*For Questions 7–14, write the letter of the correct answer on the line at the left.*

______ **7.** Fluid and small particles that leave the blood are collectively called

**A.** plasma. **C.** platelets.

**B.** lymphocytes. **D.** lymph.

______ **8.** Some of the lymph is collected in a network of vessels, nodes, and organs called the

**A.** circulatory system. **C.** respiratory system.

**B.** lymphatic system. **D.** excretory system.

______ **9.** How does lymph help protect against infection?

**A.** It screens for microorganisms.

**B.** It causes fevers when viruses are present.

**C.** It removes defective DNA from cells.

**D.** It removes toxins from the liver.

______ **10.** What moves lymph into ducts?

**A.** valves in the veins

**B.** the pumping action of the heart

**C.** pressure from skeletal muscles

**D.** the thin walls of capillaries

______ **11.** Where does lymph return to the bloodstream?

**A.** through veins just below the shoulders

**B.** through veins in the legs

**C.** through arteries in the abdomen

**D.** through capillaries in the liver

______ **12.** What nutrients does the lymphatic system pick up in the digestive tract and transport to the bloodstream?

**A.** fats and fat-soluble vitamins

**B.** water and water-soluble vitamins

**C.** water and proteins

**D.** fatty acids and cholesterol

______ **13.** Which of the following is NOT a function of lymph nodes?

**A.** pumping blood to the lungs

**B.** trapping microorganisms

**C.** collecting cancer cells

**D.** gathering debris from the body

______ **14.** Which organ of the lymphatic system stores platelets?

**A.** heart **C.** thymus

**B.** lymph node **D.** spleen

Name ________________ Class ______ Date ________

## Circulatory System Diseases

**15.** Why is the first sign of a circulatory problem an event that affects the heart or brain?

______________________________

______________________________

______________________________

**16.** What is atherosclerosis?

______________________________

______________________________

______________________________

**17.** What is angina, and what causes it?

______________________________

______________________________

**18.** What is one cause of heart failure?

______________________________

______________________________

**19.** What is a heart attack, and what causes most heart attacks?

______________________________

______________________________

______________________________

**20.** How is a stroke like a heart attack?

______________________________

______________________________

______________________________

**21.** How does high blood pressure damage the heart?

______________________________

______________________________

## Understanding Circulatory Diseases

*For Questions 22–25, complete each statement by writing the correct word or words.*

**22.** Cholesterol is transported through the body by ____________ lipoprotein and ____________ lipoprotein.

**23.** A cholesterol level in the range of ____________ is considered normal.

**24.** Cholesterol is made in the ____________, but can also be found in foods high in ____________.

**25.** High cholesterol is one of the risk factors for ____________ and heart attack.

 

Name ____________ Class ______ Date ______

**26.** Fill in the concept map to compare the path of cholesterol in normal liver cells and defective liver cells.

Normal

Defective

LDL binds to receptors on liver cell membrane and is taken into the cell

LDL cannot bind to LDL receptors

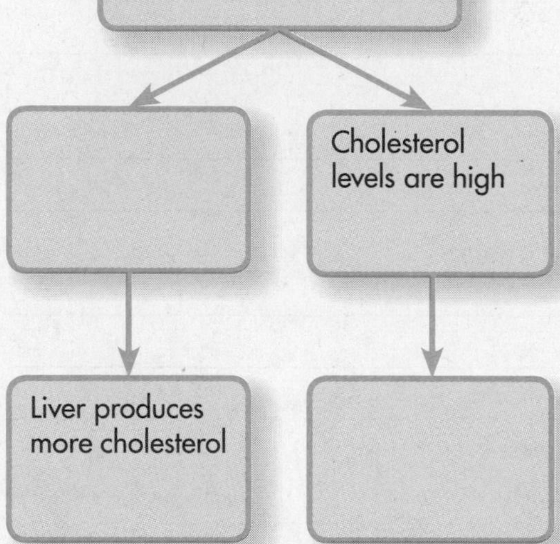
Cholesterol levels are high
Liver produces more cholesterol

**27.** What did Brown and Goldstein discover about people who eat high-fat diets?

______________________________

______________________________

______________________________

## Apply the Big idea

**28.** Heart disease, stroke, and high blood pressure are major killers in the United States, yet much can be done to prevent them. How can a healthy diet and exercise keep the circulatory system functioning properly to prevent these diseases?

______________________________

______________________________

______________________________

______________________________

 

# 33.3 The Respiratory System

- Identify the structures of the respiratory system and describe their functions.
- Describe gas exchange.
- Describe how breathing is controlled.
- Describe the effects of smoking on the respiratory system.

## Lesson Summary

**Structures of the Respiratory System** For organisms, *respiration* means the process of gas exchange between a body and the environment. The human respiratory system picks up oxygen from the air we inhale and releases carbon dioxide into the air we exhale. The structures of the respiratory system include the

- nose, where air is filtered, moistened, and warmed.
- **pharynx**, or throat, which serves as a passageway for both air and food.
- **trachea**, or windpipe, and the **larynx**, or vocal cords.
- **bronchi**, two large tubes that lead to the lungs. Each bronchus branches into smaller passageways called bronchioles that end in tiny air sacs called **alveoli** within the lungs.

**Gas Exchange and Transport** Oxygen and carbon dioxide are exchanged across the walls of alveoli and capillaries. Chemical properties of blood and red blood cells allow for efficient transport of gases throughout the body.

- Carbon dioxide and oxygen are exchanged across capillary and alveolus walls.
- Hemoglobin binds with and transports oxygen that diffuses from alveoli to capillaries. It also increases the efficiency of gas exchange.
- Carbon dioxide is transported in the blood in three ways. Most combines with water and forms carbonic acid. Some dissolves in plasma. Some binds to hemoglobin and proteins in plasma.

**Breathing** Movements of the diaphragm and rib cage change air pressure in the chest cavity during inhalation and exhalation.

- The dome-shaped muscle at the bottom of the chest cavity is the **diaphragm**. During inhalation, contraction of the diaphragm and rib muscles increases chest volume and air rushes in. In exhalation, these muscles relax and air rushes out.
- The nervous system has final control of the breathing muscles. Breathing does not require conscious control.

**Smoking and the Respiratory System** Chemicals in tobacco smoke damage structures throughout the respiratory system and have other negative health effects. Smoking causes a number of diseases, including chronic bronchitis, emphysema, and lung cancer.

# Structures of the Respiratory System

**1.** Label each of the structures indicated in this drawing of the human respiratory system.

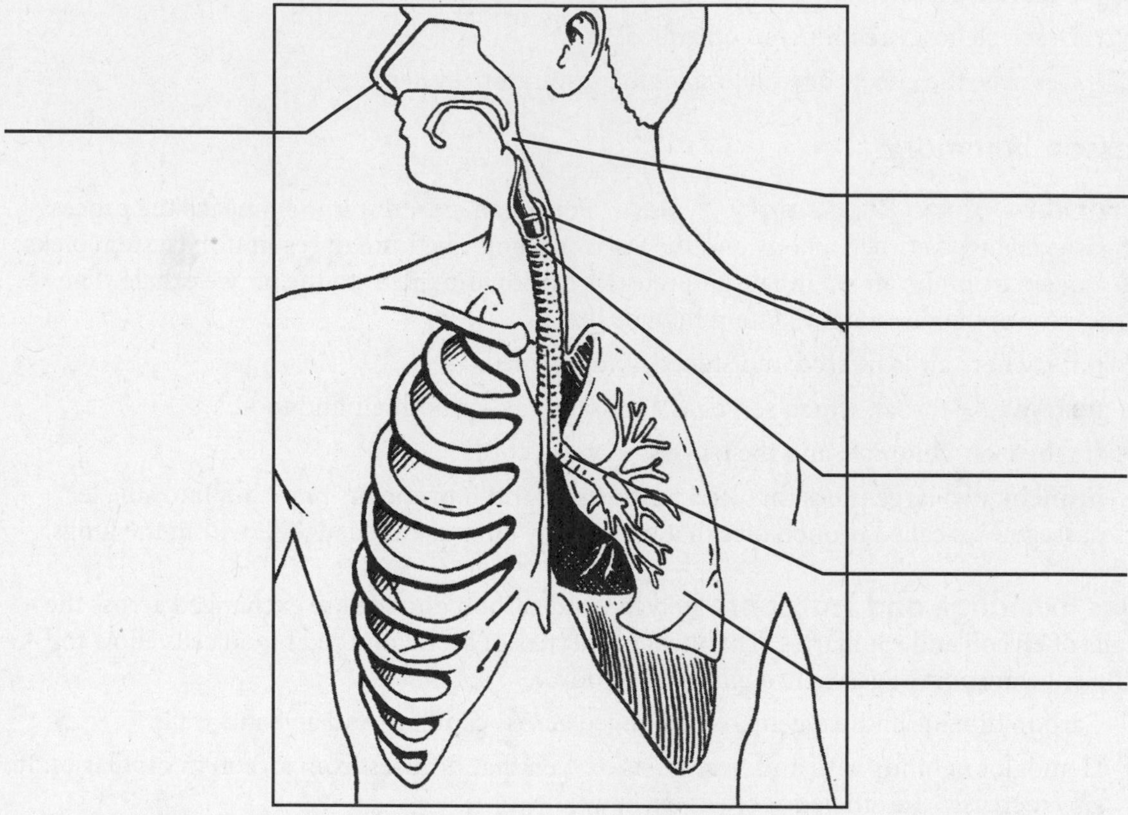

# Gas Exchange and Transport

*For Questions 2–7, complete each statement by writing the correct word or words.*

**2.** The surface area for gas exchange in the lungs is provided by the __________.

**3.** The gases exchanged in the lungs are carbon dioxide and __________.

**4.** The process that exchanges gases across the walls of capillaries is __________.

**5.** Oxygen diffuses from an area of __________ concentration to an area of lesser concentration.

**6.** __________ binds with oxygen and increases the blood's oxygen-carrying capacity.

**7.** Most carbon dioxide combines with __________ in the blood, forming carbonic acid.

 

Name ______________________ Class ______ Date ______

## Breathing

**8.** Complete the flowchart to show how breathing works.

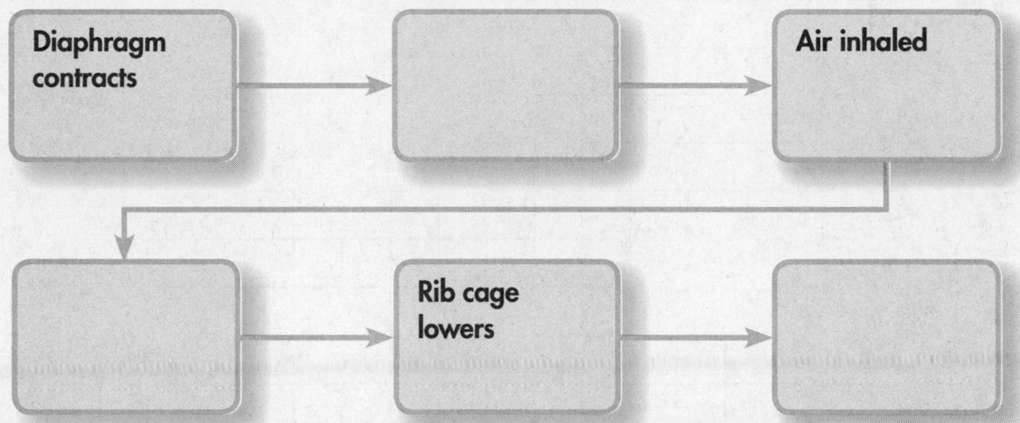


## Smoking and the Respiratory System

**9.** Complete the table to describe the health effects of three substances in tobacco smoke.

| Substance | Effect |
|---|---|
| Nicotine | |
| Carbon monoxide | |
| Tar | |

**10.** What causes smoker's cough?

______________________________________________

______________________________________________

______________________________________________

**11.** Smoking even a few cigarettes on a regular basis can lead to chronic bronchitis. What happens to people with this disease?

______________________________________________

### Apply the Big idea

**12.** Smoking and secondhand smoke damage both the respiratory system and the circulatory system. Explain how the close structural relationship of these two systems accounts for the effect of smoke on both systems.

______________________________________________

______________________________________________

______________________________________________

______________________________________________

Name ______________________ Class _____ Date ________

# Chapter Vocabulary Review

**Across**

1. the sinoatrial node of the heart
3. fluid and the small particles it contains that leaves blood cells
5. the circulation pathway that sends blood from the heart to the lungs and back to the heart
8. a muscle layer in the heart
10. the build-up of fatty deposits in artery walls
14. the smallest blood vessel
15. Leukocytes, or ______________ blood cells, guard against infection.
16. the protein in the blood that binds oxygen

**Down**

2. an upper chamber of the heart
4. the fluid portion of the blood
6. a blood vessel that returns blood from the body to the heart
7. a structure that keeps blood moving through the heart in one direction
9. a lower chamber of the heart
10. a blood vessel that carries blood from the heart to body tissues
11. Erythrocytes, or ______________ blood cells, transport oxygen.
12. the circulation that sends blood from the heart to all the body except the lungs
13. a cell fragment that makes blood clotting possible

*For Questions 17–19, complete each statement by writing the correct word or words.*

17. The throat is also called the ______________.
18. The windpipe is also called the ______________.
19. The vocal cords are in the ______________.

CHAPTER MYSTERY

IN THE BLOOD

The Chapter Mystery focused on a rare genetic disease known as familial hypercholesterolemia. Far more common are diseases that are often directly associated with cigarettes and other types of tobacco use: lung cancer and heart disease.

21st Century Learning

# Smoking, Lung Cancer, and Heart Disease: Should the FDA Regulate Tobacco?

Lung cancer and heart disease are among the nation's top killers. Together, they account for the deaths of hundreds of thousands of Americans each year.

Federal lawmakers have long debated how to best regulate tobacco products. A bill passed in the House of Representatives would require the U.S. Food and Drug Administration (FDA) to regulate cigarettes and other tobacco products if it is enacted.

Read the following statement made on the floor of the U.S. House of Representatives by Congressmember Rosa DeLauro (D-CT) urging passage of the bill, called H.R.1108:

## HOUSE OF REPRESENTATIVES, July 30, 2008

Ms. *DeLAURO*. Madam Speaker, I rise in support of H.R. 1108, the Family Smoking Prevention and Tobacco Control Act. This legislation would grant the Food and Drug Administration (FDA) long-needed authority to regulate the manufacture, sale, distribution and marketing of tobacco products.

As we all know, tobacco use contributes to the death of more than 400,000 Americans and costs the nation's health care system nearly $100 billion each year. The most tragic part of this statistic is that virtually all of these deaths are preventable. It is alarming that preventable diseases such as emphysema, heart disease and cancer all can be attributed to the use of tobacco. In addition to providing consumers with science-based information about tobacco products, granting FDA the authority to regulate tobacco will more importantly help protect our children from using these products. Approximately 90 percent of all adult smokers began their habit while in their teens, or earlier, and two-thirds become regular, daily smokers before they reach the age of 19. According to the American Medical Association, each day, about 4,000 children try smoking a cigarette for the first time and another 1,000 become new, regular, daily smokers. This means that one-third of these children will die prematurely.

Despite their claims to the contrary, the tobacco companies continue to market their products aggressively toward children. This bill will give FDA the authority to impose marketing restrictions, labeling requirements, as well as to ban candy-flavored tobacco products in order to prevent tobacco companies from addicting children to tobacco.
This bill has strong bipartisan support, and is endorsed by key groups including the American Cancer Society, the American Medical Association, the American Heart Association, the American Lung Association, and Campaign for Tobacco-Free Kids.

Continued on next page ▶

 

Name ______________________ Class ______ Date ________

## 21st Century Themes Science and Civic Literacy, Science and Health Literacy

**1.** How many deaths in the United States are directly attributed to tobacco use each year?

______________________________

**2.** How much are tobacco-related diseases estimated to cost the United States health care system annually?

______________________________

**3.** If the U.S. Food and Drug Administration (FDA) regulated tobacco products, what changes could the agency impose?

______________________________

______________________________

**4.** At what age did most adult smokers begin their habit?

______________________________

______________________________

______________________________

**5.** Do you think that bill H.R. 1108 should be passed into law? Why or why not?

______________________________

______________________________

______________________________

## 21st Century Learning Letter to Your Senator

The skills used in this activity include **critical thinking and systems thinking, information and media literacy, communication skills,** and **social responsibility.**

Using the Internet, visit the Library of Congress's powerful legislative database called "Thomas," named after the third U.S. President, Thomas Jefferson. Use the database to track the status of bill H.R. 1108. Read the bill, search for comments by other representatives, and review the economic assessment of the bill from the Congressional Budget Office. Based on this research, write a letter to your Senator voicing your opinion about whether the bill should be, or should have been, passed into law. Clearly state your reasons why or why not in your letter.

 

Name ______________________ Class ______ Date ________

# 34 Endocrine and Reproductive Systems

**Big idea** **Homeostasis**

**Q:** How does the body use chemical signals to maintain homeostasis?

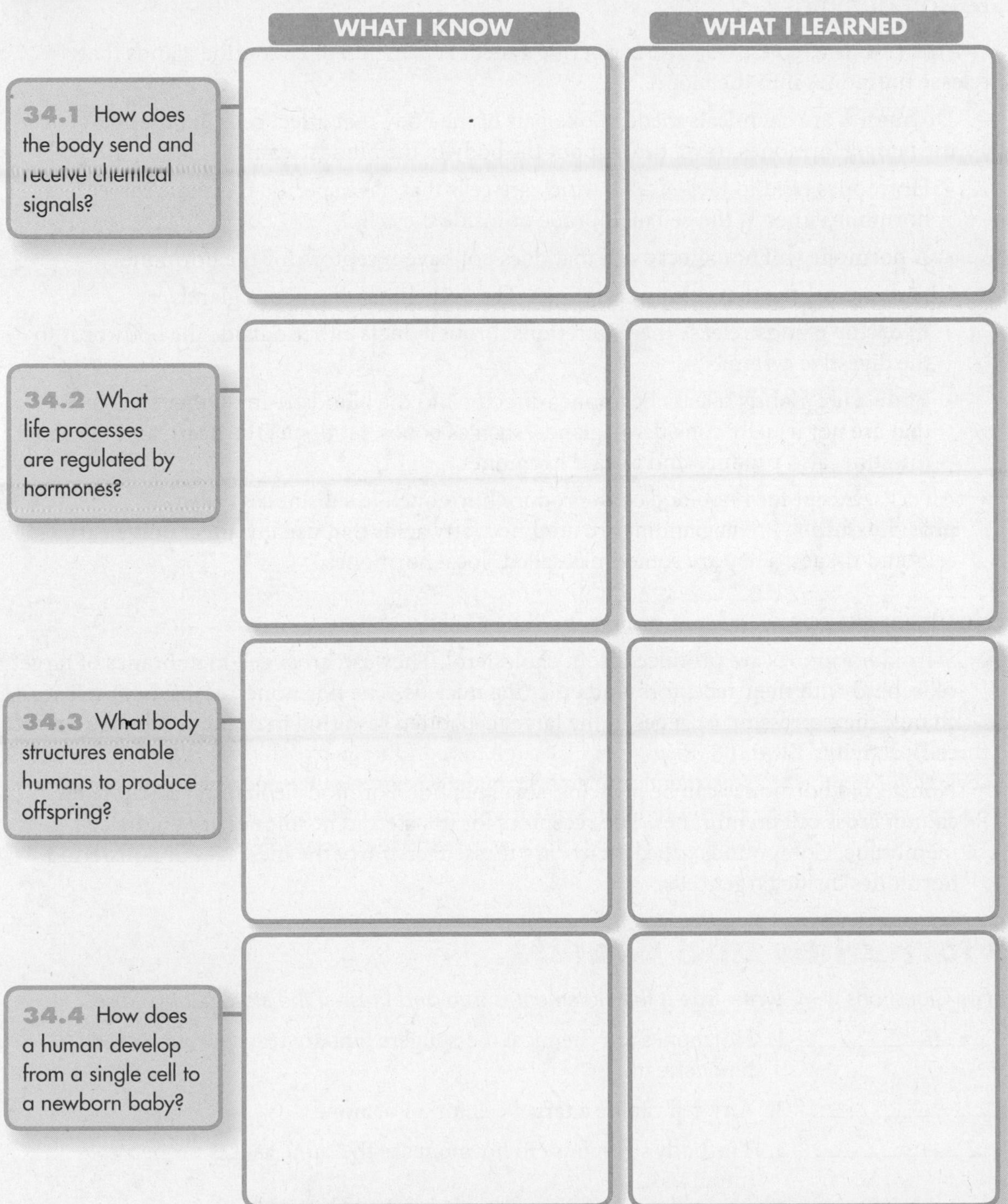

| | WHAT I KNOW | WHAT I LEARNED |
|---|---|---|
| **34.1** How does the body send and receive chemical signals? | | |
| **34.2** What life processes are regulated by hormones? | | |
| **34.3** What body structures enable humans to produce offspring? | | |
| **34.4** How does a human develop from a single cell to a newborn baby? | | |

# 34.1 The Endocrine System

## Lesson Objectives

Describe the structure and function of the endocrine system.

Explain how hormones work.

## Lesson Summary

**Hormones and Glands** The endocrine system is made up of endocrine glands that release hormones into the blood.

- **Hormones** are chemicals made in one part of the body that affect cells in other parts of the body. Hormones travel throughout the body in the bloodstream.
  - Hormones bind to **target cells**, which are cells that have specific receptors for a hormone either in the cell membrane or inside the cell.
  - A hormone will not affect a cell that does not have receptors for the hormone.
- Glands are organs that release secretions. The body has two types of glands.
  - **Exocrine glands** release their secretions through ducts either outside the body or into the digestive system.
  - **Endocrine glands** release hormones directly into the bloodstream. Other structures that are not usually considered glands, such as bones, fat tissue, the heart, and the small intestine, also produce and release hormones.
- All cells, except for red blood cells, produce hormonelike substances called **prostaglandins**. Prostaglandins are modified fatty acids that usually affect only nearby cells and tissues. They are sometimes called "local hormones."

**Hormone Action** There are two types of hormones.

- Steroid hormones are produced from cholesterol. They can cross cell membranes of target cells, bind with their receptors, and enter the nucleus. The hormone-receptor complexes change the expression of genes in the target cell, often resulting in dramatic changes in the cell's activity.
- Nonsteroid hormones can be proteins, small peptides, or modified amino acids. They cannot cross cell membranes. The receptors for nonsteroid hormones are on the cell membrane. Compounds called secondary messengers carry the messages of nonsteroid hormones inside target cells.

# Hormones and Glands

*For Questions 1–4, write True if the statement is true and False if the statement is false.*

__________ **1.** Hormones are chemical messengers that are transported by the bloodstream.

__________ **2.** Any cell can be a target cell for a hormone.

__________ **3.** The body's response to hormones is the same as it is for nerve impulses.

__________ **4.** Insulin and glucagon are two opposing hormones.

 

**5.** Complete the table that summarizes major endocrine glands of the human body.

| Gland | Hormone(s) Produced | Function |
|---|---|---|
| Parathyroid | Parathyroid hormone | |
| Pineal | | Regulates rhythmic activities |
| | Thyroxine | |
| | Corticosteroids, epinephrine, norepinephrine | |
| | | Maintains the level of glucose in the blood |
| | | Regulates formation of eggs and development of secondary female sex characteristics; prepares uterus for fertilization |
| | Testosterone | |

**6.** What are prostaglandins? How is their action different from that of hormones?

______

______

______

______

______

## Hormone Action

**7.** THINK VISUALLY Steroid and nonsteroid hormones affect their target cells in different ways. In the spaces below, draw diagrams that show how each type of hormone affects its target cells. Be sure to label the cell membrane, cytoplasm, nucleus, the hormones, and their receptors.

| How Steroid Hormones Work | How Nonsteroid Hormones Work |
|---|---|
| | |

**8.** Summarize the action of a steroid hormone on a target cell.

**9.** Summarize the action of a nonsteroid hormone on a target cell.

### Apply the Big idea

**10.** Compare the release of a hormone to the broadcast of a television commercial.

Name ______________________ Class ______ Date ______

# 34.2 Glands of the Endocrine System

## Lesson Objectives

Identify the functions of the major endocrine glands.

Explain how endocrine glands are controlled.

## Lesson Summary

**The Human Endocrine Glands** Endocrine glands are scattered throughout the body.

- The **pituitary gland** is a bean-size structure at the base of the brain. Consisting of two parts, the anterior pituitary and the posterior pituitary, it secretes hormones that regulate body functions and control the actions of other endocrine glands.
- The hypothalamus controls the secretions of the pituitary gland and is the link between the central nervous system and the endocrine system. The hypothalamus controls the posterior pituitary through neurosecretory cells. The hypothalamus produces **releasing hormones** that control the secretions of the anterior pituitary.
- An adrenal gland sits on top of each kidney. The adrenal glands make hormones that help the body prepare for and deal with stress. They consist of a cortex and a medulla.
  - The adrenal cortex produces more than two dozen **corticosteroids**, which help maintain homeostasis.
  - The adrenal medulla produces the "fight or flight" hormones **epinephrine** and **norepinephrine**, which help the body respond to stress.
- The pancreas is both an exocrine gland and an endocrine gland. As an exocrine gland, the pancreas releases digestive enzymes.
- Insulin and glucagon, hormones produced by the islets of Langerhans in the pancreas, help keep levels of glucose in the blood stable.
- The thyroid gland wraps around the trachea at the base of the neck. The four parathyroid glands are on the back surface of the thyroid gland. **Thyroxine**, produced by the thyroid gland, regulates metabolism. A hormone from the thyroid gland, **calcitonin**, and one from the parathyroid glands, **parathyroid hormone**, work together to maintain blood calcium levels.
- Reproductive glands, or gonads, make gametes and secrete sex hormones. The female gonads, ovaries, produce eggs. The male gonads, testes, produce sperm.

**Control of the Endocrine System** Feedback mechanisms involving hormones help maintain homeostasis. In feedback inhibition, increasing levels of a substance inhibit the process that produced the substance. Secretions of the hypothalamus and pituitary gland regulate the activity of other endocrine glands in this way.

- Actions of the hypothalamus and posterior pituitary gland regulate water balance. The hypothalamus signals the posterior pituitary gland to increase (in the case of dehydration) or decrease (in the case of overhydration) its release of anti-diurectic hormone (ADH). In response to ADH levels the kidneys produce less or more urine.
- The hypothalamus and anterior pituitary regulate metabolism and body temperature by controlling the amount of thyroxine produced by the thyroid gland.

 

Name ______________________________ Class _______ Date _________

# The Human Endocrine Glands

*For Questions 1–4, complete each statement by writing the correct word or words.*

**1.** The pituitary gland is located at the base of the ____________ and consists of the ____________ pituitary and the ____________ pituitary.

**2.** ________________ cells in the ________________ produce hormones that are released by the ________________.

**3.** The two hormones released from the posterior pituitary are oxytocin and ________________.

**4.** ____________ hormones secreted into blood vessels leading to the ____________ pituitary control its secretions.

*For Questions 5–9, match each pituitary hormone with its action.*

| Hormone | Action |
|---|---|
| _____ **5.** MSH | **A.** Stimulates ovaries and testes |
| _____ **6.** TSH | **B.** Stimulates the release of thyroxine |
| _____ **7.** LH | **C.** Stimulates release of hormones from adrenal cortex |
| _____ **8.** GH | **D.** Stimulates protein synthesis and growth in cells |
| _____ **9.** ACTH | **E.** Stimulates melanocytes to increase production of melanin in the skin |

**10.** Complete the table. Fill in the missing information about each adrenal gland.

| Part of the Adrenal Gland | Hormone(s) Produced | Function |
|---|---|---|
| Adrenal cortex | | |
| Adrenal medulla | | |

**11.** How does the pancreas use insulin and glucagon together to control blood glucose levels in the body?

______________________________________________________________________

______________________________________________________________________

______________________________________________________________________

**12.** What is diabetes mellitus?

______________________________________________________________________

______________________________________________________________________

 

*For Questions 13–19, write True if the statement is true. If the statement is false, change the underlined word or words to make the statement true.*

______ **13.** A major role of the thyroid gland is controlling the body's metabolism.

______ **14.** The body needs calcium in order to produce thyroxine.

______ **15.** Too little thyroxine leads to a condition called hyperthyroidism.

______ **16.** Calcitonin is a hormone produced by the thyroid gland.

______ **17.** The parathyroid glands are located on the back of the pituitary gland.

______ **18.** Parathyroid hormone promotes the proper functioning of nerves and muscles.

______ **19.** The reproductive organs are referred to as gametes.

## Control of the Endocrine System

**20.** What is feedback inhibition?

**21.** Complete the flowchart to show how feedback controls regulate the thyroid gland.

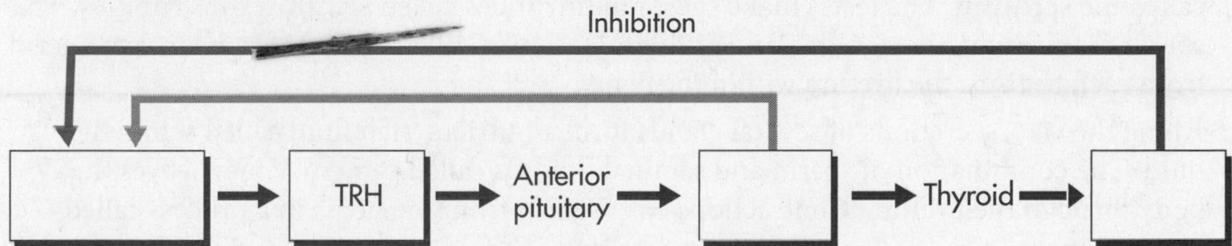


**22.** Explain how feedback control regulates the rate of metabolism.

### Apply the Big idea

**23.** Which gland, the hypothalamus or the pituitary gland, should be given the title "master gland"? Explain your choice.

 

# 34.3 The Reproductive System

## Lesson Objectives

- Describe the effects the sex hormones have on development.
- Name and discuss the structures of the male reproductive system.
- Name and discuss the structures of the female reproductive system.
- Describe some of the most common sexually transmitted diseases.

## Lesson Summary

**Sexual Development** Hormones released by the ovaries and testes cause sexual development during **puberty**, a period of rapid growth and sexual maturation that usually starts between the ages of 9 and 15. At the end of puberty, the male and female reproductive organs are fully developed and become fully functional.

**The Male Reproductive System** The main role of the male reproductive system is to make and deliver sperm.

- The **testes** are the main organs of the male system. Two testes are held in an external sac called the **scrotum**. The testes make sperm in tiny tubes called **seminiferous tubules**. The sperm mature and are stored in an **epididymis**. A tube called a **vas deferens** carries sperm from each testis to the urethra within the penis.
- Along the way, secretions of several glands form a nutrient-rich fluid called seminal fluid. The combination of sperm and seminal fluids is called **semen**. Semen leaves the body through the urethra. Contractions eject semen from the penis in a process called ejaculation.
- A mature sperm cell consists of a head that contains the nucleus, a midpiece that is packed with mitochondria, and a flagellum that propels the sperm.

**The Female Reproductive System** The main roles of the female reproductive system are to make eggs and prepare the female body to nourish an embryo.

- The **ovary** is the main organ of the female system. Each ovary has thousands of follicles, which are clusters of cells that surround an egg. A mature egg moves through the Fallopian tube to the uterus, which is connected to the outside of the body by the vagina.
- Beginning in puberty, the female body goes through a **menstrual cycle**, a series of events that prepares the body to care for a fertilized egg. The menstrual cycle has four phases:
  - Follicular phase: An egg matures in its follicle.
  - **Ovulation**: The mature egg is released from the ovary.
  - Luteal phase: The follicle develops into a structure called the **corpus luteum**.
  - **Menstruation**: The lining of the uterus falls away and leaves the body through the vagina if the egg is not fertilized.

**Sexually Transmitted Diseases** A disease spread during sexual contact is called a **sexually transmitted disease** (STD). Bacteria and viruses can cause STDs. Chlamydia, syphilis, gonorrhea, and AIDS are STDs.

Name ______________________ Class ______ Date ______

# Sexual Development

*For Questions 1–3, write the letter of the correct answer on the line at the left.*

_____ **1.** Male and female embryos are nearly identical until the

**A.** second week of development. **C.** third month of development.

**B.** seventh week of development. **D.** fifth month of development.

_____ **2.** Which hormone, when produced in an embryo, triggers a male pattern of development?

**A.** testosterone **C.** estrogen

**B.** progesterone **D.** adrenalin

_____ **3.** The period of human development that includes rapid growth and sexual maturation is called

**A.** adolescence. **C.** maturity.

**B.** childhood. **D.** puberty.

# The Male Reproductive System

*For Questions 4–8, match each structure of the male reproductive system with its description.*

| Structure | Description |
|---|---|
| _____ **4.** epididymis | **A.** External sac that holds male gonads |
| _____ **5.** scrotum | **B.** The primary male reproductive organ |
| _____ **6.** seminiferous tubule | **C.** Structure in which sperm mature |
| _____ **7.** testis | **D.** Structure in which meiosis occurs |
| _____ **8.** vas deferens | **E.** The tube through which sperm travel to the urethra |

*For Questions 9–12, complete each statement by writing the correct word or words.*

**9.** The seminal vesicles, ______________ gland, and ______________ gland produce a nutrient-rich fluid called ______________ fluid.

**10.** Sperm mixed with the seminal fluid is called ______________.

**11.** Signals from the ______________ nervous system cause sperm to be ejaculated.

**12.** The ______________ of a sperm cell contain mitochondria that supply energy to the ______________, which propels the sperm forward.

# The Female Reproductive System

*For Questions 13–16, complete each statement by writing the correct word or words.*

**13.** The primary reproductive organs of females are the ______________.

**14.** The function of a(n) ______________ is to help an egg mature.

**15.** Only about ______________ of the 400,000 eggs a female is born with develop into a mature ovum.

**16.** The structure of the female reproductive system in which the embryo develops is called the ______________.

 

*For Questions 17–20, match each phase of the menstrual cycle with the correct event.*

| Phase | Event |
|---|---|
| ______ 17. Follicular phase | A. An unfertilized egg leaves the body. |
| ______ 18. Ovulation | B. The egg travels through a Fallopian tube. |
| ______ 19. Luteal phase | C. An egg within a follicle develops. |
| ______ 20. Menstruation | D. An egg is released from an ovary. |

21. Complete the concept map to explain what the outcomes of a menstrual cycle can be.

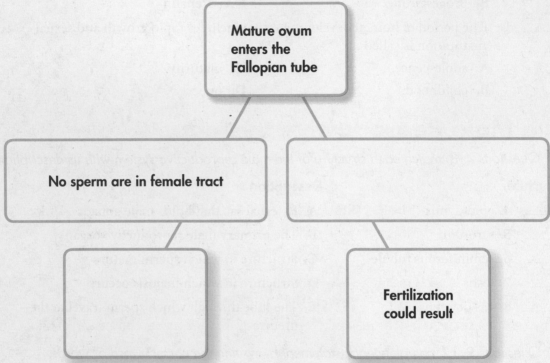

Mature ovum enters the Fallopian tube

No sperm are in female tract

Fertilization could result

## Sexually Transmitted Diseases

*For Questions 22–24, write True if the statement is true. If the statement is false, change the underlined word or words to make the statement true.*

__________ 22. <u>AIDS</u> is the most common bacterial STD.

__________ 23. Chlamydia damages the reproductive tract and can cause <u>infertility</u>.

__________ 24. Hepatitis B and genital herpes are viral STDs.

**Apply the Big idea**

25. How is the menstrual cycle an example of the body's use of negative feedback?

 

Name ________________________________ Class ______ Date ________

# 34.4 Fertilization and Development

## Lesson Objectives

- Describe fertilization and the early stages of development.
- Identify the major events of later stages of development.

## Lesson Summary

**Fertilization and Early Development** Fertilization is the joining of a sperm and an egg. Following fertilization, a series of events called development begins.

- A fertilized egg is called a **zygote**. The zygote divides and undergoes repeated rounds of mitosis and develops into a hollow ball of cells called a **blastocyst**.
- About a week after fertilization, the blastocyst attaches to the wall of the uterus in the process of **implantation**. At the same time, cells of the blastocyst start to specialize through differentiation. Some cells migrate to form two cell layers—the ectoderm and the endoderm.
- A third layer of cells is produced by a process called **gastrulation**, in which cells from the ectoderm migrate to form the mesoderm. The three layers eventually develop into the different organs of the embryo.
- During **neurulation**, the notochord and the neural tube form. The neural tube eventually develops into the brain and spinal cord.
- As the embryo develops, membranes for protection and nourishment also form. Part of one membrane combines with the uterine lining to form the **placenta**. Mother and embryo/fetus exchange gases, food, and waste products across the placenta. The umbilical cord connects the embryo/fetus to the placenta.
- After eight weeks of development, the embryo is called a **fetus**. By the end of three months, most organs are fully formed.

**Later Development** Another six months of development occurs before birth.

- During months 4–6, the fetus's tissues become specialized and organs such as the heart begin to function.
- During months 7–9, the fetus's organ systems mature as the fetus grows in size and mass. The lungs and the central nervous system complete their development.
- Childbirth occurs about nine months after fertilization, when hormones cause contractions in the mother's uterus. The contractions first push the baby out through the vagina. Then, more contractions expel the placenta and amniotic sac from the uterus. Shortly after birth, the mother's breast tissue begins to produce milk that contains everything the baby needs for the first months of life.
- The placenta is a barrier to many harmful agents, but some are able to pass through it, such as viruses that cause AIDS and German measles. Alcohol, drugs, and smoking also have negative effects on embryos and fetuses. Prenatal care and advancements in medical technology have lowered the infant mortality rate.

Name ______________________ Class ______ Date ______

# Fertilization and Early Development

*For Questions 1–4, complete each statement by writing the correct word or words.*

**1.** The fusion of a sperm with an egg is called ______________.

**2.** During implantation, the ______________ embeds itself into the lining of the uterus.

**3.** Embryonic structures called ______________ combine with the uterine lining to form the ______________.

**4.** The embryo is surrounded by fluid called the ______________ fluid.

**5.** Complete the table by identifying events and structures of early development.

| Event or Structure | What It Is |
|---|---|
| | The process in which sperm joins an egg |
| | The layer of cells that develops into the skin and nervous system |
| Gastrulation | |
| | Early stage in the development of the nervous system |
| Endoderm | |
| | Fluid-filled structure that cushions and protects the embryo |
| | Embryo's organ of respiration, nourishment, and excretion |
| Mesoderm | |
| Umbilical cord | |

# Later Development

**6.** What major changes occur in a developing fetus during months 4–6 of pregnancy?

______________________________________________

______________________________________________

**7.** What major changes occur in a developing fetus during months 7–9 of pregnancy?

______________________________________________

______________________________________________

______________________________________________

*For Questions 8–13, write the letter of the correct answer on the line at the left.*

______ **8.** The contractions of labor before childbirth are triggered by
**A.** the amniotic fluid.
**B.** the hormone oxytocin.
**C.** the umbilical cord.
**D.** the uterine wall.

______ **9.** The term "afterbirth" refers to the
**A.** amnion and the chorion.
**B.** clamping of the umbilical cord.
**C.** placenta and amniotic sac.
**D.** production of milk for the baby.

______ **10.** What is a belly button?
**A.** a structure with an unknown purpose
**B.** a scar left from the umbilical cord
**C.** remains of the notochord
**D.** the point where implantation occurred

______ **11.** Which hormone causes the mother's breast tissue to begin producing milk?
**A.** estrogen
**B.** oxytocin
**C.** progesterone
**D.** prolactin

______ **12.** Using alcohol during pregnancy can harm a developing embryo, especially its
**A.** reproductive system.
**B.** circulatory system.
**C.** endocrine system.
**D.** nervous system.

______ **13.** Which public health measure has decreased the incidence of spina bifida?
**A.** the addition of folic acid to grain products
**B.** the development of new types of baby formula
**C.** the programs aimed at reducing smoking and alcohol use
**D.** the use of a vaccine that prevents German measles

## Apply the Big idea

**14.** Women with Type 1 diabetes may face challenges controlling blood sugar levels during pregnacy. Early in pregnancy, the developing fetus removes glucose from the mother's blood at a great rate. Would this raise or lower her need for insulin?

______

______

______

 

# Chapter Vocabulary Review

*On the lines provided, label the structures of the male reproductive system that correspond to the numbers in the diagram.*

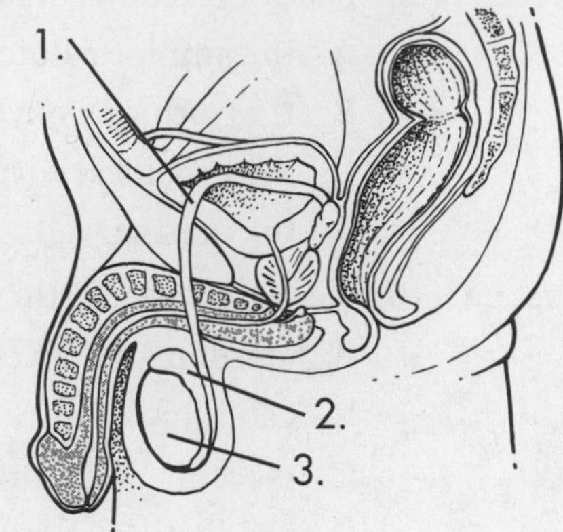


**1.** ______

**2.** ______

**3.** ______

*For Questions 4–10, match the term with its definition.*

| Term | Definition |
|---|---|
| ____ **4.** endocrine gland | **A.** Mixture of sperm and seminal fluids |
| ____ **5.** exocrine gland | **B.** Attachment of the blastocyst to the uterine wall |
| ____ **6.** gastrulation | **C.** Discharge of uterine tissue and blood from the vagina |
| ____ **7.** hormone | **D.** Chemical made in one part of the body that travels in the bloodstream to other parts |
| ____ **8.** implantation | **E.** The process that produces the three cell layers of the embryo |
| ____ **9.** menstruation | **F.** Type of gland that releases its chemicals directly into the bloodstream |
| ____ **10.** semen | **G.** Type of gland that releases its chemicals out of the body |

*For Questions 11–18, complete each statement by writing the correct word or words.*

**11.** After eight weeks of development, an embryo is called a ______.

**12.** The gland that produces hormones that regulate the secretions of other glands is the ______ gland.

**13.** Cells with receptors for a particular hormone are called ______ cells.

**14.** A fertilized egg is called a ______.

**15.** ______ are also known as "local hormones."

**16.** Oxygen and nutrients diffuse from the mother's blood to the embryo's blood through the ______.

**17.** The early stages of the brain and spinal cord form during ______.

**18.** Sperm are produced in ducts called the ______ tubules.

Name ______________________ Class _____ Date _________

# CHAPTER MYSTERY

## OUT OF STRIDE

In the Chapter Mystery, you learned about what happens when the body is not given everything it needs. Nonessential life processes, such as menstruation, may stop. In addition, the body may begin to take nutrients from organs and tissues.

21st Century Learning

## Giving Your Body What It Needs

There are many diseases associated with undernutrition. In this country, most undernutrition diseases and disorders are associated with psychological issues rather than a lack of available nutrients. One of the most common of these diseases is anorexia nervosa. This is part of the FAQs page on a Web site about anorexia nervosa.

### FAQS About Anorexia

**Q:** What is anorexia nervosa?
**A:** Anorexia nervosa is a medical condition that affects how a person thinks about food and about his or her own body.

Return to Top

**Q:** Does anorexia affect only girls and women?
**A:** It's true that 90–95% of anorexics are female, but that means that 5–10% are boys and men.

Return to Top

**Q:** What causes anorexia?
**A:** We don't know. We don't even know if there is one cause or many. But there are risk factors.

Return to Top

**Q:** What are the risk factors?
**A:** The first is culture. Anorexia almost exclusively affects people who grew up in or moved to Western cultures where they were exposed to images of the "ideal" body type for their sex. For example, Western media is full of images of flawless, thin women.

Having a relative with anorexia makes it more likely a person will develop it. It's possible that personality traits and genetic factors are involved as well.

Return to Top

**Q:** What effect does anorexia have on the human body?
**A:** The symptoms of anorexia vary depending on the severity and length of time the person has suffered from the disease. Anorexia changes the brain chemistry, causing irritability, moodiness, and difficulty thinking. The hair and nails become brittle. The blood pressure goes down and the heart rate slows. The skin becomes dry and bruises easily. Bones lose mass and break more easily. Other symptoms include kidney stones and kidney failure, anemia, yellowing of the skin, and the growth of fine hairs over the entire body. In women, anorexia stops the menstrual cycle and increases the possibility of miscarriage and low birth weight.

Return to Top

Continued on next page ▶

 

## 21st Century Themes Science and Health Literacy

**1.** What percentage of anorexics are male?

**2.** What parts of the body are affected by anorexia nervosa?

**3.** What symptoms are described both in this FAQ and in the solution to the Chapter Mystery?

**4.** What do you think some of the treatments for anorexia might be?

**5.** Suggest some ways in which the incidence of anorexia nervosa in the United States might be decreased.

## 21st Century Skills Help Wanted: Nutritionist

The skills used in this activity include **communication skills, creativity and intellectual curiosity, interpersonal and collaborative skills, accountability and adaptability,** and **social responsibility.**

An interest in nutrition could lead to a career as a nutritionist or a dietician. Nutritionists and dieticians work in hospitals, nursing homes, medical offices, schools, governmental agencies, and any number of other places. Use library or Internet resources to research the various job opportunities that involve nutrition. Then write up a help wanted ad that describes your ideal job.

*Compare your ad with those of your classmates.*

 

Name ______________________________ Class ______ Date ________

# 35 Immune System and Disease

## Homeostasis

**Q:** How does the body fight against invading organisms that may disrupt homeostasis?

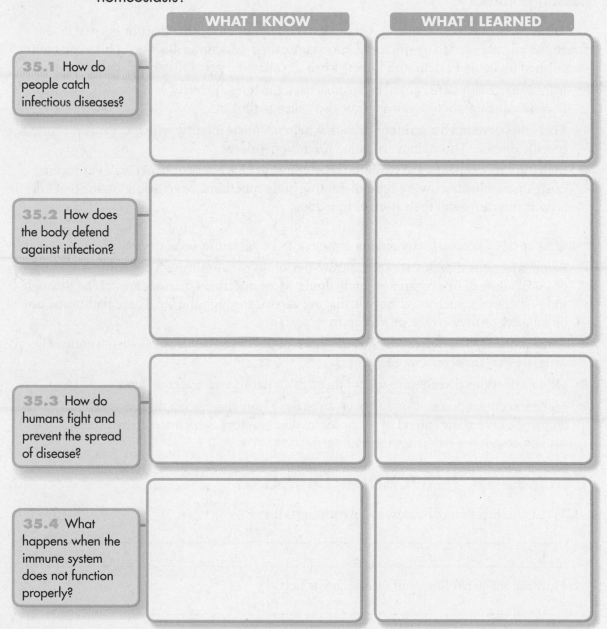

| | WHAT I KNOW | WHAT I LEARNED |
|---|---|---|
| **35.1** How do people catch infectious diseases? | | |
| **35.2** How does the body defend against infection? | | |
| **35.3** How do humans fight and prevent the spread of disease? | | |
| **35.4** What happens when the immune system does not function properly? | | |

# 35.1 Infectious Disease

## Lesson Objectives

Identify the causes of infectious disease.

Explain how infectious diseases are spread.

## Lesson Summary

**Causes of Infectious Disease** Changes to body physiology that disrupt normal body functions and are caused by microorganisms are called **infectious diseases**. This explanation, established by Louis Pasteur and Robert Koch, is called the **germ theory of disease**.

- Infectious diseases are caused by viruses, bacteria, fungi, protists, and parasitic worms. Disease-causing microorganisms are also called pathogens.
- Koch also developed a series of rules that help scientists identify which organism causes a specific disease. These rules are called **Koch's postulates**.
- Many microorganisms are symbionts that are either harmless or beneficial. Pathogens cause disease by destroying cells, disrupting body functions, or releasing toxins that kill cells or interfere with their normal functions.

**How Diseases Spread** Infectious diseases can be spread in several ways.

- Some infectious diseases are spread from person to person through coughing, sneezing, physical contact, or exchange of body fluids. Most infectious diseases are spread through indirect contact, such as pathogens that are carried through the air. These pathogens can be inhaled, or they can be picked up from surfaces.
- Some pathogens are spread by specific kinds of direct contact, such as sexual contact or drug use that involves shared syringes.
- Other infectious diseases are spread through contaminated water or food.
- Some infectious diseases spread from animals to humans. Such a disease is called a **zoonosis**. Often, the spread of zoonoses involves **vectors**, which are disease carriers that usually do not get sick from the pathogen.

## Causes of Infectious Disease

**1.** What are infectious diseases, and what causes them?

______

______

**2.** How did the germ theory of disease get its name?

______

______

**3.** What is another name that scientists use for a disease-causing agent?

______

 

*For Questions 4–12, match each type of disease with the type of disease-causing agent that causes it. Some types of disease-causing agents may be used more than once.*

| **Disease** | **Type of Disease-Causing Agent** |
|---|---|
| ______ **4.** African sleeping sickness | **A.** virus |
| ______ **5.** athlete's foot | **B.** bacterium |
| ______ **6.** botulism | **C.** protist |
| ______ **7.** chicken pox | **D.** parasitic worm |
| ______ **8.** hookworm | **E.** fungus |
| ______ **9.** influenza | |
| ______ **10.** malaria | |
| ______ **11.** trichinosis | |
| ______ **12.** tuberculosis | |

**13.** What are Koch's postulates used for?

______________________________________________________________________

______________________________________________________________________

**14.** Complete the flowchart by numbering the steps to show the order in which a researcher applies Koch's postulates.

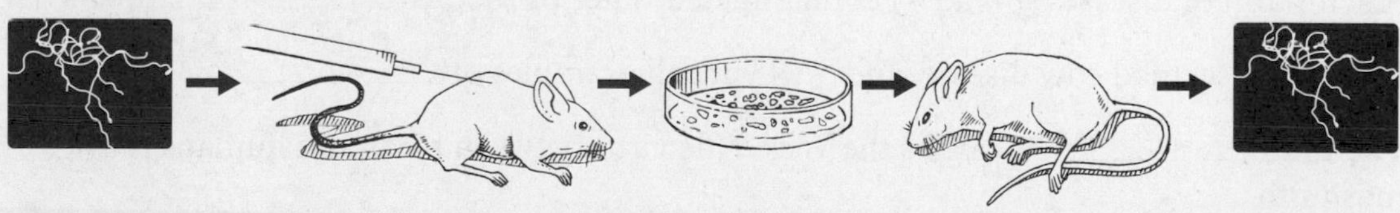
Same pathogen recovered from sick mouse
Pathogen injected into a healthy lab mouse
Pathogen grown in a pure culture
Healthy mouse becomes sick
Pathogen isolated from a dead mouse

______ ______ ______ ______ ______

**15.** Are microorganisms always harmful to the human body? Explain your answer, and give an example.

______________________________________________________________________

______________________________________________________________________

______________________________________________________________________

______________________________________________________________________

**16.** List two ways that bacteria can produce illness.

**A.** ______________________________________________________________________

**B.** ______________________________________________________________________

 

17. List three ways that parasitic worms cause disease.

A. ______

B. ______

C. ______

## How Diseases Spread

*For Questions 18–26, complete each statement by writing the correct word or words.*

18. Natural selection favors pathogens with ______ that help them spread from host to host.

19. Symptoms of disease that can spread pathogens include ______ and ______.

20. The best ways to prevent infections of the nose, throat, and respiratory tract are frequent and thorough ______ and avoiding ______ your mouth and nose.

21. ______ that cause skin infections can be transmitted by any body contact or by contact with contaminated towels or equipment.

22. ______ is spread from one host to another in body fluids exchanged during sexual activity.

23. Blood on shared syringes can spread certain forms of ______, as well as ______.

24. A symptom of diseases spread by contaminated water or food is ______.

25. Lyme disease, mad cow disease, and SARS are all examples of ______.

26. The ______ that carries the West Nile virus between birds and humans is a mosquito.

### Apply the Big idea

27. Explain how coughing and sneezing can not only spread infection, but also help protect against invading organisms.

______

 

# 35.2 Defenses Against Infection

## Lesson Objectives

- Describe the body's nonspecific defenses against invading pathogens.
- Describe the function of the immune system's specific defenses.
- List the body's specific defenses against pathogens.

## Lesson Summary

**Nonspecific Defenses** The body has many nonspecific defenses, which defend against a wide range of pathogens.

- The first line of defense is skin. Skin keeps pathogens out of the body by forming a barrier that few pathogens can get through. Mucus, saliva, and tears contain an enzyme that can kill bacteria. Mucus can also trap pathogens.
- When pathogens do enter the body, the second line of defense goes to work. These nonspecific defenses include:
  - the **inflammatory response**, in which chemicals called **histamines** cause blood vessels near a wound to expand and phagocytes to move into the tissue to fight infection.
  - the production of proteins called **interferons**, which help block the replication of viruses.
  - the release of chemicals that produce a **fever**, an increase in normal body temperature, which may slow the growth of pathogens and speed up immune response.

**Specific Defenses: The Immune System** The function of the immune system is to fight infection by inactivating foreign substances or cells that have entered the body. The specific immune response works in several ways, including:

- recognizing "self," including cells and proteins that belong to the body.
- recognizing "nonself", or **antigens**, molecules found on foreign substances. Antigens stimulate the immune system to produce cells called lymohocytes that recognize, attack, destroy, and "remember" specific pathogens.
- producing specific lymphocytes that recognize specific antigens. They work by attacking infected cells or producing **antibodies**, proteins which tag antigens for destruction by immune cells.

**The Immune System in Action** The immune response works in two ways.

- In **humoral immunity**, white blood cells, called B lymphocytes (B cells), make antibodies that attack pathogens in the blood.
- In **cell-mediated immunity** white blood cells, called T lymphocytes (T cells), find and destroy abnormal or infected cells.
- After a pathogen is destroyed, memory B cells and memory T cells stay in the body. These cells help create a faster immune response if the same pathogen enters the body again.

 

## Nonspecific Defenses

*For Questions 1–8, write the letter of the definition that best matches each term.*

| Term | Definition |
|---|---|
| ____ 1. skin | A. An increase in body temperature, which slows or stops pathogens |
| ____ 2. lysozyme | B. A secretion of the nose and throat that traps pathogens |
| ____ 3. inflammatory response | C. An enzyme found in tears and saliva that breaks down bacterial cell walls |
| ____ 4. histamines | D. Chemicals that increase blood flow to tissues |
| ____ 5. interferons | E. Combination of physical and chemical barriers that defend against pathogens |
| ____ 6. fever | F. Redness, pain, and swelling at the site of an injury |
| | G. Proteins that fight viral growth |
| ____ 7. mucus | H. The body's most important nonspecific defense |
| ____ 8. nonspecific defenses | |

## Specific Defenses: The Immune System

*For Questions 9–14, complete each statement by writing the correct word or words.*

9. The ______________ response is the body's response to specific invaders.
10. A substance that triggers the immune response is known as a (n) ______________.
11. The main role of ______________ is to tag ______________ for destruction by immune-system cells.
12. The main working cells of the immune system are two types of ______________. Their specific types are determined by a person's ______________.
13. ______________ discover antigens in body fluids.
14. ______________ defend the body against pathogens that have infected body cells.

15. **THINK VISUALLY** In the space provided, draw an example of each type of lymphocyte indicated to show a basic difference between the two types of cells.

| B Cell | T Cell |
|---|---|
| | |

 

# The Immune System in Action

*For Questions 16–22, write True or False on the line provided.*

______ **16.** Humoral immunity is a response to pathogens in blood and lymph.

______ **17.** The first response of humoral immunity to infection is much faster than the second response.

______ **18.** Plasma cells are specialized B cells.

______ **19.** Cell-mediated immunity involves antibodies.

______ **20.** Cell-mediated immunity causes infected body cells to die.

______ **21.** Cell-mediated immunity only works on viral diseases.

______ **22.** Cytotoxic T cells are a cause of rejection of transplanted organs.

**23.** Complete the table to compare how humoral and cell-mediated immunity work after a virus invades the body for the first and second times.

| Humoral Immunity vs. Cell-Mediated Immunity | |
|---|---|
| **Action of Humoral Immunity** | **Action of Cell-Mediated Immunity** |
| **Primary response:** | **Primary response:** |
| | Macrophages consume viruses and display their antigens on the cell surface. Helper T cells are activated. |
| Activated B cells grow and divide rapidly. | |
| | Helper T cells activate B cells and cytotoxic T cells and produce memory cells. |
| Plasma cells release antibodies that capture antigens and mark them for destruction. | |
| **Secondary response:** | **Secondary response:** |
| | |

## Apply the Big idea

**24.** A runny nose is a symptom of a cold. How is this evidence that the body's immune defenses are working?

______________________________________________

______________________________________________

______________________________________________

______________________________________________

Name ______________________ Class ______ Date __________

# 35.3 Fighting Infectious Disease

## Lesson Objectives

- Distinguish between active immunity and passive immunity.
- Describe how public health measures and medications fight disease.
- Describe why patterns of infectious disease have changed.

## Lesson Summary

**Acquired Immunity** You can acquire immunity without having a disease.

- **Vaccination** is the injection of a weakened or mild form of a pathogen to cause immunity.
- **Active immunity** results from vaccines or natural exposure to an antigen.
- **Passive immunity** forms when antibodies are introduced into the body. It lasts only until the immune system destroys the foreign antibodies.

**Public Health and Medications** In 2005, less than 5 percent of human deaths were caused by infectious diseases. This statistic is the result of two major factors.

- The field of public health provides services that help monitor food and water supplies and promote vaccinations and healthy behavior.
- The development and use of many new medications, particularly antibiotics and antiviral drugs, has saved many lives by helping to cure infectious diseases.

**New and Re-Emerging Diseases** Since 1980, many new diseases have appeared and several diseases once thought to have been eradicated have recurred. There are two main reasons for these changes.

- Interactions with exotic animals have increased.
- The misuse of medications has caused diseases that were once under control, such as tuberculosis and malaria, to evolve resistance to many antibiotics.

## Acquired Immunity

**1.** What was the origin of the term *vaccination*? Explain why this name was given.

______________________________________________________________________

______________________________________________________________________

______________________________________________________________________

______________________________________________________________________

**2.** How does a vaccine work?

______________________________________________________________________

______________________________________________________________________

______________________________________________________________________

______________________________________________________________________

3. What type of immunity do vaccinations produce?

_______________________________________________

4. What type of immunity does a mother pass on to her infant while breastfeeding?

_______________________________________________

5. Why is passive immunity only temporary?

_______________________________________________

6. Complete the Venn diagram comparing the two types of immunity and writing the correct word or words on the lines provided.

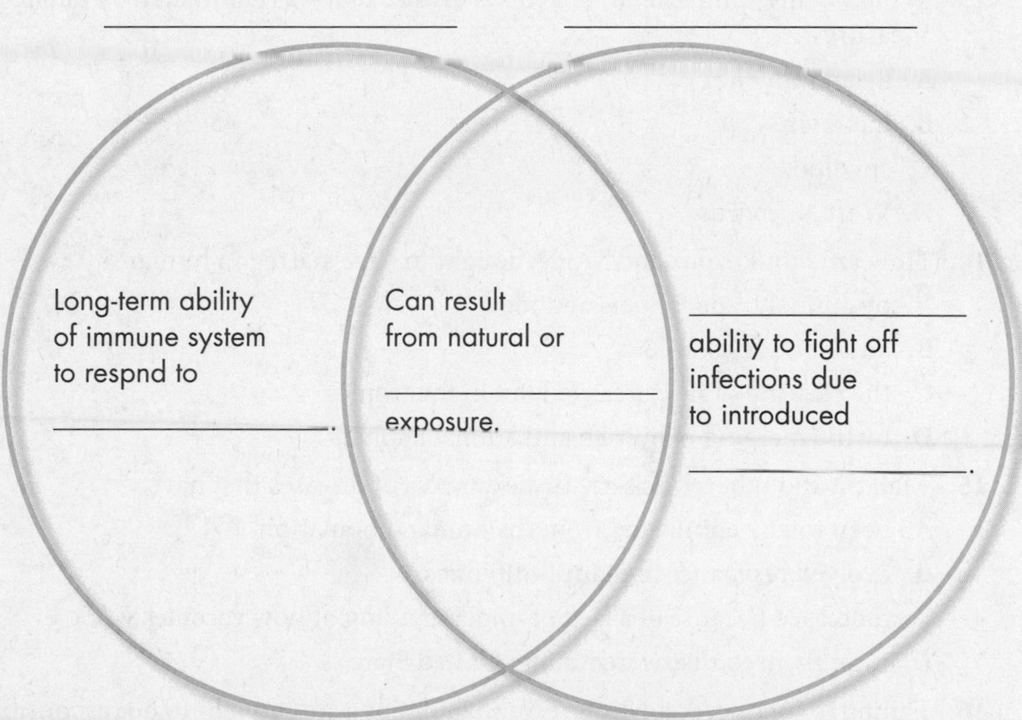

______________ ______________
Long-term ability of immune system to respnd to ______________.
Can result from natural or ______________ exposure.
______________ ability to fight off infections due to introduced ______________.

## Public Health and Medications

*For Questions 7–11, complete each statement by writing the correct word or words.*

7. Promoting childhood ______________ and providing clean drinking water are two ______________ activities that have greatly reduced the spread of many infectious diseases.

8. Compounds that kill bacteria without harming the host cells are called ______________.

9. The first antibiotic to be discovered was ______________.

10. ______________ drugs inhibit the ability of viruses to invade cells or multiply within cells.

11. How did Alexander Fleming discover the first antibiotic?

_______________________________________________

_______________________________________________

_______________________________________________

# New and Re-Emerging Diseases

*For Questions 12–16, write the letter of the correct answer on the line at the left.*

_____ **12.** Which of the following is NOT considered to be a major cause of new or re-emerging diseases?

**A.** misuse of medications

**B.** merging of human and animal habitats

**C.** vaccination

**D.** trade in exotic animals

_____ **13.** Which is an example of an infectious disease that was eliminated by public health measures?

**A.** avian influenza

**B.** hantavirus

**C.** smallpox

**D.** West Nile virus

_____ **14.** How are monkeypox and SARS thought to have started in humans?

**A.** by animal trade for pets and food

**B.** antibiotic resistance

**C.** the clearing of new areas of land in the tropics

**D.** by the merging of human and animal habitats

_____ **15.** Malaria and tuberculosis are two examples of diseases that have

**A.** been totally eliminated from the human population.

**B.** evolved resistance to many antibiotics.

**C.** increased because of a lack of understanding of how vaccines work.

**D.** recently been discovered in the United States.

_____ **16.** Failing to follow vaccination recommendations are thought to be responsible for the comeback of

**A.** Ebola.

**B.** influenza.

**C.** Lyme disease.

**D.** measles.

## Apply the Big idea

**17.** After being vaccinated, many children are treated for fever. This is not considered a danger or problem. Why might this happen?

______________________________________________________________________

______________________________________________________________________

______________________________________________________________________

______________________________________________________________________

 

# 35.4 Immune System Disorders

## Lesson Objectives

- Explain what happens when the immune system overreacts to harmless pathogens.
- Describe how HIV is transmitted and how it affects the immune system.

## Lesson Summary

**When the Immune System "Misfires"** Sometimes, the immune system overreacts to otherwise harmless antigens. Three types of disorders are caused in this way.

- The most common immune-system disorders are **allergies**, which occur when antigens enter the body and bind to mast cells. The mast cells release histamines, which increase the flow of blood and fluids to the area. This causes allergy symptoms.
- Allergic reactions in the respiratory system can cause **asthma**, a dangerous chronic disease in which the air passages narrow and breathing becomes difficult.
- When the immune system makes a mistake and attacks the body's own cells, an autoimmune disease results. Autoimmune diseases include Type I diabetes, rheumatoid arthritis, and lupus.

**HIV and AIDS** In the 1970s, clusters of cases of opportunistic diseases—diseases that attack people with weakened immune systems—led to the discovery of a new disease called acquired immunodeficiency syndrome (AIDS).

- Research revealed that AIDS is an infectious disease caused by human immunodeficiency virus (HIV). HIV attaches to receptors on helper T cells. Once inside the cells, HIV copies itself and the new viruses infect more helper T cells.
- HIV infection gradually leads to the death of more and more T cells. When a person's T cell count drops to about one-sixth the normal level, the person has AIDS.
- HIV can only be transmitted through contact with infected blood, semen, vaginal secretions, or breast milk.

# When the Immune System "Misfires"

*For Questions 1–5, complete each statement by writing the correct word or words.*

1. An overreaction of the immune system to antigens of pollen and other harmless substances is called a(n) ______________.
2. Sneezing, a runny nose, and watery eyes are symptoms of the ______________ response in the respiratory system.
3. Drugs called ______________ counteract the effects of ______________ produced by mast cells.
4. A dangerous condition that affects the respiratory system and can be caused by allergies is called ______________.
5. Examples of ______________ triggers for allergic reactions include tobacco smoke, pollution, molds, and pet dander.

**6.** What is an autoimmune disease?

______________________________

______________________________

**7.** Describe the advantage and disadvantage of treating an autoimmune illness such as lupus.

______________________________

______________________________

______________________________

**8.** Complete the table about autoimmune diseases.

| Autoimmune Diseases | |
|---|---|
| **Autoimmune Disease** | **Organ or Tissue That Is Attacked** |
| Type I diabetes | |
| | Connective tissues around the joints |
| Lupus | |

# HIV and AIDS

**9.** What does AIDS stand for?

______________________________

**10.** What is the term that describes diseases that attack people with a weakened immune system?

______________________________

**11.** List four body fluids that can transmit AIDS.

**A.** ______________

**B.** ______________

**C.** ______________

**D.** ______________

**12.** What behaviors prevent people from being infected with HIV?

______________________________

______________________________

**13.** Why is curing HIV infection so challenging? Explain your answer.

______________________________

______________________________

______________________________

 

**14.** Complete the flowchart that summarizes the HIV infection process.

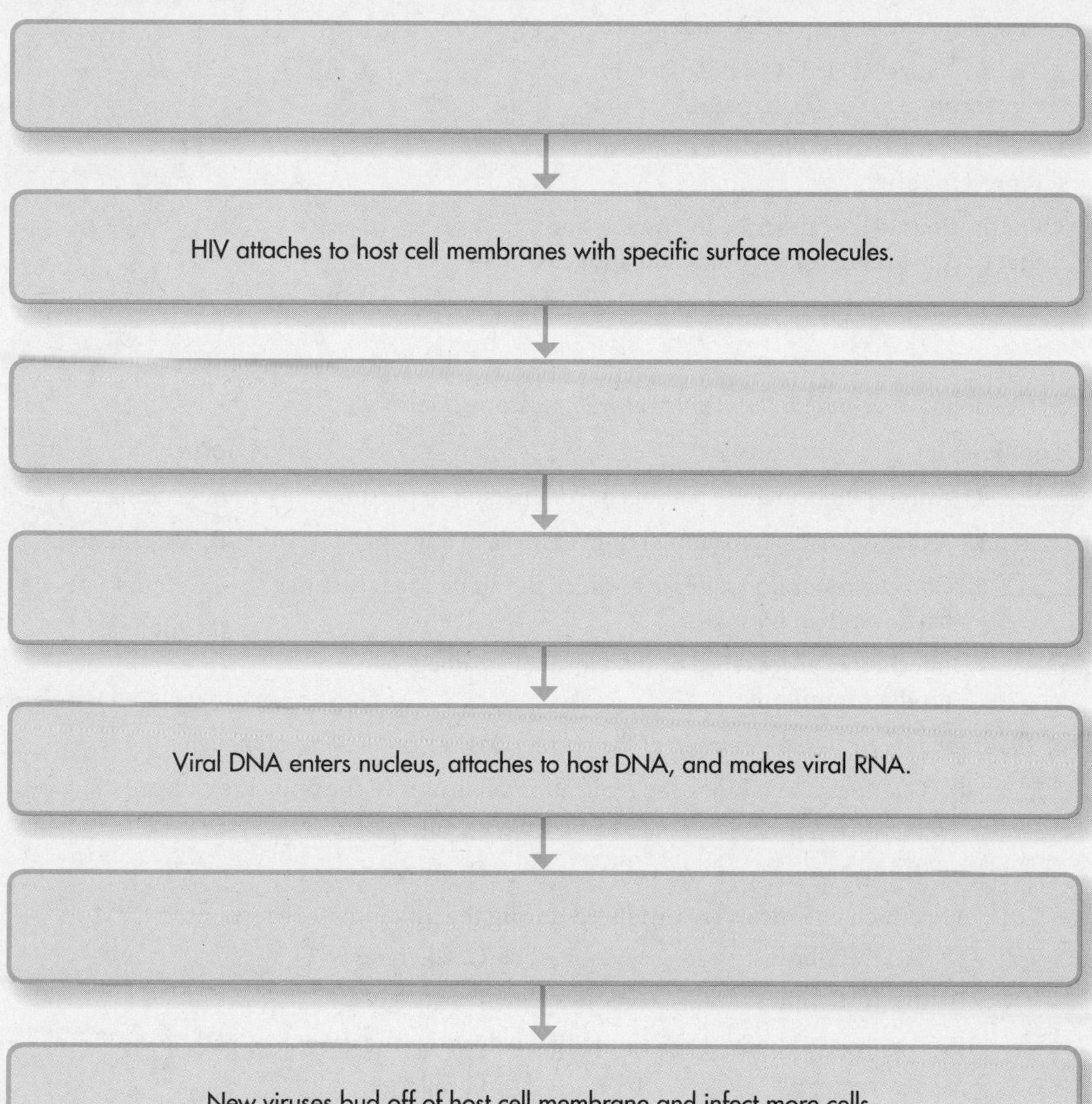
HIV attaches to host cell membranes with specific surface molecules.
Viral DNA enters nucleus, attaches to host DNA, and makes viral RNA.
New viruses bud off of host cell membrane and infect more cells.

## Apply the Big idea

**15.** What is the key difference between an immunodeficiency disease and an autoimmune disease? Provide an example of both types of disease in your response.

______________________________________________

______________________________________________

______________________________________________

______________________________________________

Name ____________ Class ______ Date ______

# Chapter Vocabulary Review

*Use the diagram to answer Questions 1–3.*

1. The structure labeled A in the diagram represents a(n) ____________.
2. The structure labeled B in the diagram represents a(n) ____________.
3. On the lines below, describe the interaction that occurs between antibodies and antigens.

____________________________________________

____________________________________________

B.

A.

*For Questions 4–7, match the definition with the correct term.*

| Definition | Term |
|---|---|
| _____ 4. Animal that carries a pathogen from person to person | A. asthma |
| _____ 5. A disease that is transmitted from animals to humans | B. vaccination |
| _____ 6. Chronic respiratory disease in which the air passages become narrower than normal | C. vector |
| _____ 7. Injection of a weakened or mild form of a pathogen to produce immunity | D. zoonosis |

*For Questions 8–10, write the letter of the correct answer on the line at the left.*

_____ **8.** Chemicals that block the replication of viruses in the body are called

**A.** interferons. **C.** allergies.
**B.** histamines. **D.** antigens.

_____ **9.** Which chemicals are produced during the inflammatory response?

**A.** interferons **C.** allergies
**B.** histamines **D.** antigens

_____ **10.** An elevated body temperature that helps stop the growth of pathogens is a(n)

**A.** vector. **C.** allergy.
**B.** zoonosis. **D.** fever.

*For Questions 11–13, complete each statement by writing the correct word or words.*

11. A change to the physiology that disrupts normal body functions and is caused by a microorganism is called a(n) ____________ ____________.
12. The part of the immune response that depends on the action of macrophages and several types of T cells is called ____________ immunity.
13. The part of the immune response that depends on the action of B cells and antibodies circulating in the blood and lymph is called ____________ immunity.

In the Chapter Mystery, you learned about a group of people in one part of Connecticut who came down with Lyme disease. Lyme disease is spread by certain kinds of ticks. But many infectious diseases are spread directly from person to person.

# Infectious Diseases in History

Smallpox is a deadly, highly-contagious disease that was once common throughout Europe, Asia, and North Africa. The war against smallpox began in the late 1700s when the British physician Edward Jenner developed a smallpox vaccine. In the 1900s, there was a worldwide effort to administer the vaccine on a global scale. By 1980, the disease had been effectively eradicated. One of the last serious smallpox outbreaks occurred in Eastern Europe in 1972. The following article describes what happened during one of the last battles against this devastatingly contagious disease.

## Smallpox's Last Stand

Every year, millions of people travel to the city of Mecca in Saudi Arabia. In 1972, on his way back from the Middle East, one man traveled through an area known to have smallpox. He returned to his village in Kosovo, Yugoslavia with the smallpox virus.

Oddly enough, the pilgrim only became slightly sick. But he indirectly passed the virus along to a man named Ljatif Muzza, who lived in a neighboring town. When Muzza became sick, he went to the local hospital, where they could not diagnose what was wrong with him. (No one recognized smallpox because there had been no outbreaks for many years.) The local hospital sent him to a larger facility, which then sent him to the main hospital in the capital city, Belgrade. Muzza died shortly thereafter. But in his journey from hospital to hospital, he had infected 38 other people with smallpox, eight of whom would die as well.

At this time, Yugoslavia was ruled by a Communist dictator named Josip Broz, who called himself "Tito." He used his dictatorial powers to take drastic measures to stop the smallpox outbreak. He declared martial law and the province in which Muzza had lived was blocked off; no one was allowed in or out. People who had been infected were quarantined in special hospitals. Anyone who had come into contact with infected individuals—10,000 people in all—were given smallpox vaccinations and quarantined in hotels, under army guard. Around the country, public events were banned and barbed wire and barricades were used to stop people from traveling—and from spreading the disease. The outbreak died out after a few weeks, and only 35 people died.

Continued on next page ▶

 

## 21st Century Themes Science and Health Literacy

**1.** How was smallpox eradicated from the global population?

**2.** Why did it take so long for doctors to recognize Muzza's disease as smallpox?

**3.** What information in the article indicates that smallpox is spread directly from person to person?

**4.** What drastic measures were taken to control the outbreak?

**5.** In the United States, children are no longer given the smallpox vaccine. Why do you think this is the case?

## 21st Century Skills Controlling an Epidemic

The skills used in this activity include **information and media literacy, communication skills, creativity and intellectual curiosity,** and **social responsibility.**

Epidemic diseases are on people's minds much more today than they were in 1972. Smallpox has been eliminated, but others, such as avian flu and SARS, are possible threats. Your state government most likely has plans in place to deal with possible epidemics or pandemics. If you live in a large city, municipal officials may have been planning as well. Interview the appropriate officials to find out what plans and procedures are in place to protect the public in the event of an epidemic. Then use the information to write a magazine article describing your government's plans.

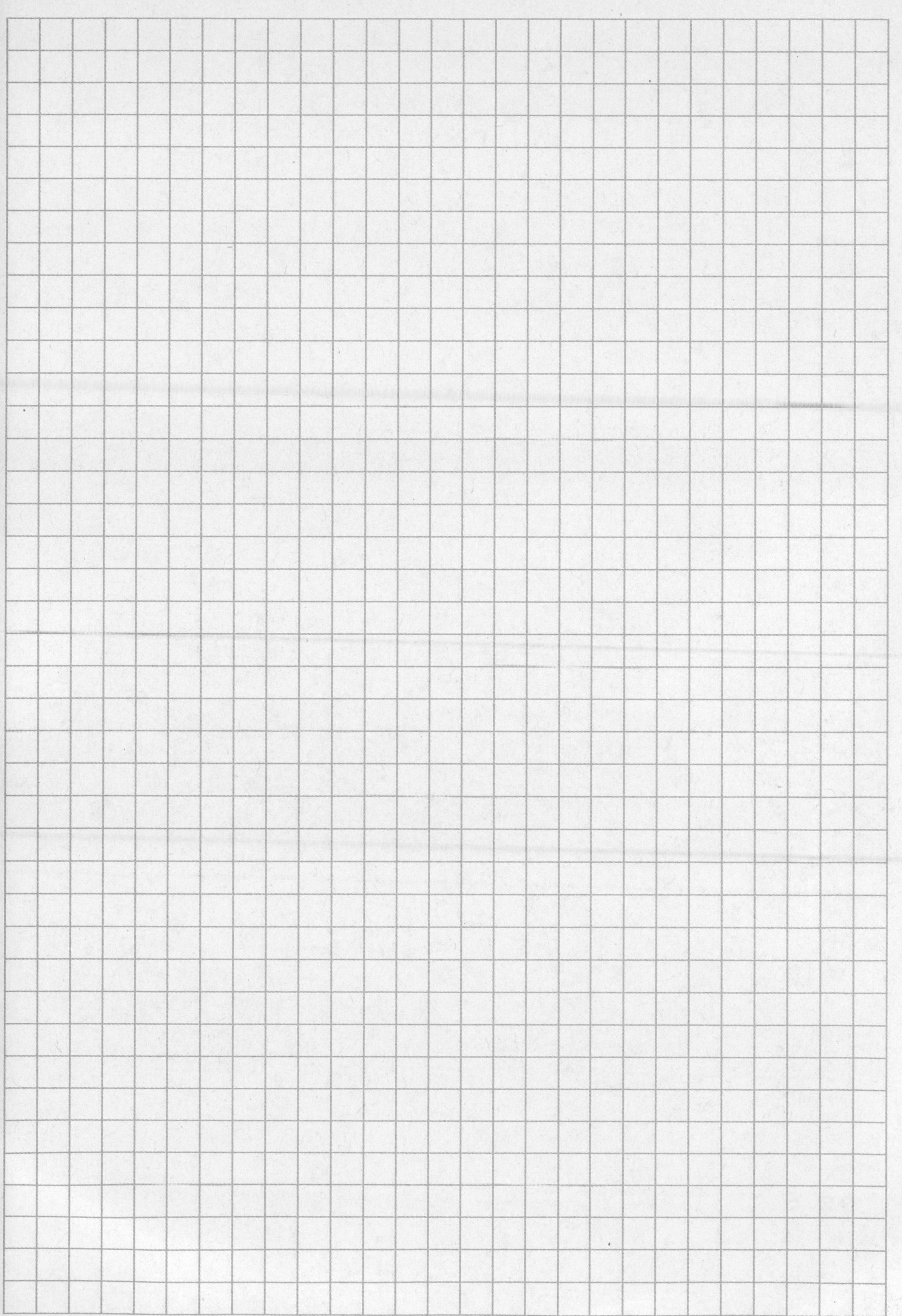

# Human Resource Management at Work

5th edition

Mick Marchington and Adrian Wilkinson
(with Lorrie Marchington for Chapters 9–11)

Chartered Institute of Personnel and Development

Published by the Chartered Institute of Personnel and Development,
151 The Broadway, London, SW19 1JQ

This edition first published 2012



Typeset by Fakenham Prepress Solutions, Fakenham, Norfolk

Printed in Great Britain by Bell & Bain, Glasgow

British Library Cataloguing in Publication Data

A catalogue of this publication is available from the British Library

ISBN 978 1 84398 267 8

Chartered Institute of Personnel and Development, CIPD House,
151 The Broadway, London, SW19 1JQ

Tel: 020 8612 6200

E-mail: cipd@cipd.co.uk

Website: www.cipd.co.uk

Incorporated by Royal Charter.

Registered Charity No. 1079797

# Contents

# Acknowledgements

It is always difficult when writing a book of this size to acknowledge all the support that has been given to make the process work, but listed below are the people with whom we have worked most closely during the last few years. We have both been fortunate to receive grants from a wide range of funding bodies and these have provided much of the data used in this book. We would therefore like to mention grants from The Economic and Social Research Council, The Department of Trade and Industry, The Department of Health, The European Regional Development Fund, The Australian Research Council, The Society of Human Resource Management, The Nuffield Foundation and The Chartered Institute of Personnel and Development.

We are both immensely lucky to have worked with such good colleagues at Manchester Business School (and before the merger in 2004 at the Manchester School of Management at UMIST), and in Adrian's case at Loughborough University Business School and at Griffith University Business School. Special thanks go to co-researchers at Manchester, especially to Jill Rubery, Damian Grimshaw and Gail Hebson, and to Fang Lee Cooke and Annette Cox who used to work there but have now moved on to other organisations, and to Peter Ackers and Stewart Johnstone at Loughborough. We are also particularly grateful to Anastasia Kynighou, an ex PhD student at Manchester, for her contribution to the thinking behind Chapter 5.

Lorrie Marchington has once again been prominently involved in the production of the manuscript, not only pulling together the references but also leading the writing of several chapters, as we note in the book. Her contribution has been significant. Perhaps the book has had an impact on Mick and Lorrie's family: Jack works in HR following a CIPD-accredited Masters in HRM and is married to Vic who is a Fellow of the CIPD, whilst after her degree Lucy opted for marketing instead – c'est la vie! At Adrian's end, Erin and Aidan are still working out whether HRM is the path to follow…

*Mick Marchington*
*Adrian Wilkinson*
*Manchester and Brisbane, November 2011*

# Acronyms and weblinks

| | |
|---|---|
| Acas | Advisory, Conciliation and Arbitration Service |
| AMO | ability, motivation and opportunity |
| BCG | Boston Consulting Group |
| BPS | British Psychological Society |
| BRIC | Brazil, Russia, India and China |
| CAC | Central Arbitration Committee |
| CBI | Confederation of British Industry |
| CEO | Chief Executive Officer |
| CIPD | Chartered Institute of Personnel and Development |
| CME | co-ordinated market economy |
| CPD | continuing professional development |
| CPI | Californian Psychological Inventory |
| CR | cost reduction |
| DB | defined benefit |
| DBIS | Department for Business, Innovation and Skills |
| DC | defined contribution |
| DOCAS | deduction of contributions at source |
| DTI | Department for Trade and Industry – now known as DBIS Department for Business, innovation and skills |
| DWP | Department for Work and Pensions |
| Ebacc | English Baccalaureate |
| EBHR | evidence-based HR |
| EDAP | Employee Development and Assistance Programme |
| EHRC | Equality and Human Rights Commission |
| EI | employee involvement |
| EIF | Employer Investment Fund |
| EIP | employee involvement and participation |
| EMA | Educational Maintenance Allowance |
| ESOL | English for speakers of other languages |
| ETUI | European Trade Union Institute |
| EU | European Union |
| EWC | European Works Councils |
| FE | further education |
| FTE | full-time equivalent |
| GDP | gross domestic product |
| HE | higher education |
| HMC | high commitment management |
| HPW | high performance working |
| HQ | headquarters |
| HRD | human resource development |
| HRIS | human resource information system |
| HRMJ | Human Resource Management Journal |
| HSE | Health and Safety Executive |
| I/C | individualism/collectivism |
| ICE | Information and Consultation Regulations |
| ICER | Information and Consultation Regulations |
| ICT | Information and Communication Technology |
| IiP | Investors in People |
| ILO | International Labour Organisation |
| IPA | Involvement and Participation Association |
| IPRP | individual performance related pay |
| JCC | joint consultative committee |
| KPI | key performance indicators |

| | |
|---|---|
| KRA | key results areas |
| L&D | learning and development |
| LEP | Local Enterprise Partnership |
| LME | liberal market economy |
| LMX | leader–member exchange |
| LSC | Learning and Skills Councils |
| LSN | Learning Skills Network |
| M/F | masculinity/femininity index (Hofstede) |
| MNC | multinational corporation |
| NAS | National Apprenticeship Service |
| NEET | not in employment, education or training |
| NFU | National Farmers Union |
| NGO | non-governmental organisation |
| NHS | National Health Service |
| NMW | National Minimum Wage |
| NQF | National Qualification Framework |
| NVQ | national vocational qualification |
| OECD | Organisation for Economic Co-operation and Development |
| OPQ | Occupational Personality Questionnaire |
| PAQ | Position Analysis Questionnaire |
| PBR | payment by results |
| PD | Power distance |
| PDI | Power distance index (Hofstede) |
| PEF | private equity firms |
| PM | performance management |
| PR | public relations |
| PRP | performance-related pay |
| QCF | Qualifications and Credit Framework |
| QE | quality enhancement |
| RBV | resource-based view |
| ROI | Return on Investment |
| SHRM | Society for Human Resource Management |
| SME | small and medium-sized enterprises |
| SSC | Shared Service Centres |
| SWOT | strengths weaknesses opportunities and threats |
| TQM | total quality management |
| TUC | Trades Union Congress |
| TUPE | Transfer of Undertaking Protection of Employment |
| UA | uncertainty avoidance index (Hofstede) |
| UK | United Kingdom |
| UKCES | UK Commission for Employment and Skills |
| ULF | Union Learning Fund |
| ULR | Union Learning Representative |
| UN | United Nations |
| VET | vocational education and training |
| VPS | variable pay systems |
| WAIS | Wechsler's Adult Intelligence Scale |
| WERS | Workplace Employment Relations Survey |
| WPS | Work Profiling System |

Websites:
www.acas.org.uk Advisory, Conciliation and Arbitration Service
www.equalityhumanrights.com Equality and Human Rights Commission
www.hse.gov.uk
www.investorsinpeople.co.uk
www.neweconomics.org The New Economic Foundation
www.oecd.org
www.UnionLearn.org.uk

# Introduction to this edition

Readers of previous editions of this book will notice quite a lot of changes in the 5th edition of *HRM at Work*. The substantive changes are designed to increase the appeal of the book to wider audiences especially at final-year undergraduate and postgraduate levels. However, the book remains ideal for students on CIPD awarded and approved programmes; that is, irrespective of whether they are on a programme overseen by the CIPD External Moderation Team or via an independent Masters course that is approved by CIPD. *HRM at Work* provides essential underpinning skills, knowledge and understanding to help embed learning across the compulsory and optional modules covered by the CIPD qualification structure at Advanced Level.

The organisation of chapters has been revised for this edition, partly to include chapters dedicated to international and comparative HRM, and HRM and performance, but also to allow more coverage of the role of HR professionals and line managers. These changes recognise key developments in the field, as well as its increasingly global character. Some chapters have additional components, again to acknowledge differences in how HRM is understood in practice. For example, sections are now included on topics such as talent management, leadership, knowledge management and employee engagement, and we try to show how these relatively new terms integrate with existing material in HRM. Some are little more than old wine in new bottles, using language that is felt to be more exciting than used previously. Yet, others do add something to HRM; engagement looks at how employees perceive their involvement at work and talent management focuses more specifically on how organisations can get the best out of their staff. At the same time, some of these terms are potentially elitist, looking to segment workers between those seen as core to the business versus those regarded as less important. This pays little regard to the role that 'ordinary' employees – such as check out staff, production operatives, truck drivers and waiters – play in the achievement and reinforcement of competitive advantage. The key point is that HRM is not simply a unitarist management philosophy but is contested at the workplace through both formal and informal means.

The first part of the book is on HRM, Strategy and the Global Context. It addresses the multiple meanings of HRM, business and corporate strategy and corporate social responsibility, and the context within which HRM operates, both at a national and a global level. It argues that HRM is shaped by a range of forces internal and external to organisations – such as globalisation, labour markets, patterns of employment, and the legal and institutional framework within which choices about HRM are made. This part of the book also reviews the principal theoretical underpinnings of HRM via the distinction between universal, contingency and resource-based views, and it questions the notion that HRM is converging across nations through an examination of home and host country effects on the HR practices of MNCs and a review of the main cultural and institutional frameworks operating in different countries. In each of these chapters, but especially Chapter 5, readers will find many more examples from different countries than were available in earlier editions of this book.

Part Two of *HRM at Work* comprises two chapters analysing the roles of HR professionals and line managers, as these groups are central to the way in which HRM policies and practices are developed and enacted in the workplace. Irrespective of how HRM is meant to work, gaps typically appear between intention, implementation and perception because intended policies may be unrealistic or not capable of being implemented in some countries/ sectors; line managers feel so pressurised by other commitments that they fail to take HRM seriously; and workers resist management plans since they challenge existing cultures and/or undermine fairness at work. HR is no longer totally or even primarily an internal function but increasingly outsourced to other organisations, something which further complicates HRM at work. However, the HR function is often measured against criteria that are developed by other managers, and reflect frameworks that privilege short-term financial returns above longer-term sustainability of organisations and their people.

The third part of the book is the largest, covering the main practice areas of HRM. We focus on resourcing and talent management – which includes HR planning, recruitment and selection; performance management; vocational education, training and skills; learning and development and knowledge management; employment relations; EIP, engagement and voice; and reward management. These chapters provide a critical analysis of HRM and essential guidance about how it works in practice, both in terms of academic underpinnings and contemporary organisational examples. We provide readers with a substantial understanding of these areas that can be used as a base for more in-depth treatments of each topic. These chapters combine a mixture of survey results and empirical research, and at all times readers are expected to draw conclusions about how HRM operates under very different employment regimes – say, between the public and private sectors, manufacturing and service, and small and large firms, as well as between different countries.

The final part of *HRM at Work* examines HRM and performance from a business perspective, and on the impact that HRM can have on business outcomes, as well as on employee attitudes and behaviours. This reviews research in the area, looking beyond statistical studies on HR practices to review HR processes and alignment, integration and consistency. The final chapter reviews research methods used in project work, using the framework in the CIPD *Investigating a Business Issue from an HR perspective* module. It offers a concise guide for final-year undergraduates and postgraduates doing a dissertation or project – whether or not they are studying for CIPD.

The pedagogical features of the book have been further enhanced in this edition. We have inserted reflective activities into the text to give readers an opportunity to review their understanding of the material, undertake exercises that require consolidation and extension of their reading, or engage in groupwork about major issues in HRM. Recommendations for further reading are provided in the form of book chapters, refereed journal articles, professional magazines and surveys. It is essential readers keep up to date with annual surveys to collect data about the extensiveness of particular techniques, as well as guidance about how these work in practice. The bibliography lists many sources for consolidating learning, but this needs to be updated by readers each year. A complete list of acronyms is provided, as well as relevant weblinks to aid further research.

The webpages accompanying the book provide a source of further information and advice to readers. Lecturers can download sets of PowerPoint slides that can help them plan sessions and enhance student learning by integrating the book and the web support. In addition, there are short introductions to how each chapter might be used and suggestions for how the mini-questions might be addressed. At the same time, we do not assume that our answers cover every possible explanation, and it is a key element of study at this level that students engage with and explore alternative solutions. After all, CIPD students are expected to act as 'thinking performers' and it goes without saying that final-year undergraduates and postgraduates should critically analyse everything they do. Our whole philosophy, which has been exemplified in each successive edition of the book, is that readers should continually review and question what is written about and what happens at work so that they improve organisational practice.

It is only by integrating the best of academic work with how HRM works in practice that gains will be made; please read and enjoy the book with this in mind.

# How to use this book

For Masters and final-year undergraduate students studying HRM as a core module, the book can quite easily be used sequentially, or readers can dip into each chapter as they stand alone as well as being part of an integrated manuscript.

Chapter 1 provides a clear discussion of the multiple meanings of HRM, the relationship between strategy and HRM, and the value of seeing strategy in terms of multiple stakeholders. This offers a very good introduction both to the subject and to how it fits with wider organisational objectives.

Chapter 2 provides a summary of the major forces shaping HRM, and this may usefully supplement ideas they have picked up from other modules on their degree. It explains clearly that institutional forces shape, but do not determine, HRM at work. There is a substantial amount of material here about globalisation, labour markets and employment relations, flexibility and employment issues across organisational boundaries, and about the role played by the law and other institutions.

In Chapters 3–5 we focus more explicitly on the principal theoretical frameworks used in HRM – the universalist high commitment paradigm, the contingency best-fit approach and the resource-based view of the firm; all of these are presented as alternative ways in which to understand the link between strategy and HRM at work. The final chapter in this section examines international and comparative HRM, and addresses key issues concerning cultural and institutional perspectives, arguments supporting convergence and divergence, and the balance between home and host country factors in HRM in MNCs. This chapter could go earlier or later in the course depending on its nature and the composition of the student body. Whilst this chapter focuses explicitly on HRM in different countries, international examples and research are peppered throughout the entire book. This section of the book also raises issues that are developed and expanded at an operational level throughout the remainder of the book – issues to do with staffing, resourcing and performance management, issues relating to learning and development, to employee relations and to reward management. These three chapters form the core of the book and they need to be understood before students embark on a more detailed analysis of specific aspects of HRM so that they are able to understand the context in which specific HR practices operate.

Chapters 6 and 7 consider who has responsibility for HRM, and examines the distinctive roles played by HR professionals and line managers, as well as reviewing alternative forms of HR service delivery through external consultants and shared service operations. We also devote several pages to discussing notions of leadership, and rather than adopting the simplistic and celebratory view taken in many books on this topic we provide a more critical evaluation of whether or not leadership really is that different from management. These chapters follow on quite naturally from the earlier chapters, but some lecturers and students may prefer to leave these until later and use them to review the role of HR professionals and line managers once they have a better understanding of detailed HR practices. They also fit well with Chapter 15 on HRM and performance.

Depending on the length of the module and its principal focus, students may find that some of the following chapters (8–14) are more useful than others and lecturers may decide to spend more time on specific aspects of HRM – such as recruitment or training – than others. Alternatively, lecturers may decide the best way to use the book is as a basis for covering all components of HRM. Apart from the regular updating that is essential for any textbook, there is also new material in each of these chapters when compared with the 4th edition. For example, new sections are included in:

- Chapter 8 on talent management
- Chapter 9 on performance management standards around the globe
- Chapter 10 on the importance of VET in its international context
- Chapter 11 on knowledge management
- Chapter 13 on employee engagement and informal EIP.

The final two chapters (15 and 16) could fit at any place in the curriculum, and indeed in the past material on HRM and performance (Chapter 15) was included with high commitment HRM. We have placed it towards the end of the book on this occasion to act as a summing-up for the main substantive chapters on HRM in the book. While this analyses how HRM can contribute to business performance, this chapter also considers how HRM is linked with wider societal objectives such as fairness, equity, social exclusion and the contribution of people as citizens. Chapter 16, on research and project management, is important for any student doing a project or dissertation.

Students on CIPD approved and awarded qualifications will find the book useful for many of the modules. The first seven chapters and Chapter 15 are especially helpful for people studying *HRM in Context: Strategy, Insights and Solutions*, whilst the whole book provides significant coverage for the *Leading, Managing and Developing People* module. Chapter 16, in particular, is essential for those undertaking a project in the *Investigating a Business Issue from a Business Perspective* module, and depending on the topic, other chapters will offer a comprehensive analysis and guide to relevant research in the area. Individual chapters also offer a concise overview of many of the other optional modules available for CIPD candidates; for example, Chapter 8 addresses the key issues for *Resourcing and Talent Management*, Chapter 9 is ideal for *Performance Management*, Chapters 10 and 11 fit well with *Learning and Talent Development*; *Designing, Delivering and Evaluating Learning and Development Provision*; and *Knowledge Management and Organisational Learning*. Chapter 12 covers the main issues in *Managing Employment Relations*, Chapter 13 *Employee Engagement*, and Chapter 14 *Reward Management*. In other words, this edition of *HRM at Work* addresses the key issues raised across most parts of the CIPD qualification structure at Advanced Level within the confines of one book.

Broadly, *HRM at Work* offers a comprehensive, analytical and systematic text to cater for the needs of students in the final year of their undergraduate studies as well as those on postgraduate courses, irrespective of whether or not they are taking CIPD examinations nationally or one that has been approved to assess locally. It deals with all the main issues and its focus throughout encourages a critical awareness of HRM. Throughout the text there are reflective activities to check understanding. Tables provide further information, as do boxes, many of which contain case studies to show how HRM works in practice in a wide variety of different settings. The cases are drawn from a range of countries. Each chapter includes a set of useful readings and the extensive bibliography provides students with pointers to further reading, as well as those that are central to the particular topic in hand. At this level, students must not rely on a textbook alone, however. It is essential they read journals to see how research is developing, visit websites and official sources of information for updating their knowledge, and engage in discussion with other class members. To achieve M-level understanding, they must eschew simple models and ideas, and consistently question both their own ideas and those of others, paying particular attention to the methods used to collect data as well as the results of research. Only by doing this are they likely to achieve an effective grounding in HRM.

# Book Map

CHAPTER 1

## HRM, strategy and the global context

LEARNING OUTCOMES

By the end of this chapter, readers should be able to:

- advise senior managers about how to recognise and respond to a wide range of stakeholder influences on business and HR strategies to enhance organisational and individual performance
- demonstrate an ethical and professional approach to HRM taking into account its multiple meanings
- contribute to recommendations about how organisations manage HR both in the UK and overseas.

In addition, readers should understand and be able to explain:

- the competing meanings of the term 'strategy', and their implications for HRM
- the nature and importance of ethics, professionalism and diversity and their contribution to the business and moral case for HRM
- the basis on which HR policies are established in multinational organisations due to the influence of home- and host-country factors.

INTRODUCTION

HRM is now often seen as the major factor differentiating between successful and unsuccessful organisations, more important than technology or finance in achieving competitive advantage. This is particularly pertinent in the service sector where workers are the primary source of contact with customers, either face-to-face in a service encounter or over the telephone or the Internet. Even in manufacturing firms the way in which human resources are managed is seen as an increasingly critical component in the production process, primarily in terms of quality and reliability. Much of this revolves around the extent to which workers are prepared to use their discretion to improve products and services. In this argument a particular style of HRM is envisaged: one that can be broadly termed the 'high commitment' model.

## Learning outcomes

Helps the student focus their learning and evaluate their progress.

Changing responsibilities for HRM 189

HRM AT WORK IN FOCUS

### Driving change through HR business partners

The Department for Work and Pensions (DWP) was formed in 2001. At the time of writing the review, the DWP employed 130,000 staff in a complex organisational structure, and in total had about 5,500 staff working on HR-related issues (a ratio of 1:24). A significant number of these staff were not officially located in HR, providing administrative support locally for dispersed units, and this made it virtually impossible to provide an integrated service across the whole business. The HR leadership team decided that organisation of the HR function was in need of major reform and that they should move to a ratio of 1:50 across the DWP.

The HR modernisation programme encompassed a wide range of activities, such as:

- developing the expertise and professionalism of HR
- implementing an effective shared services operation with direct access to allow use by line managers and staff
- introducing a new IT-enabled blended learning environment
- simplifying the HR policy framework to make it accessible to line managers
- aligning people with the business.

A key component in the change programme was the introduction of business partners who were expected, amongst other things, to focus on business goals at both a local and a strategic level, be agents for change, act as a figurehead for a more expert HR function, and improve HR service delivery through line managers. Having decided on the need for business partners, major questions arose about who would fill these posts. The Civil Service was not short of home-grown talent, but equally it was felt that the DWP could not rely solely on internal provision. Eventually, 25% of the business partners were brought in from external labour market, so inducting and socialising this group inevitably took time, as did the setting up of close working relations and effective teams.

Two years after the business partner model was implemented, the DWP was happy to note that both line managers and HR business partners felt the change had moved a long way towards the original goals, and that HR was now seen as being more aligned to business requirements as well as more accessible and more expert. Not surprisingly, there was still some way to go, particularly in relation to the operation of the shared services centres, the implementation of blended learning and the degree of understanding of how HR can support line managers. Nevertheless the Group HR director feels the business partner revolution has been worthwhile.

Ulrich's ideas have now been in the public domain sufficiently long to allow more independent analysis of whether or not they improve the HR contribution to business goals. How realistic is it to assume that HR managers have the power or the influence to have a major impact on business performance? The respondents to Guest and King's (2004) study (p.420), typically senior HR managers, were somewhat reluctant to beat their way into the boardroom 'armed only with rhetoric about people as the key resource, somewhat ambiguous evidence

## HRM at Work in focus

Provides additional information, research and case studies. Case studies give practical, real-life situations as a way of putting theory into its practical contexts. They are taken from a wide range of organisations, including public, private and voluntary sectors, manufacturing and service industries and from various countries.

Staffing and resourcing the organisation 237

REFLECTIVE ACTIVITY

Do job descriptions still exist in your organisation or one with which you are familiar?

If detailed job descriptions still exist, how well do they work?

If they have been abandoned, has it led to greater autonomy or greater stress?

Whereas *job descriptions* relate to the tasks to be undertaken, *person specifications* outline the human attributes seen as necessary to do the job. The best-known are the seven-point plan (Rodger, 1952) and its later adaptation by Fraser (1966) in the form of the five-point plan. These describe and categorise the principal features required for any job, with a differentiation between aspects that are essential to perform the job and those that, in an ideal world, are desirable. The two methods are outlined in the box below.

HRM AT WORK IN FOCUS

### A traditional view of person specifications

Rodger's seven-point plan

- *Physical make-up*: physical attributes such as the ability to lift heavy loads or differentiate between colours
- *Attainments*: educational or professional qualifications considered necessary for undertaking the work
- *General intelligence*: the ability to define and solve problems, and use initiative in dealing with issues that have arisen
- *Special aptitudes*: skills, attributes or competencies that are specifically relevant to the particular job
- *Interests*: both work-related and leisure pursuits that may be relevant to performance in the job
- *Disposition*: attitudes to work and to other members of staff and customers, as well as friendliness and assertiveness
- *Circumstances*: domestic commitments, mobility and family support.

Fraser's five-point plan

- *Impact on others*: this covers much the same sort of issues as 'physical make-up' but it is more focused on impact on other employees and customers
- *Acquired knowledge and qualifications*: see Rodger's second category above
- *Innate abilities*: see 'General intelligence' above
- *Motivation*: a person's desire to succeed in particular aspects of work and their commitment to achieve these goals
- *Adjustment*: characteristics specifically related to the job, such as the ability to cope with difficult customers or work well in a team.

## Reflective activities

These questions and activities are designed to get students reflecting critically on the topics covered and self-testing their learning progress.

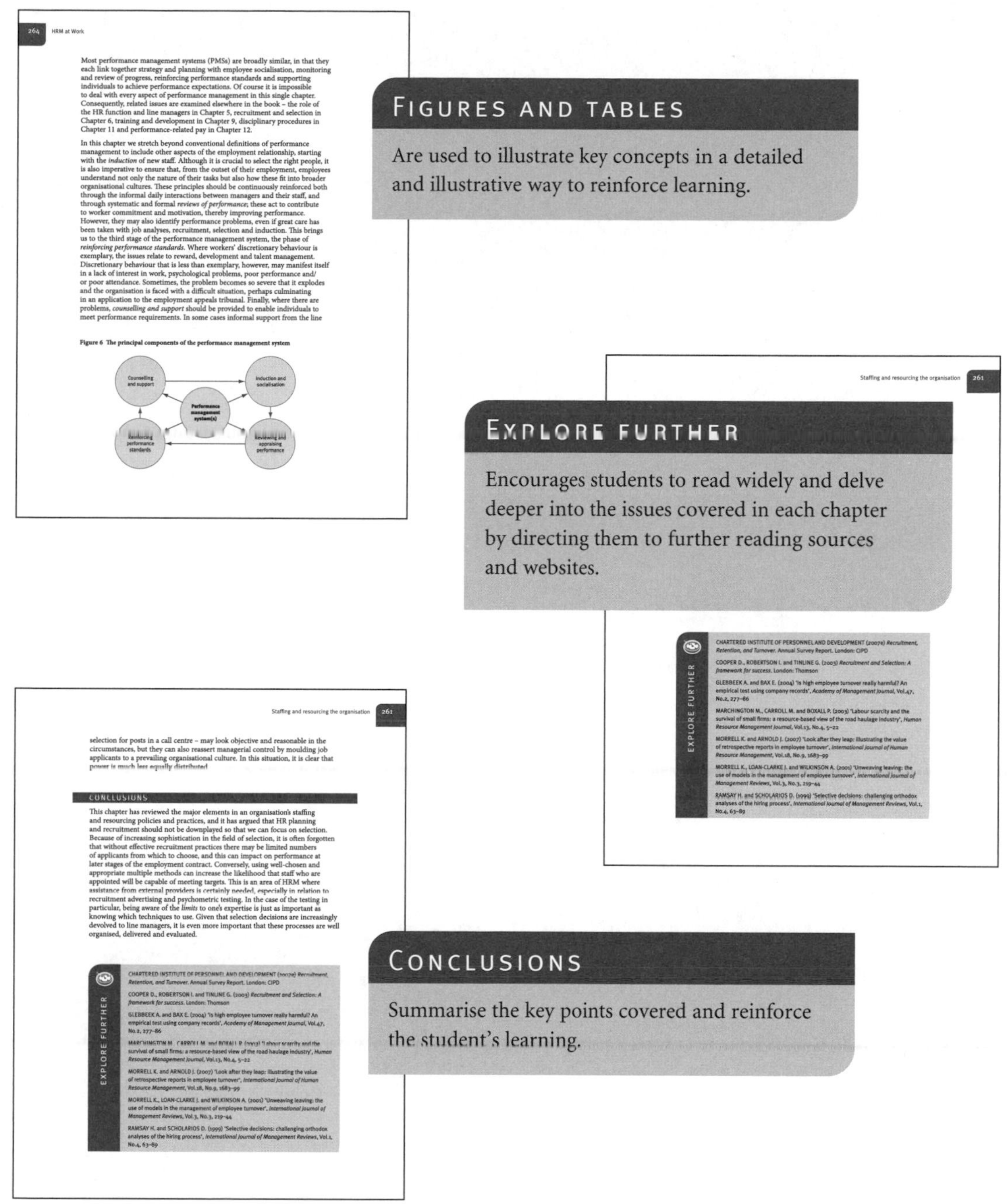

FIGURES AND TABLES
Are used to illustrate key concepts in a detailed and illustrative way to reinforce learning.
EXPLORE FURTHER
Encourages students to read widely and delve deeper into the issues covered in each chapter by directing them to further reading sources and websites.
CONCLUSIONS
Summarise the key points covered and reinforce the student's learning.


## References

A comprehensive list of references at the end of the book pulls together the main works cited in each chapter and encourages students to build on their knowledge.

## Companion Website

Comprehensive and interactive websites for students and tutors include a range of features such as lecture notes to help guide students through the book and develop their understanding. Go to www.cipd.co.uk/OLR

PART 1

# HRM, STRATEGY AND THE GLOBAL CONTEXT

CHAPTER 1

# HRM, Strategy and Corporate Social Responsibility

## LEARNING OUTCOMES

By the end of this chapter, readers should be able to:

- advise senior managers about how to recognise and respond to stakeholder influences on business and HR strategies to enhance organisational and individual performance
- advise managers as to how HR strategies can link with broader corporate strategies
- demonstrate an ethical and professional approach to HRM taking into account its multiple meanings.

In addition, readers should understand and be able to explain:

- the competing meanings of HRM, and their implications for managing people
- how strategy is conceptualised and its role in shaping patterns of HRM
- the nature and importance of ethics, professionalism and diversity and their contribution to the business and moral case for HRM.

## INTRODUCTION

HRM became a fashionable term from the mid-1980s in the UK and began to replace other terms such as 'personnel management'. Much of the interest was around the idea of HRM as a new and distinctive approach, attempting to develop and utilise the potential of human resources to the full in pursuit of the organisation's strategic objectives (Storey 2001; Redman and Wilkinson 2012) and led to talk of an HRM revolution. But HRM – as the management of employment – can take many forms in practice and it may vary between organisations and the occupational group that is targeted. HRM cannot be analysed in isolation from the wider strategic objectives of employers and measured against these, specifically the need to satisfy shareholders, or (in the public sector) government and societal demands for efficiency and effectiveness.

However, strategy is also a multidimensional concept and, despite common usage of the term, it is more complex than the simple military analogy implies. Strategies emerge within organisations rather than being set merely by senior managers (generals) and cascaded down the hierarchy by more junior managers to the workers (the troops). Moreover, strategies are also influenced by wider societal objectives, legislative and political frameworks, social and economic institutions, and a range of different stakeholder interests. Strategy is not simply about financial returns to shareholders but also involves a rather wider base of stakeholders that includes customers, local communities, the environment, and of course workers. HRM differs from other managerial functions because of its professional and moral base, so trust and integrity are important elements in how HRM is practised at work. Hence, the interest in corporate social responsibility and the idea that HRM has to be viewed in relation to organisational strategies and wider institutional forces.

## THE MEANINGS OF HUMAN RESOURCE MANAGEMENT

'People are our most valued asset' has become a very common but rather overused and trite sounding phrase (Snell *et al* 2002). Indeed, historically competitive strategies have not been based on the capabilities of employees but rather labour has been seen as a cost to be minimised, particularly in hard times when downsizing and retrenchment predominates (Cascio 2009; Mellahi and Wilkinson 2010). But more recently it has been noted that traditional sources of advantage such as access to capital, protected markets, or proprietary technologies are declining and organisations need to have the ability to innovate and learn, which puts greater emphasis on human resources (Wilkinson *et al* 2009). HRM is now often seen as the major factor differentiating between successful and unsuccessful organisations, and is considered more important than technology or finance in achieving competitive advantage. This is particularly pertinent in the service sector where workers are the primary source of contact with customers, either face-to-face in a service encounter or over the telephone or the Internet. Even in manufacturing firms, the way in which human resources are managed is seen as an increasingly critical component in the production process, primarily in terms of quality and reliability. Much of this revolves around the extent to which workers are prepared to use their discretion to improve products and services. In this argument a particular style of HRM is envisaged, one that can be broadly termed the 'high commitment' model (see Chapter 3).

Wilkinson *et al* (2009, pp.4–6) argue that HRM can be seen as having:

(a) *A human focus*. The focus on employee rights and well-being is evident in the history of HRM. That focus can be seen in the current emphasis on work design, work–life balance and equality and diversity, all of which are covered. At its core, HRM focuses on managing the employment relationship and agreements (implicit and explicit) between individuals and organisations. In some cases – as we see in Chapter 6 – HR plays the role of employee advocate in ensuring the equitable treatment of employees in order to ensure that the interests of employees as well as the organisation are protected.

(b) *A resource focus*. HRM focuses on employees as a resource in enhancing the performance of the organisation. We examine HR practices that are linked to productivity and enhancing the competitiveness of the firm by ensuring the organisation acquires employees with the ability and motivation to perform via recruitment and selection approaches, and builds capabilities by training and development and performance management. From a more macro perspective, a resource focus of HRM addresses the set of practices for managing the aggregate of human capital in organisations. Much of this literature is informed by the resource-based view of organisations (Boselie and Paauwe 2009).

(c) *A management focus*. In recent years there has been much focus on how the HR function has evolved. While the earliest roles of HR managers emerged from the administrative and transactional requirements of employment issues, the contemporary setting requires HR managers to adopt a more strategic approach that focuses on managing change, building organisational culture, and becoming a partner in the business. This requires a different set of skills, knowledge, and behaviours of HR managers.

As Morris and Snell note (2009, p.85) it is not just HR scholars that are calling for a stronger focus on the human resources inside the firm and how they are managed, but mainstream strategy scholars are also beginning to acknowledge that they need to focus on 'micro-level' factors; the value proposition of a firm is seen as relying more on knowledge and service activities, and so strategic management depends very much on what people know and how they behave. As Morris and Snell note, because no other resource possessed by a firm has free will or heterogeneity of ideas, products and services often originate in individuals making human resources, and how they are managed is a potentially unique source of strategic leverage. The increase in differentiated workforces poses added cultural, geographical and competency gaps (Becker and Huselid 2009).

HRM is still a relatively new area of study that is seeking to gain credibility in comparison with more established academic disciplines – such as economics, psychology, sociology and law – which have a much longer history. HRM is often contrasted with industrial relations and personnel management, with the former laying claim to represent the theoretical basis of the subject while the latter is viewed as the practical and prescriptive homeland for issues concerning the management of people. In addition, there are so many variants of HRM it is easy to find slippage in its use, especially when critics are comparing the apparent *rhetoric* of 'high commitment' HRM with the so-called *reality* of life in organisations that manage by fear and cost-cutting. Similarly, HRM often attracts criticism because it can never fully satisfy business imperatives nor the drive for employee well-being. As the remainder of the book explores issues such as these in depth, we focus here on a brief résumé of the main strands of the subject. In the concluding section of the chapter we outline what we see as the main components of HRM.

## THE ORIGINS OF HRM IN THE USA

There is little doubt that the HRM terminology originated in the USA subsequent to the human relations movement (Kaufman 2010). According to Kaufman (2007, pp.33–4), the term first appeared in the textbook literature from the mid-1960s, specifically in relation to the specialist function which was interchangeably termed 'personnel' or 'human resources'. What really helped HRM to take root a couple of decades later, however, was the Harvard framework developed by Beer *et al* (1985). Here, HRM was contrasted with 'personnel' and 'industrial relations'; the latter were conceptualised as reactive, piecemeal, part of a command-and-control agenda, and short-term in nature, whilst HRM was seen as proactive, integrative, part of an employee commitment perspective and long-term in focus. In line with this perspective, human resources were seen as an asset and not a cost. The Harvard framework consists of six basic components. These are:

1 *situational factors*, such as workforce characteristics, management philosophy and labour market conditions, which combine to shape the environment within which organisations operate

2 *stakeholder interests*, such as the compromises and trade-offs that occur between the owners of the enterprise and its employees and the unions. This makes the Beer *et al* framework much less unitarist than some of the other models (Bratton and Gold 2007, p.23)

3 *HRM policy choices*, in the areas of employee influence, HR flow, reward systems and work systems. Employee influence is seen as the most important of these four areas, again making this model somewhat different from some other versions of HRM

4 *HR outcomes*, in terms of what are termed the '4Cs' – commitment, competence, cost effectiveness and congruence. This incorporates issues connected with trust, motivation and skills, and it is argued that greater employee influence in the affairs of the company is likely to foster greater congruence (Beer *et al* 1985, p.37)

5 *long-term consequences,* such as individual well-being, organisational effectiveness and societal goals. Unlike many other models of HRM, this framework is explicit in recognising the role that employers play in helping to achieve wider societal goals such as employment and growth

6 *a feedback loop,* which is the final component in the framework, demonstrating that it is not conceived as a simple, unilinear set of relationships between the different components.

A key feature of the Harvard approach is that it treats HRM as an entire system, and it is the combination of HR practices that is important. As Allen and Wright (2007, p.91) note, 'this led to a focus on how the different HRM sub-functions could be aligned and work together to accomplish the goals of HRM'. This issue is taken up in detail in Chapter 3, and is often referred to as *horizontal* alignment or integration. Whilst acknowledging the role for alternative stakeholder interests – including government and the community – this framework is essentially positivist because it assumes a dominant direction of influence from broader situational and stakeholder interests through to HR outcomes and long-term consequences. In reality, the relationship is much more complex and fragmented as employers are unable to make policy choices in such a structured way, especially if they operate in networks of firms up and down supply chains or across national boundaries.

The other main school of thought which developed in the USA was the matching model (Fombrun *et al* 1984). This emphasises the links between organisational strategy and specific HR practices, concentrating on *vertical* rather than horizontal alignment. The HR practices are categorised into selection, development, appraisal and reward. The human resource cycle – as the four components are known – are tied together in terms of how effectively they deliver improved performance. In Devanna *et al*'s (1984, p.41) words:

> Performance is a function of all the HR components: selecting people who are the best able to perform the jobs defined by the structure; appraising their performance to facilitate the equitable distribution of rewards; motivating employees by linking rewards to high levels of performance; and developing employees to enhance their current performance at work as well as to prepare them to perform in positions they may hold in the future.

The focus is on ensuring that there is a 'match' or 'fit' between overall organisational goals and the way in which its people should be managed. The approach to rewards, for example, is expected to vary dependent on strategy; it is suggested that a single-product firm would deal with this in an unsystematic and paternalistic manner, while a diversified firm would operate through large bonuses based on profitability and subjective assessments about contribution to company performance. With regard to selection, the criteria used range from the subjective to the standardised and systematic depending on the strategy and structure of the firm (Devanna *et al* 1984, pp.38–9). It is essentially a unitarist analysis of HRM whereby the management of people is 'read-off' from broader organisational objectives. No account is taken of the interests of different stakeholders nor is there much room for strategic choice. This is considered more fully in Chapter 4. It should be noted at this stage that both these models were derived within the context of developed countries operating within an Anglo-Saxon business environment, thus raising questions about their applicability to very different cultures.

## THE EMERGENCE OF HRM IN THE UK

Interest in HRM in the UK – both as an academic subject and a source of interest for practitioners – developed in the late 1980s, and contributions have come from a plurality

of disciplinary backgrounds. Drawing on Bach and Sisson (2000) and developing their categorisation, it is possible to identify four different traditions:

1 *Prescriptive*: this used to be the dominant approach in the literature, stemming from the domain of personnel management, and it examined and prescribed the 'best' tools and techniques for use by practitioners. It was essentially vocational in character, although the universal prescriptions that were put forward had much greater resonance in large firms with well-staffed personnel functions. In line with the US literature, its underpinning values were essentially unitarist, assuming that workers and employers could work together, wherever possible, to achieve mutual gains within the framework of traditional hierarchical and capitalist relations. Within the prescriptive tradition personnel tended to be seen as an intermediary between the harsher extremes of cost-driven business goals and the needs and motivations of workers.

2 *Labour process*: this contrasted sharply with the benevolent, yet paternalist, image of the prescriptive tradition, and focused on HRM as an implicit or explicit device to control and subjugate labour. Whilst helping, initially at least, to introduce more critical accounts of HRM, and later providing a more nuanced and more subjective understanding of how organisations work, it tended to critique management for everything it did. In the more extreme cases it assumed that managers' sole objective in life was to control and manipulate workers, rather than meet production or service targets laid down by senior management. Whilst the HR function might appear as a human face, according to critics this made it even more dangerous because workers could be conned into meeting targets that essentially only helped the organisation to meet its goals – and ultimately operated to the detriment of workers' objectives.

3 *Industrial relations*: within this tradition, HRM was seen as 'part of a system of employment regulation in which internal and external influences shape the management of the employment relationship' (Bach and Sisson 2000, p.8). Using both detailed case study and quantitative techniques, often from the Workplace Employee Relations Surveys, students have analysed HRM *in practice* in order to develop our understanding of the main elements of the employment relationship. Whilst crucially bringing in a pluralist perspective on HRM, this tended to focus on collective aspects of the employment relationship, and in particular view all forms of employment – including non-union firms – against the template of a unionised environment.

4 *Organisational psychology*: whilst common in the USA, the contribution from this tradition has become more significant in the UK as scholars analyse HR issues connected with selection, appraisal, learning and development, and the psychological contract. As we see throughout this book, this tradition has been at the forefront of studies examining the links between various aspects of HR strategy and practice and employee outcome measures such as commitment and satisfaction. In contradistinction to the industrial relations tradition, this approach tends to downplay notions of conflict and resistance, as well as overlook the realities of HRM at the workplace.

## REFLECTIVE ACTIVITY

What does HRM mean to you?

Is it solely the specialist function or is it part of the role of every manager that has responsibility for supervising staff?

Is it realistic to conceive of HRM as potentially capable of producing mutual gains or is it merely a device to ensnare workers into accepting management plans just because they are delivered with a human face?

Work in groups to consider these questions and the contrasting traditions which underpin HRM.

The British debate initially focused on the distinction between 'hard' and 'soft' models of HRM (Storey 1989; Legge 1995; Redman and Wilkinson 2012). The 'hard' model – as with Fombrun *et al*'s (1984) approach – stresses the links between business and HR strategies and the crucial importance of a tight fit between the two. From this perspective, the human resource is seen as similar to all other resources – land and capital, for example – being used as management sees fit. Under this scenario, which stresses the 'resource' aspect of HRM, there is no pretence that labour has anything other than commodity status even though it may be treated well if the conditions are conducive, that is, when it is in short supply or it is central to the achievement of organisational objectives. Broadly, however, it would downplay the rules of industrial relations – such as procedures for dealing with redundancy – because they reduce employer flexibility to select on the basis of who they think is most/least valuable to the organisation.

By contrast, the 'soft' model focuses on the management of 'resourceful humans', assuming that employees are valued assets and a source of competitive advantage through their skills and abilities. Within this conception of HRM, there is one best way to manage staff, and this requires managers to engender commitment and loyalty in order to ensure high levels of performance. Storey (2001, p.6) defines the soft version in the following way:

> HRM is a distinctive approach to employment management which seeks to achieve competitive advantage through the strategic deployment of a highly committed and capable workforce using an array of cultural, structural and personnel techniques.

Whereas the 'hard' model allows for a range of different styles, the 'soft' variant argues that one style is superior to all others in promoting levels of employee motivation, commitment and satisfaction that are necessary for excellent performance. In short, HRM can be viewed as a particular *style* of managing that is capable of being measured and defined, as well as compared against the template of an ideal model.

The soft/high commitment version of HRM has attracted a lot of interest especially for those seeking links between HRM and performance. Although important at the time, it also stimulated what might now be seen as a series of somewhat sterile debates about whether the management of employment equates more closely with HRM or with industrial relations and personnel management. Storey (1992) compared HRM with personnel management and industrial relations, identifying 27 points of difference between the two in terms of beliefs and assumptions, strategic aspects, line management and key levers. Broadly, HRM – again seen as a distinct style – was regarded as less bureaucratic, more strategic, more integrated with business objectives, and substantially devolved to line managers; the key elements of the HRM model are outlined in the box below.

HRM AT WORK IN FOCUS

## John Storey's model of HRM

*Beliefs and assumptions*

- The human resource gives organisations a competitive edge.
- Employee commitment is more important than mere compliance.
- Careful selection and development are central to HRM.

*Strategic qualities*

- HR decisions are of strategic importance.
- Senior managers must be involved in HRM.
- HR policies need to be integrated into business strategy.

*Critical role for line managers*

- HR is too important to be left to personnel specialists alone.
- Line managers need to be closely involved as delivers and drivers of HR.

- The management of managers is critically important.

*Key levers*

- Managing culture is more important than procedures and systems.
- Horizontal integration between different HR practices is essential.
- Jobs need to be designed to allow devolved responsibility and empowerment.

Source: Adapted from Storey J. (2007, p.9).

It can be seen that a key feature of the Storey model is the role of line managers rather than the HR function, and this makes sense given that HRM is essentially embedded at workplace level in interactions between members of staff (individually or collectively) and their supervisors (Townsend *et al* 2011b). Storey argues that HRM is fundamentally concerned with the *management* of managers, with their training and development, their selection via use of sophisticated techniques, and with their performance management and career development, as opposed to that of the people who work for them (Storey 2007, p.10). Unlike some of the more positive and celebratory accounts of how HRM can make the difference, Storey (2007, p.17) accepts that 'HRM is no panacea; no set of employment practices ever will be. But, as a persuasive account of the logic underpinning choice in certain organisations and as an aspirational pathway for others, it is an idea worthy of examination'. More recent work suggests the search for HRM remains. Guest (2011) concludes that after two decades of extensive research, we are still unable to answer core questions about the relationship between HRM and performance. This is largely the result of limited longitudinal research to address the linkages between HRM and performance via the management of HR implementation. As Guest observes, 'many of the basic questions remain the same and after hundreds of research studies we are still in no position to assert with any confidence that good HRM has an impact on organisation performance' (p.11). For Thompson (2011), mainstream HRM typically pursues a myopic range of issues with little consideration of wider forces, but he equally criticises the agenda of 'critical HRM' for its distorted emphasis on identity and culture.

HRM AT WORK IN FOCUS

## Who needs workers and HRM?

The problem with employees is everything. You have to pay to hire them and you have to pay to fire them, and in between you have to pay them. They arrive with no useful skills, and once you've trained them, they leave. And don't expect gratitude! If they are not taking sick leave, they're requesting compassionate leave. They talk about unions. They want raises. They want management to notice when they do a good job. They want to know what's going to happen in the next corporate reorganisation.

The truly flexible company does not employ people at all. This is the siren song of outsourcing, the seductiveness of the sub-contract. Just try out the words – *no employees*. A company without employees would be a wondrous thing.

The above is adapted from *Company*, by Max Barry (2006), a novel about a hypothetical organisation which does things in different ways, published by Vintage Books, New York. It is a really good book to read to get an alternative view of the HR function and how organisations might operate under a different set of rules.

## THE CONTESTED NATURE OF WORK

Most writers on industrial relations and organisational behaviour see the employment relationship as comprising a mix of conflict *and* co-operation (see, for example, Noon and Blyton 2007; Blyton and Turnbull 2004; Dundon and Rollinson 2011; Wilkinson and Townsend 2011a/b). Both of these are present to differing degrees in different workplaces at any one time, and the balance between them varies over time and between countries. By contrast, it is rare for texts on other aspects of HRM (eg recruitment and selection, learning and development, reward management) to conceive explicitly of the employment relationship in such terms. Instead, discussion of motivation or commitment only tends to consider conflict in terms of management's failure to engender employee attachment to, and engagement with, the organisation. In short, conflict between buyers and sellers of labour is typically compartmentalised as an employee relations issue.

Issues of conflict and co-operation come to a head during industrial action or in collective bargaining between employers and trade unions. But these issues also pervade other aspects of HRM as well. For example, at the recruitment stage, employers increasingly want loyalty and commitment, as well as hard and skilful work, and implicitly assume workers are willing to co-operate with employers – something that is far from guaranteed. It is important to recognise that all aspects of HRM deal with how the employment relationship is negotiated, so discussions of conflict cannot be shunted off into an employee relations branch line.

Given the incompleteness of the employment contract (Cooke *et al* 2004) it is clear that all workers possess some 'tacit skills'; this is knowledge and understanding workers accumulate throughout their lives, which is typically extremely difficult to write down. Tacit skills can be seen in many areas of employment, such as in the ability to hear from the sound of a machine or a car engine that a problem is lurking. Thompson and McHugh (2002, p.187) itemise over 20 detailed activities undertaken by a waiter when taking an order, but even these overlook the less obvious interactive skills that are crucial for the effective completion of this task. Some skills can be copied by watching other people or reading manuals, but others have to be 'learned' through practice or by doing similar jobs, sometimes outside of work. The key thing, however, is that these skills and attributes are actually much more than 'simple common sense'. Tacit skills can be used in a variety of ways. First, they can be employed as a potential weapon against employers, either as part of a collective dispute or as an individual overt or covert response to management action. In these cases workers are using tacit skills and creative energies in order to 'get back' at management (Blyton and Turnbull 2004). Second, tacit skills can be used to make time at work more tolerable, but with no intention of offering employers any more than the basic minimum required to 'get by' at work; this can be seen when workers devise games to keep their minds occupied whilst at work (Burawoy 1979, pp.81–2). Finally, workers may use tacit skills to contribute actively to the achievement of employer goals by 'getting on' at work. This can take several forms, such as working hard to gain promotion, taking on extra responsibilities due to staff shortfalls, or in working hard because this is seen as the 'right' thing to do. The idea of doing a 'good job' – for example, turning out high-quality work or resolving difficult problems – is central to our socialisation and in activities undertaken beyond the workplace (Ackers and Preston 1997).

## REFLECTIVE ACTIVITY

Think about three different types of job that you have either done or about which you have some knowledge. What was the mix of 'getting back', 'getting by' and 'getting on' in these jobs, and what might have been done to increase the likelihood of workers wanting to 'get on'?

## BUSINESS AND CORPORATE STRATEGIES

### THE CLASSICAL PERSPECTIVE

Most definitions of strategy in the business and management field stem initially from the work of Chandler (1962), who argued that the structure of an organisation flowed from its growth strategy. Since then there have been major differences of opinion about the extent to which a strategy is deliberate or emergent, and about the extent to which organisations are able to determine strategies without taking into account wider societal trends and forces, and in particular the economic, legal and political frameworks within the countries in which they are located. Of course, some large multinational companies are able to exercise influence beyond national boundaries, and actually affect the development of policy within countries, but this amount of power is usually reserved for a small number of global players. The reality for most organisations is that strategic choices are shaped by forces beyond their immediate control even if they have room for manoeuvre. Rumelt (2011, p.2) notes that 'despite the roar of voices wanting to equate strategy with ambition, leadership, 'vision', planning or the economic logic of competition, strategy is none of these. The core of strategy is always the same: discovering the critical factors in a situation and designing a way of coordinating and focusing actions to deal with those factors.'

Grant (2010, p.4), in a US text, makes it clear that 'strategy is about winning ... [It] is not a detailed plan or programme of instructions; it is a unifying theme that gives coherence and direction to the actions and decisions of an individual or an organisation'. The best-known British text on the subject (Johnson *et al* 2011, p.22) defines strategy as the long-term direction of an organisation.

Drawing on these two definitions (Grant 2010, pp.7–30; Johnson *et al* 2011, pp.2–26), the principal elements of 'strategy', in the classical sense of the word, are:

1 Establishing the *long-term* direction of the organisation, looking a number of years ahead and attempting to identify the product markets and geographical locations in which the business is most likely to survive and prosper. Goals need to be simple, consistent and long-term, and they need to be pursued with a single-minded commitment. The chosen strategy has clear implications for HR policy and practice, as well as for the types of workers needed in future. Of course, shocks to the system – such as major new inventions, political upheaval or changes in the nature of the working population or demography – may disrupt strategic plans but without them organisations are likely to be rudderless. Shifts in decisions about the long-term direction of an organisation can impact heavily on HRM. For example, a move to manufacture products in a different country has major implications for future employment. Similarly, an influx of migrant workers might provide new sources of highly qualified and/or cheap labour which can lead to changes in the organisation's goals.

2 Driving the organisation forward to achieve *sustained competitive advantage*. This may emerge through the creation of new products or services or in providing better value in a way that can be sustained, even if competitors also take advantage of similar gains or move

in other equally or more profitable directions. In HR terms this may lead to decisions about whether higher levels of performance are more likely from a quality enhancement or innovation route, or one that focuses almost exclusively on cost reduction. This has implications for the type of labour that is required in the organisation, and in situations where there is a shortage of skills it may prevent employers attaining their overall goals. Moreover, as Boxall and Purcell (2008, p.37) note, other organisations do not stand still but also adapt continuously to achieve their own competitive advantage. This means that staying ahead of the game is critical.

3 Determining the *scope* of the organisation's activities, in terms of whether it chooses to remain primarily in one sector and line of business or diversify into other areas. This can be done so as to spread risk by creating a balanced portfolio or seeking success from growing markets and higher profit margin products. Decisions are also required to determine geographical market coverage. Each of these different strategies has HR implications, for example in terms of the type of staff required or the extent to which services are provided by in-house personnel or subcontracted labour. Decisions concerning scope centre on the boundaries of organisations, and ultimately power differences between organisations up and down the supply chain can have a significant impact both on business decisions and HR practices. This means that decisions about HRM may be beyond the control of an individual employer, either due to pressures from a powerful customer such as a large food retailer or because decisions are taken to set up joint ventures between organisations (Marchington *et al* 2005).

4 *Matching* their internal resources and activities to the environments in which the organisation operates so as to achieve strategic fit. This requires an assessment of internal strengths and weaknesses as well as external opportunities and threats (SWOT) in order to decide how best to design the organisation to meet current and future needs. Grant (2010, pp.12–13) argues that the best equipped strategists have a profound understanding of the competitive environment and are able concurrently to systematically appraise the resources available to them. He actually prefers the use of an internal–external categorisation to the SWOT analysis as it prevents an arbitrary classification into strengths and weaknesses versus opportunities and threats. In HR terms, major problems can occur if enough adequately qualified and trained staff have not been employed to enable the organisation to meet its strategic objectives and satisfy customer demand. However, because other organisations are also trying to achieve this match, they may poach the best staff, so compounding the problem.

5 Recognising that top-level decisions have major implications for *operational* activities, especially when there is a merger or takeover, a joint venture or public–private partnership, or even a change in the organisation's strategic direction following a review of its activities. Grant (2010) particularly emphasises the need for effective implementation, because if operational activities cannot adapt to new strategic goals, competitive advantage is hardly likely to flow. For example, deciding to grow the business through the creation of an IT-led customer service model will fail if HR issues have not been properly considered, and there are not enough staff to receive calls or they are poorly trained. One of the biggest problems in any large organisation, especially one that operates across a number of different product areas, is determining the most appropriate structures and systems to put strategies into effect.

6 Appreciating that the *values and expectations* of senior decision-makers play a sizeable part in the development of strategy because it is how they choose to interpret advice about external and internal resources that ultimately shapes strategic decisions (Lovas and Ghoshal 2000). Although many organisations within the same market choose to follow a similar path, some may decide to differentiate themselves from the competition

by adopting different strategies. This may or may not appear 'logical' from a rationalist perspective, but entrepreneurs typically mould organisations in their own image. There can be problems here as well, especially when a founder refuses to shift from their preferred position or a family-owned firm decides or is forced to bring in professional managers from outside.

Within this perspective, strategy is seen to operate at three levels. *Corporate* strategy relates to the overall scope of the organisation, its structures and financing, and the distribution of resources between its different constituent parts. *Business or competitive* strategy refers to how the organisation competes in a given market, its approaches to product development and to customers. *Operational* strategies are concerned with how the various subunits – marketing, finance, manufacturing and so on – contribute to the higher level strategies. HRM would be seen as an element at this third level, but it is rare for texts on strategy to pay much attention to HRM issues; for example, Johnson *et al* (2011) devotes only a handful of pages to managing human resources whilst Grant (2010) allocates just one page to HRM in his discussion of resources and capabilities.

Overall, the classical version of strategy relies upon an image of detached senior managers who determine the best plans for deploying workers to achieve victory over the competition in chosen market situations.

## ALTERNATIVE PERSPECTIVES ON STRATEGY

The 'classical' model is not the only way to analyse strategy, however (Hussey 1998), and an alternative approach put forward by writers such as Quinn and Mintzberg treats strategy as *emergent* rather than deliberate. Quinn (1980, p.58) regards the most effective strategies as those that tend to 'emerge step by step from an iterative process in which the organisation probes the future, experiments, and learns from a series of partial (incremental) commitments rather than through a global formulation of total strategies'. Quite rightly this casts doubt on the perspective that organisations make decisions on the basis of cold, clinical assessments in an 'objective' manner. Decisions are taken by people whose own subjective preferences and judgements clearly influence outcomes. Mistakes are made for a variety of reasons, and conditions change so as to render decisions that seemed sensible at the time totally inappropriate at a later date. Interpersonal political tensions and battles also play a major part in the outcome of decision-making processes within organisations. Mintzberg's (1987) notion of strategy being 'crafted' evokes ideas of skill and judgement, as well as people working together to make sense of confusing situations before reaching a conclusion that appears to offer a way forward. Of course, neither the classical nor the emergent perspective is correct in its entirety. Mintzberg and his colleagues (1998, p.11) have suggested that strategies are neither purely deliberate nor purely emergent as 'one means no learning, the other means no control. All real-world strategies need to mix these in some ways; to exercise some control while fostering learning'. Deliberate and emergent strategies form the poles of a continuum along which actual practice falls (Stiles 2001). Moreover, as we see below, strategy is sometimes used as a device for rationalising and legitimising decisions after they have been made.

**Figure 1 Whittington's typology of strategy**

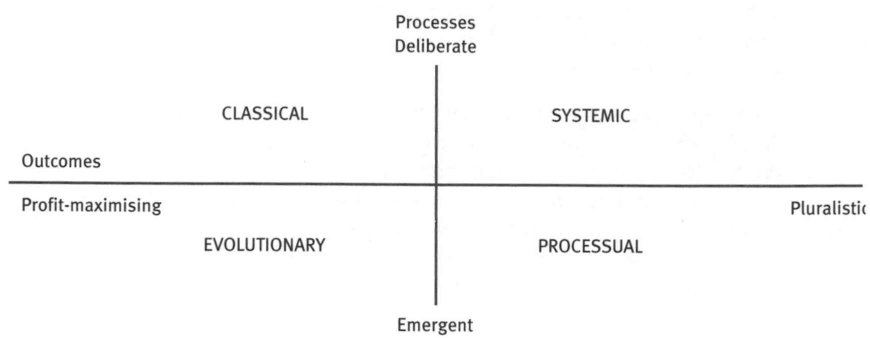


Source: Adapted from figure 1.1, page 3, chapter 1, *What Is Strategy and Does It Matter?* Whittington, R, Routledge (1993)

Whittington's (1993) fourfold typology (Figure 1) is extremely useful in helping us to understand the complex and multidimensional ways in which strategy might be conceived. It is based upon distinctions between the degree to which outcomes are perceived purely in either profit-maximising or pluralistic terms, and the extent to which strategy formulation is seen as either deliberate or emergent. The four types are:

- *Classical* (profit-maximising, deliberate) – As we have seen, under this conception, strategy is portrayed as a rational process of deliberate calculation and analysis, undertaken by senior managers who survey the external environment searching for ways in which to maximise profits and gain competitive advantage. It is characterised as non-political, the product of honest endeavour by managers who have nothing but the organisation's interests at heart, and who are able to remain above the day-to-day skirmishes that typify life at lower levels in the hierarchy. The image conveyed is that senior managers are independent professionals who make decisions in the interests of all stakeholders. Using the military analogy by separating formulation from implementation, Whittington (1993, pp.15–17) notes that 'plans are conceived in the general's tent, overlooking the battlefield but sufficiently detached for safety…the actual carrying-out of orders is relatively unproblematic, assured by military discipline and obedience'. The classical view of strategy leaves little room for choice when devising HR plans because these are operational matters, which assume there is 'one-best way' to manage people.
- *Evolutionary* (profit-maximising, emergent) – From this angle, strategy is seen as a product of market forces, in which the most efficient and productive organisations succeed. Drawing on notions of population ecology, 'the most appropriate strategies within a given market emerge as competitive processes allow the relatively better performers to survive while the weaker performers are squeezed out and go to the wall' (Legge 2005, p.136). For evolutionists 'strategy can be a dangerous delusion' (Whittington 1993, p.20). Taken to its extreme, it could be argued there is little point in planning a deliberate strategy since winners and losers will be 'picked' by a process of natural selection that is beyond the influence of senior managers. They might, however, see some advantage in keeping their options open and learning how to adapt to changing customer demands, a process that Lovas and Ghoshal (2000) refer to as 'guided evolution'. Under this scenario, the maintenance of flexible systems, whether in HRM or elsewhere, is an important component of competitive advantage. Boxall and Purcell (2008, pp.37–9) make the very useful differentiation between the problem of viability

(remaining in business) and the problem of sustained advantage (playing in the 'higher level tournament' through superior performance).

- *Processual* (pluralistic, emergent) – This view stems from an assumption that people are 'too limited in their understanding, wandering in their attention, and careless in their actions to unite around and then carry through a perfectly calculated plan' (Whittington 1993, p.4). There are at least two essential features to this perspective. First, as Mintzberg (1978) argues, strategies tend to evolve through a process of discussion and disagreement that involves managers at different levels in an organisation, and in some cases it is impossible to specify a precise strategy until after the event. Indeed, actions may only come to be defined as strategies with the benefit of hindsight, by a process of post hoc rationalisation in which events appear carefully planned in retrospect. Quinn's (1980) notion of 'logical incrementalism', the idea that strategy emerges in a fragmented and largely intuitive manner, evolving from a combination of internal decisions and external events, fits well with this perspective. Second, the processual view takes a micro-political perspective, acknowledging that organisations are beset with tensions and contradictions, with rivalries and conflicting goals, and with behaviours that seek to achieve personal or departmental objectives (Pettigrew 1973; Marchington *et al* 1993). Strategic plans may be worth little in reality but they help to give some credibility to decisions, as well as a security blanket for decision-makers who operate with severely bounded knowledge about future events. From this perspective, strategy can never be perfect and, as Whittington (1993, p.27) notes, it is 'by recognising and accommodating real world imperfections that managers can be most effective' rather than naively following a classical version of strategy that does not exist in practice.
- *Systemic* (pluralistic, deliberate) – The final perspective follows Granovetter (1985) in suggesting that strategy is shaped by the social system in which it is embedded – factors such as class, gender, legal regulations and educational systems play a major part – often subconsciously – in influencing the way in which employers and workers behave (Lane 1989; Ferner and Quintanilla 1998; Rubery and Grimshaw 2003), although at least in Germany these differences are now less clear-cut. Additionally, Whittington (1993, p.30) argues that the very notion of 'strategy' may be culturally bounded because it arose in the particular conditions of post-war North America. In other countries, the dominant perspective may be that the fate of organisations is pre-ordained and therefore unaffected by managerial actions, or it could be based upon philosophies that regard the provision of continuing work for families and local communities much more desirable than short-term gains for shareholders. A further advantage of viewing strategy from this perspective is that it highlights how – under the classical approach – management actions are legitimised by reference to external forces, so cloaking 'managerial power in the culturally acceptable clothing of science and objectivity' (ibid, p.37). Ultimately, the systemic perspective challenges the universality of any single model of strategy (and HRM for that matter) and demonstrates the importance of seeing organisational goals in the context of the countries and cultures in which they are located; 'strategy must be sociologically sensitive' (ibid, p.39).

## REFLECTIVE ACTIVITY

Discuss these competing versions of strategy with colleagues from other organisations, cultures or societies, and then try to take a fresh look at your original views.

It should be apparent that seeing strategy in different ways suggests interesting implications for how we view its links with HRM. Under the *classical* perspective this is unproblematic, merely a matter of making the right decision and then cascading this through the managerial hierarchy to shop-floor or office workers, who then snap into action to meet organisational goals. The *evolutionary* view complicates the situation, in that it puts a primacy upon market forces and the perceived need for organisations (which are seen in unitarist terms) to respond quickly and effectively to customer demands. This introduces notions of power and flexibility into the equation compared with notions of objectivity that underpin the classical perspective. The two pluralist perspectives take it for granted that organisational life is contested. The *processual* perspective demonstrate the barriers to fully fledged vertical integration in practice, whether this be due to tensions within management or to challenges which may be mounted by workers. Under this scenario, HRM styles also emerge in a fragmented and uneven manner, influenced by the relative power and influence of the HR function compared with other parts of senior management. The *systemic* perspective forces us to look beyond the level of the employing organisation and be aware that employers are not generally free to determine their own strategies in many situations. Problems are bound to arise if critical social norms or cultural traditions are ignored or it is assumed that HR practices that work in one country can be parachuted automatically into others. Indeed, as Paauwe (2004, pp.170–3) shows clearly in his study of a US firm operating in the USA and the Netherlands, planned change was typical in the former, whereas in the Dutch plants ample room was allowed for employee influence and for changes in the content of decisions during the process. Sisson (2010, p.244) also emphasises constraints – that perhaps it might be better to think of management as a systems actor rather than a strategic actor and not immune to pressures of 'path dependency', which explains why managers can get locked into a particular approach or recipe. Sisson argues that business strategy reflects the interplay between the existing structures of finance and corporate governance and the institutions, processes and rules of employment relations, both of which are deeply embedded institutions.

## STAKEHOLDERS, CORPORATE RESPONSIBILITY AND DIVERSITY

### THE BALANCED SCORECARD

Strategy is not simply about financial returns to shareholders but also involves a rather wider base of stakeholders that includes customers, local communities, the environment, and of course workers. We take a similar line to Paauwe (2004) in stressing that HRM is different from other managerial functions because of its professional and moral base, and – in some countries more than others – its rejection of the simplistic view that people are merely a means to achieve greater corporate profits and shareholder returns. This is not to deny it is important for people to make an effective contribution to organisational goals but that trust and integrity are also critically important elements in how HRM is practised at work.

In a series of publications Kaplan and Norton (2001, 2007, 2010) argue that traditional approaches to management accounting focus on short-term financial performance and shareholder value alone. Instead, firms need to take into account the longer-term needs and expectations of other stakeholders and the way in which they are linked to organisational goals. They suggest (2007) there should be a balance between four perspectives on business performance:

- how to appear to our shareholders to achieve financial success (*financial*)
- how to satisfy our shareholders and customers through the choice of excellent business processes (*internal business processes*)

- how to appear to our customers to achieve our vision (*customers*)
- how to sustain our ability to change and improve in order to achieve the vision (*learning and growth*).

It will be seen there is no specific category for employees within the scorecard but they figure principally within the learning and growth perspective. This is in terms of the strategic skills and knowledge of the workforce to support strategy, and in the cultural shifts required to motivate, empower and align the workforce behind the strategy (Boxall and Purcell 2008, p.299). In other words, the balanced scorecard does not specifically suggest that employees are stakeholders in their own right, but only in so far as they can enhance customer satisfaction and financial performance through their ability to support business strategy – not through any moral perspective. Despite this, Kaplan and Norton (2007, pp.150–1) feel the scorecard enables 'companies to track financial results while simultaneously monitoring progress in building the capabilities and acquiring the intangible assets they would need for future growth. The scorecard wasn't a replacement for financial measures; it was their complement.'

While accepting it is helpful to try and integrate 'key HR performance drivers into the strategic management framework, Boxall and Purcell (2008, pp.303–7) are concerned that the balanced scorecard approach does not go far enough in relation to HRM. There are two major concerns; first, HRM is not just about satisfying corporate objectives but also relates to social legitimacy in terms of compliance with labour laws and the provision of policies which build long-run succession and development opportunities for managers and workers. Second, the balanced scorecard tends to assume certain HR practices, in particular incentive pay systems, are universally effective in promoting better performance. By contrast, they argue that the alignment of employer and employee interests depends greatly on the circumstances and the institutional regimes within which organisations operate, and that what might appear highly appropriate in a US context could well prove counterproductive in another. Moreover, it could be argued that the balanced scorecard approach includes additional processes merely in terms of their contribution to improved performance. As such it continues to reflect management and organisational interests primarily rather than those of all stakeholders. For example, instead of arguing for greater employee engagement in organisational decisions, it suggests that managers just need to communicate with workers more effectively and educate them about the realities of organisational life. Attention is also focused on how employers can ensure that employees are aligned with the organisational vision. Similarly some of the organisations they studied were solely interested in employee morale because of its links with customer satisfaction. Nothing is wrong with these objectives, but they are hardly 'alternative' in the sense of seeking to satisfy needs for equality at work or in addressing issues of corporate responsibility. Maltz *et al* (2003, p.197) have attempted to rectify the lack of focus on the employee strand of the balanced scorecard by including a 'people development' dimension that explicitly recognises the critical role of employees in organisational success.

There have also been some attempts to develop HR scorecards as a means of measuring the return on investment in HR programmes, specifically in terms of the value created by deliverables and the control of costs through more efficient operations (Sparrow *et al* 2004, p.170). These tend to rely on a similar range of metrics to those used in other approaches, basically relying on factors that impact directly on organisational performance – such as labour turnover, absence levels and productivity. An alternative – the *real* balanced HRM scorecard – is proposed by Paauwe (2004). This starts from the stance that HR specialists cannot focus solely on organisational criteria such as efficiency, effectiveness and flexibility, and that – like Legge's deviant innovator, which we discuss in Chapter 6 – they should be prepared to risk unpopularity by questioning the short-term approaches that are so widespread in business. Paauwe argues (p.184) that 'other appropriate criteria are those of fairness (in the exchange relationship between the individual and the organisation) and legitimacy (the relation between society and organisation)'. The logic HRM scorecard that Paauwe (pp.194–208) develops consists of four components – strategic, professional, societal and delivery. The professional and societal logics comprise factors such as the following:

- providing assurance and trust about financial reporting of organisations
- maximising both tangible and intangible rewards to employees
- delivering reliable information to works council members
- offering information and individual help to employees
- safeguarding fairness in management–worker relations.

### PRIVATE EQUITY FIRMS

Whilst there are examples of organisations that are keen to be more transparent in reporting what they do, and show evidence that they are taking HRM seriously, there has also been a challenge to greater transparency and the idea of high commitment HRM by the increased role that private equity firms (PEFs) are playing. This is particularly apparent in liberal market economies (LMEs) such as the UK and USA (Wright *et al* 2009; Folkman *et al* 2009), and to some extent in Australia (Westcott 2009) following a failed takeover attempt of Qantas. Activity throughout the rest of Europe has been more limited (Watt 2008). Many of the cases have involved high-profile acquisitions, such as Southern Cross in the UK which raised major concerns about how care for the elderly would be provided for following the sell-off of land and other assets and the withdrawal from this market (Toynbee 2011a). However, authors such as Clark (2009) and Wood and Wright (2009) stress the importance of differentiating between the two main types of PEF:

1. *Insider-driven* where existing management – in some cases, jointly with workers – takes over the organisation through a buy-out and all staff tend to be offered an equity stake in the business. In these cases, management and workers often have the longer-term interests of the organisation at heart and if cuts are required they tend to be taken jointly only after serious consideration of the alternatives.
2. *Outside-driven* where an established firm is taken over by a new employer through a leveraged buy-out or a management buy-in. The pressure in the latter case is to generate high returns for external investors which often means selling off assets, reducing staff numbers and achieving efficiency gains at every corner to meet short-term expectations of the market.

Media interest has focused on the latter due to the high returns individuals gain from controlling PEFs and the low level of tax they pay. It was estimated that PEFs control firms employing vast numbers of workers in the UK; Clark (2007) estimated this at 2.8 million, about 20% of private sector employment, whilst Thornton (2007) thought it was about half this number; either way a significant number of workers are employed by these types of organisation. Some of the firms which have been owned by PEFs are household names – Alliance Boots, AA, United Biscuits, Saga, Bird's Eye – and some, such as Hertz, have been sold on. Given the downturn in economic fortunes following the global financial crisis, PEFs have found it more difficult to raise highly leveraged loans. Unlike public limited companies, PEFs are privately owned and therefore are not required to operate with the same rules of transparency and corporate governance. The business model used requires them to make rapid returns on their investment because such a large amount (typically 70%) is financed by debt rather than equity (Froud and Williams 2007). Given that PEFs operate according to short-term principles, there is bound to be less interest in high commitment HRM for their staff – especially anything which costs more to service or makes longer-term commitments. Even if they do show an interest, this will tend to be restricted to a small number of key players (Clark 2007). Trade unions have been highly critical of PEFs, arguing that workers are less well-off both financially and in terms of trade union recognition, and have lower levels of employment protection than they do in PLCs (Watt 2008), whereas the industry denies this. Indeed, Clark (2011, p.48), who has been highly critical of PEFs, concludes that the AA case was one 'where private equity owners retained union recognition and extracted value from the firm on the basis of a benign, yet superior, business model'. On the basis of evaluation across the EU, which includes both LMEs and co-ordinated market economies (CMEs), Watt (2008) provides the following evidence in Table 1:

**Table 1 How well do private equity firms do?**

| Category | Evidence |
|---|---|
| Value generation | Value is added to the firm but there is great variance and concerns that this is through value appropriation rather than value creation |
| Employment | Despite differences between studies, most independent research shows that initial restructuring leads to substantial job losses, especially in outside-driven takeovers |
| Wages and working conditions | Not much evidence available here but cuts in wages and conditions seem to be commonplace, and with no TUPE protection in these cases, that is achievable. However, would similar results have occurred if the takeover had not happened |
| Worker representation | Outcomes here depend on the institutional framework and the specific stance taken by the PEF. It is very unlikely this will increase, but also not definite that union membership will come under attack |
| Taxation | Transfer from tax payers can be a source of value creation for PEFs given subsidies and sales of assets |
| Short-termism and investment | In LMEs, as with all companies, short-termism is likely to predominate but there is limited research evidence available |
| Leverage and risk | Evidence suggests a higher rate of risk given high leverage, but then the same problems occurred following the collapse of the US sub-prime mortgage market |

Source: Adapted from Watt (2008).

REFLECTIVE ACTIVITY

Read at least one of the papers in the special issue of the *Journal of Industrial Relations* (2009, Vol.51, No.4) and draw your own conclusions about the impact that private equity firms have on HRM and employment relations.

## CORPORATE RESPONSIBILITY

In this section, we examine corporate responsibility and why it matters to HRM. The DTI definition is 'how business takes account of its economic, social and environmental impacts in the way it operates'. This usually relates to voluntary issues beyond the law and with ethical and moral behaviour. Fundamentally, it questions who should benefit from business (Brammer 2011). Since its inception, corporate responsibility has had many labels, often used interchangeably, and without accurate definition; throughout we use the phrase corporate responsibility.

Corporate responsibility involves a wide range of activities and stakeholders. Stakeholders are the groups or individuals with whom the organisation interacts, and most have vested interests. Customer issues might include quality, truthful marketing, product provenance; for the community issues include the environment, responsible/fair trade, ethical investment, donations to charity, secondments to community work, supporting Third World education and health programmes, refusal to operate in certain markets, avoidance of bribery and corruption. Its relevance to HRM is apparent in areas such as health and safety, working conditions, discrimination and harassment, reward, well-being, employee voice, training and development, child and forced labour, and concern for human rights (Ahlstrand 2010; Brammer 2011). Core labour standards in the 1998 ILO Declaration relate to basic human rights that exist without regard to level of economic development. These are:

- freedom of association
- recognition of the right to collective bargaining
- elimination of forced or compulsory labour
- abolition of child labour
- elimination of discrimination in employment.

Carroll (1991) sees corporate responsibility as a pyramid (similar to Maslow's hierarchy of needs) made up of economic, legal, ethical, and philanthropic responsibilities, with economic responsibilities at the base. The *economic* responsibility is to make a profit for shareholders. Some maintain that this is the one and only responsibility of the business community – a view initially voiced by Milton Friedman (1970). This perspective is challenged by the stakeholder model that regards business as not just about profit but also about the well-being of individuals and society.

## REFLECTIVE ACTIVITY

Bill Ford (chairman of Ford) has stated that whilst 'a good company delivers excellent products and services, a great company delivers excellent products and services and strives to make the world a better place'.

What are your views on this statement?

*Legal* responsibilities are about obeying the law whilst *ethical* responsibility involves ensuring the organisation is fair and just, and avoids harm. Finally, the *philanthropic* organisation would act to improve quality of life. The pyramid implies that the majority of organisations adhere to the Friedman view, and may even ignore legal constraints; a minority will take the ethical stance of ensuring that they do no harm; while a smaller number are philanthropic and ensure that their actions positively impact on the quality of life on the planet. The New Economics Foundation (www.neweconomics.org) in the UK, and the World Business Council for Sustainable Development (Growing Inclusive Markets Programme) both promote ethical business – that is, businesses which are set up to solve world problems whilst also making profits and offering gainful employment. Dobers and Halme (2009) provide examples such as the Grameen or Wizzit micro-finance initiatives where entrepreneurship is much more important than aid, and goes beyond fair trade. Many 'ethical pioneers' start out as SMEs and may have different forms of ownership. The field of renewable energy in the UK provides examples of community-owned co-operatives, for example Energy4All and Baywind. Others have traditional ownership (eg. Triodos Bank, cafedirect) and a number of these have been taken over by multinationals seeking to enhance their credentials (eg Body Shop, Ben and Jerry's, Green and Blacks).

Lueneburger and Goleman (2010) suggests that company behaviour confers a licence to operate and right to exist and that companies which do not engage in corporate responsibility will ultimately lose legitimacy and fail. This begs the question whether those at Carroll's base level have a licence to operate. Certainly, there are plenty of companies which have been involved in major scandals that continue (eg Dow Chemicals – Bhopal, Exxon – Exxon Valdez).

We next look at motivations for adopting corporate responsibility; looking at the business case, consumer pressure, regulatory and global pressures, and normative values.

1 The business case

For those who believe that profit is the only concern of business, increasing profits through engaging in corporate responsibility would be a major incentive. At the simplest level, profits can quickly be enhanced by reducing use of resources (heating, light, water etc), or by reusing or selling on waste products. Balanced against this is the fact that corporate responsibility typically involves resources (Shen 2011). A broader view is that corporate responsibility contributes to competitive advantage and therefore generates higher profits. This is achieved through avoidance of business risks, scandals and accidents. A good corporate image enhances customer loyalty, general acceptance by governments and local communities, and better chance of attracting, retaining and motivating staff. Furthermore, ethical companies can access ethical capital, and may be able to avoid government intervention – something that most organisations dislike. As Warren Buffett said, it takes '20 years to build a reputation and five minutes to ruin it' (*Financial Times* 2011).

2 Consumer pressure

**Box 1: Knowledgeable and empowered consumers**

Two women (green consumers) are shopping in a mall for sunscreen. They enter the first store and choose a product; on her way to the till one woman swipes the bar code into her iPhone and she receives a message back stating that the sunscreen uses materials that damage coral reefs and the packaging is difficult to recycle. Her phone knows her location and directs her to a nearby store that stocks a greener product. After buying the product, the women let their friends know through social websites what they have done. This is already possible because both GoodGuide.com and Ethical Consumer have iPhone apps that do provide information on the environmental, health, and social impact of products.

Do you think that this scenario will lead to more companies adopting corporate responsibility in order to ensure survival in a competitive market place?

Source: Adapted from Lueneberger and Goleman (2010, pp.49–55).

The scenario of ethical consumerism in Box 1 suggests that corporate responsibility could become essential for all companies operating in a competitive market. However, many consumers only care about price – and this drives a race to the bottom. Customers who do care need to have sufficient information, making it essential for corporations to ensure that stakeholders – particularly customers – are aware of differentiation (Scherer and Palazzo 2010, p.22; Brammer 2011). This involves companies listening actively to key stakeholders such as customers, government, and the community (Campbell 2007) and creates a virtuous cycle for companies attuned to stakeholder perspectives.

An example of this is Co-operative Bank which conducts in-depth communications with its stakeholders to formulate bank policy. However, it is generally agreed that the relationship between corporate responsibility and the bottom line is complex (Carroll and Shabana 2010; Crowther 2010).

3 Regulatory and global pressures
One of the main pressures is regulation, although there is ample evidence of large organisations using their power to coerce governments to weaken environmental and safety regulations, impose or raise import surcharges, to put up trade barriers through tariffs, and negotiate tax exemptions. The regulatory controls on MNCs are particularly weak and uneven (Martinez-Lucio and MacKenzie 2011). The 2008 banking crisis was seen to be caused by lax regulatory control and undue influence of city lobbyists (Hutton 2011a, pp.180–1).

Despite the ability of some to prevent or sidestep regulations, laws and rules significantly influence behaviour. In general, legislative and regulatory pressures are increasing – albeit often in response to major scandals. As well as regulations, there are international agendas to address pressing global issues of global warming, poverty, and decreasing biodiversity, through persuasion – for example, Davos and Kyoto. The UN Global Compact is one such structure which links almost 6,000 organisations with governments, labour organisations and NGOs and sets out principles around labour relations, human rights, the environment, and anti-corruption. Other organisations working towards minimally acceptable international standards include the International Labour Organisation (ILO), Organisation for Economic Cooperation and Development, World Bank and World Trade Organisation. In Europe there is the Charter of Fundamental Rights, and the Sustainability Strategy for Europe.

4 Normative values
A driving force within organisations is often the normative values of leadership whether it is from the CEO, the board and/or senior managers or the unions (Basu and Palazzo 2008; Shen 2011). Training in top business schools encourages managers to embrace corporate responsibility (Campbell 2007) and unions are increasingly linking with networks and NGOs to campaign on issues (Brammer 2011; Preuss *et al* 2009; Cooke 2011, p.585).

Bigger organisations, those operating globally and with formal strategic plans, are more likely to embrace corporate responsibility (Scherer and Palazzo 2010; Galbreath 2010). This may be because they have increased access to resources (Shen 2011). To date, there is relatively little research on developing countries, and cultural sensitivity means notions of corporate responsibility differ between MNC home countries and host countries. Where there are weak institutional frameworks, arbitrary law enforcement, corruption, tax evasion, fraud and bribery, corporate responsibility is likely to take a different form as organisations operate in lieu of the state to provide health, education, social security or environmental protection (Scherer and Palazzo 2010).

A growing number of organisations now monitor and report on corporate responsibility. Examples include: Social Accountability 8000, the Global Reporting Initiative, Global Compact, the Fair Labour Association workplace code (Rasche 2010), BITC (UK). Additionally, the EU Accounts Modernisation Directive (2005) requires non-financial reporting (reports on environment, employee, social and community issues) in directors' reports. The best organisations ensure that ethical performance covers a wide range of activities and that corporate responsibility is embedded throughout the organisation. Unfortunately, many report on only a minor part of their operations and promote them widely as a public relations exercise, leading to cynicism, especially where the organisation has reputation dents. Where responsibility for corporate responsibility rests in the public relations department, this speaks volumes. Many would argue that it fits with HRM's welfare roots and should always be located with HR (Shen 2011).

## DIVERSITY AT WORK

Discrimination is a moral issue about human rights, but it is also about addressing legal obligations, and deriving business benefit (Dickens 2007, p.468). Diversity management is important to business because of new labour market demographics, globalisation, and competitive pressures. It includes factors such as gender, age, ethnicity, political and religious belief, disability, and sexual orientation and encompasses such issues as family-related leave. The proven business benefits that can accrue to organisations that effectively manage workforce diversity include:

1 access to a wider pool of potential candidates

2 improved customer satisfaction and increased market penetration by employing a diverse workforce whose composition is similar to that of the local population

3 increased creativity and problem-solving skills

4 improved motivation, recruitment and retention because of the organisation's reputation as a 'good' employer

5 avoidance of costly discrimination cases because action has been taken to ensure the use of systematic and professional HR practices (CIPD 2010a; Dickens *et al* 2009).

Despite arguments in favour of employing a more diverse workforce, doubts remain about the likely conversion of these benefits into everyday HR practice and it is difficult to change beliefs that are deep-rooted and implicit. The business case can be fragile because it relies on the specific circumstances of each organisation, as well as changes in the wider legal, political, economic and social context, which may lead employers to downgrade equality arguments if they are not of pressing concern. Employers may have little interest in the long-term case for equality because they can gain substantially (in the short term, at least) from employing low-paid workers. Diversity may be accepted by employers in the case of professionals whose skill is scarce but ignored for casual or unskilled employees. Moreover, despite national or corporate policies supporting diversity, there can be pressure from existing staff that are male, white and able-bodied to protect their interests rather than those of disadvantaged groups. For all these reasons, diversity must be managed effectively if it is not to generate negative outcomes. As Kandola (2009) argues, diversity management needs to be systemic with a widespread and deep-rooted commitment to maximising the potential of the workforce, regardless of its profile. It is only when 'women's, disabled or black issues' are recast as 'people's issues' that any real moves towards equality can take place.

The move from anti-discrimination law towards equality has been slow, but in the UK it is hoped that the Equality and Human Rights Commission and the Equality Act 2010 will help to promote equality based on attitudes, beliefs and values. The slow rate of progress is apparent when we look at women's equality, which has been enshrined in legislation for 40 years: there remains a continuing gender pay gap of 22% (Evans 2010) and missing women in most walks of life. The UK lags behind the rest of Europe in women's participation on corporate boards (EHRC 2011a) and at the same time gender issues are declining in importance in the European Employment Strategy (Smith and Villa 2010). It will remain the case that some organisations engage in diversity management in order to comply with the law, others because of the economic benefits, whilst a relatively small number see it as part of their corporate responsibility and a moral imperative.

## REFLECTIVE ACTIVITY

Make out a case for increasing diversity at your workplace or one with which you are familiar. To what extent would you draw upon the business case to convince line managers of the value of equality provisions?

## CONCLUSIONS

In this chapter, we have provided a brief analysis of the links between strategy and HRM, paying particular attention to the main arguments and debates in the subject area. Students need to be aware that HRM does not take place in a vacuum but operates within frameworks that tie it to the strategy of the firm, as well as through influences from the wider institutional framework within which organisations are located. Morris and Snell (2009) note that the shift HR strategy has recently taken is co-evolving with the strategy literature. For the first time, they report that there are signs of the field of strategy taking cues from HR research. But they warn that many HR managers are still ill-equipped to deal with issues of knowledge and innovation in relation to globally dispersed and differentiated workforces, observing that much of the HR literature remains based in one domestic location and does not look at cross-boundary complexities. Too little is known about how an organisation might manage people who are not considered part of the official organisation, and they do not address issues of how firms might manage the increasing heterogeneity and uniqueness found across geographically dispersed workforces within a firm. As they note, addressing this requires more than rote implementation of a specific set of standardised practices (Morris and Snell 2009 p.92).

It is worth noting that many of the frameworks and models tend to assume there is a specific model of HRM – the universal, high commitment, 'best practice' model that we explore in detail in Chapter 3. Conversely, if we assume that HRM is a field of study rather than a distinct style, we can then examine how the management of employment varies between organisations and workplaces, as well as over time, because it can be shaped by the range of influences including factors external to the workplace – such as legislative, political and economic changes, which can impact differentially depending upon management choice, management–employee relations and worker attitudes and behaviours. Working with this conception of the subject means that HRM can exist just as easily in a small owner-managed sweatshop as it can in a large and sophisticated high-tech organisation. It just takes different forms.

HRM can therefore be defined as 'the management of employment', so incorporating individual and collective relations, the whole range of HR practices and processes, line management activities and those of HR specialists, managerial and non-managerial actors. It is more than just another version of the 'hard' model because it assumes management styles depend not only on business goals but also on influences from a range of different stakeholder interests. Accordingly, HRM may include a role for unions, the development of so-called leading-edge HR practices, an evident commitment to employment security and having line managers at the helm of organisational change. Conversely, HRM may be individualised, HR policies can rely on cost reduction and rationalisation, and there may be no provision for an internal HR function. Irrespective of the approach adopted, however, employers should be keen to enhance the contribution of HR practices to performance.

Four key points are central to our understanding of HRM; these continually reappear throughout the remainder of this book:

*The subject matter of HRM* – We regard HRM as those aspects of people management that need to be understood by all HR specialists and others with a major responsibility for managing people. Using Torrington's (1998) medical analogy, these are the subjects the 'general practitioner' needs to understand, and which remain critical for the specialist consultant even though he or she is not explicitly aware they are being used.

*Integration* is at the heart of HRM – This takes two forms: *vertical integration*, which refers to the links between HRM and both wider business strategies and the political, economic, social and legal forces that shape (and to some extent are shaped by) organisations; and *horizontal integration*, which refers to the 'fit' between different HR policies and practices (bundles), and the degree to which they support or contradict one another. Readers will find similar processes are addressed repeatedly in this book but this should be recognised as a positive sign of complementarity, integration and reinforcement rather than unnecessary repetition. We assume that both vertical and horizontal integration probably need to be strengthened in order to maximise the HR contribution, as well as minimise the likelihood of conflicting messages.

*Line manager involvement* – Irrespective of the role played by an internal HR function or by external agencies that provide HR support, line managers are central to the delivery of HRM at the workplace. If HRM policy and practice is to be effective, HR specialists need to gain line management commitment to and buy-in for their proposals and recommendations. It matters little that a course of action impresses other HR specialists if it fails to convince line managers – the people who have to put most policies into effect. This is not to say that HR specialists should become the servants of line managers, merely recommending what line managers want to hear in order to gain 'customer' approval. It does mean, however, that HR specialists have to be acutely aware of their audience, of the purpose of HR policies and their contribution to organisational success. On some occasions the views of line managers will need to be challenged and the basis for their perspectives questioned, while on other occasions their needs can be satisfied with clear professional judgement and sound practical advice.

*Ambiguity and tension* – Although there are increasing pressures to demonstrate added value to organisations, as we saw earlier HRM is often in an ambiguous position within employing organisations. The HR function is sometimes criticised for occupying the middle ground between management and workers, because it is dealing with issues for which it is difficult to identify a simple best option. For example, there can be conflicting and often equally strong arguments in favour of the dramatically different approaches an employer can take in relation to trade unions – for example, partnership or arm's-length relations – or to the development of skills – for example, internal or external supply. In HRM, perhaps more than in any other area of management, the choices that are made can have significant implications for the future, and lead an organisation down a path that is difficult to alter without lots of effort. Because the employment relationship is incomplete, ambiguous and contested, this means that HRM can never be a simple technical exercise, whereby answers are read off according to some scientific formula, and implemented without problem. HR professionals have to become accustomed to the fact – especially as they reach the higher echelons of the occupation – that their work is going to be fraught with tensions and contradictions, and with situations that are characterised by uncertainty, indeterminacy and competing perspectives.

EXPLORE FURTHER

AHLSTRAND, R. (2010) 'Social responsibility in connection with business closures: A study of the close-down of Ericsson Telecom facilities in Norrkoping and Lindoping', *Economic and Industrial Democracy*, Vol.31, No.4, 537–55.

BECKER, B.E. and HUSELID, M.A. (2009) 'Strategic human resource management: Where do we go from here?' in A. Wilkinson *et al* (eds) *The Sage Handbook of Human Resource Management*. London: Sage.

BOSELIE, P. and PAAWE, J. (2009) 'HRM and the resource based view', in A. Wilkinson *et al* (eds) *The Sage Handbook of Human Resource Management*. London: Sage.

GRANT, R. (2010) *Contemporary Strategy Analysis*, 7th edition. Oxford: Blackwell Publishing.

GUEST, D. (2011) 'Human resource management and performance: Still searching for some answers', *Human Resource Management Journal*, Vol.21, No.1, 3–13.

JOHNSON, G., WHITTINGTON, R. and SCHOLES, K (2011) *Exploring Corporate Strategy*, 8th edition. London: Prentice Hall.

KAUFMAN, B. (2010) *Hired Hands or Human Resources: Case Studies of HRM Programs and Practices in Early American Industry*. Ithaca, New York: Cornell University Press.

WRIGHT, M., BACON, N. and AMESS, K. (2009) 'The impact of private equity and buyouts on employment, remuneration and other HRM practices', *Journal of Industrial Relations*, Vol.51, No.4, 501–16.

CHAPTER 2

# Forces Shaping HRM at Work

## LEARNING OUTCOMES

By the end of this chapter, readers should be able to:

- implement HR policies and practices that take into account influences from networks and institutional forces beyond the organisation at a local and global level
- supply appropriate advice about patterns of employment, legal and institutional forces relevant to HRM, and guide managers to sources of specialist information
- use and interpret data from a range of internal and published sources to prepare reports about employment issues.

In addition, readers should understand and be able to explain:

- the role of globalisation, legislation and institutions in shaping HRM at work
- the implications for HRM arising from the changing nature of work and organisational structures
- the relationship between employing organisations and the economic, societal and institutional frameworks within which they operate.

## INTRODUCTION

The previous chapter examined how internal factors shape HRM, but it is crucial that practitioners appreciate that organisations also operate within wider institutional frameworks comprising global forces, patterns of work and employment, organisational networks, and legal and political forces. Whilst these may limit employer choices about how to manage employment they also provide frameworks and structures that can aid effective HRM – for example, by setting limits on working hours that can reduce accidents at work or in outlining model HR policies and procedures. We do not see these factors as determining management choice, but actually helping to shape their decisions. Accordingly, rather than treating this chapter as organisational 'context', and therefore beyond the influence of employers, we argue that it is the relationship between institutional forces and management choice that shapes HRM. Although the influence of such forces is less in the UK than in many other European countries (Rubery and Grimshaw 2003), this does not mean it can be ignored. Indeed, in some industries, employer choice is significantly influenced by the activities of employer associations and trade unions, as well as by the law (Marchington and Vincent 2004).

The remainder of the chapter proceeds as follows. First globalisation is introduced briefly to place the other forces in context, but it is discussed more fully in Chapter 5. Second, we review data on labour markets and patterns of employment, focusing on the sectoral and gendered division of labour, working time, and levels of employment and unemployment. Third, we discuss flexibility, emphasising how fragmented patterns of work and disordered hierarchies shape HRM across organisational boundaries. Fourth, we consider legal issues, both from a UK and an EU perspective, showing how this has affected employers. However, this is not done in any great detail so readers wanting more specific advice **MUST** consult specialist law texts and legal bulletins before taking action. Finally, we review a range of institutions that shape HRM at work, as well as provide details of websites and reports from which readers can access up-to-date information. Whilst this text provides a good grounding in these issues, it is critically important that readers use specialist sources as a matter of routine. For example, the CIPD undertakes a whole range of surveys annually, the UK government provides statistics on employment issues once a quarter, and the OECD and ETUI (European Trade Union Institute) do so regularly as well.

## GLOBALISATION AND GLOBAL COMPARISONS

Globalisation is a term used in a wide variety of disciplines across the social sciences. Peter Dicken (2003), a human geographer, differentiates between the 'hyper-globalists' and the 'sceptics'. The former conceive of a borderless world in which national barriers and distinctions are no longer relevant and consumer tastes are homogenised. Under this scenario, the global stage is seen as the natural order of things. An alternative – the 'sceptics' – accept that we now live an international world with lots of links between nations, but feel the latter are still important players. Indeed, he questions whether the world is now more globalised than ever due to sizeable levels of trade between Europe and Asia over one hundred years ago. Dicken (p.14) notes that 'the rhetoric of globalisation has become more powerful and persuasive, particularly in terms of what the process means for society and individuals and for the ways in which national politicians employ such rhetoric to justify why they must (or cannot) adopt certain policies'.

A contrary position is taken by Wolf (2004). He argues that 'liberal globalisation' is a movement in the direction of greater integration as barriers to international economic exchange and free trade continue to fall. His argument derives from the economic and business case for globalisation, and he sees (p.15) the consequence of globalisation as 'the increased impact of economic changes in one part of the world on what happens in others'. This could occur if greater efficiencies are achieved across the world and economic benefits trickle down from richer to poorer countries, but it can also be seen in the rapid transfer of problems following the global financial crisis from the USA to the rest of the world. Another economist – and political scientist – Stiglitz, agrees globalisation can bring benefits, for example via improvements in living standards, but his concern is that it has failed to live up to its potential. He argues (2006, p.4) that 'economics has been driving globalisation ... but politics has shaped it. The rules of the game have been largely set by the advanced industrial countries (and) they have shaped globalisation to further their own interests. They have not sought to create a fair set of rules, let alone a set of rules that would promote the well-being of those in the poorest countries of the world.' An international management perspective comes from McSweeney *et al* (2008) who are also sceptical about globalisation and especially the idea of a homogenised and uniform world. They argue (p.8) that 'barriers (institutional, cultural or otherwise) are absent or ineffective, and that prior sources of diversity have been vanquished or will readily be vanquished'. Whilst communications systems have reduced some barriers, others have been reinforced by contrasting cultural and institutional forces, and at a time of recession and crisis an increased desire to protect one's own resources. Moreover, not all services are capable of being enjoyed by people unless they are physically there – such as walks in the Peak District or swimming in the Mediterranean. This clearly limits the spread of globalisation.

Not surprisingly scholars from the HRM and employment relations fields also examine the topic. Farnham (2010) provides a very useful summary of the arguments for and against globalisation and outlines its implications for governments, MNCs and HRM. Rubery and Grimshaw (2003, pp.222–3) suggest that four major trends provide evidence of the increasing international integration of the world economy. These are: the growth in foreign trade; increasing flows of investment funds, principally between developed countries but also significant increases for developing countries; developments in information and communication technologies; and the presence and power of MNCs across the globe. Whilst they acknowledge the trends, Rubery and Grimshaw (pp.225–6) question whether globalisation is an unstoppable force, and suggest that rhetoric plays a large part in the process. They argue that 'governments will only us the globalisation agenda to help in the legitimisation of their own policy agendas. (They) will claim not be to be able to do anything against the forces of globalisation when they choose not to do so, but will take action when they consider it in their interests to do so.' Similarly, employers blame globalisation when they are trying to persuade employees to accept changes to their working conditions. Brewster and Mayrhofer (2011) also review the case for and against globalisation, but point out that in most organisations human resources are the largest single element of operating costs. In these circumstances, it is not surprising MNCs find it attractive to locate their overseas subsidiaries in low wage economies, but this depends on whether or not it is feasible or cost-effective to do so; if goods and services are required at the point of contact with customers, it is not possible, and if transportation or other costs are greater, it is not appropriate. Wailes *et al* (2011) note that globalisation, in its extreme form, is associated with a 'race to the bottom' in terms of wages and labour standards across the world. However, they argue this is too simplistic as it ignores opportunities available to governments and employers to choose what they do, or adapt policies to fit with local circumstances. Moreover, in line with the institutional theorists, they argue that national variations do persist and specific country HRM systems are unlikely to be swept away by a tide of globalisation for a whole variety of reasons.

Data compiled across a range of categories each year by the World Economic Forum helps us to address this point. The categories cover not just information relating to employment and labour markets but also to infrastructure, innovation, health and primary education, business sophistication and many institutional features such as efficiency of legal frameworks, business costs of terrorism and ethical behaviour of firms. Some of this data is relatively value-free – such as GDP and levels of tertiary education – and can be corroborated by independent analysis. Others require judgements to be made by the panel putting the data together – such as labour management co-operation, rigidity of employment and willingness to delegate authority. Moreover, some of these reflect an Anglo-American way of evaluating the world. For example, rigidity of employment tends to be viewed in terms of constraints on employers, purely from a legal or cost perspective. However, as we see later, it can also be seen – from a high commitment perspective – as a cornerstone of good HR practice and therefore an aide to sustained organisational performance.

Despite these concerns, the material is useful for comparative purposes. Table 2 provides data on ten countries chosen to reflect different business traditions (liberal market economies – LMEs – and co-ordinated market economies – CMEs) as well as the fast-growing developing BRIC countries (Brazil, Russia, India and China). These distinctions are outlined in much more detail in Chapter 5 when we examine international and comparative HRM, so readers may wish to look at this briefly before continuing. The BRIC countries have significantly lower levels of GDP than the developed countries and, apart from Russia, have much lower levels of tertiary education. Infrastructure is also lower in these countries but this is not likely to last for much longer (see, for example, Ireland and China). Levels of female participation in the labour market are not significantly different apart from in India, which is significantly below the other nine. So-called rigidity of employment is much lower in LMEs than CMEs, as one would expect, but interestingly India and China, which are often seen as highly attractive locations for employers seeking more flexible labour markets, are rated as much more rigid than the LMEs. France and Germany, so similar in many categories, are quite different in labour-management co-operation and willingness to delegate authority reflecting different cultural and institutional heritages.

**Table 2 Comparisons of GDP, infrastructure and HRM across ten countries**

| Category Country | 1 GDP (US$) | 2 Infrastructure | 3 Tertiary education (%) | 4 Labour-management co-operation | 5 Female participation rate | 6 Rigidity of employment | 7 Willingness to delegate authority |
|---|---|---|---|---|---|---|---|
| USA | 46.4 | 5.8 | 83 | 4.9 | 0.85 | 0 | 5.1 |
| UK | 35.3 | 5.3 | 57 | 5.0 | 0.85 | 10 | 4.8 |
| Ireland | 51.4 | 4.2 | 58 | 4.9 | 0.78 | 10 | 4.3 |
| Australia | 45.6 | 5.2 | 77 | 4.7 | 0.85 | 0 | 4.9 |
| France | 42.8 | 6.6 | 55 | 3.5 | 0.87 | 52 | 3.9 |
| Germany | 40.9 | 6.3 | 46 | 5.3 | 0.85 | 42 | 5.0 |
| China | 3.7 | 4.1 | 23 | 4.5 | 0.91 | 31 | 3.6 |
| India | 1.0 | 3.9 | 14 | 4.6 | 0.42 | 30 | 3.9 |
| Brazil | 8.2 | 3.8 | 34 | 4.1 | 0.76 | 46 | 3.9 |
| Russia | 8.7 | 3.6 | 77 | 3.8 | 0.90 | 38 | 3.1 |

Source: Data adapted from *Global Competitiveness Report 2010–2011* (2010) World Economic Forum, Geneva.

Notes: **Meaning of each category**

1 – GDP in US dollars

2 – quality of overall infrastructure (scale from 1 to 7, with 7 = most developed); mean = 4.3

3 – enrolment rate in tertiary education (% of current age group)

4 – labour-management co-operation (scale from 1 to 7, with 7 = highest level); mean = 4.4

5 – female participation rate in employment (ratio of women to men in work)

6 – rigidity of employment (scale from 0 to 100, with 100 = most rigid)

7 – willingness to delegate authority (scale from 1 to 7, with 7 most willing to delegate); mean = 3.7.

## REFLECTIVE ACTIVITY

Look at the Global Competitiveness Report, which is available online, and choose four countries – either from similar or different types of economies – and compare their ratings on the same categories as covered here. What does this tell you? Debate this issue in small groups.

In conclusion, rather than accept globalisation uncritically just because consumer fashion gives large chains – such as McDonalds, Nike and Primark – visibility across the world, a more measured assessment would see globalisation as just one of a series of forces that shape HRM. Key questions remain about its meaning, the accuracy of claims suggesting increasing similarity between nations, the inevitability of its spread given adaptation of wider trends and resistance to globalisation, and the use of rhetoric as a device to legitimise management actions.

## LABOUR MARKETS AND PATTERNS OF EMPLOYMENT

Over the last few decades, in most developed countries there has been a fundamental sectoral shift in employment from manufacturing and the public sector – sectors renowned for more formalised HR systems, high levels of trade union membership, and larger employment units – towards the more informal, relatively union-free, and smaller employment units of the service sector. For example, in 1985 28% of all working males were employed in the manufacturing sector, but by 2011 this had dropped to just 13% (2.15 million); the figures for females fell from 15% to 5% over the same period. In 2011, 2.5 million men and 1.5 million women worked in the public sector, a figure that is likely to fall over the next few years as public sector cuts bite harder, particularly on women. Much of the decline in the last 25 years has been in the productive public sector (eg coal) and privatisation of what were previously public service sector employers (eg gas, water, electricity and telecom), as well as contracting-out services to the private sector from healthcare and local government.

The principal growth area has been the service sector. As a whole, including both public and private services, this provides about three quarters of GDP. Indeed, numbers employed across the economy increased over the last decade, standing at around 29 million in 2011, with some of the new jobs being filled by migrant workers willing to take jobs that UK citizens do not want, either because of low pay or poor working conditions. The largest growth area up to 2008 was finance and business services, but even this has stalled due to the recession. The changing nature of employment has major implications for HRM as 'new' firms typically adopt different practices from their 'older' counterparts (Machin 2003; Edwards and Ram 2006). Table 3 shows how employment patterns have changed, most

**Table 3 Men and women in employment (millions) between 1985 and 2011**

| | 1985 | 1995 | 2000 | 2004 | 2007 | 2011 |
|---|---|---|---|---|---|---|
| **Women** | | | | | | |
| In employment | 9.73 | 11.12 | 11.92 | 13.03 | 13.37 | 13.54 |
| Full-time | 5.58 | 6.34 | 6.77 | 7.25 | 7.69 | 7.73 |
| Part-time | 4.15 | 4.78 | 5.15 | 5.78 | 5.68 | 5.81 |
| Unemployment rate (%) | 11.0 | 7.00 | 4.90 | 4.50 | 5.20 | 7.40 |
| **Men** | | | | | | |
| In employment | 13.96 | 14.11 | 15.05 | 15.28 | 15.73 | 15.63 |
| Full-time | 13.46 | 13.13 | 13.83 | 13.67 | 13.98 | 13.61 |
| Part-time | 0.50 | 0.98 | 1.22 | 1.61 | 1.75 | 2.02 |
| Unemployment rate (%) | 11.7 | 10.20 | 6.10 | 5.30 | 5.80 | 8.70 |

Source: Adapted from Office for National Statistics data from 1985 to 2011.

specifically through growing female participation in the labour market leading to major shifts in full-time and part-time work, as well as on temporary contracts.

Much of the growth has been due to the increased participation rate of *women* in the economy, which by 2011 had reached 13.5 million, up by nearly 40% since 1985, whilst the number of men in work rose over the same period by just 12%. The number of men working part-time has quadrupled from half a million in 1985 to over two million in 2011, so it would appear men are more willing to work part-time, perhaps because full-time work is less readily available. In the decade up to 2010, unemployment rates in EU27 had been higher for women than men, but this switched due to the decline in construction and manufacturing – traditional male preserves. By January 2010 the EU27 unemployment rate was 9.3% for women and 9.7% for men. The percentage of women who are in work in the UK compares well with most EU countries; in the UK, about 65% of women of working age are in employment compared to EU27 average of 59%, but still behind the participation rate in countries such as Finland and Sweden at 68% and 71% respectively. Italy has the lowest rate at 49% (Eurostat 2010). Gender and educational level play a major role in average hourly earnings with women in the EU paid 18% less than men in 2007. At a comparative level, the UK has one of the widest pay gaps among EU member states at 22% (Evans 2010), 40 years after the UK Equal Pay Act; if the gender pay gap continues to close at the same rate, it will take a further 57 years to equalise (Wilton 2011).

Whilst headline pay relativities are stark, they do not take into account different work patterns, particularly in relation to occupational choice and *part-time work*. The labour market remains heavily segmented with most women's jobs being part-time, concentrated in the service sector (public and private) and in jobs with lower pay and lower status. Levels of part-time employment increased to 18.5% of jobs in the EU, and across the EU27, of those in part time jobs, 79% are women, and of these 66% are on temporary contracts. Of those in full time employment, 40% are women and of these 43.5% are in temporary employment (Wozowczyk and Massarelli 2011). The UK is roughly on a par with Germany, Belgium and Austria, but below the Netherlands, where about three-quarters of women and one-quarter of men work part time. Part-time work helps facilitates better work–life balance, and makes it easier for workers to enter or retire from the labour market, but because it is concentrated in the service sector, it is typified by low wages. Employers tend to regard part-timers as providing more flexibility – and even being harder working – than full-timers, and it also helps them to retain skills that might otherwise be lost.

*Temporary* employment continues to grow and is now 12% across EU27. The UK has a larger proportion of temporary workers than the USA at 6.4% (Office for National Statistics 2011), but rather less than many other EU countries, such as Spain, Poland and Sweden (Wozowczyk and Massarelli 2011). The number of *agency workers* also increased over the last decade but most countries upheld the principle of equal pay for agency workers. There are severe penalties for non-compliance in some countries, including criminal liability in France, Italy and Germany, but the new UK regulations include moderate fines without legal restrictions (Hewson 2011).

Currently 91% of workers have access to some form of *flexible working* and 62% of employees take up the offer (CIPD 2011a). Opportunities include flexitime, flexible working arrangements, annualised hours, and zero-hours contracts – although the latter may be just a device to avoid paying staff when there is no demand for their work (eg in a fast-food restaurant).

## REFLECTIVE ACTIVITY

Whilst workers on temporary contracts may offer advantages in terms of cost savings and flexibility, do they add other costs for the employer (in terms of quality, productivity or commitment, for example)? What do temporary workers gain from this form of employment, if anything?

Although the composition of those in employment changed significantly since the 1970s, levels of *unemployment* remained high for much of this period, only falling back around the turn of the century and remaining low until the global financial crisis took effect. In the 1960s, unemployment typically stood at about 3 per cent (around 600,000 people) before a variety of worldwide shocks pushed the figure steadily up beyond one million by 1979. Since then changes in how unemployment is defined made it difficult to draw precise comparisons, but by the International Labour Organisation (ILO) definition it oscillated between about 1.5 and 3.5 million over the last 30 years. In percentage terms, the figure has varied from about 5% to 12%, so even at the lower levels this is higher than would have been considered reasonable in the 1960s. By 2011, it had risen to over 8%, slightly higher amongst men than women, but lower than many of the UK's main European neighbours. Of course the statistics also mask wide regional variations, and pockets of very high unemployment persist, particularly among young people in inner-city areas.

*Ethnic minority groups, the disabled and older people*, as well as women, are disadvantaged (arguably, discriminated against) in terms of employment rates and pay gaps. They have higher rates of unemployment (Walby *et al* 2008), and all ethnic minority groups earn less than white people, a disadvantage which is particularly severe for men. The picture is relatively complicated and is heavily influenced by the specific group, as well as between women and men, and by age. Only 20% of Bangladeshis, 30% of Pakistanis, and 40% of black Africans of working age are in full-time work compared with over 50% of white British people of working age (Foster 2007). Ageism has persisted in the UK, both for young people and older people (CIPD 2010b p.2) but the number of older people in the workforce was at its highest ever – having jumped from 5.5% in 1992 to 9% in 2011 (CIPD 2011b). In 2011, the UK abolished the default retirement age, resulting in reduced numbers of openings for younger people. The upside of this is that older people who do not wish to retire can remain in employment, and almost half of organisations were planning to put in place more flexible working arrangements for older workers (Brockett 2011). In future, there will be further pressures on the labour market due to an ageing population. In Britain, for example, the ratio of pensioners to the working population could rise to over 2:5 by 2030. This is not just a British problem, with estimates for Germany of over 3:5 by 2030, and for Italy of 7:10. The UK cap on non-EU *migrant workers* has led to large increases in numbers from EU, and since EU workers have unlimited access to the UK labour market, this will not help unemployed people in the UK. Meanwhile, the numbers of people from Australia, New Zealand and the USA employed in the UK decreased by up to one-third.

HRM AT WORK IN FOCUS

## Migrant workers in their employment and social context

The labour market in London has become polarised with more professionals on the one hand, but also sizeable increases in the low-wage economy which is dominated by migrants. London has high levels of unemployment, but CIPD surveys suggest migrants are preferred by employers to benefit claimants because they are seen as being more ready for work and possessing higher potential. Many have good qualifications, such as the highly skilled individuals brought in to meet skills shortages (particularly from Japan and Germany), but the majority face substantial problems once they arrive in Britain, including gaining access to work, finding housing, and building up social relationships. The papers reviewed show the main issues, with indicative quotes or case examples:

**Maximising income** in the low-pay economy. Most found it hard to survive on the minimum wage, so the majority worked overtime, or took two jobs, and moved frequently to increase income and improve working conditions. In some cases, the community helped transport goods/money back to the home country. Contrary to popular belief, the majority did not claim benefits, though almost all paid tax and National Insurance.

*'Sometimes I feel life quitting the job. I pay my rent, £300, I'll be left with £300...to pay my travel card, go shopping...and I've got a baby back home...so I have to send money back home to my mum. I'm just trying to do my best.'*

**Childcare.** In London this is prohibitively expensive and, in the absence of extended support networks, parents worked different shifts, or left children behind in their home country.

*Annabel – a 40-year-old single parent from Tanzania – worked in contract cleaning whilst studying to become an accountant. She always worked the night shift so that she was home with the children in the day, but could leave them sleeping at night. She worried about this arrangement, but could not afford childcare.*

**Work–life balance/social exclusion and isolation**. Most migrants had little time to spend with their families, and even less for a social life. Faith-based organisations provided some support, but they often differentiated on ethnic/nationality/language grounds.

*Zelu – a 35-year-old doctor from Bangladesh – came to London with his wife and child. His qualifications were not recognised in UK so he took a job as a care worker, working 40–50 hours per week. His wife worked at the weekend in a supermarket. They lived in a shared house with relatives. Childcare was shared between Zelu, his wife, and an elderly relative. He hoped to save enough money to take a postgraduate course in gastroenterology.*

Sources: Adapted from Datta, *et al* (2007); Murphy (2007a); McGovern (2007) and Philpott and Davies (2006).

The extent of strike action also illustrates the degree to which UK labour markets have changed since the 1980s. Table 4 shows how the number of working days lost to industrial action has fallen sharply from an average of about 10 million in the first half of the 1980s to a little over half a million now. The number of workers involved in stoppages also fell dramatically, and the typical figure is now about half a million per annum, under half the figure in the early 1980s. The number of recorded stoppages has also dropped by similar proportions, from nearly 1,400 per annum in the early 1980s to well under 200 now. Yet more notable is the length of stoppages, with only a handful of major strikes since the turn of the century accounting for 100,000 working days or more, several of which were one-day strikes such as the action taken in defence of public sector pensions during 2011. Godard (2011) provides a thoughtful review of whether the decline in strikes, not just in the UK but in many developed countries, is due to a triumph of capitalism, a dormant period, a shift to other forms of conflict, or whether they have morphed into poor performance, cynicism, stress and general anomie; all are likely to have played some part though the data is not precise enough to judge.

**Table 4 Yearly average for stoppages in progress in the UK, 1980–2011**

| Years | Working days lost (000s) | Working days lost per 1000 employees | Workers involved (000s) | Stoppages |
|---|---|---|---|---|
| 1980–84 | 10,864 | 457 | 1,298 | 1,363 |
| 1985–89 | 3,940 | 170 | 685 | 894 |
| 1990–94 | 824 | 37 | 223 | 334 |
| 1995–99 | 476 | 23 | 201 | 213 |
| 2000–04 | 731 | 24 | 374 | 176 |
| 2005–07 | 580 | 20 | 526 | 191 |
| 2008–11 | 573 | 19 | 467 | 156 |

Source: Adapted from Labour Market Statistics, *Labour Disputes*, 2011.

It can be seen, therefore, that employment patterns have changed dramatically over the last 30 years, and the 'traditional' image of work – principally male, full-time and permanent – no longer holds. In addition, sectoral and other shifts in employment have reshaped the character of HRM not only in the UK but also in other developed countries.

## FLEXIBILITY AND FRAGMENTATION AT WORK

Interest in workforce and organisational flexibility grew following the publication of Atkinson's work on the flexible firm in the mid-1980s (Atkinson 1984). Since then other writers have taken up the idea, notably Handy (1991) with the terminology of a 'shamrock organisation'. Both make distinctions between a core and a peripheral workforce, albeit in slightly different ways and with different foci, but Atkinson's is still widely referred to in publications. Refinements have been made over the last 25 years, notably by Ackroyd and Procter (1998), Marchington *et al* (2005) and Lepak and Snell (2007), and we revisit this via an examination of HR architecture in Chapter 4. A graphical representation of workforce flexibility is provided in Figure 2.

**Figure 2 The flexible firm**

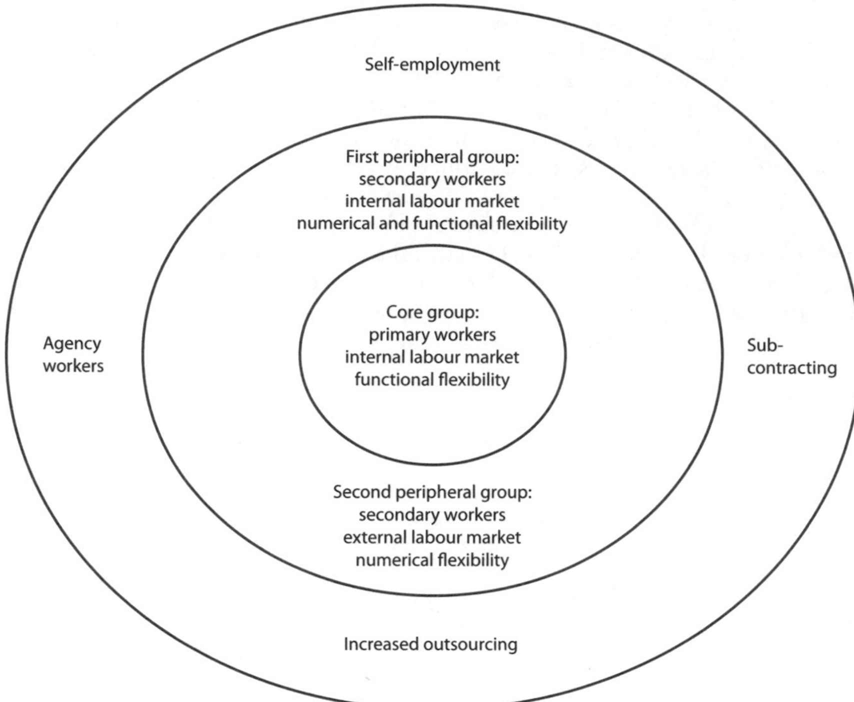


Source: Adapted from Atkinson (1984).

The core comprises workers drawn from the primary labour market, who gain security through 'permanent' (open-ended) contracts and whose skills are valued by the employer. In return, these core employees are expected to be functionally flexible by applying their skills across a wide range of tasks. Flexibility can be both vertical and horizontal. Vertical flexibility refers to employees who take on tasks that are at a higher or lower skill level than that for which they were recruited; for example, semi-skilled employees assuming responsibility for certain skilled tasks, such as making minor repairs to keep production lines running. Horizontal flexibility relates to employees doing a wider range of tasks at the same broad skill level, as for example in the case of craft workers who operate across previous skill boundaries by doing both mechanical and electrical work. Workers in chemical process teams may be vertically *and* horizontally flexible if they are responsible for a complete task (Frobel and Marchington 2005).

The periphery can be subdivided into several segments. The first group comprises workers from the secondary labour market who are employed on contracts that have some degree of permanence. They may be full- or part-time, but these workers cannot expect as much security as their colleagues from the 'core', even if they are functionally flexible. They are also numerically flexible, as they can be laid off relatively easily since applicants with similar skills can be hired quickly. The second peripheral group comprises individuals who find it hard to break into internal labour markets and have little realistic prospect of employment security. Many temporary workers fit into this category though they are sometimes hired if they are seen to do a good job and 'fit' with the organisational culture.

Beyond the second peripheral group are individuals who are clearly external to the host organisation but employed by another employer or in self-employment. This group has grown significantly as more work is subcontracted to external organisations. Agency workers – such as secretaries, nurses and teachers – fit into this category as well (Grimshaw *et al* 2003; Mitlacher 2007; Shire *et al* 2009a; Marchington *et al* 2011). Ward *et al* (2001, p.9) argue that host organisations recruit temporary workers through specialist agencies because they provide numerical flexibility and also shift the risk to agencies and the temporaries themselves. Some employers vet temporary workers to see whether or not they may be suitable for appointment to permanent positions at later dates (Forde 2001). In short, parts of recruitment and selection thus transfer to the agency, leading to the development of quasi-internal labour markets that may be useful to the employer and the agency (Rubery *et al* 2004).

Employers have developed more flexible HRM practices through the increased use of part-timers and in the growth of subcontracting and self-employment. The public sector – in particular health trusts and local authorities – has been at the forefront of these developments, with government requirements to extend outsourcing through various different vehicles over time (Colling 1999; Marchington *et al* 2011). Through the Transfer of Undertakings (Protection of Employment) Regulations (TUPE) transfers of employment are now widespread.

Despite much publicity, doubts remain about how extensive the 'flexible firm' is in reality, and some scepticism about whether or not flexibility really is the product of strategic thinking or muddling through. There are four major concerns about the model:

1 *The concept*. There are doubts about the terminology. Publications seem to veer between *descriptions* of flexibility, *predictions* that the flexible firm is the design of the future and *prescriptions* that organisations should use the model to become more successful. At times it is difficult to tell which is being used, and it has led to allegations that flexibility has been 'talked up' in order to support successive governments' ideological stance on market deregulation and 'lean' organisations (Legge 1995, p.172). It is also argued that, despite its obvious intuitive appeal, the model lacks clarity in terms of the core–periphery distinction. For example, rather than viewing part-timers as peripheral, it is clear some part-time workers are critical to organisational success given their close contact with customers or their contribution to business goals. This raises questions about whether they should be classified as core because they interface with customers or peripheral because they are part-timers (Rubery *et al* 2004).

2 *Extensiveness*. There are questions about the extent of flexibility in practice and the reasons for its growth. Robinson (1999, p.90) suggested that the more dramatic assertions about the impact of the core–periphery model are not really backed up by the data. However, earlier we presented figures on so-called 'non-standard' employment which showed that subcontracting is well established in both public and private sectors, as is the use of fixed-term contracts for staff in the public sector. WERS found temporary workers were used in about 30% of workplaces and freelancers by one in eight, though rarely in the public sector (Kersley *et al* 2006, p.80). Even though data shows over 1.5 million people in temporary work in late 2011, it is impossible to determine whether employers make use of 'atypical' work as part of a strategic HR initiative. Interestingly, Chamberlain (2011) reports that over 80% of employers planned to increase their use of temporary staff during the final months of 2011 despite changes to the law giving agency workers the same rights as direct recruits after 12 weeks in post.

3 *Costs and benefits*. There is disagreement about the costs and benefits of flexibility. It is widely assumed to be more efficient than its 'inflexible' counterpart, with part-timers, temporaries and sub-contractors offering employers advantages over secure and permanent staff. It is hard to estimate whether part-time workers are more productive than their full-time colleagues or whether they cost more due to higher levels of absenteeism and lower levels of commitment and quality. For example, there are concerns

about quality where work is done by private sector firms through sub-contracting and partnerships with the NHS and local authorities (Colling 1999; Marchington *et al* 2003a; Boaden *et al* 2008; Bach and Givan 2010). It is also queried whether core workers maintain previous levels of commitment following rationalisation due to fears for their own future security (Hebson *et al* 2003). However, it is also clear that some workers with care responsibilities may find part-time preferable to full-time work (Thompson and McHugh 2002, p.161).

4 *Single employer*. The flexible firm model is limited because it focuses on a single organisation and its HR practices, rather than taking into account inter-organisational relations (Marchington *et al* 2009, 2011a; Rubery and Urwin 2011). Even though most studies still assume a relationship between a single employing organisation and its employees, this is no longer accurate because increasingly globalised capital markets, unstable and flexible labour markets, and breakdowns and fragmentation in the world of work have dramatically altered this picture. Significant employment changes have been stimulated by adaptations in ownership patterns and state policies that have reconfigured the shape of both private and public sector organisations. Spin-off companies, joint ventures and strategic alliances have redrawn the boundaries between firms, especially in the high technology sector, and the public–private divide has become increasingly blurred. Multi-employer sites have become more common in the service sector, in particular through agency working and the expansion of franchising (Kellner *et al* 2011).

## REFLECTIVE ACTIVITY

Who do you think gains most from flexible working, and why? Put together lists for workers and employers in relation to functional and numerical flexibility before making a judgement.

It is clear that work is becoming increasingly fragmented, that boundaries between organisations are becoming blurred and that existing hierarchies are becoming disordered. In many cases work has become more pressurised and controlled rather than liberated and empowered (Delbridge 2011). So-called 'old' notions of skill, career and learning – that worked on the assumption of extended time horizons – are being replaced by new visions that rely increasingly on short-term and superficial levels of training and development where discontinuities are the norm and workers are increasingly bearing the risk for their own career development (Blyton 2011). Simultaneously, trade unions are finding their role, already weakened, is further marginalised as systems of worker representation break down following transfers of workers to other organisations (Marchington and Timming 2010; Heery 2011). Boundaries within organisations become more blurred as traditional hierarchies are dismantled, but whilst this may open up new opportunities, it can also create further insecurity and confusion for people, and often fail to deliver the improved performance expectations promised to customers or clients. The growth of inter-organisational relations also leads to a disordering of hierarchies as responsibility for the management and control of staff is diffused, and customers are increasingly seen to influence the management of employment, such as when powerful clients specifically ask for certain staff to be utilised on 'their' contracts, or where workers are rebuked following a customer-feedback survey (Marchington *et al* 2009). The increased use of agency staff means responsibility for managing staff who liaise with customers is split between employers (Rubery and Urwin 2011).

In other words, models of the flexible firm may no longer be adequate to analyse changes within and between different organisations that are tied together with a variety of commercial contracts. For example, a professional who works at the site of a client for long periods of time may be a peripheral worker so far as the client is concerned, but a core worker for the management consultancy by whom she is employed. Equally, how can the self-employed person who routinely sells his services to an agency be classified: as self-employed, as a core agency worker, or as a peripheral contract worker? Even greater confusions can occur in circumstances where several employers operate from the same site. The HRM at Work in Focus box below gives a flavour of HRM in these different organisational forms.

HRM AT WORK IN FOCUS

### Fragmenting work across organisational boundaries

Research by Marchington *et al* (2005, 2011b) analyses the management of employment in a wide range of organisational networks. Each of these took on quite different forms in practice but several features were common across the case studies.

The influence of clients over HRM at a supplier's workplace was clear in a number of cases, either through external signs – wearing the client's uniform or answering the phone using its name – or through more hidden forces, such as attempts to choose which worker was assigned to a particular contract or questioning the level and type of training offered (Rubery *et al* 2004).

Many workers were confused about who was actually their employer; something confirmed by legal cases. For example supply teachers found some aspects of their employment (for example, pay) were determined by the agency while daily control of working patterns was overseen by the headteacher in the school where they were based (Grimshaw, D *et al* 2003).

Even if there were no doubts about the status of the employer, staff transferred from the public to the private sector found difficulty in deciding where their loyalties lay – to their old employer (the NHS), to their new private sector employer, to their colleagues, to their union, to the patients or even to some wider societal goal of better health care (Hebson *et al* 2003).

Divisions within and between the workforce were also common, especially when workers were on different rates of pay depending on which business contract they were employed, when they were recruited, and which bonus system they were tied into. This also carried over into the opportunities for expressing worker voice and solidarity (Rubery *et al* 2003).

*To think about:*

*Each of these cases raises interesting issues relating to control and discipline, identity and commitment, recruitment and training, performance management and reward, as well as voice and representation. Read one of the sources quoted above and compare these findings with your own workplace or one with which you are familiar.*

## THE LEGAL FRAMEWORK FOR HRM AND EMPLOYMENT RELATIONS

This section reviews employment law to show, using examples from the UK and EU, how it shapes HRM at work. In the space available it is impossible to offer a systematic and detailed analysis of the law, so readers **MUST** seek advice from employment law books (eg, Lewis *et al* 2011; Taylor and Emir 2009) or from employment relations texts (eg, Dundon and Rollinson 2011; Gennard and Judge 2010). Legal texts are updated regularly to take account of recent changes, but reference should also be made to Factsheets or 'Employment Law' in the Topics section of the CIPD website.

## UK AND EU INFLUENCES ON HRM

### UK developments

In Britain employment law traditionally played a minor role in HRM compared with many other countries, especially the co-ordinated market economies of Europe; the system having been moulded by employers and trade unions rather than by legal enactment. 'Voluntarism' has been the prevailing philosophy with 'collective laissez-faire' (Kahn-Freund 1959, p.224) seen as the best way to resolve problems; in effect, the law has been seen as a mechanism of last resort when voluntary means fail. However, this ignores the critical role played by the law in shaping the expectations of employers and employees to make use of agreed rules rather than going to court to seek legal redress. Accordingly, assessing the impact of legal intervention should be in relation to its *desirability* as well as the likelihood of *attaining* its objectives. As with any area of legal intervention (eg speed limits or smoking bans), if this is accepted as appropriate by citizens, the more successful – and less interventionist – the law needs to be.

According to Kahn-Freund (1965, p.302), the law performs three roles in the rule-making process. First, there is the *auxiliary* role through which the state provides a statutory framework of what is called 'organised persuasion'. This provides benefits – financial or otherwise – for those observing agreements, and pressures are applied against those who do not. A good illustration of this is Acas. Second, the law has a *restrictive* role whereby it lays down rules that stipulate what is allowed and what is forbidden in the conduct of employment relations, such as in relation to strikes or picketing. Third, the law has a *regulatory* role whereby it sets a 'floor of employment rights' for employees that apply across the board; for example, in Victorian times, this provided protection to employees in mining and sweatshops, as well as to children under a certain age. Employment protection legislation expanded during the 1970s, incorporating all employees rather than just those in particular industries or working under particularly harsh conditions. Apart from direct intervention in HR issues, the law has shaped good practice; for example, the unfair dismissal legislation led to changes in recruitment and selection and disciplinary procedures during the 1970s and beyond.

Broadly, recent Labour governments have extended the regulatory role of the law, particularly via the EU with the introduction of the minimum wage and working time regulations but also through mainstreaming equality and parental rights under the banner of fairness. They also reduced the qualifying period for access to employment protection legislation. The 1997–2010 Labour governments supported a flexible labour market, underpinned by an extended but limited range of legal protections at work, largely for individuals but also, to a lesser degree, for trade unions (Dickens and Hall 2006). Yet it is noteworthy they did not seek to loosen the restrictive aspects of employment law – for example on the closed shop, picketing, secondary and unofficial action, and trade union elections (Dundon and Rollinson 2011). By contrast Conservative governments have tended to restrict trade union activities whilst leaving the floor of employment rights broadly intact, though the 2010 Conservative–Liberal Democrat coalition is proposing to extend the time period before workers can claim unfair dismissal and, more controversially, make applicants pay a fee before they are allowed to submit claims to employment tribunals. There are also suggestions that further restrictions on strike action should be introduced. Traditionally the 'market' has been used to regulate labour standards through privatisation of nationalised industries and the use of contracting-out to reduce the size of the public sector.

REFLECTIVE ACTIVITY

To what extent do you think the state should intervene in employment issues? Identify a number of arguments to support your conclusion.

## EU influences

Many of the recent initiatives have come through the EU; these include the national minimum wage, equal pay for work of equal value, the protection of employees' rights in the event of a transfer of an undertaking (TUPE), and the introduction of information and consultation machinery for a variety of situations. More recently a number of EU decisions have helped to strengthen the position of British workers who are not members of trade unions. The influence of European law is complex, making it hard to differentiate between UK-driven and European-driven developments as they continually interact (Gennard and Judge 2010). The removal of the veto by a single member state meant that HR professionals 'had to take Europe seriously because it was now possible to influence the drafting of new EU laws in a way unthinkable within national parliaments' (Gennard and Judge 2005, p.127). It brought radical changes by harmonising health and safety regulations across member states and the Working Time Directive. The UK labour market is increasingly shaped by legislation at EU level, and as employers have expanded operations into other member states this has increased the range of influences on HR managers. The model of 'flexicurity' (see Chapters 3 and 12) advocated by the Commission seeks to 'balance the employer's demand for flexibility with the employee's hopes for security. Equally important, education and training are seen not only as a way of helping individuals to become more adaptable in their present employment, but also of providing opportunities to acquire knowledge and skills so that they can find alternative employment should the number of jobs be reduced in their present workplace' (Bach and Sisson 2000, p.34). One area which has always attracted disagreement is the legislation on working hours, with some believing passionately that there should be restrictions for the good of workers and their families whilst others feel this is just an unnecessary constraint on business and individual freedom. The distribution of volunteers and conscripts amongst those working long hours has been examined by Drago *et al* (2009). The HRM at Work in Focus box shows how disagreements remain over the working time proposals.

HRM AT WORK IN FOCUS

### Battles over working time

The 1998 Working Time Regulations provide that a worker's working time (including overtime) should not exceed an average of 48 hours per week over a 17-week period. The UK took advantage of an opt-out allowing workers to 'expressly and freely' agree with their employers that the 48-hour ceiling should not apply to them. This remains the case but the coalition government has expressed its desire to withdraw from any constraint on maximum working hours, so check on the CIPD website to see whether or not this has changed. The average working hours for full-timers in 2011 was 39 hours for men and 34 hours for women, and indeed most full-timers work between 31 and 45 hours. About 5.8 million people work over 45 hours per week (Office for National Statistics 2011), a much higher rate than other developed countries, apart from the USA. Interestingly, people with second jobs average a further nine hours per week. Only four EU countries – Denmark, Ireland, the Netherlands and Sweden – have shorter average working weeks before overtime is included (Philpott 2010).

A range of issues arise here, many of which have little to do with the law. It is acknowledged there are major problems with a long-hours culture, such as higher stress levels, more accidents due to tired workers, and a reliance on using inefficient labour practices rather than investing in technology. On the other hand, the UK has always operated with higher working time than the EU in general, and it has helped to provide a decent level of income for many workers while allowing employers an easy route to meeting extra demand, especially in the short term. Two groups of people – managers and manual workers – are particularly prone to working long hours, although the reasons for doing so are generally very different. Research by Barnard *et al* (2003) showed that many workers were keen on retaining the opportunity to work long hours and it was rare for employers to pressure them into overtime. As they suggest, much of the problem has come about because UK employers have been allowed a high degree of autonomy, and high amounts of overtime have therefore become institutionalised.

*To think about:*

*As we have seen, since 1997 the Labour government took on board – sometimes reluctantly – legal provisions emanating from the EU. What do you think the 2010 Conservative–Liberal Democrat coalition will do in this area (not just working time but more generally) and how far do you think they will – and should – go in seeking to limit proposals from the EU?*

Other European developments affecting the UK include directives on race and ethnicity, equal treatment on a whole variety of grounds including religion or belief, disability, age and sexual orientation. The Human Rights Act 1998, which came into force in 2000, incorporates into UK law certain rights and freedoms set out in the European Convention on Human Rights. For further detail, please refer to Lewis *et al* (2011).

**Assessment**

The current system of employment law is thus a synthesis of competing values and traditions. It continues to accept much of the Thatcher inheritance, especially in relation to collective issues, but it has also been shaped to accommodate new beliefs. For example, there are rights to union recognition where there is a prescribed level of support, but tight restrictions on industrial action. There is now a clearer role for legislation in setting minimum standards (Taylor and Emir 2009), which has been important not only to promote improved competitiveness but also to provide greater 'fairness' at work. The 2010 Equality Act consolidated nine separate pieces of legislation.

So, how does this leave the current legal system? One view is that the period between 1997 and 2010 was a balancing act (Dickens and Hall 2006), trying simultaneously to appease employers and trade unions/workers, by tackling the worst excesses of employer behaviour (in relation to pay and discrimination, for example) while not burdening employers with too much regulation; questions about the principles behind and the actual level of the National Minimum Wage have been raised regularly (Brown 2009; Deakin and Green 2009) in this respect. The Labour government promoted 'social justice, fairness and security' via arguments supporting the business case (Dickens and Hall 2006) rather than as a moral imperative. This stance is unlikely to change with the coalition government, and if anything – apart from some commitment to family-friendly legislation – the regulatory role is likely to weaken in relation to tribunal claims. Gennard (2002, p.593) believed the Labour government from 1997 actually managed to annoy both employers and workers, and indeed their approach could be criticised for being little more than a ragbag of initiatives. On the other hand, rather than viewing the law as a constraint on business, employment regulation could be seen more positively as providing a framework of social justice that guarantees workers some minimum level of security which allows them to contribute to economic success (Dickens and Hall 2006).

## INDIVIDUAL RIGHTS AT WORK: THE EMPLOYMENT CONTRACT

Employer–worker relations are organised principally around the employment contract; for further guidance, consult either Lewis *et al* (2011) or Taylor and Emir (2009). Recently, the situation has become complex because boundaries between workers and their employers have become blurred and there is increasing flexibility built into working arrangements.

Contract law is based on common law, and because it is made by judges rather than Parliament it evolves continuously as cases are brought before the courts (Taylor and Emir 2009). Nonetheless, all employees have a contract of employment, which may or may not be written, and in practice the parties enter into a contract after the stages of advertisement, interview, offer and acceptance. Formal written contracts are desirable to avoid complications. There are several sources of contractual terms:

### Express terms

These are terms that are spelled out, either in writing or orally, to form part of the contract. They may include points in the advert, oral terms outlined at interview, or a written contract provided after the interview. The express terms may differ from what is contained in a job advert, but are clearly laid down as part of the individual contract or are expressly incorporated from a collective agreement. They take priority over all other sources (such as common law implied terms or custom and practice) but do not take priority over statutory terms. A key element is written particulars of employment to be provided within two months of starting work (see HRM at Work in Focus box); if they are not challenged by the employee, they usually form part of the contract (Lewis *et al* 2011).

HRM AT WORK IN FOCUS

### Written particulars of employment

- identity of employer and employee
- date on which the period of continuous employment commenced
- job title or description of work to be carried out
- rate of remuneration, and the interval at which it is to be paid
- terms and conditions relating to hours of work, holidays and holiday pay
- length of notice that employees are required to receive and obliged to provide
- name of persons to whom the individual employee can apply in the event of a grievance or dissatisfaction with a disciplinary decision
- place(s) of work at which the employee is required or allowed to work
- details regarding collective agreements that directly affect the

employee's terms and conditions of employment

- where the employment is temporary, the period for which it is expected to continue or, if it is for a fixed term, the date when it is to end
- arrangements where the employee is required to work outside the UK for more than a month.

The following need not be given individually; it is sufficient to make reference to them and make the information accessible:

- terms relating to pensions arrangements
- sick pay arrangements
- length of notice required
- any disciplinary rules and the name of the person who would deal with grievances.

### Terms implied by common law

These are terms assumed to be inherent in all contracts of employment. They can arise in two ways. First, they are based upon the presumed intention of the parties, either through 'the officious bystander' test – meaning that a term is so obvious it need not be stated – or 'the business efficacy' test, in which it can be presumed that this was the clear intention of both parties. Second, certain terms are implied in every contract (Lewis *et al* 2011). Under this, the employer has a duty to:

- pay wages if an employee is available for work unless there is an express term limiting this
- provide work when an employee's earnings are dependent upon it being provided, when lack of work could affect their reputation, or when employees need to practise skills continuously
- co-operate with the employee, so as not to destroy mutual trust and confidence upon which co-operation is built, for example by obligations which are impossible to comply with
- take reasonable care for workers by providing safe premises and working environments, and avoiding risks which are reasonably foreseeable.

In return, the employee also has obligations under common law. These are to:

- co-operate with the employer, by obeying lawful and reasonable instructions so as not to impede the employer's business. Complications arise when workers are asked to take on duties falling outside the scope of their contract
- be faithful to the employer, and not engage in actions which cause a conflict of interest with the employer, say by disclosing confidential information to a competitor
- take reasonable care in performing their duties so as not to put themselves or other employees at risk.

### Collective agreements

Where trade unions negotiate terms of employment, the collective agreement forms part of the contract of each individual and cannot be amended unilaterally. Pay, hours of work, holidays and conditions of service may be varied through negotiations with trade unions, or, in some circumstances, direct with employees.

### Works rules

These are unilaterally determined by the employer and can be incorporated into the contract if employees formally acknowledge this in writing or if 'reasonable notice' is given by the employer that works rules are to form part of the contract. Questions can arise about how much variation to allow and how prominently the rules have been displayed.

### Custom and practice

Before the requirement to provide written particulars, custom and practice defined the employment contract provided it was 'reasonable, certain and notorious'. 'Reasonable' means it fits with norms in the industry, 'certain' means it can be defined precisely and 'notorious' means it is well-known by those to whom it relates. Examples include bonuses and working conditions (Dundon and Rollinson 2011).

### Statute

These are terms Parliament has decreed will be put into all contracts of employment, and given that employment legislation regarding employer–worker relations has expanded considerably over the last 30 years, these cover just about every aspect of the employment relationship. Examples include awards the National Minimum Wage Act and Working Time Regulations.

## COLLECTIVE RIGHTS AT WORK

For many years, public policy encouraged the support and development of collective bargaining and emphasised voluntarism, a good example being the general duty of Acas to 'encourage the extension of collective bargaining'. Although there were no formal powers to impose changes on employers or employees, this had a positive effect on the employer–union relationship. Conservative governments during the 1980s and 1990s gradually eroded collectivism in order – from their perspective – to enhance individual freedom, protect employers from union action, and improve efficiency and competitiveness. This included restrictions on union recognition, strikes and picketing. Even though the law allowed this, not many employers took out injunctions to delay industrial action, and even fewer went beyond the injunction stage to seek damages against trade unions (Rollinson and Dundon 2007). On the other hand, the potential threat probably constrained union leaders and members, and may have prevented some deep-seated conflicts erupting as strikes.

Since the late 1990s statutes have been added covering information and consultation, recognition and representation, but the previous Conservative regime remains broadly in place (Dickens and Hall 2006). Public policy promoted partnership as a more sensible and co-operative way forward for employers and workers, as we see in Chapter 13. Continuing efforts to dismantle the closed shop – where union membership is a condition of employment – were at the forefront of the legislation, and, with some exceptions, is now more or less complete. We look at union recognition in Chapter 12, but broadly the level of membership required is set out in law, and includes assistance from Acas and application to the Central Arbitration Committee (CAC). It is now more difficult for unions to collect subscriptions at the workplace but, whilst more members now pay by direct debit, deducting contributions at source remained prominent in the majority of workplaces (Kersley *et al* 2006, p.111). In the area of collective rights, use of the law is never easy and there are concerns that employers who are hostile to recognition can find ways to undermine the union's case (Wood *et al* 2003, p.142).

The legislation on strikes and picketing gradually made it more difficult, though not impossible, for trade unions to organise industrial action and picketing because definitions of a lawful trade dispute were narrowed progressively. The dismissal of strikers has been made easier by laws prohibiting individuals dismissed during a lawful dispute from claiming unfair dismissal if all strikers at a workplace had been dismissed and none had been re-engaged within three months. The requirement to hold ballots of members before taking industrial action has been extended, and in recent years a number of strikes (for example at British Airways) have been contested due to wording on the ballot paper and incomplete membership records. It is interesting that, despite opportunities to seek damages from unions after strike action, this has been used much less than action requiring the re-run of ballots. The wording used on ballot papers has been tightened up, there are now time limits for industrial action after a ballot, and employers have to be given notice that a ballot is to be held. All of this makes it harder for trade unions to organise strikes and easier for employers to counter them.

Legislation relating to employee involvement has been in place since 2005 with the Information and Consultation (ICE) Regulations which requires employers to consult with their workers on a regular basis. The employer has to provide information and consult with workers or their representatives on issues such as the future development of the organisation, any threats to future employment, and any substantial changes in work organisation or contractual relations. In reality the low bar at which this is set makes it relatively easy for employers to comply, as we see in Chapter 13. Yet again, however, readers wanting specific and up-to-date information are advised to consult Lewis *et al* (2011) or Taylor and Emir (2009), or indeed recently published law or employment relations texts.

REFLECTIVE ACTIVITY

Do you think the ICE Regulations are useful in order to persuade employers to provide information to their staff? Why/why not?

## THE INSTITUTIONAL FRAMEWORK FOR HRM

### TRADE UNIONS AND THE TRADES UNION CONGRESS (TUC)

The British trade union movement has a long history, stretching back almost 200 years. It has helped to shape HR practice not just within those organisations where unions are – or have been – recognised, but also through its influence on employment law and government policy. Moreover, some non-union employers have introduced superior terms and conditions of employment primarily to prevent unions from gaining a foothold. Trade unions can be categorised in two ways: craft, general and industrial; or open and closed (Turner 1962). Further details can be found in Dundon and Rollinson (2011).

The earliest unions were for craftsmen (sic) who experienced high levels of autonomy in their work, and sought to maintain and extend job control by preventing dilution of their skills. These unions were based on single trades – such as printing, carpentry and milling – and were organised initially at a local and regional level. Each trade union jealously guarded its own specialist field, against other craft unions and encroachment by unskilled workers, so union strength came from the ability to regulate entry by maintaining strict controls over numbers. This led the unskilled and semi-skilled to form their own bodies – the general unions – which were very different from those of their craft-based colleagues in a number of ways. They were established in the 1880s and 1890s at national level and adopted a more overtly political stance. The final category is industrial unions, formed to represent all workers in a particular industry or sector, the most prominent being those in coal mining and the railways. Merger activity over the last 25 years has rendered this classification increasingly obsolete, and the emergence of more 'super unions' makes the categorisation even less appropriate.

The alternative classification – open and closed – has the benefit of focusing on recruitment methods and the extent to which unions seek to expand or restrict membership. Closed unions include those originally formed for craft workers or in some industries, but technological change accelerated mergers of what were once closed unions. The open unions, by contrast, seek to expand membership in order to increase their strength and influence. Trade unions can thus be categorised in terms of the degree to which they are open or closed in nature.

The number of unions declined consistently from 1,400 in 1920 to 163 in 2010, and membership is now 7.3 million compared with 13.2 million in 1979. Union density halved from 54% to around 27% of the working population over the same period, but it is still higher than the OECD average of 18%. Membership is higher in the public sector (around 56%) compared with 14% in private services; density in manufacturing is now below 18%, well below the national average, and about half the level it was in 1995. Nearly two-thirds of union members work in the public sector and union density is highest for professionals and the most highly educated – such as teachers and nurses. Women are now more likely to be union members than men (29%:24%), probably because of their dominance in the public sector (Archur 2011). The UK is not alone in seeing the density of unionisation decline, as Table 5 shows.

**Table 5 Union density in selected OECD countries in 2009/10**

| Country | Union density (%) | Country | Union density (%) |
|---|---|---|---|
| Finland | 70 | United Kingdom | 27 |
| Sweden | 68 | New Zealand | 21 |
| Denmark | 67 | Germany | 19 |
| Italy | 35 | Japan | 18 |
| Ireland | 31 | Australia | 18 |
| Canada | 28 | USA | 11 |

Source: Adapted from OECD StatExtracts, 2011.

Membership has become more concentrated, and the 10 largest unions account for 78% of trade union members, yet half of all unions have less than 1,000 members. Multi-unionism has diminished markedly over the last 30 years as mergers have created new unions which brought together some of the giants of the past – Unite being the perfect example. According to Kersley *et al* (2006, pp.111–12), 64% of workplaces employing 10 or more employees did not recognise trade unions; of those that did, the largest proportion (53%) recognised only a single trade union, and just 27% recognised more than three. Union mergers have contributed to the reduction in multi-unionism, and to the greater heterogeneity of membership of some of the larger unions. There has been pressure to create a smaller number of unions able to work together, rather than, as on some occasions, wasting resources by fighting each other. The 10 largest unions are shown in Table 6.

In the private sector, union density is closely related to the age and size of workplaces and firms; membership levels have fallen because union density is higher in 'old' declining industries and lower in areas of employment growth, and there are fewer large establishments. The public sector is now the main bastion of union membership, particularly amongst professionals.

**Table 6 Numbers of members in the largest British unions in 2010**

| | |
|---|---|
| Unite the union | 1, 572, 995 |
| UNISON | 1,374,500 |
| GMB | 601,730 |
| Royal College of Nursing of the UK | 409,801 |
| Union of Shop Distributive and Allied Workers | 386,572 |
| National Union of Teachers | 376,797 |
| National Association of School Masters and Union of Women Teachers | 326,659 |
| Public and Commercial Services Union | 301,562 |
| Communication Workers Union | 217,807 |
| Association of Teachers and Lecturers | 216,739 |

Source: Certification Officer (2011) *Annual Report of the Certification Officer, 2009–10*, London

## REFLECTIVE ACTIVITY

What is the level of union membership in your organisation (or one with which you are familiar)? To what extent has this changed recently, and what are the reasons for this?

Unlike most other Western European countries, Britain has only one main union confederation – the TUC – whose affiliates constitute the vast majority of union members. The TUC has no direct role in collective bargaining and cannot implement industrial action, largely because British unions have been keen to protect their own autonomy. Instead, the TUC's primary role is to lobby governments, although its political influence has declined (Marchington *et al* 2011b). It occasionally gets involved in trying to settle industrial disputes by putting pressure on strike leaders or in attempting to widen disputes by encouraging other unions to become involved, typically through moral and financial support. It has played a more significant role in the action to protect public sector pensions more recently. The TUC has been a keen advocate of partnership at work through its role in the Involvement and Participation Association, the Partnership Fund and its own Partnership Institute (see Chapter 13). Moreover, a more continental European-style approach has been adopted that presses for broader statutory rights for *all* employees, including non-unionised (Marchington *et al* 2011b). As well as promoting the partnership model, the TUC also sought to stem membership decline via more effective recruitment strategies and set up an Organising Academy to train a new generation of union organisers (Marchington *et al* 2011b). The need to prioritise recruitment of new members led some unions to focus on broader services to individual members, and to adopt models closer to customer 'servicing' than to the traditional ideals of collective organisation (Dundon and Rollinson 2011).

## EMPLOYERS' ASSOCIATIONS AND THE CONFEDERATION OF BRITISH INDUSTRY (CBI)

Organisations of employers have a history just as long as trade unions, but their prominence and influence has also declined. They are defined as 'any organisation of employers, individual proprietors, or constituent organisations of employers whose principal purpose includes the regulation of relations between employers and workers or between employers and trade unions' (Farnham 2000, p.42). Like trade unions, they are defined in law and registered with the Certification Officer who produces an Annual Report. Similarly, numbers have declined from well over 1,000 in the mid-1960s to about 60 in 2010 (Certification Officer 2011). In the early 1980s, about one-quarter of all workplaces were in organisations that were members of a relevant employers' association, a figure that has since declined considerably (Millward *et al* 2000, p.75; Kersley *et al* 2006, p.52).

Employers' associations differ widely in their size, structure and organisation, and can be categorised into three broad groupings (Salamon 2000, p.271). First, there are national associations or federations with local branches or affiliates, such as the National Farmers Union (NFU) and the Engineering Employers Federation, which retain key roles in the industry. Second, there are specialist bodies that represent a distinct segment of an industry, such as in printing where there are a number of different bodies for newspaper printing, book publishing and general printing. Others include the Association of Circus Proprietors of Great Britain, the England and Wales Cricket Board and the National Hairdressers Federation. Finally, there are small local associations such as the Lancaster Morecambe and South Lakeland Master Plumbers Association; the annual report provides the full list.

Historically, employers' associations played a key part in shaping employment relations in Britain. Initially at local level and then (more importantly) at national level they brought together and acted as representatives for employers in each industry, reaching agreements with unions over recognition, disputes procedures and the substantive terms and conditions to apply in member companies. This elevated the determination of basic wages, hours and other employment conditions beyond the level of individual companies. Since then, membership and influence has declined considerably, though they are still important in some industries and the public sector (Marchington *et al* 2011b).

Employers' associations have traditionally provided four major services to members:

1 *Collective bargaining with trade unions* – This role was central for many years, and is still important where collective bargaining takes place at industry level. In a small number of industries, agreements are comprehensive in scope and coverage, specifying wage rates and other terms and conditions of employment that apply broadly at each establishment. Kersley *et al* (2006, p.186) note that multi-employer bargaining covered 18% of workplaces (up from 14% six years earlier). Despite lessened penetration, nationally negotiated rates of pay – and perhaps more importantly patterns of working time – still shape HRM at workplace level in some organisations. For conglomerates whose interests span many different industries, however, the collective bargaining role offers no benefits.

2 *Assisting in the resolution of disputes* – This is where employers' associations and trade unions agree to abide by joint grievance, disputes, and disciplinary procedures if there is a 'failure to agree' at establishment or firm level. The major purpose is to allow for an independent view, by individuals with a good knowledge of the industry, and so assist the parties to reach agreement without taking unilateral action. The use of employers' associations has declined as employers have chosen to appoint their own appeals body, or seek external advice from lawyers or Acas.

3 *Providing general advice to members* – This can range from seminars for member companies on the impact of new legislation through to informal assistance in the event

of a query. This service is the most widely used, in particular for advice on health and safety, training and education, industrial relations and employment law. An increased use of lawyers, Acas, and management consultants has reduced reliance on employers' associations.

4 *Representing members' views* – This role takes two forms: first, employers' associations, and in particular the Confederation of British Industry (CBI), acts as a pressure group for employers generally, both in relation to national government and with the European Commission. Second, employers' associations also provide specialist representation for member firms at employment tribunals, although some employers now prefer to use lawyers or consultants instead.

REFLECTIVE ACTIVITY

Choose an industry-based employers' association and find out how it serves its members nowadays in terms of the four roles discussed above. In particular, assess the extent to which it shapes HR practice in the workplace.

The main national body for employers is the CBI. Its membership includes individual employers as well as employers' and trade associations. Indirectly, it claims to articulate the views of employers representing a large number of workers. It is a powerful organisation politically, and its main aim is to formulate and influence policy as it impacts on industry. As such, it shapes HRM. As well as the CBI, other organisations that speak for employer interests include the Institute of Directors and the CIPD. We look at the CIPD in Chapter 6.

### THE ADVISORY, CONCILIATION AND ARBITRATION SERVICE (ACAS)

Third-party involvement through activities such as conciliation and arbitration were provided mainly by the state until Acas was set up in 1975, bringing together duties previously handled by government departments. Acas is truly a tripartite body as its council comprises members drawn from employers' organisations (not just the CBI), employees' organisations (not just the TUC), and independent members such as lawyers and academics. Acas is independent of government, and this is seen as vital in maintaining its reputation as a genuine third-party agency which can help resolve problems at work, both of a collective and an individual nature. Acas is charged with the general duty of improving organisations and working life through better employment relations. Acas offers an independent service for dealing with disputes between groups of workers and employers, and disputes where individuals believe that their employer has denied them a legal right. Readers should update their knowledge by looking at the most recent report (www.Acas.org.uk).

Its services cover six main areas:

1 *Conciliation.* While the parties are encouraged to use their own internally agreed procedures to resolve disputes, with their agreement Acas conciliators can become involved. In 2010–11 Acas dealt with over 1,000 collective disputes, and 92,000 individual employment disputes; 91% and 90% respectively were resolved.

2 *Arbitration.* This aspect of its work is not actually conducted by Acas officials themselves, but by appointed independent experts – such as academics – or through a referral to CAC, who investigate the issue and make an award that the parties agree to accept in advance. Acas must consider whether the dispute can first be resolved through

conciliation before moving to arbitration. In 2010–11, there were 31 requests for this service.

3 *Building better employment relations.* Acas helps to prevent problems arising in the employment relations arena by getting the parties to work together more effectively. In 2010–11, over 200 workplace projects were set up.

4 *Settling complaints about employee rights.* Acas also conciliates in employment tribunal cases. A copy of all applications to the employment tribunal goes to Acas whose duty it is to achieve settlement without the case going to tribunal. In sheer volume terms, this represents one of the major aspects of Acas' work, with over 74,620 cases in 2010–11, of which only 22% went to hearing. This is probably the area in which HR practitioners have greatest contact with the service and, as with other services, this generally receives very positive feedback from users.

5 *Providing impartial information and advice.* Enquiries are the fifth broad aspect of the Acas workload, and in 2010–11 950,000 calls were answered by the national helpline and there were over 2.7 million visits to the website.

6 *Promoting good practice, advice and business solutions* with the publication of Codes of Practice, training events, services for small business and international organisations.

REFLECTIVE ACTIVITY

Download a copy of the most recent Acas Annual Report, and assess whether or not your organisation (or one with which you are familiar) is getting maximum benefit from its services.

## THE CENTRAL ARBITRATION COMMITTEE (CAC) AND OTHER BODIES

Like Acas, the CAC is not subject to ministerial direction. It is a permanent independent body with statutory powers to resolve disputes in England, Scotland and Wales under legislation relating to:

- recognition and de-recognition of trade unions
- disclosure of information for collective bargaining
- information and consultation of employees
- European Works Councils
- European Companies and Cooperative Societies, and Cross-Border Mergers.

The importance of its role cannot be estimated solely from the relatively small number of cases with which it deals, but from its influence on employers and employees in reaching settlements regarding union recognition that may not otherwise have been achieved.

The *Certification Officer* has the following areas of responsibility:

- maintaining a list of trade unions and employers' associations, and determining whether or not they can be classified as independent, ie able to continue in existence without support from the employer
- handling disputes that arise from trade union amalgamations and mergers and the administration of political funds
- ensuring that trade unions keep up-to-date membership returns for election purposes, and investigating complaints from members about the administration of elections
- dealing with complaints from members about breaches of the union's own rules relating,

for example, to ballots and the operation of the executive committee (see Lewis *et al* 2011).

Of the other bodies, *The Low Pay Commission* is probably the most relevant to HRM. It was established as a result of the National Minimum Wage Act (1998) and its main role is to advise on the level of the national minimum wage.

### EQUALITY AND HUMAN RIGHTS COMMISSION (EHRC)

The EHRC was set up in late 2007 and has a statutory remit to promote and monitor human rights, to protect, enforce and promote equality across the nine 'protected' areas of age, disability, gender, race, religion and belief, pregnancy and maternity, marriage and civil partnership, sexual orientation and gender reassignment.

The EHRC aims to help with mutual respect, freedoms, equality, dignity and fairness. It does this through monitoring the effectiveness of discrimination law, working with employers and service providers to develop best practice, undertakes research and training, produces Codes of Practice and other publications, conducts investigations, shapes public policy, and to enforces the provisions of the Equality Act 2010. It may also take up issues outside of legislation – such as how to deal with the lack of educational achievement of white, working-class boys and how to deal with and monitor hate crime of all types. Readers can get more up-to-date information from the website: www.equalityhumanrights.com.

### THE HEALTH AND SAFETY EXECUTIVE (HSE)

The HSE is an independent watchdog for work-related health, safety and illness issues. The Health and Safety at Work Act 1974 is a framework Act and through it, EU Directives are implemented. The Act establishes the general duties which employers have to employees and members of public and requires employees to protect themselves and others. The HSE ensures compliance, keeps the law under review and carries out research. It puts into effect proposals and policy and has an inspectorate to promote good practice and enforce the law. For further information refer to Lewis *et al* (2011) and HSE at www.hse.gov.uk.

## CONCLUSIONS

This chapter has reviewed the myriad of external forces and institutional factors that help to shape HRM at work. By now it should be clear that employers do not have a totally free rein in determining their HR practices due to the role played by a wide range of institutions such as trade unions and employers' organisations, Acas and other third-party agencies. Equally, EU and UK law provides a framework within which employers operate, both in terms of ensuring compliance and in shaping good employment practice. Moreover, given that workers differ from all other factors of production, employers need to be aware of their expectations from work. While keeping wages or conditions of employment at or below minimum levels may appear to save costs, as an HR strategy it can store up problems – in terms of recruitment, training and involvement, or indeed persuading staff to work harder. All these forces shape the employment relationship and the types of HR practice that employers adopt.

EXPLORE FURTHER


BLYTON, P., HEERY, E. and TURNBULL, P. (eds) (2011) *Reassessing the Employment Relationship*. Basingstoke: Palgrave Macmillan.

BROWN, W. (2009) 'The process of fixing the British national minimum wage, 1997–2007', *British Journal of Industrial Relations*, Vol.47, No.2, 429–43.

DRAGO, R., WOODEN, M. and BLACK, D. (2009) 'Long work hours: volunteers and conscripts', *British Journal of Industrial Relations*, Vol.47, No.3, 571–600.

DUNDON, T. and ROLLINSON, D. (2011) *Understanding Employment Relations*, 2nd edition. Maidenhead: McGraw-Hill Higher Education.

FARNHAM, D. (2010) *Human Resource Management in Context: Strategy, Insights and Solutions*. London: CIPD.

GENNARD, J. and JUDGE, G. (2010) *Managing Employment Relations,* 5th edition. London: CIPD.

LEWIS, D., SARGEANT, M. and SCHWAB, B. (2011) *Essentials of Employment Law*, 11th edition. London: CIPD.

MARCHINGTON, M., GRIMSHAW, D., RUBERY, J. and WILLMOTT, H. (eds) (2005), *Fragmenting Work: Blurring Organisational Boundaries and Disordering Hierarchies*. Oxford: Oxford University Press.

TAYLOR, S. and EMIR, A. (2009) *Employment Law: An Introduction*. Oxford: Oxford University Press.

CHAPTER 3

# High Commitment HRM Policy and Practice

## LEARNING OUTCOMES

By the end of this chapter, readers should be able to:

- contribute to the implementation of leading-edge HR policies and practices that can maximise the contribution of people to organisational objectives
- advise on whether high commitment HRM makes sense for all organisations irrespective of country, sector, and type of workplace
- benchmark their own organisation's HR policies and practices against those of competitors.

In addition, readers should understand and be able to explain:

- the meaning of 'best practice'/high commitment HRM, and review its application in practice
- the ways in which bundles of HR practices can be combined together and the problems which might arise if this leads to inconsistencies in application
- the major theoretical, methodological and empirical concerns about claims that 'best practice' HRM can be applied universally in all organisations irrespective of sector, country or type of organisation.

## INTRODUCTION

Much of the literature on HRM assumes there is one 'best way' to manage people, and that the approaches taken by leading-edge organisations should be copied carefully in order for others to be successful. This has led to a search for what are thought to be the best practices available, and a strong body of literature trying to examine the links between HRM and organisational performance which we review more systematically in Chapter 15.

The current chapter seeks to outline and explain which practices might be seen as 'best' in the sense of providing a high commitment model around which employers can develop their own HR policies and practices. The two terms – best practice/high commitment HRM – are used interchangeably. The list varies between publications but broadly it includes a commitment to some form of employment security and internal labour markets, sophisticated forms of recruitment and selection, extensive forms of learning and development, high levels of pay and benefits typically linked in some way with performance, and a strong focus on involving and engaging employees in organisational communications and consultation. Others have been added more recently to reflect changing circumstances – such as work–life balance and harmonisation, though the latter seems less apparent recently as disparity between the benefits accrued by top earners and other workers has increased. We also examine the notion of 'bundles' of HRM, the argument that the integration of different sets of HR practices is what makes the difference. There have been numerous attempts to define the precise bundle that has the greatest effect and thus provide what are termed 'powerful connections' as opposed to the 'deadly combinations' of HR practices (Kepes and Delery 2007) which merely lead to sub-optimal performance and inconsistencies from the workers' viewpoint.

We conclude with a critique of the high commitment model, and in particular the idea that it is universally applicable in all workplaces. This leads us nicely into Chapter 4 where 'best fit' is examined and to Chapter 5 when we review international and comparative HRM. These chapters question the notion that the HR practices used by leading (typically US and UK) firms need to be copied by all other organisations if they want to achieve success. Why, for example, would it be appropriate for a small firm in a highly competitive sector with low barriers to entry or a public sector organisation in China to adopt the same HR policies, practices and processes as a large global firm with its roots in the developed world?

## AN OUTLINE OF HIGH COMMITMENT HR POLICIES AND PRACTICES

Many years have elapsed since Pfeffer's original book on the business benefits of adopting the 'high road' approach, yet despite numerous publications on the topic we are no nearer to identifying an agreed set of HR practices that comprise the bundle (Guest 2011). Sometimes this literature refers to 'high performance work systems' (Berg 1999; Appelbaum *et al* 2000), 'high commitment' HRM (Walton 1985; Guest 2001) or 'high involvement' HRM (Wood 1999a). From the mid-1990s, a range of studies emerged from the USA examining the notion of high commitment HRM (eg Arthur 1994; Huselid 1995; MacDuffie 1995; Delaney and Huselid 1996; Delery and Doty 1996; Ichniowski *et al* 1997; Pfeffer 1998; Appelbaum *et al* 2000; Cappelli and Neumark 2001; Batt *et al* 2002; Bartell 2004). These were then supplemented by an increasing number of studies on Britain (eg Patterson *et al* 1997; Guest and Conway 1998, 2011; Wood and de Menezes 1998, 2011; Wood 1999b; Guest *et al* 2000, 2003; Purcell *et al* 2003), several being published by the CIPD. During the last few years, studies have been undertaken in a wider range of countries, such as Australia (Peretz and McGraw 2011), New Zealand (Fabling and Grimes 2010), Spain (Peña and Villasalero 2010), Turkey (Collings *et al* 2010), China (Akhtar *et al* 2008) and Korea (Lee and Lee 2009), and a number of review papers have summarised the evidence to date, such as Boselie *et al* (2005), Wall and Wood (2005), Hyde *et al* (2006) and Boxall and Macky (2009); each examines slightly different samples of work, uses different datasets and comes up with different conclusions. Some of the principal differences between the empirical studies examined relate to:

- the nature and type of HR practices examined
- the proxies for each of these practices
- the sectors in which the studies have taken place
- the methods of data collection
- the respondents from whom information was sought.

Guest (1997, p.263) argued some time ago that there is 'little additive value in these and whilst statistically sophisticated, they lack theoretical rigour'. This assessment is supported by Boselie *et al* (2005, p.81) who state 'a steady body of empirical evidence has been accumulated since the pioneering studies of the mid-1990s, yet it remains the case that no consistent picture exists on what HRM is or even what it is supposed to do'. In his recent review paper, Guest (2011) also expresses concern that we still know little about what constitutes an HR bundle but is also worried that the growing statistical sophistication in research methods might lead us down a blind alley and deter qualitative researchers from analysing HRM. Despite pleas for more theoretical models to underpin empirical research, this has not prevented yet more statistical studies taking place, and there remains concern about the strength of the conclusions that can be drawn from them. There are also more serious and deep-seated disagreements about the extent to which high commitment HRM is something all employers might wish or be able to implement, and to what extent the precise mix of practices varies between countries and types of employer, as well as whether or not it is equally attractive to workers. These issues are taken up later in the chapter.

Rather than review all of the studies mentioned above, we summarise the key high commitment HR practices identified by several sources. The list in previous editions was adapted from Pfeffer (1998) in order to make it applicable to a UK/European context, but in this edition of the book we extend the list by adding further HR practices following reviews by Boselie *et al* (2005), Hyde *et al* (2006), Wall and Wood (2005), Purcell and Hutchinson (2007a) and Boaden *et al* (2008). The box below outlines the list of HR practices.

HRM AT WORK IN FOCUS

## Key components of best practice/high commitment HRM

- employment security and internal labour markets
- selective hiring and sophisticated selection
- extensive training, learning and development
- employee involvement and participation, worker voice
- self-managed teams/team-working
- high compensation contingent on performance
- performance review, appraisal and career development
- reducing status differences/ harmonising terms and conditions
- work–life balance.

Source: Compiled from a number of sources (see above) but initially adapted significantly from Pfeffer (1998).

### EMPLOYMENT SECURITY AND INTERNAL LABOUR MARKETS

Pfeffer (1998) argues that employment security underpins the other HR practices, principally because it is regarded as unrealistic to ask employees to offer their ideas, hard work and commitment without some expectation of continued employment and career development. This is supported by studies showing the contribution a positive psychological contract makes to open and trusting employment relationships (Holman *et al* 2003) and the role that mutuality plays in partnership agreements (Johnstone *et al* 2009). The most recent WERS indicated a slight increase over the previous six years in the provision of job security guarantees to non-managerial staff, but still to no more than one-seventh of the entire sample, and in the proportion of employees feeling that their job was secure to about two-thirds of all workers (Kersley *et al* 2006, p.97). In Japan, despite a weakening of the employment security pillar of HRM over recent years, approximately two-thirds of workers still retain this type of contract, although the number of workers on non-regular employment contracts trebled between the early 1990s and 2005 (Keizer 2009).

Since then, following the global financial crisis, there are limits to any guarantee of employment security. Many manual workers have lost their jobs but it is still apparent that some organisations – such as those employing professional and qualified staff – have tried to hold on to employees for as long as they can. There have been a number of examples where employers have reached agreement with staff that everyone works reduced hours, albeit for reduced pay, rather than maintaining full hours/pay for some workers whilst others are made redundant. Similarly, some organisations have granted their staff unpaid sabbaticals so as to trim the wage bill. Both of these are viable short-term strategies because they allow employers to retain key staff, offer continuing work for those that would have been redundant and, if decisions are taken following consultation with workers, shows a degree of loyalty that might well prove beneficial in a subsequent upturn.

It should be stressed that employment security never implied employees could expect to stay in the same job for life, nor did it mean that staff whose performance was unacceptable would be kept on. The significant point is that employers try to avoid job reductions wherever possible, and that employees expect to maintain their employment, perhaps through internal transfers. Employment security can be enhanced by well-devised and forward looking systems of human resource planning (see Chapter 8) and an understanding of how organisations may be structured to achieve flexibility (see Chapter 2). The key issue is that workers are treated not as a variable cost but as a critical asset in the long-term viability and success of the organisation. As Pfeffer (1998 p.66) notes, rapid cuts in staffing 'constitutes a cost for firms that have done a good job selecting, training and developing their workforce…layoffs put important strategic assets on the street for the competition to employ'.

Proxies for employment security vary greatly, depending partly on whether information is sought about policy or practice. For example, Wood and Albanese (1995) use three measures for employment security: a policy of no compulsory redundancy; the use of temporaries primarily to protect the core workforce; and an expectation on the part of senior managers that new employees will stay with the firm until retirement. Delaney and Huselid (1996) asked managerial respondents about 'filling vacancies from within and creating opportunities for internal promotion' as a proxy for employment security. Guest *et al* (2003) ask a mix of questions about internal labour markets and organisational commitment to employment security, as well as enquiring about whether or not compulsory or voluntary redundancies have occurred in the last three years. Over half of these organisations acknowledged that compulsory redundancies had taken place during this period. Macky and Boxall (2007) asked workers in New Zealand whether their employer had a formal policy of avoiding compulsory redundancy. Research in Korea (Lee and Lee 2009) used similar measures, asking about formal commitments to employment security, guarantees that compulsory redundancies will be avoided, and whether sincere efforts are made to secure employees' jobs. These reflect Pfeffer's (1998, p.183) alternatives to compulsory lay-offs – reductions in working hours to spread the pain, job transfers, recruitment freezes and pay cuts. They are all some way short of full-blown employment security, and it is clear that such 'guarantees' are not expected to reduce corporate profitability.

The box below provides examples of employment security – flexicurity; mutuality in a partnership agreement; and key lessons for the upturn.

HRM AT WORK IN FOCUS

## Varieties of employment security

**European Commission**

Flexicurity can be defined as an integrated strategy to enhance, at the same time, flexibility and security in the labour market ... Flexibility, on the one hand, is about successful moves during one's life course: from school to work, from one job to another, between unemployment or inactivity and work, and from work to retirement ... It is about progress of workers into better jobs (and) flexible work organisations, capable of quickly and effectively mastering new productive needs and skills. Security, on the other hand, is more than just the security to maintain one's job: it is about equipping people with the skills that enable them to progress in their working lives, and helping them to find new employment. It is also about adequate unemployment benefits to facilitate transition. Finally, it encompasses training opportunities.

**Co-operatives UK**

As far as possible in a dynamic environment, the organisation will guarantee security and continuity of employment. To realise this will require flexibility and adaptability from employees to take on new duties and responsibilities whilst clearly recognising the differing levels of individual ability and competence exist. Security and continuity can only be realised if everyone makes an effective contribution and seeks continuous improvement, which will enable the organisation to be progressive and competitive by creating conditions that will achieve security.

**Preparing for the upturn; key lessons**

Firms that have managed to maintain trust, loyalty and engagement may have the competitive edge in the new business climate.

Open and honest communication with employees is essential.

How staff are treated and managed is vital when it comes to preparing for the upturn.

*To think about:*

*Looking through these extracts, discuss whether (a) it is essential to provide workers with some degree of security in order to get better quality work from them, or (b) workers perform best when they are put under pressure through temporary contracts and work intensification.*

Source: Adapted from the European Commission (2007); Bacon and Samuel (2007); Best Workplaces 2010: preparing for the upturn. www.greatplacetowork.co.uk.

## SELECTIVE HIRING AND SOPHISTICATED SELECTION

Recruitment and selection decisions are crucial for organisations that wish to develop the high commitment model, but mistakes are often made due to deficiencies in knowledge about the best techniques and poor implementation (Schmitt and Kim 2007). The recent obsession with talent management means that the right employment choice should be central to the high commitment package because it is helps to achieve sustained competitive advantage (Boxall and Purcell 2011). In terms of selection, WERS shows that about 20% of all UK workplaces employing 10 or more people routinely use personality tests and that nearly half routinely use performance tests. These were used more widely in larger workplaces, in larger organisations, where there was a specialist HR presence, and where unions were recognised (Kersley *et al* 2006, pp.75–6). Recently, interest has also grown in how to generate a strong pool of suitable talent via online recruitment (Parry and Tyson 2008).

Increasingly, employers want applicants to possess a range of social, interpersonal and team-working skills in addition to technical ability. For example, Wood and de Menezes (1998) asked about the importance of social and team-working skills as selection criteria, whilst other studies (eg Wood and Albanese 1995; Hoque 1999) found employers were keen on trainability and commitment. Indeed, in a growing number of situations, employers now feel they can provide technical training for people so long as they have the 'right' social skills, attitudes and commitment (Marchington *et al* 2003b; Warhurst and Nixon 2007; Thompson 2011), and indeed in some jobs it is the way employees look or speak that is regarded as crucial for generating customer satisfaction (Warhurst *et al* 2011).

The proxies used to measure 'selective hiring' include the following:

- the number of applicants per position (Delaney and Huselid 1996) or as many good applicants as the organisation needs (Guest *et al* 2003)
- the proportion administered an employment test prior to hiring (Huselid 1995; Guest *et al* 2003; Orlitzky 2007)
- the sophistication of (selection) processes, such as the use of psychometric tests (Patterson *et al* 1997; Schmitt and Kim 2007) and realistic job previews (Hoque 1999; Guest *et al* 2000b, 2003).

These measures capture different components of the recruitment and selection process, with some assessing the general approach taken by employers whilst others examine the precise techniques used. Moreover, some emphasise inputs rather than outputs in terms of the quality of those eventually recruited. For example, rather than being seen as a good outcome, the attraction of a large number of applicants may indicate poor HR procedures due to failures to define the job and the field adequately prior to advertising. As we see in Chapter 8, it is possible that selective hiring, especially when it focuses on how new recruits fit with the prevailing organisational culture, can lead to underrepresented groups being excluded from employment. Moreover, excessive 'cloning' of employees could be problematic if the organisation is keen to promote diversity, and counterproductive if business needs and markets change. On the other hand, there may be situations where it is hard to attract sufficient applicants due to the highly specific nature of the job (eg surgeons) or to skills shortages – as with some professional jobs in health or higher education. In these cases, the key issue is to generate a pool of potential recruits rather than finding more sophisticated ways of choosing between them.

Recruiting high quality, committed staff is seen as central to 'best practice' HRM, and the use of psychometric tests, structured interviews and work sampling is likely to increase the validity of selection decisions (Carless 2009). Competencies sought include trainability, flexibility, commitment, drive and persistence, and initiative. It is important to remember that 'best practice' selection does not necessarily involve the most sophisticated techniques but should be systematic, making use of the techniques which are appropriate for the position and the organisation, and administered by individuals who have themselves been trained.

### EXTENSIVE TRAINING, LEARNING AND DEVELOPMENT

Having recruited successfully, employers need to ensure these workers develop their skills, not only in terms of professional expertise and product knowledge but also as team members or in interpersonal relations. Boxall (1996, p.67) views this as part of 'organisational process advantage', whereby employers aim to synergise the contribution of talented and exceptional employees. There is little doubt there has been growing recognition of the importance of individual and organisational learning as a source of sustained competitive advantage as employers introduce more skills-specific forms of training and experience, continuing skills shortages in some areas. WERS showed an increase in off-the-job training between 1998 and 2004, particularly for professional and technical workers. As usual, this was more extensive at larger workplaces and organisations, and where an HR specialist was employed (Kersley *et al* 2006, p.84). These types of firm tend to recognise the value of additional training, especially where workers contribute directly to improved quality and/or customer service.

Wright and Gardner (2003, p.312) note that training, learning and development is one of the most widely quoted and important elements of high commitment HRM. The use of the word 'learning' is crucial as it shows employers encourage and facilitate the development of staff rather than just providing specific training to cover short-term crises. The focus has been at different levels, ranging from a fully fledged 'learning organisation', through to task-based and interpersonal skills training (see Chapter 11). The time and effort devoted to learning and training opportunities is important. The proxies used to measure this include the average number of days training undertaken by each worker, the proportion of workers trained, the budget set aside for training, or the establishment of agreed training targets (Castellanos and Martin 2011; Peretz and McGraw, 2011). A Canadian study by Ng and Dastmalchian (2011) used measures such as the percentage of employees that received training, worker motivation to undertake training, opportunities for employees to transfer acquired skills to their jobs, and the extent to which the organisation evaluates the effectiveness of its training. WERS used a simple absence/presence distinction for induction training and formal job training, finding that over half of all workplaces engaged in this. WERS also noted less training was provided in the private sector than the public sector in the UK (Kersley *et al* 2006) whilst the Australian study by Peretz and McGraw (2011) found no difference. West *et al* (2002) used several measures for assessing training in their study of NHS hospitals, each of which related to the amount of money spent, whilst Guest *et al* (2003) focused instead on the amount of training received by workers.

Of course, problems arise in trying to measure investment in training and learning. While it is important to establish how much time and resources employers allocate to formal training, and whether or not this covers the entire workforce, it is also crucial to identify the type of training provided. Many studies look solely at the money or time invested in training but ignore the quality or relevance of training and learning that is provided, or the impact it has on productivity. It is widely acknowledged that most workers are overqualified for the jobs they do (Grugulis 2003), and as such extra training may add little to organisational performance or worker skills. The quality of training delivered is clearly more important than a simple count of the amount provided, though it is interesting to compare time spent on formal training in several European countries (see box below). The issue of training, learning and development is explored more fully in Chapters 10 and 11.

HRM AT WORK IN FOCUS

**Average hours of formal training per year across Europe (2010)**

| | | | |
|---|---|---|---|
| Netherlands | 98 | Spain | 61 |
| Norway | 89 | UK | 60 |
| Portugal | 71 | Sweden | 51 |
| Italy | 67 | Germany | 48 |
| Ireland | 67 | France | 44 |

*To think about:*

*How does the extent of training in your organisation – or one with which you are familiar – compare with these figures? Has the training primarily been formal or informal, and does that matter? To what extent has the training been worthwhile? Do you find anything unusual in this data compared with national stereotypes?*

Adapted from Great Place to Work: the UK's best workplaces. Further information from www.greatplacetowork.co.uk

## EMPLOYEE INVOLVEMENT AND PARTICIPATION (EIP)/ WORKER VOICE

There are many reasons why EIP is a key factor in the high commitment literature. First, communication of financial performance and operational matters not only ensures workers are informed about organisational issues, it also conveys a symbolic and substantive message that they are trusted with such information. Second, for problem-solving groups to be successful, workers require information to provide a basis from which to offer their suggestions and contribute to performance improvements. Third, the use of EIP provides management with some legitimacy for its actions as ideas put forward by workers can be considered before decisions are ultimately made. As we argue throughout the book, even though management is typically more powerful than workers, the employment relationship is ill-defined and therefore open to interpretation over how it is enforced. Of course there are also arguments that workers have a moral right to EIP, but these are considered elsewhere in the book, particularly in Chapter 13.

WERS found that EIP was extensively applied – at least according to managerial respondents – in a majority of UK workplaces employing 10 or more workers. Team briefing, for example, was practised in over 90% of workplaces, the management chain was used systematically to share information in about two-thirds of these, and just under half used regular newsletters. Suggestion schemes and problem-solving groups featured at about one quarter of workplaces (Kersley *et al* 2006, p135). On-site joint consultative committees (JCCs) had become rarer (just 14% of workplaces), but this reflects the fact that small workplaces have little need for a representative committee. At multi-site workplaces, JCCs were much more likely to operate at divisional level or above than they were at the workplace (Kersley *et al* 2006, p.127).

EIP includes downward communications, upward problem-solving groups and project teams, all of which increase the involvement of individual employees at the workplace. The precise mix of EIP techniques depends upon context, but the range of measures used and the 'flexible' definition of involvement can be confusing. Some studies regard EIP as synonymous with downward communications from management to employees, and measures include the frequency of information disclosure, the regularity of team briefing, or the extent to which workers are informed or consulted about business operations or performance (Guest *et al* 2003; Lee and Lee 2009). The frequency of attitude surveys is a routine measure in many studies (eg Huselid 1995; Guest *et al* 2000a). This ties in with the growth of interest in employee engagement in recent times, not just in the UK where it has received a public policy boost through MacLeod and Clarke's (2009) report, but also in other countries as employers have sought to build employee loyalty as they address the effects of the 2008 global financial crisis (Marchington and Kynighou 2012). Leading firms now report the results of the latest employee engagement survey in their annual reports and vie to improve their reputation and attractiveness to new talent by being seen as one of the best employers in this area. For example, amongst the FTSE top 30 companies, the highest scores were gained by BT, Centrica, HSBC, Marks and Spencer, and National Grid (*The Observer* 22 August 2010). Some key points from a CIPD report on employee engagement are included in Box 2.

**Box 2 Employee engagement: strategies and outcomes**

**Key drivers of employee engagement**

- Having meaningful work is critically important.
- Senior management vision and communication is key.
- Positive perceptions of one's line manager are very important.
- Employee voice has a strong influence.
- Good HR practice is mediated by person–job fit and line management style.

**Key outcomes of employee engagement**

- Engaged employees perform better.
- Engaged employees are more innovative.
- Engaged employees are more likely to want to stay with their employer.
- Engaged employees enjoy greater levels of personal well-being.
- Excessively high levels of engagement might lead to ill-health and burnout.

Source: Adapted from Alfes, *et al* (2010).

The proxies used to measure EIP vary greatly, making it hard to draw firm conclusions about its importance to high commitment HRM. The fact that EIP is sometimes little more than information-passing means that meaningful worker contributions are unlikely. Indeed, an objective of team briefing is to reinforce the supervisor as a key figure in the management chain, and this might result in EIP being viewed as indoctrinating, emasculating and controlling, rather than educative, empowering and liberating as the terminology might imply (Marchington and Wilkinson 2005).

Most studies only examine dilute forms of EIP, but a few (eg Huselid 1995; Batt *et al* 2002; Dundon *et al* 2004; Boxall *et al* 2007) specifically include voice as a component of high commitment HRM. It could be argued workers should have an opportunity to express their grievances openly and independently, in addition to being able to contribute to management decision-making on task-related issues. Employee voice may be achieved through trade union representation and collective bargaining as well as through formally established grievance and disputes procedures, but in addition it could be through speak-up schemes, which offer employees protection if their complaints are taken badly by managers (Marchington 2007). EIP and voice has also developed in countries such as the Ukraine with no tradition of organisation-level information and consultation. Croucher's (2010) innovative study of eight comparable organisations, four of which had introduced quality management practices and four which had not, shows clearly that EIP blossomed in the former but not in the latter. Initiatives included both direct and representative forms of EIP and voice; this case is reviewed in greater depth in Chapter 13.

### SELF-MANAGED TEAMS/TEAM-WORKING

This has become more prevalent since the introduction of Japanese manufacturing practices into US and UK companies in the 1980s and 1990s as a way of pooling ideas, improving work processes and reducing costs. It has been identified as a critical component of organisational success and is a key attribute that employers seek in new recruits. Teamwork is typically seen as leading to better decision-making and the achievement of more creative solutions (Pfeffer 1998, p.76). Employees working in teams often report higher levels of satisfaction than their counterparts working under more 'traditional' regimes, although they also report working harder (Wilkinson *et al* 1997; Edwards and Wright 1998; Geary and Dobbins 2001; Batt and Doellgast 2003; Procter and Burridge 2008).

The range of measures used to assess team-working is quite narrow, generally referring to the proportion of workers in teams (MacDuffie 1995; West *et al* 2002; Guest *et al* 2003; Procter and Burridge 2008), the use of formal teams (Patterson *et al* 1997; Guest *et al* 2000a) or the design of jobs to make use of workers' abilities (Hoque 1999). However, such measures do not establish whether these teams actually are self-managed or act as autonomous groups, and much depends upon decisions concerning, inter alia, the choice of team leader, responsibility for organising work schedules, and control over quality (Frobel and Marchington 2005). A distinction is also made between off-line teams – such as quality circles – and on-line teams where workers are involved in daily decisions about work organisation (Batt 2004). WERS showed team-working was present among core employees in nearly three-quarters of workplaces employing 10 or more people, this being most extensive amongst professional workers and least likely when people worked in customer service or sales. However, this raw statistic does not tell the full story, and when respondents were questioned in more detail about exactly what team-working meant, this varied greatly. For example, whereas over 60% of these teams engaged in job/role rotation or jointly decided how work was done, only one-third set up the teams with a significant degree of autonomy and just 6% were allowed to appoint their own leaders. In short, fully autonomous teams are rare.

In contrast to the view that teams are universally good, there is a less optimistic perspective which argues they are intrusive and difficult to implement in practice, and that they strengthen – rather than weaken – management control. It may not be possible to introduce any realistic version of team-working when workers are unable to enlarge their jobs to embrace higher level skills or where there are legal, technical or safety reasons that prevent workers from making key decisions – for example, in an aircraft or a nuclear power plant. Moreover, prospects for team-working are limited where the rotation of a range of low-level jobs means that one boring job is merely swapped for another boring jobs (Marchington and Wilkinson 2005). In situations such as these, team-working may only make work more stressful and intrusive, adding nothing to the skills or discretion workers are allowed. For example, Bacon *et al* (2010, p.1245) found in their study of steel plants that teams were not made up of multi-skilled workers but that each person had a different set of skills as part of efforts to reduce costs in a wider change programme. While some might regard this as a failure of implementation, others view team-working as fatally flawed because it gives the impression of control without devolving any real power or influence. Barker (1993, p.408), for example, suggests that self-managing teams produce 'a form of control more powerful, less apparent, and more difficult to resist than that of the former bureaucracy' because it shifts the locus of control from management to workers – what he terms 'concertive control'. The consequence of this is that peer pressure and rational rules combine to 'create a new iron cage whose bars are almost invisible to the workers it incarcerates' (p.435).

REFLECTIVE ACTIVITY

What is your experience of working in teams? Do you think that peer pressure is more likely to generate better performance than supervisory control? Is team-working automatically 'positive' in your view?

## HIGH COMPENSATION CONTINGENT ON PERFORMANCE

Pfeffer (1998) outlines two elements to this component – higher than average compensation and performance-related pay (PRP) – although both send a signal to employees that they deserve to be rewarded for superior contributions. To be effective, this needs to be at a level in excess of that for comparable workers in other organisations so as to attract and retain high-quality labour. In addition, rewards should reflect different levels of worker contribution, perhaps being paid as a regular bonus or through profit sharing schemes. Despite extensive criticisms of PRP (see Chapter 14) it is included in most lists of 'best practice', particularly US studies. Given that UK researchers are more sceptical about the value of incentive pay, it might make sense to include the entire reward package in this HR practice so it is not restricted to pay alone, but includes group-wide incentive schemes, profit sharing and other benefits.

Huselid (1995) used two measures: the proportion of the workforce with access to incentive schemes and the proportion whose performance appraisals are used to determine compensation. MacDuffie (1995) refers to contingent compensation. The UK studies also focus on merit or performance-related pay. Wood and de Menezes (1998) enquired about merit pay and profit sharing, Guest *et al* (2000a) included performance related pay for non-managerial staff, whereas Hoque (1999) asked about merit pay and appraisal schemes for all staff. Macky and Boxall (2007) asked about profit sharing/employee share ownership schemes or bonuses based on individual/team performance in New Zealand, whereas Lee and Lee's (2009) interview schedule focused on fairness in pay and appraisals. In other words, measures vary between PRP both at individual and group levels, as well as profit sharing, each of which relies on quite different incentive effects.

According to WERS, some form of PRP scheme operates in about 40% of workplaces, and perhaps surprisingly these apply both to managerial and non-managerial staff in more than half these situations. Incentive systems were more common in the private than the public sector, and especially well-used in financial services and much less common in unionised workplaces. WERS also treated share ownership schemes and profit related payments as examples of variable pay systems where reward was related in some way to performance, in this case at organisational or business unit level rather than on an individual basis. Save as you earn or share incentive plans operated in about 20% of workplaces, whilst profit-related pay was found in about 30% of establishments. In other words, these forms of variable pay scheme are used in a significant minority of workplaces (Kersley *et al* 2006, pp.189–93). The proportion of large workplaces covered by these sorts of arrangement in Japan is broadly similar (Keizer 2009).

Interestingly, a European study by Arrowsmith *et al* (2010) showed that variable pay systems (VPS) were widely used in Austria, Norway, Spain and the UK – albeit in different forms. For example, whilst most of the firms studied used some form of merit pay, the UK and Spanish companies also used bonuses based on performance at group, departmental or corporate level, whilst the Norwegian organisations used profit sharing more extensively. The Austrian organisations also provided spontaneous bonuses rather than having them written into the formal system. The conclusion to the Arrowsmith *et al* (2010, p.2738) paper is that 'there are strong common tendencies in pay arrangements towards VPS, including widespread appraisal-set pay and use of bonuses, if not any move to uniform common systems of VPS. This has occurred notwithstanding the national segmentation of product markets for retail banks and differences in formal institutional structures.'

## PERFORMANCE REVIEW, APPRAISAL AND CAREER DEVELOPMENT

Performance review, appraisal and career development is also key to high commitment HRM, both in terms of defining performance expectations and in providing workers with the targets at which to aim for future employment opportunities. As we see in Chapter 9, review and appraisal is just one part of a rather wider process that starts with systematic induction into the workplace. Whilst performance review is concerned with ensuring that current levels of performance are acceptable, and instigating action if this falls below requirements, it also helps workers to plan their future and determine any future learning and training needs (see Chapter 11). In short, the results of individual performance reviews need to be aligned with those of the department and organisation as a whole if they are to be effective. Managers should be able to communicate clearly to staff, through the appraisal process, the need for vertical integration between individual activity – say, in forging stronger relationships with customers or in improving product quality – and its impact on bottom-line performance. The role played by first line managers is especially important here, given they are typically seen as 'the organisation' so far as workers are concerned, and evidence suggests that their attitudes to work are heavily influenced by the quality of this relationship (Brown and Lim 2010). The notion of leader-member exchange (LMX), which we explore more fully in Chapter 7, has been applied to the performance review process by Chen *et al* (2007) who find that high quality LMX encourages appraisees to seek critical feedback from their supervisors more frequently.

Both West *et al* (2002) and Guest *et al* (2003) focused on appraisal as a key factor; in the former, appraisal had an extremely significant impact on performance, as we see in Chapter 15. Some studies focus on specific types of appraisal, such as developmental reviews rather than those which are linked to potential pay increases (Macky and Boxall 2007), and it could be argued that this taps into a quite different mindset – eg learning and development opportunities and careers – from the situation where appraisal focuses on rewards alone. As ever, it is critically important to be aware which proxies are being for this factor in the high commitment paradigm when comparing results across different surveys. WERS finds the use of performance reviews is growing in the UK, to the extent that about three-quarters of workplaces indicated that appraisals are undertaken on a regular basis for non-managerial employees. As with other HR practices, appraisals were more common in larger workplaces and larger organisations, as well as in workplaces where at least trade unions were recognised (Kersley *et al* 2006, p.83). This finding is slightly unexpected given the criticism that appraisals are sometimes used solely as a managerial tool to control workers.

The use of performance review and appraisal in non-Anglo-Saxon countries depends greatly on the cultural and institutional arrangements in operation there – as we see in Chapters 5 and 9. In China, for example, Claus and Briscoe (2009, p.191) note that cultural factors such as face, harmony and power distance have a significant impact on what is regarded as acceptable conduct during and after performance reviews, and in particular in the acceptability and value of using 360 degree appraisal there. Activity in MNCs is likely to vary, even within the same host country, depending on whether the firm seeks to achieve greater cross-fertilisation of staff and ideas or instead attempts to maintain a clear line of separation between subsidiaries; see also Chiang and Birtch (2010).

REFLECTIVE ACTIVITY

Do you think appraisals really do offer opportunities for workers to develop their careers or are they solely a tool for managers to check up on staff and make sure they comply with organisational goals?

### REDUCING STATUS DIFFERENCES/HARMONISING TERMS AND CONDITIONS

The egalitarian principles underpinning the HR practices of firms in the co-operative sector and in some Japanese companies are meant to convey messages to lower grade staff that they are valuable assets who deserve to be treated in a similar way to their more senior colleagues. It is also seen as a way to encourage employees to offer ideas within an 'open' management culture. This could be visible through similar forms of dress (as in the case of Nissan where all staff wear uniforms), and shared canteen and car-parking facilities, but it is also achieved via the harmonisation of many terms and conditions of employment – such as holidays, sick-pay schemes, pensions, and hours of work. The purpose of single status and harmonisation is to remove artificial barriers between different groups of staff and so encourage team-working and flexibility. Extending employee share ownership to all workers is another way to reduce status differences. Indeed, Pfeffer (1998, p.38) argues that 'employee ownership, effectively implemented, can align the interests of employees with those of shareholders by making employees shareholders too'.

The proxies used to measure harmonisation and the reduction of status differentials vary greatly, encompassing both substantive and procedural factors. For example, Wood and de Menezes (1998) ask about whether or not *any* employees have to 'clock in' to work, and about the existence of employee share schemes and welfare facilities/fringe benefits. Hoque's (1999) questions relate broadly to harmonisation and single status. Guest *et al*'s (2000a, 2003) questions vary between the highly specific (harmonised holiday entitlements for all staff) through to whether the organisation has a formal commitment to achieving single status. Over 80% of the organisations in the CIPD survey (Guest *et al* 2000a) claimed to have harmonised holidays and just under half reckoned to have a formal commitment to single status. Macky and Boxall (2007) asked workers to respond to the statement 'there are few status differentials in my organisation between managers and the rest of the employees. We are all at the same level.' Those answering positively to this had significantly higher levels of job satisfaction and trust in management.

The reduction of pay differentials is arguably a key issue in this area. Some early proponents of high commitment HRM proposed a ratio between the highest paid and the median level in the organisation of about seven-to-one. Apart from firms in the co-operative sector, and especially fully worker-owned firms, where this ratio is likely to be around five-to-one, recent evidence from organisations in developed economies suggests differentials can be more than a hundred-to-one, and even more once share options, pension payments and severance payments for board members and investment bankers is taken into account. The pay of investment bankers and professional footballers can be more in one week than an average worker can earn in a decade, and despite threats from governments in many countries to put a lid on forms of executive pay which do not seem to be closely related to effort and performance, little has changed. In some countries, notably Sweden and Japan, the ratio is single figures. However, in the UK, FTSE chief executives pay is 120 times the salary of their average employee, according to the Involvement and Participation Association (Newsletter 29 June 2011). The Hutton Review (2010) into differentials in the public sector was asked to consider imposing a ratio of no more than twenty-to-one, still some distance from that suggested by the original proponents of high commitment HRM, and came up with the idea, not of a ratio but a transparent and well-communicated pay multiplier instead.

## WORK–LIFE BALANCE

Over the last decade, employers have appeared more supportive, at least in general terms, of attempts to achieve a better work–life balance for staff in their organisations. Although it could be argued that this is hardly new (Lewis *et al* 2007), business interest has been stimulated by legislation that may have forced some employers to improve their policies. It is also clear that family-friendly policies are most embedded when there is pressure on employers to offer these, for example where it is difficult to recruit and retain staff and where trade unions have pushed employers to introduce arrangements (White *et al* 2004, pp.112–13). At the same time, there has also been a growing awareness of the business case for improving work–life balance, and because more women are engaged in paid employment greater effort is needed to attract and retain female staff with responsibilities for child care (Houston 2005). Continuing gender imbalances in the domestic division of labour reinforce the 'dual burden' faced by women who have to combine paid employment with an extensive commitment to caring for other family members (Crompton *et al* 2005).

However, whilst the influx of women may have initially forced employers to offer more flexible working patterns, issues of work–life balance are not restricted merely to this group alone. For example, some men now want to be given the opportunity for career breaks or to play a bigger role in childcare, some workers have increased responsibilities for elder care, and yet others just want to devote more time to leisure activities. For the most part, however, the way in which employers tend to view the question of work–life balance, and the limited extent to which flexible patterns of working time are taken up by men, ensures that this issue remains categorised as a women's problem (Bruegel and Gray 2005, p.150). When young children are in need of care, fathers tend to work roughly twice as many hours as mothers, and although there are examples where men are house-husbands, this is still relatively rare. Recent changes to the maternity and paternity laws might help to change perceptions and practices here over the next few years, as might more role models for men to copy. Sturges (2008) notes that younger workers, men and women, value the idea of work–life balance, and in some cases specifically aim to find work that will not interfere with out-of-work commitments.

The proxies used to measure work–life balance tend to focus either on the strength of employer commitment to the practice or on the availability and take-up of specific forms of flexible working practices. In relation to the former, Heywood *et al* (2010) use both the presence of an explicit commitment from an employer and their ability to keep that commitment when it is tested. In relation to the latter, WERS (Kersley *et al* 2006, p.250) provides data on the types of working time flexibility available as a proportion of workplaces employing 10 or more staff were as follows. The first column in Table 7 shows the responses of management, the second that of employees.

This indicates that only two areas (the ability to shift from full-time to part-time or vice versa) were available at more than half of all these workplaces, whilst others (eg term-time only) were unavailable at eight out of 10 workplaces. Interestingly, when employees were asked the same question, in general much smaller proportions of respondents thought these options were available to them, and in some cases – eg the chance to reduce working hours and home working – it was considerably less. Even more worrying, case study research (Carroll *et al* 2008) suggests that people who might be in most need of these forms of flexibility are employed in workplaces where it is extremely difficult for this to be offered. For example, it is rare for care workers – who are predominantly women – to take advantage

**Table 7 Availability of flexible working arrangements, as reported by managers and employees, in workplaces employing ten or more employees**

| **Flexible working arrangement** | **Percentage of managers who say it is available (%)** | **Percentage of employees who think it is available (%)** |
|---|---|---|
| Reduced working hours | 70 | 32 |
| Increased working hours | 57 | 31 |
| Change in shift patterns | 45 | 27 |
| Job-sharing | 31 | 19 |
| Home-working | 26 | 14 |
| Term-time only | 20 | 14 |
| Compressed hours | 16 | 20 |

Source: Adapted from Kersley *et al* (2006), pp.250–52.

of time off to care for their own children because of client demands. Moreover, as Blyton (2011, p.313) notes, 'those in higher level, better paid jobs also tend to be those with greater time sovereignty, in terms of their discretion over when to start and finish work, work partly from home, and are the people most likely to be informed about work–life provisions'.

As with each aspect of high commitment HRM, other proxies could be used to measure work–life balance in organisations. These include: provision of childcare facilities at the workplace; assistance with childcare through vouchers; emergency leave for childcare or adult care; maternity and paternity leave; pay above the legal minimum. Some of these focus on processes whilst others major on outcomes.

## DIFFERENCES IN EMPLOYER TAKE-UP OF HIGH COMMITMENT HRM

In summarising this review of high commitment HRM, it is clear there are differences depending on the sector, type of firm and country where the work is located. First, high commitment HRM is generally more prevalent in the public sector than in the private, with the exception of just two areas – the use of personality tests and incentive pay systems. This runs counter to the recurrent criticism that the public sector is generally behind the private sector in adopting more innovative practices. Work–life balance in the private sector rarely comes with paid benefits. Of course, this might be explained because we are not comparing like with like, in that all public sector workplaces, no matter how small, are governed by formal policies that operate across the entire organisation whilst many private sector workplaces are single establishment and typically quite small firms.

Second, level of take-up varies greatly according to the structure and size of the organisation. For some HR practices, notably those that are required or encouraged by law, or are seen as essential to good business practice – for example, grievance procedures, equal opportunities policy, communications and team-working – a large proportion of workplaces have these in place. Whether these are properly embedded is a question we return to later in the chapter. For other practices, take-up is low, even though they are regarded as positive and forward-looking; examples of these would be personality tests where specialist knowledge and adequate resources are required to operate them effectively, or provision of childcare facilities which require both a commitment on the part of management and a workplace of adequate size. This is not to say that small firms never implement high commitment HRM. As research by Harris and Foster (2005, p.9) demonstrates, small firms often have the potential to operate in a highly informal and flexible way to retain valued members of staff.

Third, whilst research into high commitment HRM was developed initially by researchers from the USA and the UK, other Anglo-Saxon economies – such as Australia, New Zealand and Canada – soon followed. This model has since been used as the basis for research into the HRM-performance link in CMEs across Europe and in the Pacific Rim, as we saw earlier. However, Boselie *et al* (2001) remind us that high commitment practices that are discretionary in economies with relatively light levels of regulation (such as the UK) are often part of the legislative framework elsewhere; indeed they are an expected part of the HR bundle in the Netherlands. So, whilst it is relatively rare to see full-blown high commitment HRM at workplace level in the USA, in the Netherlands it would be unusual **not** to see this. In their review of low-wage work across a number of high-income countries in Northern Europe, the UK and the USA, Appelbaum and Schmitt (2009, pp.1929–30) argue that institutions – such as the legal framework and the power of organised labour – have a strong influence over the take-up of HRM. In short, high commitment HRM depends not just on employers but also on actors at the national and workplace level. This issue is considered more fully in Chapter 5.

## BUNDLES OF HUMAN RESOURCE PRACTICES

It is clear that links exist between these high commitment HR practices. For example, workers are more likely to be positive about problem-solving groups if they have employment security and their workplace is relatively well harmonised. Equally, they are more likely to show an interest in team-working if their efforts are rewarded with performance-related incentives, share ownership, work–life balance, and access to training opportunities. Similarly, if sufficient care has been taken at the recruitment and selection stage and with performance reviews – including induction – new recruits are more likely to adopt flexible working practices and welcome training opportunities, as well as strive for internal promotion. Overall, if HR practices form a coherent, synergistic and value-adding bundle, it is likely that the high commitment paradigm is deeply embedded into the culture of the workplace. Benson and Lawler (2003, p.157) note that 'research at the work unit level confirms the importance of viewing practices as complementary' and that high commitment HRM (in general) out-performed control-oriented work systems. However, the exact combination of HR practices is uncertain and industry-specific. Gooderham *et al* (2008) also note that whilst an HR bundle may influence performance, this is only one component in the mix; we take this up again in Chapter 15.

There is strong support for the idea that HR practices **should** be more effective when combined together. For example, it is easy to argue that extensive training is essential for self-managed teams to run effectively, or that higher than average rewards are likely to increase applications for jobs. An employer may be more inclined to promise employment security if selective hiring has taken place, self-managed teams are extensive throughout the organisation, and rewards are contingent upon performance. Several early research studies support this argument. For example, Wood and de Menezes (1998, p.485) find an 'identifiable pattern to the use of high commitment HR practices' and confirm that they are being used in conjunction with each other. More recently, Kepes and Delery (2007) note that, 'taken together, the (*US*) results clearly demonstrate that certain HRM activities fit with each other and form a coherent "bundle". However, the studies only investigated fit at the policy and practice levels.'

Guest (1997, p.271) categorises previous attempts to examine internal fit into three distinct groups. First, there are *criterion-specific* studies, such as Pfeffer, which outline a number of 'best practices' and suggest that the closer organisations get to this list the better their performance is likely to be. This implies it is possible to specify with some confidence what Kepes and Delery (2007) refer to as the 'powerful connections' between different HR practices so that employers could order a fixed menu of HRM. However, universal models ignore potentially significant differences between organisations, sectors and countries, and posit a particular approach – in this case, the US bundle – as the one to follow. If this is the case, all employers need to identify the right bundle and then apply this without deviation.

Second, there are two sets of *criterion-free* categories, *fit as gestalt* and *fit as bundles.* The former assumes synergies are achievable only with the adoption of **all** the practices, and if one is missing the whole effect is lost. These approaches are termed 'multiplicative' or 'synergistic' and it is assumed the whole is greater than the sum of its parts, so that breaking the chain would undermine its force (Kepes and Delery 2007). However, Macky and Boxall (2007, p.559) suggest that a particular set of HR practices – fair promotion processes, involvement in decision-making, open performance appraisal, reduction of status differentials, and information sharing – underpin fairness in the employment relationship and thus seem to have the greatest impact on worker attitudes.

In contrast to the synergistic model, *bundles* are 'additive'. Generally speaking, the more practices in place the better, so long as some distinctive core exists. In other words, it may be possible to adopt some high commitment HR practices and ignore others, but still gain from the interactive effects of those used because they form the core of a package (Boxall and Purcell 2011). Some HR practices may be central to the bundle whilst others apply to different organisations, types of workers and contexts as we see in the box below. Questions arise as to the number of practices needed to make a difference, from what areas of HRM these are drawn and whether certain practices are fundamental for synergies to work. As we see in Chapter 15, much of Guest *et al*'s research has differentiated between organisations on the basis of how many HR practices they use. Their analysis of the WERS 1998 data led them to conclude that 'despite trying a variety of approaches and combinations, we could not find any coherent pattern of bundles of practices in the private or the public sectors. The only combination that made any sense was a straightforward count of all the practices' (Guest *et al* 2000a, p.15). Provided a certain minimum number of practices are in place, it is likely (though not automatic) that high commitment HRM will exist in a range of different practices – such as selection, training, EIP and harmonisation. But this raises another issue regarding what is meant by bundles or synergies; is this to do with the combination of HR practices across the board (eg from each of recruitment, learning and development, pay, performance and appraisal, and EIP) or merely within certain components of HRM (such as recruitment and selection, or learning and development, for example) Kepes and Delery (2007) call the former inter-HRM activity fit and the latter intra-HRM activity fit, arguing that both are important for integration.

HRM AT WORK IN FOCUS

## Three perspectives on bundles of HRM

**The black box research**

Various papers by John Purcell and his colleagues focused on the link between HRM and performance, paying particular attention to the role played by line managers in converting strategy into practice. One of their papers noted that satisfaction with HR practices varied between occupational groups, and that the contribution of specific aspects of HRM to commitment varied between line managers, professionals and non-managerial staff. The results showed that rewards and recognition, communication and work–life balance were important for all three groups. In addition:

(a) line managers also valued career opportunities and involvement

(b) professionals also valued performance appraisal, involvement and openness, and

(c) non-managerial staff also valued openness.

### The NHS study

Whilst most research analyses the notion of 'fit' from the perspective of the HR practices that are intended or implemented by **employers**, recent work on the NHS (Boaden *et al* 2008) asked about 200 **workers** at a range of levels to indicate how they saw HR practices fitting together. During interviews, they were asked what they perceived as meaningful combinations of HR practices, and why. Three sets of practices routinely combined together. These were:

**(a) Professional development:** appraisal, training and career development. These were seen as important to individuals since they provided skills and learning opportunities that enabled them to do their jobs well in order to offer high levels of patient care.

**(b) Employee contribution:** communication, team-working and EIP. These were seen as important to individuals because it provided an opportunity to contribute to departmental and organisational goals and in particular to use their discretion to improve patient care.

**(c) The employee 'deal':** recruitment, pay, non-monetary rewards, work–life balance and employment security. These were seen as important to satisfy expectations that individuals had from employment, and were seen as underpinning the contract. They were essential for workers to willingly contribute to improvements in patient care.

Three quotes sum up how these 'powerful connections' work:

'To give good patient care, you've got to have training obviously, on-going training as well. And your appraisals come into that because when you have appraisals, you're discussing how you're doing your job, how you can improve etc. Any way that you can improve obviously helps with patient care.' (Health care support worker)

'We've got a very strong sense of working as a team within our own profession. The health visitors all really work together and are very supportive. How to do the job? Communication, employee involvement definitely. They are the main things you help you do your job.' (Nurse)

'Obviously pay, that's the reason everyone comes to work because they have bills to pay. Job security, again it goes along with this as you have to pay bills, you want to stay in the same place, you don't want to be moved around, you want to feel comfortable in the environment you're working in, and you want to build up your team.' (Nurse)

### The meta-analytic investigation

Based on a meta-analysis of 65 studies of the link between HR bundles and firm performance, Subramony (2009) concludes there are three distinguishable sets of HR practices that combine together. These are:

**(a) Empowerment-enhancing** bundles, which comprise employee involvement in work processes, presence of a formal grievance procedure, job enrichment, self-managed teams, employee participation in decision-making, and systems to encourage feedback from employees.

(b) **Motivation-enhancing** bundles, which comprise formal performance appraisal, group incentive plans, linking pay to performance, opportunities for internal career progression, and health and other employee benefits.

(c) **Skill-enhancing** bundles, which comprise job descriptions derived from job analysis, job-based skills training, recruiting through large applicant pools, and structured and validated selection tools.

*To think about:*

*Do any of these combinations of HR practices make sense to you, or would you put different components together instead? Why is this so? Do you think it might vary between organisations, sectors and countries – or even methods of data collection? Why?*

Sources: Adapted from Kinnie *et al* (2005); Boaden *et al* (2008); Subramony (2009).

While some authors believe employers use high commitment HRM in a consistent way across the bundle, others are not convinced this happens in reality. It is argued that contradictions between 'best practice' in one area (say, EIP) and 'worst practice' in another (say, training) will undermine the package as a whole. Workers will soon notice differences between employment practices, and are quick to spot inconsistencies between policy statements and workplace practice. There are times when a high-profile cultural change programme, for example, which has learning and development at its core, has been undermined by the announcement of mass redundancies. Similarly, new EIP policies have been introduced without first consulting employees about their shape and functions. Inconsistencies between different HR practices are likely to be even more apparent in situations where several employers operate at the same workplace or clients have a direct or indirect influence over the work of supplier organisations, either through short-term secondments of staff or through employers exercising joint responsibility for the completion of work tasks (Marchington *et al* 2005). There have also been investigations of how HRM might operate across supply chains, both between different subsidiaries within the same organisation (Koulikoff-Souviron and Harrison 2007) and between firms involved in close and continuing relationships with each other (Fisher *et al* 2008). These studies all show it is not easy to achieve consistent and integrated bundles of HRM across internal or external boundaries even if there are shared goals and long-term patterns of partnership (Marchington *et al* 2011a).

In the context of HRM within one establishment, Wood and de Menezes (1998, p.487) also find most studies indicate a lack of consistency, reporting fragmentation, a 'pick and mix' approach to managing human resources, ad hoc-ism, pragmatism and short-term-ism, rather than consistent, integrated and long-term packages of HRM. Truss *et al* (1997, pp.66–7) saw 'little evidence of any deliberate or realised coherence between HR activities. For instance, one HR Officer commented that the firm could be recruiting someone in one department and laying-off someone with a similar profile in another.' Moreover, they saw no evidence of coherence among HR activities in different parts of the organisation, and whilst the language of soft HRM was used widely, the hard model was also evident with its emphasis on financial control. Yet more worryingly, while Caldwell's (2003) survey of about 100 major organisations shows significant progress has been made in the adoption of HR practices, unfortunately most is in implementing practices that are regarded as least important and least progress with those that are most important. His respondents recognised the value of bundles but found the linkages extremely difficult to achieve for a number of reasons: it was felt there was no universal or magic formula; the size, complexity and multidivisional structure of their organisation impeded co-ordination; devolution to line managers tended to increase fragmentation; and the difficulty the HR function experienced in breaking out of its operational requirement to provide administrative efficiency rather than strategic vision (p.203). Perhaps the lack of any sizeable take-up of these HR practices should not surprise us. As Pfeffer (1998) suggests, even smart organisations do 'dumb things', failing to learn from evidence or being driven by criteria which are ultimately wide of the mark. Rousseau and Barends (2011) provide guidance on how to become an evidence-based HR practitioner, with a résumé of where to start and how to gain accurate and relevant forms of evidence; we take this up again in Chapter 16.

Although the principle of bundling may appear sound, problems can arise if the achievement of one of these practices contradicts with or undermines (some of) the others. For example, employers may make employment security conditional on an agreement that pay rates can be reduced in order to maintain that guarantee through lean times. Selective hiring on the basis of future potential rather than immediate contribution may require existing staff to work harder to induct new staff. This may be fine at the margins, but if the profit-sharing or performance-related component of rewards is a significant proportion of overall income, then it could be problematic to existing staff – as well as to customers who may have to wait longer to be served. Equally, if workers are routinely expected to work long hours, their own quality of life can be adversely affected and their own safety and that of others may be affected. Presumably, there is a point at which the value of employment security is outweighed by the need for a certain minimum salary or work–life balance. These are sometimes referred to as 'deadly combinations' (Kepes and Delery 2007) because they can automatically contradict the ability of other HR practices to work effectively – say, if one HR practice assumes individuals are motivated solely by personal factors whilst another is predicated on their performing well in teams.

Similarly, according to Pfeffer (1998, p.77), self-managed teams can remove a supervisory level from the hierarchy: 'eliminating layers of management by instituting self-managing teams saves money. Self-managed teams can also undertake tasks previously done by specialised staff, thus eliminating excess personnel.' It is not self-evident that the personnel who are 'eliminated' are actually found other jobs, so the implementation of self-managed teams – even if it does empower some workers – can result in others losing their jobs. There are further potential contradictions between the practices. For example, team-working may be undermined by the use of individual performance-related pay or by the HR practices of other firms in a network that cut across internal organisational coherence (Scarbrough and Kinnie 2003; Marchington *et al* 2011c). Similarly, Cordery (2003) cites several studies in which team-working took place against a backdrop of lay-offs and reduced pay; this is supported by Bacon *et al* (2010). It is difficult to accept that an employer's commitment to remove major status differentials or provide decent wages for lower-level staff can co-exist with the payment of substantial bonuses to senior managers especially if, as we have seen in cases where executives are paid huge sums to leave the organisation, the link between effort and reward is very tenuous.

In other words, while there is strong support for bundling in some form, there are times when it makes no sense to use a specific technique just because it is 'sophisticated' and regarded as 'best practice' as the benefits can never justify the costs. A prime example here is the use of over-designed selection systems where the additional hurdle – say, the use of an assessment centre – adds no more predictive power to the process (Boxall and Purcell 2011, p.230). It is also clear that contradictions and tensions may arise between the different HR practices in the bundle. Perhaps this is unsurprising because any notion of organisational coherence inevitably oversimplifies the contradictions at the heart of the employment relationship. This stems from the fact that 'there are multiple goals in HRM and these bring a range of strategic tensions ... for example between economic goals and the need for social legitimacy' (Boxall and Purcell 2011, p.231).

## REFLECTIVE ACTIVITY

Should it matter if there are contradictions between different components of the HR bundle which lead to perceived inconsistencies for a specific worker? How about the situation where inconsistencies and contradictions are between different segments of the labour force; is this as much of a problem?

## IS HIGH COMMITMENT HRM UNIVERSALLY APPLICABLE?

A key claim in the celebratory literature is that high commitment HRM is capable of being used in any organisation, irrespective of product market situation, industry, or workforce. Pfeffer (1998 pp.33–4) produces evidence from many industries and studies which he claims demonstrates the case for 'putting people first'. These include 'relatively low technology settings such as apparel manufacture to very high technology manufacturing processes. The results seem to hold for manufacturing and for service firms. Nothing in the available evidence suggests that the results are country-specific. The effects of high performance management practices are real, economically significant, and general – and thus should be adopted by your organisation.' Support for this argument comes from several other studies. For example, Huselid (1995, p.644) states that 'all else being equal, the use of High Performance Work Practices and good internal fit should lead to positive outcomes for all types of firms'. Delery and Doty (1996, p.828) find 'relatively strong support' for the universalistic argument and some support for other perspectives, and suggest that 'some human resource practices *always* [our emphasis] have a positive effect on performance'; these were profit sharing, results-oriented appraisals and employment security.

This perspective has been widely criticised (Guest 2011), ranging from suggestions that minor adjustments are needed through to downright rejection of the case that 'progressive' HR practices can always provide sustained competitive advantage. Youndt *et al* (1996, p.837) imply that 'the universal approach helps researchers to document the benefits of HR across all contexts, ceteris paribus, [while] the contingency perspective helps us to look more deeply into organisational phenomena to derive more situationally-specific theories and prescriptions for management practice'. Purcell (1999, p.36) is particularly sceptical of the claims for universalism, which lead us, he argues, 'down a utopian cul-de-sac'. He stresses the need to identify 'the circumstances of where and when it [high commitment management; HCM] is applied, why some organisations do and some do not adopt HCM, and how some firms seem to have more appropriate human resource systems than others'. Boxall and Purcell (2011, pp.95–6) propose an alternative here with the distinction between *surface* and *underpinning* layers of HRM. Whilst the former is likely to vary between organisations as contexts differ both between sectors and countries, the latter could reflect some general principles of labour management related to multiple goals, business pressures and the alignment of management and employee interests. We saw in the box above that workers might be interested in slightly different configurations of HRM depending on occupation, level in the hierarchy and nature of work undertaken – though of course this might reflect their realistic aspirations for what employment can deliver.

At a conceptual and empirical level, Marchington and Grugulis (2000) have argued that high commitment HRM is more likely when:

1 *Employers are able to take a long term perspective*

The high commitment model assumes that employers have the luxury of taking a long-term view or that, with a bit of foresight, they could do so. For example, they are encouraged to hire during the lean times when labour is plentiful rather than when there is a pressing demand for staff and it is harder to attract the most desirable applicants. Similarly, employers are advised to invest in workers with non-specific skills that offer most over the longer term rather than fill posts with staff that can address immediate demands even if they may not be a good long-term investment. It is also suggested that employees should be retained during downturns because it will only cost more to re-hire them when the market improves; this also reinforces employment security. Moreover, instead of cutting back on training when finances are tight, employers are urged to spend more on training during the lean times because it is easier to release employees from their work then. Of course, there are good economic and labour market reasons for employers to do these things but they all depend, to a greater or lesser extent, upon the luxury of a long-term perspective and the prospect of future market growth. We should not forget that institutional and legal forces external to the organisation might encourage employers in co-ordinated market economies, such as the Netherlands, to take a longer-term perspective and see some value in using high commitment HRM (Boselie *et al* 2001).

2 *The cost of labour is low compared with other costs*

It is easier to implement high commitment HRM when labour costs form a low proportion of controllable costs. In capital-intensive operations, such as in pharmaceuticals or life sciences, it makes little sense to cut back on essential staff that have highly specific and much-needed skills. Conversely, when labour costs represent a significant proportion of expenditure, as in many service sector organisations for example, it is much harder to persuade financiers that there are long-term benefits from investing in human capital, especially if this includes any suggestion that pay rates or levels of training would increase. We have seen in recent years that bankers in LMEs, where short-term financial interests dominate capital markets, see few benefits in a strategic HR perspective because it sacrifices short-term gains. Equally, and understandably, it is unlikely that customers will agree to slower service – except at the margins – even if the argument is made that it is helping to develop talent over the longer term (eg in the health service, pubs and restaurants). Furthermore, given an emphasis on contracting and re-contracting along supply chains, there is little incentive for employers to invest in high commitment HRM if their contracts are of limited length and they are expected to compete on the basis of reduced costs (Marchington *et al* 2005). Given one of the main reasons for contracting-out is to reduce labour costs, high commitment HRM is unlikely to figure as a goal as it costs more to implement – unless it is clear this can also lead to better quality/service and growth in sales and overall performance (Marchington and Vincent 2004).

Whilst the high commitment model does increase worker output, it also raises labour costs, and if additional costs outweigh increases in productivity or quality achieved it would be misguided for employers to invest in this approach (Cappelli and Neumark 2001). The implication is that some employers, particularly those that do not put a premium on high quality products and services, decide that an 'intensification' approach – one which takes the 'low road' or cost reduction route to higher performance – offers greater benefits than high commitment HRM. Godard (2004) argues that the proponents of high commitment HRM 'overestimate the positive effects of high levels of adoption of these practices, but also underestimate the costs'. This results in little or no overall gain in productivity.

## REFLECTIVE ACTIVITY

Bearing in mind the recent furore about contracting out manufacturing or call centres to countries where wages are low, could customers gain more from high commitment HRM – in terms of better levels of service and product quality – than they would from purchasing at the lowest price possible?

3 *Knowledge workers are expected to use their discretion*

It could be argued that high commitment HRM only applies to workers that demonstrably add value because of their skills and abilities, and in the difference they make to customer service and product quality. MacDuffie (1995, p.199) is often quoted as someone who supports the universality argument, but a closer reading of his work suggests that high commitment HRM may actually require three conditions: when employees possess more knowledge and skills than managers; when they are motivated to apply this through discretionary effort; and when the organisation's goals can only be achieved when employees contribute such discretionary effort.

This implies that the circumstances under which high commitment HRM makes a difference are quite specific. For example, employers might wish to encourage discretionary behaviour to achieve organisational goals where work systems and processes are not easily codified or overseen by managers, and when there is a shortage of qualified workers; in this situation, a case can be made for hoarding labour. In many situations, however, the time taken to train new staff is relatively short, work performance can be assessed simply and speedily, and there is a supply of substitutable labour readily available. It is hard to see why employers would adopt high commitment HRM in these circumstances. In addition, some jobs are so boring or unpleasant that it is inconceivable workers would see employment security, basic training or information sharing – for example – as a benefit. On the contrary, these workers might resent being expected to take an interest in their organisation beyond routine work performance, and find it stressful and intrusive. In short, the high commitment model may not be attractive or appropriate for all groups of workers or employers. As we saw in the box above, Kinnie *et al* (2005) found priorities differed depending on whether respondents were line managers, professionals or other workers but this distinction may not always hold and contradictions can arise. For example, research on the use of high performance work systems in adult care (Harley *et al* 2007) shows that positive outcomes are not just restricted to professional staff but can also apply to unskilled or semi-skilled workers.

4 *Organisations and workers are in a strong market position*

The previous section focused on potentially differential treatment for workers employed by the same organisation, but this issue extends to the application of high commitment HRM across organisational boundaries (Grimshaw *et al* 2006; Marchington *et al* 2011a). The psychological contract has changed and employment insecurity is more widespread now. Evidence shows that between the 1970s and the 1990s, the proportion of people who had experienced a spell of unemployment almost trebled from 7% to approximately 20% of the population (Gallie *et al* 1998, p.124). Other data reinforces the view that employees feel even more insecure than they did 20 years ago, especially since the global financial crisis of 2008 (IPA June 2011).

For example, Boaden *et al* (2008) showed that workers employed by sub-contractors chosen precisely because they offer a cheaper service tend to receive an inferior employment package due to 'differentiation' strategies. Not surprisingly, these workers are very unlikely to receive high levels of pay and rewards, training and development, employment security and career development even though the organisation to which they supply their services may treat its workers in line with the high commitment paradigm. Moreover, even when employers use an 'integration' strategy, seeking to remove differentials between staff employed by different organisations wherever possible, other factors (eg different pay systems or pension arrangements) make this hard to achieve at a strategic level and because line managers from different employers have diverse capabilities. Achieving integration and consistency in HR systems across organisational boundaries is very difficult (Marchington *et al* 2011a). Rubery and Urwin (2011) found that care workers who had responsibility for the health and well-being of older people, and therefore would be expected to use their discretion in dealing with issues that arose, were in fact subject to low wages, unsociable working hours, virtually no flexibility and limited amounts of training; that is, precisely opposite to a high commitment paradigm. This was due to contracts being agreed with very tight margins, and even if these employers had wished to utilise a high commitment approach it would have been very difficult to sustain in the circumstances. The situation did not differ greatly between providers in the private and not-for-profit sectors. The authors also note (p.134) that 'much of the responsibility for current conditions lies with the local authority contracts. These fail to cover full employment costs (and) the costs of travel, training, sick leave, recruitment and retention, and of providing services outside of standard working times.' In other words, costs pressures limited flexibility for the care workers' employer. This is taken up in Chapter 4 when we examine ideas about HR architecture and labour market segmentation within and between organisations.

## CONCLUSIONS

This chapter has focused on high commitment HRM and the way in which HR policies and practices may be used to provide coherent and comprehensive bundles. This has led to suggestions that there is one best way in which HRM should be delivered, and moreover that this has a positive impact on organisational performance. Interest remains in the high commitment HRM–performance link, and to ideas that a specific bundle of HR policies and practices is inherently superior and capable of contributing to organisational success in all workplaces, both at an organisational and a policy level, as well as to national and global firms. We have reviewed the evidence here, pointing to alternative and competing interpretations of the research findings, as well as calling for greater reflection on whether or not high commitment HRM really can be offered to all workers and all workplaces. The high commitment model has also been subject to a more radical critique which argues that research in HRM is not only limited and conservative – tending generally to be conducted within managerial terms of reference – but also fails to adopt a more critical and theoretical social science framework (Bolton and Houlihan 2007; Delbridge 2011; Thompson 2011). This is reviewed in Chapter 15 since it fits better with our discussion of the HRM–performance link.

Whilst the high commitment model might be appealing because it supports the case for implementing 'good' people management practices on both business and fairness grounds, there is also a strong theoretical and empirical basis for arguing that high commitment models cannot be – and are not being – applied in all workplaces and to all groups of staff. Having considered the 'best practice' perspective in this chapter, we are now in a position to analyse the alternative – 'best fit' – scenario in Chapter 4.

EXPLORE FURTHER

ARROWSMITH, J., NICHOLAISEN, H., BECHTER, B. and NONELL, N. (2010) 'The management of variable pay in European banking', *International Journal of Human Resource Management*, Vol. 21, No.15, 2716–40.

BOADEN, R., MARCHINGTON, M., HYDE, P., HARRIS C., SPARROW, P., PASS, S., CARROLL, M. and CORTVRIEND, P. (2008) *Improving Health Through Human Resource Management: The process of engagement and alignment*. London, Chartered Institute of Personnel and Development.

BOXALL, P. and PURCELL, J. (2011) *Strategy and Human Resource Management*. Basingstoke, Palgrave Macmillan.

GOODERHAM, P., PARRY, E. and RINGDALL, K. (2008) 'The impact of bundles of strategic human resource management practices on the performance of European firms', *International Journal of Human Resource Management*, Vol. 19, No.11, 2041–56.

HOLMAN D., WALL T., CLEGG C., SPARROW P. and HOWARD A. (2003) *The New Workplace: A guide to the human impact of modern working practices*. London, Wiley. The chapters by Wood, Batt and Doellgast, Wright and Gardner, and Legge are particularly useful.

KEPES, S and DELERY, J. 'HRM systems and the problem of internal fit', in P. Boxall, J. Purcell and P. Wright (eds) (2007) *The Oxford Handbook of Human Resource Management*, Oxford, Oxford University Press.

KINNIE, N., HUTCHINSON, S., PURCELL, J., RAYTON, B. and SWART, J. (2005) 'Satisfaction with HR practices and commitment to the organisation: why one size does not fit all', *Human Resource Management Journal*, Vol. 15, No.4, 9–29.

SUBRAMONY, M. (2009) 'A meta-analytic investigation of the relationship between HRM bundles and firm performance', *Human Resource Management*, Vol. 48, No.5, 745–68.

THOMPSON, P. (2011) 'The trouble with human resource management', *Human Resource Management Journal*, Vol. 21, No.4, 355–67.

CHAPTER 4

# Designing HRM to Align with Organisational Goals and Market Context

## LEARNING OUTCOMES

By the end of this chapter, readers should be able to:

- contribute to the choice of appropriate HR policies that can lead to enhanced organisational and individual performance in different contexts
- benchmark their own employer's approach to HRM against those of other organisations
- evaluate different types of staffing arrangements (including outsourcing) from an HR architecture perspective.

In addition, readers should understand and be able to explain:

- the benefits and limitations of best fit models linking organisational contingencies with HRM at work
- how to analyse the links between HRM, organisational goals and market context from the resource-based and institutional perspectives
- the role and nature of staffing arrangements for different groups of workers within and beyond the employing organisation.

## INTRODUCTION

Having reviewed high commitment HRM in Chapter 3, we now turn to look at contingency models which argue that external factors determine, or at least shape, the styles of HRM that an organisation adopts. This flows from the conclusions to that chapter where we questioned the extent to which high commitment HRM was universally applicable. 'Best fit' or contingency perspectives provide an alternative way of analysing HRM and assessing the extent to which there is vertical integration (external fit) with business strategy. This chapter also takes up issues raised in Chapter 1 in relation to strategy and HRM. Following a brief introduction to contingency theory in this section, we analyse three frameworks – life cycle models, Schuler's adaptation of Porter, and Delery and Doty's extension of Miles and Snow – so as to examine the links between strategy and HRM, and outline the major drawbacks of the 'best fit' approach. This is followed by a discussion of resource-based views (RBV) of HRM and strategy, and recent developments in what has been termed the 'HR architecture' approach; this allows us to consider how staffing decisions are made for different occupational groups within the organisation, as well as decisions about outsourcing work rather than retain this in-house. We conclude with a critique of RBV from the institutional perspective.

## CONTINGENCY THEORY AND BEST FIT

Contingency theory (see, for example Donaldson 2001; Watson 2007) argues that the design of HRM depends on the context in which organisations operate. In other words, HRM varies between workplaces and there is no such thing as an 'ideal' set of HR practices that could be applied across the board in order to improve organisational performance. This seemingly common sense view depends on (a) which factors in the organisational context are deemed to be important and (b) how they are seen to influence HRM. In relation to the first question, previous studies have focused on a range of factors; for example, labour markets, technology, organisation size and structure, national business and employment systems, trade union traditions, and product markets, to name a few of the more widely cited factors (see, for example Legge 1978; Marchington 1982; Kitay and Marchington 1996; Watson 2007; Boxall and Purcell 2011). The second question turns on the extent to which so-called 'external factors' *determine* management actions. Apart from 'task' contingency ideas which assume that managers are merely ciphers in the transmission of predicted HR styles, Marchington and Parker (1990) show there are several other more sophisticated ways of examining the link between contingent factors and HRM. These are:

1 The **'political contingency'** perspective, which assumes managers use their power within the organisation to make choices within a constrained range of options that are to some extent dictated by external pressures. In this scenario, choices depend on factors entirely internal to the organisation.

2 The **'strategic choice'** perspective (Child 1997) puts managerial choice centre stage both in relation to HRM and the strategic direction of the organisation in areas such as the types of product and labour markets in which to operate or which technologies to employ. For example, rather than seeing the local labour market **solely** as a determining factor, we need to consider why firms choose to locate there in the first place, and assess whether specific types of employment regimes were actually wanted.

3 The **'legitimisation'** perspective is where senior managers claim there is no alternative to their chosen HR approach due to circumstances out of their control. In this case, rather than acknowledging that senior managers have some degree of choice in how to act, external factors are used to justify chosen styles of HRM or the way that decisions are made, eg in relation to limited employee involvement in change (Marchington and Wilkinson 2005).

Table 8 identifies some key factors that shape HRM, or at least management choices about which HR systems to adopt. In terms of the *policy framework*, several chapters in this book note differences between CMEs and LMEs, and the extent to which the former is likely to promote the development of high commitment HRM; as Boselie *et al* (2001) showed in the Netherlands. *Product market* influences have been explored most in best fit analyses of HRM, as we see in the next section, but broadly these demonstrate how employers in unpredictable and unstable markets, such as those occupied by sub-contractors to large organisations, make it difficult for employers to offer the high commitment model even if they wanted to. The level of *technological sophistication* within a market also impacts on HRM, to some extent because this influences job design and rewards and/or encourages discretionary behaviour by workers, but also due to the longer-term outlook for the industry as a whole (Boxall and Purcell 2011). Finally, *labour market* factors clearly influence management styles, either in terms of broad economic characteristics such as levels of unemployment or the role of trade unions at national level, or local factors relating to skills shortages or stances taken by local union officials. There is not room to examine all of these factors here, and indeed most are covered at other points in the book (for example, policy frameworks are central to Chapter 5 and labour market issues are covered in Chapters 2 and 10). In the next section, we analyse several models derived from the literature on product markets and competitive strategy.

**Table 8 Key factors influencing the choice of HRM systems**

| Factor shaping HRM | Promoting high commitment HRM | Impeding high commitment HRM |
|---|---|---|
| Policy framework, societal regime and financial system | Co-ordinated market economies<br>Legislation supporting worker rights and voice<br>Stakeholder perspective predominant | Liberal market economies<br>Voluntarist approach to worker rights and voice<br>Shareholder perspective predominant |
| Product markets | Oligopolistic and stable product markets<br>Long-term partnerships between organisations<br>Employer dominates markets | Highly competitive and unstable product markets<br>Market driven by contracting culture/spot markets<br>Employer marginal within markets |
| Technology, skill and staffing levels | Capital-intensive systems<br>High staff-to-customer ratios | Labour-intensive systems<br>Low staff-to-customer ratios |
| Labour markets and industrial relations | High skill levels, workers hard to replace<br>Strong co-operative management–union relations | Low skill levels, workers easy to replace<br>Hostile management–union relations or aggressive non-union stance |

### REFLECTIVE ACTIVITY

Look at an organisation of your choice and apply the framework and factors outlined in Table 8 to identify how well this might *predict* HRM styles.

## 'BEST FIT' HRM, PRODUCT MARKETS AND COMPETITIVE STRATEGY

There have been several attempts to develop categorisations linking HRM with business strategy, competitive circumstances or national business systems. Many are developed from the notion of 'external fit' (Baird and Meshoulam 1988), and as Boxall and Purcell (2003, p.51) note, 'the basic recipe for HRM involves bringing HR strategy into line with the firm's chosen path in its product market (more accurately this entails matching HR practices to the competitive strategy of a business unit)'. The models used include product or organisational life cycles, the Boston Consulting Group (BCG) matrix, derivations from

Porter's ideas on competitive advantage, strategic behaviour and organisational flexibility. These include: Kochan and Barocci (1985), Schuler (1989), Marchington and Parker (1990), Delery and Doty (1996), Sisson and Storey (2000), Phelps *et al* (2007), Chow and Liu (2009), and Boxall and Purcell (2011). For the purposes of this book, we focus on three important models (Kochan and Barocci); competitive advantage (Schuler); and strategic configurations (Delery and Doty). The models are outlined in this section; we follow this with a general critique of best fit/contingency approaches.

## LIFE-CYCLE MODELS

A number of US researchers (for example, Kochan and Barocci 1985; Lengnick Hall and Lengnick Hall 1988) have attempted to apply business and product life-cycle models of strategy to HRM to explain why employer policies change or vary between organisations. Often four stages are proposed, and Leung (2003) and Rutherford *et al* (2003) have applied this to small businesses, whilst Boxall and Purcell (2011) work on the basis of three stages to the life cycle of an industry: establishment, maturity, renewal. For this book, we stick with four stages – start-up, growth, maturity and decline – since this was first used by Sisson and Storey (2000). We acknowledge there are problems with such categorisations, not least in assuming linear patterns of growth that are replicated across all types of organisation (Phelps *et al* 2007) and in determining when new stages are reached. These are taken up as part of the general critique.

### Start-up

During the early stages, it is assumed there will be strong commitment to entrepreneurialism and organisational flexibility, meaning that few rules are required if the organisation (or sub-unit) is to grow and develop. The ability to recruit and retain staff with the motivation to work long hours and engage in self-development is the key to success at this stage, and employers often use personal networks to recruit staff in the same mould as themselves (Boxall and Purcell 2011, pp.267–8). This would also help gain employee commitment to the business, and while some may be able to offer highly competitive salaries in the short-run, it is more likely employees will be encouraged to see benefits as part of a long-term investment. Formalised HRM practices are unlikely at this stage (Kim and Gao 2010), and responsibility for HRM is combined with other managerial tasks undertaken by line managers, with consultants brought in as needed. If trade unions are present, their role would be minimal. Messersmith and Guthrie (2010) found, from their survey in the USA, that high commitment HRM was used in high-technology new ventures, but generally start-ups adopt highly informal approaches to HRM (Edwards and Ram 2009).

A major problem is the assumption that start-up only relates to new businesses that are typically small in size – which is probably the case for most new firms (Edwards and Ram 2009). However, any organisation opening a new outlet faces problems of start-up, and in many cases these are extensions of existing strands of business; for example, supermarkets open many new stores each year, implementing well-developed and centrally driven HR policies. Kynighou (2010) notes that large firms investing in new outlets overseas may decide existing HR policies provide a systematic base from which to build. Decisions are then made to install expatriates to manage the process or train locals to undertake this work since they have knowledge about institutional norms in the host country environment. She also reminds us that MNCs do not always start up new outlets from scratch but often take over existing businesses that have been running independently for many years, or purchase them from other firms. In these cases, they are start-ups but brown-field sites with a history of their own; the question is whether life-cycle models should use the age of the parent company or the site in their calculations, and whether that age starts from zero when a new firm takes over an existing going concern (Kynighou 2010).

### Growth

As organisations or sub-units grow, inconsistencies in treatment arise within the management chain and calls are made for more systematic HR policies and procedures to prevent mistakes. This can also help to retain expertise and ensure that earlier levels of commitment are maintained. For example, in order to recruit staff, rather than relying on word-of-mouth and existing contacts, greater use is made of sophisticated methods for recruitment and selection, training, performance review, and pay and reward. The need for specialist expertise becomes apparent across the organisation, including recruitment of in-house HR professionals. If HRM is still informal and ad hoc, an increasing number of problems are bound to emerge because HR policies – such as grievance and discipline procedures or pay systems – are applied inconsistently.

However, the entrepreneurs who first set up the organisation may resist shifts to greater formalisation (Boxall and Purcell 2011). This is common, even in large firms such as Starbucks, where the original founder felt the organisation had lost what he saw as its informal culture as the company grew in size and geographical spread, and workers talked about joining trade unions. It is difficult for large organisations to maintain feelings of fairness across different levels in the hierarchy and between sites in a large MNC. This also shows how life cycle and organisational size/age can be conflated, with observers unable to separate their differential effects (Kim and Gao 2010).

### Maturity

As markets begin to mature, and surpluses level out, organisations are typically confronted with lower levels of growth, and even a complete flattening out of performance. By this stage, it is likely that formalised procedures, covering everything from HRM to purchasing, are in place. In the early period of this stage, it is likely organisations use high commitment HRM, and indeed publications implicitly refer to this 'golden age' where compromises are reached because market pressures allow employers to implement win–win solutions. Even during this period, relative calm and stability may be punctured by crises – such as new global pressures across economies or within the sector, political turmoil in product markets or a hostile takeover bid – which cause a rethink of existing practices. Indeed, Phelps *et al* (2007, p.16) criticise life-cycle models which assume neat, linear stages in organisational growth and suggest approaches which recognise the role of critical junctures and shifting sands in the patterns that emerge – such as during the global financial crisis.

As this stage unfolds, there is an increasing focus on the control of labour costs, something that is often hard to achieve given that employees have become accustomed to enjoying the continuing fruits of prosperity. Staff replacements are no longer automatic, training and development programmes become harder to justify, and the wage bill is kept firmly under control. Worker representatives, if unions are recognised, may find relationships start to become strained as assurances about employment security appear increasingly fragile. Staff may be encouraged to take voluntary redundancy or become more flexible in what they do, as efforts are made to improve productivity against a backcloth of weak competitive prospects (Marchington and Kynighou 2012).

### Decline (and renewal?)

Decline brings to a head the problems that emerged during late maturity. In this stage the emphasis shifts to rationalisation and redundancy, with obvious implications for HRM. Existing HR policies may be abandoned as employers try desperately to reduce costs. The specialist HR function could well be disbanded or subjected to close scrutiny, and senior managers might decide more could be gained by outsourcing some or all of the function's work or joining with other organisations or subsidiaries in a shared service provision (see Chapter 6). There might be pay cuts, training becomes focused on re-skilling and outplacement counselling, and there is a tendency to contract-out jobs that were previously undertaken in-house on cost grounds. Cultures can become tense and trade unions marginalised or derecognised.

This pattern has been reproduced in many manufacturing firms that have struggled to survive over the last 20 years, often characterised by successive plant closures, an increased tendency to use coercive comparisons between establishments to get higher levels of productivity, and soured employment relations. Of course, not all organisations continue on the road to decline and some – such as Ford – bounce back by a genuine shift to more participative management for those remaining with the new slimmed-down company (Boxall and Purcell 2003, p.200). Rather than just 'hanging-on' until things improve, a more proactive stance to 'human resource advantage in the renewal context lies in preparing for it more effectively in the mature context' (Boxall and Purcell, 2011, p.275). Following the life-cycle terminology, this could allow organisations to re-enter at one of the earlier stages. The following box provides an analysis of how the life-cycle model can be applied to small firms.

HRM AT WORK IN FOCUS

## Changes in HRM during the life cycle of small firms

There have been very few empirical studies examining how HRM might change during the organisational life cycle – in order to test the general theories advanced in this section of the chapter. Research in the USA examined the interplay of organisational life cycle and various firm characteristics in a sample of nearly 3,000 small and medium-sized enterprises so as to test the hypothesis that the principal HR problems would change as the firm develops. It was suggested that recruitment problems would be greatest during the early stage, issues to do with development would be most prominent during the growth stage and retention would become a principal concern once the firm reaches maturity. As a by-product the study also examined whether or not a four-stage model was appropriate.

The results were quite varied, with only partial support for the proposition that HR problems would change in the way suggested above. The four-stage model received support, although age of the firm was much less influential as a variable than its size. Indeed variations in the *rate of growth* proved to the most critical factor explaining the emergence of HR problems. The fastest growing firms reported the greatest problems in dealing with learning and development, something to be expected as small businesses grapple with how to formalise HRM. In contrast, high growth firms reported few retention problems, presumably because existing staff enjoyed the challenge of meeting fresh targets. The moderate growth firms reported the greatest retention problems as workers left because they had few opportunities to meet new challenges and became bored with organisational routines. Low growth firms reported few problems with either training or recruitment. Paradoxically, firms that were experiencing no growth (and presumably did not have to recruit many staff) found that recruitment was the most difficult problem they had to face, perhaps because they were unable to attract sufficiently high quality recruits in the first place.

*To think about:*

*On the basis of the research outlined above, what HR advice would you offer to a small to medium-sized business? Justify your answer with the use of examples and evidence from other types of organisation.*

Source: Adapted from Rutherford *et al* (2003).

## COMPETITIVE ADVANTAGE MODELS

Porter (1985) argues that employers have three basic strategic options in order to gain competitive advantage: cost reduction, quality enhancement and innovation. Schuler and Jackson (1987) draw out the HR implications of these strategies, and the original has been developed by Sisson and Storey (2000; see Table 9 below) and Kelliher and Perrett (2001). It has also formed the basis for studies in Spain (Sanz-Valle *et al* 1999), China (Chow and Liu 2009), France (Caroli *et al* 2010) and across the airline industry worldwide (Gittell and Bamber 2010). The research undertaken on Spanish firms, many of which employed less than 50 staff, provides support for the link between these three categories of business strategy and related HR practices. For example, cost reducers tended to provide lower levels of training, team-working and pay than the other categories, whilst the innovators were more inclined to invest in teamwork, make more use of internal labour markets and pay higher rates (Sanz-Valle *et al* 1999). The research comparing French and UK food processing firms showed that the former were more inclined to address problems in the market through low levels of employment security whilst the latter protected the core workforce to a much greater extent and used seasonal staff to cope with fluctuations in demand. In the UK, agency workers – often economic migrants – were extensively used and the managerial 'logic' was to 'make ever greater use of a cheap, pliant and insecure workforce.' The stronger and more embedded nature of national labour market institutions in France played a major part in explaining these differences (Caroli *et al* 2010). We examine the airline case in the next section.

**Cost reduction** employers compete on the basis of price, with no frills and an emphasis on minimising costs at all stages in the process – including HRM. The consequences are no systems for independent worker voice or any evidence of high commitment HRM. Recruitment and selection is likely to be ad hoc, especially for low-grade tasks, and the employer may well use agencies or subcontractors to perform much of the work (Marchington *et al* 2005). Training is likely to be poor or non-existent, with no recognition that employees should have opportunities for learning and development. Pay levels are unlikely to be much above the minimum wage, and could well be less if the employer can get away with it, for example in firms that use migrant labour and provide very basic conditions. In addition, there will be low health and safety standards, tight performance monitoring, limited employee involvement and communications, and little empathy with staff experiencing problems. It is extremely unlikely that unions will be recognised in this situation and if a specialist HR function exists, it is likely to have little influence.

Cost reducers are undoubtedly the most common form in Britain, largely because so many people work for small firms that have neither the resources nor the commitment to develop their staff. They dominate industries such as retailing, hospitality, cleaning and security, and social care. The HR problems experienced by employers were summed up by the manager of a care home who said: 'there's a new retail park going to be built in the local area … How on earth am I going to keep our employees when they do that? I haven't

**Table 9 Competitive strategies and hrm**

| HR practices | Competitive strategy | | |
|---|---|---|---|
| | **Cost reduction** | **Quality enhancement** | **Innovation** |
| Resourcing | Ad hoc methods predominate, use of agencies and sub-contractors<br>Tight performance management | Sophisticated methods of recruitment and selection<br>Comprehensive induction and socialisation | Focus on core competencies and transferable skills<br>Agreed performance outcomes |
| Learning and development | Poor or non-existent training in specific immediate skills | Extensive and long-term focus<br>Focused on learning and career development | Provided if necessary<br>Personal responsibility for learning |
| Employee relations | Little EIP or communications<br>Non-union workplace or unions tolerated | Well-developed systems for employee voice<br>Partnership arrangements | Preference for informal communication systems<br>Professional associations |
| Reward management | Low pay levels<br>No additional benefits | Competitive pay and benefits package<br>Harmonisation | Cafeteria reward system<br>Share ownership/ profit-sharing |
| HR function | Slimmed down<br>Lacking in influence | Work closely with line managers<br>Potentially large influence | Advice and support to employees<br>Potentially some influence |

Source: Adapted from Sisson and Storey (2000).

the faintest idea because they will pay them a damn sight more' (Low Pay Commission 2003, p.91). Rubery and Urwin (2011) examined HRM in social care, researching a local authority and five of its domiciliary care providers drawn from public, for-profit and not-for-profit sectors. Their findings (2011, p.134) suggest that 'employers in this sector are failing to provide minimum employment protections, let alone develop strong HR policies to promote a committed and motivated workforce. Such policies may be regarded as even more necessary given the inherent complexities and stresses of care work.' Local authorities outsourcing the work are blamed for this predicament as the basic contract fails to cover not just full employment costs but also time for moving between visits, the cost of travel and recruitment charges. All three types of employer, including the not-for-profit organisations, felt the squeeze in a similar way.

Other studies (Grimshaw and Marchington 2007) illustrate graphically the way in which flexibility for the employer – achieved through a loosely regulated labour market – translates into vulnerability for workers in these sorts of firms. Since UK nationals increasingly avoid employment in this type of firm, they had become more reliant on gang-masters for sourcing migrant labour through employment agencies. Not only did these workers suffer low rates of pay and poor working conditions, they also faced massive insecurity due to the casual nature of their employment and the failure of firms to provide training. Edwards and Ram (2006, 2010), reporting on the findings from over 120 small firms from several sectors, argue that these organisations only manage to survive due to a continued supply of labour through kinship networks and the ability of firms to operate flexibly in meeting product market opportunities. This research is reported in some more detail in the box below. However, cost reduction firms differ in their responses to difficult market conditions and externally induced crisis, with some using cut-backs to introduce more innovative HR policies as well as reduce costs (Mellahi and Wilkinson 2010).

HRM AT WORK IN FOCUS

### Low value-added firms, HRM and flexibility

Low value-added firms tend to be small, located in highly competitive sectors of the economy with low barriers to entry, low payers and typically family-owned and run. As we have already seen, small firms make up a large proportion of the UK economy, and many of these are family-run.

Three sectors illustrate this situation well. Care homes are mostly small independent operators, whose work is constrained by strict legal rules which prevent them going too far down the road of work intensification. One way to get around this problem was for managers to work very long hours, but this is clearly untenable in the long term. Clothing firms face major problems due to reductions in domestic sourcing, as large companies sub-contract work overseas to take advantage of cheaper prices, but direct competition was not possible due to requirements to pay the minimum wage in the UK. The firms responded in a number of ways, with some making greater use of family and kinship networks whilst others shifted towards quasi-legal working practices. In catering, firms responded to direct competition from other outlets in the same area by getting staff to work longer and more flexible hours, and in effect to be available as required. At the same time pay systems were also highly flexible, with little use of formal pay systems and evidence that significant 'off-the-books' working is taking place.

But the research shows that many of these firms managed to survive despite what they saw as the harsh economic and regulatory regime. In clothing and catering, they employed greater numbers of migrant and illegal workers who were prepared to accept wages below the legal minima and work long hours, sometimes in atrocious working conditions, largely because they had little alternative. In essence they became entrapped in menial jobs. Product market pressures pushed many firms to the edge of survival, but some managed to identify niche markets which allowed them relative prosperity.

Whilst at one level these findings support the competitive advantage models it would be wrong to assume that all firms used the same HR practices. Entrepreneurs operating in difficult market conditions were 'still able to exploit opportunities arising from interactions between markets and environments. The multi-faceted nature of family involvement lends distinctiveness to the management and mode of organisation in such firms' Edward and Ram 2006 (p.911).

*To think about:*

*How long can 'cost reducers' continue to recruit and retain staff if their conditions are so much worse than other employers in the same labour market?*

Source: Adapted from Edwards and Ram (2006); and Edwards and Ram (2009).

**Quality enhancement** employers adopt HR practices that are exactly opposite to the cost reducer because they produce goods and services of the highest quality in order to differentiate themselves from the competition. HRM takes the form of the 'best practice/ high commitment' model analysed in the previous chapter. This includes: systematic recruitment, selection and induction; empowerment and high-discretion jobs; high levels of EIP; extensive and continuous training and development; work–life balance; highly competitive pay and benefits packages; and a key role for performance appraisal. Schuler does not mention unions, but if they are recognised both parties try to maintain co-operative relations, perhaps through a management–union partnership. The HR function is likely to be well staffed and be proactive in shaping organisational cultures and change programmes. Close co-operation between HR and line managers is likely to improve the chances that intended HR policies are implemented consistently and in accordance with expectations.

Many large organisations offer this employment package – if only to attract and retain key staff at times of labour market shortage. However, as we see in Chapters 3 and 15, it is hard to ensure HR policy is actually converted into 'real' practice at workplace level and that commitment to employment security or equal opportunities is not jettisoned if problems arise. The extent to which quality enhancers sustain this approach during downturn and recession is open to question, as too is the ability to apply these HR practices across the entire workforce (Marchington and Kynighou 2012). Of course, some organisations use a quality enhancement approach for core staff through a process of differentiation and tightly specified business contracts on suppliers that gives the latter little option but to impose inferior terms and conditions on their workers (Marchington *et al* 2005).

**Innovative** employers are the least widespread of the three. Here, it is assumed that groups of highly trained specialists work closely together to design and produce complex and rapidly changing/adaptable products and services. Typical examples would be research scientists, professionals such as architects and lawyers, IT workers and consultants (Richter *et al* 2008; Grimshaw and Miozzo 2009; Swart and Kinnie 2010; Von Nordenflycht 2010). HR policy is similar in many respects to the quality enhancement model, but with a much greater emphasis on informality, problem-solving groups, a commitment to broadly defined goals, and flexibility. Employee development is often seen as a personal responsibility rather than the employer's obligation, and basic pay rates are likely to be supplemented by access to share ownership schemes that enable employees to link their fortunes to that of the employer. Unions are unlikely to figure prominently given the emphasis on individualism. The box below shows how the link between strategy and HRM in innovator companies is more complex than the model implies.

HRM AT WORK IN FOCUS

## How the HR function works in biotech firms

In innovative organisations, such as law firms, research agencies and high-tech start-ups, people are typically the major source of value creation, and knowing how to manage HRM in these situations is a complex issue. On the one hand, it could be argued that it is imperative to appoint an experienced HR professional to ensure the organisation recruits, motivates and retains this talent – in the same way we would expect for organisations that seek to compete on the basis of quality enhancement. On the other, given the degree of autonomy, risk-taking and individualism that characterises innovative organisations, it might be better to allow cultures to develop in a more informal and loose manner – and do without an in-house HR professional, at least in the first instance.

In order to assess this question, the authors conducted research on eight firms located in high-tech corridors in the USA and Australia. All the firms were engaged in the development of drugs or diagnostics using biotechnology, they had all been in existence for at least two years and all employed at least 10 people – thus ensuring they were beyond the initial start-up phase. The largest firm employed over 200 people.

Four different models of HR emerged, though some of these were changing as the firms grew in size and confronted new business issues.

- **No in-house HR function.** Here HRM was handled by administrators and members of the top management team depending on the issue. In one case, the CEO's prior experience had left him disillusioned about the value of HR and he was adamant that matters were handled informally as part of a 'can-do' philosophy. However as the firm grew, an external HR consultant was hired to work with the top team.
- **Tactical HR function.** This was another situation where the founders played a dominant role in developing the culture of the firm and wanted to minimise the degree of formality they felt an HR function would bring. The owners characterised the firm as one big happy family, where all staff – including one of the founders – were encouraged to maintain a work–family balance and vary their hours to fit with activities at home. Once again, pressures for co-ordination and consistency grew as the firm became larger, and the HR manager felt that the firm was likely to become a victim of its own growth.
- **Strategic HR from the outset.** This company was a little different from the others as it first identified markets for its products and then set about developing the technology. In a similar vein, the CEO decided to hire an experienced HR leader with over 20 years' experience in the sector who was aware that the HR function needed to be flexible and not become too rules-oriented if it was going to succeed in this environment.
- **HR transformation.** In common with some other high-tech start-ups, this firm hired an HR person without industry experience who did the routine administration whilst the founders retained responsibility for more strategic issues. As the firm grew, so too did the HR

problems caused by not having a more strategic HR presence, and this led to the appointment of a new HR strategist with experience in biotechnology. This resulted in attempts to create a strong and distinctive culture, including a balanced scorecard approach to strategy.

The main conclusion is that potential advantages flow from appointing a strategic HR expert as part of the leadership team, if not from the outset then soon after the firm is established. It is suggested that doing without an HR presence might reduce costs in the short term, but all this does is store up problems for the future and deny the firm any advantages that might accrue from a professional and integrated approach to HRM.

Source: Adapted from Finegold and Frenkel (2006).

It is unlikely entire organisations will be in the 'innovation' category, so this set of HR practices may be preserved for small groups of highly qualified staff or those engaged in 'leading-edge' activities. This opens up the possibility that different groups of staff may be employed on quite different terms and conditions from one another. One way to insulate these workers from others employed by the same organisation is to locate them on a different site or in a division set up specifically to develop new ideas and products, perhaps ultimately being spun off as a separate company. This separation of supplier from purchaser is common in the IT consulting sector as Grimshaw and Miozzo (2009) show in their study across four countries (the UK, Germany, Argentina and Brazil). Differences were found in HR practices – such as recruitment, skill development and job security – due to a number of factors. Clients clearly influenced HRM at the IT firms through expectations about the type of business contract and performance requirements to be provided to meet client needs. So too did the process of transfer between firms in the network, as some staff moved from the purchaser to the supplier and also between suppliers; this created additional complexities in HRM. Finally, institutional and legal factors shaped the precise development of HRM in each of the countries, ranging from relatively weak employment protection in Argentina following the crisis in 2001 to the much stronger mechanisms in Germany.

It is apparent that in many of these studies, especially the surveys, data on HR practices is supplied by single respondents, typically the HR or general manager, and their account of events. An alternative approach is to ask workers how they feel they are being treated and use that as the basis for assessing the impact of HRM on employee outcomes. Nishi *et al* (2008) asked over 4,000 workers across 95 stores in one organisation what form of HRM – quality enhancement (QE) or cost reduction (CR) – they were experiencing, and given the centralised approach taken in the company it can be assumed that the actual practices were the same, at least in terms of management intentions. The result was that those workers that felt they were receiving QE treatment held significantly more positive attitudes than those that felt they were subject to CR, that is, the way they perceived their treatment was very different.

## STRATEGIC CONFIGURATIONS

Traditional contingency theory has been criticised for its simplicity and its determinism. It is assumed that internal variables – such as specific HR practices – can be 'read-off' from so-called external factors such as product market circumstances or the firm's stage in the life cycle. As we saw earlier, choosing an alternative external factor (say, labour market circumstances) might suggest a different style altogether, and this limits the value of contingency models (Alcazar *et al* 2005). Delery and Doty (1996) address this problem via the notion of configurational perspectives which seek to identify ideal-type categories of both the HR system and the organisation's strategy. The principal point about this perspective is that it identifies an internally consistent set of HR practices that maximise horizontal integration (internal fit) and then links these to alternative strategic configurations to maximise vertical integration (external fit). Delery and Doty (p.809) do this by linking an 'internal' employment system with Miles and Snow's (1978) 'defender' strategy and a 'market-type' employment system with their 'prospector' category (see Table 10).

**Table 10 Strategic configurations and HRM**

| **HR practices** | **Strategic configuration** | |
|---|---|---|
| | **Defenders – internal employment system** | **Prospectors – market employment system** |
| Resourcing | Great care over recruitment and selection<br>Well-developed internal labour markets | Buying-in of labour to undertake specific tasks<br>Tight performance standards and expectations |
| Learning and development | Extensive and long-term focus<br>Well-defined career ladders | Likely to be extensive<br>Personal responsibility for learning and development |
| Employee relations | Emphasis on co-operation and involvement<br>Voice through grievance procedures and trade unions | Emphasis on responsibility and performance<br>Little attention paid to voice |
| Reward management | Clear grading structures and transparent pay systems<br>Employee share ownership | Pay determined by external market comparisons<br>Bonus and incentive payments |
| HR function | Well-established<br>Potentially large influence | Limited role<br>Managing external contracts |

Source: Adapted from Delery and Doty (1996).

**Defenders** concentrate on existing markets and on narrow product ranges by the use of a centralised organisation structure. They 'build' portfolios and extend their activities slowly and carefully. As such, an internal employment system offers an appropriate fit with the strategic goals and capabilities of the organisation, and it allows for the derivation of a bundle of HR practices that support each other. Recruitment, wherever possible, is through specific ports of entry and employees are promoted internally to fill higher positions. Career ladders are well defined, training and development activities are extensive, and socialisation into the dominant organisational culture is high on the managerial agenda, both through formal induction programmes and through day-to-day reinforcement. Appraisals are principally for developmental purposes, and the reward structure is geared up to long-term employment with the organisation, for example through clear grading structures and increments, as well as via employee share ownership. Employment security is high for those in core jobs, with clear opportunities for employees to exercise their voice through grievance procedures, problem-solving groups and (where recognised) trade unions. The HR function is well established and may be involved in strategic decisions because it has specific expertise about HRM within the sector. Moreover, senior HR managers are likely to be active in wider industry bodies relating to training and health and safety, or in pay clubs that share information about compensation levels and practices. It is clear that defender organisations are keen to promote not only their own performance but also the industry as a whole because it fits with their own longer-term interests.

By contrast, **prospectors** are committed to exploring new product markets and business opportunities, so are therefore less reliant on existing skills and abilities. Consequently, their HR strategies face outwards as they search the external labour market to 'buy in' staff rather than 'build' them as do the defenders. Recruitment is mainly external, with little use of internal career ladders other than for specialist core groups. Given the emphasis on external recruitment, training is likely to be much less extensive than at defender firms and typically related to short-term needs rather than long-term development. Appraisals are likely to be results-oriented, and performance-related pay schemes are prominent. Voice is not promoted particularly whilst unions are tolerated rather than encouraged. The role of the HR function is limited to administration and support rather than being a strategic business partner – unless used to manage external contracts, interpret legal issues and lead on rationalisation and change. Given that HR is not providing industry-specific expertise, much of this work could be contracted-out to specialist firms such as Capita or PwC.

## REFLECTIVE ACTIVITY

Identify a defender or a prospector firm, and find out whether or not their HR practices fit with an internal or a market employment system.

Rodriguez and Ventura (2003) examined whether the Miles and Snow model applied to HRM. Their results were mixed, although it is always hard to generalise on the basis of one country (Spain), a low response rate (5% return) and the other problems associated with survey results – such as the reliance on a single respondent and the type of proxies used for each of the practices. Broadly, the authors found that an internal HR system (defender) was linked with low levels of labour turnover and superior firm performance, but that reward practices had a negative relationship with productivity. As we suggest later in this chapter, when we examine the RBV, there may be a minimum stock of HR practices that is essential for organisational survival and continued viability, while others combine in more idiosyncratic ways to enhance sustained competitive advantage.

## LIMITATIONS OF BEST FIT/CONTINGENCY MODELS

There are clear similarities between these models, and parallels can be drawn between HR practices in some of the different categorisations, eg cost reducer and start-up, or quality enhancer and internal employment system. There are also at least six general shortcomings as we see in Table 11.

1 ***Deterministic and top-down assumptions***. All the models assume it is possible to 'read off' a preferred HR strategy and bundle of practices from an evaluation of business strategy or competitive prospects. There are several problems with this assumption. Many organisations do not have clear business strategies so it is impossible to claim there are links with HRM if no strategy exists (Boxall and Purcell 2011). In addition, the contingency approaches adopt the classical perspective on strategy, in which logical, rational decision-

**Table 11 Shortcomings in best fit/contingency models of HRM**

| | |
|---|---|
| 1 | They are deterministic and top-down, allowing no room for managerial choice. |
| 2 | Organisations are subject to multiple influences, not all of which are considered in the models. |
| 3 | Managers do not have complete power to implement precisely what they want. |
| 4 | The models are incapable of accounting for processes of change. |
| 5 | Institutional forces tend to be ignored as it assumes that organisations have autonomy to act as they choose. |
| 6 | It is difficult to apply the categorisation precisely to individual organisations. |

making takes place in an ordered and sequential manner between non-political actors. We already know from Chapter 1 that this is unrealistic. As Ritson (1999, p.170) argues, the relationship between HRM and strategy is more interactive than the classical models suggest. The models are also normative, relying on 'what ought to be' rather than 'what is', assuming there is one best way to manage people in particular situations. Empirical evidence shows HR styles vary even for organisations in similar product markets, each of which may be equally successful at the same or different periods of time.

There are several reasons why we need to be wary about these models; for example, rather than always making the right decision, senior managers can make poor choices so their organisation's approach to HRM is actually sub-optimal or even dangerously wrong. Equally, the organisation could be doing well in the short-term through existing HR practices but this could store up problems for the future because senior managers have failed to see signs of the need to change. Even if performance is strong, it could be that if senior managers had made different decisions, results could be even better. In other words, it is not possible to assess the models solely on the basis of empirical examination.

2 ***Organisations are subject to multiple influences***. Each model puts a primacy on a single – albeit different – contextual factor and assumes this *determines* patterns of HRM. Even if we accept that a particular product market context is related theoretically to a particular HR style, problems arise if different external factors suggest different types of HR strategy, or that different parts of a business operate in distinct markets. For example, a highly competitive product market might lead employers to cut labour costs wherever possible, with very tight controls on pay and other terms and conditions. However, in the same situation, if the labour market is very tight for specific grades of worker who are essential to the process, this implies that great care is needed when recruiting, developing and rewarding these staff for fear they will leave.

Moreover, as we suggested above, decisions about which HR style to adopt in each of these models is primarily influenced by factors *beyond* the employment relationship. While acknowledging that employment issues are typically lower down the decision-making hierarchy than financial or customer goals, neglecting HRM is problematic if workers can easily influence product quality or service. In service sector firms, daily interactions between front-line staff – who are often amongst the lowest paid in the organisation – and customers has a substantial impact on sales and customer satisfaction in highly competitive markets (Batt 2007). Similarly, employers in relatively high-skill sectors – such as health and education – face major problems finding well-qualified staff solely from the UK, and many are now hired from China, India and parts of Africa. Even though some of the work of nurses and teachers is now done by less-well-qualified assistants, retention has remained a major concern (Bach *et al* 2008). In short, as Boxall and Purcell (2003, p.54) note, we need to recognise that 'the strategic goals of HRM are plural. While they do involve supporting the firm's competitive objectives, they also involve meeting employee needs and complying with social requirements for labour management … The firm after all is a network of stakeholders.'

3 ***Managers do not have total control over workers.*** Each model follows traditional scientific management principles in assuming managers are omniscient (all-knowing) and omnipotent (all-powerful) in their dealings with staff. The concept of 'bounded rationality' suggests it is impossible for anyone to retain sufficient information in their head to make judgements about every possible scenario. Moreover, the models assume that once a preferred strategy has been identified by senior managers, there is no problem putting it into effect; as we see in several chapters, there are gaps between strategic intentions, its implementation by line managers and the way in which workers perceive HRM. While employers typically have greater bargaining power than employees, it is unrealistic to ignore the 'baseline needs of employees whose skills are crucial to the firm's survival' (Boxall and Purcell 2000, p.187). Even firms utilising technology to monitor performance – such as call centres – soon realise there are strict limits to managers' abilities to fully control the activities of their staff (Taylor *et al* 2002; Baldry *et al* 2007; Thite and Russell 2010).

   This is not something restricted solely to workplaces where independent worker voice exists but can apply in all types of environment, even prisoners as inmates find ways to subvert the controls imposed by wardens. It is clear from several chapters in the book that employer goals are not determined in a vacuum, but emerge through negotiations both within the managerial hierarchy and with employees/trade unions. Depending on the country and the sector, they can also be heavily shaped by governmental and institutional forces. Moreover, recent research (for example, Rubery *et al* 2004; Marchington *et al* 2009) shows how multiple influences shape HRM in any setting, but this is even more complex within networks or up and down supply chains. In a call centre, even though workers are employed at the same location, they might be supplied from various agencies, work on different contracts and have diverse terms and conditions of employment.

4 ***Static models neglect the processes of change.*** Each model relates two sets of variables together (eg life cycle and HRM) in a static way that ignores processes. Evidence suggests that organisations do not travel smoothly and seamlessly in the direction indicated by the life-cycle model, but instead move through a series of recurrent crises as they grow and develop (Phelps *et al* 2007; Grant 2008; Boxall and Purcell 2011). Assumptions tend to be made about the size, shape and structure of organisations in each of the stages and categories, so that a start-up business is typically seen as small and a mature business large. It is difficult to gauge when an organisation moves from one stage of the life cycle to the next, and at what point there *ought* to be a change in HR practice to reflect – or drive – this change. In addition, even if it was possible to identify the moment when organisations move from one stage to the next, simply adjusting the terms and conditions of staff in order to realign the business and HR strategies would not be feasible. Making wholesale changes to workers' contracts could lead not only to a worsening of management–employee relations but also to major legal claims. Accordingly, if best fit models are to be effective, a clearer focus is needed on how changes take place, on the major influences over and obstacles to change, and on the actual processes of decision-making. This may be difficult for those who are engaged in the process because they are too close to the issues to see what is happening.

5 ***HRM is shaped by institutional forces not just competitive pressures.*** The main focus of best fit models is at the level of the individual organisation, and it is assumed that employers are free agents able to make decisions merely on their own assessment of situations. This may apply to some extent for organisations in relatively unregulated Anglo-Saxon systems of employment in the UK or the USA, but it has little meaning for firms located on mainland Europe. Moreover, it ignores the role of employers' associations and trade bodies in shaping the regulatory system (Marchington and Vincent 2004). For example in chemicals, the health and safety legislation has a major impact on HR practices, while in education there are rigidly enforced standards about the minimum qualifications required of staff. There can

also be influences from the local communities in which employers are located, such as a ban on night-time deliveries which determines working hours. Similarly, factors beyond the workplace influence management decisions – such as the availability of migrant workers, the provision of local buses, and opening/closure of other employers in the district.

Rubery and Grimshaw (2003, p.39) show how the strength of institutional forces varies between countries, largely influenced by societal logics and trajectories. Perhaps this is best summed up by Boxall and Purcell (2008, p.73) who remind us that 'firms are "embedded" in societies which regulate and influence them while also providing social capital of varying quality. The firm can never be the complete author of its own HRM.' As we see in Chapter 5, research on MNCs comparing home-versus-host-country effects identifies a deeply interactive relationship between firm-level and societal-level factors (Quintanilla and Ferner 2003; Pulignano 2006; Edwards 2011; Ferner *et al* 2011; Grimshaw *et al* 2011).

6 ***Problems of categorisation***. Differences in HR practices – such as pay, employment security or union recognition – between organisations as diverse as a research-led pharmaceutical company, a service-oriented fast-food chain and a local authority are readily apparent to most intelligent observers. However, it is much harder to assess differences between two organisations in separate – or even the same – segments of the same product market. Why, for example, did General Motors develop HR policies in a certain way while Ford took a quite different stance (Mueller 1994), or why did Tesco choose to work closely with trade unions while Sainsbury's preferred to minimise union involvement? These examples call into question the ability of best fit models to wholly explain how HRM develops in organisations. Firms may also try to seek what are sometimes seen as conflicting and contradictory aims – for example, extending participation for some staff whilst cutting overall numbers employed (Boxall and Purcell 2008; Marchington and Kynighou 2012). Similarly, employer branding might lead to problems in working out which style of HRM is being pursued as Crawshaw *et al* (1994) showed with their analysis of Sainsbury's 'good food costs less' slogan; this meant the company was stuck in the middle, neither a quality enhancer nor a cost reducer. Another issue is what happens to HRM when two quite different firms merge – such as with some of the private equity purchases over the last few years or Kraft's acquisition of Cadbury through what was seen as a hostile takeover (Edwards and Rees 2006). Applying the best fit models is difficult in such circumstances without a consideration of other factors, and in the period following the change of ownership there is often so much turbulence in the system that it is hard to identify a dominant HR style.

Bird and Beechler (1995, p.40) found that organisational performance (in a sample of Japanese companies in the USA) was higher if business and HR strategies matched than when there was a mismatch. However, they suggested a more holistic approach was needed in which strategies in other functional areas – such as production, sales and R&D – were considered as well. Kelliher and Perrett (2001) applied competitive advantage models in their examination of the strategy–HRM links in 'designer restaurants.' Since these establishments stressed a quality and novel experience (using terms such as upmarket, trendy and innovative), it might be expected that a similar HR strategy would emerge. There was a strong emphasis on recruiting high quality staff, systematic performance appraisal, a high commitment to training and development, pay levels at or above that of competitors, and informal staff–management relations. However, there was little evidence that any alignment had taken place, and the dominant HR practices were hard-nosed and short-term, relying on the use of a transient workforce, particularly at the front of house, that received only average levels of pay and few other benefits (p.433). This raises questions about whether or not the restaurants were achieving maximum organisational effectiveness. From an HR perspective, the cues sent to employees about their (lack of) importance to business success could be regarded as impeding the performance of the restaurants. At the same time, certain 'key' groups of staff – notably in the kitchens – received an employment package in line with the strategy. Finally, a project on airlines (Bamber *et al* 2009; Gittell and Bamber 2010) provides a good opporunity to test best fit models. The box below summarises some key points.

HRM AT WORK IN FOCUS

## I'll fly the high road and you fly the low road: patterns of HRM in low cost airlines

The last two decades have seen a major surge in the importance of low cost airlines around the world, and the HRM and employment relations implications of this new business were considered in a 2010 special issue of the *International Journal of Human Resource Management* – see below for details. There is not the space here to do justice to the whole journal so three cases have been summarised to illustrate the range of HRM approaches taken by cost-reducer firms. The authors argue that low-cost business strategies do not necessarily mean that cost reduction HRM policies have to be used, because employers make choices about how to provide good customer service.

*Southwest Airlines* was founded in 1971 and became the largest airline serving the US domestic market. The company believes that high levels of relational co-ordination are needed to turn around planes fast and provide the service required. This led Southwest to develop a set of HR policies which supports this objective, including:

- efforts to recruit staff that demonstrate high levels of awareness of other people
- training programmes which demonstrate to staff how their role fits with that of other people
- low spans of control for first-line supervisors to enable them to support staff
- performance management systems that focus on problem-solving rather than assigning blame if things go wrong
- encouraging conflict resolution meetings rather than trying to 'hide' tensions
- a concern for work–family balance by allowing staff to take time to maintain family and community commitments
- a deliberate avoidance of lay-offs, and
- a partnership approach to trade unions.

Overall, Gittell and Bamber (2010, p.172) argue that 'rather than viewing its employees as a cost to be minimised, Southwest views its employees as partners in reducing costs and producing value. (It) therefore epitomises in many ways a high-road strategy, striving for high commitment with its employees and partnership with their union representatives.'

*Ryanair* was founded in Ireland in 1985 as an airline to provide an alternative to the Irish national carrier, Aer Lingus. It was based on the principle of low fares from the beginning and managed to break through the high levels of loyalty which customers had for Aer Lingus. From its early days, according to the authors, work practices at Ryanair already included the high stress and long working hours the company has become known for. In the early days, when only 450 people were employed, staff were given shares in the company and agreed not to join a union because they felt there would be chances to have some influence over how the company was run. At a later date, pilots were asked to accept pay cuts and changes to working conditions as well as shifting to new bases; when this was contested by the pilots that were union members there were threats to fire them. A long-working-hours culture was encouraged and seen as a sign of commitment. Subsequent attempts to activate unions have been resisted and the company's approach has been criticised in the courts. In summary, Ryanair's approach to HRM has been to enforce compliance from employees and avoid unions, though the company continues to be very successful.

*Go* began life as a low-cost subsidiary of British Airways in 1998, but was soon sold off and bought by its management team with support from a venture capital group. The brand was defined as 'energetic, passionate and tenacious', and it combined elements of the low-cost approach (cheap flights) and differentiation from the competition (with cafetiere coffee and assigned seating). From the outset Go put great emphasis on recruiting the right people, including pilots that would be comfortable with the company's philosophy, and it also made great efforts to respect flight crews' views about rosters. A job satisfaction survey of flight crew staff conducted at the company by Harvey and Turnbull (2010) showed very high levels of satisfaction with pay and a range of other employment conditions. Levels of satisfaction for pilots, a group that Go singled out for good treatment given their importance to the business, were sizeably higher here than at other UK airlines. The CEO also fostered good relations with the trade unions, which led to strong levels of mutuality between labour and management.

*To think about:*

*Why do you think different patterns of HRM emerged between these firms given their relatively similar competitive strategies?*

Sources: Adapted from Gittell and Bamber (2010); and Harvey and Turnbull (2010).

These criticisms demonstrate it is not enough to focus on one factor alone – say competitive strategy – and ignore the effect of other factors in shaping HR practice. This is not to say that contingency approaches are useless, but that key factors may vary over time. Additionally, it is the mix of factors that is critical. Moreover, within a large, diversified company, some HR practices will work well for some businesses and be inappropriate for others. Preferred HR styles may also vary between countries (Scullion *et al* 2007).

On the other hand, these models are useful for at least two reasons, especially if they are used for guidance rather than prescriptively. First, each model links HR strategies to business strategies, and at the extremes this may work quite well. For example, it can explain why so many British manufacturing companies that failed to move out of mature markets suffered so badly in the 1980s, with such disastrous consequences for employment. Equally, it is easy to see how the HR activities of new firms can be aligned with start-up or innovation business strategies. In short, it confirms that 'best practice' HRM policies are not appropriate for all employers irrespective of market fortunes or business strategies. Second, this analysis encourages HR practitioners to think more carefully about how HRM relates to organisational characteristics and how it can contribute to business goals. The case for a new HR initiative might be more successful if it is seen to 'fit' with wider organisational strategy and can be justified through a business case, albeit one that also takes into account employee needs (Boxall and Purcell 2011).

## RESOURCE-BASED VIEWS OF HRM AND THE 'ARCHITECTURE' MODEL

Three important reviews (Hoskisson *et al* 1999; Allen and Wright 2007; Boselie and Paauwe 2003) confirm the resource-based view (RBV) is a dominant framework in strategic management. Drawing on Penrose (1959), they argue that focusing on the internal resources at the disposal of the firm (and its agents) has produced a useful corrective from earlier paradigms that analysed performance in terms of external competitive forces. In simple terms, while theories of best fit take an 'outside-in' approach, those from the RBV perspective analyse strategy from the 'inside-out' (Boselie and Paauwe 2003). The former assumes that internal decisions – about recruitment or training, for example – are merely operational concerns. By contrast, these are precisely the sorts of issues that RBV regards as strategic because they influence performance (Boxall and Purcell 2008, p.87). A shortcoming we discuss later is that RBV fails to pay enough attention to external context (see Boselie and Paauwe 2003), both in terms of competitive strategies and institutional forces. RBV focuses on the mix of resources, including people, which give each firm its unique character and can produce performance improvements (Rugman and Verbeke 2002). Interestingly, a study of CEOs reported in Boxall and Purcell (2008, p.89), showed that they regarded the quality of employee know-how and their firm's reputation with customers as their most strategic assets.

RBV was rediscovered by Wernerfelt (1984) and developed into a meaningful set of concepts by Barney (1991, pp.105–6) who argued the potential for sustained competitive advantage requires four firm-specific attributes – value, rarity, imperfect imitability and a lack of substitutes. *Value* means the resource must be capable of making a difference to the organisation by adding value; if the resource does not add value and has no discernible impact on sustained competitive advantage, it cannot be classed as making a contribution to future organisational prosperity. *Rarity* means there is a shortage of these specific resources in the market so there are not enough to go around all organisations; if there was sufficient availability, all organisations could draw upon these resources and no advantage would be gained from having them. *Imperfect imitability* means it is very difficult, if not impossible, for other employers to imitate (copy) these specific rare and valuable resources, even if there were sufficient available. Holding resources which are easy to copy provides no advantage to the employer in the longer run as other organisations may soon catch up and even overtake the first mover. Finally, these resources must not be easily *substitutable* by other factors and rendered obsolete or unnecessary. Even if a resource possesses the other three factors, the fact it can be replaced by a more effective resource means no long-term advantage is gained. It is the combination of these four resources that matters.

Most often the analysis turns on barriers to imitation. There are three reasons for imperfect imitability (Barney, 1991, pp.107–11). First, unique historical conditions make it difficult for competitors to copy another firm's resources, even if they know what they are, because of its particular path through history. Allen and Wright (2007, p.98) note that the 'development and implementation of a single HR practice such as a variable pay system takes place over time including time to solicit management input and buy-in, work out discrepancies, and align the practice with current strategies as well as firm culture and needs.' Entering the market later means that initial learning has been lost and extra effort is required to catch up with leaders, although poaching key individuals could help here. Secondly, due to causal ambiguity, it is hard to identify the precise nature and mix of resources which create competitive advantage, and the ability to replicate successful HR systems requires an awareness of how the practices combine together and shape performance (Allen and Wright 2007). Moreover, due to the fact that much knowledge is tacit – that is, not open to public scrutiny – and often not apparent to those involved because it is held subconsciously, the chances of effective imitation are further reduced. Third, a firm's resources 'may be very complex social phenomena [and] beyond the ability of firms to systematically manage and influence' (Barney 1991, p.110). For example, the web of interpersonal relations that develops in an organisation, or the firm's reputation in the local labour market or the industry as a whole, is often highly complex. Informal routines are deeply embedded in the organisation's social architecture (Boxall and Purcell 2008, p.92).

While RBV potentially helps us understand why differences exist between firms in the same industry, it neglects forces for similarity in the same industry. Oliver (1997) deals with this issue well by suggesting that the potential for applying the RBV is limited because it focuses on internal resources and does not examine the social context within which resource selection decisions take place. She advocates combining the RBV with the new institutionalism of organisation theory (DiMaggio and Powell 1983; see also Boselie and Paauwe 2010). Oliver (1997, p.701) sees firms as being influenced by powerful forces for difference *and* for similarity. While internal history, culture and politics inevitably create some idiosyncrasy, pressures for similarity within industries include a mixture of external forces (for example, regulation), mimicking other successful organisations and normative traditions (created, for example, by professional networks). These forces can be formal or informal, explicit or implicit, written or unwritten; the whole point of RBV is that the most effective resources are often hidden from public view.

Similarly, Deephouse (1999) proposes what he terms 'strategic balance' theory, in which firms aim to achieve a balance between differentiation and conformity. While RBV focuses on competitive advantage through differentiation, firms that are significantly different from the rest of the industry face legitimacy challenges since they do not represent what customers expect or want (p.154). He argues that an attractive niche 'is one that is different from other firms' niches yet similar enough to be rational and understandable. In sum, the need for legitimacy limits the firm's ability to differentiate into specialised niches' (p.162). For example, whilst in many countries pharmacies are found in supermarkets and post offices are located within convenience stores, at one time this would have been unacceptable. Right now, it would be regarded as totally inappropriate to locate a doctor's surgery in a pub or have a solicitor's practice in a casino, but who knows what the future might bring! Moreover, not all organisations aspire to be market leaders; this is especially noticeable in small firms and family-owned businesses where long run survival and sufficient profits to reinvest for future generations is deemed a key goal (Gray 1992; Hunt 1995). For a broader criticism of RBV, readers are referred to Barney (2001) and Priem and Butler (2001).

Wright *et al* (1994) were the first to apply RBV to the field of HRM. Human resources are deemed to be *valuable* because they are generally heterogeneous in both supply and demand because people have varying skills and firms vary in the jobs they offer. This can change over time as societies adapt in the skills which are deemed valuable and in some cases alternative skills – such as language ability or emotional intelligence – might be the difference between success and failure. Equally, the number of vacancies in any country or sector also varies, and employers sometimes need to offer large inducements to attract people that can add value, such as medical consultants with skills in treating life-threatening illnesses. High-quality human resources are *rare* because of the well-known spread in human cognitive abilities such that some people – not necessarily those with the longest periods of training – find their skills are in short supply either across the whole economy or in specific regional labour markets.

On *inimitability*, the issue is rather less clear: human resources are potentially highly mobile, but there are often substantial costs involved in moving from one workplace to another, and if skills become firm-specific the harder this becomes. Wright *et al* (1994) (p.311) argue it is through the 'combination of social complexity, causal ambiguity and unique historical circumstances with imperfect mobility that the value created by human resources is accrued by the firm'. Finally, some human resources are seen as *non-substitutable*, even by technology, because 'they have the potential (a) not to become obsolete and (b) to be transferable across a variety of technologies, products and markets' (p.312). Accordingly, human resources can make a very substantial contribution to competitive advantage, perhaps more than other resources.

The HR architecture approach emerged from RBV (Lepak and Snell 1999, 2002, 2007). Broadly this argues that, rather than adopting a single HR style across the whole organisation, employers vary their approaches depending on occupational segmentation of the workforce. The workforce can be divided into four categories differentiated in terms of their *strategic value* to the employer and the *uniqueness of their skills* (Lepak and Snell 2007). If workers possess skills that are of high strategic value to the organisation, they tend to be employed direct, if not these skills are bought-in from other organisations. This allows for the fact that the added value of any individual worker depends on employer objectives and the sort of service/product they are offering, rather than being necessarily transferable across organisations. If worker skills are felt to be unique (rare in RBV terms), employers want to retain them in-house to prevent these skills being used by a competitor. Accordingly, four categories of worker can be identified:

1 Workers with high strategic value and unique skills are core to the organisation and treated well. This group tends to include senior managers that have shown they can make a difference ('rainmakers' in Boxall and Steeneveld 1999) to the organisation due to the specialist expertise they provide as knowledge workers or their ability to improve the performance of other staff. These are the *key workers* in Figure 3 who receive quality enhancement HRM, although in the case of senior executives or investment bankers in the finance sector they receive employment packages that are way beyond this.

2 Workers with high strategic value but with readily available skills on the external labour market are typically employed internally but treated less well (job-based employees). This group includes workers that are central to production or operations, such as front-line supervisors and manual/office workers, who used to be seen as core in the past but whose jobs are now liable for outsourcing to other countries where employment costs are less. In some cases, these parts of the organisation are floated off to other employers or become a joint venture with the original firm, as has happened in Chinese manufacturing (Cooke 2005).

3 Workers with low strategic value and readily available skills are provided by other firms (contract workers). This group includes workers whose jobs are peripheral to the organisation, such as cleaning, catering and other types of ancillary staff. The work of these groups has been outsourced for many years in developed economies (Caroli *et al* 2010) but some has to be supplied locally as it requires a physical presence at the workplace. In the UK, for example, public services are now provided by organisations in the for-profit and not-for-profit sectors as well as other public bodies. This includes services such as refuse collection, swimming pool management and care homes.

4 Workers with high skills but are not considered key to organisational goals are employed either in-house or provided by specialist partners/firms (alliance workers). This group includes well qualified and highly specialised professionals, such as IT (Grimshaw and Miozzo 2009), whose work is not core to the organisation's mission and whose services are needed intermittently. Gaining this expertise from specialist suppliers can be cost-effective and provide better quality due to their scale and critical mass. Decisions about whether to retain these groups internally rest on several factors, including the continuing availability of this expertise from the external market through the presence of specialist firms that do not increase their prices too much. Interestingly, Nesheim *et al* (2007) found in their sample of Norwegian firms that those competing on low costs used temporary help agencies for labour whilst those competing on innovation used consulting firms more widely.

Whilst this policy might provide a more integrated approach to HRM, unfortunately it also raised problems for fairness and 'among employee' consistency. This was further exacerbated because ITCo did not operate a transparent pay system; this was resented by IT staff.

*To think about:*

*What do you see as the main benefits and shortcomings for clients in outsourcing their IT work to a specialist company, and what are the principal problems that this creates for the workers themselves? How would you address these issues?*

Source: Adapted from Marchington *et al* (2009).

## APPLYING RBV AND ARCHITECTURE MODELS TO HRM

At least five important questions have emerged about the application of RBV to HRM, each of which is dealt with below:

- Are managers or workers the key human resource?
- Should the focus be on people, HR practices or HR processes?
- How important is path dependency in explaining HRM?
- How can institutional forces and networks beyond the firm help to explain HRM?
- How can issues to do with organisational survival complement questions of viability and industry leadership?

### MANAGERS OR WORKERS AS THE KEY RESOURCE

Questions arise about whether RBV relates to the entire human capital pool or just to senior managers who are not only rarer in quantity but also exert greater influence over organisational performance. Allen and Wright (2007, pp.93–4) believe it is the former because all employees are involved in making products or delivering services, and are typically less mobile. Mueller (1996, p.757) is even more convinced that the 'social architecture' (cf. Barney's 1991 'social complexity') which resides in an organisation creates the value that is dispersed throughout the workforce. This means that employers that are truly keen to encourage discretionary behaviour and reward good performance should promote an open organisational culture. Workers need to know how their actions contribute to organisational performance and see a clear link between their efforts (as individuals or in groups) and rewards. This suggests specific HR practices – such as performance management or employee involvement – are critically important to organisational success. It also shows the limits of trying to copy HR practices that are successful in other organisations without analysing whether they will work in different contextual circumstances.

### FOCUS ON PEOPLE, HR PRACTICES OR HR PROCESSES

Does RBV relate to the people (human capital), the HR practices or the HR processes used to manage employment? Boxall (1996, 1998) distinguishes between 'human capital advantage' (a stock of exceptional human talent latent with productive possibilities) and 'organisational process advantage' (causally ambiguous, socially complex, historically evolved processes – such as learning and co-operation – that are difficult to imitate). Together they form 'human resource advantage', the idea that performance depends on employing the right people *and* using better HR practices and processes. Each element is therefore important, whether it is an individual's ability to learn or their manual dexterity, or the HR policies and practices used to recruit, motivate and develop people at work. The employment of highly qualified and talented people can be useless without effective HR processes to ensure that they work well in teams and are keen to contribute to organisational goals (Wright *et al* 1994, p.320). Similarly, a bundle of high commitment HR practices is worthless if staff show no interest in using their discretion. The interdependence of people and processes, the complete bundle of HR practices that combine together, and integration with managerial systems is illustrated graphically by Leonard (1998, pp.15–16): 'Competitively advantageous equipment can be designed and constantly improved only if the workforce is highly skilled. Continuous education is attractive only if employees are carefully selected for their willingness to learn. Sending workers throughout the world to garner ideas is cost-effective only if they are empowered to apply what they have learned to production problems.'

This simple distinction suggests an important role for HRM, as well as for the management of culture. A key problem with the 'best practice' literature is that it fails to evaluate whether organisational performance is potentially improved by HR practices *or* by workers. This literature focuses on HR practices (such as sophisticated selection) which are expected to ensure the recruitment, retention and motivation of the best possible workers. However, perfectly executed selection processes cannot *guarantee* the appointment of staff able to perform at the highest levels and poorly executed HR practices do not automatically prevent the appointment of really good workers.

## REFLECTIVE ACTIVITY

Debate with colleagues – is it the people, the practices or the processes that make the biggest contribution to organisational success?

### THE IMPORTANCE OF PATH DEPENDENCY

RBV is a particularly useful for analysing HRM because it recognises the importance of historical conditions and the different paths taken in organisations over time, as well as industry movements (Boxall 1996, p.65). As we see in Chapter 15, some major studies demonstrate the importance of processes and outcomes for understanding the employment relationship. This is apposite in relation to the degree of trust (or lack of it) that develops over time between organisational actors (see, for example, Purcell 1980, Searle *et al* 2011). The informal relations occurring at workplace level – often referred to as 'the way we do things here' – are especially difficult to imitate, and HR practices may look similar to those adopted at other workplaces, but they have to combine well to produce high levels of organisational performance. This depends significantly on workers' prior expectations, as well as whether they believe managers are genuine in their actions. Research shows that, irrespective of the systems in place, the informal styles used by first-line managers has a major influence on workers (Marchington and Suter 2012).

### TACKLING THE NEGLECT OF INSTITUTIONAL FORCES AND NETWORKS BEYOND THE FIRM

Due to its 'inside-out' nature RBV downplays the significance of institutional arrangements at national, industry and network level beyond the workplace. As Boxall and Purcell (2008, p.106) note, some firms have an immediate advantage in international competition because they are located in societies that have a better educational and technical infrastructure. Also, choices about HRM are shaped not just by managers but by external forces. If strong institutional mechanisms ensure high commitment HR practices will be found at all workplaces in a particular country because they are bolstered by legal and institutional frameworks that support fair treatment, this limits the specific impact of HRM on performance because organisations are less able to differentiate themselves from the competition if HR practices are embedded in wider institutional norms (Boselie *et al* 2003). Extending this, Paauwe and Boselie (2003, pp.62–3) suggest there is greater homogeneity across organisations in terms of their HR practices in the following situations:

- The wide application of blueprints, introduced by consultants, which impact on HRM; such as psychometric tests, Investors in People and partnership agreements.
- The extent to which education and membership of professional bodies impacts on HRM; for example, more people studying HRM at universities and the influence of professional bodies and employers' organisations over legal developments.
- The degree to which legislation and directives at international and national level impact on HRM: as we saw in Chapter 2, these include national minimum wage systems, parental leave, and the information and consultation regulations.

RBV needs to recognise that individual employers do not have complete autonomy in determining their futures – much less than an 'inside-out' theory would imply. Theoretically and practically, given that networks of suppliers, customers and subcontractors are able to influence HR practices within other firms in the network, HRM has to be conceptualised beyond the confines of the single employer–employee relationship. This is apparent when people employed by agencies work at the site of another employer, but it can also take place behind the scenes when powerful customers influence HRM at supplier firms – for example, hours of work, levels of pay and trade union membership; see Rubery *et al* (2004) for work on call centres and Swart and Kinnie (2003) for knowledge-intensive firms.

## ORGANISATIONAL SURVIVAL, VIABILITY AND INDUSTRY LEADERSHIP

As with the strategic management literature on the RBV, in HRM the tendency has been to focus almost exclusively on industry leadership and competitive advantage. Boxall and Purcell (2008) urge caution in getting too obsessed with the idea of differentiation, as in order to achieve viability, some degree of similarity is required – as we saw earlier in the chapter – so as to maintain legitimacy by customers and shareholders. They suggest that a set of minimum HR investments is necessary merely to 'play the competitive game' in any industry; these are termed 'table stakes' (Hamel and Prahalad 1994, p.226) or 'enabling capabilities' (Leonard 1998, p.4). Rather than viewing these as necessary to gain competitive advantage, as a classic RBV position would, the argument is that they are critical for the firm just to *remain* in business. In other words, firm resources that are valuable, rare, imperfectly imitable and non-substitutable may well be needed merely in order to achieve satisfactory performance. In industries where significant numbers of employers go out of business each year, this may be a more appropriate way to apply RBV than to focus on the 'differentiation' route alone (Boxall and Steeneveld 1999).

Although many publications on HRM have cited RBV (Boselie and Paauwe 2010), few field studies use it as a framework. This may be due partly to methodological problems and the difficulty of analysing concepts that are hard to observe. Case studies probably offer the best way forward, although an early attempt to use the RBV to analyse HRM used questionnaires (Koch and McGrath 1996). The authors asked executives questions about HR practices such as recruitment, development and planning. The uncertainty associated with hiring decisions needed to be reduced in order to increase the likelihood that 'highly productive people' – who are relatively rare and difficult to imitate – would be recruited. Koch and McGrath (p.339) argue that 'the better an employer "knows" the labour market, in terms of workers' supply and skills distribution, for example, the better informed its hiring choices will be'.

The best RBV-informed, longitudinal case study is by Boxall and Steeneveld (1999) who examined firms in the engineering consultancy sector in New Zealand. Five firms were studied in two rounds of data-gathering over a three-year period. One firm went out of business during the 1987 share market crash but remained a research subject because staff in the surviving firms regularly drew comparisons with it. Of those remaining, there were many common elements in their approach to HRM. In particular, certain key staff ('rainmakers') who generated significant business opportunities were critical to continued viability. In their analysis, Boxall and Steeneveld make a distinction between the notion of HRM for 'credible membership in the industry' and HRM for 'industry leadership' (pp.456–9). In relation to the former, all the firms needed to recruit and retain a suitable group of 'rainmakers' merely to remain in business. The authors (p.459) conclude that their study 'affirms the point that successful firms enact those HR strategies which enable them to survive as credible members of their industry or sector ... First and foremost, HRM must support the viability of the firm as it faces the challenges of stable operation and radical change in its sector. Those firms which fail to adequately resolve these complex problems are doomed, sooner or later, to receivership or to take-over by better managed companies.' The second, and more difficult, task is to enact those HR strategies necessary for industry leadership. How to do this is neither obvious nor easy, and it is a strategic opportunity that not all firms chose to embrace.

Marchington *et al* (2003b) also demonstrated the critical importance of survival – as opposed to industry leadership – in their study of small firms in the road haulage sector. In RBV terms the drivers were valuable as they made a difference to these organisations, not only in helping their firm have more trucks on the road but also due to their interactions with customers. Drivers were rare due to shortages of qualified staff wanting to work in the industry, and companies were very reluctant to use agencies. There was no obvious substitute for drivers unless firms decided to move out of the industry altogether. The companies differentiated themselves by encouraging drivers to help recruit new staff, as well as offering additional incentives to reward their contribution.

## CONCLUSIONS

This chapter has reviewed material examining how HR strategies can be aligned with wider organisational goals. 'Best fit' HRM argues that HR practice varies between organisations depending on business strategy or product market circumstances – this is why they are termed 'outside-in' theories. The concept is useful partly because it corrects more simplistic versions of 'best practice' HRM, but also as it appears to reflect organisational reality. Whilst best fit can explain why patterns of HRM differ between sectors, it cannot really explain differences between two firms in a similar market position. The difficulty is that the models used are top-down and deterministic, driven by classical theories of strategy, whereas it is clear that several factors influence HRM at work – such as labour market context and senior management styles. By contrast, the resource-based and HR architecture models are helpful because they focus on internal resources ('inside-out') and the specific, sometimes unique, factors that enable organisations to remain viable in the market as well as achieve sustained competitive advantage. They also provide a framework for examining why some jobs remain in-house whilst others are sub-contracted or become part of a joint venture. Ultimately, HRM has to be analysed in the context of institutional forces and the role internal politics play in shaping managerial actions.

EXPLORE FURTHER

BOXALL, P. and PURCELL, J. (2011) *Strategy and Human Resource Management*, London, Palgrave Macmillan, Chapter 9.

BOXALL, P., PURCELL, J. and WRIGHT, P. (eds), (2007) *The Oxford Handbook of Human Resource Management*, Oxford, Oxford University Press, Chapters 5 and 11.

DELERY, J. and DOTY, H. (1996) 'Modes of theorising in strategic human resource management: tests of universalistic, contingency and configurational performance predictions', *Academy of Management Journal*, Vol.39, No.4, 802–35.

FINEGOLD, D. and FRENKEL, S. (2006) 'Managing people where people really matter: the management of human resources in biotech companies', *International Journal of Human Resource Management*, Vol.17, No.1, 1–24.

GITTELL, J. and BAMBER, G. (2010) 'High and low-road strategies for competing on costs and their implications for employment relations: international studies in the airline industry', *International Journal of Human Resource Management*, Vol.21, No.2, 165–79.

MARCHINGTON, M. and KYNIGHOU, A. (2012) 'The dynamics of employee involvement and participation during turbulent times', *International Journal of Human Resource Management*, forthcoming.

MARCHINGTON, M., CARROLL, M. and BOXALL, P. (2003) 'Labour scarcity and the survival of small firms: a resource-based view of the road haulage industry', *Human Resource Management Journal*, Vol.13, No.4, 5–22.

RUTHERFORD, M., BULLER, P. and MCMULLEN, P. (2003) 'Human resource management over the life cycle of small to medium sized firms', *Human Resource Management*, Vol.42, No.4, 321–33.

WILKINSON, A., BACON, N., REDMAN, T. and SNELL. S. (eds) (2010), *The SAGE Handbook of Human Resource Management*, London, Sage, Chapters 3 and 25.

CHAPTER 5

# International and Comparative HRM

## LEARNING OUTCOMES

By the end of this chapter, readers should be able to:

- contribute to decisions about which styles of HRM might be appropriate in different countries because of cultural and institutional variations in context
- advise senior management about monitoring global labour standards and how a professional and ethical stance could improve HRM and corporate reputation
- help to implement effective HRM within multinational corporations (MNCs), taking into account both home and host country influences.

In addition, readers should understand and be able to explain:

- the major models used in international and comparative HRM and the shortcomings associated with each of these approaches
- the key arguments about whether convergence or divergence is occurring in HRM across an increasingly globalised world
- the role that HRM plays in MNCs.

## INTRODUCTION

HRM is now a truly international subject of global importance, so patterns of HRM do not vary solely between employers in different sectors – or from different size-bands of organisations – within one country but are shaped and influenced by forces across the globe. Nowadays, many UK citizens are employed by foreign-owned firms such as Santander, Nestle, Starbucks and Tata; even if the location where they work is still known by its previous name or they feel allegiance to their old employer. Similarly, UK firms employ many staff in international operations, 'expatriates' who might be based in one country or move between locations gaining global experience and starting up operations in 'new' countries. Additionally, there are many trans-global firms with no clear and identifiable link with a particular country of origin – BP, Barclays or Eon, for example – because their activities are spread across the world and top management teams are drawn from many different countries.

This shift has major implications for HRM in theory and practice. It has stimulated a fierce debate about whether HRM is more likely to be shaped by the cultural characteristics of particular nation states or by the institutions (for example, financial systems, employment legislation, welfare models and education/training initiatives) where organisations are based. Yet others argue that nation states are unable to challenge the resources and power that large MNCs wield in their pursuit of global competitive advantage and preferential conditions in any one country. Threats made by leading firms to relocate to more benign tax regimes unless governments offer favourable conditions illustrate this well. Of course there is no simple answer to these questions because so much depends on the contextual conditions in each case and the willingness of nation states or large firms to take a risk in out-facing the other. Two underlying questions surface repeatedly in this chapter. First, are patterns of HRM likely to converge as MNCs extend their influence and globalisation reduces the difference between nation states? Or, conversely, does a country's cultural and institutional heritage ensure that HRM practices still diverge and depend largely on where employment is located? Second, are HR strategies and practices subject to transfer within MNCs via the spread of 'best' practice, or do subsidiaries retain the freedom to use HR policies that are appropriate to their specific context? In short the 'home versus host country' argument is central to international and comparative HRM.

This chapter is set out in the following way. First, we discuss approaches that have dominated international HRM – the cultural, institutional, universal and contingency models. Here, most space is devoted to the first two because the universal and contingency approaches were reviewed in Chapters 3 and 4. Second, we discuss arguments for convergence and divergence in HRM. Third, HRM in MNCs is examined, focusing specifically on the way in which particular HR practices – such as performance management, learning and development, and employment relations – are implemented in these organisations both at HQ (global and regional) and subsidiary level.

## INTERNATIONAL AND COMPARATIVE HRM

This section draws partly on the categorisation by Rubery and Grimshaw (2003) that three broad schools of thought and theoretical frameworks (the cultural, institutional and universal) are used when examining HRM across international boundaries. A fourth – the contingency perspective – is added because this demonstrates how divergence can be sustained both at the national and the sub-national levels. It is accepted this framework is inevitably oversimplified and potentially overlapping, but it does provide a sound basis for examining international and comparative HRM.

### THE CULTURAL PERSPECTIVE

The cultural perspective argues that clear differences between nation states are enduring and need to be recognised. This sort of thinking is implicit in television adverts stressing the importance of knowing what particular gestures or mannerisms mean in different countries, and in academic terms it is best exemplified by the work of Hofstede (1980, 1991, 2001 and 2002). His model, based on questionnaires with over 100,000 IBM employees worldwide, is very well-known; it has been widely quoted and it appears to carry enormous weight. Hofstede (1980, p.26) states that his book examines 'differences in national culture among 40 modern nations. It will show evidence of differences and similarities among the cultural patterns of countries; differences and similarities that have very old historical roots (some, for example, going back as far as the Roman Empire).' He argues that stabilising forces, such as forces of nature; geographic, demographic and genetic origins; societal norms; and consequences (such as social stratification and family patterns) reinforce existing culture and continue over time. Initially he argued there were four distinct factors which vary across national cultures:

1 *Power distance (PD)* – the extent to which societies accept that power in institutions and organisations is and should be distributed unequally. Countries with a high power distance index (PDI) include several in Latin America, Arab states, India and China,

whereas those that are low on this index include the USA, UK and Ireland as well as the Scandinavian countries, Russia and New Zealand. In the middle are a number of European countries, such as France, Greece and Hungary. In organisational terms this is reflected in degree of centralisation, length of the hierarchy and size of wage differentials (Hofstede 1980, p.135).

2 *Uncertainty avoidance (UA)* – the degree to which societies feel threatened by ambiguous situations and the extent to which they try to avoid them. Countries high on the UA index are less easily classifiable into regional stereotypes than for PD; for example, whilst Greece and Portugal score very highly on this, other southern European countries, such as Italy, are mid-way. On the other hand, Scandinavian and Anglo-Saxon countries tend to be low – with a propensity for flexibility and acceptance of more diverse views – as too are India and China. A range of quite different groups of countries tend to the middle of the ranking here – such as Brazil, Russia, Germany, Australia and Nigeria. In organisational terms low UA is reflected in fewer written rules and greater managerial openness to ideas (Hofstede 1980, p.187).

3 *Individualism/collectivism (I/C)* – the degree to which individuals are integrated into strong and cohesive groups or – conversely – have a quest for personal achievement. Where individualism is high, people are expected to take personal responsibility for their lives, as opposed to a strong familial network which would be high on collectivism. Countries high on individualism include the Anglo-Saxon economies (USA, UK, Australia and Canada) and other parts of Europe, whilst those high on collectivism are often from Central and South America, and large parts of the Pacific Rim – such as Brazil and China. Arab countries are lumped together in the middle of the range, as are India and Russia. In organisational terms high collectivism is reflected in expectations of employment security, promotion from within and high levels of employer commitment to staff, whilst high individualism is reflected in lower levels of expressed loyalty to the organisation, promotion from outside as well as inside, and lower levels of employer commitment (Hofstede 1980, pp.238–9).

4 *Masculinity/femininity (M/F)* – the extent to which dominant values are stereotypically 'male', such as assertiveness or work as a central life interest. Regional classification is difficult to establish on the basis of high masculinity; Venezuela and Mexico are towards the top of the index whilst Uruguay and Costa Rica are low. As anticipated the Scandinavian countries are more overtly feminine according to Hofstede, whereas the UK, USA, Germany and China are towards the masculine end of the index. Countries such as India, Brazil, France, Australia, Russia and Arab states occupy the middle of the range. In organisational terms, masculinity is reflected in higher levels of conflict, lower interest in work–life balance and fewer women in well-paid jobs, whilst the opposite applies for a high femininity index.

## REFLECTIVE ACTIVITY

Do these categorisations make sense to you, and do you see these attributes as typical of the country you live in or come from? Debate these ideas with colleagues from other countries or even other regions within the same country.

Readers who want to know more about this work, as well as details on specific countries, should look at Hofstede (1991), Brewster *et al* (2007, pp.22–6), Lucas *et al* (2006, pp.19–23), and Edwards and Rees (2006, pp.29–32). A fifth factor – 'Confucian dynamism' or 'long-term versus short-term orientation' – was added later specifically for Chinese populations because uncertainty avoidance was not felt to be particularly appropriate. A high score on long-term orientation indicates that a high value is placed by society on characteristics such as perseverance, recognition of status and thrift (Brewster *et al*, 2007, p.25). However, this factor has been used less widely (McSweeney 2002a).

Hofstede's work has been applied to HRM (for example, Parnell 2010) but empirical research assessing its value has been rare. Moreover, many studies have been US-based according to Chiang (2005). Her work on international reward management in the banking industry in four countries is briefly presented in the box below.

HRM AT WORK IN FOCUS

## Patterns of reward management in China, the UK, Finland and Canada

This study involved interviews with about 40 HR managers and other senior decision-makers across the four countries, and the distribution of a survey to bank employees. In total just over 1,000 completed questionnaires were received from staff in 120 banks. Responses were received from front-line, back-office, management and executive employees. Preferences for 40 different types of rewards (extrinsic and intrinsic, financial and non-financial) were measured using a five-point Likert rating scale, and control variables were put in place to account for demographic factors. Financial rewards included items such as base salary, individual incentives and annual salary increase. Extrinsic rewards covered practices such as job security, appraisal and work–life balance. Intrinsic rewards covered issues such as opportunity to use skills, job challenge and job satisfaction.

The four countries were located at different points on the four indices, with quite large variation between them in terms of individualism and masculinity, but rather less on power distance and uncertainty avoidance. Broadly the findings were as follows:

1. Irrespective of cultural orientation, intrinsic rewards were rated more highly than financial rewards, albeit to varying degrees. This refutes the hypotheses that masculine (as opposed to feminine) and individualistic (as opposed to collectivist) cultures value financial and material rewards more than non-financial rewards.
2. The hypothesis that individuals from high UA countries should prefer fixed rather than variable rewards (and vice versa for low UA countries) is not fully supported either.
3. Contrary to expectations, bank staff from Canada (high I and low PD) placed greatest value on group-oriented reward schemes, much more so than Hong Kong where the combination of low I and high PD would have predicted higher levels of interest.

The author concludes that preferences in this area of HRM may well be complicated by the complexity inherent in reward management systems and levers. This means that rather than simply adopting a cultural approach, it is important for MNCs to take into account a much wider range of factors.

Source: Adapted from Chiang (2005).

The Hofstede study is apparently highly regarded by managers, but receives little direct critique in most publications (eg Lucas *et a*l 2006; Brewster *et al* 2007). However, it has been criticised both on theoretical and empirical grounds (see for example, McSweeney 2002a, 2002b, 2008; Rubery and Grimshaw 2003; Chiang 2005; Gerhart and Fang 2005; Brewster and Mayrhofer 2011). There are at least four concerns.

*Representativeness* – As the initial research was solely on IBM employees, there are major doubts about generalising the results to a wider population within each country examined. Moreover, as the respondents were principally from sales and marketing, it is hard to see how these findings apply beyond the specific occupational groups that were surveyed within IBM and other companies in later research (Chiang 2005). Even more worryingly, the sample sizes in some countries were very low; for example there was a sample size of 37 for one of the surveys in Pakistan (McSweeney 2002a, p.94). A further question arises over the sponsorship and purpose behind the research, because it was used for development needs within IBM (McSweeney 2002a). Yet another issue is the limited number of countries where the research was done, with no material on Eastern European and less developed countries (Lucas *et al* 2006, p.20), and the fact that Arab countries are given a single score raises questions about the degree to which they can be categorised as a cohesive and coherent entity (eg the UAE compared with Saudi Arabia). Gerhart and Fang (2005, p.977) have estimated that, rather than explaining 50% of the variance between countries, Hofstede's results only explain 2–4% of the variance. This means that 'individuals vary much more *within* countries than they do *across* countries' (*our emphasis*). Gerhart and Fang's research (2005, p.983) shows that white collar workers in Taiwan (characterised as a collectivist country) are very interested in individual performance-related pay.

*Perpetuation of national stereotypes* – The research assumes cultures are longstanding and not subject to change, but this is open to question when societies adapt through the influx of different communities and traditions that could alter these scores. Moreover, the indices ignore the existence of subcultures and profoundly different sets of values in different parts of a country; even in a relatively small country such as the UK, there are likely to be major differences between groups on the basis of factors such as social class, gender and region (Rubery and Grimshaw 2003, p.36). To be fair to Hofstede (1980, p.399), however, he did accept further work was needed to see how culture might differ within countries according to regional, ethnic, organisational and occupational subcultures. Nevertheless, McSweeney (2002b, 2008) does not agree there is a single 'culture' for the USA, such as between multicultural New York and the more 'closed' populations in the deep-south or mid-west. Almond (2011) notes that legal differences between states in the USA and special economic zones in developing countries and some parts of Eastern Europe, can lead to significant sub-national variations. Edwards and Rees (2006) raise similar concerns both on empirical and theoretical grounds, something equally apparent in the UK as notions of 'British-ness' change and are adapted through processes of immigration and emigration, increasing foreign ownership and the use of migrant workers (McGovern, 2007).

*Explanatory power* – Even if the cultural data is accepted at face value, the models do not explain *why* these differences occur or why seemingly different nations might appear at similar places in the rankings (Rubery and Grimshaw 2003, p.35). This also limits analysis of how societies may adapt due to pressures from MNCs or changes in religious traditions or demography (McSweeney 2008). As Ferner and Quintanilla (1998, p.713) note, such 'approaches to differences between countries are inadequate, treating cultural variables such as "power distance" (themselves somewhat artifical constructs) in an ahistorical and static fashion as immanent properties of nations, rather than as dynamic and emerging characteristics linked to patterns of historical development and distinctive national institutions'. To take an example raised by McSweeney (2002b, pp.1368–70), industrial conflict is seen as more likely in masculine countries where people prefer to flex their muscles rather than seek co-operative solutions. Data comparing Spain (high on feminity) with the UK and Ireland (high on masculinity) supports Hofstede's hypothesis between 1961 and 1975 when there were more strikes in the latter than the former, but not between 1976 and 1990 when Spain lost many more working days than the UK and Ireland. To focus on an enduring national characteristic – difficult enough within both countries due to regional differences between England and Scotland or between Madrid and Barcelona – is bad enough, but the comparison ignores other economic or political forces such as military dictatorship, national patterns of collective bargaining or levels of unemployment.

*Complexity* – While deciding to focus on a single organisation makes sense from an experimental angle because it controls for one variable, it ignores the complexity and interaction between different factors in explaining how cultures might vary. For example, these workers are bound to have been influenced to some extent by IBM's corporate policies, in themselves the product of forces and tensions from different countries which could weaken any concept of national culture. As we see later, some MNCs are well-known for operating a similar system globally (eg McDonalds) and for seeking – as in the car industry – similar production systems worldwide. IBM is a firm that aims to create a strong internally driven corporate culture, which at the very least could compete with a so-called national culture in shaping HRM at workplace level. Moreover, access to training is also likely to vary across the sample, not just due to national differences but also the personal attributes of workers from the same country. Research on ABB shows how similarities may depend upon technological and product market factors as much as national culture (Martin and Beaumont 1998), and HRM can also vary significantly between plants in the same country (Bélanger *et al* 2003).

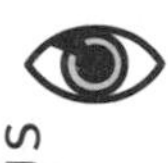

HRM AT WORK IN FOCUS

## How does the cultural perspective stand up to scrutiny in Dubai?

Using Hofstede or equivalent cultural dimensions would imply that Dubai, like all Arab countries, would be high on PDI and UA, mid-way on masculinity/femininity and low on individualism. This suggests strong hierarchical relations, a dislike of uncertainty, a strong loyalty to decisions made by close co-workers in the team (for example from similar backgrounds), and no great tendency towards either masculine or feminine styles of management. But how does this work in a multi-cultural society where workers come from contrasting cultural backgrounds? Beyond the fact that Dubai is very different from many of its Arab neighbours, most particularly Saudi Arabia and Iran, there are other reasons why it is hard to apply the cultural dimensions approach to HRM there.

Under one-sixth of the working population are Emiratis, with the remainder coming from more than 30 different countries. Prime amongst these are India, Sri Lanka, Pakistan and the Philippines, as well as other Arab countries in the Middle East and North Africa. Many firms employ managers from the UK and other Anglo-American countries, as well as from parts of Europe and Lebanon. How, given this range of nationalities and MNCs from such diverse countries, is it possible to identify a single, discrete cultural approach?

Within the private sector, much depends on the occupational group and where they come from. For example, many labourers are from South Asia, administrative and professional staff often come from India, service sector workers from the Pacific Rim, and managers from the Anglo-Saxon developed world. In this environment, is it meaningful to assume a single style in line with the cultural dimensions associated with the Arab world?

Most Emiratis work in the public sector where, arguably, it is more realistic, and potentially appropriate, to see Hofstede in action. Indeed, the institutional and cultural heritage of both managers and staff are likely to be similar, governed by a strong sense of how things should be done. Interestingly, for several years, through 'Emiritisation', there has been pressure to increase the employment of locals in private sector firms by decreeing that certain jobs – including HR – should be restricted to locals alone; this has not really taken off yet.

See also Budhwar and Mellahi (2006); Rees, Mamman and Braik (2007).

In summarising the evidence, McSweeney (2002a, p112) argues that 'Hofstede's claims are excessive because they claim far more in terms of identifiable characteristics and consequences than is justified and unbalanced because there is too great a desire to "prove" his a priori convictions rather than evaluate the adequacy of his "findings"'. Despite that, Hampden-Turner and Trompenaars (1993) agree that culture derives from differences in behaviour but argue there are seven dimensions which best account for what is perceived as culture. These are:

1 equality versus hierarchy
2 individualism versus communitarianism
3 time as sequential or synchronic
4 universalism versus particularism
5 achievement versus ascription
6 inner versus outer directed
7 analysing versus integrating.

How do scholars interpret these in terms of HRM? In effect, it can be argued that employees in some countries rely heavily on timetables and schedules, stick to plans and facts, are job-oriented and are able to emotionally separate their social and private lives. In another country, employees dislike being constrained by tight or rigid timetables, are people-oriented and emotional, interweave social and professional actions and are flexible with their plans (Lewis 2006). Support for Hofstede comes from Schneider and Barsoux (2003, p.134) who state that 'in MNCs, those at headquarters need to understand and appreciate how the local level strategy is formulated and implemented in order to best integrate it with corporate-level strategic management'. Cross-cultural research needs to appreciate that 'cultural diversity is not something that is going to go away tomorrow, enabling us to plan our strategies on the assumption of mutual understanding' (Lewis 2006, p.xvi).

## THE INSTITUTIONAL PERSPECTIVE

This perspective accepts differences between societies need to be understood and recognised but that these are the product of a wide range of forces that can either facilitate/support or hinder/undermine specific models of HRM. It rejects the universal approach for failing to acknowledge HR practices – such as selection techniques, performance review or employee voice – that are prevalent in certain countries can mean quite different things elsewhere due to institutional and societal forces. Given that so much has been based on US and UK models of HRM, or other northern European countries, it is hard to assess how these ideas can be transported into quite different regimes – such as those in Africa, South America or even Mediterranean countries. The culturalist approach is rejected because it lacks theoretical and explanatory power, but also because there is limited empirical support for its prescriptions. Differences in HRM between countries can be explained by institutional forces such as the education and training system, the legal framework, and political, social and economic factors that impinge on and influence how employers deal with employment issues. Other factors such as the organisation of family and support networks, the provision of health care and the informal economy are also important (Rubery and Grimshaw 2003, p.37). The institutional approach has been used in the international HRM literature to explain how HRM varies between countries due to differences in national business systems that shape how employers operate and are regulated by the state (Smith and Meiksins 1995; Morgan and Kristensen 2006).

Rather than try to include everything on the institutional perspective, we focus on the main players only. According to Whitley (1999), the key institutional features are the state, the financial system, skill development and control system, and trust and authority relations. For instance, it has been suggested that state and civil institutions include education and training patterns, employment relations and trade unions (Smith and Meiksins 1995). Institutions can be defined as a set of rules, norms and assumptions that shape economic and business activity on the one hand and structure the choices of organisational actors on the other, both at HQ and subsidiary level in MNCs (Edwards *et al* 2007). Whitley (1999) identifies six business types. These are:

1 fragmented
2 co-ordinated-industrial district
3 compartmentalised
4 state organised
5 collaborative
6 highly co-ordinated.

This classification reflects the degree of centralisation and hence the autonomy allowed to front-line managers. For example, the co-ordinated-industrial district type is dominated by small firms with extensive co-operation across production chains and within sectors, which in turn relies heavily on worker commitment. This type is 'limited to Italy or even northern Italian industrial districts' (Brewster 2004, p.372). In contrast, the compartmentalised type refers to models found in Anglo-Saxon economies, dominated by large firms with low levels of worker commitment and co-operation between stakeholders. American firms, for example, have high levels of individualism and are 'subject to pressures for short-term returns to shareholders' (Edwards and Ferner 2002, p.96) They also have considerable leeway in terms of HRM with freedom to operate contingent pay policies and have sole responsibility for training and development (Brewster 2004), as well as being subject to minimal influence from trade unions and multi-employer bargaining (Muller 1999). This leads US firms operating abroad to avoid co-determination whilst British firms place emphasis on relatively narrow training and formal certification of skills (Edwards and Ferner 2002). Collaborative types tend to be found in large units where stronger employer–employee partnerships are visible, such as Germany where an alliance of banks owns many firms and decisions are made on a tripartite basis between the state, the unions and employers (Hall and Soskice 2001).

Although employing a different terminology, Hall and Soskice (2001) distinguish between liberal and coordinated market economies; the former are driven by market pressures and an arm's length exchange of goods or services in a context of competition and formal contracting. Short-term profit maximisation, shareholder capitalism and market growth in fast-changing sectors dominate the system, and workers are expected to be mobile between jobs (Grimshaw *et al* 2011). Wailes *et al* (2011) add that the LMEs have well-developed capital markets, 'outsider' forms of corporate governance, little commitment from employers to employment security and the use of market mechanisms to co-ordinate relations between supplier and buyer firms. By contrast, CMEs are based on stronger employment protection, long-term investment planning and incentives to invest in skill development through stable and planned economic growth. This model relies more heavily on non-market relationships, especially those between the state, employers and trade unions, and leads to 'patient' forms of capital, 'insider' corporate governance, employment models based on long-term commitment and the use of industry associations to co-ordinate relations between suppliers and buyers (Wailes *et al* 2011). Grimshaw *et al* (2011) note the distinction between LMEs and CMEs has been used by government planners and consultants, as well as researchers.

## REFLECTIVE ACTIVITY

The distinction between LMEs and CMEs has been around for some time, and certainly before the emergence of strong and increasingly influential BRIC economies during the last decade. Discuss the LME/CME distinction with your colleagues and consider how this might apply to the following – Australia, Germany, and Brazil. Search the library and the internet to find information.

By contrast Amable (2003) proposed five different models of capitalism: market-based, social-democratic, continental Europe, Mediterranean, and Asian capitalisms. These have a geography-based denomination, as the author claims, for simplicity reasons and 'should not be taken too literally' (p.14). *Market-based* capitalism is similar to LMEs discussed above, based on labour market flexibility and deregulated financial markets, such as the USA and the UK. *Social democratic* models, like Sweden, do not aim to achieve flexibility through lay-offs or market-based adjustments but rather through moderate employment protection with mechanisms such as co-ordinated wage bargaining and easy access to retraining. France is an example of the third type – *continental European* capitalism – where a higher degree of employment protection and a less developed welfare state exist, under the umbrella a centralised financial system provides. Somewhat different is the *Mediterranean* model, which includes countries like Italy and Greece, and where more employment protection and less social protection are observed due to lower levels of product market competition. Finally, the *Asian* model is highly dependent on the large firms which collaborate with the state and a centralised financial system which, in turn, lead to phenomena like employment for life. However, since the 1990s, this has been under pressure and recent deregulation of the labour market has both decreased the proportion of workers eligible for this form of prized employment and increased the numbers governed by a more deregulated and flexible system of HRM (Suzuki and Kubo 2011). Indeed, Keizer (2008) shows how the latter has grown consistently over the last 20 years – through agency staff, contract workers and part-timers – while the proportion employed on what are termed 'regular' contracts has declined to around two-thirds now. The box below provides a brief outline of how cultural and institutional factors shape HRM in India, according to a survey of HR managers.

HRM AT WORK IN FOCUS

## Factors influencing HRM in India

These findings are based on results from a mixed method survey of senior HR managers in companies employing at least 200 people in six manufacturing industries in India: food processing; plastics; steel; textiles; pharmaceuticals; and footwear. The response rate was about 30%, with 137 completed surveys. Questions were based on the CRANET survey measures. In addition to the survey, follow-up interviews were conducted with 24 heads of HRM in the same sector.

The results show HR managers give a high priority to cultural assumptions shaping the way employees perceive the organisation, common Indian norms and values, and the way Indian managers are socialised. The main influences come from national labour laws, trade unions and educational and vocational training. From the business environment, prime importance is attached to globalisation, customer satisfaction, information and communications technology and the growth of new business arrangements such as alliances and joint ventures.

On the Hofstede dimensions, this group of Indian HR managers stressed the importance of high power distance in relationships between supervisors and their subordinates, a mix of individualism and collectivism, a strong emphasis on masculinity, and a feeling that uncertainty was inherent in life and therefore had to be expected. This fits with a sense of fatalism though it also encourages a desire for employment security.

*To think about:*

*How do these results compare with the scores for India on the Hofstede dimensions that were presented earlier in this chapter? If there are differences, which do you think makes more sense? Should you be cautious about the results from this study, and indeed Hofstede, given limited sample sizes and problems of representativeness?*

Source: Adapted from Budhwar and Singh (2009).

However, Amable (2003, p.13) admits that not only 'homogeneity within nations may be questioned' but that 'the sub-national level may be more relevant for comparative analysis'. In turn, business practices, patterns of employer organisation and the regulatory environment could differ between a single country's regions. Hence, comparative analysis between subsidiaries operating in a number of different countries need to take care when using an institutional framework. Despite this, however, it is clear that employers' decisions are influenced mainly by macro-environmental factors and institutions (Tregaskis *et al* 2001). These external pressures mean an organisation adapts both its structures and practices in order to respond to these economic and social forces (Quintanilla and Ferner 2003; Smith and Meiksins 1995). In terms of HRM, it can be argued that organisations which share the same environment may well employ similar practices and thus become 'isomorphic' with each other (Kostova and Roth 2002). These scholars believe variations in HR practices are the product of how institutions operate or how the national business system works in a specific country. For example, extensive use of downsizing in some countries is attributed to the fact that they are LMEs and therefore market-oriented, deregulated and with less state intervention, as per the USA or the UK (Hall and Soskice, 2001). Furthermore, institutional variability and complexity – in the form of financial, educational and employment systems

– limits the extent to which convergence can be achieved across nations (Quintanilla and Ferner 2003; Geppert and Williams 2006).

The institutional perspective does have shortcomings, in particular there are concerns that, just like the cultural perspective, it is static and deterministic in assuming that forces beyond the workplace are not open to influence. Rubery and Grimshaw (2003) suggest a more dynamic framework for analysing HRM. There is not the space here to examine this in detail but broadly it consists of four sets of interacting pressures: *systems* effects such as technology and global market structures; *political* systems effects felt through international trade and finance; *international transmission* of ideologies, tastes and fashions such as liberalism and deregulation; and the *power of global corporations*, through pressure on nation states to provide attractive conditions for investing in new locations (pp.43–50). We take up the final factor later in this chapter.

The criticism that institutional explanations are static has been addressed recently in several publications on Germany. Reductions in staffing levels and moves to liberalise markets have increased the pressure on stakeholder capitalism and long-standing HRM styles that are traditionally associated with CMEs; a perspective that is supported by Barry and Nienhueser's (2010) research on the airline sector and by Doellgast's (2009) on the German telecommunications industry. She argues that liberalisation of the market during the 1990s led to changes in industrial relations institutions and management strategies, specifically a fragmentation of collective bargaining structures and growing variations in pay and working conditions within and across firms. Her conclusion is that 'Germany's strong workplace-level codetermination institutions have been viewed as inter-dependent with (or complementary to) industry-level bargaining structures, distinctive financial institutions providing "patient capital" and quality-focused competitive strategies in international markets – all of which have weakened or are absent in this sector' (Doellgast 2009, p.20). Not all commentators accept the changes are quite so fundamental because, as Clark (2006, p.604) notes, the institutional framework is so embedded in Germany that the Anglo-American LME model is hard to implement due to traditions of employment protection, legal safeguards and employee voice at high levels in organisations.

Although we have considered cultural and institutional analyses as competing explanations for continuing divergence, one based on what might be called 'national characteristics', the other based on structures and the political economy of different countries, they can also be used in combination. Whilst culturalists would argue that the Chinese have a particular preference for high power-distance and high uncertainty avoidance, this is also reflected in the institutional characteristics of the country. And, given that Chinese nationals – for example – grow up under a particular institutional regime, this is bound to influence their culture.

## THE UNIVERSAL PERSPECTIVE

The universalist approach claims that certain HR practices are found to consistently lead to higher organisational performance and should be employed if an employer wants to enhance efficiency and effectiveness (Marchington and Grugulis 2000; Brewster and Mayrhofer 2011). Based on this, it could be expected that HR practices which are successful in one country should be transferred to others so that practices that are perceived globally as 'best' should be adopted across subsidiaries. We develop and critique this argument much more extensively in Chapter 3.

In the context of international HRM, ideas about implementing best practice tend to revolve around the notion of dominance effects and the role of MNCs which we deal with in more detail later in this chapter. The dominance effect argues that followers in a market attempt to copy the leader in order to improve their competitive position; this can occur either at the organisational or national level, or indeed both, but the principle is that there are superior ways of conducting HRM that can be learned from market leaders or successful nations, and then transplanted into another environment. However, this fails to take into account cultural or institutional contexts or the specific characteristics of the individual organisation (Pudelko 2005). Moreover, it tends to assume all employers use labour for the same purpose – to enhance the quality of the final product or service – which we saw in Chapter 3 is not accurate. For example, followers might be better off not using 'best practice' HRM in a developing country is this allows them to achieve lower labour costs, in which case the best performer saves money while the developing country attracts foreign direct investment. Similarly, MNCs might prefer their subsidiaries to take advantage of local working conditions and employment practices rather than using a standardised set of best practices which cost more to deliver.

A further problem with the universal approach is that the model has failed to establish its superiority over time (Coates 1999) and across very different institutional regimes. This is affected by many factors, the business cycle being one of them. Further, what constitutes 'good' and 'bad' may only be generalised within a specific cultural or institutional Anglo-Saxon mindset (Boxall and Purcell 2008). The notion there is one best way for all employers to manage their employees is both utopian and inappropriate. For example, in Russia and Poland, studies show that diffusion of best 'Anglo-Saxon' practice has been hindered by high cultural and institutional distance (D'Annunzio-Green 2002; Hetrick 2002). Further, studies in Turkey suggest that American individualistic perspectives fail because of the Turkish collectivist culture and expectations for permanent employment in an organisation (Wasti 1998). However, a recent study suggests that, despite clear differences between the USA and Turkey in their business, financial and education systems, it is possible that some HR practices can be transferred because of similarities in micro-institutional factors and commitment on the part of both home country and host country managers at subsidiary level (Sayim 2011).

## THE CONTINGENCY PERSPECTIVE

The contingency perspective states that the take-up of HR practices depends on both the external and the internal environment in which the organisation operates (Delery and Doty 1996; Evans *et al* 2002; Som 2007). Key features are the task environment, product market, size of organisation, its form and structure, and production technology (Smith and Meiksins 1995, p.242). Focusing specifically on international and comparative HRM, a key influence is the nature of the business and financial system within the country where the organisation is located – in effect whether it is an LME or CME, or other type of economy. Whilst this sets the overall context within which organisations operate, other contingent factors – such as product markets – are especially important in providing more specific drivers for HRM. In the case of a subsidiary, further factors include whether it is a green-field or brown-field location, how it was acquired, its stage in the life cycle, whether it is totally owned by one company or is a joint venture or franchise, as well as the degree of expatriate presence at the subsidiary. All these can be expected to shape HRM to some extent. So, for example, would HRM be expected to differ more because of the country in which the organisation is located, the product markets within which it competes, the labour markets from which it draws its workers, or the internal structure of the organisation as a whole? It would be bizarre to imagine that the similarities between a pharmaceutical firm and a restaurant in France, for example, would be greater than with a similar sized pharmaceutical firm in the UK, yet that is where a rigidly applied cultural or institutional framework could take us; see later in this chapter and Chapter 4 for more discussion.

## ARGUMENTS FOR CONVERGENCE AND DIVERGENCE

To what extent, then, do the preceding arguments suggest the world is converging into a single model or a small number of discrete models? Superficially, there is a view that business and HRM systems are becoming similar due to the global reach of MNCs, the spread of similar fashions and consumer goods across most of the developed world, increased levels of mobility between nations, and the role of technology in making communications much faster and more direct; globalisation seems to have made the world a smaller place. This has clear implications for HRM systems, not only because MNCs transfer practices and ways of working between subsidiaries but also because senior managers tend to be moved regularly between different firms and countries.

Some evidence supports convergence, for example in the rising number of citizens that are now moving further through the education system and to universities, and in the (overall) declining trends in union membership and collective bargaining. For example, as Grimshaw *et al* (2011, p.247) note, union membership fell between the mid-1990s and 2006–07 in Australia (from 32% to 20%), in Germany (from 29% to 20%), in France (from 9% to 8%), in Japan (from 24% to 18%), in Sweden (from 87% to 74%), in the UK (from 33% to 29%), and in the USA (from 14% to 12%). Whilst union density varies greatly between Sweden and France, for example, there has been a general downward trend over this period. Brewster and Mayrhofer (2011, p.60) report a similar trend across European countries in the strategic position of the HR function, assignment of responsibility for HRM to line managers, and in professionalisation of the HR function. Moreover, there is growing use of sophisticated HR practices in recruitment and selection, greater individualism in employment relations, increased information direct to employees, and more widespread use of contingent reward systems. Equally, there are many areas of HRM where trends do not appear to be moving in the same direction. To some extent, this is bound up with the transmission of 'new' ideas in HRM between countries and leading firms, often via consultancies or trade delegations – ideas such as lean production, quality management, performance review, non-union employment relations, knowledge management and talent development. Moreover, the power of financial markets and the role of international credit agencies have also impacted more systematically on developed countries – as Greece, Ireland and Portugal can testify during 2008–11. In relation to fair employment practices, there have been attempts by the International Labour Organisation (ILO) to persuade developing countries, in particular, to provide a floor of employment rights for all workers. Despite agreement to comply at a national level in some cases, this has not always been enforced and employers have often been able to find ways around these regulations given that many are voluntary codes. Alternatively, the optimistic scenario (Martinez-Lucio and MacKenzie (2011) is that ultimately such countries and organisations will be shamed into compliance, and Riisgaard and Hammer (2011) demonstrate how organised labour can use the power of lead firms to enforce rights for those further along the global supply chain. The box below assesses whether or not monitoring can improve labour standards, drawing on data from Nike and its suppliers.

HRM AT WORK IN FOCUS

## Learning from Nike – does monitoring improve labour standards?

The background to this case is the argument that globalised MNCs, rather than acting as a force for good in terms of extending employment into a wider range of countries, are in fact agents of exploitation that take advantage of workers in developing countries by producing low-cost goods at the expense of their welfare. Some organisations have combated this by establishing their own codes of conduct as well as mechanisms to monitor contracts aimed at enforcing compliance with these codes. The data here is drawn from a unique dataset based on factory audits in over 800 of Nike's suppliers in 51 countries.

Nike started to outsource production in the 1970s, initially with two Japanese shoe manufacturers, but as costs rose they began to cultivate relationships with suppliers in Korea, Thailand, China and Taiwan. Nike closed its remaining US factories in the early 1980s and by 1982 86% of its athletic footwear came from Korea. As costs in Korea started to rise, new links were made with firms in Indonesia, China and Vietnam. By 2004, manufacturing was taking place in over 50 countries.

Data was collected on M-audit where a score of 100 indicates complete compliance. The mean score across these suppliers was 65%, but there was considerable variation across suppliers with a high of 90% and a low of 20%. There was some variation by virtue of region, as factories in the Americas and the EMEA region (Europe, Middle East and Africa) nearly all scored in excess of 50% whilst North Asian countries (including China and Vietnam) and South Asia (including India and Indonesia) were much more variable. Much of the difference beyond the country level was due to the characteristics of each factory; for example, size, ownership, and type of product. Also important was the nature of relationships between Nike and the supplier, with (not surprisingly) the firms that entered into closer partnerships being more likely to conform than those that dealt with Nike at arm's length. Interestingly, the length of time the supplier had been working with Nike did not produce a higher M-audit score, which was explained by Nike as being due to higher levels of conformance being expected from new suppliers. Another finding was that over time, both for first-time audited suppliers and for factories that were monitored more frequently, M-audit scores improved. This would suggest, according to the authors, that monitoring works. Towards the end of the research period, Nike was making more attempts to establish collaborative relationships with suppliers, aiming to diffuse good HR practices more widely.

*To think about:*

*Do you believe that monitoring HRM along the supply chain can lead to improvements in terms and conditions (eg, pay, working hours, EIP and training)? Why/why not? Draw on the Nike case and also other material on this topic, including the paper by Riisgaard and Hammer referenced above.*

Source: Adapted from Locke, Qin and Brause (2007).

There are rather more arguments against the idea that convergence is happening; indeed several of the authors providing data to show (limited) convergence also put forward reasons for continued divergence. Brewster and Mayrhofer (2011, p.59) differentiate between directional convergence, final convergence and majority convergence. The examples above are all from the first type, where the extensiveness of particular policies/trends starts from a very different point in different countries but heads in the same direction – as the comparison of union density in France and Sweden demonstrates clearly. Final convergence allows for movement in opposite directions (say, from 60% union density to 40% in one country and from 20% to 40% in another) towards the same end-point. But this is really quite meaningless unless the figure remains at that level for a long time. Majority convergence is where organisations in one country become more alike but some move in the opposite direction; this is much harder to measure and tells us little about why changes take place and why differences remain between organisations.

A second issue is that convergence is assumed to be synonymous with change, for example if a CME adopts HR practices that are seen as more typical of LMEs (Rubery and Grimshaw 2003) – as we saw in the case of Germany earlier in this chapter. But change could be happening to all CMEs and to LMEs, without this being part of a convergence process; indeed, they could be moving further apart or proceeding in similar directions but at different speeds. It is clear that all societies and HRM systems go through periods of change, and the direction of travel may shift due to global pressures on particular countries, different economic conditions and shifts in political tastes – such as when a business-friendly government loosens employment protection or a socialist government builds up the public sector or boosts employment over time.

A third reason to cast doubt on the convergence thesis is that, despite change in some CMEs, national institutions and cultural heritage remain distinctive and can limit the likelihood of change to an LME, either partially or more significantly. Related to this, there is no reason why every country should move in the same direction as this implies one system is automatically and inevitably superior to the others. Typically, it is argued the US system leads the way and other countries are moving towards this model, partly due to the extensiveness of US MNCs worldwide but also because financial aid often depends on a willingness to make changes that more accurately reflect the US model. But, as Wailes *et al* (2011) note, there is no reason why other economies should converge around this model. Arguments could be made for the superiority of other models – such as the Scandinavian job enrichment model in the 1960s and 1970s and the Japanese lean production model in the 1980s and 1990s. Perhaps the next decade will see greater learning from HRM models in the BRIC countries.

Finally, it is also possible that some HR practices tend to converge whilst others continue to diverge (Sparrow *et al* 2004). Some practices may be so embedded in a country's institutions that they are unlikely to change. Even though there may be a growth in temporary employment and a reduction in union density in some CMEs, the key features of the long-term approach to HRM are less likely to be unravelled, especially in well-established sectors which are important for a country's competitive advantage and where workers are regarded as valuable partners. For example, there is less likely to be wholesale change in the chemical and engineering sectors in Germany than there is in retail; and if there is change in the former sectors, core staff are more likely to be insulated from change by the increased use of peripheral workers (Keller and Kirsch 2011; Shire *et al* 2009a).

A major growth area in recent times has been the emergence and extension of call centre work, either within the local country or from developed countries to emerging economies. Much of the early outsourcing was from UK operations to Indian call centres, a move which attracted plenty of criticism because it relied heavily on cost reduction and a low cost replication of the most standardised systems deployed in the UK (Bain and Taylor 2005). The data in Table 12 shows how HR practices in Indian call centres compare with the UK and Brazil.

**Table 12 Comparison of selected HR practices in call centres in three countries**

| Country<br>HR practice | UK | India | Brazil |
|---|---|---|---|
| **Annual earnings ($) and GDP per person** | 28,000<br>35,300 | 2,505<br>1,000 | 4,616<br>8,200 |
| **% use of selection tests** | 62.07 | 75.44 | 73.09 |
| **Initial training (days)** | 25.00 | 22.47 | 26.16 |
| **Ongoing training (days)** | 8.20 | 13.27 | 18.05 |
| **Flexible job descriptions (%)** | 27.02 | 3.94 | 11.86 |

Source: Batt, Holman and Holtgrewe (2009).

It is interesting that the use of selection tests and amount of training offered is broadly similar across the three countries, although in India and Brazil the amount of follow-up training is much higher. Workers in the UK are far more likely to have flexible job descriptions, whilst this is rare for Indian workers. The biggest differences across the three countries are in terms of salary, and it is obvious that firms from the developed world – such as India and to a lesser extent Brazil – pay much less than in the UK. However, once GDP is factored in, Indian workers come off much better than the average there, whilst UK and Brazilian workers are below average GDP per person. This provides a potential win-win scenario in India with employers being able to pay much lower wages whilst workers receive considerably higher than average salaries for the country. After the initial rush by UK employers to locate this work overseas, some organisations have now relocated call centre work back to the UK. The globalisation of call centre activities offers an opportunity to examine patterns of convergence and divergence, as the box below illustrates.

HRM AT WORK IN FOCUS

## Convergence and divergence in call centre work around the globe

A major project examining HRM in call centres across 17 countries reported some major findings in a special issue of *Industrial and Labor Relations Review* – see below for details. The study brought together 50 researchers from these countries, with data being collected from almost 2,500 call centres covering a workforce of almost half a million people. The countries involved included the following: LMEs – Canada, Ireland, Israel, UK, USA; CMEs – Austria, Denmark, France, Germany, Spain and Sweden; and emerging economies – Brazil, India, Poland, South Africa and South Korea. In some countries it was possible to obtain a fairly full sample of call centres given the relatively limited number of organisations engaged in this kind of work, whereas in others the sample was less but nevertheless representative of the sector. There was tight control over the questions asked in each country which, following pilots, was administered in a range of languages. Methods employed varied slightly due to logistical reasons, so while nine countries used telephone interviews, four each deployed on-site visits or a combination of mail, email and fax. The authors accept there is a slight bias towards larger, more established sites with more formalised HR systems and higher wage levels than across the sector as a whole.

The call centre sector is seen as representative of what is new in the globalisation of service work because they are located around the world, they offer remote services via technology and they often displace establishments in local or protected markets. They also require relatively little capital to start up, so may be relocated easily to other sites should economic or business conditions change. Thus, 'they are emblematic of the uncertainties created by globalisation'. Convergence to a single best-practice approach might be expected because of this and the fact that workers only require modest levels of formal education to work in this sector. Given that most countries experienced some degree of deregulation and a growth in managerial freedom to make choices about how to manage HRM, this can also propel call centres towards a common model. On the other hand, due to the widely differing cultural and institutional legacies between countries, contrasting patterns of HRM are likely to remain, and even where organisations in different countries adopt practices with the same name (such as lean management), the way they are applied is often quite different.

Rather than identifying shifts to convergence or the retention of divergence, the findings indicate a complex pattern occurs whereby in certain areas there is increased similarity (for example, in service offerings, types of technology employed and organisational structures) whilst in others divergent patterns appear – for example, in work organisation, HR practices and employment relations. The latter are more likely to be influenced by national laws and institutions, and features of industrial relations – such as trade union activity and employers' organisations. Interestingly, statistical differences differentiated CMEs from LMEs and emerging economies, particularly in work organisation, wage dispersion and collective representation. The latter were less likely to offer an HR best practice approach than the former, as would be expected if we follow institutional analysis. However, it was also apparent that organisations in CMEs were more likely to use part-time and temporary workers 'strategically as a response to employment legislation or to avoid unions, thus leading to more precarious employment patterns'. This supports other studies which show that outsourcing and fragmenting work is an effective way to pass the risk onto other employers. As such, this strategy shifts work from organisations that previously offered high commitment HRM and can lead to a change in the dominant model over time.

*To think about:*

*If this happens, do you think it can lead to greater convergence between HRM in different countries as fewer organisations retain the high commitment model in CMEs and it is increasingly undermined by shifts in employment?*

Sources: Batt, Holman and Holtgrewe, (2009); Shire, Schonauer, Valverde and Mottweiler (2009a).

## HRM IN MULTINATIONAL ORGANISATIONS

A number of typologies of MNCs have been developed to analyse how they conduct business as a whole, not just in HRM. One of the most enduring is by Bartlett and Ghoshal (1989) who classified MNCs into four groups. First is the multi-domestic company, which grows by diversification, setting up new subsidiaries that adapt to local conditions and are organised on a decentralised federal basis. Second is the international company, based on exploitation of the parent company's knowledge through professional managers as a co-ordinated federation. Third, the global corporation treats the world market as an integrated whole, operating as a centralised hub and only allowing limited autonomy for subsidiaries. Finally, the trans-national corporation combines aspects of the first three categories, being both sensitive to local conditions and developing strategies at global level. Since this type of firm is likely to have multiple centres, national units can make a distinctive and differentiated contribution to the company as a whole (Rubery and Grimshaw 2003, pp.201–2).

An alternative categorisation, by Adler and Ghadar (1990) relates the character of the organisation's development to phases in the product life cycle. Broadly, according to this approach, companies become more global as they mature and seek to penetrate new markets. A third well-known categorisation, albeit of international HRM styles and cultures rather than broader business styles, was by Perlmutter (1969). This has implications for staffing decisions in the following way:

- *ethnocentric*, where the majority of managers are recruited from the home country
- *polycentric*, where local nationals are appointed
- *geocentric*, where managers are not appointed according to their country of origin but from countries other than the host or home country.

While each of these strategies can be beneficial, they can also generate problems due to a focus on one particular approach to the exclusion of others. Also, as with any ideal type, it is difficult to determine which approach might suit organisational circumstances as so much depends on the availability of managers possessing the required qualities. Some authors focus on specific HR practices, such as expatriation or the choice of recruitment method, essentially treating these as if they are choices made internally by each firm in the light of information about the country to which staff are to be relocated. Some of the studies on specific HR practices are taken up in other chapters but readers who need to know more about the whole field should consult sources such as Bamber *et al* (2011), Brewster *et al* (2007), Edwards and Rees (2006) and Harzing and Pinnington (2011).

The remainder of this section is organised around the four influences framework (Edwards 2011) which draws on earlier work both by himself and other researchers (for example, Ferner and Quintanilla 1998; Almond 2011b; Almond *et al* 2005) to analyse the transfer of HRM within MNCs. Ferner and Quintanilla (1998) distinguish between internal and external forces in analysing the complexities of HRM across international boundaries through a focus on the source of 'isomorphic pressures' on organisations. *Isomorphism* refers to the degree of similarity in organisational practice produced by pressures to conform, such as through shared recipes of action for the same sector or through a process of mimicry by which organisations merely follow the lead of another firm in the same sector or country. It also relates to the institutional forces operating within a country (eg the legal framework) or sector (eg employers' organisations) that lead to similarity in 'choice' of HR practices.

The four influences framework differentiates between pure *home country* and pure *host country* effects at each end of the spectrum, with international pressures (*dominance effects*) and *international integration* within MNCs in between these two. We add to this framework by questioning more explicitly the notion that transfer of HR practices is primarily downward as HQs seek proactively to shape HRM at subsidiary level. Instead, it is argued there is also what might be called a 'bottom-up' effect in addition to top-down transfer (Almond 2011b; Kynighou 2010). Each of these is now discussed more fully.

### HOME COUNTRY/COUNTRY OF ORIGIN EFFECTS

The influence of home country effects is where an MNC attempts to implement HR policies and practices in its overseas subsidiaries that are derived from a distinctive management style which is deeply embedded in their country of origin. In this case, subsidiaries are expected to conform to country-of-origin HRM systems and philosophies that sit closely with the wider institutional structures in the country where the HQ is located. HR practices can therefore be different from those of similar organisations within the same sector in the host country, instead resembling those of similar firms in the home country or in other overseas subsidiaries. Much depends on the strength of country-of-origin HRM systems and the degree to which HQ decides transplants should be made in overseas locations in which the MNC operates. Harzing and Sorge (2003, p.206) suggest in this case that MNCs are best conceived as 'national firms with international operations.' Country-of-origin effects are often driven home country nationals at senior levels within these organisations. Indeed, Edwards (2011, p.274) notes 'the CEO of the vast majority of MNCs is a citizen of the original country of the firm, while the management boards are disproportionately filled by home country nationals', though the appointment of US citizens to lead companies such as Barclays and BP during 2010–11 might suggest a weakening of this stance. Earlier in the chapter we mentioned possible changes to the German system of HRM following recent developments there that have put a primacy on liberalisation which presumably acts as a stimulus for US firms to operate there, but also weakens the country-of-origin influence of firms whose home country is a CME.

Employer attitudes towards unions and collective bargaining are important here. For example, some US firms have used union-busting consultants to achieve union-free workplaces when they invest in other countries, and some German firms have been keen to develop works councils in subsidiaries where this is not part of the tradition. MNCs are likely to find it easier to implement home country policies – if they so desire – in LMEs such as the UK where there are few legal or other institutional constraints on flexible working (Geppert and Williams 2006, p.52) than in CMEs. O'Creevy *et al* (2008, p.162) report that US MNCs try to resist conceding decision-making to subsidiaries located in CMEs as this is the context where 'there is a particularly pronounced degree of inconsistency between institutional norms and the HRM concerns of US MNCs'. In contrast, other US MNCs grant autonomy to subsidiaries which have to deal with entrenched trade unions. The situation is even more complicated, as Grimshaw *et al* (2011, pp 254–55) note that US firms tend to allow union recognition in older establishments whilst pushing for a union-free environment at green-field sites, a view supported by Gunnigle *et al* (2005) on the basis of their research on US firms in Ireland. Ferner *et al*'s (2011) study of MNCs operating at UK locations provided an even more nuanced picture. They found US firms were significantly less likely to allow local discretion over HRM than companies with a CME country of origin, and that some issues (for example, performance management) were more likely to be tightly controlled by HQ than what they term 'rank and file issues' such as representation and involvement. Of course, not all US firms allow discretion to local subsidiaries, and there have been many examples of country-of-origin effects where unionisation is not supported by the company (for example, IBM and Starbucks).

However, the influence of home country effects is neither straightforward nor static. For example, the importance of the subsidiary to the MNC as a whole is critical as it is much less likely that HQ will try to force specific HR practices upon an establishment which is essential to future commercial success and that has the power to resist change (Geppert and Williams 2006; Grimshaw *et al* 2011). As Pulignano (2006, p.513) notes, 'space (is) opened up by company-specific organisational features ... to establish and pursue their group interests, but this is mediated by the institutional effects of the host country environments'. Moreover, Pudelko and Harzing (2007, p.551) do not believe all subsidiaries are expected to use the same HR practices. They suggest that '*whenever* there is no necessity to localise management practices and *whenever* home-country practices are not defining best practices, MNCs should strive for standardisation toward global best practices' (2007, p.553 – emphasis added). Therefore, they acknowledge that outcomes might differ and that *some* subsidiaries will have localised practices whilst others will not. Boxall and Purcell (2011, p.295) are less convinced that MNCs are 'desperate to export the specific HR practices used in their home country and disappointed if they can't'. Instead, they argue the evidence points to a growing international division of labour brought about by a desire to avoid some of the perceived constraints in the home country and reap the benefits from lower labour costs and less demanding regulations in developing countries. Given the number of foreign MNCs that now operate in China, either on their own or as joint ventures, the following box provides data on the diversity of approaches to HRM there.

HRM AT WORK IN FOCUS

## How MNCs from different countries treat HRM in China

During the last decade there has been considerable investment by foreign-owned MNCs in China, often via joint ventures with local firms. Previous studies have suggested there is a distinctive model of HRM including practices such as lifetime employment security, extensive welfare benefits, little wage dispersion between employees except by seniority and nepotism rather than due to explicit performance assessment. Recent years have seen signs of change (Cooke 2005) as more MNCs have moved into China, but most research has not differentiated between the home country origins of this foreign direct investment.

This case compares and contrasts how HRM has developed in Chinese subsidiaries of firms with HQs in the USA, Japan, Germany and one European-owned firm with no single home country location. *Recruitment* processes did not vary dramatically apart from the extensive use of testing by the US firms, including competency in English at some locations. All the firms invested heavily in *training*, both on-the-job and at university, in order to enhance and maintain the quality of their staff. *Pay and reward* practices appeared to be more heavily influenced by Chinese host country norms at the joint venture firms, with the traditional model to the fore, whilst the Japanese-owned companies favoured group incentives and flatter wage differentials, and the US MNCs preferred individual incentives alongside a relatively large pay differential between the top and bottom income earners. *Employment contracts* also tended to vary between the US and European firms on the one hand and the Japanese on the other, with the former going for fixed-term appointments and an individualised approach wherever possible, and the latter being keen on permanent contracts and negotiations with enterprise unions. *Employee involvement* typically took the form of top-down communications, and in the case of US firms this was all they offered. In contrast Japanese-owned companies inherited a legacy of union representation and kept this.

Apart from favouring specific HR practices, MNC parent companies exercised little direct involvement in the day-to-day affairs of their Chinese subsidiaries or joint venture partners. Instead they relied on indirect reporting via regional sub-units. This suggests an increasing segmentation of employment systems in China as foreign involvement becomes entrenched.

Source: Adapted from Walsh and Zhu (2007).

## DOMINANCE EFFECTS

This is where the MNC has a strong and essentially universal approach to HRM, to some extent free of both home and host country, drawing on what might be seen as international best practice in the sector or more generally. In this situation, HR practices central to the MNC's corporate philosophy come to be seen as so essential to its culture that they are implemented in different countries in a way that pays little attention to either the host or home countries' institutional regimes. According to Ferner and Quintanilla (1998, p.713) this can be seen as a mimetic response by copying the HR practices used by leading international competitors and effectively adopting a position that is beyond national borders; it is particularly evident in the recruitment and training of senior managers who are sought after across sectors. As Edwards (2011) notes, strong performance by a firm in one country leads to 'borrowing' by other organisations, which is reinforced by the mobility of a cadre of senior managers that take ideas from one MNC to another when they move jobs. Unlike country-of-origin effects, dominance effects can be drawn from different countries, both within the MNC itself and from other large and successful firms, as well as what are seen as more competitive economies.

This is reinforced by the building of elaborate networks within large MNCs that, even if they operate through decentralised structures, continue to provide co-ordination across the business. Boxall and Purcell (2011, p.298) illustrate how Unilever sets up networks and lateral relationships between managers in different parts of the business whilst retaining tight control over promotion and career development for this select group. These managers are moved between locations, functions and divisions to broaden their experience, and in so doing help to create a strong and potentially cohesive system that speeds up the circulation of product knowledge and preferred ways of working across the firm. The role that expatriates, drawn from a range of countries, play in this process has been widely described (for a more theoretical overview, see Reiche and Harzing 2011). However, it is hard to ignore home country effects if organisations continue to employ large numbers there and HRM is shaped by home-country institutional pressures. Moreover, financial reporting mechanisms and shareholder expectations tend to reinforce the power of home country effects. Yet, the more organisations are run by senior managers from different countries and institutional backgrounds, and the lower the number of staff employed in the home country, the easier it is for HRM to be shaped by institutional pressures at a global or regional level.

Of course it is difficult to establish where the motivation for such HR practices comes from – home country or MNC? Some large US firms have introduced new arrangements into their UK operations, such as prizes for the best team or encouragement to wear baseball caps at work, which might encounter resistance from some workers who see these as embarrassing or inappropriate to the UK culture. The move to call employees 'partners', however, does seem to have caught on more widely so lessening the opportunity for this to be a potentially unique approach.

Dominance effects can also occur through what is called 'reverse transfer'. This happens when HR practices that are seen to work well in a subsidiary in a host country are then implemented at the HQ (home country) or at a subsidiary operating either in the home country or another country altogether. In her study of a French MNC with establishments in Scotland, Thory (2008) found there was some evidence of reverse transfer; the two Scottish units of the firm were regarded as centres of excellence in HRM because they used novel HR approaches and demonstrated entrepreneurial HR behaviour. Given the distinctiveness of the French business system, there were problems in getting the HR practices that worked well at the Scottish establishments accepted back in France, to a large extent because they were so different from the expectations of French managers and workers. The box below summarises the case of a US MNC with operations in the UK and Italy.

HRM AT WORK IN FOCUS

### Contrasting approaches to HRM in different subsidiaries

This case shows how a US multinational implemented its HR practices in three Italian and two UK subsidiaries in the manufacturing sector. It offers a more developed version of the home- and host-country institutional effects by including company-specific factors as they impact on internal processes within the firm, as well as analysing how power can be derived from the subsidiary's product market position. This latter factor can be critical if the subsidiary is in a strategically important position and senior managers at local level are able to exercise influence upon the MNC to resist, amend or delay attempts to impose home country procedures.

The MNC is a significant global player with a workforce of over 300,000, which has grown consistently and has high levels of profitability. Some years ago, in order to maintain its competitive position, the company moved to a system of global sourcing with plants in different countries meeting distinct market needs. HR policy became overtly individualistic with an increased prominence for direct employee involvement and communications and performance management, with reduced emphasis on collective labour relations. However, it was also apparent that HQ varied in its implementation of these principles, with some sites being mandated whilst others were allowed to use their discretion in deciding whether or not to adopt the new HR approach in its entirety. Of course, host country factors were important in explaining this variation, and in general the greater employment protection enjoyed by workers in Italy had an impact. But, so too did the subsidiary's market position and prominence. For example, one of the Italian subsidiaries was able to deflect central HR initiatives because it was a key centre in Europe for new product development and it was well-placed geographically for large numbers of customers. Conversely, the weak competitive position of a UK establishment meant it had few resources to challenge edicts from HQ.

Source: Adapted from Pulignano (2006).

## INTERNATIONAL INTEGRATION EFFECTS

This relates to the extent to which MNCs build up stronger and closer links across borders, and attempt to achieve higher levels of integration within the organisation. Assisted by advances in communications and transportation, international co-ordination has been extended through the development of new structures for overseas operations. This has led to the emergence of regional blocks and HQs located in countries other than the original home country; in some cases it is now difficult to identify a single home for such MNCs. In the past, many operated through regional HQs at the European level – partly to separate home country HQ outside the EU from requirements to comply with European law, as well as provide a local base to co-ordinate operations in Europe. Given the spread of many MNCs to other parts of the world, blocks have emerged to cover areas such as Europe, the Middle East and Africa; Eastern Europe; Asia; and Latin America. Edwards (2011, p.278) suggests that now relatively few MNCs 'are characterised by a straightforward hierarchical relationship between HQ and operating units. Instead in most MNCs there are intermediate levels within complex multi-layered corporate structures'. Although supply chains remain **within** the same organisation, at least for the initial stages of production in a manufacturing firm, increasingly basic manufacturing or service operations further down the chain are either sub-contracted, franchised out or are joint ventures. Decisions about the transfer of HR practices therefore become more complex.

Ideas about international integration have been developed by Bjorkman and Lervik (2007) as a counter to the more widespread external focus on home or host country influences. They do not argue that institutional forces are insignificant, but suggest much more needs to be known about how transfer of HRM is implemented, internalised and integrated within MNCs. Their conceptual model comprises four factors:

1 *Governance mechanisms*, such as the degree of autonomy the subsidiary enjoys and the extent to which its performance is evaluated by HQ. If senior managers at local level believe they have to comply with head office diktats and that this is monitored by performance evaluations, conformity across locations is greater. However, this approach could also be counter-productive if local managers resent the imposition of HR practices from above.

2 *Intra-organisational social capital*, such as the degree to which informal integration mechanisms (such as short-term visits to other sites, participation in joint training exercises) exist across the organisation, the level of shared cognition and understanding, and the level of trust managers at the subsidiary enjoy with HQ staff. For example, 'ability to communicate in a shared natural language such as English or Chinese is important, as is the parties' overlap in terms of vocabulary and the meaning attached to highly specialised terms in a certain language' (Bjorkman and Lervik 2007, p.328). This aspect of international integration is reinforced by close interaction ties between managers at different locations.

3 *Subsidiary HR system*, such as the degree of satisfaction local managers have with existing practices or with the capability of HR staff at the subsidiary, also influences willingness to comply with or actively opt out of HQ initiatives. Resistance to the implementation of imported HRM might be significant if local managers feel they have ownership over the systems that are due to be replaced. Interestingly, 'subsidiaries with high-level HR capabilities are more likely to effectively acquire and assimilate the practices in their own organisation and are also more likely to exploit these in their unit' (Bjorkman and Lervik 2007, p.329).

4 *How HQ manages the process*, such as evidence of open management and due process in change programmes, is a final factor influencing the take-up of HR practices at subsidiary level. Involvement of senior managers at subsidiary level is, as with any change management programme, important in the effective transfer and implementation of HRM.

## REFLECTIVE ACTIVITY

Read the paper by Bjorkman and Lervik in the *Human Resource Management Journal*, and provide examples of how each factor works in practice. If possible, discuss this with people from other organisations to see how the transfer of HRM within MNCs might vary.

McDonnell *et al* (2010) provide an example of international integration in their examination of how knowledge is transferred within 260 MNCs in Ireland. They found over 60% of MNCs had a formal policy on learning transfer, with the most common mechanisms being the use of international networks based on informal channels, international project groups/ task forces, expatriate assignments and formal committees across the company. Secondment to other organisations was the least likely to be used. International HR linkages were found to be particularly influential in embedding these transfer mechanisms, and firms in certain sectors – such as high-tech manufacturing organisations – were significantly more inclined to adopt more of these mechanisms than those in retail, distribution, hotels and catering. Interestingly, the MNC's country of origin did not cause differences in the extensiveness of organisational learning activities. The complex and multi-faceted nature of MNCs is also confirmed by Bouquet and Birkinshaw (2008) in their survey of how nearly 300 subsidiaries in the UK, Australia and Canada 'gain attention' from corporate HQ in a positive way; that is the degree to which HQ gives credit to the subsidiary for its contribution to the MNC as a whole. They note that weight and voice play a major part in this as does the historical position of the subsidiary. Weight is assessed by factors such as the strategic significance of the local labour market and its centrality to operations within the MNC, whilst voice is assessed by the degree of initiative-taking at the subsidiary which contributes to the MNC as a whole, plus the profile it achieves through a strong track record. They also note geographical distance from HQ also matters.

In reality HR practices are rarely transferred in their original form because subsidiaries translate, mediate, refine or even ignore them (Blazejewski 2006). Four patterns of adoption are noted by Kostova and Roth (2002): (i) active, (ii) minimal, (iii) assent, and (iv) ceremonial. 'Active' subsidiaries are high on implementing and recognising the value of specific practices while in 'minimal' cases local managers tend to disregard them. In between, 'assent' sub-units believe in the HR practices but do not implement them as effectively as the 'ceremonial' subsidiaries, where it is operationalised without genuine commitment or not implemented even though local managers say they had done. Beyond this, HR practices in subsidiaries across the MNC might actually be the result of choices by local managers rather than through proactive decisions by HQ (Tempel *et al* 2006).

Subsidiaries are typically seen as units which are fully owned and controlled by the parent company. However, MNCs also expand their operations via acquisitions, joint ventures and strategic alliances (Hodgetts and Luthans 2003), which adds another layer to the picture. First, it suggests that two types of 'subsidiaries' might exist: brown-field and green-field sites. Second, the MNC might not have 100% ownership of the local unit. These have significant implications for the way in which HR practices are transferred. This means that the type of sub-unit as well as its type of ownership can also contribute to how HRM is shaped at local level. For example, brown-field subsidiaries inherit history, culture and norms from their previous owners whereas green-field sites more closely resemble a blank canvas. Other things being equal, it is easier to diffuse practices to green-field sites than to existing locations, because managers and employees might resist changes to existing HR practices. In addition, when type of ownership is considered, different approaches to HRM might be anticipated. For example, franchisees typically provide low-quality jobs, do not invest sufficiently in recruitment because of high levels of labour turnover, and pay lower wages and benefits (Cappelli and Hamori 2008). Research on automotive franchises has shown HRM 'is deployed as one of a range of tools used to create, reinforce and sustain the position of the powerful manufacturer, but also, on occasion, to subvert and rebalance this power relationship in favour of the relatively powerless dealer' (Truss 2004, p.70). To complicate matters further, some subsidiaries might be fully owned, some part of inter-organisational networks and partnerships, and others franchises. This illustrates the difficulties faced in the implementation of HRM at local level in MNCs.

## HOST COUNTRY EFFECTS

The final influence described is where subsidiaries behave like similar sorts of organisation within the host-country environment, adopting HR policies and practices that are seen as appropriate in that context. Rather than imposing country-of-origin HR practices on subsidiaries, senior managers in MNCs accept that the strength of host country institutions – such as employment legislation, trade union traditions and characteristics of the local labour market and education systems – is so great that there is little point in trying. In this case, a decision is made to fit with local norms and values even if they are contrary to those dominant in the home country or within the MNC. A good example of this was IBM's decision to deal with unions at its Irish subsidiaries even though the company – drawing on its US roots – tended to operate, wherever possible, in a union-free environment. This happened because the company realised that the role of social partners in Ireland at the time meant it would have faced difficulty operating in any other way, and that gains could be achieved by fitting in with these dominant traditions (Gunnigle *et al* 2005). Similar arguments are made about firms that have opened subsidiaries in CMEs (Almond *et al* 2005): in these countries, the strength of local institutions (eg legislation, works councils and social norms) is such that, even if the MNC wanted to adopt different HR practices, it might fall foul of the law or put off job applicants used to working in deeply embedded regimes. As Geppert and Williams (2006, p.51) note, 'the implementation of global best practices and the ability to change local practices in subsidiaries situated in highly integrated national business systems will be more restricted and less radical than in less integrated systems'. Sensitive adaptation of HR practices to the host country environment is more effective than gung-ho attempts to impose an alien culture on people working at these subsidiaries (Boxall and Purcell 2011, p.294).

Often, the host country effect is treated as a constraint which prevents MNCs implementing the HR practices that fit with their own background, particularly in the case of firms with HQs in an LME country that wishes to establish operations in a CME country. However, as Almond *et al* (2005, p.301) note, in their study of a US MNC in four European countries (France, Spain, Germany and the UK), whilst the firm was prepared to engage in collective bargaining and accept forms of employee representation, ultimately the host country practices were adapted to fit with the underlying ideology of the MNC. For example, this malleability could be seen in the 'apparent willingness of managers in Spain to overrule the views of worker representatives and risk a legal challenge, and those in Germany to opt out of the metal working collective agreement in order to deal with a moderate union'. It is more likely MNCs will accept host country HR practices if the subsidiary is strategically important, it holds a key position in the global value chain, the scope of the subsidiary market is large, it occupies a brown-field site and the share of expatriate managers from the home country is low (Grimshaw *et al* 2011, p.249).

As we saw above, whilst it might be simple to transfer certain management practices – especially technical issues such as production layout or the design of a retail outlet – to subsidiary level, this is potentially more difficult in the case of HRM. As Pudelko and Harzing (2007, p.536) note 'since HRM deals with the management of people, it is often seen as one of those functions least likely to converge across countries and where MNCs are more likely to localise practices than to export country-of-origin practices' (Pudelko and Harzing 2007, p.536). Kahancova's (2010) study of an MNC with its HQ in the Netherlands and establishments in France, Belgium, Hungary and Poland is presented in the box below; this illustrates how host country effects shaped HRM across the company.

HRM AT WORK IN FOCUS

### Patterns of HRM across Western and Eastern Europe

Electra was established over 100 years ago as a family-owned light bulb business which has now grown to be a global giant with the majority of its workforce employed in Europe and the Asia Pacific region. Despite employing over 400,000 staff in the mid-1970s, the workforce is now about one-third of that size. It is still a very large and important player, just smaller, like most other manufacturing firms. This study focused on the consumer electronics division which employed about 15,000 staff, and in particular on two sites in Eastern Europe (Hungary and Poland) and two in Western Europe (France and Belgium). Alongside the fact that quite different institutional regimes are in place in the two parts of Europe, those in the East are relatively new (under 20 years old) whilst those in the West are much older. By contrast, production systems are similar across the four sites.

Legal regulation allows Electra considerable room for manoeuvre in Hungary and Poland compared with France and Belgium, and many other features of HRM also differ. For example, employment protection, working hours, working conditions and industrial relations structures vary greatly with entrenched employment practices in the West that are not visible in the East. Even in Poland, where laws stipulating trade union rights were adopted, there are few mechanisms to enforce these, and in both countries workers are dependent on employers to support collective bargaining. Wages in the two Eastern European sites are three to five times lower than those in the West. Social rewards – such as gifts for workers on special occasions and open days for workers and their families – are provided at all four sites, with slightly more at the Polish and Hungarian factories and least at the French establishment. These fit with the paternalistic traditions of Electra and its reputation as a good employer.

Accordingly, two kinds of diversity can be seen. First, there is an East–West divide in HR practices and in how Electra adapts to host country standards. Second, there are divergences due to corporate interests in benefitting from local conditions, and the social interactions between Electra and locals at the workplace and in the regions. On the other hand, HR practices are not completely driven by host country conditions because there are some centrally determined influences from both home country and dominance effects. HQ diffuses a tightly controlled value system resulting in the appointment of subsidiary managers that internalise these ideas and clearly shape the culture at each location, yet at the same time Electra also promotes decentralisation of HRM, which gives considerable autonomy at local level. It is also apparent that Electra's sister factories engage in informal interaction and share general information, which is possible because the sites are not in direct competition with one another.

A further reason for variation in HRM between sites is that Electra hires local HR managers, observes employment legislation in each country, and maintains close links with a range of local actors. There is limited interaction between the trade unions at each site.

Source: Case adapted from Kahancova (2010).

## PULLING THE FOUR INFLUENCES TOGETHER

Bringing these four influences (home country, dominance, international integration and host country) means that market pressures and national institutional frameworks exert strong forces on the transfer of HRM, but allows room for local actors to make choices about how they operate in the context of specific conditions. In Edwards *et al*'s (2007) study, influences from the founder were apparent in attempts to change HRM and some other aspects of management to suit his own preferences and philosophy. Yet this was not achieved without amendment to the original principles, as managers and workers used political connections to prevent closure of a plant. In other words, the interplay of forces internal and external to the firm needs to be considered when seeking to explain how HR practices are implemented at subsidiaries within MNCs.

Whilst the Edwards' framework is very helpful in delineating the different forces at work, it is clear that in reality the situation is not so simple. In addition to the points already made, Quintanilla and Ferner (2003, p.364) suggest we need to pay greater attention to the sector level within countries as well as to the role of agency via the strategic choices made by managers. There are always tensions between potentially conflicting isomorphic pulls – from the home country, from the host country, from company-specific rules and operating processes, and from local actors. This can change over time so that on some occasions pressures exerted from the home country outweigh those of the host country, the MNC HQ, or local actors – and vice versa; variations can also occur between plants owned by the same MNC (Bélanger *et al* 2003). Nevertheless, we need to recall that 'strategic choice' is always shaped by factors external and internal to the organisation. Perhaps, despite what appeared at face value to be an acceptance of LME business processes by German firms operating in the UK, Ferner and Quintanilla (1998, pp.724–5) show how these are adapted to provide a German interpretation. For example, Daimler-Benz has been a major proponent of shareholder value but, unlike the British version of this philosophy, at its British plants the company was keen to emphasise medium- and long-term profitability. Similarly, German firms in the UK retain a strong commitment to employees in a way that would not figure highly in most British companies. The relationship between different influences is unstable, uneven and dynamic, subject to competing forces that put pressure on the systems employed, as we have seen with recent studies in Germany.

Even if HR practices tend towards the home or host country effect, this does not mean it is due to a **proactive** decision on the part of senior managers in the MNC. *Similarity* between HR practices at HQ and individual subsidiaries is not sufficient proof that transfer has actually taken place (Ackroyd *et al* 1988; Edwards *et al* 2007). Moreover, just because a subsidiary uses the same HR practices as host country organisations in the same sector, this does not mean HQ has made a conscious decision to allow conformance with local arrangements. This assumes a vertical process of decision-making from HQ to local subsidiary and does not allow for the fact that, especially on brown-field sites, it is likely that many HR practices were in existence before the establishment was taken over. Moreover, decisions about suitable HR systems might be taken at regional HQ – rather than MNC HQ – or at the workplace, or indeed decisions may be made in an ad hoc and less integrated way than the classical strategy literature assumes. Almond (2011) has suggested that a different approach needs to be used, which does not automatically assume a top-down perspective but acknowledges the political nature of MNCs and the opportunities for multiple sources of influence. This perspective is also supported by Kynighou (2010), in her study of MNCs in Cyprus and by other material in this chapter. Bouquet and Birkinshaw (2008, p.595) argue that transfer within MNCs comprises both a 'top down structural process whereby attention is allocated according to a subsidiary's weight' and a 'bottom-up relational process whereby attention is earned according to the subsidiary's voice in the MNC'. Senior managers at subsidiaries which want to influence HQ need – in addition to being in a favourable position within the supply chain – to shape senior managers' impressions they are reliable, credible and trustworthy and show commitment to wider organisational goals.

## REFLECTIVE ACTIVITY

Having read the material in this section on home and host country, dominance and international integration effects, find data on two large MNCs and work out the dominant approach taken in these two firms. Identify the similarities and differences between them and explain why this is the case.

## CONCLUSIONS

In this chapter we have reviewed international and comparative HRM, convergence and divergence and the role that large MNCs play in creating and developing HRM systems across the globe. This area of work has attracted some significant contributions. For example, the Hofstede and subsequent analyses have examined how culture might vary between nations, and this has been applied routinely to HRM. Similarly the distinction between LMEs and CMEs has been central to institutional analysis in the subject, recently extended to include other forms of governance as the BRIC countries and those in Eastern Europe and the Pacific Rim gain greater prominence. Arguments about convergence and divergence are central to these debates, but despite some evidence of the former, particularly due to the spread of large MNCs in food and other sectors, strong forces for divergence continue to ensure that HRM systems and practices remain distinctive. On the other hand, we see evidence from Germany and Japan where changes are taking place in some HR practices (eg, the use of temporary labour) whilst the main pillars of their systems remain intact for the majority of staff. Moreover, despite a view that large MNCs are always able to impose their own HR systems in any country where they operate, this is contradicted by evidence showing a more complex and nuanced picture. In short, whilst the study of HRM within any one country requires an acute understanding of how different forces combine together to shape HR practices, the task in understanding international and comparative HRM is even more complex and incapable of a simple answer.

EXPLORE FURTHER

ALMOND, P. (2011b) 'Re-visiting country of origin effects on HRM in multinational corporations', *Human Resource Management Journal*, Vol.21, No.3, 258–71.

BARRY, M. and NIENHUESER, W. (2010) 'Coordinated market economy/liberal employment relations: low cost competition in the German aviation industry', *International Journal of Human Resource Management,* Vol.21, No.2, 214–29.

BATT, R., HOLMAN, D. and HOLTGREWE, U. (2009) 'The globalisation of service work: comparative institutional perspectives on call centres', *Industrial and Labour Relations Review*, Vol.62, No.4, 453–88.

BJORKMAN, I. and LERVIK, J. (2007) 'Transferring HR practices within multinational corporations', *Human Resource Management Journal*, Vol.17, No.4, 32–5.

BOUQUET, C. and BIRKINSHAW, J. (2008) 'Weight versus voice: how foreign subsidiaries gain attention from corporate headquarters', *Academy of Management Journal*, Vol.51, No.3, 577–601.

EDWARDS, T., COLLING, T. and FERNER, A. (2007) 'Conceptual approaches to the transfer of employment practices in multinational companies: an integrated approach', *Human Resource Management Journal*, Vol.17, No.3, 201–17.

HARZING, A. and PINNINGTON, A. (eds) (2011) *International Human Resource Management*, 3rd edition. London: Sage. Chapters by Brewster and Mayrhofer, Grimshaw *et al*, Edwards, and Martinez Lucio and MacKenzie in particular.

LOCKE, R., QIN, F. and BRAUSE, A. (2007) 'Does monitoring improve labour standards? Lessons from Nike', *Industrial and Labour Relations Review*, Vol.61, No.1, 3–31.

McSWEENEY, B. (2008) 'Cultural diversity within nations' in C. Smith, B. McSweeney and R. Fitzgerals (eds) *Remaking Management: Between Global and Local.* Cambridge: Cambridge University Press.

PUDELKO, M. and HARZING, A. (2007) 'Country of origin, localisation or dominance effect? An empirical investigation of HRM practices in foreign subsidiaries', *Human Resource Management,* Vol.46, No.4, 535–59.

PART 2

# RESPONSIBILITIES FOR DELIVERING HRM

CHAPTER 6

# The Role of the HR Function in Changing Times

## LEARNING OUTCOMES

By the end of this chapter, readers should be able to:

- identify the most appropriate roles for the HR function in different types of organisation
- work in partnership with other stakeholders to ensure that HRM is implemented effectively
- make recommendations about whether or not to outsource some or all elements of HRM, to adopt new models of service delivery, and how to use e-HRM.

In addition, readers should understand and be able to explain:

- the different models available for analysing the role of the HR function
- the implementation of HRM by HR specialists, shared service centres and consultants, and how these interact with each other
- the contribution that HRM can make to organisational success and the measures used to evaluate this.

## INTRODUCTION

HRM originated in activities designed to some extent to address the worst effects of capitalism, and its pioneers were individuals with strong social consciences – such Rowntree and Boot. Sometimes, the HR function is regarded as the conscience of employers, there to ensure that the pursuit of more productive and efficient work does not ignore the human dimension. This ethical and professional perspective is demonstrated by what some would see as obsession with rules, compliance with legal standards or structures for employee voice. But professionalism also relates to how organisations can achieve greater productivity and efficiency through the adoption of up-to-date and proven HR practices, as well as making a contribution to societal goals such as fairness and the interests of all stakeholders. HRM is often seen as ambiguous and beset with tensions between the 'caring' and the 'control' elements of the role (Legge 1995). Both were apparent in the early days of the welfare role, whereby employees were given assistance at work, largely – though not exclusively – to ensure their contribution could be enhanced. HR practitioners are often seen as intermediaries between managers and employees, ready to listen to both but on the side of neither. However, in reality HR specialists are expected to contribute directly or indirectly to the achievement of employer objectives, something that has been reinforced by interest in metrics, measurement and quantification.

In this chapter we examine how the HR function can be structured to offer the best possible service to its internal and external customers – line managers, individual employees, the organisation and society as a whole. This includes the use of e-HRM. Recently there has also been interest in alternative forms of organisation, typically involving the outsourcing of HR work to specialist firms or the setting up of shared service centres to cover the organisation as a whole or to provide HR services to more than one organisation. In parallel, as we see in Chapter 7, many aspects of HR work are now undertaken by line managers, with HR specialists acting as advisors to support them. Irrespective of how HRM is delivered, however, it is now expected to add value, and this has led to interest in the measurement of how adequately this is being done, and concern for ways in which its services might be provided more effectively through what are sometimes referred to as 'HR metrics'.

## THE DEVELOPMENT OF HR AS A SPECIALIST FUNCTION

### THE EMERGENCE OF THE PERSONNEL FUNCTION

Several books provide potted histories of how HRM emerged, either in its historical context (for example, Farnham 1990) or from a sociological angle (Watson 1977). Both approaches illustrate that a wide range of activities is included within the boundaries of HRM. The early roots were in welfare, championed by social reformers who displayed a genuine paternalistic concern for their workers. Often driven by strong religious motivations, such as Quakerism and non-conformism, they were keen to improve working conditions and provide their employees with assistance should they fall on hard times. Nevertheless, reforms were implemented within a clear business framework, in which tight controls were maintained in relation to discipline, time-keeping, and output (Crichton 1968, p.15). Many of the earliest welfare workers were women, especially in munitions factories during the First World War. Some of the first companies to employ personnel officers were Boots, Cadbury and Rowntree – though all three have now been bought out by private equity firms; Kraft and Nestlé respectively. The history of HRM can be seen sequentially, with different aspects coming to the fore in different time periods, or it can be seen as additive, with each new set of activities representing an addition to the HR portfolio (Torrington 1998). Apart from welfare, the others are:

- *Administration* – This covers transactional work such as dealing with job applications, organising induction programmes and maintaining employee records. This has been central to HRM for years, and is important within computerised personnel information systems (Taylor 2005) and e-HRM (Bondarouk and Ruel 2009; Parry and Tyson 2011).
- *Negotiation* – This became prominent in the 1960s and 1970s, as employers faced growing trade union influence and increased workplace bargaining. It is apparent in pay negotiations but it is also seen when managers introduce new working practices and deal with grievances informally. It requires different skills from other HR work (Gennard and Judge 2005).
- *Legal expertise* – Since employment law is now more widespread in Britain, there is a greatly increased need for specialist expertise. This stimulated major changes in HR practice and now most HR professionals have a working knowledge of the law (see Lewis *et al* 2011).
- *Organisation development* – Although this attracted interest from some large companies 40 years ago, it is now much more central to HR due to the importance of change management, learning and organisation culture. It is reflected in areas such as empowerment and knowledge management (Whittington and Mayer 2002).

- *Business partner* – This is where the HR function is prominent at senior levels in the organisation. Ideas about business partners (Ulrich 1998) have attracted considerable interest (eg Brown *et al* 2004; Pritchard 2010) and critique (eg, Francis and Keegan 2006; Sparrow *et al* 2010). We examine this in the next section.

Tensions can occur between different parts of the HR function, especially if it is highly specialised and differentiated. For example, employee relations experts typically show more awareness of the ambiguity and tensions inherent in the employment relationship than their colleagues elsewhere in the HR function, and believe more in the value of structures as a key component of HRM. Issues may also fall within the province both of HR and other management functions; for example, corporate communications may be the responsibility of sales and marketing, public relations or planning, as well as HR. Given contrasting traditions, it is likely that different management functions will devise alternative 'solutions' for these activities.

How many of these aspects of HRM are evident at your place of work or one with which you are familiar? Are some more prominent than others? Why/why not?

## DEVELOPMENT OF THE PROFESSION

The first seeds of a professional body for personnel practitioners were sown in 1913 at a conference of welfare workers in York. Those present decided to form an Association of Employers 'interested in industrial betterment and of welfare workers engaged by them' (Niven 1967, p.36). By 1919, following a merger, the Welfare Workers' Institute had a membership of 700 (Farnham 1990, p.22). Since then regular changes in direction and name have led to sustained growth, differing emphasis (for example, labour management, personnel, development) and chartered status in 2000. The Chartered Institute of Personnel and Development (CIPD) has over 135,000 members, with an increasing presence in countries other than the UK; for example, a new office opened in Singapore during 2011. Table 13 shows how the function has grown since its early roots.

**Table 13 Membership of the UK professional body – selected years since 1939**

| Year | Number of members (to the nearest thousand since 1971) |
|---|---|
| 1939 | 760 |
| 1956 | 3980 |
| 1971 | 14,000 |
| 1981 | 23,000 |
| 1991 | 45,000 |
| 2001 | 110,000 |
| 2011 | 135,000 |

The CIPD is Europe's largest professional body – and second only to SHRM (the US equivalent) – for individuals specialising in HRM. It is a charity run by an executive team with committees at national and local level. A range of committees comprise experts from within the HR community plus members from local branches and staff from HQ. The local level is where most CIPD members have the chance to be involved in the work of the Institute, and this is a critical part of the whole structure, with approximately 50 branches across the country, some of which have over 4,000 members. The CIPD's mission is to:

- lead in the development and promotion of good practice in the field of the management and development of people, for application both by professional members and by their organisational colleagues
- serve the professional interests of members
- uphold the highest ideals in the management and development of people.

Does the CIPD fulfil criteria typically associated with a professional body, and do its members deserve the title 'professional'? Freidson (1973, p.22) defines professionalisation as:

> a process by which an organised occupation, usually but not always by virtue of making a claim to special esoteric competence and to concern for the quality of its work and its benefits to society, obtains the exclusive right to perform a particular kind of work, control training for and access to it, and control the right of determining and evaluating the way their work is performed.

The CIPD meets several elements in Freidson's definition well. The qualification structure provides standards (in the form of performance indicators) to be met by all aspiring members, which are then updated by continuing professional development (CPD) on a regular basis. Standards for most new entrants are maintained by a formal coursework and examination assessment scheme, which is set centrally but centres then get freedom to run their own systems following approval. According to Farndale and Brewster (2005), the vast majority of entrants to the CIPD (94%) come with some form of certificated qualification, much higher than for the US equivalent at just 15%. All CIPD members are expected to comply with the Code of Professional Conduct and failure to follow this could lead, ultimately, to expulsion from the Institute; its principal elements are:

- endeavouring to enhance the standing and good name of the profession
- continually seeking to improve performance and update skills and knowledge
- seeking to achieve the fullest possible development of people
- adopting HR processes and structures that enable their employer to achieve its goals
- maintaining fair and reasonable standards in the treatment of people
- promoting policies that remove unfair discrimination for any reason
- using due diligence and timely, accurate and appropriate standards of advice.

The CIPD therefore satisfies many of Freidson's criteria. However, despite its size the CIPD is not able to claim exclusivity in HRM because managers in the field are not *required* to gain professional qualifications before being able to practise – unlike professions such as law, medicine or dentistry. Many organisations do not employ specialist HR professionals and, of those undertaking HR work, many are not members of the CIPD. Not surprisingly, HR specialists are more likely to be found in larger organisations and workplaces, as well as in the public sector and in industries such as financial services, in electricity, gas and water, and in wholesale and retail (Kersley *et al* 2006, pp.41–2). They are least likely to work in manufacturing, construction and business services, due to the large number of smaller workplaces in these sectors. The profession contains more women than men but they tend to occupy more junior roles (Kersley *et al* 2006, p.45).

Of course, line managers also have responsibility for HRM, which further reduces the influence of HR specialists compared with some of the more established professions. However, while line managers implement HR practice, it is typically HR specialists – where present – that design the policies and procedures governing this work. Moreover, even if employers do not employ specialists, they are able to use 'good practice' which has been developed by experts in the area – either through research or the experiences of other employers that do possess specialist expertise. Apart from accountancy, however, the CIPD is stronger than most management bodies, and its research influences government and industry through fact sheets, surveys and guides across all areas of HRM.

### REFLECTIVE ACTIVITY

Read the article in *HRMJ* by Farndale and Brewster, and comment on whether HR will continue to grow as a profession similar to some of the other professional bodies.

## ANALYSING THE ROLE OF THE HR FUNCTION

### MODELS FROM VARIOUS AUTHORS

There have been several attempts to categorise the work of the HR function in order to analyse its variety, diversity and complexity. Some argue there are discrete roles which are logically distinct from one another whilst others regard the different categories

**Table 14 Models of the human resource function**

| Author/date | Categories for the HR role | Reasons for differentiation |
|---|---|---|
| Legge (1978)<br>[Guest and King (2004)] | Conformist innovator<br>Deviant innovator<br>Problem-solver | Ways to gain power and influence |
| Tyson and Fell (1986)<br>[Monks (1993)] | Clerk of the works<br>Contracts manager<br>Architect | Time span for decision-making<br>Degree of discretion<br>Involvement of HR |
| Storey (1992)<br>[Caldwell (2003)] | Handmaiden/service provider<br>Regulator<br>Adviser<br>Change-maker | Level: strategic or tactical<br>Degree of intervention |
| Wilkinson and Marchington (1994)<br>[Procter and Currie (1999)] | Facilitator<br>Internal contractor<br>Hidden persuader<br>Change agent | Level: senior or junior<br>Profile: high or low |
| Ulrich (1998)<br>Ulrich and Brockbank (2005)<br>[Francis and Keegan (2006); Keegan and Francis (2010); Hird *et al* (2010)] | Employee advocate<br>Human capital developer<br>Functional expert<br>Strategic partner<br>HR leader | Level, focus and time frame<br>Managing processes or people |

as cumulative, with each role building upon the previous one. Yet others suggest that individuals or departments display multiple roles, so it is possible for more than one category to exist in any organisation at the same time. Each of the categorisations explicitly or implicitly assesses whether or not the HR function enhances its standing within organisations. Table 14 summarises some of the major categorisations, identifying the researchers that first proposed these ideas and others that have subsequently used them.

One of the first, and arguably still one of the best, models was developed by Legge (1978) who argued that personnel managers could adopt one of three strategies to gain power and influence within their organisations. The first is *conformist innovation* whereby HR managers relate their work clearly to the dominant values and norms in the organisation in order to satisfy the expectations of senior managers. This is contrasted with *deviant innovation*, where HR subscribes to a quite different set of norms, gaining credibility and support for ideas driven by social values – such as fairness and diversity – rather than strict economic goals. Finally, there is the *problem-solver*, in which the HR contribution is assessed through its ability to identify and resolve problems for the employer.

Tyson and Fell's (1986) 'building site' analogy also identified three roles for HR, differentiated along a continuum defined by factors such as planning time, the degree of discretion exercised by the specialist function and the extent to which it shapes organisational culture. The role with least discretion is *clerk of the works*, where HR merely provides administrative and clerical support – now termed transactional work – to line managers. In the middle is the *contracts manager*, where systems and procedures are heavily formalised, and the underlying emphasis is on trouble-shooting in a highly unionised environment. The final role – *the architect* – is the most sophisticated, concerned with grand designs at a senior level and the integration of HRM into broader business plans to create the 'right' culture for the organisation. Tyson and Fell (1986, p.24) reject the assumption that HR assumes greater maturity as it develops along the continuum, but argue instead that the choice of role is contingent upon organisational circumstances and that each variant may be found anywhere in the hierarchy. This model was refined by Monks (1993) who argues the roles are cumulative rather than discrete, so in organisations where architects are present, so too are the other more operational roles.

A further categorisation is based on ideal-types differentiated along two independent axes. The best known are Storey (1992), re-examined and updated by Caldwell (2003), and Wilkinson and Marchington (1994) which has been re-tested by Procter and Currie (1999).

**Figure 4 Categorising the role of the HR function**

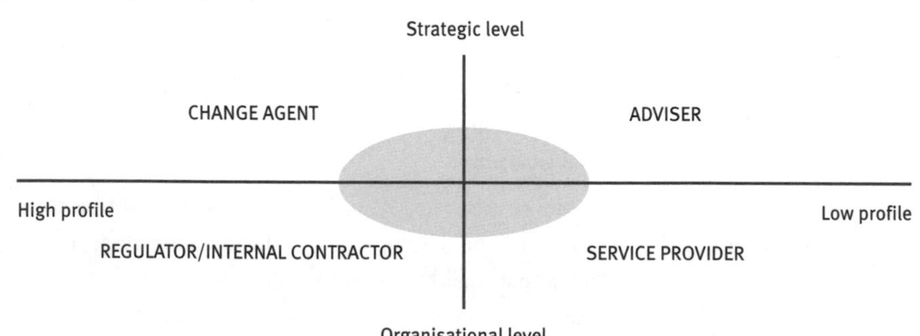


Sources: Adapted from Storey (1992); Wilkinson and Marchington (1994); Caldwell (2003).

Broadly each proposes a fourfold 'map' based on (a) the degree to which HR is strategic or operational, and (b) the extent to which it intervenes and has a high profile. The former dimension distinguishes between policy and practice, long- and short-term time horizons, and the level at which decision-making takes place. The latter dimension assesses the contribution HR specialists make to decision-making and the extent to which it is possible to measure their contribution. The labels representing these four types of HR specialist have been simplified for this book and the model is presented in Figure 4.

The most significant role is *change agent*, as this aims to create a strong and proactive HR culture and seeks ways to persuade the board to adopt new HR initiatives which improve performance. Change agents can be proponents of either soft or hard HRM, and they gain credibility by framing their proposals in ways that gain the support of senior managers. This role is likely to be particularly prominent when the organisation is going forward with a clear vision. The most common role was that of *adviser*; Caldwell (2003) found more than 80% of his respondents claimed this role was the main aspect of their work, or one of the most important roles. Advisers operate at a strategic level but tend to work behind the scenes, helping to shape HRM by the provision of 'cabinet office' support for senior managers. Third is the *service provider* role where HR responds to routine problems raised by line managers, effectively driven primarily by their needs. In the Caldwell study, this was rarely the *main* role occupied by HR specialists but it comprised a significant part of their work (p.994). Finally, the *regulator/internal contractor* works at operational level but is relatively prominent either in dealings with trade unions or with other functions internal or external to the organisation – for example, when large parts of the HR function is subcontracted. The regulator is now less significant than at the time of Storey's initial categorisation, largely due to the decline in collective employment relations, whilst the internal contractor becomes more important when HR plays a boundary-spanning role in defining and monitoring contracts with external providers (Marchington *et al* 2005); this is identified by Cunningham (2010) in purchaser-provider relations involving the voluntary sector. It bears repeating, however, that the HR function at any one site or one organisation typically occupies more than one role, as is clearly evident from the studies quoted above.

There are also dangers with each of these roles. The change agent, while potentially the most influential because of its high profile and strategic contribution, risks significant costs if problems occur due to these interventions. By taking such a visible role, HR can create enemies within the organisation, and thus attract criticism from other quarters. The problem for the adviser is entirely the opposite, since the CEO may use HR as a confidante precisely because of its assumed neutrality. Unfortunately this depends on sustained support from the CEO, and other managers may be unaware of HR's contribution. The service provider suffers in a similar way because the support HR provides to line managers is often hard to evaluate and difficult to isolate from what is typically expected. This is not a problem for the regulator/internal contractor, due to its very public role; however, the function risks being contracted-out if it is seen to cost too much or fails to meet targets. In general, even when there are strong external pressures for commonality, such as in the public sector as Truss (2009, p.734) found in her study of local authorities, the NHS and the police, that differences occurred in design and implementation due to relationships between senior managers and the choices that were made internally at local level.

## REFLECTIVE ACTIVITY

Consider whether there are circumstances (internal and external to the organisation) under which these roles are more likely to occur. Do you believe it is possible for HR practitioners and departments simply to 'choose' a role – such as change agent – they like the best?

## BUSINESS PARTNERS AND THE THREE-LEGGED STOOL

This idea owes its emergence to Ulrich (1997) and later Ulrich and Brockbank (2005). Ulrich (1997, p.124) acknowledges there is 'good reason for HR's beleaguered reputation. It is often ineffective, incompetent and costly; in a phrase, it is value-sapping'. To improve its reputation, Ulrich argued that HR needed to adopt the following five (initially four) roles:

- *Employee advocate* – HR acts as a voice for employees, representing them to senior managers, empathising with them, and working to improve their contribution, commitment and engagement. Ulrich (2005 p.26) argues this is key, covering issues such as employee involvement, managing diversity, and 'rooting out discrimination whenever it appears'. Paradoxically, the role also includes dealing with the 'removal' of employees and maintaining performance standards.
- *Functional expert* – HR possesses a body of knowledge about managing and developing people which can contribute to organisational decision-making (Ulrich and Brockbank 2005). HR has expertise in *foundational* practices such as recruitment and rewards as well as *emerging* practices which impact on people management but are not controlled by HR specialists – job design, organisation structures and internal communications. Functional experts work at multiple levels and should use IT to improve processes, even in transactional work such as pay administration and personnel records. Ulrich (1997, p.129) argues success in this role can help HR gain higher status: 'improving efficiency will build HR's credibility which, in turn, will open the door for it to become a partner in executing strategy'. It is clear that HR professionals have to become more aware of research findings by reading journals and attending conferences, as well as knowing where to seek specialist expertise (Rousseau and Barends 2011).
- *Human capital developer* – HR has to reinforce the need to see employees as critical assets and focus on practices and processes that help them develop future roles within the organisation, eg through training and learning, career development, and coaching. Whilst most of this is likely to be at an individual level, HR professionals can help shape positive team relationships, in much the same way that sports or music coaches develop both individuals and teams.
- *Strategic partner* – HR acts as a partner to line managers at all levels in strategy formulation and execution. This has three components: playing devil's advocate by posing tough questions about strategy and the organisation's ability to put this into effect; actively helping to craft strategies which help to align customer needs and organisational approaches; and leading on raising standards of strategic thinking by the management team. HR also leads on how to create 'organisational architecture', carrying out audits and renovating those areas in need of repair. In short, HR plays a significant part in building the systems and processes that help deliver organisational success.
- *HR leader* – HR leaders 'value and own' their own function, develop staff working for them, and contribute to decision-making, so gaining respect and credibility within the organisation. To do this, HR leaders need to ensure their own function operates well and shows that traditional areas of HRM – eg, hiring, training and performance management – are applied professionally within the function as well as across the whole organisation. Ulrich and Brockbank (2005, p.28) believe that HR adds greater value when structured as an integrated function rather than operating in separate silos such as training and development, recruitment and selection, reward management, and employee relations. As we saw earlier, the impact is likely to be greater if HR practices are integrated.

Although there has been a tendency to relate every recent development to Ulrich – which should not be the case (Hird *et al* 2010) – his ideas have had a major impact on the HR profession, especially in relation to the business or strategic partner role (Guest and King 2004, p.419) and the impetus to develop shared services and e-HR. A CIPD report (Brown *et al* 2004, p.9) noted that one-third of the HR specialists they surveyed stated they were performing a strategic partner role whilst over half indicated this was their aspiration. The two case studies in the box below show how changes were made to the structure and focus of the HR function in applying the Ulrich model.

HRM AT WORK IN FOCUS

## Driving change through HR business partners

**Department for Work and Pensions (DWP)**

At the time of writing, DWP employed 130,000 staff in a complex organisational structure, and had about 5,500 staff working on HR-related issues (a ratio of 1:24). Many of these were not officially located in HR, providing administrative support locally to dispersed units; this made it virtually impossible to provide an integrated service across the entire organisation. The HR leadership team decided major reform was needed, and that they should move to a ratio of 1:50. The HR modernisation programme encompassed a wide range of activities, such as:

- developing the expertise and professionalism of HR
- implementing an effective shared services operation with direct access for line managers and staff
- introducing a new IT-enabled blended learning environment
- simplifying the HR policy framework to make it accessible to line managers
- aligning people with the business.

A key element in this programme were business partners who were expected, amongst other things, to focus on business goals at local and strategic level, be agents for change, act as a figurehead for a more expert HR function, and improve HR service delivery through line managers. Major questions arose about whom would fill these posts. The Civil Service had plenty of home-grown talent, but it was felt that the DWP could not rely solely on internal provision, so 25% of the business partners were brought in from the external labour market.

Two years after the new model was implemented, DWP was happy to note that both line managers and HR business partners felt they were on track to meet the original goals, and that HR was now seen as better aligned with business requirements, and as more accessible and more expert. There was still work to be done on the operation of shared services centres, the implementation of blended learning and in understanding how HR could support line managers. Nevertheless the group HR director felt the business partner model had been worthwhile.

**Nestle**

Nestle is a massive global organisation which splits the globe into three zones: Africa Oceania and Asia; Americas; and Europe. These zones are broken down further as they cover 84 different countries and a wide range of employees. HR looks like a classic three box (legged) model at the macro level. *Shared service centres* are organised globally for services such as payroll and at zone level for personnel administration. Within Nestle this seems to be well-developed and – in line with other administrative functions elsewhere in the organisation – this has been centralised with the aim of being faster and cheaper than previous practice. The location of the shared service centres could be shifted depending on costs, say from Poland to India, at any time. *Centres of expertise* are at local or regional level but are co-ordinated centrally, and it is felt this makes sense pragmatically unless there are specific reasons to have this at local level. For example, recruitment needs to operate at different tiers – with graduates recruited on a global basis, although even here there are issues about work permits, and operator recruitment done via local schools yet overseen globally. Finally *HR business partners* are organised locally but operate within a wider global or zonal structure depending on issues. This is seen as more complex, and there is a need for business partners at different tiers within the business depending on the number of factories or locations to be covered.

Some of the key principles behind the implementation of the three box model in general are: to be consistent and simple and to provide the maximum amount of information locally; people management must be a managerial responsibility; local HR strategy sits with operational HR managers developed in conjunction with relevant elements of corporate strategy and marker/business HR. Whilst Anglo-American organisations have been more likely to follow the three box model, some continental European companies have been more cautious. However, in certain areas – notably shared service thinking – there is stronger evidence that this has been accepted and has led to changes in HR thinking. Variations in the depth of HR talent able to take on these roles, and legal and cultural differences between countries, have all impacted on the ease with which the Ulrich model can be implemented.

*To think about:*

*Discuss these ideas with colleagues, and if possible compare them with your own experiences of the business partner notion and the three-legged stool concept.*

Sources: Adapted from Brown *et al* (2004); Hird and Stripe (2010).

These ideas have now been around long enough to allow more independent evaluation of whether or not they improve the HR contribution and have the power or the influence to have a major impact on business performance. The HR managers in Guest and King's (2004) study were reluctant to move into the boardroom 'armed only with rhetoric about people as the key resource, somewhat ambiguous evidence about the impact of HRM on performance and a set of professional but widely un-welcomed bureaucratic procedures' (p.420). Caldwell (2003, p.1003) echoed this sentiment, suggesting that 'Ulrich's prescriptive vision may promise more than HR professionals can ever really deliver'. A survey of HR professionals in 118 organisations (*IRS Employment Review* 795a 2004) found administrative work was still dominant and that, despite wanting more of a strategic role, the latter took up very little of the HR function's time. Contributors to *People Management* (eg, Pickard 2005; Arkin 2007b) noted concerns about some of these ideas, arguing that HR was losing ground by failing to persuade chief executives to take the business partner role seriously, and instead putting executives from other functions (eg finance) into senior HR roles to ensure a more business-focused approach. Moreover, an obsession with developing the business or strategic partner role has led transactional work – the support function at workplace level that the HR function did for years – being done by line managers, and – in some cases – found they quite like the flexibility this has provided. Alternatively, this work is outsourced to other firms whose contribution is monitored closely. Indeed, if HR business partners are marginalised and only called upon once the bigger decisions have been made, there is a danger that rather than helping to design the new building, they are relegated to choosing the wallpaper once construction is complete!

Hird *et al* (2010, p.31) indicate that many of the attempts to implement the Ulrich HR delivery model were only partially successful because:

- off-the-shelf implementation of a new HR structure without sufficient thought as to its use
- fragmentation of HR structures due to lack of care about the boundaries between different components of the model
- insufficient attention to the new skill-sets required to run the three-legged stool structure
- lack of skill and understanding among line managers about the new model
- a gap in the middle between business partners moving on to executive work and centres of expertise to advisory work.

There is also a more deep-seated critique that HR is getting too close to business leaders and their modus operandi. Wright and Snell (2005, p.181) argue that HR leaders must 'distinguish between decisions that are driven *by* the business and decisions driven *for* the business. A focus on short-term financial returns for fickle investors may be made at the long-term cost of organisational viability ... HR leaders must be the guardians of our firm's strategic capability ... and the guardians of our ethical and moral integrity.' Similarly, Francis and Keegan (2006, p.242–3) note the employee champion role has shrunk because HR professionals have been encouraged to aspire to the role of strategic or business partner. This is not always welcomed by the individuals concerned who feel they have lost contact with the human side of their work. As one of the senior CIPD advisers they interviewed put it, 'no-one wants to be an employee champion (*employee advocate*). They think it is ideologically unsound. I think they see it as them being in opposition to the organisation ... and it suggests their management credentials are suspect.' More recently, Keegan and Francis (2010) have developed this point further with reference to the 'discursive dominance of HR business partnership'. Broadly, they argue that pressures to reduce costs, increase competitiveness and achieve a tighter alignment between business strategy and HRM have led HR to lose touch with employees. Structural shifts in the way HRM is organised means that HR specialists are not expected to devote time to employees because business partners are meant to look up the organisation to promote business goals, shared service centres are remote from any physical contact with employees as e-HR takes effect, and line managers are encouraged to be self-sufficient and lead their teams. Much like Legge's deviant innovators, the employee advocate role might be tolerated only as long as the business is performing well.

## REFLECTIVE ACTIVITY

Read the paper by Anne Keegan and Helen Francis in the *International Journal of Human Resource Management Journal* (Vol.21, No.6, 2010), and discuss with colleagues whether the emphasis on the business partner role is either achievable or desirable.

## NEW FORMS OF DELIVERY: OUTSOURCING, SHARED SERVICE CENTRES AND E-HRM

Whilst it is often assumed that a specialist, internal function deals with HR issues, some aspects – such as recruiting for specialist posts and technical training – have long been subcontracted to other providers. More recently, there has been a more explicit questioning of the need for an internal HR function or at least for substantial elements of its work. A problem with headline publications is that they conflate the different forms of alternative service delivery into one term, typically 'outsourcing'. But the move away from an internal HR function can take many forms, including: a shared service centre within a single organisation, a joint venture between organisations that combine HR resources, and a multi-client call centre providing HR services to several organisations (McEwen 2002; Cooke *et al* 2005; Woodall *et al* 2009). These are often combined with greater use of electronic forms of HRM (e-HRM). Contracts for HR services also vary from one-off or relatively short periods of duration through to deals over a five-year period which is then renewed. The expectations of both parties and their commitment to meeting shared goals are bound to vary because of this. Moreover, contracts for transactional work are staffed by agency workers, often without an HR qualification, whilst high value projects are undertaken by well-paid and experienced professionals.

### OUTSOURCING HR

Outsourcing is now a key component of HR service delivery mix compared with the situation at the beginning of this century when it was relatively rare to outsource very large parts of the HR function. The 2007 *People Management* 'Guide to HR Outsourcing' noted that despite some moves to bring HR back in-house, for example at BP, the overall market continued to grow with significant new deals at Unilever, IKEA and the BBC. This followed earlier moves when private and public sector employers chose to subcontract their transactional work to external providers through dedicated call centres or transferred all but core, strategic activity to specialist, global firms such as Accenture, ADP, Aon Hewitt, Capita and NorthgateArinso. There have been mergers in the sector and the large players have increased their domination of the market; Chynoweth (2011) reports a rise of over 10% in the total spend on HR consulting since the recession caused by the after-effects of the global financial crisis in 2008–09. Whilst many deals appear to have worked and contracts have been extended, others were terminated because anticipated improvements did not arise. *People Management* has featured articles about 'outsourcing fever' or an 'offshore boom', as well as some questioning the value of subcontracting in the first place. Similar moves have occurred in the USA according to Hewitt Associates (now Aon Hewitt). HR outsourcing is less well-developed in some other parts of the world. For example, in Belgium (Delmotte and Sels 2008), aside from payroll, training and temporary agency work, few employers make use of HR outsourcing. In Hong Kong, it is relatively rare, at around 25% of firms surveyed, limited by the lack of specialist providers there (Chiang *et al* 2010), and similar low levels of usage are found in India (Bhatnagar 2009).

Some *HR practices* are widely and routinely outsourced to other organisations, whilst others are more likely to remain in-house, a picture which Adams (1991) refers to as 'balkanisation'. The CIPD Outsourcing Report (2009a) notes that specialist activities such as pensions, payroll, legal issues, employee assistance programmes and outplacement are most likely to be fully outsourced – though even here only around one-third of the organisations responded to the survey. Training, recruitment and selection, and compensation and benefits tend to be partially outsourced with elements being retained in-house, presumably because it makes little sense to move all of this activity to external providers. The areas least likely to be outsourced are HR planning, appraisal, strategy and policy; this is hardly surprising because, in RBV terms, they are central to the organisation's mission. The US study (Hewitt Associates 2009) paints a very similar picture, showing little change from that observed in the past (Hall and Torrington 1998; Cooke *et al* 2005).

Woodall *et al* (2009, p.244) found that *transactional* work was most likely to be outsourced: 'things that can be repeated again and again to a high level of satisfaction' and those which are 'non-value adding, non-strategic, cost savings potential.' Research in North America (Klaas *et al* 2001; Klaas 2008a) shows activities such as executive search, which is not undertaken frequently, benefits from being outsourced to specialist providers. They also suggest that reliance on outsourcing depends on factors such as organisational size and complexity, product market uncertainty and the importance of HR strategy to the organisation. Klaas *et al* (2001, p.132–3) found that firms utilising idiosyncratic approaches to HRM were less likely to outsource generalist and human capital activities, presumably because contractors are less able to provide equivalent levels of support without a substantial investment in training their own staff, whereas firms whose future product market projections were uncertain were more likely to outsource generalist and transactional activities in order to reduce risk and future commitments to their own staff. Adler (2003) notes that decisions to outsource depend on the degree of risk in inter-organisational relationships and the extent to which deep-seated trust is present. The 2009 CIPD Outsourcing Report suggests other reasons for retaining activities in-house, such as already having an effective and well-resourced team, not being convinced of the benefits of outsourcing, and already using a shared service model.

The type of people and organisations involved in HR outsourcing varies greatly. As we have seen, global strategy or specialist HR firms are major suppliers, sometimes running the entire HR function or undertaking projects on discrete areas of HRM. At the same time, individual consultants offer a total HR service to small firms or offer specialist advice when needed – for example, to chair appeals against disciplinary sanctions. Acas and the Involvement and Participation Association (IPA) also provide information and advice. In general, employers looking for consultants need to be careful to avoid those lacking expertise or skills. We return to this point at the end of this section.

There are three main forces that lead employers to implement new forms of service delivery: saving costs and shifting risk; gaining external expertise unavailable in-house; and providing independent views. These are analysed below, both in terms of benefits and limitations.

### Saving costs and shifting risk

The outsourcing literature typically uses transaction costs (Williamson 1975) or the resource-based view of the firm in assessing whether to 'make or buy' on the grounds of the relative costs and benefits involved. Whilst a principal reason for HR outsourcing is to reduce costs and shift risk (Woodall *et al* 2009), in the early stages extra expenditure is incurred, in terms of time as well as money, because the parties need to understand precisely what is required. Moreover, the costs of running the HR function – or those parts which have been subcontracted – are more transparent with an outsourced service and clauses can be written into the contract to stipulate no additional payments (Cooke *et al* 2005). In theory, if employers are not happy with the service provided, it is simpler to terminate the contract with an outsourcing firm than with in-house staff.

However, depending on the type of contract, the number of credible, alternative suppliers available and the importance of achieving cost reductions, it is difficult to secure performance improvements once standards have fallen and it may be costly to terminate a contract prematurely. Although intended to increase flexibility, outsourcing can sometimes add new rigidities that are hard to shift (Greer *et al* 1999; Marchington *et al* 2005). Furthermore, if consultants are used because they are supposedly cheaper, employers need to be aware of the full financial implications. This includes both direct and opportunity costs of internal management time in putting together the tender in the first place, as well as the costs of monitoring performance with a continuing contract. All contracts require specification of agreed performance indicators, and in many cases these are tightly written – in terms of answering the telephone promptly or responding to a letter within a few days. When seen as part of a wider package, these indicators appear simple but when treated in isolation there is a danger that HR activities become distorted in order to meet certain standards while neglecting others. Moreover, KPIs typically focus on transactional criteria that are easy to define and measure, whereas HR processes critical to the business can be very difficult to define and evaluate precisely.

**Gaining external expertise not available in-house**

Outsourcing can be used to acquire specialist expertise not available internally (Klaas 2008a), either in a particular area (eg European Works Councils, executive reward or psychometric testing) or in terms of process skills. In the former, assistance is usually available from a specialist consulting firm or a leading academic. One of the respondents to the Greer *et al* (1999) study summed it up well by saying 'you outsource when someone else can perform the activity better than you'. Smaller firms may use an ex-HR manager with plenty of experience but is no longer in full-time employment, or perhaps someone from an interim management agency. In the case of process consultancy, help can be provided to implement cultural change or improve teamwork amongst board members, for example. This argument utilises the principle that organisations should specialise in areas they regard as core to their mission, and consider using commercial contracts for other work. Consultancy firms have the resources to set up extensive databases of information, to offer benchmarking and – in the case of the large, multinational firms – provide support on a global basis (Brewster *et al* 2007). This is not available in all countries as the Hong Kong study (Chiang *et al* 2010) found. Outsourcing has been used extensively for transactional work that relies on expensive IT systems staffed by people who do not need expertise in HRM; subcontracting these activities is meant to free internal HR professionals to engage in strategic decisions (Ulrich 1998; Woodall *et al* 2009).

However, contracting-out HR means that expertise is no longer retained in-house, and there is a loss of internal synergy if large parts of the function are outsourced. Adler (2003) argues this is risky because dependence on an outside provider reduces the capability of HR within the organisation. Moreover, retaining an in-house function provides opportunities for internal teams to learn across the organisation. Tacit skills that are difficult to codify and formalise are lost when outsourcing takes place (Klaas *et al* 2001) and organisations can become dependent on external providers to maintain service quality and professional standards. While this may not be problematic initially if experienced staff continue working on the contract, it is hard to sustain if the subcontractor fails to maintain skills or employs agency staff to reduce costs. Having lost their own internal staff, it is difficult for employers to negotiate lower prices at subsequent contract renewals, especially if the market is dominated by a few large organisations. Additionally, a good way to develop HR practitioners is to plan their careers so they have experience of different aspects of HR and the business as a whole by moving them between jobs and functions; this also helps to gain legitimacy. This is impossible if large blocks of HR work are externalised (Hall and Torrington 1998; Kelly and Gennard 2007).

**Independence from internal pressures**

Consultants are regarded as independent from the organisation and consequently able to provide an expertise that is theoretically free from internal influence. This could be very useful in complex and multifaceted situations, as well as beneficial in providing an alternative and fresh perspective on issues, as an outsider's view can help to resolve problems which had previously seemed intractable. This can be helpful because consultants are able to use the language of independence, objectivity and so-called 'rational' solutions (Baxter 1996). If attitude surveys are undertaken by independent consultants, for example, this may increase their acceptability with a range of stakeholders.

Being external to the organisation, however, is not necessarily advantageous because there is less understanding of workplace culture and past traditions. While consultants may have greater access to wider knowledge and contemporary developments, they do not know what has been tried before and failed, they lack insight into the politics that permeate any organisation, and they lack knowledge of organisational products and services. Much depends on what is acceptable to the parties involved; this proved to be a major problem in BP's experience with outsourcing (Higginbottom 2001). There are also limits to benchmarking, and sometimes external consultants have 'solutions looking for problems' (Baxter 1996; Fincham and Evans 1999). This suggests that consultants often recommend HR systems which have worked effectively elsewhere, and assume they can be implemented in quite different contexts, sectors and situations; this is dubious as we see in Chapters 3 and 5.

An example of HR outsourcing between Kimberly-Clark and ResourceBank is outlined in the following box.

HRM AT WORK IN FOCUS

## Outsourcing recruitment for increased strength

The partnership between Kimberly-Clark and ResourceBank to deal with recruitment began when K-C's learning and development director realised that only 30% of their European staff were located in the UK, but nearly 75% of the recruitment budget was spent there. This included all graduate recruitment, which at the time was done by a number of external agencies.

The decision was made to use a firm called ResourceBank, whose staff sit alongside K-C employees at their Brighton headquarters, to do all recruitment. The company had worked with ResourceBank in the past and was impressed that their presentations for the tender were done by HR people who would actually do the work, rather than sales people. The contract was initially for two years, with a shorter get-out clause, but it was later extended to five years. The system operated through a series of KPIs – such as filling a vacancy within six to eight weeks – and during the first year, 80% of the vacancies were filled within this period. The companies chose not to use a system of fines or bonuses but instead talked over the issues and sought improvements within the next three months.

Several factors increased the effectiveness of the deal. For example, one of the K-C team worked with staff from ResourceBank to develop closer contacts and address issues, decisions were made about joint IT systems, and no staff were made redundant from K-C. It was felt the recruitment process improved dramatically, as costs came down, service was enhanced, and line managers (one of the major customers of the service) were much more satisfied.

*To think about:*

*Debate with your colleagues whether or not it makes sense to outsource the HR function, either in specific areas such as recruitment or more widely. Make use of the arguments outlined here, as well as others, and find contemporary examples to support your case.*

Source: Adapted from *People Management*, 'HR Guide to Outsourcing', February 2007, 28–29.

## SHARED SERVICE CENTRES (SSCS)

An alternative which has similarities with outsourcing but retains HR in-house, or at least within a network of partner employers, is the shared service centre, a model which derives from the finance function in the USA (Quinn *et al* 2000; Cooke 2006). SSCs are made up of a small group of HR professionals at corporate level that drive the strategic vision of the organisation while a call centre is set up to give advice to line managers, and in many cases individual workers, on administrative issues such as employee records, recruitment services and relocation. It takes three broad forms:

1. an in-house function that operates solely as an internal market for the provision of HR services across a multi-site organisation. These can either cover HR advice within a single country or across a range of countries within a large MNC (Brewster *et al* 2007). In the latter, a global 24-hour service can be offered by staff located around the world (Sparrow *et al* 2004, p.66)
2. an in-house unit providing services to staff *within* the organisation but also operating on the *open market* to other organisations looking for an HR service (Cooke 2006). This can also results in the setting up a specialist, stand-alone HR firm which is then floated off from the original employer
3. a specialist firm providing advice to several employers that cooperate due to geographical proximity or prior organisational links. The latter is now quite common in the public sector, where a number of NHS Trusts or schools pool resources to provide a joint service, in particular for transactional HR work. The case of schools is particularly interesting due to greater freedom from local authority controls, and although individual schools are able to appoint their own HR staff, it is unlikely they have the resources to do so.

An example of a shared service centre in the NHS (Redman *et al* 2007) is outlined in the box below.

HRM AT WORK IN FOCUS

### Pooling human resources in the NHS

Despite being characterised as having low credibility within the NHS, policy changes over the last decade have given HR an opportunity to become more central to strategic change within each Trust. Most people think of the NHS as a series of hospitals, either engaged in accident and emergency or in various forms of palliative care, but primary care plays a critical role in improving patient care. These units employ much fewer people than a hospital and they are dispersed across the community. It is therefore much more difficult to staff an internal HR function in this context.

Primary care units either opted to share an HR function with their NHS neighbours or contract services from another NHS organisation. In this case four different employers, which employed about 1,500 staff between them, decided to pool a number of corporate services, including HR. In total, 16 staff were employed on this work, and one of the employers acted as the host for the service. Each of the senior HR leads took responsibility for a different component of HRM across the four organisations, and in order to reduce complexity and bureaucracy it was agreed not to operate a system of cross-charging.

The rationale for setting up the SSC was similar to the reasons put forward above – lower costs, higher levels of quality/expertise, and a more integrated approach to change. There was also an element of expediency given so many other structural changes were on the agenda, and an SSC seemed the simplest thing to do. Each employer could have opted to set up their own HR function or outsource completely but these were rejected on grounds of cost and quality at the time. This was not ruled as a future solution if existing arrangements failed to work.

In evaluating progress so far, senior managers in each organisation (CEOs and HR leaders) agreed the emphasis had been on transactional aspects of HRM rather than on strategic developments. There were some anxieties that resourcing was too tight and that the limited number of staff employed (ratio of 1:125) made it difficult to get everything done. The staff working in the SSC saw advantages in terms of service delivery but expressed concerns about conflicting priorities in the face of competing demands from the four employers. Questions of organisational identity (eg who was their employer?) also loomed large. This study also found differences between the staff who were co-located and those that had to move between employers in line with business needs, with the former reporting much higher levels of satisfaction and lower intentions to quit than the latter. For such arrangements to work effectively in the future, the authors suggest rather more attention should be paid to the SSC staff themselves and the roles they are expected to fulfil.

Source: Adapted from Redman *et al* (2007).

## REFLECTIVE ACTIVITY

Identify the organisational and business circumstances where an SSC might be most useful. Think about things to do with product markets, labour markets and geographical location.

SSCs have a number of advantages according to Reilly (2000), Cooke (2006), Redman *et al* (2007), Farndale *et al* (2009) and Torrington *et al* (2011). Major gains include: more efficient processes and economies of scale in staffing and resources; higher customer satisfaction ratings; more integrated 'total solutions' to problems; better management information systems; better monitoring of HR contribution due to transparency of costs; improved levels of inter-group learning; and overall a more strategic contribution from HR to business goals. In the Netherlands' study by Farndale *et al* (2009), the reasons for using the SSC were to increase customer focus and professionalism; cost reduction came some way down the list of drivers.

In practice, according to Reilly (2000), Cooke (2006), Brewster *et al* (2007) and Farndale *et al* (2009), SSCs have also hit problems, such as:

- lower levels of customer satisfaction due to less face-to-face contact with HR staff, less interesting work and reduced career opportunities for HR staff, leading to lower levels of staff morale, especially in the early days of its operation
- higher than expected costs, and especially the duplication of posts and services both in the SSC and at specific locations

- lack of performance data and weak collaboration making it hard to assess benefits, and
- transfer of jobs from high wage to low wage economies.

In addition, Cooke (2006, p.218) notes that line managers, who were expected to use the service, reported their own work had increased and their teams felt there was a lack of structure for dealing with HR issues. This was amplified due to IT problems which led to difficulties in getting access to an HR person in the call centre. In short, Cooke (2006, p.224) suggests that 'the transition from a traditional HR delivery model to an HR shared services model involves major organisational change and careful management ... firms should not expect a high cost saving in the first few years of setting up an SSC'.

## ELECTRONIC HRM (E-HRM)

The use of e-HRM has become much more extensive over the last decade, often alongside SSCs and external providers. This has resulted in several special issues of journals and plenty of material from the providers. E-HRM has been defined as 'an umbrella term covering all possible integration mechanisms and contents between HRM and information technologies aimed at creating value within and across organisations for targeted employees and management' (Bondarouk and Ruel 2009, p.507). The authors break this down into four aspects:

1. *content*: any form of HR practice that is supported by IT, either of a transactional or transformational nature, which makes use of the Internet or intranet
2. *implementation*: this covers the adoption and appropriation of e-HRM by organisational members
3. *targeted employees and managers*: although initially e-HRM was directed principally to the HR department, it is now focused on employees – including potential recruits – and line managers to a great extent. It is a key component of the support that line managers receive in many organisations
4. *consequences*: this relates to the goals that have been set for e-HRM and the extent to which they are achieved in practice.

Parry and Tyson (2011) argue there are three sets of goals for e-HRM. *Operational* or *transactional* goals relate to the idea of improving efficiency or reducing costs (Martin *et al* 2008; Marler 2009) via speedier processing, releasing HR professionals from administrative work, and cutting back on headcount. *Relational* goals refer to the provision of remote access to HR information for employees and line managers so that they can perform HR work themselves – such as updating personal data and locating terms and conditions on-line rather than having to print them off. *Transformational* goals relate to opportunities for communication across geographical boundaries to support virtual teams and network organisations. There is some disagreement about whether these goals can be achieved via e-HRM; most researchers conclude it is most appropriate for transactional activities and that it leads merely to the externalisation of HR staff, but Parry (2011) – looking at data from countries across Europe – found there was a link between the use of e-HRM and a more strategic HR function. Parry and Tyson's research on 10 organisations noted that e-HRM had disparate goals and varying levels of success. Three of these cases are outlined in the box below.

HEM AT WORK IN FOCUS

## Achieving the goals for e-HRM in three organisations

*BOC* is a large manufacturer of industrial gases based in 50 countries, which employs approximately 2,000 staff. It has five functional HR teams plus central support. It uses a SAP HR system which gives line managers access to HR data from their desktops on issues relating to absence, bonus ratings and salary review dates. An e-recruitment system was introduced in 2003 and this is now linked to career centres. The two main goals of e-HRM were to improve (1) the visibility of spend, reduce headcount and advertise more quickly; this led to savings in recruitment fees and in staff costs, and (2) service delivery by getting information to job candidates more quickly; this has improved the accuracy of HR data but also depersonalised the process.

*Cancer Research UK* is a charity that employs 3,500 staff and has HR teams in the areas of resourcing and employee relations which provide advice on transactional issues. The organisation has an end-to-end e-recruitment system and a comprehensive HR information system, and at the time of the case study it was planning to introduce a self-service e-HR portal. As with BOC, the two main goals of e-HRM were to (1) improve recruitment processes and achieve cost reductions; this has led to a speeding-up of calculations, reduced headcount and saved on paper consumption, and (2) improve the credibility of the HR function and accuracy of data entry; the latter is now much more transparent and accessible both for employees and for applicants.

*IBM* is a large global IT company employing 20,000 people around the world. HR is organised globally, both in geographical regions and by country, and there is an SSC. As would be expected, technology is used widely for communicating with a dispersed workforce, HR information is on the intranet, and there is a range of self-service tools for managers. Once again cost formed a key part of the reason for using e-HRM, and headcount in HR has been reduced as has the extent of manual input of new data and cycle times. The IBM example showed that other goals were also important: increasing the strategic orientation of the HR function was achieved through business partners being able to focus more on high-level and forward-looking issues, whilst managers and employees have been empowered through greater access to HR knowledge.

*To think about:*

*What are the main conclusions to be drawn from these cases and others outlined in the Parry and Tyson paper? Do you see any downsides from the development of e-HRM, aside from the loss of HR jobs within the organisations?*

Source: Adapted from Parry and Tyson (2011).

E-HRM has been most widely used for transactional HRM as Farndale *et al* (2009) illustrate in their study of how 15 organisations in the Netherlands used self-service applications in SSCs. Highest usage was found for absence management, holiday leave and expenses, whilst there were extensive plans to use e-HRM for personal data, performance management and general information via a dashboard system. Amongst their sample it was rare for e-HR to be used for material relating to stock option plans and exit interviews. Interestingly,

Bondarouk and Ruel (2009) identified that e-HR had been used for career development and internal mobility in a government department also in the Netherlands. Managers found it useful for appraisal records although – as usual – there were irritations with the system whilst employees felt the 'mobility bank' provided quality information. They also believed the use of e-HRM increased the speed of searching and applying for new posts, though many still printed off the material in order to read it. Employees also felt that many barriers remained in the area of career development, though blame for this was attributed to lack of support from their managers and bureaucratic rules rather than e-HRM.

## CAREERS FOR HR SPECIALISTS IN THE FUTURE

It is clear the role of HR specialists has changed since the emergence of the business partner model and the three-legged stool configuration. On the one hand, the future looks positive for those able to reach the senior echelons of the organisation and command a place on the board or its equivalent. On the other, the growth of SSCs and HR outsourcing firms that do transactional work, especially if these are in call centres staffed by administrators without HR qualifications, does not augur well for the profession. Whilst each extreme is possible, it is more likely the HR profession will continue to reconfigure itself in a range of forms. In the past, not all HR staff were architects or change agents, and in most organisations a variety of roles are undertaken by HR professionals at different stages in their working lives.

However, there is little doubt the traditional model of the HR career – where staff remained in the same organisation for many years, moving through the ranks from assistant to officer to manager to director – is now rare. In its place, people zig-zag between functions and organisations, gaining experience in a variety of HR and non-HR roles. Time might be spent in an SSC, at corporate HQ, in a specialist HR role (such as reward management or employee relations) and as a line manager, or even in a totally different function such as marketing. Whilst this might offer more rewarding career routes for some, it could also lead to uncertainty and insecurity for others, especially if they find it hard to gain business partner positions (Tamkin *et al* 2006). A CIPD survey, drawing on data supplied by more than 1,800 respondents, suggests the situation for those at early stages in their HR career is rather more optimistic and complex than alarmists would indicate (see box below).

HRM AT WORK IN FOCUS

### Myths and realities in HR?

**People are parachuted into top HR jobs from outside the profession**: research shows that HR directors have worked in the profession for an average of 20 years and only 3% have been in HR less than five years.

**Academic qualifications do not matter**: 86% of directors have a degree and nearly two-thirds have a postgraduate qualification.

**The top jobs are filled by headhunting**: the most likely way into a top HR job is via an application, with less than a quarter of directors and senior executives found by headhunters.

**People in HR do not understand the business**: 83% of the respondents had experience working outside of HR, and business awareness was recognised as a very important factor in getting to the top.

Source: Adapted from Jarvis and Robinson (2005).

Whilst much of the literature looks at HR specifically, Kelly and Gennard's (2007) study is useful because it includes finance and marketing directors as well as HR. Results showed that directors from all three groups felt they were required to combine a high level of functional expertise with business awareness and social and political skills. Their functional expertise was essential in providing a necessary baseline for one of the top roles, but on its own this was not sufficient. Individuals were required to demonstrate, according to Kelly and Gennard (2007, p.112), 'the possession of wider business knowledge and understanding coupled with well-developed interpersonal skills. The effective director thus manages across the business in multi-functional teams as well as carrying out a core functional specialism.'

## ASSESSING THE CONTRIBUTION OF THE HR FUNCTION

Whilst it is now common for employers to use HR metrics, there are very few publications which have evaluated the role of the HR function in improving organisational performance. Indeed, the CIPD *Shaping the Future* report (2011c) notes that assessment and evaluation is less developed than would be expected for an area that is considered a priority. This is surprising given the increased tendency for organisations to use alternative forms of HR delivery and the enduring obsession with cost reduction, as well as views that HR has minimal impact – summed up by Skinner's quote that the personnel function is just 'big hat and no cattle' (Guest 1991; Guthrie *et al* 2011). HR specialists are often critical of their contribution to organisational goals in a way that does not appear to concern other specialist functions (Torrington 1998). Three reasons can be suggested for this (Guest and Hoque 1994a). First, HR has always been in an ambiguous position, and on cost grounds alone its presence can be questioned. Second, doubts about the value of HR are reinforced by a UK national culture that puts a primacy on financial control and short-termism to the neglect of longer term considerations (see Chapter 5). Third, the contribution of HR specialists has always been hard to quantify because they work closely with line managers and are dependent on them to put policies into effect. Consequently, although it is argued that 'we may be able to identify the impact of personnel decisions, we cannot always be sure whether the personnel specialists contributed towards them' (p.41). This raises doubts about the appropriateness of using 'hard' metrics – such as levels of absence or employee engagement – to assess the value of the HR function if HR practices are not implemented by line managers or done so ineffectively. It also shows the value of 'soft' measures which ask for views of stakeholders instead. In this section we evaluate the HR contribution by examining four sets of factors: board membership/influence on strategy; views of key stakeholders; benchmarking against external data; internal evaluation via service level agreements.

### BOARD MEMBERSHIP/INFLUENCE ON STRATEGY

It has been argued that in order to ensure issues are taken seriously, HR needs to have a presence on the board. Millward *et al* (2000, p.76) found that by the late 1990s, 64% of workplaces in the private sector were located in organisations where there was a specialist presence on the board, particularly in organisations which dealt with trade unions. Unfortunately the 2004 WERS did not ask this question, so it is hard to assess how things have changed since the late 1990s. Despite using a less representative sample, and surveying organisations rather than workplaces, IRS conducted annual surveys for many years. These found (Crail 2007) that just over two-thirds of the sampled organisations had a director responsible for HR alone (43%) or for HR and other issues (25%); this was at about the same level as the year before and slightly higher than in 2003. Not surprisingly, HR directors were more likely in larger organisations and, whilst there was little variation between sectors, 85% of public sector organisations had a director either solely for HR, or for HR and other issues.

Researchers such as Hope-Hailey *et al* (1997) and Torrington (1998) do not believe an HR presence on the board guarantees that HRM is taken seriously or that the function has greater influence. Indeed, it is possible for HRM to be treated as a strategic issue *without* a specialist presence but this only occurs if the Chief Executive is convinced of the value of HRM and these values are embedded throughout the entire organisation via line managers. Moreover, Kelly and Gennard (2007, pp.107–8) suggest that because strategy is more often formulated at a sub-group of the board and merely approved by the latter, a presence at the former is very important. This is not confined just to HR; other functions, such as marketing, are in a similar position. As we saw earlier, HR directors are usually appointed because they make an overall contribution to the business rather than just speak on HR (Caldwell 2001; Guest and King 2002; Kelly and Gennard 2007).

## VIEWS OF KEY STAKEHOLDERS

A second way to assess the effectiveness of HR is to ask key 'customers' – line managers, chief executives and non-managerial staff – what they think about HR delivery (Guest and Peccei 1994; Wilkinson and Marchington 1994; CIPD 2006; Guest and Conway 2011; Guthrie *et al* 2011).

The services and support valued by *other managers* depends on their level in the hierarchy. Buyens and de Vos (2001) asked senior managers, line managers and HR managers to indicate (a) the value of various HR practices to the organisation and (b) the value that the HR function added to the organisation in general. Using Ulrich's original model, the senior managers in their study valued HR's role principally in the areas of change and transformation, whereas line managers were not really bothered about HR as a strategic partner but felt that added value came from administrative expertise, managing costs and delivering core HR services such as recruitment and training. The HR managers felt the role of employee champion added the greatest value – both in terms of regarding employees as 'the heartbeat of the organisation' and providing a bridge between different interest groups. They were valued just as much for problem-solving ability as for their strategic contribution. Other surveys (for example, Crail 2006b) note that HR specialists tend to be more positive about their own contribution to HRM than did the line managers working with them. Yet, about half of the line managers reckoned HR was either extremely or very approachable, and performed best in the areas of grievance and discipline, general administration, training and occupational health. On the downside, HR was rated poor or average in terms of succession planning, performance management, job evaluation, and change management.

The assessments made by *directors and general managers* about the HR contribution are clearly very important if HR wants to make an impact. Guest and King (2002) interviewed 48 directors, finding that rather more were positive than negative about the contribution of the HR function, and indeed the most critical were the HR directors themselves. Views were split on whether there should be an HR presence on the board. One chief executive suggested that, without an HR presence on the board, the message given out would be that people management is not as important as other activities. In contrast, one of the operations directors felt there was no need for specific HR representation on the board because this was the responsibility of all members. If present, HR directors were expected to operate as 'thinking partners'. Guthrie *et al* (2011) report that general managers are inclined to be more positive about HR when the organisation is pursuing high commitment HRM because human capital is so important in this situation.

Because there are hardly any published surveys seeking the views of *employees* about the HR function, and this data is quite old, it is hard to assess what they think nowadays. Gibb's (2001) survey of over 2,600 employees in 73 organisations found HR tended to do best in areas concerning interpersonal relations (such as being approachable, helpful and prompt) and professionalism and knowledge (such as confidentiality and advice). Interestingly, members of staff in the HR department were seen in a more positive light than HR practices. This is interesting because as HR departments have become more distant from employees due to the growth of call centres, e-HRM and devolution of HRM to line managers, it is unlikely this is still the case. In a sense, the more that HR looks up the organisation for legitimacy, the less that employees value its role (Marchington 2010).

## BENCHMARKING AGAINST EXTERNAL COMPARISONS

There is much talk about the value of external benchmarking where HR professionals compare their own policies with other organisations in the sector via industry clubs, consultants and employers' organisations. Little has been published on this topic over the last few years so again we depend on slightly dated material. The CIPD report on *The Changing HR Function* (CIPD 2006) estimated that over 1,000 human capital indices had been used as benchmarks, though there is no one single measure that adequately assesses the complete HR contribution. To make matters worse, many metrics are subject to external as well as internal influence, and thus vary between sectors, regions and occupational group, as well as over time depending on the state of the external labour market. Some of the most widely used metrics are listed in Table 15.

**Table 15 Benchmarking the HR function**

| HR measures | Value of this measure | Limitations of this measure |
|---|---|---|
| Labour turnover | Can indicate level of commitment to organisation | Influenced by availability of jobs at other organisations |
| Absence rate | Can indicate level of commitment to organisation | Influenced by absence management policies and line management style |
| Expenditure or days devoted to training | Can indicate management commitment to building skills | Tells us nothing about the quality or relevance of the training |
| Employee satisfaction | Can indicate level of commitment to organisation | Influenced by other factors such as work–life balance and short-term actions at organisation |
| Employee engagement | Can indicate level of commitment to organisation | Influenced by other factors such as work–life balance and short-term actions at organisation |
| Cost to fill vacancies | Can indicate use of effective channels of recruitment | Tells us nothing about the quality of the people selected |
| Time to fill vacancies | Can indicate use of effective channels of recruitment | The best employees often take longer to hire as they are in demand |
| HR costs as percentage of total costs or profits | Can indicate a well-run function that is cost-efficient | Tells us nothing about quality of provision and depends on sector and extent of HR outsourcing |
| Response time for employee grievances | Can indicate effective and well-oiled procedures | Tells us nothing about whether grievances resolved effectively |

An IRS survey (Crail 2008) confirmed the extensive use of indicators such as absence figures, employee engagement surveys, data on grievances and disciplinary incidents, staff turnover and feedback from exit interviews. The study showed that hard measures – for example, levels of labour turnover, days lost to absence and expenditure on training costs – are the most widely used, although soft measures such as employee satisfaction levels/ opinion surveys are not far behind. Productivity assessments are rarely employed according to this survey. The most effective are absence and labour turnover figures, followed by employee satisfaction. Other frequently used measures are:

- ratio of HR staff to full-time equivalent employees
- percentage of employees involved in training
- percentage of employees receiving formal appraisals
- ratio of salaries and wages to those of competitors
- speed and effectiveness of response to employee grievances.

As we see from Table 15, incredible care should be taken with benchmarking to ensure the measures used are appropriate and accurately measured. For example, the time and the costs of recruiting and training vary considerably across occupations, and much depends on whether new starters arrive with pre-established skills. Levels of absenteeism and labour turnover differ significantly between sectors and much depends on the nature of the external labour market. Equally, figures for absence levels can vary depending on whether or not all forms of absence are included. Levels of satisfaction show differences between countries, industries and occupations, as well as between men and women (Rose 2003). Even if we can be sure the comparisons are valid, many of the measures used relate to costs rather than value-added. As we saw in Chapter 3, additional costs can be offset by, or contribute to, higher levels of performance over time. In addition, a single, blanket figure for the costs of replacing a member of staff assumes that all employees are worth retaining because they perform at or above expectations, whereas it may be more cost-effective for some staff whose performance is sub-standard to leave the organisation. Complexities like undermine these indicators.

Pfeffer (1997, p.360) questions whether benchmarking exercises have much value because 'what is easily measurable and what is important are often only loosely related'. For example, consider the ratio of permanent HR staff to number of employees. IRS Benchmarking Surveys (Crail 2007, 2008) show this ratio varies sizeably between sectors, and between organisations of different sizes, often due to whether or not there was an internal HR function. For example, in 2007, the median ratio was 1:118 across all sectors, with the public sector lowest (or highest depending on one's perspective) at 1:94 compared with manufacturing at 1:156. By 2008, the ratios had changed and private sector services were lower. However, these median figures concealed large differences within sectors; for example, the upper quartile figures for the public sector were 1:186 compared with 1:250 in the private sector and 1:253 in manufacturing whilst the lower quartile figures were respectively 1:76, 1:63 and 1:69. In other words, many manufacturing companies had lower ratios than their public sector equivalents. It is therefore difficult to draw firm conclusions from this data. Moreover, if an organisation is above average, does this justify a reduction in HR staff without any consideration of how these people operate and the value added by their contribution?

## REFLECTIVE ACTIVITY

Write a short report for your manager outlining the benefits and limitations of using these sorts of metrics to evaluate the contribution of the HR function.

## INTERNAL EVALUATION VIA SERVICE LEVEL AGREEMENTS

A final option is to focus on *internal* evaluations, perhaps by drawing up service-level agreements. These cover a range of HR practices such as payroll management, recruitment advertising and induction. Service-level agreements offer several advantages to employers, not least in enabling a more specific statement of service provision against which performance can be assessed (Mayo 1995). This approach has also been used by large multinational corporations such as Shell (Sparrow *et al* 2004, pp.165–6). Although the precise list of items varies, some of the more typical are:

- preparing offer and contract letters within one day
- providing advice on disciplinary matters within two days
- advising staff on terms and conditions of employment within five days
- preparing, disseminating and analysing absence and labour turnover data to line managers on a monthly basis
- evaluating training provision on an annual basis.

There are also dangers with this approach as the HR function can find that in trying to satisfy internal customers, it becomes their servant instead. Allowing HRM to be defined by line managers undervalues the judgement of HR professionals and encourages short-term action to the neglect of longer term considerations about sustainable HRM (Marchington 2010). By attempting to quantify its contribution, HR basically succumbs to the accountants' vision of how organisations are meant to operate. As Armstrong (1989, p.160) cautioned many years ago, this cedes too much to 'the dominant accounting culture and may also, in the end, achieve little security for the personnel function'. Pfeffer (1997, pp.363–4) argues that HR is unlikely ever to win the numbers game because other departments have much more experience of this – and they also set the rules! He warns that 'if all HR becomes is finance with a different set of measures and topic domains, then its future is indeed likely to be dim' (p.364). Alternatively, Toulson and Dewe (2004, p.88) suggest that HR managers need to 'become conversant with different accounting practices, experienced in using a range of analytic tools and capable of providing an alternative view'. To focus solely on costs is too narrow, and it is better to identify how the HR function can add value; figures used with sensitivity and discretion may help HR improve its service to stakeholders.

HRM AT WORK IN FOCUS

### Have you got an effective HR function?

Is there any advice to offer HR directors that are looking for ways in which to make the function more effective? Accepting there are limitations in generalising from the IRS sample, as well as in trying to draw causal connections between factors, Crail (2006b, p.20) offers the suggestion that 'effective HR departments are more likely to:

- be headed by a director who is solely responsible for HR who reports directly into the Chief Executive
- have a documented HR strategy explicitly linked to organisational strategy
- measure their own effectiveness, particularly through benchmarking and absence data
- exert tight control over their budgets
- view a wider range of activities as the shared responsibility of HR and line managers.'

*To think about:*

*How well does your organisation, or one with which you are familiar, fare against this checklist? What might you do to increase the effectiveness of the HR function and how might you overcome barriers to the achievement of a more strategic role for HRM?*

## CONCLUSIONS

In this chapter, we have reviewed the changing nature of work undertaken by HR departments. There has been substantial interest in the notion that HR needs a presence on the board in order to make a more meaningful and sustained contribution, and that this may be best achieved via a business or strategic partner role. Whilst there are aspirations aplenty to take on a more strategic role, there is limited evidence this has occurred in many organisations, although it is clear that high commitment HRM is more likely in workplaces that have a specialist presence. However, the tendency to outsource HR work, either in its entirety or piecemeal, or to set up SSCs, has become more extensive, and this has raised questions about whether the HR function will prosper in the future. The increased use of e-HRM, especially if line managers and employees have direct access to HR data, has also affected the visibility of internal HR functions. Whether employees feel empowered, as some of the literature suggests, is more contentious, and some organisations accept that a human presence is still desired, rather than a 24-7 portal without specialists. The desire to seek quantitative assessments of HR work exacerbates the problem because many indicators are inappropriate or too simplistic to allow a full evaluation. Although management is dominated by accountancy versions of performance, it is important to be aware that models are limited because they focus on easily measurable, cost-driven indicators which do not fit with the assumption that HRM – especially the high commitment variant – provides greater benefits over the longer term.

## EXPLORE FURTHER

ADLER, P. (2003) 'Making the HR outsourcing decision', MIT Sloan Management Review, Fall, pp.53–60.

CALDWELL R. (2003) 'The changing roles of personnel managers: old ambiguities, new uncertainties', *Journal of Management Studies*, Vol.40, No.4, 983–1004.

CHARTERED INSTITUTE OF PERSONNEL AND DEVELOPMENT (2009a) *HR Outsourcing and the HR Function: threat or opportunity.* London: CIPD.

FRANCIS, H. and KEEGAN, A. (2006) 'The changing face of HRM: in search of balance', *Human Resource Management Journal*, Vol.16, No.3, 231–49.

KEEGAN, A. and FRANCIS, H. (2010) 'Practitioner talk: the changing text-scape of HRM and emergence of HR business partnership', *International Journal of Human Resource Management*, Vol.21, No.6, 873–98.

KELLY, J. and GENNARD, J. (2007) 'Business strategic decision making: the role and influence of directors', *Human Resource Management Journal*, Vol.17, No.2, 99–117.

KLAAS, B. (2008a) 'Outsourcing and the HR function: an examination of trends and developments within North American firms', *International Journal of Human Resource Management*, Vol.19, No.8, 1500–14.

PARRY, E. and TYSON, S. (2011) 'Desired goals and actual outcomes of e-HRM', *Human Resource Management Journal*, Vol.21, No.3, 335–54.

PFEFFER, J. (1997) 'Pitfalls on the road to measurement: the dangerous liaison of human resources with the idea of accounting and finance', *Human Resource Management*, Vol.36, No.3, 357–65.

REDMAN, T., SNAPE, E., WASS, J. and HAMILTON, P. (2007) 'Evaluating the human resource shared services model: evidence from the NHS', *International Journal of Human Resource Management*, Vol.18, No.8, 1486–506.

ULRICH, D. and BROCKBANK, W. (2005) *The HR Value Proposition*. Boston: Harvard Business School Press.

CHAPTER 7

# Line Managers, Leadership and HRM

## LEARNING OUTCOMES

By the end of this chapter readers should be able to:

- provide appropriate levels of support to line managers to enable them to undertake the HRM parts of their role effectively and consistently
- advise their own organisation (or one with which they are familiar) on how to address the barriers which prevent line managers from doing HR work effectively
- contribute to the development of leadership styles and skills that are suitable for a range of different operating environments.

In addition, readers should be able to understand and explain:

- the reasons why specific areas of HR work are devolved to line managers and the support that they need to do this effectively
- why line managers face difficulties in taking responsibility for HRM and the ways in which these might be overcome
- the different meanings of leadership at the front-line/middle management level and their interactions with staff in terms of HRM.

## INTRODUCTION

It should be clear from earlier chapters that responsibility for HRM does not reside solely or even primarily with specialist HR managers, despite the important role they play in devising policies and procedures in the organisations where they are employed. In large organisations where there is an active HR function, certain aspects of HR work are undertaken by external providers and/or shared service centres. Whatever their role, such specialists provide support for line managers that have day-to-day responsibility for HRM in relation to the staff that work for them, and are centrally involved in the implementation of HR policies operating within the organisation. In smaller organisations without a specialist presence, line managers take on even greater responsibility for HR issues, often without much guidance or any great knowledge of professional and legal standards governing the employment of people. In these situations, with the best will in the world, mistakes are bound to occur and inconsistencies appear in the treatment of individual staff. Recently, the emphasis has shifted so that supervisors are expected not just to manage their staff but also show leadership capabilities that bring out the best in those that work for them, encourage them to work harder and smarter, and discourage them from adopting attitudes and behaviours that undermine 'strong HR systems'. In addition to having appropriate levels of technical and project management skills, line managers are now urged to become transformational leaders as well. This sets the scene for this chapter which explores (1) the growing HR responsibility of line managers, (2) the blockages and barriers that prevent them from fulfilling this role successfully, (3) the actions that can be taken to minimise these problems, in particular relating to skills, consistency and support from the HR function, and (4) the part that leadership skills can play in the performance of line managers.

## INCREASING LINE MANAGEMENT RESPONSIBILITY FOR HRM

Line managers have criticised the contribution HR specialists make to organisational performance in at least four ways (Whittaker and Marchington 2003; Kulik and Perry 2008; Hutchinson and Purcell 2010; Sanders and Frenkel 2011). First, HR practitioners are regarded as out of touch with commercial realities, not really aware of how the business operates or its customer needs, but instead applying principles – such as welfare or employee rights – that could be seen to conflict with business goals. This criticism might lose some of its sting as business partners grow in numbers and HR professionals show greater understanding of and allegiance to organisational goals; even if this becomes more widespread, past legacies are often hard to dispel. Second, HR is often felt to constrain the autonomy of line managers to make decisions they feel are in the best interests of the business. Frustration is most apparent in relation to what are seen as constraints brought about by legal restrictions and trade union constraints on managerial prerogative, or in having to work with what might be seen as new-fangled policies – such as in the area of work–life balance – that provide opportunities for workers to have some degree of flexibility in how they work. The third criticism is that HR managers are unresponsive and slow to act, always wanting to check options thoroughly rather taking action immediately in support of line managers' recommendations. As we see later, this is where inconsistencies in HR implementation are most prone to arise and where there is an explicit clash between the objectives of different stakeholders – for example, in hiring a new member of staff to cope with an urgent business need without having to go through fair and transparent procedures. Finally, HR practitioners are criticised for promoting policies that may be fine in theory but hard to put into effect, or inappropriate for their particular workplace. For example, while line managers may support the principle of appraisal they are often annoyed by the practical requirement to keep records of meetings. The HR function is caught in a cleft stick, criticised both for being too interventionist and too remote. Watson's classic book (1986, p.204) still has a strong resonance today:

> If personnel specialists are not passive administrative nobodies who pursue their social work, go-between and fire-fighting vocations with little care for business decisions and leadership, then they are clever, ambitious power-seekers who want to run organisations as a kind of self-indulgent personnel playground.

Legge (1995, pp.27–28) terms this the 'vicious circle in personnel management'. Because senior managers do not involve the HR function at an early stage, this results in 'people' issues being ignored or downplayed during the decision-making process. Problems inevitably arise with new initiatives or with routine business issues because HR has not been involved – difficulties such as poor recruits, inadequately trained staff or stoppages of work. When this happens, HR is asked to help resolve the crisis and the short-term solutions they provide merely store up trouble for the future because they are rushed through. Accordingly HR gets the blame for not being able to resolve the problem, and so continues to be excluded from major decisions, thus completing the vicious circle.

In order to address these concerns, line managers have been encouraged to take on greater responsibility for HR activities – although in one sense this has always been the case because line managers operate a key people management role at the workplace all the time. It is argued that, rather than having to wait for an 'answer' from the HR department, they can resolve issues instantly. Moreover, line managers believe their 'solutions' are typically more in tune with business realities, and therefore contribute more overtly to improved performance. Being given more explicit responsibility for HRM also enhances line management ownership of these ideas and should increase their commitment to integrating HR with other objectives. Despite suggestions that HR should be disbanded altogether, a more realistic option is for line managers and HR professionals to work together as partners (Ulrich 1998; Whittaker and Marchington 2003; Purcell and Hutchinson 2007a). Indeed, a cross-country study using the CRANET data showed that shared decision-making between HR specialists and line managers led to increases in organisational performance whilst too much reliance on one or the other had no impact (Dany *et al* 2008).

There is little doubt line managers have significant responsibility for HRM, typically in conjunction with HR practitioners where they are employed. A review of empirical studies in the UK and other developed countries shows how the line's role in HRM has increased over the last 20 years; see, for example, Storey (1992); Hutchinson and Wood (1995); Hall and Torrington (1998); Renwick (2003); Purcell and Hutchinson (2007a); Dany *et al* (2008); Brandl *et al* (2009); Sanders and Frenkel (2011). There are few areas in which the HR function makes decisions on its own, except in relation to wider company policies and procedures, and in most cases first-line managers typically make decisions in conjunction with HR specialists. Results from an IRS survey are presented in Table 16.

**Table 16 Responsibility for HRM**

| Responsibility Area of work | HR department | Shared | Line manager | Other |
|---|---|---|---|---|
| Training | 56 | 30 | 5 | 9 |
| Administration | 47 | 42 | 8 | 3 |
| Equal opportunities | 43 | 40 | 12 | 5 |
| Staffing | 42 | 50 | 6 | 2 |
| Health and safety | 15 | 28 | 15 | 42 |
| Performance appraisal | 14 | 33 | 53 | 0 |

Source: Adapted from Crail (2007).

Notes: n = 117 respondents. Figures are percentages of organisations responding.

These indicate that major responsibility for HR issues resides with the HR department more than with line managers, but in many cases it is shared. Involvement of HR specialists tends to remain highest in policy formulation where issues of consistency and specialist expertise are most important and lowest when line managers are responsible for putting plans into effect. Maxwell and Watson's (2006) research at Hilton International's UK hotels showed that line managers felt they were most heavily involved in the following activities: motivation and morale of their staff; team briefings and communications; health and safety; identifying training needs; employee selection; and performance appraisal. For the most part, the HR specialists working with these line managers had a similar interpretation, though they felt the line managers had substantially underestimated their role in disciplinary and grievance procedures, and in employee induction. Both the CIPD (CIPD 2006) and IRS surveys (Crail 2008) indicated that partnership between HR and the line manager was more common in resourcing and in training and development but more likely to be done mainly by HR specialists in employee relations and reward management. Hutchinson and Purcell (2007) examined line manager involvement in learning and development in more detail in their study of 663 organisations; this found that line managers were assumed to have the main responsibility for conducting performance appraisals, agreeing personal development plans and planning the training and development needs of staff, some responsibility for induction, the provision of informal training, and coaching, and very limited involvement in formal training. This confirms other studies where line manager involvement was most significant in areas requiring the implementation of HR policies.

Interesting tensions arise for front-line managers in contexts where professional and clinical work is being done. For example, research on ward managers in hospitals shows how the HR aspects of their role have increased substantially whilst their clinical duties have remained critically important, particularly if staff are absent or crises arise on the ward. This leads to a feeling that they are overworked and under-resourced (Hutchinson and Purcell 2010), not surprisingly given the average size of the teams under their supervision is over 25, more than double the ratio suggested by Acas as ideal. They were responsible for much HR work, the most widespread being communication, listening to staff, absence management, discipline and grievance handling, and informal training. They had much less involvement in decisions relating to pay and grading, but nevertheless even here over half the sample felt this was part of their role. Similar findings emerge from studies on ward managers in Canada (Armstrong-Stassen and Schlosser 2010) and Australia (Townsend *et al* 2012); in the latter, it is clear that these managers found difficulty implementing HRM because of the mixed messages received from senior management.

Nevertheless, it is apparent from these studies that HR specialists and line managers tend to work in conjunction with each other on many HR issues. In terms of line manager involvement, the following sums up the situation well:

- *major responsibility* – leading team briefings, problem-solving groups and informal communications; performance review; team/staff development; managing employee absence
- *shared responsibility* – selection decisions; induction and ongoing training; disciplinary cases; flexible working patterns
- *little responsibility* – performance-related pay; recruitment advertising, applications and initial search; promotions; welfare; organisation development.

The study undertaken for the CIPD by Purcell and his team (Purcell *et al* 2003; Purcell and Hutchinson 2007a; Hutchinson and Purcell 2007) takes this a stage further by analysing the relationship between first-line managers and HR activities in terms of the difference they make to performance and employee attitudes. Based on over 600 interviews with employees, as well as many others with managers, six activities seem to be particularly influential: performance appraisal; training, coaching and guidance; involvement and communication; openness (the ability to express grievances or raise concerns); work–life balance; recognition. If these are done well, positive benefits accrue, but unfortunately the evidence shows they are often done badly. For example, employees felt performance appraisals suffered due to lack of clarity in targets and measurements and system complexity, and that many of the problems could be directly linked to the behaviour of managers. The box below examines the difference that line managers can make to HRM in practice, and to employee outcomes.

HRM AT WORK IN FOCUS

## How line managers can make a difference

The research that John Purcell and his colleagues undertook for the CIPD has major implications for the roles of line managers and HR specialists. Based on interviews with 608 workers in 12 organisations over a two-year period, including repeat interviews following the introduction of changes, they concluded that line managers could make a real difference to employee attitudes and behaviour. Managers who were good at 'front-line leadership' – things such as keeping people up to date and giving them a chance to comment on proposed changes, responding to suggestions, dealing with problems and treating employees fairly – also had team members with high levels of satisfaction, commitment, motivation and discretion.

One of the organisations involved in the research was the Selfridges store at Trafford Park near Manchester. About 650 people worked at the store, comprising a mix of directly employed and concessionary (franchised) staff, but both present an identical image to the customer. Results from the first survey undertaken at the store showed that workers displayed high levels of organisational commitment, much higher than the average for retail staff generally. The survey also uncovered some less positive views, in particular in relation to appraisal and the role played by front-line managers in the process. There was a gap between intended policies and implemented practices, with about half the sample reporting poor leadership behaviour by their team leaders, and the HR manager was concerned that supervisory behaviour was not in line with company expectations.

Following the feedback of these results, Selfridges focused on making improvements to the team leader role: this included a clearer role definition, the introduction of a new process whereby team leaders reapplied for their positions, a revamping of the performance appraisal system for team leaders which linked it more with career development opportunities. Following the introduction of these changes, a second attitude survey was undertaken a year later, and this showed marked improvements in employee attitudes, organisational commitment, worker satisfaction and job influence. The researchers feel that, since no other changes had taken place to the job role of sales associates, the changes the way front-line managers did their jobs offered the best explanation for the change in attitudes. This was also supported by interview responses from sales associates. More significantly perhaps, store performance also improved, with sales increasing by nearly a quarter compared with the previous year, payroll costs were reduced by 5% and labour turnover also declined.

Because senior store managers also attributed the improvements to changes in the front-line managers' roles, it was decided to continue to focus on this group of staff and provide yet more training so they could do the HR aspects of the job better. A whole series of formal and informal interventions took place to increase the people management content of the team leaders' roles. This led one of the senior managers at the store to comment this had forced the team leaders 'to be more disciplined, more planned and forcing them to be less reactive ... partly because the HR team are no longer available on-site to wipe their back sides.'

*To think about:*

*Have any changes to the role of front-line managers taken place at your workplace or one with which you are familiar, and if so, what were the results? Can you think of any other factors beyond the change to the team leader role that might help to explain these very positive outcomes at this Selfridges' store?*

Source: Adapted from Purcell and Hutchinson (2007a).

Of course, much depends on the respective power bases of line managers and HR practitioners, and the degree to which senior managers believe that HRM is important within the organisation. A study by Lupton (2000) provides a useful corrective for HR specialists believing that decisions about devolution rest solely with them. He examined the role played by the personnel function in the selection of doctors, and concluded that it was little more than 'pouring the coffee' and acting as an administrative support while the consultants made decisions. In this situation, the HR professionals were on low grades and had little opportunity to influence the highly paid and very influential consultants who made it clear that they resented any interference at all. Sometimes consultants short-circuited the formal procedures, as well as making it clear to candidates that they felt questions asked by the personnel officer were of little importance (p.62). Zhu *et al*'s (2008) study of devolving HRM to line managers in China reinforces that point about power; this shows senior and middle managers having significant responsibility for HRM in recruitment and selection, pay and benefits, performance assessments and job design, front-line managers had virtually no involvement. The HR function continued to play a major role in most of these areas with the exception of job design. The authors suggest there is likelihood of devolution to front line managers until they have acquired more support in the form of training and ongoing advice.

HRM AT WORK IN FOCUS

## Danish women think HRM is more important than men!

Julia Brandl and her colleagues undertook a survey on the HR duties of line managers in Denmark, in an attempt to determine the extent to which these activities were important in comparison with other aspects of their jobs. Overall, nearly 700 line managers completed the survey, drawn from across sectors, levels in the hierarchy, and both males and females. The areas of activity involved were: staff well-being; communication; training and development; coaching; motivation; delegation; team building; conflict resolution; and information handling.

Unlike some other studies these HR duties focus more on what might be regarded as 'soft' and informal issues. The overall results show that 'motivating others' was seen as the most important HR activity, followed closely by staff well-being, and then some distance behind came communication and staff development. Line managers in the public sector seemed to regard these HR duties as more important than their private sector counterparts, whilst those in more junior positions regarded them as least important. Interestingly, on every single issue, female managers were felt that HRM was more important than male managers did, and this was particularly marked for staff well-being, staff development and communication. Given that other research on Danish organisations suggests that the role of the HR function has declined considerably, questions can be asked about whether HRM is safe in the hands of line managers.

*To think about:*

*How can you explain this finding? Is it to do with cultural stereotypes of the HR function, the greater awareness of gender in Scandinavian countries, the type of questions asked, or something else altogether?*

Source: Adapted from Brandl *et al* (2009).

## PROBLEMS WITH DEVOLVING HRM TO LINE MANAGERS

The arguments for devolving HRM to front-line and middle managers assume people-management decisions should be made as close to the workplace as possible. As we have seen, there is plenty of evidence to support this in principle. But there are also problems with devolution, particularly if the decision has been taken in order to cut costs by getting rid of HR support staff that are not felt to contribute directly to product quality or customer service. The problem with this argument, however, is that it assumes HRM is a relatively minor add-on to any line manager's job which can be undertaken during existing working time and without specialist training. In this section, we review the evidence on this issue, especially in relation to front-line and middle managers. Broadly we argue that they:

1 have conflicting goals and do not automatically identify with organisational goals
2 have competing priorities and suffer from work overload when they are asked to take on HR responsibilities in addition to their existing jobs
3 lack the knowledge and skills to undertake HR duties when appointed, and find organisations rarely provide them with sufficient training and support to do HRM effectively
4 have little respect for HR work, regarding it as 'soft' and value-sapping, and they view HR professionals with disdain
5 behave inconsistently when implementing HR policies because they wish to retain flexibility in dealing with staff and are not always fully aware of what they are expected to do.

### LACK OF IDENTIFICATION WITH EMPLOYER GOALS

Front-line and middle managers sometimes find it difficult to identify closely with employer goals, but instead view themselves as quite distinct from senior managers (Thompson and McHugh 2002; Gleeson and Knights 2008; Wilkinson and Dundon 2010). Following on from Scase and Goffee's (1989, p.186) conceptualisation of 'reluctant managers', those that have been promoted from a more junior position might feel that they have escaped from the working class, but are not accepted into the managerial class, to some extent stuck in the middle and unable or unwilling to align themselves either with workers or with managers. This notion of being an 'in-between' recurs consistently in studies, particularly in knowledge-based organisations where front-line managers retain elements of professional work and have loyalties to their profession as well as their employer. For example, Gleeson and Knights (2008) reported that managers in further education establishments were highly sceptical of the ideas put forward by senior managers to bring about change, often referring to them as 'the latest fad', and were keen to maintain connection with their subject matter, their students and their own pedagogic values. This perspective is also apparent in other countries. Benn and Moore (2009) noted the same sorts of issues arose for library managers in Australia, whilst McCann *et al* (2010) found many similarities between the positions occupied by line managers in the UK, USA and Japan despite very different cultural and institutional frameworks. These managers experienced work overload, increased intensity of work and a decline in career prospects, and to make matters worse this happened alongside feeling increasingly distanced from senior managers who were a world away from the shop floor. One of the ward managers in Townsend *et al*'s (2012) Australian hospitals study summed this up well: 'You just end up being the sandwich in the middle ... keeping the relationship with my boss on a good keel because I am sticking to my budget ... but then I get flack from the nurses'.

Line managers also doubt the validity of some senior management's ideas espousing employee involvement which are often regarded as akin to soft management (Dundon *et al* 2004; Wilkinson and Dundon 2010). Whilst the language of team working and empowerment might be attractive to senior managers, it can appear threatening to first-line managers whose authority has been built on technical expertise and the restriction of information to the shop floor (Marchington and Wilkinson 2005).

Feelings of role conflict/ambiguity and insecurity are reinforced if front-line and middle managers find their existing skills are no longer needed or their numbers are reduced in the organisation. Though written some time ago, Scase and Goffee's (1989, p.191) conclusion is perhaps even more apposite during times of global financial crisis when employers seek cuts at all levels: 'corporations may succeed in cultivating "cultures of excellence" and introducing more flexible organisational forms, but predominant practice [in Britain] will tend, we suspect, to lead mainly to the *compliance* of reluctant managers'. Front-line and middle managers often receive little genuine support from senior managers, being left to fend for themselves when things go wrong or even disciplined when their attempts to maintain production or customer service misfire. Currie and Procter (2005, p.1337) found that first-line managers rarely saw their senior colleagues because the latter preferred to remain within the HQ building rather than seeing staff in their own departments; this led to feelings of isolation and distance, certainly not to any conception of shared interests. Anxieties about their role are further fuelled as their own job security is lessened and they find little attempt to 'involve' them in management decisions (Rubery *et al* 2003; McCann *et al* 2008). Studies in the UK, Italy and Ireland have all shown it is rare for line managers to be given responsibility and authority during change programmes even though this could be seen as good practice (Fenton O'Creevy 2001; Giangreco and Peccei 2005; Conway and Monks 2011). In each case, middle and first-line managers faced a challenge because they were the agents of change (carriers) on behalf of the organisation *and also* its victims (targets) because changes usually affected them negatively.

### COMPETING PRIORITIES AND WORK OVERLOAD

Brewster *et al*'s (1983) distinction between espoused and operational policies offers a framework for analysing the notion of competing priorities. *Espoused* policy is a 'summation of the proposals, objectives and standards that top-level management hold and/or state they hold for establishing the organisation's approach to its employees' (p.63). These are often little more than broad philosophical assumptions about how senior management feel towards staff – such as mission statements stating that 'employees are our most important resource'. If they are committed to paper, the phraseology used is very general, and is capable of interpretation in different ways depending on circumstances. In contrast, *operational* policy describes 'the way senior management are seen to *order* industrial relations (and human resource) priorities vis-à-vis those of other policies' (p.64). This may be done overtly or subconsciously since it is reflected in managerial value systems and is clearly moulded by issues arising on a daily basis. If two policies are seen to conflict – say, a commitment to staff development and to be customer-responsive – then HR policies typically take a lower priority. Many examples can be found from different industries illustrating the way in which espoused policies are ignored, amended or downgraded in the face of conflicting pressures. For example, Boaden *et al* (2008, p.51) note that nurse managers complained about the difficulty of squeezing all their HR and clinical responsibilities into the time available. Given pressure to improve patient care, this is hardly surprising, but it does raise questions about how committed employers are to staff development.

Several studies confirm line managers feel other goals take priority over managing human resources. For example, at the 'leading edge' organisations studied by Gratton *et al* (1999), line managers did not feel any institutional support or targets – in the form of key performance indicators – to consider HRM issues seriously because they were low on their list of priorities, and HR issues did not appear in formal key performance indicators. The study at Hilton Hotels (Maxwell and Watson 2006) noted that both line managers and HR specialists felt that pressure of work, over the short or longer term, was the biggest barrier to line manager involvement in HRM. These managers feel over-burdened by their HR work because it is *in addition to* their other tasks, thus making them reluctant to accept responsibility for these issues (Hutchinson and Purcell 2007). In a sense, HR duties are seen as 'an extra' beyond the main aspects of the role and balancing between competing priorities leads to HR being ignored or left until later because it is seen as less urgent (Whittaker and Marchington 2003). Some studies suggest this is understood by senior managers, suggesting they are not that bothered about HRM being low priority. For example, Hutchinson and Purcell (2010) note that 'ward managers had huge people management responsibilities and exceptionally large spans of control ... Given the increasing evidence of a link between HRM and the quality of patient care, the criticality of their role is evident. The reality was, however, that HRM was afforded a low priority as the more clinical aspects of the role took precedence. Indeed, senior managers believed that clinical work should and did dominate.' Line managers report frustration they cannot devote sufficient time to HR issues because 'harder' priorities are paramount; for example, in Boaden *et al*'s (2008) study, one of the managers told us 'as far as I'm concerned, patient care comes first, and if I'm late doing a personal development review, then I'm afraid that's tough. I have to give priority to the patients'. HR acknowledged that they were realistic enough to know which priorities came first.

Fenton O'Creevy (2001) argues that continual de-layering and job loss put even greater pressures on line managers, but rather than treating them as scapegoats, as is often the case, he questions whether reward and appraisal mechanisms encourage positive behaviours or if there is sufficient time left in the working day for HRM. It is hardly surprising that line managers concentrate on achieving targets they know will be used to assess them in appraisals (Bach 2005a). If the priority at appraisals is to meet production deadlines, have zero defects or reduce queue lengths rather than holding regular team briefings, developing staff or keeping absence levels low, they are bound to focus on the former. First-line managers pick up signals from senior management about the ordering of priorities rather than follow the vague messages within formal mission statements (McCann *et al* 2008).

## REFLECTIVE ACTIVITY

Does this state of affairs resonate with your own experiences? If so what has been done about it in your organisation or one with which you are familiar? Could the HR function do more to persuade line managers that their HR responsibilities should be given greater priority?

### LACK OF KNOWLEDGE AND SKILLS AND INSUFFICIENT TRAINING

A common complaint is that line managers do not possess the skills and competencies necessary to perform the HR aspects of their jobs effectively (Renwick 2003; Maxwell and Watson 2006; Hutchinson and Purcell 2010; Teague and Roche 2012) because their knowledge of motivation theory or pay systems is typically based on personal experience or deeply held personal beliefs about why people work. Given so few line managers, especially those at workplace level, have undertaken any formal study in HRM, this is a potential problem, and many authors have argued that the low educational and technical base of line managers in Britain is a significant constraint on devolution. Even those with degrees rarely had any management component in the subjects they studied, though that is improving nowadays. At the workplace, changes typically occur rapidly leaving insufficient time for training to be done properly or systematically, and line managers are left to pick things up as they go along. Moreover, the faddish nature of many new initiatives means that line managers fail to take new ideas seriously because they expect these to be jettisoned when the next fashion appears (Marchington and Wilkinson 2005).

When asked, line managers typically feel they have sufficient skills to succeed. For example, in the hotel studied by Maxwell and Watson (2006), just 17% of the line managers felt they were lacking in communication skills whilst nearly 80% of the HR specialists reported this as a problem. At the same time, many line managers recognise they need support from HR if they are to be effective. As one of the respondents to Renwick's study (2003, p.268) noted, grievance handling 'is done by the line manager but during all this you are getting advice, comment and support from personnel'. Another acknowledged it was crucial to take on board HR's ideas because they had the training and the professional back-up.

An IRS study (Rankin 2006a) on line manager training for recruitment and selection noted that whilst most programmes tended to be compulsory, they were also short, lacking in depth, and too reliant on 'talk and chalk' rather than role plays and practical learning situations. Our own studies of employee involvement show that training in how to run a quality circle, for example, could consist of little more than a half-hour session on 'how not to communicate' followed by an amusing video illustrating how things went wrong elsewhere. Occasionally, a speaker may be invited from another organisation to explain their approach and answer questions, but there is little attempt to give line managers an opportunity to practise their skills (Marchington and Wilkinson 2005). In Ireland, Teague and Roche (2012) noted about half the firms in their sample agreed line managers were trained in how to handle conflict at the workplace but compared this with the fact they were *required* to engage in conflict resolution; that is, half the sample were not trained for the tasks they were meant to do. Hutchinson and Purcell (2010) also found that training, where provided, was often for clinical needs rather than for the HR aspects of the line manager role, and over a third had received no management training at all during the previous 12 months. In short, not only do many line managers lack expertise in HRM when appointed, they also tend to receive minimal levels of training in HR once in these roles.

### DISDAIN FOR HR WORK

This is a problem because most studies suggest line managers need training in HRM if they are to be effective (Cunningham and Hyman 1995; Hutchinson and Purcell 2007; Teague and Roche 2012). However, some feel this is not necessary – as we saw above – because HR competence is gained not through training or a specialist qualification, but from a mixture of common sense and experience; after all, HRM is straightforward. Whilst some managers acknowledge the value of working with HR, many others are negative about its contribution and about HR policies; quite contrasting views are apparent from two line managers who took part in the Boaden *et al* (2008, p.51) study:

> Staff that I work with don't always see why we need this or that policy. It seems redundant to them because it doesn't actually affect or impact on their work.

> HR is the biggest priority in my job because obviously a key part of the job is managing staff and that is all about HR management.

Such disdain for learning and development is worrying as it contrasts sharply with line managers' beliefs about what is needed for people working in their work roles, especially if this is a technical area where knowledge and skills in science or engineering, for example, are considered essential. By contrast it is often assumed that the skills held by HR specialists are either irrelevant – because this is all common sense – or inappropriate because they are derived from models of human behaviour that are seen as naïve and idealistic. This is apparent in small organisations without a specialist HR presence where this work is undertaken by people without any training and whose main responsibility is to ensure that wages are paid correctly and on time. The case of doctor recruitment mentioned above (Lupton 2000, p.56) is also a clear, albeit extreme, example of how HR can be marginalised in the workplace even if it is required as part of the organisation's policy. Doctors refused to use person specifications, feeling that they could 'spot a good doctor' when they saw one without any interference from personnel. Moreover, the consultants chairing panels undermined personnel officers who tried to stop improper questions being asked. Employee involvement is an area where line managers have raised major doubts about the need for training, regarding it as 'soft' management and pandering to worker needs. However, Cox *et al*'s (2009) analysis of WERS data showed that employees who reckon line managers are good at seeking their views, responding to their suggestions and involving them are also significantly more satisfied at work and committed to their employers.

### INCONSISTENCIES IN APPLICATION OF HR POLICIES

Without specialist HR support and clear procedures to follow, inconsistencies in application are likely to arise, particularly for compliance with employment legislation. Earnshaw *et al*'s (2000) research on discipline and dismissal in small firms demonstrates clearly the potential problems that can occur. Dismissals arose after 'heated rows' at the workplace or due to personality clashes, without following any procedure whatsoever. Evidence, due process and the opportunity to appeal were typically lacking. Moreover, action taken on one occasion with one member of staff was ignored subsequently in relation to another worker who was liked or valued, and dismissals were deferred until after the completion of an urgent order or a replacement was available. Inconsistencies arise in other HR activities as well, such as absenteeism or performance appraisal. These issues are taken up again in subsequent chapters (see Marchington *et al* 2011a, for example) but inconsistencies in relation to performance appraisal, especially if it is tied into reward, are particularly serious. As two managers said (Hutchinson and Purcell 2003, p.29):

> It seems rather subjective. There are concerns that if you've got problems and you raise them, you're perceived as being negative.

> The pay aspect is down to line manager discretion rather than based on actual information. It depends on how well you get on with your line manager.

Inconsistencies can also arise if HR specialists and line managers have quite different views about the importance of particular HR activities; for example, in the Hilton study (Maxwell and Watson 2006), whilst line managers ranked motivation and morale, team briefings and communications, and employee selection as their top three, HR staff saw motivation as rather less important. By contrast, although selection and communications also ranked highly for HR specialists, what they regarded as the other most important activities (employee budgeting and forecasting, and maintenance of HR processes) were towards the bottom of the list for line managers. This is problematic, according to the authors, because higher levels of convergence between different groups of managers in their ranking correlate with higher levels of hotel performance. This is supported by Khilji and Wang's (2006) research on the banking industry in Pakistan. They found that consistent implementation of HR practices increases employee satisfaction with HRM, which is then positively related to high levels of organisational performance. We take up the intention-implementation-perception chain again in Chapter 15 when we look at HRM and performance.

So, how can we explain why inconsistency in the application of HRM remains a perennial problem in organisations? Part of the problem is that line managers prefer to have some flexibility in how they operate and favour informal styles of management wherever possible (Marchington and Suter 2012). This allows them to choose how to interpret rules and procedures and thus provide some leeway to reward or discipline workers on a selective basis. This can work not only to reinforce managerial control over employees, but also show leniency or provide a negotiating counter as appropriate (Brown 1973). But having discretion in dealing with employees, for example by allowing some flexibility (say, in taking time off) in return for them working harder or staying late at work to complete a rush job, also leads to inconsistencies between different workers and over time depending on the issue (Marchington *et al* 2011). An alternative explanation for why line managers do not act consistently in HRM is that they may not be aware they are failing to implement HR policies as intended (Brown 1973), for example if they are supervising staff that are employed by another organisation in a public-private partnership (Grimshaw *et al* 2010) or at a call centre (Rubery *et al* 2004). In the employment relations area, senior managers may agree to requests that undermine previous agreements made by a line manager, so creating awkward precedents. What makes acts of omission so hard to manage is that they often go unnoticed until a later date when they are used to support a case against disciplinary action, for example (Earnshaw *et al* 2000).

How can HR practitioners convince line managers that it is worth using procedures and that they can make a contribution to organisational success? Renwick (2006) argues that all managers need to be trained to handle grievance and discipline cases so that they can draw a distinction between unjustified employee complaints and those that are justified under the organisation's procedure, collective agreement or works rule. The benefits and costs of greater line management involvement in HRM are set out in the box below.

HRM AT WORK IN FOCUS

## Benefits and costs of greater line management involvement in HRM

*Benefits of adoption*

- HR problems are solved at source and receive a business focus
- better change management is achieved and there is increased speed of decision-making
- more time for HR managers to focus on strategic HRM
- line managers 'own' HR issues, are aware of them and thus cannot ignore them, and are more likely to be committed to their 'own' HR decisions
- reduces costs
- promotes the case that HRM cannot always be transferred to specialists.

- *Costs of adoption*
- increased pressure to train and/or reskill line managers in HRM to improve capability and confidence
- a need for strict auditing in order to address problems of inconsistency in decision-making
- risk of falling standards or abuse of position (discrimination)
- potential for the HR/ER management role to be marginalised
- little time for line to perform HR duties due to operational demands on them
- risks of job overload/stress as line manager workloads are increased.

Source: Adapted from Renwick (2006).

## DEVELOPING LINE MANAGERS TO PROVIDE EFFECTIVE HRM

Given that line managers now take responsibility for key elements of HRM in many organisations, and have total responsibility in others (either because they are too small to employ a specialist HR manager or decisions have been taken to devolve HRM as a whole), it is important to identify ways in which to improve their contribution. Broadly there are three areas where action can be identified: selection, appraisal and training of line managers; the use of procedures to enhance consistency in decisions; support from the HR function. These are now explored in turn.

### SELECTION, APPRAISAL AND TRAINING OF LINE MANAGERS

Given that most studies suggest that line managers lack the skills to undertake HRM aspects of their role effectively, employers need to provide clearer job descriptions and person specifications for these critical roles. As we have seen already, the focus is primarily on technical rather than people management skills, and it is hardly surprising that line managers often struggle with the HR aspects of their role, and if they are successful it is often down to chance. In professional and knowledge work, it is understandable there is such an emphasis on technical expertise as most people that eventually take on management roles start their careers on the ground – say, as a probation officer, a research chemist or a university lecturer – and need to show strengths there before they are considered for promotion. Attempts to parachute a manager without requisite qualifications and experience into a leadership role have happened in the health service and in universities, with fairly unsatisfactory results. However, it is possible to combine both technical and people management goals into a person specification in order to ensure that both are taken seriously; see Chapter 8 on resourcing and talent management for much more on this topic. In other sectors, it is feasible to define a set of performance criteria which does focus more on people management skills because technical mastery does not matter quite so much; for example, restaurant managers do not have to be top chefs in order to qualify for their posts, nor do television producers need to be high-profile actors before being appointed.

Without explicit proactive support from senior managers, and recognition and rewards for their work in the HR area, it is easy to understand why line managers do not take this part of their job too seriously. Hutchinson and Purcell (2007) argue this is a major issue to which insufficient attention has been paid; for example, little time is spent trying to gain line manager engagement with the principles of reward systems that have been designed by the HR function and other senior managers, and not surprisingly questions raised by employees about the operation of the scheme are deflected with a shrug of the shoulders and transference of blame to the door of the HR function. One obvious way in which to address this problem is to establish effective appraisal systems for line managers which give sufficient emphasis to HRM, and which are treated as important by more senior staff (see Chapter 9). Another is to provide proper training which helps to deliver skills, rather than short, sharp bouts of exposure to the latest initiative that is being rolled out in the organisation. See Chapter 11 for discussion of management development programmes and other forms of learning such as coaching.

The box below outlines the key skills that RestaurantCo seeks in its branch managers and the management capability framework that is used to select and appraise them.

HRM AT WORK IN FOCUS

### What a branch manager needs to do in order to work at RestaurantCo

Branch managers are given a wide range of responsibilities for members of staff, customers, property and finances. Key amongst these are: the day-to-day running of the restaurant; developing and motivating their teams; taking disciplinary action as needed; ordering and controlling stock and supplies; looking after finances; operating the payroll system; ensuring food safety; and reinforcing product quality and service standards. This shows that HRM forms only a small part of their role. The most important qualities sought in branch managers are:

- a keen service mentality
- the ability to work autonomously
- strong self-motivation
- the capacity to think strategically
- first-rate leadership skills
- a flexible approach to your own work
- the ability to relate to people.

Branch managers are encouraged to adopt an informal style wherever possible and this forms a key part of their performance reviews. It is monitored via the management capability framework which includes the following:

- inspiring leadership and the ability to create confident, performing teams
- harnessing potential so that the company gets the best possible from its staff
- creating a sense of belonging whereby the team works well together
- innovation to ensure the company remains a leader in the industry.

Source: Adapted from Suter and Marchington (2012).

## USING PROCEDURES TO ENHANCE CONSISTENCY

As we have seen, in practice operational targets tend to take priority over HR considerations, and directives from HR specialists tend to have less force than those coming from a production director. This helps to explain why line managers are often hostile to rules handed down from HR specialists who are castigated for not 'living in the real world'. Thus, an HR policy that is well formulated, embodies the basic rules of good management practice, and ensures uniformity and consistency may appear very differently when viewed from the position of the line manager. It might be seen as a bureaucratic hurdle over which they need to jump merely to satisfy a third party who does not know the details of the case confronting them. In short, procedures of any kind can be seen as the problem rather than a potentially valuable way of channelling disagreements through an agreed route.

Under such circumstances, HR specialists need to be able to persuade line managers that procedures are valuable tools rather than millstones. One argument might be that the procedures are no more than the codification of good practice. So, for example, the disciplinary procedure represents a helpful prompt for managers, encouraging them to follow actions they should take in any case. Moreover, by not following procedure they potentially lay themselves and their employer open to the likelihood of appeals, time spent at an employment tribunal, and ultimately financial penalties. A second argument might be that, by breaking rules or condoning new custom and practice, this merely lays down the seeds of greater trouble. For example, if line managers concede demands to employees in exchange for greater co-operation to meet a production target, this can create an expectation that all extra effort will be so rewarded. Thirdly, the observance of procedures sets the tone for dealing with other issues in the workplace. If managers are seen to be fair and prepared to follow procedures, it is much more likely that employees will behave likewise if they are unhappy with some aspect of management behaviour. Rather than taking industrial action to settle differences, employees are encouraged to ensure that procedures are exhausted first. This allows employers to maintain production or services while resolving problems at work.

Procedures therefore have a role in giving line managers a clear perspective on the direction in which the organisation is moving, its objectives, and the general standards applied in relation to all aspects of the employment relationship. While line managers may not have the time to become experts in all these matters, they should know the broad parameters of actions, as well as where and when to look for advice. HR specialists clearly play a key role both in providing information and acting as a sounding board. IRS research into managing discipline at work (Welfare 2006) demonstrated that line managers increasingly take responsibility for disciplinary procedures and that almost nine out of 10 organisations trained line managers to deal with grievance and disciplinary issues, with coaching from HR staff as a popular option. Over half of the 46 respondents (20 in the public sector and 26 in the private sector) reported that line managers spent up to 5% of their time on disciplinary issues, and about one-fifth estimated that line mangers spent about 10% of their time on disciplinary issues. Despite this, discipline still makes up a significant portion of the workload of HR staff. Over half of the respondents estimated that it took up 5% and approximately one-fifth that it took up 20% or more of HR staff time.

## SUPPORT FROM THE HR FUNCTION

Because HR issues are increasingly dealt with by line managers, this has implications for the type of work undertaken by HR professionals – beyond the fact that less might be employed in future. New skills are likely to become more important. For example, they might play a larger part in the formulation of HR policies and procedural frameworks – such as in recruitment or grievance handling – to ensure adherence to corporate policy and legal requirements. They might also provide expert advice and guidance on all HR matters, either through shared service centres or web-based manuals. Finally, there is likely to be an even greater demand to train line managers so that they have sufficient skills to devise a job description, conduct an interview, or deal with a request from a member of staff to change their working hours. This new role is likely to be strengthened by the effective use of information technology in areas such as absence monitoring, spreadsheets and personal records.

Hutchinson and Purcell (2007, pp.29–34) review the supportive conditions that are necessary for effective line management involvement. These include the following:

1 The HR function needs to understand that policies are implemented and brought to life by line managers and therefore there ought to be some line manager involvement in their design.

2 Training and development courses need to be taken more seriously and made compulsory, and the action points need to be embedded at the workplace to make them effective.

3 Appraisal processes could include a wider range of stakeholders, such as with 360 degree review, and self-assessment tools could help line managers to monitor their own progress.

4 The creation of a strong positive organisational culture which puts a primacy on integration of HR practices and alignment between strategic goals and the workplace.

5 A focus on key staff following the ideas developed in Chapter 4 about HR architecture.

6 Support from and active commitment of senior managers in role modelling behaviours that are important for the organisation and to line managers in particular.

In order to convince line managers to take HR more seriously, two sets of arguments can be used, both of which require HR managers to acquire better financial awareness and the ability to cost their recommendations. The first argument relates to the cost of getting things wrong and it is worthwhile estimating the financial implications of mistakes. Examples include the cost of a tribunal case for an unfair dismissal, a lapse in safety awareness resulting in an accident or the cost of lost orders due to a strike because an employee relations issue was badly handled. Organisations with a poor public relations profile can suffer costs at the recruitment stage through a lack of high quality applicants or because staff leave since the organisation has not met their expectations. Costs should also be viewed in 'softer' motivational terms reflected in low levels of productivity, unsatisfactory customer service and inadequate quality standards, or through poor levels of attendance, high levels of labour turnover, stress, and general dissatisfaction.

The second argument is about the benefits of getting it right, many of which are the converse of those outlined above. Financial benefits can accrue through the higher value that is added from each well-motivated and productive employee while public relations benefits can improve the reputation of the employer and attract high-quality applicants. Moreover, 'softer' motivational benefits can flow from low levels of absenteeism, from the positive impact on customers, and from higher levels of productivity and quality associated with high commitment HRM. Reality of course is never quite so simple and the box below raises a number of practical issues and questions about how the partnership between line managers and the HR function might be strengthened.

HRM AT WORK IN FOCUS

## Obstacles to the effective delivery of HRM

**This case concerns a local authority department, and it demonstrates that major problems can arise without clear lines of accountability and a systematic framework for relations between the HR function and line managers.**

The organisation in question has a personnel presence both at corporate and at departmental level, with some element of dotted line relationships between the two. Broadly, however, the personnel function in each department is left to get on with its own work within a framework that applies to the council as a whole. The head of HR for the department has no previous personnel experience but had worked as a line manager in the service for many years and was well-known to staff there. The chief officer for the department felt that one of his strengths was HR and was therefore keen to run this himself; indeed, he made a point of stressing that he wanted 'someone who knew the service, rather than an expert in human resources'. The other HR staff in the department were on low grades and part way through their CIPD courses at the local college. Accordingly, they had little experience of HRM beyond their current jobs but they were aware of the main professional issues.

The department was run in a very hierarchical way, and all decisions had to be approved by senior managers. Line managers were allowed relatively little freedom to make decisions, and this often resulted in long delays. Many of the front-line staff in the department had been transferred from other jobs in the council, as they were on the 'at-risk register' and had to be redeployed internally. Unfortunately, some were renowned for being difficult to manage. This led to several issues at workplace level, set within a context of an increasingly problematic employment relations agenda at national level.

During the past year, there have been problems with time-keeping, with poor performance and with fraudulent use of the council's property. In some cases, the evidence is clearly available while in others it is more difficult due to varying interpretations of the situation. The line managers have tried to address these issues, but on each occasion the matter has to be referred up the chain for a decision. It has not been unusual for there to be delays of several months whilst senior management worked out what to do. As the head of HR in the department knows so many of the staff, and had worked there himself for so long, he finds it difficult to take a hard line on disciplinary issues. This inertia is also reinforced by the fact that some of the senior managers are in a similar position.

The authority of the line managers is also undermined because long-serving front-line staff – and in particular the redeployed workers – go direct to the senior manager if they have problems and effectively short-circuit the management chain. They also ensure their views about line managers are made known across the authority. The head of department always expects to be involved in HR decisions, so this causes yet more problems. The junior HR staff – the only ones that have any professional training in the subject – are on low grades and find it difficult to gain acceptance for their views on the situation. Indeed, this lack of influence has led several of the partly qualified staff to leave the organisation in frustration.

*To think about:*

*Clearly, the situation depicted in the*

*department is a mess. What would you do to address these issues, and what advice would you provide about (a) the organisation of the HR function, (b) the authority to be vested in line managers and (c) the quality of the relationship between line managers and the HR function?*

## LEADERSHIP

Over the last decade there has been increasing interest in leadership (Mumford 2011) and how it might differ from management, certainly in the area of HRM. What is the difference between management and leadership, and does it matter? Leadership is variously seen as linked to change, transformation, culture, vision, and looking to the future, whereas management is seen as concerned with internal organisational issues such as efficiency, planning, procedures, and keeping an eye on the bottom line. In short, leadership is typically seen as doing the right thing, and management as doing things right (Iles *et al* 2010, p.256; Watson and Adamson 2010). This would imply that organisations need both managers and leaders, although in practice, individuals switch between management and leadership routinely. Christy (2010) distinguishes between strategic leadership and managerial leadership: strategic leadership involves the development of organisational strategy – this involves both vision and mission – and subsequently ensuring resources are available to achieve strategy. Management carries out the strategy and managerial leadership involves the 'creation, maintenance and development of an appropriate infrastructure for business operations, including that which involves organising the work of other people' (p.78).

In the literature, leadership is portrayed as much more exciting than management, something which initiates change and transformation in organisations, rather than a process which focuses on day-to-day activities that contribute to the achievement of shorter-term targets. This sounds very clear and simple but as ever reality is more complex (Storey 2004). There are as many theories of leadership as there are of management, and the spectrum of approaches means the former are often little different from the latter. Moreover, sceptics feel the differences are exaggerated because leadership tends to be viewed as positive and inspirational whereas management is seen as routine and mundane; this is a very superficial and inaccurate assumption.

Many publications on leadership tend to list the range of perspectives used in the literature, which is helpful but it tends towards historical description and does not attempt to categorise these more conceptually (see, for example, Bass and Bass 2009; Christy 2010). Drawing on Kempster (2009) and Cowsill and Grint (2008), we examine leadership from three perspectives: (1) those focusing solely on the traits or attributes of leaders; (2) those focusing on exchange relations between leaders and their teams; and (3) those that regard leadership as varying depending on context or situation. Of course elements of all three are relevant and Kempster (2009) argues that an integrative approach is needed, whilst Cowsill and Grint (2008) note that leaders need to be both upward and downward-facing to achieve success. In this chapter we focus on front-line and middle managers rather than CEOs/ senior managers as this is where HR practices are put into operation.

### LEADERS ARE BORN AND NOT MADE

Many of the earliest models of leadership focused on the characteristics of leaders themselves, the best known being trait-based theories (Bass and Bass 2009). These were derived from close observations of the qualities shown by well-known leaders, from politics as well as business, in order to identify the attributes that characterised their style. This approach led to a number of different models with little in common aside from a few key characteristics such as self-confidence and intelligence which appeared more frequently in these lists (Christy 2010); interestingly, this would probably be termed evidence-based management nowadays as it relies on what appear to be successful role models. In any era, different names fill these lists, but one of the most frequently quoted in recent times is Richard Branson, who combines a mixture of personal charm, entrepreneurial spirit and slightly eccentric behaviours in his approach to business. These are the qualities which managers are expected to show in their approach to work and in managing their teams, something which is quite hard to do in the context of a structured production line or fast-food chain. In brief, trait theories are based on the assumption that leaders are born and have personal characteristics that are immutable: such as charisma, inspiration, transformative ability, drive, passion, integrity and heroism.

There have been many criticisms of trait-based theories. First, by focusing on the attributes of existing leaders they tend to conservatism and do not allow space for other styles of leadership that are less visible – and possibly equally effective in practice – but take longer to have an impact. Given the desire to specify these traits and improve leadership theory, little attention was paid to the performance of these people over the longer-term. Second, since the majority of leaders have been men, they overlook any of the attributes that women may bring to bear, and especially the 'softer', more inclusive and emotionally aware skills that typically characterise their styles (Broadbridge and Hearn 2008; Alimo-Metcalfe 2010). However, some women that make it to the top of organisations have tended to adopt more masculine ways of leadership in order to progress in a male-dominated world, so perhaps not a lot can be learned here. Third, trait theories relied primarily on research undertaken in the USA and were assumed to be directly transportable to other countries and cultures; whilst there might be some purchase in this argument in the UK or other LMEs, this is highly dubious in quite different institutional and cultural regimes, as we saw in Chapter 5. As Storey (2004, p.19) notes,

> this individualised interpretation is fuelled by the media (as) business magazines are especially prone to focus on the supposed crucial impact of top managers ... Certain chief executives become lionised and company fortunes are deemed to be closely linked to the actions of these figures.

Finally, as should be apparent by now, these sorts of leadership models are totally acontextual and assumptions are made that a 'good' leader has attributes which will be successful irrespective of the situation in which they are operating; we still see examples of this when senior managers that have been successful in a private sector environment are parachuted into the public sector to turn it around, and show little awareness of the external – and often government-led – factors which shape HRM in these circumstances.

An even more serious concern is that 'heroic' or charismatic leaders may not be quite so fantastic to work for, and given their profile depends on being confident about their approach, they are unlikely to admit further development is needed. Preece and Iles (2009) illustrate that charismatic leaders are not always the heroes portrayed, but have uncertainties in relation to their work and their ability to perform in leadership development programmes. A study of Enron in which lauded leaders displayed spectacularly inappropriate behaviours – bullying and corruption – which led to the downfall of the organisation shows how emphasis on the leaders (rather than leadership) can be unhelpful (Iles *et al* 2010, p.259). There are some concerns that charismatic leaders might also be narcissistic, which can lead them to be destructive, but little is known about this as so much of the emphasis has been on their heroic displays (Padilla *et al* 2007; Mumford 2011). Based on her research, Pelletier (2010) identifies a set of dimensions which characterise toxic leader behaviour, including:

- attacks on followers' self-esteem (demeaning, ridiculing, mocking)
- lack of integrity (being deceptive, blaming others for leader's mistakes)
- abusiveness (displaying anger, coercing)

- social exclusion (excluding individuals from social functions)
- divisiveness (ostracising employees, inciting one employee to chastise another)
- promoting inequity (exhibiting favouritism, being selective in promotions)
- threats to followers' security (being aggressive, threatening employee's job security)
- laissez-faire approach (ignoring ideas, disengagement, being rigid).

REFLECTIVE ACTIVITY

Think of leaders in the business field – what names do you come up with? What attributes would you assign to them? Do you think that leaders can be successful in any situation?

How about the dark side of charismatic leaders – have you ever experienced any of these behaviours and if so were you able to do anything about it?

## LEADERS AND FOLLOWERS WORK TOGETHER IN AN EXCHANGE RELATIONSHIP

Kempster (2009, p.39) sums up this approach well with the statement, 'you cannot have a leader without followers'. Unlike trait-based theories of leadership, this approach takes the view that the relationship between a leader and those that work for them (followers) is key to assessing the value of leadership. Thus, context is considered at the micro level in relation to teams of people. In this situation, much depends on the physical and psychological make-up of the team and the way in which they interact; two approaches are considered here: transactional and transformational leadership, and leader–member exchange (LMX).

Within the field, most emphasis has been placed on the former (Storey 2004; Bass and Bass 2009; Kempster 2009). *Transactional leadership* is where leaders seek to gain commitment through the negotiation of appropriate follower behaviours comprising rewards and punishments, with the assumption that worker motivation will be achieved if the rewards are sufficiently generous. This may take the form of material/monetary rewards or positive behaviours which make people feel they have done well. Punishments are meant to be strong enough to deter employees from working against departmental goals, and take the form of disciplinary warnings and dismissals or more subtle forms of control. Given that transactional leadership relies on instrumental factors, this is only capable of generating calculative and relatively weak forms of identification which are soon lost if material rewards are no longer available – as in many organisations following the global financial crisis or when the psychological contract has broken down (Guest 2007).

By contrast, *transformational leadership* aims to develop motivation and commitment by generating and communicating a clear vision where the focus is on higher values. Transformational leaders are supposed to be able to inspire their teams to achieve higher levels of performance and encourage them to accept (or even embrace) change (Nemanich and Keller 2007). As such it may have both direct and indirect influences on work outcomes and be effective in a range of different settings. For example, Purvanova and Bono (2009) found that transformational leaders were even more effective with virtual teams than they were with face-to-face encounters, though it must be noted that their research was undertaken with college students in a laboratory setting rather than in a real-world business. The leadership scales developed by Avolio and Bass (2002) relating to transformational leadership are summarised in Fukushige and Spicer's (2011) study of Japanese and UK managers. These are:

- *Idealised influence attributed*: leaders have socialised charisma, they are perceived as being confident and powerful and viewed as focusing on higher-order ideals and ethics.

- *Idealised influence behaviours*: leaders' behaviour is centred on values, beliefs and a sense of mission, and they consider the needs of others and share risks with them.
- *Inspirational motivation*: this is done by providing meaning and challenge at work, team spirit is aroused, and enthusiasm and optimism is displayed.
- *Intellectual stimulation*: followers are encouraged to be innovative and creative by questioning assumptions, reframing problems and approaching 'old' situations in new ways.
- *Individualised consideration*: special attention is paid to each team member so as to aid achievement and growth by two-way communication and 'management by walking about'.

Despite being much more realistic than the trait models, transformational leadership also comes in for criticism. First, it is idealised and predicated upon a specific type of organisational setting where followers are expected to question assumptions and seek input into decision making and where leaders accept that they do not have all the answers. Whilst this might work well in a knowledge-based organisation, it is hard to see how such an open and participative style could function in a traditional manufacturing or service setting where rules and conformance to standards are essential. Imagine asking team members for their views about how to sort out a nuclear meltdown once it has erupted or the pilot asking the crew what they think is the best way to deal with engine failure. Second, as with other leadership approaches, these behaviours are implicitly drawn from organisations in the developed world. This seems dated when we consider pushes for globalisation, knowledge sharing, and de-layering of organisations which disperse leadership – operating at all levels of an organisation and even across global and inter-organisational boundaries. Abdalla and Pinnington's (2012) comparison of transactional and transformational leadership in the UAE public sector shows the latter did deliver some immediate benefits – such as enhanced employee commitment and improved performance – in this different cultural and institutional context. However, as the programme continued, employees reported seeing no great difference between the two styles, and indeed claimed that the transactional contingent reward scheme was the main driving force in motivating them to improve performance. Third, even though followers are taken into account in these theories of leadership, the emphasis is still on leaders and their behaviour rather than equally focused on followers and leaders (Kellerman 2008). Moreover, assumptions are made that all followers are keen to take part in decision-making, which may not be the case in many organisations, and that they are all treated in an equal, albeit different, fashion. More recent research on LMX addresses this better.

*Leader–member exchange theory* states that it is the quality of the relationship between an employee and their immediate line manager which impacts on employee outcomes and performance rather than supervisor–follower relations being exactly the same across the whole group (see, for example, Wayne and Green 1993; Liden *et al* 2004; Ilies *et al* 2007). This explains why employees in the same team or organisation might have different experiences of HRM and their supervisor since it is argued that the quality of relationships between employees (members) and their line managers (leaders) vary (Ma and Qu 2010). The relationship between the two is thought of as an exchange between two parties or 'dyad', whereby some employees have closer relationships with their supervisors than others. They therefore experience high LMX which gives them access to higher levels of resources, support and advice from their line managers; in return, this elicits desirable discretionary behaviours and attitudes from employees. High LMX relationships are characterised by a strong degree of trust and interaction, support, and formal and informal rewards according to Ilies *et al*'s (2007) meta-analysis of 50 independent samples covering over 9,000 respondents. Similarly, Gerstner and Day (1997) showed in their meta-analysis that the quality of the LMX relationship was positively and significantly related to employee job performance, satisfaction and commitment. Other studies show links between high LMX, favourable employee attitudes and higher levels of engagement in collaborative problem-solving (Liu and Ipe 2010), with organisational citizenship behaviour (Ilies *et al* 2007) and with organisational justice (Piccolo *et al* 2008), among other factors. This seems to hold across different samples and countries, as the box below shows.

HRM AT WORK IN FOCUS

## High LMX pays off for expatriates in different ways

**MNCs in China**

Given the growth of Western-owned MNCs that now operate in China, it is important to assess the role that leadership plays in generating commitment for expatriates based in the host country. This study investigated the influence of high LMX on 162 expatriates working for 37 subsidiaries in China who had worked there for an average of nearly two years. The majority of the expatriates were from other parts of the Pacific Rim, though a handful has been moved from the USA. The findings showed that high LMX had a significant impact on the affective commitment of expatriates, both directly and in moderating the influence of perceived organisational support from the parent company. The implications from this study are that supervisors are critically important, and along with programmes to support expatriates during transition, MNCs should also look into coaching supervisors on how to build stronger relationships with new staff from other countries. Training on cross-cultural awareness could also be valuable to ensure that expatriates are better prepared for the challenges that face them in a different country.

**Expatriates from US-owned MNCs**

This study compared the roles that different leaders, from the host and the home country, played in the life of 206 expatriates. High LMX was found to be important for both sets of relationships, that is, between the expatriate and their host **and** home country supervisors, but in different ways. Relations with the former were particularly important for local (short-term) goals of expatriate assignments, such as settling in and adjusting to work in a foreign location, whilst the latter were critical in longer-term issues concerning job fit, career growth and performance whilst overseas. This is interesting because it shows how LMX can relate to an individual's relationship with more than one supervisor. In order to minimise tensions between these different supervisory relationships and goals, employers need to ensure that both sets of supervisors are aware of the wider purpose of expatriation, and the fact that it should be seen as just one stage in an individual's career.

Sources: Adapted from Liu and Ipe (2010); Benson and Pattie (2009).

Furthermore, Liden *et al* (2004) argue that line managers play a very important role in socialising employees, not simply by ensuring they understand the formal content of their job description but also in initiating them into group cultures, introducing them to contacts within their own social network and shaping their understanding of the cultural norms of the workplace. LMX theory has also been used to explain how transformational leaders can generate increased task performance from employees, to some extent because 'they are sensitive to follower contributions … and reciprocate in ways that build follower self-worth … Effective leaders link achievement of organisational goals to follower fulfilment of self-development goals, with the former advancing the latter' (Wang *et al* 2005, p. 430). In HRM, LMX theory seems to have caught on as a way to analyse the relationships between managers and their teams in a range of different areas of practice. For example, Lam *et al* (2007) used LMX to consider performance management and feedback-seeking behaviours from their supervisors, Kang and Stewart (2007) linked LMX with human resource development, whilst Cox *et al* (2009), Farndale *et al* (2011) and Marchington and Suter (2012) have used this idea in their analyses of EIP and voice. In the case of the latter, it was found that informal EIP was closely connected with the branch managers' willingness to promote open relations and to seek advice from certain trusted employees.

As with other leadership theories, LMX is not immune from criticism. Like trait and exchange theories, it focuses on the micro level and therefore ignores wider forces that shape and privilege certain leadership styles over others depending on context. Second, because it links leader behaviour directly with the attitudes and performance of their teams, strong LMX could promote high levels of employee commitment to their supervisors with no knock-on effect to the organisation level. In other words, the attachment and identification of workers is to their line manager rather than to the organisation as a whole, which could be fine in the short-term but raise problems were the supervisor to leave. The third concern is the most worrying. Since LMX refers to dyadic relations, and it is accepted that the quality of these can vary between individual workers and their manager, some workers are likely to benefit from preferential treatment whilst others suffer from weaker – and perhaps negative – interpersonal relations. This can lead to accusations of favouritism with the in-group receiving support from their supervisor whilst members of the out-group are in danger of being marginalised, and even losing their jobs (Ma and Qu 2010). Moreover, LMX could be seen to explicitly challenge principles of equality and consistency which are important for social harmony and essential for well-being and satisfaction, as well as being morally desirable. This could result in low status workers (in LMX terms) disliking and distrusting high status workers, who in return start to reject and show disrespect for their lower status colleagues (Hooper and Martin 2008).

## LEADERSHIP IS SHAPED BY SITUATION RATHER THAN BEING AN ENDURING QUALITY

We have already illustrated how the trait and exchange models overlook the contextual pressures that shape leadership, and for this reason they are deficient in at least some respects. It is unlikely that the leadership skills needed for surviving in the desert or negotiating access through a violent country would be similar to those deemed appropriate for leading a group of scientists or lawyers. Yet more worrying is that some of the research which examines leadership uses college students as subjects, in the worst cases allocating them roles before setting up short-term tasks that act as proxies for real-world experience. To use such methods for topics as complex as leadership, which depend on relationships developed over time, is bizarre at best and unreliable at worst given the contexts within which leadership takes place.

There is a range of contingent factors which can influence appropriate leadership styles, similar to those that were examined in Chapters 4 and 5. Some of the most important factors are:

1 *Differences between institutions and cultures in different countries.* As we saw in Chapter 5, there are major differences between countries that can influence what are deemed

acceptable styles of leader behaviour and leader–follower relations. Countries that are high on power distance or collectivism are likely to favour leaders that use a more directive style as opposed to countries that are low on these indices where supportive leadership styles tend to be more prevalent; see Wendt *et al* (2009) for an evaluation of this issue using data from 80 countries. Legal and institutional norms can also influence leadership; for example, leadership is likely to vary dramatically between countries where there is strong legal support for managerial prerogatives and those where industrial democracy is enshrined in law.

2 *Differences between sectors*: this mirrors the debate about high and low road styles of HRM, with leadership in quality enhancement (QE) organisations tending towards involvement of staff whilst in cost reduction (CR) organisations it is likely to be more directive. To some extent this relates to the competitive pressures which organisations in different market segments face but it also has a cost element. Differences can also arise between private and public sector organisations due to more direct pressures from central government in the latter compared with the former (Currie *et al* 2009). Any study of leadership in the public sector which ignores this wider environment lacks credibility.

3 *Differences between organisations due to structure, size and CEO*: leadership styles are bound to vary due to these factors, not least because the larger the organisation the harder it is to promote informal and participative leadership, in much the same way as style depends on the size and complexity of the team being managed (Hutchinson and Purcell 2010). At the same time the CEO might be able to champion a style and reinforce this through targeted recruitment and selection, appraisal and training policies.

4 *Differences due to labour market conditions and occupational groups being led*: leadership needs to take into account the qualifications and experience of followers and their knowledge and expectations at the workplace. Whilst in broad terms, transformational leaders are likely to be more successful in situations that call for significant employee input and transactional leaders in situations where rules need to be followed, external labour market conditions can also cause shifts in what is perceived as appropriate leadership. If the labour market is tight and quality replacements are hard to find, then a more participative style which recognises followers' concerns would be more likely to keep labour turnover down and generate support and engagement from staff.

## CONCLUSIONS

This chapter has focused on the role of line managers who are now expected to take significant responsibility for HRM, even in organisations with well-staffed HR functions. There are good reasons why this makes sense, not least because HRM comes to life at the supervisory interface and it is here that, irrespective of the quality of HR policies, many of the mistakes are made. Part of the problem is that line managers have often been given responsibilities without sufficient consideration of the skills they possess, the amount of work they are expected to do in areas other than HRM, and regularly without much training in people management. On some occasions they are not even interested in or committed to the HR policies that their organisation uses, viewing them as inappropriate, irrelevant or nonsensical. Support is needed to ensure that line managers are either appointed with requisite skills or are given proper training in HRM which is embedded in the organisation, rather than short sessions on the latest fad that hits the business press. Recent times have seen the rise of leadership as a concept which, for all its exciting and positive undertones, differs little from management in many key respects, and often focuses solely on leaders rather than their relationship with followers. Indeed, at its worst, this literature presents images of heroic leaders achieving nirvana with the wave of a magic wand, until an external shock to the system blows them off course.

EXPLORE FURTHER

BENSON, G. and PATTIE, M. (2009) 'The comparative roles of home and host country supervisors in the expatriate experience', *Human Resource Management*, Vol.48, No.1, 49–68.

CONWAY, E. and MONKS, K. (2011) 'Change from below: the role of middle managers in mediating paradoxical change', *Human Resource Management Journal*, Vol.21, No.2, 190–203.

HUTCHINSON, S. and PURCELL, J. (2010) 'Managing ward managers for roles in HR in the NHS: overworked and under-resourced', *Human Resource Management Journal*, Vol.20, No.4, 357–74.

KELLERMAN, B. (2008) *Followership: how followers are creating change and changing leaders*. Boston: Harvard University Press

KEMPSTER, S. (2009) *How Managers have Learnt to Lead: exploring the development of leadership practice*. Basingstoke: Palgrave Macmillan. Chapters 1 and 2 in particular.

KHILJI, S. and WANG, X. (2006) '"Intended" and "implemented" HRM: the missing linchpin in strategic human resource management research', *International Journal of Human Resource Management*, Vol.17, No.7, 1171–89.

McCANN, L., MORRIS, J. and HASSARD, J. (2008) 'Normalised intensity: the new labour process of middle management', *Journal of Management Studies*, Vol.45, No.2, 343–71.

PELLETIER, K. (2010) 'Leader toxicity: an empirical investigation of toxic behaviour and rhetoric', *Leadership*, Vol.6, No.4, 373–89.

PURCELL, J. and HUTCHINSON, S. (2007a) 'Front-line managers as agents in the HRM-performance causal chain: theory, analysis and evidence', *Human Resource Management Journal*, Vol.17, No.1, 3–20.

TOWNSEND, K., WILKINSON, A. and ALLAN, C. (2012) 'Mixed signals in HRM: the HRM role of hospital line managers', *Human Resource Management Journal*, forthcoming.

PART 3

# HRM PRACTICES AND PROCESSES

CHAPTER 8

# Resourcing and Talent Management

## LEARNING OUTCOMES

By the end of this chapter, readers should be able to:

- undertake the main aspects of resourcing and talent management processes
- operate, support and evaluate cost-effective processes for recruiting and retaining the right calibre of staff in their own organisation
- contribute to the design, implementation and evaluation of selection decisions.

In addition, readers should understand and be able to explain:

- links between human resource planning, talent management, recruitment and selection and other aspects of HRM
- the nature of the recruitment process and its principal components
- the major advantages and disadvantages of the most important selection methods, and their contribution to organisational effectiveness.

## INTRODUCTION

Resourcing and talent management is a critical feature of HRM in all organisations irrespective of their size, structure, sector or country location (Cappelli 2008; Collings and Mellahi 2009; Taylor 2010). It incorporates a range of different aspects of HRM including decisions about HR planning, job descriptions and person specifications, recruitment and selection. Performance can be improved as decisions made during these stages of the employment contract have a major impact on how new employees fit within the organisation and contribute thereafter to the achievement of its goals. Whilst the literature on HR planning is limited and relatively technical compared with that available in the burgeoning area of talent management, the former is crucial in ensuring the right number of staff is available at any one time. Similarly, whilst material on selection is relatively widespread and sophisticated due to contributions from organisational psychologists seeking ways to improve the reliability and validity of decisions, the literature on recruitment is limited and often very practical in nature. Again, this is slightly strange given selection decisions rely totally on the employer being able to generate a pool of suitable applicants from which to choose the right candidate. Thus, each area of resourcing and talent management is vital to reduce the chances of poor selection decisions and prevent having to deal with their implications in terms of high levels of labour turnover, recruitment and retention costs, poor interpersonal relations and problems with product quality and customer service. These can occur not only by recruiting someone who is under-qualified but also by hiring overqualified staff that soon become bored. Selecting the *right* person for the task is what matters. This chapter reviews resourcing and talent management, paying particular attention to recruitment and selection, from HR planning through to appointment. Care is needed at each stage to ensure the organisation continues to convey the message it wants to in order to maintain its reputation in the market place; corporate advertising in general and for recruits in particular has an impact upon applications (Collins and Han 2007).

## HUMAN RESOURCE PLANNING, TURNOVER AND RETENTION

At a time when world markets were more stable and predictable, HR planning was a prominent feature of HRM. There was an extensive literature on the topic and leading organisations planned future employment needs, especially of managers, in a systematic way. This was referred to as the 'golden age of manpower planning', and the techniques in favour at the time drew heavily upon statistical techniques (Bowey 1975; Bramham 1994; Sisson and Timperley 1994). While some HRM texts still include a chapter on HR planning (for example, Taylor 2010), the majority (for example, Boxall *et al* 2007a; Storey 2007; Wilkinson *et al* 2010) no longer bother. In the context of 'flexible and agile' organisations, HR planning conveys images of bureaucracy, rigidity, and a failure to comprehend the limitations of planning in an uncertain environment – and events since 2008 would reinforce the view that that planning is not viable in a turbulent competitive environment. As Taylor (2005, p.98) reports, the problem with forecasting is 'its reliance on past experience to predict future developments (and) the extrapolation of past trends' to predict future scenarios.

There is a danger that this can be used to justify ad hoc solutions, but as Taylor (2010) reminds us planning remains critically important during turbulent times, if only to ensure that employers have staff of the right quality and quantity available at the right time. The decision by many firms not to lay off key staff during the recession but to retain them on reduced hours or allow sabbaticals shows there were concerns about having to re-recruit at a future time when demand outstripped the supply of suitable labour. Moreover, pressures to control labour costs and protect profit margins at the same time as engaging the workforce in a more agile and scalable way (Nijjsen and Paauwe 2012) could imply an increased emphasis on HR planning by employers, both in terms of their own employees and those employed by sub-contractors down the supply chain (Marchington and Kynighou 2012).

### REFLECTIVE ACTIVITY

Do you believe HR planning is worthwhile in your organisation (or one with which you are familiar)? What do you see as the organisational benefits of spending time making plans about future employment projections?

HR planning can be regarded as important for the following reasons:

1 *Clear links between business and HR plans* – This linkage can be seen in two ways. First, in terms of HRM 'fitting' with broader strategic plans, and HR delivering precisely what the business requires. Second, the relationship between corporate and HR plans can be seen interactively with a recognition that longer term business goals can be disrupted through shortages of labour. Either way, HR planning is a major facilitator of competitive advantage.

2 *Better control over staffing costs and numbers employed* – Employers need to know about anticipated staffing needs, irrespective of whether these are expected to grow or decline.

This helps to match supply and demand so management can decide whether to recruit from the external labour market, relocate staff, or prepare for cutbacks to control staff costs (Taylor 2010). For example, if future demand is uncertain or known to be highly variable, greater use might be made of subcontracting or temporary contracts to shift the risk to agencies and protect their own staff from redundancy and redeployment (Cooke *et al* 2004).

3 *Better informed judgements about the skills and attitude mix in the organisation* – While it is important to employ the right number of staff, it is also critical to achieve the right skills mix among the workforce. Choices about the skill mix can be linked to decisions about the future shape of the business, and adjustments planned in advance. For example, if an organisation wants to become more customer-oriented, decisions are required about whether existing staff can be retrained or new recruits are needed, or indeed if work could be subcontracted instead.

4 *Maintain a profile of current staff* – Without accurate figures on staff employed and their breakdown by grade and position, it is impossible for employers to decide how equality targets can be achieved (Liff 2000; p.103). This can provide profiles in terms of gender, ethnic origin, age and disability, a task made easier by the use of ICT packages.

'Hard' HR plans have been applied to three areas: forecasts of future demand for labour; forecasts of internal supply; and forecasts of external supply. Each is considered below, with a particular focus on forecasts of internal supply since this has been where HR has contributed most.

## FORECASTING FUTURE DEMAND

There are two techniques for assessing future demand for labour: the objective and the subjective. The former relies upon projection of past trends but also takes into account shifts brought about by changes in technology and organisational goals. Past ratios are extrapolated to indicate how much or what type of labour is required in the future, say in relation to demand for customer service staff at different times of the day, or the use of part-time rather than full-time posts. In schools, for example, norms have been established for the number of full-time equivalent (FTE) students per member of staff, or class sizes deemed ideal for effective learning. Arguments for replacements typically use established figures, and comparisons made with schools in similar situations. However, technological change can alter demand for some occupations and governments introduce policies which undermine the value of simple extrapolations.

Fears that 'objective' systems are not responsive to customer needs have fuelled arguments that subjective methods are more useful. At its simplest, this may be no more than managerial judgement about future needs and even speculation based on limited data. Subjective approaches can be either 'top-down' or 'bottom-up', or a mixture of both. A top-down approach relies heavily on estimates from senior managers who ought to have a clear idea about the direction in which the organisation is moving. In bottom-up systems, conversely, departmental managers estimate future requirements based upon their experience and judgement at the front end of the organisation (Walker 1992); this is susceptible to 'inflated' demands for fear of losing out. In reality, both methods are combined to arrive at meaningful estimates of future demand.

Forecasting demand relies on product market projections, a task rarely undertaken by HR specialists but more likely involving business planners or finance managers. It is much easier to forecast future demand in certain sectors than in others. For example, based upon past projections, reasonable assumptions can be made about *overall* levels of demand for health care, primary school education or food products in the next five years, thus allowing for relatively sensible estimates of future labour demand. However, even in these relatively simple cases it is still difficult to estimate the numbers of patients, schoolchildren or shoppers anticipated at a *specific* hospital, school or supermarket, given mobility patterns and, in principle, a wider degree of choice for consumers. Since classes at school are run in broad unit sizes (say, 30), problems arise if an extra 10 children are enrolled across two age groups. This can also have major implications for facilities, buildings and infrastructure. In addition, the growing fragmentation of education and healthcare systems is making future estimates more untenable, whilst in more uncertain markets, decisions made by MNCs to shift subsidiaries and employment around the globe makes long-term planning of labour needs even more difficult. The 2011 CIPD survey indicated the steps taken by employers to cope with the recession (see Table 17).

**Table 17 Resourcing and talent practices**

| **Sample of practices implemented in 2011 by 582 organisations** | **Respondents using this practice (%)** |
|---|---|
| Developing more talent in-house | 66 |
| Continuing to recruit key talent in niche areas | 59 |
| Reducing reliance on recruitment agencies | 47 |
| Redeploying people into new roles | 44 |
| Taking actions to improve ways of identifying quality candidates | 35 |
| Increasing the number of interim/contract staff recruited | 29 |
| Offering sabbaticals, career breaks and additional holidays | 12 |
| Reducing graduate recruitment | 8 |

Source: Adapted from Chartered Institute of Personnel and Development/Hays (2011d).

## REFLECTIVE ACTIVITY

Discuss these findings with colleagues to identify why you think these approaches are being taken by employers. Does this bear any resemblance to the approach taken by your own employer or one with which you are familiar?

### FORECASTING INTERNAL SUPPLY

Once forecasts are made about potential demand for labour, decisions are needed about the balance between external recruitment and internal staff development or, if appropriate, workforce reductions. The principal techniques relate to internal job/grade movements and wastage/labour turnover, and these can highlight a range of organisational problems. Although important to calculate labour flows within the organisation, few employers chart these changes carefully in order to assess where gaps are likely to appear in the future; this can be done by a process called system dynamics (Grössler and Zock 2010) used by a large German service sector employer, but most firms use less sophisticated approaches. Data on labour turnover is collected by most large organisations but sometimes not used effectively, whilst small organisations rarely have such data to hand. High levels of labour turnover, for example, can indicate problems with just about any HR practice – inadequate recruitment and selection methods, poorly designed or uncompetitive pay systems, and ineffective grievance and disciplinary procedures. External factors, such as competition for labour in the area or poor public transport provision, also contribute to these problems.

Two schools of thought dominate research on turnover: the labour market/economic and the psychological (Morrell *et al* 2001; Morrell and Arnold 2007). The former focuses on external forces – sometimes referred to as 'pull' factors – such as the level of unemployment and the availability of alternative jobs locally, nationally or globally depending on the occupation in question; some of these are beyond the control of the employer or can only be tackled through an employers' organisation or by government policy; we explore these below when external supply of labour is addressed. The latter focuses on individuals and their decisions to quit, often termed 'push' factors, which relate labour turnover to factors such as satisfaction, commitment and job insecurity, as well as to occupational characteristics (Batt *et al* 2002; Taplin *et al* 2003). Laine *et al* (2009) sampled over 32,000 nurses in 10 European countries to establish whether or not intention to quit was related to job insecurity; this was found to hold across the sample aside from Poland and Slovakia. Smith *et al* (2011) examined the relationship between HR practices and turnover, using both British and Australian data. They found a very positive relationship between employee retention and (a) learning and training, (b) employee voice and (c) flexible working time practices. Unlike most studies, low pay did not seem to increase turnover and high pay did not aid retention.

Most authors agree neither school is capable on its own of providing satisfactory explanations of or predictions for labour turnover. The approach taken by Morrell and Arnold (2007, pp.1689–91) is interesting as they use a *retrospective* procedure to differentiate between the primary (P) and any other (O) reasons for turnover, as well as factors that might have prevented the person quitting (A). For example, in one of their cases, P was boredom, O was no chance of promotion and A was that something could have been done to increase pay. In another case, P was the inability to work three days per week, O was dissatisfaction with their immediate manager, whilst A was an agreement to allow part-time working. This can highlight why people leave and how this could have been avoided.

Two measures are typically used to calculate rates of labour turnover. First is the **wastage rate**, which divides the number of staff leaving in a given period by the number of staff employed overall. In Figure 5 below both the numerator and the divisor can include different elements. For example, leavers may refer solely to those quitting voluntarily, or it can include those made redundant, those at the end of fixed-term contracts or those dismissed, each of which inflates the numerator. The divisor can be calculated on the basis of the number employed at the beginning of the year, at the end, or the average of the two figures. Because comparisons are inevitably complicated by this, it is essential to know how these statistics are derived before drawing conclusions. Exit interviews may shed some light on the problem but people are often unwilling to provide an honest answer to explain their resignation. A more serious problem with these indices, however, is that they do not differentiate between leavers in terms of their length of service, grade or gender. As Morrell *et al* (2001, p.222) note, 'this is because any single-figure measure of turnover will be inadequate in so far as it treats all those who leave as a homogenous group'.

**Figure 5 Indices of labour turnover**

$$\text{Wastage rate} = \frac{\text{Number of staff leaving in one year}}{\text{Average number employed in year}} \times 100$$

$$\text{Stability rate} = \frac{\text{Number of staff with at least one year's service at date}}{\text{Number of staff employed exactly one year before}} \times 100$$

The second measure is the **stability index**. Here, the number of staff with at least one year's service at a certain date is divided by overall numbers employed one year earlier; Figure 5 also shows this calculation. Stability indices identify the proportion of long-term staff and the extent to which the turnover problem is specific to new recruits. This latter phenomenon is referred to as the 'induction crisis' as it occurs within the first few months of employment when people find the job is rather different from what they expected, or that their previous post may not have been that bad after all. Overall, about 20% of workers leave within the first six months and one-third within the first two years, a figure which varies across employment, so it is important that HR practitioners are aware of the rate for their industry, occupational group and type of firm, for example. Taplin *et al* (2003, p.1044) found a turnover rate of 26.5% in the US clothing industry, with 45% leaving during the first three months and only one-third lasting beyond a year; small workplaces suffered most.

The annual CIPD Resourcing and Talent Planning Surveys provide useful information about current levels of labour turnover. In 2011, this was just 12.5% compared with 25% in 2000 and 18% in 2007. Most people left voluntarily, rather than being forced to leave through the ending of a fixed-term contract, dismissal or redundancy, but that is likely to change significantly as the public sector cuts take effect from the latter part of 2011. Table 18 shows how rates of labour turnover vary; for example both in 2007 and 2011, private sector services and voluntary, community and not-for-profit organisations had the highest rates whilst manufacturing and production and public sector services were lower. It is also apparent that voluntary turnover dropped dramatically over this period due to insecurity and the lack of alternative jobs following the global financial crisis. Data on variations in labour turnover by occupation stopped in 2009; at that time, senior managers and directors were least likely to leave whilst all other groups had similar rates of turnover. The 2011 survey does, however, indicate how difficult it was to retain different groups of staff as Table 18 shows clearly; managers and professional staff were hardest to retain whilst manual workers, administrative and secretarial staff and senior managers were less of a problem. Costs of replacing people that left also vary between occupations, and once again managerial and professional staff were much more expensive to replace. It is important for employers to take into account the full cost of labour turnover; this includes not only recruitment costs such as advertising and agency fees but also cover for vacancies, selection panels and induction for new staff. Given these costs, we would expect employers to take actions to retain staff. Table 18 shows the most widely used approaches were to improve line managers' people skills, improve induction, increase learning and development opportunities, extend employee involvement, improve selection techniques and improve pay. These are addressed both in this chapter and elsewhere in the book.

**Table 18 Labour turnover fact file**
**Labour turnover (voluntary and all leavers) differentiated by sector (2007 and 2011)**

| Industry sector | % all leavers (2007 data in brackets) | % voluntary turnover (2007 data in brackets) |
|---|---|---|
| Manufacturing and production | 9.3 (13.4) | 3.7 (8.7) |
| Voluntary, community and not for profit | 13.1 (15.2) | 7.0 (12.9) |
| Private sector services | 13.8 (22.6) | 8.7 (14.5) |
| Public sector services | 8.5 (13.7) | 3.4 (7.8) |

n = 173 for 2011 UK employers, 235 for 2007 for UK and Irish employers

Have labour turnover rates changed recently? What factors might help to explain this and how should organisations respond to this situation? Look at CIPD surveys to update these figures.

Whilst assessing costs might be useful for budget control, it is crucial to recognise the limitations in these calculations. The most problematic is that all cases of labour turnover are treated in the same way, with no allowance for performance levels and potential of the employees who leave compared with those who stay at the organisation. Clearly, managers may be happy if a poor performer were to leave, and there are suggestions that employers actually encourage turnover if future demand is uncertain so they do not end up 'carrying' staff (Smith *et al* 2004, p.375). However, if turnover is high among high-flyers or those with experience, and those who remain are all poor performers or lack ambition, this can have serious consequences for the organisation. If the objective is to reduce costs, a high rate of labour turnover could actually be advantageous because employers can use temporary employment agencies rather than recruit their own staff direct (Rubery *et al* 2004; Smith *et al* 2004). Another question is whether there is an optimum level of labour turnover, just

**Retention difficulties by occupational category (%) in 2011**

| Occupational group | % reporting difficulties |
|---|---|
| Senior managers and directors | 7 |
| Managers and professionals/specialists | 28 |
| Administrative and secretarial | 9 |
| Technical | 21 |
| Services (customer, personal, protective and sales) | 13 |
| Manual/craft | 6 |

n = 601; base = UK

Source: Adapted from Chartered Institute of Personnel and Development/Hays (2011d).

**Steps taken specifically to address staff retention (%) in 2010**

| Step taken by employer | Used in 2010 (%) | Most effective (%) |
|---|---|---|
| **Most widely used and effective** | | |
| Improve line managers' people skills | 39 | 31 |
| Increase learning and development opportunities | 38 | 34 |
| Improve induction process | 38 | 22 |
| Improve employee involvement | 34 | 24 |
| Improve selection techniques | 30 | 25 |
| Improve pay | 27 | 23 |
| **Least widely used and effective** | | |
| Created clearer career paths | 18 | 2 |
| Redesigned jobs to make them more satisfying | 11 | 8 |
| Improved physical working conditions | 15 | 7 |

n = 559; base = UK

Source: Adapted from Chartered Institute of Personnel and Development/Hays (2011d).

sufficient to 'churn' the internal labour market and keep new recruits coming in, or whether the costs of turnover make most cases expensive and unwanted (Glebbeek and Bax 2004). A range between 6 and 10 per cent is quoted but it is neither sensible nor worthwhile to rely on quantitative information without analysing the characteristics of leavers.

### FORECASTING EXTERNAL SUPPLY

Most texts on HR planning devote little attention to forecasts of external supply and it probably explains why so many employers are shocked to discover there are skill shortages or a lack of suitably qualified staff when recruiting. The so-called 'demographic time-bomb' in the 1990s was a good illustration of this (Taylor 2005). Due to a decline in the birth rate in the late 1970s, it was apparent that the number of school and college leavers entering the labour market in the early to mid-1990s would be significantly lower than in previous years. This stimulated recruitment and advertising schemes designed to attract school leavers, but also new policies to retain existing female and elderly staff, and employment of individuals past the normal age of retirement. Since 2009, the problem is an oversupply of labour, particularly school leavers and recent graduates.

Several factors shape supply from the external labour market, both at a local and a national/EU level, and most developed economies have seen a rise in migrant workers who do jobs unable to attract sufficient numbers of applicants from the indigenous population. In addition, shortages of skilled workers mean that migrant workers fill gaps in the economy at higher levels as well. Local labour market information is important when recruiting manual or office workers whereas national and global trends and educational developments matter more for managers and professionals. Broadly, the major factors influencing external labour supply *locally* include:

- levels of unemployment and qualified staff in the travel-to-work area
- opening or closure of other workplaces which compete for the same types of labour
- cost of housing and availability of transport to and from work
- reputation of the employer compared with that of others in the area, measured by such things as wage levels, working conditions, and general public relations image.

The major factors influencing labour supply at a *national* level, and by implication locally, include:

- levels of unemployment in general, and in particular occupations
- number of graduates in general, and in specific fields
- UK and EU legal frameworks governing issues such as working time, equal opportunities and employment protection
- government and industry-wide training and development schemes.

## TALENT MANAGEMENT

Although talent management currently attracts significant interest, it seems to be a catch-all for so many different areas of HRM. It is seen as critical for growth and competitiveness and is a key priority for MNCs that recognise the importance of having sufficient global managers with the right skills (Collings and Mellahi 2009; McDonnell *et al* 2010a). There is also agreement that talent needs to be retained during recession to ensure sustainability, but organisations do not always identify their most talented employees. Drawing on the work of Beardwell *et al* (2010) and Scullion and Collings (2011), the main reasons for the growth of interest in talent management are:

- emphasis on talent for competitive edge and future survival
- lack of leadership talent, particularly of managers that can work across cultural/geographic boundaries

- aging populations and loss of baby boomers means loss of experience
- changed values and attitudes of younger workers and the concept of boundary-less careers results in less loyalty to organisations.

Talent management is about the identification, nurture, progress, reward, and retention of key individuals who can aid the development of organisational sustainability. Talent management therefore impacts on a wide range of resourcing decisions, such as HR planning, recruitment and selection, employee retention and outsourcing. Moreover, it can be seen to impact on HRM as a whole as recruiters see talent management in terms of getting the best candidates, trainers regard it as concerned with development, and reward experts link it with performance management. Broadly there is a distinction between the exclusive and the inclusive definitions of talent management:

1 The *exclusive* view. This derives from work at McKinsey where the term the 'war for talent' was first used (Michaels *et al* 2001) in anticipation of shortages in leadership talent. They saw talent management as identifying a small number of individuals who could make a big impact on organisations. Employees are graded from A to C, and typically the top 20% would be graded 'A' and resources focused on them. Many organisations subscribe to this approach and target senior managers or those with high potential as part of succession planning.

2 The *inclusive* view. This is concerned with the opportunity for ***all*** employees to reach their full potential, and is used synonymously with HRM focusing in particular on recruitment, leadership, career development, and workforce planning. Even though this focuses on all employees, it also ignores key elements of HRM such as employment relations and pluralist views of the employment relationship.

Collings and Mellahi (2009, p.304) define strategic talent management as 'activities and processes that involve the systematic identification of key positions which differentially contribute to the organisation's sustainable advantage, the development of a talent pools of high potential and high performing incumbents to fill these roles, and the development of a differentiated human resource architecture to facilitate filling these positions with competent incumbents and to ensure their continued commitment to the organisation'; see Chapter 4 for discussion of HR architecture.

There are obvious dangers in adopting the exclusive model and lavishing scarce resources upon the few as, whether talent is sourced externally or internally, mistakes can be made. Recruitment and selection, and performance management systems do not always accurately determine individuals' potential for inclusion in the talent pool. Internally, those who make a difference may be missed as it is not always easy to identify pivotal strategic positions in the organisation. Where a few employees are favoured over the majority, this limits the development of social capital and undermines teams, networks and trust relations in the organisation (Beardwell *et al* 2010). Favours given to an elite group can reduce motivation and commitment elsewhere with negative consequences for equality and diversity as Harris and Foster (2010) show, with tensions between talent management and an embedded ethos of equality, diversity and fairness in the public sector. Although the role of talent pools was recognised, this was counterbalanced by the need to promote positive action in relation to women, ethnic minorities and those with disabilities. Similarly, if the training budget is being squeezed, decisions have to be made whether to apply resources to the few, or maintain commitment to spending on all; focusing this on a few talented individuals may be counterproductive, especially for front-line managers who are being asked to meet more stretching targets. Furthermore, getting rid of 'C' graded personnel is naturally fraught, as is a policy of filling all positions with 'A' performers. Both would be unrealistic for many organisations and actually non-strategic when, for many jobs, adequate performance is enough (Lewis and Heckman 2006). The case of Enron, seen as a shining example of one of the best talent companies by McKinsey, shows how dangerous it can be to focus on A-grade performers.

Talent management is a key priority for MNCs (Collings and Mellahi 2009) because leadership skills are scarce, a problem which is exacerbated by requirements for people to be geographically mobile and to have cultural awareness as well as a global perspective. MNCs can choose between expatriates, host-country based or internationally mobile professionals, or a mix of all three (Harvey and Moeller 2009). The choice is determined partly by supply and demand for talent (for example, a limited pool of prepared expatriates) but worsened by poor succession planning. For example, home versus host country cultural issues need to be addressed because managing talent across subsidiaries is particularly difficult and performance reviews may need to take on board both short- and long-term issues which are seen differently at the centre than they are at the subsidiary (Benson and Pattie 2009). Identification of key talent is fraught, partly because those at the centre may not have accurate information (Mellahi and Collings 2010), and the social and geographic distance that separates subsidiaries from HQ means that talent at the centre is much more visible and able to engage in personal networking than those in distant subsidiaries. Vaiman and Holden's (2011) research in Central and Eastern Europe uncovered considerable arrogance and prejudice by home employers to host country staff. Furthermore, managers at subsidiaries are reticent to lose their best performing team members to a global talent pool or they may resent having 'talent' foisted upon them if they are from another country and need training (Burbach and Royle 2010). The task is further complicated when MNCs aim to build a talent pool capable of transfer across several countries (Sparrow *et al* 2011). As seen in Chapter 5, do MNCs use home country talent, so that HQ control and uniformity is assured; or do they develop host country talent so that local needs and culture are accommodated? And is development organised through international assignments or locally? If MNCs do not develop international talent pools, they are less likely to thrive, especially in emerging markets (Sparrow *et al* 2011). For further material on global talent management with specific reference to India, the Middle East, China, Central and Eastern Europe see the Journal of World Business Special Issue edited by Scullion and Collings (2011). The following box shows an example of global talent management.

HRM AT WORK IN FOCUS

## Global talent management in German and Irish subsidiaries of a US multinational

USCo is an MNC employing 38,000 people in 120 countries in five product divisions. The research into global talent management took place at sites in Ireland and Germany. HR strategy is centrally decided by a council made up of 10 senior vice presidents. Belief in talent management is one of the organisation's core values and, as such, it is endemic throughout the HR architecture. USCo uses a HR partnership model which comprises four stages: talent management and acquisition; culture change; reward and recognition; and employee commitment.

Talent management strategy includes recruitment and selection, succession planning, talent profiles and pipelines, performance management, and individual development plans. Each employee is required to complete and maintain a ***talent profile*** which are accessed by line managers to be used in a ***talent review*** – the means by which talent is identified and categorised. USCo uses nine categories from 'low performer' to 'strategic star' – the better performers enter a '***talent pipeline***'. There are four stages in the pipeline from 'early contributor' to 'executive' and key talent progresses through use of appropriate ***development opportunities***, provided by mentor feedback, courses, individual learning, or movement into more challenging tasks and posts.

USCo uses a number of tools and systems to support talent management, many of which were incorporated into the HRIS (human resource information system); these include

- talent planning
- management succession summary
- organisation chart and future organisation chart
- leadership pipeline.

In practice, there were glitches in the system. The HRIS was developed in the US and failed to recognise German qualifications. In addition, in Germany, important data relating to the talent reviews got lost in the HRIS. Employees and managers were pressured to complete profiles and reviews by threats (for example, withdrawal of promotion, pay rises, or bonuses). Despite these sanctions, not all profiles and reviews were completed. One senior manager had not heard of the talent management system, and other line managers interviewed were uninterested, stating that they went through the process to 'keep management happy' (p.425). Line managers were required to use forced ranking of employees (from one to five), but these were interpreted differently, or not universally used, meaning that USCo did not have a complete picture of its global talent. European subsidiaries had little power within the US council and its decision-making process, demonstrating how country of origin can be an important factor in implementation. There was no evidence that the USCo was measuring return on investment from the development of talent.

Despite the company's centrist approach, talent management was delivered differently in each subsidiary, partly due to local cultures in the host country. Additionally, there was lack of support for the system because local managers were not involved when the system was unveiled. Power relations also came into play as larger and more important subsidiaries were able to influence procedures more than the smaller establishments.

*To think about:*

*Why do you think so many things went wrong in this case? Was it more to do with the value systems held by senior management in the USA, the way in which the system was implemented, or problems at the host country level?*

Source: Adapted from Burbach and Royle (2010).

## DEFINING JOBS AND CREATING PERSON SPECIFICATIONS

### JOB AND ROLE ANALYSIS

This helps to identify tasks new recruits are expected to undertake (Searle 2003). In organisations that recruit regularly, it is not necessary to re-analyse jobs every time a vacancy occurs but it is useful to examine whether or not existing job descriptions, person specifications or competency profiles are appropriate for future needs. This may conclude there is no need for further recruitment or that the type of job and person required has changed. Job analysis refers to 'the process of collecting, analysing and setting out information about the contents of jobs in order to provide the basis for a job description and data for recruitment, training, job evaluation and performance management' (Armstrong 1989, p.190). The emphasis on gathering information about the purpose of the role is what differentiates job analysis from job descriptions, with the latter being seen as an output of the former.

The methods used to analyse jobs and roles vary in terms of their sophistication, cost, convenience and acceptability; all these need to be borne in mind when choosing a method (Taylor 2010). The issue of cost is pertinent, as benefits always need to be weighed against the time, effort and money expended. Similarly, methods need to be acceptable to the staff involved. No method is inherently superior so choices should be made on the basis of the jobs to be analysed and the context in which this takes place. For example, sophisticated techniques are not cost-effective for a small number of low skill jobs where it is better to use simple methods than employ untrained staff for a sophisticated analysis. There are four main techniques: observation, diaries, interviews, and questionnaires. The first three are relatively simple and are the most widely used. Readers needing more detail should consult Cooper *et al* (2003), Searle (2003) and Taylor (2010).

- *Observation* is the most straightforward and readily available method, often used with other techniques. It is also cheap, and if there are problems clarification can be sought direct from the job-holder. On the other hand, it can be difficult to interpret precisely what is being done, especially if there is a high cognitive content to the job, and the fact that someone is being observed can impact on job behaviour.
- *Work diaries* are also used regularly. Here job-holders record their activities over a period of time – say, each hour during a week, or every time they move onto a new task. This requires a high degree of co-operation from the job-holder, being willing to spend time explaining items in the diary. It relies on job-holders keeping a comprehensive record of their activities, and not excluding items that seem unimportant or are done frequently.
- *Interviews* range from the relatively unstructured – in which job-holders describe their job while the interviewer probes for detail – through to more standardised formats where similar questions are asked of each job-holder. The major advantages are cost, convenience and the chance for interaction between interviewer and interviewee. The major disadvantages relate to bias and reliability, and interviewer skills. A more sophisticated variant is repertory grid analysis, though to be effective this requires skilled analysts (Searle 2003; Taylor 2010).
- *Questionnaires and checklists* often make use of computer packages to analyse data. The best known techniques are the Position Analysis Questionnaire (PAQ) and the Work Profiling System (WPS). Readers wanting more information should consult Searle (2003, pp.39–41) where PAQ is used to analyse the work of firefighters, and Cooper *et al* (2003, pp.36–7) for WPS.

Using several techniques together can reduce the likelihood of a poor person specification, but there are other problems with job analysis, in particular its stability over time, given that jobs change. Searle (2003, p.53) is also concerned that because job analysis focuses specifically on precisely what people **do** at work, it can separate workers from the context in which they work – for example their role in teams – as well as assuming there is one best way to do each job. It is simplistic to imagine that job roles exist in an unchanging manner, not affected by the people who fill them.

## JOB DESCRIPTIONS

The results from job analysis provide the basis for job descriptions. These can be very specific or relatively broad in character, but the tendency has been to focus on the skills that employers need not just in the short-term, but over a longer time frame. Job descriptions of some form are used by most organisations, particularly large employers and in the public sector. These typically include:

1 *Job title*: a clear statement is all that is required, such as transport manager or customer service assistant
2 *Location*: department, establishment, name of organisation
3 *Responsible to*: job title of supervisor to whom member of staff reports
4 *Responsible for*: job titles of members of staff who report directly into the job-holder, if any
5 *Main purpose of the job*: a short and unambiguous statement indicating precisely the overall objective and purpose of the job, such as 'assist and advise customers in a specific area', 'to drill metals in accordance with manufacturing policy'
6 *Responsibilities/duties*: a list of the main and subsidiary elements in the job, specifying what is required, such as maintaining records held on computer system or answering queries
7 *Working conditions*: a list of the major contractual agreements relating to the job, such as pay scales and fringe benefits, hours of work and holiday entitlement, and union membership if appropriate
8 *Other matters*: information such as geographical mobility and performance standards
9 *Any other duties* that may be assigned by the organisation.

Despite extensive usage, job descriptions are criticised for being outmoded and irrelevant to modern times, symptomatic of what is seen as a collectivist, inflexible and rules-oriented culture. It is argued that workers should not be concerned with the precise definition of 'standard' behaviour but rather with how 'value' can be added through personal initiative. Instead of 'working to contract' and abiding by explicit rules, staff should be encouraged to work 'beyond contract' under a regime of 'high-performance work systems' and 'blame-free cultures'. Consequently, specific job descriptions have been overtaken by more generic and concise job profiles or accountability statements that are short – say, less than one page – and focused on outcomes rather than detailed components. Another alternative is to use role definitions and 'key result area' statements (KRAs) that relate to the critical performance measures for the job. Examples of KRAs are: 'prepare marketing plans that support the achievement of corporate targets for sales revenue'; or 'provide an accurate, speedy and helpful word-processing service to internal customers'.

Given the criticisms, it is surprising that job descriptions or role profiles are still used. However, they do provide recruits with information about the organisation and their potential role, and without them people would apply for jobs without any form of realistic job preview. Vague and 'flexible' accounts of jobs only store up trouble if there are subsequent concerns about whether people are doing what is expected of them or how they fit into the role. This is particularly important for workers due to go on overseas assignments; as Richardson *et al* (2008) note in their study of knowledge workers it can provide information about local culture and opportunities for spouses to find work in the region or for children to go to school. As studies of expatriates show, non-work issues are often as important as those relating to the job when posted overseas. In addition, requirements to outline accountability profiles can help managers decide if a post must be filled, and if so in what form and at what level.

## REFLECTIVE ACTIVITY

Do job descriptions still exist in your organisation or one with which you are familiar? If they have been abandoned, has this led to greater autonomy or greater stress? If detailed job descriptions still exist, how well do these work?

### PERSON SPECIFICATIONS AND COMPETENCY FRAMEWORKS

Whereas *job descriptions* relate to the tasks to be undertaken, *person specifications* outline the human attributes seen as necessary to do the job. The best known are the seven-point plan (Rodger 1952) and the five-point plan (Fraser 1966). These describe and categorise the principal features required for any job, with a differentiation between essential and desirable aspects to perform the job. These are outlined in the box below.

HRM AT WORK IN FOCUS

## A traditional view of person specifications

**Rodger's seven-point plan**

- *Physical make-up*: physical attributes such as ability to lift heavy loads or differentiate between colours.
- *Attainments*: educational or professional qualifications considered necessary for undertaking the work.
- *General intelligence*: ability to define and solve problems, and use initiative in dealing with issues that have arisen.
- *Special aptitudes*: skills, attributes or competencies that are specifically relevant to the particular job.
- *Interests*: both work-related and leisure pursuits that may be relevant to performance in the job.
- *Disposition*: attitudes to work and to other members of staff and customers, as well as friendliness and assertiveness.
- *Circumstances*: domestic commitments, mobility and family support.

**Fraser's five-point plan**

- *Impact on others*: this covers much the same sort of issues as 'physical make-up' but it is more focused on impact on other employees and customers.
- *Acquired knowledge and qualifications*: see Rodger's second category above.
- *Innate abilities*: see 'general intelligence' above.
- *Motivation*: a person's desire to succeed in particular aspects of work and their commitment to achieve these goals.
- *Adjustment*: characteristics specifically related to the job, such as ability to cope with difficult customers or work well in a team.

*To think about:*

*Before moving on to the next part of this chapter, on competency frameworks, analyse the two plans outlined above in a little more detail. Focus in particular on the specifications that are used, explain what they are looking for and assess how easily and effectively these can be measured. What are the major shortcomings of these approaches?*

Both methods are still used, often in an adapted form (Newell 2005; Beardwell 2010; Taylor 2010). The problem is that they were devised at a time it was considered acceptable to ask questions about people's domestic circumstances or private life. Although the framework may be valid, it is now unethical, inappropriate and potentially discriminatory to probe too deeply into some of these areas. Moreover, unless specific technical expertise is critical, it makes no sense to restrict applications to people with specific qualifications or experience.

Both the Rodger and Fraser frameworks rely heavily on personal judgement to specify the human qualities associated with successful performance (Newell 2005, p.120). Accordingly, the traditional person specification is giving way to competency frameworks which focus on the *behaviours* of job applicants. This reduces the subjectivity inherent in recruitment and selection (Suff 2006b), and limits the tendency to make inferences about the personal qualities that underpin behaviour (Newell 2006). Job descriptions and person specifications can exist alongside competency-based approaches (Taylor 2010), not least because they set a framework within which subsequent HR practices – such as performance management, learning and development, and pay bands – can be placed. In addition, competencies can relate to specific performance outcomes rather than potentially vague processes, such as disposition or interests outside of work. Moreover, these approaches avoid using criteria just because they are easy to measure – for example, educational qualifications or length of service – but might not relate closely with job effectiveness. Some of the commonly used competencies are team orientation, communication, customer focus, results orientation and problem-solving. Strangely, ethical behaviour, responsibility, enthusiasm and listening are less widely used.

Roberts (1997, pp.71–2) differentiates between four types of competency. These are:

1 *natural competencies* – the 'big five' dimensions of personality: extraversion/intraversion, emotional stability, agreeableness, conscientiousness and openness to experience
2 *acquired competencies* – knowledge and skills acquired through work or other avenues
3 *adapting competencies* – the ability to adapt natural talents and acquired skills to a new situation
4 *performing competencies* – comprising observable behaviours and outputs.

These focus on 'softer' customer service skills rather than 'harder' technical skills, as employers seek positive employee attitudes – such as a preparedness to work flexibly, a willingness to change and a responsiveness to customers. A book by Ted Johns (2007) outlines a range of, often amusing, ways in which customers fail to get the service they expect, and occasions when they do. One particularly pertinent example of great customer service was at Pret A Manger where an employee arrived at work, opened up and served a customer who was waiting, even though the shop was not fully operational. He even gave the coffee for free because the tills were not set up!

There has been much interest in how the service economy alters and shapes employee behaviour, often through the concept of 'emotional labour'. This puts primacy on the need to manage emotions in the workplace so as to 'satisfy' customers' needs and expectations (eg, Bolton 2005, Korczynski 2005) and provide them with the service they feel is appropriate. Other work (eg, Bishop and Hoel 2008) raises the question of what action employers should take if workers are bullied by customers into doing things which are beyond the realms of acceptability, and there are now signs in reception areas and on trains and buses specifying that bullying will not be tolerated. This is the danger with a philosophy that treats the customer as 'king', which can have enormous implications for recruitment if organisations do not support their staff or allow grievances to be raised at work. Some years ago, Royle (1999) argued that McDonalds was keen to recruit an acquiescent workforce unlikely to resist management by targeting people in weak labour market positions with minimal work experience. A recent emphasis to 'aesthetic' labour – recruiting on the basis of attitude, looks and sound – is now more important in the service sector, particularly in call centres and in fashion retailing. Once appointed, workers can then be trained up in technical skills (Callaghan and Thompson 2002; Nickson *et al* 2011; Warhurst *et al* 2011). However, eventually customers might find the soothing tones of the customer service operator do not compensate for the poor quality service provided by the train company or the call centre that is operating with inadequately trained staff or suboptimal staffing levels merely to save costs. The box below provides an example of aesthetic labour.

HRM AT WORK IN FOCUS

### Good looks, nice voice, lousy product

It has become part of modern business language that employers recruit staff in some sectors who have the right attitude in face-to-face interactions or 'smile' down the telephone rather than have well-developed technical skills. Several projects led by Nickson and Warhurst have investigated this issue in the retail sector both in the UK and in Australia. They report that workers are being selected on the basis of their looks and clothes or their voices. This is referred to as 'the commercial utility of aesthetic labour' where image and design pervade the new economy. For example, about three-quarters of the Manchester retailers and nearly 90% of the Sydney employers surveyed rated appearance as very important or essential. Specifically this related to personal hygiene and general tidiness, clothing style and personal grooming. This was argued to be important to maintain brand image. Interestingly, having the right personality and appearance were rated much higher than prior experience or qualifications. Warhurst *et al* (2011), conclude that 'as employer strategies to control workers' feelings complement strategies to control workers' heads, these are now complemented by other strategies centred on controlling workers' bodies'. The implication of this is that certain people who are overweight or speak in the wrong dialect may be excluded from an increasing range of employment opportunities.

*To think about:*

*Does it make commercial sense to focus so much on attitudes and appearance rather than technical skills, or do you think that the latter can be taught effectively once people have been appointed? What would the person specification contain in the cases outlined above? Do you find this approach discriminatory in any way?*

Sources: Adapted from Warhurst and Nickson (2007); Nickson, Hurrell, Warhurst and Cammander (2011); Warhurst, van den Broek, Nickson and Hall (2011).

## RECRUITMENT METHODS

Watson (1994a, p.203) argued some time ago that 'recruitment provides the candidates for the selector to judge. Selection techniques cannot overcome failures in recruitment; they merely make them evident.' Because of this it is surprising that recruitment typically attracts much less interest than selection, with little evidence of theoretical underpinnings (Breaugh and Starke 2000) other than the use of RBV by Orlitzky (2007). Recruitment can be crucial if applicants are in a more powerful position than prospective employers, and energy has to be expended trying to persuade individuals to apply in the first place. In some cases, it is difficult to recruit knowledge workers, so employers need to make jobs appealing, challenging and worthwhile to encourage genuine interest.

Decisions need to be made about the sources from which to recruit, at what cost, and by which media. In relation to the latter, the documentation used presents images of organisations, their products and overall philosophy whilst legal issues are critical when recruiting, particularly in design and wording of adverts and through online channels (Orlitzky 2007; Taylor 2010). Moreover, if it generates too few applications, or too many that are unsuitable, the process is expensive. Choosing a cost-effective recruitment method therefore depends on organisational needs and type of vacancy. Table 19 provides data from CIPD surveys that differentiates recruitment into closed and open searches. Given CIPD did not ask which methods were used beyond 2009 we are reliant on slightly dated material for this, and from 2010 the survey asked about effectiveness, so findings are not comparable over time.

**Table 19 Types of external recruitment methods used by employers and their effectiveness**

| **Recruitment methods used by employers** | **Percentage of organisations using method (2009)** | **Most effective method (2011)** |
|---|---|---|
| *Closed searches and responsive methods* | | |
| Speculative applications/word-of-mouth | 46 | 25 |
| Links to schools, colleges and universities | 34 | 13 |
| Recruitment agencies | 76 | 54 |
| Search consultants | 31 | 15 |
| *Open searches* | | |
| Local newspaper adverts | 70 | 32 |
| Adverts in specialist press | 55 | 27 |
| National newspaper adverts | 31 | 11 |
| Jobcentre Plus and predecessors | 43 | 25 |
| Employer's website | 78 | 59 |
| Radio or TV adverts | 7 | Not specified |

Sources: Chartered Institute of Personnel Development (2009b); Chartered Institute of Personnel and Development/Hays (2011d).

## INTERNAL RECRUITMENT

The 2011 CIPD survey reported that just over a quarter of vacancies are filled internally, a figure that rises in line with organisation size to 53% for those employing more than 5,000 staff. Public sector organisations are most likely to recruit for new posts internally

(45%) compared with 19% of voluntary, community and not-for-profit organisations, and about a quarter of private sector firms. Internal recruitment also becomes more prevalent during periods of rationalisation. If posts are filled following a search of employee records, and staff are redeployed from one area to another, this could assist career development and the effective use of skills and abilities as part of a wider HR plan. However, if external recruitment is frozen, this may simply entail shifting staff onto a redeployment register and then moving them between departments, with the consequence that employees become demotivated because they are not really wanted anywhere. Transfers from temporary posts to open-ended contracts can give employers a chance to observe people before they commit to more secure employment (Rubery *et al* 2004). This is very prevalent in small firms (Edwards *et al* 2009).

### CLOSED SEARCHES

Although these use the external labour market, it is limited to workers the employer knows in some way. It includes 'word-of-mouth' recruitment or referral by existing staff that recommend friends and/or may have worked with before; in the Nickson *et al* (2011) study, two-thirds of employers used this method. CIPD surveys show that word-of-mouth recruitment and employee referrals are quite widely used (46% of employers use them), but only 25% regarded them as particularly effective. Organisations sometimes offer 'bounties' or referral payments to staff who recommend a friend who then remains in employment for more than a set period of time; amounts depend on the post but could be £250–£500. A major advantage of referrals is that employees are unlikely to recommend friends they deem to be unsuitable or would not 'fit' with the culture (Nickson *et al* 2011). All the firms investigated by Carroll *et al* (1999, p.244) used this method, often alongside formal approaches, and two-thirds had rehired former employees. Whilst this can be cheap as recruits are readily available and known to existing staff, Acas and the EHRC worry that such 'ring-fencing' reinforces existing imbalances (gender, race and disability) and thwarts attempts to achieve greater diversity. However, in some cultures, for example in the Gulf, this method is widely used as family and friends are felt to be more reliable than unknown applicants, a policy aiding Emiritisation of the workforce (Forstenlechner 2010). Similarly, in China, network-based recruiting gives priority to the children of existing staff (provided they are qualified) and graduate students with internship experience, with wide use being made of employee referrals (Han and Han 2009).

## REFLECTIVE ACTIVITY

Debate with your colleagues the justification for employing 'word-of-mouth' recruitment and employee referrals and their implications for performance and ethical standards.

Closed searches also make use of external contacts at schools, colleges and universities to identify suitable candidates, a method which can aid recruitment of younger workers. Use of this method has declined in recent times, from half of all respondents to the CIPD 2004 survey to about one-third in 2009. It was not felt to be particularly effective either by the 2011 respondents. Nevertheless, graduates are still recruited through campus visits, sponsored and ex-placement students, although open methods – such as national adverts and company websites/job boards – are used extensively. Judging by the number of firms visiting the leading universities each year, and now sponsoring degrees as well, this method remains vital for recruiting graduates. It is interesting that recruitment techniques might be viewed quite differently by employers and applicants; the 2011 CIPD survey found employers regarded their own websites as very effective whereas research on MBA students in the USA (Cable and Yu 2006) found careers fairs and campus visits were seen as much richer and more credible than company websites and bulletin boards.

Recruitment agencies and search consultancies are also a key source of applicants, typically because they have access to better databases of suitable staff, many of whom may not have applied through open searches. This applies particularly for executive posts where confidentiality is critical for both parties in the initial stages of the process; head-hunters are expensive but generally tend to be very professional in their approach. Agencies now occupy a central place in the recruitment market, and are also found to be effective in generating a good pool of applicants (CIPD 2011d), particularly in the field of professional, secretarial and administrative posts (Grimshaw *et al* 2003; Purcell *et al* 2004; Suff 2009; Taylor 2010). According to IRS (Suff 2005), the principal reasons employers outsource recruitment is to speed up the process, gain greater access to expertise, and provide a more flexible and responsive service. Cost is an issue in decisions not to outsource but there are anxieties that recruitment is too important to hand over to a third party. Employers need to be clear about what agencies are used for as the recruitment process contains a number of different activities. Suff (2005) reports that agencies are used more extensively in the early stages – advertising, managing the applications process and arranging interviews – rather than when decisions are made about job offers or the running of assessment centres. The box below shows how two organisations had different approaches to recruitment outsourcing depending on the circumstances.

HRM AT WORK IN FOCUS

## New approaches to agency use taking off

Rolls-Royce employs nearly 40,000 staff in 50 countries, about 20,000 of whom work in the UK. HR is provided via a shared service centre, and the move to this new system provided an opportunity to cut back on the number of agencies with whom the company had links. There are six preferred suppliers, compared with 280 a few years ago, and this has allowed closer ties to develop between Rolls-Royce and the agencies. There are quarterly strategic reviews of agency performance but this is not just a one-way exercise and the company has been able to tap into agency expertise to generate applications from Eastern Europe. Rolls-Royce has been able to gain a cheaper service alongside more effective sourcing of candidates for the business.

By contrast, 16 London boroughs came together to form a shared recruitment service. Initial discussions commenced two years prior to the launch, at the instigation of Sutton, when it was clear that requirements for modernisation made it too expensive to continue with existing in-house and one-off arrangements. Contracts were awarded to different firms for specific parts of the process: recruitment advertising went to Barkers; Tribal dealt with areas such as online short-listing; and three organisations covered executive search and selection. Each council pays for its specific use of the services. The scheme has to be flexible as each local authority has different needs.

Source: Adapted from Johnson (2007).

## RESPONSIVE METHODS

These differ from closed methods because employers interview casual callers or former applicants whose names and addresses are on file, and shops, bars and restaurants advertise vacancies inside the establishment to generate applications. Case studies suggest this is prevalent in SMEs. Carroll *et al* (1999) found over half their case study organisations contacted former applicants if a vacancy arose, and a similar proportion had offered work to casual callers; see also Edwards and Ram (2006), Harney and Dundon (2006) and Edwards *et al* (2009). This method is not totally 'closed' because it relies on people making the effort to search for work rather than merely responding to an invitation from a friend or ex-colleague, but it is less 'open' than adverts in the local paper. It could be argued that responsive methods encourage initiative and drive, and in customer-facing firms can also create synergies between customers and workers that could lead to increased sales.

## OPEN SEARCHES

This covers the largest number of techniques. Advertisements in local papers remain very popular for manual workers and office staff, whilst the trade press is used for specialist posts. By contrast, radio and TV adverts are rarely used now, although there have been campaigns trying to persuade people to undergo teacher training or nursing at times of shortage. Employers using adverts in the national press has halved over the last decade. Job centres or their equivalent are relatively popular. It is also typical for organisations to use more than one method at a time, and in most cases employer websites play an important part in attracting candidates (CIPD 2011d).

Online recruitment has become much more significant in the last few years, as Table 19 showed, with much greater usage of employer websites now than at the turn of the century. The 2011 CIPD survey also suggests it is one of the most effective sources of new recruits according to employers. Other research in the UK confirms this. Parry and Tyson (2008) draw on results from a quarterly survey of HR managers to show how widely corporate and commercial websites were used, and that they were just as, if not more, successful than other methods of recruitment. Despite this, there are some anxieties that online recruitment is resource-intensive compared with agencies that sift applications for the company, as well as issues to do with equality in relation to access to these systems. It was also acknowledged that online recruitment was harder to establish in small firms. In follow-up research, Parry and Wilson (2009) suggest that 'subjective norms' – the likelihood of online recruitment being particularly suited to certain sectors and applicants, for example in the high technology area – could also lead to exclusion of some candidates that might be suitable. Table 20 summarises the main advantages and disadvantages of online recruitment. From this it can be seen that employers have to address questions about cost, internal HR

**Table 20 The merits and shortcomings of online recruitment**

| Main advantages to employers | Main disadvantages to employers |
|---|---|
| • reduced costs of recruitment<br>• improved corporate image if website well-designed<br>• reduced administration<br>• shorter recruitment cycle<br>• wider pool of applicants, including from overseas<br>• easier process for candidates to complete. | • too many unsuitable applicants<br>• technical problems with website<br>• not enough information about job or organisation<br>• the impersonal nature of the process<br>• applicants can be put off if website poorly designed. |

resources, the width or narrowness of the net, the use of agencies and the design of websites before deciding how to proceed.

US research has demonstrated that website design and orientation has a major impact on users' perceptions of how attractive the company is to work for, and consequently on the number of high-quality applications (Feldman and Klaas 2002; Williamson *et al* 2003). Pfieffelmann *et al* (2010) found that women's interest in applying for jobs via corporate websites was influenced by the degree to which they found the site usable and whether or not they saw a strong person–organisation fit from what they read; but this did not apply to men. Selden and Orenstein (2011) found that both the content and the usability of e-recruitment sites had an impact on numbers applying for government jobs (higher) and on the level of voluntary quits (lower) after appointment; this was seen as a highly effective outcome across all 50 states in the USA. Positive results such as this led Llorens and Kellough (2007) to suggest that the success of online systems mean that it could be rolled out beyond recruitment to the whole selection process in the future, though they do raise concerns about how this might impact upon equal employment initiatives. The box below presents key findings about applicant perceptions of web based recruitment procedures in a large financial services firm.

HRM AT WORK IN FOCUS

### The attractiveness of webs for recruiting staff

This study examined the reactions of 1,360 applicants for posts in the UK, Netherlands and Belgian operations of a large MNC in the financial services sector. The company employs over 100,000 staff and is in the top 20 world-wide. Applicants searched for data on the company website and could collect ideas about the organisation's culture, structure, development opportunities and profiles of co-workers. The website facade was unified showing consistency in the use of colours, shapes and textures, and videos and links were integrated into the process. The main findings were:

1 Applicants reported generally favourable reactions to the web-based procedures used by the organisation.

2 Perceived efficiency is the most important predictor of applicant satisfaction with online applications, with user-friendliness coming second. What might seem quite superficial features of the website have been found to influence applicant perceptions strongly.

3 Perceptions of fairness seem to matter less than efficiency and user-friendliness on websites in terms of influencing applicant satisfaction with the process.

4 No significant differences were found on the basis of gender, age or ethnic group in applicant perceptions of the on-line process, though those that classed themselves internet-savvy were more positive.

Source: Adapted from Sylva and Mol (2009).

Choice of method depends on the vacancy to be filled and the resources the employer is prepared to commit. The state of the external labour market also matters, and the most appropriate methods vary depending upon local and/or national levels of unemployment, on specific skill shortages, and on competition in the labour market. For example, a company recruiting manual or clerical workers might target a job centre and put adverts in local newspapers at relatively little cost. Conversely, recruitment for technical and professional jobs is more likely to involve specialist trade magazines, schools and further education colleges to generate a suitable pool of applicants. Moreover, it is common to use executive search agencies to recruit senior managers. Interestingly, Turban and Cable (2003, p.746) show that 'good' employers tend to receive a higher quantity and quality of applicants for posts, which illustrates the value of employer branding (Lievens and Chapman 2010).

## CHOOSING THE MOST APPROPRIATE SELECTION METHODS

### OVERVIEW

Employers have many different selection methods from which to choose, and it is impossible to do justice to all these in a few pages of a general HRM text. Therefore, following a general overview, we focus on interviews and tests given their widespread usage; for other techniques, Taylor (2010) or Lievens and Chapman (2010) are helpful, and for continuing up-to-date material it is worth looking at the *International Journal of Selection and Assessment* and other specialist HR journals that are appropriate for the region in which they operate. For example, papers on assessment centres have been published recently by the International Task Force on Assessment Centre Guidelines (2009) and Melchers *et al* (2010). Before progressing, it has to be noted that no single method, regardless of how well it is designed and administered, is capable of producing perfect selection decisions that predict individual performance with certainty.

The popularity of different selection methods can be gauged from the results of annual CIPD surveys over a number of years shown in Table 8.6. Interviews remain very popular in 2011, even in their traditional form (after submission of an application form or CV and supported with references) but competency-based interviews have become more widespread over the last few years to become the most popular form of all. Telephone interviews have

**Table 21 The popularity of different selection methods**

| Method used by organisations | 2004 | 2009 | 2011 |
|---|---|---|---|
| Traditional interview | 66 | 68 | 63 |
| Structured interview (panel) | 55 | 59 | 56 |
| Competency-based interview | 62 | 69 | 70 |
| Telephone interview | 26 | 38 | 43 |
| General ability tests | 53 | 44 | 23 |
| Literacy and/or numeracy tests | 48 | 39 | 38 |
| Tests for specific skills | 60 | 50 | 49 |
| Online tests (selection/self-selection) | 6 | 17 | 25 |
| Personality questionnaires | 46 | 35 | 35 |
| Assessment centres | 43 | 35 | 35 |

Source: Chartered Institute of Personnel and Development (2004a); Chartered Institute of Personnel Development (2009b); Chartered Institute of Personnel and Development/Hays (2011d).

grown in extensiveness, which makes sense given the greater number of people involved in call centres and/or employed away from the location where most staff are employed where these skills are more important. Tests appear to have declined in popularity since 2004, apart from online tests which are increasingly being used as a pre-selection device and are now used by one-quarter of all organisations that responded to the 2011 survey. This presumably relates to administration costs and the availability of qualified staff able to run them. Assessment centre use is down from 2004 but still used in at about one-third of organisations. Use of these methods also varies between sectors. For example, traditional interviews are used more in the private sector whilst panel interviews are more common in the public and not-for-profit sectors. Tests for specific job-related skills are more widely used in public and not-for-profit organisations whilst telephone interviews are principally a private sector phenomenon. Assessment centres and personality questionnaires are only really used for managerial and professional jobs, while there is little variation between occupations for the other methods.

The use of selection techniques also varies between countries. Newell and Tansley (2001) found that interviews were most extensive in Britain and North America, graphology in France (and French companies in other countries), and assessment centres in Britain, Germany and the Netherlands. Tests in general were used more widely in France and Belgium, and integrity tests in the USA although only to a limited extent. Brewster *et al* (2007) note personal or governmental connections matter greatly in some cultures (eg in Mexico and the Middle East), being a graduate from an elite university is critical in parts of the Pacific Rim (as well as in France), and there are limits to open recruitment and selection in countries with strong ethnic, gender or age distinctions (eg China or Malaysia). Ispas *et al* (2010) found that work sampling was the most widely used technique in Romania, followed by interviews and ability tests, whilst in the German-speaking part of Switzerland interviews were used by 99% of respondents, with personality tests used by a third of the sample (Konig *et al* 2010). It is clear societal, cultural and institutional factors are important when choosing which technique to use, especially with the number of people now employed by MNCs as expatriates (Lievens and Chapman 2010). Also, female and ethnic minority applicants may be disadvantaged due to the samples used in validating certain techniques (Schmitt and Chan 1999; Searle 2003).

Robertson and Smith (2001) suggest most techniques have very low levels of accuracy in producing effective selection decisions (see the box below). For individual techniques, work sampling offers the highest likelihood of success, closely followed by intelligence tests and structured interviewing. References score fairly low on accuracy levels, and graphology is regarded by some as hardly better than random selection. Schmidt and Hunter (1998, p.270) argue it is not the characteristics of writing that leads to different estimates of people's abilities and personalities but its content – which is clearly quite different. Bangerter *et al* (2009) reviewed five studies of graphology and concluded all were based on myth, partly because subsequent references to original work did not take into account the small and unrepresentative sample sizes used. Moreover, practitioners were sometimes persuaded to use graphology because they thought it was widely used – when it is not! In this respect, Carless (2009) criticises managers for not making sufficient use of evidence-based research, often adopting methods for purely historical reasons.

HRM AT WORK IN FOCUS

## Accuracy of selection methods

| | |
|---|---|
| 1.0 | perfect selection |
| 0.65 | intelligence tests and integrity tests |
| 0.63 | intelligence tests and structured interviews |
| 0.60 | intelligence tests and work sampling |
| 0.54 | work sample tests |
| 0.51 | intelligence tests |
| 0.51 | structured interviews |
| 0.41 | integrity tests |
| 0.40 | personality tests |
| 0.37 | assessment centres |
| 0.35 | biodata |
| 0.26 | references |
| 0.18 | years of job experience |
| 0.10 | years of education |
| 0.02 | graphology |
| 0.0 | selection with a pin |

Source: Adapted from Robertson and Smith (2001).

It is also clear that combining techniques greatly increases accuracy; for example, the combination of intelligence tests with structured interviews, integrity tests or work sampling leads to a substantial improvement in validity (Schmidt and Hunter 1998, p.272). Moreover, no single method offers a panacea, so decisions have to be made about the most appropriate technique for each situation. There is little guidance here despite the voluminous literature on selection; as Wilk and Cappelli (2003, p.122) note 'virtually no research has been done on the determinants of the selection process itself, on the employer's choices'. They found more sophisticated methods were used where work was more complex because traditional methods were unable to capture the range of attributes sought, whilst multiple methods provided alternative perspectives. In addition, failures for this group were more catastrophic for the organisation. However, choice does depend on the situation; for example, call centre staff could be selected by telephone screening, secretarial staff through work sampling and management consultants via presentations, along with other methods as appropriate. The criteria for assessing each method are practicability, sensitivity, reliability and validity.

- *Practicability*, according to Cooper *et al* (2003, p.94), is a very important criterion. The method has to be acceptable to all parties – managers, candidates, statutory bodies (such as the EHRC) and professional organisations (such as the CIPD and the BPS). It also has to be cost-effective, not take up too much time and be within the capabilities of those running the selection process. Cost is particularly critical; there is little point using a complex personality test if just one candidate applies or if it is for a temporary post.
- *Sensitivity* is key to choice of selection methods. This represents the ability of the technique to discriminate between candidates in terms of their ability to do the job. Care is needed to ensure it is not simply a smokescreen for making employment decisions that disadvantage or exclude applicants on grounds of race, gender, age or disability.
- *Reliability* refers to 'the consistency of a method used to select individuals' (Newell 2005, p.126). It is assessed in relation to (1) different raters for the same person, (2) if the same technique is used over time, and (3) between different selection methods (Cooper *et al* 2003, pp.50–2). Inter-rater reliability is crucial to ensure consistency between several interviewers, and tests are deficient if applicants can improve their performance over time.
- *Validity* refers to the correctness of the inferences drawn from the selection method. Newell (2005, p.127) defines this as 'the relationship between the predictors (the results from the selection method used) and the criterion (performance on the job)'. The key attributes and skills demonstrated by high (or satisfactory) performers are identified

and then used as a benchmark against which to assess applicants. This is not always easy as it is hard to find proxies for characteristics such as effectiveness in leading teams or managing change. It is also hard to draw inferences about future job performance at the selection stage because this is influenced by many factors, some of which occur outside of work. However, following a review of existing research, Salgado (2002) found correlations between the Big Five personality factors and subsequent levels of labour turnover, theft and disciplinary problems.

## INTERVIEWS

Interviews are widely used for selection but they are also roundly condemned (Macan 2009). Whilst being relatively cheap to conduct, they are criticised for unacceptable levels of reliability, poor predictive validity and low sensitivity. Many legal issues surround interviews, in terms of equal opportunities, data protection and confidentiality, as well as human rights (Leighton and Proctor 2001). However, interviews are often blamed for poor outcomes when the real problem is that they have been conducted by untrained and inadequately prepared interviewers. This can be reduced by training interviewers properly before letting them loose on applicants or making sure interviews are only used in conjunction with other methods. Nevertheless, there are deeper questions about the purpose of the interview; is it a two-way decision-making process involving both the organisation and the applicant, or is it an attempt to achieve perfect selection with high predictive validity?

### REFLECTIVE ACTIVITY

Consider ***two*** interviews – one you think was well handled and one that was poorly handled – in which you have taken part, either as an interviewer or as an applicant. Identify the reasons for the differences between them. What can you learn from this to improve the validity of interviews as a selection device?

Selection interviews take a number of forms (Cook 1998; Cooper *et al* 2003; Taylor 2010). Firstly they can be *one-to-one*, which has the advantage of relative informality, encouraging rapport and potentially generating more frank and open discussions. However, they are prone to interviewer bias (both the 'halo' and the 'satan' effects), low levels of reliability, and lack of coverage of the subject matter. This type of interview is liable to the accusation that interviewers make up their minds about applicants in the first few minutes, and then spend the rest of the time finding reasons to justify their view. The sequential interview is a slight adaptation of this in that candidates are seen by a series of managers in one-to-one situations, with each probing for evidence about different aspects of the job.

The second type is the *small group* or tandem interview, where a few people see a candidate together, making judgements on the basis of the same interaction. They may explore different aspects of the job or take on specific roles during the interview. In the case of a supervisory appointment, for example, a line manager and an HR specialist can interview together to examine both technical skills and management style. This can be beneficial because at least two people to observe the candidate first-hand to reach (hopefully) a joint decision.

The final type is the *panel*, typically comprising between three and five interviewers drawn from different parts of the organisation undertaking – if roles have been allocated beforehand – different duties. Panel interviews for senior academics may involve 12 or more people – in which case the interview really does become something of a ritual or trial, depending upon which side of the table one is sitting. Arguments in favour of panels are similar to the small group interview. Several people can see the candidate together, it minimises the potential for overt bias and it ensures – in theory at least – that decisions are made by those closely related to the post. The disadvantages are also well known. It is more difficult for interviewers to build up rapport, some interviewees may be extremely nervous about the prospect of facing lots of people in a formal setting, and panel members often lack training in how to interview. Bias can occur because some panel members exert a sizeable influence over the decision, yet this is often hidden and covert.

Most commentators agree that selection interviews are problematic due to the nature of the interview process and the skills of interviewers. Plumbley's (1991, p.103) comments are still relevant here: interviewing is 'an everyday occurrence and is the most widely used assessment technique. It is part of the popular vocabulary. It looks easy, and everyone is inclined to believe they are good at it. Therein lies the danger and the confusion.' Mostly, this can be explained by attribution theory, the view that applicants are defined as 'good' if they obey the rules of the interview and 'bad' if they do not (Cooper *et al* 2003, p.104). Similarly, interviewers tend to select candidates displaying attributes they regard as important, behaving/looking like others for whom they have positive feelings, or saying things with which the interviewer agrees (Taylor 2010). The converse also applies, leading to rejection of candidates who do not 'fit' with stereotypical expectations. A common problem is that interviewers have highly selective memories, typically picking up on points supporting their predetermined opinion while ignoring contraindications (Taylor 2010).

*Structured interviews* can improve the validity and reliability of selection decisions (Cooper *et al* 2003; Macan 2009). Several features differentiate them from traditional interviews: questions should be developed from the job analysis; each candidate should be asked standard, though not necessarily identical, questions; and a systematic scoring procedure should be used, preferably based upon a behaviourally anchored rating scale. Nikolaou's (2011) research in Greece showed note-taking and other systematic techniques are important in structured interviews. In the public sector, as part of the drive to ensure that selection decisions are free from gender and race bias, applicants might even be asked precisely the same questions – which are agreed in advance – in the same order, and answers are rated in a systematic manner. On the other hand structured interviews may not be acceptable to senior decision-makers because they prefer to avoid rigid, fixed and standardised processes. They do improve reliability but problems remain with validity. For example, some applicants are good at impression management (Posthuma *et al* 2002; Searle 2003, p.120; Macan 2009), articulating their achievements with ease but poor at putting plans into effect. Conversely, others may be very good at their jobs but fail to convey this at the interview. A slight variant of the structured interview is the behavioural or situational interview where candidates are asked to describe how they have acted in the past and what they would do if a particular issue arose. Evidence from organisations using behavioural interviews (Barclay 2001, p.88) suggest they appear to produce better decisions due to improved quality of information, which offsets the additional training costs incurred.

The ritualistic nature of interviews is more important than is often admitted and in many cultures hiring decisions are only made via face-to-face contact (Macan 2009), though at times of shortage teachers and nurses have been recruited from overseas on the basis of written documentation and references. Greater use is now made of video-conferencing instead of face-to-face interviews, but it is hard to gain a feel for the dynamics of the interview situation and, even if the images are relatively clear and no technical glitches occur, it is impossible to observe other interviewers without multiple cameras. Taylor (2010) feels interviews are popular because, in addition to relatively low costs, they provide a chance for the parties to interact, to negotiate issues before appointment and as a public relations exercise; these differ from the conventional view that reliability and validity matter most.

## SELECTION TESTING

As we saw in Table 21, selection tests are popular because employers seek higher levels of validity in choosing between candidates, and whilst not used as widely as interviews, a significant number of organisations use them in some way. In this section, we provide an insight into the major types of tests available, their principal merits and shortcomings, and their part in selection decisions. It must be stressed this is *not* designed to enable readers to design, administer and interpret tests, and it is crucial that HR practitioners recognise the limits of their own expertise and when to seek advice on test usage, and from which suppliers. Readers needing more detail should consult Cook (1998), Cooper *et al* (2003), Morgeson *et al* (2007), Taylor (2010), CIPD and BPS.

Smith and Robertson (1993, p.161) have defined psychological tests as: 'carefully chosen, systematic and standardised procedures for evoking a sample of responses from a candidate, which can be used to assess one or more of their psychological characteristics by comparing the results with those of a representative sample of an appropriate population.' This means that tests:

1 should be chosen carefully and be appropriate for the situation

2 should be applied systematically in a standard manner

3 should be capable of comparison with norms for the particular group in question.

CIPD stresses that tests must be supported by strong evidence and statistical data that demonstrates their validity in a particular occupational setting, legal and organisational context. Wolf and Jenkins (2006, p.204) indicate that personality tests are much more widely used if a specialist HR manager is in post, the organisation has Investors in People (IiP) status and there is a strong commitment to diversity. However, it is also higher if there has been a tribunal complaint in the previous 12 months. Similar factors explain the use of competency and ability tests, which suggest the main driver is a mix of professional HR policies and a desire to protect the organisation against complaints in the future. Wolf and Jenkins (2006, p.209) remind us that whilst 'academic evidence demonstrates the predictive validity of *appropriate* testing, it also underlines the critical importance of context...and of selecting the correct test.' Major questions arise about the validity of tests that have been tested in specific countries and whether they can be used elsewhere (Lievens and Chapman 2010).

Cooper *et al* (2003, p.126) distinguish between two broad categories of test. ***Cognitive tests*** are designed to measure mental ability, and take several different forms. First, tests of *achievement* purport to measure the degree of knowledge and/or skill a person has acquired at the time the test is administered, such as school examinations. Second, tests of *general intelligence* are designed to assess 'the capacity for abstract thinking and reasoning within a range of different contexts' (Toplis *et al* 1994, p.17), an example of which is Wechsler's Adult Intelligence Scale (WAIS). The third set of cognitive tests measure special *aptitudes or abilities*, such as assessment of verbal, numerical or spatial ability, and manual dexterity. These include tests for clerical speed and accuracy, computer aptitudes, or sales skills, which can be compiled into batteries of tests for organisations. Cook (1998, p.135) argues that 'validity generalisation analysis has proved that tests of natural ability predict work performance very well. For a vast range of jobs, the more able worker is the better worker.' Others (for example Stairs *et al* 2000, p.28) argue these techniques are most appropriate for managers.

HRM AT WORK IN FOCUS

## Performance interviews which make a difference

A major criticism of selection techniques is that they are not suitable proxies for work performance. That does not apply to work sampling or skills tests which identify suitable candidates on the basis of how well they actually do the job. In this study of an engine components supplier to the auto industry in the USA, the employee committee suggested that paper and pencil tests of job knowledge were ineffective so it would be much better to conduct the interview at workplace level, watch someone perform and ask them questions. This led to the development of a performance interview primarily by employees (associates) at the company in conjunction with their team leaders and some experts. Subsequent analysis confirmed there were strong links between the selection technique and superior job performance across all departments, as well as between men and women and between different racial groups. Whilst it was acknowledged this was a more costly process than traditional interviews, the authors felt this was offset by skill levels being raised in the organisation.

Source: Adapted from Morgeson *et al* (2009).

The second broad grouping – ***personality tests*** – are based around 'trait' or 'type' theories, involving 'the identification of a number of fairly independent and enduring characteristics of behaviour which all people display but to differing degrees' (Toplis *et al* 1994, p.28). The Big Five personality factors are agreed by the scientific community as generally applicable across all contexts but this does not mean that all the factors are applicable in all situations and for all occupations, nor does it mean that the correlations between these factors and performance is strong in every situation (Cooper *et al* 2003, pp.131–2). For example, Barrick *et al* (2001) show that conscientiousness and emotional stability seem to be relevant for selection decisions in all occupations, whereas other factors – agreeableness, extraversion and openness to experience – are more specific to particular jobs and situations; extraversion appears to be useful in predicting managerial performance.

Choosing an appropriate test should be judged against evidence in similar situations and perceived organisational needs. There are many tests on the market, some designed and tested solely in the USA which therefore need to be treated with caution if they are to be used in other cultures. Among the best-known personality questionnaires are Cattell's 16PF, the SHL Occupational Personality Questionnaire (OPQ), the Myers–Briggs Type Indicator and the Californian Psychological Inventory (CPI). There are also interest questionnaires (such as the Rothwell-Miller Interest Blank and many SHL questionnaires for different levels), values questionnaires, and work behaviour questionnaires. Most of these have been available for at least 25 years. As so many tests are available, listing them alone would cover several pages, so look at the sources above for further information.

Not surprisingly, increased usage has highlighted problems, particularly in the choice of tests and in their deployment. CIPD and BPS warn against disreputable providers and using untrained assessors who do not know how to interpret results. In addition, there are anxieties that some tests discriminate against particular groups, most notably ethnic minorities and women (Schmitt and Chan 1999; Searle 2003). Ng and Sears (2010) sampled 154 organisations across Canada and found the use of cognitive ability tests is associated with lower levels of minority group representation, especially in managerial positions, whilst personality tests are associated with higher levels of minority representation. Firms covered by employment equity legislation were less inclined to use cognitive ability tests. It is also observed that financial pressures may lead to employers taking short cuts in test usage, leading to inconsistencies. Used in isolation, tests are not particularly good predictors of future job behaviour (Newell 2005) because strong situational pressures lead to alternative solutions in practice. Moreover many jobs, especially those with discretionary potential, can be done perfectly well in more than one way. Problems can also arise if individuals fake their responses to present an image that increases the chance of being selected (Arthur *et al* 2001, pp.665–6), but also note that applicants providing a 'true' answer to a trick question – say, about never having stolen anything – are penalised because it is assumed everyone will have stolen something during their lives (p.668). In their review of personality tests, Morgeson *et al* (2007) accept faking takes place but do not believe attempts to detect it improves validity.

Tests have a role to play in selection decisions for certain jobs provided they are used properly and in tandem with other tests or selection methods. Points to consider when choosing and using tests are:

- Tests need to be reliable and valid, and provide evidence they do not unfairly disadvantage certain groups.
- Tests should only be sold to qualified users, carried out under standard conditions, and only released after adequate research.
- Candidates need to understand the place of tests in the selection process, see their relevance to the job in hand, and be convinced of their accuracy.
- Test administrators must be qualified to use tests and be able to interpret the inferences drawn from them, and candidates need to be reassured about this.
- Candidates should not be coached for tests.
- The results should be confidential and results should be fed back to candidates.

REFLECTIVE ACTIVITY

Which selection techniques would you advise using for the appointment of (a) a worker in a call centre, (b) a chef in a busy restaurant and (c) a research scientist? Justify your answer.

## DIFFERING PARADIGMS OF SELECTION

The discussion thus far has intimated there are competing paradigms within the field of selection – for the most part implicit rather than explicit. Broadly there are four perspectives, though the distinctions are not always clear-cut. These are: scientific rationality; social exchange; socialisation; and socially constructed reality.

### SCIENTIFIC RATIONALITY

This is the dominant perspective, focusing on employer goals and the role of validity and reliability in the selection process. It reflects the influence that psychology has over this element of HRM and emphasises that selection can become more scientific by using structured interviews, tests and work sampling (Posthuma *et al* 2002; Morgeson *et al* 2007). This perspective follows a simple sequence of premises (Newell and Shackleton 2001, p.24):

1 Excellent job performance can be identified and codified.

2 There is one best way to work.

3 Competencies can be derived and used to define the key characteristics of a post.

4 Selection techniques can be devised to assess these competencies.

5 Validity and reliability can be improved by sticking to certain methods.

Newell and Shackleton (2001, p.32) term this the 'actuarial method' of selection because 'it is based purely on a numerical calculation of the collected data'. However, the notion of rationality implicit in psychometric ideas is a myth 'because it is based on assumptions that there is one best way to do a job'. Moreover they claim (p.42) that the 'psychological perspective simply hides behind a façade of objectivity so it remains easy to perpetuate discrimination while presenting the whole process as fair'. Confidence in testing can be undermined by inappropriate and poorly applied tests, whilst the idea that selection techniques can be 'objective' is problematic, as the exercise is always open to management choice; for example, in terms of which test to use, the items contained within it, perceived validity for the job and the cultural norms implicit in the test (McDaniel 2009). The use of standard tests may lead to cloning and limit workforce diversity. Searle (2003, p.263) is particularly scathing; she argues that 'the psychometric approach reflects a Western context, which is based on a capitalistic premise of the dominance of profit and the market place as regulator.'

## SOCIAL EXCHANGE

Given that interviews are the most popular method, it is clear that selection is not just devised with one party – the employer – in mind. It has even been likened to 'a controlled conversation with a purpose', that being to 'collect information in order to predict how successfully the individual would perform in the job for which they have applied, measuring them against predetermined criteria' (Torrington *et al* 2002, p.242). The idea of a conversation, albeit controlled, conjures up images of a pleasant chat and downplays the fact selectors are typically in a more powerful position, especially at times of high unemployment. But, there is some substance to this view. After all, applicants decide whether they want to work for an organisation, and if labour markets are tight or in jobs where it is hard to attract people, this can be a relatively equal exchange. Potential applicants may decide after reading the literature from an organisation they will not bother applying. Similarly, candidates may decide not to attend an interview or turn down a job after it has been offered. Newell (2005, p.139) portrays the process as a series of episodes in which the parties exchange increasing amounts of information to decide whether or not they are compatible with each other. Contrary to the literature examining selection from an employer perspective, however, there is little on applicant satisfaction with interviews (Küskü and Ataman 2011). Social exchange can also be manipulative if applicants 'create and maintain impressions of themselves which they believe the assessor is looking for' (Newell 2006, p.78), thus undermining the validity of selection decisions; see the earlier discussion of faking. This can also occur if selectors try to persuade someone to work for the organisation and give unrealistic job previews in order to tempt them. These points show selection is not just a scientific and economic decision but is shaped by interpersonal and institutional factors such as organisational self-promotion and legal/cultural factors in the country involved (Konig *et al* 2010).

## SOCIALISATION

This is where selection is seen as part of HRM, rather than being viewed in isolation, and constitutes the first stage in person–job–organisation fit (Anderson and Ostroff 1997). From this perspective, 'selection and socialisation are more accurately conceived as stages in a single, longitudinal process of newcomer integration…socialisation begins during selection as the applicant experiences the organisation's formal procedures for the first time' (p.413). Socialisation includes:

- *information provision* – extent and accuracy of communications

- *preference impact* – procedural and distributive justice and personal liking for methods
- *expectational impact* – assumptions about organisational climate and psychological contract
- *attitudinal impact* – degree of investment in the selection process
- *behavioural impact* – the extent to which the selection methods create/affect subsequent behaviour.

### SOCIALLY CONSTRUCTED REALITY

This looks behind the *practice* of selection and considers it as part of a wider process serving other purposes within and beyond the organisation. For example, Bozionelos (2005) feels that selection is often a political arena which houses wider power games between organisational actors, such as when there are battles over scarce resources and each department seeks to appoint the person they want rather than the one who is rated more highly in scientific tests. Similarly, McDaniel (2009) examines the role that gerrymandering plays within selection decisions in order to get preferred candidates appointed; this can take place in relation to the methods chosen, the scoring and in choosing between candidates that meet the criteria for appointment. Brannan and Hawkins (2007) argue that whilst role playing a telephone call for people applying for a job in a call centre may look objective and reasonable in the circumstances, it can also assert managerial control by moulding job applicants to a prevailing organisational culture. In addition, selection decisions are not shaped solely within organisations but by wider societal frameworks (Ramsay and Scholarios 1999). This includes knowledge and power, social structures and expected norms. Consequently, 'an integrated model of selection should accommodate the subjective, discursive, power-laden, contested, negotiated and transient nature of each aspect of the process' (p.77). This contrasts starkly with the notion of scientific rationality and objective decisions, and it helps us to understand why choices about selection methods vary so much between countries and organisations.

## CONCLUSIONS

This chapter has reviewed the major components of resourcing and talent management, and has argued that all stages in this process – HR planning, talent management, recruitment and selection – play a key part in the process. Often, recruitment and HR planning are downplayed to focus on selection, and more recently talent management. Because of greater sophistication in selection, it is often forgotten that without effective recruitment practices the numbers of applicants from which to choose can be limited and can therefore impact on subsequent performance. Conversely, using well-chosen and appropriate multiple methods can increase the likelihood that successful candidates are capable of meeting targets and have a more positive psychological contract. This is an area of HRM which is routinely outsourced, especially recruitment advertising and psychometric testing, and being aware of the *limits* to one's expertise is just as important as knowing which techniques to use. Given that selection decisions are increasingly devolved to line managers, it is critical these processes are well organised, delivered and evaluated.

EXPLORE FURTHER

CHARTERED INSTITUTE OF PERSONNEL AND DEVELOPMENT/HAYS (2011d) *Resourcing and Talent Planning: annual survey report*. London: CIPD.

COOPER D., ROBERTSON I. and TINLINE, G. (2003) *Recruitment and Selection: A framework for success*. London: Thomson.

KONIG, C., KLEHE, U., BERCHTOLD, M. and KLEINMANN, M. (2010) 'Reasons for being selective when choosing personnel selection procedures', *International Journal of Selection and Assessment*, Vol.18, No.1, 17–27.

MACAN, T. (2009) 'The employment interview: a review of current studies and directions for future research', *Human Resource Management Review*, Vol.19, 203–18.

MORRELL, K. and ARNOLD, J. (2007) 'Look after they leap: illustrating the value of retrospective reports in employee turnover', *International Journal of Human Resource Management*, Vol.18, No.9, 1683–99.

MORRELL, K., LOAN-CLARKE, J. and WILKINSON, A. (2001) 'Unweaving leaving: the use of models in the management of employee turnover', *International Journal of Management Reviews*, Vol.3, No.3, 219–44.

ORLITZKY, M. (2007) 'Recruitment strategy', in P. Boxall, J. Purcell and P. Wright (eds), (2007a) *The Oxford Handbook of Human Resource Management*. Oxford: Oxford University Press.

RAMSAY, H. and SCHOLARIOS, D. (1999) 'Selective decisions: challenging orthodox analyses of the hiring process', *International Journal of Management Reviews*, Vol.1, No.4. 63–89.

SYLVA, H. and MOL, S. (2009) 'E-recruitment: a study into applicant perceptions of an on-line application system', *International Journal of Selection and Assessment*, Vol.17, No.3, 311–23.

TAYLOR, S. (2010) *Resourcing and Talent Management*. London: CIPD.

CHAPTER 9

# Performance Management

WITH LORRIE MARCHINGTON

## LEARNING OUTCOMES

By the end of this chapter, readers should be able to:

- design systematic induction programmes for employees
- advise line managers about the key issues involved in handling performance review /appraisal
- tackle poor performance using appropriate techniques.

In addition, readers should understand and be able to explain:

- the contribution that effective performance management systems can make to the achievement of organisational goals
- the way that cultural and contextual factors impact on performance review globally
- the role that attendance management can play in a comprehensive HR strategy.

## INTRODUCTION

It should be clear that horizontal and vertical integration are key themes in HRM, and nowhere is the concept of integration more important than in the management of performance. As we see below, performance management (PM) is a continuous process that links together performance, motivation, individual goals, departmental purpose, and organisational objectives. It incorporates central HRM issues, from recruitment, induction, training and development, reward management, through to capability procedures and termination (Boxall and Purcell 2008, pp.171–2). Indeed, it has been argued that performance management is synonymous with the totality of day-to-day management activity because it is about how work can be organised to achieve the best possible results.

Most performance management systems are broadly similar, in that they link together strategy and planning with employee socialisation, monitoring and review of progress, reinforcing performance standards and supporting individuals to achieve performance expectations. Of course it is impossible to deal with every aspect of performance management in this single chapter. Consequently, related issues are examined elsewhere in the book – the role of the HR function in Chapter 6, line managers in Chapter 7, recruitment and selection in Chapter 8, training and development in Chapter 10 and performance-related pay in Chapter 14.

## PERFORMANCE MANAGEMENT SYSTEMS

In this chapter we stretch beyond conventional definitions of performance management to include other aspects of the employment relationship, starting with the *induction* of new staff. It is crucial to select the right people, but also imperative to ensure that from day one, employees understand the nature of their tasks and how these fit into broader organisational cultures. These principles should be continuously reinforced both through informal daily interactions between managers and their staff, and through systematic and formal *performance review*; this contributes to worker commitment and motivation, thereby improving performance. However, review may also identify performance problems, even if great care has been taken with job analyses, recruitment, selection and induction. This brings us to the third stage of the performance management system, the phase of *reinforcing performance standards*. Where workers' discretionary behaviour is exemplary, then issues relate to reward, development and talent management. Where performance slips, it may manifest itself in a lack of interest in work, psychological problems, poor performance, and/or poor attendance. Sometimes, the problem becomes so severe that it explodes and the organisation is faced with a difficult situation, perhaps culminating in an application to employment appeal tribunal. Finally, where there are problems, *support* should be provided to enable individuals to meet performance requirements. In some cases informal support from the line manager may be enough, in other cases professional help may be necessary using occupational health, or counselling services. It should be noted that the terms 'performance review' and 'appraisal' are both used widely, so we use them interchangeably in this chapter.

Armstrong and Baron (2007, p.2) see performance management as a natural process of management and state that 'PM aims to make the good better, share understanding about what is to be achieved, develop the capacity of people to achieve it, and provide the support and guidance people need to deliver high performance and achieve their full potential to the benefit of themselves and the organisation'. More specifically, a performance management system:

- communicates the organisation's vision and objectives to all employees
- sets departmental and individual performance targets linked to organisational objectives
- uses formal review procedures to communicate performance requirements
- conducts formal review of progress
- uses the review process to identify training, development and reward outcomes
- evaluates the whole process.

**Figure 6 The principal components of the performance management process**

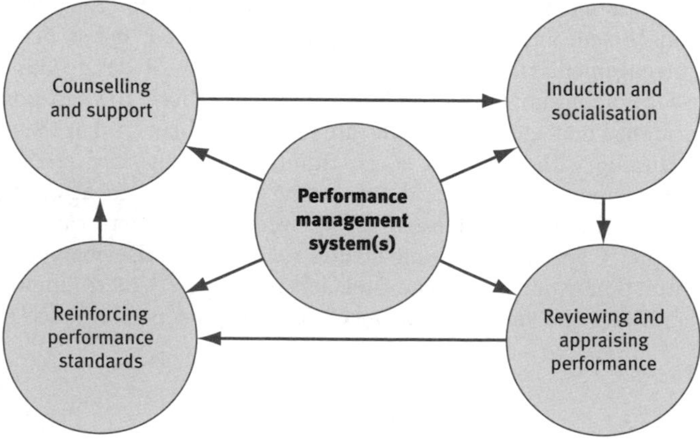

As outlined in Chapter 3, performance management is linked to most HR polices (Purcell *et al* 2003) and the Ability, Motivation and Opportunity (AMO) framework has major relevance because performance depends on a mix of ability, motivation and opportunity. This begs the question, what is it that makes employees go the extra mile? Is it simply reward in its many forms, fear of discipline or dismissal, or more subtle factors?

REFLECTIVE ACTIVITY

Think about what motivates you to work hard and go the extra mile. Identify the key factors.

Think about someone with whom you have worked who is not motivated to work hard. What are the factors that might have a bearing on their lack of motivation?

The best performance management systems operate in organisations with effective and endemic communication channels (see box below), and where the system links with learning and development (L&D) and with reward, while recognising that development in itself is a reward (Purcell *et al* 2007, p.39).

HRM AT WORK IN FOCUS

**Communications and Performance Appraisal at KPMG**

KPMG recognise the importance of 'dialogue' (the name which they give to their appraisal scheme): 'Dialogue encourages development and matches the career aspirations and talent of our people with our business needs. It fosters an environment of ongoing communication between individuals and performance managers, helping to ensure everyone meets their goals and maximises potential as individuals and as a firm.'

Source: Adapted from the KPMG website www.kpmgcampus.com

As with many issues, the **role of the line manager** is important because employee commitment often hinges on this (Purcell and Hutchinson 2007b; Latham *et al* 2007, pp.364–5), yet there is often a gap between HR policy and what is delivered by front-line managers. 'Poorly designed or inadequate polices can be "rescued" by good management behaviour in much the same way as "good" HR practices can be negated by poor front line manager behaviour or weak leadership' (Purcell and Hutchinson 2007b, p.4). Barriers for front-line managers include lack of time, work overload, lack of interest, conflicting priorities or because of political behaviour, dysfunctional managerial behaviour and personality syndromes (Boxall and Purcell 2008). It is typically assumed that line manager training will put right many of the problems, but much depends on the quality of the organisation's performance management system; this is particularly so in relation to induction.

## INDUCTION AND EMPLOYEE SOCIALISATION

Organisations spend billions on recruitment and selection yet often neglect induction and socialisation. Most texts stress that induction is a process that starts with recruitment and leads into continuous development. New recruits are briefed about performance standards and expectations, with learning needs established, and attempts are made to socialise them into the organisation. Typically, this is expressed through mission statements that articulate organisational goals, which are transcribed into departmental/divisional objectives. Much of the literature on performance management assumes this phase of the process is concerned with corporate communications, job descriptions and key accountabilities, each of which are considered elsewhere in this book. Induction training and initial socialisation into employment are rarely mentioned, but this is a critical time for establishing understanding about, and commitment to, wider corporate and departmental goals. Acas (2010a) suggests that 'the benefits of a good induction programme are a more settled employee, a more effective response to training, lower labour turnover, and improved industrial relations'. A formal induction need not be expensive, and the huge benefits gained from a systematic process far outweigh the costs of recruiting new staff if large numbers of people leave at the time of the 'induction crisis'.

Almost one in five new starters leaves an organisation within six months (CIPD 2009b). Induction is also important to the psychological contract as new employees consider whether their employer owes them more than agreed, and how much they owe the employer. In balancing this reciprocity of promises, if the employee concludes that the employer does in fact owe them more, this has obvious implications on their commitment and hence on performance and discretionary effort.

Irrespective of whether or not a structured programme is in place, all employees go through an induction phase. In many organisations, especially those that do not have a specialist HR manager, this may be little more than a rudimentary greeting before being shown to their place of work. New recruits may be told to ask questions if they need assistance and they are left to get on with the job, as it is assumed they have the required technical or administrative skills to cope. The rite of passage may consist of practical jokes ('go and find a left-handed screwdriver') and there may be little attempt to explain anything about the company mission, philosophy or policies. Even information about health and safety, disciplinary rules and company procedures may be dealt with informally, despite their importance in setting the tone of the workplace and defining acceptable behaviours. The problems associated with such informality are obvious. Employees may feel isolated and confused, unaware of rules and procedures and they may struggle to learn how to do the job. Low morale and commitment are likely to result if they end up breaking safety or disciplinary rules, and they may leave. Each of these problems represents a cost to the employer, either in direct financial terms (lengthening the amount of time it takes for the newcomer to be productive, poor-quality work, time spent on disciplinary issues, re-advertising jobs) or in public relations terms. Additionally, where new starters feel uncomfortable, they will not be honest about their training and development needs. In such circumstances, it is hardly surprising that employees question the depth of employers' commitments to people as their most important resource.

HRM AT WORK IN FOCUS

## Nippon CTV induction

At Nippon CTV, all new recruits received a two-day induction, which lays down the company rules. The first person to speak was the personnel officer. Rather than enthusing about the company, she seemed cynical and often referred to the company as 'them'. She explained, 'we have to make sure you know the rules and things so that you can't say that you didn't know if you don't do something right . . . Nippon CTV is harsh and strict, but that is the rule. If you are away three times in three months then it may well be that we'll be letting you go', and 'procedures can be very short'. She advised people to come in if they felt unwell and see the doctor in work: 'don't be ill, it's easier that way' and 'people do get ill, though Nippon CTV doesn't believe it'. All calls are logged so that workers cannot allege that they have called in sick. After the session with the personnel officer, recruits were shown a video and given general information about the company. Throughout emphasis was placed on the company rules and who to turn to with problems – usually the individual's team leader. On day 2 of induction much of the talk concentrated on training and there was a talk by the chief union shop steward. He explained that the union had signed a no-strike deal and did not get involved in collective bargaining, but that it was useful in handling grievances.

Source: Adapted from Delbridge R (1998).

Planning induction is a balancing act, and is not simple. Empathetic understanding of the stressful nature of being a new employee should mean that it is taken seriously. Although there is a considerable amount of information to get across, new recruits do not want data overload, and they also want to settle into their personal workspace and be given meaningful tasks. To ensure interest and relevance, the induction programme needs to be individually tailored in recognition of the experience and job specification of the newcomer. This usually translates into a combination of group and one-to-one activity paced over a period of time and may include an element of self-accessed online information. The line manager should play an important part as building a positive relationship at this stage will set the scene for future interaction. Sadly, line managers all too often regard induction as a chore, and few organisations give guidance on its importance. Others likely to be involved in induction include HR specialists, health and safety officers, IT staff, peer group, chief executive/MD and possibly trade union representatives (Acas 2010a).

HR specialists typically maintain quality assurance standards and deliver parts of the induction programme – such as information about welfare, wage and salary administration, grievance and disciplinary procedures. Specialists can aid line managers by designing policies and training in conjunction with them, and monitoring their effectiveness. Data on labour turnover crisis points, on the results of exit interviews, and on evaluating the experiences of recent recruits should all feed back into the process.

A successful induction profile:

- An initial short intensive programme on basic orientation and health and safety, followed by a longer tailored programme.
- Line managers take major responsibility for delivery and are given support to ensure that they have the appropriate motivation, skills and knowledge.

- Induction is integrated with training systems.
- Induction is evaluated to monitor its delivery and overall effectiveness.
- The programme has been updated within the previous two years.

REFLECTIVE ACTIVITY

Using the Acas documents on *Induction* work together in small groups to plan an induction programme for a particular individual and job role with which you are familiar. Be prepared to justify your scheme.

The content can be divided into three broad perspectives on the nature and purpose of the process. The first views it as an *administrative* exercise, designed to give information about the job, procedures and the organisation. The key point is what to include, when, so as to prevent information overload. Typically the following is covered:

- physical orientation – where everything is located
- orientation – how the person fits into the structure
- health and safety information (required by law in UK)
- terms and conditions of employment
- culture and history of the organisation, corporate social responsibility
- job/role requirements.
- company rules and policies, eg disciplinary and grievance procedures, equal opportunities policies, site speed limits, energy conservation
- employee development opportunities and sports and social amenities.

The second and third perspectives analyse the underlying philosophy of the process and its interpretation. The *social integration perspective* assumes that informal groupings have a powerful influence on how quickly a newcomer settles in and feels loyalty and commitment. An example of a successful induction programme is found in the box below.

HRM AT WORK IN FOCUS

**The Merchant Hotel, Belfast**

The Merchant Hotel is a small independent hotel Belfast. Its aim was to be the best hotel in Ireland catering for the top end of the market; it also aimed to be very different with unusual décor and a distinctive style of dealing with guests.

Its induction programme comprised three days off-site and two in the hotel and was mainly about teambuilding and establishing the style of the hotel through service delivery. Day one included a tour of the city; information about the history and geography of the region and the hotel site, as well as a talk from a famous butler on his experiences. Day two included words to use when talking to guests, how to greet guests, and grooming. Particular emphasis was given to dealing with complaints and turning them into opportunities. Day three centred on policies and procedures. The theme focus was on morale and motivation, and on the business vision. Day three ended with crazy golf as a teambuilding exercise. The last two days in the hotel concentrated on administration, health and safety, and meeting heads of department. All staff were invited to dine and stay one night in the hotel.

The result was turnover at 24% – low compared with the industry norm – and more importantly, the hotel's reputation as an excellent employer was established early on, resulting in a continuous stream of enquiries about vacancies.

Source: Adapted from CIPD (2007b).

Some organisations allocate a buddy to help new recruits socially as well as professionally. In some cases contact is made before the employee starts work and this enables help and advice to be offered where appropriate, eg with relocation. Picking the right person for this is obviously important, and would usually exclude the line manager. Someone of similar age and status with a good grounding in the work would be ideal (Taylor 2010, p.290). There are obvious advantages in introducing new starters to a range of people across a variety of functions. Similarly, there are advantages in having a buddy within the work team, as they are then on hand to help with queries about the work role, essentially acting as a mentor. There may be groups of workers for whom some cosseting is particularly appropriate, such as school-leavers, long-term unemployed, employees with disabilities, or new recruits from another culture (Acas 2010a). Buddies may need some training and support, particularly where they are supporting special groups.

The final perspective, *cultural control*, or *employee branding* makes use of various techniques to 'educate' employees about the company values and ethos, aiming to integrate them with existing organisational cultures. This perspective is associated with Japanese and US companies, exemplified by uniforms, badges, baseball caps and company credit cards. This *cultural control perspective* is often dismissed, but induction can be a powerful device for integrating new employees, gaining their commitment and inculcating them with a sense of belonging and identity, which forms a basis for effective performance 'beyond contract'. There is a fine line between cultural control and what some see as 'indoctrination'.

## REFLECTIVE ACTIVITY

Do you think there is any substance to the view that induction can be interpreted as indoctrination?

For workers who are relocating internationally to a new organisation, business and national culture, induction is even more critical, and yet it is often neglected. Web-based learning can be an asset here (Chu and Chu 2011). Apart from settling into a new organisation, many issues arise when adapting to an unfamiliar country, finding schools, and accommodation. Activities for spouses and children are of particular importance as their experiences are unstructured, but if they don't settle the international assignment may fail. Induction is more complicated and more critical for international expatriates as, financially, the costs of recruitment, relocation and training is usually extremely high and failed assignments generate negative publicity.

An effective induction programme enables new employees to become productive quickly, improves motivation and commitment, and ensures new starters get the same information. Essentially, induction is the start of the employee's development, in which the line manager plays a critical role. It is important to ensure that programmes are updated regularly to embrace new developments and to keep up to date with the law and internal procedures; however, many organisations allow their induction programmes to stagnate.

## PERFORMANCE REVIEW

Whilst induction sets out performance standards and expectations, review of these is the second stage of the performance management process. Performance review comprises a meeting between the employee and line manager with formal review taking place on an annual or more frequent basis, with more frequent informal meetings in between. The process should be continuous, but often the ongoing and unsolicited support (such as the telephone call or the 'chance' conversation just to check that all is going well) is overlooked. The 'review interview' then becomes the sole event when staff are praised or criticised, and when training and development needs are identified. Not that informal meeting should replace the formalised PR when adequate time is devoted to overview all performance issues in a structured and focused manner.

Ideally, the review should be an honest and open conversation between colleagues which summarises what has happened since the last review, based on fact rather than opinion. There should be no surprises, as issues should have been dealt with as they arose. Learning from mistakes and motivations arising from successes are both more likely if they are immediate. The manager uses counselling skills to actively listen and to offer constructive feedback, as well as to agree on future aims, career and personal development plans. In terms of self-development, every phase should be done jointly between the appraiser and appraisee and it is most effective if it includes self-assessment. The employee's involvement is especially important when determining objectives to ensure that these are appropriate and owned by the individual. The interview may also give employees an opportunity to comment on leadership, support and guidance from their managers. Increased informal feedback generates trust and confidence in line managers, and ultimately in the review process (Chiang and Birtch 2010).

The way in which appraisal is introduced is important to shaping attitudes towards it. There should be wide-ranging consultation; senior managers should be committed to the idea and ensure that time, training and resources are available; the scheme should be as simple as possible; timetables should be agreed for implementation; adequate training provided; a check should be made that appraisals are carried out and the system should be monitored and modified accordingly (Acas 2010b).

The main purposes and benefits of appraisal according to Gold (2007), Kuvaas (2011, 2008) and Chiang and Birtch (2010) are:

- clarification of performance expectations and standards
- allocation of rewards
- identification of learning and development needs
- career management
- counselling
- discipline
- planning remedial actions
- setting goals and targets
- improved motivation and morale
- improved employee productivity and quality
- job satisfaction
- increased trust
- improved communication.

Performance reviews are now widespread, particularly in the public sector and there has been an increase in use with non-managerial staff.

## MEASUREMENT AND RATING SYSTEMS

Reviews rely on clarity of the standards expected, particularly when they determine retention, reward, training, promotion and demotion (Latham *et al* 2007, p.265; Brown and Lim 2010). But ensuring validity in decision-making is not easy.

The first decision concerns **what to measure**. Whatever the system, there are likely to be problems in terms of meaningfulness, objectivity, accuracy, validity and equity. What is meaningful may not be measurable. For example, advice that covers all angles – on the basis that the customer does not know what they do not know – may be difficult to measure. Whereas answering the telephone within five rings may be measurable, but not very meaningful. Clearly, it is more important to be doing the right thing, rather than doing the wrong thing well. Where surveys are used, questions may be poorly worded, or open to wide interpretation, for example, 'Does the manager deal with problems in a flexible manner?' Setting SMART (Specific, Measurable, Achievable, Realistic and Time-bound) objectives is thought to ease measurement and eliminate some subjectivity, although this may be difficult. Over time, a variety of systems have been used to overcome problems of validity.

**Competencies** have been increasingly used for selection and L&D and they have spilled over into the field of performance management. Competencies are useful for identifying areas for improvement and provide appropriate language for feedback (Redman 2006, p.165). In theory, where competencies which are critical to good job performance are identified, it should be relatively simple to assess an individual's position in relation to each competency; in practice it is more difficult.

**Objective setting** is used by a majority of organisations although these may be influenced by factors outside the control of the worker/team; they often do not take into account the process and encourage outcome at any cost ignoring other elements. Additionally, in a rapidly changing climate is it difficult to continuously adjust objectives.

In response to the above problems, schemes appraising behaviours have become popular and this fits with theories that employees and their behavioural traits are valued above outcomes. Workers with emotional, practical and intuitive intelligence – displaying traits such as creativity, teamworking skills, perception and judgement, commitment, enthusiasm, loyalty, and using initiative – are likely to be the most effective workers (CIPD 2010d). However, measurement of behaviour is still more difficult and subject to bias. **Behavioural observation scales** and **behaviourally anchored schemes** are two such schemes. Behavioural observation scales allow raters to state the frequency with which they have observed specific job-related behaviours. Gold (2007, p.300) gives an example from a financial services company under the heading 'developing people'. Observed behaviour might include 'gives praise where it is due to others in the team'; 'provides constructive feedback to colleagues'; 'shares best practice with others'. Ratings may be on a 1–5 scale from Never to Always. Behaviourally anchored schemes are similar to competencies in that they are descriptions of key job behaviours 'anchored' to a rating scale. These scales are produced by getting those familiar with the job to write descriptions of effective and ineffective performance indicators (Gold 2007, p.299). Both are meant to facilitate communications and self-appraisal, and the former is slightly less open to bias (Gold 2007, p.300). However, both have low reliability, and are subject to bias and challenge from appraisees, leading to questions about the legality of their use in US and UK (Latham *et al* 2007, p.67).

**Electronic performance monitoring** can be used to give second-by-second tracking and provides fact-based performance review. Although this reduces theft and absenteeism, it leads to increased stress and labour turnover and debases trust between employer and employee (Latham *et al* 2007, p.370).

HRM AT WORK IN FOCUS

## Use of forced rankings

General Electric was among the first companies to use forced rankings, and other high-profile organisations, like Microsoft, have followed suit. They identify under-performers and suggest that the bottom 10% should be removed every year because they demotivate top performers and create inertia. Sun Microsystems ranks employees into 'superior' – the top 20%; 'standard' – the next 70%; and 'under-performers' – the bottom 10%. The latter are given one-to-one coaching and are expected to improve or leave. The idea is that such systems force managers to take tough decisions which they would otherwise avoid. In the UK, the Civil Service has adopted its use. It categorises senior managers into a top rank (top 25%), a middle rank (next 65–70%) and a bottom rank of 5–10% with pay linked to ranking.

Source: Adapted from: Michaels *et al* (2001); Arkin (2007b); and Redman (2006).

The advantage of forced ranking is that it increases productivity and motivation of those at the top, and as Pfeffer and Sutton (2006) remind us, 'the best performance comes in organisations where as many people as possible are treated as top dogs'. However, it is unlikely to motivate those at the bottom and questionable whether it would motivate the 70% labelled 'standard' at Sun Microsystems (see box above). Choice of usage of numerical, alphabetical, or verbal labels is important here. Using feedback, Orange adjusted its ratings from numbers to names. In the past it had a scale form 1–5, with many employees being rated '3'. People rated '3' felt that it meant that they had not met objectives. The 1–5 scale became 'exceptional', 'excellent', (three became) 'great stuff', 'getting there', and 'unacceptable' (Johnson 2006, p.57–60). A further advantage of forced ranking is that it aids budgetary control. If you know that 10% get a 5% increase, 20% a 4% increase etc, you can calculate costs, whereas this is not possible when using absolute performance, particularly as managers tend to push people into higher rankings (Arkin 2007b, p.28). Organisations that value knowledge workers and internal competition might use rankings rather than ratings (Latham *et al* 2007, p.371). A further example of use of forced ranking is given later in the chapter (Standard Chartered Bank).

There are obvious problems with this approach, particularly demotivation of lower-ranked employees. It has structural faults too, as 'under-performers' in high ranking sections are better than 'standard' employees in poorly performing sections; it belittles team-working, and sets up a competitive rather than co-operative culture; it may be subject to legal challenge as unions believe that appeals against such subjective decisions are almost impossible. Finally, its use is particularly hard on line managers who have to implement the scheme, although good processes for supporting underperformers may ameliorate this. Latham *et al* (2007) provide detail on rating systems and their validity.

## REFLECTIVE ACTIVITY

Think about an organisation with which you are familiar. Do you think that the adoption of forced rankings would improve performance, or reduce motivation?

For a detailed answer, refer to Latham *et al* (2007).

## WHO GENERALLY DOES PERFORMANCE REVIEWS?

The typical model is the individual performance review – usually conducted by line managers, although others may be involved. Choices about who should appraise depend on international location, nationalities involved, organisational cultures, and the group to be appraised. Options include: self-assessment, peer assessment (colleagues at the same grade/level), upward assessment (the appraisee's subordinates), external assessors (such as consultants or assessment centres), internal or external customers for the individual's services.

*Reviews conducted by the immediate supervisor* are appropriate where reward is linked to performance, and where control is one of the aims; however, it is also prevalent where the aim is developmental. This method ideally results in strengthening relationships, but only where the relationship is already sound, and where the manager has the appropriate skills. If the aim is developmental, both the organisational culture and the managers' approach are critical, as a 'control' focus is likely to stifle open discussion. It is the relationship between the parties that has the single most powerful influence on success, and is one of the major problems. Disagreements may well arise and the process can quickly break down where neither party subscribes to the goals or philosophy of the system, or where mutual trust is lacking. Where reward is involved the manager must balance control/judgement and support/development, while acting as both judge and helper. In recent years there has been a shift away from relying predominantly on managers' reviews, as we see below.

*Self-assessment* is often combined with other forms of assessment. Research indicates that most self-assessments are reasonably accurate, although there can be problems with over-inflation and down-rating. Where rewards depend on the outcome of appraisal, it can be a powerful incentive to over-inflate. On the other hand, research has shown that some groups (women in particular) tend to rate themselves lower than men and further problems arise when cultural differences are involved (Fletcher 2008, p.83).

*Upward review* is increasingly being adopted by UK companies, although this may be very threatening and/or undermining for managers. Employees comment on their manager's performance, usually through an anonymous questionnaire. This relies on employees not feeling intimidated, nor using the opportunity to register unjustified complaints against their supervisors, factors that may explain lack of widespread use in the UK (Brown and Lim 2010).

*Peer assessment* involves colleagues, and is particularly suited to team review, although when used outside of small teams it can lead to problems of selection.

*Team review*: it would seem logical that the team should appraise its own work, since teams are often given responsibility for allocating work, selecting new staff, and reward. In some cases the team leader responsible for the review allocates each team member the same rating, and the team deals internally with issues regarding competency and development of individual team members.

*Customer review* is becoming increasingly widespread, sometimes feeding into the setting of performance targets, especially if service guarantees involve compensation to customers. Customer surveys might include a wide variety of techniques, including electronic surveillance, and it is now common for call centres to record a random sample of conversations. A more controversial means is the use of individuals posing as customers to check quality of service.

## 360-DEGREE PERFORMANCE APPRAISAL

Because of problems with other forms of review, 360-degree, or multi-source, performance appraisals have been growing in popularity, but the extent of its use is in question with wildly differing estimations. Typically, it incorporates voluntary feedback from peers, subordinates and supervisors, and is particularly useful if customer feedback is included. It is usually confidential, self-determining and learning-oriented, rather than linked to assessment. However, there is a range of types and purposes for 360-degree feedback. Its use is based on two assumptions: first that self-awareness increases when feedback is based on a number of assessments and second, that self-awareness is a prerequisite for improved performance.

360-degree appraisals are particularly popular as they encourage self-awareness, multi-rater assessment provides greater validity; it encourages open communications; provides a framework for development of poor performers, and aids strategic planning (Fletcher 2008; Bach 2005a, p.307):

It may be more appropriate for more open organisational forms because:

- It fosters continuous improvement.
- It aligns with the shift from management-driven to employee-driven performance management processes. With flatter organisations and greater spans of control it is more difficult for any one manager to appraise a large number of staff with any degree of accuracy or knowledge.
- The concept fits well with employee involvement and empowerment and open organisational cultures.
- Involving staff in upward reviews enhances their commitment. Subordinates are often in closer contact with their managers than senior staff and are on the receiving end of his or her actions.
- An open system in which employees have access to their personal files lessens the likelihood of legal action.
- It is suited to the service sector when customer feedback is included.

REFLECTIVE ACTIVITY

What do you see as the major problems with 360-degree performance review? How might they be overcome?

Two of the main drawbacks are cost and the production of what might be an overwhelming amount of information. As with all forms of feedback, there remain questions about whether the data is consistent, accurate, valid, or even useful to the organisation. Its success is dependent on effective pre- and post-communication to convince those involved of its usefulness, validity, and to assure anonymity. Training is needed in analysing the information, giving and receiving feedback, and on developing effective self-appraisal (Fletcher 2008; Redman 2006, p.162; Latham *et al* 2005). Since many of these elements are missing, it is hardly surprising that there are some reports of only small improvements resulting from 360-degree feedback (Smither *et al* 2005; Fletcher 2008, p.84).

### PROBLEMS WITH PERFORMANCE REVIEW

Reviewing staff performance is the most disliked of line managers' activities (Redman 2006, p.165) perhaps because of problems around validity, conflicts of purpose and fundamental questions over whether or not it is effective.

#### Validity

The first major issue relates to validity. Grint's classic work (1993) describes common assessment distortions. The '**halo**' effect occurs when the appraiser notes desirable traits and allows these to spread to all other attributes. The '**horn**' effect is the reverse and results in a lower assessment than might otherwise be expected. The '**crony**' effect is caused by closeness of the personal relationship between appraiser and appraisee. The '**Veblen**' effect results in central tendencies, so-named after the tutor's habit of giving all his students C grades irrespective of their quality. Finally, the '**doppelganger**' effect occurs when appraisers reward similarities between themselves and appraisee, whereas differences lead to adverse ratings. There are clear equal opportunities implications (Latham and Mann 2006) and in local government research (Rana 2003, p.11) senior managers' performance ratings of ethnic minority managers were lower than ratings given by peers. Other distortions include the '**recency**' effect where only events that have happened recently are remembered and commented on. Personal idiosyncrasies may feature too. For example, the manager who manipulates ratings for their own ends by downgrading graduates to 'show them that they didn't know everything' or gives high ratings in order to get rid of weak performers (Redman 2006, p.166). Added to these is the '**confirmation bias**' – where the appraiser looks for information that confirms their pre-conceived evaluation of the employee (Latham *et al* 2007, p.377) and the '**impression effect**' where employees use effective impression management to hoodwink the appraiser into believing their performance is better than it actually is (Redman 2006, p.166). There is a range of distortions relating the complex motives of appraiser and appraisee with some line managers acting politically or dysfunctionally, as where they are intimidated and jealous of high-fliers (Brown and Lim 2010; Boxall and Purcell 2008, p.182).

As we saw earlier, problems over measurements are endemic, and development of objective ratings systems has proved elusive, particularly when attempting measurement of behaviour or personality traits.

### Conflict of purpose

Where the primary purpose of the review is reward, the employee is unlikely to openly discuss performance problems. Furthermore, review for reward tends to be backward-facing, and future development needs may be overlooked. Despite these problems, there is ample evidence that review commonly incorporates both developmental and reward aims, and many are top-down.

It is generally agreed that it makes sense to reward the best performers. However, research has shown that a majority of those in an organisation believe that their work merits reward and if this reward is not forthcoming, they feel demotivated. Similarly, it is unlikely to motivate those with major development needs (Purcell *et al* 2007). Cumulative financial penalties are also a major issue; most workers are unaware of the impact of financial penalties over their lifetime, but if they calculated them, they are likely to be extremely discontented (see box below).

HRM AT WORK IN FOCUS

#### Financial penalties associated with performance review

For those who, perhaps for just one year, get a zero increase in salary, this has long-term implications. For example, a 40-year-old worker who received a zero rise one year would lose out a total of £30–40,000 in pay and pension where there is a final salary pension scheme, when compared with someone getting a 3% rise, if this shortfall is never made up during their working life.

Source: adapted from Attwood (2005).

Employees are more likely to trust a performance-related pay system which they see as fair, equitable, consistent and transparent (Armstrong and Baron 2007, p.110). This would imply some form of rating system, but just over half of organisations operating performance-related pay did not have a rating system and in any case, as we saw earlier, ratings systems are never totally objective (Armstrong and Baron 2007). Some organisations separate pay and developmental review meetings. For further details on employee reward, refer to Chapters 12 and 13.

### Control or commitment?

Redman (2006, p.159) believes that there is a shift away from using review for career planning and determining future potential to one of control and manipulation with 'screw your buddy' peer review systems, and 'failed' managers who are dispensed with. Bach (2005a, p.306) sees review as a 'form of disciplinary gaze' in reference to Foucault's concept of power. This is particularly apparent in customer service work where technological monitoring of performance is commonplace.

### The culture is not conducive to its introduction

A developmental framework for performance review will only be successful if it is introduced into an open culture of trust. It cannot be expected to provide a universal panacea for motivating disaffected employees or those with low levels of trust in their managers.

### Does it work?

The process assumes that individuals will accept feedback and amend behaviour accordingly, although this is not guaranteed. Not all appraisees react in the same way to performance review. Satisfaction and work performance is mediated by individual work motivation; those with high intrinsic motivation have a positive relationship, and those with low intrinsic motivation have a negative relationship (Kuvaas 2006, 2007, 2011). Furthermore, **developmental** review can demotivate the best employees who already perform well autonomously and are highly committed and motivated (Kuvaas 2007). They may feel that the time and resources deployed are unnecessary and that they are more than capable of self-assessment.

Where there are disagreements between the parties involved, or where the appraisee is not allocated rewards, appraisal is not likely to be successful even where the process is managed well. Even among the best employers, best practice is not always evident (Armstrong and Baron 2005; Redman 2006). To a large extent, success is determined by the attitudes and aims of those involved rather than the quality of the paperwork (Brown and Lim 2010; Fletcher 2008, pp.90–1), as the local government case study discussed later in the chapter demonstrates.

### Bureaucracy

Reviews are often seen as a bureaucratic, expensive, time-consuming and irksome exercise carried out to satisfy the HR function; the event can become meaningless to all parties, but the paperwork is duly completed and filed. Where review is not seen to add value, and appraisers are not rewarded for conducting them on time, then the system often peters out. Conversely, where the system works well, managers will adopt review as a key contributor to a high-commitment performance-oriented culture. Many organisations have acted to reduce the bureaucracy, and most continually adjust systems.

**Table 22 General views on employee review**

| Organisation | Comments |
|---|---|
| TRW Aeronautical Systems | *'TRW has a well-established web-based approach that incorporates performance management and employee development.'* |
| Plymouth City Council | *'Feedback on under-performance must be timely – otherwise it might be too late for the organisation, and the individual.'* |
| North Tyneside Council | *'If carried out properly, the appraisal process is a valuable management tool. It can improve performance, morale and commitment ... Done badly and we have got problems.'* |
| Budgens Stores | *'The importance of quality one-to-one time is the key, and the skills of the individual managers to achieve open and honest conversations determines the effectiveness of the appraisal.'* |
| Warburtons | *'Valuable tool if fully integrated vertically with business strategy and cascaded appropriately.'* |

Source: Adapted from *IRS Employment Review* 769a (2003).

## LINE MANAGER TRAINING AND SKILLS

Line managers are usually given the responsibility for performance review, and their training is as important as choice of rating system (Latham *et al* 2007, p.368). Research from Purcell and Hutchinson (2007a, p.13) at Selfridges demonstrated that most dissatisfaction related to the line manager's role – in this case only 58% of respondents were satisfied with the appraisal system. Particular problems related to inconsistency and not being asked for their views (pp.19–25).

Feedback is one of the most important components, but it is also the most difficult to do well. Managers may feel embarrassed about commenting on standards and broaching personal/behavioural traits. Where weak performance leads to loss of earnings or dismissal, avoidance is a typical response; negative feedback needs to be handled sensitivity if it is not to result in demotivation. One result of this is ratings drift where large numbers end up with above-average ratings. Particular problems arise where there are personality conflicts, or 'bizarre' personalities. Appraisers may be ill-prepared, talk too much, base discussion on third-party complaints and rely on 'gut feelings'. Other managers may find it difficult to hand over ownership of the process to the appraisee. Without training, managers may not be competent or confident to tackle underperformance. Apart from lack of training, as systems become more complex, and line managers have an increasing number of tasks, time to carry out appraisal is a major issue, and where line managers have no faith in the system, they are unlikely to engage with it.

## THE FUTURE OF PERFORMANCE REVIEW

Few would state that appraisal is objective, rational and systematic, but, despite problems, it is here to stay because of its centrality to day-to-day management and its integral role in the high commitment bundle (refer to Chapter 3 for more on this). When performance review works well, it aids self-determination, motivation, personal development and growth, as well as increasing confidence and job satisfaction. Developmental reviews fit with the current trends away from control to high performance, autonomous working and, under the new psychological contract employees expect such treatment. Over recent years, a number of changes have overcome problems.

Performance review is becoming more **universal** and now covers most of the workforce including blue collar, secretarial, and admin staff, rather than just managerial levels; additionally, post-Higgs Report (2003), it includes directors. The increased **use of technology** has helped remove some bureaucracy and aids feedback by suggesting appropriate wording and r**atings systems** have improved validity and reliability scores.

Nonetheless, however objective the ratings, employees have their own opinions of their performance, the rewards they deserve, and the development opportunities which they seek. Raters typically want systems to be easy to use and result in changing attitudes and behaviours, whereas employees want clear links between behaviour and reward (Latham *et al* 2007, p.371). Where employees disagree, their behaviour is unlikely to change and negative feedback can demotivate them. There is a need for constant evaluation to ensure that systems are operating as they should, as well as continuous coaching/training of line managers who are doing performance reviews (Latham *et al* 2005).

As we saw earlier, there are many questions about how effective review really is. It is expensive, generates conflict, contains too many distortions, and does not enhance the strategic management of the organisation. It only works well when it is well-resourced and well-led, leading Boxall and Purcell (2008, p.182) to suggest that small firms might be better advised to stick with informal methods. Nor is it a management panacea. Just as we have individual learning styles, so too we each have different motivational styles and values. Not all workers are easily motivated and committed to organisational goals and some may have personality traits that preclude effective social skills and team-working. The psychological literature puts emphasis on contexts, the personality, beliefs and opinions of those involved. Although performance reviews might motivate committed workers it must be remembered that it is but one tool in the management kitbag, and may not produce the desired outcome with every individual, however well managed, as the case study in the box below demonstrates.

HRM AT WORK IN FOCUS

## Janet as appraiser and appraisee – a local authority case study

Janet was newly appointed to a local authority post, line managing 20 staff. She quickly discovered that there had been a long history of laissez-faire management, and that two previous women managers had left the post after lengthy periods of stress having tried to put some structure into the service.

**Rose and Janet**

Rose had worked with the authority for some years and was used to working in her own way. People at all levels in the organisation 'trod around' her with great care. She could work hard and well when she wanted to, but she seemed to have little interest in the aims of the organisation and refused all training. At about the same time as Janet was appointed new management systems were introduced, including performance appraisal. Rose resented what she saw as an encroachment on her usual ways of working, and resented Janet's role. Janet initially tried to harness Rose's motivation by using positive feedback and giving her a high degree of autonomy, but Rose refused to change her work practices to accommodate changes in the service needs, and in review meetings she was sullen. Janet maintained an open style through appraisal, but felt that she would eventually have to use these reviews to set targets based on control rather than equality.

**Salina and Janet**

Salina was a dynamic, self-motivated single parent who was keen to stretch herself by taking on responsibilities and training. Janet and Salina met regularly to discuss work issues. Notes were taken at the meetings and Salina's development was often discussed. Salina was on a clerical grade, but took on professional-level responsibilities to cover when her line manager was absent for a long period. She enrolled on a part-time HNC, but since the authority would not help with this, she paid for the course herself and attended in her own time. Annual appraisals provided quality time to discuss issues that had been skated over in their more regular meetings.

**Janet and John**

John had been in the service for many years and line-managed Janet. Janet felt under constant pressure when she joined the service, mainly because of the laissez-faire management style she had inherited that had lead to entrenched staff attitudes. She took her problems to John and on one occasion said that she desperately needed proactive support. John responded by saying that he always gave support when he was asked for it, and suggested that Janet attend a stress management course. Janet did not think that this was the answer, and began to realise that unless she took her own solutions to the meetings, John would not be able to help. John never initiated meetings, and often neglected to produce records of the meetings that took place. The reviews became increasingly irregular and Janet put less effort into preparation for them.

*To think about:*

*Do you agree that the main aims of PM are to motivate and value workers? Do you think that performance review was an effective motivator for people in the case study?*

## PERFORMANCE MANAGEMENT SYSTEMS AROUND THE GLOBE

Although many MNCs export their home-country performance management system across the globe and expect them to fit, this will not work without taking into account cultural and contextual factors which create differences between and within countries (Varma *et al* 2008; Chiang and Birtch 2010; Claus and Briscoe 2009). This may be due to home-country ethnocentrism, possibly combined with lack of respect or indifference to expatriate experiences. Commonly, performance management systems are Western in origin and rooted in US values of equity and procedural justice (Chiang and Birtch 2010). Cultural norms, values, and beliefs affect how performance is viewed and the way employees are motivated as issues of equity, expectations and justice differ. Expatriates or those on international assignments deal with employees from different cultures, religions, nationalities with particular traditions, technology, and historical backgrounds; and it is important that they understand the motivations and expectations of other expatriates and country nationals. There are endless permutations: an expatriate manager may have to manage those from the parent company, host country nationals, and third country nationals. Examples might include the UK manager operating in Japan and acting as appraiser for managers from Finland, or the Chinese manager working in US acting as appraiser of Indian workers. Much of the theoretical work on culture is based on the work of Hofstede (see Chapter 5 for more on this), but context is as important, and the two are intricately linked. Contextually, the size of the company and the type of firm ownership (MNC, joint venture, private family, public sector, private sector) are important (Sharma *et al* 2008; Barzantny and Festing 2008; Claus and Briscoe 2009). There are often huge differences between HQ and overseas subsidiaries in terms of what is valued, and perceptions of behaviour, plus communications from home country may be misunderstood (not only because of language differences) and often there is a lack of effective performance goals for the overseas operation (Briscoe and Claus 2008). Since many expatriates are provided with inadequate induction, this exacerbates problems (Claus and Briscoe 2009).

Cultural and contextual issues are exacerbated in relation to performance review. There is often **ratings bias** when managers from different cultures judge behaviour of subordinates, and subordinates may rate their own behaviour differently. Examples might include a modesty bias common to Asia, or a bias towards family or community members – 'guanxi' in China (Claus and Briscoe 2009). Indian and Chinese managers tend to give employees they like higher ratings. Claus and Briscoe (2009) cite the example of Japanese expatriates working in the US; here Japanese subordinates were rated higher than American subordinates, but only when evaluated by a Japanese manager. Training obviously helps eliminate rater bias, but research indicates that even in the best global organisations, less than half provide such training (Biron *et al* 2011).

In those countries with high power distance, **360 degree feedback** would not be welcomed (Cooke 2005, p.178; DeNisi *et al* 2008, p.260; Varma *et al* 2008; Chiang and Birtch 2010; Claus and Briscoe 2009). This is evidenced in the box below. In collectivist cultures group-based feedback and goal setting is more common. China, South Korea, Japan, Brazil, Greece, and Saudi Arabia are categorised as collectivist cultures, whereas Netherlands and US are categorised as individualistic (Barzantny and Festing 2008). Open frank discussions about performance would not happen in China or Asian countries where loss of face is important (Chiang and Birtch 2010). Feedback is likely to be top-down, control-oriented, formal and infrequent, and used to determine reward. In such cases, less trust is generated in the process and this becomes a vicious cycle (Chiang and Birtch 2010). Peer evaluations, too, may be unacceptable, and the more hierarchical the setting, the less likely that upward feedback is used (eg India). This compares to the US culture which tends towards egalitarianism, reduced hierarchy, and low power distance between workers. These features facilitate open discussion, especially where reward is tied into PM – as is common in Finland and Sweden (Pulakos *et al* 2008).

**Motivation and uncertainty avoidance** are other variables. In Mexico, appraisal is rarely used as a motivational tool and managers tend to employ benevolent paternalism (as in India) to protect their staff. This leads to overrating of appraisees and workers can become dependent (Briscoe and Claus 2010; Varma and Budhwar 2011; Sharma *et al* 2008). Countries such as Belgium, Portugal and Israel are rated highly on uncertainty avoidance and US, China and India are rated low (Barzantny and Festing 2008).

Even in countries which one would expect to be similar in outlook, such as Germany and France, there are differences. They are similar in that both model their performance management systems on the USA, and often use the balanced scorecard. In contrast to the USA, both display pluralist and collectivist traditions with emphasis on social welfare and responsibility towards the more disadvantaged in society; social partnership; stronger legal environment; and differences in ownership and governance. They differ from each other as they have different histories, cultures, and environments, which impact on their understanding of performance management. The French approach is couched in conflictual industrial relations and the legal requirement that French organisations invest 1.6% of payroll on training. There is emphasis on employee involvement, governance, and well-being. In contrast with Germany, the French system leans more towards control, whereas in Germany emphasis is on co-ordination and co-operation. The German system is legalistic, and there is lower power distance in Germany (Barzantny and Festing 2008, p.160).

HRM AT WORK IN FOCUS

## Performance management in China

History has a bearing on culture, and this has a bearing on performance management systems. In China, prior to the end of the Cultural Revolution in 1976, the state controlled numbers employed, who they were, and pay rates, and around 75% of urban employees worked for state-owned organisations. Wages were low and there were small differentials between grades, but jobs were for life, regardless of performance. From the late 1970s, a number of factors decreased state control, in particular inward foreign investment and privatisation, and there was mass movement from agriculture and heavy industry. Chinese performance review existed but it was mainly used for attendance and skill grading, or to select and promote cadres. From the 1980s, new systems were introduced by incoming organisations, although most made adjustments to suit Chinese culture. Performance-related reward was brought in to motivate ordinary workers (often rural migrants) by supplementing extremely low wages to compensate for long hours, and determine job security. Appraisal for managers and professionals were usually annual, more sophisticated, and sometimes included self-appraisal. A peer appraisal/collective meeting was commonly followed by the supervisor signing forms and sending them to HR. Such systems became part of government and civil service organisations where four main performance indicators are typically used: morality, competence/ability, obedience/diligence/work attitude, and achievement. Some organisations add honesty/non-corrupted. Some managers and professionals working for MNCs welcomed the emphasis on development and feedback.

There was a significant shift from political affiliation to outcomes, and the inclusion of behaviours such as morality, honesty and obedience, is very Confucian. Other cultural features include:

- respect for age and seniority
- collectivist rather than individually focused
- sensitivity over loss of 'face' (mianzi)
- importance of guanxi (connections – often family)
- harmony as opposed to conflict is paramount
- high power distance factors.

The practical impact of these cultural features is that feedback and goal-setting tend to be to the group rather than to the individual; egalitarianism means that workers do not want to be singled out for reward/prizes and often prizes are shared between colleagues, or rotated. Negative feedback is avoided to save face and to retain harmony; it would be particularly inappropriate to criticise elders or those more senior, and modesty and self-discipline affect self-evaluation. Whether or not guanxi is involved, appraisal is likely to be highly subjective. It is typically highly formalised, top-down, lacking transparency, with limited employee participation. Work attitudes such as obedience, effort and conscientiousness may be rewarded above performance outcomes and the trait of avoiding criticism leads to tolerance of poor work, which can demotivate the best workers. Where ratings are used, the result is a broad band.

A conversation reported by Cooke (2008, p.206) brings this alive:

> *It is an annual joke for us. When we appraised ourselves, we all said we had been performing adequately and had tried our best. But there was still room for improvement and we would like to receive more criticism and guidance from our leaders and colleagues in order to improve ourselves next year. We would then give one or two examples of very trivial areas which we have identified as targets for improvement. Of course, we were not going to disclose or admit to any major failures because, apart from being face losing, they would go on your personnel record. It would give others excuses for allocating you to a lower category for the annual bonus... When it came to the appraisal of our chief, nobody dared say anything negative about him no matter how much we hated him, as we don't want him to take revenge on us. But we had to find some negative points to say about him to help him improve next year just as a formality. After a long silence, I made the speech. I praised the leader highly at first and then said, 'the only shortcoming of our leader is that he worked too hard and did not pay sufficient attention to his own health'.*

There is small wonder that the system becomes no more than an administrative exercise. Apart from these problems, there may also be structural issues: such as absence of organisational strategic goals, making it hard to align performance management systems; undeveloped information systems to support the system; review introduced without complete understanding of performance indicators; focus on reward rather than development; managers lacking skills and training and not accepting the system, making for a lack of alignment of outcomes and reward.

Source: Adapted from Cooke (2008); Varma and Budhwar (2011); Chiang and Birtch (2010); DeNisi *et al* (2008).

There is evidence of some movement towards westernised systems (more egalitarian, increased participation and use of feedback, etc) particularly in large organisations and MNCs. This can be seen in India, China, Japan and South Korea where merit is increasing in importance relative to age and seniority (Claus and Briscoe 2009; DeNisi *et al* 2008; Chiang and Birtch 2010; Sharma *et al* 2008). Economic maturity is an important dimension – possibly as important as culture – so as economies become more 'sophisticated' the performance management system places increased emphasis on individual performance and merit (DeNisi *et al* 2008, p.257). This may or may not be a good thing. The aim is for performance management systems to be globally consistent and locally appropriate (Varma and Budhwar 2011, p.458) and this means removing ethnocentric blinkers so as to understand both the culture and context of the host country, including a range of variables such as the state of technology, legal and political frameworks (Varma and Budhwar 2011; Chiang and Birtch 2010). Performance review is always one of the most difficult management tasks, and when it operates across borders the need for effective induction, training and evaluation to ensure cultural and contextual alignment is particularly important (DeNisi *et al* 2008).

## REINFORCING PERFORMANCE STANDARDS

### DEVELOPMENT AND TALENT MANAGEMENT

Most reviews encourage employees to think about their needs for training, either to enhance their current jobs, or to assist them with career progression. The review provides data for succession planning, as can be seen from the Standard Chartered Bank case study in the box below.

HRM AT WORK IN FOCUS

#### Talent Management at Standard Chartered Bank

Standard Chartered Bank has its HQ in London, but the bulk of its profits are from work in Asia, Africa, and the Middle East. It operates in over 50 countries and its 60,000 employees are made of 100 different nationalities. Because it works in a competitive field, it has to work hard to retain the best talent. Its performance management systems are informed by hard data which are analysed by country, by team, by type of employee etc. There are certain standards to which all parts of the organisation adhere (such as six-monthly performance appraisal), but there are options offered within this. For example, managers can choose whether to adopt 360-degree appraisal (common in Africa), or 180-degree (more common in China). The system is used to categorise employees into high-potentials – those who would rise quickly; critical resources – people who have potential to improve; core contributors – those who are probably working to their capacity; underachievers who need help to improve; and, finally, underperformers who are 'in the wrong job and should be moved into another role or managed out'. Controversially, people are not told how they are classified; but the information is used by managers. The categorisations are analysed centrally, allowing the bank to look strategically at its talent by comparing one country with another. Recently the bank realised that it was losing a lot of new recruits, and, as a result, rolled out a global induction programme.

The talent management scheme identifies senior managers whose leadership skills it wishes to enhance. These top managers are profiled to increase self-awareness and offered coaching. In addition, all managers can access self-help tools such as 'conversations that matter', which helps managers develop the skills needed to conduct performance appraisal.

Adapted from Syedain (2007).

### MANAGING POOR PERFORMANCE

Much of the HRM literature describes situations in which workers have used initiative to work well beyond their contractual obligations. Examples include the secretary who redrafted a letter to incorporate new information while his boss was away, or the production worker who ignored instructions and changed a machine setting to override a fault.

Although such examples are quoted regularly, they are probably less extensive than the number of cases where employees fall short of targets or, worse still, fail to turn up for work at all.

Performance management generally tends to be seen in terms of positive reinforcement and identification of weaknesses to aid setting development targets. In the past, there has been relatively little focus on ineffective performance and those who are unable or unwilling to meet standards required, although reviews are bound to expose poor performance. Where this is exposed, much of the literature emphasises organisational inadequacies that contribute to ineffective performance. Examples include problems relating to recruitment and selection, promotion, work conditions, inadequate job descriptions, poor managers, work overload, stress and work organisation, and lack of appropriate training and development. Organisations are paying increasing attention to under-performance; as through the use of ratings systems that remove the bottom 10%. The issue of managing poor performance is considered below in relation to capability and ill-health, then attendance/absence is discussed.

### Use of capability procedures and dismissal

It is acknowledged that mistakes can be made at the initial interview, or when people are promoted. However, where the problem is capability, use of procedures leading to dismissal can be used. According to Lewis *et al* (2011, p.241), 'capability' is assessed by reference to 'skill, aptitude, health or any other physical or mental quality' with inflexibility or lack of adaptability included under 'aptitude and mental qualities'.

Stress is placed on the importance of early identification of problems and informality to begin with, as well as an investigation into the causes of poor performance. Acas (2010b) suggests that at interview, or point of promotion, it should be made clear what standards of work will be expected and any conditions attached to probationary periods should be explained. Where poor performance is identified the procedure should be:

- The employee should be asked for an explanation and the explanation checked.
- Where the reason is lack of the required skills, the employee should, wherever possible, be helped through training and given reasonable time to reach the required standards.
- Where the employee is then unable to reach the required standards, it should be considered whether alternative work could be found.
- Where alternative work is not available, the position should be explained to the employee before dismissal proceedings begin (Acas 2011).

Workers should not normally be dismissed because of poor performance unless warnings and a chance to improve have been given. Moreover, if the main cause of poor performance is the changing nature of the job, employers should assess whether the situation should be dealt with through redundancy rather than capability. Where individuals are not prepared to work as required – as opposed to not being able to – the case is likely to be dealt with as misconduct. Refer to Acas Code of Practice for Disciplinary and Grievance for more on this.

In practice, many managers avoid capability issues, maybe by moving the person to another department, or having a quiet word about inadequate performance and the prospect of capability/disciplinary proceedings in the hope that the person will leave.

REFLECTIVE ACTIVITY

How are capability issues dealt with in your organisation (or one with which you are familiar)? How should such issues be addressed?

**Ill-health**

Where the problem relates to ill-health, the basic issue is whether the employer could be expected to wait any longer for the employee to recover, as well as whether the contract has been frustrated. In cases of long-term illness, the *Acas Guide* recommends the following:

- The employee and employer should maintain regular contact.
- The employee should be kept informed if employment is at risk.
- The employee's GP/consultant should be asked when a return to work is likely and what sort of work the employee might be capable of.
- Using the GP's report, the employer should consider whether alternative work is available.
- The employer is not expected to create a special job, but to take action on the basis of the medical evidence.
- Where there is doubt about the ill-health, the employee should be asked if they are willing to be examined by a medical expert employed by the company.
- Where an employee refuses to co-operate in providing medical evidence or to be examined, the employee should be told in writing that a decision will be taken on the basis of the information available and that this could result in dismissal.
- Where the employee's job can no longer be kept open and no suitable alternative work is available the employee should be informed of the likelihood of dismissal.
- Where dismissal takes place, the employee should be given the period of notice to which they are entitled and informed of right of appeal.

When there are intermittent absences owing to ill-health, the employer does not necessarily have to rely on medical evidence, but can take an overview of the worker's employment history. This should take into account factors such as the type of illness and likelihood of recurrence, lengths of absence, the employer's need for that particular employee, the impact of the absences on the workforce and how far the employee was made aware of their position. In such cases dismissal may take place at a time when the employee is fit and in work (Lewis *et al* 2011, p.242). Decisions to dismiss are based on individual circumstances; for example, where an employer cannot manage without the post-holder, a decision to dismiss may take place after a short space of time. However, if it is possible to arrange cover for the post-holder, the employer may wait for the employee's return. Critical questions are whether the employee could return to work if they were given help, or if more suitable alternative employment was available.

Where the illness is the result of disability, the **Disability Discrimination Act** (DDA) 1995 applies. Under the Act employers discriminate unlawfully if they do not make 'reasonable adjustments' for disabled employees. Section 1(1) of the Act states: 'A person has a disability if they have a physical and mental impairment which has a substantial and long-term adverse effect on their ability to carry out normal day-to-day activities.' The Act covers a wide range of physical and mental conditions. For further information refer to specialist law texts such as Lewis *et al* (2011) and to Acas (2010c).

## MANAGING ATTENDANCE

Absence is a measure of corporate health as it may indicate low morale and conflict at work, and it is intrinsically linked with retention. Employers are increasingly aware of their 'duty of care' for employees, whilst attendance is seen as a major business risk. Acas estimates that the average worker is absence for 8.4 days per year, roughly an annual cost of £598 per employee, and the cost to the UK economy is estimated to be £10–12 billion (Acas 2010d, p.4). Financial costs are not the only factor in the management of attendance as other workers feel aggrieved when colleagues get away with regular absences for no apparent reason. The indirect costs of poor levels of attendance are seen in inadequate levels of customer service, cancelled commuter trains, unanswered telephone calls, and overworked staff that cover for absent colleagues, only to run into problems when attempting to complete their own work on time.

The majority of employers believe it is possible to reduce absence and, according to the latest CIPD Survey (2011e), almost all organisations have written attendance management policies and most record absence rates and reasons for absence. Better recording systems typically lead to increases in recorded short-term absence because they were not logged previously, whereas reductions in absence result from tightened policies for reviewing absence. These include absence monitoring, return-to-work interviews, raising the profile of absence management with managers, and changing recording methods.

More recently, reductions in absence levels have been due to the economic climate and the threat of redundancy. Half of organisations surveyed by CIPD (2011e) report they use absence as one criterion when selecting for redundancy; this frequently leads to presenteeism, when employees come into work, but do not function at full capacity because of ill-health. There has always been concern over people turning up for work, but doing very little (Bolchover 2005), and we mentioned elsewhere situations in which mental ill-health was involved, but during times of recession when people are fearful of losing their jobs, absence rates decline, and presenteeism rises. Over one-quarter of organisations have reported increases in this (CIPD 2011e), and some estimate that presenteeism costs organisations almost twice as much as absence, in part because it is more common among more highly paid staff (Smedley 2011). The better organisations train line managers to tell people to go home, and come back when they are better. The UK has a particularly poor health record. A recent government review reported that eight out of 10 workers are overweight or have long-term illness that limits their productivity; only one in five of British full-time workers are in optimal health. The cost of this is estimated to be at least £21.5 billion (Brindle 2011).

Much of the research on absence management concentrates on what is seen as 'preventable' short-term absence. It is generally assumed that long-term absence is more likely to be genuine, although this is not always the case. The number of long-term absences are relatively small, but account for a disproportionate amount of lost time with increased stress-related illness pushing this up.

HRM AT WORK IN FOCUS

## How sickness absence was reduced in Shepway Council

In 2005 the annual sickness absence rate was 12.2 days per person, and 13 people (out of 480) had long-term health problems. The cost of this was almost £1m per year and impacted on service delivery. A new head of HR was concerned that managers did not take responsibility for absence and hard-working employees were demoralised by others playing the system. An absence management policy was devised which specified responsibilities and the council's ill-health capability procedures; this was agreed with the unions and all staff were informed.

The key change was a cultural one. All staff had to personally telephone their managers on the first day of absence and managers were responsible for return-to-work interviews and monitoring absence. A training programme for managers included role play of return-to-work interviews, information on medical advice, and how to question workers who rang in sick. In addition, an employee assistance programme (EAP) was initiated, provided by an outsourced occupational healthcare provider. The aim was to prevent long-term absences; the EAP provided 24-hour access to telephone help as well as face-to-face counselling. A close relationship with the healthcare provider was built up, and this involved joint case conferences and telephone discussions in order to ensure that individuals were given the maximum support to get back to work. It was seen as important that the occupational health provider understood the organisation's needs.

The results were that of those on long-term absences, a number were helped back to work by providing suitable adjustments to working arrangements, some took ill-health retirement, and two resigned. Flexible working policies to help those with homecare responsibilities reduced short-term absence. Overall, the annual absence rate reduced from 12.2 to 6.5 days.

Source: Adapted from Wolff (2007a).

### Stress at work

It can be seen from Tables 23 and 24 that stress is a major cause of short- and long-term absence, and rates continue to increase, with threats of redundancy exacerbating this. In the CIPD 2011 Absence Management Survey, stress-related absence had increased, with the main causes attributed to workloads, management style, external factors such as relationships and family, relationships at work and organisational change. Three-fifths of organisations were taking action to reduce stress in the workplace. Common ways to identify and reduce stress involved use of surveys, training, flexible working and improved work–life balance. Two-thirds of public-sector and one-third of private-sector respondents have an employee well-being strategy in place. Typically these offer counselling, stop-smoking support and employee assistance programmes (CIPD 2011e). The Health and Safety Executive (HSE) stress management standards are particularly useful for managing stress.

## STRATEGIES TO DEAL WITH ABSENCE

The majority of employers believe it is possible to reduce absence levels (CIPD 2011e), yet many do not know the level of sickness absence in their organisation, and still less calculate the cost. According to the CIPD 2011 Survey, just under half of the respondents set targets for reducing absence levels. Once sickness absence figures are collected, it is possible to define the problem and to set up effective management systems. Absence measures do not normally include anticipated and legitimate spells away from work – such as holidays or jury service. Other forms of absence are divided between authorised and unauthorised. Broadly, the former deals with situations in which employees are genuinely unwell and have a valid medical certificate. The latter refers to cases in which it is not clear if the employee is actually unwell or has an acceptable reason for being away from work. For example, if an employee has been absent for a series of single days over a specified period, a quiet word may lead to improved attendance patterns. Conversely, if an employee has been off with a serious health problem, different measures are needed.

The actual causes of absence are sometimes hard to ascertain, as workers are unlikely to report low morale, alcoholism, mental ill-health or personal problems as valid reasons for absence. Travel difficulties, family and home commitments all act to pull the employee away from work. Factors that push the employee away might include low morale, job insecurity, long hours and the work culture – including an entitlement view. Overlaid upon these are personality traits.

Disciplinary approaches are widely used despite the fact that its perceived effectiveness is relatively low – see Tables 23 and 24 below. According to the CIPD 2011 Survey, around

**Table 23 Short-term absence**

| Main causes of short-term absence | Top six tools used | Top six most effective tools |
|---|---|---|
| Minor illness (cold, flu, stomach bugs) | Return-to-work interviews | Return-to-work interviews |
| Stress | Trigger mechanisms to review absence | Trigger mechanisms to review absence |
| Musculoskeletal injuries eg strains and repetitive strain injury | Sickness absence information provided to line managers | Disciplinary procedures for unacceptable absence |
| Back pain | Disciplinary procedures for unacceptable absence | Restricting sick pay |
| Home and family responsibilities | Line managers take primary responsibility | Line managers take primary responsibility |
| Recurring medical conditions such as asthma, angina and allergies | Leave for family circumstances | Managers are trained in absence-handling |

Source: Adapted from Chartered Institute of Personnel and Development (2011e).

Table 24 Long-term absence

| Main causes of long-term absence (over 20 days) | Top six tools used | Top six most effective tools |
|---|---|---|
| Stress | Return-to-work interviews | Occupational Health involved |
| Acute medical conditions such as stroke, heart attack, cancer | Occupational health involvement | Return to work interviews |
| Musculoskeletal injuries eg strains and repetitive strain injury | Sickness absence information provided to line managers | Trigger mechanisms to review attendance |
| Mental ill-health | Trigger mechanisms to review attendance | Rehabilitation programme |
| Back pain | Risk assessment to aid return to work | Changes to working patterns or environment |
| Injuries/accidents not related to work | Flexible working | Restricting sick pay |

Source: Adapted from Chartered Institute of Personnel and Development (2011e).

three-quarters of organisations refer to the disciplinary procedure in relation to persistent absence. Delbridge's work in Nippon CTV referred to earlier describes how absenteeism is not tolerated there. This is clearly far from ideal, but for those organisations determined to use the ultimate sanction, dismissals for sickness absence can be fair and reasonable in certain conditions and where procedures are followed. Case study material, however, points to softer approaches being prevalent with line managers given a wide degree of discretion. Such approaches might include informal chats, counselling, return-to-work interviews, and the provision of medical support services.

The most common causes of, tools used, and the most effective tools for managing short- and long-term absence are detailed in Tables 23 and 24. The most effective methods for reducing short-term absence are: return-to-work interviews, trigger mechanisms to review attendance, sickness absence information given to line managers, disciplinary procedures, giving line managers responsibility for managing absence, and giving leave for family circumstances.

Bradford points or similar triggering systems are useful to identify persistent short-term absences. Using this system, one can distinguish between the effect of a single long-term absence and the more significant effect of many short absences, even though the total number of days may be the same. It does this by awarding points according to the formula: A × A × D where A is the number of absences, and D is the total number of days' absence taken over one year. It does this by awarding points according to the formula:

*One absence of 10 days amounts to (1 × 1 × 10) = 10 points.*

*Ten absences of one day amounts to (10 × 10 × 10) = 1,000 points.*

*Two five-day absences amounts to (2 × 2 × 10) = 40 points.*

*Five two-day absences amounts to (5 × 5 × 10) = 250 points.*

Using this system it is easy to identify those with persistent short-term absence records.

The main strategies for dealing with long-term absence include: return to work interviews, occupational health involvement, trigger mechanisms, rehabilitation programmes, risk assessment for return to work, changes to working patterns or environment (CIPD 2011e).

The return to work interview is effective for managing short-term and long-term absence, and line managers are frequently involved. For best results, the line manager needs accurate data about past absences, and details of past interviews. The interview provides the opportunity to enquire about the reasons for absence, to follow up any serious problems, to suggest further assistance if required (Acas 2010d). Where this is caused by caring or domestic emergencies, the employee may be willing to be honest where the employer offers flexible work arrangements. Absences due to time off to deal with family responsibilities are increasing, possibly because it is now more acceptable to be open about them. The interview also signals that the absence has been noticed, helping to generate an attendance culture in which genuine illness is acknowledged but malingering is dealt with severely. As with all people management issues, this message is important not only for the individual concerned but also for other workers, who may suffer the consequences of colleagues' absence.

### USE OF FINANCIAL PENALTIES AND REWARDS

Restricting sick pay is an effective tool for addressing both short-term and long-term absence, but relatively few public service organisations do this – possibly because they effectively pay employees twice for turning up for work, although organisations with particular problems find that the financial investment is worthwhile (Rankin 2007d).

HRM AT WORK IN FOCUS

## Case studies in how to tackle absence

*BMW* uses a mix of absence management strategies including: training for managers, ensuring procedures are clear, well-being support, and flexible working opportunities. All managers are trained in absence management, and it maintains a high profile through weekly use of a balanced scorecard that shows absence targets and corresponding figures across the business. Audits ensure that return-to-work interviews are used. There is a trigger mechanism whereby employees with three absences within 12 months are called for an 'absence review' with their manager. If they are off again within 13 weeks, they receive a warning letter. Subsequent absences (two or more within 26 weeks) lead to a second written warning. If there are further absences in the following 52 weeks, the company may terminate employment. Throughout this, the company offers maximum support for health problems as well as flexibility with work–life balance. Manual workers are on annualised hours, and leave for family reasons can be taken at short notice. There is an occupational health centre and all employees have access to counselling services. Well-being strategies include an in-house gym, healthy eating in the canteen, and occupational sick pay for up to two years.

*Robinson Brothers*, a medium-sized chemical company, had an average absence rate of 5.8 days per year. Most staff achieved 100% attendance and it was decided to reward these. The reward for one years' 100% attendance was a voucher worth £250; two years' 100% attendance was rewarded with a £500 voucher, and three years earned vouchers worth £1,000. The Bradford points scheme was introduced and the score was set at 125 for 12-month periods. Employees who triggered this target were referred to HR for an interview and warned that the issue could become one of conduct if there were no special circumstances. Of the employees referred, 80% improved their attendance and absence fell from 5.8 days in 2002 to 4.6 days in 2004.

*Royal Mail* also introduced an incentive scheme, and increased attendance by almost 11%. Those with no absence over a one-year period were entered into a lottery. In the first draw, 37 workers won a new car, 75 won holiday vouchers worth £2,000, and more than 90,000 workers won £150 in holiday vouchers.

*Richmondshire District Council* introduced an incentive scheme in 1998 and offered an extra day's leave for those with 100% attendance during the previous year. Since its introduction the number of staff gaining the extra day rose each year. Time off for hospital treatment and pregnancy-related sickness absence were not included as sick leave.

Source: Adapted from: CIPD (2007c); Silcox (2005a).

REFLECTIVE ACTIVITY

Look at the case studies above as well as the most recent CIPD survey on employee absence. Work in groups to devise strategies for the management of short-term and long-term absence.

Reporting of sickness absence information to **line managers** and involving them in absence management are widely employed strategies. However, line managers are often not supported (online or via HR) to deal with difficult cases, particularly as stress and mental health problems are increasing and typically complex (CIPD 2011e).

### REHABILITATION AND WELL-BEING, HEALTH MANAGEMENT AT WORK

An increasing number of organisations are introducing well-being strategies – with nearly half of CIPD respondents doing so (CIPD 2011e). Nearly three-quarters of organisations provide access to counselling services and more than two-thirds offer employee assistance programmes to all employees. Access to counselling services, EAPS and stop-smoking support are the most commonly provided benefits, with others available only to certain grades eg private medical insurance. Health screening was provided to all employees by around one-third of employees. The public sector was most likely to provide services such as counselling, stop-smoking support, advice on healthy eating, access to physiotherapy etc within the workplace, whereas the private sector was more likely to provide insurances. The results to the CIPD 2011 Survey identified increases in mental health problems, such as anxiety and depression, and this was often linked to increased risk of redundancies, indicating that organisations at risk need to increase focus on employee well-being.

Where rehabilitation relates to mental health, issues are complex, yet according to the Office for National Statistics, around one in six adults suffer from mental illness at some time in their lives and 40% of the 2.6 million claiming incapacity benefit are those suffering mental health problems (Chubb 2007). Attitudes play a major role here, and sufferers are often reluctant to disclose that they have a problem and to seek help. Depression, anxiety, and panic attacks are the most common types of mental ill-health, although some employees have more severe conditions (Murphy 2007d). Dealing with mental ill-health is particularly difficult, yet most line managers are not trained in this (Murphy 2007d), and this is compounded by prejudice and negative attitudes towards sufferers. The support of occupational health and counselling services, typically available through EAPs, are especially useful in these cases.

There is much to be learned from countries that have successfully adopted strategies to get workers back to work quickly, thereby reducing the proportion of workers reliant on state sickness benefits. In Sweden employers must assess needs quickly and arrange rehabilitation. In the Netherlands employers must report to the social security agency within 13 weeks details of rehabilitation plans for employees who are incapacitated (James *et al* 2002). The government is pushing employers to recruit from the long-term sick and help those with health problems to stay in work for longer. Additionally, changes to pension schemes make it increasingly difficult for employers to use early retirement as a way of managing ill-health. All of these changes signal increased importance of occupational health services and well-being schemes.

## CONCLUSIONS

Performance management systems are now much more widespread than they were and are seen as synonymous with new ways of managing human resources. They revolve around three stages: defining performance standards, reviewing and appraising performance, and reinforcing performance standards. Several of these issues are taken up in later chapters of the book, for example in our analysis of learning organisations and performance-related pay. Each stage of performance management is important, but often too little attention is paid to the critical role which induction can play in creating the right cultural expectations among new recruits. Employers who are serious about performance management need to realise that this stage of the cycle makes a significant contribution to the socialisation of new staff, and it is much more than a routine administrative exercise. Systems also need to be designed to fit the cultures and context of the organisation operating in the global marketplace. Continuous monitoring is often overlooked but it is important to check that the system is effectively aligning individual and corporate objectives, especially in times of rapid change

### EXPLORE FURTHER

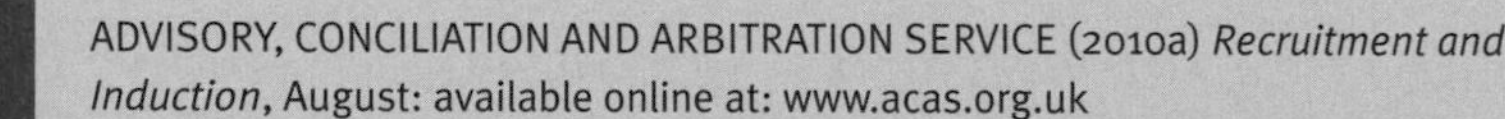


ADVISORY, CONCILIATION AND ARBITRATION SERVICE (2010a) *Recruitment and Induction*, August: available online at: www.acas.org.uk

ADVISORY, CONCILIATION AND ARBITRATION SERVICE (2011) *The Acas Guide: Discipline and grievances at work*, available online at: www.acas.org.uk

ARMSTRONG, M., and BARON, A. (2007) *Managing Performance: Performance management in action*. London: CIPD.

BIRON, M, FARNDALE, E. and PAAUWE, J. (2011) 'Performance Management Effectiveness: lessons from world-leading firms', *International Journal of Human Resource Management*, Vol.22, No.6, 1294–311.

CIPD (2011e) *Absence Management Survey: Annual Survey Report*. London: CIPD.

LATHAM, G., SULSKY, L.M. and MACDONALD, H. 'Performance Management', in P. Boxall, J. Purcell and P. Wright (eds) (2007), *The Oxford Handbook of Human Resource Management*. Oxford: Oxford University Press.

LEWIS D., SARGEANT M. and SCHWAB B. (2011) *Employment Law: The Essentials* 11th Edition. London: CIPD.

PURCELL, J. and HUTCHINSON, S. (2007a) 'Front-line managers as agents in the HRM-performance causal chain: theory, analysis and evidence', *Human Resource Management Journal*, Vol.17, No.1, 3–20.

VARMA, A. and BUDHWAR, P. (2011) 'Global Performance Management' in A-W. Harzing and A.H. Pinnington (eds), *International Human Resource Management*. London: SAGE.

CHAPTER 10

# Vocational Education, Training and Skills

WITH LORRIE MARCHINGTON

## LEARNING OUTCOMES

By the end of this chapter, readers should be able to:

- advise their organisations on the value of training initiatives such as NVQs, apprenticeships and IiP
- work with trade unions to encourage non-traditional learners to take advantage of training opportunities
- assess the contribution of VET to the enhancement of worker skills and organisational performance.

In addition, readers should understand and be able to explain:

- why the government is concerned to shift the economy from its low-skills equilibrium
- the way in which governments influence the provision of VET and its rationale
- the major barriers to VET increasing skill levels.

## INTRODUCTION

This chapter examines the ways in which government intervention shapes vocational education and training (VET) in order to maximise the skills and contributions of people; wherever possible international comparisons are made. There is a section outlining some of the change to education and training and the major influences on workplace learning; namely National Vocational Qualifications (NVQs), apprenticeships, Investors in People (IiP), and the Trade Union Learning Representatives. Consideration is given to how far workplaces are moving towards the ideal of the learning organisation and using high-performance working. The main thrust of the chapter analyses how far government strategies of increasing skills is triggering a shift from the low-skills equilibrium to a high-skill economy and whether the government's spiralling investment has been successful in increasing employers' demand for training; and questioning whether it is realistic to believe that government aims will be fulfilled by employers without compulsion.

## THE IMPORTANCE OF VET AND THE INTERNATIONAL CONTEXT

In the fast-moving global economy, it is generally agreed that a highly skilled and flexible workforce is needed for economic competitiveness. The National VET (NVET) system is seen to be the means by which to increase skills, and address issues of social inclusion and mobility. There are many external factors that impact on NVET strategy: social, economic, environmental, as well as cultural and historical. These include globalisation, expansion of ICT, rising global population, emigration, immigration, age demography and shift to flexible labour markets. Of particular importance is the position of competitors, whether BRIC, developing, or developed countries. In the UK, competitiveness depends on skills alone rather than natural resources. UK policy is affected by the EU and the European Employment Strategy which aims to build comparative advantage utilising high skills as well as dealing with social issues of gender inequality, age distribution and participation, and migrant labour (Stewart and Rigg 2011, p.56). In the UK traditional workplaces have disappeared from industrial heartlands, and been largely replaced by a service economy. The labour market is fragmented and the UK competes on high-level skills, as well as on low-level skills – on price and quality. The UK VET system has a number of fundamental problems: English technical education is relatively weak; and there is an entrenched attitude that vocational education is second best and therefore suitable for the less able (Stewart and Rigg 2011). Wolf (2011) reports that vocational routes from 30 or 40 years ago offered better and more secure prospects than those available at the present time. Of skills-shortage vacancies in 2009, 30% were attributed to literacy problems (UKCES 2010). It is accepted that the individual, the employer and the state all gain from investment in VET, but what has not been clarified is who pays for the investment. In periods of high unemployment, most governments swing towards intervention, although the UK has persisted with a voluntarist stance whereby the government expects organisations and individuals to take responsibility. Training levies to support learning and development (L&D) were abandoned in the UK in the 1980s, whereas in France, there has been a training levy as a proportion of payroll from the 1970s.

In comparison with its major competitors, the UK has a poor record of investment in VET. Most of Europe has a dual educational system in which academic study and practical skills are intrinsically linked and equally regarded. Students in vocational and technical training spend around half of their time in college, and half with employers for between two to four years. Training is regulated by the state with legal underpinning for collective behaviour in order that the cost is shared. Using Germany as an example, Chambers of Commerce are central to training for all workers and all firms are required to be members of their local Chamber and to pay a membership fee. In France, employers pay a levy to support training and apprenticeships; in Austria, Denmark, Germany, The Netherlands and Switzerland successful apprenticeship systems often link to a 'licence to practise'. As we saw in Chapter 5, co-ordinated market economies make investment funds available to organisations to stoke innovation, and investors look to the longer term. In comparison, the UK and USA operate deregulated liberal market economies in which investors look for short-term gains, which act against long-term L&D strategies, thereby neglecting weaker students (Hall and Soskice 2001; Watson 2010, p.311; Bosch and Charest 2008). Australia is similar to the UK in many respects, and has seen high levels of youth unemployment and a declining apprenticeship system, but using state funding has managed to increase the numbers of trainees and apprenticeships fourfold (Stewart and Rigg 2011, p.68). VET systems are context-specific and incorporate cultural and historic backgrounds (Bosch and Charest 2008; Stewart and Rigg 2011, p.67). For example, the Czech Republic has very high rates of post-compulsory education and training – reflecting the historic value placed on education. In the USA there is state autonomy for VET, and California has increased state intervention, used employment training taxes, and a large number of colleges to make its VET successful (Bosch and Charest 2008). Although we can learn from overseas systems, cultural and historic contexts may make it difficult for wholesale adoption of practices from other countries.

We begin by looking at the English education system, in particular for post-16s and higher education, before moving on to look at the workplace. Note that the systems in Scotland, Wales, and Northern Ireland develop in a different way.

## THE EDUCATION SYSTEM

### SCHOOLS AND FURTHER EDUCATION

The education system is the first building block for a culture of lifelong learning and skill enhancement. Those who experience success at school are likely to be natural lifelong learners, and are able to cope with rapid change. In the UK, there is a class ceiling with a chasm between the knowledge-rich and the knowledge-poor. This starts and widens through school with the class system influencing access to higher educational opportunities and thereby to better careers that bring additional learning opportunities. In comparison, those with poor educational experiences are most likely to be found in marginalised employment in the low pay, low-skill sector of the labour market without access to training and development. Employers frequently bemoan the fact that the educational system does not provide the skills and knowledge they want and schools system suffers from under-achievers, poor standards, too many providers, inadequate resources, and a wide gap between academic and vocational routes (Harrison 2009, p.61).

From the late 1980s education became increasingly centralised as the Local Education Authorities' role was decreased in order to open up education to market forces. Since 1985 there have been continuous changes aimed at improving quality, coherence, and attempting to give vocational pathways some prestige. The Tomlinson Report (2004) critiqued curriculum, assessment and qualifications and identified a key problem of non-academic children being turned off at school and leaving with few qualifications. This report heralded a plethora of reforms and new vocational qualifications. In 2006 the White Paper (*Further Education, Raising Skills, Improving Life Chances*) addressed perceived problems within further education (FE) and emphasised links with business and working to industry-set standards. Also in 2006 came the Leitch Review which set out the appalling state of skills and qualification levels in the UK compared to competitors, and reiterated the view that the UK cannot compete internationally on labour costs, but can compete using people skills. The report emphasised strengthening employer voice through the creation of a demand-led system in which the needs of employers take priority through the Sector Skills Councils. Leitch criticised adult skills and reiterated Tomlinson's call for an integrated, rationalised 14–19 system with reduced bureaucracy and ambitious targets. One of the main instruments for this reform was the development of the 14–19 Diplomas.

HRM AT WORK IN FOCUS

### Reinventing vocational qualifications at 14–19

The 14–19 Diplomas were set up as result of the Tomlinson Review (2004) which recommended a single qualification covering all learning for those aged 14–19 years of age. They combine academic and vocational learning, and aim to prepare for both HE and employment. Diplomas comprised sector-related knowledge and skills; functional skills in English, maths and IT combined with a project, personal and learning skills, and additional units which could be taken from the National Qualifications Framework eg A levels, BTEC. The size was determined by level, and the Advanced Level would be equal to 3.5 A levels. Five vocational 'lines' were available from September 2008 with 14 lines being available from 2010. There were plans to introduce a final three lines from 2012, but these were axed in 2011.

From the start there were problems; the government did not want one qualification so academic qualifications (GCSE and A level) were retained, immediately removing the original aims of a simplified, single system. There was a warning that unless the Diplomas were viewed as on par with A levels, they would be seen as second rate qualifications for inferior students. By 2011, the tinkering became tampering and there were four major changes: schools would not be obliged to offer Diplomas; individual components could be offered outside of the framework of the Diploma; no requirement for approval from the Department for Education to deliver Diploma subjects; and the final three lines were dropped.

Such changes weakened the Diplomas. There had been confusion over purpose and delivery since the start, and criticism of low uptake, understanding, recognition, and complexity continue (Hodgson and Spours 2010; Richardson and Haynes 2009). They compete with well established, understood, and prestigious vocational and general qualifications such as BTECs, City and Guilds and A levels. Similar qualifications (General National Vocational Qualifications and Advanced Vocational Certificate of Education) had all failed and were short-lived (Golden *et al* 2011). With all such qualifications, the main problem is competing with the gold standard of A levels for progression to higher education (HE). The best universities placed restrictions on accepting Diplomas and others were ignorant about them; although teaching-led institutions were more supportive and knowledgeable (Richardson and Haynes 2009). Initial evaluation showed that students taking Diplomas reported benefits, and the CIPD 2010 *Resourcing and Talent Planning Survey* showed that employers felt they were relevant to their workplace, with only apprenticeship being regarded more highly. There now remain three main routes (general, broad vocational, apprenticeships) for 14–19-year-olds and these will enable the government to raise school leaving age to 18 years by 2015.

*To think about:*

*The past is littered with failed attempts to confer prestige onto vocational qualifications; do you think that the 14–19 Diplomas will succeed? If so, why?*

One aim of the government is to eliminate the 'class ceiling' and narrow the gap in attainment between those from poorer and more affluent backgrounds, and ensure that all young people in the age range 16–19 are in education and training from 2015. The latter proposal has met with criticism, in part because research showed that those who are forced to stay on at school are less likely to gain qualifications, and more likely to become disenchanted (CIPD Press release, 8 January 2008). Much depends on the relevance and variety of alternatives to the academic route and whether the system can offer sufficient interest and diversity for each child to find an appropriate niche. New developments include the establishment of Studio Schools which will provide project-based, practical learning alongside academic study. Students will be allowed to enrol in college from the age of 14, and work with local employers and a personal coach to follow a curriculum designed to give them employability skills. Some thought has also gone into new qualifications, including the English Baccalaureate (Ebacc). It was hoped that the Ebacc would encourage students from low-income areas to take traditional subjects, and improve their chances of getting into top universities. Quite why it was thought that this would help was not clear and its introduction was hastily dropped (Shepherd 2011). Also, from 2011, vocational qualifications that do not provide progression to further study after the age of 16 are to be removed from schools league tables – examples include NVQ 2 in hairdressing or OCR L2 in travel and tourism. At the moment more than 4,800 qualifications count towards school results and this only adds to confusion (Vasagar 2011a). The Qualifications and Credit Framework (see box below) identifies qualification levels and it can be seen that the HE, professional and school sectors are not integrated, and it lacks flexibility. Lester (2010) suggests that there are much better examples overseas. Nor does the UK model fit with the European Qualifications Framework which is looking to harmonise models (Winterton 2009; Rauner 2008). Further reforms to school education are expected in a forthcoming 2011 White Paper. It remains to be seen whether the speed and scale of educational reforms will detract from their purpose (Harrison 2009).

Funding became a major issue from 2011, as the coalition government scrapped Educational Maintenance Allowances (EMAs) that provided up to £30 per week for students aged 16–19 from low income households to study full time. The EMA continues in Wales, Scotland and Northern Ireland. In England, a 16–19 Fund is supposed to help support young people from disadvantaged backgrounds with a discretionary bursary of up to £1,200 per year. Many believe that this will cut the number of young people from poor families being able to study, and in some colleges, 70% of students rely on EMA (Toynbee 2011). It is difficult to see how raising the school leaving age to 18 will engage the least academic students and give them a meaningful transition from education to work, without abandoning them to a lifetime on social benefits (Harrison 2009). In late 2011, almost one million young British are without a job and the issue has some urgency as English inner cities are full of disenfranchised youths, with little hope of gaining qualifications or jobs.

The VET system for the post-16s, including further education (FE) and higher education (HE) has been subjected to continuous and radical reforms. Dearing (1997) and Foster (DfES 2006) criticised complexity and quality in comparison with the rest of Europe. From 2000 onwards, emphasis has been on increasing the influence of employers. There continues to be concern about young adults entering the labour market; compared with the rest of the EU, the numbers were high, and the majority enter vulnerable jobs with low pay – reflecting low levels of productivity compared with older workers.

Learning and Skills Councils (LSC) and Sector Skills Councils were established in 2001–2. In 2003 the 'Skills Strategy' was launched, aiming 'to ensure that employers have the right skills to support the success of their businesses, and individuals have the skills they need to be both employable and personally fulfilled'. The government backed its strategic push with targets – one of which is that by 2010 employers would not be able to say that education and training failed to meet its needs. Money was made available to provide free training to Level 3 for those aged 19–25; Train to Gain involved employers; and Business in the Community gave advice on accessing government funding. The LSC budget was £11.1 billion for 2007–8.

HRM AT WORK IN FOCUS

## Qualifications by level across the National Qualification Framework (NQF) and Qualifications and Credit Framework (QCF)

| Level | Examples of NQF qualifications | Examples of QCF qualifications |
|---|---|---|
| **Entry** | – English for Speakers of Other Languages (ESOL)<br>– Skills for Life<br>– Functional Skills (English, maths and ICT) | – Awards, Certificates, and Diplomas at entry level<br>– Foundation Learning at entry level<br>– Functional Skills at entry level |
| **1** | – GCSEs grades D–G<br>– BTEC Introductory Diplomas and Certificates<br>– OCR Nationals<br>– Key Skills at Level 1 | – BTEC Awards, Certificates, and Diplomas at Level 1<br>– Functional Skills at Level 1<br>– NVQs at Level 1 |
| **2** | – GCSEs grades A*–C<br>– Key Skills Level 2<br>– Skills for Life | – BTEC Awards, Certificates, and Diplomas at Level 2<br>– OCR Nationals<br>– NVQs at Level 2 |
| **3** | – A levels<br>– GCE in applied subjects<br>– International Baccalaureate<br>– Key Skills Level 3 | – BTEC Awards, Certificates, and Diplomas and NVQ L3<br>– BTEC Nationals<br>– OCR Nationals |
| **4** | – Certificates of Higher Education | – BTEC Professional Diplomas Certificates and Awards<br>– HNCs<br>– NVQs at Level 4 |
| **5** | – HNCs and HNDs<br>– Other higher diplomas | – HNDs<br>– BTEC Professional Diplomas, Certificates and Awards<br>– NVQs at Level 5 |
| **6** | – National Diploma in Professional Production Skills<br>– BTEC Advanced Professional Diplomas, Certificates and Awards | – BTEC Advanced Professional Diplomas, Certificates and Awards |
| **7** | – BTEC Advanced Professional Diplomas, Certificates and Awards | – BTEC Advanced Professional Diplomas, Certificates and Awards |
| **8** | – Specialist awards | – Award, Certificate and Diploma in strategic direction |

**Framework for HE qualifications**

Somewhat confusingly, there is a separate framework for the higher education sector which broadly corresponds with Levels 4 to 8 of the framework above.

| Level | Examples of qualifications |
|---|---|
| 4 | – HE certificates<br>– higher national certificates |
| 5 | – HE diplomas<br>– foundation degrees<br>– higher national diplomas |
| 6 | – bachelors degrees<br>– Professional Graduate Certificate in Education |
| 7 | – masters degrees<br>– postgraduate certificates |
| 8 | – doctoral degrees |

Source: http://www.direct.gov.uk/en/EducationAndLearning/QualificationsExplained/DG_10039017 (accessed 19 September 2011).

The UK still lags behind its competitors – estimates put UK labour productivity at around 20% below that of Northern Europe (Bevan 2010, p.3; CIPD 2010e, p.26), with little evidence that the continuous reform over the previous decades had produced results. The coalition government of 2010 swept away much of the previous infrastructure, targets, and finance and the UKCES Review of Employment and Skills proposed a more integrated service and emphasis on local solutions rather than imposition of national top-down targets. A further white paper (DBIS 2010) promised to reduce confusion whilst prioritising young people and those with literacy and numeracy problems. The paper talks of stronger communities, stimulus to private sector growth, social mobility, social inclusion, environmental sustainability, as part of the coalition governments' 'Big Society' idea. It dispensed with Leitch's (2006) 2020 targets, and promised not to change the system whilst announcing a plethora of changes, including:

- employers work with UKCES to increase investment in the skills
- increased diversity of provision, as where FE colleges offer HE courses
- increased information available on quality of provision through an all-age careers service
- the Qualifications and Credit Framework to be developed by business, with the Sector Skills Councils updating national occupational standards
- free training for basic skills, and for first Level 2 qualifications for those under the age of 24
- Lifelong Learning accounts for every adult (self-funded) with loans available
- end of Level 2 funding for adults over the age of 24 and of English for Speakers of Other Languages (ESOL); Train to Gain and Regional Development Agencies abolished
- 25% reduction in adult FE and skills budget over three years; 20–30% cut to Sector Skills Councils; 25% cuts to Department for Business, Innovation and Skills; 25% cut to FE budget.

(UnionLearn Newsletter 2011a; DBIS 2010; Payne and Keep 2011.)

A relatively small amount of government money (£5 million) was available through an Employer Investment Fund (EIF) to raise skills and promote high performance working. SME support was cut back as Business Link regional offices were replaced by a national website and call centre. The Skills Funding Agency and the Young People's Learning Agency were established in 2009. The former regulates adult FE and skills training in England as part of the Department for Business, Innovation and Skills (DBIS) with the mission of ensuring that people and employers can access the skills training they need. They have a £4 billion annual budget to invest in colleges and training organisations, and also run the National Apprenticeship Service. State financial support was considerably reduced, with emphasis instead on individuals and employers taking responsibility for investing in skills. UKCES priorities from 2011 were: increased investment in skills; enhancing value and accessibility of vocational training, especially apprenticeships; galvanising industries and sectors to improve skills; and working with employers to maximise opportunities for the unemployed and disadvantaged groups (UKCES 2011a).

It was not made clear how employers would be galvanised to invest, and given the current economic climate and past experience (for example finding employer and individual co-funding for Train to Gain) of failure, it is highly unlikely that employers will invest. In the past, such failures have resulted in the government increasing subsidy as employers became adept at obtaining public money for training they would have provided anyway (Payne and Keep 2011). Ideologically, the coalition government is averse to alternatives such as using labour market regulation to cut off low-value, low-skills products and services using a cheap and marginalised workforce (for example by raising the minimum wage, making it harder to sack people) and to shift from short-term shareholder returns which act against longer term investments,. The coalition is also averse to regulatory measures and is in favour of reduced business taxes. It has no incentives to offer employers, and so, if the government persists in attempting to push the supply-side of skills, it will have to fund initiatives itself (Payne and Keep 2011).

There is at last some recognition of the importance of utilisation of skills, employee engagement, and moving to higher performance workplaces. The government hopes to work with a wider range of agencies (including TUC, IiP, Acas and CIPD) to improve leadership and management to raise skills and promote high performance working (HPW).

Much emphasis is put on innovation to haul the UK out of the economic doldrums. There is £50 million available to the Growth and Innovation Fund and £200 million to set up a network of Technology and Innovation Centres with the aim of linking university research centres to commercialise research and innovations. This compares unfavourably with Germany where institutes have a budget of 1.6 billion euros (much of which is from research contracts with industry) or Finland, where national workplace development programmes aim to improve productivity and the quality of working life, and funding through state or social partners. £200 million is very little to create the 'elite network' especially when employers are not as actively involved as European comparators (Payne and Keep 2011, p.33). Government emphasis is also on local economic development but the Regional Development Agencies have been abolished and replaced with Local Enterprise Partnerships (LEPs); the new bodies have an exceedingly wide brief, but no powers; there are complaints about the geographic areas covered; for example in the Peak District National Park, which generates jobs and millions in revenue, has to negotiate with six LEPs, and only one of these provides a board seat. The chair of the Campaign for National Parks also accused LEPs of only being interested in economic growth, but not sustainable environmental growth. Nor is the LEP system joined up with the system of Technology and Innovation Centres, and there are questions over how areas without a Technology and Innovation Centres fit into the whole. Payne and Keep (2011) question how neo-liberal, free market policies can allow UK to compete with BRIC countries; they conclude that UK is urgently in need of a modern industrial policy, similar to those in France, Japan, and Germany.

## REFLECTIVE ACTIVITY

Do you think that the governments changes will increase social mobility, increase skill development, and generate the growth of good jobs?

Justify your answer.

## HIGHER EDUCATION

In the past, HE had been mainly accessible to the upper classes. Even now, certain groups are extremely under-represented (House of Commons 2009; Syedain 2011). There was change from the 1960s when the Robbins Report (1963) made university education available to all of those with the ability and qualifications to benefit. With the provision of full means-tested grants more working class children got into HE, although at this time, only a small proportion (well under 10%) of young people did so. From 1997, the new Labour government pushed to increase participation rates to 50% by 2010 in order to increase supply-side skills, although HE expansion doesn't equate to increased productivity (Keep and Mayhew 2010). Significant changes to financial arrangements were announced with the hope of securing adequate funding for the sector at the same time as increasing and widening participation. From 2006 deferred tuition fees of £3,000 per annum were introduced for home students together with a system of student loans and bursaries. Fees were introduced in part because the government felt unable to bear the costs of rapid expansion, justified by the fact that average students gained substantially increased salaries over their lifetimes. From 2011 the fee arrangements in England changed, with universities allowed to charge up to £9,000 per annum in fees for home students. Over one-third of English universities decided to charge the full amount, making the cost of a three-year degree £27,000 in tuition fees alone. Loans covering tuition and living costs are to be paid back after graduation when earning over £21,000 per annum (DBIS 2011).

Expansion has meant that not all graduates are able to find graduate-level jobs, and individual rates of return on degrees have fallen (Keep and Mayhew 2010). This makes the high cost of HE extremely risky, particularly for those with less prestigious degrees from less highly regarded institutions. Parents from poor social-economic backgrounds are not likely to know about such differences in prestige, nor about the availability of financial support that has been built into the system (Aynsley and Crossouard 2010). HE is not desirable for all, and for many working class children, university is an alien concept rather than a normal choice. Instead, working class cultural norms prefer debt-avoidance, and entering gainful employment as soon as possible (Aynsley and Crossouard 2010). It seems highly likely that the cost and system of loans will deter non-traditional students, resulting in less social mobility and diversity.

Increasing the supply of graduates has meant that many are employed in jobs that do not require degree-level skills; graduates take up 'new graduate jobs' that formerly did not need degrees, and are likely to be under-employed. This is not a cost-efficient way to increase skills, and there is insufficient evidence that increasing the number of graduates results in up-skilling through job redesign, even though it may keep young people out of unemployment in recession or downturns (Elias and Purcell 2004; Holmes and Mayhew 2010). A further likely outcome is that students will be picky about their degree and will choose those which are likely to result in employability. A further result of over-supply of graduates has been the expansion of internships – and this tends to favour young people with good connections and money to support themselves (see box below).

HRM AT WORK IN FOCUS

## Who gains from internships?

In theory at least, internships are being used by young people to gain work experience, and by employers to help poorer individuals by giving them opportunities in desirable professions. In reality, they are criticised, with employers exploiting interns as free labour and because they favour 'wealthy people in the south east' (CIPD 2011g). Malpractice even includes US-style auctions of places, and there is debate about the degree of exploitation. Graduate Fog (which campaigns against unpaid internships) believes that the majority are unpaid, particularly those in SMEs which do not have the resources to pay. CIPD supports this view as in 2010 there were around 250,000 internships, the majority of which were unpaid. Other sources suggest that about a fifth of British businesses use unpaid interns to 'get work done more cheaply, particularly during the recession' (Malik 2011). On the other hand, the Association of Graduate Recruiters maintains that 95.8% of its members now pay their interns, while adding that they mainly constitute large organisations sensitive to reputation dents (Snowdon 2011). Even in paid and well structured programmes, the quality of experience varies widely: some offer very little meaningful experience and others are given impossible tasks.

Using unpaid interns is illegal where the intern qualifies as a 'worker' under the national minimum wage (NMW) legislation. The definition of 'worker' is someone with a contract of employment carrying out genuine work. Genuine voluntary work can be unpaid, but of course this makes for a lot of confusion. In order to ameliorate the situation a voluntary code of best practice was established in 2011 (Common Best Practice Code for High-Quality Internships) in the hope of reducing exploitation and improving diversity and social mobility.

The government is keen to improve university–industry collaboration and the White Paper on HE (June 2011 led by Sir Tim Wilson) went so far as to suggest that employers could become degree-awarding bodies. Newer universities in particular are working closely with local employers, and the evidence shows that graduates from such courses find work and utilise their specialist training (Chillas 2010 cited by Holmes and Mayhew 2010). Of course, if such degrees meet the needs of employers, this again raises the question of who should pay. Some employers (examples include KPMG, Morrisons Supermarkets, Barclays and Logica) are sponsoring degrees (employing students and meeting full costs of university) so that they can pick the best students and the most suitable undergraduate courses that meet their needs. Employers hope for greater involvement in course design and mention widening access, although, as ever with high levels of competition, when you target the best you *usually* get the most privileged (Syedain 2011). Sponsorship is attractive to universities as it brings in more students outside of their quota, and helps with employability statistics, although most will be keen to preserve academic freedoms.

## REFLECTIVE ACTIVITY

What can be done to increase the proportion of young people from poorer backgrounds going on to HE? What can be done to encourage students to apply for courses that fill the longer term skills shortages (such as languages, science and engineering)?

All governments have been keen to widen access to HE and provide vocational routes. Foundation degrees and University Technical Colleges are both attempting to meet these aims. Foundation degrees were introduced in 2001 to help people on vocational routes into HE. These work-related degrees were developed in conjunction with employers and Sector Skills Councils and were deemed equivalent to the first two years of an honours degree. It was hoped that foundation degrees would help with social mobility and provide progression from vocational routes. However, the numbers on tried and tested HNDs fell as those taking foundation degrees rose; under half of those with Level 3 progressed to HE (these are mostly confined to specialist subjects such as maths and computing, business, arts and design); and a large proportion of working class men do not progress (Aynsley and Crossouard 2010). From 2011, University Technical Colleges have been set up to offer progression routes to HE or apprenticeships. These colleges are for those aged 14–19 and aim to integrate academic study with practical learning, GCSE and technical qualifications. Specialist subjects, such as engineering or construction, will run alongside ICT and business skills. They hope to confer status on craft skills, and provide a more relevant curriculum for the disengaged. However, such ideas have been tried in the past, and Estelle Morris (previous Education Secretary) wonders what the impact will be on secondary schools and whether it will re-establish the tripartite system of grammar, secondary, and vocational with selection at 14 (Morris 2011).

Overseas, similar debates and changes to HE are taking place. In Europe, the Bologna Declaration (1999) and the Copenhagen Declaration (2002) aimed for harmonisation, standardisation, comparability and transparency through the development of a unitary framework of qualifications and competences with credit transfer. In particular, Germany and France have seen substantial increases in provision and take-up of vocational HE (Giret 2011; Powell and Solga 2010). In Australia, the system is similar to that in UK, where the aim is to merge vocational and academic routes and to raise the prestige of vocational qualifications. Pilot work on dual HE qualifications (vocational and academic) has met with some success, and may be replicated across the system (McLaughlin and Mills 2011).

## ESTABLISHING A CULTURE OF LIFELONG LEARNING IN THE WORKPLACE

The creation of many products and services is increasingly dependent on human capital, and much of the literature cites examples of organisations responding to shortages by maximising the skills and contributions of people, in recognition of this fact. It is assumed that employees need high levels of education and skills in order to meet increasingly rigorous demands. They need to use IT; continuously learn and update skills; take responsibility for their own learning; understand their role in the organisation; be able to work autonomously; and have the ability to solve problems, change and anticipate the future. It is argued that L&D professionals have responded to this challenge and become involved with teaching people how to learn, and encouraging them to become lifelong learners, as part of a business strategy to retain competitive advantage.

In particular, the idea of the learning organisation has attracted interest. Pedler *et al* (1991, p.1) define it as 'an organisation which facilitates the learning of all its members and continuously transforms itself'. This includes re-organising work so that it facilitates learning, linking it to skills utilisation and high performance working. Evidence shows that learning organisations that continuously change and learn are likely to maintain competitive advantage – particularly in times of economic restraint (Elliott *et al* 2009).

There is debate about how far organisations are moving towards the ideal type of the learning organisation. Research shows a paucity of evidence and within so-called high-skills sectors it is a minority of workers who are given access to learning, and there is plenty of evidence that many employers do not value the potential of their workforce (Keep 2000). Moreover, the learning organisation assumes empowerment of workers, whereas evidence points to the continued existence of 'command and control' styles of management. The concept of the learning organisation is complemented by theories of knowledge management, high performance working, and of the knowledge worker which are dealt with elsewhere in the book. Despite the rhetoric about these idealised forms of work organisation, it remains the case that in many workplaces, access to training and development remains inadequate and partial. In the absence of employer investment, the government has increasingly been involved in VET.

## GOVERNMENT INITIATIVES TO DEVELOP SKILLS

As we saw earlier, government interventions shape VET through the education system and through training initiatives. Currently, the main initiatives which push employers to increase investment in skills are National Vocational Qualifications, apprenticeships, and Investors in People. We examine each in turn before looking at trade unions' contribution.

### NATIONAL VOCATIONAL QUALIFICATIONS AND SCOTTISH VOCATIONAL QUALIFICATIONS

National Vocational Qualifications (NVQs) and the Scottish version (SVQs) were developed in the late 1980s with the aim of establishing a wide range of employer-led vocational qualifications that covered most occupations and offered qualifications from the most basic levels, to the most sophisticated.

NVQs are based on National Occupational Standards, which describe what competent people in a particular job are expected to do. They cover all the main aspects of an occupation and the knowledge and understanding that underpin competent performance. While NVQs may require employees to be trained to reach a set of standards, it is not a training programme, nor is there a prescribed learning method. The NVQ concept is based on four main principles: it is industry-led; it is based on performance on the job rather than entirely on knowledge; accessibility; and finally, the qualifications are flexible and transferable because they are unit-based and include Accreditation of Prior Learning.

There have been refinements over time, although criticisms remain about the process, content and outcomes. The unwieldy nature of building portfolios is laborious, and assessment can be inconsistent. Work by Lewis *et al* (2008) showed that within the retail sector both students and management were unhappy with NVQs, partly because the assessment procedures led to uncertainty about the actual level of skills of those with NVQ qualifications. There are questions over whether a competence gained in one context is transferable to another. Grugulis (2000, pp.95–6) believes that the relevance of competence-based qualifications is based on bureaucratisation and routinisation of what are often the less important elements of work. Using teachers as an example, emotional elements of the work, such as enthusing students and conveying ideas, are excluded in favour of trivial (more measurable) competences and, consequently, the meaningful element of the work is lost. Grugulis (2007) and Cox (2007) suggest that the qualifications are not as rigorous as the ones they replaced, and skill levels are lower in construction, hairdressing, management, electrical engineering and plumbing than they were under former qualifications regimes. Grugulis (2007) believes that lower level NVQs confer few financial benefits, although this is true for most low-level vocational qualifications, and that the failure to provide the consistent and high-level skills development seen overseas is partly because of the focus on accreditation and auditing rather than the content and syllabi. CIPD (2010f) reported that NVQ is not suitable for some employers as it is costly, and resource intensive; there was a need to redesign the structure, in particular, focussing on line managers as coaches rather than assessors.

### REFLECTIVE ACTIVITY

Find out about NVQs/SVQs in an occupation of your choice, and assess how effective they are in providing an appropriate and relevant qualification structure for that occupation.

Despite criticism, Cox (2007) maintains that NVQs play a valuable role in stimulating learning, but only where there is an 'expansive' orientation to L&D in the workplace (making reference to the work of Fuller and Unwin 2006). She points to research in the public healthcare sector where employers and lower-grade staff were enthusiastic about NVQs and the qualification led to increased knowledge and skill, as well as increased levels of confidence and career progression. Success was put down to sustained emotional and practical support for the learners and the organisation ensured appropriate job design and career progression; the learning was high quality and fitted specific needs of both learners and the organisation. Research in the NHS (McBride *et al* 2006; Cox 2007) demonstrates that NVQs are particularly useful for those working at lower levels, who lack prior educational success and confidence (see box below). In contrast, those working in more senior roles, particularly at managerial levels, were highly critical of NVQs (McBride *et al* 2006). Other research that supports these findings include Rainbird *et al* (2004b, pp.47–8), Sargeant (2000), and Roe *et al* (2006).

HRM AT WORK IN FOCUS

### Reporting back on the NHS skills escalator

*'An immigrant who started work in the UK as a cleaner is now fulfilling her dream of becoming a nurse. The woman who was on her nursing degree secondment... paid her way through college to gain L2 NVQ, got a job as a nursing auxiliary and completed NVQ L3 to access nurse training.'*

The NHS Skills Escalator was developed to help the NHS recruit, improve efficiency, and offer career development opportunities to all staff. An 'expansive' learning environment was developed in which all staff were given L&D opportunities. Manchester Business School researchers found that the most common approach was for managers to set up projects to meet their own particular needs, and roles were redesigned to promote staff development. The best impact was where lower-grade staff were encouraged to gain qualifications. Managers and staff were pleased with the results in terms of recruitment and retention, motivation heightened skills usage and knowledge, and increased levels of self-confidence. Two large urban trusts were able to solve recruitment problems using the escalator to 'tap into large pools of latent talent among ethnic minority groups'. HR professionals worked closely with line managers and L&D professionals to find funding and high-quality learning providers.

The NHS case studies showed how NVQs enhanced the skills and knowledge of workers, and gave them greater self-confidence to undertake further training opportunities.

Managers were actively involved in encouraging staff and ensured external tuition was of high quality and appropriate content. Action was taken if standards slipped, and close relationships with providers was maintained. Such support generated a 'community of trust' which conferred credibility onto the NVQ system. Learners reported good experiences when tutors, managers and peers encouraged their learning. Managers worked with HR to define learning needs and support career development, in some cases by the creation of new roles. The majority of the learners were enthusiastic about NVQs and the knowledge and skills acquired, particularly as taking the qualifications necessitated taking on different job tasks.

Based on Cox and McBride (2007) and Cox (2007).

It remains the case that those with NVQs are still a minority of the workforce, and that there is a patchy spread across occupations and a concentration in lower skilled jobs, particularly in the service sector. Although they are continuously criticised, NVQs have provided a different form of qualification and one that would seem highly successful in certain circumstances. Specifically, where those lacking in confidence and qualifications were supported to take NVQs, they proved useful in bridging the gap between formal and informal qualifications.

## APPRENTICESHIPS

Apprenticeships have historic and international recognition as a model of learning occupational and social skills. For an overview of the history of apprenticeships see Fuller and Unwin (2009). Prior to the 1970s, apprenticeships were controlled by employers who commissioned off-the-job training from further education (FE) colleges, typically with trade union involvement. Large employers, or groups of employers took on dozens of apprentices annually. This model was entrenched in local communities and apprenticeships were both well understood and respected.

Mass youth unemployment in the 1970s changed this as training schemes subsumed some apprenticeships and reduced the time involved. Training was taken from employers and colleges and handed to private sector providers which ran the schemes using work placements. Many employers took on trainees to replace more expensive workers, or they relabelled employees as 'apprentices' (Fuller and Unwin 2009). Trainees could get NVQs, for work they were already doing, much training was on-the-job, and some taking NVQ level 3 already held higher level qualifications. The focus was on keeping the numbers of young people not in employment, education or training (NEETs) down and hitting government targets; employers' needs were not necessarily taken into account.

Other factors also affected the apprenticeship model. The UK manufacturing base had reduced; few employers took on large numbers of apprentices and labour market deregulation led to erosion of boundaries between jobs and organisations (Brockmann *et al* 2010; Fuller and Unwin 2009). The close links between employers, FE colleges, and the local community almost disappeared and apprenticeships became restricted to a small number of occupational areas. For the government's VET policy to work, more able young people needed to take the vocational route; this did not happen; the less able took the vocational route, but few of these were able to attain Level 3. Instead, young people were encouraged to stay on in education, even those unsuited to academic study. This resulted in a high proportion dropping out and ending up in low-paid, low-skill jobs with virtually no access to training (Fuller and Unwin 1998). This compared unfavourably with North European systems.

Criticism of apprenticeships included low completion rates, bureaucracy, content, quality and flexibility. By 2008, there were 220 types of apprenticeship in over 80 sectors. In sectors with the largest numbers (retail, hospitality and business administration), there was no apprenticeship tradition and low demand for Level 3. Only 63% operated at Level 2 (CIPD 2011f). New-sector companies commit to apprenticeship to obtain subsidies, without committing to the philosophy. Typically, they have low completion rates, and prefer bespoke training, with some developing their own training. For example, Tesco developed its own Level 2 training and this was accredited to become eligible for public funding.

As well as government-supported apprenticeships there are a number that operate outside of government funding. Typically, these are where the 'apprentice' is not eligible for government funding or there is no suitable framework matching the specialist skill needs of the organisation (Ryan *et al* 2006). We follow the practice of Ryan *et al* (2006) and term government sponsored schemes 'Apprenticeship', and all others 'apprenticeship'.

There is considerable demand for quality higher level Apprenticeships (L3 and L4) and evidence that higher level Apprenticeships work well for some sectors (Ryan *et al* 2006). Higher level Apprenticeship is successful in sectors with Apprenticeship tradition, in larger organisations, and where there is a genuine need for L3 and L4 training. Engineering and telecommunications are good examples; typically 5 GCSEs grade A*–C including English and maths are required, and there are progression routes to Higher Nationals or degrees. In many such sectors, there is associated community of practice and an institutional infrastructure similar to the European models (Brockmann *et al* 2010; Ryan *et al* 2006; Fuller and Unwin 2009). Apprenticeships are lauded, and result in: increased loyalty, productivity, reduced labour turnover, enhanced reputation, improved competitiveness, and increased earning capacity of trainees. These schemes are equal to academic routes and detractions, such as high costs, risk of poaching, and dislike of certain elements (like key skills) did not stop companies from offering Advanced Apprenticeships. Furthermore, it is evident that they would provide quality schemes, *with or without* government support and funding.

## REFLECTIVE ACTIVITY

In order to fill the intermediate skills gap (at L3), vocational routes must become as attractive as academic routes to able young people. Do you agree with this statement? Do you think that Apprenticeships will achieve this aim? If not, why not?

HRM AT WORK IN FOCUS

## Getting apprenticeships at McDonalds

McDonalds pledged to take on around 10,000 Apprentices from 2010, and was one of the largest government-supported providers. The 12-month Apprenticeship was L2 Multi-skilled Hospitality Services. Each Apprenticeship consists of three elements: a competence-based element at L2: a knowledge-based element at L2 and key skills. Apprentices must complete two key skill units (application of number and communications) at L1, and nine further units. Of the nine units, two are mandatory (hygiene and secure working environment; and giving customers a good impression of oneself and the organisation). Of the remaining seven options, Apprentices can choose three at L1. This means that six of the eleven units could be at L1, even though the Apprentice is awarded a L2 qualification. McDonalds advertisements state that the Apprenticeship is combined with GCSE equivalent in maths and English, without specifying the level. There has to be a question mark over whether this is an L2 Apprenticeship when the majority of units can be taken at L1.

In any case, it is highly probable that McDonalds' employees would all go through the same process of induction and training, whether or not they are 'Apprentices'. Given that the 2007 rate for 16–18-year-olds completing NVQ2 Apprenticeship in Hospitality (Food Processing) was £3,682, this would mean that McDonalds received over £22 million of taxpayers' money in 2009.

Source: Adapted from James (2010).

The McDonalds case shows how the Apprenticeship standard can be diluted. The confusion about qualification levels makes it understandable that employers prefer good GCSEs over NVQs (remembering that L2 should equate to five A–C GCSEs); such confusions do nothing to aid progression routes (James 2010).

Following criticism, a new Apprenticeship programme was launched in 2009. The National Apprenticeship Service (NAS) was set up to support, fund, and co-ordinate delivery and there was to be a statutory entitlement to Apprenticeship for all 'suitably qualified' young people from 2013. Numbers were to be increased to 200,000 a year by 2014/15 with L3 the level to which all should aspire. Apprenticeships would include a technical knowledge qualification, functional skills, and take from one to four years. A limited number of Adult Apprenticeships for those aged 25+ would be supported although those with L3 qualifications already would still be eligible. Young people who refuse places could be prosecuted, and a National Minimum Wage of £2.50 per hour was introduced for those aged 16–18. The hope is that all Apprentices will be employed and paid the minimum wage appropriate for the age range.

By 2011 85,000 employers were offering schemes at three levels:

- Intermediate Level – work towards NVQ Level 2, functional skills, and possibly BTEC.
- Advanced Level – work to NVQ Level 3, functional skills, and usually relevant knowledge based qualification such as BTEC. For entry, a young person would need 5 GCSEs (grade C and above) or Intermediate Level Apprenticeship.
- Higher Apprenticeships – work towards NVQ Level 4, and in some cases a knowledge-based qualification such as a foundation degree.

Additionally, there is a fourth level – Access to Apprenticeships, which helps those aged 16–24 who need extra support.

The changes are ambitious, and aim to solve a host of problems with one initiative:

- tackle massive youth unemployment
- broaden coverage to almost all sectors
- address equality issues – gender, race, and disability
- increase numbers of adult Apprenticeships (19–30 age) at L3
- clear progression to L3 Advanced Apprenticeships and increase L4 opportunities
- clear progression routes to L3 and L4 with HE tariff points
- piloting Honours and Masters Schemes.

Even before the new Apprenticeship scheme was put in place, there was cynicism. Historically, demand for apprentices in UK remains comparatively low, often because they were not appropriate for the organisation (CIPD 2010f). Nonetheless, by 2011, the numbers rose dramatically although this included large numbers of older workers, which does nothing to ameliorate record levels of unemployed youth, and many of those aged over 25 were already in work and enrolled on Apprenticeships lasting as little as 12 weeks (Vasagar 2011b).

Under the new arrangements, employers share the costs by employing Apprentices with the government funding the training element. The government should pay for training those who leave school without qualifications to raise employability and help them to avoid low-paid, vulnerable work. What is in dispute is whether the government should subsidise training which employers would have provided in any case, especially when they get cheap labour at £2.50 per hour.

Many of the new Apprenticeships are at lower levels (Fuller and Unwin 2009, Brockmann *et al* 2010) and polarisation between high and low skills is developing (CIPD 2011f; Brockmann *et al* 2010; LSN 2011). The problem is that at low levels (L2), Apprenticeships offer on the-job training that employers provide anyway (CIPD 2011f); examples include Tesco and McDonalds. It will be tempting for employers to use the ready supply of substitute cheap labour when the NMW for 16–18 olds is £2.50 per hour, with Apprentices leaving once they reach 18 and commanding a higher NMW. Many are 'conversions' ie employees relabelled as apprentices, other retake levels of qualifications that they already have, or gain NVQ for work that they are already doing competently and where jobs previously 'unskilled' jobs become Apprenticeships; this can debase kudos and brand (Fuller and Unwin 2009). Ryan *et al* (2007) question the aim to spread across all sectors rather than targeting sectors in which there is high demand and a need for high level skills (L3+) such as engineering, construction, and telecommunications. Of course, this would not solve the problems of the not in employment, education or training (NEETs).

Kudos can only be retained by pushing attainment at higher levels and ensuring progression routes to HE. However, less than one-fifth are offered at the advanced level. The Learning and Skills Network (LSN 2011) believes that policy in relation to higher level Apprenticeships is both confused and confusing vis-à-vis aims for HE. At a time of increased demand for HE and reduced supply, it is likely that the most prestigious courses and institutions will prefer A levels. Since qualification levels are not aligned (the full undergraduate degree is L6 whereas foundation degrees are at L4/5) and undergraduate L4 Apprenticeships are not yet developed, there remains some confusion as to how it will all fit together (LSN 2011). CIPD (2011f) is calling for the system of funding, allocation, and delivery, to be simplified with more intelligible and effective marketing. Those organisations (often SMEs) which offer little or no training continue to remain hard to reach and it is unclear how current proposals will ameliorate this situation.

All Apprentices should be employed, although as employers reach saturation point (LSN 2011), it is not clear what will happen to the guarantee of a place for all young people. As unemployment among young people rises, there may be a repeat of 1980s-style training schemes using temporary work placements – something that gave schemes a bad reputation, particularly as those without an employer were disproportionately women or from ethnic minority groups.

The UK Apprenticeship system is often compared with European models and found lacking in terms of participation rates and quality (Ryan *et al* 2010; Fuller and Unwin 2009). Germany, Switzerland, Denmark, and Netherlands retain higher numbers of apprentices (Fuller and Unwin 2009). In Germany and Switzerland participation rates are around two-thirds and three-quarters respectively, whereas England hopes to raise this to one-fifth by 2020 (Ryan *et al* 2010). Content is generally higher quality, with Apprentices in Germany and Switzerland spending one or two days a week in formal college education, and engineering Apprentices spending the first nine months off-the-job (Ryan *et al* 2010), and in most of Europe the standard is L3, whereas in Britain, most are L2 with standards varying widely (Brockmann *et al* 2010; Ryan *et al* 2010). Across Europe, the term Apprenticeship is legally defined, whereas, in the UK Apprentices cannot clearly be differentiated from other trainees and employees (Ryan *et al* 2010). The UK system is narrowly based on skill and prescribed tasks at a satisfactory level rather than an occupational model with high status. An example of the difference can be seen by comparing bricklaying in UK with Germany, France and Scandinavia. In the latter, the Apprenticeship covers maths, physics and a range of related occupations so that bricklayers can work autonomously and co-ordinate work across a range of contexts (Brockmann *et al* 2010). Notwithstanding the high reputation of German Apprenticeships, there is some evidence that organisations (almost one in five) are following a substitution strategy, ie replacing unskilled or semi-skilled workers with cheaper Apprentices. This is particularly prevalent in the service sector where there is lower capital equipment, absence of works councils, higher share of white-collar workers, and smaller companies. In other sectors, German organisations generally accept the cost of training, taking a longer-term investment view than those of UK companies (Mohrenweiser and Backes-Gellner 2010). The government could learn from European models which provide an equitable funding system based on social agreements between employers, unions, the government and educators with quality underpinned by legislation.

The nuanced work by Ryan *et al* (2006) shows how organisations make decisions about apprenticeship training based upon their own specific circumstances. Where their needs align with government, formal Apprenticeships are offered and the organisations work around elements which they do not like. On the other hand, where their interests do not align, then provision is made without government funding. Organisations continue to provide high quality craft skills training with progression routes, usually in traditional skill areas; these retain high prestige whether they are government funded Apprenticeships or not. The mass provision in sectors with no tradition, and low demand for L3 skills, downgrades the brand as a whole. Apprenticeships are unlikely to prove to be the silver bullet to simultaneously save NEETs from becoming another 'lost generation'; to drive up intermediate skill levels; and to provide prestigious vocational routes to HE (LSN 2011). For it all to work, there has to be parity of esteem between the vocational and academic routes, and this has not proved easy in the past.

## INVESTORS IN PEOPLE (IIP)

IiP was set up in 1991 as a national quality standard for good L&D practice; the government hoped that it would cajole employers to invest in L&D. The focus has moved to management, and leadership, as well as skills development, and the framework acts as a business tool to assess how people are managed and where improvements can be made. The standard is based on 39 evidence requirements under three headings: Planning Strategy (Business, L&D, People Management, and Leadership and Management); Action (Management

Effectiveness, Recognition and Reward, Involvement and Empowerment, Learning and Development), and Review (Performance Measurement, and Continuous Improvement). Approaches to health and well-being at work are being piloted (Bevan 2010).

The government aims to work alongside the TUC, Acas, Business in the Community, the National Enterprise Academy and CIPD to improve leadership and management, and IiP is 'the improvement tool of choice for businesses wishing to grow through ... use of skills' (DBIS 2010). From 2009 IiP became part of UKCES and was relaunched under 'The New Choices Approach'. The aim was to utilise IiP to help UKCES to attain its objectives – to promote economic growth through building a more strategic, agile and demand-led employment and skills system; raise skill levels by increasing employer investment in skills, and create more and better jobs (Gloster *et al* 2011). It was hoped that more flexibility would increase numbers signing up to IiP. At the same time, extension levels of award were added – Bronze, Silver and Gold and advisors and assessors were given more of a consultancy role (UKCES 2011b).

According to IiP (www.investorsinpeople.co.uk), the standard improves profitability, helps organisations meet their strategic goals, aids managing change in a downturn, aids retention, and provides a benchmark for good management practice. Several pieces of independent research (Hoque 2003; Grugulis 2007; Bourne and Franco-Santos 2010; Walsh *et al* 2011; Gloster *et al* 2010) also confirm that the majority of accredited organisations benefit from the IiP standard:

- increased productivity
- improved profitability
- better customer service
- reduction in workforce turnover
- improved employee motivation
- better L&D practice
- management and leadership improvements.

Critics point to the uneven distribution of IiP, its inability to reach SMEs and new employers, and the lack of concrete proof of benefits. IiP accreditation is most likely in larger organisations; in the public sector; in unionised workplaces, and there is an imbalance across industrial sectors with concentration on professionals and managers (Kersley *et al* 2006, p.65; Rainbird and Munro 2003a, p.36; Hoque *et al* 2005; Walsh *et al* 2011; Gloster *et al* 2010). Research also questions whether there are proven benefits in reduced absenteeism, labour turnover, and workforce injuries. Most studies seem to confirm that there are improvements in employee attitudes, particularly motivation and morale, but much of this relies on employers' responses rather than those of employees and tangible evidence is difficult to find (Grugulis and Bevitt 2002). Hill and Stewart (1999), Ram (2000), and Hoque (2003) all believe that a large number of organisations, particularly those in the initial waves of accreditation, already had good HR systems and procedures in place, so gaining IiP was nothing more than a 'badging' process, and training reverts to what it had been in the past once the award had been achieved. More recent research (Gloster *et al* 2011) links the learning capacity of employers and high performance working practices with take-up of IiP, which could indicate that those organisations accredited would be doing the good work with or without IiP ratification.

## REFLECTIVE ACTIVITY

Is your own organisation IiP accredited? If yes, evaluate the advantages that it has brought. If not, do you feel that it should be, and can you list the potential advantages?

To address criticisms, the standard was reviewed in 2004 and again in 2010. By 2011, IiP had over 21,000 recognised organisations (IiP Customer Services), and in 2010 26% of the workforce was employed in IiP accredited organisations; but, over the last decade, the majority of work has been with re-accreditations (Gloster *et al* 2010).

It is early days since the launch of 'The New Choices Approach', but initial research by UKCES (2011a) reports that the new scheme is better-suited to organisational needs, although it is still not reaching small employers and new organisations. It is agreed that SMEs take training seriously, but that the informal, reactive and ad hoc nature of training in small firms is not suited to IiP and is not always recognised because it is uncertified and hidden (Ram 2000; Kitching 2007). The burden of costs, time, and perception of the amount of paperwork deters SMEs and they are less likely to have specialist HR managers to push IiP forward (UKCES 2011a; Gloster *et al* 2010).

UKCES is considering financial incentives and improved and targeted marketing to increase take-up by organisations new to IiP, particularly SMEs (Hoque *et al* 2005; Walsh *et al* 2011). IiP centres and consultants tend to work primarily with those already accredited, because they are more profitable and easier to engage with. Financial incentives could be used to promote working with SMEs, and those outside the scheme, or who have dropped out prior to accreditation. Other ideas mooted (Walsh *et al* 2011; Gloster *et al* 2011) include making more use of champions to market IiP such as CIPD, Chambers of Commerce, CBI, Sector Skills Councils, and LEPs, particularly its relevance through a downturn. However, it is anticipated that the economic downturn will reduce numbers of public and voluntary sector organisations investing, and may deter committed organisations from signing up to bronze, silver and gold awards. Finally, although there is now stretch at the top end, with the extension awards, more needs to be done at the bottom end to aid accreditation. UKCES needs to continue research in the impact of changes, particularly on employer engagement and investment in skills, and whether IiP can attract a broader church, particularly small businesses.

## TRADE UNIONS, LEARNING AND DEVELOPMENT

Throughout the 1960s and 1970s Britain operated a model under which trade unions, employers, the government and educationalists were all involved in VET. This disappeared during the Thatcher years but since 1997 the UK has moved slightly closer to the EU social partnership model, something required by the 1997 Treaty of Amsterdam. As we saw earlier, lifelong learning and VET is seen as a priority for economic growth, social inclusion, and high employment levels. In common with the ILO and OECD, the EU places emphasis on VET policy, and delivery is through partnership models involving trade unions (OECD 2010; Stuart and Wallis 2007).

In the UK, the TUC established its Learning Service in 1994 with the mission 'to represent all employee interests in securing the learning and skills they require to maintain their employability, enhance their career progression and guarantee social inclusion' and 'to create a learning culture in every workplace and for every worker to be a lifelong learner'. The Union Learning Fund (ULF) was set up in 1998 and training provided for union learning representatives (ULRs) became a statutory right from 2003. UnionLearn was set up in 2006. The ULRs role was defined by legislation ensuring entitlement for time off in order to: assess learning and training needs; provide information, advice and guidance; arrange learning; promote the value of learning; consult with the employer about learning; and undergo relevant training. Every worker in a union-recognised workplace is entitled to access to a ULR, whether they are union members or not. The government at the time welcomed union involvement and described the TUC's strategy as 'an inexpensive source of advice for employers'. In recognition, the government contribution to the ULF was £9 million in 2003, rising to £21 million for 2011–12. By 2008, 847 learning centres were established, 1,557 learning agreements were signed and over 600,000 learning opportunities had been assessed, and in the 12 years up to 2011 more than 26,000 ULRs had been trained (Stuart *et al* 2010; UnionLearn 2011b).

Overall, the model has been successful, for the government, the employer, the unions, as well as the learners. According to UnionLearn (2011c) the result is:

- increased learning needs assessment
- higher quality and levels of L&D provision
- improved take-up of job-related training
- improved qualification levels of employees
- fewer skills gaps
- improved operating measures and business outcomes
- positive impact on union–employer relations
- enhanced equality of access to L&D
- success in attracting non-participants, eg older males, those from lower socio-economic groups. (Stuart *et al* 2011).

There is much written about the difficulty in attracting non-traditional learners (NIACE), and ULRs have been particularly effective in reaching those with little experience of successful learning (migrant workers, those at lowest levels and in contingent employment), and giving them the confidence to return to learning (Stuart *et al* 2011; Findlay and Warhurst 2011; Rainbird and Stewart 2011). Most employees would not wish their employer to know about their basic skills problems, but will discuss these with a colleague (Cassell and Lee 2009). Research has shown there is only a small amount of deadweight (people who would have taken another type of learning opportunity if UnionLearn had not been available).

Once learners experience success, improved confidence hooks them in and more than 80% wanted more union learning – particularly those from lower socio-economic levels working in caring and service occupations. According to UnionLearn (2011b), of the almost 250,000 involved in L&D in 2009–10; 5,000 were on degree level courses, 22,000 on L3, and 40,000 on L2, and UnionLearn typically exceeded targets of numbers going for NVQ levels 2 and 3. Of those continuing, almost half improved by two levels; and almost 10% by three levels; quite an achievement, as even moving to Level 2 creates an estimated £3,113 annual gross value-added (Stuart *et al* 2011). The increased demand for higher levels of L&D (to L3 and above) and evidence of progression contributed to government skills strategy and is particularly welcome. Unions hope to embed what they have achieved through building infrastructure, in terms of learning centres, partnerships, committees and agreements (Rainbird and Stewart, 2011; Stuart *et al* 2011). The box below gives examples of work by ULRs.

HRM AT WORK IN FOCUS

### ULR of the year 2010

Bharti works on the till in Primark. She was shop steward, equalities rep and became a ULR for USDAW in 2007. Since then she has introduced courses such as English for speakers of other languages, and maths, and developed a skills swap-shop in the staff canteen. As well as encouraging fellow workers to return to learn, she has encouraged many to join the union, and persuaded management to pay for all staff to take NVQs.

Adapted from UnionLearn (2011).

**UnionLearn in recession**

Chamberlin and Hill, a manufacturer of steel castings, suffered hugely in the recession and production was reduced from 5.5 days per week to 3 days per fortnight. The workplace used the spare time available to employees to offer L&D at the on-site learning centre which had been opened in partnership with Unite union and the local college.

The company is now back to full capacity, as it has won contracts, in part because of its improved efficiency and quality. The managing director believed that Union learning had helped the company and employees come through the recession 'in a better position to move forwards'.

Source: Adapted from Stuart *et al* (2011).

In addition to the success stories above, there are times when legislation dictates a minimum qualification level, for example when the care sector required all workers to have a minimum of NVQ L2; or in redundancy situations (Cassell and Lee 2009; Stuart and Wallis 2007). Where several unions are involved in a sector, a number of unions might combine, for example four unions collaborated to form the Rail Union Learning Project (Cassell and Lee 2009).

## REFLECTIVE ACTIVITY

How might ULRs be able to help with the training renaissance, especially for the 'skills poor'?

Employers gain, and one-third make direct funding available. Other employers offer 'in kind' donations such as time off for training and support for workplace learning committees. Although around 90% of employers commit to continue with union learning activities, sustainability is tied to funding. To date, most ULF-financed projects have been supported again, but only one-fifth of employers may continue in the absence of UnionLearn funding (Stuart and Cook 2011). Not all employers welcome union involvement in L&D, and unions may not be accorded equal partnership rights. Although the 2002 Act made provision for statutory rights of ULRs, there was no right to negotiate with the employer on training, and as a result, negotiating rights are determined by the strength of the union locally. There is ample evidence of employers blocking unions:

- insufficient time allowance for UnionLearn activities
- only one in five ULRs are given cover for their regular job
- lack of negotiation and consultation with managers on decisions over learning
- less than half ULRs felt that senior managers valued their activity
- around a quarter of union members that ULRs represent are given no training by the employer (UnionLearn 2011b; Saundry *et al* 2010).

Of course, where the employer does not allow adequate time off, or no cover, colleagues may have to pick up on the work and this leads to resentment (Cassell and Lee 2009). In practice, UnionLearn delivery is determined locally by the characteristics of the union, the infrastructure, and organisational priorities, as well as differences across sectors (Rainbird and Stuart 2011; Bacon and Hoque 2010).

A major spin-off for the unions has been increased trade union membership; improved relations with members; and increased recruitment of new activists to the ULR role – particularly among women, younger people and those from minority ethnic groups (Findlay and Warhurst 2011; Stuart *et al* 2011; UnionLearn 2011; Cassell and Lee 2009;

Saundry *et al* 2010). Overall, UnionLearn has been a major fillip for unions, even though there may be opportunity costs for unions in carrying out this work. Despite positives, some believe that unions should not become instruments of the state, because unions are not accorded equal status and have little influence over strategic skills policy, nor should they fund and initiate L&D that employers themselves should provide (Cassell and Lee 2009).

As with most initiatives, there are difficulties in reaching the self-employed and SMEs – almost half of all workplaces with more than 25 employees are non-union (DTI 2007). Despite problems, the government and the unions are optimistic about union-led initiatives to stimulate co-investment in L&D to increase the contribution from employers through Collective Learning Funds (CLFs). There is also talk of union involvement pushing high performance work practices – something that has happened already in Scotland (Green 2010). In England, the biggest challenge will be gaining employer financial support in the absence of external sources of funding and without compulsory contributions to learning (Bacon and Hoque 2010). Once again, the European culture of social partnership is more conducive to partnership arrangements for L&D and results in agreements at all levels with national, regional and sectoral regulatory frameworks (Stuart and Wallis 2007).

## ASSESSING THE CONTRIBUTION OF VET TO SKILL IMPROVEMENT

### DEMAND FOR AND USAGE OF SKILLS

In terms of the demand for and usage of skills, UK employers remain in the low skills equilibrium (Finegold and Soskice 1988), relying on low prices, rather than high quality, for competitive advantage. The result is low demand for employees with high skills, under-employment of existing skills and low priority given to L&D. The prevailing view is that the UK must make the shift from the low-skills equilibrium position to high-skills, high-value-added system based on a more highly educated and flexible workforce in order to compete internationally. As we have seen, the government's strategy has been to use a variety of means (short of legislation) to improve skill levels and to cajole companies to increase levels of L&D and skill utilisation. A number of issues relating to this are discussed below.

HRM AT WORK IN FOCUS

#### Looking to the future

Sloman (2007b) analysed the data from the 2006 survey on work skills and concluded that the scenario for the future might be:

'as the economy advances, higher-value products will demand greater commitment and greater skills from the workforce. These "modern economy" skills involve the extensive use of technology and the deployment of influencing skills. The former is acquired by discretionary learning; the acquisition and deployment of the latter is another discretionary activity. This requires a motivated, engaged and committed workforce. However, an increasing proportion of our workforce feel themselves overqualified for the job, and the amount of discretion that people are allowed is at best remaining at the same level. These findings are hardly consistent with the increased engagement we seek, and the constraints of the job may indeed be demotivating.'

*To think about:*

*Is Sloman's analysis still accurate? Justify your answer.*

## DEFINITION – THE SKILLS DEBATE

In the past it has been difficult to gain an accurate picture of skill levels, and only recently has there been a coherent attempt to evaluate sectoral skill levels and predict those needed for the future based on the opinions of employers. Keep (2002) believes that employers are often vague, confused and contradictory and since most organisations lack any HR planning, accuracy is difficult. As he says (p.463), 'skill strategies and forecasts are only as good as the weakest data upon which they are founded'. There remain enormous problems of accurate measurement; one is that skills are not the same as qualifications (qualifications usually being proxy for skills), and are not easily quantified, leading employers to maintain that there is more going on than is recognised (Kitching 2007), particularly in service work (Korczynski 2005, p.11).

Another major problem lies with definitions of 'skill'. Keep E (2001) gives the example of shop workers who are now defined as 'skilled', whereas 20 years ago they would have been 'unskilled'. Questions arise about whether or not they really are more skilled, and whether we get a better service. Warhurst and Thompson (1998, p.5) cite examples in the financial sector in which 'knowledge workers' in call centres have to use 'standardised quality' responses so that their work is routinised, and lacks autonomy. The switch from manufacturing to the service sector has seen the demand for aesthetic or soft skills increase. Sturdy *et al* (2001, pp.186–7) showed that Glasgow residents were not 'posh' enough for 'style' jobs which were taken by students and suburban commuters to the exclusion of inner city youth. These personal attributes and traits, such as appearance, accent and self-confidence, may not be amenable to training. Moreover, they are subjective, making them vulnerable to prejudice on the basis of race, gender, class, accent, or appearance, as for example where women's soft skills are not accorded the same importance as those of men. At higher levels, soft skills such as practical intelligence (PI), emotional intelligence (EI) and intuitive intelligence (II) (CIPD 2010d) are seen as critical for effective leadership and management and employers bemoan the lack of such skills, even from graduates of highly rated business schools (Lucas and Claxton 2010).

## SUPPLY AND DEMAND FOR SKILLS, AND SKILLS UTILISATION

Fundamentally, there are questions whether raising the supply of skills will shift the UK from its low-skill equilibrium. In the global skills race, the focus has been on increasing the supply of skills, although it is now recognised that this is insufficient; there needs to be increased demand and utilisation of skills and a shift to high performance working (Payne and Keep 2011; Felstead *et al* 2007; Keep and Mayhew 2010; Lloyd and Mayhew 2010). Evidence from Scotland, which increased supply of high-level skills, showed that there was little or no impact on productivity and from 2007, the Scottish government concentrated on addressing demand and utilisation (Green 2010).

Many UK employers gain competitive advantage through low value goods and services using low skilled, low waged workforce; they neither need nor want a skilled workforce. Lloyd's (2005) work in the fitness industry demonstrated this. UK employers typically ask for lower educational qualifications for labour maricet entry than other European countries (Preston and Green 2008). Although the government takes the view that low skilled, 'bad' jobs are disappearing, the evidence suggests that the number of jobs not requiring qualifications for entry are growing – in retail, hotels, food processing, cleaning and servicing (Lloyd and Mayhew 2010).

In such jobs, little training is needed; where it is given, it is mostly on-the-job and the sort of qualifications offered (L2) offer limited opportunity for progression or movement to other employers, and do not solve issue of low wages. Furthermore, this level is seen as the minimum for employability (Lloyd and Mayhew 2010; Payne and Keep 2011).

Employers train as much as they need to, particularly to promote employees, but often it is in-house and unaccredited, and part-time workers (typically women) miss out. There is also a reluctance to invest in higher level training (L3/L4) as it is cheaper to recruit from outside and some employers fear that if they train an employee they will leave. There is some evidence that employer training has been falling and this amounts to a waste of talent and potential, but because of the large supply of labour this does not affect employers (Lloyd and Mayhew 2010).

Furthermore, increasing the supply of higher skills does not always result in employers' upgrading their goods and services, nor increasing productivity, nor does it result in 'bad' jobs disappearing (Keep and Mayhew, 2010; Payne and Keep, 2011). Instead of relying on skills to shift people out of bad jobs, there is a need to reduce the number of bad jobs through interventions such as raising the NMW, stricter regulation of working time, job redesign and initiatives to move to high performance working.

There is evidence that rising skill levels on the supply side (particularly the number of graduates entering the labour market) results in under-utilisation of these skills and under-employment (Felstead *et al* 2007; Sutherland 2009; Payne and Keep 2011). This issue also applies to low-paid workers in the public sector – particularly women and part-time workers (Rainbird and Munro 2003a).

The situation is complex, with both fragmentation and stability in the labour market (Nolan and Wood 2003), disagreement over the proportion of jobs demanding highly skilled workers, and the speed at which demand is developing (Keep *et al* 2006). Felstead *et al* (2007) found evidence that usage of job skills has risen and the number of jobs needing L4 qualifications had gone up. However, there are few high-skills export sectors in the UK, the main ones being information technology, pharmaceuticals, some branches of chemicals, aircraft manufacture and some aspects of insurance and finance, but together these account for a small proportion of UK exports. Even in these industries, highly skilled workers may only be required in R&D, design and product management roles, and training is frequently only available to a small number of employees who are difficult to replace. In most of the developed world, the main employers of highly educated and trained employees are in the public sector in health, education and welfare and in these sectors high-level skills are not needed by a majority of staff, nor are they exported.

CIPD research shows that the use of skills is more effective when linked to job appraisal, reward, job design, flexible working and effective staff communication, with the role of line manager being particularly important. In short, high performance working should be given as much attention as investment in skills (CIPD 2010f). The challenge is to encourage employers to move to high-performance working where human capital, and their skills, are valued and used, and workers gain pride and development as part of the job (Gold *et al* 2010, p.57). UKCES (2009a, p.10) has just started to look at demand and utilisation, seeing that the 'UK has too few high performance workplaces, too few employers producing high quality goods and services, and too few businesses in high value added sectors'.

Three case studies illustrating the importance of work organisation and context to training are given in the box below.

HRM AT WORK IN FOCUS

## The importance of work organisation and context to training

**NHS sterilisation and disinfection unit**

Workers in this unit were low skilled and low paid with little potential for skill development. Many had qualifications although none were required for the work – women in particular had a range of skills that were not used in the job. Workers were attracted to the job because of flexibility of hours (numbers and timing). There was no opportunity for formal training, nor career progression (except to supervision), and little opportunity to acquire skills that would be marketable outside the workplace.

**The housing department**

The housing department was responsible for the maintenance of housing stock and sheltered accommodation. Staff numbers had been radically cut and there were intense budgetary pressures. Work was redesigned so that managers' jobs were generic. Each manager was responsible for all issues to do with 350 houses, often in sink estates. The work was on the front line and exceedingly stressful as it involved a huge workload and dealing with irate tenants. Initial training was given before staff took on generic roles. However, the timing and amount of training was deemed inadequate. It was specifically targeted at ability to do the job, rather than for personal development or training for future need. For all of these reasons, the training was viewed negatively, and morale was low.

**The local government cook-freeze centre**

This is a small factory unit contracted by Social Services. The work is 'repetitive, boring and low skilled'. Despite this, turnover was low, and workers said that they were proud to be able to help others. All were encouraged by management to train; they were given time off and, wherever possible, the opportunity to use the skills they learned. It was thought that management's support in taking external courses helped motivate and retain workers, even though most courses did not contribute to work role.

Source: Adapted from Rainbird *et al* (2004b).

The case studies in the box above demonstrate the importance of work organisation, job design and context. In the cook-freeze unit, the work was low-skill and boring, with little opportunity for change to the situation. Nonetheless, staff were encouraged to train for their personal development and motivation levels were high, with low turnover. In comparison, in the housing department, highly skilled workers were trained to cope with generic working, but the training was job-specific, and other aspects of work organisation lead to extremely low morale. In the NHS example, the majority of employees' existing qualifications are not used and they were offered no opportunity for development. It can be seen that even where the government is the employer, commitment to 'high skills' work organisation and approaches to HRM and training and development is likely to be almost accidental rather than strategic (Rainbird and Munro 2003b). Such case studies demonstrate the conflict between individual and organisational training and development needs.

It is clear that the issues of HRM practices, line management involvement and the opportunity to practice skills are as important as the product specification in developing skills (Hansson 2007).

REFLECTIVE ACTIVITY

How far is your organisation along the road to becoming a learning organisation and what more needs to be done to embed a culture of learning?

## LABOUR MARKET MOBILITY

Where people increase their employability, this may be at the expense of someone else in a zero-sum game of social mobility. For example, as the numbers of graduates have increased, many take jobs that previously did not require a degree and displace those with lower level qualifications. Internationally, as developing countries gain higher skills, numbers of high skilled jobs in the UK may decline (Payne and Keep 2011; Keep and Mayhew 2010).

A further factor is the belief that technological growth drives up demand for skilled labour, without recognising that it may increase demand for both good jobs and bad jobs. Since many routine jobs that can be replaced are in the middle of the labour market this leaves a hollowing-out with demand at the top for skills, and demand at the bottom for non-routine jobs such as cleaning or shelf stacking (Nolan and Wood 2003). This is known as the polarisation or hourglass economy and is based on the idea that technology is complementary to skilled labour and a substitute for unskilled labour. Technological progress increases demand for skilled workers and lessens demand for unskilled labour (who perform routine tasks that are replaced by technology). The decrease in middle jobs may mean that semi-skilled workers in routine jobs find themselves out of work, and have to drop down to unskilled non-routine jobs. This interrupts career moves to high quality work, as people usually move up in small steps and careers are developed slowly, with one job allowing access to better jobs through the skills and experience developed on each step up. If this theory is correct, then the position of those in low-skilled non-routine occupations is bleak, and focus on giving more skills to those in the middle may not work if these skills are under-utilised. The only surety is that those with L4 and above has increased access to professional occupations but vocational qualifications below Level 4 have little effect on mobility after displacement from the labour market (Holmes 2011).

The government can influence skills development and usage through persuasion, money and regulation. The main method has been persuasion, and the Labour government invested huge amounts of money, but by 2011 resources were reduced as austerity measures were introduced to cope with the after-effects of the banking crisis, and resources are being cut back. The coalition government emphasised market forces, private investment and reduced government input. There is a small amount (£50 million per year) in the Growth and Innovation Fund to encourage employers to promote high performance working, but support for SMEs was reduced. The assumption is that employers will invest in skills, even though employers have not been willing to do so in the past. Payne and Keep (2011) believe that employers know that if they do not support L&D, the government does so, and many are adept at obtaining public money for training they would have provided anyway.

An alternative strategy is for the government to tackle the flexible, deregulated labour market to cut off low-cost competitive strategies using a cheap and marginalised workforce, through moving away from the neo-liberal, free market policies. There would need to be a clear industrial policy, similar to those of France, Japan or Germany, to reduce bad jobs, support long-term investment, and to promote innovation (Keep and Mayhew 2010). This would entail a shift from short-term shareholder returns (which act against longer term investments), reformed corporate governance and increased accountability, industrial relations, support for job redesign, raising the minimum wage, and making it harder to sack people (Payne and Keep 2011; Keep and Mayhew 2010; Green 2010). In England, it is highly unlikely that there will be training levies nor license to practice arrangements except where a majority of employers in any one sector want this (Payne and Keep 2011). Ideologically the coalition government is not likely to consider these options; preferring to concentrate on skills as the solution (Keep and Mayhew 2010, p.567).

### INTERNATIONAL COMPARISONS

It is useful to look overseas for examples of good practice, particularly from similar economies, even though ideas cannot always be lifted wholesale to the UK context. For example, the prerequisites for creating high-skill ecosystems in California include increased funding for basic research and pre-venture capital, more courses on starting up new businesses – especially for scientists and engineers – strategies to retain the talents of overseas students, and increased regional networks (including research universities) to promote sector clusters and sector networks (Finegold 1999, p.79). Technology and Innovation Centres may create a similar stimulus, but it is also important to be alert to new global opportunities. If we take the energy renewables industry as an example, the government funding strategies have been weak, leaving Germany to steal the initiative on development and design, as well as skills for fitting and maintenance. Such markets need pump-priming through subsidising purchases or through investment funds; in 'co-ordinated market economies' such as Germany, France and Japan, this happens. In comparison, the voluntarist, 'free-market model' of UK and USA largely leaves decisions to employers and individuals. A pilot in Australia (Eddington and Eddington 2010) has shown how a shift can be made to high skills equilibrium that can deal with change, produce decent and sustainable work in a carbon-constrained economy, but only when industry promotes its own skill ecosystem through demand in attracting, developing, utilising and retaining skills. Winterton (2007) makes the point that rather than looking to Anglo-American strategies for inspiration, the UK needs to turn to other regions such as Asia and the Middle East. The Tiger economies of South Korea, Singapore and Taiwan demonstrate how the strategic role of state can successfully make change happen through adopting the longer-term view, and making decisions based on robust information about skill needs; and VET providers are given both targets and financial incentives (Gold *et al* 2010, p.58).

Although BRIC countries compete on both low-skill and high-skill, the context is very different. Taking China as an example, even though it has one of the largest workforces in the world, there are low levels of L&D offered – even to graduates (Cooke 2005, p.88). Although some larger firms – particularly MNCs – invest heavily in L&D to compete, there is an overall lack of coherence and funding is mainly provided by individuals or employers. Here too, there is an urgent need for increased state funding to increase the skills levels (Cooke 2011b).

## CONCLUSIONS

The government's stated aim is to meet the needs of employers and individuals to push the economy from its low-skills equilibrium. It also aims to promote social cohesion and inclusion through equal access to decent employment that offers quality training, particularly as the deregulative approach in the UK and USA makes it easy to dispose of workers without skills who find themselves marginalised, drifting in and out of low-paid work. The hope has been that increasing the *supply* of skills will provide impetus for change, but too few UK organisations live up to the image of the 'learning organisation' and where decisions are left to firms, training tends to be limited to the essentials, with major inequalities in access. Many employers achieve competitive advantage through low-skill equilibrium; this makes short-term economic sense but perpetuates the cycle. Some of the larger organisations do think longer term, but it is a major challenge to engage with SMEs. The issue of formal versus informal learning is related to this, and although the government prefers formal learning (presumably because of ease of measurement), informal learning is likely to grow because it is flexible, and therefore more attractive, particularly to smaller firms. Similarly, promoting high quality training, while at the same time meeting social aims, is difficult without establishing a two-tier system of poorer provision for those less skilled and qualified. Increasing the supply of skills is only one part of the solution – and the easiest to effect. Rather more difficult is to ensure that firms *demand* and *utilise* skills, as well as provide the opportunity for continual learning for *all*. There is no point in training people if they then find themselves in a workplace that neither values nor utilises skills.

In its continuing search to increase skills, the government has handed employers a significant amount of power over VET, and even over parts of the education system. But the needs of industry are not the same as those of government, and it is unlikely that they will deliver the systemic spread of training that the government is looking for. As the work of Ryan *et al* (2006, 2007) on Apprenticeship training demonstrated, firms act in a rational, economic way in relation to the amount and type of training they offer. Firms push for finance for bespoke qualifications and firm-specific training that they would presumably deliver without government intervention. Nor is there evidence that employers are the best judges of longer-term skill needs for their own employees, let alone for the country as a whole (TUC 2007). Furthermore, employers are not accountable to the electorate, and do not have the expertise to make critical decisions about nation-wide VET (including parts of the education system) and the UK's longer-term economic future.

Keep E (2003) believes the government's non-interventionist view, its refusal to look at alternative models (particularly European), and its wish to avoid conflict with employers are the major problems. The UK system remains far removed from the European social partnership model in which trade unions, employers and educationalists are actively involved in developing strategy and the cost of training is shared. There is little evidence that employers will fund training in the absence of regulation (Payne and Keep 2011; Grugulis 2007), but will continue to poach or outsource. The coalition government is unlikely to move from voluntarism; meantime, it has slashed budgets hoping that employers and individuals will invest in skills at this difficult economic time. Unless the government grasps the nettle of compulsion, investment in skills will fall and England will fall further behind in the global skills race (Payne and Keep 2011). There is an urgent need for a coherent industrial policy that is effectively communicated to interested parties (CIPD 2010c, p.29). Finally, VET has been overly influenced by the economy and there is a need to consider social and environmental issues, to focus on the concept of fairness, particularly in the aftermath of recent riots in England (Payne and Keep 2011). It is still the case that the class ceiling ensures that the wealthy and middle classes get into the best schools and universities and into the best jobs, while the gap between them and those at the bottom of the labour market are increasingly marginalised – something that the VET system must address (Lloyd and Mayhew 2010).

EXPLORE FURTHER

AYNSLEY, S. and CROSSOUARD, B. (2010) 'Imagined futures: why are vocational learners choosing not to progress to HE?' *Journal of Education and Work*, Vol.23, No.2, 129–43.

COX, A. (2007) *Re-visiting the NVQ Debate: 'Bad' Qualifications, Expansive Learning Environments and Prospects for Upskilling Workers.* SKOPE Research Paper No.71. Oxford/Cardiff: SKOPE/ESRC. Available from: www.skope.ox.ac.uk

DBIS (2010) *Government Skills Strategy: Skills for Sustainable Growth*. London: Department for Business, Innovation and Skills.

GLOSTER, R., SUMPTION, F., HIGGINS, T., COX, A. and JONES, R. (2010) *Perspectives and Performance of Investors in People: A Literature Review.* Evidence Report 24. London, UK: Commission for Employment and Skills.

GOLD, J., STEWART, J. and ILES, P. (2010c) 'National HRD Policies and Practice', in J. Gold, R. Holden, P. Iles, J. Stewart and J. Beardwell *Human Resource Development: Theory and Practice.* Basignstoke: Palgrave Macmillan.

HOLMES, C. and MAYHEW, K. (2010) *UK Higher Education in Recession.* SKOPE Research Paper No.24. University of Oxford: SKOPE.

INVESTORS IN PEOPLE UK. www.iipuk.co.uk.

LLOYD, C. and MAYHEW, K. (2010) 'Skill: the solution to low wage work?', *Industrial Relations Journal*, Vol.41, No.5 429–45.

PAYNE, J. and KEEP, E. (2011) *One Step Forward, Two Steps Back? Skills Policy in England under the Coalition Government.* SKOPE Research Paper No.102. Cardiff University: SKOPE.

RYAN, P., GOSPEL, H. and LEWIS, P. (2007) 'Large employers and apprenticeship training in Britain', *British Journal of Industrial Relations*, Vol.45, No.1, 127–53.

CHAPTER 11

# Learning and Development and Knowledge Management

WITH LORRIE MARCHINGTON

## LEARNING OUTCOMES

By the end of this chapter, readers should be able to:

- utilise evidence-based arguments to identify L&D and knowledge management priorities
- design and deliver L&D initiatives to support organisational goals in different international contexts
- evaluate the effectiveness of L&D initiatives both for the organisation and for individuals.

In addition, readers should understand and be able to explain:

- the differences between education, training, learning, skills and competency
- the methods used to deliver L&D (e-learning, coaching, management development and continuing professional development) and their relevance to specific situations
- the role of L&D in relation to knowledge management.

## INTRODUCTION

The lack of learning and development (L&D) in most organisations is due both to the short-termism of employers and an imperfect understanding of how adults learn. Many learners are themselves wary about L&D opportunities, perhaps due to unsatisfactory experiences in formal educational settings. Equally, many line managers regard the provision of learning opportunities for manual workers or clerical staff as pampering the workforce, and an unwarranted distraction from their targets and duties. As a result, L&D may be used as a punishment or a reward, rather than a means to improve performance. Senior managers might view human resource development (HRD) as essential for professional and managerial staff, but as an unnecessary expense for the rest.

Traditionally, organisations used to employ specialists whose job was to train people how to work more efficiently; now the strategic value of L&D is critical, with emphasis on meeting current and future corporate objectives (Stewart *et al* 2010; Collin 2010). Additionally, the emphasis has moved from training to learning, both from the standpoint of the individual and from the organisation. This is what Sloman (2003, p.xiii) calls the new paradigm: whereby responsibility for learning falls on the individual with the organisation facilitating and supporting learners. This is not philanthropic, but to improve productivity, performance and knowledge development and as a strategy for retaining key staff. For individuals the benefits are increased personal competence, adaptability and the likelihood of continuous employability. The shift involves moving from delivering courses (training) to facilitating individual learning, often through supporting line managers. More organisations recognise the value of a learning culture whereby workers enhance their skills and knowledge, where creativity and initiative are fostered in the drive for continuous improvement. As we see in the section on talent management, where rare skills are involved, investment in human capital is particularly critical, and organisations increasingly recognise the value of development of global leaders and of L&D in bad times as well as good (Debrah and Rees 2011; Stewart and Rigg 2011).

As globalisation increases, so too does the demand for international L&D. There are two main areas; the first focuses on the development of global leaders – those who develop global strategies; integrate global activities; and manage geographically dispersed and globally diverse teams (Caligiuri 2006) and expatriates – those working on assignments overseas. These two groups of people need specific competences to deal with the challenges associated with global operations.

In this chapter we examine learning theories, the training cycle – which involves identification of learner needs, design, delivery, and evaluation – as well as the importance of business strategy and line managers for the promotion of learning. Current trends are analysed (coaching and e-learning) together with continuing professional development, management development, the international context for L&D, and knowledge management.

## DEFINITIONS AND TERMINOLOGY

Although terms such as training, learning and education are often used interchangeably, we need to be aware of the major distinctions between them, although such distinctions are blurred. For example, the educational process ought to involve learning, hopefully leads to development, and may contain training in specific techniques. As the use of competences spreads, the distinction between education and training is likely to become even more blurred.

*Education* develops intellectual capability, conceptual and social understanding and work performance through the learning process. *Training* is usually instructor-led, content-based, and skills-related. The differences are not always obvious, and because a two-day course in negotiating skills takes place away from the employer's premises, this does not qualify as education unless it comprises part of a wider product, such as a professional qualification or an MBA. Similarly, full-time students on a Masters' programme in HRM or an outdoor-based development programme undertake this as part of their education even though the course is run by trainers. Education and training typically refer – albeit implicitly – to the process by which an individual's attitudes, behaviour or performance is changed. *Learning* is self-directed, and focuses on the changes which take place in the individual's skill, attitude or knowledge. Examples of attitudes mediated through the learning process might include confidence-building, recognising and dealing with prejudices, or adopting socially responsible mores. Formalised learning has purpose, typically measured by outcomes, as is evident from the standards for the CIPD Professional Development Scheme. *Development* is an umbrella term and covers both training and learning. It may cover a long period of enhancing skills, and knowledge through a wide range of techniques – whether training, coaching, education, or informal interventions. For example, 'management development' includes everything to do with enhancing the performance of managers. *Skills* are aspects of behaviour which are developed through practice, and which individuals need to perform at an acceptable level in order to do the job satisfactorily. They include motor skills, manual dexterity, social and interpersonal skills, technical skills, and analytical skills. They are frequently seen as a hierarchy, in which the lower levels are prerequisites for the higher levels; for example, Bloom's taxonomy (reproduced in Gibb 2008, pp.51–2) views learning as a series of building blocks:

1 *knowledge* – simple knowledge of facts, terms, theories, etc
2 *comprehension* – understanding the meaning of this knowledge
3 *application* – ability to apply this knowledge and comprehension in new situations
4 *analysis* – breaking down material into constituent parts and seeing relationships between them
5 *synthesis* – reassembling the parts into a new and meaningful relationship
6 *evaluation* – the ability to judge the value of the material.

Understanding and knowledge, and the ability to explain things to other people, are therefore incorporated within the term 'skill'. For most people, however, skill typically connects with lower levels, and is seen in the application of motor skills rather than the powers of analysis, synthesis and evaluation.

*Tacit skills* are harder to define. These refer to the ability to perform a task without necessarily being aware of how it is done. For example, female home-care staff often undervalue their acquired skills and knowledge, regarding them as instinctive and natural. Since this know-how is typically acquired through experience, rather than formal instruction, it can be hard to specify and quantify. Yet tacit skills can explain high performance in business and, because they are unique to the people of the particular organisation, they give competitive advantage (CIPD 2010d).

## REFLECTIVE ACTIVITY

Do you think it is possible for people to learn without being aware they are learning? Do they need to consolidate this learning or relate it to abstract principles for learning to be effective?

*Competency* is a newer term than 'skill' and has grown in importance since the publication of *The Competent Manager* by Boyatsis in 1982, but there remains much confusion about the terminology. *Competence and competences* relate to the ability to perform up to a minimal standard in employment (Griggs *et al* 2010, p.111). *Competency and competencies* relate to behaviours needed to perform to high levels of performance. A competency framework describes the behaviours that an employee must have, or acquire, to achieve high levels of performance. These frameworks are an effective means to benchmark and review performance and potential and are therefore useful when looking to future L&D needs. A majority of organisations now use competency frameworks and these cover over three-quarters of the workforce. Because competencies allow workers to clearly see what superior and inferior performance looks like, they link new paradigm where learners take responsibility for their own development. In the majority of cases, frameworks are available electronically (Sloman 2007b, p.20).

## THE PROCESS OF LEARNING

The way that people learn is important for HR professionals, given its centrality to most aspects of organisational life. Learning process theories are based in psychology and explain how learning takes place. Here we briefly overview some of the main ideas.

Theories fall into two categories, behaviourist and cognitive. The *behaviourist* theories are based on conditioning and reinforcing desired behaviours. The first approach relates to the work of B.F. Skinner and incorporates signal and stimulus–response learning. Signal learning is exemplified by the Pavlovian dog experiment – for example, when a pet runs into the kitchen when it hears its dish being filled (Gagne 1977, p.77). This might translate to the smile on a salesperson's face as a customer walks through the door. Conditioning can be either classical (whereby the stimulus automatically leads to a response) or operant, in which case a desired response is rewarded and reinforced after it has been delivered. In the latter case, behaviour is often learned by trial and error. In organisations, operant conditioning can be seen in the recognition given to high-quality performance – this acts as a powerful reinforcement. These theories formed the basis for training for a long time; the trainer/teacher was in control of the process. Cybernetics forms part of conditioning theory; where learning is an information-processing system in which a signal containing information is passed along a communication channel. All messages are subject to external factors that interfere with the transmission process. There are limits to the amount of information that can be transmitted along a channel and feedback is important to these models (Gibb 2008, p.125; Harrison 2009, p.98).

*Cognitive* theories are based on studies of the brain as a machine and relate to perception, memory, thinking and learning (Harrison 2009, p.97). They are based on stimulus–stimulus connections, with the idea of insight being central. The pleasure of gaining an insight acts as a powerful reinforcement of learning and stimulus to memory. Good examples of this are case studies, which help link theories and practical applications, or group problem-solving. Whereas stimulus–response might be suitable for practical skills, cognitive learning is more appropriate for mental skills. These types of theory rely on learners connecting together different concepts or actions to form a chain of stimuli.

Both behaviourist and cognitive theories are inadequate on their own to account for learning and need to be mediated by social theories in recognition that teaching does not necessarily lead to learning and that there are a great many external factors at play, many based on the social aspects of learning. Gibb (2008, pp.122–6) here refers to 'wisdom literature' that is written largely by practitioners on how best to deliver L&D interventions. Social theories recognise that learners are not empty tin cans that need filling with knowledge/skills delivered by a trainer/teacher but 'communities of practice' whereby learning is transferred from networks of people who share knowledge and skills and support learning through experience. Social and interpersonal skills can be learned through this process, and are often acquired without the individual being aware that learning has actually taken place. One of the major problems with social learning, which does not incorporate feedback or evaluation, is that people may learn inefficient ways of working or fail to decipher some of the tacit skills used by experienced workers. There are also dangers that individuals learn inappropriate behaviour society by imitation – for example, bullying or aggressive behaviour, fiddles and scams, racism and sexism.

## REFLECTIVE ACTIVITY

Keep a diary for a week noting all the times when you learned something new. Categorise these learning experiences according to the different theories outlined above. Make sure that you include all learning events, not just those taking place at work or in a formal situation.

Much mainstream psychology literature focuses on 'traditional' learning – the importance of building blocks, hierarchies of skills, and reinforcing theory with examples. This is appropriate to formal educational situations and child development, but is less so for adults who come to the situation with very different motivations, experiences, and perspectives. Carl Rogers (1969, p.5) is the major proponent of experiential learning, which has the following components: personal involvement, self-initiation, pervasiveness and evaluation by the learner. The essence of experiential learning resides in its meaning to the learner. This makes it exciting for employees who left school early and feel threatened by the classroom situation. Because it puts the responsibility for learning on the individual employee it can require skilful management; as Mumford (1988, pp.171–2) warns, experiential learning can be 'a very inefficient, hit-or-miss operation . . . guidance helps the process to be both quicker and easier'. Experiential learning has been developed by Kolb and Honey and Mumford and is critical for continuing professional development. Kolb *et al* (1995, p.49) view the learning process as both active and passive, concrete and abstract. This model is displayed in Figure 7.

**Figure 7 The learning process**

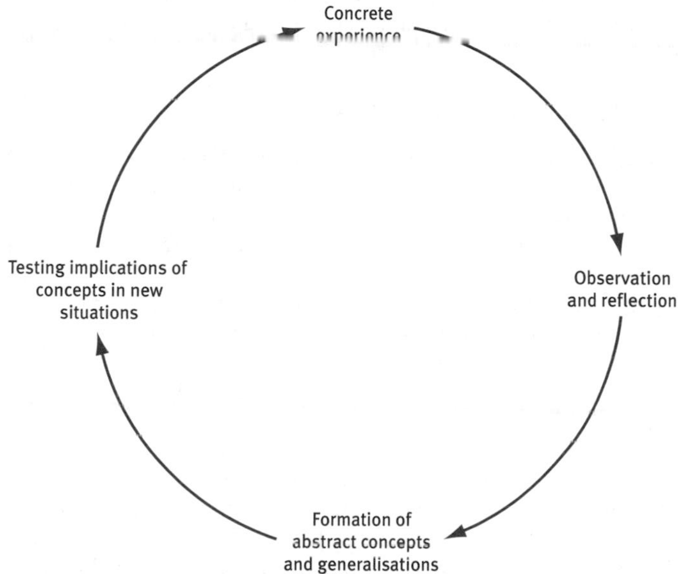


Source: Kolb *et al* (1995).

Kolb argues that effective learners rely on four different learning modes, and each individual has an orientation towards one or more of these: concrete experience, reflective observation, abstract conceptualisation and active experimentation. Honey and Mumford's learning styles classification (Mumford and Gold 2004, pp.97–8) is similar:

- *Activists* – learn best by active involvement in concrete tasks, and from relatively short tasks such as business games and competitive teamwork exercises.
- *Reflectors* – learn best by reviewing and reflecting upon what has happened in certain situations, where they are able to stand back, listen and observe.
- *Theorists* – learn best when new information can be located within the context of concepts and theories, and who are able to absorb new ideas when they are distanced from real-life situations.
- *Pragmatists* – learn best when they see a link between new information and real-life problems and issues, and from being exposed to techniques that can be applied immediately.

This has major implications for the L&D process, and for the choice of methods, although its application should be flexible given that the four categories represent 'ideal types'. People do not conform to a single learning style, and they may be strong on two apparently dissimilar axes. The precise questions asked of individuals are also capable of differing interpretations, depending upon the context. For example, an individual may be a reflector in response to certain questions or situations, and a pragmatist in others. Moreover, the combination of people in a working group may lead individuals to adopt different styles than those in a formal learning situation. For example, a group of theorists may be cajoled into action, or a set of activists encouraged to reflect. Also people's preferred learning styles may alter over time rather than remaining static. For the L&D practitioner, it is appropriate to adopt a number of formats to accommodate all learners' preferences.

## THE TRAINING CYCLE

The basis for most L&D is the training cycle which comprises three main steps: (1) identifying learning needs; (2) design and delivery; and (3) evaluating outcomes (Griggs *et al* 2010, p.107).

### (1) IDENTIFYING LEARNING NEEDS

The first stage is identification of needs (skills, knowledge and behaviours/attitudes) and is often reviewed in conjunction with learning needs analysis (LNA) which determines how needs might be met. An L&D need exists when there is a gap between the requirements of the job and the current capabilities of the incumbent; this links with performance management.

We have to be certain, however, that training represents the best or only solution as it is not a panacea for all organisational ills. The problem may reside elsewhere, and there are dangers that employers prescribe training as a universal solution ('training is the answer irrespective of the question') without considering alternatives such as job redesign, better systems of communication and involvement, or adjustments to organisational cultures and structures. It may make sense to do nothing as there are dangers in providing too much training as in providing too little. Excessive levels of training cost valuable resources, and may result in job dissatisfaction if employees are unable to practise newfound skills in their jobs, or become frustrated by spending time on unnecessary training and then have to catch up on work left undone. Furthermore, the opportunity cost of meeting short-term needs through training might not satisfy longer-term needs, thereby causing major problems for organisations (Gibb 2008, p.34). Sadly, the focus is often on short-term needs, possibly because they are much simpler to define.

Learning needs can be identified at three different levels – organisational, job/occupational and personal. Identifying learning needs is the most important step in the effectiveness of training, and should be top-down and bottom-up. Where a learning need is identified, responses could be at the organisational, job, or individual level or at all three levels simultaneously.

It makes sense to start with a review of organisational learning needs in order to establish how L&D contributes to broader strategic goals. This is central to the IiP standard and involves consideration of which organisational goals are facilitated through L&D. The main method is a 'global' review in which the organisation's short- and longer term goals are examined to determine appropriate skills and knowledge needed to meet corporate objectives, then each employee is assessed against the skills and knowledge criteria. This is very time-consuming, and unsuited to organisations working with rapid change, or those that outsource. In effect this approach presumes that an organisation is the sum of its individuals and their skills, and this is a doubtful assumption. The second technique is 'competence and performance management approaches'. Job descriptions are used to draw up competences against which performance is measured. The line manager reviews performance using the competence framework and is expected to access appropriate training. The third technique is 'critical incident or priority problem analysis': the main problem areas which require a L&D response are identified. This fits with the concept of total quality management (TQM), but L&D might be only one component when addressing problem areas.

Each job is placed under the microscope in order to identify its component parts, and specify what has to be learned in terms of knowledge, skills, or attitude for effective delivery. There are four common job training analyses:

1 Comprehensive – detailed analysis of every job. This is time-consuming and generally only used for simple repetitive tasks. The process usually results in a job description, personnel specification, and a job training specification showing the skills, knowledge and attitudes needed, and the required standards of performance (Griggs *et al* 2010, p.119).

2 Key task analysis – detailed analysis of the most important tasks within any job. As above, the result is a job description, and a job training specification, but this only relates to key tasks within the job. This is useful where a job has changed and so gives rise to a training need.

3 Problem-centred analysis – focus on problems.

4 Competency – use of competency framework to analyse training need.

Person-level analysis shares characteristics with the methods discussed above. This frequently involves the use of interviews and questionnaires, observation and work sampling, testing the knowledge of job-holders on specific issues, and performance appraisal and assessment centres. If employees are encouraged to acknowledge that areas of their work are not being performed at full capacity, or with inadequate knowledge or skills, then appraisal interviews help to identify L&D needs. However, where appraisal is linked to rewards, they are unlikely to unearth L&D needs (see Chapter 9 for more on appraisals).

It is generally assumed that all three levels can be integrated, although conflict is inevitable, particularly where learning is self-managed. All levels are important, and each feeds into the other so that 'bottom-up needs assessment' from performance review can mesh with top-down analysis of future organisational needs. However, the idea of pulling together the three levels assumes perfect information and unlimited resources, neither of which is generally available, making errors in analysis almost inevitable. The result may be meeting perceived needs or wants rather than actual needs and limited resources mean that it is impossible to meet all current and future needs, even if future needs could be accurately forecast (Gibb 2008, p.33).

There are advantages in using structured and sequential models for analysing the training cycle. However, it over-simplifies the extreme complexity which comes into play when dealing with individuals and organisations and confines the HRD role to 'passive provider' rather than 'change agent' (Smith and Sadler-Smith 2006, pp.204–5). Certainly, it represents an 'ideal' state of affairs rather than conveying an accurate and realistic picture of organisational practice. The idea that L&D follows this logical and sequential cycle is open to question, and – as with other aspects of HRD – there is likely to be more ad hoc and reactive management of L&D than planned and proactive. A more serious concern is that learning and development often lapses into a 'closed' cycle, in which there are few, if any, links with other aspects of HR, let alone broader business plans and objectives. This can result in efficient rather than effective training. In other words, the effectiveness is assessed against the training needs identified by the trainers themselves, and not measured in relation to their contribution to business goals.

The narrow focus and inability to predict and meet future need can be remedied by developing a culture of learning and giving all employees a training allowance to use at their discretion – with support from line and senior management. However, this does not ensure linkage to strategic plans (Griggs *et al* 2010, pp.124–5).

## REFLECTIVE ACTIVITY

For an organisation with which you are familiar, design a training cycle.

## (2) DESIGNING AND DELIVERING TRAINING AND LEARNING

The learning needs analysis enables consultation and prioritisation to take place; the next stage is the development of a learning plan. The traditional approach is to determine clear **aims** (why the learning event is taking place); **objectives** (specifying attitudinal, behavioural or performance outcomes); and **targets** (for example, number of trainees). Aims are expressions of general intent. Objectives are more precise and give measurable outcomes; the clearer the objectives, the better the chance of success, as they aid students' understanding and facilitate evaluation. Examples of an aim might be to improve customer service, and one objective may be to decrease customer complaints by 10% (Gibb 2008, p.49). Objectives should be SMART (specific, measurable, achievable, realistic, and bound within a time frame). L&D resources are wasted where learning needs are not adequately identified and the design and delivery is weak (Glaister *et al* 2010, p.133).

Major considerations when planning design and delivery of L&D are: how people learn, characteristics of learners, barriers to learning transfer, and choice of appropriate methods of delivery, cost, and strategic goals and culture of the organisation. Evaluation and planning should link from the outset, so that design and delivery takes account of past evaluation, and links with organisational strategic aims. Anderson's partnership model of learning clearly demonstrates this (see Figure 8 below). Choice of method is determined by a range of factors including costs, benefits, likelihood of learning transfer to the work situation, profile of the learner group, applicability of method.

When devising plans it is the characteristics of the learners that are critically important. Their 'baggage' may include prior experiences, ability, knowledge, skills, attitudes, confidence, motivations, expectations and personality. The person who has been successful in prior educational experiences and who has asked for training, will have a different attitude to someone who is temperamentally difficult, has not previously experienced a positive learning event, and who has been told to attend. Additionally, culture and social class have huge bearing on attitudes to learning; there may be variations in the extent to which trainees have been briefed beforehand about the learning event or in the amount of preparation undertaken before the workshop gets under way. It is always useful for the HRD expert if they can know something about the profile of the learners, the nature of the organisational culture, and the work environment – for example, whether learners will be supported to use their new knowledge back in their job. Some of the most salient considerations are:

- content, carefully structured and sequenced
- learners receive feedback
- reward and reinforcement
- learner is actively involved
- check for understanding

- meaningful in terms of job responsibilities
- learning transfer back to the job and opportunity to use

There are a multitude of methods that can be used to develop staff, both on- and off-the-job, ranging from the relatively unstructured and informal – such as 'sitting next to Nellie' – through to the carefully structured – such as the lecture. Most texts provide lists of methods, their nature and meaning, their advantages and shortcomings. While useful at one level, lists are lacking in two respects. First, they are not organised into any coherent conceptual framework that differentiates between techniques according to learning principles or the characteristics of the learning situation. This makes it difficult for readers to 'locate' different methods within a structure. Secondly, while lists describe the key features of different methods, there is little attempt to identify the conditions under which particular techniques may be appropriate.

Of course, no one method is inherently superior to any other, but different methods are suitable for different sets of circumstances. Choosing which method to use, and why, is more important than being able to note the advantages and disadvantages of each method in the abstract. While the lecture may be inappropriate for most training situations, it may be the best way for a marketing director to open the annual sales conference; e-learning can be effective for reinforcing basic language skills but it offers rather less towards the development of team-working and group problem-solving.

Rather than produce yet another list, here we review training methods in four distinct categories, differentiated according to the main approach, and whether the training is individual or group-based. Snape *et al* (1994, p.73) make the distinction between andragogical and pedagogical approaches to learning and development. The former, more accurately titled 'auto-didactic', is self-directed and participative, with the trainer in a facilitative or supportive role. The latter, by contrast, is largely trainer-driven and allows little room for student input into the learning situation. The second distinction is between individual and group-based training. This categorisation is illustrated in Figure 8, with an example of each type of training for illustrative purposes.

**Figure 8 Categories of training and learning methods**

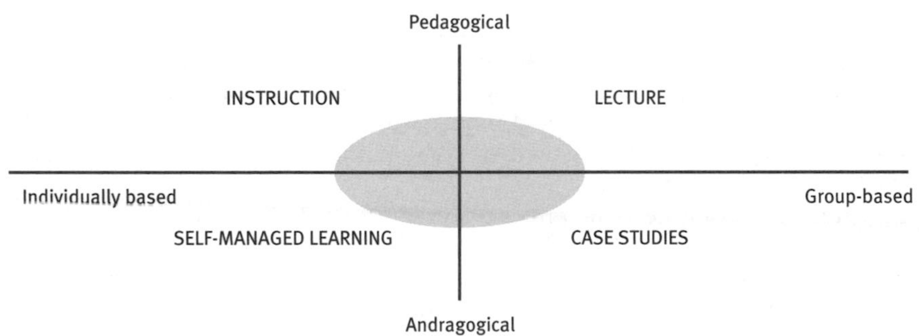


The top left-hand quadrant in Figure 8 includes methods that are principally *pedagogically oriented and individually based*, such as one-to-one instructional techniques and simulations. These are particularly useful for the acquisition of standard programmable skills, for the transfer of routine information and ways of working, but which also require practice and application in real-life situations. At one extreme might be simulators for trainee pilots; at the other extreme might be assembly operation or standardised call-centre scripts. The major point is that there is little room for discretion or creativity; only when employees become more experienced might there be room for autonomy and use of initiative. The basic principles of these kinds of L&D are of the 'tell–show–do–review' variety, in which skills, knowledge and operating routines are transferred progressively to trainees until they have mastered the task. There is no room for vagueness or confusion in the instruction but this may lead to motivational problems if the employees concerned feel that they already have the required skills or they do not share senior management's commitment to them.

The top right-hand quadrant includes methods that are *pedagogically and group-based*, such as lectures, presentations and videos, and these are particularly appropriate in situations when a large number of people need to be given information at the same time, and/or it is cost-effective to deliver training in this way. Most learners are used to lectures, and know the limits to the amount that can be retained during a session. Estimates vary, but typically less than a quarter is remembered, and the maximum concentration span is usually less than 20 minutes. Despite this, it is cost-effective, although whether it represents a cost-effective way of learning depends on the way it is delivered. Most of us will have listened to an individual speak for an hour or more, and been enthralled. Some management gurus can keep audiences transfixed for a couple of hours using few, if any, visual aids. But for most lecturers it is essential to use PowerPoint, and litter the talk with examples and anecdotes and even discussion in small groups, to ensure that some retention takes place. Enthusiasm and knowledge of the subject matter are essential, as is an awareness of learner needs, an ability to present information in a clear and concise manner, with varying tone and cadence to maintain attention.

One of the major problems with lectures and presentations is that they are often used inappropriately, transmitting information that can more easily be distributed electronically or as written documents or videos. These also can provide a useful interlude in the training programme to facilitate learning. But there are dangers with these techniques. They have to be chosen carefully to ensure that they fit the issue in hand, are realistic and relevant, not dated, and are contextualised in the programme with specific learning outcomes attached to them.

The bottom right-hand quadrant is the *andragogical/group-based category*, which includes case studies, projects, group role-playing exercises and business games. These are essentially team-oriented and allow the group to propose their own solutions with minimum trainer intervention. The trainer supports the team, helps it to arrive at conclusions, and facilitates learning through a sharing of ideas. In effect, learning takes place through a process of induction, in which examples and incidents are generalised to arrive at a better understanding of the principles and processes that underpin management issues. These methods aid the development of core competencies that are central to a manager's job such as: decision-making, planning and time management, drive and persistence, ability to work under pressure, oral and written communication, flexibility and adaptability, self-confidence and persuasiveness.

Case studies provide 'real-life' problem-solving, for working out solutions in teams and for presenting recommendations. Like other training techniques, they need to be well managed, have clear learning outcomes, and be relevant to the needs and abilities of the learners. They need to be an appropriate length and degree of difficulty for the group, as well as containing sufficient information and flexibility to allow for competing solutions between different teams. Problems with group-based training include the possibility of conflict, or one or more individuals dominating discussion and excluding others. Getting the right amount of information is also important – there may be too much to analyse in the time, or too little to make a recommendation.

The final set of methods is the *self-directed* category. This group of techniques includes e-learning and use of language laboratories. These are self-managed and can be taken at a pace, time and possibly location to suit the individual. Self-management of learning is especially appropriate for acquiring impersonal techniques (such as accounting or computing), basic language skills, and for gathering information for reports. Although these techniques have been used for interpersonal skills training, it is unlikely that their use will become extensive given the importance of face-to-face contact for improving such skills. In this sort of situation, role-playing offers a much better solution to learning how to cope, say with an aggressive senior manager or in counselling a poor performer. *Self-managed learning* fits with Sloman's 'new paradigm' and changes the HRD role away from planning and delivering training, to facilitating. The advantage is that learners can choose the delivery method that suits their learning styles and personal circumstances. Not all provision is work-related, as with Ford's Employee Development and Assistance Programmes (EDAPs). The resources invested in learning for personal goals (as opposed to departmental/organisational) are tied up with the psychological contract and interest in retaining and motivating key employees. Despite the fact that EDAPs fit with the paradigm of placing responsibility with learners, their popularity is declining (Gibb 2008, pp.151–2).

## REFLECTIVE ACTIVITY

In a small group, brainstorm those factors that have facilitated and hindered learning for you. Compile the results and compare these with those presented by Mumford and Gold (2004, p.109).

Traditional off-the-job learning methods remain the most common, despite the fact that learner-centred techniques allegedly represent the future. This may because they are familiar, having been used over decades and are simple, fast, cheap, and easily evaluated – the danger is that this may be evidence of a lack of initiative on the part of HRD. A list of common delivery methods, together with advantages and disadvantages, appears in Glaister *et al* (2010, pp.144–8).

### (3) EVALUATING THE OUTCOMES OF LEARNING AND DEVELOPMENT

Whatever delivery method is used, evaluation is critical to establish strategic alignment and value – value for the organisation, for the team/department, for the learner, and its durability over time. Despite its importance, evaluation is frequently neither comprehensive nor systematic. Typical excuses are that it is difficult to carry out effectively and efficiently, it is resource-heavy, and managers at all levels are often not interested in evaluative data. The CIPD 2011 Survey showed that one in six respondents did not evaluate learning; and just under half did not assess whether there would be benefit from L&D before instigating L&D; nor was there any discussion with line managers and coaches about the organisation's expectation of L&D interventions; subsequently, half of respondents did not discuss an individual's learning at appraisal. Typically, evaluation consists of informal feedback rather than tests or formal evaluations conducted some time after the L&D has been completed. In other words, as with many other aspects of HRM, the extent of formal and systematic evaluation is limited, despite its known worth.

Once it is established *why* evaluation is being undertaken, it should then be possible to determine *what* should be evaluated, and *when* and *how*. Most ideas stem from the work of Kirkpatrick (1967), who differentiated between four levels of evaluation: reaction, immediate, intermediate, and ultimate; a fifth has been added: return on investment. The most important level of evaluation differs according to the circumstances and stakeholders' needs. For example, while trainers will be interested in how well they performed, the finance director will focus on cost-effectiveness and return on investment, while the departmental manager will want to assess impact on job performance.

**Reaction level – level 1**

This is the most usual form of evaluation and is used by 93% of organisations (CIPD 2011f). This 'smile sheet' is commonly used at the course end and assesses the performance of trainers in both absolute and relative terms from the point of view of the learners. These views are useful, provided trainers see them as valuable and are prepared and able to act upon them. There are many concerns about 'smile sheets', including worries that students react to the quality of the performance, the lecturer's ability to maintain surface-level interest or tell jokes to the class, rather than actual learning. Nor do smile sheets evaluate L&D in its wider context, as part of a broader educational programme, or its relevance to future performance in work. Finally, research suggests that there is a very poor relationship between positive reaction-level assessments, learning, changes in job performance, and the transfer of learning into the workplace (Devins and Smith 2010).

**Immediate level – level 2 – learning**

This attempts to measure outcomes in terms of knowledge, skills and attitudes. Techniques include tests, examinations, projects, structured exercises and case studies, as well as discussion.

**Intermediate level – level 3 – transfer to performance**

This refers to the impact on job performance and how effectively learning has been transferred back into the workplace. Intermediate-level evaluation takes many forms, including interviews, self-report questionnaires, diaries, observation and feedback from line managers – the latter is seen as one of the more effective methods (Wolff 2007d). Evaluation at this level is much less common than at the first two levels, because it is harder to undertake and to isolate the impact of training from the effect of other variables. According to the CIPD 2011 L&D survey, stories and testimonials were used by 56% of organisations.

**Ultimate-level evaluation – level 4 – strategic impact on organisation**

This attempts to assess the impact on departmental or organisational performance, and on the individual's total job. The distinction between intermediate- and ultimate-level evaluation is somewhat blurred, but the former usually refers to performance in a particular task for which L&D has been provided, whereas the latter evaluates impact on overall organisational results. The best indicators for ultimate-level evaluation vary depending upon the key performance indicators which should be measured before and after training (XpertHR 2007; Wolff 2007b). Examples might include:

- number of customer complaints; customer retention
- level of sales, turnover or productivity
- number of accidents or lost employment tribunal cases
- level of unauthorised absenteeism or labour turnover
- increased morale in the workplace.

As the name implies, ultimate-level evaluation is the most difficult to measure. In some situations there may be no clear and simple measures, or data may not be collected in a form that allows evaluation to take place. There are factors other than training that could affect outcomes, especially at higher levels in the organisation when external influences can have a significant impact – for example, the influence of unemployment on labour turnover. In addition, only a small proportion of staff within a department or establishment might have been trained, and although their performance may have improved, this may have relatively little overall effect. As we saw in the previous chapter, learning organisations attempt to satisfy organisational and personal demands at the same time, and organisations claiming to practise high commitment HRM look for links between L&D and other areas of people management, as well as assessing its impact on performance. The CIPD found that 42% of organisations assess the impact of business key performance indicators (CIPD 2011f).

**An additional level – return on investment – level 5**

A fifth level of evaluation has been added to the original four – return on investment (ROI). Again this is not easy to carry out, particularly where 'soft' skills are involved. As a result, under half of organisations use ROI (CIPD 2011f). Being aware of *costs and benefits* is important although it is often not carried out. It is easy to reel off lists of general benefits from L&D, but less easy to quantify them financially. It is hard to demonstrate unequivocally that learning has a measurable impact on organisational performance, although people often make this claim. Yet organisational economic circumstances impact on learning and it is critical that L&D professionals can fight their corner by reference to the bottom line. Political skills help to identify measures relevant to business objectives, but it might prove difficult to sell general solutions on more than one occasion, or to convince senior managers who want hard estimates of costs and benefits.

Costs are easier to calculate than benefits, although much depends on what is included. Typically, fixed costs include accommodation or training equipment; salaries and on-costs; the cost of developing training materials and evaluation tools. Finally, there are costs which vary according to the amount of training undertaken, and include the costs of travel, of delegates attending the event, either as a pro rata salary or the costs of replacements.

Calculating the opportunity costs of not training is more complex. These costs may include wasted materials or the time spent in dealing with problems caused by untrained staff. In other words, to consider the costs of training fully we need to be aware of the costs of *not* training, and of relying on informal, ad hoc and potentially inefficient methods for improving performance. Benchmarking the amount spent by similar organisations can be useful. Employers in Britain spend relatively little on training compared with many foreign competitors, but comparisons should be made with similar types of organisation in the same sector or area of the country. If figures are low, this information may prove help HR professionals to justify training expenditure.

It is not usually viable to evaluate at all five levels, and judicious choice of the appropriate level is necessary, as can be seen from the BBC case study in the box below.

HRM AT WORK IN FOCUS

## BBC develops new ways to evaluate learning and development

BBC L&D was not linked to the strategic aims of the organisation because it was locally run and the main form of evaluation was 'smile sheets'.

When reviewing evaluation, the BBC first looked at the value that it should add to the business, the activities that should be assessed, and who should receive the results of evaluation. It agreed that:

1 L&D providers need feedback for continuous improvement.
2 Information must be provided on how far development activities impact on organisational performance.
3 ROI calculations should be made where possible.
4 The organisation needs insights into how it uses and supports learning.

An evaluation framework was developed loosely based on

Kirkpatrick's model and including ROI and 'inputs' (what was delivered, when, to whom, cost) and 'process' (key performance indicators and evaluation of progress against forecast). Evaluation was pitched at differing levels. All training programmes used **'reaction level'** questionnaires, but only more strategically important training was evaluated at higher levels. Each training activity was categorised into three groups: 1. 'strategic' – L&D that influenced the way the BBC works; 2. 'maintenance' – L&D that helped maintain current performance; and 3. 'informal' – L&D such as mentoring and work shadowing. Informal interventions were not covered by evaluation.

**Reaction level** evaluation made use of electronic questionnaires sent out between 7–14 days after the event. Questions related to quality of content, learning as a result, quality of trainers and facilitation, and whether the learners were adequately prepared beforehand. The emphasis was on ensuring that learners took responsibility and that line managers were fully involved. The electronic package saved time as it generated analytical reports.

**Transfer level of learning** is again assessed electronically, and 20–30% of L&D is covered at this level. It covers training which alters the way that people work and enhances the organisational strategic aims. Typically, an online questionnaire is sent out after three months and is often used in conjunction with a pre-course questionnaire.

The BBC recognises that **line managers** are instrumental to the transfer of learning and a random sample is asked for feedback; in time this would be included in performance review.

At the **strategic level**, approximately 20% is evaluated with design based on learning aims. For example, one of the L&D programmes aimed to increase collaboration across programme teams in order to pump prime collaborative projects. Evaluation was measured by the number of delegates who fostered working relationships across teams, as well as the number of collaborative projects and their success.

Approximately 5% of training is measured in terms of **ROI** using methods promoted by the Return on Investment Institute (www.roiinstitute.net).

An overview of evaluation reports goes to the executive board and more comprehensive reports go to the learning board, which decides on future L&D initiatives and funding levels.

The changes made to evaluation led to a **culture change** within the BBC, effectively closing the loop between L&D planning and strategic business goals.

Source: Adapted from Wolff (2006b).

As seen in the BBC case study, strategic evaluation of L&D should not solely be left to HRD professionals. The CIPD Partnership Model of Learning emphasises this, as well as the interconnections and responsibilities of the line manager, learner, senior management and HRD professional (see Figure 9). Using this model, all stakeholders are involved and the focus is on ensuring that learning and organisational strategies are aligned. As stated earlier, CIPD see the purpose of evaluation as establishing strategic alignment and reinforcing learning with concentration on four main areas of evaluations (Anderson 2007):

a Efficiency of the learning function (are L&D activities effective in developing the productivity of the workforce and supporting critical success factors – are they aligned with the organisations strategic aims).

b Key performance indicators and benchmark measures (internal and external benchmarking of levels of spends on L&D).

c Return on investment.

d Return on expectations.

**Figure 9 The CIPD's Partnership of Learning Model**

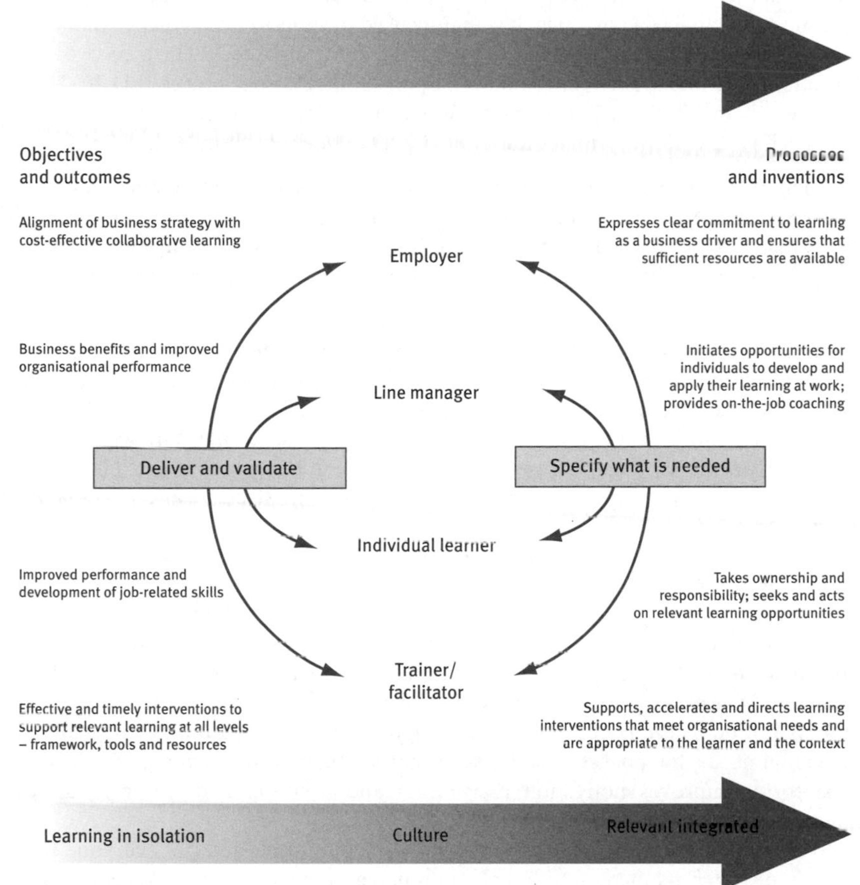


Source: Anderson (2007).

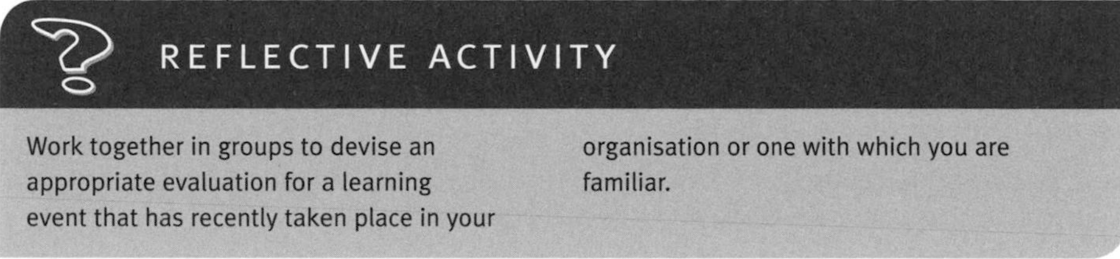

## REFLECTIVE ACTIVITY

Work together in groups to devise an appropriate evaluation for a learning event that has recently taken place in your organisation or one with which you are familiar.

## KEY TRENDS IN LEARNING AND DEVELOPMENT

Time pressure remains a major barrier to learning and in response there has been increased interest in flexible, just-in-time learning methods, including coaching, e-learning and bite-sized provision (modular learning offered in shorter chunks of time). We now turn to examine two types of learning that have experienced a doubling of provision – coaching and mentoring and e-learning – as well as considering the role of continuing professional development (CPD).

### COACHING AND MENTORING

According to the CIPD 2011 Survey, eight out of 10 organisations use coaching, probably as it is the most effective L&D practice. It is mainly used to support performance management (43%), preparing for leadership roles (33%), and supporting L&D (21%). In two-fifths of organisations line managers have the main responsibility for coaching (CIPD 2011f).

There exists much confusion over definitions and a great deal of overlap when people talk of coaching, mentoring, and counselling. CIPD defines coaching as (2010h):

> Developing a person's skills and knowledge so that their job performance improves, hopefully leading to the achievement of organisational objectives. It targets high performance and improvement at work although it may also have an impact on an individual's private life. It usually lasts for short period and focuses on specific skills and goals.

The emphasis is on specific skills with measurable outcomes in order to differentiate between colleagues chatting and 'sitting next to Nellie'. Clutterbuck and Megginson (2005, p.19) define a coaching culture as being both a method for L&D, as well as a management style: 'where a commitment to grow the organisation is embedded in a parallel commitment to grow the people in the organisation'. Gibb (2008, p.172) emphasises fit with talent management, and leadership as it promotes problem solving, strategic and personal insight in complex environments.

In comparison, *mentoring* involves the more holistic, longer term 'development' of an individual or group, as for example in career development. Typically, it is about someone more experienced being counsellor and friend to support an individual – perhaps a new recruit or minority member (eg women in management). Ideally the mentor and mentee are matched in terms of temperament and profile. The relationship works best where the arrangement is voluntary – for this reason, it may not always work with line manager as mentor as power relations come into play. Support may include meeting organisational and personal needs, but goal setting is less formalised than with coaching. Evidence shows that mentoring improves motivation, recruitment and retention, and promotes knowledge management (Stewart and Rigg 2011, p.206).

Both *coaching* and *mentoring* draw on soft counselling skills and not everyone is suited to the role of coach or mentor, although training can ameliorate this. For either to work the coachee/mentee will be psychologically well and the aim is to improve performance; this differentiates from professional counselling which is therapeutic in nature. Problems in work are often caused by those with some psychological problems (the grey zone between good and poor mental health) and/or lack of self-evaluation skills, but neither coaching nor mentoring will work with such people (Stewart and Rigg 2011).

*Coaching practice* is about ways in which the individual is assisted with personal growth – for example to set and implement goals (for more on this see Stewart and Rigg 2011, pp.201–2). The attributes of coaching:

- It is based on counselling skills and is non-directive, non-judgmental, uses active listening, summative feedback, and it is challenging.

- It improves performance through development of self-awareness and analytical skills.
- It aids the identification of personal L&D needs.
- It is an effective learning tool and involves reciprocal learning.
- It offers feedback on strengths and weaknesses and tackles underperformance.
- There are individual and organisational goals.
- It impacts on the bottom line and improves productivity.

(Clutterbuck and Megginson 2005; Harrison 2009, p.171; CIPD 2010h.)

For coaching to work effectively, supervision of coaches, adequate resources (especially time), piloting of new initiatives, clear expectations established of all involved (organisation, line manager, coachee) and robust evaluation are all essential. Evaluation is a thorny issue, as only one-third evaluates it (CIPD 2011f). Line managers frequently – in two-fifths of organisations (CIPD 2011f) – carry the main responsibility for coaching yet there are many barriers to their effectiveness. They include lack of time, the organisational culture, equity issues, lack of skills and confidence – particularly when dealing with difficult people (CIPD 2009d). There is also the issue of ownership of feedback: who can access it and will it be used for development, reward, or discipline?

HRM AT WORK IN FOCUS

### Mentoring in professional service firms

DeLong *et al* (2008) make an effective case for mentoring in the highly competitive field of professional service firms (PSFs). In the past, mentoring was common practice and all junior partners were mentored by senior partners. As PSFs have become larger and more bureaucratic, this system has withered and this has led to high rates of attrition. Given that PSFs' competitive advantage relies on their employees, it is essential that firms retain their talent and where partners re-engage with junior staff and provide them with feedback; this can be a powerful way to ensure retention.

PSFs often concentrate energy and resources on 'A' players, generating discord among those lower down the pecking order. 'B' players typically make up 70% of the staff and are the solid citizens of any organisation. They should be included in mentoring programmes (for more on this see the section on Talent Management) as they are typically more loyal to the organisation (downplaying personal goals), stay longer, and are therefore critical to the build-up of institutional knowledge. Over time, the yield from investment in A players may not produce as many gains as investment in B players, particularly where the B players are given opportunities to interact with high fliers through team-working. Mentoring plays a significant role in motivating, recruiting, and retaining the intellectual capital that is organisational lifeblood of PSFs.

Source: Adapted from DeLong *et al* (2008).

*Executive coaching* initially involved external coaches with responsibility subsequently transferred internally to L&D professionals or line managers. Where external coaches are used now, they tend to be specialists who meet particular needs. The advantages of using external coaches are that they draw on experience from other organisations and provide a different insight. However, they are more costly, and not as effective relative to coaching by line managers (CIPD 2010f).

Coaching is seen to be extremely effective when it has adequate support, clear goals, supervision of coaches, and robust evaluation. It works best where there is a coaching policy and it is used generically rather than focusing on senior managers with questionable performance or dealing with difficult people. Coaching is popular and powerful, but it has to be remembered that it is not a panacea, but one of many L&D methods and, as with all methods, it is important to know when it is the most effective and efficient intervention. Its use seems certain to expand, with a greater integration between coaching, organisational development and performance management to drive organisational change (CIPD 2011f; Anderson *et al* 2009).

## E-LEARNING

CIPD (Factsheet 2009c) defines e-learning as 'learning that is delivered, enabled, or mediated by electronic technology, for the explicit purpose of training in organisations'. Its use is increasing, with 62% of organisations using it in 2010 (CIPD L&D Survey) despite the fact that it is not highly rated for its effectiveness. Cynically, some put the rise in its usage down to the role of vendors of e-learning although there are a range of factors at play (Stewart 2010, p.339).

The main advantages of e-learning are that it can be accessed at times and locations to suit learners who work at their own pace; it accommodates employees who work shifts, who like to work alone or who prefer to learn in antisocial hours. Additionally, the training is consistent and methodical and does not rely on variations between trainers. It is particularly useful for multinationals where new knowledge has to be quickly disseminated worldwide and/or across many sites. It can be used for standard information or for rapidly changing complex information and can be personalised for each learner. Finally, it is ideally suited to learner-centred development and once workers can use the technology, e-learning increases access to a large and expanding amount of information, and the learners themselves can become knowledge producers (Gibb 2008, p.211). The top three factors which have the greatest impact on e-learning effectiveness are motivation, appropriate support and time to learn.

A decade ago, it was predicted that e-learning would increase more rapidly than it has. Barriers to its use include lack of access to computers, lack of familiarity, and lack of face-to-face support. To some extent, learning centres ameliorate such problems, although these are not always well used; in part, because some employees prefer to access materials through their desktops, although they are then unable to get away from frequent interruptions. Other problems – not exclusive to e-learning – include lack of instructor time to prepare, lack of organisational support, difficulties with evaluating ROI, and it can be dull (Weekes 2007). Low opinion of e-learning is generally put down to its misuse or because it is evaluated as a standalone method. When mixed with traditional methods involving personal interaction (blended learning), it proves both popular and highly effective (Weekes 2007; Brown *et al* 2006). Complex skills development is possible, and simulations are now available for many situations, even surgical procedures (Stewart and Rigg 2011, p.209). Technology moves on apace, and developments of mobile phones with PC capabilities, and Web 2.0 technologies (for example, blogs, social networking, Wikis) have all ensured increased access and familiarity. In general, users familiar with technology find e-learning more enjoyable than paper-based learning; as older workers are replaced by younger ones, its use will accelerate.

For some organisations, e-learning is very cost-effective; whereas in others, costs may increase where e-learning is additional to existing training methods (hardware and development of software are expensive). In SMEs particularly, perceptions about cost can be a barrier to its use. However, training time can be reduced by one-quarter (as well as saving time and carbon use in travel) and direct costs (such as premises, course fees) are reduced significantly where large numbers of learners access materials (Gibb 2008, p.215). Although picking up generic materials may not fit the need, they can be used as a basis for developing in-house materials.

CIPD respondents reported it was extremely difficult to assess whether e-learning was more effective than face-to-face learning, a view upheld by Sambrook (2003 cited in Stewart 2010).

According to the CIPD, e-learning is most effectively used where:

- the content is largely concerned with knowledge, for example company procedures
- there is a long-term training need and thus a sufficient period to recoup investment
- trainees are scattered geographically
- large numbers have to be trained in a relatively short time
- unusual, expensive or dangerous situations need to be simulated.

Situations in which it may not be appropriate include where:

- it is not the most cost-effective solution
- lead times are short
- learners are not comfortable using computers
- learning styles are more attuned to learning with others in groups
- it may not be suitable for teaching practical, hands-on skills.

E-learning usage continues to expand as technology advances and the future lies with highly effective blended learning.

REFLECTIVE ACTIVITY

How can e-learning be used to improve worker skills and organisational performance?

## CONTINUING PROFESSIONAL DEVELOPMENT (CPD)

In a world of rapid change, it is essential to ensure that skills, knowledge and experiences are regularly updated – and this is particularly pertinent for professionals. Emphasis on this is underpinned by terms such as 'reflective practitioners' and the 'learning organisation' and increasingly, by CPD.

> *Without reflection you may have lots of experience, but you do not have the means to generalise from them and to apply learning to other situations.*
>
> Megginson and Whittaker (2003, p.29)

CPD is a planned process which involves reflecting on learning from experiences and problems, and applying that learning in subsequent situations. It is about setting goals for self-development, and charting progress towards them. The process of reflection on learning soon becomes a habit, and can become subliminal. As with all L&D, it is cyclical: assess needs; carry out development activities; evaluate; assess needs.

The essential principles of CPD are that it should:

- be continuous
- be owned and managed by the individual learner
- be driven by the individual's needs and current state of development
- have clear learning outcomes that satisfy individual and/or organisational needs
- evaluates learning rather than merely describes what has taken place
- be seen as an essential part of professional and personal life, not an optional extra.

This latter point is important; when CPD is seen as an optional extra on top of a heavy workload, it is unlikely to be completed. Organisational support aids CPD, and for an increasing number of professions, it is compulsory.

Gold and Smith (2010) estimate that around one-fifth of UK workers hold or are working towards professional qualifications, and most professions now use CPD in recognition that all professionals are in need of continuous updating.

HRM AT WORK IN FOCUS

### Developing lawyers

The Law Society has a compulsory requirement for 16 hours per year CPD, of which one-quarter must be Law Society accredited training courses. In common with other professions, CPD is supported by *online* communities which are custom-built for those working both in the UK and overseas to meet the requirements of the Solicitors' Regulation Authority, The Bar Council and ILEX. One such resource for the legal profession is CPDcast.com which is custom-built for those working both in the UK and overseas to meet the requirements of the Solicitors' Regulation Authority, The Bar Council, and ILEX.

CPD is also a compulsory aspect of the Professional Development Scheme for CIPD members; evidence of CPD is required from those seeking an upgrade. The sort of activity that can be put forward for CPD breaks down into three broad areas. First, evidence related to an ongoing qualification, such as research for course work, group activities and role-playing, and presentations. Second, there are work-related activities such as projects or assignments, report-writing, attending training courses and secondments. Finally, there are personal development activities such as learning a new language, acting as a school governor, and organising sports or social events. A much longer and indicative list is available from CIPD, but the key point to stress is that CPD can be achieved via a range of different routes provided that learning takes place.

It is generally assumed that employees are motivated to learn in order to ensure employability and career development. This implies a narrow view of CPD as being undertaken for instrumental reasons, whereas *personal* development is also important. Where personal development unrelated to the job is included, it may be viewed by employers as a waste, or a threat in that it can contribute to labour turnover. In some instances, this may be true as learning can lead to unanticipated and unplanned outcomes. However, research tells us that *all* development opportunities link with retention as well as increased motivation and commitment. As Megginson and Whitaker (2003, p.17) note, even where CPD is unrelated to work, those undertaking it 'appear to be more engaged, less stressed, more interested in new opportunities and open to working with new colleagues'.

The advantages of undertaking CPD for CIPD members are:

- build confidence, job satisfaction, and credibility
- track learning – document achievements for appraisals, CV, promotion etc
- manage self-development and keep up to date
- develop reflective skills and the ability to transfer learning from one situation to another – become a 'thinking performer'
- aids professional recognition.

## REFLECTIVE ACTIVITY

Not all professionals value CPD as highly as others, and of those that do, not all engage with it. What motivates you to engage with CPD, and what are the barriers? Analyse the activities you engage in and consider whether there are others that might be useful to you.

The spread of CPD through most professions demonstrates its importance, though there is a danger when it is imposed that it could degenerate into a box-ticking exercise. It is usually included in performance management and there is a need to check that learning transfer takes place into work practice, although this begs the question of who judges what can and cannot count as CPD (Gold and Smith 2010, p.391).

## MANAGEMENT DEVELOPMENT ACROSS THE GLOBE

### MANAGEMENT DEVELOPMENT

In part, the problems relating to management development revolve around definitions of 'management'. Mumford and Gold (2004, p.2) define 'management' as a description of managers' activities, but this begs the question, what do managers do? Despite numerous attempts to analyse managers' roles, difficulties remain. Managers operate at a multitude of levels and situations – junior, senior management, line managers, professionals, working in SMEs and multinationals, and there are a range of specialist areas such as HRM, HRD, finance, and marketing. Overlaid on this is continuous and increasingly rapid change, with change initiatives often sinking because of management faults (Burnes 2003). The main management skill gaps are leading and managing change and performance management (CIPD 2010f; Gold *et al* 2010a). Management development is set in unique social, organisational and economic contexts, and is expected to deal with individuals with different development needs; in recognition of this, organisations differ in their approaches. Generally, management development aims to improve efficiency and productivity, to promote innovation and facilitate change. It is specifically a long-term investment and results may not be seen for many years – and this complicates evaluation.

As with all L&D, management development should align with organisational strategy and ethics; although such alignment is difficult to achieve (Anderson 2009). Choice of the beneficiaries and defining needs may involve audits, development/assessment workshops, and appraisal systems. The main methods used include formal education such as the MBA or undergraduate management degrees; internal or externally provided training courses, outdoor development, coaching and mentoring, as well as more exotic, creative learning methods. *Performance Review* is a critical component of any form of management development. *Competences* are often used as tacit skills such as practical intelligence, emotional intelligence and intuition are increasingly seen as critical for the best managers (CIPD 2010d). The Management Standards Centre (MSC) has established national standards of competence for managers at all levels within four roles – managing operations, finance, people, and information. *Coaching and mentoring* are seen as particularly effective as they are tailored to the individual situation and, combined with feedback and performance review, managers are assisted to determine their own development needs. *Action learning, secondments, shadowing and project work* are based on live issues in the work setting and may involve learning from colleagues as well as line managers; they fit well with the model of the learning organisation; and are commonly used within SMEs.

*Formal education and training* remains a mainstay with business schools increasingly tailoring executive education, jointly planned, often modularised, to ensure that it is innovative, and reflects organisational and individual needs. Use of business schools allows for networking of ideas, and enables participants to gain an external perspective, although many organisations have developed corporate universities. Subsequent to formal education and training, it is important to support learning transfer through coaching and reviews.

*Outdoor development* is popular for team-building and problem-solving, despite criticism that some providers include extreme and dangerous activities (Reid *et al* 2004, p.239). Many organisations use more unusual forms of L&D to boost soft skills, such as dancing days, or sing-a-longs of opera, for teambuilding (John Lewis) and presentation skills (Deloitte, Barclays) respectively.

As with all L&D, evaluation is important, but proving its worth is not easy. Research by Mabey and Ramirez (2005) across six European countries demonstrates that management development can improve competitive advantage, so long as it is couched in a strategic approach to HRM, with senior and line-manager buy in. Without such support, it did not greatly improve organisational performance. Mabey and Terry (2007) comment that management development still operates in a blinkered way, and question why organisations continue to spend huge amounts on it without robust evaluation. Debates about management development continue and there remains dissatisfaction with provision (despite large amounts of money invested in it) partly because organisations remain unsure of what is needed, and many managers remain unable to take up what training is on offer. The future is likely to see an extension of self-development generating demand for an ever-broader range of management development options.

## GLOBAL MANAGEMENT DEVELOPMENT

It is generally stated that organisations globally are hampered by a lack of good managers, and that management development is a good thing for business performance. China has recognised the need for professional L&D for managers and has funded institutes and business schools for this purpose since the 1980s (Cooke 2011, p.135). There is a proliferation of management courses of various types and levels, but also concerns about quality of provision. The CIPD 2010 Survey reflected interest in international L&D by including questions about it for the first time: 64% of survey respondents felt that L&D was a key driver for international competitiveness with management and leadership skills seen as most important followed by intercultural, then people management skills. Despite this finding, many organisations do not offer international L&D. Dowling *et al* (2008) report that only 13% of European organisations provide cross-cultural training to expatriates, although 47% offered briefings for potentially problematic international placements. Presumably many organisations do not offer international L&D because they assume that management skills are generic and transferable.

Indeed, many skills required for the international arena are generic (Brownell 2006; Swart *et al* 2007), but intercultural skills (cultural sensitivity, cultural intelligence and a global mindset) are critical to the international context. For a full analysis of current research on typologies of global leaders see Debrah and Rees (2011) or Osland *et al* (2006). Global mindset is the ability to communicate and work within different cultures, to manage uncertainty and global complexity. Complexity includes environmental issues that differ widely from one region or country such as the economic, social, political, religious and legal influences. Working globally requires an enhancement of political skills and the ability to build up and sustain relationships and networks (McDonnell and Collings 2011, p.59).

In common with management development, the first step is to assess what it is that global leaders do that differentiates their work from that of domestic managers (particularly since the latter do not always succeed in international roles). The next step is to identify the behaviours associated with the roles in order to determine behaviourally linked competences. As with leadership development, there is a conflict of views in the literature as to whether *all* managers can be trained to become global leaders, or whether global leaders have particular personal traits (for example, openness and flexibility) that cannot be emulated. Those that believe in the trait theory would suggest that the first stage would be to screen for those personal characteristics, and to offer international L&D opportunities only to those selected.

According to Debrah and Rees (2011), development opportunities may include:

- international assignments
- membership of international/global teams
- travel overseas
- action learning
- attendance at international meetings and forums
- L&D focused on international issues.

*Expatriates* are appointed to live and work outside their home country, and their development needs are different from those of global leaders. Since expatriates operate as agents for knowledge transfer across geographical boundaries, their development is particularly important. L&D is also important for their families to lessen failure rates.

The majority of organisations rely almost entirely on pre-departure training programmes which would typically include the following (Debrah and Rees 2011):

- expatriate training tailored to individual and their destination
- short term overseas assignments
- coaching and mentoring
- assessment centres
- e-learning
- international job rotation
- personal security (health and safety, terrorist threats).

## KNOWLEDGE MANAGEMENT

A great deal has been written about knowledge management since the 1980s because it is thought that *knowledge* and highly talented people generate competitive advantage; in the past this was generated by physical or financial capital (Boxall and Purcell 2011; Gold *et al* 2010b). Employees are now contracted for their ability to apply knowledge through their experience and skill development. Academic interest focuses on how such an ill-defined concept as knowledge can be identified, harnessed, manipulated and incorporated into organisational structures and norms.

Knowledge is hard to define, in part because most knowledge incorporates explicit and tacit elements. **Explicit knowledge** is that which is easily accessed as it is contained in written materials, making it easily transmitted from one person to another. **Tacit knowledge**, on the other hand, is hard to transmit, as individuals themselves may not be aware that they hold such knowledge. It is often termed 'know-how', and is typically acquired through experience rather than formal instruction, making it hard to specify, quantify, capture, and transfer. Despite this, tacit knowledge is seen as critical to competitive advantage, as it can generate high performance and may be unique to individuals within a specific organisation, whilst being hard to transfer and capture.

Even with the differentiation between explicit knowledge and tacit knowledge, there are further issues. The first is separating out IT from knowledge, and differentiating between high-quality knowledge and low-quality knowledge. Spender (2008) examines the knowledge management and organisational learning literature and his work illuminates nuances by referring to knowledge as data; knowledge as meaning; and knowledge as practice. Practice is 'richer and more complex than the mere execution of cognition, and cannot be theorised within a framework of rationality and goal-seeking' (p.164). This is self-evident when we compare a student finishing a law or architecture degree with a professional in the field with 20 years of experience. Recent graduates have the information, and the cognitive ability, but they lack the experience that comes through practice. Collectively knowledge is variously known as **intellectual capital** or **human capital**.

Swart (2007, p.452) defines knowledge workers as 'employees who apply their valuable knowledge and skills (developed through experience) to complex, novel, and abstract problems in environments that provide rich collective knowledge and relational resources'. They may be working in a wide range of fields, such as science, biotechnology, engineering, pharmaceuticals, IT, media, advertising, academia, professional services, lawyers, scientists, stockbrokers, biotechnology, or consultancies. A profile of typical knowledge workers might be:

- Commitment to the job rather than the organisation.
- Intrinsic motivation tied up with the work, although likely to command high salaries.
- Look for work that offers challenge and opportunities for self-development.
- Network with peers and clients outside of the employing organisation.
- High degrees of autonomy and organise own work (or within teams).
- High degree of power relative to the employing organisation.
- Resistant to control.
- Typically follow a boundaryless career.

(Donnelly 2011; Swart 2007; Boxall and Purcell 2011.)

This profile does not tell us how many within an organisation might be designated as 'knowledge workers'. Are we talking about all professional workers, or just a few senior staff whose experience has made them invaluable to the organisation? Within most fields we can think of individuals whose stardust makes them household names, but this would be too narrow a category, and within most leading-edge organisations there will be many knowledge workers with professional qualifications engaged in relatively mundane tasks, whether in a laboratory, or manipulating data at a computer. Swart (2007, p.456) adds an organisational context for knowledge production. She suggests that knowledge workers are found in dynamic, fast-changing, unstable environments, with innovative structures, dealing with ambiguous client demands, compared to more traditional, slow-growing organisations.

**Social capital** refers to knowledge shared through networks of relationships – these may be within (working in teams, mentoring and coaching) or outside the organisation (clients, external colleagues). The social aspect of knowledge creation and transfer necessitates trust, co-operation, and reciprocity, especially where knowledge workers are transferred to an outsourced organisation and bought back in (Grimshaw and Miozzo 2009) or where there are alliances forged for cutting-edge knowledge creation with two or more corporations (Meier 2010). Trust is important in relation to quality – there needs to be some guarantee that knowledge transferred is of high quality, ie accurate and reliable (Spender 2008). Problems associated with knowledge generation are greater in the transnational setting. Tregaskis *et al* (2010) examined MNCs and concluded that competitive advantage is retained through social capital. There are many ways to maximise knowledge sharing: transnational project teams, committee and governance groups, social networks, horizontal networking, development, expatriate assignments, cross-functional groups, shared management frameworks, job rotation, staff exchanges, cross-national forums, and training offered by one part of the business to another (p.473). Best practice would link local knowledge with corporate knowledge transferred through expatriates (Li and Scullion 2010).

The trick for organisations is to retain key knowledge holders, harness their knowledge for use by others in the organisation, and, ultimately, to lock this into the organisational processes and behaviours (Swart and Kinnie 2010). The hope is that a symbiotic relationship between organisational needs and individual needs develops in the process of creating, transferring, and applying knowledge so that workers remain loyal. The dilemma is that knowledge work typically involves project work, broad networks and teams working closely with the client, and the boundaries between the client and employing organisation become permeable (Marchington *et al* 2005). This presents dangers as workers identify with those external to the organisation and decide to move on. Where knowledge workers are not paid enough or little loyalty is engendered, they may transfer allegiance and contract with the client, or to others within their personal network.

In SMEs, where the owner/manager is present, it is easier to engender loyalty but in larger organisations this is more difficult, and as many tactics as possible are needed to be used to ensure commitment. As the case study work by Donnelly (2011) shows, brand reputation is important in attracting the best clients who can offer cutting-edge work at high market rates, and this helps to attract and retain key knowledge workers. HRM has a key role in meeting knowledge workers' needs for autonomy, challenge, and opportunities for self-development, whilst simultaneously facilitating sharing of knowledge. As we saw in Chapter 4, Lepak and Snell (2007) suggest that a specific HR system is needed to deal with knowledge workers – one which provides high investment in motivation, empowerment and development. Examples of ways in which this can be achieved include: job and leadership rotation, secondments, inter-disciplinary team-working; mentoring; shared training opportunities and conferences; relatively low levels of monitoring and managerial control; and the creation of highly specialist units of knowledge workers who can work together and share knowledge in fluid project teams. Performance management systems should reward meeting strategic and organisational aims, and knowledge sharing should be rewarded (Taylor 2010, p.458; Swart 2007, p.457).

HRM AT WORK IN FOCUS

## Consultants as knowledge workers

Donnelly's case study throws light on theories of knowledge management. It was conducted in the Netherlands and the UK with a large multinational consultancy firm. Consultants are the archetypical knowledge workers as they market intellectual work, created and captured from tacit knowledge and organisational capital.

To the company, value is locked in individuals' tacit knowledge combined with social capital gained through working with clients and in teams. Counterbalancing this, the knowledge workers, especially those in junior positions, are highly dependent on the brand and organisational capital. They rely on the firm's systems and databases to provide a service to clients, as well as the expertise available from more senior colleagues. Senior consultants generally have more power and therefore autonomy, and may leave to join rival consultancy firms, possibly taking clients with them. However, they too are dependent on the brand capital which accrues to the international high status of the firm – it is this that enables them to command high salaries. Self-employment was generally not an option as clients, particularly large PLCs, are generally not interested in commissioning individuals, regardless of the relationship which may have developed between them. Large clients prefer to put their trust in the reputation and range of expertise offered by big consultancy companies. The result is a delicate balance of power between the firm and the knowledge workers. Each is reliant on the other. Individuals are expected and supported to stay abreast of key developments, but they rely on the social capital and organisational capital which is locked into the firm's systems and procedures. Although the firm uses techniques to ensure knowledge sharing (such as project based and teamwork), there is a tension between senior consultants making available their knowledge, and retaining it to ensure personal competitive advantage. Some will try to keep skills and knowledge to themselves to help their career trajectory.

The case study shows that these knowledge workers do not follow boundary-less careers in networked organisations. Instead, the consultancy firm is hierarchical, and workers have little control over hours worked, locations, and choice of clients. The firm relies on the tacit knowledge of individual employees, on the social capital generated by interaction with clients and teams; and the consultants rely on the firm for high calibre work and colleagues. A tension arises from the power and influence of the client in dictating terms and conditions of employment so that there is a triangular relationship with diffuse ownership of knowledge.

*To think about:*

*How does Donnelly's case study work fit with the archetypical definitions of knowledge workers and the companies which employ them?*

Source: Adapted from Donnelly (2008) and Donnelly (2011).

Knowledge occurs in a wide variety of contexts, in differing organisational forms and across international geographic and cultural boundaries, and HR responses vary accordingly. Outsourcing as a means of knowledge management is investigated in Grimshaw and Miozzo's (2009) research into two global IT services firms operating in Germany, the UK, Argentina and Brazil. Their work demonstrated how HR responses varied according to a range of factors, including client relations and the outsourcing contracts; knowledge flows; and the economic and institutional context. Meier (2010) explores how expatriates enhance knowledge transfer across geographical/cultural distances and ways that alliances are forged between organisations to create new knowledge – examples include R&D alliances in software development, biotechnology and pharmaceuticals. His work shows that high trust, effective communications, and use of expatriates all facilitate knowledge transfer, although there is some reluctance on the part of those with cutting-edge knowledge to transfer to alliance partners freely. Winch (2008) explores ways that large international French and British architectural organisations operate differently according to the practices of the host country and home culture when organising knowledge transfer. Use may be made of internationally mobile professionals, expatriate managers, and networking with professionals in the host country, the more diverse the talent pool, the higher the likelihood of knowledge creation.

Knowledge management does not fit one stereotyped profile – it may occur in hierarchical organisations, in strategic alliances or voluntary arrangements between firms, across international boundaries, and it can be outsourced. It follows that HR cannot be one-dimensional, but must reflect the diversity of circumstances – including clients, industrial relations, environment, partners and suppliers. Knowledge workers are important to competitive advantage, but they are not irreplaceable and their worth is intrinsically tied to social and organisational capital. There is a need to identify who are the core knowledge workers – those whose loss would make a difference to the organisation, who own unique, superior knowledge that is not easily imitated.

## PROMOTING A LEARNING AND DEVELOPMENT CULTURE

In order to promote an L&D culture, employers need to be supportive, provide adequate resources, capture management enthusiasm, and facilitate line managers' support. Barriers to L&D are lack of time, resources, organisational culture, lack of commitment from senior and line managers, followed by poor motivation (CIPD 2007d). Sadly, too few organisations take into account L&D implications when organisational strategies are developed. To remedy this, Jennings (2007) stresses the need for L&D professionals to become proactive and position themselves as business partners in order to be involved in strategy at the initial stages, rather than merely responding to requests. As mentioned earlier, L&D professionals need to be political and able to provide hard data on the value of learning in achieving organisational objectives. Without such hard data and written L&D strategies aligned to business aims, the positioning of HRD in business partnership remains unlikely.

## THE LINE MANAGER'S ROLE

Line managers are increasingly important to delivery of HRM, and we emphasise their HRD role here. The CIPD 2011 Survey showed that in 29% of organisations line managers had the main responsibility for L&D, and in 58% of cases, they had some involvement. This was expected to increase in the future. Purcell and Hutchinson (2007a) believe that line managers' behaviour is critical because their involvement provides a wide range of benefits including: increased levels of commitment, satisfaction and motivation, a willingness to undertake L&D, and line managers can ensure that learning is directly linked to workplace activities. They are ideally placed to implement strategic organisational and individual learning priorities through their roles in induction, review, supervision, facilitating knowledge-sharing and problem-solving, job rotation and secondments. In addition, they are in the best position to evaluate outcomes of learning, both to the individual and the organisation (Purcell and Hutchinson 2007b).

**Figure 10 Who has the main responsibility for determining the L&D needs of the organisation?**

| | |
|---|---|
| L&D specialist | 56% |
| Senior managers | 39% |
| HR department | 30% |
| Line manager | 29% |
| Employees/learners | 14% |
| External consultants | 2% |

n= 589.

Source: Adapted from CIPD (2011f).

However, not all line managers are competent, motivated, and confident learners and they may see time taken out for learning as an unnecessary interruption, and not see L&D as part of their job. Obstacles to assuming responsibility for L&D include lack of time, senior management commitment, resource implications, and lack of understanding about the impact of L&D. Lack of training was also a problem, because they may refuse offers of training due to work pressures, lack of commitment, or because the training is deemed insufficient on its own (Purcell and Hutchinson 2007b). Line managers need confidence that they have the right skills for the job, and this relies on adequate HR support and feedback through effective performance management, offering reward for development of their staff. It helps if responsibility for L&D is included in job descriptions (Hutchinson *et al* 2007; Hutchinson 2007, p.7). As long as L&D is seen as an optional extra for line managers, it will remain marginalised. One major problem is that giving discretion to line managers can lead to equity issues, in terms of how much access to opportunities individual managers give (see box below).

HRM AT WORK IN FOCUS

### John Lewis Partnership

John Lewis Partnership is a successful chain of partnership department stores. It places importance on the way partners feel about the brand, as this is seen as essential to the success of the business and the happiness of staff. HRD is important to this, and ownership of L&D is placed with partners, with support from line managers.

The company has developed an appraisal framework using competences, against which performance can be measured and personal development planned. All partners were involved in the development of the frameworks – rather than outside consultants. Both section and department managers were responsible for the review process and, as part of John Lewis Partnership's succession planning and talent management programme, a new training programme for managers and non-managers has been developed.

*To think about:*

*Using the John Lewis Partnership case study, identify possible barriers to maintaining a programme of learning and development.*

Source: Adapted from Purcell and Hutchinson (2007b).

## CONCLUSIONS

In this chapter we have stressed the importance of having a systematic and well-organised structure for managing L&D. Although there are a number of models and frameworks that can be used, each covers broadly the same cycle: identify learning needs, design and plan delivery and evaluation. It is worth reiterating that there is no single best approach to L&D since the most suitable method depends on purpose, subject matter, the size and make-up of the learners, and the finance available. HR practitioners need to be able to choose the approach that is most appropriate for specific circumstances, while drawing on learning theories to inform their choice. Robust evaluation is critical, especially in assessing transfer back to the workplace. Perhaps most important of all, HR professionals must be at the forefront in establishing an organisational culture in which learning is allowed to flourish, and this usually necessitates becoming political and financially astute. As with other components of HRM, L&D is becoming increasingly strategic, with emphasis shifting from training to learning, and with increasing responsibility delegated to line managers. Coaching and e-learning continue to attract attention and action is being taken to ensure better efficacy. Management development retains its high profile, having become increasingly international and global in nature. Knowledge management is seen as essential for the achievement of competitive edge. However, here too is a need for robust evaluation, and an awareness that learning needs must be reflected in the provision of the right sort of L&D, offered at the right time. It is also worth remembering that some of the new ideas and methods are not growing as fast as the literature might lead us to believe, and traditional training methods remain the mainstay of L&D opportunities.

EXPLORE FURTHER

ANDERSON, V. (2007) *The Change Agenda. The value of learning: A new model of value and evaluation.* London: CIPD. Available at: http://www.cipd.co.uk/changeagendas

CIPD (2011f) *Learning and talent development: Annual Survey Report 2011.* London: Chartered Institute of Personnel and Development

DEBRAH, Y.A. and REES, C.J. (2011) 'The development of global leaders and expatriates', in A-W. Harzing and A.H. Pinnington (eds) *International Human Resource Management* 3rd edition. London: Sage.

DONNELLY, R. (2011) 'The ambiguities and tensions in creating and capturing value: views from HRM consultants in a leading consultancy firm', *Human Resource Management*, Vol.50, No.3, 429–44.

GIBB, S. (2008) *Human Resource Development: Process, practices and perspectives.* London: Palgrave Macmillan.

GOLD, J., HOLDEN, R., ILES, P., STEWART, J. and BEARDWELL, J. (2010d) *Human Resource Development: Theory and Practice.* Basingstoke: Palgrave Macmillan.

MEIER, M. (2010) 'Knowledge management in strategic alliances: a review of empirical evidence', *International Journal of Management Reviews*, Vol.13, No.1, 1–23.

PURCELL, J. and HUTCHINSON, S. (2007a) 'Front-line managers as agents in the HRM-performance causal chain: theory, analysis, and evidence', *Human Resource Management Journal*, Vol.17, No.1, pp.3–20.

STEWART, J. and RIGG, C. (2011) *Learning and Talent Development*, London: Chartered Institute of Personnel and Development.

SWART, J. (2007) 'HRM and knowledge workers', in P. Boxall, J. Purcell and P. Wright (eds) *The Oxford Handbook of Human Resource Management.* Oxford: Oxford University Press.

CHAPTER 12

# Managing Employment Relations

## LEARNING OUTCOMES

By the end of the chapter, readers should be able to:

- provide advice to management on employment relations objectives appropriate for their own organisation
- design an employment relations policy explaining how trade unions and collective bargaining will be dealt with, or how a non-union strategy will be developed
- contribute to the design and evaluation of effective procedures for disciplinary issues, grievances and disputes.

In addition, readers should understand and be able to explain:

- the way in which effective employment relations can contribute to increased employee potential and commitment and organisational goals
- the processes of union recognition and derecognition
- the nature and meaning of collective bargaining within the employment relations framework.

## INTRODUCTION

The management of employment relations is central to HRM. Different approaches have gained prominence in line with a variety of internal and external pressures on the employing organisation; these include the growth and decline of trade unionism, changing product and employment market conditions, labour law and new technology (Blyton and Turnbull 2004; Gennard and Judge 2010; Wilkinson *et al* 2009; Wilkinson and Townsend 2011). 'Employee' or 'employment relations' are typically used more or less interchangeably with the term 'industrial relations'. Both terms go back to the World War One period in the Anglo-American literature. For most of the twentieth century the industrial relations term was the more popular but in the last decade or so usage has shifted, in part because it tended to be associated with a blue-collar 'smokestack' image and was seen largely as dealing with unions (Kaufman 2011). Sisson (2010, p.4) defines employment relations as the study of 'the institutions involved in governing the employment relationship, the people and organisations that make and administer them, and the rule making processes that are involved, together with their economic and social outcomes'. As he points out much of the work in the 1960s and 1970s focused on the role of trade unions and collective bargaining, and the profile of the strikes and other forms of industrial action that often accompanied them. But as Sisson (2010, p.5) notes more recently, there has been a return to examining the employment relationship in general, with it being characterised less as a psychological or legal relationship but more of a managerial one – with all the potential for conflict that such a relationship entails:

- The basis of the exchange is security and flexibility – employees receive rewards (tangible and intangible) in return for which employers acquire the right to direct them (Sisson 2010).
- The nature of the exchange is indeterminate, continuous, contradictory and exploitative, (Sisson 2010, p.5; see also Ackers 2011).

Whether or not trade unions are recognised, the process of exchange is political, involving ongoing negotiation against an unequal power relationship. As Sisson (2010, p.5) notes, while the employment relationship is by definition one between an employee and an employer, it is not exclusively private, as for the great majority of employees, employment is a collective activity – with employees tending to be found working in groups, and some may also belong to trade unions/professional organisations. As he comments, in practice, managers tend not to differentiate much between individual employees because of the costs, and as a result most contracts of employment take a 'standard' form.

The purpose of this chapter is to examine management's role in employment relations, focusing in particular on union recognition and the nature of union and non-union workplaces, as well as collective bargaining and procedures.

## EMPLOYMENT RELATIONS IN ITS HISTORICAL AND COMPARATIVE CONTEXT

While the institutions of collective bargaining have declined in most developed countries, it is important to note that this is not the only institution with which employment relations are concerned (Wilkinson and Wood 2012). An 'institution' can be law, custom and practice, as well as substantive rules that cover the 'what' of the employment relationship and procedural rules that deal with the 'how' (Dundon and Rollinson 2011). As Sisson (2010, p.7) observes, managers make rules and employees are expected to obey them, and despite complaints about the burden of regulation, it is management that has been providing new sets of institutions; such as appraisal and target setting, individual performance pay, and share option schemes for senior executives.

During the 1970s employers were encouraged to recognise and work with trade unions, required to improve the floor of employment rights for workers, and prompted to conciliate with, rather than confront, staff. However, during the 1980s, the climate became more hostile for unions and changes in the political and legal context removed much of their statutory support, leaving many workers with little employment protection by continental standards. Moreover, the government encouraged employers to reassert their control, and high levels of unemployment in the UK contributed to the shift in the balance of power (Ackers and Wilkinson 2003; Gospel and Wood 2003). Hence, some commentators talked of a 'new employee relations' and the transformation of the British workplace (Towers 2003, p.18). The late 1990s marked a shift in the pattern of employee relations as the Labour government was more sympathetic to trade unions (although it did not undo the Thatcher settlement), and this was reflected in a statutory recognition procedure. The policy environment also became more animated with notions of employee rights (or in the EU case, citizenship) supported by new legal regulations (Brown 2011; Ewing 2003). While the Labour government remained committed to labour flexibility and considerable management 'choice' regarding employment practices, it was prepared both to regulate independently on behalf of employees and to commit the UK to European social policy.

The current coalition government has argued that 'red tape' – based on the notion the labour market is overregulated – needs to be minimised. In fact OECD measures suggests the UK is, next to the USA, the weakest in employment protection legislation and the belief that employment rights are not compatible with efficiency is equally misplaced (Coats 2009); there is more than one route to performance. But as Coats notes, the common complaint might be explained by a view that all employers everywhere prefer fewer to more regulatory obligations. While employees may have more rights than ever before, issues to do with the ability to access these is problematic (Coats 2009, p.110). The modernisation agenda promoted by the Conservatives does provide some distancing from the neo-liberal emphasis on anti-unionism and some accommodation with New Labour themes (Williams and Scott 2010) but in practice, the priority on cutting budgets and reform of the public sector have been more significant (Nolan 2011).

As we saw in Chapter 2, the decline in union membership has contributed significantly to the new employment relations terrain (Wilkinson and Townsend 2011). Collective bargaining now has lower levels of coverage and scope than at any time since the 1930s, and trade unions have lost their national prominence and voice to an extent that would not have been thought possible in the 1970s (Brown 2011). In addition, the extent of industrial action has also fallen dramatically, with days lost through strikes at a very low level, and a whole generation of HR managers now unaccustomed to dealing with collective disputes at work. For example, in the latest WERS, managers in only 5% of workplaces reported some collective dispute of any kind in the previous year in contrast to the situation when the public was accustomed to consuming strikes with its cornflakes (Lane and Roberts 1971, p.232). But the problems of employment relations are less to do with industrial action and more to do with quality of work relations, work organisation and effective management (Coats 2009, p.14).

There has been a major growth in legislation in the UK over the past 30 years, and lawyers have played an increasingly important role in setting the parameters within which employee relations is enacted (Gennard and Judge 2010, pp.98–132). For the vast majority of employers, the most immediate and obvious influence on their activities, especially in the area of employment rights, comes from the employment tribunal system; but the employment tribunals are themselves overseen and explicitly influenced by the Employment Appeals Tribunal and higher level courts. Increasingly, this includes European legal institutions – such as the European Court of Justice – whose influence over the adjudication of employment rights has grown enormously over the last 20 years, and has led to major changes in employment law.

It is worth noting that employment relations tends to be context-specific because of different national systems and laws that reflect different institutional and cultural contexts; thus, legislative and other forms of regulation vary considerably across counties (Wilkinson and Wood 2012). An example is Australia's industrial relations system. Developed as a hybrid system that set a floor of minimum standards via awards, it provided widespread protection for many workers but also enabled collective bargaining where unions had sufficient market power. Australia's central, and most distinctive institutional actor, the Arbitration Commission, was insulated from direct political interference and was independent, although it was required to take into account the views of employers and unions – and government – in making its decisions. Over the years the state's institutional architecture, most notably the arbitral model, has changed dramatically (Wilkinson *et al* 2009). Equally, India and China, both emerging economies, have quite different traditions of labour law (see box below).

HRM AT WORK IN FOCUS

## Labour law in India and China

Fang Lee Cooke compares the law in China and India. She notes that over 60 major pieces of labour legislation have been enacted by the central legislature in India and these are in addition to over 150 labour regulations enacted by the state legislatures which are specific to the needs of the state concerned. Some of these laws were introduced prior to India's independence, although some amendments have been made to bring these laws up to date. While the laws are seen as being supportive of labour they are also regarded as being 'among the most restrictive and complex in the world' and 'seen as having constrained the growth of the formal manufacturing sector where these laws have their widest application' (The World Bank 2006, p.3). In short, it is felt that legislation aimed at providing an enhanced level of labour protection may actually prove to be counterproductive, especially when the laws are only applicable to certain sectors. Restrictions on lay-offs may have not only led to inefficiency, but also discouraged employers from creating employment rather than better job quality in the formal sector, trapping millions into poor jobs in the informal sector. Cooke notes, however, that this pro-labour government stance has not been equally applied across all groups of employees; notably those in the public sector providing public services. Herein lies the tension, caused by the multiple role of the Indian government as an employer, an economic manager, and a legislator and policy maker.

Contrary to India's complex and detailed labour legislative framework, the regulation of the labour market and employment relations in China has until recently relied primarily on administrative regulations and policy guidelines issued at the central, regional (provincial) and local (municipal and township) level. She points out that the *Enterprise Minimum Wage Regulation* (enacted in 1993, revised in 2004) was essentially a national administrative regulation to provide a framework; local governments, however, determined the level of minimum wage and coverage. The first major piece of labour legislation was only passed in 1994, followed by three major laws in 2007. Unlike India, the laws generally apply to all employing organisations and groups of workers, but regional and local governments often develop local policy guidelines to modify the impact of the laws so as to prioritise their economic development agenda. It has been argued that, with 'the major exception of freedom of association', the labour standards established by the series of labour laws and regulations of China 'are not markedly inferior to those of comparable countries and indeed many developed nations' (Cooney 2007, p.674). But what remains problematic is the lack of effective enforcement and the confusing channels through which workers can seek to secure compliance of laws.

Source: Adapted from Cooke (2011a); see also Cooney (2007).

More broadly, globalisation and changes in technology have increased the mobility of capital, work, and workers thereby weakening the influence of national laws, institutions, and norms in shaping employment relationships and outcomes. As Kochan and Bamber (2009 p.318) note in the early twentieth century, labour costs are under intense competition, but today labour markets are international. This reflects not so much the international mobility of labour, but rather an increasingly clear international division of labour including more 'offshoring' of manufacturing (eg to China) and services (eg to India) (Kochan and Bamber 2009; Townsend and Wilkinson 2011; Wilkinson and Townsend 2011).

## MANAGEMENT'S ROLE IN EMPLOYMENT RELATIONS

The centrepiece of employment relations is the relationship between employers and employees, with its common and divergent interests (Edwards 2003; Sisson 2010). It is in neither party's interest for the organisation to perform poorly with consequent negative effects on profits (for the employer) or wages (for the employee). However, while there are clearly common goals there are also divergent interests. In simple terms, the employer is likely to wish to buy labour at the lowest possible price or cost so as to maximise profits, whereas employees wish to sell their labour at the highest possible price. This produces a conflict of interest, which not necessarily results in open conflict, but means that the arrangements reached may be unstable depending on relative bargaining power. Because employees are usually relatively weaker than employers, employees are likely to gain from organising themselves into trade unions so as to boost bargaining power (Budd and Bhave 2008). Budd (2004) argues that the objective of the employment relationship is to achieve a balance between efficiency, equity and voice, and that extreme positions are both undesirable and unsustainable. He suggests that while economic performance is clearly important, this has to be balanced with 'equity', defined as fair employment standards and treatment, and 'voice', defined as meaningful input into decisions (see also Chapter 13). In Europe, the 'flexicurity model' has been influential (see box below).

HRM AT WORK IN FOCUS

### Common principles of flexicurity

The origin of the word 'flexicurity' goes back to a Dutch discussion resulting in a law on flexibility and security. This law made it easier for employers to use flexible forms of employment while it also provided for better protection of workers on such contracts. The term has appeared as a 'win–win' solution, accommodating both workers and employers.

The common principles of flexicurity were adopted in late 2007 by the EU Council, but the main basis is outlined below:

- *Flexible and secure contractual arrangements and work organisation*, both from the perspective of the employer and the employee, through modern labour laws and modern work organisation.
- *Active labour market policies* which effectively help people to cope with rapid change, unemployment spells, reintegration and, importantly, transitions to new jobs – ie the element of *transition security.*
- *Reliable and responsive lifelong learning systems* to ensure the continuous adaptability and employability of all workers, and enable firms to keep up productivity levels.
- *Modern social security systems* that provide adequate income

support and facilitate labour market mobility. These include provisions that help people combine work with private and family responsibilities such as childcare.

As a process variable, this definition includes: *the involvement of the social partners in the design and implementation of flexicurity policies through social dialogue and collective bargaining*, with public authorities retaining an overall responsibility.

Source: Adapted from Auer and Chatani (2011); see also Vandenberg (2010).

Thus, employment relations is characterised by both conflict and cooperation. Some people regard it as inextricably linked with conflict, since this is the only time employment relations obtains much media coverage. It is now accepted that the so-called 'British disease' of industrial conflict in the 1970s was largely a myth, as Britain had a record no worse than many other developed countries.

## REFLECTIVE ACTIVITY

Write **two** lists, one specifying the common interests of employers and employees, and the other the divergent interests. Apply this to an organisation you are familiar with and see if it helps you to evaluate the quality of employee relations there.

However, the notion of two sides is also too simplistic. First, because neither side is consistently unified, much bargaining and disagreement takes place within each party as well as between them. Within management there are likely to be conflicting objectives between different functions and between different levels; for example, the objectives of the sales team may conflict with those of the production function. Similarly, the demands placed upon line managers in terms of adherence to procedure agreements may cause conflict between them and the HR function. To some extent, though, the overriding objective of companies to secure profitability can help integrate the various sub-objectives. On the union side, matters are even more complex, with conflict between members in different departments and in different trade unions, as well as between different levels in the shop steward hierarchy. There may also be differences between different trade or interest groups or between the leadership and the ordinary rank and file members.

It is also inappropriate to conceive of only two parties in employee relations because of third-party governmental intervention (Hayes and Clark 2012) and Civil Society Organisations (Williams *et al* 2011). The state performs several roles. For example, UK legislation on employee relations has developed considerably since the 1960s and it played a key role during the 1980s – legislation on the closed shop, industrial action and ballots, for example. The government has also played a role in pay regulation since the Second World War. This has either been through a formal mechanism – such as incomes policy during the 1960s and 1970s, or the imposition of cash limits for the public sector in the 1980s and the establishment of the minimum wage in 1998. In addition, via the agencies of independent tripartite bodies such as Acas, it has played a role in the resolution of disputes in both the public and private sectors. Furthermore, the government is a key employer, with a managerial function. As Hayes and Clarke (2012) note, while globalisation may have muted the role of individual governments, the state retains a strong influence and globalisation is just one of the forces at work creating new multiple centres and levels of power, with private equity firms another transnational force complicating the lives of employment legislators.

Before looking at employment relations objectives, we need to remind ourselves of the nature of management itself, and especially the sharply differing contexts within which employment relations are enacted. Three aspects are worthy of mention. First, there is the distinction between different types of sectors (for example, manufacturing or service) and ownership (private or public). This leads to a categorisation of four types of employing organisation: private businesses, public corporations, public services and voluntary bodies (Farnham 2000). Second, there are major differences between employment in large, multi-establishment enterprises and small single-unit firms. Third, we need to be aware of the influence of employment relations decisions compared with other corporate-level issues (Sisson and Marginson 2003, pp.176–82). The 'strategic choice' model whereby employers are seen as the key movers of change, and industrial relations policies are seen as strategic in that they form part of a long-term plan has been influential (Kochan *et al* 1986; Bacon 2008). This is important in recognising both the element of choice management faces and the extent to which management is able to set the agenda to which other actors – eg trade unions – then react (Boxall and Purcell 2008).

It might be expected that employment relations objectives would be in line with corporate strategy but often employers just muddle through. Even if we assume that employers have some idea about what they are doing, and why, their objectives may be implicit rather than explicit, and in many cases not committed to paper. In any event, employment relations objectives typically include the following:

- reducing unit labour costs, though not necessarily wages
- achieving greater stability in employee relations by channelling discontent through agreed procedures
- increasing productivity and the utilisation of labour
- increasing cooperation and commitment so as to increase the likely acceptance of change
- increasing control over the labour process
- minimising disruption at work and reducing the likelihood of overt conflict.

Some of these objectives do not make sense in isolation. For example, while management clearly wants to minimise disruption this should not be at the expense of high productivity. It could well be that the latter could be achieved in the long term by engineering a strike so as to confront inefficient working practices. Equally, some objectives may be more appropriate for certain stages in an organisation's development, or for some types of employer.

It has been argued that management must adopt a more strategic approach to employment relations, largely because fire-fighting is seen as leading to problems as short-term, ad hoc solutions merely store up trouble for the future. By way of contrast, a clearly devised strategy could prove more successful because it would increase consistency and harness commitment (Donovan 1968; Thurley and Wood 1983; Schuler *et al* 2001). However, research suggests that managers adopt opportunistic and pragmatic approaches to managing employees rather than the strategic approaches extolled by the human resource management texts (Bach 2005b; Boxall and Purcell 2008; Morris and Snell 2009; Becker and Huselid 2009) and HR issues tend to be considered at the implementation stage, rather than at the point where initial decisions are formulated.

In trying to understand management's approach to employment relations, it is useful to draw upon the 'frames of reference' developed by Alan Fox (1966) in his research paper for the Donovan Commission. These embody the main selective influences that cause managers to supplement, omit and structure what they see. Thus, two people may see the same event in a completely different manner and may judge its meaning, significance and outcomes in contrasting ways. The *unitary* frame of reference sees the organisation as a team (like a football team), with all employees striving towards a common goal. All members of the team are assumed to work to the best of their ability, accept their place in the hierarchy, and follow their appointed leader with no reason for factions. Given that unions are unnecessary (since everyone is on the same side), conflict is seen as pathological or abnormal, the result of misunderstanding and trouble makers. In contrast, *pluralism* conceives of the organisation as comprising varied interest groups with common and divergent interests, with management's job to balance these competing demands. Trade unions may be seen as a natural reflection of varied interests, rather than a cause of conflict. Conflict is not regarded as illegitimate, but needs to be channelled or managed through rules and procedures (Ackers 2002a, 2002b).

In simple terms, the two frames of reference have different perspectives on management prerogatives (Bacon 2006; Gennard and Judge 2010, pp.46–8). Managers with a unitary perspective would trust employees to make the 'correct' decision, and since everyone supposedly has the same interests, there should be no conflict between what is best for the company and what is best for employees. In contrast, the pluralist accepts the union role and believes in a policy of gaining the support of unions and employees to achieve an 'acceptable' solution. Pluralists believe in union consultation about changes that may have a fundamental effect on employees. On many occasions the substantive outcome of joint decision making may be little different from that achieved by direct management action. However, the procedural element is critical.

HRM AT WORK IN FOCUS

## The changing role of unions in China

Before the wave of economic reform in China that began in 1978, unions were mandated in the state-owned enterprises but were subordinate to the ruling party. The main role was to help the government manage peaceful employment relations. However, with the reform process the non-state sector grew and became larger than the state sector. In this sector, unions are not mandatory and have needed to find a role. Yi et al suggest that conflicting interest are more pronounced in the non-state sector and unions have to balance their role between harmonising and representing worker interests. Their research indicates that while unions may not contribute to wage increases they do assist worker benefits and the formalisation of employment contracts, hence creating better relations. They suggest that their ability to promote worker interests and harmonious industrial relations explains why MNCS seem receptive to their operations. They note almost all Fortune 500 companies allow unions in their operations. There is an irony in that some US companies are now denying US-based workers representation while acceding to collective bargaining in China and Western business. People also complain that the Chinese enforce laws against overseas employers while ignoring local ones.

*To think about:*

*Does the absence of strikes indicate that employees are content? How do employees show their discontent? How can discontent be monitored and handled?*

Source: Adapted from Yi *et al* (2010) and; McDermott (2011).

Individual managers vary in their willingness to accept a curbing of managerial rights, depending on the subject matter under consideration. For example, managers may be willing to negotiate on matters relating to payment methods, job design and work practices, but be unwilling to consult about matters such as investment and pricing policy, and product development. In any event, while management may be willing to consult, involve, and even bargain they also insist that they have a 'prerogative' to make the final decision. Hence, in certain areas of employee relations – such as promotion and training – management prerogative is the norm. In organisations where unions are absent, management is more able to vary terms and conditions of employment at will. The box below outlines how the role of unions has changed over time in China.

As Dundon (2011, pp.26–32) points out, conflict is quite normal because managers and workers can have very divergent interests and competing priorities. For example, managers may require increased flexibility from amongst its employees in order to carry out a whole range of job tasks while workers may be concerned that flexible work practices may dilute their skill and weaken their position in the labour market. Conflict in employment relations conflicts is often *vertical* in nature (Dundon and Rollinson 2011) so when workers question employer decisions, this symbolises a visible challenge to managerial authority. As individual employees tend to be powerless in contrast to the power of resources available to an employer, conflicts are commonly pursued as collective forms of action (Dundon and Rollinson 2011). Strike action has diminished in many countries, and Godard (2011) advances four possible reasons why this has occurred. First, strikes may have been diverted into other forms such as individual manifestations of conflict associated with the rise in individual rights; the evidence does not necessarily support this as Kersley *et al* (2006, p.277) report that only 8% of workplaces experienced a tribunal claim in 2004. Second, there is a view that capitalism has triumphed and industrial conflict has simply disappeared as a major issue, particularly because of the decline of manufacturing, less alienating work organisation and better employer practices. Third, conflict has become embedded in other, broader societal dysfunctions. Fourth, collective action is simply dormant as workers 'just get on' rather than challenging management, but resurgence may take place (see Chapter 2 also).

Dundon and Rollinson (2011) argue it is plausible that conflict has taken other forms, demonstrated as 'flight' rather than that of 'fight'. In other words, workers may engage in *unofficial*, *unorganised* and even individualised forms of conflictual behaviours. In this regard, Bryman (2004) distinguishes between *passive* and *active* forms of conflict, which may have a greater relevance among many of the smaller and non-unionised service sector companies (Dundon and Rollinson 2011). Passive protest occurs when employees mentally 'switch-off' from their job or to use the modern parlance of engagement, workers just become 'disengaged' (see also Chapter 13). The box below provides an illustration of this.

HRM AT WORK IN FOCUS

## Conflict, resistance and misbehaviour in the workplace

Frozone is an organisation, established to develop frozen meals for airlines and with the intent to change from the past and use new technologies and management practices, including teamwork. One objective was the removal of all physical barriers, while still ensuring the safety and integrity of the cooking and storage processes. Management wanted a plant design that would provide an efficient use of time: a plant layout where employees are not required to move far from their workspace would limit the possibility of employee 'loafing' and avoid the temptation of employee 'theft of time'.

The worksite is divided into three main areas. The first a non-food preparation area including administrative workspaces, canteen and changing areas/toilets. The second a 'low-risk' area of the building where food safety standards were less problematic as the food was still to be cooked; low-risk rooms are painted green and employees are required to wear green uniforms and hairnets in this area. The third area of the processing plant is the 'high-risk' area, where food contamination, through poor hygiene or work practices, is more likely and potentially very dangerous. This area includes the catchment area where food is removed from the cookers in the 'low-risk' area, and the assembly area, where cooked ingredients are assembled into the individual serves and sent through the freezing process.

The management team set about establishing a pathway to reaching the 'vision' for the new entity and employed the services of a consultant. The manager of operations explains that the consultant was employed to assist in the 'de-programming' of the new management so they could 'forget about all the things we thought we knew about managing people and running a business'. The management group was determined to create a business where they could instil 'self-responsibility' and create semi-autonomous, high-performance work teams.

While some employees enthused about the team spirit and the new working environment, others were more cynical. One employee summed up the feelings of many at Frozone:

> 'The thing we all hate most is the manipulation. Talking about equality, everyone's equal in this place and you can see that because even the boss doesn't have an office, you know? I say bullshit – when you try living on $390 a week then come back and talk to me about equality because at the moment equality is bullshit, mate.'

What became apparent is that not all employees could see 'the vision' before them. For managers, it was one thing to supervise and guide people who shared the vision and embraced the culture but it was a very different matter managing people who did not.

There is little doubt that many Frozone employees worked very hard, but when some did not, conflict began to creep in. As one employee states:

> '... we could be working flat out, you know, 100 per cent and a few people could be slackening off so someone has to pick up the slack. So the choice is either to work at 130 per cent or tell these guys to get their act together.'

Even one team leader was not immune to slackening off according to some employees:

> 'We call him Heidi because he's always hiding from the real work.'

*To think about:*

*Why is it hard to instil a culture in the workplace?*

Source: Adapted from Townsend (2011).

## THE EXTENT AND NATURE OF UNION RECOGNITION

The issue of union recognition lies at the heart of employment relations, and policies and practices in this area have changed more than most in the last three decades in the UK. As noted earlier, employment relations systems vary between countries because of varied historical, legal and institutional contexts (Wilkinson and Wood 2012). In the UK in the mid-1970s it was assumed that most employers would recognise and deal with trade unions, support their activities in the workplace, and attempt to build close working relationships so as to lubricate relations at work and minimise the likelihood of disruption. By the 1990s many employers introduced new working patterns without even consulting, let alone negotiating with, union representatives (Brown 2011). While derecognition was not widespread, the lack of new recognition deals is seen as more significant (Cully *et al* 1998, p.16). Until 1999 there was no legally enforceable route for unions and employers to follow in order to grant recognition, which made the British system different from those operating in many other industrialised countries in Europe and North America. In theory it meant that if they so desired, British employers could choose to grant recognition to a union with no members in the workplace. Indeed, this is precisely what happened at some green-field sites when deals with a single union were signed before employees were recruited, as at Nissan (Wickens 1987, pp.129–37). Conversely, employers could choose not to recognise a union at a workplace where all employees are union members, although this is more hypothetical and, in practice, would be difficult to sustain. In other words, the ultimate decision to grant recognition remained the prerogative of management. The *Employment Relations Act 1999* changed this by making legal provision for statutory trade union recognition through a number of possible routes (Smith and Morton 2001; Dickens and Hall 2003; Gennard and Judge 2010).

Gall (2004) has argued that the *Employment Relations Act 1999* marked a change in fortunes for the unions in terms of increasing recognition. There were many gains under the tranche of new recognition agreements, even though the majority are voluntary and the process and outcomes under post-recognition arrangements have delivered 'improvements for members'. The WERS data shows that the decline in union recognition has ceased since 1998, at least in workplaces with 25 or more employees, and there was even a rise in union recognition rates in the shrinking private manufacturing sector.

There seems to be a distinction between workplaces where (a) unions have maintained a presence and where they appear to be supported by management, (b) they are being edged out and (c) non-union workplaces. The critical importance of management attitudes is shown graphically by the WERS data. Where management had a positive attitude towards union membership, around 60% of employees were union members whereas where the managers' attitudes were negative it was around 5% (Kersley *et al* 2006, p.114). We now examine these three options.

## WORKING WITH THE UNIONS

The proportion of workplaces in Britain that recognise a union continued to fall between 1994 and 2004 for the purposes of negotiating pay and conditions, although there is still substantial sector variation (Kersley *et al* 2006, p.118). For example, 16% of all private sector organisations recognise a trade union, whereas in the public sector this is almost universal (90%). Union recognition is also a function of organisational size. Six per cent of workplaces with 100 or less employees recognised unions as opposed to 62% for those with over 10,000. It is also important to note that recognition varies in both scope and depth (Brown *et al* 1998) and employers recognise unions for specific activities, such as discipline, grievance or health and safety representation but not necessarily full-blown collective bargaining.

There are a number of reasons why employers should choose to **work with**, rather than against, unions at the workplace:

1 Management may regard trade union representatives as an essential part of the communication and voice process in larger workplaces (Gomez *et al* 2010). Rather than being forced to establish a system for dealing with all employees, or setting up a non-union representative forum, trade unions are a channel that allows for the effective resolution of issues concerned with pay bargaining or grievance handling. Reaching

agreement with union representatives, in contrast to imposing decisions, can provide legitimacy and perhaps lead to 'better' decisions. Even if it appears more time-consuming than the imposition of change, less time is spent trying to correct mistakes or persuade employees after the event of the efficacy of management ideas.

2 Employers may decide that it is more important to achieve long-term stability in employment relations even though their power advantage might allow them to impose changes on the unions. It is argued that management is more able to persuade unions to observe procedures if they have also conformed to previous agreements. As a quid pro quo, employers have to be prepared to use procedures themselves for resolving differences at work, especially in the area of disciplinary matters. Indeed, it can be argued that 'responsible' workplace union organisation and 'responsive' management is mutually reinforcing.

3 Some employers take the view that unionisation is inevitable because of the nature of their workforce, the industry, and the region in which establishments are located. The recognition procedure means that where there is sufficient support for a union, employers may feel it is far better to reach an agreement with a preferred union from the outset rather than suffer both poor employment relations and employee morale where there is defiance.

4 Even if employers wanted to reduce the role of unions, they may lack the power to carry through their intentions because of local constraints. For example, skill shortages may make wholesale dismissals unrealistic, as may fears that the tacit skills of workers will be lost, with the consequence of less effective organisations. Moreover, it is often forgotten that trade unions perform a number of functions in the workplace that can assist the management of employment relations. In a non-union organisation following complete derecognition, the onus falls upon management to perform an even greater range of tasks, and it may prove difficult to sustain alternative representation arrangements, as well as satisfy employee expectations. It is also important to keep the trade union issue in perspective. Employers have many concerns other than those relating to trade unions and, provided the latter do not present a major obstacle to the realisation of more important goals, union presence can be tolerated.

Most people join trade unions primarily for instrumental reasons – for example, for protection against arbitrary management decisions or for insurance against accidents (Charlwood 2003) – or peer-group pressure – and they may not necessarily believe in the notion of collective action. The predominantly instrumental attitude partially explains why participation increases considerably if there is a problem or employee relations issue (Waddington and Whitson 1997). It also explains why unions tend to be seen in local and economic terms. This 'local' perspective helps us understand why people agree that 'unions in general are too strong' and at the same time feel 'that unions at the [individual's] workplace are not strong'.

Millward *et al* (2000, p.89) note a reduced willingness to join a union even in situations where the employer encourages unionism and there is a growing number of younger workers who have never been union members or been exposed to trade unions. Despite unions being a force for fairness in the workplace, narrowing the pay distribution, boosting family-friendly policies and reducing accidents (Metcalf 2005), some 14 million workers are neither members nor have their pay and conditions set by collective bargaining: most of these have never been a union member. Around a fifth of these say they either desire union representation or would be very likely to join a union if one were available – this suggests a 'representation gap' of some 2.8 million employees. As Metcalf (2005, p.22) notes, in order to achieve recognition these employees need to be concentrated by firm or workplace or there will never be a union available to join. However, MSF-Amicus (now UNITE) signed up some Church of England clergy who had no employment rights as their employer was held to be divine, not earthly, and the GMB managed to recruit lap dancers. In the USA the 'justice for janitors' campaign generated much attention (Erickson *et al* 2002) as did the case of casino workers and car wash workers also in Los Angeles.

More recently, there has been a revival of interest in notions of 'partnership' (Johnstone *et al* 2009). This refers to the situation in which management is prepared to support the activities of the trade union(s), and for their part, employees are more likely to regard union membership as an important aspect of their employment conditions (see Chapter 13).

## EDGING OUT THE UNIONS

While some employers have sought to develop their relationship with unions, others have opted for marginalisation or derecognition. In these situations, employers believe that their objectives are more likely to be achieved by reducing or removing the union presence. Disputes may have arisen that slowed down or blocked changes in working practices, or managers may have doubts about whether they can work with trade unions. Others may simply have taken advantage of a superior power base to remove or restrict the activities of unions, to reduce wage costs, and enforce a stricter managerial regime, perhaps in line with some deep-seated antagonism among senior managers towards unions. Some reduction in union influence has been part of a broader management strategy rather than an attack on unions as such, and the removal of the union is undertaken in conjunction with a shift to more direct methods of EIP. For example, some employers place emphasis on individualism and performance-related pay schemes rather than collectively negotiated rates.

Even when trade unions are marginalised they can still retain a presence in the workplace, and maintain the right to collective bargaining. In these situations, even though the institutions of collective employee relations remain in place, they represent a much less important aspect of HRM (Simms and Charlwood 2009). A number of changes are typically associated with marginalisation:

- substantial reductions in the number of shop stewards at establishment level
- restrictions on access to time off for trade union activities and facilities for undertaking union-related work
- withdrawal of full-time shop steward positions, often subsequent to the dismissal (usually through redundancy or early retirement) of the existing role-holders
- lack of support for deduction of contributions at source (DOCAS)
- a lower priority accorded to collective bargaining with unions and the upgrading of consultative committees
- a greater emphasis on individualism and direct communications from line managers to all employees.

Certainly in recent years, as unions have become less able and willing to take industrial action, employers have pruned the collective bargaining agenda and relied more heavily on written and oral communications to all staff as opposed to going through union channels alone. As the production director at a carpet manufacturer reflected on changes: 'It's crazy when you think back. We used to not talk to our employees; only through a union representative' (Marchington *et al* 2001, p.64). In short, management is seeking to deny, rather than legitimise, the unions and this led to increased emphasis on direct communication (see Table 25).

**Table 25 Arrangements for direct communication, by sector of ownership**

| Type of communication | Private sector (%) | Public sector (%) | All workplaces (%) |
|---|---|---|---|
| *Face-to-face meetings* | | | |
| Meetings between senior managers and the whole workforce | 77 | 89 | 79 |
| Team briefings | 68 | 81 | 71 |
| Any face-to-face meetings | 90 | 97 | 91 |
| *Written two-way communication* | | | |
| Employee surveys | 37 | 66 | 42 |
| Email | 36 | 48 | 38 |
| Suggestion schemes | 30 | 30 | 30 |
| Any written two-way communication | 62 | 84 | 66 |
| *Downward communication* | | | |
| Notice boards | 72 | 86 | 74 |
| Systematic use of management chain | 60 | 81 | 64 |
| Regular newsletters | 41 | 63 | 45 |
| Intranet | 31 | 48 | 34 |
| Any downward communication | 80 | 97 | 83 |

Base: All workplaces with 10 or more employees.

Source: Adapted from Kersley *et al* (2006).

WERS 2004 confirmed that the trend to 'hollow out' collective agreements was continuing. The percentage of workplaces engaging in any collective bargaining over pay fell from 30% in 1998 to 22% in 2004 although the decline was largely found in the private sector (Kersley *et al* 2006, p.182). Managers in many workplaces appear to regard certain HR issues as 'off limits' to union representatives and do not even involve unions by providing information to them (Bacon 2006). It is increasingly apparent that even where unions are recognised, employers are setting up non-union voice structures (Gomez *et al* 2010).

Employers can derecognise unions but it is important to appreciate at the outset that this is not a homogeneous concept (Dundon and Rollinson 2011). In its most straightforward form derecognition refers to the complete withdrawal of collective bargaining rights and trade union organisation for some or all employees at a workplace or throughout a complete employing organisation. In other words, no trade union is recognised for the employees involved, even though by law employees retain the right to join unions of their choice. Alternatively, derecognition can mean the removal of bargaining rights for one or more unions in a multi-union environment, while allowing for, and even encouraging, the transfer of membership to other unions in the workplace. In this situation management might seek to simplify existing arrangements and reduce the number of unions with which it deals, and the end result could well be levels of union membership little different from before the derecognition. While one union loses, another gains.

The extent of union derecognition is difficult to gauge. WERS shows that the decline in union membership cannot be explained by the marginal rise in derecognition and it is insignificant compared to other sources of membership decline – such as shifts in employment from areas of high to low union density. Furthermore, it is important to note that a number of problems often occur after derecognition, including increased workloads for line managers, particularly responsibility for communications and consultation.

What are the advantages and disadvantages of union recognition for employers?

## MANAGING WITHOUT UNIONS

As with derecognition, discussions of non-union firms did not receive much attention in publications prior to the 1980s (Gollan 2010; Kaufman and Taras 2010). It was well known that there were large numbers of small, usually independent, companies which did not recognise or deal with trade unions, but they were generally labelled as 'traditionalist', 'unitarist' or 'sweatshop' employers, and castigated (usually quite rightly) for their poor treatment of staff. It was only with the growing awareness of what Beaumont (1987, p.117) refers to as the 'household name' group – companies such as IBM, Marks and Spencer and Hewlett Packard that managed without unions (Colling 2003). These companies were praised for their HR policies, which were designed to offer employees more than could be achieved by trade unions through negotiations. It appeared that non-union firms could feel proud of their approach to employee relations, and these companies later began to be seen as fertile ground for the development of HRM in the UK. Today non-unionism is close to the norm. Gomez *et al* (2010) point to a larger category of never members; that is, generations of people who have never been in a union. This is very apparent in the USA where overall figures mask the 8% union coverage in the private sector (Slinn and Hurd 2011).

Non-unionism is more extensive in certain parts of the country (such as the south-east of England) and in certain sectors of the economy (such as retailing, professional services, and hotels and catering) than in others. Younger and smaller establishments are also more likely to be non-union. But non-unionism can take many different forms, varying from the sophisticated and pleasant employment practices (eg the household-name group) through to the sweatshops and 'bleak houses' (Sisson 1993) of 'Dickensian' employers. One of the problems with studies of non-union firms has been the lack of differentiation between them. Guest and Hoque (1994a) argue that the term 'non-unionism' is actually limiting, in that firms are only analysed in relation to unionisation. They suggest a categorisation of non-union firms into the good, the bad, the ugly and the lucky – here we focus on the first three of these.

First, there are employers who are leaders in their product market, who would be classified by Guest and Hoque (1994b) as 'good'. These are often large employers, who have a clear strategy for managing people and operate with a wide range of HR policies. These employers often operate a 'union substitution' policy (Dundon and Rollinson 2004; Blyton and Turnbull 2004) that offers a complete employment package intended to be seen by employees as an attractive alternative to trade union membership. Such an approach might include:

- a highly competitive pay and benefits package, typically in excess of those offered by other firms in the same labour market

- a comprehensive battery of recruitment techniques (including psychometric tests) designed to select individuals who 'match' organisational norms and discard those who do not fit with the company profile (eg those with a history of union activism)
- a high priority accorded to induction programmes, which are geared up to socialising employees into the company ethos
- a stress on training and development opportunities, related both to the employees' work and more broadly to their role in the company and society (eg employee development and assistance programmes and career counselling)
- a focus on employee communications and information-sharing within the enterprise, such as through team-briefing
- a system (such as speak-up) enabling employee concerns and anxieties to be dealt with by management (rather than a union), as well as for contributing ideas which may help to improve organisational efficiency
- a commitment to providing secure and satisfying work while employed by the organisation, often involving regular moves to different types of job
- single status and harmonised employment policies between blue- and white-collar employees
- an individualised pay and appraisal system differentiating between staff in terms of previous performance and future potential, designed to reward those who contribute most to organisational success (eg performance-related or merit pay).

HRM AT WORK IN FOCUS

## Consultancy Co.: a non-union company

Consultancy Co. was founded in the mid-1990s as a micro company and it now employs 150 staff with offices in three countries. The company provides consultancy services in technology software, radio communications and security systems to a range of blue-chip companies and national and local governments. At the time of the research, financial turnover was in excess of £3 million per year.

Management emphasise 'success through people' and 'employee control' with non-traditional (ie non-bureaucratic) surveillance systems. A variety of sophisticated HRM and EI techniques seek to win employee 'hearts and minds'. Initiatives range from social bonding and team-building activities to self-managed/task-based involvement. Consultants regularly present papers at international business and technology conferences, work independently and in teams which are capable of determining their own work schedules. There is a paternalistic attitude to management and repeated attempts to engender a 'fun' side to work.

In an attempt to preserve this distinctive culture, when the number of employees grew beyond the limits of a single social circle, the owner-manager appointed a full time 'culture manager' and allocated 2% of company turnover (about £250,000) to culture management. The preservation of this cultural identity took several forms. Once recruited, management techniques sought to develop workers in line with the company's 'culture statement'. Top of the list includes having 'fun at work', which was actively encouraged. There was a strong emphasis on mutual 'trust and respect' both inside and outside the workplace, with employees at all levels on first-name terms. These ideas were underpinned by social activities funded from the culture budget, including weekend trips to Dublin, white-water canoeing in Wales, and a river cruise-cum-office party. There were regular inter-company football tournaments among staff when the men played and the women dressed as American-style cheer-leaders. More serious matters were also mixed with humour to encourage an informal atmosphere. Individual appraisal interviews and group inductions for new staff were regularly held as social events at the company's expense. At Consultancy Co. the whole approach was strongly influenced by the founding owner's ideas of paternalism and a desire to maintain a 'small firm culture'. Here social activities were not organic informal responses, as might be found in ties of friendship, but carefully designed to try to engender an attachment to Consultancy Co. and to persuade workers to 'work beyond contract'. One office employee remarked:

> 'It's a happy office, everyone's approachable, you're never left on your own and being a good team member is regarded as an important thing. I mean, there's no problem having a laugh with anyone. [The founding owner] is approachable as anyone.'

There was also a considerable emphasis placed on personal and professional development. All 12 directors were studying for the Institute of Directors professional examination, another 30 staff had attained the Institute of Electronic Engineers membership, four had doctorates and several were working toward MBAs. In addition, two separate company-wide training days were held each year when the whole workforce would be taken to a hotel to discuss new projects and receive company information. Management were keen to encourage two-way communication:

> 'Voice is about having opinions and observations heard. How voice is realised, recognised and acted upon is what matters. There is no "real" voice if it is not listened to.' (General Manager, Consultancy Co.)

Many employees were enthusiastic advocates of employee involvement. Most valued their in-house friendships and many enjoyed the social events. But tensions and problems still existed. Pay was set by the owner and no formal criteria on how individual performance was evaluated were published. This research was conducted when the company was performing well and the majority of employees were extremely well satisfied with the pay awards. However, clerical employees expressed concern about the lack of paid overtime, and other employees lower down the hierarchy were critical of both the long hours and difficulties achieving a performance pay award, as few worked exclusively on client (fee-earning) projects. Consultants were engaged in interesting and responsible work but taking ownership for decisions, actively negotiating contracts with clients and participating in social activities often demanded long hours at work.

To think about:

*The HR practices used by 'good' firms such as Constultancy Co. and those mentioned in Chapter 3 certainly look attractive to employees. Do they represent a cost-effective alternative to trade unions?*

Source: Adapted from Wilkinson *et al* (2007).

However, such organisations have not escaped criticism. It could be argued that 'sophisticated' employment practices are merely an illusion designed to obscure the true nature of HRM regimes, or that workers are merely 'conned' by their overt appeal into working harder, not for their own benefit but for that of the company. Similarly, it has been suggested that employers may continue to provide superior employment practices only under favourable economic and competitive conditions, and that product market problems will lead to their permanent or temporary withdrawal. In other words, the supposed employer commitment to employees as their 'most valuable resource' is both superficial and trite. In the case of a steel plant that widely publicised the introduction of a HRM approach and subsequently derecognised trade unions, employee gains proved illusory, with managerial strategy geared towards compliance, work intensification and the suppression of any counterbalancing trade union activity (Bacon 1999). Gollan's work (2002, 2006) on News International argued that attempts to have a substitution or union avoidance strategy with non-union representation structures failed as the body lacked legitimacy and power thus leading to employee dissatisfaction. There is also an argument that these sophisticated non-union organisations offer good benefits only because of the previous and continuing efforts of trade unions across the economy as a whole.

The second type of non-union firm is the traditional, sweatshop employer, often a small independent single-site company operating as a supplier to one of the sophisticated non-union organisations mentioned above. Managements deliberately depriving workers

**Table 26 Non-union management control approaches**

| Non-union approach | Type of anti-union behaviour and control |
|---|---|
| Fear stuff[1] | Union suppression: Employer behaviour here includes blatant intimidation of workers, the objective to instil a 'fear' (real or otherwise) of managerial reprisals to possible unionisation. |
| Sweet stuff[1] | Union substitution: Management argues that unions are unnecessary, with better terms and conditions and sophisticated employee voice channels to resolve any grievances. |
| Evil stuff[1] | Ideological opposition to unions: Management articulates the view that unions are 'reds under the beds', and will be destructive to the company performance. |
| Fatal stuff[1] | Blatant refusal: Employer behaviour here includes refusal to recognise a union, or at best refusal to 'bargain in good faith'. |
| Awkward stuff[2] | Stonewalling: Managers create what appear to be legitimate obstacles to union recognition, effectively employing 'delaying' tactics. |
| Tame stuff[2] | Damage limitation: Employer behaviour can take the form of 'sweetheart' deals, partly recognising 'moderate' unions or creating internal (managerially controlled) staff associations. |
| Harm stuff[2] | By-passing: Employer behaviour seeks to effectively marginalise collective employee voice, often through specific non-union communication channels. |

[1]Roy's (1980) original classification. [2]Gall's (2001) additional typologies.

Source: Adapted from Dundon, T. (2002b) 'Employer opposition and union avoidance in the UK', *Industrial Relations Journal*, Vol.33, No.3, 236, John Wiley and Sons Ltd

of their rights are categorised as 'ugly', whereas those offering poor terms and conditions without such manipulative intentions is referred to as 'bad'. The subordinate role many of these small suppliers have with a larger company – dependent, dominated and isolated – leaves them with little control over their own destiny and places a primacy on labour flexibility. These firms are under considerable pressure to control costs and enhance flexibility, goals many of these employers believe to be unachievable with interference by trade unions. Typically, pay rates are low, while formal fringe benefits and welfare arrangements are non-existent. The regime tends to be highly personalised (Scott *et al* 1989, p.42; Dundon and Wilkinson 2003; Scase 2003) and recruitment practices likely to reflect the owner/managers' deep distrust of unions. The lack of formal disciplinary procedures means that employee protection is haphazard and arbitrary at best, totally absent at worst (Wilkinson 1999). Guest and Conway (1999) termed firms without a union presence or high commitment HRM as 'a black hole', noting the lack of satisfaction and commitment and high propensity of employees to quit. In a study by Dundon *et al* (1999, pp.258–62) a personnel manager took the view that 'communicating to employees can be a dangerous thing. The current system of withholding information is a strategy that has been built up over the years and is used to keep employees on their toes.' At the same firm, an employee noted that the 'the firm is run by "family-men". What they say goes. It's as simple as that…and I can't see them giving that control up.' Of course not all small firms are run by sweatshop-type employers, and diversity a feature of the sector (see Edwards and Ram 2009). The range of non-union management approaches are summarised in Table 26.

## COLLECTIVE BARGAINING

Collective bargaining was a significant component of British employment relations from the end of the First World War through to the 1980s. It was the principal method by which wages and conditions were determined for a majority of the workforce although it has been described as a 'hollow shell' (Hyman 1997). Collective bargaining outcomes (in terms of wage levels, hours worked and holiday entitlements, for example) also influenced the terms and conditions of employees whose pay was determined by management alone. One reason suggested why paternalist employers offer superior terms and conditions of employment to those negotiated by trade unions, is to ensure that they remain union-free. In recent years, however, the prominence of collective bargaining has declined.

Collective bargaining is by no means restricted to formal confrontation. Indeed, negotiations take place continually between shop stewards, supervisors/line managers and personnel managers at workplace level on a wide range of matters concerned with working conditions, health and safety, discipline and grievance cases, and welfare/social concerns. It is an all pervasive social process that may be overt or covert, and informal or formal (Gospel and Palmer 1993, p.180). Thus, collective bargaining is a process occurring principally – in terms of the time involved and the number of issues dealt with – at workplace level through unwritten deals and custom and practice. Conversely, some of the more important and long-term decisions about pay and working conditions are the subject of infrequent company-wide or multi-employer negotiations.

It is also concerned with both **substantive** (what is determined) and **procedural** issues (how decisions are made) (Dundon 2011). Many of the blockages in bargaining occur not because of disputes about substantive matters (such as marginal increases in pay), but are due to disagreements about how employee relations are to be managed in the future – for example, over union de-recognition. In short, collective bargaining is both an adversarial and a co-operative process, one in which employees not only oppose managerial plans with which they disagree, but may also wish to improve management decisions that they feel are inadequate. In rare circumstances, unions may unilaterally set the rules, the other side of the coin to management prerogative. This was seen historically with the craft societies, which imposed their own employment rules on employers, for example by insisting on a specific period of apprenticeship or requiring all new workers to have a union card. It is also evident today in professions, such as lawyers and accountants, whose bodies operate in a similarly restrictive fashion.

The extensiveness of formal collective bargaining can be estimated from the WERS data. Seventy per cent of workplaces set pay for at least some of their employees unilaterally by management, but 27% set pay for at least some of their employees through collective bargaining with unions. But workplace size is an important factor with 65% of workplaces with 500 or more employees setting some pay through collective bargaining. In the public sector collective bargaining is found in over 80% of public sector workplaces (Kersley *et al* 2006, p.179). Sweeping changes in the political and legal environment in the last 20 years, together with changes in employment across sectors, have had a major impact on workplace union organisation such that the distinctive British system of adversarial collective bargaining is no longer characteristic of the economy as a whole. As Gospel and Wood (2003, p.5) point out, 'collective bargaining is no longer the dominant method of conducting employment relations' (see Table 27).

**Table 27 Joint regulation of terms and conditions**

| Issue | Per cent of workplaces | | | |
|---|---|---|---|---|
| | Nothing | Inform | Consult | Negotiate |
| Pay | 70 (16) | 6 (10) | 5 (13) | 18 (61) |
| Hours | 71 (18) | 5 (10) | 8 (20) | 16 (53) |
| Holidays | 71 (19) | 9 (17) | 5 (13) | 15 (52) |
| Pensions | 73 (22) | 11 (25) | 6 (16) | 10 (36) |
| Staff selection | 78 (42) | 10 (26) | 9 (23) | 3 (9) |
| Training | 75 (36) | 10 (24) | 13 (31) | 3 (9) |
| Grievance procedure | 69 (15) | 9 (20) | 14 (36) | 9 (28) |
| Disciplinary procedure | 69 (15) | 9 (21) | 13 (35) | 8 (29) |
| Staffing plans | 75 (33) | 11 (26) | 12 (34) | 3 (7) |
| Equal opportunities | 72 (22) | 10 (23) | 14 (40) | 5 (15) |
| Health and safety | 69 (17) | 9 (19) | 17 (49) | 5 (15) |
| Performance appraisal | 75 (33) | 9 (20) | 12 (33) | 4 (14) |

Base: All workplaces with 10 or more employees.

Source: Adapted from Kersley *et al* (2006).

The shape and character of collective bargaining varies considerably between workplaces, particularly in relation to the level at which bargaining takes place and the size/structure of the organisation covered by any agreement. The concept of bargaining level refers to the point(s) at which collective bargaining takes place, and it can range from workplace/section through to establishment, division, company and industry/multi-employer. In many cases terms and conditions are the subject of negotiation at more than one level in the hierarchy;

for example, the setting of holiday entitlements at industry level, pension arrangements at the company level, and wages and flexibility issues locally. In other words, bargaining can take place both on a multi- and a single-employer basis, as well as at a range of levels within a multi-establishment organisation. Since the 1980s managements (Sisson and Storey 2000) have been more prepared to make use of their superior bargaining power. Multi-employer bargaining has been replaced by single-employer bargaining, and decentralised unit-specific arrangements are more common. In these systems the role of the union may be marginalised as the employer focuses on direct communication with individual employees, and HR practices, such as performance-related pay, are managerially determined. In short, the scope of managerial prerogative has been extended (Tailby and Winchester 2000; Kessler and Purcell 2003; Sisson 2010). The impact of international competition on local collective bargaining is seen as an important factor as the scope for collective bargaining is seen as reduced given global market constraints (Brown *et al* 2009). The Boeing case in the USA shows how collective bargaining rights and business imperatives can be seen as conflicting.

HRM AT WORK IN FOCUS

## Boeing and the unions

In the USA in 2010, Boeing was accused of setting up a non-union production line in South Carolina as a way of retaliating against the striking of unionised workers in Washington State. While it is illegal to retaliate against workers for striking (or threatening workers in order to discourage strikes), companies are permitted to locate production in another state if it is seen as making business sense. Production stability is a legitimate business rationale. Boeing claimed it wished to diversify its assembly production to make it less vulnerable to disruptions caused by potential future strikes. Boeing also claimed that opening the line in South Carolina would not lead to lay-offs in Washington, where it is adding jobs. This wider issue raises a debate over labour protections in the USA in that while there is a right to collective bargaining, companies are able to work around this by going to another state, especially 'right-to-work' states, where workers cannot be required to join a union.

According to reports in the *New York Times* a labour board's lawyer says Boeing's decision to move the operation to South Carolina constituted illegal retaliation against Boeing's unionised workers in Washington for engaging in their legally protected right to strike, including a 58-day walkout in 2008.

Boeing has acknowledged that the fear of labour disruptions factored into its thinking, but it said the main reason for moving the line was South Carolina's lower production costs with pay at the South Carolina plant lower than that in Washington.

So the debate ranges from, on the one hand, the labour board being accused of trying to sabotage right-to-work states as well as the fundamental right of corporate managers to decide how and where to run their businesses while, on the other hand, it is seen as an attack on the rights of bargaining.

Source: Adapted from Greenhouse (2011); and Editorial (2011) 'Boeing and the N.L.R.B: is a move to South Carolina a way to avoid unions or retaliation against them?', *New York Times*. 26 April, A24.

## REFLECTIVE ACTIVITY

To what extent has the collapse of collective regulation removed employee influence in relation to setting terms and conditions?

For a large part of the twentieth century, multi-employer bargaining was considered to be the norm, and in some industries there was very little difference between the nationally negotiated wage rate and an individual's actual pay (Brown *et al* 2003). The last 30 years have seen a significant reduction in the extent of multi-employer bargaining. This has been influenced by pressures from increasingly competitive international product markets, the growth in large multidivisional corporations with profit and cost centre management and means to develop internal labour markets (Sisson and Storey 2000, p.197), and the fact that trade unions have been less able to resist moves to decentralise negotiations. Within the private sector as a whole, the decline has been pronounced with most pay being set at enterprise level by managers rather than by joint regulation (Terry 2003; Brown 2011).

A second trend has been the shift away from centralised bargaining arrangements towards on-site and unit-level negotiations (Gennard and Judge 2010, p.343). The aim has been to encourage units to take decisions themselves reflecting devolved responsibility for financial control (Sisson and Marginson 2003), although Sisson and Storey (2000, p.201) note that such control is often an illusion, as key issues of employment policy may be decided at high levels in the organisation.

## POLICIES AND PROCEDURES: ESSENTIAL OR OUTMODED?

### THE ROLE OF PROCEDURES IN EMPLOYMENT RELATIONS

Policies and procedures are defined as 'formal, conscious statements' that support organisational goals. They are the official way companies disseminate their policies as the leitmotif of acceptable practice (Sisson and Storey 2000). However, there is a difference between a 'policy' and a 'procedure'. As Dundon (2002a, pp.196–7) notes:

> Policies are written documents that outline defined rules, obligations and expectations for managers and employees. Typically, policy statements cover areas such as discipline, grievance, redundancy, reward, recruitment or promotion. The policy may be a statement of intent, such as 'it is the policy of this company to promote and reward high achievers'.

Procedures outline the details of how to enact a policy. For example, having a policy of 'rewarding high achievers' would require some guidance on how managers implement the policy, such as the criteria for promotion or how much they can reward an individual. Similarly, a discipline procedure would outline possible sanctions, areas of conduct and so on. Rules are there to see both sides play fair. As Dundon and Rollinson (2011, p.164) note, 'if one party to the employment situation fails to abide by the rules of the relationship, the other party can bring a procedure into play to attempt to get the offending party to adjust his/her behaviour; managers can use disciplinary procedures, and employees can use grievance mechanisms'. The scope and depth of HR policies and procedures can be used as a proxy for management style. The absence of policies and procedures can indicate an informal managerial approach, whereas very detailed policies and procedures could point to a formalised managerial style. Procedures are often seen as a product of the employee relations environment of the 1960s and 1970s in which there was a more explicit struggle for control at the workplace. This had two principal effects. First, it produced the need for clear procedures so that all employees were aware of works rules and the action that could be taken against them if rules were flouted. Second, it made for greater clarity and consistency in management action.

In contrast, the environment today is one in which trade unions are weaker, and managers have greater freedom to avoid some rules that supposedly constrain their ability to manage. Moreover, as the principal activities of many HR practitioners have shifted away from employment relations to employee development, resourcing and reward, the main guides to management action are seen as business need, flexibility and commitment rather than adherence to rules and procedures (Storey 2007; Lewin 2008). Previous appeals to consistency, compromise and regulations have been displaced by a new language of competitiveness, customers and commitment. As Lewin (2008) notes, strategic human resource theory envisions management creating a positive voice mechanism in which conflict either does not occur or, may occur but can be anticipated and dealt with 'proactively'. This is carried out through teams or joint labour management committees or informal discussions between supervisors and employees, employee forums, online chat rooms or even through grievance mediation. Human resource theory thus emphasises early stage conflict manifestation and resolution, in contrast to most other conflict theories that emphasise relationship deterioration and a reactive search for organisational justice. Storey's classic research (1992, p.178) highlighted the following criticisms of procedures:

> From the hard side [of HRM] comes the criticism that the long drawn out appeals and referrals are simply inappropriate in a fiercely competitive and fast-changing climate. From the soft side ... the regulator's arguments about due process and about honouring agreements and observing custom and practice are anathema.

However, this interpretation contains a number of problems. It is by no means obvious that emphasis on rules and procedures is outdated. Indeed, a belief in consistency and fairness is central to gaining employees' commitment (Bott 2003). What may appear as flexibility to managers may seem unfair and arbitrary treatment to an employee. As Gennard and Judge (2010, p.457) observe:

> every grievance, whether genuine or unfounded, is important to the individual concerned and has to be treated on its merits. When management receives a complaint which appears frivolous, it is not good practice to reject it without at least an investigation into how it has arisen. If this reveals the employee's complaint to be ill-founded, this must be explained to the individual. By acting on the basis of just cause after investigation and then behaving in a fair, reasonable, and consistent manner, management demonstrates to its employees that both unfounded and genuine complaints are treated seriously and in a businesslike manner.

Despite the rhetoric of high commitment management, which assumes workers are motivated to use discretionary effort, managers from different sectors report an extensive list of problem behaviour (Klaas 2008). This list includes such issues as chemical dependency, employees with weak ethical standards, managers who are personally abusive, employees whose performance spirals downward for no obvious reason, and employees who are unwilling to change their behaviour in response to changing conditions (Wheeler *et al* 2004). As Klaas (2008) notes, problem behaviour is a feature of organisational life and it rarely lends itself to easy solutions. Managers struggle with questions about whether they should look the other way, give the employee a chance to improve, and whether treating a problem employee fairly puts the organisation at undue risk (Butterfield *et al* 1996). From an employee point of view, 42 per cent of respondents reported a problem at work in the last five years (DTI 2006). In another DTI report (2007) more than two million British employees said they had experienced discrimination, bullying, sexual harassment or other unfair treatment at work in the previous two years and bullying alone affected almost one million employees. The most common reason given for unfair treatment was age, followed by long-term illness (both reported by 0.8% of employees). Next was 'accent or the way I speak' (0.5%), followed by race and ethnic group, disability, 'physical appearance', gender, 'being pregnant', nationality, and 'the way I dress' (all 0.4%). Union membership, religion and 'colour of skin' were reported by 0.3% of employees (Grainger and Fitzner 2007, p.3). The box below shows the scale of workplace conflict.

HRM AT WORK IN FOCUS

## Conflict and procedures

CIPD survey findings show the scale of workplace conflict. Of those who used each method, almost half say their organisation has increased its use of disciplinary action (49.5%), grievance procedures (47.7%) and mediation (49.4%) in the last two years. A high proportion of respondents said their organisation makes more use of mediation; also noteworthy is the number making increased use of training line managers in handling difficult conversations.

Two in three respondents (65.3%) say that troubleshooting by the HR department has gone up, reflecting the increased volume of disciplinary and grievance cases. We see only small percentages say that use of any of the methods listed has gone down (2011, p.2).

The number of days of management and HR time spent on managing both disciplinary and grievance cases has gone up since 1997 from 13 to 18 days (disciplinary) and nine to 14.4 days (grievance). There are however significant differences between sectors with the public sector taking more number of days in management time spent on handling grievances (nine days); this is two-thirds as high again as that in private services (five and a half days).

The great majority of discipline and grievance cases are resolved internally (85%), but the lower figure for the public sector (81%) suggests a somewhat greater willingness by employers and employees in that sector to call on outside help to resolve disputes.

Source: Adapted from CIPD (2011g).

Small firms are less likely to have formal policies in place, probably because owners rarely possess the specialist knowledge to construct such policies or the inclination/resources to employ professionals for this task (Wilkinson 1999; Edwards and Ram 2009). The owner is likely to work in close proximity to employees as well as managing the employment relationship (Ram 1994). This creates an environment of 'teamwork' (Goss 1991), but the team analogy is vulnerable when ownership authority must be reinforced. Evidence indicates that, rather than risk disruption of the 'team' environment, small-firm owners resist using formal policy or practice, preferring a negotiated solution to employment-related issues, which avoids overt conflict or workplace dissonance (Marlow 2002). As we saw above, this informality is now being tested by European Directives and recent employment legislation (Kersley *et al* 2006, p.234).

## REFLECTIVE ACTIVITY

How well does informality work in resolving workplace problems? Has such an approach been effective in your organisation or one with which you are familiar? Why do you think it was successful or unsuccessful in the circumstances?

Some procedures provide an automatic role for third-party intervention from the Advisory, Conciliation and Arbitration Service (Acas), whereas others may be tied to an agreement between employers' organisations and trade unions. Yet others make use of an independent arbitrator on an ad hoc basis. Intervention by a third party can be in one of three forms: conciliation, mediation and arbitration. With conciliation and mediation, assistance is provided when the parties have reached an impasse, but the parties themselves must resolve the issue. With conciliation, the third party must confine itself to facilitating discussion, while with mediation they come up with specific recommendations. Arbitration involves the third party (such as Acas) coming up with a decision to resolve the issue. It should be noted that Acas should not be used as a substitute for the establishment of joint union–management procedures for dispute resolution as this allows the parties to avoid taking responsibility and employee relations can be damaged if commitment to agreed procedures withers away (refer to Chapter 2 for more information on Acas).

### DISCIPLINARY PROCEDURES

The concept of unfair dismissal was first introduced by the *Industrial Relations Act 1971* and amended subsequently in the *Employment Protection (Consolidation) Act 1978 (EPCA)* and the *Employment Rights Act (ERA) 1996*. The *ERA 1996* obliges employers to ensure the principal statement of employment conditions makes reference to rules, disciplinary and appeals procedures (Gennard and Judge 2010, p.417). The 2002 *Employment Act* introduced a standard procedure but this had some unintended consequences. It appeared the statutory dispute resolution procedures, while introducing clarity about the formal steps required in pursuing grievance and discipline, has discouraged early resolution of problems:

> Rather than encouraging early resolution, the procedures have led to the use of formal processes to deal with problems which could have been resolved informally. This means that problems escalate, taking up more management time. Employees find themselves engaged in unnecessarily formal and stressful processes, which can create an expectation that the dispute will end in a tribunal. The complexity of the procedures and the penalties for failing to follow them mean that both employers and employees have tended to seek external advice earlier (Gibbons 2007, p.8).

The *Act* was subsequently repealed and replaced by a new Acas code in 2009. While breach of the code is not unlawful, tribunals do take account of the code in their cases (Gennard and Judge 2010, pp.416–24). The *Acas Guide to Discipline and Grievances at Work* (Acas 2009b, p.13) states: 'disciplinary procedures should be used primarily to help and encourage employees to improve rather than just a way of imposing punishment'. Organisational procedure should conform as closely as possible to the code of practice formulated by Acas (2009a) and its associated guide to good practice (2009b) (see also Suff 2010a, 2010b). Clearly, actions must be appropriate to the circumstances, so minor misconduct is usually dealt with by informal warning. Being five minutes late for example, is unlikely to lead to dismissal. Managers should not look simply to punish employees but to counsel them. For example, if performance is not up to standard, then management should investigate the reasons rather than just deal with the 'offence'. Employee performance may vary for many reasons such as lack of training, or problems at home and employees should be supported to improve rather than simply be punished. As we saw in Chapter 7, counselling should be seen as a positive rather than punitive action. Procedures should be designed to provide managers with the tools necessary to address problem behaviour, to help employees see the consequences of failing to comply with organisational expectations and understand that managerial actions are driven by standards of justice (Klaas 2008; Wheeler *et al* 2004). But this is premised on long-term relationships whereas other models may be based on more fluid labour markets that stress efficiency and managerial prerogative (Colvin 2003). They are much less concerned with due process and improving behaviour and more interested in quick fix hire and fire approaches.

Where employees feel that they have been dismissed unfairly, they can refer the case to an employment tribunal that determines whether or not the dismissal is automatically fair, automatically unfair, or potentially fair (Taylor and Emir 2009). The potentially fair reasons at the time of writing are:

- lack of capability
- misconduct
- redundancy
- a statutory requirement
- retirement of an employee
- some other substantial reason of a kind to justify the dismissal of an employee holding the position which that employee held (eg reorganisation of business).

Once the substantive case has been established, the question of whether the dismissal was fair or unfair can be determined, having regard to the reason shown by the employer. Fairness depends on whether in the circumstances – which include the size and administrative resources – the employer acted reasonably. Although the legislation provides for unfairly dismissed employees to be reinstated or re-engaged, in practice they tend to be awarded compensation. This normally comprises a basic compensatory award although where dismissal is for whistle-blowing or raising health and safety issues the compensatory award has no ceiling.

**REFLECTIVE ACTIVITY**

Think of an attempt at disciplinary action by an employer that went wrong, and explain why this occurred? What could have been done to stop this from going wrong?

It should also be recognised that discipline at work can have wider ramifications for the management of employee relations as dismissal and other disciplinary measures can be a cause of strike action. It is important to appreciate that discipline at work also involves self-discipline and peer discipline as well as managerial discipline, and that the first two have been given greater attention in recent years (Edwards 2000; Dunn and Wilkinson 2002; Parkin 2009; Macdonald 2010).

## GRIEVANCE AND DISPUTES PROCEDURES

A grievance is a complaint made by an employee about management behaviour (Gennard and Judge 2010; Wilkinson 2011). In the UK, grievances tend to be used widely and embrace both collective and individual issues reflecting the idea that the line between grievance (individual) and dispute (collective) can sometimes be a blurred one. However, in general, grievance procedures are used for handling individual issues, while collective issues are usually dealt with by disputes procedures. In practice some organisations have a combined procedure reflecting the fact that grievances are often likely to affect more than one employee, and others allow for grievances to be referred to the collective disputes procedure.

The types of grievances most commonly raised can be seen from Table 28. Clearly, pay and conditions come out highest with relations with supervisors/line managers next. Working time and working conditions are also prominent. However, it is particularly interesting to note that many managers (over half of all workplaces in 2004) reported no grievances has been raised over the previous year.

**Table 28 Types of grievances raised in 1998 and 2004**

| **Subject matter of grievance raised** | **Per cent of workplaces** | |
|---|---|---|
| | **1998** | **2004** |
| Pay and conditions | 25 | 18 |
| Relations with supervisors/line managers (ie unfair treatment/victimisation) | 16 | 16 |
| Work practices, work allocation or the pace of work | 14 | 12 |
| Working time, annual leave or time off | 13 | 10 |
| Physical working conditions or health and safety | 12 | 10 |
| Promotion, career development or internal transfers | 14 | 8 |
| Bullying at work | 3 | 7 |
| Job grading or classification | 13 | 6 |
| Performance appraisal | 7 | 4 |
| No grievances raised formally in past twelve months | 44 | 53 |

Base: all workplaces with 10 or more employees.

Source: Adapted from Kersley *et al* (2006).

In the USA, as Klaas (2009) notes, by providing employees with an effective voice mechanism, employers are able to reduce the appeal of unionisation. Use of procedures such as peer review has been found to be more likely in firms thought to be facing a greater threat of unionisation (Colvin 2004). In addition to these external pressures, firms are also likely to be motivated by internal factors. Providing employees with voice to challenge management decisions regarding discipline and other matters is generally viewed as consistent with high commitment work practices as it enhances employees' perceptions of procedural justice which may positively impact on employee motivation and commitment (Greenberg 2006; Coyle-Shapiro and Densha-Kahlon 2011; Wilkinson 2011).

The aim of a grievance procedure is to prevent issues and disagreements leading to major conflict and to prevent employees leaving. Even if an employee's grievance is the result of a fellow employee's action – as in racial or sexual harassment – the grievance is taken against management for failing to provide protection. As with discipline, the spirit with which the grievance procedure is approached is significant. It may be easy for management simply to follow the letter of the procedure, making it a hollow sham, but once this is known employees will not bother to refer issues to the procedure. Consequently, it is important that HR professionals encourage the proper use of procedures to uncover any problems, particularly where line managers wish to hide them because of fear that it shows them in a bad light. Open-door systems operate in some organisations that allow workers to take up grievances with managers directly rather than follow a lengthy procedure. However, this relies on managers taking the system seriously and being prepared to devote time and effort to keep it going.

Disputes procedures specify how collective grievances should be dealt with. The chain of complaint may go from the supervisor, or immediate line manager, to the departmental manager or personnel manager to senior management. It may provide for matters to be referred to a third party such as Acas if matters are not resolved. It is also important that the procedure is efficient and relatively quick. Clearly there is a balance between the time needed to reflect on the issue at hand, while ensuring that it is not 'lost' in the process because of the length of time involved.

## REFLECTIVE ACTIVITY

Get a copy of **two** organisations' grievance and disputes procedures, and compare them. What are the major differences between them and why? How might they be improved?

The *Employment Act 2002 (Dispute Resolution) Regulations 2004* imposed statutory procedures for the handling of disciplinary and grievance cases assists in the resolution of workplace disputes although merely following the minimum procedures did not necessarily ensure a dismissal is fair (Gaymer 2004, p.17). All employers were obliged to follow a statutory dismissal and disciplinary procedure (unless the existing procedures exceed the requirements of the acts). However, this was repealed by the *Employment Act 2008* which made the Acas code of Practice on *Discipline and Grievance* the main plank of disciplinary and grievance procedures although it is not legally binding (Gennard and Judge 2010, p.465). Dispute resolution mediation has taken on a more significant role with CIPD and Acas procedures being important in this regard.

In Table 29 below we see the different methods of dealing with workplace conflict in the UK.

**Table 29 Use of different methods of dealing with workplace conflict in last two years**

| | Increased | Decreased | Stayed the same |
|---|---|---|---|
| Disciplinary action | 49.5 | 8.6 | 41.9 |
| Grievance procedures | 47.7 | 10.3 | 42.1 |
| Internal or external mediation | 49.4 | 3.5 | 47.1 |
| Independent arbitration | 10.3 | 6.6 | 83.1 |
| Early neutral evaluation | 7.5 | 8.3 | 84.2 |
| Training line managers to handle difficult conversations | 61.5 | 6.9 | 31.6 |
| Troubleshooting by HR department | 65.3 | 7.3 | 27.5 |

Source: CIPD (2011g) *Conflict Management*. Survey Report. London, CIPD.

In conclusion, Lewin (2005) provides an interesting finding about grievance procedures. His research indicates that the *presence* or availability of a grievance procedure is positively associated with organisational performance, whereas actual *use* of a grievance procedure (grievance activity) is negatively associated with organisational performance. It appears that having a procedure may provide some reassurance and confidence to employees of the type of workplace in which they are working, but usage of the procedure may be seen as evidence of a breakdown in relationships.

## CONCLUSIONS

It is important to reiterate that employment relations, like all aspects of HRM, is characterised by conflict and co-operation. At certain times, and in certain workplaces, one of these can predominate. This sometimes gives the misguided impression that at one site or one point in time employment relations is solely conflict-based, whereas at another establishment or time it is seen as co-operative. Furthermore, just because conflict is not expressed overtly, this does not mean it is absent and the workplace is a haven of consent. It would appear that employment relations is becoming increasingly bifurcated, not so much between union and non-union organisations, but within each of these broad categories. Given the degree to which labour markets have been deregulated over the last 20 years, employers now have greater flexibility in choosing appropriate styles and structures for managing employment relations, as well as a greater opportunity to integrate human resource strategies with those shaping the business as a whole. To do this effectively, however, employers must embrace a more strategic approach to the management of employment relations, be aware of the techniques adopted by other employers, and disregard fads and fashions if these are inappropriate for their own workplace. How they do this, of course, is another question.

In this chapter we have emphasised how employment relations vary greatly between workplaces and organisations, and that HR managers are able to influence their eventual shape. In order to do this, however, HR practitioners need to be aware of the mix of different types of arrangement and their suitability for particular organisational contexts in order to make informed decisions about what is appropriate for each employment situation. We have also focused on the UK more than any other country but this is not meant to imply the UK is representative of what is happening elsewhere in the world – see Chapters 2 and 5 for more detail. Despite the convergence thesis from the 1950s which was given impetus by the forces of globalisation, we still see widespread diversity in employment relations practices across countries (Bamber *et al* 2011).

EXPLORE FURTHER

ACAS (2009a) *Discipline and Grievance at Work*. London: Acas.

ACAS (2009b) *Code of Practice 1: Disciplinary and Grievance Procedures*. London: Acas.

BACON, N. (2006) 'Employee relations', in T. Redman and A. Wilkinson (eds), *Contemporary Human Resource Management*. London: Financial Times/Prentice Hall, pp.188–208.

BAMBER, G., LANSBURY, R. and WAILES, N. (eds) (2011) *International and Comparative Employment Relations: Globalisation and change*, 5th edition. Crows Nest: Allen and Unwin.

BLYTON, P. and TURNBULL, P. (2004) *The Dynamics of Employee Relations*, 3rd edition. London: Macmillan.

BROWN, W. (2011) 'Industrial relations in Britian under New Labour, 1997–2010: a post mortem', *Journal of Industrial Relations*, Vol 53, No 3, 402–13.

DUNDON, T. and ROLLINSON, D. (2011) *Understanding Employment Relations*, 2nd edition. London: McGraw Hill.

GENNARD, J. and JUDGE, G. (2010) *Employee Relations*, 5th edition. London: CIPD.

KERSLEY, B., ALPIN, C., FORTH, J., BRYSON, J., BEWLEY, H. and OXENBRIDGE, S. (2006) *Inside the Workplace: Findings from the 2004 Workplace Employment Relations Survey*. London: Routledge.

MARCHINGTON, M., WILKINSON, A., ACKERS, P. and DUNDON, A. (2001) *Management Choice and Employee Voice*. London: CIPD.

CHAPTER 13

# Employee Involvement and Participation: Creating Engagement and Voice in the Workplace

## LEARNING OUTCOMES

By the end of the chapter, readers should be able to:

- provide advice to management on forms of employee involvement and participation (EIP) which might be appropriate for their own organisational context
- design an overall EIP system – including direct, indirect and informal practices as appropriate – and embed this into organisations
- provide advice on how employee engagement can be developed and measured within their own organisation.

In addition, they should understand and be able to explain:

- the role that direct and indirect forms of EIP play within organisations and more broadly in society
- the meaning of employee engagement and how this can harnessed to contribute to increased employee potential and commitment
- the ways in which informal and formal EIP interact and its implications for HRM.

## INTRODUCTION

The nature of employee participation in the UK has changed over the last 30 years. The 1970s model of participation reached its high point with the 1977 Bullock Report on 'Industrial Democracy', which addressed the question of how workers might be represented at board level. This emerged in a period of strong union bargaining power and the Labour government's 'Social Contract'. The Bullock Committee's approach to industrial participation had several distinctive features. It was partly union-initiated, through the Labour Party, and based on collectivist principles that saw trade unions playing a central part in future arrangements. In addition, it was wedded to the general principle of employee rights established on a statutory basis (Ackers *et al* 2006). Participation can be seen as a fundamental democratic right for workers to extend a degree of control over managerial decision-making in an organisation. This also brings in notions of free speech and human dignity (Budd 2004). Indeed the argument is that workplace democracy allows for the development of skills and values, which then have a role in broader society (Foley and Polyani 2006).

More recently we have seen a rather different animal – employee involvement and participation (EIP). The context initially was reduced union power and an anti-corporatist Thatcher government, which resisted statutory blueprints and encouraged firms to evolve the arrangements that best suited them. This agenda differed from that of the 1970s in several ways. First, it was management-initiated, often from outside the industrial relations sphere, and with scant reference to trade unions. Second, it was more individualist, and stressed direct communications with individual employees. Third, it was driven by business criteria concerning economic performance and the 'bottom line', with an emphasis on employee motivation and commitment (Ackers and Wilkinson 2000). Dutiful compliance and following rules no longer described the 'good worker'; instead, management demanded employee commitment, working beyond contract and exercising initiative (Smethurst 2003). The notion of high commitment HRM (see Chapter 3) made the case that long-term competitive advantage could only be achieved through people (Wood 2010; Wilkinson *et al* 2011).

Voice is also used in the literature in this area sometimes interchangeably with EIP. The academic concept of 'employee voice' was popularised by Freeman and Medoff (1984) who argued that it made good sense for both company and workforce to have a 'voice' mechanism. This had both a consensual and a conflictual image: on the one hand, employee voice could lead to a beneficial impact on quality and productivity; while on the other, it could identify and deal with problems (Gollan and Wilkinson 2007). Trade unions were seen as the best or indeed only agents to provide voice as they were independent. A variation of this strand has also looked at representative voice but taking account of non-union forms (Gollan 2010).

One way to make sense of the terminology is to see voice as an **outcome** of EIP processes. The debate on workers losing their voice was originally premised on union decline, but loss of union presence does not necessarily mean employees have a reduced appetite for voice or EIP. Voice does indeed extend beyond competiveness into shaping the psychological and economic well-being of employees and indeed the health of families as well as the quality of a country's democratic process (Budd and Zagelmeyer 2010). In countries such as the Ukraine, the lack of democratic experience at political level is reflected in EIP and voice at the organisational level (see box below).

HRM AT WORK IN FOCUS

## EIP in Ukrainian companies

Croucher examines the development of EIP in Ukrainian manufacturing and service companies. EIP was seen as central to improving the historically comparatively low quality of products and services in post-Soviet countries, and with foreign markets demanding increased quality from Ukrainian companies, it was apparent that the traditional command and control modes of operations and bureaucratic structures traditional in the former Soviet Union were barriers to improved performance.

In Ukraine, levels of employee autonomy in carrying out job tasks are low and the notion of involvement was largely unknown in Soviet enterprises. The main priority concern was with fulfilling the planned outputs by use of coercive measures, and workers whose outputs could be identified as falling short of quality standards were disciplined. In Ukraine, HRM is much closer to an American than a European version since it is more reliant on external than internal labour markets and envisages little role for unions. It is based on employees being in a weak bargaining position in relation to employers. Involvement and voice are issues raised by trade unions but their role of 'protecting workers' interests', is seen more as a 'watchdog' role rather than in mobilisation or bargaining terms. Workplace collective agreements are rarely reached by anything resembling collective bargaining and union functions are centred on employee welfare.

Western-style quality improvement schemes were a driver of limited forms of EIP. While the external and bureaucratic nature of the driver places limits on the depth of involvement, these companies remain innovative in the Ukrainian context. The strong perception in Ukraine that poor service and product quality hinders their efforts in global markets has created a strong view within many companies that employee involvement in production must be greatly improved. Moreover, the changes were driven by the most senior managers and both of these factors mean that the changes are likely to be permanent. Management hierarchy was reorganised emphasising the enterprise as a collective rather than as a hierarchy. Workers appeared to welcome these developments as it improved managers' understandings of the production process and the difficulties that they faced with regard to outmoded equipment and processes. But managements also ensured against allowing involvement to spill over into a strengthening of workers' collective voice.

Source: Adapted from Croucher.

The rest of this chapter reviews the notion of EIP and the varieties it can take in practice. Following an outline of the terminology, we consider direct EIP through the most recent idea in management parlance – employee engagement – before moving on to examine indirect EIP; this reviews the social partnership debate, and brings in material relating to European Works Councils (EWCs) and the Information and Consultation of Employees Regulations (ICER). We conclude by analysing the links between formal and informal EIP, as well as the advantages that employers can gain from embedding EIP more effectively within their HRM and organisational systems. We use the terminology of EIP to refer to practices and processes, whilst voice is treated as an outcome of EIP.

## THE MEANING OF EMPLOYEE INVOLVEMENT AND PARTICIPATION (EIP)

Unlike notions of industrial democracy, which are rooted in employee rights, EIP stems from an economic efficiency argument. It is seen to make business sense to involve employees, as a committed workforce is likely to understand better what the organisation is trying to do and be more prepared to contribute to its efficient operation. But management decides whether or not employees are to be involved and how they will be involved. EIP in its most limited forms could be characterised as a move away from 'you will do this' to 'this is why you will do this' (Wilkinson *et al* 1993, p.28). There is no doubt the sizeable growth in direct EIP and communications during the 1980s as management stepped up their communication with employees as a whole and WERS confirmed the growth in EIP and communication (Gomez *et al* 2010). However this tells us relatively little about the character of EIP as experienced by ordinary employees.

EIP systems allow for workers to have a say (or voice) which potentially allows staff to influence events at work, and can bring together collective and individual techniques into one framework. HR managers typically play an important role in the choices made about

EIP in identifying the options available, forming alliances with line managers and devising strategies for implementation. Generally, a broad mix of factors shape management choice. For some, rational choice is about satisfying employee expectations, particularly when faced with tight labour markets; others equate choice with their own understanding of corporate and organisational objectives. In smaller and family-run enterprises this often relates to the personal styles and characteristics of owner-managers. Some managers may feel that they have no choice, either because employees demand 'a say' or due to market pressures and new legislative requirements (Dundon *et al* 2004). On the whole, however, management decide whether or not workers have a say, and it is managers rather than employees who decide what EIP mechanisms to utilise. Thus the main aim of this approach to EIP reflects a management agenda concerned with increasing understanding and commitment from employees and securing an enhanced contribution to the organisation. Thus, while some forms may provide employees with new channels through which their influence is enhanced, facilitating employee voice via EIP systems does not involve any *de jure* sharing of authority or power (Kaufman and Taras 2010).

External influences also shape management choice, evident across large and small as well as single and multi-site organisations. Legislation for trade union recognition or the requirement to establish an EWC (see below) means that choices are made to comply with legislation. Much of the extant research is about how EIP structures are established and the motivation for them and how they operate in practice. Other research takes a largely institutional view – that is failure is the decline or collapse of the structure. The assumption is that setting up a structure of itself sorts the problem (Dietz *et al* 2009). But many EIP systems have 'deaf ears' and frustration can arise (Harlos 2001), as we can see in the case of the Bundaberg Hospital (see box below).

HRM AT WORK IN FOCUS

## Dr Death at Bundaberg Hospital – EIP systems failure

At Bundaberg EIP processes failed. This made international news in 2005 after a doctor at the hospital was estimated to have caused at least 18 deaths through negligence. While medical tragedies (and errors) are by no means novel, the case revealed that a number of staff had raised concerns over the doctor on a range of incidents spanning two years prior to his departure but these had not been acted upon. In the end a nurse acted as a whistle-blower and went outside the formal EIP system and approached a member of parliament to ensure action was taken.

As in many hospitals there was an array of EIP structures including incident reports, the complaint management system and grievance procedures. But these procedures can be time-consuming. During Doctor Patel's two years of employment there were no fewer than 20 complaints made against him relating to competence, unnecessary surgery, performing surgery beyond his skills and hygiene. But none of these complaints were acted upon and Patel even won employee of the month with his contract extended.

The hospital had a multiplicity of EIP channels and staff were professionally trained and motivated. This was not a group dealing with widgets or car parts. They had a strong professional and ethical background, and helping patients was at the cornerstone of their values. The matters being dealt with could not be more serious. But the EIP system appeared not to be taken seriously or given priority. First, managers were ill-trained and not prepared to operate the system, so EIP was overridden by the need to stick to some sense of professional etiquette and courtesy. Second, there was some uncertainty as to which processes should be used. Third, there was a concern that any EIP process exercised would be ignored, which undermined the process further. Fourth, EIP process was one thing but action was another, and in the complex world of hospitals it was not clear who was to take responsibility for action. The critical lynchpins were line managers. The testimony of staff spoke about the perception that managers did not have time for their complaints, and that other issues took priority. Here we see staff reading between the lines. They read the culture as one where staff should be encouraged by senior management if the latter wanted them to express views.

It was also hard for management to 'look at the big picture'. When all the isolated incidents were put together it was easier to see Patel's incompetence. But information was fragmented across various EIP channels. Staff either felt they could not use the channels as management had not given their blessing to do so, or argued that the vehicle was wrong. A culture of blame existed in the hospital which was deep rooted with nurses willing to complete incident report forms for faulty equipment, but not for clinical error.

While there appeared a plentiful array of EIP structures, in practice the system was a patchwork of disparate channels and dead ends. So managers heard voices via the EIP systems but under pressure of time and resources as well as being sensitive to issues of power and professionalism, discounted some voices or set the bar so high that single voices were ignored unless there was corroborating data, but then never sought to access such data. In practice, much voice was deemed illegitimate; so neither formal nor informal EIP system proved effective in this case.

Source: Adapted from Florens (2006); Forster (2005) and Wilkinson *et al* (2011).

It is important to unpick the purpose, meaning and subsequent impact of employee participation and to this end a fourfold framework can be used; including the 'degree', 'level', 'scope' and 'form' of participation schemes in practice (Marchington *et al* 1992; Marchington and Wilkinson 2005; Wilkinson *et al* 2011).

First is the *degree* of say that employees have about organisational decisions (Marchington and Wilkinson 2005). A greater degree may be when employees, either directly or indirectly, can influence those decisions that are normally reserved for management. The other end of the continuum may be a shallow degree, evident when employees are simply informed of management decisions (see Figure 11 below).

Second is the *level* at which participation takes place. This can be at a work group, department, plant or corporate level. What is significant here is whether the schemes adopted take place at an appropriate managerial level. For example, involvement over future strategy would in most incidences be inappropriate given that most team leaders would not have the authority to redesign organisational strategy.

Third is the *scope* of participation, that is, the topics on which employees can contribute. This ranges from relatively minor – such as car parking spaces – to more substantive issues, such as future investment or plant relocation.

Finally is the *form* that participation takes, which can a combination of direct, indirect, informal and financial schemes:

- *Direct EIP* is where employees are personally involved in a formal practice – such as team briefing, upward problem-solving and suggestion schemes. Evidence suggests that these forms of EIP were amongst the most extensive in Europe (Kessler *et al* 2004) and the Anglo-American world (Freeman *et al* 2007).
- *Indirect* EIP is where workers are represented by one of their co-workers or trade union officials on a formal committee, such as for joint consultation (JCC) or health and safety. JCCs occupied a prime place in the UK employment relations system, operating either as an adjunct to collective bargaining or as a potential alternative (Marchington and Cox 2007), but now they are much less extensive; for example WERS found that JCCs were present in just 14% of workplaces where more than 25 people were employed compared with over one-third 30 years ago. Partnership agreements have become more widespread, as we see later in the chapter, and there has been increased use of European Works Councils and Company Boards in UK firms that operate in a range of countries (Dobbins and Gunnigle 2009; Johnstone *et al* 2009; Lavelle *et al* 2010; Hall *et al* 2011).
- *Informal* EIP is less well-researched as most studies focus on formal EIP, but given the decline in union presence in many countries and growth in customer-facing service sector firms it has been seen either as a substitute for or a supplement to formal schemes (Marchington and Suter 2012). It also fits with the notion of employee engagement and the idea that processes are more important than formal structures (MacLeod and Clarke 2009).
- *Financial involvement* encompasses schemes that link part of an individual's reward to the success of the unit or enterprise as a whole and has been the object of much attention since the 1980s. This takes a variety of forms, ranging from profit-sharing and employee share ownership through to ESOPs (employee share ownership plans) (Kessler 2010). Financial involvement assumes that employees with a financial stake in the overall success of the unit/enterprise are more likely to work harder for its ultimate success; this is covered in Chapter 14.

**Figure 11 The Degree of EIP**

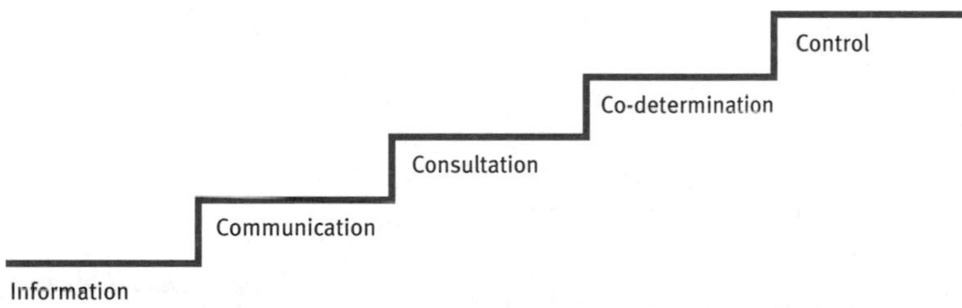


Source: Marchington *et al* (1992)

Taken together this framework provides a description, not only of the type of involvement and participation schemes in use, but the extent to which they empower employees (Wilkinson *et al* 2011). It shows that involvement and participation is more complex than a straightforward continuum from no involvement (information) to extensive worker participation (control) and that schemes can overlap and co-exist. For example, the use of collective bargaining and joint consultation does not mean that management abandons other communication techniques. Power in the employment relationship is an important variable, and systems can be differentiated by the methods used (direct or indirect classifications), the level at which participation takes place (individual or board-room level), and the extent to which any particular technique is employee or management-centred).

EIP schemes can be seen as a rejection of the classical school of management which emphasised a strict division of labour, with workers as 'machine minders', carrying out fragmented and repetitive jobs (Wilkinson 1998). They imply a neo-unitarist, win-win approach, which is moralistic in tone, and is 'represented as squaring the circle of organisational needs for high levels of employee performance and employees' demands for autonomy and self-expression in work' (Claydon and Doyle 1996, p.13). An example of a company where EIP has been successfully implemented is given in the box below.

HRM AT WORK IN FOCUS

## Midbank

Midbank is a clearing bank with regional roots, employing around 4,000 staff in over 100 locations in the UK. Like most financial institutions, the company provides HR support from a centralised base although many HR processes have been devolved to line managers. The small size of the branches facilitates a more informal atmosphere than in the call centres. New performance management tools have recently been agreed with the union for the call centres and their introduction has provided better terms and conditions, and resulted in reduced turnover, increased productivity and improved career progression.

A single union has sole negotiating rights for staff and membership is well over 70%. Union presence in the workplace is in the form of local representatives as well as one full-time seconded representative. National joint partnership meetings are held monthly, supported by local and departmental partnership forums between the union and management representatives. These local forums concentrate on resolving local business-related matters, thereby enabling the national partnership team to concentrate on wider issues. A separate consultation forum is the company's Staff Council, which enables elected representatives from all areas of the business to meet with senior managers to discuss bank-wide business related matters. There is also a well established quarterly company newspaper, to which staff are encouraged to contribute. Attitude surveys, focus groups and suggestion schemes – one member of staff recently received £25,000 – are also regular features. Midbank's partnership approach commits it to measuring and reporting on issues that staff themselves identify as important.

As a result, Midbank won a *Sunday Times* award for its commitment to best practice HRM and employee involvement.

*To think about:*

*What purpose do these different forms of EIP serve? Identify ways in which these practices could be improved.*

There is a danger that these programmes are viewed solely in a positive manner, ignoring the contested and mundane nature of much participation. For example, rather than leading to autonomy and self-management, it may merely produce greater work intensification, increased stress levels and redundancies (Wilkinson 2002; Martinez-Lucio 2010). There is a fear that employers are exchanging strong union-centred forms of participation for EIP initiatives that are 'weak on power'. As one HR manager noted, 'there are plenty of vehicles for staff to have a voice, but the question is whether his voice is being heard and whether action is being taken as a result of this. And that's debatable' (Marchington *et al* 2001, p.24). As we have seen, EIP can vary by degree, scope, level and form. Some forms are purposely designed to give workers a very modest role in decision-making, while others are intended to give the workforce a substantial amount of power in organisational governance.

The rise of EIP has coincided with the decline of indirect, representative participation such as JCCs which are built upon the notion of indirect participation and worker representation in joint management–employee meetings. The scope of joint consultation is typically wider than collective bargaining – and may for instance, include financial matters – although the issues discussed are not formally negotiated. For some, they represent a diluted form of collective bargaining, and the shift in interest towards consultation reflects a decline in collectivism. However, JCCs can take a number of forms, often contrasting sharply with each other in terms of their objectives, structures and processes. Some researchers suggest that joint consultation has been revitalised in order to cover issues traditionally dealt with through collective bargaining, and involve stewards more closely with management issues in order to convince them of the 'logic' of their decisions. Others have argued that the committees have largely been concerned with trivia and are thus marginal to the employee relations processes of the organisation. In some organisations, JCCs can act as a safety valve (ie an alternative to industrial action) through which deep-seated employee grievances are addressed, while in others they are used to hinder the recognition of trade unions or undermine their activities in highly unionised workplaces. Elsewhere they may be irrelevant to management–employee relations, merely debating trivia. The relationship between collective bargaining and joint consultation in unionised workplaces can be a source of tension, particularly if management is trying to 'edge out' the unions and there has been a failure to engage in meaningful consultations.

## REFLECTIVE ACTIVITY

How does an organisation choose which EIP structures are appropriate for its employees? In practice, how effective are such structures? What are seen as the main barriers?

Research by Dundon *et al* (2004) found that EIP systems could impact positively in three general ways. The first is valuing employee contributions. This might lead to improved employee attitudes and behaviours, loyalty, commitment and co-operative relations. The second impact relates to improved performance, including productivity and individual performance, lower absenteeism and (in a few cases) new business arising from the usage of EIP. The final impact relates to improved managerial systems. This incorporates the managerial benefits from tapping into employee ideas, the informative and educational role of EIP along with improved relations with recognised trade unions.

## FROM DIRECT EIP TO EMPLOYEE ENGAGEMENT

Direct EIP is now far and away the most extensively used form, taking in a range of different methods and practices, not just in the UK but also in many other countries (Marchington and Kynighou 2012). For ease of analysis these can be separated into downward communications, upward problem-solving and task-based participation. Each of these is briefly reviewed below:

- *Downward communication* from managers to employees, the principal purpose of which is to inform and 'educate' staff so that they accept management plans. This represents the most dilute form of EIP and includes techniques such as team briefing, formal written media such as employee reports, house journals or company newspapers, and videos used to convey messages about the organisation's financial performance or to publicise some new managerial initiative. These techniques provide employees with greater amounts of information from managers than most enjoyed previously. In theory, employers gain because employees are 'educated' about the needs of the business and utilise their greater knowledge base to improve customer service or product quality, so helping to sustain competitive advantage (Wilkinson *et al* 2012). The principles behind direct EIP are simple. They rely on bringing together small 'natural' groups of staff at pre-determined times (eg, once a week or four times per annum) to hear about new developments direct from their supervisor. Information is cascaded down the organisational hierarchy, either through face-to-face meetings or via written or electronic means. For the most part, methods such as team briefing are one-way but there is usually an opportunity for employees to raise issues that can be taken back up the management chain (Marchington and Wilkinson 2005).

- *Upward problem-solving* is designed to tap into employee knowledge and opinion, either at an individual level or through small groups. The objective is to increase the stock of ideas within an organisation, to encourage co-operative relations at work, and to legitimise change. These include quality circles, or action teams, suggestion schemes and attitude surveys (Marchington and Cox 2007). Problem-solving groups are what is termed 'off-line', that is when groups of managerial and non-managerial staff discuss issues related to quality and other work-related questions away from their immediate workplace, perhaps in a meeting room. They sometimes include experts from specific areas that come along to advise the problem-solving group on how to tackle an issue or the resources that might be required to make a recommendation work. Attitude surveys and suggestions schemes are more overt in asking for employee views; in the case of the former in response to a set of predetermined questions which **should** then be used to address concerns – though this does not always happen – whilst the latter is a device used to get ideas from workers for which they are paid a token amount (Marchington and Cox 2007). In theory these schemes offer employees the prospect of greater opportunities to contribute to work-related issues, and employers the possibility of higher levels of productivity and quality (Geary 2003; Wilkinson 2007).
- *Task participation and teamworking*, in which employees are encouraged or expected to extend the range and type of tasks undertaken at work. As with the previous categories, these are individualist in nature, and some have their roots in quality of working life experiments from the 1960s and 1970s (Procter and Mueller 2000). Examples of task participation are horizontal job redesign, job enrichment and teamworking, each of which featured in a number of chemical and vehicle components companies that operate production systems on a relatively autonomous teamwork basis (Delarue *et al* 2007). Task-based participation is probably the most innovative method of EIP, given that it encompasses the whole job. In addition, unlike team briefing or quality circles, which can be viewed as additional or incidental to working arrangements, this is integral to work itself (Geary and Dobbins 2001; Wilkinson and Dundon 2010). This is taken up again towards the end of Chapter 14.

'Engagement' has been the latest buzzword to excite the pulses of practitioners, if not academics, in the area of participation. The CIPD (2011) define it as 'a combination of commitment to the organisation and its values, plus a willingness to help out colleagues. It goes beyond job satisfaction and is not simply motivation. Engagement is something the employee has to offer: it cannot be "required" as part of the employment contract.'

A number of reports suggest there is value in engaging staff more widely. A Watson Wyatt study (2009) indicated that a company with highly engaged employees achieves a financial performance four times better than those with poor engagement. Other reports also excitedly report on potential gains with Gallup finding more highly engaged staff take an average of 2.5 days sick days per year whereas disengaged staff take 6.2 days per year (Harter *et al* 2006). Welbourne (2011) reports how at a recent Conference Board meeting on employee engagement, the audience was asked how their organisations defined employee engagement; they actually provided definitions by relating the concept to traditional academic areas of work (eg job satisfaction, job involvement, commitment, organisation citizenship), to emotional descriptors (eg when employees love the company), to statements about well-being and fairness (eg people bring their 'whole selves' to work) and lastly to company-specific programs (eg inspiration, innovation, creativity, caring for the community). She points out that authors also have attempted to break employee engagement up into various parts, such as psychological state engagement, behavioural engagement, and trait engagement (Macey and Schneider 2008). But it has not been without criticism. As she notes, a Forbes writer Luisa Kroll (2005), quoting Randall MacDonald

**Table 30 The words of employee engagement**

| **Authors** | **Theories or other literature cited when discussing definitions of employee engagement** |
|---|---|
| Macey and Schneider (2008) | Involvement, commitment, attachment, mood, citizenship behaviour, effort, pro-social behaviour, disposition, loyalty, productivity, ownership, job satisfaction, and at some point they point out that it could be 'some combination of the above' |
| Saks (2006) | Organisational commitment, organisational citizenship, emotional and intellectual commitment, discretionary effort, attention, absorption, antithesis of burnout, energy, involvement, efficacy, cynicism, exhaustion, state of mind, vigour, dedication, absorption |
| Ferrer (2005) | Job satisfaction, enthusiasm, motivation for work, positive attitude, feeling involved and valued, organisation commitment |
| Report to the UK government by MacLeod and Clarke (2009) | Commitment, energy, potential, creativity, personal attachment to work, positive attitude, authentic values, trust, fairness, mutual respect, discretionary effort, job satisfaction |
| The Conference Board report on Employee Engagement (2006) | Cognitive commitment, emotional attachment, connection, discretionary effort, emotional drivers (pride, relationships with manager), rational drivers (pay and benefits), satisfaction. Focus on drivers of engagement, which include trust and integrity, nature of the job, line of sight between individual and company performance, career growth, pride, co-worker and team relationships, employee development, and relationship with one's manager |
| Kular *et al* (2008) | Role performance, intellectual and emotional commitment, discretionary effort, passion for work, job involvement, flow, organisation citizenship behaviours |

Source: Welbourne (2011).

of IBM saying, 'Soon we'll be talking about marrying all those employees to whom we're engaged'. Welbourne (2011) suggests that the beauty of employee engagement is that it can be everything to everybody, and most people think it sounds good. As she points out, employee engagement speaks to something most social scientists, employees and managers truly believe, and that is the fact that when employees go 'above and beyond' and are not robots just doing a simple, repetitive job, then organisations do better. It is worth noting that much of the literature about employee engagement can be found in practitioner journals where it is the latest fad. See Table 30 which illustrates how broad and all-encompassing employee engagement has become.

In the UK, the Macleod report entitled *Engaging for Success* was designed to open a national discussion on the subject but the assumption behind this was not to debate the merits of the idea but to work out how best to implement it given a recognition that one size does not fit all. But while his may be the case, Purcell (2010) shows there are key common factors linking the experience of work to organisational commitment and engagement for most employees. Drawing from the WERS data he notes that it is possible to divide between eight main occupational groups and find the factors significantly linked to positive commitment for all or most occupations. These are:

- employee trust in management (significant for all occupations)
- satisfaction with the work itself (significant for seven of the eight occupations)
- satisfaction with involvement in decision-making at the workplace (significant for six of the eight occupations)
- quality of relationships between management and employees, sometimes called 'employee relations climate' (significant for five of the eight occupations)
- satisfaction with the amount of pay received (significant for five of the eight occupations)
- job challenge (significant for five of the eight occupations)
- satisfaction with sense of achievement from work (significant for four of the eight occupational groups).

Trust in management was highly significant for all occupations, closely followed by job satisfaction and involvement in decision-making. These factors can be seen as the basic building blocks for employee engagement. From the WERS data not all employees appear engaged and, indeed, the number who are 'fully engaged', defined as scoring highly on every dimension, is often less than one in five. On a scale of one to five, where one is 'fully disengaged' and five is 'fully engaged' with three meaning 'neither engaged nor disengaged', the expectation would be that the bulk of employees in a well-functioning firm would be 'engaged' (ie score four) and the median score would be over three. Lower levels of engagement are also more likely to be found where there is perceived unfairness in rewards, where there is bullying and harassment and where people believe they are stuck in their jobs and feel isolated from open communications. All this clearly has implications for line managers (Purcell 2010, p.4).

The Macleod report notes that the same four broad enablers or drivers were cited as being critical to employee engagement (see box below).

HRM AT WORK IN FOCUS

### The enablers of engagement

*Leadership* 'provides a strong strategic narrative which has widespread ownership and commitment from managers and employees at all levels. The narrative is a clearly expressed story about what the purpose of an organisation is, why it has the broad vision it has, and how an individual contributes to that purpose. Employees have a clear line of sight between their job and the narrative, and understand where their work fits in. These aims and values are reflected in a strong, transparent and explicit organisational culture and way of working.'

*Engaging managers* 'are at the heart of this organisational culture – they facilitate and empower rather than control or restrict their staff; they treat their staff with appreciation and respect and show commitment to developing, increasing and rewarding the capabilities of those they manage.'

*Voice* 'An effective and empowered employee voice – employees' views are sought out; they are listened to and see that their opinions count and make a difference. They speak out and challenge when appropriate. A strong sense of listening and of responsiveness permeates the organisation, enabled by effective communication.'

*Integrity* 'Behaviour throughout the organisation is consistent with stated values, leading to trust and a sense of integrity.'

Source: Adapted from MacLeod and Clarke (2009).

A CIPD study by Truss *et al* (2006, pp.30–37) found that whilst one third of their respondents could be described as actively engaged, over half were only moderately engaged; less than 10% were actively disengaged. This is reflected in a series of other questions; for example, about half the sample would recommend their organisation to someone who sought their advice about a job opportunity or would encourage friends and relatives to do business with the organisation compared with around 20% disagreeing with these statements. Equally, about 60% felt emotionally engaged with their own job, in terms of really putting their heart into it or getting excited when they perform well. In addition, whilst quite a few respondents had actively searched for another job, almost 20% had never even thought of doing so and over 50% had never actually made any effort to quit their present employment.

Alfes *et al* (2010) find the main drivers for engagement in were meaningful work, voice, senior management communication style and vision, supportive work environment, person–job fit and line management style. They also reported that engagement was clearly associated with high levels of performance, reduced intent to quit and raised levels of personal well-being. One issue in this area relates to the reciprocity of engagement. One can see why employers would like to get employees working harder or smarter because they are engaged, but what is the return for employees? Or what can employers provide to support employees better? Another neglected dimension is whether engagement is always a good outcome.

## REFLECTIVE ACTIVITY

What can organisations do to get workers to be more engaged at work? Is it a win-win for managers and workers? Can staff be too engaged? How about the issue of work–life balance?

## REPRESENTATIVE PARTICIPATION

### SOCIAL PARTNERSHIP

The public policy context has changed markedly through the development of social partnership, which has led to a revival in representative participation. The European Union concept of social dialogue centres on partnership between employers and employees, through representative bodies, such as trades unions and works councils. It also advocates participation as an extension of employee citizenship rights. Ferner and Hyman (1998) suggest social partnership has three characteristics: it acknowledges that workers have different interests from managers, it encourages their representation, and it believes such an approach can be effective in regulating work and the labour market. Partnership can also be viewed at different levels – for example, European, national, state, sectoral and enterprise level – but the focus here is at enterprise level, because the UK lacks the institutional and legislative support afforded in most other Western European nations. The idea of

**Table 31 Elements of social partnership**

| Partnership element | IPA | TUC | Classification |
|---|---|---|---|
| A joint declaration of commitment to organisational success | ✓ | ✓ | Values Commitment |
| Mutual recognition of the legitimate role and interests of management, employees and trade unions where present | ✓ | ✓ | Values Commitment |
| Commitment and effort to develop and sustain trust between the organisation's constituencies | ✓ | | Values Commitment |
| Means for sharing information [IPA]/Transparency [TUC] | ✓ | ✓ | Process |
| Consultation and employee involvement, with representative arrangements for an 'independent employee voice' [IPA]/Transparency [TUC] | ✓ | ✓ | Process |
| Policies to balance flexibility with employment security [IPA/TUC] | ✓ | ✓ | Outcome |
| Sharing organisational success [IPA] | ✓ | | Outcome |
| Adding value [TUC] | | ✓ | Outcome |
| Improving the quality of working life [TUC] | | ✓ | Outcome |

Source: Adapted from Johnstone *et al* (2009) John Wiley & Sons Ltd.

employment relationship with goals, rather than concentrating on the largely economic implications for employees. But the value of Budd's framework is that it explicitly sets out the three dimensions that have run through a long debate in the field of employment relations. First, efficiency matters because it creates stable employment at the company level and growth at national level, for the benefit of shareholders, employees and society. Second, equity matters because employees and society care about the distribution of benefits. Third, EIP systems and voice matter because in a democratic society employees should have some say over how decisions are made.

Budd's call for 'balance' has caused controversy, as it could be perceived as suggesting the achievement of some kind of stable equilibrium, and raises concerns as to whether this is actually achievable. Adams (2005, p.115) proposes a slightly modified objective: 'optimality within minimally accepted bounds ... societies should attempt to optimise efficiency, equity and voice – but the result might not be an equal weighting of all three objectives'. In other words, the aim should be to achieve sufficient levels of voice and equity compatible with high levels of efficiency. Budd (2005) acknowledges this criticism, and suggests that 'balance' need not necessarily be thought of as an *equal* weighting between the three dimensions, but rather as 'the search for arrangements that enhance one or more dimensions without undue sacrifices in other dimensions' (Budd 2005, p.196). He suggests that they can usefully be viewed more as a 'regulative ideal' even if they are never realised or cannot be easily measured. The point is that employment relations in a socially regulated, liberal democratic, capitalist society should modify the goal of efficiency by equity and voice (Johnstone *et al* 2011).

## EUROPEAN INITIATIVES TO INCREASE EIP AND VOICE

The *European Works Council (EWC) Directive* requires employers to set up an EWC or equivalent information and consultation procedure if they have at least 1,000 employees in order to ensure that employees are informed and consulted within the organisations where they work. There is scope for the negotiation of customised agreements, but in the event of failure to agree, a standard package will apply. In broad terms, this provides a template for the composition of the EWC and its remit, as well as a stipulation that an annual meeting should take place. The EWC is informed and consulted about the enterprise's progress and prospects in a number of areas, including the broad financial and employment situation, as well as trends in employment and substantial changes in working methods.

Some see this Directive as one of the most far-reaching and important developments in European industrial relations, while others regard it as far too weak to make any substantial difference. On the positive side, EWCs have been seen as an opportunity for management to communicate corporate strategy, to facilitate discussion of change, to encourage international contact, to facilitate employee identification with the company, build a 'European' culture, and to enhance management–union partnerships. Trade unions and employee representatives in turn gain access to useful company information to facilitate collective bargaining (Cressey 1998). Trade union criticisms have centred on the limited capacity of EWCs to effectively influence managerial prerogative in multinational companies (Gumbrell-McCormick and Hyman 2010). Timming (2007) shows a darker side to managerial strategies in a UK-based European Works Council (EWC), but from the perspective of workers' representatives it shows how employers' representatives in central management were proactively fragmenting worker voice, arguably in order to convert the EWC into a business-friendly instrument and to assert managerial control. However, he found no suggestion that such tactics yield organisational benefits with the employer's strategies reflecting the traditional cultural antagonisms within the particular sector in which the firm is embedded.

More recent developments have created a policy dialectic that shapes management choice for EIP and voice (Ackers *et al* 2005). The broader environment is supportive of both neo-liberal policies and flexible markets, yet at the same time seems sympathetic to issues concerning union recognition, individual employment rights as well as emergent collective-type regulations (Ewing 2003). The UK government transposed the European Employee Information and Consultation Directive with the statutory *ICE 2004 Regulations* that provide **all** employees (union and non-union) with the right to receive information and to be consulted on a range of employment and business-related matters.

The implications of these regulations were potentially far-reaching. For the first time employees in the UK have the legal right to be informed and consulted on a range of business and employment matters, should they wish. Crucially, the ICE Regulations define employee *information* as 'data transmitted by the employer to the information and consultation representative; or, in the case of a negotiated agreement, directly to employees'. Running alongside this *consultation* is defined as 'the exchange of views and establishment of dialogue between the information and consultation representative and employer; or, in case of a negotiated agreement, the employee and employer'. The *scope* of information and consultation relates to three specific areas, and each area progressively increases the *degree* to which employees may exercise a greater influence over managerial decisions. First, employers are obliged to share 'information pertaining to the economic situation of the organisation'. Second, an employer must 'inform and consult on the structure and probable development of employment, including threats to employment'. The final area is potentially the most significant, where an employer must 'inform and consult, with a view to reaching agreement, on decisions likely to lead to changes in work organisation or contractual relations'.

We already know that the form, scope, degree and level of EIP is linked with managerial power. Consequently this new statutory framework for information and consultation could lead to a shift in power relations because it provides both potential levers for employees to exert pressure as well as giving a new normative framework where expectations may change the baseline of acceptable practice (Dundon *et al* 2006). However, recent research suggests that the impact on UK employment relations has not been very significant although the regulations have prompted considerable voluntary activity in terms of reviewing, modifying and introducing information and consultation arrangements, but all this has been largely employer-led. Trade unions have shown ambivalence towards the legislation and there has been low uptake of its provisions by employees (Hall 2010).

### REFLECTIVE ACTIVITY

What impact has the directive had on your organisation or one with which you are familiar?

## LINKS BETWEEN INFORMAL AND FORMAL EIP

There is now an increased awareness that formal EIP systems – whether direct or indirect – can never be sufficient on their own to embed voice at the workplace, or ensure that workers believe it is meaningful (Marchington and Cox 2007). Without active support from line managers, EIP systems are likely to fall into disrepute, and have little meaning for workers whose voice they are meant to be catching. For example, team briefing sessions might be postponed or abandoned because line managers believe they have more important priorities than communicating a formal message to their staff or seeking their views about quality. Similarly, even if the briefing system does operate according to plan, this has only limited effect if, in between these sessions, managers make it clear they do not value workers' opinions. In such situations, unless workers have access to independent representative voice through trade unions, they have little opportunity to hear about company plans or articulate their ideas to management. Although there has been research into the relationship between direct and indirect EIP (Marchington *et al* 1993; Dundon *et al* 2004; Bryson 2004; Cox *et al* 2007; Freeman *et al* 2007), the links between formal and informal EIP, especially in organisations with limited formal systems, has not really been explored.

Several authors (Boxall *et al* 2007; Mohr and Zoghi 2008; Townsend *et al* 2011a; Marchington and Suter 2012) have suggested that informal EIP is an important component of the mix of EIP practices that operate at workplace level. Whilst formal EIP relates to prearranged and regular practices / concrete structures – the practices that are typically captured in most studies and surveys – informal EIP refers to ad hoc or non-programmed interactions between managers and their staff which provide opportunities for information-passing, consultation and the seeking of ideas. Relatively little attention has been paid to informal EIP, and most definitions refer to methods, mechanisms and structures rather than processes and face-to-face dialogue (for example, Dundon and Rollinson 2004; Wilkinson *et al* 2010). Strauss (1998, p.15) defines informal participation as 'the day-to-day relations between supervisors and subordinates in which the latter are allowed substantial input into decisions … a process which allows workers to exert some influence over their work and the conditions under which they work.' 'Substantial input' accords rather too great a degree of influence to informal EIP, and the Strauss definition fails to include information-passing which is a major component of EIP in most organisations, but at least this has the virtue of looking beyond formal practices. Strauss (1998, pp.17–18) acknowledges the distinction is not always clear; he suggests that 'a boss may meet her subordinates around a table to discuss work problems in pursuance of a written quality circle plan; this is formal participation. Or the individuals may gather informally to discuss the same problems around a water cooler; this is informal participation'.

Managers appear to find informal EIP valuable. They can use informal interactions to let workers hear about new developments in work organisation and provide opportunities for them to discuss issues with their manager. As Purcell and Georgiadis (2007, p.197) note, 'employers who want to gain the maximum value from voice systems would do well to note that all the evidence points to the need for direct face-to-face exchange with employees at their work stations and in groups'. This is attractive to line managers because it provides them with opportunities to explain issues directly to workers and some choice about whether or not to accept their ideas (Marchington *et al* 2001). It also allows them to develop closer relationships with some employees more than with others (Liden *et al* 2004).

In the study of RestaurantCo by Marchington and Suter (2012), all the branch managers believed that informal EIP was critical to effective operations in restaurants where close teamworking and interaction with customers was pivotal. The notion of devolved decision-making came up regularly, especially where it had implications for how staff worked together and it could improve operations; for example, seeking ideas on how to design seating plans in the restaurant, or taking over responsibility for how tips were distributed and tables handed over to the next shift. Managerial preference for informal, rather than formal, EIP came across very strongly during the interviews as well, with views that one-to-one discussions achieved a lot more than formal meetings, partly because employees felt uncomfortable speaking in large groups but also it was seen as a more effective way to solve problems. Another branch manager reported that informal chats accounted for the vast majority of what he learned about the restaurant. In short, managers regarded informal EIP as crucial to the generation of worker commitment to the goals of the restaurant, as well as helping to make it a more pleasant environment in which to work. In another study, managers in hotels also liked informal EIP (Townsend *et al* 2011a; see Box 13.6 below).

Workers also seem to like informal EIP. For example, Gollan (2006) notes that email and word-of-mouth were cited as particularly valuable, whereas Kessler *et al* (2004, pp.528–9) found, from their study of different EU countries, that one-to-one meetings and informal discussions proved much more useful than arm's-length forms of communication such as newsletters or notice boards. Marchington and Suter (2012) found that workers preferred informal to formal EIP, and that the former, with the exception of team briefing, had a stronger and more consistent association with commitment and satisfaction than did formal practices.

Links obviously occur between formal and informal EIP. First, they can operate in parallel, with each being used for different issues and/or for different degrees of involvement. Formal systems may be more useful if senior managers wish to cascade information down the hierarchy and ensure it reaches the maximum number of staff possible. In a situation where there are diverse staffing patterns, this can only really be done by written communications via notice boards or newsletters. To be effective, however, these formal methods need to be updated regularly and placed in locations where they are visible. One of the managers in the Marchington and Suter (2012) study suggested 'there are some things for the notice-board, some things that have to be said individually and some things that need to be said in a meeting'. Whilst written formal communications tend to be used for information-passing, informal interactions are used when managers feel consultation is needed.

Second, formal systems act as a safety net for informal EIP to ensure that a wide cross-section of workers receives information or have the chance to offer their views at team briefings. Whilst informal EIP might be preferred, it can be overlooked if managers are busy with operational issues; again one of the restaurant managers in the Marchington and Suter (2012) study was adamant that some back-up via formal systems is required. He said: 'when it comes to being informal, sometimes it is hard for a manager to be really involved with your staff because you are busy and pre-occupied. Before you realise it they have already left, so having the newsletter and the notice-board means they are going to see that.'

Third, and most significantly, formal and informal EIP can interact sequentially to lubricate the wheels of participation. Managers tend to use informal EIP to ask what employees think about new ideas or changes that are being planned before these are raised via the formal machinery, because it offers a chance to reflect before they are formally discussed. The informal system can also act to follow up on formal announcements, particularly when these are likely to raise concerns. Managerial preference for informality is clear but it is tempered by a realisation that formal practices offer additional support that helps to sustain EIP.

HRM AT WORK IN FOCUS

## Formal and informal EIP in hotels

Many aspects of the service industry operate on a continuous production model – servicing the customer 24 hours a day, seven days a week. While the increase in data management can provide managers with better expectations of managing line balance in service sectors, unexpected pressures brought about by sudden surges in customer demand remain. As such, planning formal meetings can be difficult and furthermore having large proportions of often casual and part time staff available in a continuous service operation presents substantial practical difficulties. These pressures have an impact on the success of any formal EIP mechanisms. As such, informal processes often fill the gaps left between the occasional formal mechanisms.

The hotel researched operates with a moderate degree of *formal EIP*.

On a daily basis, employees within each section will be involved in a 'team brief /changeover meeting' where the workload for the day will be discussed and employees given an opportunity to speak about issues that concern them. Employees have an electronic 'suggestion box' to direct ideas and concerns, and each of the departments also has monthly departmental meetings. Again, this forum is primarily about department heads and senior managers communicating to the employee's information that they feel is required, for example, upcoming specials within the hotel, major functions for the month, and overall hotel performance data. Employees have the opportunity to ask for items to be included on the agenda, or to raise them from the floor; however, this was very rare. On an annual basis the employees complete an 'Employee Opinion Survey' (EOS). Given the low propensity for employees to use other voice mechanisms at this hotel, this is just one more forum for employees to have a say; there is adequate evidence to suggest that there are substantial benefits to the formal voice mechanism.

Overall, because formal structures within the hotel are not adequate in providing the employees the opportunities they need to have a say over what affects them in their work, *informal EIP* was critically important. Managers made it clear that the service component of their organisation meant that continual meetings to allow employees to have a say was simply not possible and they needed to capture the thoughts and requirements of employees in other ways. When we consider a full-time employee's standard 40 hours of work each week or eight hours a day, it is clear that with all the formal mechanisms in place, on average, employees experience opportunities for formal voice for just a few minutes each day. It is therefore critical for employees and managers alike to have other avenues to address concerns about work and the way the work is performed.

Without exception, employees and managers in this hotel provide support for informal EIP and the central role it plays in the workplace. Starting from the top of the hierarchy, the general manager explains the informal approach in his hotel:

'Ninety-nine per cent of the stuff will be done informally, yes you will tick your boxes on workplace health and safety (meetings) and yes you will have your (formal) audit ... But 99 per cent of the stuff is solved outside, ... and we can address so much there before that cancerous feeling goes throughout your hotel ... People are not formal and people don't want to be tied up in meetings ... and to be honest, they (line staff) know the business far better than we do, without a doubt in the world.'

He later adds, 'my view again is that informality is king'. This view is embraced by line managers and employees alike who value the capacity to voice their opinions and concerns informally.

Source: Adapted from Townsend *et al* (2011a).

## EMBEDDING EIP AT WORK

Increasingly, research suggests that employers have a range of EIP structures (Bryson *et al* 2010), and there is evidence that employees want a range of channels. Equally, while there is talk of EIP systems, much of the data suggest employers have ad hoc practices reflecting history rather than a fine-tuned employee EIP strategy. So, EIP systems are not always embedded in the workplace and can be fragile both in terms of the structure but also the efficacy (Cox *et al* 2009). Pyman *et al* (2006) argue that a critical issue is the configuration of multiple channels rather than a single channel. Furthermore, they question how and why different channels complement each other and under what conditions multiple arrangements are sustainable. They conclude that the interaction and co-existence of multiple channels and plurality of arrangements are most effective and legitimate from an employee's perspective in achieving organisational outcomes. Similarly, Handel and Levine (2004, p.14) point out that bundles should be more effective than the simple sum of effects for the individual practices, and hence the existence of EIP schemes may tell us little about the quality of the process (Wilkinson and Fay 2011).

Comparing countries, the provision for EIP varies considerably (Lansbury and Wailes 2008). Thus in European countries, government policy and legislation provides for a statutory right to voice in certain areas among both union and non-union establishments; this is by no means typical. Other countries, including the USA and Australia, have much less emphasis on statutory provisions for EIP, with more emphasis on the preferences of managers and unions to establish their own arrangements. In many organisations the result is a mixed cocktail of direct and indirect EIP. It is also worth noting that depending on the societal regime within which employee voice is situated, the benefits tend to be seen from rather different perspectives. Thus, in liberal market economies, EIP and voice is seen in terms of contribution to profit and shareholder value at the organisational level and in customer service, and product quality and staff retention at the workplace level. Issues to do with worker commitment, job satisfaction and alignment with organisational goals are often the proxies used to measure the success of EIP schemes, but in themselves these may tell us little about the impact of particular schemes on the bottom-line or the consolidation of management prerogative.

In CMEs, the focus is longer-term and more widely defined in terms of a range of stakeholder interests including that of the government, employers, trade unions and workers. The focus is on peak level institution representation. In other words, in these situations the expectation is more likely to be of mutual gains, either at the level of the individual employing organisation or more broadly in terms of citizenship and long-term social cohesion (Wilkinson *et al* 2010a). As Budd and Zagelmeyer (2010) remind us, voice is not necessarily a private affair and it is not simply about improving economic performance.

Cox *et al* (2006, 2009) illustrate that many studies of EIP use measures of absence and presence alone to provide a measure of EIP, rather than examining how these practices are *implemented and perceived* at workplace level. This is a very narrow way to evaluate the significance of EIP for a number of reasons. First, relying on questions about absence or presence takes no account of *how* these schemes work in practice; for example, one organisation may hold problem-solving groups every six months whilst at another it happens every morning as a prelude to work or every week to allow for staff training. Similarly, a briefing scheme in one organisation may just be a vehicle for supervisors to inform staff about developments with little or no chance for them to ask questions or engage in discussion, whilst in another it may have been designed specifically to incorporate an opportunity for debate. Second, asking questions about absence or presence, without any follow-up about the proportion of workers involved, overlooks the possibility that only a minority of those employed are able to take advantage of the scheme. Finally, questions about extensiveness tell us nothing about the importance of particular EIP practices within an organisation. A technique may have been in operation for many years but be marginal to everything that occurs in the workplace; for example, a JCC could be a tangential, albeit rather pleasant, talking shop or a briefing group only to tell workers information they already know or are not interested in. Cox *et al* (2006, 2009) used the concept of embeddedness (Granovetter 1985) to assess how individual EIP practices and the system as a whole are configured within organisations and developed this to analyse the *breadth* and *depth* of EIP, which have now been used by several authors (for example, Butler 2009; Danford *et al* 2009) in more recent work.

*Breadth* can be measured by the number of EIP practices operating at the workplace. Single EIP practices are likely, other things being equal, to have less effect than a number of practices operating together because they lack reinforcement. They can be more easily dismissed as 'bolted-on' or out of line with other HR practices, and not taken seriously by workers. Combinations of EIP provide the potential for employees to be involved in different ways. For example, employees can receive information from and ask questions of their line managers through team briefings, give their views on aspects of work via surveys, resolve issues about quality through problem-solving groups and interact with their representatives who can exercise collective influence at establishment level through meetings with senior managers. Information received in one forum can be used in others, and influence on decision-making at a more senior level can help to shape employment relations at workplace level. If managers show they value employee views and share information, this helps to build trust.

*Depth* can be assessed, amongst other things, by the frequency with which meetings take place, the opportunity for employees (or their representatives) to raise issues and the relevance and importance of subjects considered at meetings. The more frequently meetings take place, and the more that employees are directly involved in the process – for example, via their contribution to team briefings or to problem-solving groups – then the more embedded the practice, and potentially the stronger and more positive its association with employee perceptions. Without regular meetings to discuss views, issues may be forgotten and without opportunities for upward communication, employees may assume their views are not sincerely valued. Conversely, regular and frequent use of EIP helps build expertise and familiarity with their operations among managers and employees so both parties may commit more to, and gain more from, the process. Survival of the mechanisms in an organisation over time may indicate commitment to making them worthwhile and useful. Greater depth reduces the possibility that techniques will be regarded as superficial. The box below provides an example of how EIP can be embedded within an organisation to achieve organisational gains.

HRM AT WORK IN FOCUS

## EIP at Delta Airlines

Delta Airlines' employment strategy focused on customer service and positive employment practices in order to foster co-operation through non-union relations. In the 1990s competitive pressures led to wage cuts and downsizing. Out of this crisis came an EIP programme designed to provide pilots with a non-voting seat on the board in exchange for contract concessions. While EIP had not been originally part of the paternalistic family model it became central to the new competitive strategy.

The employee involvement (EI) infrastructure has three main components:

1 At the top level is the Delta Board Council, which provides employee input at the board and top executive level on the entire spectrum of

business and HR issues facing the company.

2 The middle level is composed of five division-level employee councils. Each forum/council deals with issues that affect operations and employees of the specific division (such as on-board passenger service, work schedules for flight attendants, training requirements and engine overhaul cycle time for mechanics).

3 At the bottom of the organisational pyramid are two major EI groups. The first is over 100 small-scale 'continuous improvement teams', which are convened as needed by either management or employees. They are usually six to 10 people in size, and focus on work-process improvements. Team members volunteer and rotate on an informal basis. Complementing these, but with a broader focus and mandate, are employee councils at the individual base, station or hub facility.

The Delta EI programme is supplemented with a variety of other initiatives. For example, twice a year a large group – including 200 frontline employees – from around the world are invited to attend a 'State of the Company Leadership Meeting'. The president and the top executive team attend and are available to answer questions following presentations. Other important events include the monthly CEO forum at which eight employees get to talk to the president for 90 minutes; and a monthly presidential breakfast at which the president and CEO provide a company update and answers questions for 80 employees.

This case illustrates profound changes in the way companies are structured and managed. Few companies have developed EIP programmes with the breadth and depth as Delta's. High-level EIP changes the way a company does business, and has both benefits and costs that have to be carefully considered. The response of airline companies to the events of 9/11 illustrates this clearly. Because of the dramatic drop in passenger traffic, every major airline had to reduce capacity and cut costs. Whilst most acted quickly and unilaterally to avoid major lay-offs, Delta did not lay-off, but partnered with its employees and, with their help, two months later rolled out a voluntary leave programme. In the short run, Delta's business model cost it money that other airlines were able to bring down to the bottom line. However, the other companies also ended up with a demoralised, angry and insecure workforce and a business operation that a year later had badly deteriorated, threatening several with bankruptcy. In contrast, Delta employees, while reeling from events, nonetheless came together stronger than ever and worked as a committed, unified team to save the company.

In 2009 Delta merged with North Western airlines (which had a union history) and a key question was whether the new North Western employees would tip the balance towards a majority vote for a union. In fact in 2010, flight attendants, in the largest union election in more than 30 years, chose by 9,500 to 8,700 to have NO union.

Source: Adapted from Kaufman (2003) and Kaufman (2012).

## CONCLUSIONS

It is clear there are competing visions and expectations of EIP that vary between organisations and countries depending on motives and underlying philosophical stances. Whilst some employers might support forms of representative participation, such as partnership, others prefer to restrict EIP to direct and informal mechanisms. While EIP has important democratic implications, given a choice most managers tend only to be interested if there is a perceived pay-off. That might be seen in terms of avoiding problems due to the early warning system EIP can offer, or it could represent a more positive role in terms of contributing to the better running of organisations. However, for EIP to have legitimacy it needs to offer more than managerial concepts of efficiency and added value.

EIP does not exist in a vacuum and choice is likely to be affected by other components of HRM and management style, as well as external factors. Informal EIP often plays a role but is not always embedded in the EIP system effectively (Marchington and Suter 2012). Wood and de Menezes (2008, p.676) conclude that management's *overall orientation* to EIP can be more significant than the installation of any specific practice. Equally, Bryson *et al* (2006, p.438) believe that managerial responsiveness to the process of participation at shop-floor level is just as important for labour productivity as the existence of a formal EIP regime. Just as with HRM in general, EIP may need to be bundled and then embedded to produce a pay-off. Once implemented, there seems to be a life cycle in relation to specific schemes because EIP is a fragile plant which needs care and attention to allow it to flourish. Management behaviour lies at the heart of its success.

EXPLORE FURTHER


ALFES, K., TRUSS, C., SOANE, E.C., REES, C. and GATENBY, M. (2010) *Creating an Engaged Workforce*. Wimbledon: CIPD.

BOXALL, P., FREEMAN, R.B. and HAYNES, P. (2007) *What Workers Say: Employee Voice in the Anglo-American Workplace*. Ithaca: Cornell University Press.

BRYSON, A., GOMEZ, R. and WILLMAN, P. (2010) 'Voice in the Wilderness: The shift from union to non union voice in Britain', in A. Wilkinson, P. Gollan, M. Marchington and D. Lewin (eds) *The Oxford Handbook of Participation in Organisations*. Oxford: Oxford University Press.

COX, A., MARCHINGTON, M. and SUTER, J. (2009) 'Employee involvement and participation: developing the concept of institutional embeddedness', *International Journal of Human Resource Management*, Vol.20, No.10, 2150–68.

DIETZ, G., WILKINSON, A. and REDMAN, T. (2009) 'Involvement and participation' in A. Wilkinson, N. Bacon, T. Redman and S. Snell (eds) *The Sage Handbook of Human Resource Management*. London, Sage.

GEARY J. and TRIF A. (2011) 'Workplace Partnership and the Balance of Advantage: A Critical Case Analysis', *British Journal of Industrial Relations*, Vol.49, 44–69.

JOHNSTONE, S., ACKERS, P. and WILKINSON, A. (2009) 'The British partnership phenomenon: A ten year review', *Human Resource Management Journal*, Vol.16, No.3, 260–75.

MACEY, W.H. and SCHNEIDER, B. (2008) 'The meaning of employee engagement', *Industrial and Organisational Psychology*, Vol.1, 3–30.

MACLEOD, D. and CLARKE, N. (2009) *Engaging for success: Enhancing performance through employee engagement*, report to the government. Department for Business, Innovation and Skills.

MARCHINGTON, M. and SUTER, J. (2012) 'Where informality really matters: patterns of employee involvement and participation in a non-union firm', *Industrial Relations*.

WILKINSON, A., GOLLAN, P., MARCHINGTON, M. and LEWIN, D. (eds) (2010) *The Oxford Handbook of Employee Participation in Organisations*. Oxford: Oxford University Press.

CHAPTER 14

# Reward Management

## LEARNING OUTCOMES

By the end of this chapter, readers should be able to:

- advise management on the circumstances under which different payment systems may be appropriate for their organisation
- outline the case for and against the introduction of performance-related pay and specify the conditions under which it is appropriate
- understand the advantages and disadvantages of different methods of job evaluation.

In addition, readers should understand and be able to explain:

- the importance of linking pay schemes to wider organisational goals and other HR strategies
- how well-devised reward management practices can contribute to enhanced employee motivation and satisfaction at work
- the principal characteristics of other elements of the benefits package and their implications for HR practice.

## INTRODUCTION

The sight of employees sprinting away from the workplace at the end of the day suggests many workers are not that well-motivated. Studies also show that even where labour turnover – a widely used indicator of employee satisfaction – is limited, this may obscure deep-rooted discontent as employees feel they have little choice but to remain with their current employer because of the economic situation or their lack of transferable skills. The term used in the USA for this area, 'compensation', is telling. You get compensation for something bad which has happened – an accident, death or disaster. So work is seen as a similarly traumatic event which is inflicted on one who has to earn a crust. Compensation is required to take account of the terrible experience you have when you go to work. This explains the traditional emphasis on money in the reward literature.

Certainly money is a factor that can motivate people at work, but even here things are not straightforward. Many people are motivated to work hard regardless of financial reward, and for some the level of monetary reward is important symbolically – as recognition of worth (Fay 2011a). Clearly there are other benefits from being at work as well as money – such as activity, variety, status and social contacts. In recent years there has been a growing emphasis in the literature that reward should be utilised as a strategic tool to manage corporate performance and to influence corporate values and beliefs (Lawler 2000; Kessler 2007; Perkins and White 2011), rather than just as a technique to recruit, retain and motivate staff. Reward strategy as a concept moves rewards away from being a procedural issue concerned with the technicalities of complex pay structures and job evaluation (Fay 2011b).

In this chapter we examine reward management in context as well as a range of different pay schemes. It is important the reward philosophy reflects the overall objectives of the employer, and that different elements of the package send a clear and consistent message to employees. Moreover, as organisations become flatter and promotion opportunities are reduced, even more emphasis is placed on the recognition and reward elements of the pay system. We also discuss job evaluation and equal value, as well as look at benefits other than pay – including non-financial recognition.

## REWARD MANAGEMENT IN CONTEXT

Reward management is a key element in the strategic approach to HRM for a number of reasons. First, it is a mechanism by which employers aim to elicit effort and performance; second, the actual payment system may require adjustment to develop motivation; and third, it is often a significant part of the employer's financial strategy (Hendry 1994, p.343). Such an approach ties in well with the HRM ideal, which sees policies designed around strategic choices rather than simply reflecting environmental pressures. This means that there is unlikely to be a state-of-the-art, 'one size fits all' set of practices suitable for all organisations, and managers need to develop a 'fit' between remuneration policies and the strategic objectives of the organisation (Fay 2011b; Storey 2007; White and Druker 2008; Perkins and White 2011). However, the extent to which remuneration is used as a strategic tool in practice is more open to doubt. Management tend to assess or reassess one part of the remuneration package but often fail to analyse the whole system. The notion of 'total reward' (Bremen and McMullen 2010) is more myth and hype than reality. Furthermore, management tends to have a whole host of objectives for remuneration policy but these sometimes contradict one another, and their wider implications are not always clearly thought through.

When examining the reward package as a whole, however, it is important to consider other benefits – financial and non-financial – that provide the total reward experience for employees. If we take into account the various schools of thought on motivation and reward it is clear that pay is only one element of the total reward package and benefits are not usually seen in a strategic way but taken as 'givens'. Expectancy theory however, suggests that a more contingent view needs to be taken, and that it may make sense to individualise rewards, a notion that has led to considerable interest in 'cafeteria' benefits.

In the reward management literature most attention has been focused on pay since this is often seen as a key lever of change, and much less attention has been devoted to benefits such as pensions and sick pay. Indeed, other benefits have often been seen as fixed, despite the fact that many employers pay above the statutory minimum. The benefits package has itself been subject to fads and fashions, with many employers merely reacting by adjusting benefits to address short-term problems such as recruitment and retention, rather than adopting a long-term approach (Corby *et al* 2008). In the field of pensions, probably the largest item in the benefits package, there has been an absence of strategic thinking (Taylor 2008; Fay 2011d), yet it should be apparent from our discussion of motivation that terms and conditions beyond pay can be very significant in the overall reward package.

The employment relationship assumes that employees will give their time to the organisation in return for a reward, which will include money but may also include other factors such as status or job satisfaction. However, this is by no means a simple process as work is not precisely specified and / or different employees may expect different rewards. Because many factors are not specified in the contract – work intensity and supervision for example – the effort bargain can only be established over time by custom and practice. However, the effort bargain is potentially unstable because factors change, and the relationships may come to be perceived by one party as compromised. For example, at a time of recession managers may attempt to change working practices to increase

**Table 32 Driving reward strategy forward**

| Reformed reward strategy driver | Relationship to reward strategy |
|---|---|
| More competitive product markets | Greater employee productivity needs to be generated through making it a key driver of reward strategy |
| More competitive product markets dictating need for greater cost control | Greater emphasis upon cash bonuses (eg in team pay or IPRP schemes) which are not consolidated into base pay |
| The drive for more customer-focused organisational cultures | Greater need for reward strategies which emphasise the demonstration of customer-focused behaviours as a key performance criterion |
| More competitive product markets in key occupations | Reward strategies which are designed to attract and retain key employees (eg paying for competence acquisition, high performance) (see Schuster and Zingheim 1999) |
| Low inflation economies | Greater need for self-financing reward mechanisms, eg output-related performance-related pay, gain sharing |
| Adoption of new technologies | Reward strategies which are designed to pay employees for acquiring new competences become more important |
| Increase in flexible organisation structures and work practices | Enhanced importance of flexible reward practices |
| Flatter organisation structures resulting in fewer promotion opportunities | Alternative ways of rewarding employees who are effective need to be adopted (eg IPRP) |
| Changing career expectations of employees | Declining likelihood of employees staying with organisations most of their careers mean loyalty less important than effectiveness so rewards schemes need to reflect individual effectiveness. Less attention paid to service-related pay |
| The decline of collective bargaining | Less emphasis upon across-the board pay settlements to apply to all employees means greater opportunity for managers to differentiate between the pay of individuals and teams |
| The rise of HRM and high commitment work practices | Increase in initiatives such as employee involvement and teamwork lead to search for reward initiatives which complement these |

Source: Lewis, D. (2006) 'Reward Management', in T. Redman and A. Wilkinson (eds), *Contemporary Human Resource Management*. London, Pearson Education Ltd.

productivity, whereas workers may perceive this as a breach of custom and practice, so leading to potential conflict (Baldamus 1961). The achievement of fairness is central to the issue of payment, and however well bonus schemes are devised it is unlikely to be effective if it is perceived to be unfair and undermine the psychological contract. As Brown and Walsh (1994, p.443) observe, 'the prudent personnel manager devotes far less time to devising new pay incentives than to tending old notions of fairness'. However, as they point out 'there is nothing absolute about fairness in pay', as it is 'a normative idea' based on comparison (p.443). Equity theory suggests people will be better motivated if they feel they are treated equally and demotivated if they are treated unequally. This has been referred to as the 'felt-fair' principle (Armstrong 2002, p.61). Fair is, of course, subjective. People doing the same work may have different notions of 'felt fairness' (Jaques 1962). The effects of underpayment may be dissatisfaction: eg lateness, lack of co-operation, absence. The issue of felt-fairness raises the question of 'fair in relation to what?' All employees derive their judgement of what feels fair from comparisons with other individuals and groups. These comparisons at an individual level may be related to the qualifications and experience of a colleague, or to the level of performance which the employee thinks the colleague delivers (Lewis 2006, p.130).

Thus, when people compare wages, it tends to be with people close to themselves, rather than with Premiership football stars or paupers. As a result the most intense rivalry is **within** organisations (and sometimes within families), although in many organisations salaries are kept secret. In families, it has been found that the more your spouse earns, the less satisfied you are with your own job. People are concerned about their relative income and not simply its absolute level (Layard 2003, p.8).

When trying to understand the strategic choices made by management about reward policies, the broader *political and economic context* is important. Lewis (2006, p143) sets out key drivers for reform in reward strategy in Table 32.

There are several factors which can influence salary and wage levels. First, job 'size' has traditionally been the main determinant of pay. This includes factors such as responsibility, level in the organisational hierarchy, knowledge, skills or competencies, external contacts, complexity and decision-making. Hence, the individual's hierarchical position in large organisations has been central to the design of internal pay structures, with performance rewarded by promotion. However, job size is now seen as less important than individual contribution. In other words, having a large staff or control of larger budgets does not in itself indicate a significant contribution that merits extra reward. Second, individual characteristics – such as age, experience, qualifications and special skills, contribution and performance – are also significant factors. Third, labour market factors – such as the supply and demand of particular skills both locally and the 'going rate' in the particular labour market – are important. Fourth, product market conditions and the employer's cost structure – such as its position in the market, profitability and market ambitions and strategies – have a major influence on pay strategy. Finally, the remuneration philosophy of the organisation also has an influence on wage and salary levels. An organisation with the reputation for being a 'good employer', and wishing to attract the most able staff, is likely to offer higher wages than one where staff are valued less positively.

Reward systems can influence a number of HR processes and practices, which in turn impact on organisational performance (Lawler 2000; Guthrie 2007; Shields 2010; Perkins and White 2011), as follows:

1 Rewards influence recruitment and retention. High wages attract more applicants, which allows greater choice over selection and hiring decisions, which in turn may reduce labour turnover. In addition, better performers generally need to be rewarded more highly than poor performers. The type of payment system – not just the level of rewards – also has an effect on recruitment and retention, so performance-based systems are more

likely to attract high performers. The 'efficiency wage hypothesis' explains why it may make sense to pay above market wages. First it reduces performance or shirking issues as staff wish to maintain their post. Second, it reduces turnover. Third, employees may increase effort out of a sense of fairness. Furthermore a better pool of applicants may be attracted (Guthrie 2007, p.356).

2 The way in which employees are rewarded has a major influence on corporate culture. For example, reward systems that provide benefits to long-serving staff are likely to shape the existing culture into one where loyalty is seen as central to the corporate ideology. In contrast, a system that rewards innovative behaviour is more likely to help create a creative and innovative culture.

3 Cost is a key factor in reward systems, and for service-sector organisations labour costs are a significant proportion of their overall costs. The employer might wish to achieve flexibility so that labour costs can be brought down if the organisation is under financial pressure. Having a lower cost ratio than competitors might be another aim. However, lower wages do not always lead to reduced labour costs because productivity may be lower whereas the cost of paying higher wages may be more than offset by higher levels of performance (Pfeffer 1998, pp.195–202).

4 Employees see reward systems as signalling the importance the employer places on various activities or behaviours. Hence, reward systems have a motivational impact and need to be integrated with the corporate behaviour being sought. A key strategic issue is how to use the reward system to overcome the tendency towards short-termism. If rewards are tied too closely to annual performance, managers may not devote time and energy to long-term objectives and may 'mortgage the future for present performance'.

## INTEGRATION OR CONTRADICTION IN REWARD STRUCTURES

The fact that management aims may conflict with or contradict each other is a particular danger if those responsible for remuneration policy are unclear about its specific objectives. The latest CIPD survey reports that organisations have a range of reward priorties (see Table 33).

**Table 33 Top five reward priorities**

| Reward priorities | Per cent of respondents from all sectors |
|---|---|
| Alignment with business strategy | 58.5 |
| Mareket competitiveness | 41.1 |
| Alignment / individual performance | 40.3 |
| Ensure internal equity | 35.2 |
| Cost minimisation | 32.6 |

Source: Adapted from CIPD (2011i).

Another potential problem is that there may well be differences in the expectations of different groups of workers from the payment system, as we saw from the discussion on expectancy theory earlier in this chapter. While much of the literature discusses the functional and dysfunctional role of reward systems, it is not always matched by discussion of the strategic role of such systems. It is usual to regard the reward system as dependent on the business strategy and the management style of the organisation concerned. However, as we have seen from the previous section, existing human resources and reward systems may also exercise a constraint on corporate strategy, so the relationship is not simply one way.

'New Pay' is Lawler's term for an approach that asserts the need for an understanding of the organisation's goals, values and culture and the challenges of a global economy when formulating reward strategy. This has now become the orthodoxy in pay ideas (Schuster and Zingheim 1992; Lawler 2000). The business strategy of the organisation determines the behaviours employees need to demonstrate in order to ensure that goals may be implemented effectively. These behaviours may, in part, be affected through the reward strategy (Lewis 2006). However, Lewis (2006) points out that there a number of assumptions underlying the model. First, it assumes business strategy is a rational top-down process and that HR goals can be simply matched to this (see Chapter 1). Second, the model is 'essentially unitarist' in that it assumes employees will endorse business strategy and demonstrate the behaviours it implies. Third, it is deterministic – assuming that an effective reward strategy will have a direct impact upon organisational performance. Fourth, it assumes pay will motivate employees to behave in a way in which they may not otherwise do (see also Richbell and Wood 2009). As Lewis (2006, p106) observes:

> Caution needs to be exercised in assuming that the implementation of strategic reward management will lead to a reward strategy that automatically changes employee behaviours in line with the organisation's business strategy. There are far too many variables which may conspire against such a straightforward cause–effect relationship. However, it would be foolish to abandon the possibility that reward strategy may play a role in contributing to organisational change.

Nevertheless, there are choices managers make in their design of reward systems (Gerhart 2009) which have a major impact on organisational strategy. There are two dimensions to consider in the strategic design of reward systems (Lawler 2000). First, there is a structural content dimension (formal procedures and practices) and second, there is a process dimension (communication and decision process parts). In relation to *structural decisions*, there are several issues to address:

- *Basis for rewards* – Are people to be paid for the jobs they do (ie through job evaluation techniques) or for their skills or competencies? Skills-based pay is seen as more appropriate for those organisations that have a flexible, relatively permanent workforce that is oriented towards learning.
- *Pay for performance* – Should staff be paid on the basis of seniority or performance? Because of the problems in implementing performance-based schemes, some believe individual pay should be based on seniority, as in Japan, with motivation to be achieved through other means (such as personal growth or recognition). If management decides to pursue the performance route, then decisions need to be made on the behaviours to be rewarded and how they should be rewarded (for example, by individual or group plans).
- *Market position* – The market position and stance of an organisation will influence organisational climate. If management feels it is important to be a leading player with pay levels set above those of competitors, there is likely to be a different reward system from one in which staff are seen as less critical to business success.
- *Internal–external pay comparisons* – Management needs to decide the extent to which it values internal equity – someone doing similar work is paid the same even if they may be in different regions or in different businesses – or external equity, which focuses on the labour market as the key determinant of levels of pay. This issue depends on the extent to which the organisation wishes to have an overall corporate identity (eg everyone working for a multinational chemical company to have similar conditions of service) or product market differentiation (bulk chemicals and pharmaceuticals to be seen as distinct business or product lines).

- *Centralised–decentralised reward strategy* – Organisations with a centralised strategy usually have a corporate HR department that develops standardised pay and wage guidelines. This creates a feeling of internal equity and shared values. In decentralised organisations flexibility allows for local options.
- *Degree of hierarchy* – Management can choose whether it employs a hierarchical approach to reward – where people are rewarded according to their position in the hierarchy and are often also provided with symbols of their status – or a more egalitarian approach where the climate is more team-based and there are fewer status symbols.
- *Reward mix* – This refers to the type of rewards given to individuals (benefits, status symbols etc) or indeed the choice employees are given through a cafeteria-style approach where individuals can make up their own package. Again, the form of rewards should reflect the culture or climate the employer wishes to create and reinforce.

## REFLECTIVE ACTIVITY

Examine the strategic reward system of an organisation with which you are familiar and assess where the organisation fits with regard to the structural issues raised by Lawler.

Do they support or contradict one another? How might greater horizontal and vertical integration be achieved?

In relation to the *process dimensions* of reward systems there are two key issues:

- *Communication policy* – How far the employer wants to have an open or closed policy on rewards depends on its philosophy. In some organisations disclosure of salary is a dismissible offence although in the UK the *Equality Act 2010* made any pay secrecy clauses in a contract of employment unenforceable in relation to discussing pay within an organisation.
- *Decision-making practices* – The issue here is whether or not to involve employees in system design and administration. Involvement can lead to important issues being raised and expertise being provided, which is not always the case if a top-down approach is taken. Moreover, involving employees and their representatives helps the acceptance of any changes since there is a greater sense of legitimacy bestowed on decisions. Cox (2000, p.363) presents the argument for involvement in pay scheme design as follows:

> *Seeking information from employees may provide a fuller perspective on whatever problems exist in the operation of the current pay scheme, thus increasing the chance that they will be resolved in the design of the new system. Furthermore, this may also ensure that the rewards offered are commensurate in timing and kind with the rewards employees desire. Full explanations of the reasons for changing the system may make employees more likely to accept the new system. The consultation process may allow the opportunity to identify any individuals or groups likely to be adversely and unfairly affected and to take action to prevent this before the scheme is implemented. Some authors argue that the process itself of involving as many parties as possible in the development of a new scheme makes them more committed to its success.*

Moreover, reward systems need to fit with the HR system as a whole, as well as the culture and systems used in the organisation. Unless 'fit' exists, the organisation will be replete with conflicts and, to a degree, the reward system practices will potentially be cancelled out by the practices in other areas. In short, a contingency approach – which takes into account particular organisational and environmental factors – is likely to be superior to an off-the-shelf solution that reflects current fads and fashions (Brown 2001; Corby *et al* 2009).

Much of the literature in the field tends to be prescriptive. We are told how management **should** tackle the subject of reward management but not what actually happens in practice (Richbell and Wood 2009). A major concern is that few managements attempt to evaluate their pay schemes in any real depth (Armstrong *et al* 2011). They appear not to have clear criteria against which the schemes can be evaluated, but rather tend to rely on a 'gut feel' assessment that, for example, because of its performance emphasis, a performance-related pay (PRP) system must be conducive to good performance (Sisson and Storey 2000). Conversely, any contraindications or problems are dismissed as mere 'teething problems' relating to issues of implementation. Corby *et al* (2008) argue that because new pay systems take time to develop and implement there are strong political pressures not to disturb arrangements if there is no negative anecdotal information; managers assume 'no news is good news'.

## TYPES OF PAYMENT SCHEMES

According to Torrington *et al* (2011), since the 1940s arrangements for payment have had one or two underlying philosophies. First the *service* philosophy, which emphasises the acquisition of experience; this implies that people become more effective as they remain in a job so that their service is rewarded through incremental pay scales. These scales are typically of five to eight points, encouraging people to continue in the post for several years as there is still some headroom for salary growth. Second is the *fairness* philosophy, which emphasises getting the right structure of differentials. The progressive spread of job evaluation from the 1960s onwards was an attempt to cope with the problems of relative pay levels that were generated by increasing organisation size and job complexity. Legislation on equal value in the 1970s gave further impetus to this approach.

Accompanying the growth of pay systems emphasising service and fairness, was a steady decline in incentive schemes. These had been developed almost entirely for manual workers from the early part of this century until the late 1960s, but declined due to years of battling with union representatives, employees using their ingenuity in outwitting the work study officer, and changes in production technology. More recently there has been a return to the incentive idea and a new performance philosophy has arisen. Length of service is useful, fairness is necessary, but what really matters is the *performance* of the employee (Torrington *et al* 2011).

It is important that HR professionals see the payment system not solely as something in its own right, but also to consider the links with organisation strategy and other human resource practices. By simply selecting a scheme just because it is seen as the latest fad is likely to lead to failure. Nor should management regard the adoption of a payment system as the complete and final solution to problems of pay policy. Indeed, there is a view that every scheme which is implemented, however satisfactory, contains the seeds of its own destruction (Watson 1986, pp.182–3). As individuals or groups bring their own interests to bear on the system, this means that subsequently it becomes very difficult to manage as interests become embedded, and the system serves certain groups rather than the organisation as a whole. Furthermore, as technology, business objectives, work organisation and labour supply alter, systems may need to be re-evaluated. In short, pay systems do not last forever (Shields 2007; Corby *et al* 2008). Accordingly attention needs to be paid to the conditions under which schemes operate and the messages sent to various audiences.

### TIME RATES

These are usually expressed as an hourly rate, a weekly or monthly wage, or an annual salary. They are widely used although less popular today. In 1984, 47% of firms had no incentive scheme at all but by 2004 this was down to less than a third (Pendleton *et al* 2009, p.279).

Some employees are paid on pure time rates although in some cases a payment by results component may be added. There are two forms of time rate. The first is a flat rate per period of time, while the second incorporates fixed scales, with increases based on length of service (Lynch 2000, p.275). Such schemes are simple and cheap to administer, easily understood by employees, and unlikely to cause disputes in themselves. On the other hand they are limited in providing work incentives (Acas 2006). Time rates are often found in managerial and white-collar work, although many managers put in more than their contractual hours, or in complex and process industries (such as in chemicals) where it is difficult to measure individual contributions to performance. With time-based systems, work effort and work quality has to be guaranteed by supervisory control or through well-established systems of custom and practice (Kessler 2007).

There has been a shift from simple wage systems, with a single rate attached to all jobs of the same description, to salary systems where there is a range of pay for each job grade. Salary systems with pay progression reflect a view that experience is important and should be rewarded, so progression through salary scales is based on length of service or age (Thompson 2000, p.127). However, there have been problems with traditional incremental systems – which in theory can provide both 'carrot and stick' by withholding or offering increments. In practice, the lack of a systematic appraisal system and high employee expectations means that automatic increments tend to be the norm. This means that staff bunch at the top of a grade, so making it expensive for employers to fund. While time rates should be simple, in practice additional payments for overtime add complexity.

## PAYMENT BY RESULTS

The philosophy with payment by results (PBR) is to establish a link between reward and effort as a motivational factor. Such schemes reflect the ideas of F.W. Taylor, the father of scientific management who, by standardising work processes through time and motion studies, laid the groundwork for such schemes to operate. As we saw earlier, views that workers are motivated solely by money led to payment schemes being designed to reflect this.

Individual PBR schemes vary in practice, and they can relate either to the whole of the employee's pay or be part of an overall pay package. They may involve payment varying according to output, or payment of a fixed sum on the achievement of a particular level of output. Most schemes have fallback rates and guarantee payments for downtime. The principal advantage of individual PBR schemes is that the incentive effect should be strong as workers can see a direct link between individual effort and earnings. By way of contrast, the major disadvantages of individual PBR are that they are expensive to install and maintain, often requiring a dedicated team to establish the system. Moreover, standards are often disputed and considerable effort is spent on both sides to apply the appropriate standards, or renegotiate in the light of any changes, such as new technology or problems with components supplied. Finally, there is often friction between employees because of the emphasis on personal performance as external factors are likely to impact on performance, but are not within their own control.

The most popular form of individual PBR is piecework. Such schemes have a long tradition in British industry, in particular in the textiles, footwear and engineering industries. They are based upon work-study methods whereby the employee is simply paid a specific rate or price per unit (ie piece) of output. Some studies show significant positive impacts. Lazear (1999), in his study of windshield installers, reported a productivity improvement of 44% after the introduction of a piece-rate plan with half the result of an incentive effect and the rest due to 'sorting' (the impact on retention and attrition). Although piecework survives in some industries – such as clothing – few new schemes are being introduced and their importance has declined over the last 30 years as such schemes do not fit with the emphasis

on team-based forms of work organisation, for example cellular manufacturing (Perkins and White 2011). Outside of the production arena, PBR was common in commission paid to sales staff in insurance and estate agencies. However, commission-based pay was badly hit by scandals over the mis-selling of pensions in the 1990s because this form of payment was seen as a major contributor to problems. More recently, this issue was evident in the deregulated telephone directory enquiries services, where the bonus system was based on reducing call time and it was reported that operators were providing wrong numbers so as to meet targets and receive bonus payments. Arrowsmith and Marginson (2010) suggest the decline of PBR can be linked to workplace modernisation and associated with a wider change agenda.

REFLECTIVE ACTIVITY

Can you think of any jobs for which a form of PBR might be suitable? Why?

## PLANT /ENTERPRISE-BASED SCHEMES

While PBR can be effective for particular industries or groups, it may do little for overall performance, especially if there is friction between different groups. Enterprise- or plant-wide bonus schemes (sometimes called *gain-sharing*) encourage staff to identify more widely with the organisation as a whole, attempting to make work appear as a win–win situation with both employees and the organisation deriving direct financial success from the operation (Bowey 2000, p.330; Ferrin and Dirks 2003; Lewis 2006). Gain-sharing (a minority practice in the UK) differs from profit-sharing schemes in that it takes account of the fact that profits may be affected by external factors such as interest rates or increased price of raw material. It therefore recognises that profits may not be directly related to productivity gains. Employees are rewarded for their improved performance and this helps them to see the link between their efforts and the achievement of corporate objectives (Morley 2002a, pp.93–4; Acas 2006).

In general such schemes have the advantage that employees see their contribution to the total effort of the enterprise and do not see themselves as individual units. In this way it can facilitate achievement of corporate identity. As this form of financial participation is often part of a wider consultation process, this can lead to a greater understanding of business issues as employees take more interest in the overall performance of the enterprise. There may be a greater willingness on the part of employees to accept and even push for change; managers may feel more able to discuss issues with workers; and greater productivity and efficiency can be achieved.

Set against the advantages, there are some potential disadvantages. First, while gain-sharing plans are implemented on the assumption that employees can see the connection between their own efforts and the rewards generated by the scheme (Kim and Arthur 2005), in many cases they have little control over the size of the bonus. External factors – such as increased costs of raw materials or services – may limit the bonus, as may management decisions to delay an increase in prices due to competitive pressures. Second, rather than encouraging co-operation between different groups in the organisation, the schemes may increase inter-group hostility and recriminations if the bonus levels fail to meet employee expectations. Most important of all, some schemes may fail because managers are not prepared to accept a modified role, listen to employee suggestions for improvements, and act upon these ideas, and reassertion of managerial prerogatives is likely to undermine employee commitment to the scheme.

## PERFORMANCE-RELATED PAY

For the last two decades, private and public sector employers have put much greater emphasis on 'paying for performance' and attempting to 'incentivise' remuneration in order to improve individual and organisational performance and create a new performance-based culture; see Chapter 9 for more discussion of performance management. PRP schemes provide individuals with rewards linked to an assessment of performance, usually in relation to agreed objectives (for example, sales targets or customer satisfaction) (Perkins and White 2011). This reflects a move towards rewarding output (rather than input), using qualitative (rather than quantitative) judgements in assessing performance, a focus on working objectives (rather than personal qualities) and an end to general annual across-the-board pay increases (Fowler 1988). Over 40% of all workplaces in Britain operate some form of PRP (Kersley *et al* 2006, p.190).

According to Armstrong (2010), PRP offers the following potential benefits:

- It motivates people and therefore improves individual and organisational performance.
- It acts as a lever for change.
- It delivers a message that performance generally or in specified areas is important and good performance is paid more than poor performance.
- It links reward to the achievement of specified results that support the achievement of organisational goals.
- It helps the organisation to attract and retain people through financial rewards and competitive pay, and reduces the 'golden handcuff' effect of poor performers staying with employers.
- It meets a basic human need: to be rewarded for achievement.

### REFLECTIVE ACTIVITY

What are the principal benefits that employer and employees gain from PRP? Does this general list correspond with experience in your own organisation?

PRP is now used in a large number of organisations particularly for managers and professional staff. In many sectors it has replaced traditions systems of reward that valued seniority and long service, but not performance. It is widely used in the public sector (for example, local government, the NHS, the Civil Service and teachers; see box below) where governments of both political complexions have promoted the concept. This is not just a UK phenomenon either, as companies in Asian countries are using individual performance incentives more widely, even Japan which has traditionally emphasised seniority pay (Chang 2006; Keizer 2009).

HRM AT WORK IN FOCUS

## Do bonuses in schools work?

In the USA, a scheme paying bonuses to schools who in turn paid money to teachers was evaluated, and the students' achievements suggest that the programme did not achieve its goal of improving student performance, with the progress no better than those that were not rewarded. The researchers discuss four possible explanations for this result. First, the newness of the programme could have been a factor. However, if newness were the explanation, some positive effects should have emerged by year three, but that was not the case. Second, it is possible that several factors important for pay-for-performance programmes (eg understanding of the programme, buy-in for bonus criteria, and perceived value of the bonus) did not take root in all participating schools, which might have weakened the motivational effects of the bonus. Third, the theory underlying school-based pay-for-performance programmes may be flawed. Motivation alone might not be sufficient. Even if the bonus here had inspired teachers to improve, they might have lacked the capacity or resources – such as school leadership, expertise, instructional materials, or time – to bring about improvement. Finally, the lack of observed results could have been due to the low motivational value of the bonus relative to other accountability incentives that applied to all the schools.

Many teachers and other staff acknowledged that other accountability pressures, such as receiving high Progress Report grades or achieving Adequate Yearly Progress targets, held the same if not greater motivational value as the possibility of receiving a financial bonus. While the bonus might have been another factor motivating staff members to work hard or change their practices, they would probably have been similarly motivated without it because of the high level of accountability pressure on all schools and their staffs.

Source: Marsh *et al* (2011).

PRP is different from the types of incentive scheme discussed so far in that many traditional schemes in manufacturing are collectively negotiated and based on standard formulae, whereas PRP is designed on an individual and personal basis. Accordingly, some workers do better than others – and some do worse – and it is this that makes PRP for manual workers a recent phenomenon. A common approach has been to have PRP on top of a

**Table 34 Typical PRP distribution**

| Rating | General increase/cost of living plus performance pay |
|---|---|
| Exceptional | General + 5% |
| Highly effective | General + 4% |
| Effective | General + 2% |
| Less than effective | General |
| Unacceptable | No increase |

general award, so that, say, 2% is awarded to all employees to cover inflation, and additional payments are made to reward above-average performance. Alternatively, there may be no across-the-board increase but all pay increases are dependent on performance. Typical PRP distribution is shown in Table 34.

It is hard to find definitive evidence to measure the achievements of PRP. Indeed, isolating one aspect of HR and linking it to performance is problematic (Perry *et al* 2009). While PRP has been widely promoted and practitioners in particular seem to retain great faith in its merits, in recent years there has been a more cautious, and indeed critical, evaluation of the ideas behind PRP. A good 'proxy' indicator is likely to be employee reactions. As Lewis (1998, p.74) notes:

> if employees are generally in agreement with both the principle and practice of PRP, then they will be motivated to better job performance and beneficial organisational outcomes will follow. Conversely, if they are not in agreement with either the principle or the practice of PRP, then they will not be motivated to perform more effectively in their jobs and such organisational outcomes will not follow.

PRP is most commonly awarded on the basis of individual performance appraisal, by each employee's line manager, against pre-agreed objectives. Since the first performance pay schemes in the Inland Revenue in the late 1980s, appraisal has moved away from evaluation against a standard set of criteria for all employees, and towards setting individual objectives in line with those of the organisation as a whole (Marsden 2010). Marsden (2010) notes the *anticipated* consequence of performance-related pay – to improve the motivation of public servants – has proved elusive. But the *unintended* or *unanticipated consequence* was that although performance appears to have improved in several cases, it did so by other means than motivation. He argues that it came about because of the emergence of processes facilitating convergence between goal setting at the individual and organisational levels. These have supported a renegotiation of performance standards and priorities at the individual level. This did not come about overnight, but progressively as successive governments and generations of managers grappled with the need to make PRP work in a public service environment. The notion of a renegotiation of the work–effort bargain rather than a more direct motivating effect was also evident in research on PRP in the German public sector (Schmidt *et al* 2011). They show that enhancing employee motivation is not the only objective pursued by the collective actors in the introduction of PRP. Also evident are the corrosive effect on employee motivation of appraisals that employees feel are not a fair reflection of their performance. The problems associated with performance management are also covered in Chapter 9.

Although discussions of PRP for top executives and sales staff tend to focus on the incentive effect of additional rewards, the experience of ordinary public employees suggests that the strength of marginal financial incentives is weak. Likewise, the damage done by poorly conducted appraisals outweighs the benefits of additional financial incentives and this puts the emphasis on the skills and motivation of line managers and suggests the need for them to have ownership of the process. Where PRP motivates employees positively, their workplace performance, as judged by line managers, was better. Where it demotivates employees, line-manager judgements of workplace performance were less favourable. It is difficult to grade performance in a way that staff find acceptable. One of the chief lessons from the work by Marsden *et al* (2000) is that the success of PRP is dependent upon the way that employees are allocated into different performance grades; wherever the line is drawn, it is likely to be controversial, especially when employees are suspicious of both management's intentions and its competence to appraise fairly. Finally, many staff felt that they were unable to improve their performance.

There are many other criticisms of PRP – the difficulty of formulating objectives, the risk of bias or perceived bias, the inevitable inflationary tendency, the high costs of administration, the dubious impact on performance, the problems associated with a focus on the individual and the difficulty of organising and delivering the necessary degree of managerial commitment (Perkins and White 2011). Furthermore, performance pay stimulates high expectations. People respond to it because there is the prospect of more money, but it has to be significantly more money if it is to be effective. Therefore, management often introduces the scheme by indicating how much one can expect. An enthusiastic, performance-enhancing response (which is the sole purpose of the exercise) will bring with it a widespread expectation of considerably more money. A theme echoed widely in the PRP literature is that people think it is a good practice in principle, and indeed it is difficult to object to the view that hard-working and effective employees should get more than those who are less hard-working or effective. However, the 'Lake Wobegone effect' – that almost all staff perceive their performance to be above average – creates problems (Guthrie 2006). Thus, they are likely to disagree with how the scheme operates in practice, a factor that may lead to continual changes. Other concerns include the fact that managers are unhappy at marking staff below average, feeling that all their own staff are above average. One way to prevent this is to allocate quotas for each category, to avoid ratings clustering at a central point, but this can seem arbitrary (Perkins and White 2011). As Purcell (2000, p.41) notes:

> most people in receipt of IPRP (Individual Performance Related Pay) are in the middle range of performance. We can expect 10 per cent of staff to be in the top-performing bracket and 5 per cent to be in the poor-performer category. The rest, all 85 per cent of them, will get average awards that are similar to the going rate. Most of them have no prospect of getting into the top bracket next year, so the incentive is minimal. We could live with this if the outcome of the pay system was neutral, but often it is negative, costing more than any benefit achieved.

Assessment of performance lies at the heart of individual PRP, but there are complaints about subjectivity and inconsistency (leading to accusations of favouritism). This is often compounded by lack of attention to the training of managers in carrying out appraisal and to the administrative procedures for monitoring arrangements. Furthermore, the links between performance and the level of pay are not always clear and effective. It is also apparent that individual PRP sits rather uneasily with a number of other policies that managers profess to be pursuing – especially the emphasis on teamwork. Research on American multinationals show clearly that many local managers are unhappy with forced distribution – given the implications of poor ratings (see box below).

HRM AT WORK IN FOCUS

## Pay as a vehicle of change in the UK and China

**American multinationals and PRP**

A study of American multinationals operating in the UK found that all the subsidiaries operated a PRP system that covered most staff. It was believed that linking pay and performance was of strategic importance and needed to follow corporate-wide logic. The system mixed hard objectives (such as sales targets) with softer ones (eg co-operation within the team). A forced ranking was used, to prevent assessors rating subordinates above average. This made assessors allocate a percentage of staff into specified categories. Poor ratings led to job insecurity as staff with poor ranking were dismissed, or threatened with dismissal. In other cases, they were most likely to be the victims of downsizing. Almond notes that both approaches are legally questionable in the UK and that line managers there often resisted forced distribution practices.

**Benefits in China**

Since the reforms in 1978, China has been undergoing significant change in HRM including in relation to reward systems. Prior to the reforms the major principle was to maintain egalitarianism with little emphasis on individual incentives. There were a number of mandatory social insurance benefits. However, more autonomy has become available to Chinese enterprises and there is evidence that management styles have been influenced by western management philosophies, and they deal with the war for talent with the enhanced globalisation of the economy and the problems of labour turnover. They conclude that the present benefit types in China have become more varied and more attractive to employees compared to those in the planned economy period. They included employee stock ownership plans (ESOPs), profit-sharing, travel incentive and flexible benefit plans. They also note that the provision of employee benefits was generally perceived to have an impact on organisational outcomes. They had a role in attracting and retaining people at work.

*To think about:*

*Compare and contrast the role of rewards in these two very different contexts.*

Source: Adapted from Almond *et al* (2006); Zhaihing *et al* (2010).

There is concern that PRP reflects a short-termist approach where individuals look for quick returns from small scale projects rather than addressing more fundamental problems. Of course, it is possible to argue that this simply suggests that care needs to be exercised in the choice of performance objectives. If sales targets are seen as the only real objective, then it is likely that long-term customer relationships, as well as management–staff relations, may be threatened. On the other hand, if the latter are highlighted as key priorities, the issue of measurement may be problematic.

Furthermore, Heywood (2007) notes the inability to reward every type of productive activity can result in counterproductive behaviour. Thus, an emphasis on individual performance can actually lower performance as workers cut back on productive behaviour in which they would have otherwise engaged but for which they are now not rewarded (see box below).

HRM AT WORK IN FOCUS

### The damaging effect of poorly designed PRP

H.J. Heinz Company only paid a bonus to managers in individual areas if they managed to improve their profits in the previous year. In response to this plan, managers manipulated profits so that they could always show a year-on-year improvement. They did this by delaying or accelerating deliveries to customers, thus securing payment for activities that had not actually been performed yet. Although in this way the managers were able to secure a pay raise for themselves, it also meant that the future flexibility of the company was severely restricted, thus reducing long-term growth and compromising the value of the company.

At Sears, a badly designed compensation system had even more critical consequences. Mechanics working for the company's car repair operation were paid according to the profits earned on repairs requested by customers. With this incentive in mind, the mechanics talked customers – with some success – into commissioning unnecessary repairs. When this dishonesty was exposed, the Californian authorities threatened to close down all the Sears car repair shops in the state. The company abandoned this type of performance-related compensation.

Source: Adapted from Frey and Osterloh (2002).

The cultural dimension is often neglected because most research on PRP is based in the USA or UK. However, in more communitarian cultures, the Anglo-Saxon notion of pay for performance may be less popular. As Gannon (2000, p.5) notes 'employers may not accept that individual members of the group should excel – a way that reveals the shortcomings of other members'. An 'outstanding individual' may be defined as one who benefits others. Customers in more communitarian cultures also take offence at a 'quick buck' mentality, preferring to build up and maintain relationships. Another cultural insight is provided by Schneider and Barsoux (1997, p.14):

> While it would be unthinkable for most American managers to consider implementing a system at home where the amount that family members are given to eat is related to their contribution to the family income, at work the notion of pay for performance seems quite logical. In contrast, in many African societies a collective logic prevails; the principles applied to family members also apply to employees. One multinational, in an effort to improve the productivity of the workforce by providing nutritious lunches, met with resistance and the demand that the cost of the meal be paid directly to the workers so that they could feed their families. The attitude was one of 'How can we eat while our families go hungry?'

Nevertheless, other studies have found a more positive reception to the introduction of PRP into other cultures. Du and Choi (2010) report an association in China with conscientiousness at an individual level but note organisational commitment and interpersonal helping was reduced, which they suggest relates to the impact of cultural distance manifesting itself at a collective, rather than individual level.

Concerns regarding the potential limitations of IPRP, combined with the shift towards a culture of team-working in many organisations, have led to interest in team reward. Team reward is a broad term, used to refer to a wide range of schemes aiming to reward employees collectively on the basis of their performance, and in turn intending to increase employee contribution and improve productivity. A team may be defined as a small group of employees, all employees at a particular plant or location, or all employees in the organisation. Accordingly, specific schemes range from bonus rewards for small teams, to gain-sharing and company- or plant-wide bonus schemes. Theoretically, team reward offers several advantages by providing an incentive to improve performance, encouraging teamwork and co-operation, clarifying team goals and aligning objectives of individual teams with the wider organisational strategy. It may also encourage low performers to improve to meet the team standards. Team reward may be introduced as part of a broader culture change programme. In practice, however, implementation and administration of team reward schemes may be difficult, and the use of team reward remains a minority practice.

Some alternatives in approaches to rewards might be learnt from the Swedish Bank, Handelsbanken. With no volume or profit goals other there is no great emphasis on executive reward. Amid controversy that the CEO of Royal Bank of Scotland received a £7.7 million salary-and-bonus package in 2011 despite leading a bank that made a £1 billion loss, at Handelsbanken the incentive scheme is one where everyone (from the chairman to the cashier), gets the same (Adapted from Hennessey 2011, with kind permission from The Irish Times).

## FINANCIAL PARTICIPATION AND EMPLOYEE SHARE OWNERSHIP

Financial participation is 'a mechanism by which employees are provided with a stake in the performance or ownership of an organisation' (Kessler 2010). Since the 1980s there has been a substantial growth in the field of financial participation (sometimes termed people's capitalism) fuelled by a number of developments in the area. It included the Conservative government's interest in extending financial involvement on a voluntary basis as opposed to other more radical forms of participation. In addition, the Social Chapter makes reference to employee participation in the capital or profits/losses of the European company. Unlike current British provisions, however, it goes further in requiring a scheme to be negotiated between the management board of the enterprise and the employees or their representatives. There are a number of objectives behind the introduction of financial involvement – such as education, motivation, recruitment and retention, performance and paternalistic ideas – although it is likely that several of these are combined (Hyman 2000, pp.180–81; Gamble *et al* 2002, p.10; Lewis 2006).

There was a major growth in employee share ownership schemes in the 1990s, which can be attributed partly to tax incentives in order to make them more attractive to companies. Some 2,000 companies operate all employee share plans covering around 3 million employees (Cohen 2006). WERS reported that 21% of workplaces had at least one of following: share incentive schemes, Save as you Earn, enterprise management incentives and company share option plans (Kersley *et al* 2006, p.191). Such payments are on the increase in Europe with British companies leading the way (Kaarsemaker 2010) and there is some evidence suggesting that organisations in which employees have a financial stake perform better (Freeman 2001; Bryson and Freeman 2006).

A number of problems are apparent in profit-sharing and employee share ownership schemes. First, schemes do not usually provide any real control because employees are unable to influence to any great extent the level of profits or the quality of management decision-making within the enterprise. Second, investing savings in the firms for which they work can increase employee insecurity. If the employer goes out of business or suffers cutbacks, individuals not only stand to lose their jobs, they might also lose some or all of their savings (Heery 2000, p.65). Marconi staff facing redundancy in 2002 found the values of shares held in the company reduced by 97% over the previous 12 months (CIPD 2006). A further major problem with financial involvement is that it does not link effort to reward in a clear and unambiguous manner, nor is the payout made at regular enough intervals to act as a motivator (Kessler 2010). Because profits or share prices are affected significantly by factors other than employee performance, it is clearly not linked with effort. Indeed, due to factors beyond the control of employees, an individual who has worked extra hard during the year may be 'rewarded' with a negligible profit share, or vice versa.

**REFLECTIVE ACTIVITY**

Can profit-sharing make organisations more democratic?

### NEW PAYMENT INITIATIVES

Skills-based pay (sometimes referred to as competence-based pay or pay-for-knowledge) schemes have become more prominent (Hastings 2000; Guthrie 2007; Perkins and White 2011). This approach emerged from the USA in the 1980s to provide incentives for technical staff. Core competencies or skills are built into the pay system, and rewarded according to the standard or level achieved, so inputs and outputs are considered rather than just the latter – one criticism of PRP – and it is forward-looking rather than retrospective. Such an approach encourages skill development and should widen and deepen the skills base of the organisation. Furthermore, it may increase job satisfaction, break down rivalries between groups or units, and increase flexibility as well. This in turn could reduce the costs of absenteeism. Competence-based pay is actually wider than skills-based pay as it incorporates behaviour and attributes, rather than simply skills alone and some writers suggest that skills-based pay is suited to manual work, while competency pay suits white-collar work. In many respects this system represents a rejection of the concept of job evaluation as it evaluates the person rather than the job. There are potential problems with such systems, in that management needs projected need for future skills some years ahead, and it may create high and unfulfilled expectations among employees if they reach the top of the skills-based pay structure. Competence-based pay is applicable for organisations experiencing rapid technical change and where a high degree of involvement already exists, so that the new scheme can be introduced with the co-operation of employees and the exchange of information which is necessary (Cox 2000).

**REFLECTIVE ACTIVITY**

Before reading the remainder of this chapter, gather information about the pay levels for a sample of **five** occupations – for example, Member of Parliament, train driver, checkout operator, nurse, HR manager. Place these in rank order. Do you consider these pay levels to be fair in relation to each other? Why/why not? Discuss with your colleagues notions of fairness and differentials.

## JOB EVALUATION

Job evaluation can be defined as a process whereby jobs are placed in a rank order according to overall demands placed upon the job-holder. It therefore provides a basis for a fair and orderly grading structure, but it is best regarded as a systematic rather than a scientific process. It is a method of establishing the relative position of jobs within a hierarchy, which is achieved by using criteria drawn from the content of the jobs (Acas 2010). However, there is sometimes considerable confusion concerning the process. Writing job descriptions (which is covered in Chapters 2 and 8) is central to job evaluation, but this is not designed to evaluate the person or job-holder on his or her performance, or to establish the pay for the job. Job evaluation has existed since the 1920s but was given considerable impetus in the 1960s and 1970s because of government incomes policies. Job evaluation has a number of benefits. It provides a formula for dealing with grievances about pay, and decisions are likely to be more acceptable if there is a formal system rather than ad hoc ways of dealing with pay issues. The WERS data shows that 22% of workplaces with 25 or more staff had a job evaluated pay structure (Kersley *et al* 2006, p.245).

According to Arthurs (2002b, pp.131–2), employers normally have some or all of the following objectives in seeking to introduce job evaluation:

- to establish a rational pay structure
- to create pay relationships between jobs, which are perceived as fair by employees
- to reduce the number of pay grievances and disputes
- to provide a basis for settling the pay rate of new or changed jobs
- to provide pay information in a form which enables meaningful comparisons with other organisations (see also Armstrong 2002, p.107).

In broad terms job evaluations fall into two types of scheme – non-analytical and *analytical. Non-analytical schemes* use a simple ranking method, with jobs placed in rank order, and no attempt is made to evaluate or compare parts of each job (Perkins and White 2011, pp.120–3). They have declined in favour in recent years, as they are unlikely to be a defence in an equal value claim. There are various forms of non-analytical scheme.

## JOB RANKING

Under this system, job descriptions or titles are placed in a rank order or hierarchy to provide a league table. It is a very simple method as the job is considered as a whole rather than broken down into constituent parts. It is usually seen as suitable for small organisations where the evaluation team is likely to know all the jobs. It is simple and cheap to implement but tends to be very subjective. Furthermore, while job Y can be identified as more difficult than job X, it is not clear how much more difficult it is (Duncan 1992, p.277; Smith and Nethersell 2000, p.219; Perkins and White 2011, pp.124–5; Acas 2005, p.10). For example, the box below shows a simple ranking system.

**Box 3 job grades**

Grade 1 Supervised manual labour.
Grade 2 Unsupervised manual labour following prescribed procedures.
Grade 3 Tasks involving interpretation of procedures.
Grade 4 Tasks involving interpretation of procedures and responsibility for work groups.

## PAIRED COMPARISON

This approach is similar to the above but more systematic in that each job is compared with every other job, and points are allocated depending on whether it is less than, equal to, or more than the other jobs. The points are added up to provide a league table. It is more objective than job ranking but can be time-consuming unless there is computer support, given the comparisons that need to be made (Acas 2005, p.10; Perkins and White 2011, pp.127–8).

## JOB CLASSIFICATION

This is the reverse of the above process in that, under this technique, the number of grades is first decided upon, and a detailed grade definition is then produced. Benchmark (representative) jobs are evaluated with non-benchmark jobs before being slotted in on the basis of the grade definitions. The main drawbacks are that complex jobs may be difficult to assess as they may stretch across grade boundaries, and given it works best in cohesive, stable and hierarchical organisations its appeal today is limited (Smith and Nethersell 2000, p.219; Acas 2005, pp.10–11).

The main drawback of these 'whole job' approaches is that they are highly subjective. Given that they are not analysed systematically, it is likely that implicit assumptions about the worth of jobs may be left unquestioned. Physical strength, for example, may be given extra weight and this has significant implications for equal opportunities, as 'women's' jobs may be rated lower than 'men's' jobs for historical reasons.

By contrast, *analytical schemes* involve a systematic analysis of jobs by breaking them down into constituent factors. There are two principal categories of analytical scheme.

## POINTS RATING

This is the most popular technique. It involves breaking down jobs into a number of factors, usually between three and 12, to include factors such as skill, judgement, knowledge, experience, effort, responsibility and pressure. Each factor receives weighting, which is then converted to points, with the total points determining the relative worth of a job. It is more objective than non-analytical methods, and by breaking down the jobs helps overcome the danger that people are assessed rather than jobs (Smith and Nethersell 2000, p.220; Acas 2005, pp.11–12). However, it is a time-consuming process that is prone to grievances as small changes in job content can lead to regrading issues. Examples of factors commonly assessed include:

- knowledge and skills
- people management
- communication and networking
- decision-making
- working environment
- impact and influence
- financial responsibility. (CIPD 2010i)

## FACTOR COMPARISON

This attempts to rank jobs and attach monetary values simultaneously. Jobs are analysed in terms of factors (mental and physical requirements, responsibility etc) and benchmark jobs are examined, one factor at a time, to produce a rank order of the job for each factor. The next step is to check how much of the wage is being paid for each factor. Where employees are shown to be overpaid for the job they do, the usual practice is red-circling, which protects the individual's pay in the post (sometimes for a set period of time), but a successor would be paid the newly evaluated (lower) rate. This system is not popular in Britain, partly because the allocation of cash values to factors is seen as too arbitrary and it assumes that a pay structure already exists. Factor comparison was the basis of the development of the Hay Guide chart profile method, the most widely used around the world (Smith and Nethersell 2000, p.221; Perkins and White 2011 pp.126–7).

Despite the growth of more 'scientific' forms of job evaluation, ultimately the process is subjective, as assumptions are made about the design of the scheme, the factors and weights chosen, as well as the judgement of those doing the evaluating. Because of this, employee involvement in the scheme is important to lend credibility to something that would otherwise be seen as management-driven.

There are a number of reasons why job evaluation is in a transitional phase. Firstly, equal pay legislation has meant that it has been necessary to re-examine schemes to ensure they are analytical and gender-neutral. Second, new technology is changing roles, eliminating job differences and introducing new skills – for example, by reducing the emphasis on physical skills and increasing the relevance of more conceptual skills. Third, there is now greater flexibility in working arrangements and a growth in team-working, for example. Fourth, de-layering meaning that decisions are being made by employees lower down the hierarchy. Hence, more is being demanded of employees, and their horizons may be narrowed rather than widened by job descriptions that define a single job. Fifth, labour market pressures due to skill shortages can lead to comparisons based on external relativities rather than internal relativities. Finally, the notion of individual contribution is now more important, especially in relation to PRP schemes (Armstrong and Murlis 1998; CIPD 2011i; Perkins and White 2011, pp.122–3).

## REFLECTIVE ACTIVITY

What are the main strengths and weaknesses of analytical and non-analytical schemes of job evaluation?

Traditional criticisms of job evaluation have pointed to its costly and bureaucratic nature as well as its lack of flexibility (Arthurs 2002a; Watson 2005). It is argued that job descriptions assume stability and hierarchy in the world of work – a situation that no longer appears to exist – and that job evaluation may not be compatible with employers' attempts to develop high performance workplaces (Rubery 1995). We have already noted that formal job evaluation processes began in the 1960s and 1970s, when, for many organisations, the main interest was in establishing internal equity, with a focus on jobs rather than on people. External labour markets were regarded as relatively homogeneous, and individual performance was an optional extra, or accommodated by highly structured systems in which employees gained automatic progression. In addition, traditional job evaluation has difficulties in coping with jobs based on knowledge work and team-working, as well as with flatter structures. Conventional job evaluation was seen as exaggerating small differences in skill and responsibility by the attachment of points in a way that impeded flexibility. Management stressed the need to evaluate employees and not just jobs. However, rather than abandoning job evaluation, it appears there is a movement to make it more flexible so as to reflect internal and external worth (CIPD 2011i; Perkins and White 2011, p.123).

There is some evidence that employers are developing more flexible forms of work organisation **and** systems of job evaluation simultaneously (Kessler 2005). This is being done by creating generic job descriptions and broad-bands; the development of career progression linked to attainment of key skills or competencies; the development of 'growth structures' involving clear career paths; and the integration of manual and non-manual structures.

Broad-banding involves the compression of a hierarchy of pay grades or salary ranges into a number of wider bands. Each of the bands normally span the pay opportunities previously covered by several separate grades and pay ranges but broad-banding has not replaced analytical job evaluation as job evaluation can define band boundaries (Armstrong and Brown 2001, p.55; Kessler 2005, pp.339–40). It is driven by twin pressures of the need to replace complex pay structures and organisational changes in structure and is now the leading approach to pay structure (Thompson and Milsome 2001). Not all employees will be enthusiastic because it adds uncertainty to pay determination, unlike the transparency and predictability of service-related increments.

The key features of broad-banding, according to Armstrong and Brown (2001, p.61) are:

- typically no more than five or six bands for all employees covered by the structure, although some organisations describe their structures as being broad-banded when they have as many as eight or nine grades
- wide pay spans, which can be 80% or more above the minimum rate in the band
- emphasis on external relativities; market pricing may be used to define reference points or 'target rates' for roles in the band, and to place jobs in the band
- less reliance on conventional and rigidly applied analytical job evaluation schemes to govern internal relativities
- focus on lateral career development and competence growth
- increased devolution of pay decisions to line managers who can be given more freedom to manage the pay of their staff in accordance with policy guidelines and within their budgets by reference to information on market rates and relativities within their departments
- less emphasis on hierarchical labels for bands
- less concern for structure and rigid guidelines, and more concern for flexibility and paying for the person rather than the job.

Research indicates that *competence-based factors* are being added to existing points factor schemes and/or replaced existing factors (Simon 2006). Job descriptions are being replaced by generic role definitions setting out core competencies. If a role requires a particular level of competence, this can then be translated into a standard of competence performance for the individual in that role. A 'family' of closely related jobs – such as research scientists for example – can be constructed as a hierarchy of levels with employees paid according to the range and depth of their competencies (Armstrong 2002, pp.197–9; Perkins and White 2011 p.117). However, management is interested in outputs such as bottom-line results or employee contributions, and not just inputs such as competency levels.

## EQUAL VALUE CONSIDERATIONS

A variety of legal changes – from *The Equal Pay Act 1970* to *The Equality Act 2010* – have made this a key area of pay system design, which is now dealt with by The Equality and Human Rights Commission. Accordingly, if a woman is doing work of the same value as a man, even if it is a different job, she can claim equal pay (Equality and Human Rights Commission 2011a, p.21). This means that women performing jobs in which traditionally few men have been employed are now within the scope of the recent *Act* (or the reverse – the *Act* gives the same rights to men). Prior to this, women could not claim equal pay because they were doing jobs not done by men employed by the same employer. Equal value claims can be made across sites, provided employees are deemed to be in the same employment (that is, working for the same or an associated employer). This raises major questions when workers employed by several different employers are engaged in the same form of work – for example – at a call centre – but subject to different contractual arrangements (Earnshaw *et al* 2002a; Grimshaw and Rubery 2007).

Grimshaw and Rubery (2007, p.ix) note segregation makes it difficult to compare the relative skills or contributions of women and men directly. Segregation may disguise the influence of gender on wage differentials between sectors and organisations and on pay and grading hierarchies within firms. These influences are:

- Visibility – women's skills are often simply not visible, as their jobs tend to be aggregated into large and undifferentiated pay and grading bands.

- Valuation – women's skills may not be valued, since pay and grading structures are still often based on male-type skills.
- Vocation – women's skills are often treated as 'natural', deriving from women's essence as mothers and carers, and are considered to provide opportunities for high levels of job satisfaction that justify the provision of low pay.
- Value added – women are more likely than men to be found in low-value-added or labour-intensive occupations.
- Variance – women's lives follow different patterns to men's. This variance from a male norm promotes the notion that women's work (eg part-time work) occupies a separate sphere that is non-commensurate with that of men's.

Equal pay regulations have far-reaching implications for organisations and their pay systems, and many employers have sought to introduce a new scheme or reassess their existing job evaluation system. Clearly job evaluation systems should reflect published objective criteria which enable the employer to justify why particular rates are being paid to men and women. However, it is important to ensure that schemes do not reflect discriminatory values, perhaps by overrating 'male' characteristics such as strength.

However, it has been argued that job evaluation may serve to reinforce existing hierarchies. This is partly the result of the aims of job evaluation, which tend to emphasise stability and acceptability, and hence do not disrupt established differentials (Armstrong 2002). Non-analytical schemes are particularly prone to bias because they produce a 'felt-fair' rank order that can be based on stereotypes. However, even with analytical schemes, problems can occur in factor choice and weighting. For example, tacit skills such as those involved in caring and human relations are often missed or misunderstood (Perkins and White 2011).

An employer can justify differences in pay only where the variation between the terms and conditions is due to a 'material' (ie significant and relevant) factor, and not difference in gender. That is, even when 'like work' is proved, a woman has no right to equal pay if an employer can show there is a material difference (not based on sex) between the two employees, which justifies the differences in payment. Material factors which can be used to justify a difference in pay are personal differences between the workers concerned such as experience and qualifications, geographical differences (such as London weighting) and unsocial hours (see Equality and Human Rights Act 2011 pp.28–9; Taylor and Emir 2009). However, this is to be evaluated on a one-by-one basis, as experience may be deemed relevant in one instance but irrelevant in another. For example, if a man is being paid more than the comparator because of certain skills he has which the applicant does not, it needs to be shown that these are necessary for the job and do not represent, for example, a past pay agreement. The gender pay gap remains an issue (see Chapter 2) but equal pay reviews and monitoring can be used to ensure the system delivers equal pay; involving the workforce in such exercises is seen as good practice. Thus Wright (2011) questions whether job evaluation can achieve pay equality objectives because the labour market tends to favour male-dominated jobs.

## NON-PAY BENEFITS AS PART OF THE PACKAGE

### PENSIONS

Pensions can be seen as a form of deferred pay and just under half of UK's employees take up occupational pensions (Taylor and Emir 2009; Perkins and White 2011, pp.279–300). They remain a widespread fringe benefit and the most costly element of the remuneration package especially for older workers, despite the fact that the reward management literature shows little interest in this area (Taylor 2008). Occupational pensions were developed during the nineteenth century as part of a broader paternalistic-driven personnel policy in gas and public-service organisations, in conjunction with various other benefits such as paid leave, sickness and accident benefits. Paternalism was not simply the act of benevolent employers, but it was seen initially as a means of managing retirement, and later for attracting and retaining a good loyal labour force (Smith 2000a, pp.154–6). After the Second World War, pension schemes began to develop as more employees became liable to tax, thus making the tax relief aspects of pensions especially attractive. The legislation covering pensions is now extremely complex subsequent to a growth in UK and European legislation; additionally there are three regulatory bodies overseeing provision as a result of major scandals where company pension funds have become insolvent (Taylor and Emir 2009).

There are two main types of pension scheme: defined benefit (DB) schemes, where the level of pension is calculated as a percentage of the retiring individual's final salary, and defined contribution (DC) money-purchase schemes, where regular payments are made (by employee and employer) to a pension fund which are then invested – with the employee receiving a pension based on the value of the investment; these represent just a few schemes. Legislation during the 1980s meant employees are no longer required to join a scheme and there are reduced penalties for leaving. Those who do leave can take their pension with them – hence the terminology of 'portable' pensions. The incentive to stay with a particular firm is reduced, although in practice final salary revaluation tends to result in a pension that is less than they would have received if they had remained (Taylor 2008).

The pressures of an ageing population, greater flexibility in working patterns and retirement age, the decline in equity markets, the changing balance between private and public pension provision and increased pension regulation are all having an impact on traditional ideas about pension provision, and there is a clear shift towards DC with many employees winding up their DB schemes as there is talk of a pensions crisis. DB schemes have virtually ended in the private sector (CIPD 2011i) and in the public sector there have been significant moves to a life-time career average as the basis for pensions in the future, as well as an increase in the contributions made by workers.

### FLEXIBLE BENEFITS

There are many other benefits which employees may value – such as sick pay, company cars, health insurance and holidays, but there is not the space to review each of these here. Perhaps one of the most valued benefits in these uncertain times is job security. While few organisations today guarantee such benefits, some prescribe a lengthy process to be followed before redundancies are invoked, and this may provide some reassurance that terms will be fair and generous (for a wider discussion on benefits, see Armstrong 2002, pp.401–15).

In recent years there has been great interest in the notion of 'cafeteria' and flexible benefits (Perkins and White 2011 pp.271–7; Towers Perrin 2007; Tulip 2003). The main reason for such an approach is to maximise flexibility and choice amongst a diverse workforce, particularly in the area of fringe benefits, which can make up a high proportion of the total remuneration package. Under this system staff are provided with 'core' benefits – including salary – and are offered a menu of other costed benefits (company car, health insurance, childcare, length of holiday entitlement etc) from which they can construct a package of benefits, up to a total value. The emphasis is on employee choice. Such schemes have been popular in the USA, but have not been widely taken up in the UK as a result of administrative complexity and taxation issues, as well as inertia within organisations. Some of the ideas on 'cafeteria' benefits sit well with the motivation literature, which stresses that different individuals have different needs and expectations from work but studies suggest that only a small minority of organisations currently operate a flexible benefits package.

Family-friendly benefits (such as childcare vouchers, subsidised and crèche facilities, enhanced maternity/paternity leave) are a current trend.

REFLECTIVE ACTIVITY

Do you think 'cafeteria' benefits are a good idea? What would make an ideal package for you?

## NON-FINANCIAL REWARDS AND RECOGNITION

According to Herzberg (1987, p.30), 'managers do not motivate employees by giving them higher wages, more benefits, or new status symbols. Rather, employees are motivated by their own inherent need to succeed at a challenging task. The manager's job, then, is not to motivate people to get them to achieve; instead, the manager should provide opportunities for people to achieve so they will become motivated.' It is therefore important to consider the role which non-financial rewards and recognition play in motivating staff and in this section we examine a number of these. Semler's (1993) story of his company and management style in Brazil is a good example of how employees accept responsibility when treated in a way that shows they are obviously valued. The desire of many individuals to seek opportunities for personal growth through their work is very powerful (Giancola 2011). Gratton (2004) argues that reward themes should emphasise both monetary and non-monetary rewards, and include opportunity to participate in decisions about working time and job design.

How do job characteristics combine to motivate, reward and recognise good employee performance? A 'job characteristics model', developed by Hackman and Oldham (1976), incorporates the five core job characteristics they believe are involved in job satisfaction and motivation. These characteristics are:

- *skill variety* – the range of skills and talents required
- *task identity* – the extent to which the completion of a whole piece of work is required
- *task significance* – the impact of the task on others
- *autonomy* – freedom and discretion in selecting methods and hours of work
- *feedback* – clear information provided on performance.

According to these writers, if jobs are designed in a way that maximises these core dimensions, three psychological states can occur:

- *experienced meaningfulness at work* – the result of skill variety, task identity and task significance
- *experienced responsibility for work outcomes* – the result of autonomy
- *knowledge of results of work activities* – the result of feedback.

Where these occur, work motivation and job satisfaction will be high and other behavioural outputs – such as attendance – may also be positively affected (Rollinson *et al* 1998, pp.244–6). Equally, employees with high 'growth-need strength' are more likely to experience changes in their psychological contract when core job dimensions are improved. It is also important to realise that simply having a highly motivated employee does not necessarily equate with good job performance. Employees also need the necessary skills, tools and materials to do a good job. Obviously, a motivated but unskilled employee is unlikely to do a job to the required standard, but neither is a motivated and skilled employee who has had inadequate training or is provided with inappropriate raw materials. This has similarities with the AMO (performance = ability × motivation × opportunity) concept covered elsewhere in the book. The box below illustrates that pay may not be as effective as encouraging creativity and providing opportunities for personal growth.

HRM AT WORK IN FOCUS

### Is pay the answer?

Although many firms offer big cash incentives to employees in order to stimulate creativity, this is not always effective. Thompson and Heron (2006) showed that among UK high technology firms, there was an increased use of short-term rewards such as bonuses and performance pay to stimulate innovation. This was despite the fact that research shows that use of such rewards is not effective in encouraging creativity among R&D professionals.

The key to an innovative workforce is the linking of reward strategy to other HR strategies. Successful practices include:

- an emphasis on long-term decentralised pay determination and employee participation in pay system design
- allowing employees opportunities for personal and professional growth and development. One reward practice, that of providing employees with the opportunity to work on projects of their own interest in firm's time and using the firm's resources
- collaboration, involvement, information-sharing, teamwork and the development of the employee's own skills and professional standing
- job design which encourages team work speeds up innovation through the sharing of ideas.

Big bonuses may seem a quick fix, but could have the unwelcome result of encouraging a more individual approach to work.

Source: Adapted from Thompson and Heron (2006).

#### RECOGNITION AND FEEDBACK

Employees' work needs to be valued by employers and hence recognised by them, a line taken up by a number of the TQM gurus such as Crosby and Deming. According to Crosby (1980, p.218), 'people really don't work for money. They go to work for it, but once the salary has been established, their concern is appreciation. Recognise their contribution publicly and noisily, but don't demean them by applying a price tag to everything.' He argues that it is much more important to recognise achievements through symbolic awards and prizes. However, Kohn (1993, p.55) argues that research shows that tangible rewards, as well as praise, can actually lower the level of performance, particularly in jobs requiring creativity. According to him, studies show that intrinsic interest in a task (the sense that it is worth doing for its own sake) tends to decline when the individual concerned is given an external reason for doing it. Extrinsic motivation is not only less effective than intrinsic motivation, it can also corrode the latter. People who work in order to get a reward tend to be less interested in the task than those who are not expecting to be rewarded. According to Kohn (p.55), when we are led to do something in order to get a prize, we feel that the goal of the prize controls our behaviour and this deprivation of self-determination makes tasks seem less enjoyable. Moreover, the offer of an inducement sends a message that the task cannot be very interesting otherwise it would not be necessary to bribe us to do it. As Pfeffer notes (1998, p.217):

> All this is not to say that pay is unimportant to people. If individuals are not treated fairly, pay becomes a symbol of the unfairness and a source of discontent. If the job, or the organisation, or both, are basically unpleasant, boring, or unchallenging, then pay may be the only source of satisfaction or motivation in the work environment. But, creating a fun, challenging, and empowered work environment in which individuals are able to use their abilities to do meaningful jobs for which they are shown appreciation is likely to be a more certain way to enhance motivation and performance – even though creating such an environment may be more difficult and take more time than merely turning the reward lever.

Others have argued that providing praise for good work, rather than criticism for poor work, is important. Managers should 'catch staff doing it right'. Token prizes/awards can also play a role as they have symbolic worth even if they are low in financial value (Crosby 1980, p.218). Over 25% of organisations operate individual non-monetary recognition rewards although fewer use group-based ones (CIPD 2011i).

The HRM literature stresses that employees should have the opportunity to satisfy their needs for involvement, autonomy and responsibility through work, perhaps through participation in quality circles or merely by increasing involvement in day-to-day matters. When they agree policy and practice, they are likely to be more positive about implementation. Obviously, management styles are critical to this. How might these states be achieved? Some of these aspects of management can be integrated into day-to-day management activity, and recognition and feedback can be made part of the corporate culture. Others might be achieved via *job redesign*. Job redesign is concerned with the allocation of task functions among organisational roles, and has been defined as 'any attempt to alter jobs with the intent of increasing the quality of work experience and productivity' (Wilson 1999, p.13). While early work in this area was largely concerned with matters of efficiency and rationalising work, breaking it down into tiny components in line with Taylor's ideas, modern job redesign has broader aims and looks to balance efficiency and job-satisfaction goals. As there has been increasing recognition that extrinsic rewards (such as pay) are insufficient on their own to motivate employees, more emphasis has been put on intrinsic factors such as job content. Drawing on expectancy theory, the aim is to design jobs that satisfy employee needs so that the work can be performed to a high standard, hence enabling both employee and organisational goals to be satisfied (Buchanan and Huczynski 2004, pp.253–4).

## CONCLUSIONS

It is clear there are fads and fashions in reward management which are influenced by prevailing theories of motivation, as well as external and internal contingencies (Perkins and White 2011; Trevor 2011). However, as Kessler (2007) observes, pay rhetoric outpaces actual change in pay practice because making changes to existing pay systems is a complex and potentially problematic process. In this chapter we reviewed the way in which dominant reward philosophies tend to reflect the views of leading management writers who make significantly different assumptions about what motivates workers. Accordingly, incentive schemes are typically founded upon the assumption that money is the sole motivating force, while time-based systems are more likely to reflect the view that employees have hierarchies of needs. By way of contrast, some of the process theorists argue that motivation is a highly personal concept, and therefore reward policies need to be flexible, allowing for cafeteria-style benefits and individualised packages. Factors external to the organisation – such as incomes policies, taxation systems, and the management of the economy and local labour market factors – also have an important influence over the choice of appropriate reward systems, as does the employer's overall business strategy and position in the product market (Greene 2010; Richbell and Wood 2009).

But we also need to recall that the reward package is somewhat more than a payment system alone, incorporating a range of financial and non-financial benefits. Also, it is not enough simply to install the system because it needs to be monitored and reviewed to ensure that it operates in the way that was intended, and is judged against established criteria (Shields 2010). Given that all reward systems tend to have unintended consequences and decay over time, regular review is critical; there is no such thing as an ideal scheme that can operate for many years without modification.

EXPLORE FURTHER


ADVISORY, CONCILIATION AND ARBITRATION SERVICE (2010) *Job evaluation: considerations and risks*. Advisory booklet. London: Acas.

ARROWSMITH, J. AND MARGINSON, P. (2010) 'The decline of incentive pay in British manufacturing', *Industrial Relations Journal*, Vol.41, No.4, 289–311.

BRYSON, A., PENDLETON, A. and WHITEFIELD, K. (2009) 'The changing use of contingent pay at the modern British workplace', in W. Brown, A. Bryson, J. Forth and K. Whitfield (eds) *The Evolution of the Modern Workplace*. Cambridge: Cambridge University Press.

CHARTERED INSTITUTE OF PERSONNEL AND DEVELOPMENT (2011i) *Reward Management*. Annual Survey Report. London: CIPD.

GUTHRIE, J. (2007) 'Remuneration pay effects and work', in P. Boxall, J. Purcell and P. Wright (eds) *Oxford Handbook of Human Resource Management*. Oxford: Oxford University Press.

KESSLER, I. (2007) 'Reward choices: Strategy and equity', in J. Storey (ed) *Human Resource Management: A Critical Text*, 3rd edition. London: Thomson.

LEWIS, P. (2006) 'Reward management', in T. Redman and A. Wilkinson (eds) *Contemporary Human Resource Management*, 2nd edition. London: Financial Times/ Pearson.

PENDLETON, A., KAARSEMAKER, E. and POUSTAMA, E. (2010) 'Employee participation and share ownership', in A. Wilkinson, M. Marchington, P. Gollan and D. Lewin (eds), *Oxford Handbook of Participation in Organisations*. Oxford: Oxford University Press.

PERKINS, S. and WHITE, G. (2011) *Reward Management*. London: CIPD.

PART 4

# HRM AND PEFORMANCE FROM A BUSINESS PERSPECTIVE

CHAPTER 15

# Examining the Links between HR Practices and Processes and Organisational Performance

## LEARNING OUTCOMES

By the end of this chapter, readers should be able to:

- contribute to the implementation of appropriate HR policies and practices that maximise the contribution of people to organisational objectives
- advise on the role that HR processes (strong HR systems, implementation of intended HR practices and aligned, integrated and consistent HRM) can play in their own organisation
- benchmark their own organisation's HR policies, practices and processes against those of other organisations.

In addition, readers should understand and be able to explain:

- the contribution of 'best practice'/high commitment HRM to the achievement of high performance outcomes at both an individual and an organisational level, and how this might vary between countries
- the contribution of HR processes (strong HR systems, implementation of intended HR practices and aligned, integrated and consistent HRM) to improved individual and organisational performance
- theoretical, methodological, empirical and ethical concerns about how studies on the links between HRM and performance are conducted.

## INTRODUCTION

There have been a large number of studies since the early 1990s investigating the links between HRM and organisational performance. These have focused on the extent to which – if at all – high commitment/best practice HRM leads to improvements in employee outcomes and organisational performance. This was stimulated initially by the work of a number of US academics but it has developed significantly elsewhere since then, firstly in the UK and then in a range of other countries, most notably Australia, New Zealand, The Netherlands, Spain and China (for example, Paauwe 2004; Akhtar *et al* 2008; Boxall and Macky 2009). The basic idea is that particular bundles of HR practices have the potential to contribute improved employee attitudes and behaviours, lower levels of absenteeism and labour turnover, and higher levels of productivity, quality and customer service in all types of organisation. This, it is argued, ultimately generates higher levels of profitability. Since the HR practices that supposedly contribute to an improved bottom line performance are generally perceived as 'good' for workers – for example, employment security, training and development, information and consultation, higher levels of pay, and work–life balance – this looks like an attractive scenario for employers and workers alike.

However, not all the studies report such glowing and positive links between HRM and performance. There are some doubts about the precise sorts of HR practices that comprise the high commitment bundle, about their supposed synergy with one another, about their attractiveness to workers and employers, and about their universal applicability. Some would argue that the 'high commitment bundle' is actually little more than a device to persuade staff to work even harder for very little more. Even if an association is found between high commitment HRM and performance, questions remain about directions of causality and the processes that underpin and drive these linkages; research sponsored by the CIPD, undertaken by teams of researchers at Bath (Purcell *et al* 2003) and at Manchester Business School (Boaden *et al* 2008), provides further analysis of the make-up of this so-called 'black box'. It is argued that much of the research tended to focus on HR *practices* alone, whereas it is equally important to examine the *processes* that accompany managerial initiatives. Here, we draw on several publications to examine the role of HR processes. These are by Purcell *et al* (2003), Purcell and Hutchinson (2007a), Khilji and Wang (2006), Bowen and Ostroff (2004) and Marchington *et al* (2011).

Together these show there are often substantial gaps between rhetoric used by senior management and the operational reality of HRM at workplace level. We have seen in several chapters that when trying to assess how workers *perceive* HRM, the role played by HR specialists and line managers has a major impact on whether and how *intended* HR policies are actually *implemented* at the workplace. Yet there is also a more radical critique which argues that employers are not actually that interested in trying to invest in high commitment HRM, but merely use this as a cloak behind which to hide their real intentions – which is to extract as much surplus value from labour as possible. For example, Willmott (1993), Legge (2005) and Delbridge (2011) have made major contributions to this more critical assessment on HRM, and Thompson (2011) has reviewed its significance.

Guest (2011) suggests that research into the links between HRM and performance has been through six phases, though there are inevitably overlaps between them. These are:

1 During the 1980s, the initial phase worked on the idea that HRM was a new way of looking at people management, with data drawn primarily from case studies and anecdotal evidence, as part of a semi-prescriptive agenda.

2 The first set of survey-based studies emerged during the 1990s, primarily from the USA, and often focused on particular sectors in order to provide some form of evidence base.

3 Subsequent to the rush to collect data, the third phase questioned the theoretical basis on which the research had been designed, as well as the measures used for both HRM and performance. At the same time, there was a backlash, primarily from the UK, which raised doubts about whether or not best practice HRM delivered gains for workers as it had been suggested.

4 This phase centred on conceptual refinement and attempts to use more sophisticated theoretical frameworks to address the HRM-performance link. As we see later this included the ability–motivation–opportunity (AMO) model and the use of institutional approaches that recognised the way in which legal and financial systems in countries can shape HRM.

5 Soon after, there was an increasing awareness that a 'black box' existed which mediated the link between HR practices and organisational performance research – as we see later when we look at HR processes and the key role played by workers in delivering product and service quality.

6 The most recent phase has sought to increase yet further the sophistication of research methods and theoretical development. This has stimulated studies that seek multiple sources of information and use more complex statistical techniques.

Yet, many of the original questions remain unanswered, but Guest (2011, p.6) raises a concern that 'by raising the bar in terms of complexity of research methods and statistical analysis, a growing number of researchers may feel excluded from the field. There is also a risk that research ceases to be accessible to practitioners and policy makers.' The remainder of this chapter aims to present the main issues from these studies in a form that does not require specialist statistical training.

## EXAMINING LINKS BETWEEN HIGH COMMITMENT HRM AND PERFORMANCE

Analysing the links between high commitment HRM and performance is a major area of interest for research and policy. Originally, this stemmed from work in the USA, but there have now been several studies in the UK, most notably by David Guest and his colleagues. Before reviewing some of this work in more detail, it is worth reminding readers of some of the earlier studies that claimed to establish a link between HRM and performance. Huselid (1995) drew his conclusions from a survey of nearly 1,000 US organisations. He divided high commitment work practices into two broad groupings: employee skills and organisational structures, and employee motivation. The former included items such as the proportion of workers taking part in attitude surveys, the number of hours training received in the previous year and the proportion of workers taking an employment test as part of the selection process. The latter included items such as the proportion of the workforce with performance appraisals linked to compensation and the number of applicants for those posts where recruitment took place most frequently. Output measures included labour turnover, productivity and corporate financial performance. Huselid (p.667) concludes that 'the magnitude of the returns for investments in [what he calls] high performance work practices is substantial. A one per cent standard deviation increase in such practices is associated with a 7.05 per cent decrease in labour turnover and, on a per employee basis, 27,044 US dollars more in sales and 18,641 US dollars and 3,814 US dollars more in market value and profits respectively.' Appelbaum and colleagues (2000) also argued that high performance work systems paid off. Their research was conducted in a number of different industries (steel, apparel and medical electronic instrument), and in each they were 'large enough to be important to the companies in our study but not so large as to strain credulity' (p.19). Importantly, they also found (p.20) that high performance work practices increased workers' trust, job satisfaction and commitment, and notably no evidence of 'speed up' (work intensification) and higher levels of stress. A key factor, as we see later when we look at the work of Purcell *et al* (2003), is that having the opportunity to participate enhances workers' discretion and effort.

The survey by Patterson *et al* (1997) published by the Institute of Personnel and Development (now CIPD) was based on longitudinal studies of 67 UK manufacturing that were mainly single site and single product operations. It was claimed – on the basis of this research – that HRM had a greater impact on productivity and profits than a range of other factors including strategy, R&D and quality. For example, it was argued that 17% of the variation in company profitability could be explained by HRM practices and job design, as opposed to just 8% from research and development, 2% from strategy and 1% from both quality and technology. Similar results were indicated for productivity. This produced some forceful claims about the impact of high commitment HRM on performance (Wall and Wood 2005). A CIPD report (2001) argued that the economic and business case for good people management has now been proved. It noted (2001, p.4) that 'more than 30 studies carried out in the UK and the US since the early 1990s leave no room to doubt that there is a correlation between people management and business performance, that the relationship is positive, and that it is cumulative'. Since, it is argued, senior personnel practitioners now agree that the case for HRM impacting on organisational performance is proven, the key question is how to make it happen (Caulkin 2001). From a US perspective, Pfeffer (1998, p.306) agrees that best practice HRM has the potential to have a positive impact on all organisations, irrespective of sector, size or country. It was argued that organisations are just leaders possessing both insight and courage to generate the large economic returns available from high commitment HRM. Many of the studies have focused on manufacturing but Batt and Doellgast (2003, p.306) also suggest that 'a growing number of studies show that collaborative forms of work organisation predict better performance in the service sector'.

Many studies have been published since, a sample of which is outlined in Table 35. These are presented in chronological order, showing that studies are now being undertaken in many countries other than the USA and the UK, and that understanding of HRM has moved from being solely about high commitment HRM to one that envisages different patterns dependent on country and organisational context (see also Chapters 4 and 5).

## REFLECTIVE ACTIVITY

In reading through this list of studies, try to identify similarities and differences in what has been done. In particular, look at the samples used, the respondents, the HR practices chosen for examination, the measures of performance, and the links between HRM and performance. Review your ideas again at the end of this section before moving on to the next section.

**Table 35 A sample of studies examining links between HR practices and performance**

| Empirical studies | Sample – country, sector and respondents | Nature of study |
|---|---|---|
| **Classic studies in the early years** | **USA and UK** | |
| Arthur (1994) | USA: 30 mini-mills in the steel industry | Cross-sectional |
| Huselid (1995) | USA: 968 US-owned firms with more than 100 employees | Cross-sectional |
| MacDuffie (1995) | USA: 62 automotive plants | Cross-sectional |
| Delery and Doty (1996) | USA: 114 banks | Cross-sectional |
| Youndt *et al* (1996) | USA: 97 manufacturing plants | Longitudinal |
| Patterson *et al* (1997) | UK: 67 manufacturing firms employing less than 1,000 | Longitudinal |

| Empirical studies | Sample – country, sector and respondents | Nature of study |
|---|---|---|
| Wood and de Menezes (1998) | UK: use of data from WERS (1990) and Employers' Manpower and Skills Practice Survey – approximately 2,000 workplaces with more than 25 employees, all sectors | Cross-sectional |
| Guest *et al* (2000b) | UK: 835 private sector companies with more than 50 employees, interviews with HR professionals and CEOs | Cross-sectional |
| Appelbaum *et al* (2000) | USA: 40 manufacturing plants in steel, apparel and medical electronics and imaging | Cross-sectional |
| West *et al* (2002) | UK: 61 NHS acute hospital trusts, interviews and questionnaires mainly with HR directors | Cross-sectional |
| Guest *et al* (2003) | UK: 610 private sector companies both from services and manufacturing, telephone interviews with head of HR | Longitudinal |
| **Some more recent studies** | **Range of other countries** | |
| Akhtar *et al* (2008) | China: 465 enterprises, responses from general managers and HR directors in each case | Cross-sectional |
| Apospori *et al* (2008) | Northern and Southern Europe (21 countries): 3,541 respondents from private sector firms with 150 employees or more | Cross-sectional |
| Som (2008) | India: 69 organisations from all sectors, 196 respondents from different functions in these firms | Cross-sectional |
| Zhang and Li (2009) | China: 136 pharmaceutical firms, responses from general managers, HR, marketing and finance managers | Cross-sectional |
| Collings *et al* (2010) | Turkey: 340 responses from CEOs of private sector firms employing more than 20 people | Cross-sectional |
| Fabling and Grimes (2010) | New Zealand: 2,147 private sector firms employing at least six people, single response for each firm | Cross-sectional |
| Peña and Villasalero (2010) | Spain: 86 banks from across the sector, responses from HR managers | Cross-sectional |
| Chi and Lin (2011) | Taiwan: 74 high technology and 86 traditional manufacturing firms, responses from head of HR | Cross-sectional |
| Razouk (2011) | France: responses from managers at 275 small and medium-sized firms | Longitudinal |
| **Review articles** | **Source** | |
| Wood (1999a) | *International Journal of Management Reviews*, Vol.1, No.4 | |

| Empirical studies | Sample – country, sector and respondents | Nature of study |
|---|---|---|
| Wright and Gardner (2003) | Holman *et al* (eds), *The New Workplace: A guide to the human impact of modern working practices*. London, Wiley | |
| Godard (2004) | *British Journal of Industrial Relations*, Vol.42, No.2 | |
| Boselie *et al* (2005) | *Human Resource Management Journal*, Vol.15, No.3 | |
| Wall and Wood (2005) | *Human Relations*, Vol.58, No.4 | |
| Boxall and Macky (2009) | *Human Resource Management Journal*, Vol.19, No.1 | |
| Kim *et al* (2010) | *Asia Pacific Journal of Human Resources*, Vol.48, No.1 | |

The best way to gain a decent understanding of research on links between HRM and organisational performance is to examine several studies separately rather than try to summarise them all. Below, we look at six studies in more detail, three from the classic work in the USA and the UK, and three from the more recent international studies.

1 **David Guest** and colleagues (2000b) analysed data on links between HRM/employment relations and performance. They put forward a path model linking together business and HR strategies on the one hand and performance outcomes on the other. The latter included measures like financial performance, quality and productivity, as well as employee outcomes in terms of competence, commitment and flexibility. The overall framework is glued together by a number of HR practices covering all the usual areas of HRM, as well as by HR effectiveness. The HR practices include job security, recruitment and selection, induction, appraisal, training and development, EI and teamwork, pay and rewards, harmonisation and equal opportunities. The inclusion of a factor assessing effectiveness is particularly important because this allows us to evaluate how well the practices are seen to be working, in addition to whether or not they are present.

A key finding was that a very small proportion of organisations actually use more than three quarters of the HR practices outlined. At the other extreme, an equally small proportion use less than a quarter. In general, those organisations in the public sector and with trade union involvement utilise more practices than those in the private sector and non-union firms, and indeed nearly 60% reported using less than half of the whole list of HR practices. These HR practices are typically less widespread in the private sector, but the same practices emerge as most widespread apart from the fact that appraisal appears to be used in more organisations. The least extensive HR practices are job security guarantees, the use of quality circles and preference being given to internal candidates when filling vacancies. What the data is unable to show, given that it relies on a straight number count, is whether or not specific HR practices are essential for the bundle to work.

However, even if organisations utilise many HR practices, this is no guarantee they are applied effectively or they have any impact on workers or managers. For example, while it is important to know whether or not an employer makes use of regular appraisals or provides information about performance targets, we have no clue as to whether the appraisals make any difference or the information is supplied in a meaningful and timely fashion. This is where measures of effectiveness can be useful. In this survey, managing directors and HR professionals were asked to assess the effectiveness of each practice area, and in most cases they were judged to be either slightly or highly effective. There were relatively small differences between the respondents, with the HR professionals being slightly more circumspect about the effectiveness of the practices.

2 Connected with this, research by **Michael West** *et al* (2002) investigated the links between a set of HR practices and performance in the NHS, data being gathered through interviews/questionnaires with HR managers in 61 separate Trusts. They found that three particular HR practices – training, teamworking and appraisal – had a very strong impact on performance. A number of measures were used to assess HR practices, as indicated in Chapter 3. Measures of performance included information about mortality rates, waiting times, complaints and financial outcomes. It is important to note that the data was gathered by different researchers to prevent any possibility of conscious or subconscious influence on the conclusions. The analysis 'reveals a strong relationship between HRM practices and mortality' (2002, p.1305), with appraisal having the strongest influence of all. These results have been widely quoted because of the massive potential impact on policy but also because of the finding that 'better' HRM might lead to lower mortality rates.

Drawing on this and other research, West *et al* (2002, p.1309) suggest that 'it may be possible to influence hospital performance significantly by implementing sophisticated and extensive training and appraisal systems, and encouraging a high percentage of employees to work in teams.' However, the authors do urge caution in assuming any direction of causality, and agree that it could be argued there is less pressure on staff when the hospital is already achieving low mortality rates – and so more time can be devoted to investments in high commitment HRM (West *et al* 2002, p.1308). On the other hand, questions could be raised about the choice of mortality as an indicator of performance, and quality of life subsequent to operations might be a better indicator even if it is harder to measure.

3 Subsequent work by **Guest *et al*** (2003) provided a further twist to the debate. Rather than being broadly positive about the links between HRM and performance, this study (p.307) concluded that 'the results are very mixed and on balance predominantly negative. The tests of association show a positive relationship between the use of more HR practices and lower labour turnover and higher profitability, but show no association between HR and productivity. The test of whether the presence of more HR practices results in a change in performance shows no significant results.' Moreover, despite some evidence there are links between high commitment HRM and performance, Guest *et al* (p.311) state that this study 'fails to provide any convincing indication that greater application of HRM is likely to result in improved corporate performance'.

The key point is that choice of measures can have a major impact on results. When subjective performance measures are used, there is a consistently positive message, whereas the associations are less strong and consistent if objective measures of performance are employed. This leads the authors to suggest, contrary to some of their earlier conclusions, that reverse causality is a plausible explanation; that is, rather than regarding good HRM as driving better performance, it is possible that profitable organisations have the scope to introduce more high commitment HR policies than their less successful counterparts – we return to this later in the chapter.

4 **Collings *et al*** (2010) examined links between HRM and three separate performance outcomes in their study of 340 firms in Turkey. Although requests were sent to CEOs of each of these firms, only just over 40% were in fact completed by these people and the remainder were filled in by other managers, in particular their deputies and HR managers. The sample comprised a wide range of organisations, with the vast majority employing more than 50, roughly equal proportions from manufacturing and services, and the average age of the firms was 24 years. HRM was measured using training, appraisal, performance-based compensation, merit-based promotion, communications, and empowerment, but unlike many other studies there was also a measure of external fit between strategy and HRM. Controls were put in place in relation to firm size, age and industry. The three outcome measures were employee skills and abilities, employee motivation, and organisational financial performance. The first two of these mirror those used in some of the early studies whilst the latter was a subjective estimate of performance from the respondent.

At the level of individual HR practices, none showed a statistically significant relationship with all three outcome measures, though two of the hypotheses – relating to compensation and appraisal – were supported in terms of employee outcomes, but not with the performance measure. Interestingly, there was much stronger support for the link between external fit and all three outcome measures, leading the authors to conclude (2010, p.2607) that 'where organisations made an explicit effort to align business and HRM strategies, involved the HRM department in the strategic planning process and viewed HR managers as partners in the management of the business, this had a positive and significant impact on all three outcomes'. They also suggested that the Turkish cultural context (high scores on collectivism, power distance and uncertainty avoidance – see Chapter 5) and institutional features make it difficult for so-called Western HR practices to be applied there. This reinforces comments made in earlier chapters about the US–UK axis in HRM though not all studies on Turkey concur with this view (Sayim 2011).

5 Given the growing importance of China in the global economy and the massive surge in HRM research there, it is useful to include the **Akhtar *et al*** (2008) study of former state-owned Chinese and foreign-owned enterprises here. They sampled 465 firms in three major cities in China and thus acknowledge their results are likely not to be totally representative of China given how much of its population lives in rural areas. Data on company performance was collected from general managers in these organisations who were asked to estimate how their own organisation compared with the competition, once again relying on subjective rather than objective measures of performance. The HR managers provided information on a range of seven core HR practices. These were training; participation; employment security; job descriptions; results-oriented appraisal; internal career opportunities; and profit sharing. It will be apparent that these differ to some extent from those covered in many other studies of HRM (for example, contingent pay, teamworking and work–life balance are missing), though it is relevant – given traditions in China – to note that job security formed a key part in the survey.

The results show that, apart from profit-sharing, all the other HR practices were estimated to have significant effects on product/service performance, though as usual we have to infer that from the results as the study was cross-sectional and not capable of ascribing causality. In terms of links between HRM and performance, foremost amongst the HR practices were training, participation, results-oriented appraisals and internal career opportunities. Yet they also note (2008, p.28) that 'it is rare for Chinese employees to cross boundaries and to take the initiative to give critical feedback and suggest improvements'. The authors also recognise their results might have limited generalisability because many of the sample were foreign-owned or foreign-invested organisations that are likely to be trendsetters within the Chinese economy.

6 A comparative study using the CRANET data was conducted by **Stavrou *et al*** (2010) on 14 EU countries in order to test whether there were regional differences in the HRM-performance link between countries and across different sets of HR practices. This followed the general CRANET view that HRM has to be seen in its cultural and institutional context because that shapes the way in which employers manage the people working for them. In this case, 1,273 manufacturing and service sector firms formed the sample, with data collected through the most senior HR person at the organisation (ie, this is different from WERS where data is collected at the establishment level). The questions used were comparable across countries, though they had to be translated to make them meaningful. HR practices were distinguished into five bundles – training and development; compensation and benefits; staffing (which includes recruitment and selection); communication and participation; and human resource planning. Organisational performance was established by asking the respondents for their views on three different indicators: profitability, productivity, and service quality.

The main findings were that the EU could be divided into three broad clusters in terms of HRM practices: a *North-West* region of Sweden, Finland, Denmark, the Netherlands, Germany and Austria; an *Anglo-Irish* region of the UK and Ireland; and a *Central-Southern* region covering Greece, Spain, Portugal, Italy, France and Belgium. There is little doubt that most commentators would put the UK and Ireland in a similar group despite some traditional differences between them (for example in the degree of social partnership), and a plausible case could be made for the North-West cluster as the countries have quite a lot in common with each other. However, it is harder to see how northern EU countries such as France and Belgium can be combined with the southern states totally in the Mediterranean and Iberia (see Chapter 5) due to a range of differences, not the least of which is economic strength as the global financial crisis has shown graphically. These three clusters do, however, show clear differences in relation to specific HR practices. Links between performance and training and development, and with planning are highest in the Anglo-Irish region, those with compensation and benefits, and with communications and participation are highest in the North-West, and the staffing bundle seems uniformly related to performance across the whole sample. Of course there are more specific differences within these regional clusters as well which are often the result of legislation; for example, profit-sharing in France. The authors conclude (2010, p.953) by acknowledging that 'the link between HRM and organisational performance is inevitably complex. Exploring the link across national borders adds extra complexity ... (also) it seems that the "best fit" and "best practice" approaches are not necessarily mutually exclusive'.

## REFLECTIVE ACTIVITY

Find a copy of one of these publications and analyse the links between high commitment HRM and performance. Prepare a presentation specifying the key components of the project and identify the business benefits (eg more reliable/better quality products; increased sales; improved patient care or community support) that might be gained from investing in high commitment HRM. What are the major lessons learnt from this study and what are its major limitations? Do you think that these ideas would persuade your organisation to change the HR practices it uses at present?

## RAISING QUESTIONS ABOUT THE HRM–PERFORMANCE LINK

Persuasive as they might be to HR professionals keen to demonstrate they contribute to the business, studies arguing high commitment HRM leads to improved performance have not escaped criticism, including – as we have seen – some by the authors themselves. Drawing on several sources (eg Holman *et al* 2003: Wright and Gardner 2003; Godard 2004; Boselie *et al* 2005; Wall and Wood 2005; Gardner and Wright 2009; Sengupta and Whitfield 2011), the major concerns are set out below.

### QUESTIONS ABOUT THE DIRECTION OF CAUSALITY, LINEAR RELATIONSHIPS AND THE 'BLACK BOX'

It should be apparent that the direction of causality is a key concern (Sengupta and Whitfield 2011, p.100), and much depends on the theoretical framework adopted by the researcher. Some would argue the most likely explanation is that high commitment HR practices motivate workers – through models such as AMO, for example – to increase their individual or team performance, and that this ultimately leads to improved organisational performance. This has an attractive ring to it, especially for HR specialists keen to justify their value to the organisation. Conceptually, the alternative is equally plausible: that is, high commitment HRM is most likely if it can be financed by high levels of organisational performance that allow firms to invest in a bundle of sophisticated HR practices. Under this scenario, the high commitment organisation is likely to be rare so there is little point in the majority of employers copying other organisations with which they have little in common. Of course a further argument is that the link is iterative, so that more profitable firms are the only ones able to implement high commitment HRM because of the cost but equally these are organisations which rely heavily on their staff – especially knowledge workers – to provide high levels of service and performance (McClean and Collins 2011). A yet more complex argument, dealt with in Chapter 4, is that employers do not adopt a universal HR style that is appropriate for everyone but instead segment staff according to their organisational value and scarcity in the labour market, varying HRM to suit (Lewin 2011; Marchington and Kynighou 2012).

One way to overcome the problem about direction of causality is to use longitudinal research but, as we saw in Table 35, this is relatively rare. Of course there are major problems in trying to undertake such a project: employers are not keen to allow access for the years it takes to do this properly and academics depend increasingly on publishing their results within a relatively short-term timeframe, both to enable universities to capture funding through research assessment exercises and to further their own careers. Gaining access to multiple respondents is more difficult than sending a survey to just one manager at each organisation, and problems arise if some respondents fail to complete the survey if it relies on all these being returned. It also makes sense to ask HR specialists about HRM and general or finance managers about performance to ensure they are able to provide an authoritative answer, and that views about one area are not influenced by the other (Gardner and Wright 2009; Sengupta and Whitfield 2011).

The review undertaken by Wright *et al* (2005) is particularly enlightening. They found 70 studies which had found some link between high commitment HRM and performance, of which 50 had actually taken a measure of performance from a period **before** data was collected on HR practices, thus making it impossible to argue that HRM had impacted positively on performance! Of the others, some collected data on HR practices retrospectively by asking respondents to recall the HR practices that had existed a few years ago, leaving only about 10 that actually used a design that was capable of assessing the direction of causality. This led Wright *et al* (2005) to design a project examining a number of business units within the same organisation in order to address the question; the findings are interesting in as much as they provide further twists to the argument. They confirm a relationship between HRM and performance but agree this is iterative because HR practices tend to change little over time and could therefore be linked both to past and future performance. They also warn against a quick-fix HR solution: 'high performance cultures that are supported by HR practices tend to exhibit high performance, but simply transplanting a set of HR practices into a low performance culture or under an ineffective leader may not have the intended effect' (Wright *et al* 2005, p.435).

Most studies assume there is a linear relationship between HRM and performance, so that the more HRM is practised (for example, in terms of more practices from the bundle or a better embedded system) the higher performance will be. Chi and Lin (2011) use data from 160 firms in Taiwan to argue that the returns from high performance work systems diminish because there is an inherent limit to the gains that can be made from adopting this form of HRM due to increased costs of implementation (Cappelli and Neumark 2001). High technology organisations are particularly susceptible to this problem, with an inverted-U pattern (a curvilinear relationship between HRM and performance) whilst traditional manufacturing firms are not because they start from a lower base, they are less innovative and they are built around stable production technologies. The proposition about high technology firms was supported, but in traditional manufacturing firms HPWS was not significantly related to performance. The implication for practitioners in high technology firms is that a cost-benefit analysis would establish the precise point at which investments in HRM no longer provide any additional benefits for the organisation. However, as Boxall and Purcell (2011) repeatedly make clear, most employers have interests beyond pure economic and financial goals.

Questions are bound to remain until there is more longitudinal research and greater efforts to open up the 'black box' by tracking organisational changes via case studies. This issue is taken up later in the chapter when we examine HR processes in an attempt to understand how intended HR practices are implemented by line managers and perceived by employees. It is also necessary to understand how employee outcomes – such as commitment and satisfaction – translate into higher levels of organisational performance.

## LITTLE CONSISTENCY IN THE HR PRACTICES INCLUDED IN THE BUNDLE

The number of HR practices in each list varies substantially (from six to 20-plus) as does the inclusion or exclusion of specific techniques. Boselie *et al* (2005) noted the HR practices quoted most often were training and development, contingent pay and reward, performance management (including appraisal) and careful recruitment and selection. Hyde *et al* (2006), drawing on a different sample of papers, found that training, pay and selection figured in their list of HR practices used, but also noted the widespread inclusion of EIP and voice, and teamworking. Indeed, many of the papers on high performance work systems regard this as central to the notion. Exclusion of HR practices is the other side of the coin. For example, despite the importance attached to employment security by Pfeffer, this does not always appear (eg Delaney and Huselid 1996; Patterson *et al* 1997; Wood and de Menezes 1998), although it formed a key part of the practices examined by Akhtar *et al* (2008) in their study on China. Perhaps this does not matter if we are clear as to why certain HR practices should be included but, as Wood (2003, p.280) argues, identifying an underlying orientation for integrated management or high commitment HRM is more important than devoting energy to finding a specific set of practices that might be appropriate across all workplaces. However, often the lists are developed on the basis of individual preference, looking at what other researchers have used or by constructing clusters of practices on the basis of factor analysis, and then attempting to impose some theoretical justification for this ex-post facto.

Several studies have a clear theoretical model to underpin their approach, but even then it is not always clear why certain practices are included and others are not. For example, Huselid (1995, pp.645–7) used two groups of practices: (1) 'employee skills and organisational structures' covering job design, enhanced selectivity, formal training, various forms of participation, and profit-sharing, and (2) 'employee motivation' which included performance appraisal linked to compensation and a focus on merit in promotion decisions. It seems strange that participation and profit-sharing should be in the first grouping rather than the second given the supposed importance of these as techniques that enhance employee motivation. Patterson *et al* (1997) also emerge with two groups of practices, subtitled 'acquisition and development of employee skills' and 'job design', and on this occasion, participation and teamworking find their way into the second grouping rather than the first. Subramony (2009) identified three HR bundles, termed empowerment-enhancing (which centred on EIP, the chance for workers to ask questions and raise concerns), motivation-enhancing (appraisal, compensation and benefits), and skill-enhancing (including recruitment and selection, job descriptions and training). Collings *et al* (2010) used two groups: employee skills and abilities; employee motivation. A simple count of HR practices does not tell us a great deal, and it is hard to assess the meaning of high commitment HRM without some attention being paid to the configuration of the overall HR system and the degree to which synergies are achievable through 'powerful connections' or undermined by 'deadly combinations' (Marchington and Zagelmeyer 2005).

REFLECTIVE ACTIVITY

What are the most important HR practices in your organisation, or one with which you are familiar? How do these compare with the high commitment bundles?

## VARIATIONS IN THE PROXIES USED TO MEASURE HRM PRACTICES

The studies use a range of different proxies for the same HR practice. As Boselie *et al* (2005) note, there are three variants: yes/no or absence/presence type measures; percentage of workforce covered; intensity of implementation and the degree to which particular practices are key in the organisation. Absence/presence is relatively easy to define, although this glosses over major doubts about whether or not the HR practice is actually implemented as intended in the organisation concerned (Khilji and Wang 2006). We return to this issue later in this chapter. When surveys ask for the percentage of the workforce covered by a particular aspect of HRM – such as PRP, proportions vary between studies with, say 25% in one and 90% in another. Worse still, they vary within a particular study between different items. Differences in how practices are counted as present has a major effect on the construction of the overall bundle, and it is rare for there to be an explicit explanation about why certain levels have been set; unusually, Guest *et al* (2000a) do openly explain why they chose 90% in some of their questions. Intensity can be measured by a range of proxies, which probably explains why this is rarely followed up in surveys because it would lead to extremely long lists of questions. This was measured, using the WERS data, by Cox *et al* (2006, 2009) to assess how deeply EIP was embedded in organisations. Proxies for depth included items such as regularity of meetings, proportion of time given over to workers' questions, and influence over management decisions.

The most widely used approach to assess HRM is to ask simply whether a particular practice is used without any consideration of how it is implemented or its impact on employees. Take the example of grievance procedures; these are almost universal in UK organisations, so a proxy based around their absence or presence tells us nothing about how people take up grievances, how many they take up, and whether they regard the processes as open and reasonable – arguably more important as a differentiator. A similar point arises in relation to days spent on training. Knowing that the typical employee is trained for about five days per annum is hardly evidence of high commitment HRM if they are trained merely in how to conform to strict rules and procedures. Moreover, problems also arise when compiling scores of high commitment HRM as to whether or not each practice should be weighted equally. This is clearly inadequate where there are more measures of a particular item than others, for example as often occurs with EIP. This makes it possible for the overall measure to give too much weight to one factor compared with others. Moreover, what happens when, as in the WERS analysis, one practice – such as a formal statement on equal opportunities – is widely used whilst another, such as job security, is rarely provided? Should these be equal in importance or is the use of a relatively rare practice something that differentiates organisations from their competitors?

## VARIATIONS IN THE PROXIES USED TO MEASURE PERFORMANCE

A major problem arises due to the different types of performance measure used, in particular whether they are based on objective or subjective assessments. Many of the studies have focused on the former, using measures of organisational performance such as profitability and share price that have little direct linkage with the efforts of individual workers, even though ultimately this is what matters to organisations. Purcell and Kinnie (2007, pp.536–7) reckon these measures are too far removed from HRM influence – too distal – and that we ought to focus on measures that are closer to and more meaningful (proximal) for workers – as we see below. More seriously, there are questions about whether or not profitability and financial performance is a relevant measure, especially given the emphasis in Anglo-Saxon economies on shareholder value and short-term financial indicators.

The use of distal financial measures is also problematic in multi-plant organisations within the same industry, and even more complicated in conglomerates that operate across a range of sectors and countries, as well as in public–private partnerships and inter-organisational networks where it is hard to establish identifiable boundaries between them. Questions also arise about the appropriateness of measures used to assess performance; as we saw in the West *et al* (2002) study one measure was the number of deaths following hip surgery. Clearly, death during surgery is a major problem – not least to the patient – but a better measure could be how well the person felt a few months later. A large number of studies use subjective measures by asking HR managers or managing directors to estimate how well their organisation is doing compared with others in the same sector. This relies on respondents knowing this information, which is not always the case, and also in them being honest and not overestimating their own organisation's performance; as was evident in the WERS surveys. Given that most self-assessment results in people saying they are doing better than they are in reality, this is a major problem (Gardner and Wright 2009). Although Wall *et al* 2004) found consistency between objective and subjective assessments, Guest *et al* (2003) found no association between them, so the jury is out on that issue.

Many of the studies relate HRM to employee outcomes such as labour turnover, absence rates, job satisfaction, organisational and supervisory commitment as well as, or instead of, wider performance measures (see for example, Guest 2007; Wright and Kehoe 2008; Searle *et al* 2011). Some of the intermediate employee outcome measures are simple to quantify but not easy to interpret. For example, it may be important for an organisation to have low labour turnover or absence levels compared with the average for the industry as a whole, but there are questions about whether or not a zero figure is actually indicative of good HRM (see Chapter 9). Work may be so pleasant and relaxing that few people ever want to leave but if productivity levels are poor, this is hardly effective HRM. Similarly, absence levels may be low because people are scared to take a day off for fear of reprisal or because they have so much work they feel it is impossible to stay at home even when they are ill. A related problem arises with measures of job satisfaction; employees that are relatively well-treated at work, but have recently experienced a dip in expectations, tend to report they are dissatisfied, whilst those who expect little from work may be deliriously happy they are no longer treated quite so badly. Clearly, what appears initially as an operational problem of measurement actually obscures rather more serious conceptual weaknesses in defining and assessing performance.

An interesting alternative definition of performance is proposed by Sengupta and Whitfield (2011, pp.116–18). They suggest including measures that relate to each of the major stakeholders in the organisation so that we move away from shareholder concepts such as return on investment and the promotion of economic growth. An employee-management indicator could be average pay relative to industry standards, an environmental indicator could relate to overall energy consumption, and a community indicator could be perception of the company's performance on human rights. This would certainly extend the current list and bring in a more rounded stakeholder perspective.

### DANGERS IN RELYING ON SELF-REPORT SCORES FROM A SINGLE MANAGEMENT RESPONDENT

The vast majority of surveys rely on a single respondent for all the information, but whilst this makes data collection easier, it hardly provides a deep understanding of what happens in the organisation as a whole, or even the establishment if this is the point of data collection as in WERS. Several problems emerge. Questions have to be simple to allow for coding, and because most surveys are undertaken over the telephone they require instant judgements from respondents, and cannot be checked for accuracy. This has a number of implications. For example, questions assume that there is one style of HRM across all employee groups in an organisation, which as we saw in Chapters 4 and 5 is highly unlikely, or in the case of WERS questions specifically relate to the largest occupational group (Kim *et al* 2010). More worryingly, in most studies, non-managerial employees are not asked for their views. It is therefore hard to take seriously results that rely on management estimates of employee views (for example, about the state of management–employee relations, or about engagement) without independent corroboration. This raises substantial doubts about how 'objective' some measures of performance really are.

Relatedly, a single respondent is unlikely to have sufficient knowledge to answer questions across the board. For example, asking HR specialists, who are the respondents in most surveys, about the competitive strategies used by their organisations and the proportion of sales derived from these strategies, lacks validity because it is not normally within their area of expertise. Similarly, asking managing directors about the detail of HR practice is also problematic as they are not likely to know such details (Gardner and Wright 2009). Asking HR directors from large firms questions about HRM at workplace level – as some studies do – makes little sense because they have little direct knowledge. It is interesting to note that no less than 60% of the studies examined by Wall and Wood (2005) used estimates of performance provided by the same person who had given information about HR practices, whereas these two pieces of data should come from different sources to minimise bias. At least the Guest *et al* (2003) and Akhtar *et al* (2008) studies overcame some of these limitations by including managing directors *and* HR professionals in their sample, but they were unable to get opinions from employees themselves. Anxieties such as these mean that considerable caution is needed when interpreting conclusions from these quantitative studies.

### DOUBTS ABOUT HOW MUCH AUTONOMY ORGANISATIONS HAVE IN HR DECISION-MAKING

It is implicitly assumed that organisations operate as free agents, able to choose precisely which HR practices they wish to employ without considering any forces beyond their own organisational boundaries. As we have seen from Chapters 2 and 5, in particular, every organisation is subject to forces that shape its HR policies, in terms of legal and institutional arrangements or through the pressure exerted by clients or industry bodies. This is apparent in how the high commitment HRM package might be applied in different countries, and we should not assume the Anglo-Saxon model (based principally on North American and UK research) is easily transferable to other countries. Boselie *et al* (2001, p.1122) make it clear that 12 of Pfeffer's original list of 16 practices are common in the Netherlands, whereas very few UK organisations could boast anything like this many. Because of the legal, political and social infrastructure, certain HR practices are deemed necessary in the Netherlands, whereas they are not required by law in many other countries. Indeed, some of the fastest developing economies in the world have few legal controls on employment and source their labour from other countries. In these circumstances, when a disciplinary case arises, rather than go through lengthy procedures with a view to improving performance, it is simpler to rescind their work permit and send them home. The cases reported earlier by Collings *et al* (Turkey) and Akhtar *et al* (China), as well as in Chapter 5, show clearly that institutional and cultural factors play a key role not only in shaping HRM at organisational level but also influence which measures of performance are important in different countries.

It is not correct to say that employers in LMEs are completely free from industry regulation or informal norms that govern behaviour. In some sectors, Codes of Practice or industry guidance are regarded as part of the 'way we do things around here' and it may be assumed that – via a process of 'nudging' rather than compelling employers to introduce certain HR practices – that all employers would come to see the benefit of adopting high commitment HRM as opposed to a low-cost or bleak-house philosophy. However, firms competing in tight product markets that feel little need to employ committed, enthusiastic workers who wish to exercise their discretion to improve performance might see little advantage from the high commitment model. Indeed, even organisations using 'best practice' models for their own employees often pressurise suppliers to cut costs so there is little chance these subcontractors can invest in high commitment HRM even if they wanted to (Marchington *et al* 2011c). Rather than seeking to achieve higher levels of integration and consistency between partners in a network, employers may be much more interested in a differentiation strategy where labour is provided at the cheapest possible price, and the headache of finding suitably qualified workers can be borne by somebody else. In this case, as we saw in Chapter 3, the high commitment paradigm may become a preserve of the better-off (Marchington and Zagelmeyer 2005).

## REFLECTIVE ACTIVITY

Look back at Table 35 and choose three of these studies to review more carefully. Which of the limitations noted in this section are most apparent in these three studies, and how serious are they in causing you to question the quality of the findings? Apply the principles of an evidence-based practitioner (Rousseau and Barends 2011) in doing this.

## THE ROLE OF HRM PROCESSES IN TRANSLATING POLICY INTO PRACTICE

The vast majority of research into HRM and performance has focused on the part played by HR **practices** in motivating workers to contribute to organisational goals. This is understandable as it is difficult to gain commitment from staff that are paid poorly, receive minimal benefits from their employer, have no job security, and are not given chance to be involved in decision-making at their organisation. On the other hand, superior or even 'decent' substantive rewards alone are not sufficient to achieve highly committed and hard-working employees because so much depends on the HRM climate in organisations. Consequently, attention has now turned to look more systematically at HRM **processes** (Guest 2011). In this section, we examine the key contributions to this area, starting with attempts to 'open-up' the black box between HRM and high performance in the work of Purcell *et al* (2003, 2007), and Khilji and Wang's (2006) contribution on the distinction between intended and implemented HRM. This is followed by a review of 'strong' HR systems (Bowen and Ostroff 2004) and attempts to develop these ideas through empirical work before finally we discuss the notion that employers seek alignment, integration and consistency in HRM (Marchington *et al* 2011). To use the words of Parkes *et al* (2007), 'it ain't what you do; it's the way that you do it'!

## OPENING-UP THE BLACK BOX: FROM INTENDED POLICIES TO IMPLEMENTED PRACTICES

Whilst much of the survey research does demonstrate links between HRM and performance, it cannot explain *why* these associations occur. Research by Purcell and colleagues (Purcell *et al* 2003; Kinnie *et al* 2005; Purcell and Hutchinson 2007a) has sought to open up this 'black box', and we briefly review some of the major findings here that relate to high commitment HRM and performance; discussion on the role of line managers is covered more extensively in Chapter 7. The Purcell study was undertaken over a 30-month period in 12 organisations drawn from different sectors and comprising quite a wide range of employment contexts; the sample included household names such as Tesco, PricewaterhouseCoopers, Selfridges, Jaguar, Siemens and the Royal United Hospital at Bath. Interviews were conducted with HR and line managers, as well as non-managerial staff both at professional and manual/clerical levels in these organisations, generally on two separate occasions during the research period. The research also involved close liaison with these organisations.

This produced some significant findings that extended previous work investigating the links between high commitment HRM and performance. First, the researchers used the *AMO model* (Appelbaum *et al* 2000), which argues that in order for people to perform better, they must:

- Have the ability and necessary knowledge and skills, including how to work with other people (A). This is influenced by HR practices such as sophisticated recruitment and selection, and effective training, learning and develoment.
- We motivated to work and want to do well (M). This is influenced by HR practices such as employment security, performance review, appraisal and career development, high compensation related to peformance, harmonisation, and a feeling of work–life balance.
- Be given the opportunity to deploy their skills on the job and more broadly contributing to work group and organisational success (O). This is influenced by HR practices such as employee involvement and participation, teamworking and job design.

Second, each case study organisation was used a 'big idea', a feature or way of working that served to glue together all the different attempts to make the organisation successful. The 'big idea' was embedded within the organisation, it connected different activities together, it was seen as enduring, and it was collectively shared. Moreover, performance against or progress towards the big idea was measured and managed in an ongoing basis (Purcell *et al* 2003, p.13). Third, line managers were identified as critical to the achievement of high performance working as they provide the principal point of contact with non-managerial staff and are in a position to strengthen, ignore or even undermine the messages conveyed through the big idea. Finally, measures of performance were adapted to be relevant for the organisation concerned; for example, at Tesco these included data on queue lengths, stock availability, theft and stock errors as well as financial data relating to the store (op cit, pp.53–4). The decision to collect this type of data at unit level makes sense as it is a more meaningful measure of how workers might be able to contribute to improved performance than – as we have seen – some distant measure of profitability over which most workers have little influence. It is also appropriate to vary the measures of high commitment HRM because workers stress different practices depending on their occupational status, age or gender for example.

Another important contribution to this debate stems from the work of Khilji and Wang (2006) on 'intended' and 'implemented' HRM. Drawing on data collected from 12 banks in Pakistan, they examined whether or not there was a gap between the intentions of senior managers and the way in which these were implemented by lower level managers, and if so how this was related to HR satisfaction. Data was collected from 195 interviews, 508 surveys and inspections of company documentation. Intended HRM was assessed via interviews with senior managers and HR professionals, whilst data on implemented HRM came from interviews with managers and non-managerial staff. Whilst there was a close fit between intentions and implementation in a few banks, 'implementation of practices so eloquently described during the first phase of interviews (with senior and HR managers) was sketchy at best in nine of the twelve organisations' (p.1180). Employees at the organisations where HRM was rated as low on implementation revealed they were not even aware of intended practices or they were criticised for being unrealistic or vague.

Summarising these various approaches leads to a simple path model similar to the one put forward by Purcell and Kinnie (2007, p.541):

**Figure 12 A simple graphic representation of the HRM–performance link**

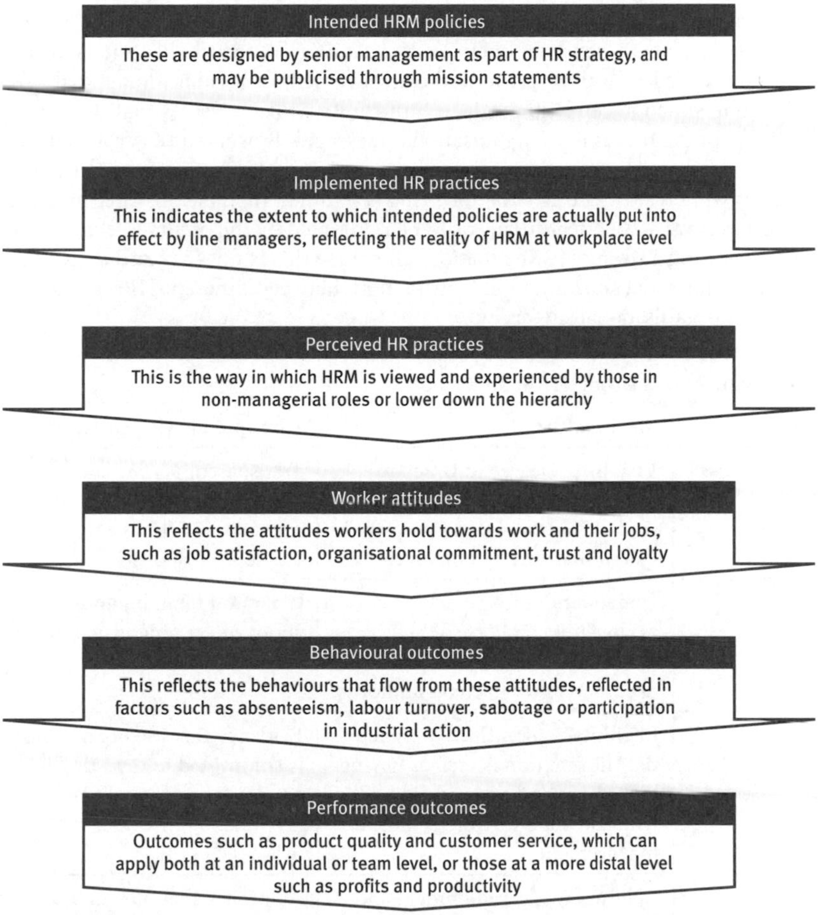

**Intended HRM policies**
These are designed by senior management as part of HR strategy, and may be publicised through mission statements

**Implemented HR practices**
This indicates the extent to which intended policies are actually put into effect by line managers, reflecting the reality of HRM at workplace level

**Perceived HR practices**
This is the way in which HRM is viewed and experienced by those in non-managerial roles or lower down the hierarchy

**Worker attitudes**
This reflects the attitudes workers hold towards work and their jobs, such as job satisfaction, organisational commitment, trust and loyalty

**Behavioural outcomes**
This reflects the behaviours that flow from these attitudes, reflected in factors such as absenteeism, labour turnover, sabotage or participation in industrial action

**Performance outcomes**
Outcomes such as product quality and customer service, which can apply both at an individual or team level, or those at a more distal level such as profits and productivity

## REFLECTIVE ACTIVITY

Drawing on your own experience, how well do you think the organisation(s) you have worked for – in a full-time, part-time, or temporary position – managed to translate intended HRM policies into practice? Where did any blockages occur in the process?

## 'STRONG' HR SYSTEMS

As an alternative to the many projects examining HR **practices**, a newer stream of studies have focused instead on HR **processes**. Prime amongst these is a conceptual paper by Bowen and Ostroff (2004). For them a strong system is one in which 'individuals share a common interpretation of what behaviours are expected and rewarded. The strength of the HRM system can explain how individual employee attributes accumulate to affect organisational effectiveness' (Bowen and Ostroff 2004, p.203). The authors differentiate between content and process. The former refers to the set of practices adopted to help achieve organisational goals, eg selection techniques, induction methods and pay systems. The latter refers to how the HR system can be designed and administered effectively to ensure that it can create shared meaning about content that might ultimately impact on organisational performance. This relates to the symbolic and actual messages used within the organisation that help workers make sense of their work situation so they believe it is worthwhile contributing their effort and expertise to the achievement of organisational goals. In other words, a strong situation can help produce conformity whilst a weak situation can result in ambiguity about the meaning of organisational messages. Bowen and Ostroff (2004, p.208) propose that when an HRM system 'is perceived as high in distinctiveness, consistency and consensus, it will create a strong situation'. This is outlined in Table 36. The three concepts are interrelated in that each feature needs to be reinforced by the others in order for it to be effective in creating a strong HRM situation. Of course this is not easy and there is massive room for ambiguity and contradiction to arise, both between different HR practices and up and down the organisational hierarchy.

**Table 36 Features of a strong HRM situation**

| Concept | Meta-feature | Example of HR practice/process |
|---|---|---|
| **Distinctiveness** | **Visibility**. Degree to which the HR practices are salient and readily observable, and perceived in a similar way by employees. | Transparent *performance criteria* required to construct shared expectations about appropriate employee response. |
| | **Understandability**. Lack of ambiguity and ease of comprehension of HRM practice needed in order to create authority. | Clear and unambiguous messages about *career progression* in order to avoid confusion. |
| | **Legitimacy of authority**. When the HR function is seen as having high status and high credibility with and support from senior management. | Evidence that the organisation is committed to investing in employees and involvement of *HR function* in strategic planning process. |
| | **Relevance**. Clear alignment and congruence between individual and organisational goals, and evidence that line managers act in a way which supports this link. | Assurance that *line managers* believe in, promote and adhere to organisational policies about work–life balance. |
| **Consistency** | **Instrumentality**. Establishing an unambiguous perceived cause–effect relationship between the goals of HRM systems and the associated employee consequences. | Close links over time between management assertions that workers are our principal asset and maintenance of *employment security* guarantees. |

| Concept | Meta-feature | Example of HR practice/process |
|---|---|---|
| | **Validity**. HRM practices must display consistency between what they purport to do and what they actually do in order to help create a strong situation. | *Selection tests* must be a valid screen for personal attributes that are essential for human capital development. |
| | **Consistent HRM messages.** These need to convey compatibility and stability in the signals sent about HRM down the organisational hierarchy, between different HR practices and over time. | *Communications* about issues need to convey the same message about what is important in terms of objectives and requisite behaviour by employees. |
| **Consensus** | **Agreement among principal HRM decision-makers.** This is necessary to ensure that employees receive similar messages about organisational goals and values from different managerial functions. | Clear vision and mission from *top management* that is seen to have support across the board. |
| | **Fairness.** This is a composite of employee perceptions of whether HRM practices adhere to the principles of different forms of organisational justice. | The willingness of employees to take 360 degree *appraisals* seriously depends on whether feedback shapes subsequent management behaviour. |

Source: Developed from Bowen and Ostroff (2004).

The authors (2004, p.214) are aware that the creation of a single 'strong' HRM system may not be either achievable or desirable in all situations, and acknowledge that sub-systems are likely exist in large conglomerates operating in different sectors or countries, where different business pressures and institutional forces are apparent. There is also acceptance that a strong HRM system could be potentially inflexible and resistant to change. Moreover it could be counterproductive and stifle creativity if employers want workers to use their discretion to solve problems or encourage them to voice their concerns about issues to do with, for example, bullying and harassment.

Pavlou (2011) used the Bowen and Ostroff framework to assess HRM in a Cypriot bank, which is well-known for providing amongst the best benefits available in the country. He also compared responses from senior managers, line managers and non-managerial respondents. For the most part, senior managers believed a strong HR system existed in all its features, but that is hardly surprising given they had been its architects in the first place. Line managers were generally sceptical of how well this had been embedded in the organisation. For example, they felt that HR policies, though they might exist, were not communicated well to staff, that the bank typically failed to motivate its employees well, and that it was not clear how the supposed bundle of HR practices actually fitted together. Non-managerial employees were predominantly negative about the HRM system, describing it as lacking in visibility and augmenting managerial power through retention of vital information, as well as failing to motivate and engage employees despite its stated intentions (see Nishi *et al* 2008). Appraisal practices were seen as especially problematic, lacking in substance and not being taken seriously. In addition, the HR function was seen to lack authority and credibility. The problem is exacerbated by the situation at the firm; on the one hand, bank employees do very well in terms of material rewards and levels of employment security, whilst at the same time they do not feel their initial enthusiasm at being selected from a very strong pool of applicants has been reinforced through subsequent career development and engagement opportunities. In short, whilst the system is seen as strong by those at the top, it is perceived as weak by those in the workforce as a whole.

Other studies have also used Bowen and Ostroff's framework. Whilst broadly supportive, Haggerty and Wright (2010, p.101) propose a reconceptualisation of the strong HR system as 'signals from management to employee groups and individuals' which are reflected in HR practices and bundles, rather than being about the HR practices themselves; this is contrary to the understanding adopted in this book. Given that messages are likely to be interpreted in different ways by different groups of workers, employers need to be careful that the desired signals are received by the employees for which they are intended. Thus, they argue (p.107) – in line with the architecture ideas presented in Chapter 4 – that 'attempts to broadly disseminate information about practices that are not relevant will most likely result in significantly less attention to chosen media over time, weakening the organisational situation'. Since HR practices vary between occupational groups – for example, between senior executives, professionals, hourly paid workers and sub-contractors – it is better to create a range of 'strong' HRM systems appropriate for the group concerned. Stanton *et al* (2010) applied the framework in their study of HRM in three Australian hospitals, finding some support for the principles underpinning Bowen and Ostroff (2004) but noting that a strong HR system was hard to achieve in practice. They conclude their study (2010, p.580) by reiterating how important the CEO is in encouraging 'all levels of the managerial hierarchy to "sing the same song". This requires high level leadership based on within group agreement that uses its authority to transmit relevant, consistent and valid HRM messages and information across the organisation.' Guest and Conway (2011) tested Bowen and Ostroff's idea of consensus as part of a 'strong' HR system in their analysis of HR effectiveness with data from 237 matched pairs of senior line managers and HR practitioners. Interestingly, their hypothesis that consensus between these two sets of managers would be more strongly associated with subjective and objective measurements of performance than a high score from either one was not supported by the evidence. The authors argue therefore that consensus is not an important component of a strong HR system. These studies raise doubts about how the strong HR systems approach might work in practice.

HRM AT WORK IN FOCUS

### How employees interpret HR practices: attribution theory

Nishi *et al* (2008) build upon the work of Bowen and Ostroff (2004) by proposing that employees' perceptions of HR practices are also important, primarily through why they think employers have introduced these practices in the first place. They argue (p.505) that employees may share 'climate perceptions based on the HR practices they experience ... but disagree about why those HR practices were put into place to create that climate'. For example some believe that management has concerns for employee well-being whilst others believe they are motivated by a desire solely to cut costs. They use the word 'attributions' to mean 'the causal explanations that employees make regarding management's motivations for using particular HR practices and argue that employees HR attributions have important consequences for their commitment and satisfaction' (pp.507–8).

The study was undertaken across 362 departments in 95 stores of a large retailer which had standard HR practices applied centrally. It comprised a survey of 1,010 departmental managers and 4,208 employees. In addition, the researchers checked their survey with 25 scholars with expertise in the area, and at company level with focus groups prior to it being administered; this led to some questions being changed to confirm understanding. The authors acknowledge the HR practices they surveyed may not be appropriate for all settings but they made sense in their organisational context. As an aside, the procedures used here were very impressive, showing how high-quality research should be conducted.

In line with their expectations, the researchers found that HR practices which employees felt were motivated by a concern for employee well-being and enhancing service quality were positively related to employee attitudes, whilst an attribution focused on reducing costs and exploiting employees was negatively associated with attitudes. The implication is clear: whilst HR practices are important, employees' **perceptions** of employer goals for pursuing these practices are also critically important for achieving desired organisational outcomes. This demonstrates clearly that employers cannot hoodwink employees into believing they are regarded as valued assets without substantial evidence they mean what they say.

*To think about:*

*On the basis of these research findings, what advice would you give to an employer about how to ensure employees interpret messages in the way they are intended? Use ideas from the whole book to draw up a list of ideas.*

Source: Adapted from Nishi *et al* (2008).

## ALIGNMENT, INTEGRATION AND CONSISTENCY IN HRM

The final framework we examine combines processes and practices, mirroring the reviews of HRM which focus on notions of external and internal fit. External (or vertical) fit refers to the development of links between organisational goals/strategies and HRM (Allen and Wright 2007), that is, processes. Alignment and integration are the terms more widely used in the literature and in practitioner publications. In addition, a key HR objective is to achieve consistency in actions, both at the level of policy and practice. The alignment–integration–consistency framework has been examined both in the context of single employers and in partnerships and alliances across organisational boundaries by Marchington *et al* (2011).

*Alignment* relies on achieving links which lead to the development of employee commitment and allegiance to organisational goals (Kepes S and Delery J 2007). Alignment is considered desirable because there is a higher likelihood of congruence and shared meanings up and down the hierarchy if HR practices support organisational goals, person–organisation fit is tight and workers are strongly committed to their organisation (Bowen and Ostroff 2004). Even where an organisation deploys differential HRM systems, alignment may still be achievable if a strong organisational climate can be developed to provide the glue to unify the workforce and to help create 'a deep emotional commitment that makes employees believe they are part of a unique bond with other employees and the whole organisation' (Kepes and Delery 2006, p.59). Alignment could be bolstered through the development of 'employer branding'. Kepes and Delery (2007) argue that brands may help create a unique bond even when there are differential HR systems in place. However, once organisations move beyond a single establishment, alignment is harder to achieve, especially if the organisation operates across divisions and product ranges, and even more so if it takes place across different countries.

*Integration* requires complementary HR policies and practices both between (eg between recruitment and reward) and within different HR policy areas (eg within employee voice between communication and team-working policies). As we saw earlier, such connections are typically termed 'bundles' and high levels of *integration* across the bundle should promote synergies that enhance organisational effectiveness (Benson and Lawler 2003). 'Powerful connections' reinforce a common organisational message, thereby helping to avoid potential contradictions that could produce 'deadly combinations' (Kepes and Delery 2007).

*Consistency* relates to whether or not workers perceive the implementation of HR policies to be fair and reasonable compared with their colleagues and also over time. Guest (2007) further argues that employee perceptions of fair treatment are essential for the operation of the psychological contract and consistently applied rules reduce the likelihood that workers will harbour perceptions of unfair treatment. Baron and Kreps (1999) refer to three types of consistency: single employee; among employee; and temporal. 'Single employee' consistency occurs where an individual worker perceives the HRM system to be sending consistent and complementary messages; for example, in a high commitment organisation, s/he might be consulted about some decisions, receive high levels of pay, and be given opportunities for promotion where possible (Kepes and Delery 2007). 'Among employee' consistency is when individuals that work together are treated similarly; this can fail across multi-divisional teams or even be caused by inconsistencies in management treatment of different workers on the same team. As we saw in Chapter 7, there are many reasons why line managers operate inconsistently, either by design so as to reward star performers or by omission because circumstances change or because they are unaware that some staff are receiving preferential treatment. 'Temporal consistency' is where workers receive 'messages' that remain the same over time, but problems arise if an organisation shifts from a long-standing no-redundancy policy to one of voluntary severance as a way to combat market decline.

Marchington *et al* (2011) applied this framework to how HRM is shaped across multi-employer networks which are instigated to improve customer service. Efforts to achieve *alignment* encountered problems when partner organisations differ in their goals and expectations, and tensions arose in the search for shared long-term goals, particularly if one partner operates under pressure to maximise shareholder value while the other is measured against achievement of social objectives. The potential for conflict is high in collaborations between private and public sector organisations because, in attempting to satisfy their own objectives, each may adopt different HRM styles (Boxall and Purcell 2008). Though employer branding might work within the same organisation, in multi-employer networks the presence of competing and potentially incongruent brands makes this much harder to achieve. Shared experiences are unlikely if employees work closely with teams at a client site for months, or even years at a time. The longer they are absent from the site of their own employer, the more likely they are to 'live the brand' of the client. However, George and Chattopadhyay's (2005) research on contract workers in IT found that identification with their client depended greatly on personal relations, such as high trust in their supervisors and positive relationships with colleagues.

Achieving *integration* of HR practices across multi-employer networks is problematic if there are few similarities between partners' goals, but if groups of staff from partner organisations work more closely with one another than with colleagues from their own employer, there is a stronger case for seeking to move towards integration by reducing differences between the HRM policies used by employers in the network (Kepes and Delery 2007; Lepak and Snell 2007). However, integration across the network may undermine fit with strong organisation-specific HR systems, and this could – for example – limit career prospects within the home organisation's internal labour market. Additionally, as we have seen, much depends on line managers implementing HRM in accordance with senior management's intentions. This is more difficult in multi-employer networks because people often work at the site of another employer – and are thus distanced from their own organisation – and/or because they are supervised by managers employed by a different organisation.

*Consistency* is particularly hard to achieve across multi-employer networks. For example, single employee inconsistency can arise if a performance review is undertaken using the approach of a partner employer in the network, while access to training – which is a frequent outcome of such reviews – may be dependent on their own employer's policies and practices. This can affect commitment to organisational and/or network goals. Multi-employer networks also raise problems for 'among employee' consistency if workers employed alongside each other are subject to different HR practices that result in significant variations in how they are treated. Organisation A may pay employees with similar skills and experience more than Organisation B – due to historical reasons, to different HRM policies or simply because Organisation A can afford more than Organisation B. The application of disciplinary rules is probably the area where perceptions of fair treatment are most overtly compromised by inconsistencies (Grimshaw *et al* 2003; Walsh and Deery 2006) as different workers are subject to decisions which might have internal legitimacy within their own organisation but may create major tensions between workers in a multi-employer network (Kuvaas 2008). Finally, temporal consistency in HRM policies and practices is hard to maintain if there are efforts to integrate HR systems to create 'among employee' consistency. Moreover, client-specific contracts may require specific working time arrangements, different disciplinary standards, or a requirement that the workforce does not join trade unions; all of which can undermine the delivery of temporal consistency. Segmentation according to client needs may be resolved, however, by separating work groups by client but this then restricts mobility across the organisation (Lepak and Snell 2007).

## THE RADICAL CRITIQUE: WHERE IS THE 'H' IN HUMAN RESOURCE MANAGEMENT?

Whilst the previous sections highlight limitations in the research on the link between HRM and performance, there is a more radical critique that questions whether high commitment HRM is actually beneficial for workers. Ramsay *et al* (2000) propose an alternative, labour process explanation that suggests that higher levels of organisational performance are achieved not through 'progressive' employment practices but instead through work intensification. Basically, both the high commitment and the labour process versions agree that a distinctive set of HR practices may well contribute to improved levels of organisational performance. However, as Ramsay *et al* (p.505) argue, 'it is at this point that the two approaches part company. The labour process critique holds that, while high performance work systems practices may provide enhancements in discretion, these come to employees at the expense of stress, work intensification and job strain, the latter being a key explanatory factor in improved organisational performance'. This interpretation is quite different therefore, mirroring the discussion about competing versions of EIP and teamworking in Chapters 3 and 13. In order to test their proposition, they used the 1998 WERS material, focusing in particular on employee outcomes. They included other factors in their analysis related to job strain and work intensification – measured by questions about the lack of time to complete work, worrying about work outside working hours, and changes in productivity (p.527). Their conclusions contrast with those of the high commitment school as little support is found for the idea that positive performance outcomes flow from positive employee outcomes. At the same time, however, the labour process interpretation is not supported either.

This approach has been reviewed by Thompson and Harley (2007) who argue that much depends on the societal systems and organisational circumstances within which the high commitment paradigm is located. As we have stressed repeatedly, in LMEs which put a primacy on shareholder value and financial markets, HRM is likely to suffer more than in CMEs where workers are less likely to be treated as disposable commodities. In relation to skill formation for example, the argument that jobs are being consistently upgraded within a knowledge society – one component of high commitment HRM – provides a highly distorted account of what is happening. As they note (2007, p.158) 'there is the inconvenient fact that the largest actual and projected job growth in the USA and the UK is at the lower end of the labour market. Most are in routine jobs in hospitality and retail, or in personal services in the private and public sectors.' However, this does not negate the possibility of pockets of high commitment HRM within certain firms or in particular occupations, as we saw earlier in the book. Godard (2004) reaches similar conclusions, and hypothesises that in Canada high performance programmes might be fragile and short-lived due to decisions – say, in relation to redundancies or major structural change – that are made on financial grounds by senior managers, but which undermine the coherence of HRM and dissipate the trust workers have in their employers.

Moving yet further into the critique takes us to the post-modern perspective. This argues that by adopting 'softer' techniques, employers merely create yet more sophisticated ways of exploiting workers. From this angle, high commitment HRM is even more insidious than its Taylorist counterpart, precisely because it offers the illusion that managers are seeking co-operative ways of working. This is a strategy which gets workers to agree to changes that are not, ultimately, to their own benefit (see, for example, Willmott 1993). Of course, real-life situations are more complicated than this, partly because workers are not 'cultural dopes', like putty in the hands of skilful managers, but also because employers are rarely able to implement HR practices as originally intended (Thompson and Harley 2007). Nevertheless this does question whether HRM has actually anything to do with humans, for example in relation to flexibility, skill development or diversity management (Bolton and Houlihan 2007). As an example, work–life balance policies struggle hard to make an impact against a backcloth of the 'long hours' culture, time pressures and the deployment of domestic care by dual career families who choose to outsource family responsibilities in order to maintain their own professional lifestyles. Delbridge (2011) makes the case for 'Critical HRM' by arguing that mainstream approaches are too dependent on management perspectives and the dominant ideology which supports shareholder goals and government direction. This critique raises important questions about HRM, not least the use of performance indicators that are narrowly defined – profitability, productivity, commitment, labour turnover – within a managerial discourse. However, this underestimates the wide range of approaches taken in 'mainstream' HRM, and leads Thompson (2011) to conclude little will be gained from the establishment of a 'Critical HRM' ghetto which focuses on a narrow research agenda populated by like-minded scholars rather than continuing with a wider approach using a range of social science traditions.

## CONCLUSIONS

Despite a wealth of research and publications on the links between HRM and performance (Guest 2011), we are still no nearer to a definitive view on this issue. Part of the problem has been that researchers have tended to adopt varying definitions of and measures for what is meant by HRM and performance, and there has been little direct replication of studies because fault has been found, in one way or another, with them. Take definitions of HRM as an example: some studies have focused on practices that comprise the high commitment paradigm whilst others have compared different conceptions of HRM, such as cost reduction, quality enhancement and innovation. At the level of detail, similar problems arise about what comprises the bundle of practices examined as well as the proxies used as indicators of HRM. Similar problems arise with measures of performance, with some studies opting for subjective measures whilst others aim to get objective measures; both have shortcomings, and studies suggest there is often little agreement between them. Just to complicate matters further there are contrasting views on whether high commitment HRM generates benefits both for employers and employees, as the mainstream literature implies. Proponents of Critical HRM believe this not to be the case, and argue that employers are only interested in developing even more subtle ways of controlling workers – the iron fist under the illusion of a velvet glove. Whilst it is important to retain a critical perspective on HRM, it is too simplistic to assume that managers are automatically and implicitly conditioned to control workers at all times.

Recent interest in HRM processes, stimulated by – amongst others – Bowen and Ostroff with their conception of strong HRM systems, and by Purcell and his colleagues who have attempted to open up what is known as the black box has opened up new avenues. This has shown that whilst specific HR practices may be important to gain employee commitment, the **way** these are implemented and supported also matters significantly. As we saw in earlier chapters, employee perceptions of HRM has a major impact on their success, and it is perfectly feasible for two employers to adopt the same bundle of HR practices yet have quite different employee outcomes. Alignment, integration and consistency are crucial here, as is the degree to which HR practices are embedded and underpinned in any organisation. Since the first edition of this book in the mid-1990s, the role of line managers has become even more important in translating HRM policies into practice and the HR function has taken on a more wide-ranging and varied role in the management of people at work.

EXPLORE FURTHER

BOWEN, D. and OSTROFF, C. (2004) 'Understanding HRM-firm performance linkages: the role of the "strength" of the HRM system', *Academy of Management Review*, Vol.29, No.2, 203–21.

BOXALL, P. and MACKY, K. (2009) 'Research and theory in high performance work systems: progressing the high involvement stream', *Human Resource Management Journal*, Vol.19, No.1, 3–23.

GARDNER, T. and WRIGHT, P. (2009) 'Implicit human resource management theory: a potential threat to the internal validity of human resource practice measures', *International Journal of Human Resource Management*, Vol.20, No.1, 57–74.

GODARD, J. (2004) 'A critical assessment of the high performance paradigm', *British Journal of Industrial Relations*, Vol.42, No.2, 349–78.

GUEST, D. (2011) 'Human resource management and performance: still searching for answers', *Human Resource Management Journal*, Vol.21, No.1, 3–13.

GUEST, D., MICHIE, J., CONWAY, N. and SHEEHAN, M. (2003) 'Human resource management and performance', *British Journal of Industrial Relations*, Vol.41, No.2, 291–314.

KHILJI, S. and WANG, X. (2006) '"Intended" and "implemented" HRM: the missing linchpin in strategic human resource management research', *International Journal of Human Resource Management*, Vol.17, No.7, 1171–89.

MARCHINGTON, M., RUBERY, J. and GRIMSHAW, D. (2011) 'Alignment, integration and consistency in HRM across multi-employer networks', *Human Resource Management*, Vol.50, No.3, 313–39.

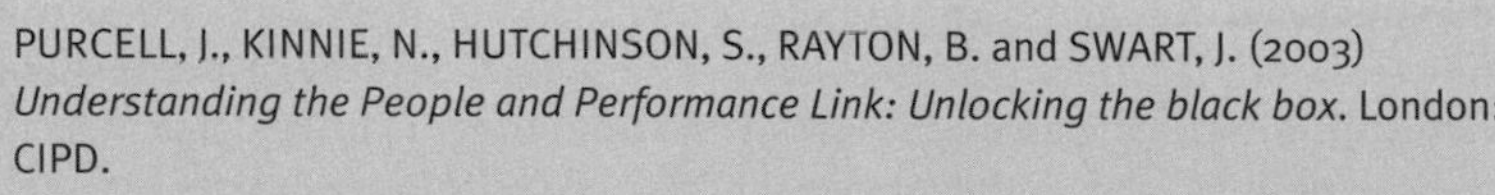

PURCELL, J., KINNIE, N., HUTCHINSON, S., RAYTON, B. and SWART, J. (2003) *Understanding the People and Performance Link: Unlocking the black box*. London: CIPD.

WEST, M., BORRILL, C., DAWSON, J., SCULLY, J., CARTER, M., ANELAY, S., PATTERSON, M. and WARING, J. (2002) 'The link between the management of employees and patient mortality in acute hospitals', *International Journal of Human Resource Management*, Vol.13, No.8, 1299–310.

CHAPTER 16

# Research Skills and Project Management

## LEARNING OUTCOMES

By the end of this chapter, readers should be able to:

- contribute effectively to the planning, design and implementation of projects
- make appropriate and correct use of different techniques in gathering data for a management project
- draw realistic conclusions from evidence-based research and present these in a logical and systematic manner.

In addition, readers should understand and be able to explain:

- the advantages and disadvantages of a range of research methods and their relevance to different situations
- the structure and contents of a management research report, including the role of realistic and appropriate recommendations
- how to develop and present a persuasive business report on an HR issue.

## INTRODUCTION

HR specialists are often involved in investigating business issues and project work with other managers and achieving outcomes through the actions of other people. The skills needed in order to do this include interviewing, communication, presentation, assertiveness, time management, negotiating, influencing and persuading. In addition to these general transferable skills, for any project work to be successful a wide range of analytical skills need to be deployed. These include identifying key issues, planning and organising work individually or in teams, information search and retrieval, and data analysis. Project work forms a critical part of the HR manager's job, and provides the means by which HR impacts on broader management agendas. The 2011 CIPD standards make it clear that qualified HR professionals should be able to research relevant topics and write reports that can persuade key stakeholders in the organisation to change or adopt a particular policy and practice. The applied nature of the report requires a combination of academic research and business report writing skills, as well as awareness of how HR issues relate to business strategy (see Chapter 1). There has been increasing interest in how an HR practitioner can make better-quality decisions and use HR practices that actually work. This is evidence-based HR (EBHR), which is explained more fully in the box below, and is informed by a much wider application of evidence-based ideas particularly in medicine. As Rousseau and Barends (2011) note, faulty practices and decision-making are common in HR. Sometimes an HR practitioner lacks the scientific knowledge but the key problem is the absence of a questioning mindset and the failure to think critically. This means exploring alternatives, seeking understanding and testing assumptions about the effectiveness of one's own professional decisions and activities. Imitation or reliance on fads or copycat practices from other companies is not critical thinking as it fails to take account of what is likely to work in a particular organisation (Pfeffer and Sutton 2006). Anderson (2004, p.6) defines research in HR as 'finding out things in a systematic way in order to increase knowledge about people and processes involved in the management of work organisation'.

HRM AT WORK IN FOCUS

## Becoming an EBHR practitioner

**What EBHR means**

EBHR combines four features into everyday management practice and decision-making:

1. use of the *best available scientific evidence* from peer-reviewed sources
2. systematic gathering of *organisational facts, indicators and metrics* to better act on the evidence
3. *practitioner judgement* assisted by procedures, practices and frameworks that reduce bias, improve decision quality and create more valid learning over time
4. ethical *considerations* weighing the short- and long-term *impacts of decisions on stakeholders and society*

*Best available research evidence* – this refers to findings from published scientific (peer reviewed) research.

*Organisational facts, metrics and assessments* – an HR practitioner needs to take into account the facts of the situation in order to identify what kinds of research findings are likely to be useful. So they need to understand the context.

*Practitioner reflection and judgement* – effective use of evidence depends on there being not only good scientific knowledge informed by organisational facts, but also mindful decision-making with people aware that they are prone to bias in making decisions and taking steps to avoid this.

*Consideration of affected stakeholders* – HR decisions and practices have both direct and indirect consequences for an organisation's stakeholders. This includes employees, executives and managers as well as stakeholders outside of the organisation, including suppliers, shareholders or indeed the public at large.

*Developing a questioning mindset* – unfreezing old habits of mind means questioning traditional assumptions, and checking whether beliefs are facts. This critical habit of mind is known as 'mindfulness'. EBHR practitioners need to learn to question things and not feel like they are rocking the boat.

*Make your decisions more explicit* – in EBHR, decisions are made explicit to reduce decision neglect (not making a decision that needs to be made), to avoid making decisions on auto-pilot (important actions are taken without deliberation) and to increase mindful, deliberate decision-making. The process of making decisions explicit has two parts. The first aspect is developing decision awareness, recognising the numerous micro-choices made every day, all with potential to be informed by evidence. The second feature of making decisions explicit means to actually begin paying attention to how a decision is made: with whom and with what evidence.

Source: Adapted from Rousseau and Barends (2011).

This chapter looks at good practice in carrying out investigating business issues via a research project and introducing change into organisations. We examine research design and method, structure and layout, as well as considering the role of the HR manager and the skills required to implement projects. This chapter is somewhat different from the rest of the book, as it provides guidance on producing a research project and implementing recommendations. Naturally, this will be particularly helpful to those who have limited experience, but it should also be a useful reminder for more experienced practitioners. The word 'researcher' is used throughout but this also covers 'project manager', 'student' and 'change management specialist' as well.

A sequence proposed by Howard *et al* (2002) is commonly used when planning projects. This is illustrated in Figure 13 and is used as a framework for the remainder of the chapter. We have added to this an implementation stage (incorporating change management) – something that would be required of the HR manager. Each step in the sequence should be given sufficient attention if time is to be saved in the longer term. A common error is to give insufficient attention to defining clearly the topic to be investigated (Gill and Johnson 2010, p.24). This is similar to answering the wrong question in an examination – still the most common reason for failure. As a result the project may be too broad, take up too much time, and the recommendations be difficult to justify or do not flow from the content of the report.

**Figure 13 Sequence for a project**

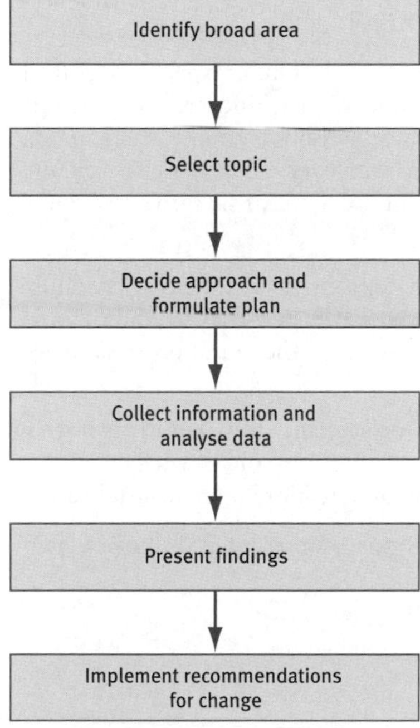


Source: Adapted from Howard *et al* (2002).

## IDENTIFYING THE BROAD TOPIC AREA

A number of issues are important when identifying the broad area. These include terms of reference, access and collaboration. The terms of reference indicate what the researcher is being asked to do and what access and budget are provided. If the report is a CIPD Management Report, the terms of reference will normally be a part of the brief. Clarifying the terms of reference shows what the report is about – and what it is not about. In short, it delineates the boundaries of the report (Johns 1996).

The prospect of gaining access and the type of access are very important issues (Saunders *et al* 2009, pp.162–98). Topics concerned with, for example, redundancy, competitive product markets or managerial stress – although potentially interesting and useful research areas – may be difficult to study (Gill and Johnson 2010, p.25). Similarly, topics which are politically sensitive – such as executive pay for senior managers – may make access to information difficult. For those already employed in the HR function, access to the organisation itself may not be a problem but access to data and people may be more difficult. For researchers who are starting 'cold', one common approach is to send a project proposal (no more than two pages) to targeted organisations, and then follow this up with further letters or telephone calls. It is often difficult to gain access, and luck tends to play a large part in this.

The next issue is collaboration and research partners. As projects often depend heavily on working closely with prospective respondents and practitioners, it might be useful to involve them in the definition and management of research. This very often brings an immediate relevance to the work (practitioners are likely to have many 'hot' topics they need researching) and the findings can be disseminated quickly across user networks. However, work must be theoretically grounded in a way that makes its contribution to knowledge obvious and this cannot be traded off in the interests of 'practical utility'. If working within an employing organisation, it is similarly important to ensure that the needs of the researcher match organisational needs; otherwise it is possible to end up doing two quite different projects. Additionally, there are confidentiality and ethical issues. As Brewerton and Millward (2001, p.4) note:

> The researcher must be conscious of and respect any ethical issues raised. Research projects involving participants of any kind are likely to raise expectations, or have other implications for the organisation or the participants involved. Confidential information gained from whatever source must remain confidential, and the researcher must retain a high degree of integrity in conducting research within a 'live' setting.

The choice and definition of topic is determined by a number of issues, including the amount of time available as well as the personal capabilities and interests of the researcher (Anderson 2004, pp.33–7). Amongst the questions that need to be addressed are the following:

- What is the purpose of the project and how realistic is it to investigate?
- Will it usefully add to the existing store of knowledge?
- Will the subject chosen for investigation be manageable and not be too open-ended?

Some further important questions are presented in the box below.

HRM AT WORK IN FOCUS

## Checklist of attributes of a good research topic

1. Does the topic fit the specifications and meet the standards set by the examining institution?
2. Is the topic something with which you are really fascinated?
3. Does your research topic contain issues that have a clear link to theory?
4. Do you have, or can you develop within the project time frame, the necessary research skills to undertake the topic?
5. Is the research topic achievable within the available time?
6. Is the research topic achievable within the financial resources?
7. Are you reasonably certain of being able to gain access to the required data?
8. Are you able to state your research question(s) and objectives clearly?
9. Will your proposed research be able to provide fresh insights on this topic?
10. Does the research topic match your career goals?

Source: Adapted from Saunders *et al* (2009).

The general purpose of the project needs to be clear. It is important to have several ideas and be flexible over the choice and treatment of the research topic. Where possible, it is important to choose something interesting with enough depth, without it being too broad. For example, 'what impact does organisational change have on the everyday life of employees?' is far too vague, whereas 'what is organisational change?' needs a clearer definition in terms of strategy, structure and culture (Thietart *et al* 2001, pp.44–5). In short, the topic should be manageable, precise and achievable in the time period. It is better to say a lot about a relatively specific problem, than a little about a very broad issue. Another trap is what Silverman (1993) terms 'tourism'; that is only examining innovative or novel aspects and ignoring routine issues.

*Time management* is a crucial consideration. With limited time available there may be a temptation to select a topic before doing the preliminary groundwork. This is short-sighted as time will not be saved in the long run. It is generally the case that the time taken to accomplish a piece of research is underestimated. This can be lengthened by delays, illness or job pressures (Gill and Johnson 2010, p.24). External factors may have a bearing on the time needed, especially when relying on the goodwill of others who may prove difficult to pin down in practice. Additionally, there may be unforeseen organisational changes that make it difficult to carry out the original project.

A *research plan* showing the phases of the research and dates for completion can assist in the management of unforeseen delays. It is useful to keep a research diary including targets, progress and ideas, and to review these regularly. In the business and management world it is often very difficult to plan ahead precisely, but that does not mean such planning should be avoided. Few research projects are as elegant and unproblematic as their eventual published form suggests. Companies may drop out, people go on holiday and circumstances change – this is part of the normal process of research. There is a danger of assuming all research projects are undertaken with fully articulated objectives at the commencement of the study, an error compounded by the rational and logical way in which results are written up after the event! As Pettigrew (1985, p.222) honestly admits, 'it is more easily characterised in the language of muddling through, incrementalism and political process' rather than a rationally contrived act. Similarly, access is often assumed to be unproblematic, with researchers having total freedom to inquire into the exact details in the precise location where their theoretical preconceptions lead them. Unfortunately, reality rests more on good fortune and opportunism; for example, making contact at a time when the 'gatekeeper' in the organisation wants outside intervention, or in not 'losing' sites through closure or takeover. As Buchanan *et al* (1988, p.53) observe:

> Fieldwork is permeated with the conflict between what is theoretically desirable on the one hand and what is practically possible on the other. It is desirable to ensure representativeness in the sample, uniformity of interview procedures, adequate data collection across the range of topics to be explored, and so on. But the members of the organisations block access to information, constrain the time allowed for interviews, lose your questionnaires, go on holiday, and join other organisations in the middle of your unfinished study. In the conflict between desirable and the possible, the possible always wins.

Gill and Johnson (2010, p.24) point out that a researcher with strong capabilities in the behavioural sciences but low numeracy skills should hesitate before choosing a topic involving complex statistical analysis. Similarly, a researcher with poor analytical and writing skills might be unwise to embark on an ethnographic study. If possible, projects should make use of existing skills, and of course, it helps greatly if the topic is of particular interest to the researcher. Finally, the value of the project is important. Gill and Johnson (p.24) suggest that motivation and interest is higher if the work is clearly making a contribution to the solution of a significant problem. There are a number of techniques that can be used to generate and refine research ideas (see box below).

HRM AT WORK IN FOCUS

### Frequently used techniques for generating and refining research ideas

| **Rational thinking** | **Creative thinking** |
|---|---|
| Examining your own strengths and interests | Keeping a notebook of ideas |
| Looking at past projects | Exploring personal preferences |
| Discussion | Using past projects |
| Searching the literature | Relevance trees |
| | Brainstorming |

Source: Saunders *et al* (2009) *Research Methods for Business Students*, 4th edition. London, Financial Times/Pearson Education Ltd.

## DETERMINING THE APPROACH AND FORMULATING THE PLAN

Writing a project proposal is an important first step, whether it is going before a managerial meeting, a research committee, or a student's tutor. It is a process that repays very careful attention (Saunders *et al* 2009, p.38). For example, writing can be a good way of clarifying thoughts and ideas, and it can also help organise ideas into a coherent statement of research intent. The proposal must convince the audience that the objectives are achievable in the timeframe allowed. If asked to carry out a project for a client or one's own organisation, researchers need a clear proposal to submit for approval. Acceptance of the proposal by the client forms part of the contract, and implies that the proposal is satisfactory (Saunders *et al* 2009, pp.38–9).

The struggle to finish on time often comes about because ideas were not focused at the earliest stage or the viability was not thoroughly investigated. A proposal should have the following:

- *Title* – Should reflect the content of the proposal, even if this title is provisional.
- *Rationale* – Why the research is important and worth the effort?
- *Objectives* – A precise statement of what is hoped to achieve.
- *Themes / issues* – The ideas that will be used to guide the project research and a statement of what will be investigated and why. If it is expected that the research will prove or disprove hypotheses, then these should be stated.
- *Existing literature* – A brief discussion of existing work on the topic, demonstrating how the proposed research will fit in.
- *Methodology* – A brief account of how the work might be carried out, an indication of the proposed sources of information, the research approach and methods (justified in the light of project objectives) and an indication of analytical or statistical tools to be used. The research design and data collection phases are both important. The latter is more concerned with detail of how the data is collected (for example, how many interviews are to be carried out and their length).
- *Proposed timetable* – A provisional outline of how the research will be completed over a period of time, suggesting how many days/weeks will be spent on each of the various stages involved – always assume it will take longer than you first think.
- *Potential problems* – An indication of any problems the researcher is likely to meet. Resources may be an issue here: to what extent does one have the resources, time, money, assistance in collecting data, software packages etc to carry out the project? Another key issue relates to access. If you are suggesting interviewing every personnel director in all the major competitors in the region you might want to think whether this is viable.

See Figure 14 by Tony Watson (1994b), which is useful in crafting research projects.

## REFLECTIVE ACTIVITY

Think about a potential (or actual) project that you are doing. Write down four key questions that the project seeks to address. Which of these is central to the question?

**Figure 14 The process – a 'what, why and how' framework for crafting research**

| | |
|---|---|
| What?<br>What puzzles/intrigues me?<br>What do I want to know more about/understand better?<br>What are my key questions? | Why?<br>Why will this be of enough interest to others to be published as a thesis, book, paper, guide to practitioners or policy-makers?<br>Can the research be justified as a 'contribution to knowledge'? |
| How – conceptually?<br>What models, concepts and theories can I draw on/develop to answer my research questions?<br>How can these be brought together into a basic conceptual framework to guide my investigation? | How – practically?<br>What investigative style and techniques shall I use to apply my conceptual framework (to both gather material and analyse it?)<br>How shall I gain and maintain access to information sources? |

Source: Adapted from Watson, Managing, Crafting and Researching in British Journal of Management, John Wiley & Sons Ltd.

The project needs to be mapped out into clear stages, eg planning and preparation, project design, project implementation, data analysis/interpretation, report and various sub-stages. This might include meeting with contacts, seeking feedback on methods, acquiring ethical approval, and agreeing logistics. In addition measurable milestones need to be provided, although it is sensible to build in contingency times (Brewerton and Millward 2001, pp.23–4). There are different ways of documenting the time-planning, but one of the best is by using a Gantt chart as shown in Figure 15.

**Figure 15 Gantt Chart**

| Activity/task | Jan | Feb | Mar | Apr | May | Jun | Jul |
|---|---|---|---|---|---|---|---|
| Literature review | ■ | ■ | | | | | |
| Complete access interviews | | ■ | | | | | |
| Finalise questionnaire/interviews | | | ■ | | | | |
| Undertake interviews/questionnaires | | | | ■ | | | |
| Analyse responses | | | | ■ | ■ | | |
| Preliminary report | | | | | | ■ | ■ |

Methodology is about choosing the most appropriate methods of research to fit the aims and projected outcomes. It provides a rationale for the particular methods utilised. Methods are the practical techniques used by researchers to test their methodological and theoretical assumptions (Ackroyd and Hughes 1992). A distinction is often made between quantitative and qualitative research with the former concerned with figures and the latter with words (Miles and Huberman 1984).

Quantitative research refers to studies concerned with measurement and quantification of data to answer research questions. To be useful, data needs to be analysed and interpreted using quantitative analysis techniques. The archetypal approach is the application of a formula: a statement or hypothesis to be tested; an account of sampling and methods; and, finally, a description of results and a discussion of the implications. With quantitative work, the process of data collection becomes distinct from analysis (Easterby-Smith *et al* 2008, pp.234–67).

Qualitative research is more fashionable than in the past when there was greater stress on 'objectivity' and 'reliability' and an attempt to impose scientific use of theory (Silverman 2010). Qualitative research puts emphasis on individuals' interpretation of behaviour and their environment. The emphasis tends to be on understanding what is going on in organisations in participants' own terms rather than those of the researcher. As Fineman and Mangham (1983, p.296) observe: 'if behaviour is viewed as situationally-specific, idiosyncratic, multivariate or holistic, then a "richer", more descriptive analysis may well be taken to be worthwhile'. The scientific model has been criticised on the grounds that research in the real world does not fit the textbook model. In contrast, qualitative research tends to generate data in a non-standard fashion and hence has been described as 'an attractive nuisance' (Miles 1979, p.590).

In practice the differences between quantitative and qualitative approaches can be exaggerated, and both can be equally useful (Silverman 2010). Qualitative material can be generated from quantitative data – for example, interviews and surveys can incorporate open-ended questions that allow for qualitative analysis to be used (Easterby-Smith *et al* 2008, p.116). Both approaches are frequently used together. For example, research into best practice in teacher capability procedures involved quantitative research (analysis of questionnaires sent to head-teachers) as well as qualitative data (analysis of interviews with head-teachers). The conclusions and recommendations resulting from the research were informed by both sets of data (Earnshaw *et al* 2002b).

Glaser and Strauss (1967) have emphasised the evolutionary nature of research, especially in the fieldwork phase. They stress the limitations of sticking to a prescribed research plan when events unfold that highlight different issues which are much more important than those originally identified. Mintzberg (1979, p.587) is particularly critical of quantitative researchers who never 'go near the water' or collect data from a distance 'without anecdote to support them'. He argues that this may lead to 'difficulty explaining interesting relationships'. His focus on inductive research comprises two parts. Firstly, there is detective work, which involves tracking down patterns and seeing how pieces fit together. Secondly, there is the 'creative leap', which effectively requires researchers to generalise beyond their data in order to describe something new. However, he warns that this kind of research can tend to be haphazard and harder to plan than testing simple hypotheses in the relative security of the laboratory.

An understanding of theory and related research is an essential part of a good project and it is important to present the theoretical background to a project. This is the sum of what is already known about a subject area, and its related problems, in general terms. It should outline and provide a critique of the generally accepted models on which general understanding is based. This may provide a rationale for the proposed project, where it supplements existing theory, or fills a gap in theoretical knowledge. A critical review of other researchers' published work can be included as a part of a discussion of the general theoretical background. In most projects it is necessary to make comparisons with similar studies or similar problems in some detail. It is necessary to identify and discuss the key studies in the field, so their implications can be considered in the choice of research approach and method, and their results and conclusions can be compared.

There are generally accepted methods for choosing research sites, making data observations, collection, and analysis. Usually they depend upon on some common consensus held by a research community about what they think they know, and what constitutes a subject area, as well as appropriate research styles and approaches. It is important to take care over the sources of data and literature to identify the studies closest to the project. The research should relate to these studies, and if different findings emerge, explanations need to be found. Sometimes, however, it happens that there are competing schools of thought, or different research and theoretical traditions, so it is important to establish the state of knowledge. The researcher needs to state the perspective to be adopted in the project and an explanation about how the research fits into the general picture. The research should then be designed with research methods to match this. It is important to state the reasons for the choice of approach and later, perhaps in the project discussion, state something about the validity of methods (Witcher and Wilkinson 2002).

### REFLECTIVE ACTIVITY

Critically assess the research approach, sample and methods used in a project that has been carried out in your organisation or in a paper in one of the main academic journals.

Research hypotheses are often necessary to guide and direct the research process. Often, however, they do much more than this; they dictate quite precisely the nature of the research process itself. Many accounts of how to carry out research suggest the following process:

1 read other people's work
2 construct a general model
3 propose hypotheses
4 design a survey and/or questionnaire to operationalise the hypothesis
5 process the results to see if the hypothesis is confirmed
6 assess the results in terms of implications for the usefulness of the model.

The role and purpose of different research styles, and the methodologies they suggest, constitute a major subject area in itself and would take too long to outline here. However, it is important to note that while, in principle, this general approach is correct, in practice it can often prove too simplistic. Research is often messy and plans continually change, perhaps because of unforeseen changes in the organisation being studied. Perfection and planning are difficult to achieve in practice, and the researcher should be aware that while taking a systematic approach is important, analytical quality in a project is also crucial. It can be difficult in management and organisational studies to prove or disprove hypotheses. The level of required theoretical abstraction is often too high, and the results are too specific to be meaningful for statements of theory that have a general application. Research in organisations is typically exploratory as well as investigative in its nature. Often, it is based around 'solving' a practical and clearly defined problem. Solving a problem or issue in one particular case means that the emphasis is on achieving insights rather than about

**Figure 16 Planning the methodology**

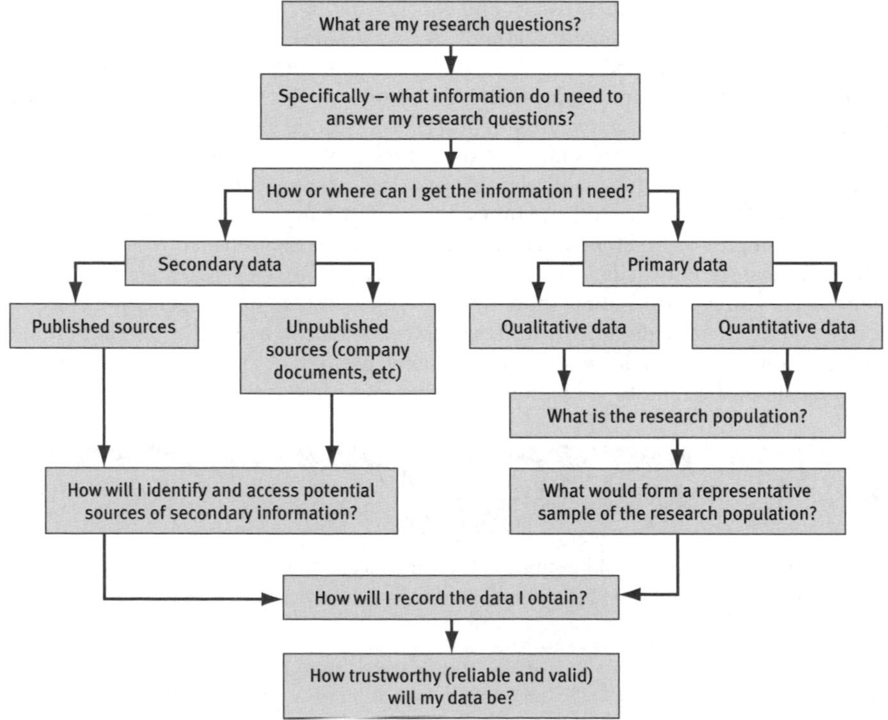


Source: Andersen (2004).

formulating general theoretical statements. Where hypothesis-directed research is going to be used in its narrow and strict sense, such as to prove or disprove ideas, it needs to be clear how the research hypotheses will be operationalised in terms of data collection and quantitative analysis (Witcher and Wilkinson 2002). The flow chart in Figure 16 will help you plan your methodology.

## COLLECTING INFORMATION AND ANALYSING DATA

### LITERATURE SEARCH AND REVIEW

Data that has already been collected is normally referred to as secondary data. There is always a huge amount of secondary data available from newspapers, government departments, trade organisations and professional bodies. They publish a huge volume of information, statistics, and official reports, much of which is available on the web. For example, the CIPD website has continuously updated material on a wide range of issues, written from an HR perspective. Some data is held by companies and is not always accessible. Basic factual data on companies is easily available through annual reports and web sites but some data – such as company minutes and reports – may be much more difficult to access. Look at Saunders *et al* (2009, pp.64-95) for advice on identifying literature and information. When carrying out the literature search, it is useful to look for work that has used theory and methods similar to those identified for the project. Classification of sources of organisational evidence is given in Table 37.

The *literature review* has been referred to as 'a means of thought organisation' (Brewerton and Millward 2001, p.36) and the most common approach is to start broad and then narrow down when a more specific focus is achieved (Anderson 2004, p.68). It is important to be reflective and think critically. For example, if investigating a new topic, say knowledge management, one can look exclusively at books covering this subject. However, if examining the management of quality, this is by no means new and could be traced back to the building of the pyramids. Rather than assuming a so-called 'hot topic' is new, it may make sense to contextualise it by looking at other relevant literature rather than to restrict focus at the start. Reinventing wheels can be a needless task. Today, literature searches can be undertaken much more quickly and efficiently using computerised databases – such as AB Inform – that provide considerable detail on management topics. It is important to keep a good list of references and also to try to write up notes before the box files of material become too large. Writing notes helps to make sense of the material gathered and how it fits together rather than simply collecting it in an unfocused way. The danger otherwise is 'mountains of facts piled up on plains of human ignorance'. The literature should generate issues and questions to help choose the main objective. Once the main objective has been decided, it may then be possible to derive more specific questions.

### RESEARCH APPROACHES

There is no one single model for project research, but a number of different approaches. Here we briefly examine three: the experiment, the case study and the survey. Each has its own advantages and disadvantages and it is important to identify what is most appropriate for the project. All three can be used for exploratory, descriptive or explanatory research (Yin 2009, p.8). The type of research question (ie who, what, where, how, why) influences the choice of strategy. A survey may be the best approach for 'what'-type questions, whereas 'how' and 'why' questions are more appropriately addressed through exploratory and case study research. Table 38 outlines these different research strategies and the types of questions they are designed to address.

**Table 37 Different sources of organisational evidence**

| **Primary sources** | | **Secondary sources** |
|---|---|---|
| **Examples of evidence produced internally for internal use** | **Examples of evidence produced internally for external use** | **Examples of evidence produced externally using internal sources of evidence** |
| Administrative sources:<br>personnel records<br>safety records<br>production/service records | Organisational Internet sites | Newspaper cuttings |
| Business records:<br>agendas<br>notes from meetings<br>progress reports<br>project proposals | Corporate brochure(s) (for clients/potential investors etc) | TV/radio transcripts/ recordings |
| Operational records:<br>letters<br>memos<br>emails<br>handwritten note | Corporate video/DVD (for PR purposes) | Books and journal articles featuring the organisation |
| Policy documents and procedures:<br>HR<br>purchasing and supply<br>finance and accounting<br>marketing | Marketing information | |
| Other internal 'artefacts':<br>briefing notes<br>induction presentations<br>corporate videos (for staff and associates)<br>maps, plans and drawings<br>process diagrams | Published diaries/ memoirs of key people | |

Source: Andersen (2004).

**Table 38 Relevant situations for different research strategies**

| Strategy | Form of research question | Requires control over behavioural events? |
|---|---|---|
| Experiment | How?<br>Why? | Yes |
| Survey | Who?<br>What?*<br>Where?<br>How many?<br>How much? | No |
| Case study | How?<br>Why? | No |

* 'What' questions, when asked as part of an exploratory study, pertain to all strategies.

Source: Adapted from Yin (2009).

### THE EXPERIMENT

This is the common 'classical' approach in the physical sciences (Saunders *et al* 2009, p.136). The researcher sets up a project in a laboratory with a number of variables (usually controllable) and conducts the experiment by altering one variable at a time, so they can study the relationship between the different variables (Bryman and Bell 2011, p.39). The researcher controls the independent (or input) variables while measuring the effect on the dependent (or output) variables and keeping intervening factors constant (Bennett 1983). The social experiment takes place in a field setting where the researcher follows the above pattern by treating different groups of people in different ways. For example, evaluating the effect of a training course on a group of managers will involve measurement of knowledge or attitudes before and after the course and a comparison of their responses with a group of similar managers who did not attend the course. This assumes nothing 'happens' to the 'control' group (those not on the course). Easterby-Smith *et al* (2008, pp.37–8) note that this is naïve and provide the example of a course which they evaluated. While the course was ongoing those not on the course (the control group) took the opportunity to improve relationships with their bosses and strengthen their political standing – in effect shutting out some of those who were absent because they were on the course. This meant that the original topic – assessing the impact of a course – was rendered meaningless by changes elsewhere in the organisation.

## REFLECTIVE ACTIVITY

To what extent is it possible to draw meaningful conclusions from studies that have used laboratory experiments – for example, on sleep patterns of students in order to predict the effects of shiftwork on long-term health?

### CASE STUDIES

In this situation, research is carried out in an organisation to examine a particular topic or event (Bryman and Bell 2011, p.53). Case studies have formed an essential plank of research in a variety of disciplines, from medicine and psychology through to political science. According to Yin (2009, p.18) the case study is 'an empirical enquiry that investigates a contemporary phenomenon in depth and within its real life context especially when the boundaries between phenomenon and context are not clearly evident'. Mitchell (1983, p.191) describes the case study as 'a detailed examination of an event (or series of related events) which the analyst believes exhibits (or exhibit) the operation of some identified general theoretical principle'. In short, the case study method tries to capture the whole, is intensive in nature, and is open-ended and flexible at all stages of the research process. A comparative case approach could involve the researcher in examining a particular topic via visits to several different organisations to interview staff and collect data. For example, this approach could be used to examine the impact of a particular pay system on employees in different organisational contexts. It has been argued that the technique utilised by case study researchers can lead to bias in the results, either via the inherent limitations of any single method (Denzin 1970, p.13) or due to the effect of the researcher on the situation itself (see discussion on interviews below).

### SURVEYS

This is also one of the most widely adopted approaches in social science and business and management research and HR projects are no exception (Anderson 2004, p.208). Surveys are cheap, quick to administer, and provide a much wider coverage than say an experiment or case study (Bennett 1983). The main method of data collection is via the questionnaire (see below) although other survey methods include structured observation. The main aim of the survey is to collect information from, or about, a defined group or 'population' (Easterby-Smith *et al* 2008, pp.86–87). The data is standardised so allows for comparison. Saunders *et al* (2009, pp.138–9) notes that the data is less wide ranging than that collected by qualitative methods as there is a limit to the number of questions that can be asked. An example of this would be WERS surveys that collected data from a representative sample of 2000 workplaces on various aspects of employee relations (Kersley *et al* 2006).

## RESEARCH METHODS

Having decided on a broad approach, a number of different techniques can be used to collect data, particularly in case study research.

### OBSERVATION

According to Ackroyd and Hughes (1992, p.127) 'the most well-known of the observational methods is participant observation, which requires researchers to involve themselves in the lives of those being studied – looking, listening, enquiring, recording, and so on'. Observations are directed towards an understanding of how interaction patterns are linked – with symbols and meanings used to understand behaviour – rather than the frequency and distribution of events. Participant observation, according to Denzin's wider meaning of the term, is a method of qualitative analysis that requires observer submersion in the data and uses analytical induction and theoretical sampling as the main strategies of analysis and discovery. A major advantage is that it allows the 'simultaneous generation and verification of theory' since the researcher tries to share his/her life with those being studied (Denzin 1978, p.187). There are four variants of participant observation:

- Complete participant – In this role the researcher aims to become an ordinary member of the group and their full intent is not revealed. Perhaps the researcher may need to collect information without revealing their identity for fear that this would either undermine access or affect the results. An example of this might be a study looking at the extent to which companies observe minimum wage or health and safety legislation.
- Participant as observer – The role of observer is made clear to the research subjects. Although the researcher undertakes the same tasks as the people being observed – as in the work on assembly lines undertaken by Delbridge (1998) – their reason for being there is made explicit.
- Observer as participant – In this role the contact is brief and tends to take the form of interviews with no attempt to create a longer-term relationship. This is probably the most typical of research situations in the HR area.
- Complete observer – The researcher is removed completely from interaction with his/her subjects, and merely administers questionnaires or observes their behaviour – perhaps through a one-way mirror as in some psychology research.

A balance between involvement and distance is needed. The researcher needs to get close enough to the subjects in order to empathise with them, but maintain enough distance to retain a theoretically informed and detached viewpoint (Pettigrew 1985, p.228) and avoid 'going native'.

## INTERVIEWS

Interviews have been defined by Ackroyd and Hughes (1992, p.100) as 'encounters between a researcher and a respondent in which the latter is asked a series of questions relevant to the subject of the research. The respondent's answers constitute the raw data analysed at a later point in time.' It is based on the assumption that the answers offered by respondents are valid indicators of the subject under investigation, and these answers provide access to observable and reportable behaviour. Put another way, the information collected is 'presentational data' – based upon symbolic projections and appearances – rather than 'operational data', which is behaviour actually observed by the researcher. This analytical distinction is critically important for interpretation, since there is a danger that 'the presentational data will literally swamp the operational data, thus masking the difference between fact and fiction in the findings' (van Maanen 1979, pp.542–3). Questions asking line managers how they have handled grievance and disciplinary cases is presentational data, whereas, with operational data, their handling of actual cases would be observed. By using multiple triangulation (see next section) and longitudinal research, as well as a degree of common sense, researchers can remain aware of any potential shortcomings in their analysis and interpretation of results, and can minimise this by using a range of techniques.

The interview may be classified into three major forms/types, according to the degree of standardisation or structuring (Brewerton and Millward 2001, pp.70–1; Bryman and Bell 2011, p.119; Saunders *et al* 2009, p.311). The most rigid and formalised is the schedule or *standardised form*, in which there is strict adherence to a prearranged schedule both in terms of the wording of the questions and the order in which questions are put to respondents. In addition, other features of the situation are also standardised across different interviews, such as location, in order to minimise the possibility of variance between responses (Ackroyd and Hughes 1992, p.103). Rigidity is relaxed in the second type, the *non-schedule standardised or semi-structured interview*. In this type, the researcher aims to elicit certain information from all respondents, but the phrasing of questions and their order is varied in order to allow for the special characteristics of each respondent, and to maintain rapport throughout the interaction. However, the same sorts of questions are posed to each interviewee. Finally, there is the *non-standardised (unstructured) interview*, which is sometimes compared with a conversation (Denzin 1970, p.126; Ackroyd and Hughes 1992, p.103). In this situation the interviewer can work from a list of topics, indicating broad areas in which issues are to be pursued, or the interaction can be totally free of prearranged sets of questions. The principal advantage of this latter type of interview is that it does not attempt to fit respondents into predetermined categories, and so enables the interviewer to explore issues as they arise. The interviewer is free to adopt whatever mode of behaviour seems appropriate in the circumstances in order to elicit information from the respondent. This type of interview is particularly useful at the commencement of the research, and with more senior managers who could amplify their views with examples, especially when the researcher 'plays dumb' (Denzin 1970, p.131). It may be less effective in situations where the respondents felt less at ease in the interviews, or where the range of their experiences (in relation to the research) was more limited.

One of the principal criticisms of the interview, and especially the non-standardised variety given its less rigid and more open structure, is that bias can invalidate the results from the research process. Bias can enter into the process at a number of stages:

- in the construction of interview questions, their precise order and wording and the context in which they are posed (Ackroyd and Hughes 1992, pp.110–20; Brewerton and Millward 2001, p.71) and in the extent to which the interviewer poses leading or bland questions
- due to physical characteristics of the interviewer, such as age, gender, class and colour, which cannot usually be removed in the typical research programme. Other factors – such as mode of dress or gestures – are more easily controlled, although it should be remembered that whatever the interviewer's characteristics, these always create some impression with the respondents (Denzin 1970, pp.140–1)
- through respondents not conforming with the rules governing the interview – for example by telling lies or by providing answers that they imagine the researcher wants to hear
- the situation in which the interview takes place, its location and timing, and the way in which this may limit or facilitate rapport in the interaction. It is often assumed that good rapport is an essential precondition of a successful interview, to the extent that the researcher must communicate trust, avoid technical language, and adapt to the type of interviewee (Brewerton and Millward 2001, p.71). However, while good rapport may be a necessary requirement for successful interviews in most cases, it is not sufficient to guarantee such an outcome. Indeed, it may actually be counterproductive in some instances, leading to over-identification between researcher and respondent
- in the recording and interpretation of results. Data from the interview can either be recorded by hand, relying upon rough notes taken verbatim by the interviewer(s), or by tape recording the proceedings and later transcribing the findings. Tape recording has been used in a variety of research studies and has the principal advantage of ensuring that everything the respondent says is noted, so that the transcript can be reanalysed to tease out the meanings and subtleties in the interviewee's responses. Of course, it also has the associated disadvantages that transcription takes a considerable amount of time and the presence of a tape recorder may inhibit the respondent from providing open answers. Taking notes during the interview is a more manageable process, and can ensure relatively full accounts of the interview, particularly if the notes are written up very soon after the interaction, and the notes are kept in case they need to be re-examined. It is possible to recall with some precision the words used by respondents, so that these can be used as verbatim quotes to supplement the argument of the research report. Nonetheless, there is still the danger that the interviewer consciously – or more likely unconsciously – fails to report accurately the respondents' words or nuances in the write-up, thus introducing another source of bias into the process.

## REFLECTIVE ACTIVITY

Assess what can be done to minimise the effect of bias on the results gathered from a set of interviews.

*Focus groups* are a specific form of interview that simultaneously uses multiple respondents to generate data. It is used to get close to participants' understanding and perspectives of issues and more appropriate as a technique for generating ideas rather than testing hypotheses (Brewerton and Millward 2001, pp.80–1). It can either be used as a self-contained means of data collection or a supplementary approach. However, results must be interpreted in the context of group dynamics.

### DOCUMENTARY DATA

In addition to the techniques described above, data can be collected via the inspection of documentary information produced by individuals within the organisation involved. Personnel departments can provide a range of statistics and information to go alongside the material that emerges from the use of other techniques. Minutes of meetings can also be inspected. However, it is foolhardy to rely too heavily upon such data for a number of reasons. They do not provide a detailed account of meetings; they are not sensitive enough to capture the nuances which generally lie behind specific items; and they tend to represent one version of reality – that of management as they are usually responsible for their completion. However, recognising these limitations, minutes are of some value in that they can help the researcher appreciate the kind of issues that have arisen over time, and the arena in which they were raised, as well as the manner in which they were subsequently formally resolved. If combined with observation of current-day meetings, the adequacy or comprehensiveness of previously recorded minutes can also be assessed, and their worth evaluated with a little more precision.

### QUESTIONNAIRES

Questionnaires are perhaps the most widely used research tool in social sciences and management studies. They are attractive as they require minimal resources, do not cost much but can provide a large sample. However, Saunders *et al* (2009, pp.354–99) warn that questionnaires are not easy to design, administer and interpret. It is important to ensure that precise data can be collected to answer the specific research questions and it is not usually easy to go back to respondents if one realises the questionnaire is badly designed or inappropriate. Broadly speaking three types of data can be collected: (1) demographic or background data; (2) behavioural data; (3) attitudinal data (Brewerton and Millward 2001, pp.99–108).

The main decisions in questionnaire design relate to the type of questions to be used and the overall format of the questionnaire (Easterby-Smith *et al* 2008, p.227–31). It is important to distinguish between questions of 'fact' and questions of 'opinion'. Biographical data such as age, length of service or job title are factual and capable of a 'correct' answer, although there are sometimes problems with the last of these as people may define the job in a different way. Other questions may ask for opinions such as 'do you think you have enough say in decisions made at your work?' The answers to these sorts of question can vary significantly across a sample.

There is also a distinction between 'closed' (or forced-choice) and 'open' questions. The former – as in the question above – can be answered with a yes/no response. However, if the question is phrased as 'what do you see as the main functions of management development?' then the answer could be several lines long. Once all the data has been collected, it needs to be coded by assigning numbers to each answer category so that common answers can be aggregated (Bryman and Bell 2011, pp.156–8). One of the problems with open questions (and unstructured interviews) is that when coding, the researcher has no idea whether omissions are deliberate or simply forgotten. For example, using the above question, where respondents omit to mention implementation of corporate strategy, it is not clear whether it is not regarded as one of the main functions, or whether the respondent forgot to include this in their answer.

With closed questions, yes/no responses may be rather crude and a Likert scale is commonly used providing some idea of the strength of opinion. A statement – such as 'do you think you have enough say in decisions made at your work?' – is provided and respondents are asked to indicate their views by choosing from the options available. Typically, a five-point Likert scale, or a six- or seven-point variant, would be used:

Strongly agree → Agree → Undecided → Disagree → Strongly disagree

There are certain general principles to follow when drafting a questionnaire (Easterby-Smith *et al* 2008, p.227–31; Brewerton and Millward 2001, pp.104–8; Bryman and Bell 2011, pp.146–50), and it is essential to ensure that:

1 questions are clear and unambiguous
2 questions are short
3 questions avoid jargon or specialist language
4 'double-barrelled' questions, in which the respondent is asked about two things in one question, are avoided
5 'leading' questions and 'presuming' questions that suggest indirectly what the right answer might be are avoided
6 personal questions are avoided unless essential to the research.

It is normal for questionnaires to begin with relatively simple, non-threatening and closed questions, before moving on to questions that are more involved, complex or 'open' towards the end of the document (Thietart *et al* 2001, p.174). This is done to ensure that respondents are not discouraged from continuing with the questionnaire. There are also a number of issues relating to layout that are important in terms of achieving comprehensibility. Amongst the key issues identified by Brewerton and Millward (2001, pp.107–8) are the following:

- the instructions and covering letter need to be clear, outlining the background and aims of research, explaining why the respondent's involvement is important, as well as stressing confidentiality and anonymity
- the questionnaire should normally be able to be completed in no more than 45 minutes, and not be more than 10 pages in length
- the font type and size needs to be readable. Having tiny fonts to keep the number of pages down is not a good approach
- correct spelling and grammar are critical to reassure the respondent that the researcher is competent and professional.

It is essential to 'pilot' the draft questionnaire to check that respondents are able to understand all the questions and that they make sense. It is also vitally important to ensure that respondents are able to answer questions in the way that was intended and that their replies are meaningful. If a large number of questionnaires are to be distributed, it is necessary to use statistical packages such as SPSS to help with the analysis. In this case, issues of scaling are also critically important. These need to be sorted out during the drafting of the questionnaire so as to avoid problems at a later stage in the analysis. It is impossible in this book to provide details of all the issues relating to questionnaire design and analysis, so researchers are referred to the standard texts indicated in the useful reading section.

REFLECTIVE ACTIVITY

Consider the last time that you filled in a questionnaire, and try to recall how you felt about this. Does this experience help you to design questionnaires?

## TRIANGULATION

Denzin's (1970, p.13) commitment to multiple triangulation is clear: 'if each method leads to different features of empirical reality, then no single method can ever completely capture all the relevant features of that reality'; hence, there is a need to 'learn to employ multiple methods in the analysis of the same empirical events'. There are four basic types of triangulation: data, investigator, theory and methodology. By *data triangulation* he means that information should be collected from different people, at different times, and in different places, in order to create a fuller picture of a single event. At the same time, data needs to be drawn from a range of levels as well. *Investigator triangulation* is fairly straightforward, meaning that more than one researcher should be employed, wherever possible, on the data collection parts of a project so as to remove the potential bias that comes from a single person, and ensures greater reliability in observations. *Theoretical triangulation* requires researchers to approach the study with multiple perspectives and hypotheses in mind. In addition, it permits the widest possible use of theoretical findings. Finally, there is *methodological triangulation*, which can be within an individual method – for example by using separate scales in a questionnaire for measuring the same construct (say personality) – or between methods. Denzin (1970, p.308) regards the latter as essential because 'the flaws of one method are often the strengths of another and by combining methods, observers can achieve the best of each, while overcoming their unique deficiencies'. In sum, *multiple triangulation* combines all the features (data, investigator, theory, methods) simultaneously in analysing the same set of events.

Qualitative data is not always easy to analyse (Cassell and Symon 2004). Often large amounts of qualitative data are collected, but the researcher needs to make sense of it. Facts don't always speak for themselves, they have to be interpreted. Too often researchers/ students simply reproduce un-regurgitated quotes that report a frequency (eg 80% of senior staff are male) without any comment. All too often projects contain a large amount of such *description* and too little *analysis*, yet it is the analysis that is the most important element, and should carry greater weight. Much relevant information can be presented in appendices, devoting more space to discussion and analysis in the main body of the report. Data needs to be linked with theory and the research questions. The first objective needs to be to reduce information and have a sense of control over what one has collected (Anderson 2004, p.169). Analysis is a process of thought that enables you to understand the nature of what is being investigated, the relationship between different variables in the literature, and the likely outcomes of particular actions or interventions. Analysis therefore involves finding answers to your research questions using the data you have gathered by asking questions such as 'what', 'why' and 'how' (Anderson 2004, p.169). Figure 17 gives an overview of the process of qualitative data analysis.

**Figure 17 Overview of the process of qualitative data analysis**

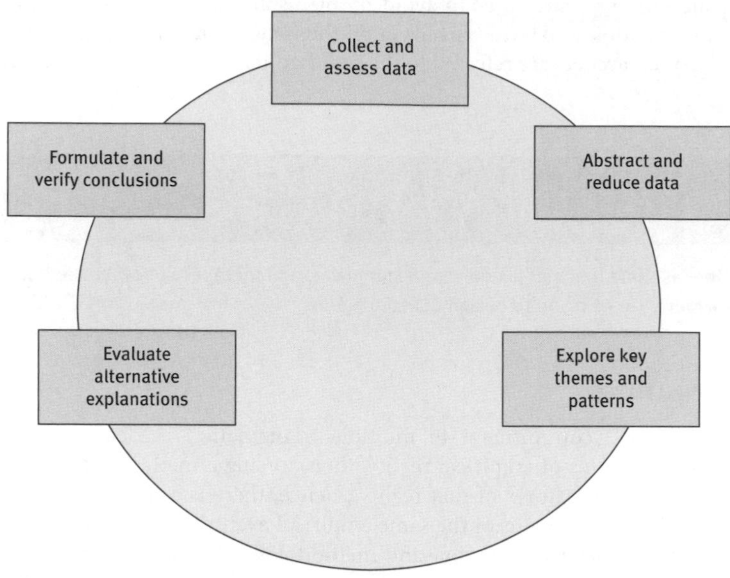


Source: Anderson (2004).

In short, one needs to transform the nature of the data one has collected in order to:

1 comprehend and manage them
2 merge related data drawn from different transcripts and notes
3 identify key themes or patterns from them for further exploration
4 develop and/or test hypotheses based on these apparent patterns or relationships and
5 outline and verify conclusions (Saunders *et al* 2009, p.382).

To reduce the volume of data one must attempt to categorise or code it. These categories/codes may come from the research questions, the literature or the researcher's own experience while gathering the data and could be about subject matter, attitudes, methods of work, characteristics of people and so on (Anderson 2004, p.177). For example, if explaining attitudes to and the implementation of performance-related pay, issues could be categorised as (a) the principles of performance-related pay and (b) its practice in operation. These may result in further categories such as management attitudes, training issues and so on. By reducing data to categories the processes of interpreting the data and determining emerging themes is simplified. This process may lead to re-examination of some categories and may result in their being integrated or combined. The process is complex and iterative, with some themes being apparent from early on, others emerging later. This analysis will then lead on to drawing up of conclusions, and it is important to look for alternative explanations at this stage. For example, are employees positive about performance-related pay as a principle, or because it resulted in £2,000 extra for most workers? Do employees welcome team briefing as an opportunity to engage in meaningful discussions about the organisation or because it results in half an hour off their normal work?

There are two basic ways of analysing such data: content analyses, with an emphasis on numbers and frequency, and grounded theory (see earlier) where the emphasis is on feel and intuition aiming to produce common or contradicting patterns as the basis for interpretation (Easterby-Smith *et al* 2008, pp.86–87).

According to Cresswell (2003, pp.191–4) there are six steps to data analysis:

1 Organise and prepare the data for analysis. This involves transcribing interviews, material, typing up field notes and arranging the data into different types depending on the sources of information.

2 Read through all the data, obtain a general sense of the information and reflect on its overall meaning. What general ideas are being expressed? What is the general impression of the overall depth, credibility and use of the information?

3 Begin detailed analysis with a coding process. Coding is the process of organising material into 'chunks' before bringing meaning to these. It involves taking text data, segmenting paragraphs into categories and labeling those categories. Researchers should analyse their data for material that can yield codes that address topics that readers would expect to find, codes that are surprising, and codes that address a larger theoretical perspective in the research. Obviously, there is an enormous range of codes that could be used depending on the research; they could include processes, activities, people's perceptions etc. The coding process can be enhanced by the used of computer qualitative software programs.

4 The coding process generates a description of the setting or people as well as categories or themes for analysis. Description involves a detailed rendering of information about people, places or events in a setting. Researchers can generate codes for this description. The coding can then be used to generate a small number of themes or categories.

5 Explain how the description and themes will be represented in the narrative. A story is needed to convey the findings of analysis, including a chronology of events, discussion of several themes and a discussion with interconnecting themes.

6 A final step in data analysis involves making an interpretation of the data including the lessons learned (Lincoln and Guba 1985).

## PRESENTING THE FINDINGS: THE STRUCTURE OF THE REPORT

The precise form of the report obviously depends upon the subject matter, the individual writer and the terms of reference. The introduction would typically include something on terms of reference or hypotheses, and maybe a discussion of research methods, and a rough balance should be achieved between subsequent sections. It needs to be remembered that the report – especially if commissioned – can be seen as an exercise in persuasion and the researcher needs to do everything possible to ensure its presentation maximises impact. A typical format would be:

- *Executive summary* – A short report to management or the sponsoring organisation summarising the key points and recommendations. This is particularly pertinent where the report is to be presented to several audiences, some of which might not read the report in its entirety. For example, it would be hoped that senior management of the organisation in which the research took place and academics assessing the work would read it very carefully. On the other hand, managers at other organisations may wish only to consult the executive summary. Since the executive summary is likely to reach the widest possible audience, it is very important that it is well presented, clear and unambiguous.
- *Introduction* – A clear statement of the terms of reference for the project, and its principal objectives. This should indicate the way in which the topic has been formulated, the issues connected with the project, and how these have been interpreted and clarified. A

summary of the structure of the report is helpful to the reader. It may be necessary at an early stage in the project to acquaint the reader with some background information that is relevant to a full understanding of the project argument. This may include some complex issues. If such information is detrimental to a fluent reading of the text, it could be presented as an appendix.

- *Literature review* – A concise and critical review of the relevant literature, appreciation of the range of theoretical bases upon which the study has drawn and an awareness of current practice in the matter being investigated. The review is not a separate part of the report; it should inform the research approach and needs to be re-examined in the conclusions so as to locate the findings within the wider body of knowledge about the subject.
- *Methodology* – An account of, and justification for, the methods (for example, qualitative and/or quantitative) selected. The writer should be able to demonstrate an understanding of the different methods and an appreciation of which methods are appropriate in particularly sets of circumstances. The influence of different methods on the results emerging from their investigations should be explained. For example, different results may be obtained by asking personnel managers and employees about the success of performance-related pay. The former may have designed and implemented the scheme whereas employees have it applied to them.
- *Data description and background* – An account of the investigation stating what has actually been done. It is crucial that data is presented in a concise and logical manner, and makes appropriate use of tables, statistics, quotations and observations, so as to guide the reader through the mass of information in the report. It is important not to mix together evidence and analysis in the same place but to deal with these things separately. Other people's work can provide evidence, but it must be clear which is their own project work, and which is the work and findings of others. It is better to present project findings first, and then bring in other evidence in a separate analysis of these findings, and discussion of them.
- *Analysis and discussion* – This is the most important part of the report. It is about the significance of findings in terms of the overall project argument. It involves evaluating the project findings as well as the theoretical literature and other published work. Discussion is wider and more speculative, as the wider meaning of the findings are analysed and interpreted to achieve different ways of understanding. It is important to be original and show initiative and imagination in the work, and not to hide 'ifs' and 'buts'. Also, when discussing findings from the fieldwork, it should be clear what the researcher is concluding and what others have claimed. In other words, if a company says it has implemented TQM, equal opportunities or empowerment, make it clear that this is what *they* claim, not necessarily what the researcher believes. Beware of using confidential, sensitive or personal material obtained from respondents, especially via the interview process.
- *The conclusion* – This draws together the evidence from the investigation, and explains it with reference to the introduction and the literature survey and relates findings to the hypotheses or terms of reference for the project. There should be an explicit statement indicating the value of the investigation, and the way in which it supplements, refines or disputes existing wisdom. Researchers should also show their awareness of the limitations of the study, and indicate what they have personally learned from their investigation. This process of reflection is vital for researchers and it can help with CPD because it may prevent similar mistakes being made.
- *Recommendations* – Recommendations are usually presented as simple statements of follow-up actions. It is important to be specific, especially if asked to provide these. Vague statements about 'a need to review x and y', 'more thought needs to be given to z' or 'we should involve people more' are not really very helpful. If recommending greater

involvement of staff then suggestions as to how to operationalise this are important. Also bear in mind that recommendations exist in a context: issues of practicality and affordability always need to be considered. If there are recommendations then these should not be confused with conclusions.

- *References* – These need to be appropriate, accurate and easy to follow. They should provide details of the sources used, and they can help to provide the reader with a good understanding of the approach that has been taken as well as an indication of other sources that have been useful to the project.
- *Appendices* – These can be used for information which is necessary to provide a fuller understanding of the research, but would be a distraction to the key arguments if it were put in the main body of the text. Typically such material would be organisational documents, forms or internal publications central to the research, but which are not the researchers' own work. The status of such material should be clearly stated. However, information put into an appendix should not be there just for padding.

## CONCLUSIONS

This chapter has examined how to investigate and report on an HR issue from a business perspective. This is important if HR managers are to move beyond acting simply as administrative agents or 'clerks of the works' (see Chapter 6) but increasingly play a role in devising strategy. Research has a vital role to play in this, and it is usually linked to a wider change management role. In carrying out research projects, the parameters are often defined by those outside the function, but it is dangerous to allow 'customers' to be the sole arbiters of how HRM should be defined (Wilkinson and Marchington 1994). If customer needs assume HR plays a narrow conformist role, where needs are defined by line managers, advice from HR function is more likely to be rejected. In such circumstances, HR can do no more than reflect the competencies and values of line managers who expect it to adopt a passive role. A paradigm in which 'hard data' or meeting contractual obligations is required to justify personnel activity means that HR can lose its distinctive role. Thus, we would argue that much depends on HR adopting a creative role in organisations. Simply responding to the requests of line managers may provide short-term credibility but in the longer run makes little contribution to organisational goals. The HR function is regarded by some managers as free from the typical conflicts that take place between production, marketing and design, and thus more likely to be 'objective' in its approach to managing change. Alongside the use of evidence-based arguments and the use of high quality research, this could offer real opportunities for HR to help define the agenda.

EXPLORE FURTHER

ANDERSON, V. (2004) *Research Methods in Human Resource Management*. London: CIPD.

BRYMAN, A. and BELL, E. (2011) *Business Research Methods*, 3rd edition. Oxford: Oxford University Press.

CASSELL, C. and SYMON, G. (2004) *Essential Guide to Qualitative Methods in Organisational Research*. London: Sage.

EASTERBY-SMITH, M., THORPE, R. and LOWE, A. (2008) *Management Research: An introduction*, 3rd edition. London: Sage.

GILL, J. and JOHNSON, P. (2010) *Research Methods for Managers*. London: Sage.

PFEFFER, J. and SUTTON, R. (2006) *Hard Facts, Dangerous Half-Truths and Total Nonsense: Profiting From Evidence-Based Management*. Cambridge: Harvard Business School Press.

ROUSSEAU, D. and BARENDS, E. (2011) 'Becoming an evidence-based HR practitioner', *Human Resource Management Journal*, Vol.21, No.3, 221–35.

SAUNDERS, M., LEWIS, P. and THORNHILL, A. (2009) *Research Methods for Business Students*, 5th edition. London: Financial Times/Prentice Hall.

SILVERMAN, D. (2010) *Doing Qualitative Research*, 3rd edition. London: Sage.

YIN, R. (2009) *Case Study Research: Design and methods*, 4th edition. London: Sage.

BACH, S. and SISSON, K. (eds) (2000) *Personnel Management: A comprehensive guide to theory and practice*. Oxford: Blackwell.

BACH, S., KESSLER, I. and HERON, P. (2008) 'Role redesign in a modernised NHS: the case of health care assistants', *Human Resource Management Journal*, Vol. 18, No. 2, 171–87.

BACON, N. (1999) 'Union derecognition and the new human relations: a steel industry case study', *Work, Employment and Society*, Vol. 13, No. 1, 1–17.

BACON, N. (2006) 'Employee relations', in T. REDMAN and A. WILKINSON (eds) *Contemporary Human Resource Management*. London: Financial Times/Prentice Hall.

BACON, N. (2008) 'Management strategy and industrial relations' in P. BLYTON, N. BACON, J. FIORITO and E. HEERY (eds) *The Sage Handbook of Industrial Relations*. London: Sage.

BACON, N. and HOQUE, K. (2010) 'Exploring the relationship between union learning representatives and employer-provided training in Britain', *International Journal of Human Resource Management*, Vol. 21, No. 5, 720–41.

BACON, N., BLYTON, P. and DASTMALCHIAN, A. (2010) 'The impact of organisational change in steelworkers in craft and production occupational groups', *Human Relations*, Vol. 63, No. 8, 1223–48.

BAIN, P. and TAYLOR, P. (2005) 'India calling to far away towns: the call centre labour process and globalisation', *Work, Employment and Society*, Vol. 19, No. 2, 261–82.

BAIRD, L. and MESHOULAM, I. (1988) 'Managing two fits of strategic human resource management', *Academy of Management Review*, Vol. 13, No. 1, 116–28.

BALDAMUS, W. (1961) *Efficiency and Effort*. London: Tavistock.

BALDRY, C., BAIN, P., TAYLOR, P., HYMAN, J., SCHOLARIOS, D., MARKS, A., WATSON, A., GILBERT, K., GALL, G. and BUNZEL, D. (2007) *The Meaning of Work in the New Economy*. London: Palgrave.

BAMBER, G., GITTELL, J., KOCHAN, T. and VON NORDENFLYCHT, A. (2009) *Up in the air: how airlines can improve performance by engaging their employees*. Ithaca: Cornell University Press.

BAMBER, G., LANSBURY, R., and WAILES, N. (eds) (2011) *International and Comparative Employment Relations: Globalisation and Change,* 5th edition. Crows Nest: Allen and Unwin.

BANDURA, A. (1977) *Social Learning Theory*. Englewood Cliffs: Prentice Hall.

BANGERTER, A., KONIG, C., BLATTI, S. and SALVISBERG, A. (2009) 'How widespread is graphology in personnel selection practice? A case study of a job market myth', *International Journal of Selection and Assessment*, Vol. 17, No. 2, 219–30.

BARCLAY, J. (2001) 'Improving selection interviews with structure: organisations' use of "behavioural" interviews', *Personnel Review*, Vol. 30, No. 1, 81–101.

BARKER, J. (1993) 'Tightening the iron cage: concertive control in self-managing teams', *Administrative Science Quarterly*, Vol. 38, 408–37.

BARNARD, C., DEAKIN, S. and HOBBS, R. (2003) 'Opting out of the 48-hour week: employer necessity or individual choice?' *Industrial Law Journal*, Vol. 32, No. 4, 223–52.

BARNEY, J. (1991) 'Firm resources and sustained competitive advantage', *Journal of Management*, Vol. 17, No. 1, 99–120.

Barney, J. (2001) 'Is the resource-based "view" a useful perspective for strategic management research? Yes', *Academy of Management Review*, Vol. 26, No. 1, 41–56.

Baron, J. and Kreps, D. (1999) *Strategic Human Resources*. New York: John Wiley & Sons.

Barrick, M., Mount, M. and Judge, A. (2001) 'Personality and performance at the beginning of the new millennium: what do we know and where do we go next?' *International Journal of Selection and Assessment*, Vol. 9, No. 1–2, 9–30.

Barry, M. (2006) *Company*. New York: Vintage Books.

Barry, M. and Nienhueser, W. (2010) 'Coordinated market economy/liberal employment relations: low cost competition in the German aviation industry', *International Journal of Human Resource Management*, Vol. 21, No. 2, 214–29.

Bartell, A. (2004) 'Human resource management and organizational performance: evidence from retail banking', *Industrial and Labor Relations Review*, Vol. 5, No. 2, 181–203.

Bartlett, C. and Ghosal, S. (1989) *Managing Across Borders: The transnational solution*. Boston: Harvard Business School Press.

Barzantny, C. and Festing, M. (2008) 'Performance management in France and Germany', in A. Varma, P.S. Budhwar and A. DeNisi *Performance Management Systems: A Global Perspective*. Abingdon, Oxon: Routledge.

Bass, B. and Bass, R. (2009) *The Bass Handbook of Leadership: theory, research and managerial applications*. New York: Free Press.

Basu, K. and Palazzo, G. (2008) 'Corporate social responsibility: a process model of sensemaking', *Academy of Management Review*, Vol. 33, No. 1, 122–36.

Batt, R. (2004) 'Who benefits from teams? Comparing workers, supervisors and managers', *Industrial Relations*, Vol. 43, No. 1, 183–212.

Batt, R. (2007) 'Service strategies: marketing, operations, and human resource practices', in P. Boxall, J. Purcell and P. Wright (eds) *The Oxford Handbook of Human Resource Management*. Oxford: Oxford University Press.

Batt, R. and Doellgast, V. (2003) 'Organizational performance in services', in D. Holman, T. Wall, C. Clegg, P. Sparrow and A. Howard (eds) *The New Workplace: A guide to the human impact of modern working practices*. London: John Wiley & Sons.

Batt, R., Colvin, A. and Keefe, J. (2002) 'Employee voice, human resource practices, and quit rates: evidence from the telecommunications industry', *Industrial and Labor Relations Review*, Vol. 55, No. 4, 573–94.

Batt, R., Holman, D. and Holtgrewe, U. (2009) 'The globalisation of service work: comparative institutional perspectives on call centres', *Industrial and Labour Relations Review*, Vol. 62, No. 4, 453–88.

Baxter, B. (1996) 'Consultancy expertise: a post-modern perspective', in H. Scarbrough (ed.) *The Management of Expertise*. London: Macmillan.

Beardwell, J. (2010), 'Talent management', in J. Beardwell and T. Claydon (eds) *Human Resource Management: A Contemporary Approach*, 6th edition. London: Financial Times/Prentice Hall.

Beardwell, J. and Claydon, T. (eds) (2007) *Human Resource Management: A contemporary approach*, 5th edition. London: Financial Times/Prentice Hall.

Beardwell, J., Gold, J., Iles, P., Stewart, J., and Holden, R. (2010) 'The future of human resource development', in J. Gold, R. Holden, P. Iles, J. Stewart and J. Beardwell *Human Resource Development: Theory and Practice.* Basingstoke: Palgrave Macmillan.

Beaumont, P. (1987) *The Decline of Trade Union Organisation*. London: Croom Helm.

Becker, B.E. and Huselid, M.A. (2009) 'Strategic human resource management: where do we go from here?' in A. Wilkinson, N. Bacon, T. Redman and S. Snell (eds) *The SAGE Handbook of Human Resource Management*. London: Sage.

Beer, M., Spector, B., Lawrence, P., Quinn Mills, D. and Walton, R. (1985) *Human Resource Management: A general manager's perspective.* Glencoe: Free Press.

Bélanger, J., Giles, A. and Grenier, J. (2003) 'Patterns of corporate influence in the host country: a study of ABB in Canada', *International Journal of Human Resource Management*, Vol. 14, No. 3, 469–85.

Benn, J. and Moore, R. (2009) 'Growing next generation library managers: are new librarians reluctant to step into management?' in J. Varlejs, L. Lewis and G. Walton (eds) *Strategies for regenerating the library and information provision*. Berlin and New York: De Gruyter.

Bennett, R. (1983) *Research Guides for Higher Degree Students*. Oxford: Thomson Publications.

Benson, G. and Lawler, E. (2003) 'Employee involvement: utilization, impacts, and future prospects', in D. Holman, T. Wall, C. Clegg, P. Sparrow and A. Howard, A. (eds) *The New Workplace: A guide to the human impact of modern working practices*. London: Wiley.

Benson, G. and Pattie, M. (2009) 'The comparative roles of home and host country supervisors in the expatriate experience', *Human Resource Management,* Vol. 48, No. 1, 49–68.

Berg, P. (1999) 'The effects of high performance work practices on job satisfaction in the United States steel industry', *Relations Industrial/Industrial Relations*, Vol. 54, 111–35.

Beswick, J., Gore, J. and Palferman D. (2006) *Bullying at Work: A review of the literature.* HSE, available online at: www.hse.gov.uk/research

Bevan, S. (2010) *The Business Case for Employee Health and Wellbeing. A Report prepared for Investors in People.* London: The Work Foundation.

Bhatnagar, J. (2009), 'Human resource information systems and HR outsourcing in India', in P. Budhwar and J. Bhatnagar (eds) *The changing face of people management in India.* London: Routledge.

Bird, A. and Beechler, S. (1995) 'Links between business strategy and HRM strategy in US-based Japanese subsidiaries: an empirical investigation', *Journal of International Business Studies*, First quarter, 23–46.

Biron, M, Farndale, E. and Paauwe, J. (2011) 'Performance management effectiveness: lessons from world-leading firms', *The International Journal of Human Resource Management*, Vol. 22, No. 6, 1294–311.

Bishop, V. and Hoel, H. (2008) 'The customer is always right? Exploring the concept of customer bullying', *Journal of Consumer Behaviour*, Culture, Vol. 8, pp.341–367.

Bjorkman, I. and Lervik, J. (2007) 'Transferring HR practices within multinational corporations', *Human Resource Management Journal*, Vol. 17, No. 4, 320–35.

BLAZEJEWSKI, S. (2006) 'Transferring value-infused organisational practices in multinational companies', in M. GEPPERT and M. MAYER (eds) *Global, National and Local Practices in Multinational Companies*. London: Palgrave MacMillan.

BLYTON, P. (2011) 'Working time, work-life balance and inequality', in P. BLYTON, E HEERY and P. TURNBULL (eds) *Reassessing the Employment Relationship*. London: Palgrave Macmillan.

BLYTON, P. and TURNBULL, P. (2004) *The Dynamics of Employee Relations*, 3rd edition. London: Palgrave Macmillan.

BLYTON, P., HEERY, E. and TURNBULL, P. (eds) (2011) *Reassessing the Employment Relationship*. Basingstoke: Palgrave Macmillan.

BOADEN, R., MARCHINGTON, M., HYDE, P., HARRIS, C., SPARROW, P., PASS, S., CARROLL, M. and CORTVRIEND, P. (2008) *Improving Health through Human Resource Management: The process of engagement and alignment*. London: CIPD.

BOLCHOVER, D. (2005) *The Living Dead*. Chichester: Capstone.

BOLTON, C. and HOULIHAN, M. (eds) (2007) *Searching for the Human in Human Resource Management*. London: Palgrave Macmillan.

BOLTON, S. (2005) *Emotion Management in the Workplace*. Basingstoke: Palgrave Macmillan.

BONDAROUK, T. and RUEL, H. (2009) 'Electronic human resource management: challenges in the digital era', *International Journal of Human Resource Management*, Vol. 20, No. 3, 505–14.

BOSCH, G. and CHAREST, J. (2008) 'Vocational training and the labour market in liberal and coordinated economies', *Industrial Relations Journal*, Vol. 39, No. 5. 428–47.

BOSELIE, P. and PAAWE, J. (2009) 'HRM and the resource based view', in A. WILKINSON *et al* (eds) *The Sage Handbook of Human Resource Management*. London: Sage.

BOSELIE, P. and PAAUWE, J. (2010) 'Human resource management and the resource-based view', in A. WILKINSON, N. BACON, T. REDMAN and S. SNELL (eds) *The SAGE Handbook of Human Resource Management*. London: Sage.

BOSELIE, P., DIETZ, G. and BOON, C. (2005) 'Commonalities and contradictions in HRM and performance research', *Human Resource Management Journal*, Vol. 15, No. 3, 67.

BOSELIE, P., PAAUWE, J. and JANSEN, P. (2001) 'Human resource management and performance: lessons from the Netherlands', *International Journal of Human Resource Management*, Vol. 12, No. 7, 1107–25.

BOSELIE, P., PAAUWE, J. and RICHARDSON R. (2003) 'Human resource management, institutional and organisational performance: a comparison of hospitals, hotels and local government', *International Journal of Human Resource Management*, Vol. 14, No. 8, 1407–29.

BOTT, D. (2003) 'Employment relations procedures', in B. TOWERS (ed.) *The Handbook of Employment Relations, Law and Practice*, 4th edition. London: Kogan Page.

BOUQUET, C. and BIRKINSHAW, J. (2008) 'Weight versus voice: how foreign subsidiaries gain attention from corporate headquarters', *Academy of Management Journal*, Vol. 51, No. 3, 577–601.

BOURNE, M. and FRANCO-SANTOS, M. (2010) *Investors in People, Managerial Capabilities and Performance*. A study conducted by the Centre for Business Performance, Cranfield School of Management for IiP.

Bowen, D. and Ostroff, C. (2004) 'Understanding HRM–firm performance linkages: the role of the "strength" of the HRM system', *Academy of Management Review*, Vol. 29, No. 2, 203–21.

Bowey, A. (1975) *A Guide to Manpower Planning*. London: Macmillan.

Bowey, A. (2000) 'Gainsharing', in R. Thorpe and G. Homan (eds) *Strategic Reward Systems*. London: Financial Times/Prentice Hall.

Boxall, P. (1996) 'The strategic HRM debate and the resource-based view of the firm', *Human Resource Management Journal*, Vol. 6, No. 3, 59–75.

Boxall, P. (1998) 'Achieving competitive advantage through human resource strategy: towards a theory of industry dynamics', *Human Resource Management Review*, Vol. 8, No. 3, 265–88.

Boxall, P. and Macky, K. (2009) 'Research and theory in high performance work systems: progressing the high involvement stream', *Human Resource Management Journal*, Vol. 19, No. 1, 3–23.

Boxall, P. and Purcell, J. (2000) 'Strategic human resource management: where have we come from and where are we going?' *International Journal of Management Reviews*, Vol. 2, No. 2, 183–203.

Boxall, P. and Purcell, J. (2003) *Strategy and Human Resource Management*. Basingstoke: Palgrave Macmillan.

Boxall, P. and Purcell, J. (2008) *Strategy and Human Resource Management*. Basingstoke: Palgrave Macmillan.

Boxall, P. and Purcell, J. (2011) *Strategy and Human Resource Management*. New York: Palgrave Macmillan.

Boxall, P. and Steeneveld, M. (1999) 'Human resource strategy and competitive advantage: a longitudinal study of engineering consultancies', *Journal of Management Studies*, Vol. 36, No. 4, 443–63.

Boxall, P., Freeman, R.B. and Haynes, P. (2007) *What Workers Say: Employee Voice in the Anglo-American Workplace*. Ithaca: Cornell University Press.

Boxall, P., Purcell, J. and Wright, P. (eds) (2007a) *The Oxford Handbook of Human Resource Management*, Oxford: Oxford University Press, Chapters 5 and 11.

Boyatsis, R. (1982) *The Competent Manager: A model for effective performance*. New York: Wiley.

Bozionelos, N. (2005), 'When the inferior candidate is offered the job: the selection interview as a political and power game', *Human Relations*, Vol. 58, No. 12, 1605–31.

Bramham, J. (1994) *Human Resource Planning*. London: Institute of Personnel and Development.

Brammer, S. (2011) 'Employment relations and corporate social responsibility', in K. Townsend and A. Wilkinson (eds) *The Handbook of Work and Employment Relations*. London: Edward Elgar, pp.296–318.

Brandl, J., Madsen, M. and Madsen, H. (2009) 'The perceived importance of HR duties to Danish line managers', *Human Resource Management Journal*, Vol. 19, No. 2, 194–210.

Brannan, M. and Hawkins, B. (2007) 'London calling: selection as a pre-emptive strategy for cultural control', *Employee Relations*, Vol. 29, No. 2, 178–91.

Bratton, J. and Gold, J. (2007) *Human Resource Management: Theory and practice*, 3rd edition. Basingstoke: Palgrave Macmillan.

Breaugh, J. and Starke, M. (2000) 'Research on employee recruitment: so many studies', *Journal of Management*, Vol. 26, No. 3, 405–34.

Bremen, J.M. and McMullen, T. (2010) 'A decade of total rewards', *Workspan*, Vol. 53, No. 6, 20–5.

Brewerton, P. and Millward, L. (2001) *Organisational Research Methods: A guide for students and researchers*. London: Sage.

Brewster, C. (2004) 'European perspectives on human resource management', *Human Resource Management Review*, Vol. 14, No. 4, 365–82.

Brewster, C. and Mayrhofer, W. (2011) 'Comparative human resource management', in A. Harzing and A. Pinnington (eds) *International Human Resource Management*, 3rd edition. London: Sage.

Brewster, C., Gill, C. and Richbell, S. (1983) 'Industrial relations policy: a framework for analysis', in K. Thurley and S. Wood (eds) *Industrial Relations and Management Strategy*. Cambridge: Cambridge University Press.

Brewster, C., Sparrow, P. and Vernon, G. (2007) *International Human Resource Management*, 2nd edition. London: CIPD.

Brindle, D. (2011) 'Eight out of 10 workers overweight or have long-term illness – study', *The Guardian*, 30 September, p.28.

Briscoe, D.R. and Claus, L.M. (2008) 'Employee performance management', in A. Varma, P.S. Budhwar and A. DeNisi (2008) *Performance Management Systems: A Global Perspective.* Abingdon, Oxon: Routledge.

Broadbridge, A. and Hearn, J. (2008) 'Gender and management: new directions in research and continuing patterns in practice', *British Journal of Management*, Vol. 19, No. 1, s38–s49.

Brockett, J. (2011) 'DRA abolition "to deny young workers opportunities"', *People Management online.* Available at: http://peoplemangement.co.uk/ (accessed 7 October 2011).

Brockmann, M and Clarke, L. (2009) 'Competence and competency in the EQF and in European VET systems', *Journal of European Industrial Training*, Vol. 33, No. 8/9, 787–99.

Brockmann, M., Clarke, L., and Winch, C. (2010) 'The Apprenticeship framework in England: a new beginning or a continuing sham?' *Journal of Education and Work*, Vol. 23, No.2, 111–27.

Brown, D. (2001) *Reward Strategies: From intent to impact*. London: CIPD.

Brown, D. and Armstrong, M. (1999) *Paying for Contributions*. London: Kogan Page.

Brown, D., Caldwell, R., White, K., Atkinson, H., Tansley, T., Goodge, P. and Emmott, M. (2004) *Business Partnering: A new direction for HR*. London: CIPD.

Brown, L., Murphy, E. and Wade, V. (2006) 'Corporate e-learning: human resource development implications for large and small organizations', *Human Resource Development International*, Vol. 9, No. 3, 415–27.

BROWN, M. and LIM, V.S. (2010) 'Understanding Performance, Management and Appraisal: Supervisory and Employee Perspectives', in A. WILKINSON, N. BACON, T. REDMAN, and S. SNELL (eds) *The Sage Handbook of Human Resource Management.* London: SAGE, pp.191–209.

BROWN, W. (1973) *Piecework Bargaining*. London: Heinemann.

BROWN, W. (2000) 'Putting partnership into practice in Britain', *British Journal of Industrial Relations*, Vol. 38, No. 2, 299–316.

BROWN, W. (2009) 'The process of fixing the British national minimum wage, 1997–2007', *British Journal of Industrial Relations*, Vol. 47, No. 2, 429–43.

BROWN W. (2011) Industrial Relations in Britain Under New Labour, 1997–2010: A Post Mortem', *Journal of Industrial Relations*, 2011, pp 1–12.

BROWN, W. and WALSH, J. (1994) 'Managing pay in Britain', in K. SISSON (ed.) *Personnel Management*, 2nd edition. Oxford: Blackwell.

BROWN, W., BRYSON, A. and FORTH, J. ( 2009) 'Competition and the retreat from collective bargaining', in W. BROWN, A. BRYSON, J. FORTH and K. WHITFIELD (eds) *The Evolution of the Modern Workplace.* Cambridge: Cambridge University Press.

BROWN, W., DEAKIN, S., HUDSON, M., PRATTEN, C. and RYAN, P. (1998) *The Individualisation of Employment Contracts in Britain*, DTI Employment Relations Research Series, No. 4. London: DTI.

BROWN, W., MARGINSON, P. and WALSH, J. (2003) 'Management of pay', in P. EDWARDS (ed.) *Industrial Relations*, 2nd edition. Oxford: Blackwell.

BROWNELL, J. (2006) 'Meeting the competency needs of global leaders: a partnership approach', *Human Resource Management*, Vol. 45, No. 3, 309–36.

BRUEGEL, I. and GRAY, A. (2005) 'Men's conditions of employment and the division of childcare between parents', in D. HOUSTON (ed.) *Work-Life Balance in the Twenty-First Century*. Basingstoke: Palgrave Macmillan.

BRYMAN, A. (2004) *The Disneyisation of Society*. London: Sage.

BRYMAN, A. and BELL, E. (2011) *Business Research Methods*, 3rd edition. Oxford: Oxford University Press.

BRYSON, A. (2004) 'Managerial responsiveness to union and non-union worker voice in Britain', *Industrial Relations*, Vol. 43, No. 1, 213–41.

BRYSON, A. and FREEMAN, R. (2006) *Doing the Right Thing. Does fair share capitalism improve workplace performance?*, Employment Relations Research Series, No. 8. London: DTI.

BRYSON, A., CHARLWOOD, A. and FORTH, J. (2006) 'Worker voice, managerial response and labour productivity: an empirical investigation', *Industrial Relations Journal*, Vol. 37, No. 5, 438–55.

BRYSON, A., GOMEZ, R. and WILLMAN, P. (2010) 'Voice in the wilderness: the shift from union to non-union voice in Britain', in A. WILKINSON, P. GOLLAN, M. MARCHINGTON and D. LEWIN (eds) *The Oxford Handbook of Participation in Organisations.* Oxford: Oxford University Press.

BRYSON, A., PENDLETON, A. and WHITEFIELD, K. (2009) 'The changing use of contingent pay at the modern British workplace', in W. BROWN, A. BRYSON, J. FORTH, and K. WHITFIELD (eds) *The Evolution of the Modern Workplace*. Cambridge: Cambridge University Press.

BUCHANAN, D. and HUCZYNSKI, A. (2004) *Organizational Behaviour: An introductory text*, 5th edition. London: Financial Times/Prentice Hall.

BUCHANAN, D., BODDY, D. and MCCALLUM, J. (1988) 'Getting in, getting on, getting out and getting back', in A. BRYMAN (ed.) *Doing Research in Organisations*. London: Routledge.

BUDD, J. (2004) *Employment with a Human Face: Balancing efficiency, equity and voice*. Ithaca: ILR Press, an imprint of Cornell University Press.

BUDD, J. and ZAGELMEYER, S. (2010) 'Public policy and employee participation', in A. WILKINSON, P. GOLLAN, M. MARCHINGTON and D. LEWIN (eds) *The Oxford Handbook of Participation in Organisations*. Oxford: Oxford University Press.

BUDD, J.W. and BHAVE, D. (2009) 'The employment relationship', in A. WILKINSON, T. REDMAN, S. SNELL and N. BACON (eds) *Handbook of Human Resource Management*. London: Sage.

BUDD, J.W.C. (2005) 'Employment with a human face: the author responds', *Employee Responsibilities and Rights Journal*, Vol. 17, No. 3, 191–9.

BUDHWAR, P. and MELLAHI, K. (eds) (2006) *Managing Human Resources in the Middle East*. London: Routledge.

BUDHWAR, P. and SINGH, V. (2009) 'Factors influencing Indian HRM policies and practices', in P. BUDHWAR and J. BHATNAGAR (eds) *The Changing Face of People Management in India*. London: Routledge.

BURAWOY, M. (1979) *Manufacturing Consent: Changes in the labour process under monopoly capitalism*. Chicago: University of Chicago Press.

BURBACH, R. and ROYLE, T. (2010) 'Talent on demand? Talent management in the German and Irish subsidiaries of a US multinational corporation', *Personnel Review*, Vol. 39, No. 4, 414–31.

BURNES, B. (2003) 'Managing change and changing managers from ABC to XYZ', *Journal of Management Development*, Vol. 22, No. 7, 627–42.

BURNES, B. (2004) *Managing Change*, 4th edition. London: Pitman.

BUTLER P. (2009) '"Riding along on the crest of a wave": tracking the shifting rationale for non-union consultation at FinanceCo', *Human Resource Management Journal*, Vol. 19, No. 2, 176–93.

BUTTERFIELD, K., TREVINO, L. and BALL, G. (1996) 'Punishment from the manager's perspective: a grounded investigation and inductive model', *Academy of Management Journal*, Vol. 39, No. 6, 1479–512.

BUYENS, D. and DE VOS, A. (2001) 'Perceptions of the value of the HR function', *Human Resource Management Journal*, Vol. 11, No. 3, 53–89.

CABLE, D. and YU, K. (2006) 'Managing job seekers' organisational image beliefs: the role of media richness and credibility', *Journal of Applied Psychology*, Vol. 91, No. 4, 828–40.

CALDWELL, R. (2001) 'Champions, adapters, consultants and synergists: the new change agents in HRM', *Human Resource Management Journal*, Vol. 11, No. 3, 39–52.

CALDWELL, R. (2003) 'The changing roles of personnel managers: old ambiguities, new uncertainties', *Journal of Management Studies*, Vol. 40, No. 4, 983–1004.

CALIGIURI, P.M. (2006) 'Developing global leaders', *Human Resource Management Review*, Vol. 16, 219–28.

CALLAGHAN, G. and THOMPSON, P. (2002) '"We recruit attitude": the selection and shaping of routine call centre labour', *Journal of Management Studies*, Vol. 39, No. 2, 233–55.

CAMPBELL, J.L. (2007) 'Why would corporations behave in socially responsible ways? An institutional theory of corporate social responsibility', *The Academy of Management Review*, Vol. 32, No. 3, 946–67.

CAPPELLI, P. (2008) *Talent on Demand*, Boston: Harvard Business School.

CAPPELLI, P. and HAMORI, M. (2008) 'Are franchises bad employers?' *Industrial and Labour Relations Review*, Vol. 61, No. 2, 147–62.

CAPPELLI, P. and NEUMARK, D. (2001) 'Do "high-performance" work practices improve establishment-level outcomes?' *Industrial and Labor Relations Review*, Vol. 54, No. 4, 737–76.

CARLESS, S. (2009) 'Psychological testing for selection purposes: a guide to evidence-based practice for human resource professionals', *International Journal of Human Resource Management*, Vol. 20, No. 12, 2517–32.

CAROLI, E., GAUTIE, J., LLOYD, C., LAMANTHE, C. and JAMES, S. (2010) 'Delivering flexibility: contrasting patterns in the French and the UK food processing industry', *British Journal of Industrial Relations*, Vol. 48, No. 2, 284–309.

CARROLL, A. (1991) 'The pyramid of corporate social responsibility: towards the moral management of organizational stakeholders', *Business Horizons*, Vol. 34, No. 4, 39–48.

CARROLL, B.C. and SHABANA, K.M. (2010) 'The business case for corporate social responsibility: a review of concepts, research and practice', *International Journal of Management Reviews*, Vol. 12, No. 1, 85–105.

CARROLL, M., MARCHINGTON, M., EARNSHAW, J. and TAYLOR, S. (1999) 'Recruitment in small firms: processes, methods and problems', *Employee Relations*, Vol. 21, No. 3, 236–50.

CARROLL, M., SMITH, M., OLIVIER, G. and SUNG, S. (2008) 'Recruitment and retention in front-line services: the case of childcare', *Human Resource Management Journal*, Vol. 18, No. 4.

CASCIO, W. (2009) 'Downsizing', in A. WILKINSON, N. BACON, T. REDMAN and S. SNELL (eds) *The SAGE Handbook of Human Resource Management*. London: Sage.

CASSELL, C. and LEE, B. (2009) 'Trade Union learning representatives: progressing partnership?' *Work, Employment and Society*, Vol. 23, No. 2, 213–30.

CASSELL, C. and SYMON, G. (2004) *Essential Guide to Qualitative Methods in Organisational Research*. London: Sage.

CASTELLANOS, R. and MARTIN, Y. (2011) 'Training as a source of competitive advantage: performance impact and the role of firm strategy, the Spanish case', *International Journal of Human Resource Management*, Vol. 22, No. 3, 574–94.

CAULKIN, S. (2001) 'The time is now', *People Management*, 30 August, 32–4.

CERTIFICATION OFFICER (2007) *Annual Report of the Certification Officer, 2006–7*. London, Certification Office for Trade Unions and Employers' Associations.

Certification Officer (2011) *Annual Report of the Certification Officer, 2009–10*, London.

Chamberlain, L. (2011) 'Demand for temporary workers remains high as Agency Worker Regulations loom', *Personnel Today*, 23 September.

Chandler, A. (1962) *Strategy and Structure: Chapters in the history of the American industrial enterprise*. Cambridge: MIT Press.

Chang, E. (2006) 'Individual pay for performance and commitment HR practices in South Korea', *Journal of World Business*, Vol. 41, 368–81.

Charlwood, A. (2003) 'Willingness to Unionize Amongst Non-Union Workers' in Howard Gospel and Stephen Wood (eds.) *Representing Workers: Trade Union Membership and Recognition in Britain*, London: Routledge, pp. 51–71.

Chartered Institute of Personnel and Development (2001) *Performance through People: the new people management*. London: CIPD, chapter 15.

Chartered Institute of Personnel and Development (2004) *Recruitment, Retention, and Turnover: A survey of the UK and Ireland*. London: CIPD, chapter 8.

Chartered Institute of Personnel and Development (2005) *HR: Where is your career heading?* Survey Report. London: CIPD, chapter 6.

Chartered Institute of Personnel and Development (2006) Change Agenda: *The Changing HR Function*. London: CIPD chapter 6.

Chartered Institute of Personnel and Development (2007a) 'HR guide to outsourcing', *People Management*, 28–9 February.

Chartered Institute of Personnel and Development (2007b) *Recruitment, Retention, and Turnover: A survey of the UK and Ireland*. London: CIPD, chapter 9.

Chartered Institute of Personnel and Development (2007c) *Absence Management*. Annual Survey Report. London: CIPD, chapter 9.

Chartered Institute of Personnel and Development (2007d) *Learning and Development*. Annual Survey Report. London: CIPD, chapter 11.

Chartered Institute of Personnel and Development (2009a) *HR outsourcing and the HR function: threat or opportunity*. London: CIPD, chapter 6.

Chartered Institute of Personnel Development (2009b) *Recruitment, Retention and Turnover*. Annual Survey Report. London: CIPD, chapters 8, 9.

Chartered Institute of Personnel Development Factsheet (2009c) *E-learning: progress and prospects*. London: CIPD, chapter 11.

Chartered Institute of Personnel Development Factsheet (2009d) *Coaching at the Sharp End: The role of managers in coaching at work*. London: CIPD, chapter 11.

Chartered Institute of Personnel Development (2010a) *Diversity in the Workplace: an overview*. London: CIPD, chapter 1.

Chartered Institute of Personnel Development (2010b) *Labour Market Outlook*, Autumn, 2. London: CIPD, chapter 2.

Chartered Institute of Personnel and Development (2010c) *People Management Guide to Recruitment Marketing*. London: CIPD, chapter 8.

CHARTERED INSTITUTE OF PERSONNEL DEVELOPMENT (2010d) *Research Report: Using the head and heart at work: A business case for soft skills.* London: CIPD, chapter 9.

CHARTERED INSTITUTE OF PERSONNEL DEVELOPMENT (2010e) *Skills for sustainable growth: Submission to the Department for Business, Innovation and Skills.* London: CIPD, chapter 10.

CHARTERED INSTITUTE OF PERSONNEL DEVELOPMENT (2010f) *Resourcing and Talent Planning Survey.* London: CIPD, chapter 10.

CHARTERED INSTITUTE OF PERSONNEL DEVELOPMENT (2010g) *Learning and Talent Development: Annual Survey Report 2010.* London: CIPD, chapter 11.

CHARTERED INSTITUTE OF PERSONNEL DEVELOPMENT FACTSHEET (2010h) *Coaching and Mentoring.* London: CIPD, chapter 11.

CHARTERED INSTITUTE OF PERSONNEL DEVELOPMENT (2010i) *Market Pricing and Job Evaluation Factsheet.* London: CIPD, chapter 14.

CHARTERED INSTITUTE OF PERSONNEL AND DEVELOPMENT (2011) *Employee Engagement.* Factsheet. London: CIPD.

CHARTERED INSTITUTE OF PERSONNEL AND DEVELOPMENT (2011a) *Flexible Working Factsheet.* London: CIPD, chapter 2.

CHARTERED INSTITUTE OF PERSONNEL AND DEVELOPMENT (2011b) 'Diversity', *People Management*, 16 August, chapter 2.

CHARTERED INSTITUTE OF PERSONNEL AND DEVELOPMENT (2011c) *Shaping the Future.* London: CIPD, chapter 6.

CHARTERED INSTITUTE OF PERSONNEL AND DEVELOPMENT/HAYS (2011d) *Resourcing and Talent Planning.* Annual Survey Report. London: CIPD.

CHARTERED INSTITUTE OF PERSONNEL AND DEVELOPMENT (2011e) *Absence Management Survey.* Annual Survey Report. London: CIPD.

CHARTERED INSTITUTE OF PERSONNEL AND DEVELOPMENT (2011f) *Learning and talent development.* Annual Survey Report. London: CIPD.

CHARTERED INSTITUTE OF PERSONNEL DEVELOPMENT (2011g) *Conflict Management.* Survey Report. London: CIPD, chapter 12.

CHARTERED INSTITUTE OF PERSONNEL DEVELOPMENT (2011h) *Reward Management.* Annual Survey Report. London: CIPD, chapter 14.

CHARTERED INSTITUTE OF PERSONNEL AND DEVELOPMENT (2011i) *Engagement Factsheet.* London: CIPD, chapter 13.

CHARTERED INSTITUTE OF PERSONNEL DEVELOPMENT (2011g) 'Internships', *People Management*, 10–11 August.

CHEN, Z., LAM, W. and ZHONG, J. (2007) 'Leader–member exchange and member performance: a new look at individual level negative feedback-seeking behaviour and team level empowerment climate', *Journal of Applied Psychology*, Vol. 92, No. 1, 202–12.

CHI, N. and LIN, C. (2011) 'Beyond the high performance paradigm: exploring the curvilinear relationship between high performance work systems and organisational performance in Taiwanese manufacturing firms', *British Journal of Industrial Relations*, forthcoming.

Chiang, F. (2005) 'A critical examination of Hofstede's thesis and its application to international reward management', *International Journal of Human Resource Management*, Vol. 16, No. 9, 1545–63.

Chiang, F., Chow, I. and Birtch, T. (2010) 'Examining HR outsourcing in Hong Kong', *International Journal of Human Resource Management*, Vol. 21, No. 15, 2762–77.

Chiang, F.F.T. and Birtch, T.A. (2010) 'Appraising performance across borders: an empirical examination of the purposes and practices of performance appraisal in a multi-country context', *Journal of Management Studies*, Vol. 47, No. 7, 1365–93.

Child, J. (1997) 'Strategic choice in the analysis of action, structure, organisations and environment: retrospect and prospect', *Organisation Studies*, Vol. 18, No. 1, 43–76.

Chillas, S. (2010) 'Work-readiness: what employers really want from graduate employees', Paper presented to the International Labour Process Conferences, Rutgers University, New Jersey cited in Holmes, C. and Mayhew, K. *UK Higher Education in Recession*. SKOPE Research Paper No. 24. University of Oxford: SKOPE.

Chow, I. and Liu, S. (2009) 'The effect of aligning organisational culture and business strategy with HR systems on firm performance in Chinese enterprises', *International Journal of Human Resource Management*, Vol. 20, No. 11, 2292–311.

Christy, G. (2010) 'Leadership', in G. Rees and R. French (eds) *Leading, Managing and Developing People*. London: CIPD.

Chu, A.Z-C. and Chu, R.J-C. (2011) 'The intranet's role in newcomer socialization in the hotel industry in Taiwan – technology acceptance model analysis' *The International Journal of Human Resource Management*. Vol. 22, No. 5, 1163–79.

Chubb, L. (2007) 'Attitudes to mental health staff return-to-work plans', *People Management*, 29 November.

Chynoweth, C. (2011) 'Small but perfectly informed', *People Management*, July.

CIPD *see* Chartered Institute of Personnel and Development.

Clark, I. (2006) 'Another third way? VW and the trials of stakeholder capitalism', *Industrial Relations Journal*, Vol. 37, No. 6, 593–606.

Clark. I. (2007) 'Private equity and HRM in the British business system', *Human Resource Management Journal*, Vol. 17, No. 3, 218–26.

Clark, I. (2009) 'Private equity in the UK: job regulation and trade unions', *Journal of Industrial Relations*, Vol. 51, No. 4, 489–500.

Clark, I. (2011) 'Private equity, union recognition and value extraction at the Automobile Association: The GMB as an emergency service?' *Industrial Relations Journal*, Vol. 42, No. 1, 36–50.

Claus, L. and Briscoe, D. (2009) 'Employee performance management across borders: A review of relevant academic literature', *International Journal of Management Reviews*, Vol. 11, No. 2, 175–96.

Claydon, T. (1998) 'Problematising partnership: the prospects for a co-operative bargaining agenda', in P. Sparrow and M. Marchington (eds) *Human Resource Management: The new agenda*. London: Financial Times/Pitman.

Claydon, T. and Doyle, M. (1996) 'Trusting me, trusting you? The ethics of employee empowerment', *Personnel Review*, Vol. 25, No. 6, 13–25.

Clutterbuck, D. and Megginson, D. (2005) *Making Coaching Work: Creating the coaching culture*. London: CIPD.

Coates, D. (1999) 'Models of capitalism in the New World Order', *Political Studies*, Vol. 47, No. 4, 643–60.

Coats, D. (2009) *Time to cut the Gordian Knot: The case for consensus and the reform of the UK's employment relations system*. London: The Smith Institute.

Cohen, S. (2006) *Employee Share Ownership Plans: Supporting business performance*. CIPD Briefing.

Collin, A. (2010) 'Contextualising HRM: developing critical thinking', in J. Beardwell and T. Claydon, *Human Resource Management: A Contemporary Approach*, 6th edition. Harlow: Pearson Education Ltd.

Colling T. (1999) 'Tendering and outsourcing: working in the contract state?' in S. Corby and G. White (eds) *Employee Relations in the Public Services*. London: Routledge.

Colling, T. (2003) 'Managing without unions', in P. Edwards (ed.) *Industrial Relations*, 2nd edition. Oxford: Blackwell.

Collings, D. and Mellahi, K. (2009) 'Strategic talent management: a review and research agenda', *Human Resource Management Review*, Vol. 19, 304–13.

Collings, D., Demirbag, M., Mellahi, K. and Tatoglu, E. (2010) 'Strategic orientation, human resource management practices and organisational outcomes: evidence from Turkey,' *International Journal of Human Resource Management*, Vol. 21, No. 14, 2589–613.

Collins, C. and Han, J. (2007) 'Exploring pool applicant quantity and quality: the effects of early recruitment practice strategies, corporate advertising and firm reputation', *Personnel Psychology*, Vol. 57, 685–717.

Colvin, A. (2003) 'Institutional pressures, human resource strategies and the rise of nonunion dispute resolution procedures', *Industrial and Labor Relations Review*, Vol. 56, No. 3, 375–92.

Colvin, A. (2004) 'The relationship between employee involvement and workplace dispute resolution', *Relations Industrielles*, Vol. 59, No. 4, 681–704.

Conference Board (2006) 'Employee Engagement, A Review of Current Research and Its Implications'. NY: The Conference Board.

Conference Board, The (2010) *Senior Corporate Communications Management Conference*. Los Angeles, CA, Davidson Conference Center on the Campus of USC, 3–5 November.

Conway, E. and Monks, K. (2011) 'Change from below: the role of middle managers in mediating paradoxical change', *Human Resource Management Journal*, Vol. 21, No. 2, 190–203.

Cook, M. (1998) *Personnel Selection: Adding value through people*, 3rd edition. Chichester: John Wiley & Sons.

Cooke, F.L. (2005) HRM, Work and Employment in China, Abingdon: Routledge.

Cooke, F.L. (2005) *Work and Employment in China*. London: Routledge.

Cooke, F.L. (2006) 'Modeling an HR shared services center; experience of an MNC in the United Kingdom', *Human Resource Management*, Vol. 45, No. 2, 211–27.

COOKE, F.L. (2008) 'Performance management in China', in A. VARMA., P.S. BUDHWAR and A. DENISI *Performance Management Systems: A Global Perspective*. Abingdon, Oxon, Routledge.

COOKE, F.L. (2011) 'Employment relations in China and India', in M. BARRY and A. WILKINSON (eds) *Research Handbook on Comparative Employment Relations*. Cheltenham: Edward Elgar, pp. 183–213.

COOKE, F.L. (2011a) 'Social responsibility, sustainability and diversity of Human Resources', in A-W. HARZING and A.H. PINNINGTON *International Human Resource Management*, 3rd edition. London: Sage Publications.

COOKE, F.L. (2011b) 'Talent management in China', in H. SCULLION and D.G. COLLINGS *Global Talent Management*. New York and Abingdon: Routledge.

COOKE. F.L., EARNSHAW, J., MARCHINGTON, M. and RUBERY, J. (2004) 'For better and for worse: transfer of undertaking and the reshaping of employment relations', *International Journal of Human Resource Management*, Vol. 15, No. 2, 276–94.

COOKE, F.L., SHEN, J. and MCBRIDE, A. (2005) 'Outsourcing HR as a competitive strategy? A literature review and an assessment of implications', *Human Resource Management*, Vol. 44, No. 4, 413–32.

COONEY, S. (2007) 'China's labour law, compliance and flaws in implementing institutions', *Journal of Industrial Relations*, Vol. 49, No. 5, 673–86.

COOPER, D., ROBERTSON, I. and TINLINE, G. (2003) *Recruitment and Selection: A framework for success*. London: Thomson.

CORBY, S., PALMER, S. and LINDOP. E. (eds) (2009) *Rethinking Reward*. Basingstoke: Palgrave.

CORDERY, J. (2003) 'Teamwork', in D. HOLMAN, T. WALL, C. CLEGG, P. SPARROW and A. HOWARD (eds) *The New Workplace: A guide to the human impact of modern working practices*. London: John Wiley & Sons.

COUPAR, W. and STEVENS, S. (1998) 'Towards a new model of industrial partnership: beyond the HRM versus industrial relations argument', in P. SPARROW and M. MARCHINGTON (eds) *Human Resource Management: The new agenda*. London, Financial Times/Pitman.

COWSILL, R. and GRINT, K. (2008) 'Leadership, task and relationship: Orpheus, Prometheus and Janus', *Human Resource Management Journal*, Vol. 18, No. 2, 188–95.

COX, A. (2000) 'The importance of employee participation in determining pay effectiveness', *International Journal of Management Reviews*, Vol. 2, No. 4, 357–72.

COX, A. (2007) 'Re-visiting the NVQ Debate: 'bad' qualifications, expansive learning environments and prospects for upskilling workers', SKOPE Research Paper No. 71. Oxford/Cardiff, SKOPE/ESRC. Available online at: www.skope.ox.ac.uk (accessed 04/01/2012)

COX, A. and MCBRIDE, A. (2007) 'What goes up…', *People Management*, 17 May, 36–8.

COX, A., MARCHINGTON, M. and SUTER, J. (2007) *Embedding the Provision of Information and Consultation in the Workplace: A longitudinal analysis of employee outcomes in WERS 1998 and 2004*. Department of Trade and Industry Employment Relations Research Series No. 72.

COX, A., MARCHINGTON, M. and SUTER, J. (2009) 'Employee involvement and participation: developing the concept of institutional embeddedness', *International Journal of Human Resource Management*, Vol. 20, No. 10, 2150–68.

Cox, A., Zagelmeyer, S. and Marchington, M. (2006) 'Embedding employee involvement and participation at work', *Human Resource Management Journal*, Vol. 16, No. 3, 250–67.

Coyle-Shapiro, J. and Dhensa-Kahlon, R. (2011) 'Justice in the 21st century organisation' in K. Townsend and A. Wilkinson (eds) *Research Handbook on Work and Employment Relations*. Cheltenham: Edward Elgar, pp. 385–404.

Crail, M. (2006a) 'In the round: a 360-degree appraisal for HR', *IRS Employment Review* 857, 20 October, 20–3.

Crail, M. (2006b) 'What are the attributes of an effective HR function?' *IRS Employment Review* 841, 17 February, 18–20.

Crail, M. (2007) 'Roles and responsibilities, 2007: benchmarking the HR function', *IRS Employment Review* 863, 6–12.

Crail, M. (2008) 'HR roles and responsibilities: benchmarking the HR function', *IRS Employment Review* 888.

Crawshaw, M., Davis, E., and Kay, J. (1994) '"Being stuck in the middle" or "good food costs less at Sainsbury's"', *British Journal of Management*, Vol. 5, No. 1, 19–32.

Cressey, P. (1998) 'European works councils in practice', *Human Resource Management Journal*, Vol. 8, No. 1, 67–79.

Cresswell, J. (2003) *Research Design: Qualitative, quantitative, and mixed methods approaches*, 2nd edition. London: Sage.

Crichton, A. (1968) *Personnel Management in Context*. London: Batsford.

Crompton, R., Brockmann, M. and Lyonette, C. (2005) 'Attitudes, women's employment and the domestic division of labour: a cross-national analysis in two waves', *Work, Employment and Society*, Vol. 19, No. 2, 213–33.

Crosby P. (1980) *Quality is Free*. New York: Mentor.

Croucher, R. (2010) 'Employee involvement in Ukranian companies', *International Journal of Human Resource Management*, Vol. 21, No. 14, 2659–76.

Crowther, D. (2010) 'Corporate Social Responsibility', *Human Resources*, March, 35–8.

Cully, M., Woodland, S., O'Reilly, A., Dix, G., Millward, N., Bryson, A. and Forth, J. (1998) *The 1998 Workplace Employee Relations Survey: First findings*. London: Department of Trade and Industry.

Cunningham, I. (2010) 'The HR function in purchaser-provider relationships: insights from the UK voluntary sector', *Human Resource Management Journal*, Vol. 20, No. 2, 189–205.

Cunningham, I. and Hyman, J. (1995) 'Transforming the HRM vision into reality: the role of line managers and supervisors in implementing change', *Employee Relations,* Vol. 17, No. 8, 5–20.

Currie, G. and Procter, S. (2005) 'The antecedents of middle managers' strategic contribution: the case of a professional bureaucracy', *Journal of Management Studies*, Vol. 42, No. 7, 1325–56.

Currie, G., Lockett, A. and Suhomlinova, O. (2009) 'Leadership and institutional change in the public sector: the case of secondary schools in England', *The Leadership Quarterly*, Vol. 20, 664–79.

D'Annunzio-Green, N. (2002) 'An examination of the organisational and cross-cultural challenges facing international hotel managers in Russia', *International Journal of Contemporary Hospitality Management,* Vol. 14, No. 6, 266–73.

Danford, A., Durbin, S., Richardson, M., Tailby, S. and Stewart, P. (2009) '"Everybody's talking at me": The dynamics of information disclosure and consultation in high-skill workplaces in the UK', *Human Resource Management Journal*, Vol. 19, No. 4, 337–54.

Danford, A., Richardson, M., Stewart, P., Tailby, S. and Upchurch, M. (2003) 'Partnership, mutuality and the one-way street: A case study of aircraft workers', Labour Process Conference, Bristol.

Dany, F., Guderi, Z. and Hatt, F. (2008) 'New insights into the link between HRM integration and organisational performance: the moderating role of influence distribution between HR specialists and line managers', *International Journal of Human Resource Management*, Vol. 19, No. 11, 2095–112.

Datta, K, McIlwaine, C., Evans, Y., Harbert, J, May, J. and Wills, J. (2007) 'From coping strategies to tactics: London's low-pay economy and migrant labour', *British Journal of Industrial Relations*, Vol. 45, No. 2., 404–32.

DBIS (2010) *Investing in Skills for Sustainable Growth.* London: Department for Business, Innovation and Skills.

DBIS (2011) *Higher Education: Students at the Heart of the System.* June. London: Department for Business, Innovation and Skills.

De Vos, A., Buyens, D. and Schalk, R. (2003) 'Psychological contract development during organizational socialization: adaptation to reality and the role of reciprocity', *Journal of Organizational Behaviour*, Vol. 24, 537–59.

Deakin, S. and Green, F. (2009) 'One hundred years of British minimum wage legislation', *British Journal of Industrial Relations*, Vol. 47, No. 2, 205–13.

Deakin, S., Hobbs, R., Konzellman, S. and Wilkinson, F. (2004) 'Working corporations: corporate governance and innovation in labour–management partnerships in Britain', in M. Stuart and M. Martinez-Lucio (eds) *Partnership and Modernisation in Employment Relations.* London: Routledge.

Dearing R. (1997) *The National Committee of Inquiry into Higher Education.* London: DfES.

Debrah, Y.A. and Rees, C.J. (2011) 'The development of global leaders and expatriates', in A-W. Harzing and A.H. Pinnington *International Human Resource Management*, 3rd edition. London: Sage.

Deephouse, D. (1999) 'To be different, or to be the same? It's a question (and theory) of strategic balance', *Strategic Management Journal*, Vol. 20, 147–66.

Delaney, J. and Huselid, M. (1996) 'The impact of human resource management practices on perceptions of organisational performance', *Academy of Management Journal*, Vol. 39, 349–69.

Delarue, A., van Hootegem, G., Procter, S. and Burridge, M. (2007) 'Teamworking and organizational performance: a review of survey-based research', *International Journal of Management Reviews*, Vol. 9, No. 4.

Delbridge, R. (1998) *Life on the Line in Contemporary Manufacturing: The workplace experience of lean production and the 'Japanese' model.* Oxford: Oxford University Press.

Delbridge, R. (2011) 'The critical future of human resource management', in P. Blyton, E. Heery and P. Turnbull (eds) *Reassessing the Employment Relationship*. London: Palgrave Macmillan.

Delery, J. and Doty, H. (1996) 'Modes of theorising in strategic human resource management: tests of universalistic, contingency and configurational performance predictions', *Academy of Management Journal*, Vol. 39, No. 4, 802–35.

Delmotte, J. and Sels, L. (2008) 'HR outsourcing: threat or opportunity?' *Personnel Review*, Vol. 37, No. 5, 543–63.

DeLong, T.J., Gabarro, J.J. and Lees, R.J. (2008) 'Why mentoring matters in hypercompetitive world', *Harvard Business Review*, Vol. 86, No. 1, 115–21.

DeNisi, A., Varma, A. and Budhwar, P.S. (2008) 'Performance Management: what have we learned?' in A. Varma., P.S. Budhwar and A. DeNisi *Performance Management Systems: A Global Perspective.* Abingdon, Oxon: Routledge.

Denzin, N. (1970) *The Research Act*. Chicago: Aldine.

Denzin, N. (1978) *Sociological Methods: A sourcebook*. New York: McGraw-Hill.

Department of Trade and Industry (2006) *Women at Work Commission: Shaping a fairer future.* London: DTI.

Department of Trade and Industry (2007) *Trade Union Membership 2006.* London: DTI. Available online at: www.dti.gov.uk/publications (accessed 04/07/2012).

Devanna, M., Fombrun, C. and Tichy, N. (1984) 'A framework for strategic human resource management', in C. Fombrun, N. Tichy and A. Devanna (eds) *Strategic Human Resource Management*. New York: Wiley.

Devins, D. and Smith, J. (2010) 'Evaluation of HRD', in J. Gold, R. Holden, P. Iles, J. Stewart and J. Beardwell *Human Resource Development: Theory and practice.* Basingstoke: Palgrave Macmillan.

DfES (2006) *Foster Review: Further Education: Raising Skills, Improving Life Chances.* London: DfES.

Dicken, P. (2003) *Global Shift: Reshaping the Global Economic Map in the 21st Century*, 4th edition. London: Sage.

Dickens, L. (2007) 'The road is long: thirty years of equality legislation in Britain', *British Journal of Industrial Relations*, Vol. 43, No. 3, 463–94.

Dickens, L. and Hall, M. (2003) 'Labour law and industrial relations: a new settlement', in P. Edwards (ed.) *Industrial Relations*, 2nd edition. Oxford: Blackwell.

Dickens, L. and Hall, M. (2006) 'Fairness – up to a point. Assessing the impact of New Labour's employment legislation', *Human Resource Management Journal*, Vol. 16, No. 4, 338–56.

Dickens, S., Mitchell, M., and Creegan, C. (2009) *Research Paper: Management handling of sexual orientation, religion and belief in the workplace.* London: Acas/CIPD.

Dietz, G. (2004) 'Partnership and the development of trust in British workplaces', *Human Resource Management Journal*, Vol. 14, No. 1, 5–24.

Dietz, G., Wilkinson, A. and Redman, T. (2009) 'Involvement and participation' in A. Wilkinson, N. Bacon, T. Redman and S. Snell (eds) *The Sage Handbook of Human Resource Management*. London: Sage.

DiMaggio, P. and Powell, W. (1983) 'The iron cage revisited: institutional isomorphism and collective rationality in organisational fields', *American Sociological Review*, Vol. 48, 147–60.

Dobbins, T. and Gunnigle, P. (2009) 'Can voluntary workplace partnership deliver sustainable mutual gains?,' British Journal of Industrial Relations, 47(3): 546–570.

Dobers, P. and Halme, M. (2009) 'Corporate social responsibility and developing countries', *Corporate Social Responsibility and Environmental Management*, Vol. 16, 237–49.

Doellgast, V. (2009), 'Still a coordinated model: market liberalisation and the transformation of employment relations in the German telecommunications industry', *Industrial and Labour Relations Review*, Vol. 63, No. 1, 3–23.

Donaldson, L. (2001) *The Contingency Theory of Organisations*. London: Sage.

Donnelly, R. (2008) 'Careers and temporal flexibility in the new economy: an Anglo-Dutch comparison of the organisation of consultancy work', *Human Resource Management Journal*, Vol. 18, No. 3, 197–215.

Donnelly, R. (2009) 'The knowledge economy and the restructuring of employer: the case of consultants', *Work, Employment & Society*, Vol. 23, No. 2, 323–28.

Donnelly, R. (2011) 'The ambiguities and tensions in creating and capturing value: views from HRM consultants in a leading consultancy firm', *Human Resource Management*, Vol. 50, No. 3, 429–44.

Donovan Report (1968) 'Royal Commission on Trade Unions and Employers Associations 1965–68', Report Cmnd 3623. London: HMSO.

Dowling, P.J., Festing, M. and Engle, A.D. (2008) *International Human Resource Management: Managing People in a Multinational Context*. London: Cengage/South-Western.

Drago, R., Wooden, M. and Black, D. (2009) 'Long work hours: volunteers and conscripts', *British Journal of Industrial Relations*, Vol. 47, No. 3, 571–600.

Du, J. and Choi, J.N. (2010) 'Pay for performance in emerging markets: insights from China', *Journal of International Business Studies*, Vol. 41, 671–89.

Duncan, C. (1992) 'Pay, payment systems and job evaluation', in B. Towers (ed.) *A Handbook of Industrial Relations Practice*, 3rd edition. London: Kogan Page.

Dundon T. (2011) 'Conflict Management', in C. Rowley and K. Jackson (eds), *Human Resource Management: the key concepts.* London, Routledge p 26–32

Dundon, T. (2002a) 'Policies and procedures', in T. Redman and A. Wilkinson (eds) *The Informed Student Guide to Human Resource Management*. London: Thomson Learning.

Dundon, T. (2002b) 'Employer opposition and union avoidance in the UK', *Industrial Relations Journal*, Vol. 33, No. 3, 234–45.

Dundon, T. (2011a) 'Collective bargaining', in C. Rowley and K. Jackson (eds) *Human Resource Management: the key concepts*. London: Routledge, pp. 15–21.

Dundon, T. (2011b) 'Conflict Management', in C. Rowley and K. Jackson (eds) *Human Resource Management: the key concepts*. London: Routledge, pp. 26–32.

Dundon, T. and Rollinson, D. (2004) *Employment Relations in Non-union Firms*. London: Routledge.

Dundon, T. and Rollinson, D. (2011) *Understanding Employment Relations*, 2nd edition. London: McGraw Hill.

Dundon, T. and Wilkinson, A. (2003) 'Employment relations in SMEs', in B. Towers (ed.) *Handbook of Industrial Relations*. London: Kogan Page.

Dundon, T., Curran, D. and Maloney, M. (2006) 'Conceptualising the dynamics of employee information and consultation: evidence from the Republic of Ireland', *Industrial Relations Journal*, Vol. 37, No. 5, 492–512.

Dundon, T., Grugulis, I. and Wilkinson, A. (1999) 'Looking out of the black-hole: non-union relations in an SME', *Employee Relations*, Vol. 21, No. 3, 251–66.

Dundon T, Grugulis, I. and Wilkinson, A. (2001) 'New management techniques in small and medium-sized enterprises', in T. Redman and A. Wilkinson (eds) *Contemporary Human Resource Management*. London: Financial Times/Prentice Hall.

Dundon, T., Wilkinson, A., Marchington, M. and Ackers, P. (2004) 'The meaning and purpose of employee voice', *International Journal of Human Resource Management*, Vol. 15, No. 6, 1149–70.

Dunn, C. and Wilkinson, A. (2002) 'Wish you were here: managing absence', *Personnel Review*, Vol. 31, No. 2, 228–46.

Earnshaw, J., Marchington, M. and Goodman, J. (2000) 'Unfair to whom? Discipline and dismissal in small establishments', *Industrial Relations Journal*, Vol. 31, No. 1, 62–73.

Earnshaw, J., Ritchie, E., Marchington, L., Torrington, D. and Hardy, S. (2002b) *Best Practice in Undertaking Teacher Capability Procedures*. London: DfES.

Earnshaw, J., Rubery, J. and Cooke, F.L. (2002c) *Who is the Employer?* London, Institute of Employment Rights.

Easterby-Smith, M., Thorpe, R. and Lowe, A. (1996) *Management Research: An introduction*. London: Sage.

Easterby-smith, M., Thorpe, R. and Lowe, A. (2008) *Management Research: An introduction*, 3rd edition. London: Sage.

Eddington, N. and Eddington, I. (2010) *Methods and Instruments for the Evaluation and Monitoring of VET systems*. SCOPE Research Paper 98.

Edwards, P. (2000) 'Discipline: towards trust and self-discipline', in S. Bach and K. Sisson (eds) *Personnel Management*, 3rd edition. Oxford: Blackwell.

Edwards, P. (2003) 'The employment relationship and the field of industrial relations', in P. Edwards *Industrial Relations: Theory and Practice*. Oxford: Blackwell pp.1–36.

Edwards, P. and Ram, M. (2006) 'Surviving on the margins of the economy: working relationships in small, low-wage firms', *Journal of Management Studies*, Vol. 43, No. 4, 895–916.

Edwards, P. and Ram, M. (2009) 'HRM in small firms: respecting and regulating informality', in A. Wilkinson, N. Bacon, T. Redman, and S. Snell (eds) *The Sage Handbook of Human Resource Management*. London: Sage.

Edwards, P. and Wright, M. (1998) 'Human resource management and commitment: a case study of teamworking', in P. Sparrow and M. Marchington (eds) *Human Resource Management: The new agenda*. London: Pitman.

Edwards, P., Sengupta, S. and Tsai, C. (2009) 'Managing low-skill workers: a study of small UK food manufacturing firms', *Human Resource Management Journal*, Vol. 19, No. 1, 40–58.

Edwards, T. (2011) 'The transfer of employment practices across borders in multinational companies', in A. Harzing and A. Pinnington (eds) *International Human Resource Management*, 3rd edition. London: Sage.

Edwards, T. and Ferner, A. (2002) 'The renewed "American Challenge": a review of employment practice in US multinationals', *Industrial Relations Journal*, Vol. 33, No. 2, 94–111.

Edwards, T. and Rees, C. (2006) *International Human Resource Management: Globalisation, national systems and multinational companies*. Harlow: FT/Prentice Hall.

Edwards, T., Colling, T. and Ferner, A. (2007) 'Conceptual approaches to the transfer of employment practices in multinational companies: an integrated approach', *Human Resource Management Journal*, Vol. 17, No. 3, 201–17.

EHRC (2011) *Equal Pay 2010 Statutory Code of Practice*. London: Equality and Human Rights Commission.

EHRC (2011a) *Sex and Power*. London: Equality and Human Rights Commission.

Elias, P. and Purcell, K. (2004) 'Is mass higher education working? Evidence from the labour market experiences of recent graduates', *National Institute Economic Review*, No. 190, October.

Elliott, M., Dawson, R. and Edwards, J. (2009) 'Providing demonstrable return-on-investments for organisational learning and training', *Journal of European Industrial Training*, Vol. 33, No. 7, 657–70.

Erickson, C., Fisk, C., Millkman, R., Mitchell, D. and Wong, K. (2002) 'Justice for janitors in Los Angeles: Lessons from three rounds of negotiations', *British Journal of Industrial Relations*, Vol. 40, No. 3, September, 543–67.

European Commission (2007) *Towards Common Principles of Flexicurity: More and better jobs through flexibility and security*. Green Paper. Commission of the European Communities

Eurostat (2010) http://epp.eurostat.ec.europa.eu/cache/ITY_PUBLIC/1-05032010-AP/EN?1-05032010-AP-EN.PDF (accessed 6.10.11.)

Evans, J. (2010) 'Ladies in waiting' *People Management*, 30 September, 18–22.

Evans, P., Pucik, V. and Barsoux, J. (2002) *The Global Challenge: Frameworks for international human resource management*. New York: McGraw Hill.

Ewing, K. (2003) 'Labour law and industrial relations', in P. Ackers and A. Wilkinson (eds) *Understanding Work and Employment: Industrial relations in transition*. Oxford: Oxford University Press.

Fabling, R. and Grimes, A. (2010) 'HR practices and New Zealand firm performance: what matters and who does it?' *International Journal of Human Resource Management*, Vol. 21, No. 4, 488–508.

Farndale, E. and Brewster, C. (2005) 'In search of legitimacy: personnel management associations worldwide', *Human Resource Management Journal*, Vol. 15, No. 4.

Farndale, E., Paauwe, J. and Hoeksema, L. (2009) 'In-sourcing HR: shared service centres in the Netherlands', *International Journal of Human Resource Management*, Vol. 20, No. 3, 544–61.

Farndale, E., Van Ruiten, J., Kelliher, C. and Hope-Hailey, V. (2011) 'The influence of perceived employee voice in organisational commitment: an exchange perspective', *Human Resource Management*, Vol. 50, No. 1, 113–29.

Farnham, D. (1990) *Personnel in Context*. London: Institute of Personnel Management.

Farnham, D. (2000) *Employee Relations in Context*, 4th edition. London: CIPD.

Farnham, D. (2010) *Human Resource Management in Context: Strategy, insights and solutions*. London: CIPD.

Fay, C. (2011a) 'Motivation and rewards' in C. Rowley and K. Jackson (eds) *Human Resource Management: the key concepts*. London: Routledge.

Fay, C. (2011b) 'Compensation strategies', in C. Rowley and K. Jackson (eds) *Human Resource Management: the key concepts*. London: Routledge

Fay, C. (2011c) 'Pensions and other benefits', in C. Rowley and K. Jackson (eds) *Human Resource Management: the key concepts*. London: Routledge

Fay, C. (2011d) 'Pensions and other benefits', in C. Rowley and K. Jackson (eds) *Human Resource Management: the key concepts*. London: Routledge

Feldman, D. and Klaas, B. (2002) 'Internet job-hunting: a field study of applicant experiences with online recruiting', *Human Resource Management*, Vol. 41, No. 2, 175–92.

Felstead, A., Gallie, D., Green, F. and Zhou, Y. (2007) *Skills at work 1986–2006*. Oxford/ Cardiff: SKOPE/ESRC. Available online at www.skope.ox.ac.uk

Fenton O'Creevy, M. (2001) 'Employee involvement and the middle manager: saboteur or scapegoat?' *Human Resource Management Journal*, Vol. 11, No. 1, 24–40.

Ferner, A. and Hyman, R. (eds) (1998) *Industrial Relations in the New Europe*. Oxford: Blackwell.

Ferner, A. and Quintanilla, J. (1998) 'Multinational, national business systems and HRM: the enduring influence of national identity or a process of Anglo-Saxonisation', *International Journal of Human Resource Management*, Vol. 9, No. 4, 711–31.

Ferner, A., Tregaskis, O., Edwards, P., Edwards, T. and Marginson, P. (2011) 'HRM structures and subsidiary discretion in foreign multinationals in the UK', *International Journal of Human Resource Management*, Vol. 22, No. 3, 483–509.

Ferrer, J. (2005) 'Employee engagement: is it organisational commitment renamed?' *Victoria University Working Paper Series*.

Ferrin, D. and Dirks, K. (2003) 'The use of rewards to increase and decrease trust: mediating processes and differential effects', *Organizational Science*, Vol. 14, No. 1, 18–31.

*Financial Times* (2011) 'Buffett and the value of trust', Financial Times Editorial, 5 April. p.12.

FINCHAM, R. and EVANS, M. (1999) 'The consultants' offensive: re-engineering – from fad to technique', *New Technology, Work and Employment*, Vol. 14, No. 1, 32–44.

FINDLAY, P and WARHURST, C. (2011) 'Union Learning Funds and trade union revitalisation: A new tool in the toolkit?' *British Journal of Industrial Relations*, Vol. 49, Special Issue, June, 115–34.

FINEGOLD, D. (1999) 'Creating self-sustaining high-skill ecosystems', *Oxford Review of Economic Policy*, Vol. 15, No. 1, 60–79.

FINEGOLD, D. and FRENKEL, S. (2006) 'Managing people where people really matter: the management of human resources in biotech companies', *International Journal of Human Resource Management*, Vol. 17, No. 1, 1–24.

FINEGOLD, D. and SOSKICE, D. (1988) 'The failure of training in Britain: analysis and prescription', *Oxford Review of Economic Policy*, Vol. 15, No. 1, 60–80.

FINEMAN, S. and MANGHAM, I. (1983) 'Data meanings and creativity', *Journal of Management Studies*, Vol. 20, No. 3, 295–300.

FISHER, S., WASSERMAN, M., WOLF, P. and WEARS, K. (2008) 'Human resource issues in outsourcing: integrating research and practice', *Human Resource Management*, Vol. 47, No. 3, 501–23.

FLETCHER, C. (2008) *Appraisal, Feedback and Development*, 4th edition. London: CIPD.

FLORENS, P. (2006) *Why Won't Anyone Listen? Employee Voice at the Bundaberg Hospital Fiasco*, unpublished Honours thesis. Brisbane, Department of Employment Relations, Griffith University.

FOLEY, J. and POLANYI, M. (2006) 'Workplace democracy: why bother?' *Economic and Industrial Democracy*, Vol. 27, No. 1, 173–91.

FOLKMAN, P., FROUD, J., JOBAL, S. and WILLIAMS, K. (2009) 'Private equity: levered on capital or labour?' *Journal of Industrial Relations*, Vol. 51, No. 4, 517–28.

FOMBRUN, C., TICHY, N. and DEVANNA, M. (eds) (1984) *Strategic Human Resource Management*. New York: Wiley.

FORDE, C. (2001) 'Temporary arrangements: the activities of employment agencies in the UK', *Work, Employment and Society*, Vol. 15, No. 3, 631–44.

FORSTENLECHNER, I. (2010) 'Workforce localisation in the emerging Gulf economies: the need to fine-tune HRM', *Personnel Review*, Vol. 39, No. 1, 135–52.

FORSTER, P. (2005) *Queensland Health Systems Review: Forster Report*. Available online at

FOSTER REVIEW (2005) *Realising the potential: a review of the future of FE colleges*. London, DfES.

FOSTER, C. (2007) 'Ethnic minorities in the labour market', *IRS Equal Opportunities Review* 165, available online at: www.xperthr.co.uk

FOWLER, A. (1988) 'New directions in performance-related pay', *Personnel Management*, Vol. 20, No. 11, 30–4.

FOX, A. (1966) *Industrial Sociology and Industrial Relations*. Royal Commission Research Paper No. 3. London: HMSO.

FRANCIS, H. and KEEGAN, A. (2006) 'The changing face of HRM: in search of balance', *Human Resource Management Journal*, Vol. 16, No. 3, 231–49.

Fraser, M. (1966) *Employment Interviewing*. London: McDonald & Evans.

Freeman, R. (2001) 'Upping the stakes', *People Management*, 8 February, 24–9.

Freeman, R. and Medoff, J. (1984) *What do unions do?* New York: Basic Books.

Freidson, E. (ed.) (1973) *The Professions and their Prospects*. London: Sage.

Frey, B. and Osterloh, M. (2002) *Successful Management by Motivation*. Berlin: Springer-Verlag.

Friedman, M. (1970) 'The social responsibility of business is to increase its profits', *The New York Times Magazine*, 13 September 1970.

Frobel, P. and Marchington, M. (2005) 'Teamworking structures and worker perceptions: a cross-national study in pharmaceuticals', *International Journal of Human Resource Management*, Vol. 16, No. 2, 90–110.

Froud, J. and Williams, K. (2007) *Private Equity and the Culture of Value Extraction*. Centre for Research in Socio-cultural Change, Working Paper No. 31. University of Manchester.

Fukushige, A. and Spicer, D. (2011) 'Leadership and followers' work goals: a comparison between Japan and the UK', *International Journal of Human Resource Management*, Vol. 22, No. 10, 2110–34.

Fuller, A. and Unwin, L. (1998) 'Reconceptualising apprenticeship: exploring the relationship between work and learning', *Journal of Vocational Education and Training*, Vol. 50, No. 2, 153–73.

Fuller, A. and Unwin, L. (2006) 'Expansive and restrictive learning environments', in K. Evans, P. Hodkinson, H. Rainbird and L. Unwin (eds) *Improving Workplace Learning*. London: Routledge.

Fuller, A. and Unwin, L. (2009) 'Change and continuity in apprenticeship: the resilience of a model of learning', *Journal of Education and Work*, Vol. 22, No. 5, 405–16.

Gagne, R. (1977) *The Conditions of Learning*. New York: Holt Saunders.

Galbreath, J. (2010) 'Drivers of corporate social responsibility: the role of formal strategic planning and firm culture', *British Journal of Management*, Vol. 21, 511–25.

Gall, G. (2004) 'Trade union recognition in Britain 1995–2002: turning a corner?' *Industrial Relations Journal*, Vol. 35, No. 3, 249–70.

Gallie, D., White, M., Cheng, Y. and Tomlinson, M. (1998) *Restructuring the Employment Relationship*. Oxford: Oxford University Press.

Gamble, J., Culpepper, R. and Blubaugh, M. (2002) 'ESOPs and employee attitudes: the importance of empowerment and financial value', *Personnel Review*, Vol. 31, No. 1, 9–26.

Gannon, M. (2000) *Understanding Global Cultures*. London: Sage.

Gardner, T. and Wright, P. (2009) 'Implicit human resource management theory: a potential threat to the internal validity of human resource practice measures', *International Journal of Human Resource Management*, Vol. 20, No. 1, 57–74.

Gaymer, J. (2004) 'Making a molehill out of a mountain', *People Management*, 26 February, 17.

Geary, J. (2003) 'New forms of work organisation', in P. Edwards (ed.) *Industrial Relations*, 2nd edition. Oxford: Blackwell.

Geary, J. and Dobbins, A. (2001) 'Teamworking: a new dynamic in the pursuit of management control', *Human Resource Management Journal*, Vol. 11, No. 1, 3–23.

Geary, J. and Trif, A. (2011) 'Workplace partnership and the balance of advantage: a critical case analysis', *British Journal of Industrial Relations*, Vol. 49, 44–69.

Gennard, J. (2002) 'Employee relations public policy developments 1997–2001: a break with the past?' *Employee Relations*, Vol. 24, No. 6, 581–94.

Gennard, J. and Judge, G. (2005) *Employee Relations*, 4th edition. London: CIPD.

Gennard, J. and Judge, G. (2010) *Employee Relations*, 5th edition. London: CIPD.

George, E. and Chattopadhyay, P. (2005) 'One foot in each camp: the dual identification of contract workers', *Administrative Science Quarterly*, Vol. 50, 68–99.

Geppert, M. and Williams, K. (2006) 'Global national and local practices in multinational corporations: towards a socio-political framework', *International Journal of Human Resource Management*, Vol. 17, No. 1, 49–69.

Gerhart B. (2009) 'Compensation', in A. Wilkinson, N. Bacon, T. Redman and S. Snell (eds), *Handbook of Human Resource Management*. London, Sage.

Gerhart, B. and Fang, M. (2005) 'National culture and human resource management: assumptions and evidence', *International Journal of Human Resource Management*, Vol. 16, No. 6, 971–86.

Gerstner, C. and Day, D. (1997) 'Meta-analytic review of leader–member exchange theory: correlates and construct issues', *Journal of Applied Psychology*, Vol. 82, No. 6, 827–44.

Giancola, F. (2010) 'Examining the job as a source of employee motivation', *Compensation and Benefits Review*, January/February 2011, Vol. 43, No. 1, 23–9.

Giangreco, A. and Peccei, R. (2005) 'The nature and antecedents of middle manager resistance to change: evidence from an Italian context', *International Journal of Human Resource Management*, Vol. 16, No. 10, 1812–29.

Gibb, S. (2001) 'The state of human resource management: evidence from employees' views of HRM systems and staff', *Employee Relations*, Vol. 23, No. 4, 318–36.

Gibb, S. (2008) *Human Resource Development: Process, practices and perspectives.* London: Palgrave Macmillan.

Gibbons, M. (2007) *Better Dispute Resolution: A review of employment dispute resolution in Great Britain*. London: DTI.

Gill, J. and Johnson, P. (2010) *Research Methods for Managers*. London: Sage.

Giret, J-F. (2011) 'Does vocational training help transition to work? The "New French Vocational Bachelor Degree"', *European Journal of Education*, Vol. 46, No. 2.

Gittell, J. and Bamber, G. (2010) 'High and low-road strategies for competing on costs and their implications for employment relations: international studies in the airline industry', *International Journal of Human Resource Management*, Vol. 21, No. 2, 165–79.

Glaister, C., Holden, R., Griggs, V. and Mccauley, P. (2010) 'The design and delivery of training', in J. Gold, R. Holden, P. Iles, J. Stewart and J. Beardwell, *Human Resource Development: Theory and Practice*. Basingstoke: Palgrave Macmillan.

Glaser, B. and Strauss, A. (1967) *The Discovery of Grounded Theory: Strategies for qualitative research.* New York: Adline De Gruyter.

Glebbeek, A. and Bax, E. (2004) 'Is high employee turnover really harmful? An empirical test using company records', *Academy of Management Journal*, Vol. 47, No. 2, 277–86.

Gleeson, D. and Knights, D. (2008) 'Reluctant leaders: an analysis of middle managers' perceptions of leadership in further education in England', *Leadership*, Vol. 4, No. 1, 49–72.

Gloster, R., Higgins, T., Cox, A. and Jones, R. (2011) *Exploring Employer Behaviour in relation to Investors in People.* Evidence Report 27. London: UK Commission for Employment and Skills.

Gloster, R., Sumption, F., Higgins, T., Cox, A. and Jones, R. (2010) *Perspectives and Performance of Investors in People: A Literature Review.* Evidence Report 24. London: Commission for Employment and Skills.

Godard, J. (2004) 'A critical assessment of the high-performance paradigm', *British Journal of Industrial Relations*, Vol. 42, No. 2, 349–78.

Godard, J. (2011) 'What has happened to strikes?' *British Journal of Industrial Relations*, Vol. 49 No. 2, 282–305.

Gold, J. (2007) 'Performance management and appraisal', in J. Bratton and J. Gold (eds) *Human Resource Management Theory and Practice.* Basingstoke: Palgrave Macmillan.

Gold, J. and Smith, J. (2010) 'Continuing Professional Development and lifelong learning', in J. Gold, R. Holden, P. Iles, J. Stewart and J. Beardwell, *Human Resource Development: Theory and Practice.* Basingstoke: Palgrave Macmillan.

Gold, J. Holden, R., Griggs, V., and Kyriakidou, N. (2010) 'Workplace learning and Knowledge Management', in J. Gold, R. Holden, P. Iles, J. Stewart and J. Beardwell, *Human Resource Development: Theory and Practice.* Basingstoke: Palgrave Macmillan.

Gold, J. Holden, R., Griggs, V., and Kyriakidou, N. (2010b) 'Workplace learning and Knowledge Management', in J. Gold, R. Holden, P. Iles, J. Stewart and J. Beardwell, *Human Resource Development: Theory and Practice.* Basingstoke: Palgrave Macmillan.

Gold, J., Holden, R., Iles, P., Stewart, J. and Beardwell, J. (2010d) *Human Resource Development: Theory and Practice.* Basingstoke: Palgrave Macmillan.

Gold, J., Smith, J., and Burrell, C. (2010a) 'Management development', in J. Gold, R. Holden, P. Iles, J. Stewart and J. Beardwell, *Human Resource Development: Theory and Practice.* Basingstoke: Palgrave Macmillan.

Gold, J., Stewart, J., and Iles, P. (2010c) 'National HRD policies and practice', in J. Gold, R. Holden, P. Iles, J. Stewart, and J. Beardwell, *Human Resource Development: Theory and Practice.* Basingstoke: Palgrave Macmillan.

Golden, S., Mccrone, T., Wade, P., Featherstone, G., Southcott, C. and Evans, K. (2011) *National Evaluation of Diplomas: Cohort 1 – the second year.* London: Department for Education.

Gollan, P. (2002) 'So what's the news? Management strategies towards non union employee representation at News International', *Industrial Relations Journal*, Vol. 33, No. 4, 316–31.

Gollan, P. (2006) 'Editorial: consultation and non-union employee representation', *Industrial Relations Journal*, Vol. 37, No. 5, 428–37.

GOLLAN, P. (2010) 'Employer strategies towards non-union collective voice', in A. Wilkinson, P. GOLLAN, M. MARCHINGTON and D. LEWIN (eds) *The Oxford Handbook of Participation in Organisations*. Oxford: Oxford University Press.

GOLLAN, P. and WILKINSON, A. (2007) 'Developments in Information and Consultation', *International Journal of Human Resource Management*, Vol. 18, No. 7, 1133–45.

GOLLAN, P. and WILKINSON, A. (2007) 'The EU Information and Consultative Directive and the future of employee consultation', *International Journal of Human Resource Management*, Vol. 18, No. 7, 1145–58.

GOMEZ, R., BRYSON, A. and WILLMAN, P. (2010) 'Voice in the wilderness: the shift from union to non union voice', in A. WILKINSON, P. GOLLAN, M. MARCHINGTON and D. LEWIN (eds) *The Oxford Handbook of Participation in Organisations*. Oxford: Oxford University Press, pp. 383–406.

GOODERHAM, P., PARRY, E. and RINGDALL, K. (2008) 'The impact of bundles of strategic human resource management practices on the performance of European firms', *International Journal of Human Resource Management*, Vol. 19, No. 11, 2041–56.

GOSPEL, H. and PALMER, G. (1993) *British Industrial Relations*, 2nd edition. London: Routledge.

GOSPEL, H. and WOOD, S. (eds) (2003) *Representing Workers: Union recognition and membership in Britain*. London: Routledge.

GOSS, D. (1991) *Small Business and Society*. London: Routledge.

GRAINGER, H. and FITZNER, G. (2007) *The First Fair Treatment at Work Survey: Executive Summary – updated*. Employment Relations Research Series, No. 63. London: DTI.

GRANOVETTER, M. (1985) 'Economic action and social structure: the problem of embeddedness', *American Journal of Sociology*, Vol. 91, No. 3, 481–510.

GRANT, R. (2008) *Contemporary Strategy Analysis*, 6th edition. Oxford: Blackwell.

GRANT, R. (2010) *Contemporary Strategy Analysis*, 7th edition. Oxford: Blackwell.

GRATTON L. (2004) 'More than money', *People Management*, 29 January, 23.

GRATTON, L. (2004) 'The democratic organisation', *Financial Times*.

GRATTON, L., HOPE-HAILEY, V., STILES, P. and TRUSS, C. (1999) *Strategic Human Resource Management*. Oxford: Oxford University Press.

GRAY, C. (1992) 'Growth orientation and the small firm', in K. CALEY, E. CHELL, F. CHITTENDEN and C. MASON (eds) *Small Enterprise Development and Policy and Practice in Action*. London: Paul Chapman.

Great Place to Work (2010) *UK's best Workplaces: special report*. May.

GREEN, F. (2010) *Unions and Skills Utilisation*, available at www.UnionLearn.org

GREENBERG, J. (2006) 'Losing sleep over organizational injustice: attenuating insomniac reactions to underpayment inequity with supervisory training in interactional injustice', *Journal of Applied Psychology*, Vol. 91, No. 1, 58–69.

GREENE, R.J. (2010) 'Evaluating the ongoing effectiveness of rewards strategies and programs', *World at Work Journal*, Vol. 19, No. 2, Second Quarter, 58–66.

GREENHOUSE, S. (2011) 'Boeing Labor battle is poised to go before judge', *New York Times*. 13 June.

GREER, C., YOUNGBLOOD, S. and GRAY, D. (1999) 'Human resource management outsourcing: the make or buy decision', *Academy of Management Executive*, Vol. 13, No. 3, 85–96.

GRIGGS, V., MCCAULEY, GLAISTER C., HOLDER R. (2010) 'The identification of training needs', in J. GOLD, R. HOLDEN, P. ILES, J. STEWART and J. BEARDWELL, *Human Resource Development: Theory and Practice*. Basingstoke: Palgrave Macmillan.

GRIMSHAW, D. and MARCHINGTON, L. (2007) 'United Kingdom: persistent inequality and vulnerability traps', in F. EYRAUD and D. VAUGHAN-WHITEHEAD (eds) *The Evolving World of Work in the Enlarged EU*. Geneva: International Labour Organisation.

GRIMSHAW, D. and MIOZZO, M. (2009) 'New human resource management practices in knowledge-intensive business service firms: the case of outsourcing with staff transfer', *Human Relations*, Vol. 62, No. 10, 1521–50.

GRIMSHAW, D. and RUBERY, J. (2007) *Undervaluing Women's Work*. Equal Opportunities Commission Working Paper Series, No. 53.

GRIMSHAW, D., EARNSHAW, J. and HEBSON, G. (2003) 'Private sector provision of supply teachers: a case of legal swings and professional roundabouts', *Journal of Education Policy*, Vol. 18, No. 3, 267–88.

GRIMSHAW, D., MARCHINGTON, M. and RUBERY, J. (2006) 'The blurring of organisational boundaries and the fragmentation of work', in G. WOOD and P. JAMES (eds) *Institutions, Production and Working Life*. Oxford: Oxford University Press.

GRIMSHAW, D., RUBERY, J. and ALMOND, P. (2011) 'Multinational companies and the host country environment', in A. HARZING and A. PINNINGTON (eds) *International Human Resource Management*, 3rd edition. London: Sage.

GRIMSHAW, D., RUBERY, J. and MARCHINGTON, M. (2010) 'Managing people across hospital networks in the UK: multiple employers and the shaping of HRM', *Human Resource Management Journal*, Vol. 20, No. 4, 407–23.

GRINT, K. (1993) 'What's wrong with performance appraisals? A critique and a suggestion', *Human Resource Management Journal*, Vol. 3, No. 3, 61–77.

GRÖSSLER, A. and ZOCK, A. (2010) 'Supporting long-term workforce planning with a dynamic aging supply chain model: a case study from the service industry', *Human Resource Management*, Vol. 49, No. 5, 829–48.

GRUGULIS, I. (2000) 'The management NVQ: a critique of the myth of relevance', *Journal of Vocational Education and Training*, Vol. 52, No. 1, 79–99.

GRUGULIS, I. (2003) 'The contribution of National Vocational Qualifications to the growth of skills in the UK', *British Journal of Industrial Relations*, Vol. 41, No. 3, 457–75.

GRUGULIS, I., (2007) Skills, *Training and Human Resource Development: A critical text*. Basingstoke: Palgrave Macmillan.

GRUGULIS, I. and BEVITT, S. (2002) 'The impact of Investors in People: a case study of a hospital trust', *Human Resource Management Journal*, Vol. 12, No. 3, 44–60.

GUEST, D. (1991) 'Personnel management: the end of orthodoxy?' *British Journal of Industrial Relations*, Vol. 29, No. 2, 149–75.

GUEST, D. (1997) 'Human resource management and performance: a review and research agenda', *International Journal of Human Resource Management*, Vol. 8, No. 3, 263–76.

GUEST, D. (2001) 'Human resource management: when research confronts theory', *International Journal of Human Resource Management*, Vol. 12, No. 7, 1092–106.

GUEST, D. (2007) 'HRM and the worker: towards a new psychological contract?' in P. Boxall, J. Purcell and P. Wright (eds), The Oxford Handbook Resource Management. Oxford, Oxford University Press.

GUEST, D. (2011) 'Human resource management and performance: still searching for some answers', *Human Resource Management Journal*, Vol. 21, No. 1, 3–13.

GUEST, D. and CONWAY, N. (1998) *Fairness at Work and the Psychological Contract: Issues in people management.* London: CIPD.

GUEST, D. and CONWAY, N. (1999) 'Peering into the black hole: the downside of the new employment relations in the UK', *British Journal of Industrial Relations*, Vol. 37, No. 3, 367–89.

GUEST, D. and CONWAY, N. (2011) 'The impact of HR practices, HR effectiveness and a "strong HR system" on organisational outcomes: a stakeholder perspective', *International Journal of Human Resource Management*, Vol. 22, No. 8, 1686–1702.

GUEST, D. and HOQUE, K. (1994a) 'Yes, personnel does make a difference', *Personnel Management*, November, 40–4.

GUEST, D. and HOQUE, K. (1994b) 'The good, the bad and the ugly: employment relations in new non-union workplace', *Human Resource Management Journal*, Vol. 5, No. 1, 1–14.

GUEST, D. and KING, Z. (2002) *Voices from the Boardroom: Senior executives' views on the relationship between HRM and performance*. London: CIPD.

GUEST, D. and KING, Z. (2004) 'Power, innovation and problem-solving: the personnel managers' three steps to heaven?' *Journal of Management Studies*, Vol. 41, No. 3, 401–23.

GUEST, D. and PECCEI, R. (1994) 'The nature and causes of effective human resource management', *British Journal of Industrial Relations*, Vol. 32, No. 2, 219–42.

GUEST, D. and PECCEI, R. (2001) 'Partnership at work: mutuality and the balance of advantage', *British Journal of Industrial Relations*, Vol. 39, No. 2, 207–36.

GUEST, D., MICHIE, J., CONWAY, N. and SHEEHAN, M. (2003) 'Human resource management and performance', *British Journal of Industrial Relations*, Vol. 41, No. 2, 291–314.

GUEST, D., MICHIE, J., SHEEHAN, M. and CONWAY, N. (2000a) *Employment Relations, HRM and Business Performance: An analysis of the 1998 Workplace Employee Relations Survey*. London: CIPD.

GUEST, D., MICHIE, J., SHEEHAN, M., CONWAY, N. and METOCHI, M. (2000b) *Effective People Management: Initial findings of the Future of Work study*. London: CIPD.

GUMBRELL-MCCORMICK, R. and HYMAN, R. (2010) 'Works councils: the European model of industrial democracy?' in A. WILKINSON, P. GOLLAN, M. MARCHINGTON and D. LEWIN (eds) *The Oxford Handbook of Participation in Organisations.* Oxford: Oxford University Press, 286–314.

GUNNIGLE, P., COLLINGS, D. and MORLEY, M. (2005) 'Exploring the dynamics of industrial relations in US multinationals: evidence from Ireland', *Industrial Relations Journal*, Vol. 36, No. 3, 241–56.

GUTHRIE, J. (2007) 'Remuneration pay effects and work', in P. BOXALL, J. PURCELL and P. WRIGHT (eds) *The Oxford Handbook of Human Resource Management*. Oxford: Oxford University Press.

GUTHRIE, J., FLOOD, P., LIU, W., MACCURTAIN, S. and ARMSTRONG, C. (2011), 'Big hat, no cattle? The relationship between use of high-performance work systems and managerial perceptions of HR departments', *International Journal of Human Resource Management*, Vol. 22, No. 8, 1672–85.

HACKMAN, J. and OLDHAM, G. (1976) 'Motivation through the design of work: test of a theory', *Organisation Behaviour and Human Performance*, Vol. 16, 250–79.

HAGGERTY, J. and WRIGHT, P. (2010) 'Strong situations and firm performance: a proposed re-conceptualisation of the role of the HR function', in A. WILKINSON, N. BACON, T. REDMAN and S. SNELL (eds) *The Sage Handbook of Human Resource Management*. London: Sage.

HALL, L. and TORRINGTON, D. (1998) 'Letting go or holding on – the devolution of operational personnel activities', *Human Resource Management Journal*, Vol. 8, No. 1, 41–55.

HALL, M., HUTCHINGTON, S., PURCELL, J., TERRY, M. and PARKER, J. (2011) 'Promoting effective consultation? Assessing the impact of the ICE regulations', *British Journal of Industrial Relations. Doi: 10:10.1111/j.1467-8543.2011.00870.x*

HALL, M.J. (2010) 'EU regulation and the UK employee consultation framework', *Economic and Industrial Democracy*, Vol. 31, 55–69.

HALL, P. and SOSKICE, D. (2001) *Varieties of Capitalism: The institutional foundations of comparative advantage*. Oxford: Oxford University Press.

HAMEL, G. and PRAHALAD, C.K. (1994) *Competing for the Future*. Boston: Harvard Business School Press.

HAMPDEN-TURNER, C. and TROMPENAARS, F. (1993) *The Seven Cultures of Capitalism*. London: Piatkus.

HAN, J. and HAN, J. (2009) 'Network-based recruiting and applicant attraction in China: insights from both organizational and individual perspectives', *International Journal of Human Resource Management*, Vol. 20, No. 11, 2228–49.

HANDEL, M. and LEVINE, D. (2004) 'The effects of new work practices on workers', *Industrial Relations*, Vol. 43, No. 1, 1–43.

HANDY, C. (1991) *Inside Organisations: 21 ideas for managers*. London: BBC Books.

HANSSON, B. (2007) 'Company-based determinants of training and impact of training on company performance: results from an international HRM survey', *Personnel Review*, Vol. 36, No. 2.

HARLEY, B., ALLEN, C. and SARGENT, L. (2007) 'High-performance work systems and employee experience of work in the service sector: the case of aged care', *British Journal of Industrial Relations*, Vol. 45, No. 3, 607–33.

HARLOS, K. (2001) 'When Organisational Voice Systems Fail: More on the Deaf-Ear Syndrome and Frustration Effects, *The Journal of Applied Behavioural Science*, Vol. 31, No. 3, 324–42.

HARNEY, B. and DUNDON, T. (2006) 'Capturing complexity: developing an integrated approach to analysing HRM in SMEs', *Human Resource Management Journal*, Vol. 16, No. 1, 48–73.

Harris, L. and Foster, C. (2005) *'Small, Flexible and Family-friendly': Work practices in service sector business*. Employment Relations Research Series, No. 47.

Harris, L. and Foster, C. (2010) 'Aligning talent management with approaches to equality and diversity: Challenges for UK public sector managers'. *Equality, Diversity and Inclusion: An International Journal,* Vol. 29, No. 5, 422–35.

Harrison, R. (2009) *Learning and Development*, 5th edition. London: CIPD.

Harter, J.K., Schmidt, F.L., Killham, E.A. and Asplund, J.W. (2006). *Q12 Meta-Analysis.* Omaha, NE: Gallup.

Harvey, G. and Turnbull, P. (2010) 'On the Go: walking the high road at a low cost airline', *International Journal of Human Resource Management*, Vol. 21. No. 2, 1230–41.

Harvey, M. and Moeller, M. (2009) 'Expatriate managers: a historical review', *International Journal of Management Reviews*, Vol. 11, No. 3, 275–96.

Harzing, A. and Pinnington, A. (eds) (2011) *International Human Resource Management*, 3rd edition. London: Sage. Chapters by Brewster and Mayrhofer, Grimshaw *et al*, Edwards, and Martinez Lucio and MacKenzie in particular.

Harzing, A. and Sorge, A. (2003) 'The relative impact of country of origin and universal contingencies on internalisation strategies and corporate control in multinational companies; world wide and European perspectives', *Organisation Studies*, Vol. 24, No. 2, 187–214.

Hastings, S. (2000) 'Grading systems and estimating value', in G. White and J. Druker (eds) *Reward Management: A critical text.* London: Routledge.

Hayes, J. and Clark, I. (2012) 'The state and employment relations', in A. Wilkinson and K. Townsend (eds) *New Directions in Employment Relations.* London: Palgrave Macmillan.

Haynes, P. and Allen, M. (2001) 'Partnership as a union strategy: a preliminary evaluation', *Employee Relations*, Vol. 23, No. 2, 164–87.

Health and Safety Executive (2004) *Management Standards for Work-related Stress.* London: HSE. Available online at: www.hse.gov.uk/stress/standards/

Hebson, G., Grimshaw, D. and Marchington, M. (2003) 'PPPs and the changing public sector ethos: case study evidence from the health and local authority sectors', *Work, Employment and Society*, Vol. 17, No. 3, 483–503.

Heery, E. (2000) 'Trade unions and the management of reward', in G. White and J. Druker (eds) *Reward Management: A critical text.* London: Routledge.

Heery, E. (2011) 'Assessing voice: the debate over worker representation', in P. Blyton, E. Heery and P. Turnbull (eds) *Reassessing the Employment Relationship.* Basingstoke: Palgrave Macmillan.

Hendry, C. (1994) *Human Resource Management: A strategic approach to employment.* London: Butterworth.

Hennessey, M. (2011) 'Massive bonuses for bankers? Not for these equitable Swedes', *The Irish Times*. 21 April.

Herzberg, F. (1987) 'Workers' needs: the same around the world', *Industry Week*, 21 September, 29–32.

HETRICK, S. (2002) 'Transferring HR ideas and practices; globalisation and convergence in Poland', *Human Resource Development International*, Vol. 5, No. 3, 333–51.

HEWITT ASSOCIATES (2009) *HR Outsourcing Trends and Insights 2009*. Illinois: Hewitt Associates.

HEWSON, C. (2011) 'UK plays catch up on AWD' *People Management on line*, available at: http://peoplemangement.co.uk/ 20 September, (accessed 7.10.11.)

HEYWOOD, S. (2007) 'A comparative view of unions, involvement and productivity'. Miegunyah Public Lecture, University of Melbourne, August.

HEYWOOD, J., SIEBERT, W. and WEI, X. (2010) 'Work–life balance: promises made and promises kept', *International Journal of Human Resource Management*, Vol 21, No. 11, 1976–95.

HIGGINBOTTOM, K. (2001) 'BP learns outsourcing lesson', *People Management*, 8 November.

HILL, R. and STEWART, J. (1999) 'Investors in People in small organisations: learning to stay the course?' *Journal of European Industrial Training*, Vol. 23, No. 6, 286–99.

HIRD, M. and STRIPE, M. (2010) 'Nestle: reflections on the HR structure debate', in P. SPARROW, M. HIRD, A. HESKETH and C. COOPER (eds) *Leading HR*. London: Palgrave Macmillan.

HIRD, M., SPARROW, P. and MARSH, C. (2010) 'HR structures: are they working?' in P. SPARROW, M. HIRD, A. HESKETH and C. COOPER (eds) *Leading HR*. London: Palgrave Macmillan.

HM GOVERNMENT (2010) *Local Growth: Realising Every Place's Potential*. CM7961. London: HMSO.

HODGETTS, R. and LUTHANS, F. (2003) *International Management, Culture, Strategy and Behaviour*, 15th edition, New York: McGraw Hill.

HODGSON, A. and SPOURS, K. (2010) 'Vocational qualifications and progression to higher education: the case of the 14–19 Diplomas in the English system', *Journal of Education and Work*, Vol. 23, No. 2, March, 95–110.

HOFSTEDE, G. (1980) *Culture's Consequences: International differences in work-related values*. London: Sage.

HOFSTEDE. G. (1991) *Cultures and Organizations: Software of the mind*. London: McGraw-Hill.

HOFSTEDE, G. (2001) *Cultures and Organizations*, 2nd edition. Thousand Oaks: Sage.

HOFSTEDE, G. (2002) 'Dimensions do not exist; a reply to Brendan McSweeney', *Human Relations*, Vol. 55, No. 11, 1355–61.

HOLMAN, D., WALL, T., CLEGG, C., SPARROW, P. and HOWARD, A. (2003) *The New Workplace: A guide to the human impact of modern working practices*. London: Wiley. The chapters by WOOD, BATT and DOELLGAST, WRIGHT and GARDNER, and LEGGE are particularly useful.

HOLMES, C. (2011) *Implications of polarisation for UK policymakers*. SKOPE Research Paper No. 26. University of Oxford: SCOPE.

Holmes, C. and Mayhew, K. (2010) *UK Higher Education in Recession*. SKOPE Research Paper No. 24. University of Oxford: SKOPE.

Hooper, D. and Martin, R. (2008) 'Beyond personal leader-member exchange quality: the effects of perceived LMX variability in employee reactions', *The Leadership Quarterly*, Vol. 19, 20–30.

Hope-Hailey, V., Gratton, L., McGovern, P., Stiles, P. and Truss, C. (1997) 'A chameleon function? HRM in the 90s', *Human Resource Management Journal*, Vol. 7, No. 3, 5–18.

Hoque, K. (1999) 'Human resource management and performance in the UK hotel industry', *British Journal of Industrial Relations*, Vol. 37, No. 3, 419–43.

Hoque, K. (2003) 'All in all, it's just another plaque on the wall', *Journal of Management Studies*, Vol. 40, No. 2, 543–71.

Hoque, K., Taylor, S. and Bell, E. (2005) 'Investors in People: market-led voluntarism in vocational education and training', *British Journal of Industrial Relations*, Vol. 43, No. 1, 135–53.

Hoskisson, R., Hitt, M., Wan, W. and Yiu, D. (1999) 'Theory and research in strategic management', *Journal of Management*, Vol. 25, No. 3, 417–56.

Houldsworth, E. (2007) 'In the same boat', *People Management*, 25 January, 35–6.

House of Commons (2009) *Widening Participation in Higher Education*, 4th report of session 2008–9. London: Stationery Office.

Houston, D. (ed.) (2005) *Work–Life Balance in the Twenty-First Century*. Basingstoke: Palgrave Macmillan.

Howard, K., Sharp, J. and Peters, J. (2002) *The Management of a Student Research Project*, 3rd edition. London: Gower/Open University, available at http://www.health.qld.gov.au/health_sys_review/final/qhsr_final_report.pdf, (accessed 30 June 2006). Forster R (2005) Queensland Health System Review 'The Forster Report'.

Hunt, S. (1995) 'The resource-advantage theory of competition', *Journal of Management Inquiry*, Vol. 4, No. 4, 317–32.

Huselid, M. (1995) 'The impact of human resource management practices on turnover, productivity and corporate financial performance', *Academy of Management Journal*, Vol. 38, No. 3, 635–72.

Hussey, D. (1998) *Strategic Management: From theory to implementation*. Oxford: Butterworth-Heinemann.

Hutchinson, S. (2007) *Latest Trends in Learning, Training, and Development: Reflections on the 2007 Learning and Development survey*. London: CIPD.

Hutchinson, S. and Purcell, J. (2003) *Bringing Policies to Life: The vital role of front line managers in people management*. London: CIPD.

Hutchinson, S. and Purcell, J. (2007) *Line Managers in Reward, Learning and Development: Research into practice*. London: CIPD.

Hutchinson, S. and Purcell, J. (2010) 'Managing ward managers for roles in HR in the NHS: overworked and under-resourced', *Human Resource Management Journal*, Vol. 20, No. 4, 357–74.

Hutchinson, S. and Wood, S. (1995) 'The UK experience', in Institute of Personnel and Development, *Personnel and the Line: Developing the new relationship*. London: IPD.

Hutchinson, S., Purcell, J. and Winkler, V. (2007) 'Golden gate', *People Management*, 19 April, 38–40.

Hutton, W. (2011a) *Them and Us*. London: Abacus.

Hutton, W. (2011b), *Review of Fair Pay in the Public Sector: final report*. London: Crown Copyright.

Hyde, P., Boaden, R., Cortvriend, P., Harris, C., Marchington, M., Pass, S., Sparrow, P. and Sibbald, B. (2006) *Improving Health Through Human Resource Management*. London: CIPD.

Hyman, J. (2000) 'Financial participation schemes', in G. White and J. Druker (eds) *Reward Management: A critical text*. London: Routledge.

Hyman, R. (1997) 'The future of employee representation', *British Journal of Industrial Relations*, Vol. 35, No. 3, 309–36.

Hyman, R.M. (2005) 'Striking a balance? Means, ends and ambiguities', *Employee Responsibilities and Rights Journal*, Vol. 17, No. 2, 127–30.

Ichniowski, C., Shaw, K. and Prennushi, G. (1997) 'The effects of human resource management practices on productivity: a study of steel finishing lines', *American Economic Review*, Vol. 87, 291–313.

Iles, P., Meetoo, C. and Gold, J. (2010) 'Leadership Development', in J. Gold, R. Holden, P. Iles, J. Stewart and J. Beardwell *Human Resource Development: Theory and Practice*. Basingstoke: Palgrave Macmillan.

Ilies, R., Nahrgang, J. and Morgeson, F. (2007) 'Leader-member exchange and citizenship behaviours: a meta-analysis', *Journal of Applied Psychology*, Vol. 92, No. 1, 269–77.

International Task Force on Assessment Centre Guidelines (2009) 'Guidelines and ethical considerations for assessment centre operations', *International Journal of Selection and Assessment*, Vol. 17, No. 3, 243–52.

Investors in People UK. www.iipuk.co.uk.

Involvement and Participation Association (1997) *Towards Industrial Partnership*. London: IPA.

Involvement and Participation Association (2011) 'Cable to push for reform of private sector executive pay', *IPA Newsletter*, June.

*IRS Employment Review* 769a (2003) 'Time to talk: how and why employers conduct appraisals', 7 February, 8–14.

*IRS Employment Review* 795a (2004) 'HR roles and responsibilities: climbing the admin mountain', 5 March, 9–15.

Ispas, D., Ilie, A., Ilescu, D., Johnson, R. and Harris, M. (2010) 'Fairness reactions to selection methods: a Romanian study', *International Journal of Selection and Assessment*, Vol. 18, No. 1, 102–10.

James, P., Cunningham, I. and Dibben, P. (2002) 'Absence management and the issues of job retention and return to work', *Human Resource Management Journal*, Vol. 12, No. 2, 82–94.

JAMES, S. (2010) 'What is Apprenticeship?' SKOPE.

JAQUES, E. (1962) *Measurement of Responsibility*. London: Bradford & Dickens.

JARVIS, J. and ROBINSON, D. (2005) 'Watch your step', *People Management*, 27 October.

JENNINGS, C. (2007) *Latest Trends in Learning, Training and Development: Reflections on the 2007 Learning and Development survey.* London: CIPD.

JOHNS, T. (1996) *Report Writing as an Exercise in Persuasion*. London: CIPD.

JOHNS, T. (2007) *Tales of the Unexpected, the Unbelievable and the Unforgivable: stories about customers and customer service experiences*. London: Institute of Customer Service.

JOHNSON G., WHITTINGTON, R. and SCHOLES, K, (2011) *Exploring Corporate Strategy*, 8th edition. London: Prentice Hall.

JOHNSON, R. (2006) 'Orange blossoms', *People Management*, 26 October, 57–60.

JOHNSON, R. (2007) 'Sharing the load', *People Management*, 9 August, 40–2.

JOHNSTONE, S. (2010) *Labour and Management Cooperation.* London: Gower.

JOHNSTONE, S., ACKERS, P. and WILKINSON, A. (2009) 'The British partnership phenomenon: a ten year review', *Human Resource Management Journal*, Vol. 16, No. 3, 260–75.

JOHNSTONE, S., ACKERS, P. and WILKINSON, A. (2010) 'Better than nothing: is non-union partnership a contradiction in terms?' *Journal of Industrial Relations*, Vol. 52, No. 2, 151–68.

JOHNSTONE, S., WILKINSON, A. and ACKERS, P. (2011) 'Applying Budd's model to partnership', *Economic and Industrial Democracy*, Vol. 32, No. 2, 207–38.

KAARSEMAKER, E.C.A., PENDLETON, A. & POUTSMA, F. (2010). Employee Share Ownership. In A. WILKINSON, P.J. GOLLAN, M. MARCHINGTON & D. LEWIN (Eds.), *The Oxford Handbook of Participation in Organizations* (pp. 315–337). Oxford, UK: Oxford University Press.

KAHANCOVA, M. (2010) *One Company, Diverse workplaces: the social construction of employment practices in Western and Easter Europe.* Basingstoke: Palgrave Macmillan.

KAHN-FREUND, O. (1959) 'Labour law', in M. GINSBERG (ed.) *Law and Opinion in England in the Twentieth Century*. London: Stevens.

KAHN-FREUND, O. (1965) 'Industrial relations and the law: retrospect and prospect', *British Journal of Industrial Relations*, Vol. 7, 301–16.

KANDOLA, B. (2009) *The Value of Difference: Eliminating bias in organisations.* Oxford: Pearn Kandola.

KANG, D. and STEWART, J. (2007) 'Leader-member exchange theory and human resource development', *Leadership and Organisation Development Journal*, Vol. 28, No. 6, 531–51.

KAPLAN, R. and NORTON, D. (2001) *The Strategy-focused Organisation: how balanced scorecard companies thrive in the new business environment.* Boston: Harvard Business School Press.

KAPLAN, R, and NORTON, D.P. (2007) 'Using the balanced scorecard as a strategic management system', *Harvard Business Review*, July–August, 150–61.

KAPLAN, R. and NORTON, D.P. (2010) *Kaplan and Norton on Strategic Management.* Harvard: Harvard Business Publishing.

Kaufman, B. (2003) 'High-level employee involvement in Delta Airlines', *Human Resource Management*, Vol. 42, No. 2, 175–90.

Kaufman, B. (2007) 'The development of HRM in historical and international perspective', in P. Boxall, J. Purcell and P. Wright (eds) *The Oxford Handbook of Human Resource Management*. Oxford: Oxford University Press.

Kaufman, B. (2010) *Hired Hands or Human Resources: Case Studies of HRM Programs and Practices in Early American Industry*. Ithaca, New York: Cornell University Press.

Kaufman, B. (2011) 'The future of employment relations: insights from theory', in K. Townsend and A. Wilkinson (eds) *Research Handbook on the Future of Work and Employment Relations*. Cheltenham: Edward Elgar.

Kaufman, B. (2012) 'Employee Councils at Delta Air Lines' in P. Gollan, B. Kaufman, D. Taras and A. Wilkinson (eds) *Voice and Involvement at Work: Experience with Non-Union Representation*, London: Taylor and Francis.

Kaufman, B. and Taras, D. (2010) 'Employee participation through non-union forms of employee representation' in A. Wilkinson, P. Gollan, M. Marchington and D. Lewin (eds) *The Oxford Handbook of Participation in Organisations*. Oxford: Oxford University Press.

Keegan, A. and Francis, H. (2010) 'Practitioner talk: the changing text-scape of HRM and emergence of HR business partnership', *International Journal of Human Resource Management*, Vol. 21, No. 6, 873–98.

Keep, E. (2000) 'Learning organisations, lifelong learning and the mystery of the vanishing employers', *Economic Outlook*, Vol. 24, No. 4, 18–26.

Keep, E. (2001) 'If it moves, it's a skill: the changing meaning of skill in the UK context. Paper presented at ESRC seminar 'The Changing Nature of Skills and Knowledge, UMIST, Manchester 3–4 September.

Keep, E. (2002) 'The English vocational education and training debate – "fragile technologies" or opening the "black box": two competing visions of where we go next', *Journal of Education and Work*, Vol. 15, No. 4, 457–79.

Keep, E. (2003b) 'The State and Power: An elephant and a snake in the telephone box of English VET policy'. Paper presented to the ESRC Seminar Series on the history and philosophy of VET, University of Greenwich, London, 27 November.

Keep, E. and Mayhew, K. (2010) 'Moving beyond skills as a social and economic panacea', *Work, Employment and Society*, Vol. 24, No. 3, 565–77.

Keep, E., Mayhew, K. and Payne, J. (2006) 'From skills revolution to productivity miracle – not as easy as it sounds?' *Oxford Review of Economic Policy*, Vol. 22, No. 4, 539–59.

Keizer, A. (2008) 'Non-regular employment in Japan: continued and renewed dualities', *Work, Employment and Society*, Vol. 22, No3, 407–25.

Keizer, A. (2009) 'Transformations in and outside the internal labour market: institutional change and continuity in Japanese employment practices', *International Journal of Human Resource Management*, Vol. 20, No. 7, 1521–35.

Keller, B.K. and Kirsch, A. (2011) 'Employment relations in Germany', in G.J. Bamber, R.D. Lansbury and N. Wailes *International and Comparative Employment Relations: Globalisation and Change*, 5th edition. Crow's Nest: Allen and Unwin.

KELLERMAN, B. (2008) *Followership: how followers are creating change and changing leaders*. Boston: Harvard University Press.

KELLIHER, C. and PERRETT, G. (2001) 'Business strategy and approaches to HRM: a case study of new developments in the UK restaurant industry', *Personnel Review*, Vol. 30, No. 4, 421–37.

KELLNER, A., TOWNSEND, K. and WILKINSON, A. (2011) 'Franchise firms: changing employment relations', in A. WILKINSON and K. TOWNSEND (eds) *The Future of Employment Relations: New paradigms, new approaches*. Basingstoke: Palgrave Macmillan.

KELLY, J. (2004) 'Social partnership arrangements in Britain', *Industrial Relations*, Vol. 43, No. 1, 267–92.

KELLY, J. and GENNARD, J. (2007) 'Business strategic decision making: the role and influence of directors', *Human Resource Management Journal*, Vol. 17, No. 2, 99–117.

KEMPSTER, S. (2009) *How Managers have Learnt to Lead: exploring the development of leadership practice*. Basingstoke: Palgrave Macmillan.

KEPES, S and DELERY, J. (2007) 'HRM systems and the problem of internal fit', in P. BOXALL, J. PURCELL and P. WRIGHT (eds) *The Oxford Handbook of Human Resource Management*. Oxford: Oxford University Press.

KERSLEY, B., ALPIN, C., FORTH, J., BRYSON, J., BEWLEY, H and OXENBRIDGE, S. (2006) *Inside the Workplace: Findings from the 2004 Workplace Employment Relations Survey*. London: Routledge.

KESSLER, I. (2005) 'Remuneration systems', in S. BACH and K. SISSON (eds) *Managing Human Resources: Personnel management in transition*, 4th edition. Oxford: Blackwell.

KESSLER, I. (2007) 'Reward choices: strategy and equity', in J. STOREY (ed) *Human Resource Management: A Critical Text*, 3rd edition. London: Thomson.

KESSLER, I. (2010) 'Financial participation', in A. WILKINSON, P. GOLLAN, M. MARCHINGTON and D. LEWIN (eds) *Oxford Handbook of Employee Participation*. Oxford: Oxford University Press.

KESSLER, I. and PURCELL, J. (2003) 'Individualism and collectivism', in P. EDWARDS (ed.) *Industrial Relations*, 2nd edition. Oxford: Blackwell.

KESSLER, I., UNDY, R. and HERON, P. (2004) 'Employee perspectives on communication and consultation: Findings from a cross-national survey', *International Journal of Human Resource Management*, Vol. 15, No. 3, 512–32.

KHILJI, S. and WANG, X. (2006) '"Intended" and "implemented" HRM: the missing linchpin in strategic human resource management research', *International Journal of Human Resource Management*, Vol. 17, No. 7, 1171–89.

KIM, D.O. and ARTHUR, J. B. (2005) 'Gainsharing and knowledge-sharing, the effects of labour management cooperation', *International Journal of Human Resource Management*, Vol. 16, No. 9, 1564–82.

KIM, S., WRIGHT, P. and SU, Z. (2010) 'Human resource management and firm performance in China: a critical review', *Asia Pacific Journal of Human Resources*, Vol. 48, No. 1, 58–85.

KIM, Y. and GAO, F. (2010) 'An empirical study of human resource management practices in family firms in China', *International Journal of Human Resource Management*, Vol. 21, No. 12, 2095–119.

Kinnie, N., Hutchinson, S., Purcell, J., Rayton, B. and Swart, J. (2005) 'Satisfaction with HR practices and commitment to the organisation: why one size does not fit all', *Human Resource Management Journal*, Vol. 15, No. 4, 9–29.

Kirkpatrick D. (1967) 'Evaluation of training, in R. Craig and L. Bittell (eds) *Training and Evaluation Handbook*. New York: McGraw-Hill.

Kitay, J. and Marchington, M. (1996) 'A review and critique of workplace industrial relations typologies', *Human Relations*, Vol. 49, No. 10, 1263–90.

Kitching, J. (2007) 'Regulating employment relations through workplace learning: a study of small employers', *Human Resource Management Journal*, Vol. 17, No. 1, 42–57.

Klaas, B. (2008) 'Outsourcing and the HR function: an examination of trends and developments within North American firms', *International Journal of Human Resource Management*, Vol. 19, No. 8, 1500–14.

Klaas, B. (2009) 'Grievance and discipline', in A. Wilkinson, N. Bacon, T. Redman and S. Snell (eds) *Handbook of Human Resource Management*. London: Sage.

Klaas, B., McClendon, J. and Gainey, T. (2001) 'Outsourcing HR: the impact of organizational characteristics', *Human Resource Management*, Vol. 40, No. 2, 125–38.

Koch, M. and McGrath, R. (1996) 'Improving labour productivity: human resource management policies do matter', *Strategic Management Journal*, Vol. 17, No. 5, 335–53.

Kochan, T. and Barocci, T. (1985) *Human Resource Management and Industrial Relations*. Boston: Little Brown.

Kochan, T. and Osterman, P. (1994) *The Mutual Gains Enterprise*. London: Harvard Business School Press.

Kochan, T., Katz, H. and Cappelli, R. (1986) *The Transformation of American Industrial Relations*. New York: Basic Books.

Kochan, T.A. and Bamber, G.J. (2009) 'Industrial relations and collective bargaining', in A. Wilkinson, N. Bacon, T. Redman and S. Snell (eds) *The Sage Handbook of Human Resource Management*. London: Sage.

Kohn, A. (1993) 'Why Incentive plans cannot work', *Harvard Business Review*, September/October, 54–63.

Kolb, D., Osland, J. and Rubin, I. (1995) *Organisational Behaviour: An experiential approach*, 6th edition. New Jersey: Prentice Hall.

Konig, C., Klehe, U., Berchtold, M. and Kleinmann, M. (2010) 'Reasons for being selective when choosing personnel selection procedures', *International Journal of Selection and Assessment*, Vol. 18, No. 1, 17–27.

Korczynski, M. (2005) 'Skills in service work: an overview', *Human Resource Management Journal*, Vol. 15, No. 3, 3–14.

Kostova, T. and Roth, K. (2002) 'Adoption of an organisational practice by subsidiaries of multinational corporations: institutional and relational effects', *Academy of Management Journal*, Vol. 45, No. 1, 215–33.

Koulikoff-Souviron, M., and Harrison, A. (2007) 'The pervasive human resource picture in interdependent supply relationships', *International Journal of Operations and Production Management*, Vol. 27, No1, 8–17.

KROLL, K. (2005) 'No employee left behind', *Forbes online*, 15 September.

KULAR, S., GATENBY, M., REES, C., SOANE, E. and TRUSS, K. (2008) *Employee Engagement: A Literature Review*. Kingston Hill, UK: Kingston University.

KULIK, C. and PERRY, E. (2008) 'When less is more: the devolution of HR's strategic role and construed image', *Human Resource Management*, Vol. 47, No. 3, 541–58.

KÜSKÜ, F. and ATAMAN, B. (2011) 'Employment interview satisfaction of applicants within the context of a developing country: the case of Turkey', *International Journal of Human Resource Management*, Vol. 22, No. 11, 2463–83.

KUVAAS, B. (2006) 'Performance appraisal satisfaction and employee outcomes: mediating and moderating roles of motivation', *International Journal of Human Resource Management*, Vol. 17, 504–22.

KUVAAS, B. (2007) 'Different relationships between perception of developmental performance appraisal and work performance', *Personnel Review*, Vol. 30, 378–97.

KUVAAS, B. (2008) 'An exploration of how the employee-organisation relationship affects the linkage between perception of developmental human resource practices and employee outcomes', *Journal of Management Studies,* Vol. 45, 1–25.

KUVAAS, B. (2011) 'The interactive role of performance appraisal reactions and regular feedback' *Journal of Management Psychology*, Vol. 26, No. 2, 123–37.

KYNIGHOU, A. (2010) *Analysing the interplay of factors affecting the implementation of HRM within service sector MNCs: the case of Cypriot sub-units*, unpublished PhD thesis, Manchester Business School.

LAINE, M., VAN DER HIEJDEN, B., WICKSTROM, G., HASSELHORN, H, TACKENBURG, P. (2009) 'Job insecurity and intent to leave the nursing profession in Europe', *International Journal of Human Resource Management*, Vol. 20, No. 2, 420–38.

LAM, W., HUANG, X. and SNAPE, E. (2007) 'Feedback-seeking behaviour and leader-member exchange: do supervisor-attributed motives matter?' *Academy of Management Journal*, Vol. 50, No. 2, 348–63.

LANE, C. (1989) *Management and Labour in Europe*. Aldershot: Edward Elgar.

LANE, T. and ROBERTS, K. (1971) *Strike at Pilkingtons*. London: Fontana.

LANSBURY, R. and WAILES, N. (2008) 'Employee involvement and direct participation' in P. BLYTON, N. BACON, J. FIORITO and E. HEERY (eds) *The Sage Handbook of Industrial Relations*. London: Sage.

LATHAM, G., SULSKY. L.M. and MACDONALD, H. (2007) 'Performance management', in P. BOXALL, J. PURCELL and P. WRIGHT (eds) *The Oxford Handbook of Human Resource Management*. Oxford: Oxford University Press.

LATHAM, G.P. and MANN, S. (2006) 'Advances in the science of performance appraisal: implications for practice', in G.P. HODGKINSON and J.K. FORD (eds) *International Review of Industrial and Organizational Psychology*, Vol. 21, 295–338.

LATHAM, G.P., ALMOST, J., MANN, S. and MOORE, C. (2005) 'New developments in performance management', *Organizational Dynamics*, Vol. 34, 77–87.

LAVELLE, J., GUNNIGLE, P. and MCDONNELL, A. (2010) 'Patterning employee voice in multinational companies', *Human Relations*, Vol. 63, March, 395–418.

LAWLER, E. (2000) *Rewarding Excellence: Pay strategies for the new economy*. New York: Jossey-Bass.

LAYARD, R. (2003) 'Happiness: Has social science a clue?' Lionel Robbins Memorial Lecture. London, London School of Economics, 3–5 March.

LAZEAR (1999) LAZEAR, EDWARD P., 2000a, "Performance Pay and Productivity," *American Economic Review*, 90(5), 1346–1361.

LEE, J. and LEE, D. (2009) 'Labour management partnership at Korean firms', *Personnel Review*, Vol. 38, No. 4, 432–52.

LEGGE, K. (1978) *Power, Innovation and Problem-Solving in Personnel Management*. London: McGraw-Hill.

LEGGE, K. (2005/1995) *Human Resource Management: Rhetorics and realities*. London: Palgrave Macmillan.

LEIGHTON, P and PROCTOR, G. (2001) *Legal Essentials: Recruiting within the law*. London: CIPD.

LEITCH, S. (2006) *Prosperity for All in the Global Economy – world-class skills*. HM Treasury, December.

LENGNICK HALL, C. and LENGNICK HALL, M. (1988) 'Strategic human resource management: a review of the literature and a proposed typology', *Academy of Management Review*, Vol. 13, No. 3, 454–70.

LEONARD, D. (1998) *Wellsprings of Knowledge: Building and Sustaining the Sources of Innovation*. Boston, MA: Harvard Business School Press cited in P. BOXALL and J. PURCELL (2011) *Strategy and Human Resource Management*. New York: Palgrave Macmillan.

LEPAK, D. and SNELL, S. (1999) 'The human resource architecture: toward a theory of human capital allocation and development', *Academy of Management Review*, Vol. 24, No. 1, 31–48.

LEPAK, D. and SNELL, S. (2002) 'Examining the Human Resource Architecture: The relationships among human capital, employment, and human resource configurations', *Journal of Management*, Vol. 28, No. 4, 517–43.

LEPAK, D. and SNELL, S. (2007) 'Employment sub-systems and the "HR architecture"', in P. BOXALL, J. PURCELL and P. WRIGHT (eds) *The Oxford Handbook of Human Resource Management*. Oxford: Oxford University Press.

LESTER, S. (2010) 'The UK Qualifications and Credit Framework: a critique', *Journal of Vocational Education and Training*, Vol. 63, No. 2, 205–16.

LEUNG, A. (2003) 'Different ties for different needs: recruitment practices of entrepreneurial firms at different developmental phases', *Human Resource Management*, Vol. 42, No. 4, 303–20.

LEWIN, D. (2005) 'Unionism and employment conflict resolution', *Journal of Labor Research*, Vol. 26, No. 2, 209–39.

LEWIN, D. (2008) 'Resolving conflict', in N. BACON, P. BLYTON, J. FIORITO and E. HEERY (eds) *Handbook of Industrial and Employment Relations*. London: Sage.

LEWIN, D. (2010) 'Employee Voice and Mutual Gains', in A. WILKINSON, P. GOLLAN, M. MARCHINGTON and D. LEWIN (eds) *Oxford Handbook of Employee Participation*. Oxford: Oxford University Press.

LEWIN, D. (2011) 'High performance human resources', in A. WILKINSON and K. TOWNSEND (eds) *The Future of Employment Relations*. London: Palgrave.

LEWIS, D., SARGEANT, M. and SCHWAB, B. (2011) *Employment Law: The Essentials*, 11th edition. London: CIPD.

LEWIS, P. (1998) 'Managing performance-related pay based on evidence from the financial service sector', *Human Resource Management Journal*, Vol. 8, No. 2, 66–77.

LEWIS, P. (2006) 'Reward management', in T. REDMAN and A. WILKINSON (eds) *Contemporary Human Resource Management*, 2nd edition. London: Financial Times/Pearson.

LEWIS, P., GOSPEL, H. and RYAN, P. (2008) 'A hard sell? The prospects for apprenticeship in British retailing', *Human Resource Management Journal*, Vol. 18, No. 1.

LEWIS, R. (2006) *When Cultures Collide: Leading Across Cultures*, 3rd edition. London: Nicholas Brealey International.

LEWIS, R. and HECKMAN, R. (2006) 'Talent Management: A critical review', *Human Resource Management Review*, Vol. 16, 139–154.

LEWIS, S., GAMBLES, R. and RAPOPORT, R. (2007) 'The constraints of a "work–life balance" approach: an international pespective', *International Journal of Human Resource Management*, Vol. 18, No. 3, 360–73.

LI, S. and SCULLION, H. (2010) 'Developing the local competence of expatriate managers for emerging markets: a knowledge-based approach', *Journal of World Business*, Vol. 45, No. 2, 190–96.

LIDEN, R., BAUER, T. and ERDOGAN, B. (2004) 'The role of leader–member exchange in the dynamic relationship between employer and employee: implications for employee socialization, leaders, and organisations', in L. SHORE, S. TAYLOR, J. COYLE-SHAPIRO and L. TETRICK (eds) *The Employment Relationship: Examining psychological and contextual perspectives*. Oxford: Oxford University Press.

LIEVENS, F. and CHAPMAN, D. (2010) 'Recruitment and selection', in A. WILKINSON, N. BACON, T. REDMAN and S. SNELL (eds) *The SAGE Handbook of Human Resource Management*. London: Sage.

LIFF, S. (2000) 'Manpower or human resource planning: what's in a name?' in S. BACH and K. SISSON (eds) *Personnel Management: A comprehensive guide to theory and practice*. Oxford: Blackwell.

LINCOLN, Y. and GUBA, E. (1985) *Naturalistic Inquiry*. California: Sage.

LIU, Y. and IPE, M. (2010) 'The impact of organisational and leader–member support on expatriate commitment', *International Journal of Human Resource Management*, Vol. 21, No. 7, 1035–48.

LLORENS, J. and KELLOUGH, J. (2007) 'A revolution in public personnel administration: the growth of web-based recruitment and selection processes in the federal service', *Public Personnel Management*, Vol. 36, No. 3, 207–21.

LLOYD, C. (2005) 'Training standards as a policy option? The regulation of the fitness industry', *Industrial Relations Journal*, Vol. 36, No. 5, 367–85.

LLOYD, C. and MAYHEW, K. (2010) 'Skill: the solution to low wage work?' *Industrial Relations Journal*, Vol. 41, No. 5, 429–45.

LOCKE, R., QIN, F. and BRAUSE, A. (2007) 'Does monitoring improve labour standards? Lessons from Nike', *Industrial and Labour Relations Review*, Vol. 61, No. 1, 3–31.

LOVAS, B. and GHOSHAL, S. (2000) 'Strategy as guided evolution', *Strategic Management Journal*, Vol. 21, No. 9, 875–96.

LOW PAY COMMISSION (2003) *The National Minimum Wage*: 4th annual report. London: The Stationery Office.

LSN (The Learning and Skills Network) (2011) *Apprenticeships and higher education: good sound-bites, bad policy making.* LSN: London.

LUCAS, B. and CLAXTON, G. (2010) *New Kinds of Smart: How the Science of Learning Intelligence is Changing Education.* Maidenhead: Open University Press/McGraw Hill Education.

LUCAS, R., LUPTON, B. and MATHIESON, H. (2006) *Human Resource Management in an International Context*. London: CIPD.

LUENEBURGER, C. and GOLEMAN, D. (2010) 'The change leadership sustainability demands', *MIT Sloan Management Review*, Summer, Vol. 51, No. 4, 49–55.

LUPTON, B. (2000) 'Pouring the coffee at interview? Personnel's role in the selection of doctors', *Personnel Review*, Vol. 29, No. 1, 48–68.

LYNCH, P. (2000) 'Time-based pay', in R. THORPE and G. HOMAN (eds) *Strategic Reward Systems*. London: Financial Times/Prentice Hall.

MA, L. and QU, Q. (2010) 'Differentiation in leader-member exchange: a hierarchical linear modelling approach', *The Leadership Quarterly*, Vol. 21, 733–44.

MABEY, C. and TERRY, R. (2007) 'The manager in the mirror', *People Management*, 12 July, 38–40.

MABEY, C. and RAMIREZ, M. (2005) 'Does management development improve organizational productivity? A six-country analysis of European firms', *International Journal of Human Resource Management*, Vol. 16, No. 7, 1067–82.

MACAN, T. (2009) 'The employment interview: a review of current studies and directions for future research', *Human Resource Management Review*, Vol. 19, 203–18.

MACDONALD, L.A.C. (2010) *Managing discipline*. Surrey, UK: Wolters Kluwer.

MACDUFFIE, J. (1995) 'Human resource bundles and manufacturing performance: Organisational logic and flexible production systems in the world auto industry', *Industrial and Labor Relations Review*, Vol. 48, 197–221.

MACEY, W.H. and SCHNEIDER, B. (2008) 'The meaning of employee engagement', *Industrial and Organisational Psychology*, Vol. 1, 3–30.

MACHIN, S. (2003) 'Trade union decline, new workplaces and new workers', in H. GOSPEL and S. WOOD (eds) *Representing Workers: Union recognition and membership in Britain.* London: Routledge.

MACKENZIE, R. and FORDE, C. (2009) 'The rhetoric of the "good worker" versus the realities of employers' use and experience of migrant workers', *Work Employment and Society*, Vol. 23, No. 1, 142–59.

MACKY, K. and BOXALL, P. (2007) 'The relationship between "high-performance work practices" and employee attitudes: an investigation of additive and interaction effects', *International Journal of Human Resource Management*, Vol. 18, No. 4, 537–67.

MacLeod, D. and Clarke, N. (2009) *Engaging for Success: Enhancing performance through employee engagement*. London: Department for Business, Innovation and Skills.

Malik, S. (2011) 'Almost one in five British businesses admin using interns as cheap labour', Guardian.co.uk, 28 April, (accessed 20 July 2011).

Maltz, A., Shenhar, A. and Reilly, R. (2003) 'Beyond the balanced scorecard: refining the search for organisational success measures', *Long-Range Planning*, Vol. 36, No. 2, 187–204.

Marchington, M. (1982) *Managing Industrial Relations*. Farnborough: McGraw-Hill.

Marchington, M. (2005) 'Employee involvement: patterns and explanations', in B. Harley, J. Hyman and P. Thompson (eds) *Participation and Democracy at Work: Essays in honour of Harvie Ramsay*. London: Palgrave.

Marchington, M. (2007) 'Employee voice system', in P. Boxall, J. Purcell and P. Wright (eds) *The Oxford Handbook of Human Resource Management*. Oxford: Oxford University Press.

Marchington, M. (2010), 'Where next for HRM? Rediscovering the heart and soul of people management', Institute for Employment Studies, 40th Anniversary Paper, Brighton.

Marchington, M. and Cox, A. (2007) 'Employee involvement and participation: structures, processes and outcomes', in J. Storey (ed) *Human Resource Management: A critical text*. London: Thompson.

Marchington, M. and Grugulis, I. (2000) '"Best practice" human resource management: perfect opportunity or dangerous illusion?' *International Journal of Human Resource Management*, Vol. 11, No. 4, 905–25.

Marchington, M. and Kynighou, A. (2012) 'The dynamics of employee involvement and participation during turbulent times', *International Journal of Human Resource Management*.

Marchington, M. and Parker, P. (1990) *Changing Patterns of Employee Relations*. Hemel Hempstead: Harvester Wheatsheaf.

Marchington, M. and Suter, J. (2012) 'Where informality really matters: patterns of employee involvement and participation in a non-union firm', *Industrial Relations*.

Marchington, M. and Timming, A. (2010) 'Participation across organisaional boundaries', in A. Wilkinson, P.J. Gollan, M. Marchington and D. Lewin (eds) *The Oxford Handbook of Participation in Organisations*. Oxford: Oxford University Press.

Marchington, M. and Vincent, S. (2004) 'Analysing the influence of institutional, organisational and interpersonal forces in shaping inter-organisational relations', *Journal of Management Studies*, Vol. 41, No. 6, 1029–56.

Marchington, M. and Wilkinson, A. (2005) 'Direct participation', in S. Bach and K. Sisson (eds) *Personnel Management: A comprehensive guide to theory and practice*. Oxford: Blackwell.

Marchington, M. and Zagelmeyer, S. (2005) 'Foreword: Linking HRM and performance – a never-ending search?' *Human Resource Management Journal*, Vol. 15, No. 4, 3–8.

Marchington, M., Carroll, M. and Boxall, P. (2003b) 'Labour scarcity and the survival of small firms: a resource-based view of the road haulage industry', *Human Resource Management Journal*, Vol. 13, No. 4, 5–22.

Marchington, M., Cooke, F. and Hebson, G. (2003a) 'Performing for the "customer": managing housing benefit operations across organisational boundaries', *Local Government Studies*, Vol. 29, No. 1, 51–74.

Marchington, M., Goodman, J., Wilkinson, A. and Ackers, P. (1992) *New Developments in Employee Involvement.* Sheffield: Department of Employment.

Marchington, M. Grimshaw, D., Rubery, J., Carroll, M and Pass, S. (2009) *Managing People in Networked Organisations*. London: CIPD.

Marchington, M., Grimshaw, D., Rubery, J. and Willmott, H. (eds) (2005) *Fragmenting Work: Blurring organisational boundaries and disordering hierarchies*. Oxford: Oxford University Press.

Marchington, M., Hadjivassiliou, K., Martin, R. and Cox, A. (2011c) 'Employment relations across organisational boundaries', in A. Wilkinson and K. Townsend (eds) *The Future of Employment Relations*. London: Palgrave Macmillan.

Marchington, M., Rubery, J. and Grimshaw, D. (2011a) 'Alignment, integration and consistency in HRM across multi-employer networks', *Human Resource Management*, Vol. 50, No. 3, 313–39.

Marchington, M., Waddington, J. and Timming, A. (2011b) 'Employment relations in Britain' in G. Bamber, R. Lansbury and N. Wailes (eds) *International and Comparative Employment Relations: Globalisation and Change*, 5th edition. Crows Nest: Allen and Unwin.

Marchington, M., Wilkinson, A., Ackers, P. and Dundon, A. (2001) *Management Choice and Employee Voice*. London: CIPD.

Marchington, M., Wilkinson, A., Ackers, P. and Goodman, J. (1993) 'The influence of managerial relations on waves of employee involvement', *British Journal of Industrial Relations*, Vol. 31, No. 4, 543–76.

Marler, J. (2009) 'Making human resources strategic by going to the net: reality or myth?' *International Journal of Human Resource Management*, Vol. 20, No. 3, 515–27.

Marlow, S. (2002) 'Regulating labour management in small firms', *Human Resource Management Journal*, Vol. 12, No. 3, 1–25.

Marsden, D., French, S. and Kubo, K. (2000) 'Why does Performance Pay De-motivate? Financial incentives versus performance appraisal'. Discussion Paper. London, LSE Centre for Economic Performance.

Marsden, D. (2010) 'The paradox of performance-related pay systems: why do we keep adopting them in the face of evidence that they fail to motivate?' in H. Margetts, P. and C. Hood (eds) *Paradoxes of Modernization: Unintended Consequences of Public Policy Reforms*. Oxford, Oxford University Press, pp. 185–202.

Marsh, J.A., Springer, M.G., McCaffrey, D.F., Yuan, K., Epstein, S., Koppich, J., Kalra, N., DiMartino, C. and Peng, X. (2011) 'A Big Apple for educators: New York City's experiment with school-wide performance bonuses: Final Evaluation Report', Santa Monica: Rand Corporation.

Martin, G. and Beaumont, P. (1998) 'Diffusing "best practice" in multinational firms: prospects, practice and contestation', *International Journal of Human Resource Management*, Vol. 9, No. 4, 671–95.

MARTIN, G., REDDINGTON, M. and ALEXANDER, H. (2008) *Technology, Outsourcing and Transforming HR*. Oxford: Elsevier.

MARTINEZ-LUCIO, M. (2010) 'Labour process and Marxist perspectives on employee representation', in A. WILKINSON, P.J. GOLLAN, M. MARCHINGTON and D. LEWIN (eds) *The Oxford Handbook of Participation in Organisations*. Oxford: Oxford University Press, pp. 105–131.

MARTINEZ-LUCIO, M. and MACKENZIE, R. (2011) 'Regulation and change in global employment relations', in A-W. HARZING and A.H. PINNINGTON (2011) *International Human Resource Management*, 3rd edition. London: Sage Publications.

MARTINEZ-LUCIO, M. and STUART, M. (2005a) 'Partnership and new industrial relations in a risk society: an age of shotgun weddings and marriages of convenience?' *Work, Employment and Society*, Vol. 19, No. 4, 797–817.

MARTINEZ-LUCIO, M. and STUART, M. (eds) (2005b) *Partnership and Modernisation in Employment Relations*. London: Routledge.

MAXWELL, G.A. and WATSON, S. (2006) 'Perspectives on line managers in human resource management: Hilton International's UK hotels', *International Journal of Human Resource Management*, Vol. 17, No. 6, 1152–70.

MAYO, A. (1995) 'Economic indicators of human resource management', in S. TYSON (ed.) *Strategic Prospects for Human Resource Management*. London: Institute of Personnel and Development.

MCBRIDE, A., MUSTCHIN, S., COX, A., HYDE, P., ANTONACOPOULOU, E., WALSHE, K. and WOOLNOUGH, H. (2006) *Developing Skills in the NHS*. Report to the Department of Health. Manchester Business School.

MCCANN, L., HASSARD, J. and MORRIS, J. (2010) 'Restructuring managerial labour in the USA, the UK and Japan: challenging the salience of "varieties of capitalism"', *British Journal of Industrial Relations*, Vol. 48, No. 2, 347–74.

MCCANN, L., MORRIS, J. and HASSARD, J. (2008) 'Normalised intensity: the new labour process of middle management', *Journal of Management Studies*, Vol. 45, No. 2, 343–71.

MCCLEAN, E. and COLLINS, C. (2011) 'High commitment HR practices, employee effort and firm performance: investigating the effects of HR practices across employee groups within professional service firms', *Human Resource Management*, Vol. 50, No. 3, 341–63.

MCDANIEL, M. (2009) 'Gerrymandering in personnel selection: a review of practice', *Human Resource Management Review*, Vol. 19, 263–70.

MCDERMOTT, P. (2011) 'Industrial relations in China: ball of confusion?' in K. TOWNSEND and A. WILKINSON (eds) *Research Handbook on Work and Employment Relations*. Cheltenham: Edward Elgar, pp. 319–44.

MCDONNELL, A. and COLLINGS, D.G. (2011) 'Identification and evaluation of talent in MNEs', in H. SCULLION and D.G. COLLINGS *Global Talent Management*. New York and Abingdon: Routledge.

MCDONNELL, A., GUNNIGLE, P. and LAVELLE, J. (2010) 'Learning transfer in multinational companies: explaining inter-organisational variation', Human Resource Management Journal, Vol. 20, No. 1, 23–43.

MCDONNELL, A., LAMARE, R., GUNNIGLE, P., and LAVELLE, J. (2010a) 'Developing tomorrow's leaders – evidence of global talent management in multinational enterprises', *Journal of World Business*, Vol. 45, 150–60.

McEwen, N. (2002) 'Transforming HR: the practitioner's perspective', *Strategic HR Review*, Vol. 2. No. 1, 18–23.

McGovern, P. (2007) 'Immigration, Labour markets and employment relations: problems and prospects', *British Journal of Industrial Relations*, Vol. 45. No. 2, 217–35.

McLaughlin, P. and Mills, A. (2011) 'Combining vocational and higher education studies to provide dual parallel qualifications', *Journal of Further and Higher Education*, Vol. 35, No. 2. 233–45.

McSweeney, B. (2002a) 'Hofstede's model of national cultural differences and their consequences: a triumph of faith – a failure of analysis', *Human Relations*, Vol. 55, No. 1, 89–118.

McSweeney, B. (2002b) 'The essentials of scholarship: a reply to Geert Hofstede', *Human Relations*, Vol. 55, No. 11, 1363–72.

McSweeney, B. (2008) 'Cultural diversity within nations' in C. Smith, B. McSweeney and R. Fitzgerals (eds) *Remaking Management: Between Global and Local*. Cambridge: Cambridge University Press.

McSweeney, B., Smith, C. and Fitzgerald, R. (2008) 'Remaking management: between global and local', in C. Smith, B. McSweeney and R. Fitzgerals (eds) *Remaking Management: Between Global and Local*. Cambridge: Cambridge University Press.

Megginson, D. and Whitaker, V. (2003) *Continuing Professional Development*. London: CIPD.

Meier, M. (2010) 'Knowledge management in strategic alliances: a review of empirical evidence', *International Journal of Management Reviews*, Vol. 13, No. 1, 1–23.

Melchers, K., Kleinmann, M. and Prinz, M. (2010) 'Do assessors have too much on their plates? The effects of simultaneously rating multiple assessment centre candidates on rating quality', *International Journal of Selection and Assessment*, Vol. 18, No. 3, 329–41.

Mellahi, K. and Collings, W. (2010) 'The barriers to effective global talent management: the example of corporate elites in MNEs', *Journal of World Business*, Vol. 45, 143–9.

Mellahi, K. and Wilkinson, A. (2010) 'Slash and burn or nip and tuck? Downsizing, innovation and human resources', *International Journal of Human Resource Management*, Vol. 21, No. 13, 2291–305.

Messersmith, J. and Guthrie, J. (2010) 'High performance work systems in emergent organisations: implications for firm performance', *Human Resource Management*, Vol. 49, No. 2, 241–64.

Metcalf, D. (2005) 'British unions: resurgence or perdition?', The Work Foundation, *Provocation Series*, Vol. 1, No1. Available from: http://theworkfoundation.co.uk/assets/docs/publications/68_British%20Unions.pdf.

Michaels, E., Handfield-Jones, H. and Axelrod, B. (2001) *The War for Talent*. Boston: Harvard Business School Press.

Miles, M. (1979) 'Qualitative data as an attractive nuisance: the problem of analysis', *Administrative Science Quarterly*, Vol. 12, No. 4, 590–601.

Miles, M. and Huberman, A.M. (1984) *Analysing Qualitative Data: A source book for new methods*. London: Sage.

Miles, R. and Snow, C. (1978) *Organisational Strategy, Structure and Process*. New York: McGraw-Hill.

Millward, N., Bryson, A. and Forth, J. (2000) *All Change at Work: British employment relations 1980–1998, as portrayed by the Workplace Industrial Relations Survey series*. London: Routledge.

Mintzberg, H. (1978) 'Patterns in strategy formation', *Management Science*, Vol. 24, No. 9, 934–48.

Mintzberg, H. (1979) 'An emergent strategy of direct research', *Administrative Science Quarterly*, Vol. 24, No. 4, 582–9.

Mintzberg, H. (1987) 'Crafting strategy', *Harvard Business Review*, July–August, 66–75.

Mintzberg, H., Ahlstrand, B. and Lampel, J. (1998) *Strategy Safari: A guided tour through the wilds of strategic management*. London: Prentice Hall.

Mitchell, J. (1983) 'Case and situation analysis', *Sociological Review*, Vol. 31, No. 2, 187–211.

Mitlacher, L. (2007) 'The role of temporary agency work in different industrial relations systems: a comparison between Germany and the USA', *British Journal of Industrial Relations*, Vol. 45, No. 3, 581–606.

Mohr, R. and Zoghi, C. (2008) 'High involvement work design and job satisfaction', *Industrial and Labour Relations Review*, Vol. 61, No. 3, 275–96.

Mohrenweiser, J and Backes-Gellner, U. (2010) 'Apprenticeship training: for investment or substitution?' *International Journal of Manpower*, Vol. 31, No. 5, 545–62.

Monks, J. (1998) 'Trade unions, enterprise and the future', in P. Sparrow and M. Marchington (eds) *Human Resource Management: The new agenda*. London: Financial Times/Pitman.

Monks, K. (1993) 'Models of personnel management: a means of understanding the diversity of personnel practices?' *Human Resource Management Journal*, Vol. 3, No. 2, 29–41.

Morgan, G. and Kristensen, P. (2006) 'The contested space of multinationals: varieties of institutionalism, varieties of capitalism', *Human Relations*, Vol. 59, 1467–90.

Morgeson, F., Campion, M., Dipboye, R., Hollenbeck, J., Murphy, K. and Schmitt, N. (2007) 'Reconsidering the use of personality tests in personnel selection contexts', *Personnel Psychology*, Vol. 60, No. 3, 683–729.

Morgeson, F., Campion, M. and Levashina, J. (2009) 'Why don't you just show me? Performance interviews for skill-based promotions', *International Journal of Selection and Assessment*, Vol. 17, No. 2, 203–18.

Morley, M. (2002a) 'Gainsharing', in T. Redman and A. Wilkinson (eds) *The Informed Student Guide to Human Resource Management*. London: Thomson Learning.

Morrell, K. and Arnold, J. (2007) 'Look after they leap: illustrating the value of retrospective reports in employee turnover', *International Journal of Human Resource Management*, Vol. 18, No. 9, 1683–99.

Morrell, K., Loan-Clarke, J. and Wilkinson, A. (2001) 'Unweaving leaving: the use of models in the management of employee turnover', *International Journal of Management Reviews*, Vol. 3, No. 3, 219–44.

Morris, E. (2011) 'Time to ask the tricky questions about university technical colleges', *The Guardian*, 26 April.

Morris, S. and Snell, S. (2009) 'The evolution of HR strategy: adaptations to increasing global complexity', in A. Wilkinson, N. Bacon, T. Redman, and S. Snell (eds) *The SAGE Handbook of Human Resource Management*. London: Sage.

Mueller, F. (1994) 'Societal effect, organisation effect and globalisation', *Organisation Studies*, Vol. 15, 407–28.

Mueller, F. (1996) 'Human resources as strategic assets: an evolutionary resource-based theory', *Journal of Management Studies*, Vol. 33, No. 6, 757–85.

Muller, M. (1999) 'HRM under institutional constraints: the case of Germany', *British Journal of Management*, Vol. 10, No. 1, 31–44.

Mumford, A. (1988) 'Enhancing your learning skills – a note of guidance for managers', in S. Wood (ed.) *Continuous Development*. London: Institute of Personnel Management.

Mumford, A. and Gold, J. (2004) *Management Development: Strategies for action*. London: CIPD.

Mumford, M. (2011) 'A hale farewell: the state of leadership research', *The Leadership Quarterly*, Vol. 22, 1–7.

Murphy, N. (2007a) 'An introduction to employing migrant workers', XpertHR, *IRS Employment Review* 874.

Murphy, N. (2007d) 'Managing mental ill health in the workplace', *IRS Employment Review* 879, 20 August.

Negandhi, A. (1983) 'Cross cultural management research: trends and future directions', *Journal of International Business Studies*, Vol. 14, No. 2, 17–28.

Nemanich, L. and Keller, R. (2007) 'Transformational leadership in an acquisition: a field study of employees', *The Leadership Quarterly*, Vol. 18, 49–68.

Nesheim, T., Olsen, K. and Kalleberg, A. (2007) 'Externalising the core: firms' use of employment intermediaries in the information and communication technology industries,' *Human Resource Management*, Vol. 46, No. 2, 247–64.

*New York Times* Editorial (2011) 'Boeing and the N.L.R.B: is a move to South Carolina a way to avoid unions or retaliation against them?' *New York Times*, 26 April, A24.

Newell, S. (2005) 'Recruitment and selection', in S. Bach (ed.) *Managing Human Resources*, 4th edition. Oxford: Blackwell.

Newell, S. (2006) 'Selection and assessment', in T. Redman and A. Wilkinson (eds) *Contemporary Human Resource Management*. Harlow: Pearson Education.

Newell, S. and Shackleton, V. (2001) 'Selection and assessment as an interactive decision-action process', in T. Redman and A. Wilkinson (eds) *Contemporary Human Resource Management*. London: Financial Times/Prentice Hall.

Newell, S. and Tansley, C. (2001) 'International uses of selection methods', *International Review of Industrial and Organisational Psychology*, Vol. 16, 195–213.

Ng, E. and Sears, G. (2010) 'The effect of adverse impact in selection practices on organisational diversity: a field study', *International Journal of Human Resource Management*, Vol. 21, No. 9, 1454–71.

Ng, I. and Dastmalchian, A. (2011) 'Perceived training benefits and training bundles: a Canadian study', *International Journal of Human Resource Management*, Vol. 22, No. 4, 829–42.

Nickson, D., Hurrell, S., Warhurst, C. and Cammander, J. (2011) 'Labour supply and skills demand in fashion retailing, in I. Grugulis and O. Bozkurt (eds) *Retail Work*. Basingstoke: Palgrave Macmillan.

Nijssen, M. and Paauwe, J. (2012) 'HRM in turbulent times: how to achieve organizational agility?' *International Journal of Human Resource Management*.

Nikolau, I. (2011) 'Core processes and applicant reactions to the employment interview: an exploratory study in Greece', *International Journal of Human Resource Management*, Vol. 22, No. 10, 2185–201.

Nishi, L., Lepak, D. and Schneider, B. (2008) 'Employee attributions of the "why" of HR practices: their effects on employee attitudes and behaviours, and customer satisfaction', *Personnel Psychology*, Vol. 61, No. 3, 503–45.

Niven, M. (1967) *Personnel Management, 1913–1963*. London: Institute of Personnel Management.

Nolan, P. (2011) 'Money, markets, meltdown: the 21st-century crisis of labour', *Industrial Relations Journal*, Vol. 42, No. 1, 2–17.

Nolan, P. and Wood, S. (2003) 'Mapping the future of work', *British Journal of Industrial Relations*, Vol. 41, No. 2, 165–74.

Nonaka, I. (1994) 'A dynamic theory or organizational knowledge creation', *Organization Science*, Vol. 5, No. 1, 14–37.

Nonaka, I., Toyama, R. and Konno, N. (2000) 'SECI, BA and Leadership: a unified model of dynamic knowledge creation', *Long Range Planning*, Vol. 33, 5–34.

Noon, M. and Blyton, P. (2007) *The Realities of Work*. London: Macmillan Business.

O'Creevey, M., Gooderham, P. and Nordhaug, O. (2008) 'Human resource management in US subsidiaries in Europe and Australia: centralisation or autonomy?' *Journal of International Business Studies*, Vol. 39, 151–66.

OECD (2010) *Local Economic and Employment Development Working Papers*, 2010/4. OECD Publishing.

Office for National Statistics (2011) *Labour Force Survey*. London: ONS.

Oliver, C. (1997) 'Sustainable competitive advantage: combining institutional and resource-based views', *Strategic Management Journal*, Vol. 18, No. 9, 697–713.

Orlitzky, M. (2007) 'Recruitment strategy', in P. Boxall, J. Purcell and P. Wright (eds) *The Oxford Handbook of Human Resource Management*. Oxford: Oxford University Press.

Osland, J.S., Bird, A., Mendenhall, M. and Osland, A. (2006) 'Developing global leadership capabilities and global mindset: a review', in G.K. Stahl and I. Bjorkman (eds) *Handbook of Research in International Human Resource Management*. Cheltenham: Edward Elgar.

Oxenbridge, S. and Brown, W. (2004). 'Achieving a new equilibrium? The stability of cooperative employer-union relationships', *Industrial Relations Journal*, Vol. 35, No. 5, 388–402.

Oxenbridge, S. and Brown, W. (2005) 'Developing partnership relationships: a case of leveraging power', in M. Martinez-Lucio and M. Stuart (eds) *Partnership and Modernisation in Employment Relations*. London: Routledge.

Paauwe, J. (2004) *HRM and Performance: Achieving long term viability*. Oxford: Oxford University Press.

Paauwe, J. and Boselie, P. (2003) 'Challenging "strategic HRM" and the relevance of the institutional setting', *Human Resource Management Journal*, Vol. 13, No. 3, 56–70.

Padilla, A., Hogan, R. and Kaiser, R. (2007) 'The toxic triangle: destructive leaders, susceptible followers and conducive environments', *The Leadership Quarterly*, Vol. 18, 176–94.

Parkes, C., Scully, J., West, M. and Dawson, J. (2007) '"High commitment" strategies: it ain't what you do, it's the way that you do it', *Employee Relations*, Vol. 29, No. 3, 306–18.

Parkin, M. (2009) *The Employer's Guide to Grievance and Discipline Procedures: Identifying, addressing and investigating employee misconduct*. London: Kogan Page.

Parnell, J. (2010) 'Propensity for participative decision making in Latin America, Mexico and Peru', *International Journal of Human Resource Management*, Vol. 21, No. 13, 2323–38.

Parry, E. (2011) 'An examination of the e-HRM as a means to increase the value of the HR function', *International Journal of Human Resource Management*, Vol. 22, No. 5, 1146–62.

Parry, E. and Tyson, S. (2008) 'An analysis of the use and success of online recruitment methods in the UK', *Human Resource Management Journal*, Vol. 18, No. 3, 257–74.

Parry, E. and Tyson, S. (2011) 'Desired goals and actual outcomes of e-HRM', *Human Resource Management Journal*, Vol. 21, No. 3, 335–54.

Parry, E. and Wilson, H. (2009) 'Factors influencing the adoption of on-line recruitment', *Personnel Review*, Vol. 38, No. 6, 655–73.

Patterson, M., West, M., Lawthom, R. and Nickell, S. (1997) *The Impact of People Management Practices on Business Performance*. London: Institute of Personnel and Development.

Pavlou, F (2011) 'Human resource management in the banking sector in Cyprus: intention, implementation and perception', unpublished PhD thesis, Manchester Business School.

Payne, J. and Keep, E. (2011) *One Step Forward, Two Steps Back? Skills Policy in England under the Coalition Government*. SKOPE Research Paper No. 102. Cardiff University: SKOPE.

Pedler, M., Burgoyne, J. and Boydell, T. (1991) *The Learning Company: A strategy for sustainable development*. London: McGraw-Hill.

Pelletier, K. (2010) 'Leader toxicity: an empirical investigation of toxic behaviour and rhetoric', *Leadership*, Vol. 6, No. 4, 373–89.

Peña, I. and Villasalero, M. (2010) 'Business strategy, human resource systems and organisational performance in the Spanish banking industry', *International Journal of Human Resource Management*, Vol. 21, No. 15, 2864–88.

Pendleton, A. (2009) 'Employee participation in employee share ownership: an evaluation of the factors associated with participation and contributions in Save-As-You-Earn plans', *British Journal of Management*, Vol. 21, No. 2, 555–70.

PENROSE, E. (1959) *The Theory of the Growth of the Firm*. Oxford: Blackwell.

PERETZ, M. and MCGRAW, P. (2011) 'Trends in Australian human resource practice, 1996–2009', *Asia Pacific Journal of Human Resources*, Vol. 49, No. 1, 36–54.

PERKINS, S. and WHITE, G. (2011) *Reward management*. London: CIPD.

PERLMUTTER, H. (1969) 'The tortuous evolution of the multinational corporation', *Columbia Journal of World Business*, Vol. 4, 9–18.

PERRY, J.L., ENGBERS, T.A. and JUN, S.Y. (2009) 'Back to the Future? Performance-related pay, empirical research, and the perils of persistence', *Public Administration Review*, Vol. 69, 39–51.

PETTIGREW, A. (1973) *The Politics of Organisational Decision-Making*. London: Tavistock.

PETTIGREW, A. (1985) 'Contextualist research and the study of organisational change processes', in E. LAWLER (ed.) *Doing Research that is Useful in Theory and Practice*. New York: Jossey-Bass.

PFEFFER, J. (1997) 'Pitfalls on the road to measurement: the dangerous liaison of human resources with the idea of accounting and finance', *Human Resource Management*, Vol. 36, No. 3, 357–65.

PFEFFER, J. (1998) *The Human Equation: Building profits by putting people first*. Boston: Harvard Business School Press.

PFEFFER, J. and SUTTON, R. (2006) *Dangerous Half-Truths and Total Nonsense*. Boston: Harvard Business Press.

PFIEFFELMANN, B., WAGNER, S. and LIBKUMAN, T. (2010) 'Recruiting on corporate websites: perceptions of fit and attraction', *International Journal of Selection and Assessment*, Vol. 18, No. 1, 40–47.

PHELPS, R., ADAMS, R. and BESSANT, J. (2007) 'Life cycles of growing organisations: a review with implications for knowledge and learning', *International Journal of Management Reviews*, Vol. 9, No. 1, 1–30.

PHILPOTT, J. (2010) *Working Hours in the Recession*. London: CIPD.

PHILPOTT, J. and DAVIES, G. (2006) 'No turning back?' *People Management*, 14 September, 26–30.

PICCOLO, R., BARDES, M., MAYER, D. and JUDGE, T. (2008) 'Does high quality leader-member exchange accentuate the effects of organisational justice?' *European Journal of Work and Organisational Psychology*, Vol. 17, No. 2, 273–98.

PICKARD, J. (2005) 'Part, not partner', *People Management*, 27 October.

PINNINGTON, A.H. (2011) 'Leadership development: applying the same leadership theories and development practices to different contexts?' *Leadership*, Vol. 7, No. 3, pp.335–65.

PLUMBLEY, P. (1991) *Recruitment and Selection*. London: Institute of Personnel Management.

PORTER, M. (1985) *Competitive Advantage: Creating and sustaining superior performance*. New York: Free Press.

POSTHUMA, R., MORGESON, F. and CAMPION, M. (2002) 'Beyond employment interview validity: a comprehensive narrative review of recent research and trends over time', *Personnel Psychology*, Vol. 55, No. 1, 1–81.

POWELL, J.J.W. and SOLGA, H. (2010) 'Analyzing the nexus of higher education and vocational training in Europe: a comparative-institutional framework', *Studies in Higher Education*, Vol. 35, No. 6, 705–21.

PREECE, D. and ILES, P. (2009) 'Executive development: assuaging uncertainties through joining a leadership academy' *Personnel Review*, Vol. 38, No. 3, 286–306.

PRESTON J. and GREEN A. (2008) *Modernising vocational education and training. Fourth report on vocational education and training research in Europe: background report Volume 1*. Luxembourg: Office for Official Publications of the European Communities (Cedefop Reference series).

PREUSS, L., HAUNSCHILD, A. and MATTEN, D. (2009) 'The rise of CSR: implications for HRM and employee representation', *The International Journal of Human Resource Management*, Vol. 20, No. 4, 953–73.

PRICE, R. and PRICE, L. (1994) 'Change and continuity in the status divide', in K. SISSON (ed.) *Personnel Management in Britain*. Oxford: Blackwell.

PRIEM, R. and BUTLER, J. (2001) 'Is the resource-based "view" a useful perspective for strategic management research?' *Academy of Management Review*, Vol. 26, No. 1, 22–40.

PRITCHARD, K. (2010) 'Becoming an HR strategic partner: tales of transition', *Human Resource Management Journal*, Vol. 20, No. 2, 175–88.

PROCTER, S. and BURRIDGE, M. (2008), 'Teamworking and performance: the extent and intensity of teamworking in the 1998 UK workplace employee relations survey', *International Journal of Human Resource Management*, Vol. 19, No. 1, 153–68.

PROCTER, S. and CURRIE, G. (1999) 'The role of the personnel function: roles, perceptions and processes in an NHS Trust', *International Journal of Human Resource Management*, Vol. 10, No. 6, 1077–91.

PROCTER, S. and MUELLER, F. (eds) (2000) *Teamworking*. London: Macmillan.

PUDELKO, M. (2005) 'Cross national learning from best practice and the convergence–divergence debate in HRM', *International Journal of Human Resource Management*, Vol. 16, No. 11, 2047–76.

PUDELKO, M. and HARZING, A. (2007) 'Country of origin, localisation or dominance effect? An empirical investigation of HRM practices in foreign subsidiaries', *Human Resource Management*, Vol. 46, No. 4, 535–59.

PULAKOS, E.D., MUELLER-HANSON, R.A. and O'LEARY, R.S. (2008) 'Performance management in the United States', in A. VARMA, P.S. BUDHWAR and A. DENISI *Performance Management Systems: A Global Perspective.* Abingdon, Oxon: Routledge.

PULIGNANO, V. (2006) 'The diffusion of employment practices of US-based multinationals in Europe; a case study comparison of British- and Italian-based subsidiaries', *British Journal of Industrial Relations*, Vol. 44, No. 3, 497–518.

PURCELL, J. (1980) *Good Industrial Relations: Theory and practice.* London: Macmillan.

PURCELL, J. (1999) 'The search for best practice and best fit in human resource management: chimera or cul-de-sac?' *Human Resource Management Journal*, Vol. 9, No. 3, 26–41.

PURCELL, J. (2000) 'After collective bargaining? Acas in the age of human resource management', in B. TOWERS and W. BROWN (eds) *Employment Relations in Britain: 25 years of the Advisory, Conciliation and Arbitration Service.* Oxford: Blackwell.

PURCELL, J. (2010) *Building employee engagement*, Acas policy discussion paper. Available online at: www.acas.org.uk

PURCELL, J. and GEORGIADIS, K. (2007) 'Why should employers bother with worker voice?' in R. FREEMAN, P. BOXALL and P. HAYNES (eds) *What Workers Say: Employee voice in the Anglo-American workplace*. Ithaca: Cornell University.

PURCELL, J. and HUTCHINSON, S. (2007) 'Front-line managers as agents in the HRM-performance causal chain: theory, analysis and evidence', *Human Resource Management Journal*, Vol. 17, No. 1, 3–20.

PURCELL, J. and HUTCHINSON, S. (2007a) *Learning and the Line: The role of the line manager in learning and development*. London: CIPD. Available online at: http://www.cipd.co.uk/onlineinfodocuments

PURCELL, J. and KINNIE, N. (2007) HRM and Business Performance in P. BOXALL, J. PURCELL and P. WRIGHT (eds) *The Oxford Handbook of Human Resource Management*. Oxford: Oxford University Press.

PURCELL, J., HUTCHINSON, S. and COTTON, C. (2007) 'Controlling interest', *People Management*.

PURCELL, J., KINNIE, N., HUTCHINSON, S., RAYTON, B. and SWART, J. (2003) *Understanding the People and Performance Link: Unlocking the black box*. London: CIPD.

PURCELL, J., PURCELL, K. and TAILBY, S. (2004) 'Temporary work agencies: here today, gone tomorrow?' *British Journal of Industrial Relations*, Vol. 42, No. 4, 705–25.

PURVANOVA, R. and BONO, J. (2009) 'Transformational leadership in context: face-to-face and virtual teams', *The Leadership Quarterly*, Vol. 20, 343–57.

PYMAN, A., COOPER, B., TEICHER, J. and HOLLAND, P. (2006) 'A comparison of the effectiveness of employee voice arrangements in Australia', *Industrial Relations Journal*, Vol. 37, No. 5, 543–59.

QUINN, B., COOKE, R. and KRIS, A. (2000) *Shared Services: Mining for corporate gold*. London: Pearson Education.

QUINN, J. (1980) *Strategies for Change: Logical incrementalism*. Homewood, IL: Irwin.

QUINTANILLA, J. and FERNER, A. (2003) 'Multinationals and human resource management: between global convergence and national identity', *International Journal of Human Resource Management*, Vol. 14, No. 3, 363–8.

RAINBIRD, H. and MUNRO, A. (2003a) 'Workplace learning and the employment relationship in the public sector', *Human Resource Management Journal*, Vol. 13, No. 2, 30–44.

RAINBIRD, H. and MUNRO, A. (2003b) 'Professional standards: how do people learn?' *People Management*, 20 November, 52.

RAINBIRD, H. and STUART, M. (2011) 'The state and the union learning agenda in Britain', *Work, Employment and Society*, Vol. 25, No. 2, 202–17.

RAINBIRD, H., FULLER, A. and MUNRO, A. (2004a) *Workplace Learning in Context*. London: Routledge.

RAINBIRD, H., MUNRO, A. and HOLLY, L. (2004b) 'Exploring the concept of employer demand for skills and qualifications: case studies from the public sector', in C. WARHURST, E. KEEP and I. GRUGULIS (eds) *The Skills That Matter*. Basingstoke: Palgrave.

Ram, M. (1994) *Managing to Survive: Working lives in small firms*. Oxford: Blackwell.

Ram, M. (2000) 'Investors in People in small firms', *Personnel Review*, Vol. 29, No. 1, 69–89.

Ramsay, H. and Scholarios, D. (1999) 'Selective decisions: challenging orthodox analyses of the hiring process', *International Journal of Management Reviews*, Vol. 1, No. 4, 63–89.

Ramsay, H., Scholarios, D. and Harley, B. (2000) 'Employees and high-performance work systems: testing inside the black box', *British Journal of Industrial Relations*, Vol. 38, No. 4, 501–31.

Rana, E. (2003) 'Council appraisals discriminate', *People Management*, 23 January, 11.

Rankin, N. (2006a) 'In the hiring line: boosting managers' recruitment skills', *IRS Employment Review* 846, 5 May.

Rankin, N. (2007d) 'The most effective ways of managing absence', *IRS Employment Review* 872, 8 May.

Rasche, A. (2010) 'The limits of corporate responsibility standards', *Business Ethics: A European Review*, Vol. 19, No. 3, 280–90.

Rauner, F. (2008) 'European vocational education and training: a prerequisite for mobility?' *Journal of European Industrial Training*, Vol. 32, Nol.2/3, 85–98.

Rausch, E., Sherman, H. and Washbush, J.B. (2002) 'Defining and assessing competencies for competency-based, outcome-focused management', *Journal of Management Development*, Vol. 21, No. 3/4, 184–201.

Razouk, A. (2011) 'High performance work systems and performance of French small- and medium-sized enterprises: examining causal order', *International Journal of Human Resource Management*, Vol. 22, No. 2, 311–30.

Redman, T. (2006) 'Performance appraisal', in T. Redman and A. Wilkinson (eds) *Contemporary Human Resource Management: Text and cases*. Harlow: Pearson Education.

Redman, T. and Wilkinson, A. (2012) 'Human resource management: a contemporary perspective', in T. Redman and A. Wilkinson (eds) *Contemporary Human Resource Management: Text and Cases*, 3rd edition. Harlow: Pearson.

Redman, T., Snape, E., Wass, J. and Hamilton, P. (2007) 'Evaluating the human resource shared services model: evidence from the NHS', *International Journal of Human Resource Management*, Vol. 18, No. 8, 1486–506.

Rees, C., Mamman, A. and Braik, A. (2007) 'Emiritisation as a strategic HRM change initiative: case study evidence from a UAE petroleum company', *International Journal of Human Resource Management*, Vol. 18, No. 1, 33–53.

Reiche, B. and Harzing, A. (2011) 'International assignments' in A. Harzing and A. Pinnington (eds) *International Human Resource Management*. 3rd edition. London: Sage.

Reid, M., Barrington, H. and Brown, M. (2004) *Human Resource Development: Beyond training interventions*. London: CIPD.

Reilly, P. (2000) *HR Shared Service and the Realignment of HR*. Report 368. London: Institute of Employment Studies.

Renwick, D. (2003) 'Line manager involvement in HRM: an inside view', *Employee Relations*, Vol. 25, No. 3, 262–80.

RENWICK, D. (2006) 'Line managers', in T. REDMAN and A. WILKINSON (eds) *Contemporary Human Resource Management*, 2nd edition. Harlow: Pearson.

RICHARDSON, J., MCBEY, K. and MCKENNA, S. (2008) 'Integrating realistic job previews and realistic living conditions previews: realistic recruitment for internationally mobile knowledge workers', *Personnel Review*, Vol. 37, No. 5, 490–508.

RICHARDSON, W. and HAYNES, G. (2009) *National Evaluation of Diplomas: Findings from the 2008 Survey of higher education institutions on their implementation and impact.* DCSF Research Report RR 145. London: DCSF.

RICHBELL, S. and WOOD, G. (2009) "Reward Management" in COLLINGS, D.G. and WOOD, G. (eds.) *Human Resource Management: A Critical Approach*, Routledge, London, pp. 208–221.

RICHTER, A., DICKMAN, M. and GRAUBNER, M. (2008) 'Patterns of HRM in consulting firms', *Personnel Review*, Vol. 37, No. 2, 184–202.

RIGGS, V., MCCAULEY, P., GLAISTER, C., HOLDEN, R. and GOLD, J. (2010) 'The identification of training needs' in J. GOLD, R. HOLDEN, P. ILES, J. STEWART and J. BEARDWELL *Human Resource Development: Theory and Practice.* Basingstoke: Palgrave Macmillan.

RIGIO, R., CHALEFF, I. and LIPMAN-BLUMEN, J. (eds) (2008) *The Art of Followership: How great followers create great leaders and organisations.* San Francisco: Jossey-Bass.

RIISGAARD, L. and HAMMER, N. (2011) 'Prospects for labour in global value chains: Labour standards in the cut flower and banana industries', *British Journal of Industrial Relations*, Vol. 49, No. 1, 168–90.

RITSON, N. (1999) 'Corporate strategy and the role of HRM: critical cases in oil and chemicals', *Employee Relations*, Vol. 21, No. 2, 159–75.

ROBERTS, G. (1997) *Recruitment and Selection: A competency approach.* London: Institute of Personnel and Development.

ROBERTSON, I. and SMITH, M. (2001) 'Personnel selection', *Journal of Occupational and Organizational Psychology*, Vol. 74, No. 4, 441–72.

ROBINSON, P. (1999) 'Explaining the relationship between flexible employment and labour market regulation', in A. FELSTEAD and N. JEWSON (eds) *Global Trends in Flexible Labour.* London: Macmillan.

ROCHE, W. and GEARY, J. (2002) 'Advocates, critics and union involvement in workplace participation', *British Journal of Industrial Relations*, Vol. 40, No. 3, 659–88.

RODGER, A. (1952) *The Seven Point Plan.* London: National Institute for Industrial Psychology.

RODRIGUEZ, J. and VENTURA, J. (2003) 'Human resource management systems and organisational performance: an analysis of the Spanish manufacturing industry', *International Journal of Human Resource Management*, Vol. 14, No. 7, 1206–26.

ROE, P., WISEMAN, J. and COSTELLO, M. (2006) *Perceptions and Use of NVQs: A survey of employers in England.* Research Report 714. London: Department for Education and Skills.

ROGERS, C. (1969) *Freedom to Learn.* Ohio: Charles & Merrill.

ROLLINSON, D. and DUNDON, T. (2007) *Understanding Employment Relations.* Maidenhead: McGraw-Hill Higher Education.

ROLLINSON, D., BROADFIELD, A. and EDWARDS, D. (1998) *Organisational Behaviour and Analysis*. London: Addison-Wesley.

ROMANI, L. (2011) 'Culture in IHRM', in A-W HARZING and A.H. PINNINGTON *International Human Resource Management*, 3rd edition. London: Sage.

ROSE, M. (2003) 'Good deal, bad deal? Job satisfaction in occupations', *Work, Employment, and Society*, Vol. 17, No. 3, 503–30.

ROUSSEAU, D. and BARENDS, E. (2011) 'Becoming an evidence-based HR practitioner', *Human Resource Management Journal*, Vol. 21, No. 3, 221–35.

ROYLE, T. (1999) 'Recruiting the acquiescent workforce: a comparative analysis of McDonald's in Germany and the UK', *Employee Relations*, Vol. 21, No. 6, 540–55.

RUBERY, J. (1995) 'Performance-related pay and the prospects for gender equity', *Journal of Management Studies*, Vol. 35, No. 5, 637–54.

RUBERY, J. and GRIMSHAW, D. (2003) *The Organisation of Employment: An international perspective*. London: Palgrave.

RUBERY, J. and URWIN, P. (2011) 'Bringing the employer back in: why social care needs a standard employment relationship', *Human Resource Management Journal*, Vol. 21, No. 2, 122–37.

RUBERY, J., CARROLL, M., COOKE, F.L., GRUGULIS, I. and EARNSHAW, J. (2004) 'Human resource management and the permeable organisation: the case of the multi-client call centre', *Journal of Management Studies*, Vol. 41, No. 7, 1199–222.

RUBERY, J., COOKE, F.L., EARNSHAW, J. and MARCHINGTON, M. (2003) 'Inter-organisational relations and employment in a multi-employer environment', *British Journal of Industrial Relations*, Vol. 41, No. 2, 265–89.

RUBERY, J., MARCHINGTON, M., GRIMSHAW, D., CARROLL, M. and PASS, S. (2009) 'Employed under different rules: the complexities of working across organisational boundaries', *Cambridge Journal of Regions, Economy and Society*, Vol. 2, No. 3, 413–28.

RUGMAN, A. and VERBEKE, A. (2002) 'Edith Penrose's contribution to the resource-based view of strategic management', *Strategic Management Journal*, Vol. 23, No. 8, 769–80.

RUMELT, R. (2011) *Good strategy, Bad strategy; the difference and why it matters*. London: Profile Books.

RUTHERFORD, M., BULLER, P. and MCMULLEN, P. (2003) 'Human resource management over the life cycle of small to medium sized firms', *Human Resource Management*, Vol. 42, No. 4, 321–33.

RYAN, P., GOSPEL, H. and LEWIS, P. (2007) 'Large employers and apprenticeship training in Britain', *British Journal of Industrial Relations*, Vol. 45, No. 1, 127–53.

RYAN, P., GOSPEL, H., LEWIS, P. and FOREMAN, J. (2006) *Large Employers and Apprenticeship Training*. London: CIPD.

RYAN, P., WAGNER, K., TEUBER, S. and BACKES-GELLNER, U. (2010) 'Corporate ownership and initial training in Britain, Germany, and Switzerland', Where? SKOPE.

SAKS, A.M. (2006) 'Antecedents and consequences of employee engagement', *Journal of Managerial Psychology*, Vol. 21, No. 7, 600–19.

SALAMON, M. (2000) *Industrial Relations: Theory and practice*, 4th edition. Harlow: Financial Times/Prentice Hall.

SALGADO, J. (2002) 'The big five personality dimensions and counterproductive behaviours', *International Journal of Selection and Assessment*, Vol. 10, No. 1/2, 117–25.

SAMUEL, P. and BACON, N. (2010) 'The contents of partnership agreements in Britain, 1990–2007: modest aims of limited ambition?' *Work, Employment and Society*, Vol. 24, No. 3, 430–48.

SANDERS, K. and FRENKEL, S, (2011) 'HR-line management relations: characteristics and effects', *International Journal of Human Resource Management*, Vol. 22, No. 8, 1611–17.

SANZ-VALLE, R., SABATER-SANCHEZ, R. and ARAGON-SANCHEZ, A. (1999) 'Human resource management and business strategy links: an empirical study', *International Journal of Human Resource Management*, Vol. 10, No. 4, 655–71.

SARGEANT, A. (2000) 'An exploratory study of the effects of progression towards National Vocational Qualifications on the occupational knowledge and care practice of social care workers', *Social Work Education*, Vol. 19, No. 6, 639–66.

SAUNDERS, M., LEWIS, P. and THORNHILL, A. (2009) *Research Methods for Business Students*, 5th edition. London: Financial Times/Prentice Hall.

SAUNDRY, R., HOLLINRAKE, A., and ANTCLIFF, V. (2010) *Learning works: report of the 2009 survey of Union learning reps and their managers*. London: UnionLearn. (ULR Research 12).

SAYIM, K. (2011) 'Policy transfer from advanced to less-advanced institutional environments: labour market orientations of US MNEs in Turkey', *Human Relations*, Vol. 64, No. 4, 573–97.

SCARBROUGH, H. and KINNIE, N. (2003) 'Barriers to the development of teamworking in UK firms', *Industrial Relations Journal*, Vol. 34, No. 2, 135–49.

SCASE, R. (2003) 'Employment relations in small firms', in P. EDWARDS (ed.) *Industrial Relations*, 2nd edition. Oxford: Blackwell.

SCASE, R. and GOFFEE, R. (1989) *Reluctant Managers: Their work and lifestyles*. London: Unwin Hyman.

SCHERER, A.G. and PALAZZO, G. (2010) 'The new political role of business in a globalized world: a review of a new perspective on CSR and its implications for the firm, governance, and democracy', *Journal of Management Studies*, 30 April.

SCHMIDT, F. and HUNTER, J. (1998) 'The validity and utility of selection methods in personnel psychology: practical and theoretical implications of 85 years of research findings', *Psychological Bulletin*, Vol. 124, No. 2, 262–74.

SCHMIDT, W., TRITTEL, N. and MÜLLER, A. (2011) 'Performance-related pay in German public services: the example of local authorities in North Rhine-Westphalia', *Employee Relations*, Vol. 33, No. 2, 140–58.

SCHMITT, N. and CHAN, D. (1999) 'The status of research on applicant reactions to selection tests and its implications for managers', *International Journal of Management Reviews*, Vol. 1, No. 1, 45–62.

SCHMITT, N. and KIM, B. (2007) 'Selection decision-making' in P. BOXALL, J. PURCELL and P. WRIGHT (eds) *The Oxford Handbook of Human Resource Management*. Oxford: Oxford University Press.

Schneider, S. and Barsoux, J. (1997) *Managing Across Cultures*. London: Financial Times/ Prentice Hall.

Schneider, S. and Barsoux, J. (2003) *Managing across Cultures*, 2nd edition. New York: Prentice Hall.

Schuler, R. (1989) 'Strategic human resource management and industrial relations', *Human Relations*, Vol. 42, No. 2, 157–84.

Schuler, R. and Jackson, S. (1987) 'Linking competitive strategies with human resource management', *Academy of Management Executive*, Vol. 1, No. 3, 207–19.

Schuler, R., Jackson, S. and Storey, J. (2001) 'HRM and its link with strategic management', in J. Storey (ed.) *Human Resource Management: A critical text*, 2nd edition. London: Thomson Learning.

Schuster, J. and Zingheim, P. (1999) *The New Pay: Linking employee and organisational performance*. New York, Lexington.

Scott, M., Roberts, I., Holroyd, G. and Sawbridge, D. (1989) *Management and Industrial Relations in Small Firms*. Department of Employment Research Paper No. 70. London: HMSO.

Scullion, H. and Collings, D. (2011) 'Global talent management', *Journal of World Business*, Vol. 45, 105–8.

Scullion, H., Collings, D.G. and Gunnigle, P. (2007) 'International HRM in the 21st century: emerging themes and contemporary debates', *Human Resource Management Journal*, Vol. 17, 309–19.

Searle, R. (2003) *Selection and Recruitment: A critical text*. Milton Keynes: Open University Press.

Searle, R., Den Hartog, D., Weibel, A., Gillsepie, N., Six, F., Hatzakis, T. and Skinner, D. (2011) 'Trust in the employer: the role of high-involvement work practices and procedural justice in organisations', *International Journal of Human Resource Management*, Vol. 22, No. 5, 1069–92.

Selden, S. and Orenstein, J. (2011) 'Government e-recruiting websites: the influence of e-recruitment content and usability on recruiting and hiring outcomes in US state governments', *International Journal of Selection and Assessment*, Vol. 19, No. 1, 31–40.

Semler, R. (1993) *Maverick!* London: Arrow Business Books.

Sengupta, S. and Whitfield, K. (2011) 'Ask not what HRM can do for performance but what HRM has done to performance', in P. Blyton, E, Heery and P. Turnbull (eds) *Reassessing the Employment Relationship*. London: Palgrave Macmillan.

Sharma, T., Budhwar, P.S. and Varma, A. (2008) 'Performance management in India' in A. Varma, P.S. Budhwar and A. DeNisi *Performance Management Systems: A Global Perspective*. Abingdon, Oxon: Routledge.

Shen, J. (2011) 'Developing the concept of socially responsible international human resource management', *The International Journal of Human Resource Management*, Vol. 22, No. 6, 1351–63.

Shepherd, J. (2011) 'English Baccalaureate is flawed and does not help poor pupils' prospects, say MPs', *The Guardian*, 28 July, p.2.

Shields (2010); Managing Employee Performance and Rewards Cup.

Shields, J. (2007) *Managing Employee Performance and Reward.* New York: Cambridge University Press.

Shire, K., Mottweiler, H., Schonauer, A. and Valverde, N. (2009) 'Temporary work in coordinated market economies: evidence from front-line service workers', *Industrial and Labour Relations Review*, Vol. 62, No. 4, 602–17.

Shire, K., Schonauer, A., Valverde, M. and Mottweiler, H. (2009a) 'Collective bargaining and temporary employment in contracts in call centre employment in Austria, Germany and Spain', *European Journal of Industrial Relations*, Vol. 15, No. 4, 437–56.

Silcox, S. (2005a) 'Attendance incentives are on the HR agenda once again', *IRS Employment Review* 832, 30 September, 18–20.

Silverman, D. (2010) *Doing Qualitative Research*, 3rd edition. London: Sage.

Simms, J. (2005) 'Better by design', *People Management*, 29 September, 24–9.

Simms, M. and Charlwood, A. (2009) 'Trade unions: power and influence in a changed context', in T. Colling and M. Terry (eds) *Industrial Relations*. Oxford: Blackwell.

Simon, M. (2006) 'Competencies, job evaluation and equal pay', *Competency and Emotional Intelligence*, Vol. 14, No. 1, Autumn, 35–8.

Simons, P., Germans, J. and Ruijters, M. (2003) 'Forum for organisational learning: combining learning at work, organisational learning and training in new ways', *Journal of European Industrial Training*, Vol. 27, No. 1, 41–9.

Sisson, K. (1993) 'In search of human resource management', *British Journal of Industrial Relations*, Vol. 31, No. 2, 201–10.

Sisson, K. (2010) *Employment relations matter.* Available at: http://www2/warwick.ac.uk/fac/soc/wbs/research/irru

Sisson, K. and Marginson, P. (2003) 'Management: systems, structure and strategy', in P. Edwards (ed.) *Industrial Relations*, 2nd edition. Oxford: Blackwell.

Sisson, K. and Storey, J. (2000) *The Realities of Human Resource Management*. Milton Keynes: Open University Press.

Sisson, K. and Timperley, S. (1994) 'From manpower planning to strategic human resource management?' in K. Sisson (ed.) *Personnel Management: A comprehensive guide to theory and practice in Britain*. Oxford: Blackwell.

Slinn, S. and Hurd, R. (2011) 'Employment relations in Canada and the US', in M. Barry and A. Wilkinson (eds) *Research Handbook on Comparative Employment Relations*. Cheltenham: Edward Elgar, pp. 153–183.

Sloman, M. (2003) *Training in the Age of the Learner*. London: CIPD.

Sloman, M. (2007a) 'Skills at work', *Impact*, Issue 20, August.

Sloman, M. (2007b) *Latest Trends in Learning, Training, and Development. Reflections on the 2007 Learning and Development survey*. London: CIPD.

Smedley, T. (2011) 'Unwanted presence' *People Management*, January. London: CIPD.

Smethurst, S. (2003). Empowerment; blood simple *People Management*, 20 March, 22–24.

Smith, A., Oczkwoski, E. and Selby-Smith, S. (2011) 'To have and to hold: modeling the drivers of employee turnover and skill retention in Australian organizations', *International Journal of Human Resource Management*, Vol. 22, No. 2, 395–416.

Smith, C. and Meiksins, P (1995) 'System, society and dominance effects in cross-national organisational analysis', *Work, Employment and Society*, Vol. 9, No. 2, 241–67.

Smith, C., Daskalaki, M., Elger, T. and Brown, D. (2004) 'Labour turnover and management retention strategies in new manufacturing plants', *International Journal of Human Resource Management*, Vol. 15, No. 2, 371–96.

Smith, I. (2000a) 'Benefits', in G. White and J. Druker (eds) *Reward Management: A critical text*. London: Routledge.

Smith, M. and Robertson, I. (1993) *The Theory and Practice of Systematic Personnel Selection*. Basingstoke: Macmillan.

Smith, M. and Villa, P. (2010) 'The ever-declining role of gender equality in the European Employment Strategy', *Industrial Relations Journal*, Vol. 41, No. 6, 526–43.

Smith, P. and Morton, G. (2001) 'New Labour's reform of Britain's employment law: the devil is not only in the detail but in the values and policy too', *British Journal of Industrial Relations*, Vol. 39, No. 1, 119–38.

Smith and Nethersell (2000) Job evaluation in R. Thorpe and G. Holman (eds) Strategic Rewards Systems, Harlow, FT Prentice Hall.

Smith, P. and Sadler-Smith, E. (2006) *Learning in Organizations: Complexities and diversities*. Abingdon: Routledge.

Smither, J., London, M. and Reilly, R. (2005) 'Does performance improve following multisource feedback?' *Personnel Psychology*, Vol. 58, 33–66.

Snape, E., Redman, T. and Bamber, G. (1994) *Managing Managers: Strategies and techniques for human resource management*. Oxford: Blackwell.

Snell A., Shadur, M.A. and Wright, P.M. (2002) 'Human resources strategy: the era of our ways', in Michael A. Hitt, R. Edward Freeman and Jeffrey S. Harrison (eds) *Blackwell Handbook of Strategic Management*. Oxford: Blackwell.

Snowdon, G. (2011) 'Are the days of the unpaid intern over?' The Guardian.co.uk, 15 July, (accessed 28.7.11.)

Som, A. (2007) 'What drives the adoption of innovative SHRM practices on Indian organisations?' *International Journal of Human Resource Management*, Vol. 18, No. 5, 808–28.

Som, A. (2008) 'Innovative human resource management practice and corporate performance in the context of economic liberalisation in India', *International Journal of Human Resource Management*, Vol. 19, No. 7, 1278–97.

Sparrow, P., Brewster, C. and Harris, H. (2004) *Globalizing Human Resource Management*. London: Routledge.

Sparrow, P., Hird, M., Hesketh, A. and Cooper, C. (2010) *Leading HR*. London: Palgrave Macmillan.

Sparrow, P., Scullion, H. and Farndale, E. (2011) 'Global Talent Management: new roles for the corporate HR function?' in H. Scullion and D. Collings (eds) *Global Talent Management*. New York: Routledge.

Spender, J.-C. (2008) 'Organizational learning and knowledge management: whence and whither?' *Management Learning*, Vol. 39, No. 2, 159–176.

Stairs, M., Kandola, B. and Sandford-Smith, R. (2000) 'Slim picking', *People Management*, 28 December, 28–30.

Stammers, R. and Patrick, J. (1975) *The Psychology of Training*. London: Methuen.

Stanton, P., Young, S., Bartram, T. and Leggat, S. (2010) 'Singing the same song: translating HRM messages across management hierarchies in Australian hospitals', *International Journal of Human Resource Management*, Vol. 21, No. 4, 567–81.

Stavrou, E., Brewster, C. and Charalambous, C. (2010) 'Human resource management and firm performance in Europe through the lens of business systems: best fit, best practice or both?' *International Journal of Human Resource Management*, Vol. 21, No. 7, 933–62.

Stewart, J. (2010) 'E-learning' in J. Gold, R. Holden, P. Iles, J. Stewart and J. Beardwell, *Human Resource Development: Theory and Practice*. Basingstoke: Palgrave Macmillan.

Stewart, J. and Rigg, C. (2011) *Learning and Talent Development*. London: CIPD.

Stewart, J., Iles, P., Gold, J., Holden, R., Rodgers, H., and Kershaw-Solomon, H. (2010) 'Strategic HRD and the learning and development function', in J. Gold, R. Holden, P. Iles, J. Stewart and J. Beardwell, *Human Resource Development: Theory and Practice*. Basingstoke: Palgrave Macmillan.

Stiglitz, J. (2006) *Making Globalisation Work*. London: Penguin.

Stiles, P. (2001) 'The impact of the board on strategy: an empirical investigation', *Journal of Management Studies*, Vol. 38, No. 5, 627–50.

Storey, J. (ed.) (1989) *New Perspectives on Human Resource Management*. London: Routledge.

Storey, J. (1992) *Developments in the Management of Human Resources*. Oxford: Blackwell.

Storey, J. (ed.) (2001) *Human Resource Management, a critical text*, 2nd edition. London: Thomson.

Storey, J. (2004) 'Changing theories of leadership and leadership development', in J. Storey (ed.) *Leadership in Organisations: Current issues and key trends*. London: Routledge.

Storey, J. (ed.) (2007) *Human Resource Management: a critical text*, 3rd edition. London: Thomson.

Strauss, G. (1998) 'Participation works – if conditions are appropriate', in F. Heller, E. Pusic, G. Strauss and B. Wilpert (eds) *Organisational Participation: Myth and Reality*. Oxford, Oxford University Press, pp. 190–219.

Strauss, G. (2006) 'Worker participation – some under-considered issues', *Industrial Relations*, Vol. 5, No. 4, 778–803.

Stuart, M., Cook, H. and Cutter, J. (2010) *Evaluation of the union learning fund and union learn. Preliminary findings*. London: UnionLearn.

Stuart, M. and Cook, H. (2011) 'Sustaining ULF activity: findings from the Union Project Office follow-on survey. London: UnionLearn.

Stuart, M., Cutter, J., Cook, H. and Winterton, J. (2011) *Union Learning – Adding Value: An evaluation of the UnionLearn and the Union Learning Fund*. London: UnionLearn with the TUC.

Stuart, M. and Wallis, E. (2007) 'Partnership approaches to learning: a seven country study', *European Journal of Industrial Relations*, Vol. 13, No. 3, 301–21.

Sturdy, A., Grugulis, I. and Willmott, H. (eds) (2001) *Customer Service: Empowerment and entrapment*. London: Palgrave.

Sturges, J. (2008) 'All in a day's work? Career self management and the management of the boundary between work and non-work', *Human Resource Management Journal*, Vol. 18, No. 2, 118–34.

Subramony, M. (2009) 'A meta-analytic investigation of the relationship between HRM bundles and firm performance', *Human Resource Management*, Vol. 48, No. 5, 745–68.

Suff, R. (2005) 'Outsourcing recruitment: a minority pursuit?' *IRS Employment Review* 830, 26 August, 42–8.

Suff, R. (2006) 'Using competencies in selection and recruitment', *IRS Employment Review* 853, 45–8.

Suff, R. (2009) 'Employers' use of employment agencies and recruitment agencies 2009', *Industrial Relations Services* 921, May.

Suff, R. (2010a) 'IRS 2010 dispute resolution survey: grievances and the new Acas Code of Practice', *IRS Employment Review*, 12 April, p.8.

Suff, R. (2010b) 'IRS 2010 dispute resolution survey: managing discipline', *IRS Employment Review*, 26 April, p.10.

Suter, J. and Marchington, M. (2012), 'The role of line managers and employee voice in the restaurant industry', in T. Dundon and A. Wilkinson (eds) *Case Studies in People Management, Strategy and Innovation*. Prahran, Victoria: Tilde University Press.

Sutherland, J. (2009) 'Skills and training in Great Britain: further evidence', *Education and Training*, Vol. 51, No. 7. 541–54.

Suzuki, H. and Kubo, K. (2011) 'Employment relations in Japan', in G. Bamber, R. Lansbury and N. Wailes (eds) *International and Comparative Employment Relations: Globalisation and Change*, 5th edition, Crows Nest: Allen and Unwin.

Swart, J. (2007) 'HRM and knowledge workers', in P. Boxall, J. Purcell, and P. Wright (eds) *The Oxford Handbook of Human Resource Management*. Oxford: Oxford University Press.

Swart, J. and Kinnie, N. (2003) 'Knowledge-intensive firms: the influence of the client on HR systems', *Human Resource Management Journal*, Vol. 13, No. 3, 37–55.

Swart, J. and Kinnie, N. (2010) 'Organisational learning, knowledge assets and HR practices in professional service firms', *Human Resource Management Journal*, Vol. 20, No. 1, 64–79.

Swart, J., Kinnie, N., and Rabinowitz, J. (2007) *Managing Across Boundaries: Human Resource Management Beyond the Firm*. London: CIPD.

Syedain, H. (2007) 'A talent for numbers', *People Management*, 14 June, 36–8.

Syedain, H. (2011) 'The futures market', *People Management*, August. London: CIPD, pp. 24–7.

Sylva, H. and Mol, S. (2009) 'E-recruitment: a study into applicant perceptions of an on-line application system', *International Journal of Selection and Assessment*, Vol. 17, No. 3, 311–23.

Tailby, S. and Winchester, D. (2000) 'Management and trade unions: towards social partnership', in S. Back and K. Sisson (eds) *Personnel Management*, 3rd edition. Oxford: Blackwell.

Tamkin, P., Reilly, P. and Hirsh, W. (2006) *Managing and Developing HR Careers*. Research Report. London: CIPD.

Taplin, I., Winterton, J. and Winterton, R. (2003) 'Understanding labour turnover in a labour-intensive industry: evidence from the British clothing industry', *Journal of Management Studies*, Vol. 40, No. 4, 1021–46.

Taylor, P., Hyman, J., Mulvey, G. and Bain, P. (2002) 'Work organisation, control and the experience of work in call centres', *Work, Employment and Society*, Vol. 16, No. 1, 133–50.

Taylor, S. (2005) *People Resourcing*. London: CIPD.

Taylor, S. (2008) 'Occupational pensions', in G. White and J. Druker (eds) *Employee Reward: A critical text*. London: Routledge.

Taylor, S. (2010) *Resourcing and Talent Management*, 5th edition. London: CIPD.

Taylor, S. and Emir, A. (2009) *Employment Law: an introduction*. Oxford: Oxford University Press.

Teague, P. and Roche, W. (2012) 'Line managers and the management of workplace conflict: evidence from Ireland', *Human Resource Management Journal*, forthcoming.

Tempel, A. and Walgenbach, P. (2007) 'Global standardisation of organisational forms and management practices? What new institutionalism and the business systems approach can learn from each other', *Journal of Management Studies*, Vol. 44, No. 1, 1–24.

Tempel, A., Wachter, H. and Wangenbach, P. (2006) 'The comparative institutional approach to human resource management in multinational companies', in M. Geppert and M. Mayer (eds) *Global, National and Local Practices in Multinational Companies*. London: Palgrave MacMillan.

Terry, M. (2003) 'Can "partnership" reverse the decline of British trade unions?' *Work, Employment and Society*, Vol. 17, No. 3, 459–72.

The World Bank (2006) *India Country Overview 2006*. The World Bank.

Thietart, R. *et al* (2001) *Doing Management Research*. London: Sage.

Thite, M. and Russell, R. (2010) 'Work organisation, human resource practices and employee retention in Indian call centres', *Asia Pacific Journal of Human Resources*, Vol. 48, No. 3, 356–74.

Thompson, M. (2000) 'Salary progression schemes', in G. White and J. Druker (eds) *Reward Management: A critical text*. London: Routledge.

Thompson, M. and Heron, P. (2006) 'Relational quality and innovative performance in R&D-based science and technology firms', *Human Resource Management Journal*, Vol. 16, No. 1, 28–47.

Thompson, P. (2011) Provocation Series Paper 'The trouble with human resource management', *Human Resource Management Journal*, Vol. 21, No. 4, pp.*355–67*.

Thompson, P. and Harley, B. (2007) in P. Boxall, J. Purcell and P. Wright (eds) *The Oxford Handbook of Human Resource Management*. Oxford: Oxford University Press.

THOMPSON, P. and MCHUGH, D. (2002) *Work Organisations: A critical introduction*, 3rd edition. London: Palgrave.

THOMPSON, P. and MILSOME, S. (2001) *Reward Determination in the UK*. Research Report. London: CIPD.

THORNTON, I. (2007) *Inside the Dark Box: Shedding light on private equity*. London: The Work Foundation.

THORY, K. (2008) 'The internationalisation of HRM through reverse transfer: two case studies of French multinationals in Scotland', *Human Resource Management Journal*, Vol. 18, No. 1, 52–69.

THURLEY, K. and WOOD, S. (eds) (1983) *Industrial Relations and Management Strategy*. Cambridge: Cambridge University Press.

TIMMING, A.R. (2007) 'European Works Councils: the dark side of managing worker voice', *Human Resource Management Journal*, Vol. 17, No. 3, 248–64.

TOPLIS, J., DULEWICZ, V. and FLETCHER, C. (1994) *Psychological Testing: A manager's guide*. London: Institute of Personnel Management.

TORRINGTON, D. (1998) 'Discipline', in M. POOLE and M. WARNER (eds) *IEBM Handbook of Human Resource Management*. London: International Thomson Press.

TORRINGTON, D., HALL, L. and TAYLOR, S. (2002) *Human Resource Management*. London: Prentice Hall.

TORRINGTON, D., HALL, L., TAYLOR, S. and ATKINSON, C. (2011) *Human Resource Management*, 8th edition. London: FT Prentice Hall.

TOULSON, P. and DEWE P. (2004) 'HR accounting as a measurement tool', *Human Resource Management Journal*, Vol. 14, No. 2, 75–90.

TOWERS, B. (2003) 'Overview: the changing employment relationship', in B. TOWERS (ed.) *The Handbook of Employment Relations, Law and Practice*. London: Kogan Page.

TOWERS, PERRIN. (2007) 'Flexible benefits research', *Employee Benefits*, January.

TOWNSEND, K. (2012) 'Conflict, resistance and misbehaviour in the workplace', in T. DUNDON and A. WILKINSON (eds) *Case Studies in People Management, Strategy and Innovation*. Victoria: Tide University Press.

TOWNSEND, K. and WILKINSON, A. (2011) 'New directions in employment relations', in A. WILKINSON and K. TOWNSEND (eds) *The Future of Employment Relations: New Paradigms, New Approaches*. London: Palgrave Macmillan.

TOWNSEND, K., WILKINSON, A. ALLAN, C. and BAMBER, G. (2012) 'Mixed signals in HRM: the HRM role of hospital line managers', *Human Resource Management Journal*, forthcoming.

TOWNSEND, K., WILKINSON, A. and BURGESS, J. (2011a) 'Filling the gaps: patterns of formal and informal voice', *Working Paper Series, Centre for Work, Organisation and Wellbeing*. Brisbane: Griffith University.

TOWNSEND, K., WILKINSON, A., BAMBER, G., and ALLAN, C. (forthcoming 2011b) 'Mixed signals in human resources management: the HRM role of hospital line managers', *Human Resource Management Journal*.

Toynbee, P. (2011) 'Moral outrage fixes nothing: the only remedies are liberal', *The Guardian*, 13 August.

Toynbee, P. (2011a) 'Public tolerance has now been tested to destruction', *The Guardian*, 4 June.

Trades Union Congress (1997) *Partners for Progress*. London: TUC.

Trades Union Congress (1999) *Partners for progress: next steps for the new unionism*. London: TUC.

Trades Union Congress (2002) *Partnership Works*. London: TUC.

Trades Union Congress (2007) *Post-16 Skills Training*. Available online at: www.tuc.org.uk/skills/tuc-12876-f0.cfm

Tregaskis, O., Edwards, T., Ferner, A. and Marginson, P. (2010) 'Transnational learning structures in multinational firms: organizational context and national embeddedness', *Human Relations*, Vol. 63, No. 4, 471–99.

Tregaskis, O., Heraty, N. and Morley, M. (2001), 'HRD in multinationals: the global/local mix', *Human Resource Management Journal*, Vol. 11, No. 2, 34–56.

Trevor, J. (2011) *Can Pay be Strategic? A critical exploration of strategic pay in practice*. London: Palgrave Macmillan.

Truss, C. (2004) 'Who's in the driving seat? Managing human resources in a franchise firm', *Human Resource Management Journal*, Vol. 14, No. 4, 57–75.

Truss, C., Gratton, L., Hope-Hailey, V., McGovern, P. and Styles, P. (1997) 'Soft and hard models of human resource management: a reappraisal', *Journal of Management Studies*, Vol. 34, No. 1, 53–73.

Truss, C., Soane, E., Edwards, C., Wisdom, K., Croll, A. and Burnett, J. (2006) *Working Life: Employee attitudes and engagement, 2006*. London: CIPD.

Truss, K. (2009) 'Changing HR functional forms in the UK public sector', *International Journal of Human Resource Management*, Vol. 20, No. 4, 717–37.

TUC *see* Trades Union Congress

Tulip, S. (2003) 'Just rewards', *People Management*, 10 July, 42–6.

Turban, D. and Cable, D. (2003) 'Firm reputation and applicant pool characteristics', *Journal of Organizational Behavior*, Vol. 24, No. 6, 733–51.

Turner, H. (1962) *Trade Union Growth, Structure and Policy: A comparative study of the cotton unions*. London: Allen & Unwin.

Tyson, S. and Fell, A. (1986) *Evaluating the Personnel Function*. London: Hutchinson.

UKCES (2010) *National Employer Skills Survey for England 2009, Key Findings Report*. London: UK Commission for Employment and Skills.

UKCES (2011a) *Business Plan and Strategic Objectives 2011–12*. London: UK Commission for Employment and Skills.

UKCES (2011b) *Investors in People: Research on the New Choices Approach*. London: UK Commission for Employment and Skills.

Ulrich, D. (1997) *Human Resource Champions: The next agenda for adding value and delivering results*. Boston: Harvard Business School Press.

ULRICH, D. (1998) 'A new mandate for human resources', *Harvard Business Review*, Jan–Feb, 125–34.

ULRICH, D. (2005) 'Role call', *People Management*, 16 June.

ULRICH, D. and BROCKBANK, W. (2005) *The HR Value Proposition*. Boston: Harvard Business School Press.

UNIONLEARN (2011) 'Working for learners: a handbook for unions and their union learning representatives' Third edition, April 2011.

UNIONLEARN (2011a) Learning and Skills Policy Newsletter, 30 January.

UNIONLEARN (2011b) 'UnionLearn lead organisation promoting higher level learning to working people' UnionLearn press release, 8 June.

UNIONLEARN (2011c) *Working for learners: a handbook for unions and their union learning representatives*, 3rd edition, April

VAIMAN, V. and HOLDEN, N. (2011) 'Talent management in Central and Eastern Europe', in H. SCULLION and D. COLLINGS (eds) *Global Talent Management*. New York: Routledge.

VAN MAANEN, J. (1979) 'The fact of fiction in organisational ethnography', *Administrative Science Quarterly*, Vol. 24, No. 4, 539–50.

VANDENBERG, P. (2010) 'Is Asia adopting flexicurity?' *International Labour Review*, Vol. 49, No. 1, 31–58.

VARMA, A. and BUDHWAR, P. (2011) 'Global performance Management' in A-W. HARZING and A.H. PINNINGTON (eds) *International Human Resource Management*. London: SAGE.

VARMA, A., BUDHWAR, P.S. and DENISI, A. (2008) *Performance Management Systems: A Global Perspective*. Abingdon, Oxon: Routledge.

VASAGAR, J. (2011a) 'Vocational subjects will not count for league tables', *The Guardian*, 21 July, p.10.

VASAGAR, J. (2011b) 'Over-25s help coalition to apprenticeship target', *The Guardian*, 15 August, p.10.

VON NORDENFLYCHT, A. (2010) 'What is a professional services firm? Toward a theory and taxonomy of knowledge-intensive firms', *Academy of Management Review*, Vol. 35, No. 1, 155–74.

WADDINGTON, J. and WHITSON, C. (1997) 'Why do people join unions in a period of membership decline?' *British Journal of Industrial Relations*, Vol. 35, No. 4, 515–46.

WAILES, N., BAMBER, G., and LANSBURY, R. (2011) 'International and comparative employment relations: an introduction' in G. BAMBER, R. LANSBURY, and N. WAILES (eds) *International and Comparative Employment Relations: Globalisation and Change*, 5th edition. Crows Nest: Allen and Unwin.

WALBY, S., ARMSTRONG, J., and HUMPHREYS, L. (2008) *Review of Equality Statistics*. London: Equality and Human Rights Commission.

WALKER, J. (1992) *Human Resource Strategy*. New York: McGraw-Hill.

WALL, T. and WOOD, S. (2005) 'The romance of human resource management and business performance, and the case for big science', *Human Relations*, Vol. 58, No. 4, 429–62.

WALL, T., MICHIE, J., PATTERSON, M., WOOD, S., SHEEHAN, M., CLEGG, C. and WEST, M. (2004) 'On the validity of subjective measures of company performance', *Personnel Psychology*, Vol. 57, 95–118.

WALSH, J. and DEERY, S. (2006) 'Refashioning organisational boundaries: outsourcing customer service work', *Journal of Management Studies*, Vol. 43, No. 3, 557–82.

WALSH, J. and ZHU, Y. (2007) 'Local complexities and global uncertainties: a study of foreign ownership and human resource management in China', *International Journal of Human Resource Management*, Vol. 18, No. 2, 249–67.

WALSH, K., LANZ, S., BERRY-LOUND, D, and LUANAIGH, A.N. (2011) *Investors in People Research on the New Choices Approach*. London: UKCES.

WALTON, R. (1985) 'From control to commitment in the workplace', *Harvard Business Review*, Vol. 63, March–April, 76–84.

WANG, H., LAW, K., HACKETT, R., WANG, D. and CHEN, Z. (2005) 'Leader–member exchange as a mediator of the relationship between transformational leadership and followers' performance and organisational citizenship behaviour', *Academy of Management Journal*, Vol. 48, No. 3, 420–32.

WARD, K., GRIMSHAW, D., RUBERY, J. and BEYNON, H. (2001) 'Dilemmas in the management of temporary work agency staff', *Human Resource Management Journal*, Vol. 11, No. 4, 3–21.

WARHURST, C. and NICKSON, D. (2007) 'Employee experience of aesthetic labour in retail and hospitality', *Work, Employment and Society*, Vol. 21, No. 1, 103–20.

WARHURST, C. and THOMPSON, P. (1998) 'Hands, hearts and minds: changing work and workers at the end of the century', in P. THOMPSON and C. WARHURST (eds) *Workplaces of the Future*. London: Macmillan.

WARHURST, C., VAN DEN BROEK, D., NICKSON, D., and HALL, R. (2011) 'Employee looks and lookism', in A. WILKINSON and K. TOWNSEND (eds) *The Future of Employment Relations*. London: Palgrave.

WARHURST, C., VAN DEN BROEK, D., NICKSON, D., and HALL, R. (2011a) 'Heads, hearts and now bodies: employee looks and lookism at work', in A. WILKINSON and K. TOWNSEND (eds) *The Future of Employment Relations: New Paradigms, New Developments*. New York: Palgrave Macmillan.

WASTI, S. (1998) 'Cultural barriers in the transferability of Japanese and American human resource practices to developing countries: the Turkish case', *International Journal of Human Resourced Management*, Vol. 9, No. 4, 608–31.

WATSON, G. and ADAMSON, I. (2010) 'Leadership and team dynamics', in G. WATSON and S. REISSNER (eds) *Developing Skills for Business Leadership*. London: CIPD.

WATSON, G. and REISSNER, S.C. (2010) *Developing Skills for Business Leadership*. London: CIPD.

WATSON, M. (2010a) 'Management and leadership development', in J. BEARDWELL and T. CLAYDON, *Human Resource Management: A contemporary approach*, 6th edition. Harlow: Pearson Education Limited.

WATSON, M. (2010b) 'Human resource development: the organisational and national framework', in J. BEARDWELL and T. CLAYDON *Human Resource Management: A contemporary approach*, 6th edition. Harlow: Pearson Education Limited.

WATSON, S. (2005) 'Is job evaluation making a comeback – or did it never go away?' *Benefits and Compensation International*, Vol. 34, No. 10, June, 8–12, 14.

WATSON, T. (1977) *The Personnel Managers: A study in the sociology of work and employment*. London: Routledge & Kegan Paul.

WATSON, T. (1986) *Management, Organisation and Employment Strategy*. London: Routledge & Kegan Paul.

WATSON, T. (1994a) 'Recruitment and selection', in K. SISSON (ed.) *Personnel Management: A comprehensive guide to theory and practice in Britain*. Oxford: Blackwell.

WATSON, T. (1994b) 'Managing, crafting and researching: words, skill and imagination in shaping management research', *British Journal of Management*, Vol. 5, Special issue, June, 80.

Watson, T. (2007) 'Organisational theory and HRM', in P. BOXALL, J. PURCELL and P. WRIGHT (eds) *The Oxford Handbook of Human Resource Management*. Oxford: Oxford University Press.

WATSON, W. (2009) *Continuous Engagement: The Key to Unlocking the Value of Your People during Tough Times*, Work Europe Survey 2008–2009.

WATT, A. (2008) 'The impact of private equity on European companies and workers: key issues and a review of the evidence', *Industrial Relations Journal*, Vol. 39, No. 6, 548–68.

WAYNE, S. and GREEN, S. (1993) 'The effects of leader-member exchange on employee citizenship and impression management behaviour', *Human Relations*, Vol. 46, No. 12, 1431–40.

WEEKES, S. (2007) 'E-ureka. Online learning comes of age', *Personnel Today*, 24 July, available online at: www.xpertHR.co.uk

WELBOURNE, T. (2011) 'Engaged in what? So what? A role-based perspective for the future of employee engagement', in A. WILKINSON and K. TOWNSEND (eds) *The Future of Employment Relations: New Paradigms, New Approaches*. London: Palgrave Macmillan.

WELFARE, S. (2006) 'Grievances and discipline: taking a proactive approach', *IRS Employment Review* 849, 23 June.

WENDT, H., EUWEMA, M. and VAN EMMERIK, I. (2009) 'Leadership and team cohesiveness across cultures', *The Leadership Quarterly*, Vol. 20, 358–70.

WERNERFELT, B. (1984) 'A resource-based view of the firm', *Strategic Management Journal*, Vol. 5, No. 2, 171–80.

WEST, M., BORRILL, C., DAWSON, J., SCULLY, J., CARTER, M., ANELAY, S., PATTERSON, M. and WARING, J. (2002) 'The link between the management of employees and patient mortality in acute hospitals', *International Journal of Human Resource Management*, Vol. 13, No. 8, 1299–310.

WESTCOTT, M. (2009) 'Private equity in Australia', *Journal of Industrial Relations*, Vol. 51, No. 4, 529–42.

WHEELER, H., KLAAS, B. and Mahony, D. (2004) *Workplace Justice without Unions*. Kalamazoo: Upjohn Institute.

WHITE, G. and DRUKER, J. (eds) (2008) *Reward Management: A critical text*, 2nd edition. London: Routledge.

White, M., Hill, S., Mills, C. and Smeaton, D. (2004) *Managing to Change? British workplaces and the future of work*. Basingstoke: Palgrave.

Whitley, R. (1999), *Divergent Capitalisms*. Oxford: Oxford University Press.

Whittaker, S. and Marchington, M. (2003) 'Devolving HR responsibility to the line: threat, opportunity or partnership?' *Employee Relations*, Vol. 25, No. 3, 245–61.

Whittington, R. (1993) *What is Strategy and Does It Matter?* London: Routledge.

Whittington, R. and Mayer, M. (2002) *Organising for Success in the Twenty-first Century*. London: CIPD.

Wickens, P. (1987) *The Road to Nissan: Flexibility, quality, teamwork*. London: Macmillan.

Wilk, S. and Cappelli, P. (2003) 'Understanding the determinants of employer use of selection methods', *Personnel Psychology*, Vol. 56, No. 1, 103–24.

Wilkinson, A., Townsend, K. and Graham, T. (2011) 'Deaf Ear Syndrome – Doctor Death and the Failure of Employee Voice Systems at Bundaberg Hospital', Working Paper.

Wilkinson, A. (1998) 'Empowerment: theory and practice', *Personnel Review*, Vol. 27, No. 1, 40–56.

Wilkinson, A. (1999) 'Employment relations in SMEs', *Employment Relations*, Vol. 1, No. 3, 206–17.

Wilkinson, A. (2002) 'Empowerment', in M. Warner (ed.) *International Encyclopaedia of Business and Management*, 2nd edition. London: Thomson.

Wilkinson, A. (2007) 'Industrial relations', in S. Clegg and J. Bailey (eds) *International Encyclopedia of Organisation Studies*. New York: Sage.

Wilkinson, A. (2011) 'Grievance and disciplinary procedures', in C. Rowley and K. Jackson (eds) *Human Resource Management: the key concepts*. London: Routledge, pp. 87–93.

Wilkinson, A. and Dundon, T. (2006) 'Employee participation', in T. Redman and A. Wilkinson (eds) *Contemporary Human Resource Management*. London: Financial Times/ Pitman.

Wilkinson, A. and Dundon, T. (2010) 'Direct employee participation', in A. Wilkinson, P. Gollan, M. Marchington and D. Lewin (eds) *The Oxford Handbook of Participation in Organisations*. Oxford: Oxford University Press, pp. 167–85.

Wilkinson, A. and Fay, C. (2011) 'New times for employee voice?' *Human Resource Management*, Vol. 50, No. 1, 65–74.

Wilkinson, A. and Marchington, M. (1994) 'Total quality management: instant pudding for the personnel function?' *Human Resource Management Journal*, Vol. 5, No. 1, 33–49.

Wilkinson, A. and Townsend, K. (2011) 'The changing face of work and industrial relations', in K. Townsend and A. Wilkinson (eds) *Research Handbook on Work and Employment Relations*. Cheltenham: Edward Elgar, pp. 1–10.

Wilkinson, A. and Townsend, K. (eds) (2011) *New Directions in Employment Relations*. Basingstoke: Palgrave.

Wilkinson, A. and Wood, G. (2012) 'Institutions and employment relations: the state of the art', *Industrial Relations*.

WILKINSON, A., BACON, N., REDMAN, T. and SNELL, S. (2009c) 'The field of human resource management', in A. WILKINSON, N. BACON, T. REDMAN and S. SNELL (eds) *The SAGE Handbook of Human Resource Management*. London: Sage.

WILKINSON, A., BACON, N., REDMAN, T. and SNELL, S. (eds) (2009) *The SAGE Handbook of Human Resource Management*. London: Sage.

WILKINSON, A., BAILEY, J. and MOURELL, M. (2009) 'Australian industrial relations in transition', *Industrial Relations Journal*, Vol. 40, No. 5, 358–71.

WILKINSON, A., DUNDON, T. and GRUGULIS, I. (2007) 'Information, not consultation', *International Journal of Human Resource Management*, Vol. 18, No. 7, 1279–97.

WILKINSON, A., DUNDON, T. and MARCHINGTON, M. (2012) 'Employee involvement and voice', in S. BACH and M. EDWARDS (eds) *Managing Human Resources.* Oxford: Blackwell.

WILKINSON, A., DUNDON, T., MARCHINGTON, M. and ACKERS, P. (2004) 'Changing patterns of employee voice', *Journal of Industrial Relations*, Vol. 46, No. 3, 297–321.

WILKINSON, A., GODFREY, G. and MARCHINGTON, M. (1997) 'Bouquets, brickbats and blinkers: total quality management and employee involvement in practice', *Organisation Studies*, Vol. 18, No. 5, 799–819.

WILKINSON, A., GOLLAN, P., MARCHINGTON, M. and LEWIN, D. (2010a) 'Conceptualising employee participation in organisations', in A. WILKINSON, P. GOLLAN, M. MARCHINGTON and D. LEWIN (eds) *The Oxford Handbook of Participation in Organisations*. Oxford: Oxford University Press, pp. 1–25.

WILKINSON, A., GOLLAN, P., MARCHINGTON, M. and LEWIN, D. (eds) (2010) *The Oxford Handbook of Employee Participation in Organisations*. Oxford: Oxford University Press.

WILKINSON, A., MARCHINGTON, M. and ACKERS, P. (1993) 'Strategies for human resource management: issues in larger and international firms', in R. HARRISON (ed.) *Human Resource Management*. London: Addison-Wesley.

WILKINSON, A., REDMAN, T., SNELL, S. and BACON, N. (2009) 'The field of human resource management', in A. WILKINSON. N. BACON, T. REDMAN, and S. SNELL (eds) *The SAGE Handbook of Human Resource Management*. London: Sage.

WILLIAMS, S. and SCOTT, P. (2010) 'Shooting the past? The modernisation of Conservative Party employment policy under David Cameron', *Industrial Relations Journal*, Vol. 41, No. 1, 4–18.

WILLIAMS, S., ABBOTT, B. and HEERY, E. (2011) 'New and emerging actors in work and employment relations: the case of civil society organisation', in K. TOWNSEND and A. WILKINSON (eds) *Research Handbook on Work and Employment Relations*. Cheltenham: Edward Elgar, pp. 130–49.

WILLIAMSON, I., LEPAK, D. and KING, J. (2003) 'The effect of company recruitment website orientation on individuals' perceptions of organisational attractiveness', *Journal of Vocational Behaviour*, Vol. 63, 242–63.

WILLIAMSON, O. (1975) *Markets and Hierarchies: Analysis and antitrust implications*. New York: Free Press.

WILLMOTT, H. (1993) 'Strength is ignorance; slavery is freedom: managing culture in modern organisations', *Journal of Management Studies*, Vol. 30, No. 4, 515–52.

WILSON, F. (1999) *Organisational Behaviour: An introduction*. Oxford: Oxford University Press.

WILTON, P. (2011) *Gender Pay Gap – Where now for workplace equality?* eGov Monitor. Available at: http://www.egovmonitor.com/node/43725 (accessed 7.10.11)

WINCH, G.M. (2008) 'Internationalisation strategies in business-to-business services: the case of architectural practice', *The Service Industries Journal*, Vol. 28, No. 1, 1–3.

WINTERTON, J. (2007) 'Training, development, and competence', in P. BOXALL, J. PURCELL and P. WRIGHT (eds) *The Oxford Handbook of Human Resource Management*. Oxford: Oxford University Press.

WINTERTON, J. (2009) 'Competence across Europe: highest common factor or lowest common denominator?' *Journal of European Industrial Training*, Vol. 33, No. 8/9, 681–700.

WITCHER, B. and WILKINSON, A. (2002) *What a Research Thesis Should Look Like*. Department of Management Working Paper. Norwich: University of East Anglia.

WOLF, A. (2011) *Wolf Review of Vocational Education: Government Response*. London: Department for Education.

WOLF, A. and JENKINS, A. (2006) 'Explaining greater test use for selection: the role of HR professionals in a world of expanding regulation', *Human Resource Management Journal*, Vol. 16, No. 2, 193–213.

WOLF, M. (2004) *Why Globalisation Works*, New Haven and London: Yale University Press.

WOLFF, C. (2006b) 'BBC gets wider view on learning', *IRS Employment Review* 859, 17 November, 16–19.

WOLFF, C. (2007a) 'Cultural change halves sickness absence at Shepway Council', *IRS Employment Review* 874, 4 June; available online at: www.xperthr.co.uk/viewarticleprint.asp?id=75982

WOLFF, C. (2007b) 'Survey: workplace training – budgets and challenges, 2007', *IRS Employment Review* 882, 8 October.

WOLFF, C. (2007d) 'Training evaluation – the secrets of success', *IRS Employment Review* 874, 4 June.

WOOD, G. and WRIGHT, M. (2009) 'Private equity: a review', *International Journal of Management Reviews*, Vol. 11, No. 4, 361–80.

WOOD, S. (1999a) 'Human resource management and performance', *International Journal of Management Reviews*, Vol. 1, No. 4, 367–413.

WOOD, S. (1999b) 'Getting the measure of the transformed high-performance organisation', *British Journal of Industrial Relations*, Vol. 37, No. 3, 391–418.

WOOD, S. (2003) 'Organisational performance and manufacturing practices', in D. HOLMAN, T. WALL, C. CLEGG, P. SPARROW and A. HOWARD (eds) *The New Workplace: A guide to the human impact of modern working practices*. London: Wiley.

WOOD, S. (2010) 'High involvement management and performance', in A. WILKINSON, P. GOLLAN, M. MARCHINGTON and D. LEWIN (eds) *The Oxford Handbook of Participation in Organisations*. Oxford and New York: Oxford University Press.

Wood, S. and Albanese, M. (1995) 'Can we speak of a high-commitment management on the shop floor?' *Journal of Management Studies*, Vol. 32, No. 2, 1–33.

Wood, S. and de Menezes, L. (1998) 'High-commitment management in the UK: evidence from the Workplace Industrial Relations Survey and Employers' Manpower and Skills Survey', *Human Relations*, Vol. 51, No. 4, 485–515.

Wood, S. and de Menezes, L. (2008) 'Comparing perspectives on high Iivolvement management and organisational performance across the British economy', *International Journal of Human Resource Management*, Vol. 19, No. 4, 639–83.

Wood, S. and de Menezes, L. (2011) 'High involvement management, high performance work systems and well-being', *International Journal of Human Resource Management*, Vol. 22, No. 7, 1586–610.

Wood, S. and Fenton O'Creevy, M. (1999a) 'Channel hopping', *People Management*, 25 November, 42–5.

Wood, S., Moore, S. and Ewing, K. (2003) 'The impact of the trade union recognition procedure under the Employment Relations Act 2000–2', in H. Gospel and S. Wood (eds) *Representing Workers: Union recognition and membership in Britain*. London: Routledge.

Woodall, J., Scott-Jackson, W., Newham, T. and Gurney, M. (2009) 'Making the decision to outsource human resources', *Personnel Review*, Vol. 38, No. 3, 236–52.

Wozowczyk, M. and Massarelli N. (2011) *European Union Labour Force Survey – Annual Results, 2010*. Luxembourg: Eurostat.

Wright, A. (2011) '"Modernising" away gender pay inequality? Some evidence from the local government sector on using job evaluation', *Employee Relations, Vol. 33, No. 2,* 159–78.

Wright, M., Bacon, N. and Amess, K. (2009) 'The impact of private equity and buyouts on employment, remuneration and other HRM practices', *Journal of Industrial Relations*, Vol. 51, No. 4, 501–16.

Wright, P. and Gardner, T. (2003) 'The human resource–firm performance relationship: methodological and theoretical challenges', in D. Holman, T. Wall, C. Clegg, P. Sparrow and A. Howard (eds) *The New Workplace: A guide to the human impact of modern working practices*. London: Wiley.

Wright, P. and Kehoe, R. (2008) 'Human resource practices and organisational commitment: a deeper examination', *Asia Pacific Journal of Human Resources*, Vol. 46, No. 6, 6–20.

Wright, P. and Snell, S.A. (2005) 'Partner or guardian? HR's challenge in balancing value and values', *Human Resource Management*, Vol. 44, No. 2, 177–82.

Wright, P., Gardner, T., Moynihan, L. and Allen, M. (2005) 'The relationship between HR practices and firm performance: examining causal order', *Personnel Psychology*, Vol. 58, No. 2, 409–46.

Wright, P., McMahon, G. and McWilliams, A. (1994) 'Human resources and sustained competitive advantage: a resource-based perspective', *International Journal of Human Resource Management*, Vol. 5, No. 2, 301–26.

XpertHR (2007) 'The measure of all things soft', *Training and Coaching Today*, 1 July.

Yi, L., Zhigang, T. and Yijiang, W. (2010) 'Union effects on performance and employment relations: evidence from China', China Economic Review, Vol. 21, No. 1, 202–10.

Yin, R. (2009) *Case Study Research: Design and methods*, 4th edition. London: Sage.

Youndt, M., Snell, S., Dean, J. and Lepak, D. (1996) 'Human resource management, manufacturing strategy, and firm performance', *Academy of Management Journal*, Vol. 39, 836–66.

Zhaihing, L., Trenberth, L. and Kelly, J. (2010) 'The development and implications of China's employee benefit scheme', *Asia Pacific Journal of Human Resources*, Vol. 48, No. 3, 287–301.

Zhang, Y. and Li, S. (2009) 'High performance work practices and firm performance: evidence from the pharmaceutical industry in China', *International Journal of Human Resource Management*, Vol. 20, No. 11, 2331–48.

Zhu, C., Cooper, B., De Cieri, H., Thomson, B. and Zhao, S. (2008) 'Devolvement of HR practices in transitional economies: evidence from China', *International Journal of Human Resource Management*, Vol. 19, No. 5, 840–55.

# Index